THE GREAT TRADITION

THE GREAT TRADITION

*Classic Readings on What It Means to
Be an Educated Human Being*

edited by Richard M. Gamble

*To Michael and Patti Mahan —
Thank you for carrying forward the
great tradition of liberal learning.*

*Richard M. Gamble
Spring 2018*

ISI BOOKS

Wilmington, Delaware

The great tradition : classic readings on what it means to be an educated human being / [edited by] Richard M. Gamble. — 1st ed. — Wilmington, DE : ISI Books, 2007.

    p. ; cm.

    ISBN-13: 978-1-933859-25-5
    ISBN-10: 1-933859-25-3
    An anthology of classic writings on education.
    Includes bibliographical references.

    1. Education—History. I. Gamble, Richard M.

LA7 .G74 2007   2007923892
370.9—dc22   0708

book design by Beer Editorial and Design

ISI Books
Intercollegiate Studies Institute
Post Office Box 4431
Wilmington, DE 19807-0431
www.isibooks.org

To Thomas J. St. Antoine,

a teacher with the courage to make students unfit

for the modern world

⚮

Table of Contents

Acknowledgments

Credit for this anthology belongs to the authors included herein. My task as compiler and editor has been merely to reap a harvest that others have sown and tended over millennia. I can offer no better thanks to the faithful teachers within the Great Tradition than to pass on their legacy to others.

This project began while I was on sabbatical leave from Palm Beach Atlantic University in the spring of 2003. The board of trustees and then-president Paul Corts awarded me the inestimable privilege of time away from the daily duties of teaching simply to think, to read, and to begin piecing together what I only vaguely knew as the Great Tradition. A generous grant from the H. B. Earhart Foundation enabled me to spend my sabbatical at Cambridge University. I am indebted to several friends and institutions in Cambridge who welcomed me into their venerable academic community that semester. Bruce Winter, at that time warden of Tyndall House, provided me with an appointment as reader, a comfortable home, a quiet library, and the companionship of an international group of scholars. His generous assistance also opened the way to my appointment as visiting scholar at St. Edmund's College. There is no more hospitable college in all of Cambridge. Also, two dear friends, Chad and Emily Van Dixhoorn, always made room for me in their growing family.

At ISI Books, editor in chief Jeremy Beer guided this project from the time it was barely a mental sketch. His enthusiasm, good humor, and attention to detail make it an ongoing privilege to work with him. Managing editor Jennifer Connolly hunted down copyright holders and brought order and coherence to an unwieldy mass of material. In every facet of its operations, ISI Books blends professionalism and informality in a way that makes an author feel at home.

If this anthology has any single point of origin, it is in the vibrant conversation that took place among the faculty and students in the honors program at Palm Beach Atlantic University. Together, in rare camaraderie, my former colleagues and I struggled to reassemble the liberal arts tradition, to teach ourselves in a comprehensive and systematic way what many of us had been taught only in fragments. The simple joy of discovery sustained us through years of hard work. Our students patiently endured our earnest attempts to teach ourselves in the guise of teaching them. But it was the students, of course, who gave it all meaning and enduring significance. By singling out the program's current director, Tom St. Antoine, to whom this volume is dedicated, I wish to express my indebtedness to all my former colleagues and students. May they continue to give what they have received.

HILLSDALE, MICHIGAN
JUNE 2007

Introduction

Evelyn Waugh's gently satirical *Scott-King's Modern Europe* follows the declining career of a classics teacher at Granchester, a fictional English public school. Granchester is "entirely respectable" but in need of a bit of modernizing, at least in the opinion of its pragmatic headmaster, who is attuned to consumer demands. The story ends with a poignant conversation between Scott-King and the headmaster:

> "You know," [the headmaster] said, "we are starting this year with fifteen fewer classical specialists than we had last term?"
>
> "I thought that would be about the number."
>
> "As you know I'm an old Greats man myself. I deplore it as much as you do. But what are we to do? Parents are not interested in producing the 'complete man' any more. They want to qualify their boys for jobs in the modern world. You can hardly blame them, can you?"
>
> "Oh yes," said Scott-King. "I can and do."
>
> "I always say you are a much more important man here than I am. One couldn't conceive of Granchester without Scott-King. But has it ever occurred to you that a time may come when there will be no more classical boys at all?"
>
> "Oh yes. Often."
>
> "What I was going to suggest was—I wonder if you will consider taking some other subject as well as the classics? History, for example, preferably economic history?"
>
> "No, headmaster."

"But, you know, there may be something of a crisis ahead."

"Yes, headmaster."

"Then what do you intend to do?"

"If you approve, headmaster, I will stay as I am here as long as any boy wants to read the classics. I think it would be very wicked indeed to do anything to fit a boy for the modern world."

"It's a short-sighted view, Scott-King."

"There, headmaster, with all respect, I differ from you profoundly. I think it the most long-sighted view it is possible to take."[1]

And there ends the story of Scott-King's misadventures in the modern world. Any teacher who has endured a similar conversation sympathizes instinctively with poor Scott-King. His dignified but stubborn resistance to the wickedness of making students fit for the modern world speaks to the heart of teachers who, like Scott-King, take the long view. It is to these teachers, then—and to like-minded students, parents, and administrators—that this anthology of classic writings on education is addressed. This collection from what has been called the "Great Tradition" is intended to supply an arsenal of the liberal arts for those who would wage war—covertly or openly—on the side of an education rooted in the classical and Christian heritage. It will, I hope, inspire modern misfits who seek to initiate themselves and their students into an ancient way of teaching and learning much larger than themselves, and who recognize that their task is chiefly formative rather than instrumental. Readers looking for up-to-the-minute advice about innovative teaching methods and classroom technology, or about how to prepare students for the "real world" and tomorrow's top-ten careers, will be gravely disappointed.

By design, this anthology offers nothing new. As C. S. Lewis remarked in his preface to *The Problem of Pain*, any originality here is unintentional. Furthermore, this anthology is meant neither to be a documentary history of education in the West nor a comprehensive survey of competing philosophies of education. It excludes utilitarians, romantics, and progressives; there is nothing here by John Locke, Jean-Jacques Rousseau, or John Dewey. Instead, it follows the trail of an older, more noble, and continual conversation about what it means to be a truly educated human being.

More than two hundred years ago, the utilitarians disconnected themselves from liberal education and the Great Tradition, redefining and redirecting the "useful" away from that which forms the "complete man," and toward that which primarily promotes man's material well-being. Of course, education has always aimed to be useful. The question has been, and continues to be, useful to what end? The modern age, often with good intentions, has defined educational usefulness as that which leads to material results that can be weighed and measured and counted. Thus, it is no surprise that it has been darkened by the spiritual "eclipse" that Saint Augustine warned us against so long ago in his *Confessions*. The Great Tradition, in contrast, anchored in the classical and Christian humanism of liberal education, has taken the broader view that what is useful is that which helps men and women to flourish in nonmaterial ways as well—in other words, that which helps

---

1. From an abridged version originally published in 1947 in the *Cornhill* magazine and reprinted in *The Complete Stories of Evelyn Waugh* (Boston: Little, Brown, 1999), 328–76.

them to be happy. Indeed, what the Great Tradition has meant by the words "humanism," "liberal," and "education" will emerge from the full context—spanning a breathtaking twenty-four centuries—of the remarkably intelligible, unified, and coherent conversation that unfolds in these pages.

Of course, the writers anthologized here do not always speak with one voice. No group of statesmen, philosophers, schoolmasters, historians, theologians, architects, and critics could possibly reach unanimity. There are tensions and inconsistencies within the Great Tradition. Indeed, a few of these authors would be surprised to find themselves in each other's company, at a loss to guess what strange principle of selection had landed them all in one book. This is especially true for Protestant Reformers and their Catholic adversaries, such as John Calvin and the Jesuits, respectively. But this anthology attempts to recover an *educational* legacy, not a theological one. It takes no position on matters of theology. It draws wisdom from the Eastern and Western church, from Catholics and Protestants and also Jews, but it claims no ecumenical synthesis in matters of faith; its only ecumenism is built on the ground of respect for liberal learning, an ecumenism so broad that for the sake of this task it embraces pagans, skeptics, and agnostics as well. So, whenever possible, these authors have been allowed to choose their compatriots, in the hope that a transgenerational conversation would emerge organically from the selections themselves.

In fact, this anthology explicitly struggles against the modern tendency to value the past merely as a precursor to the present. Typically, ancient and medieval writers on education have been praised (and anthologized) not for their own sake but for the degree to which they anticipate the future. They have been held to matter only insofar as in their writings one is able to catch a prophetic glimpse of Bacon or Rousseau or Dewey. Too often, we praise only those authors who most resemble us or prefigure an imagined future, never allowing the wisdom of the past to sit in judgment on our own prejudices and activities. The great twentieth-century Cambridge historian Herbert Butterfield described this progressive habit; his warning should be heeded by anyone attempting to understand educational theory and practice: "The curious fact is that the historian has to learn—and he has had to learn it consciously by discovering that the alternative method produces unsatisfactory results—that the generations of the past are not to be dismissed as subordinate to the later ones, mere stepping-stones to the present day, merely preparations or trial shots for authentic achievement that was still to come." Striking even closer to the fallacy that this anthology seeks to correct, Butterfield warned nationalist Britons to "stop regarding the Anglo-Saxons as mere links in a chain leading to us, mere precursors, significant only because of what they contributed to the modern world."[2]

The authors anthologized here are indeed links in a chain, but they are not simply links that derive their truth and significance from what comes next in the sequence. The Great Tradition has no desire to escape from the past, recognizing instead the continuity of a world larger than the momentary self. It willingly accepts the present's obligation to pass on what it has received. It fears that if it "wipes the slate clean" it will in turn be swept away

---

2. *Christianity and History* (New York: Charles Scribner's Sons, 1950), 65. The brief essay "Kafka and His Precursors," by Jorge Luis Borges, offers a literary take on nearly the same point. It is included in *Labyrinths: Selected Stories & Other Writings*, ed. by Donald A. Yates and James E. Irby (New York: New Directions, 1964), 199–201.

by some future generation armed with an equal zeal for innovation. (Readers who find their appreciation for the past enhanced by this anthology may wish to go beyond the brief biographical essays that introduce each selection and reconnect these links into a narrative whole. If so, two books will be particularly helpful: Arthur F. Holmes's *Building the Christian Academy* and Christopher Dawson's *The Crisis of Western Education*, especially the first few chapters.)

This sense of obligation to both the past and the future is an inescapable feature of the Great Tradition. It was captured well in the fifth century by Macrobius's advice to his son Eustachius. In the preface to *The Saturnalia*, he wrote, "This, then, is what I would have this present work to be: a repository of much to teach and much to guide you, examples drawn from many ages but informed by a single spirit, wherein—if you refrain from rejecting what you already know and from shunning what you do not—you will find much that it would be a pleasure to read, an education to have read, and of use to remember. . . ."[3] In the twelfth century, John of Salisbury wrote that the same spirit animated his own teacher, Bernard of Chartres: "Our own generation enjoys the legacy bequeathed to it by that which preceded it. We frequently know more, not because we have moved ahead by our own natural ability, but because we are supported by the [mental] strength of others, and possess riches that we have inherited from our forefathers. Bernard of Chartres used to compare us to [puny] dwarfs perched on the shoulders of giants. He pointed out that we see more and farther than our predecessors, not because we have keener vision or greater height, but because we are lifted up and borne aloft on their gigantic stature."[4] The "single spirit" that Macrobius detected in authors "from many ages" unified the Great Tradition in the Middle Ages and continued to do so for centuries. John Henry Newman spoke of "a continuous historical tradition."[5] Herbert Butterfield wrote, "Whether our establishment is a new one or an old one, we ought to have the sense of belonging to a single great tradition."[6]

The Great Tradition is so vast that this anthology could have comprised an entirely different set of authors, or at least different excerpts from these same authors. No doubt some readers' favorite writers and passages are missing. But this anthology is not an end in itself. It must not replace the reading of these authors and their works as a whole. Rather, I hope that it will whet readers' appetites, inviting them to further exploration and reflection. This invitation goes out to all teachers, parents, and students who seek ways to defend liberal learning from the onslaught of careerism, utilitarianism, and numbing technique that threatens public and even private and Christian education, who seek to reconnect themselves with an ancient yet living tradition. The Great Tradition embraces an enduring community of learning that values liberal education for its own sake; desires to educate for wisdom and virtue, not power and vanity; finds tiresome the present age's preoccupation with utility, speed, novelty, convenience, efficiency, and specialization; and refuses to justify education as a means to wealth, power, fame, or self-assertion. The Great Tradition is a gift to be received and passed on to the future, not the imagined "Future" of progressive fantasy, but the real human future of our posterity.

3. *The Saturnalia*, trans. by Percival Vaughan Davies (New York: Columbia University Press, 1969), 28.
4. *The Metalogicon of John of Salisbury: A Twelfth-Century Defense of the Verbal and Logical Arts of the Trivium*, trans. by Daniel D. McGarry (Berkeley, CA: University of California Press, 1955), 167.
5. *The Idea of a University*, ed. by Martin J. Svaglic (Notre Dame, IN: University of Notre Dame Press, 1982), 83.
6. *The University and Education Today* (London: Routledge & Kegan Paul, 1962), 26–27.

In the 1930s, Albert Jay Nock nearly despaired "that our American society will ever return to the Great Tradition."[7] But he also laughed at those who thought their own meager contributions to its survival were indispensable: "We can do nothing for the Great Tradition; our fidelity to it can do everything for us."[8] The Great Tradition patiently endures, ready to speak on its own behalf, ready to challenge narrow prejudices, ready to examine those with the courage to be interrogated by it, ready to teach those who are willing to be made unfit for the modern world.

---

7. *The Theory of Education in the United States* (New York: Harcourt, Brace and Company, 1932), 159.
8. Ibid., 155.

THE GREAT TRADITION

Plato

C. 427–347 B.C.

Neither must we cast a slight upon education, which is the first and fairest thing that the best of men can ever have.

THE LAWS

For many centuries, the Greek standard of excellence in education was embodied in Homer's epic poetry. The Greeks revered the relationship between Athena (in the form of Mentor) and Telemachus in *The Odyssey* and between Phoenix and Achilles in *The Iliad*. The philosophical tradition in classical education, however, begins with Plato. Plato founded his Academy in Athens in 387, and Aristotle was among his students and later faculty. Plato's developing reflections on education can be found in the *Republic*, *Statesman*, *Phaedrus*, *Sophist*, *Gorgias*, *Laches*, *Protagoras*, and *The Laws*. Few of Plato's dialogues fail to touch in some way on education. He spoke mostly through the voice of his teacher Socrates; indeed, most of what people think they know about Socrates comes from his most famous student. Socrates himself left behind no treatise and no dialogue, but through Plato he shaped the West's enduring conception of education. In Werner Jaeger's summary of Socrates' teaching, "Education is not the cultivation of certain branches of knowledge. . . . The real essence of education is that it enables men to reach the true aim of their lives" *(Paideia, II, 69)*. That "true aim" requires turning toward the unseen realm of the good, the true, and the beautiful. The twentieth-century political philosopher Eric Voegelin noted that for Plato "education is the art of *periagoge*, of turning around" (see the reading from Voegelin found later in this anthology). Education is properly understood as the care and perfection of the soul. Excellence *(arete)* is not primarily excellence of skill but excellence of virtue.

THE SELECTIONS

Plato's *Republic* as a whole contemplates the nature of justice and the well-ordered city, but nearly every page also comments on education in the ideal state. Choosing a representative sample from the *Republic* is almost impossible. The end of Book V through the beginning of Book VI (included here) differentiates between true knowledge and mere opinion and consequently between true and false philosophers. The well-known "Allegory of the Cave" from Book VII summarizes many of Plato's presuppositions and introduced into history a powerful metaphor of sight that would shape educational discourse for centuries to come. While the *Republic* is concerned with justice in the literal city, it is primarily concerned with justice in the city of the soul, an inner city attuned with the order of the heavenly city. The *Laws*, a work from late in Plato's career, returns to the persistent questions about the nature and purpose of *paideia*—an untranslatable word that encompasses the total formation of a human being. In the excerpt from Book VII included here, the "Athenian" and Cleinias discuss reverence for tradition and regulations for the education of young boys. The Athenian is speaking.

A fuller estimation of Plato's contribution to the West's philosophy of education must include the dialogues *Laches* and *Protagoras*. In both of these, Socrates takes up the question of whether virtue can be taught. Socrates urges "that every one of us should seek out the best teacher whom he can find, first for ourselves, who are greatly in need of one, and then for the youth, regardless of expense or anything. But I cannot advise that we remain as we are. And if anyone laughs at us for going to school at our age, I would quote to them the authority of Homer, who says, that 'Modesty is not good for a needy man.' Let us, then, regardless of what may be said of us, make the education of the youths our own education" (*Laches*, 201).

from the Republic

BOOK V

Once more [said Socrates] let me ask: Does he who desires any class of goods, desire the whole class or a part only?

The whole.

And may we not say of the philosopher that he is a lover, not of a part of wisdom only, but of the whole?

Yes, of the whole.

And he who dislikes learning, especially in youth, when he has no power of judging what is good and what is not, such an one we maintain not to be a philosopher or a lover of knowledge, just as he who refuses his food is not hungry, and may be said to have a bad appetite and not a good one?

Very true, he said.

Whereas he who has a taste for every sort of knowledge and who is curious to learn and is never satisfied, may be justly termed a philosopher? Am I not right?

Glaucon said: If curiosity makes a philosopher, you will find many a strange being will have a title to the name. All the lovers of sights have a delight in learning, and must therefore be included. Musical amateurs, too, are a folk strangely out of place among philosophers, for they are the last persons in the world who would come to anything like a philosophical discussion, if they could help, while they run about at the Dionysiac festivals as if they had let out their ears to hear every chorus; whether the performance is in town or country— that makes no difference—they are there. Now are we to maintain that all these and any who have similar tastes, as well as the professors of quite minor arts, are philosophers?

Certainly not, I replied; they are only an imitation.

He said: Who then are the true philosophers?

Those, I said, who are lovers of the vision of truth.

That is also good, he said; but I should like to know what you mean?

To another, I replied, I might have a difficulty in explaining; but I am sure that you will admit a proposition which I am about to make.

What is the proposition?

That since beauty is the opposite of ugliness, they are two?

Certainly.

And inasmuch as they are two, each of them is one?

True again.

And of just and unjust, good and evil, and of every other class, the same remark holds: taken singly, each of them is one; but from the various combinations of them with actions and things and with one another, they are seen in all sorts of lights and appear many?

Very true.

And this is the distinction which I draw between the sight-loving, art-loving, practical class and those of whom I am speaking, and who are alone worthy of the name of philosophers.

How do you distinguish them? he said.

The lovers of sounds and sights, I replied, are, as I conceive, fond of fine tones and colours and forms and all the artificial products that are made out of them, but their mind is incapable of seeing or loving absolute beauty.

True, he replied.

Few are they who are able to attain to the sight of this.

Very true.

And he who, having a sense of beautiful things has no sense of absolute beauty, or who, if another lead him to a knowledge of that beauty is unable to follow—of such an one I ask, Is he awake or in a dream only? Reflect: is not the dreamer, sleeping or waking, one who likens dissimilar things, who puts the copy in the place of the real object?

I should certainly say that such an one was dreaming.

But take the case of the other, who recognises the existence of absolute beauty and is able to distinguish the idea from the objects which participate in the idea, neither putting the objects in the place of the idea nor the idea in the place of the objects—is he a dreamer, or is he awake?

He is wide awake.

And may we not say that the mind of the one who knows has knowledge, and that the mind of the other, who opines only, has opinion?

Certainly.

But suppose that the latter should quarrel with us and dispute our statement, can we administer any soothing cordial or advice to him, without revealing to him that there is sad disorder in his wits?

We must certainly offer him some good advice, he replied.

Come, then, and let us think of something to say to him. Shall we begin by assuring him that he is welcome to any knowledge which he may have, and that we are rejoiced at his having it? But we should like to ask him a question: Does he who has knowledge know something or nothing? (You must answer for him.)

I answer that he knows something.

Something that is or is not?

Something that is; for how can that which is not ever be known?

And are we assured, after looking at the matter from many points of view, that absolute being is or may be absolutely known, but that the utterly non-existent is utterly unknown?

Nothing can be more certain.

Good. But if there be anything which is of such a nature as to be and not to be, that will have a place intermediate between pure being and the absolute negation of being?

Yes, between them.

And, as knowledge corresponded to being and ignorance of necessity to not-being, for that intermediate between being and not-being there has to be discovered a corresponding intermediate between ignorance and knowledge, if there be such?

Certainly.

Do we admit the existence of opinion?

Undoubtedly.

As being the same with knowledge, or another faculty?

Another faculty.

Then opinion and knowledge have to do with different kinds of matter corresponding to this difference of faculties?

Yes.

And knowledge is relative to being and knows being. But before I proceed further I will make a division.

What division?

I will begin by placing faculties in a class by themselves: they are powers in us, and in all other things, by which we do as we do. Sight and hearing, for example, I should call faculties. Have I clearly explained the class which I mean?

Yes, I quite understand.

Then let me tell you my view about them. I do not see them, and therefore the distinctions of figure, colour, and the like, which enable me to discern the differences of some things, do not apply to them. In speaking of a faculty I think only of its sphere and its result; and that which has the same sphere and the same result I call the same faculty, but that which has another sphere and another result I call different. Would that be your way of speaking?

Yes.

And will you be so very good as to answer one more question? Would you say that knowledge is a faculty, or in what class would you place it?

Certainly knowledge is a faculty, and the mightiest of all faculties.

And is opinion also a faculty?

Certainly, he said; for opinion is that with which we are able to form an opinion.

And yet you were acknowledging a little while ago that knowledge is not the same as opinion?

Why, yes, he said: how can any reasonable being ever identify that which is infallible with that which errs?

An excellent answer, proving, I said, that we are quite conscious of a distinction between them.

Yes.

Then knowledge and opinion having distinct powers have also distinct spheres or subject-matters?

That is certain.

Being is the sphere or subject-matter of knowledge, and knowledge is to know the nature of being?

Yes.

And opinion is to have an opinion?

Yes.

And do we know what we opine? or is the subject-matter of opinion the same as the subject-matter of knowledge?

Nay, he replied, that has been already disproven; if difference in faculty implies difference in the sphere or subject-matter, and if, as we were saying, opinion and knowledge are distinct faculties, then the sphere of knowledge and of opinion cannot be the same.

Then if being is the subject-matter of knowledge, something else must be the subject-matter of opinion?

Yes, something else.

Well then, is not-being the subject-matter of opinion? or, rather, how can there be an opinion at all about not-being? Reflect: when a man has an opinion, has he not an opinion about something? Can he have an opinion which is an opinion about nothing?

Impossible.

He who has an opinion has an opinion about some one thing?

Yes.

And not-being is not one thing but, properly speaking, nothing?

True.

Of not-being, ignorance was assumed to be the necessary correlative; of being, knowledge?

True, he said.

Then opinion is not concerned either with being or with not-being?

Not with either.

And can therefore neither be ignorance nor knowledge? That seems to be true.

But is opinion to be sought without and beyond either of them, in a greater clearness than knowledge, or in a greater darkness than ignorance?

In neither.

Then I suppose that opinion appears to you to be darker than knowledge, but lighter than ignorance?

Both; and in no small degree.

And also to be within and between them?

Yes.

Then you would infer that opinion is intermediate?

No question.

But were we not saying before, that if anything appeared to be of a sort which is and is not at the same time, that sort of thing would appear also to lie in the interval between pure being and absolute not-being; and that the corresponding faculty is neither knowledge nor ignorance, but will be found in the interval between them?

True.

And in that interval there has now been discovered something which we call opinion?

There has.

Then what remains to be discovered is the object which partakes equally of the nature of being and not-being, and cannot rightly be termed either, pure and simple; this unknown term, when discovered, we may truly call the subject of opinion, and assign each to their proper faculty,—the extremes to the faculties of the extremes and the mean to the faculty of the mean.

True.

This being premised, I would ask the gentleman who is of opinion that there is no absolute or unchangeable idea of beauty—in whose opinion the beautiful is the manifold—he, I say, your lover of beautiful sights, who cannot bear to be told that the beautiful is one, and the just is one, or that anything is one—to him I would appeal, saying, Will you be so very kind, sir, as to tell us whether, of all these beautiful things, there is one which will not be found ugly; or of the just, which will not be found unjust; or of the holy, which will not also be unholy?

No, he replied; the beautiful will in some point of view be found ugly; and the same is true of the rest.

And may not the many which are doubles be also halves?—doubles, that is, of one thing, and halves of another?

Quite true.

And things great and small, heavy and light, as they are termed, will not be denoted by these any more than by the opposite names?

True; both these and the opposite names will always attach to all of them.

And can any one of those many things which are called by particular names be said to be this rather than not to be this?

He replied: They are like the punning riddles which are asked at feasts or the children's puzzle about the eunuch aiming at the bat, with what he hit him, as they say in the puzzle, and upon what the bat was sitting. The individual objects of which I am speaking are also a riddle, and have a double sense: nor can you fix them in your mind, either as being or not-being, or both, or neither.

Then what will you do with them? I said. Can they have a better place than between being and not-being? For they are clearly not in greater darkness or negation than not-being, or more full of light and existence than being.

That is quite true, he said.

Thus then we seem to have discovered that the many ideas which the multitude entertain about the beautiful and about all other things are tossing about in some region which is half-way between pure being and pure not-being?

We have.

Yes; and we had before agreed that anything of this kind which we might find was to be described as matter of opinion, and not as matter of knowledge; being the intermediate flux which is caught and detained by the intermediate faculty.

Quite true. . . .

BOOK VI

And thus, Glaucon, after the argument has gone a weary way, the true and the false philosophers have at length appeared in view.

I do not think, he said, that the way could have been shortened.

I suppose not, I [Socrates] said; and yet I believe that we might have had a better view of both of them if the discussion could have been confined to this one subject and if there were not many other questions awaiting us, which he who desires to see in what respect the life of the just differs from that of the unjust must consider.

And what is the next questions? he asked

Surely, I said, the one which follows next in order. Inasmuch as philosophers only are able to grasp the eternal and unchangeable, and those who wander in the region of the many and variable are not philosophers, I must ask you which of the two classes should be the rulers of our State?

And how can we rightly answer that question?

Whichever of the two are best able to guard the laws and institutions of our State—let them be our guardians.

Very good.

Neither, I said, can there be any question that the guardian who is to keep anything should have eyes rather than no eyes?

There can be no question of that.

And are not those who are verily and indeed wanting in the knowledge of the true being of each thing, and who have in their souls no clear pattern, and are unable as with a painter's eye to look at the absolute truth and that original to repair, and having perfect vision of the other world to order the laws about beauty, goodness, justice in this, if not already ordered, and to guard and preserve the order of them—are not such persons, I ask, simply blind?

Truly, he replied, they are much in that condition.

And shall they be our guardians when there are others who, besides being their equals in experience and falling short of them in no particular of virtue, also know the very truth of each thing?

There can be no reason, he said, for rejecting those who have this greatest of all great qualities; they must always have the first place unless they fail in some other respect.

Suppose then, I said, that we determine how far they can unite this and the other excellences.

By all means.

In the first place, as we began by observing, the nature of the philosopher has to be ascertained. We must come to an understanding about him, and, when we have done so, then, if I am not mistaken, we shall also acknowledge that such an union of qualities is possible, and that those in whom they are united, and those only, should be rulers in the State.

What do you mean?

Let us suppose that philosophical minds always love knowledge, of a sort which shows them the eternal nature not varying from generation and corruption.

Agreed.

And further, I said, let us agree that they are lovers of all true being; there is no part whether greater or less, or more or less honourable, which they are willing to renounce; as we said before of the lover and the man of ambition.

True.

And if they are to be what we were describing, is there not another quality which they should also possess?

What quality?

Truthfulness: they will never intentionally receive into their mind falsehood, which is their detestation, and they will love the truth.

Yes, that may be safely affirmed of them.

"May be," my friend, I replied, is not the word; say rather "must be affirmed:" for he whose nature is amorous of anything cannot help loving all that belongs or is akin to the object of his affections.

Right, he said.

And is there anything more akin to wisdom than truth? How can there be?

Can the same nature be a lover of wisdom and a lover of falsehood?

Never.

The true lover of learning then must from his earliest youth, as far as in him lies, desire all truth?

Assuredly.

But then again, as we know by experience, he whose desires are strong in one direction will have them weaker in others; they will be like a stream which has been drawn off into another channel.

True.

He whose desires are drawn towards knowledge in every form will be absorbed in the pleasures of the soul, and will hardly feel bodily pleasure—I mean, if he be a true philosopher and not a sham one.

That is most certain.

Such an one is sure to be temperate and the reverse of covetous; for the motives which make another man desirous of having and spending, have no place in his character.

Very true.

Another criterion of the philosophical nature has also to be considered.

What is that?

There should be no secret corner of illiberality; nothing can be more antagonistic than meanness to a soul which is ever longing after the whole of things both divine and human.

Most true, he replied.

Then how can he who has magnificence of mind and is the spectator of all time and all existence, think much of human life?

He cannot.

Or can such an one account death fearful?

No indeed.

Then the cowardly and mean nature has no part in true philosophy?

Certainly not.

Or again: can he who is harmoniously constituted, who is not covetous or mean, or a boaster, or a coward—can he, I say, ever be unjust or hard in his dealings?

Impossible.

Then you will soon observe whether a man is just and gentle, or rude and unsociable; these are the signs which distinguish even in youth the philosophical nature from the unphilosophical.

True.

There is another point which should be remarked.

What point?

Whether he has or has not a pleasure in learning; for no one will love that which gives him pain, and in which after much toil he makes little progress.

Certainly not.

And again, if he is forgetful and retains nothing of what he learns, will he not be an empty vessel?

That is certain.

Labouring in vain, he must end in hating himself and his fruitless occupation?

Yes.

Then a soul which forgets cannot be ranked among genuine philosophic natures; we must insist that the philosopher should have a good memory?

Certainly.

And once more, the inharmonious and unseemly nature can only tend to disproportion?

Undoubtedly.

And do you consider truth to be akin to proportion or to disproportion?

To proportion.

Then, besides other qualities, we must try to find a naturally well-proportioned and gracious mind, which will move spontaneously towards the true being of everything.

Certainly.

Well, and do not all these qualities, which we have been enumerating, go together, and are they not, in a manner, necessary to a soul, which is to have a full and perfect participation of being?

They are absolutely necessary, he replied

And must not that be a blameless study which he only can pursue who has the gift of a good memory, and is quick to learn,—noble, gracious, the friend of truth, justice, courage, temperance, who are his kindred?

The god of jealousy himself, he said, could find no fault with such a study.

And to men like him, I said, when perfected by years and education, and to these only you will entrust the State. . . .

BOOK VII

And now, I [Socrates] said, let me show in a figure how far our nature is enlightened or un-enlightened:—Behold! human beings living in an underground den, which has a mouth open towards the light and reaching all along the den; here they have been from their childhood, and have their legs and necks chained so that they cannot move, and can only see before them, being prevented by the chains from turning round their heads. Above and behind them a fire is blazing at a distance, and between the fire and the prisoners there is a raised way; and you will see, if you look, a low wall built along the way, like the screen which marionette players have in front of them, over which they show the puppets.

I see.

And do you see, I said, men passing along the wall carrying all sorts of vessels, and statues and figures of animals made of wood and stone and various materials, which appear over the wall? Some of them are talking, others silent.

You have shown me a strange image, and they are strange prisoners.

Like ourselves, I replied; and they see only their own shadows, or the shadows of one another, which the fire throws on the opposite wall of the cave?

True, he said; how could they see anything but the shadows if they were never allowed to move their heads?

And of the objects which are being carried in like manner they would only see the shadows?

Yes, he said.

And if they were able to converse with one another, would they not suppose that they were naming what was actually before them?

Very true.

And suppose further that the prison had an echo which came from the other side, would they not be sure to fancy when one of the passers-by spoke that the voice which they heard came from the passing shadow?

No question, he replied.

To them, I said, the truth would be literally nothing but the shadows of the images.

That is certain.

And now look again, and see what will naturally follow if the prisoners are released and disabused of their error. At first, when any of them is liberated and compelled suddenly to stand up and turn his neck round and walk and look towards the light, he will suffer sharp pains; the glare will distress him, and he will be unable to see the realities of which in his former state he had seen the shadows; and then conceive some one saying to him, that what he saw before was an illusion, but that now, when he is approaching nearer to being and his eye is turned towards more real existence, he has a clearer vision,—what will be his reply? And you may further imagine that his instructor is pointing to the objects as they pass and requiring him to name them,—will he not be perplexed? Will he not fancy that the shadows which he formerly saw are truer than the objects which are now shown to him?

Far truer.

And if he is compelled to look straight at the light, will he not have a pain in his eyes which will make him turn away to take refuge in the objects of vision which he can see, and which he will conceive to be in reality clearer than the things which are now being shown to him?

True, he said.

And suppose once more, that he is reluctantly dragged up a steep and rugged ascent, and held fast until he is forced into the presence of the sun himself, is he not likely to be pained and irritated? When he approaches the light his eyes will be dazzled, and he will not be able to see anything at all of what are now called realities.

Not all in a moment, he said.

He will require to grow accustomed to the sight of the upper world. And first he will see the shadows best, next the reflections of men and other objects in the water, and then the objects themselves; then he will gaze upon the light of the moon and the stars and the spangled heaven; and he will see the sky and the stars by night better than the sun or the light of the sun by day?

Certainly.

Last of all he will be able to see the sun, and not mere reflections of him in the water, but he will see him in his own proper place, and not in another; and he will contemplate him as he is.

Certainly.

He will then proceed to argue that this is he who gives the season and the years, and is the guardian of all that is in the visible world, and in a certain way the cause of all things which he and his fellows have been accustomed to behold?

Clearly, he said, he would first see the sun and then reason about him.

And when he remembered his old habitation, and the wisdom of the den and his fellow-prisoners, do you not suppose that he would felicitate himself on the change, and pity them?

Certainly, he would.

And if they were in the habit of conferring honours among themselves on those who were quickest to observe the passing shadows and to remark which of them went before, and which followed after, and which were together; and who were therefore best able to draw conclusions as to the future, do you think that he would care for such honours and glories, or envy the possessors of them? Would he not say with Homer,

> Better to be the poor servant of a poor master,

and to endure anything, rather than think as they do and live after their manner?

Yes, he said, I think that he would rather suffer anything than entertain these false notions and live in this miserable manner.

Imagine once more, I said, such an one coming suddenly out of the sun to be replaced in his old situation; would he not be certain to have his eyes full of darkness?

To be sure, he said.

And if there were a contest, and he had to compete in measuring the shadows with the prisoners who had never moved out of the den, while his sight was still weak, and before his eyes had become steady (and the time which would be needed to acquire this new habit of sight might be very considerable), would he not be ridiculous? Men would say of him that up he went and down he came without his eyes; and that it was better not even to think of ascending; and if any one tried to loose another and lead him up to the light, let them only catch the offender, and they would put him to death.

No question, he said.

This entire allegory, I said, you may now append, dear Glaucon, to the previous argument; the prison-house is the world of sight, the light of the fire is the sun, and you will not misapprehend me if you interpret the journey upwards to be the ascent of the soul into the intellectual world according to my poor belief, which, at your desire, I have expressed—whether rightly or wrongly God knows. But, whether true or false, my opinion is that in the world of knowledge the idea of good appears last of all, and is seen only with an effort; and, when seen, is also inferred to be the universal author of all things beautiful and right, parent of light and of lord of light in this visible world, and the immediate source of reason and truth in the intellectual; and that this is the power upon which he who would act rationally either in public or private life, must have his eye fixed.

I agree, he said, as far as I am able to understand you.

Moreover, I said, you must not wonder that those who attain to this beatific vision are unwilling to descend to human affairs; for their souls are ever hastening into the upper world where they desire to dwell; which desire of theirs is very natural, if our allegory may be trusted.

Yes, very natural.

And is there anything surprising in one who passes from divine contemplations to the evil state of man, misbehaving himself in a ridiculous manner; if, while his eyes are blinking and before he has become accustomed to the surrounding darkness, he is compelled to fight in courts of law, or in other places, about the images or the shadows of images of justice, and is endeavouring to meet the conceptions of those who have never yet seen absolute justice?

Anything but surprising, he replied.

Any one who has common sense will remember that the bewilderments of the eyes are of two kinds, and arise from two causes, either from coming out of the light or from going into the light, which is true of the mind's eye, quite as much as of the bodily eye; and he who remembers this when he sees any one whose vision is perplexed and weak, will not be too ready to laugh; he will first ask whether that soul of man has come out of the brighter life, and is unable to see because unaccustomed to the dark, or having turned from darkness to the day is dazzled by excess of light. And he will count the one happy in his condition and state of being, and he will pity the other; or, if he have a mind to laugh at the soul which comes from below into the light, there will be more reason in this than in the laugh which greets him who returns from above out of the light into the den.

That, he said, is a very just distinction.

But then, if I am right, certain professors of education must be wrong when they say that they can put a knowledge into the soul which was not there before, like sight into blind eyes.

They undoubtedly say this, he replied.

Whereas, our argument shows that the power and capacity of learning exists in the soul already; and that just as the eye was unable to turn from darkness to light without the whole body, so too the instrument of knowledge can only by the movement of the whole soul be turned from the world of becoming into that of being, and learn by degrees to endure the sight of being, and of the brightest and best of being, or in other words, of the good.

Very true.

And must there not be some art which will effect conversion in the easiest and quickest manner; not implanting the faculty of sight; for that exists already, but has been turned in the wrong direction, and is looking away from the truth?

Yes, he said, such an art may be presumed.

And whereas the other so-called virtues of the soul seem to be akin to bodily qualities, for even when they are not originally innate they can be implanted later by habit and exercise, the virtue of wisdom more than anything else contains a divine element which always remains, and by this conversion is rendered useful and profitable; or, on the other hand, hurtful and useless. Did you never observe the narrow intelligence flashing from the keen eye of a clever rogue—how eager he is, how clearly his paltry soul sees the way to his end; he is the reverse of blind, but his keen eye-sight is forced into the service of evil, and he is mischievous in proportion to his cleverness?

Very true, he said.

But what if there had been a circumcision of such natures in the days of their youth; and they had been severed from those sensual pleasures, such as eating and drinking, which, like leaden weights, were attached to them at their birth, and which drag them down and turn the vision of their souls upon the things that are below—if, I say, they had been released from these impediments and turned in the opposite direction, the very same faculty in them would have seen the truth as keenly as they see what their eyes are turned to now.

Very likely.

Yes, I said; and there is another thing which is likely, or rather a necessary inference from what has preceded, that neither the uneducated and uninformed of the truth, nor yet those who never make an end of their education, will be able ministers of State; not the former, because they have no single aim of duty which is the rule of all their actions, private as well as public; nor the latter because they will not act at all except upon compulsion, fancying that they are already dwelling apart in the islands of the blest.

Very true, he replied.

Then, I said, the business of us who are the founders of the State will be to compel the best minds to attain that knowledge which we have already shown to be the greatest of all—they must continue to ascend until they arrive at the good; but when they have ascended and seen enough we must not allow them to do as they do now.

What do you mean?

I mean that they remain in the upper world: but this must not be allowed; they must be made to descend again among the prisoners in the den, and partake of their labours and honours, whether they are worth having or not.

But is not this unjust? he said; ought we to give them a life, when they might have a better?

You have again forgotten, my friend, I said, the intention of the legislator, who did not aim at making any one class in the State happy above the rest; the happiness was to be in the whole State, and he held the citizens together by persuasion and necessity, making them benefactors of the State, and therefore benefactors of one another; to this end he created them, not to please themselves, but to be his instruments in binding up the State.

True, he said, I had forgotten.

from the Laws

BOOK I

Ath. . . . At the outset of the discussion, let me define the nature and power of education; for this is the way by which our argument must travel onwards to the God Dionysus.

Cle. Let us proceed, if you please.

Ath. Well, then, if I tell you what are my notions of education, will you consider whether they satisfy you?

Cle. Let us hear.

Ath. According to my view, any one who would be good at anything must practise that thing from his youth upwards, both in sport and earnest, in its several branches: for example, he who is to be a good builder, should play at building children's houses; he who is to be a good husbandman, at tilling the ground; and those who have the care of their education should provide them when young with mimic tools. They should learn beforehand the knowledge which they will afterwards require for their art. For example, the future carpenter should learn to measure or apply the line in play; and the future warrior should learn riding, or some other exercise, for amusement, and the teacher should endeavour to direct the children's inclinations and pleasures, by the help of amusements, to their final aim in life. The most important part of education is right training in the nursery. The soul of the child in his play should be guided to the love of that sort of excellence in which when he grows up to manhood he will have to be perfected. Do you agree with me thus far?

Cle. Certainly.

Ath. Then let us not leave the meaning of education ambiguous or ill-defined. At present, when we speak in terms of praise or blame about the bringing-up of each person, we call one man educated and another uneducated, although the uneducated man may be sometimes very well educated for the calling of a retail trader, or of a captain of a ship, and the like. For we are not speaking of education in this narrower sense, but of that other education in virtue from youth upwards, which makes a man eagerly pursue the ideal perfection of citizenship, and teaches him how rightly to rule and how to obey. This is the only education which, upon our view, deserves the name; that other sort of training, which aims at the acquisition of wealth or bodily strength, or mere cleverness apart from intelligence and justice, is mean and illiberal, and is not worthy to be called education at all. But let us not quarrel with one another about a word, provided that the proposition which has just been granted hold good: to wit, that those who are rightly educated generally become good men. Neither must we cast a slight upon education, which is the first and fairest thing that the best of men can ever have, and which, though liable to take a wrong direction, is capable of reformation. And this work of reformation is the great business of every man while he lives. . . .

BOOK VII

Ath. Education has two branches,—one of gymnastic, which is concerned with the body, and the other of music, which is designed for the improvement of the soul. And gymnastic has also two branches—dancing and wrestling; and one sort of dancing imitates musical recitation, and aims at preserving dignity and freedom, the other aims at producing health, agility, and beauty in the limbs and parts of the body, giving the proper flexion and extension to each of them, a harmonious motion being diffused everywhere, and forming a suitable accompaniment to the dance. As regards wrestling, the tricks which Antaeus and Cercyon devised in their systems out of a vain spirit of competition, or the tricks of boxing which Epeius or Amycus invented, are useless and unsuitable for war, and do not deserve to have much said about them; but the art of wrestling erect and keeping free the neck and hands and sides, working with energy and constancy, with a composed strength, and for the sake of health—these are always useful, and are not to be neglected, but to be enjoined alike on masters and scholars, when we reach that part of legislation; and we will desire the one to give their instructions freely, and the others to receive them thankfully. Nor, again, must we omit suitable imitations of war in our choruses; here in Crete you have the armed dances of the Curetes, and the Lacedaemonians have those of the Dioscuri. And our virgin lady, delighting in the amusement of the dance, thought it not fit to amuse herself with empty hands; she must be clothed in a complete suit of armour, and in this attire go through the dance; and youths and maidens should in every respect imitate her, esteeming highly the favour of the Goddess, both with a view to the necessities of war, and to festive occasions: it will be right also for the boys, until such time as they go out to war, to make processions and supplications to all the Gods in goodly array, armed and on horseback, in dances, and marches, fast or slow, offering up prayers to the Gods and to the sons of Gods; and also engaging in contests and preludes of contests, if at all, with these objects. For these sorts of exercises, and no others, are useful both in peace and war, and are beneficial alike to states and to private houses. But other labours and sports and exercises of the body are unworthy of freemen, O Megillus and Cleinias.

I have now completely described the kind of gymnastic which I said at first ought to be described; if you know of any better, will you communicate your thoughts?

Cle. It is not easy, Stranger, to put aside these principles of gymnastic and wrestling and to enunciate better ones.

Ath. Now we must say what has yet to be said about the gifts of the Muses and of Apollo: before, we fancied that we had said all, and that gymnastic alone remained; but now we see clearly what points have been omitted, and should be first proclaimed; of these, then, let us proceed to speak.

Cle. By all means.

Ath. Let me tell you once more—although you have heard me say the same before—that caution must be always exercised, both by the speaker and by the hearer, about anything that is very singular and unusual. For my tale is one which many a man would be afraid to tell, and yet I have a confidence which makes me go on.

Cle. What have you to say, Stranger?

Ath. I say that in states generally no one has observed that the plays of childhood have a great deal to do with the permanence or want of permanence in legislation. For when plays are ordered with a view to children having the same plays, and amusing themselves after the same manner, and finding delight in the same playthings, the more solemn institutions of the state are allowed to remain undisturbed. Whereas if sports are disturbed, and innovations are made in them, and they constantly change, and the young never speak of their having the same likings, or the same established notions of good and bad taste, either in the bearing of their bodies or in their dress, but he who devises something new and out of the way in figures and colours and the like is held in special honour, we may truly say that no greater evil can happen in a state; for he who changes the sports is secretly changing the manners of the young, and making the old to be dishonoured among them and the new to he honoured. And I affirm that there is nothing which is a greater injury to all states than saying or thinking thus. Will you hear me tell how great I deem the evil to be?

Cle. You mean the evil of blaming antiquity in states?

Ath. Exactly.

Cle. If you are speaking of that, you will find in us hearers who are disposed to receive what you say not unfavourably but most favourably.

Ath. I should expect so.

Cle. Proceed.

Ath. Well, then, let us give all the greater heed to one another's words. The argument affirms that any change whatever except from evil is the most dangerous of all things; this is true in the case of the seasons and of the winds, in the management of our bodies and the habits of our minds—true of all things except, as I said before, of the bad. He who looks at the constitution of individuals accustomed to eat any sort of meat, or drink any drink, or to do any work which they can get, may see that they are at first disordered by them, but afterwards, as time goes on, their bodies grow adapted to them, and they learn to know and like variety, and have good health and enjoyment of life; and if ever afterwards they are confined again to a superior diet, at first they are troubled with disorders, and with difficulty become habituated to their new food. A similar principle we may imagine to hold good about the minds of men and the natures of their souls. For when they have been brought up in certain laws, which by some Divine Providence have remained unchanged during long ages, so that no one has any memory or tradition of their ever having been otherwise than they are, then every one is afraid and ashamed to change that which is established. The legislator must somehow find a way of implanting this reverence for antiquity, and I would propose the following way:—People are apt to fancy, as I was saying before, that when the plays of children are altered they are merely plays, not seeing that the most serious and detrimental consequences arise out of the change; and they readily comply with the child's wishes instead of deterring him, not considering that these children who make innovations in their games, when they grow up to be men, will be different from the last generation of children, and, being different, will desire a different sort of life, and under the influence of this desire will want other institutions and laws; and no one of them reflects that there will follow what I just now called the greatest of evils to states. Changes in bodily fashions are no such serious evils, but frequent changes in the praise and censure of manners are the greatest of evils, and require the utmost prevision.

Cle. To be sure.

Ath. And now do we still hold to our former assertion, that rhythms and music in general are imitations of good and evil characters in men? What say you?

Cle. That is the only doctrine which we can admit.

Ath. Must we not, then, try in every possible way to prevent our youth from even desiring to imitate new modes either in dance or song? nor must any one be allowed to offer them varieties of pleasures.

Cle. Most true.

Ath. Can any of us imagine a better mode of effecting this object than that of the Egyptians?

Cle. What is their method?

Ath. To consecrate every sort of dance or melody. First we should ordain festivals,—calculating for the year what they ought to be, and at what time, and in honour of what Gods, sons of Gods, and heroes they ought to be celebrated; and, in the next place, what hymns ought to be sung at the several sacrifices, and with what dances the particular festival is to be honoured. This has to be arranged at first by certain persons, and, when arranged, the whole assembly of the citizens are to offer sacrifices and libations to the Fates and all the other Gods, and to consecrate the several odes to Gods and heroes: and if any one offers any other hymns or dances to any one of the Gods, the priests and priestesses, acting in concert with the guardians of the law, shall, with the sanction of religion and the law, exclude him, and he who is excluded, if he do not submit, shall be liable all his life long to have a suit of impiety brought against him by any one who likes.

Cle. Very good.

Ath. In the consideration of this subject, let us remember what is due to ourselves.

Cle. To what are you referring?

Ath. I mean that any young man, and much more any old one, when he sees or hears anything strange or unaccustomed, does not at once run to embrace the paradox, but he stands considering, like a person who is at a place where three paths meet, and does not very well know his way—he may be alone or he may be walking with others, and he will say to himself and them, 'Which is the way?' and will not move forward until he is satisfied that he is going right. And this is what we must do in the present instance:—A strange discussion on the subject of law has arisen, which requires the utmost consideration, and we should not at our age be too ready to speak about such great matters, or be confident that we can say anything certain all in a moment.

Cle. Most true.

Ath. Then we will allow time for reflection, and decide when we have given the subject sufficient consideration. But that we may not be hindered from completing the natural arrangement of our laws, let us proceed to the conclusion of them in due order; for very possibly, if God will, the exposition of them, when completed, may throw light on our present perplexity.

Cle. Excellent, Stranger; let us do as you propose.

Ath. Let us then affirm the paradox that strains of music are our laws [νόμοι], and this latter being the name which the ancients gave to lyric songs, they probably would not have very much objected to our proposed application of the word. Some one, either asleep or awake, must have had a dreamy suspicion of their nature. And let our decree be as follows:—No one in singing or dancing shall offend against public and consecrated models, and the general fashion among the youth, any more than he would offend against any other law. And he who observes this law shall be blameless; but he who is disobedient, as I was saying, shall be punished by the guardians of the laws, and by the priests and priestesses. Suppose that we imagine this to be our law.

Cle. Very good.

Ath. Can any one who makes such laws escape ridicule? Let us see. I think that our only safety will be in first framing certain models for composers. One of these models shall be as follows:—If when a sacrifice is going on, and the victims are being burnt according to law,—if, I say, any one who may be a son or brother, standing by another at the altar and over the victims, horribly blasphemes, will not his words inspire despondency and evil omens and forebodings in the mind of his father and of his other kinsmen?

Cle. Of course.

Ath. And this is just what takes place in almost all our cities. A magistrate offers a public sacrifice, and there come in not one but many choruses, who take up a position a little way from the altar, and from time to time pour forth all sorts of horrible blasphemies on the sacred rites, exciting the souls of the audience with words and rhythms and melodies most sorrowful to hear; and he who at the moment when the city is offering sacrifice makes the citizens weep most, carries away the palm of victory. Now, ought we not to forbid such strains as these? And if ever our citizens must hear such lamentations, then on some unblest and inauspicious day let there be choruses of foreign and hired minstrels, like those hirelings who accompany the departed at funerals with barbarous Carian chants. That is the sort of thing which will be appropriate if we have such strains at all; and let the apparel of the singers be, not circlets and ornaments of gold, but the reverse. Enough of all this. I will simply ask once more whether we shall lay down as one of our principles of song

Cle. What?

Ath. That we should avoid every word of evil omen; let that kind of song which is of good omen be heard everywhere and always in our state. I need hardly ask again, but shall assume that you agree with me.

Cle. By all means; that law is approved by the suffrages of us all.

Ath. But what shall be our next musical law or type? Ought not prayers to be offered up to the Gods when we sacrifice?

Cle. Certainly.

Ath. And our third law, if I am not mistaken, will be to the effect that our poets, understanding prayers to be requests which we make to the Gods, will take especial heed that they do not by mistake ask for evil instead of good. To make such a prayer would surely be too ridiculous.

Cle. Very true.

Ath. Were we not a little while ago quite convinced that no silver or golden Plutus should dwell in our state?

Cle. To be sure.

Ath. And what has it been the object of our argument to show? Did we not imply that the poets are not always quite capable of knowing what is good or evil? And if one of them utters a mistaken prayer in song or words, he will make our citizens pray for the opposite of what is good in matters of the highest import; than which, as I was saying, there can be few greater mistakes. Shall we then propose as one of our laws and models relating to the Muses—

Cle. What?—will you explain the law more precisely?

Ath. Shall we make a law that the poet shall compose nothing contrary to the ideas of the lawful, or just, or beautiful, or good, which are allowed in the state? nor shall he be permitted to communicate his compositions to any private individuals, until he shall have shown them to the appointed judges and the guardians of the law, and they are satisfied with them. As to the persons whom we appoint to be our legislators about music and as to the director of education, these have been already indicated. Once more then, as I have asked more than once, shall this be our third law, and type, and model—What do you say?

Cle. Let it be so, by all means.

Ath. Then it will be proper to have hymns and praises of the Gods, intermingled with prayers; and after the Gods prayers and praises should be offered in like manner to demigods and heroes, suitable to their several characters.

Cle. Certainly.

Ath. In the next place there will be no objection to a law, that citizens who are departed and have done good and energetic deeds, either with their souls or with their bodies, and have been obedient to the laws, should receive eulogies; this will be very fitting.

Cle. Quite true.

Ath. But to honour with hymns and panegyrics those who are still alive is not safe; a man should run his course, and make a fair ending, and then we will praise him; and let praise be given equally to women as well as men who have been distinguished in virtue. The order of songs and dances shall be as follows :—There are many ancient musical compositions and dances which are excellent, and from these the newly-founded city may freely select what is proper and suitable; and they shall choose judges of not less than fifty years of age, who shall make the selection, and any of the old poems which they deem sufficient they shall include; any that are deficient or altogether unsuitable, they shall either utterly throw aside, or examine and amend, taking into their counsel poets and musicians, and making use of their poetical genius; but explaining to them the wishes of the legislator in order that they may regulate dancing, music, and all choral strains, according to the mind of the judges; and not allowing them to indulge, except in some few matters, their individual pleasures and fancies. Now the irregular strain of music is always made ten thousand times better by attaining to law and order, and rejecting the honeyed Muse—not however that we mean wholly to exclude pleasure, which is the characteristic of all music. And if a man be brought up from childhood to the age of discretion and maturity in the use of the orderly and severe music, when he hears the opposite he detests it, and calls it illiberal; but if trained in the sweet and vulgar music, he deems the severer kind cold and displeasing. So that, as I was saying before, while he who hears them gains no more pleasure from the one than from the other, the one has the advantage of making those who are trained in it better men, whereas the other makes them worse.

Cle. Very true.

Ath. Again, we must distinguish and determine on some general principle what songs are suitable to women, and what to men, and must assign to them their proper melodies and rhythms. It is shocking for a whole harmony to be inharmonical, or for a rhythm to be unrhythmical, and this will happen when the melody is inappropriate to them. And therefore the legislator must assign to these also their forms. Now both sexes have melodies and rhythms which of necessity belong to them; and those of women are clearly enough indicated by their natural difference. The grand, and that which tends to courage, may be fairly called manly; but that which inclines to moderation and temperance, may be declared both in law and in ordinary speech to be the more womanly quality. This, then, will be the general order of them.

Let us now speak of the manner of teaching and imparting them and the persons to whom, and the time when, they are severally to be imparted. As the shipwright first lays down the lines of the keel, and thus, as it were, draws the ship in outline, so do I seek to distinguish the patterns of life, and lay down their keels according to the nature of different men's souls; seeking truly to consider by what means, and in what ways, we may go through the voyage of life best. Now human affairs are hardly worth considering in earnest, and yet we must be in earnest about them,—a sad necessity constrains us. And having got thus far, there will be a fitness in our completing the matter, if we can only find some suitable method, of doing so. But what do I mean? Some one may ask this very question, and quite rightly, too.

Cle. Certainly.

Ath. I say that about serious matters a man should be serious, and about a matter which is not serious he should not be serious; and that God is the natural and worthy object of our most serious and blessed endeavours, for man, as I said before, is made to be the plaything of God, and this, truly considered, is the best of him ; wherefore also every man and woman should walk seriously, and pass life in the noblest of pastimes, and be of another mind from what they are at present.

Cle. In what respect?

Ath. At present they think that their serious pursuits should be for the sake of their sports, for they deem war a serious pursuit, which must be managed well for the sake of peace; but the truth is, that there neither is, nor has been, nor ever will be, either amusement or instruction in any degree worth speaking of in war, which is neverthe-less deemed by us to be the most serious of our pursuits. And therefore, as we say, every one of us should live the life of peace as long and as well as he can. And what is the right way of living? Are we to live in sports always? If so, in what kind of sports? We ought to live sacrificing, and singing, and dancing, and then a man will be able to propitiate the Gods, and to defend himself against his enemies and conquer them in battle. The type of song or dance by which he will propitiate them has been described, and the paths along which he is to proceed have been cut for him. He will go forward in the spirit of the poet:—

Telemachus, some things thou wilt thyself find in thy heart, but other things God will suggest; for I deem that thou wast not born or brought up without the will of the Gods.[1]

And this ought to be the view of our alumni; they ought to think that what has been said is enough for them, and that any other things their Genius and God will suggest to them—he will tell them to whom, and when, and to what Gods severally they are to sacrifice and perform dances, and how they may propitiate the deities, and live according to the appointment of nature; being for the most part puppets, but having some little share of reality.

Meg. You have a low opinion of mankind, Stranger.

Ath. Nay, Megillus, be not amazed, but forgive me:—I was comparing them with the Gods; and under that feeling I spoke. Let us grant, if you wish, that the human race is not to be despised, but is worthy of some consideration.

Next follow the buildings for gymnasia and schools open to all; these are to be in three places in the midst of the city; and outside the city and in the surrounding country, also in three places, there shall be schools for horse exercise, and large grounds arranged with a view to archery and the throwing of missiles, at which young men may learn and practise. Of these mention has already been made; and if the mention be not sufficiently explicit, let us speak further of them and embody them in laws. In these several schools let there be dwellings for teachers, who shall be brought from foreign parts by pay, and let them teach those who attend the schools the art of war and the art of music, and the children shall come not only if their parents please, but if they do not please; there shall be compulsory education, as the saying is, of all and sundry, as far as this is possible; and the pupils shall be regarded as belonging to the state rather than to their parents. My law would apply to females as well as males; they shall both go through the same exercises. I assert without fear of contradiction that gymnastic and horsemanship are as suitable to women as to men. Of the truth of this I am persuaded from ancient tradition, and at the present day there are said to be countless myriads of women in the neighbourhood of the Black Sea, called Sauromatides, who not only ride on horseback like men, but have enjoined upon them the use of bows and other weapons equally with the men. And I further affirm, that if these things are possible, nothing can be more absurd than the practice which prevails in our own country, of men and women not following the same pursuits with all their strength and with one mind, for thus the state, instead of being a whole, is reduced to a half, but has the same imposts to pay and the same toils to undergo; and what can be a greater mistake for any legislator to make than this?

Cle. Very true; yet much of what has been asserted by us, Stranger, is contrary to the custom of states; still, in saying that the discourse should be allowed to proceed, and that when the discussion is completed, we should choose what seems best, you spoke very properly, and I now feel compunction for what I have said. Tell me, then, what you would next wish to say.

---

1. Homer, *Odyssey*, iii. 26 foll.

Ath. I should wish to say, Cleinias, as I said before, that if the possibility of these things were not sufficiently proven in fact, then there might be an objection to the argument, but the fact being as I have said, he who rejects the law must find some other ground of objection; and, failing this, our exhortation will still hold good, nor will any one deny that women ought to share as far as possible in education and in other ways with men. For consider;—if women do not share in their whole life with men, then they must have some other order of life.

Cle. Certainly.

Ath. And what arrangement of life to be found anywhere is preferable to this community which we are now assigning to them? Shall we prefer that which is adopted by the Thracians and many other races who use their women to till the ground and to be shepherds of their herds and flocks, and to minister to them like slaves?—Or shall we do as we and people in our part of the world do—getting together, as the phrase is, all our goods and chattels into one dwelling, we entrust them to our women, who are the stewards of them, and who also preside over the shuttles and the whole art of spinning? Or shall we take a middle course, as in Lacedaemon, Megnius—letting the girls share in gymnastic and music, while the grown-up women, no longer employed in spinning wool, are hard at work weaving the web of life, which will be no cheap or mean employment, and in the duty of serving and taking care of the household and bringing up children, in which they will observe a sort of mean, not participating in the toils of war; and if there were any necessity that they should fight for their city and families, unlike the Amazons, they would be unable to take part in archery or any other skilled use of missiles, nor could they, after the example of the Goddess, carry shield or spear, or stand up nobly for their country when it was being destroyed, and strike terror into their enemies, if only because they were seen in regular order? Living as they do, they would never dare at all to imitate the Sauromatides, who, when compared with ordinary women, would appear to be like men. Let him who will, praise your legislators, but I must say what I think. The legislator ought to be whole and perfect, and not half a man only; he ought not to let the female sex live softly and waste money and have no order of life, while he takes the utmost care of the male sex, and leaves half of life only blest with happiness, when he might have made the whole state happy.

Meg. What shall we do, Cleinias? Shall we allow a stranger to run down Sparta in this fashion?

Cle. Yes; for as we have given him liberty of speech we must let him go on until we have perfected the work of legislation.

Meg. Very true.

Ath. Then now I may proceed?

Cle. By all means.

Ath. What will be the manner of life among men who may be supposed to have their food and clothing provided for them in moderation, and who have entrusted the practice of the arts to others, and whose husbandry, committed to slaves paying a part of the produce, brings them a return sufficient for men living temperately; who, moreover, have common tables in which the men are placed apart, and near them are the common tables of their families, of their daughters and mothers, which day by day, the officers, male and female, are to inspect—they shall see to the behaviour of the company, and so dismiss them; after which the presiding magistrate and his attendants shall honour with libations those Gods to whom that day and night are dedicated, and then go home? To men whose lives are thus ordered, is there no work remaining to be done which is necessary and fitting, but shall each one of them live fattening like a beast? Such a life is neither just nor honourable, nor can he who lives it fail of meeting his due; and the due reward of the idle fatted beast is that he should be torn in pieces by some other valiant beast whose fatness is worn down by brave deeds and toil. These regulations, if we duly consider them, will never be exactly carried into execution under present circumstances, nor as long as women and children and houses and all other things are the private property of individuals; but if we can attain the second-best form of polity, we shall be very well off. And to men living under this second polity there remains a work to be accomplished which is far from being small or insignificant, but is the greatest of all works, and ordained by the appointment of righteous law. For the life which may be truly said to be concerned with the virtue of body and soul is twice, or more than twice, as full of toil and trouble as the pursuit after Pythian and Olympic victories, which debars a man from every employment of life. For there ought to be no bye-work interfering with the greater work of providing the necessary exercise and nourishment for the body, and instruction and education for the soul. Night and day are not long enough for the accomplishment of their perfection and consummation; and therefore to this end all freemen ought to arrange the way in which they will spend their time during the whole course of the day, from morning till evening and from evening till the morning of the next sunrise. There may seem to be some impropriety in the legislator determining minutely the numberless details of the management of the house, including such particulars as the duty of wakefulness in those who are to be perpetual watchmen of the whole city; for that any citizen should continue during the whole of any night in sleep, instead of being seen by all his servants, always the first to awake and get up—this, whether the regulation is to be called a law or only a practice, should be deemed base and unworthy of a freeman; also that the mistress of the house should be awakened by her handmaidens instead of herself first awakening them, is what the slaves, male and female, and the serving-boys, and, if that were possible, everybody and everything in the house should regard as base. If they rise early, they may all of them do much of their public and of their household business, as magistrates in the city, and masters and mistresses in their private houses, before the sun is up. Much sleep is not required by nature, either for our souls or bodies, or for the actions which they perform. For no one who is asleep is good for anything, any more than if he were dead; but he of us who has the most regard for life and reason keeps awake as long as he can, reserving only so much time for sleep as is expedient for health; and much sleep is not required, if the habit of moderation be once rightly formed. Magistrates in states who keep awake at night are terrible to the bad, whether enemies or citizens, and are honoured and reverenced by the just and temperate, and are useful to themselves and to the whole state.

A night which is passed in such a manner, in addition to all the above-mentioned advantages, infuses a sort of courage into the minds of the citizens. When the day breaks, the time has arrived for youth to go to their schoolmasters. Now neither sheep nor any other animals can live without a shepherd, nor can children be left without tutors, or slaves without masters. And of all animals the boy is the most unmanageable, inasmuch as he has the fountain of reason in him not yet regulated; he is the most insidious, sharp-witted, and insubordinate of animals. Wherefore he must be bound with many bridles; in the first place, when he gets away from mothers and nurses, he must be under the management of tutors on account of his childishness and foolishness; then, again, being a freeman, he must be controlled by teachers, no matter what they teach, and by studies; but he is also a slave, and in that regard any freeman who comes in his way may punish him and his tutor and his instructor, if any of them does anything wrong; and he who comes across him and does not inflict upon him the punishment which he deserves, shall incur the greatest disgrace; and let the guardian of the law, who is the director of education, see to him who coming in the way of, the offences which we have mentioned; does not chastise them when he ought, or chastises them in a way which he ought not; let him keep a sharp look-out, and take especial care of the training of our children, directing their natures, and always turning them to good according to the law.

But how can our law sufficiently train the director of education himself; for as yet all has been imperfect, and nothing has been said either clear or satisfactory? Now, as far as possible, the law ought to leave nothing to him, but to explain everything, that he may be an interpreter and tutor to others. About dances and music and choral strains, I have already spoken both as to the character of the selection of them, and the manner in which they are to be amended and consecrated. But we have not as yet spoken, O illustrious guardian of education, of the manner in which your pupils are to ace those strains which are written in prose, although you have been informed what martial strains they are to learn and practise; what relates in the first place to the learning of letters, and secondly, to the lyre, and also to calculation, which, as we were saying, is needful for them all to learn, and any other things which are required with a view to war and the management of house and city, and, looking to the same object, what is useful in the revolutions of the heavenly bodies—the stars and sun and moon, and the various regulations about these matters which are necessary for the whole state—I am speaking of the arrangements of days in periods of months, and of months in years, which are to be observed, in order that seasons and sacrifices and festivals may have their regular and natural order, and keep the city alive and awake, the Gods receiving the honours due to them, and men having a better understanding about them: all these things, O my friend, have not yet been sufficiently declared to you by the legislator. Attend, then, to what I am now going to say:—We were telling you, in the first place, that you were not sufficiently informed about letters, and the objection was to this effect,—that you were never told whether he who was meant to be a respectable citizen should apply himself in detail to that sort of learning, or not apply himself at all; and the same remark holds good of the study of the lyre. But now we say that he ought to attend to them. A fair time for a boy of ten years old to spend in letters is three years; the age of thirteen is the proper time for him to begin to handle the lyre, and he may continue at this for another three years, neither more nor less, and whether his father or himself like or dislike the study, he is not to be allowed to spend more or less time in learning music than the law allows. And let him who disobeys the law be deprived of those youthful honours of which shall hereafter speak. Hear, however, first of all, what the young ought to learn in the early years of life, and what their instructors ought to teach them. They ought to be occupied with their letters until they are able to read and write; but the acquisition of perfect beauty or quickness in writing, if nature has not stimulated them to acquire these accomplishments in the given number of years, they should let alone. And as to the learning of compositions committed to writing which are not set to the lyre, whether metrical or without rhythmical divisions, compositions in prose, as they are termed, having no rhythm or harmony—seeing how dangerous are the writings handed down to us by many writers of this class—what will you do with them, O most excellent guardians of the law? or how can the lawgiver rightly direct you about them? I believe that he will be in great difficulty.

Cle. What troubles you, Stranger? and why are you so perplexed in your mind?

Ath. You naturally ask, Cleinias, and to you and Megillus, who are my partners in the work of legislation, I must state the more difficult as well as the easier parts of the task.

Cle. To what do you refer in this instance?

Ath. I will tell you. There is a difficulty in opposing many myriads of mouths.

Cle. Well, and have we not already opposed the popular voice in many important enactments?

Ath. That is quite true; and you mean to imply that the road which we are taking may be disagreeable to some but is agreeable to as many others, or if not to as many, at any rate to persons not inferior to the others, and in company with them you bid me, at whatever risk, to proceed along the path of legislation which has opened out of our present discourse, and to be of good cheer, and not to faint.

Cle. Certainly.

Ath. And I do not faint; I say, indeed, that we have a great many poets writing in hexameter, trimeter, and all sorts of measures—some who are serious, others who aim only at raising a laugh—and all mankind declare that the youth who are rightly educated should be brought up in them and saturated with them; some insist that they should be constantly hearing them read aloud, and always learning them, so as to get by heart entire poets; while others select choice passages and long speeches, and make compendiums of them, saying that these ought to be committed to memory, if a man is to be made good and wise by experience and learning of many things. And you want me now to tell them plainly in what they are right and in what they are wrong.

Cle. Yes, I do.

Ath. But how can I in one word rightly comprehend all of them? I am of opinion, and, if I am not mistaken, there is a general agreement, that every one of these poets has said many things well and many things the reverse of well; and if this be true, then I do affirm that much learning is dangerous to youth.

Cle. How would you advise the guardian of the law to act?

Ath. In what respect?

Cle. I mean to what pattern should he look as his guide in permitting the young to learn some things and forbidding them to learn others. Do not shrink from answering.

Ath. My good Cleinias, I rather think that I am fortunate.

Cle. How so?

Ath. I think that I am not wholly in want of a pattern, for when I consider the words which we have spoken from early dawn until now, and which, as I believe, have been inspired by Heaven, they appear to me to be quite like a poem. When I reflected upon all these words of ours, I naturally felt pleasure, for of all the discourses which I have ever learnt or heard, either in poetry or prose, this seemed to me to be the justest, and most suitable for young men to hear; I cannot imagine any better pattern than this which the guardian of the law who is also the director of education can have. He cannot do better than advise the teachers to teach the young these words and any which are of a like nature, if he should happen to find them, either in poetry or prose, or if he come across unwritten discourses akin to ours, he should certainly preserve them, and commit them to writing. And, first of all, he shall constrain the teachers themselves to learn and approve them, and any of them who will not, shall not be employed by him, but those whom he finds agreeing in his judgment, he shall make use of and shall commit to them the instruction and education of youth. And here and on this wise let my fanciful tale about letters and teachers of letters come to an end. . . .

Xenophon

c. 428–c. 354 B.C.

*Is it not clear . . . that through self-knowledge men come to much good,
and through self-deception to much harm? For those who know
themselves, know what things are expedient for themselves and
discern their own powers and limitations.*

MEMORABILIA

Xenophon, Greek soldier, historian, and prolific essayist, was born in Athens and studied under Socrates. Socrates' trial and execution turned Xenophon against his native city. He fought in the Peloponnesian War, served with the mercenary Greek forces that fought under Persia's Cyrus the Younger, and campaigned with the Spartans against Persia and then against his own Athens (which had banished him for his oligarchic views). Once Athens allied itself with Sparta against Thebes, it lifted Xenophon's banishment. His historical works include an account of the mercenaries under Cyrus (the *Anabasis*) and a continuation of Thucydides' history of the Peloponnesian War (the *Hellenica*). Xenophon was widely read and admired later by the Romans. His *Anabasis* was translated and published in most European languages in the sixteenth and seventeenth centuries.

THE SELECTION

In the *Memorabilia*, Xenophon pays tribute to his teacher Socrates, providing a different perspective from Plato's better-known account of their mentor. Book IV, excerpted here, demonstrates Socrates' wit and dialectical method. Socrates leads his student, destined for leadership, through the painful process of self-examination, turning him away from smug satisfaction with the mere appearance of wisdom and insisting that he follow the Delphic injunction to "know thyself." Socrates also warns against the potential distractions in other kinds of knowledge. Xenophon's educational ideals are also found in his *Cyropaedia* (Education of Cyrus the Great) and *Economics*.

from the Memorabilia
Book IV

Socrates was so useful in all circumstances and in all ways, that any observer gifted with ordinary perception can see that nothing was more useful than the companionship of Socrates, and time spent with him in any place and in any circumstances. The very recollection of him in absence brought no small good to his constant companions and followers; for even in his light moods they gained no less from his society than when he was serious.

Thus he would often say he was "in love"; but clearly his heart was set not on those who were fair to outward view, but on those whose souls excelled in goodness. These excellent beings he recognised by their quickness to learn whatever subject they studied, ability to remember what they learned, and desire for every kind of knowledge on which depend good management of a household and estate and tactful dealing with men and the affairs of men. For education would make such beings not only happy in themselves, and successful in the management of their households, but capable of conferring happiness on their fellow-men and on states alike. His method of approach varied. To those who thought themselves possessed of natural endowments and despised learning, he explained that the greater the natural gifts, the greater is the need of education; pointing out that thoroughbreds by their spirit and mettle develop into serviceable and splendid creatures, if they are broken in as colts, but if unbroken, prove intractable and sorry jades; and high-bred puppies, keen workers and good tacklers of game, make first-rate hounds and useful dogs, if well trained, but, if untrained, turn out stupid, crazy, disobedient brutes. It is the same with human beings. The most highly gifted, the youths of ardent soul, capable of doing whatever they attempt, if educated and taught their duty grow into excellent and useful men; for manifold and great are their good deeds. But untrained and untaught, these same become utterly evil and mischievous; for without knowledge to discern their duty, they often put their hand to vile deeds, and through the very grandeur and vehemence of their nature, they are uncontrollable and intractable: therefore manifold and great are their evil deeds.

Those who prided themselves on riches and thought they had no need of education, supposing that their wealth would suffice them for gaining the objects of their wishes and winning honour among men, he admonished thus. "Only a fool" he said, "can think it possible to distinguish between things useful and things harmful without learning: only a fool can think that without distinguishing these he will get all he wants by means of his wealth and be able to do what is expedient: only a simpleton can think that without the power to do what is expedient he is doing well and has made good or sufficient provision for his life: only a simpleton can think that by his wealth alone without knowledge he will be reputed good at something, or will enjoy a good reputation without being reputed good at anything in particular.

I will now show his method of dealing with those who thought they had received the best education, and prided themselves on wisdom. He was informed that Euthydemus, the handsome, had formed a large collection of the works of celebrated poets and professors, and therefore supposed himself to be a prodigy of wisdom for his age, and was confident of surpassing all competitors in power of speech and action. At present, Socrates observed, he did not enter the Market-place owing to his youth, but when he wanted to get anything done, he would be found sitting in a saddler's shop near the Market. So, to make an opening, Socrates went to this shop with some of his companions.

At the first visit, one of them asked: "Was it by constant intercourse with some wise man or by natural ability that Themistocles stood out among his fellow-citizens as the man to whom the people naturally looked when they felt the want of a great leader?"

In order to set Euthydemus thinking, Socrates said:

"If in the minor arts great achievement is impossible without competent masters, surely it is absurd to imagine that the art of statesmanship, the greatest of all accomplishments, comes to a man of its own accord."

Some time afterwards, meeting Euthydemus again, he saw that he was reluctant to join the circle and anxious not to betray any admiration for the wisdom of Socrates: "Well, gentlemen," said he, "when our friend Euthydemus has attained his full powers, and some question of policy is before the Assembly, he won't be backward in offering advice: that is obvious from his behaviour. I fancy he has prepared a noble exordium to his addresses, with due care not to give the impression that he is indebted to anyone for his knowledge. No doubt he will begin his speech with this introduction:

"'Men of Athens, I have never yet learnt anything from anyone, nor when I have been told of any man's ability in speech and in action, have I sought to meet him nor have I been at pains to find a teacher among the men who know. On the contrary, I have constantly avoided learning anything of anyone, and even the appearance of it. Nevertheless I shall recommend to your consideration anything that comes into my head.'

"This exordium might be adapted so as to suit candidates for the office of public physician. They might begin their speeches in this strain:

"'Men of Athens, I have never yet studied medicine, nor sought to find a teacher among our physicians; for I have constantly avoided learning anything from the physicians, and even the appearance of having studied their art. Nevertheless I ask you to appoint me to the office of a physician, and I will endeavour to learn by experimenting on you.'"

The exordium set all the company laughing.

Now when it became evident that Socrates had gained the attention of Euthydemus, but that Euthydemus still avoided breaking silence himself, and thought that he assumed an air of prudence by remaining dumb, Socrates wanted to put an end to that affectation. "How strange it is," he said, "that those who want to play the harp or the flute, or to ride or to get skill in any similar accomplishment, work hard at the art they mean to master, and not by themselves but under the tuition of the most eminent professors, doing and bearing anything in their anxiety to do nothing without their teachers' guidance, just because that is the only way to become proficient: and yet, among those who want to shine as speakers, in the Assembly and as statesmen, there are some who think that they will be able to do so on a sudden, by instinct, without training or study. Yet surely these arts are much the harder to learn; for many more are interested in them and far fewer succeed. Clearly then these arts demand a longer and more intense application than the others."

For a time, then, Socrates continued to talk in this strain, while Euthydemus listened. But on finding him more tolerant of his conversation and more attentive, Socrates went alone to the saddler's; and when Euthydemus had taken a seat beside him, he said: "Tell me, Euthydemus, am I rightly informed that you have a large collection of books written by the wise men of the past; as they are called?"

"By Zeus, yes, Socrates," answered he, "and I am still adding to it, to make it as complete as possible."

"By Hera," retorted Socrates, "I do admire you for valuing the treasures of wisdom above gold and silver. For you are evidently of opinion that, while gold and silver cannot make men better, the thoughts of the wise enrich their possessors with virtue."

Now Euthydemus was glad to hear this, for he guessed that in the opinion of Socrates he was on the road to wisdom. But Socrates, aware that he was pleased with his approbation, went on to say: "Tell me, Euthydemus, what kind of goodness do you want to get by collecting these books?"

And as Euthydemus was silent, considering what answer to give, "Possibly you want to be a doctor?" he guessed: "Medical treatises alone make a large collection."

"Oh no, not at all."

"But perhaps you wish to be an architect? One needs a well-stored mind for that too."

"No, indeed I don't."

"Well, perhaps you want to be a good mathematician, like Theodorus?"

"No, not that either."

"Well, perhaps you want to be an astronomer?" And as he again said no, "Perhaps a rhapsodist, then? They tell me you have a complete copy of Homer."

"Oh no, not at all; for your rhapsodists, I know, are consummate as reciters, but they are very silly fellows themselves."

Then Socrates exclaimed: "Surely, Euthydemus, you don't covet the kind of excellence that makes good statesmen and managers, competent rulers and benefactors of themselves and mankind in general?"

"Yes, I do, Socrates," answered Euthydemus, "that kind of excellence I greatly desire."

"Why," cried Socrates, "it is the noblest kind of excellence, the greatest of arts that you covet, for it belongs to kings and is dubbed 'kingly.' However," he added, "have you reflected whether it be possible to excel in these matters without being a just man?"

"Yes, certainly; and it is, in fact, impossible to be a good citizen without justice."

"Then tell me, have you got that?"

"Yes, Socrates, I think I can show myself to be as just as any man."

"And have just men, like carpenters, their works?"

"Yes, they have."

"And as carpenters can point out their works, should just men be able to rehearse theirs?"

"Do you suppose," retorted Euthydemus, "that I am unable to rehearse the works of justice? Of course I can,—and the works of injustice too, since there are many opportunities of seeing and hearing of them every day."

"I propose, then, that we write J in this column and I in that, and then proceed to place under these letters, J and I, what we take to be the works of justice and injustice respectively."

"Do so, if you think it helps at all."

Having written down the letters as he proposed, Socrates went on: "Lying occurs among men, does it not ?"

"Yes, it does."

"Under which heading, then, are we to put that?"

"Under the heading of injustice, clearly."

"Deceit, too, is found, is it not?"

"Certainly."

"Under which heading will that go?"

"Under injustice again, of course."

"What about doing mischief?"

"That too."

"Selling into slavery?"

"That too."

"Then we shall assign none of these things justice, Euthydemus?"

"No, it would be monstrous to do so."

"Now suppose a man who has been elected general enslaves an unjust and hostile city, shall we say that he acts unjustly?"

"Oh no!"

"We shall say that his actions are just, shall we not?"

"Certainly."

"And what if he deceives the enemy when at war?"

"That too is just."

"And if he steals and plunders their goods, will not his actions be just?"

"Certainly; but at first I assumed that your questions had reference only to friends."

Then everything we assigned to injustice should be assigned to justice also?"

"Apparently."

"Then I propose to revise our classification, and to say: It is just to do such things to enemies, but it is unjust to do them to friends, towards whom one's conduct should be scrupulously honest."

"By all means."

"Now suppose that a general, seeing that his army is downhearted, tells a lie and says that reinforcements are approaching, and by means of this lie checks discouragement among the men, under which heading shall we put this deception?"

"Under justice, I think."

"Suppose, again, that a man's son refuses to take a dose of medicine when he needs it, and the father induces him to take it by pretending that it is food, and cures him by means of this lie, where shall we put this deception?"

"That too goes on the same side, I think."

"And again, suppose one has a friend suffering from depression, and, for fear that he may make away with himself, one takes away his sword or something of the sort, under which heading shall we put that now?"

"That too goes under justice, of course."

"You mean, do you, that even with friends straightforward dealing is not invariably right?"

"It isn't, indeed! I retract what I said before, if you will let me."

"Why, I'm bound to let you; it's far better than getting our lists wrong. But now, consider deception practised on friends to their detriment: we mustn't overlook that either. Which is the more unjust deception in that case, the intentional or unintentional?"

"Nay, Socrates, I have lost all confidence in my answers; for all the opinions that I expressed before seem now to have taken an entirely different form. Still I venture to say that the intentional deception is more unjust than the unintentional."

"Do you think there is a doctrine and science of the just, as there is of letters?"

"Yes."

"Which, in your judgment, is the more literate, the man who intentionally blunders in writing and reading, or the man who blunders unintentionally?"

"The one who blunders intentionally, I presume; for he can always be accurate when he chooses."

"May we not say, then, that the intentional blunderer is literate and the unintentional is illiterate?"

"Indeed we must."

"And which knows what is just, the intentional liar and deceiver, or the unintentional?"

"The intentional, clearly."

"You say, then, as I understand, that he who knows letters is more literate than he who is ignorant of them?"

"Yes "

"And he who knows what is just is more just than he who does not know?"

"Apparently; but here again I don't feel sure of my own meaning."

"Now come, what do you think of the man who wants to tell the truth, but never sticks to what he says; when he shows you the way, tells you first that the road runs east, then that it runs west; and when he casts up figures, makes the total now larger, now smaller?"

"Why, I think he shows that he doesn't know what he thought he knew."

"Are you aware that some people are called slavish?"

"Yes."

"To what do they owe the name, to knowledge or to ignorance?"

"To ignorance, obviously."

"To ignorance of the smiths' trade, shall we say?"

"Certainly not."

"Ignorance of carpentry perhaps?"

"No, not to that either."

"Of cobbling?"

"No, to none of these: on the contrary, those who are skilled in such trades are for the most part slavish."

"Then is this name given to those who are ignorant of the beautiful and good and just?"

"That is my opinion."

"Then we must strain every nerve to escape being slaves."

"Upon my word, Socrates, I did feel confident that I was a student of a philosophy that would provide me with the best education in all things needful to one who would be a gentleman. But you can imagine my dismay when I realise that in spite of all my pains I am even incapable of answering a question about things that one is bound to know, and yet find no other way that will lead to my improvement."

Hereupon Socrates exclaimed: "Tell me, Euthydemus, have you ever been to Delphi?"

"Yes, certainly; twice."

"Then did you notice somewhere on the temple the inscription 'Know thyself'?"

"I did."

"And did you pay no heed to the inscription, or did you attend to it and try to consider who you were?"

"Indeed I did not; because I felt sure that I knew that already; for I could hardly know anything else if I did not even know myself."

"And what do you suppose a man must know to know himself, his own name merely? Or must he consider what sort of a creature he is for human use and get to know his own powers; just as those who buy horses don't think that they know the beast they want to know until they have considered whether he is docile or stubborn, strong or weak, fast or slow, and generally how he stands in all that makes a useful or a useless horse?"

"That leads me to think that he who does not know his own powers is ignorant of himself."

"Is it not clear too that through self-knowledge men come to much good, and through self-deception to much harm? For those who know themselves, know what things are expedient for themselves and discern their own powers and limitations. And by doing what they understand, they get what they want and prosper: by refraining from attempting what they do not understand, they make no mistakes and avoid failure. And consequently through their power of testing other men too, and through their intercourse with others, they get what is good and shun what is bad. Those who do not know and are deceived in their estimate of their own powers, are in the like condition with regard to other men and other human affairs. They know neither what they want, nor what they do, nor those with whom they have intercourse; but mistaken in all these respects, they miss the good and stumble into the bad. Furthermore, those who know what they do win fame and honour by attaining their ends. Their equals, are glad to have dealings with them; and those who miss their objects look to them for counsel, look to them for protection, rest on them their hopes of better things, and for all these reasons love them above all other men. But those who know not what they do, choose amiss, fail in what they attempt and, besides incurring direct loss and punishment thereby, they earn contempt through their failures, make themselves ridiculous and live in dishonour and humiliation.

"And the same is true of communities. You find that whenever a state, in ignorance of its own power, goes to war with a stronger people, it is exterminated or loses its liberty."

"Socrates," answered Euthydemus, "you may rest assured that I fully appreciate the importance of knowing oneself. But where should the process of self-examination begin? I look to you for a statement, please."

"Well," said Socrates, "I may assume, I take it, that you know what things are good and what are evil?"

"Of course, for if I don't know so much as that, I must be worse than a slave."

"Come then, state them for my benefit."

"Well, that's a simple matter. First health in itself is, I suppose, a good, sickness an evil. Next the various causes of these two conditions—meat, drink, habits—are good or evil according as they promote health or sickness."

"Then health and sickness too must be good when their effect is good, and evil when it is evil."

"But when can health possibly be the cause of evil, or sickness of good?"

"Why, in many cases; for instance, a disastrous campaign or a fatal voyage: the able-bodied who go are lost, the weaklings who stay behind are saved."

"True; but you see, in the successful adventures too the able-bodied take part, the weaklings are left behind."

"Then since these bodily conditions sometimes lead to profit, and sometimes to loss, are they any more good than evil?"

"No, certainly not; at least so it appears from the argument. But wisdom now, Socrates,—that at any rate is indisputably a good thing; for what is there that a wise man would not do better than a fool?"

"Indeed! have you not heard how Daedalus was seized by Minos because of his wisdom, and was forced to be his slave, and was robbed of his country and his liberty, and essaying to escape with his son, lost the boy and could not save himself, but was carried off to the barbarians and again lived as a slave there?"

"That is the story, of course."

"And have you not heard the story of Palamedes? Surely, for all the poets sing of him, how that he was envied for his wisdom and done to death by Odysseus."

"Another well-known tale!"

"And how many others, do you suppose, have been kidnapped on account of their wisdom, and haled off to the great King's court, and live in slavery there?"

"Happiness seems to be unquestionably a good, Socrates."

"It would be so, Euthydemus, were it not made up of goods that are questionable."

"But what element in happiness can be called in question?"

"None, provided we don't include in it beauty or Strength or wealth or glory or anything of the sort."

"But of course we shall do that. For how can anyone be happy without them?"

"Then of course we shall include the sources of much trouble to mankind. For many are ruined by admirers whose heads are turned at the sight of a pretty face; many are led by their strength to attempt tasks too heavy for them, and meet with serious evils: many by their wealth are corrupted, and fall victims to conspiracies; many through glory and political power have suffered great evils."

"Well now, if I am at fault in praising even happiness, I confess I know not what one should ask for in one's prayers."

"But perhaps you never even thought about these things, because you felt so confident that you knew them. However, as the state you are preparing yourself to direct is governed by the people, no doubt you know what popular government is?"

"I think so, certainly."

"Then do you suppose it possible to know popular government without knowing the people?"

"Indeed I don't."

"And do you know, then, what the people consists of?"

"I think so."

"Of what do you suppose it to consist?"

"The poorer classes, I presume."

"You know the poor, then?"

"Of course I do."

"And you know the rich too?"

"Yes, just as well as the poor."

"What kind of men do you call poor and rich respectively?"

"The poor, I imagine, are those who have not enough to pay for what they want; the rich those who have more than enough."

"Have you observed, then, that some who have very little not only find it enough, but even manage to save out of it, whereas others cannot live within their means, however large?"

"Yes, certainly—thanks for reminding me—I know, in fact, of some despots even who are driven to crime by poverty, just like paupers."

"Therefore, if that is so, we will include despots in the people, and men of small means, if they are thrifty, in the rich."

"I am forced to agree once more," cried Euthydemus, "evidently by my stupidity. I am inclined to think I had better hold my tongue, or I shall know nothing at all presently." And so he went away very dejected, disgusted with himself and convinced that he was indeed a slave.

Now many of those who were brought to this pass by Socrates, never went near him again and were regarded by him as mere blockheads. But Euthydemus guessed that, he would never be of much account unless he spent as much time as possible with Socrates. Henceforward, unless obliged to absent himself, he never left him, and even began to adopt some of his practices. Socrates, for his part, seeing how it was with him, avoided worrying him, and began to expound very plainly and clearly the knowledge that he thought most needful and the practices that he held to be most excellent. . . .

I think that I have said enough to show that Socrates stated his own opinion plainly to those who consorted with him: I will now show that he also took pains to make them independent in doing the work that they were fitted for. For I never knew a man who was so careful to discover what each of his companions knew. Whatever it befits a gentleman to know he taught most zealously, so far as his own knowledge extended; if he was not entirely familiar with a subject, he took them to those who knew. He also taught them how far a well-educated man should make himself familiar with any given subject.

For instance, he said that the study of geometry should be pursued until the student was competent to measure a parcel of land accurately in case he wanted to take over, convey or divide it, or to compute the yield; and this knowledge was so easy to acquire, that anyone who gave his mind to mensuration knew the size of the piece and carried away a knowledge of the principles of land measurement. He was against carrying the study of geometry so far as to include the more complicated figures, on the ground that he could not see the use of them. Not that he was himself unfamiliar with them, but he said that they were enough to occupy a lifetime, to the complete exclusion of many other useful studies.

Similarly he recommended them to make themselves familiar with astronomy, but only so far as to be able to find the time of night, month and year, in order to use reliable evidence when planning a journey by land or sea, or setting the watch, and in all other affairs that are done in the night or month or year, by distinguishing the times and seasons aforesaid. This knowledge, again, was easily to be had from night hunters and pilots and others who made it their business to know such things. But he strongly deprecated studying astronomy so far as to include the knowledge of bodies revolving in different courses, and of planets and comets, and wearing oneself out with the calculation of their distance from the earth, their periods of revolution and the causes of these. Of such researches, again he said that he could not see what useful purpose they served. He had indeed attended lectures on these subjects too; but these again, he said, were enough to occupy a lifetime to the complete exclusion of many useful studies.

In general, with regard to the phenomena of the heavens, he deprecated curiosity to learn how the deity contrives them: he held that their secrets could not be discovered by man, and believed that any attempt to search out what the gods had not chosen to reveal must be displeasing to them. He said that he who meddles with these matters runs the risk of losing his sanity as completely as Anaxagoras, who took an insane pride in his explanation of the divine machinery.

For that sage, in declaring the sun to be fire, ignored the facts than men can look at fire without inconvenience, but cannot gaze steadily at the sun; that their skin is blackened by the sun's rays, but not by fire. Further, he ignored the fact that sunlight is essential to the health, of all vegetation, whereas if anything is heated by fire it withers. Again, when he pronounced the sun to be a red-hot stone, he ignored the fact that a stone in fire neither glows nor can resist it long, whereas the sun shines with unequalled brilliance for ever.

He also recommended the study of arithmetic. But in this case as in the others he recommended avoidance of vain application; and invariably, whether theories or ascertained facts formed the subject of his conversation, he limited it to what was useful.

He also strongly urged his companions to take care of their health. "You should find out all you can," he said, "from those who know. Everyone should watch himself throughout his life, and notice what sort of meat and drink and what form of exercise suit his constitution, and how he should regulate them in order to enjoy good health. For by such attention to yourselves you can discover better than any doctor what suits your constitution."

When anyone was in need of help that human wisdom was unable to give he advised him to resort to divination; for he who knew the means whereby the gods give guidance to men concerning their affairs never lacked divine counsel.

Isocrates

436–338 B.C.

*Who does not know that words carry greater conviction when spoken
by men of good repute than when spoke by men who live under a cloud,
and that the argument which is made by a man's life is of more
weight than that which is furnished by words?*

ANTIDOSIS

I socrates lived in Athens during the time when it reached the pinnacle of its cultural achievement. But he also experienced the upheaval of the Peloponnesian War, which divided the Greek city-states against themselves. He founded his school of rhetoric in 393 B.C., predating Plato's Academy by six years. Technically a "sophist" (literally, a teacher of wisdom), he nevertheless criticized the notorious sophists of his day who had rightly earned a bad reputation for valuing oratorical showmanship over truth. He knew Socrates, and the two seem to have shared a degree of mutual respect. In Plato's *Phaedrus* (279a–b), Socrates foretold Isocrates' eminence as a teacher of rhetoric and predicted that one day "a more divine impulse will lead him to greater things; for . . . something of philosophy is inborn in his mind." Such a compliment extended from the philosopher to the orator was no small thing, and the tribute was later remarked upon by the Roman statesman Cicero, upon whom Isocrates exercised a profound influence (*The Orator,* xiii, 41; *De Oratore* ii, 94). It is worth pondering the relative influence of Isocrates and Plato in their own time. Historian H. I. Marrou claimed that "on the whole it was Isocrates, not Plato, who educated fourth-century Greece and subsequently the Hellenistic and Roman worlds."[1] Beyond ancient Greece and Rome, moreover, Isocrates' influence extended to modern Europe. In the sixteenth century, his works were translated into German, French,

---

1. *A History of Education in Antiquity,* trans. by George Lamb (New York: Sheed and Ward, 1956), 79.

and English. In Renaissance England, Juan Luis Vives translated Isocrates' *Areopagitica* and *Nicocles,* and Thomas Elyot translated *To Nicocles* (a book on leadership) under the title *Doctrinal of Princes* (1531).

THE SELECTIONS

Isocrates' reflections on education are scattered throughout a long lifetime of letters, treatises, and speeches. True to the oratorical tradition, "his aim was to train citizens for success in their own private life and in public affairs."[2] Two short excerpts follow from *Against the Sophists* and the *Panathenaicus* and one extended section of *Antidosis,* written when Isocrates was a vigorous eighty-two. Crafted as a courtroom defense but never delivered, the *Antidosis* parallels Socrates' *Apology.* Like his more famous contemporary, Isocrates had to defend himself against charges of corrupting the youth of Athens. A fuller acquaintance with Isocrates' views on education must include *To Nicocles.*

from Against the Sophists

If all who are engaged in the profession of education were willing to state the facts instead of making greater promises than they can possibly fulfil, they would not be in such bad repute with the lay-public. As it is, however, the teachers who do not scruple to vaunt their powers with utter disregard of the truth have created the impression that those who choose a life of careless indolence are better advised than those who devote themselves to serious study.

Indeed, who can fail to abhor, yes to contemn, those teachers, in the first place, who devote themselves to disputation, since they pretend to search for truth, but straightway at the beginning of their professions attempt to deceive us with lies? For I think it is manifest to all that foreknowledge of future events is not vouchsafed to our human nature, but that we are so far removed from this prescience that Homer, who has been conceded the highest reputation for wisdom, has pictured even the gods as at times debating among themselves about the future—not that he knew their minds but that he desired to show us that for mankind this power lies in the realms of the impossible.

But these professors have gone so far in their lack of scruple that they attempt to persuade our young men that if they will only study under them they will know what to do in life and through this knowledge will become happy and prosperous. More than that, although they set themselves up as masters and dispensers of goods so precious, they are not ashamed of asking for them a price of three or four minae! Why, if they were to sell any other commodity for so trifling a fraction of its worth they would not deny their folly; nevertheless, although they set so insignificant a price on the whole stock of virtue and happiness, they pretend to wisdom and assume the right to instruct the rest of the world. Furthermore, although they say that they do not want money and speak contemptuously of wealth as "filthy lucre" they hold their hands out for a trifling gain and promise to make

---

2. Aubrey Gwynn, *Roman Education from Cicero to Quintilian* (Oxford: Oxford University Press, 1926), 47.

their disciples all but immortal! But what is most ridiculous of all is that they distrust those from whom they are to get this money—they distrust, that is to say, the very men to whom they are about to deliver the science of just dealing—and they require that the fees advanced by their students be entrusted for safe keeping to those who have never been under their instruction, being well advised as to their security, but doing the opposite of what they preach. For it is permissible to those who give any other instruction to be exacting in matters open to dispute, since nothing prevents those who have been made adept in other lines of training from being dishonourable in the matter of contracts. But men who inculcate virtue and sobriety—is it not absurd if they do not trust in their own students before all others? For it is not to be supposed that men who are honourable and just-dealing with others will be dishonest with the very preceptors who have made them what they are.

When, therefore, the layman puts all these things together and observes that the teachers of wisdom and dispensers of happiness are themselves in great want but exact only a small fee from their students, that they are on the watch for contradictions in words but are blind to inconsistencies in deeds, and that, furthermore, they pretend to have knowledge of the future but are incapable either of saying anything pertinent or of giving any counsel regarding the present, and when he observes that those who follow their judgements are more consistent and more successful than those who profess to have exact knowledge, then he has, I think, good reason to contemn such studies and regard them as stuff and nonsense, and not as a true discipline of the soul.

But it is not these sophists alone who are open to criticism, but also those who profess to teach political discourse. For the latter have no interest whatever in the truth, but consider that they are masters of an art if they can attract great numbers of students by the smallness of their charges and the magnitude of their professions and get something out of them. For they are themselves so stupid and conceive others to be so dull that, although the speeches which they compose are worse than those which some laymen improvise, nevertheless they promise to make their students such clever orators that they will not overlook any of the possibilities which a subject affords. More than that, they do not attribute any of this power either to the practical experience or to the native ability of the student, but undertake to transmit the science of discourse as simply as they would teach the letters of the alphabet, not having taken trouble to examine into the nature of each kind of knowledge, but thinking that because of the extravagance of their promises they themselves will command admiration and the teaching of discourse will be held in higher esteem—oblivious of the fact that the arts are made great, not by those who are without scruple in boasting about them, but by those who are able to discover all of the resources which each art affords.

For myself, I should have preferred above great riches that philosophy had as much power as these men claim; for, possibly, I should not have been the very last in the profession nor had the least share in its profits. But since it has no such power, I could wish that this prating might cease. For I note that the bad repute which results therefrom does not affect the offenders only, but that all the rest of us who are in the same profession share in the opprobium.

But I marvel when I observe these men setting themselves up as instructors of youth who cannot see that they are applying the analogy of an art with hard and fast rules to a creative process. For, excepting these teachers, who does not know that the art of using letters remains fixed and unchanged, so that we continually and invariably use the same letters for the same purposes, while exactly the reverse is true of the art of discourse? For what has been said by one speaker is not equally useful for the speaker who comes after him; on the contrary, he is accounted most skilled in this art who speaks in a manner worthy of his subject and yet is able to discover in it topics which are nowise the same as those used by others. But the greatest proof of the difference between these two arts is that oratory is good only if it has the qualities of fitness for the occasion, propriety of style, and originality of treatment, while in the case of letters there is no such need whatsoever. So that those who make use of such analogies ought more justly to pay out than to accept fees, since they attempt to teach others when they are themselves in great need of instruction.

However, if it is my duty not only to rebuke others, but also to set forth my own views, I think all intelligent people will agree with me that while many of those who have pursued philosophy have remained in private life, others, on the other hand, who have never taken lessons from any one of the sophists have become able orators and statesmen. For ability, whether in speech or in any other activity, is found in those who are well endowed by nature and have been schooled by practical experience. Formal training makes such men more skilful and more resourceful in discovering the possibilities of a subject; for it teaches them to take from a readier source the topics which they otherwise hit upon in haphazard fashion. But it cannot fully fashion men who are without natural aptitude into good debaters or writers, although it is capable of leading them on to self-improvement and to a greater degree of intelligence on many subjects.

But I desire, now that I have gone this far, to speak more clearly on these matters. For I hold that to obtain a knowledge of the elements out of which we make and compose all discourses is not so very difficult if anyone entrusts himself, not to those who make rash promises, but to those who have some knowledge of these things. But to choose from these elements those which should be employed for each subject, to join them together, to arrange them properly, and also, not to miss what the occasion demands but appropriately to adorn the whole speech with striking thoughts and to clothe it in flowing and melodious phrase—these things, I hold, require much study and are the task of a vigorous and imaginative mind: for this, the student must not only have the requisite aptitude but he must learn the different kinds of discourse and practise himself in their use; and the teacher, for his part, must so expound the principles of the art with the utmost possible exactness as to leave out nothing that can be taught, and, for the rest, he must in himself set such an example of oratory that the students who have taken form under his instruction and are able to pattern after him will, from the outset, show in their speaking a degree of grace and charm which is not found in others. When all of these requisites are found together, then the devotees of philosophy will achieve complete success; but according as any one of the things which I have mentioned is lacking, to this extent must their disciples of necessity fall below the mark.

Now as for the sophists who have lately sprung up and have very recently embraced these pretensions, even though they flourish at the moment, they will all, I am sure, come round to this position. But there remain to be considered those who lived before our time and did not scruple to write the so-called arts of oratory. These must not be dismissed without rebuke, since they professed to teach how to conduct law-suits, picking out the most discredited of terms, which the enemies, not the champions, of this discipline might have been expected to employ—and that too although this facility, in so far as it can be taught, is of no greater aid to forensic than to all other discourse. But they were much worse than those who dabble in disputation; for although the latter expounded such captious theories that were anyone to cleave to them in practice he would at once be in all manner of trouble, they did, at any rate, make professions of virtue and sobriety in their teaching, whereas the former, although exhorting others to study political discourse, neglected all the good things which this study affords, and became nothing more than professors of meddlesomeness and greed.

And yet those who desire to follow the true precepts of this discipline may, if they will, be helped more speedily towards honesty of character than towards facility in oratory. And let no one suppose that I claim that just living can be taught; for, in a word, I hold that there does not exist an art of the kind which can implant sobriety and justice in depraved natures. Nevertheless, I do think that the study of political discourse can help more than any other thing to stimulate and form such qualities of character.

But in order that I may not appear to be breaking down the pretensions of others while myself making greater claims than are within my powers, I believe that the very arguments by which I myself was convinced will make it clear to others also that these things are true. . . .

⸙⧫⸮

from the Panathenaicus

. . . Now in fact, so far from scorning the education which was handed down by our ancestors, I even commend that which has been set up in our own day—I mean geometry, astronomy, and the so-called eristic dialogues, which our young men delight in more than they should, although among the older men not one would not declare them insufferable. Nevertheless, I urge those who are inclined towards these disciplines to work hard and apply themselves to all of them, saying that even if this learning can accomplish no other good, at any rate it keeps the young out of many other things which are harmful. Nay, I hold that for those who are at this age no more helpful or fitting occupation can be found than the pursuit of these studies; but for those who are older and for those who have been admitted to man's estate I assert that these disciplines are no longer suitable. For I observe that some of those who have become so thoroughly versed in these studies as to instruct others in them fail to use opportunely the knowledge which they possess, while in the other activities of life they are less cultivated than their students—I hesitate to say less cultivated than their servants. I have the same fault to find also with those who are skilled in oratory and those who are distinguished for their writings and in general with all who have superior attainments in the arts, in the sciences, and in specialized skill. For I know that the majority even of these men have not set their own house in order, that they are insupportable in their private intercourse, that they belittle the opinions of their fellow-citizens, and that they are given over to many other grave offences. So that I do not think that even these may be said to partake of the state of culture of which I am speaking.

Whom, then, do I call educated, since I exclude the arts and sciences and specialties? First, those who manage well the circumstances which they encounter day by day, and who possess a judgement which is accurate in meeting occasions as they arise and rarely misses the expedient course of action; next, those who are decent and honourable in their intercourse with all with whom they associate, tolerating easily and good-naturedly what is unpleasant or offensive in others and being themselves as agreeable and reasonable to their associates as it is possible to be; furthermore, those who hold their pleasures always under control and are not unduly overcome by their misfortunes, bearing up under them bravely and in a manner worthy of our common nature; finally, and most important of all, those who are not spoiled by successes and do not desert their true selves and become arrogant, but hold their ground steadfastly as intelligent men, not rejoicing in the good things which have come to them through chance rather than in those which through their own nature and intelligence are theirs from their birth. Those who have a character which is in accord, not with one of these things, but with all of them—these, I contend, are wise and complete men, possessed of all the virtues. . . .

❧

from the Antidosis

I suppose that you are not unaware of the fact that the government of the state is handed on by the older men to the youth of the coming generation; and that since the succession goes on without end, it follows of necessity that as is the education of our youth so from generation to generation will be the fortune of the state. Therefore, you must not let the sycophants have control of a thing so momentous, nor punish those who refuse to pay them money, while permitting those from whom they have received it to do whatever they please. But if philosophy has an influence which tends to corrupt our youth, you ought not merely to punish the occasional offender whom some sycophant hales into court but to banish all who are engaged in teaching it. If, however, it has the opposite effect and helps and improves and makes better men of its devotees, then you should call a halt on those who load this study with abuse; you should strip the sycophants of their rewards, and counsel our young men to occupy themselves with this pursuit above all others.

I would have given a good deal, assuming that I was doomed by fate to defend myself against this charge, if I could have faced this trial in the fullness of my vigour; for in that case I should have felt no misgiving but should have been better able both to protect myself from my accuser and to champion the cause of liberal education. Now, however, I am afraid that, although I have been enabled by this education to speak well enough on other themes, I may find that I have discoursed less ably upon this subject than upon matters which should have concerned me less. And yet I would rather lay down my life this day—for you shall have the truth even though the words be inept—after having spoken adequately upon this theme and persuaded you to look upon the study of eloquence in its true light, than live many times my allotted span and see it continue to fare among you as it now does.

My aspiration, then, is much greater than my power to do the subject justice; but yet I shall try as best I can to explain what is the nature of this education, what is its power, what of the other arts it is akin to, what benefit it is to its devotees, and what claims I make for it. For I think that when you know the truth about this you will be in a better position to deliberate and pronounce judgement upon it. But I beg of you, if I appear to carry on the discussion in a manner far removed from that which is customary here, not to be impatient but to bear with me, remembering that when a man is defending himself on a charge unlike any other, he must resort to a kind of pleading which is out of the ordinary. Be patient, therefore, with the manner of my discourse and with my frankness of speech; permit me to use up the time allotted to my defence; and then cast your ballots as each of you thinks is right and in accordance with the law.

In my treatment of the art of discourse, I desire, like the genealogists, to start at the beginning. It is acknowledged that the nature of man is compounded of two parts, the physical and the mental, and no one would deny that of these two the mind comes first and is of greater worth; for it is the function of the mind to decide both on personal and on public questions, and of the body to be servant to the judgements of the mind. Since this is so, certain of our ancestors, long before our time, seeing that many arts had been devised for other things, while none had been prescribed for the body and for the mind, invented and bequeathed to us two disciplines, physical training for the body, of which gymnastics is a part, and, for the mind, philosophy, which I am going to explain. These are twin arts—parallel and complementary—by which their masters prepare the mind to become more intelligent and the body to become more serviceable, not separating sharply the two kinds of education, but using similar methods of instruction, exercise, and other forms of discipline.

For when they take their pupils in hand, the physical trainers instruct their followers in the postures which have been devised for bodily contests, while the teachers of philosophy impart all the forms of discourse in which the mind expresses itself. Then, when they have made them familiar and thoroughly conversant with these lessons, they set them at exercises, habituate them to work, and require them to combine in practice the particular things which they have learned, in order that they may grasp them more firmly and bring their theories into closer touch with the occasions for applying them—I say "theories," for no system of knowledge can possibly cover these occasions, since in all cases they elude our science. Yet those who most apply their minds to them and are able to discern the consequences which for the most part grow out of them, will most often meet these occasions in the right way.

Watching over them and training them in this manner, both the teachers of gymnastic and the teachers of discourse are able to advance their pupils to a point where they are better men and where they are stronger in their thinking or in the use of their bodies. However, neither class of teachers is in possession of a science by which they can make capable athletes or capable orators out of whomsoever they please. They can contribute in some degree to these results, but these powers are never found in their perfection save in those who excel by virtue both of talent and of training.

I have given you now some impression of what philosophy is. But I think that you will get a still clearer idea of its powers if I tell you what professions I make to those who want to become my pupils. I say to them that if they are to excel in oratory or in managing affairs or in any line of work, they must, first of all, have a natural aptitude for that which they have elected to do; secondly, they must submit to training and master the knowledge of their particular subject, whatever it may be in each case; and, finally, they must become versed and practised in the use and application of their art; for only on these conditions can they become fully competent and pre-eminent in any line of endeavour. In this process, master and pupil each has his place; no one but the pupil can furnish the necessary capacity; no one but the master, the ability to impart knowledge; while both have a part in the exercises of practical application: for the master must painstakingly direct his pupil, and the latter must rigidly follow the master's instructions.

Now these observations apply to any and all the arts. If anyone, ignoring the other arts, were to ask me which of these factors has the greatest power in the education of an orator I should answer that natural ability is paramount and comes before all else. For given a man with a mind which is capable of finding out and learning the truth and of working hard and remembering what it learns, and also with a voice and a clarity of utterance which are able to captivate the audience, not only by what he says, but by the music of his words, and, finally, with an assurance which is not an expression of bravado, but which, tempered by sobriety, so fortifies the spirit that he is no less at ease in addressing all his fellow-citizens than in reflecting to himself—who does not know that such a man might, without the advantage of an elaborate education and with only a superficial and common training, be an orator such as has never, perhaps, been seen among the Hellenes? Again, we know that men who are less generously endowed by nature but excel in experience and practice, not only improve upon themselves, but surpass others who, though highly gifted, have been too negligent of their talents. It follows, therefore, that either one of these factors may produce an able speaker or an able man of affairs, but both of them combined in the same person might produce a man incomparable among his fellows.

These, then, are my views as to the relative importance of native ability and practice. I cannot, however, make a like claim for education; its powers are not equal nor comparable to theirs. For if one should take lessons in all the principles of oratory and master them with the greatest thoroughness, he might, perhaps, become a more pleasing speaker than most, but let him stand up before the crowd and lack one thing only, namely, assurance, and he would not be able to utter a word. . . .

. . . A little while ago I said that many good men had been misled about philosophy, and are consequently harshly disposed toward it. Now, however, I have assumed that the arguments which I have presented are so plain and evident to all that no one, it seems to me, can misapprehend its power or accuse me of corrupting my disciples or have any such feeling as I imputed to them a little while ago. Nevertheless, if I am to speak the truth and say what has now come into my mind, I am of the opinion that while all those who are envious of my success covet the ability to think and speak well, yet they themselves neglect to cultivate it, some because they are indolent, some because they discredit their own powers, and some on other pretexts (and these are legion); but when other men take great pains and show a desire to attain what they themselves covet, then they grow irritated, jealous, perturbed in spirit, and are much in the same state of mind as lovers are. Indeed, how could one more aptly explain their condition? They envy the good fortune of those who are able to use words eloquently; yet they reproach the youth who aspire to win this distinction. There is no one of them who would not pray the gods to bestow the power of eloquence upon himself, first of all, and failing that, upon his sons and his own kin; yet when men strive through work and study to accomplish for themselves what these people would like to have as a gift from the gods, they accuse them of going utterly astray. At one moment they make believe to mock at them as dupes and victims; and then again, for no reason at all, they change about and denounce them as adepts in grasping their own advantage. When any danger threatens the city, they seek counsel from those who can speak best upon the question at issue and act upon their advice; but when men devote their efforts to preparing themselves to serve the state in just such crises, they think it proper to traduce them. And they reproach the Thebans and our other enemies for their ignorance; yet when men seek by every means to escape from that malady, they never cease maligning them.

But as a symptom, not only of their confusion of mind, but of their contempt for the gods, they recognize that Persuasion is one of the gods, and they observe that the city makes sacrifices to her every year, but when men aspire to share the power which the goddess possesses, they claim that such aspirants are being corrupted, as though their desire were for some evil thing. But what is most astonishing of all is that while they would grant that the mind is superior to the body, nevertheless, in spite of this opinion, they look with greater favour upon training in gymnastics than upon the study of philosophy. And yet how unreasonable it is to give higher praise to those who cultivate the less than to those who cultivate the greater thing, and that too when everyone knows it was not through excellence of body that Athens ever accomplished any noteworthy thing, but that through wisdom of men she became the most prosperous and the greatest of Hellenic states.

It would be possible to bring together many more contradictions than the above in the views of these people, but that is a task for those who are younger than I and who are free from anxiety about the present occasion. For example, one might put the following questions on this very subject: Suppose the case of men who, having inherited large fortunes from their ancestors, used their wealth, not to render themselves serviceable to the state, but to outrage their fellow-citizens and to dishonour their sons and their wives; would anyone venture to put the blame upon the authors of their wealth instead of demanding that the offenders themselves be punished? Again, suppose the case of men who, having mastered the art of war, did not use their skill against the enemy, but rose up and slew many of their fellow-citizens; or suppose the case of men who, having been trained to perfection in the art of boxing or of the pancration, kept away from the games and fell foul of the passers-by; would anyone withhold praise from their instructors instead of putting to death those who turned their lessons to an evil use?

We ought, therefore, to think of the art of discourse just as we think of the other arts, and not to form opposite judgements about similar things, nor show ourselves intolerant toward that power which, of all the faculties which belong to the nature of man, is the source of most of our blessings. For in the other powers which we possess, as I have already said on a former occasion, we are in no respect superior to other living creatures; nay, we are inferior to many in swiftness and in strength and in other resources; but, because there has been implanted in us the power to persuade each other and to make clear to each other whatever we desire, not only have we escaped the life of wild beasts, but we have come together and founded cities and made laws and invented arts; and, generally speaking, there is no institution devised by man which the power of speech has not helped us to establish. For this it is which has laid down laws concerning things just and unjust, and things honourable and base; and if it were not for these ordinances we should not be able to live with one another. It is by this also that we confute the bad and extol the good. Through this we educate the ignorant and appraise the wise; for the power to speak well is taken as the surest index of a sound understanding, and discourse which is true and lawful and just is the outward image of a good and faithful soul. With this faculty we both contend against others on matters which are open to dispute and seek light for ourselves on things which are unknown; for the same arguments which we use in persuading others when we speak in public, we employ also when we deliberate in our own thoughts; and, while we call eloquent those who are able to speak before a crowd, we regard as sage those who most skilfully debate their problems in their own minds. And, if there is need to speak in brief summary of this power, we shall find that none of the things which are done with intelligence take place without the help of speech, but that in all our actions as well as in all our thoughts speech is our guide, and is most employed by those who have the most wisdom.

But without reflecting at all on these truths, Lysimachus has dared to attack those who aspire to an accomplishment which is the source of blessings so many and so great. But why should we be surprised at him when even among the professors of disputation there are some who talk no less abusively of the art of speaking on general and useful themes than do the most benighted of men, not that they are ignorant of its power or of the advantage which it quickly gives to those who avail themselves of it, but because they think that by decrying this art they will enhance the standing of their own.

I could, perhaps, say much harsher things of them than they of me, but I refrain for a double reason. I want neither to descend to the level of men whom envy has made blind nor to censure men who, although they do no actual harm to their pupils are less able to benefit them than are other teachers. I shall, however, say a few words about them, first because they also have paid their compliments to me; second, in order that you, being better informed as to their powers, may estimate us justly in relation to each other; and, furthermore, that I may show you clearly that we who are occupied with political discourse and whom they call contentious are more considerate than they; for although they are always saying disparaging things of me, I shall not answer them in kind but shall confine myself to the simple truth.

For I believe that the teachers who are skilled in disputation and those who are occupied with astronomy and geometry and studies of that sort do not injure but, on the contrary, benefit their pupils, not so much as they profess, but more than others give them credit for. Most men see in such studies nothing but empty talk and hair-splitting; for none of these disciplines has any useful application either to private or to public affairs; nay, they are not even remembered for any length of time after they are learned because they do not attend us through life nor do they lend aid in what we do, but are wholly divorced from our necessities. But I am neither of this opinion nor am I far removed from it; rather it seems to me both that those who hold that this training is of no use in practical life are right and that those who speak in praise of it have truth on their side. If there is a contradiction in this statement, it is because these disciplines are different in their nature from the other studies which make up our education; for the other branches avail us only after we have gained a knowledge of them, whereas these studies can be of no benefit to us after we have mastered them unless we have elected to make our living from this source, and only help us while we are in the process of learning. For while we are occupied with the subtlety and exactness of astronomy and geometry and are forced to apply our minds to difficult problems, and are, in addition, being habituated to speak and apply ourselves to what is said and shown to us, and not to let our wits go wool-gathering, we gain the power, after being exercised and sharpened on these disciplines, of grasping and learning more easily and more quickly those subjects which are of more importance and of greater value. I do not, however, think it proper to apply the term "philosophy" to a training which is no help to us in the present either in our speech or in our actions, but rather I would call it a gymnastic of the mind and a preparation for philosophy. It is, to be sure, a study more advanced than that which boys in school pursue, but it is for the most part the same sort of thing; for they also when they have laboured through their lessons in grammar, music, and the other branches, are not a whit advanced in their ability to speak and deliberate on affairs, but they have increased their aptitude for mastering greater and more serious studies. I would, therefore, advise young men to spend some time on these disciplines, but not to allow their minds to be dried up by these barren subtleties, nor to be stranded on the speculations of the ancient sophists, who maintain, some of them, that the sum of things is made up of infinite elements; Empedocles that it is made up of four, with strife and love operating among them; Ion, of not more than three; Alcmaeon, of only two; Parmenides and Melissus, of one; and Gorgias, of none at all. For I think that such curiosities of thought are on a par with jugglers' tricks which, though they do not profit anyone, yet attract great crowds of the empty-minded, and I hold that men who want to do some good in the world must banish utterly from their interests all vain speculations and all activities which have no bearing on our lives.

Now I have spoken and advised you enough on these studies for the present. It remains to tell you about "wisdom" and "philosophy." It is true that if one were pleading a case on any other issue it would be out of place to discuss these words (for they are foreign to all litigation), but it is appropriate for me, since I am being tried on such an issue, and since I hold that what some people call philosophy is not entitled to that name, to define and explain to you what philosophy, properly conceived, really is. My view of this question is, as it happens, very simple. For since it is not in the nature of man to attain a science by the possession of which we can know positively what we should do or what we should say, in the next resort I hold that man to be wise who is able by his powers of conjecture to arrive generally at the best course, and I hold that man to be a philosopher who occupies himself with the studies from which he will most quickly gain that kind of insight.

What the studies are which have this power I can tell you, although I hesitate to do so; they are so contrary to popular belief and so very far removed from the opinions of the rest of the world, that I am afraid lest when you first hear them you will fill the whole court-room with your murmurs and your cries. Nevertheless, in spite of my misgivings, I shall attempt to tell you about them; for I blush at the thought that anyone might suspect me of betraying the truth to save my old age and the little of life remaining to me. But, I beg of you, do not, before you have heard me, judge that I could have been so mad as to choose deliberately, when my fate is in your hands, to express to you ideas which are repugnant to your opinions if I had not believed that these ideas follow logically on what I have previously said, and that I could support them with true and convincing proofs.

I consider that the kind of art which can implant honesty and justice in depraved natures has never existed and does not now exist, and that people who profess that power will grow weary and cease from their vain pretensions before such an education is ever found. But I do hold that people can become better and worthier if they conceive an ambition to speak well, if they become possessed of the desire to be able to persuade their hearers, and, finally, if they set their hearts on seizing their advantage—I do not mean "advantage" in the sense given to that word by the empty-minded, but advantage in the true meaning of that term; and that this is so I think I shall presently make clear.

For, in the first place, when anyone elects to speak or write discourses which are worthy of praise and honour, it is not conceivable that he will support causes which are unjust or petty or devoted to private quarrels, and not rather those which are great and honourable, devoted to the welfare of man and our common good; for if he fails to find causes of this character, he will accomplish nothing to the purpose. In the second place, he will select from all the actions of men which bear upon his subject those examples which are the most illustrious and the most edifying; and, habituating himself to contemplate and appraise such examples, he will feel their influence not only in the preparation of a given discourse but in all the actions of his life. It follows, then, that the power to speak well and think right will reward the man who approaches the art of discourse with love of wisdom and love of honour.

Furthermore, mark you, the man who wishes to persuade people will not be negligent as to the matter of character; no, on the contrary, he will apply himself above all to establish a most honourable name among his fellow-citizens; for who does not know that words carry greater conviction when spoken by men of good repute than when spoken by men who live under a cloud, and that the argument which is made by a man's life is of more weight than that which is furnished by words? Therefore, the stronger a man's desire to persuade his hearers, the more zealously will he strive to be honourable and to have the esteem of his fellow-citizens.

And let no one of you suppose that while all other people realize how much the scales of persuasion incline in favour of one who has the approval of his judges, the devotees of philosophy alone are blind to the power of good will. In fact, they appreciate this even more thoroughly than others, and they know, furthermore, that probabilities and proofs and all forms of persuasion support only the points in a case to which they are severally applied, whereas an honourable reputation not only lends greater persuasiveness to the words of the man who possesses it, but adds greater lustre to his deeds, and is, therefore, more zealously to be sought after by men of intelligence than anything else in the world.

I come now to the question of "advantage" the most difficult of the points I have raised. If any one is under the impression that people who rob others or falsify accounts or do any evil thing get the advantage, he is wrong in his thinking; for none are at a greater disadvantage throughout their lives than such men; none are found in more difficult straits, none live in greater ignominy; and, in a word, none are more miserable than they. No, you ought to believe rather that those are better off now and will receive the advantage in the future at the hands of the gods who are the most righteous and the most faithful in their devotions, and that those receive the better portion at the hands of men who are the most conscientious in their dealings with their associates, whether in their homes or in public life, and are themselves esteemed as the noblest among their fellows.

This is verily the truth, and it is well for us to adopt this way of speaking on the subject, since, as things now are, Athens has in many respects been plunged into such a state of topsy-turvy and confusion that some of our people no longer use words in their proper meaning but wrest them from the most honourable associations and apply them to the basest pursuits. On the one hand, they speak of men who play the buffoon and have a talent for mocking and mimicking as "gifted"—an appellation which should be reserved for men endowed with the highest excellence; while, on the other hand, they think of men who indulge their depraved and criminal instincts and who for small gains acquire a base reputation as "getting the advantage," instead of applying this term to the most righteous and the most upright, that is, to men who take advantage of the good and not the evil things of life. They characterize men who ignore our practical needs and delight in the mental juggling of the ancient sophists as "students of philosophy," but refuse this name to whose who pursue and practise those studies which will enable us to govern wisely both our own households and the commonwealth—which should be the objects of our toil, of our study, and of our every act.

It is from these pursuits that you have for a long time now been driving away our youth, because you accept the words of those who denounce this kind of education. Yes, and you have brought it about that the most promising of our young men are wasting their youth in drinking-bouts, in parties, in soft living and childish folly, to the neglect of all efforts to improve themselves; while those of grosser nature are engaged from morning until night in extremes of dissipation which in former days an honest slave would have despised. You see some of them chilling their wine at the "Nine-fountains"; others, drinking in taverns; others, tossing dice in gambling dens; and many, hanging about the training-schools of the flute-girls.

And as for those who encourage them in these things, no one of those who profess to be concerned for our youth has ever haled them before you for trial, but instead they persecute me, who, whatever else I may deserve, do at any rate deserve thanks for this, that I discourage such habits in my pupils.

But so inimical to all the world is this race of sycophants that when men pay a ransom of a hundred and thirty minae for women who bid fair to help them make away with the rest of their property besides, so far from reproaching them, they actually rejoice in their extravagance; but when men spend any amount, however small, upon their education, they complain that they are being corrupted. Could any charge be more unjust than this against our students? For, while in the prime of vigour, when most men of their age are most inclined to indulge their passions, they have disdained a life of pleasure; when they might have saved expense and lived softly, they have elected to pay out money and submit to toil; and, though hardly emerged from boyhood, they have come to appreciate what most of their elders do not know, namely, that if one is to govern his youth rightly and worthily and make the proper start in life, he must give more heed to himself than to his possessions, he must not hasten and seek to rule over others before he has found a master to direct his own thoughts, and he must not take as great pleasure or pride in other advantages as in the good things which spring up in the soul under a liberal education. I ask you, then, when young men have governed themselves by these principles, ought they not to be praised rather than censured, ought they not to be recognized as the best and the most sober-minded among their fellows?

I marvel at men who felicitate those who are eloquent by nature on being blessed with a noble gift, and yet rail at those who wish to become eloquent, on the ground that they desire an immoral and debasing education. Pray, what that is noble by nature becomes shameful and base when one attains it by effort? We shall find that there is no such thing, but that, on the contrary, we praise, at least in other fields, those who by their own devoted toil are able to acquire some good thing more than we praise those who inherit it from their ancestors. And rightly so; for it is well that in all activities, and most of all in the art of speaking, credit is won, not by gifts of fortune, but by efforts of study. For men who have been gifted with eloquence by nature and by fortune, are governed in what they say by chance, and not by any standard of what is best, whereas those who have gained this power by the study of philosophy and by the exercise of reason never speak without weighing their words, and so are less often in error as to a course of action.

Therefore, it behoves all men to want to have many of their youth engaged in training to become speakers, and you Athenians most of all. For you, yourselves, are pre-eminent and superior to the rest of the world, not in your application to the business of war, nor because you govern yourselves more excellently or preserve the laws handed down to you by your ancestors more faithfully than others, but in those qualities by which the nature of man rises above the other animals, and the race of the Hellenes above the barbarians, namely, in the fact that you have been educated as have been no other people in wisdom and in speech. So, then, nothing more absurd could happen than for you to declare by your votes that students who desire to excel their companions in those very qualities in which you excel mankind, are being corrupted, and to visit any misfortune upon them for availing themselves of an education in which you have become the leaders of the world.

For you must not lose sight of the fact that Athens is looked upon as having become a school for the education of all able orators and teachers of oratory. And naturally so; for people observe that she holds forth the greatest prizes for those who have this ability, that she offers the greatest number and variety of fields of exercise to those who have chosen to enter contests of this character and want to train for them, and that, furthermore, everyone obtains here that practical experience which more than any other thing imparts ability to speak; and, in addition to these advantages, they consider that the catholicity and moderation of our speech, as well as our flexibility of mind and love of letters, contribute in no small degree to the education of the orator. Therefore they suppose, and not without just reason, that all clever speakers are the disciples of Athens.

Beware, then, lest it make you utterly ridiculous to pronounce a disparaging judgement upon the reputation which you have among the Hellenes even more than I have among you. Manifestly, by such an unjust verdict, you would be passing sentence upon yourselves. It would be as if the Lacedaemonians were to attempt to penalize men for training themselves in preparation for war, or as if the Thessalians a saw fit to punish men for practising the art of horsemanship. Take care, therefore, not to do yourselves this wrong and not to lend support to the slanders of the enemies of Athens rather than to the eulogies of her friends.

I think that you are not unaware that while some of the Hellenes are hostile to you, some are extremely friendly, and rest their hopes of security upon you. These say that Athens is the only city, the others being mere villages, and that she deserves to be termed the capital of Hellas both because of her size and because of the resources which she furnishes to the rest of the world, and most of all because of the character of her inhabitants; for no people, they insist, are more kindly or more sociable, nor could anyone find any people with whom he could spend all his days in friendlier intercourse. Indeed, so extravagant are they in their praise that they do not even hesitate to say that they would rather suffer injury at the hands of an Athenian gentleman than benefit through the rudeness of people from another city.

There are, on the other hand, those who scoff at this praise, and, dwelling upon the cruel and iniquitous practices of the sycophants, denounce the whole city as savage and insupportable.

It is, therefore, the duty of intelligent judges to destroy those who heap infamy upon the city and to reward those who are responsible in some degree for the tributes paid to her, more than you reward the athletes who are crowned in the great games, seeing that they win for the city a greater and more fitting glory than any athlete; for in contests of the body we have many rivals; but in the training of the mind everyone would concede that we stand first. And men with even a slight ability to reason ought to show the world that they reward those who excel in those activities for which the city is renowned, and they ought not to envy them nor hold an opinion of them which is the opposite of the esteem in which they are held by the rest of the Hellenes.

But you have never troubled yourselves to do this; nay, you have so far mistaken your true interests that you are more pleased with those who cause you to be reviled than with those who cause you to be praised, and you think that those who have made many people hate the city are better friends of the demos than those who have inspired good will toward Athens in all with whom they have had to deal.

If, however, you are wise, you will put an end to this confusion, and you will not continue, as now, to take either a hostile or a contemptuous view of philosophy; on the contrary, you will conceive that the cultivation of the mind is the noblest and worthiest of pursuits and you will urge our young men who have sufficient means and who are able to take the time for it to embrace an education and a training of this sort. And when they are willing to work hard and to prepare themselves to be of service to the city, you will make much of them; but when they give themselves to loose living and care for nothing else than to enjoy riotously what their fathers left to them, you will despise them and look upon them as false to the city and to the good name of their ancestors. For it will be hard enough, even though you show such an attitude of mind in either case, to get our youth to look down upon a life of ease and be willing to give their minds to their own improvement and to philosophy.

But reflect upon the glory and the greatness of the deeds wrought by our city and our ancestors, review them in your minds and consider what kind of man was he, what was his birth and what the character of his education, who expelled the tyrants, brought the people into their own, and established our democratic state; what sort was he who conquered the barbarians in the battle at Marathon and won for the city the glory which has come to Athens from this victory; what was he who after him liberated the Hellenes and led our forefathers forth to the leadership and power which they achieved, and who, besides, appreciating the natural advantage of the Piraeus, girded the city with walls in despite of the Lacedaemonians; and what manner of man was he who after him filled the Acropolis with gold and silver and made the homes of the Athenians to overflow with prosperity and wealth: for you will find if you review the career of each of these, that it was not those who lived unscrupulously or negligently nor those who did not stand out from the multitude who accomplished these things, but that it was men who were superior and pre-eminent, not only in birth and reputation, but in wisdom and eloquence, who have been the authors of all our blessings. . . .

Aristotle

384–22 B.C.

It is clear . . . that there are branches of learning and education which we must study with a view to the enjoyment of leisure, and these are to be valued for their own sake; whereas those kinds of knowledge which are useful in business are deemed necessary,and exist for the sake of other things.

POLITICS

Aristotle was born in Macedonia, where his Greek father was royal physician to the king. After his father's death, he traveled to Athens and studied under Plato. He excelled beyond his peers at the Academy and eventually taught rhetoric there. Philip of Macedon engaged Aristotle as a tutor for his son, the future Alexander the Great. According to Plutarch, Aristotle taught Alexander ethics and politics and the more abstract philosophical disciplines. Aristotle also gave his pupil a copy of Homer's *Iliad* corrected in his own hand, a treasure which Alexander, imagining himself a new Achilles, kept under his pillow at night—along with a dagger. During Alexander's military campaigns, Aristotle returned to Athens and founded his own school, the Lyceum, a rival to Plato's Academy in its scope and influence. He amassed a large library, collected specimens, engaged in scientific research, and pondered the nature of the heavens and the earth.

THE SELECTIONS

Aristotle explores education, character, and virtue in the *Nicomachean Ethics*, a short selection from which (most of Book X.ix) follows. The abrupt ending links the *Ethics* to the *Politics*. Aristotle scatters comments on education throughout the *Politics* (especially in Book VII), but nearly all of Book VIII concerns the proper education of youth and why the city should care. Aristotle's emphasis on the state's compelling interest in education may be controversial, but he has a profound grasp of the relationship between education and the political health of the commonwealth. Aside from these practical legislative questions, the *Politics* values education for its own sake, as an end in itself, and not for its instrumental subservience to physical necessity or utilitarian ends. True education aims at freedom and nobility and delight: "To be seeking always after the useful does not become free and exalted souls." The *Politics* identifies themes that unified the Great Tradition of the liberal arts for more than two millennia: the formation of character, the cultivation of the intellect, the development of judgment, and the inspiration of delight in the right things. A detailed study of Aristotle's philosophy of education should include his *Rhetoric*.

from the Nicomachean Ethics
Book X

. . . We must therefore by some means secure that the character shall have at the outset a natural affinity for virtue, loving what is noble and hating what is base. And it is difficult to obtain a right education in virtue from youth up without being brought up under right laws; for to live temperately and hardily is not pleasant to most men, especially when young; hence the nurture and exercises of the young should be regulated by law, since temperance and hardiness will not be painful when they have become habitual. But doubtless it is not enough for people to receive the right nurture and discipline in youth; they must also practise the lessons they have learnt, and confirm them by habit, when they are grown up. Accordingly we shall need laws to regulate the discipline of adults as well, and in fact the whole life of the people generally; for the many are more amenable to compulsion and punishment than to reason and to moral ideals. Hence some persons hold, that while it is proper for the lawgiver to encourage and exhort men to virtue on moral grounds, in the expectation that those who have had a virtuous moral upbringing will respond, yet he is bound to impose chastisement and penalties on the disobedient and ill-conditioned, and to banish the incorrigible out of the state altogether. For (they argue) although the virtuous man, who guides his life by moral ideals, will be obedient to reason, the base, whose desires are fixed on pleasure, must be chastised by pain, like a beast of burden. This indeed is the ground for the view that the pains and penalties for transgressors should be such as are most opposed to their favourite pleasures.

But to resume: if, as has been said, in order to be good a man must have been properly educated and trained, and must subsequently continue to follow virtuous habits of life, and to do nothing base whether voluntarily or involuntarily, then this will be secured if men's lives are regulated by a certain intelligence, and by a right system, invested with adequate sanctions. Now paternal authority has not the power to compel obedience, nor indeed, speaking generally, has the authority of any individual unless he be a king or the like; but law on the other hand is a rule, emanating from a certain wisdom and intelligence, that has compulsory force. Men are hated when they thwart people's inclinations, even though they do so rightly, whereas law can enjoin virtuous conduct without being invidious. But Sparta appears to be the only or almost the only state in which the lawgiver has paid attention to the nurture and exercises of the citizens; in most states such matters have been entirely neglected, and every man lives as he likes, in Cyclops fashion "laying down the law For children and for spouse."

The best thing is then that there should be a proper system of public regulation; but when the matter is neglected by the community, it would seem to be the duty of the individual to assist his own children and friends to attain virtue, or even if not able to do so successfully, at all events to make this his aim. But it would seem to follow from what has been said before, that he will be more likely to be successful in this if he has acquired the science of legislation. Public regulations in any case must clearly be established by law, and only good laws will produce good regulations; but it would not seem to make any difference whether these laws are written or unwritten, or whether they are to regulate the education of a single person or of a number of people, any more than in the case of music or athletics or any other form of training. Paternal exhortations and family habits have authority in the household, just as legal enactments and national customs have authority in the state, and the more so on account of the ties of relationship and of benefits conferred that unite the head of the household to its other members: he can count on their natural affection and obedience at the outset. Moreover individual treatment is better than a common system, in education as in medicine. As a general rule rest and fasting are good for a fever, but they may not be best for a particular case; and presumably a professor of boxing does not impose the same style of fighting on all his pupils. It would appear then that private attention gives more accurate results in particular cases, for the particular subject is more likely to get the treatment that suits him. But a physician or trainer or any other director can best treat a particular person if he has a general knowledge of what is good for everybody, or for other people of the same kind: for the sciences deal with what is universal, as their names imply. Not but what it is possible no doubt for a particular individual to be successfully treated by someone who is not a scientific expert, but has an empirical knowledge based on careful observation of the effects of various forms of treatment upon the person in question; just as some people appear to be their own best doctors, though they could not do any good to someone else. But nevertheless it would doubtless be agreed that anyone who wishes to make himself a professional and a man of science must advance to general principles, and acquaint himself with these by the proper method: for science, as we said, deals with the universal. So presumably a man who wishes to make other people better (whether few or many) by discipline, must endeavour to acquire the science of legislation—assuming that it is possible to make us good by laws. For to mould aright the character of any and every person that presents himself is not a task that can be done by anybody, but only (if at all) by the man with scientific knowledge, just as is the case in medicine and the other professions involving a system of treatment and the exercise of prudence.

Is not then the next question to consider from whom or how the science of legislation can be learnt? Perhaps, like other subjects, from the experts, namely the politicians; for we saw that legislation is a branch of political science. But possibly it may seem that political science is unlike the other sciences and faculties. In these the persons who impart a knowledge of the faculty are the same as those who practise it, for instance physicians and painters; but in politics the sophists, who profess to teach the science, never practise it. It is practised by the politicians, who would appear to rely more upon a sort of empirical skill than on the exercise of abstract intelligence; for we do not see them writing or lecturing about political principles (though this might be a more honourable employment than composing forensic and parliamentary speeches), nor yet do we notice that they have made their own sons or any others of their friends into statesmen. Yet we should expect them to have done so had they been able, for they could have bequeathed no more valuable legacy to their countries, nor is there any quality they would choose for themselves, and therefore for those nearest to them, to possess, in preference to political capacity. Not that experience does not seem to contribute considerably to political success; otherwise men would never have become statesmen merely through practical association with politics; so it would appear that those who aspire to a scientific knowledge of politics require practical experience as well as study. On the other hand those sophists who profess to teach politics are found to be very far from doing so successfully. In fact they are absolutely ignorant of the very nature of the science and of the subjects with which it deals; otherwise they would not class it as identical with, or even inferior to, the art of rhetoric. Nor would they imagine that it is easy to frame a constitution by making a collection of such existing laws as are reputed to be good ones, on the assumption that one can then select the best among them; as if even this selection did not call for understanding, and as if to judge correctly were not a very difficult task, just as much as it is for instance in music. It is only the experts in an art who can judge correctly the productions of that art, and who understand the means and the method by which perfection is attained, and know which elements harmonize with which; amateurs may be content if they can discern whether the general result produced is good or bad, for example in the art of painting. Laws are the product, so to speak, of the art of politics; how then can a mere collection of laws teach a man the science of legislation, or make him able to judge which of them are the best? We do not see men becoming expert physicians but those from a study of medical handbooks. Yet medical writers attempt to describe not only general courses of treatment, but also methods of cure and modes of treatment for particular sorts of patients, classified according to their various habits of body; and their treatises appear to be of value for men who have had practical experience, though they are useless for the novice. Very possibly therefore collections of laws and constitutions may be serviceable to students capable of studying them critically, and judging what measures are valuable or the reverse, and what kind of institutions are suited to what national characteristics. But those who peruse such compilations without possessing a trained faculty cannot be capable of judging them correctly, unless they do so by instinct, though they may very likely sharpen their political intelligence.

As then the question of legislation has been left uninvestigated by previous thinkers, it will perhaps be well if we consider it for ourselves, together with the whole question of the constitution of the State, in order to complete as far as possible our philosophy of human affairs.

We will begin then by attempting a review of any pronouncements of value contributed by our predecessors in this or that branch of the subject; and then on the basis of our collection of constitutions we will consider what institutions are preservative and what destructive of states in general, and of the different forms of constitution in particular, and what are the reasons which cause some states to be well governed and others the contrary. For after studying these questions we shall perhaps be in a better position to discern what is the best constitution absolutely, and what are the best regulations, laws, and customs for any given form of constitution. Let us then begin our discussion.

from the Politics
Book VIII

1. No one will doubt that the legislator should direct his attention above all to the education of youth, or that the neglect of education does harm to states. The citizen should be molded to suit the form of government under which he lives. For each government has a peculiar character which originally formed and which continues to preserve it. The character of democracy creates democracy, and the character of oligarchy creates oligarchy; and always the better the character, the better the government.

Now for the exercise of any faculty or art a previous training and habituation are required; clearly therefore for the practice of virtue. And since the whole city has one end, it is manifest that education should be one and the same for all, and that it should be public, and not private,—not as at present, when every one looks after his own children separately, and gives them separate instruction of the sort which he thinks best; the training in things which are of common interest should be the same for all. Neither must we suppose that any one of the citizens belongs to himself, for they all belong to the state, and are each of them a part of the state, and the care of each part is inseparable from the care of the whole. In this particular the Lacedaemonians are to be praised, for they take the greatest pains about their children, and make education the business of the state.

2. That education should be regulated by law and should be an affair of state is not to be denied, but what should be the character of this public education, and how young persons should be educated, are questions which remain to be considered. For mankind are by no means agreed about the things to be taught, whether we look to virtue or the best life.

Neither is it clear whether education is more concerned with intellectual or with moral virtue. The existing practice is perplexing; no one knows on what principle we should proceed—should the useful in life, or should virtue, or should the higher knowledge, be the aim of our training; all three opinions have been entertained. Again, about the means there is no agreement; for different persons, starting with different ideas about the nature of virtue, naturally disagree about the practice of it.

There can be no doubt that children should be taught those useful things which are really necessary, but not all things; for occupations are divided into liberal and illiberal; and to young children should be imparted only such kinds of knowledge as will be useful to them without vulgarizing them. And any occupation, art, or science, which makes the body or soul or mind of the freeman less fit for the practice or exercise of virtue, is vulgar; wherefore we call those arts vulgar which tend to deform the body, and likewise all paid employments, for they absorb and degrade the mind.

There are also some liberal arts quite proper for a freeman to acquire, but only in a certain degree, and if he attend to them too closely, in order to attain perfection in them, the same evil effects will follow. The object also which a man sets before him makes a great difference; if he does or learns anything for his own sake or for the sake of his friends, or with a view to excellence, the action will not appear illiberal; but if done for the sake of others, the very same action will be thought menial and servile. The received subjects of instruction, as I have already remarked, are partly of a liberal and partly of an illiberal character.

3. The customary branches of education are in number four; they are—(1) reading and writing, (2) gymnastic exercises, (3) music, to which is sometimes added (4) drawing. Of these, reading and writing and drawing are regarded as useful for the purposes of life in a variety of ways, and gymnastic exercises are thought to infuse courage. Concerning music a doubt may be raised—in our own day most men cultivate it for the sake of pleasure, but originally it was included in education, because nature herself, as has often been said, requires that we should be able, not only to work well, but to use leisure well; for, as I must repeat once and again, the first principle of all action is leisure. Both are required, but leisure is better than occupation; and therefore the question must be asked in good earnest, what ought we to do when at leisure? Clearly we ought not to be amusing ourselves, for then amusement would be the end of life. But if this is inconceivable, and yet amid serious occupations amusement is needed more than at other times (for he who is hard at work has need of relaxation, and amusement gives relaxation, whereas occupation is always accompanied with exertion and effort), at suitable times we should introduce amusements, and they should be our medicines, for the emotion which they create in the soul is a relaxation, and from the pleasure we obtain rest. Leisure of itself gives pleasure and happiness and enjoyment of life, which are experienced, not by the busy man, but by those who have leisure. For he who is occupied has in view some end which he has not attained; but happiness is an end which all men deem to be accompanied with pleasure and not with pain. This pleasure, however, is regarded differently by different persons, and varies according to the habit of individuals; the pleasure of the best man is the best, and springs from the noblest sources.

It is clear then that there are branches of learning and education which we must study with a view to the enjoyment of leisure, and these are to be valued for their own sake; whereas those kinds of knowledge which are useful in business are to be deemed necessary, and exist for the sake of other things. And therefore our fathers admitted music into education, not on the ground either of its necessity or utility, for it is not necessary, nor indeed useful in the same manner as reading and writing, which are useful in money-making, in the management of a household, in the acquisition of knowledge and in political life, nor like drawing, useful for a more correct judgment of the works of artists, nor again like gymnastic, which gives health and strength; for neither of these is to be gained from music. There remains, then, the use of music for intellectual enjoyment in leisure; which appears to have been the reason of its introduction, this being one of the ways in which it is thought that a freeman should pass his leisure; as Homer says—

How good it is to invite men to the pleasant feast,

and afterwards he speaks of others whom he describes as inviting

The bard who would delight them all.

And in another place Odysseus says there is no better way of passing life than when

> Men's hearts are merry and the banqueters in the hall, sitting in order, hear the voice
> of the minstrel.

It is evident, then, that there is a sort of education in which parents should train their sons, not as being useful or necessary, but because it is liberal or noble. Whether this is of one kind only, or of more than one, and if so, what they are, and how they are to be imparted, must hereafter be determined. Thus much we are now in a position to say that the ancients witness to us; for their opinion may be gathered from the fact that music is one of the received and traditional branches of education. Further, it is clear that children should be instructed in some useful things,—for example, in reading and writing,—not only for their usefulness, but also because many other sorts of knowledge are acquired through them. With a like view they may be taught drawing, not to prevent their making mistakes in their own purchases, or in order that they may not be imposed upon in the buying or selling of articles, but rather because it makes them judges of the beauty of the human form. To be seeking always after the useful does not become free and exalted souls. Now it is clear that in education habit must go before reason, and the body before the mind; and therefore boys should be handed over to the trainer, who creates in them the proper habit of body, and to the wrestling-master, who teaches them their exercises.

4. Of these states which in our own day seem to take the greatest care of children, some aim at producing in them an athletic habit, but they only injure their forms and stunt their growth. Although the Lacedaemonians have not fallen into this mistake, yet they brutalize their children by laborious exercises which they think will make them courageous. But in truth, as we have often repeated, education should not be exclusively directed to this or to any other single end. And even if we suppose the Lacedaemonians to be right in their end, they do not attain it. For among barbarians and among animals courage is found associated, not with the greatest ferocity, but with a gentle and lion-like temper. There are many races who are ready enough to kill and eat men, such as the Achaeans and Heniochi, who both live about the Black Sea; and there are other inland tribes, as bad or worse, who all live by plunder, but have no courage. It is notorious that the Lacedaemonians, while they were themselves assiduous in their laborious drill, were superior to others, but now they are beaten both in war and gymnastic exercises. For their ancient superiority did not depend on their mode of training their youth, but only on the circumstance that they trained them at a time when others did not. Hence we may infer that what is noble, not what is brutal, should have the first place; no wolf or other wild animal will face a really noble danger; such dangers are for the brave man. And parents who devote their children to gymnastics while they neglect their necessary education, in reality vulgarize them; for they make them useful to the state in one quality only, and even in this the argument proves them to be inferior to others. We should judge the Lacedaemonians not from what they have been but from what they are; for now they have rivals who compete with their education; formerly they had none.

It is an admitted principle, that gymnastic exercises should be employed in education, and that for children they should be of a lighter kind, avoiding severe regimen or painful toil, lest the growth of the body be impaired. The evil of excessive training in early years is strikingly proved by the example of the Olympic victors; for not more than two or three of them have gained a prize both as boys and as men; their early training and severe gymnastic exercises exhausted their constitutions. When boyhood is over, three years should be spent in other studies; the period of life which follows may then be devoted to hard exercise and strict regimen. Men ought not to labor at the same time with their minds and with their bodies; for the two kinds of labor are opposed to one another, the labor of the body impedes the mind, and the labor of the mind the body.

5. Concerning music there are some questions which we have already raised; these we may now resume and carry further; and our remarks will serve as a prelude to this or any other discussion of the subject. It is not easy to determine the nature of music, or why any one should have a knowledge of it. Shall we say, for the sake of amusement and relaxation, like sleep or drinking, which are not good in themselves, but are pleasant, and at the same time "make care to cease," as Euripides says? And therefore men rank them with music, and make use of all three,—sleep, drinking, music,—to which some add dancing. Or shall we argue that music conduces to virtue, on the ground that it can form our minds and habituate us to true pleasures as our bodies are made by gymnastic to be of a certain character? Or shall we say that it contributes to the enjoyment of leisure and mental cultivation, which is a third alternative? Now obviously youth are not to be instructed with a view to their amusement, for learning is no pleasure, but is accompanied with pain. Neither is intellectual enjoyment suitable to boys of that age, for it is the end, and that which is imperfect cannot attain the perfect or end. But perhaps it may be said that boys learn music for the sake of the amusement which they will have when they are grown up. If so, why should they learn themselves, and not, like the Persian and Median kings, enjoy the pleasure and instruction which is derived from hearing others? (for surely skilled persons who have made music the business and profession of their lives will be better performers than those who practice only to learn). If they must learn music, on the same principle they should learn cookery, which is absurd. And even granting that music may form the character, the objection still holds: why should we learn ourselves? Why cannot we attain true pleasure and form a correct judgment from hearing others, like the Lacedaemonians? For they, without learning music, nevertheless can correctly judge, as they say, of good and bad melodies. Or again, if music should be used to promote cheerfulness and refined intellectual enjoyment, the objection still remains—why should we learn ourselves instead of enjoying the performance of others? We may illustrate what we are saying by our conception of the Gods; for in the poets Zeus does not himself sing or play on the lyre. Nay, we call professional performers vulgar; no freeman would play or sing unless he were intoxicated or in jest. But these matters may be left for the present.

The first question is whether music is or is not to be a part of education. Of the three things mentioned in our discussion, which is it?—Education or amusement or intellectual enjoyment, for it may be reckoned under all three, and seems to share in the nature of all of them. Amusement is for the sake of relaxation, and relaxation is of necessity sweet, for it is the remedy of pain caused by toil, and intellectual enjoyment is universally acknowledged to contain an element not only of the noble but of the pleasant, for happiness is made up of both. All men agree that music is one of the pleasantest things, whether with or without song; as Musaeus says,

Song is to mortals of all things the sweetest.

Hence and with good reason it is introduced into social gatherings and entertainments, because it makes the hearts of men glad: so that on this ground alone we may assume that the young ought to be trained in it. For innocent pleasures are not only in harmony with the perfect end of life, but they also provide relaxation. And whereas men rarely attain the end, but often rest by the way and amuse themselves, not only with a view to some good, but also for the pleasure's sake, it may be well for them at times to find a refreshment in music. It sometimes happens that men make amusement the end, for the end probably contains some element of pleasure, though not any ordinary or lower pleasure; but they mistake the lower for the higher, and in seeking for the one find the other, since every pleasure has a likeness to the end of action. For the end is not eligible, nor do the pleasures which we have described exist, for the sake of any future good but of the past, that is to say, they are the alleviation of past toils and pains. And we may infer this to be the reason why men seek happiness from common pleasures. But music is pursued, not only as an alleviation of past toil, but also as providing recreation. And who can say whether, having this use, it may not also have a nobler one? In addition to this common pleasure, felt and shared in by all (for the pleasure given by music is natural, and therefore adapted to all ages and characters), may it not have also some influence over the character and the soul? It must have such an influence if characters are affected by it. And that they are so affected is proved by the power which the songs of Olympus and of many others exercise; for beyond question they inspire enthusiasm, and enthusiasm is an emotion of the ethical part of the soul. Besides, when men hear imitations, even unaccompanied by melody or rhythm, their feelings move in sympathy. Since then music is a pleasure, and virtue consists in rejoicing and loving and hating aright, there is clearly nothing which we are so much concerned to acquire and to cultivate as the power of forming right judgments, and of taking delight in good dispositions and noble actions. Rhythm and melody supply imitations of anger and gentleness, and also of courage and temperance and of virtues and vices in general, which hardly fall short of the actual affections, as we know from our own experience, for in listening to such strains our souls undergo a change. The habit of feeling pleasure or pain at mere representations is not far removed from the same feeling about realities; for example, if any one delights in the sight of a statue for its beauty only, it necessarily follows that the sight of the original will be pleasant to him. No other sense, such as taste or touch, has any resemblance to moral qualities; in sight only there is a little, for figures are to some extent of a moral character, and (so far) all participate in the feeling about them. Again, figures and colors are not imitations, but signs of moral habits, indications which the body gives of states of feeling. The connection of them with morals is slight, but in so far as there is any, young men should be taught to look, not at the works of Pauson, but at those of Polygnotus, or any other painter or statuary who expresses moral ideas. On the other hand, even in mere melodies there is an imitation of character for the musical modes differ essentially from one another, and those who hear them are differently affected by each. Some of them make men sad and grave, like the so-called Mixolydian, others enfeeble the mind, like the relaxed harmonies, others, again, produce a moderate and settled temper, which appears to be the peculiar effect of the Dorian; the Phrygian inspires enthusiasm. The whole subject has been well treated by philosophical writers on this branch of education, and they confirm their arguments by facts. The same principles apply to rhythms: some have a character of rest, others of motion, and of these latter again, some have a more vulgar, others a nobler movement. Enough has been said to show that music has a power of forming the character, and should therefore be introduced into the education of the young. The study is suited to the stage of youth, for young persons will not, if they can help, endure anything which is not sweetened by pleasure, and music has a natural sweetness. There seems to be in us a sort of affinity to harmonies and rhythms, which makes some philosophers say that the soul is a harmony, others, that she possesses harmony.

6. And now we have to determine the question which has been already raised, whether children should be themselves taught to sing and play or not. Clearly there is a considerable difference made in the character by the actual practice of the art. It is difficult, if not impossible, for those who do not perform to be good judges of the performance of others. Besides, children should have something to do, and the rattle of Archytas, which people give to their children in order to amuse them and prevent them from breaking anything in the house, was a capital invention, for a young thing cannot be quiet. The rattle is a toy suited to the infant mind and (musical) education is a rattle or toy for children of a larger growth. We conclude then that they should be taught music in such a way as to become not only critics but performers.

The question what is or is not suitable for different ages may be easily answered; nor is there any difficulty in meeting the objection of those who say that the study of music is vulgar. We reply (1) in the first place, that they who are to be judges must also be performers, and that they should begin to practice early, although when they are older they may be spared the execution; they must have learned to appreciate what is good and to delight in it, thanks to the knowledge which they acquired in their youth. As to (2) the vulgarizing effect which music is supposed to exercise, this is a question (of degree), which we shall have no difficulty in determining, when we have considered to what extent freemen who are being trained to political virtue should pursue the art, what melodies and what rhythms they should be allowed to use, and what instruments should be employed in teaching them to play, for even the instrument makes a difference. The answer to the objection turns upon these distinctions; for it is quite possible that certain methods of teaching and learning music do really have a degrading effect. It is evident then that the learning of music ought not to impede the business of riper years, or to degrade the body or render it unfit for civil or military duties, whether for the early practice or for the later study of them.

The right measure will be attained if students of music stop short of the arts which are practiced in professional contests, and do not seek to acquire those fantastic marvels of execution which are now the fashion in such contests, and from these have passed into education. Let the young pursue their studies until they are able to feel delight in noble melodies and rhythms, and not merely in that common part of music in which every slave or child and even some animals find pleasure.

From these principles we may also infer what instruments should be used. The flute, or any other instrument which requires great skill, as for example the harp, ought not to be admitted into education, but only such as will make intelligent students of music or of the other parts of education. Besides, the flute is not an instrument which has a good moral effect; it is too exciting. The proper time for using it is when the performance aims not at instruction, but at the relief of the passions. And there is a further objection; the impediment which the flute presents to the use of the voice detracts from its educational value. The ancients therefore were right in forbidding the flute to youths and freemen, although they had once allowed it. For when their wealth gave them greater leisure, and they had loftier notions of excellence, being also elated with their success, both before and after the Persian War, with more zeal than discernment they pursued every kind of knowledge, and so they introduced the flute into education. At Lacedaemon there was a Choragus who led the chorus with a flute, and at Athens the instrument became so popular that most freemen could play upon it. The popularity is shown by the tablet which Thrasippus dedicated when he furnished the chorus to Ecphantides. Later experience enabled men to judge what was or was not really conducive to virtue, and they rejected both the flute and several other old-fashioned instruments, such as the Lydian harp, the many-stringed lyre, the "heptagon," "triangle," "sambuca," and the like—which are intended only to give pleasure to the hearer, and require extraordinary skill of hand. There is a meaning also in the myth of the ancients, which tells how Athene invented the flute and then threw it away. It was not a bad idea of theirs, that the Goddess disliked the instrument because it made the face ugly; but with still more reason may we say that she rejected it because the acquirement of flute-playing contributes nothing to the mind, since to Athene we ascribe both knowledge and art.

Thus then we reject the professional instruments and also the professional mode of education in music—and by professional we mean that which is adopted in contests, for in this the performer practices the art, not for the sake of his own improvement, but in order to give pleasure, and that of a vulgar sort, to his hearers. For this reason the execution of such music is not the part of a freeman but of a paid performer, and the result is that the performers are vulgarized, for the end at which they aim is bad. The vulgarity of the spectator tends to lower the character of the music and therefore of the performers; they look to him—he makes them what they are, and fashions even their bodies by the movements which he expects them to exhibit.

7. We have also to consider rhythms and harmonies. Shall we use them all in education or make a distinction? And shall the distinction be that which is made by those who are engaged in education, or shall it be some other? For we see that music is produced by melody and rhythm, and we ought to know what influence these have respectively on education, and whether we should prefer excellence in melody or excellence in rhythm. But as the subject has been very well treated by many musicians of the present day, and also by philosophers who have had considerable experience of musical education, to these we would refer the more exact student of the subject; we shall only speak of it now after the manner of the legislator, having regard to general principles.

We accept the division of melodies proposed by certain philosophers into ethical melodies, melodies of action, and passionate or inspiring melodies, each having, as they say, a mode or harmony corresponding to it. But we maintain further that music should be studied, not for the sake of one, but of many benefits, that is to say, with a view to (1) education, (2) purification (the word "purification" we use at present without explanation, but when hereafter we speak of poetry, we will treat the subject with more precision); music may also serve (3) for intellectual enjoyment, for relaxation and for recreation after exertion. It is clear, therefore, that all the harmonies must be employed by us, but not all of them in the same manner. In education ethical melodies are to be preferred, but we may listen to the melodies of action and passion when they are performed by others. For feelings such as pity and fear, or, again, enthusiasm, exist very strongly in some souls, and have more or less influence over all. Some persons fall into a religious frenzy, whom we see disenthralled by the use of mystic melodies, which bring healing and purification to the soul. Those who are influenced by pity or fear and every emotional nature have a like experience, others in their degree are stirred by something which specially affects them, and, all are in a manner purified and their souls lightened and delighted. The melodies of purification likewise give an innocent pleasure to mankind. Such are the harmonies and the melodies in which those who perform music at the theater should be invited to compete. But since the spectators are of two kinds—the one free and educated, the other a vulgar crowd composed of mechanics, laborers, and the like—there ought to be contests and exhibitions instituted for the relaxation of the second class also. And the melodies will correspond to their minds; for as their minds are perverted from the natural state, so there are exaggerated and corrupted harmonies which are in like manner a perversion. A man receives pleasure from what is natural to him, and therefore professional musicians may be allowed to practice this lower sort of music before an audience of a lower type. But, for the purposes of education, as I have already said, those modes and melodies should be employed which are ethical, such as the Dorian; though we may include any others which are approved by philosophers who have had a musical education. The Socrates of the *Republic* is wrong in retaining only the Phrygian mode along with the Dorian, and the more so because he rejects the flute; for the Phrygian is to the modes what the flute is to musical instruments—both of them are exciting and emotional. Poetry proves this, for Bacchic frenzy and all similar emotions are most suitably expressed by the flute, and are better set to the Phrygian than to any other harmony. The dithyramb, for example, is acknowledged to be Phrygian, a fact of which the connoisseurs of music offer many proofs, saying, among other things, that Philoxenus, having attempted to compose his Tales as a dithyramb in the Dorian mode, found it impossible, and fell back into the more appropriate Phrygian. All men agree that the Dorian music is the gravest and manliest. And whereas we say that the extremes should be avoided and the mean followed, and whereas the Dorian is a mean between the other harmonies (the Phrygian and the Lydian), it is evident that our youth should be taught the Dorian music.

Two principles have to be kept in view, what is possible, what is becoming: at these every man ought to aim. But even these are relative to age; the old, who have lost their powers, cannot very well sing the severe melodies, and nature herself seems to suggest that their songs should be of the more relaxed kind. Wherefore the musicians likewise blame Socrates, and with justice, for rejecting the relaxed harmonies in education under the idea that they are intoxicating, not in the ordinary sense of intoxication (for wine rather tends to excite men), but because they have no strength in them. And so with a view to a time of life when men begin to grow old, they ought to practice the gentler harmonies and melodies as well as the others. And if there be any harmony, such as the Lydian above all others appears to be, which is suited to children of tender age, and possesses the elements both of order and of education, clearly (we ought to use it, for) education should be based upon three principles—the mean, the possible, the becoming, these three.

Cicero

106–43 B.C.

*Only those are men who are perfected in the arts appropriate to
humanity.*

Republic

❧

Marcus Tullius Cicero, Roman lawyer, statesman, and peerless orator, defended the traditions of the Roman Republic first against Catiline and then against Julius Caesar. His remarkable career ended tragically when he was beheaded by Marc Antony's henchmen in the civil wars following Caesar's assassination. His surviving letters, dialogues, and treatises set the standard of literary Latin in antiquity and later among the Renaissance humanists. At the time of the Roman Empire, according to H. I. Marrou, "being educated meant, to a Latin, knowing Virgil and Cicero."[1] Cicero helped bridge the Greek and Roman intellectual worlds (it was quipped that he taught Plato to speak Latin). Marrou writes that in Cicero "Latin Hellenism reaches its perfection. Cicero not only knew Greek perfectly, but he had assimilated all the Greek culture of his day. In Athens and in Rhodes he had studied rhetoric and philosophy as deeply as any Greek. His culture was profound, not as a superficial veneer, not as an affectation."[2] He endured around him, however, shallow Romans for whom cultivation was such a veneer and affectation. In the *Tusculan Dialogues* he wrote, "We Romans have gone to school in Greece; we read their poets and learn them by heart, and then we think ourselves scholars and men of culture" (ii.27). Cicero occupied himself with the true cultivation of the ideal orator. An orator in the Roman world was more than a highly skilled public speaker or courtroom

1. *A History of Education in Antiquity,* trans. by George Lamb (New York: Sheed and Ward, 1956), 259.
2. Ibid., 258.

attorney; he was a statesman. In several of his works, Cicero ponders the best education of the consummate public servant, a man possessing both eloquence and wisdom held in fruitful balance. His ideal leader combined action with reflection, practical experience with the learned arts, and fidelity to tradition with "the foreign learning which originated with Socrates" (Cicero's *Republic,* III.iii).

THE SELECTIONS

Pro Archia Poeta (62 B.C.) is Cicero's moving tribute to a beloved teacher and friend. The speech is a patriotic defense of the Greek poet Archias's right to Roman citizenship (against the counterclaims of the prosecuting attorney Gratius). The dialogue *De Oratore* (On the Orator) dates from 55 B.C. and is central to Cicero's mature thinking on education. In Aubrey Gwynn's estimation, *De Oratore* is "a masterpiece which may not unfairly be called the orator's programme of educational reform," a work that embodies "the fullest statement of Cicero's educational theory."[3] Through the mouth of Crassus, his former rhetoric teacher, Cicero offers a penetrating discourse on the proper relationship between philosophy and oratory, or between the contemplative life of academic leisure and the active life of public service. Cicero tries to maintain a workable real-world synthesis between the two that would produce the rare combination of learned orator and eloquent philosopher. *The Orator* (46 B.C.) is a prose work in which Cicero addresses some of the same themes, concluding "that whatever ability I possess as an orator comes, not from the workshop of the rhetoricians, but from the spacious grounds of the Academy" (iii.12), and that "the foundation of eloquence, as of everything else, is wisdom" (xx.70). Finally, two additional works directly concern education as the cultivation of wisdom and virtue: the dialogue *De Partitione Oratoria* (On the Parts of Oratory), written about 46 B.C., and the profound and influential treatise *De Officiis* (On Duties), written in 44 B.C. in the grim days after Caesar's assassination. These were written for Cicero's son Marcus as he began his university studies in Athens.

from Pro Archia Poeta

. . . You will no doubt ask me, Gratius, to account for the deep interest I feel in my friend. It is because he provides refreshment for my spirit after the clamour of the courts, and repose for senses jaded by their vulgar wrangling. Do you think that I could find inspiration for my daily speeches on so manifold a variety of topics, did I not cultivate my mind with study, or that my mind could endure so great a strain, did not study too provide it with relaxation? I am a votary of literature, and make the confession unashamed; shame belongs rather to the bookish recluse, who knows not how to apply his reading to the good of his fellows, or to manifest its fruits to the eyes of all. But what shame should be mine, gentlemen, who have made it a rule of my life for all these years never to allow the sweets of a cloistered

---

3. Aubrey Gwynn, *Roman Education from Cicero to Quintilian* (Oxford: Oxford University Press, 1926), 81.

ease or the seductions of pleasure or the enticements of repose to prevent me from aiding any man in the hour of his need? How then can I justly be blamed or censured, if it shall be found that I have devoted to literature a portion of my leisure hours no longer than others without blame devote to the pursuit of material gain, to the celebration of festivals or games, to pleasure and the repose of mind and body, to protracted banqueting, or perhaps to the gaming-board or to ball-playing? I have the better right to indulgence herein, because my devotion to letters strengthens my oratorical powers, and these, such as they are, have never failed my friends in their hour of peril. Yet insignificant though these powers may seem to be, I fully realize from what source I draw all that is highest in them. Had I not persuaded myself from my youth up, thanks to the moral lessons derived from a wide reading, that nothing is to be greatly sought after in this life save glory and honour, and that in their quest all bodily pains and all dangers of death or exile should be lightly accounted, I should never have borne for the safety of you all the brunt of many a bitter encounter, or bared my breast to the daily onsets of abandoned persons. All literature, all philosophy, all history, abounds with incentives to noble action, incentives which would be buried in black darkness were the light of the written word not flashed upon them. How many pictures of high endeavour the great authors of Greece and Rome have drawn for our use, and bequeathed to us, not only for our contemplation, but for our emulation! These I have held ever before my vision throughout my public career, and have guided the workings of my brain and my soul by meditating upon patterns of excellence.

"But," an objector may ask, "were these great men, whose virtues are perpetuated in literature, themselves adepts in the learning which you describe in such fulsome terms?" It would be difficult to make a sweeping and categorical reply, but at the same time I have my answer ready. Many there have been, no doubt, exceptionally endowed in temperament and character, who, without any aid from culture, but only by a heaven-born light within their own souls, have been self-schooled in restraint and fortitude; I would even go so far as to say that natural gifts without education have more often attained to glory and virtue than education without natural gifts. Yet I do at the same time assert that when to a lofty and brilliant character is applied the moulding influence of abstract studies, the result is often inscrutably and unapproachably noble. Such a character our fathers were privileged to behold in the divine figure of Scipio Africanus; such were those patterns of continence and self-control, Gaius Laelius and Lucius Furius; such was the brave and venerable Marcus Cato, the most accomplished man of his day. These surely would never have devoted themselves to literary pursuits, had they not been aided thereby in the appreciation and pursuit of merit. But let us for the moment waive these solid advantages; let us assume that entertainment is the sole end of reading; even so, I think you would hold that no mental employment is so broadening to the sympathies or so enlightening to the understanding. Other pursuits belong not to all times, all ages, all conditions; but this gives stimulus to our youth and diversion to our old age; this adds a charm to success, and offers a haven of consolation to failure. In the home it delights, in the world it hampers not. Through the night-watches, on all our journeying, and in our hours of country ease, it is our unfailing companion. . . .

from De Oratore

IV. . . . But the truth is that this oratory is a greater thing, and has its sources in more arts and branches of study, than people suppose.

V. For, where the number of students is very great, the supply of masters of the very best, the quality of natural ability outstanding, the variety of issues unlimited, the prizes open to eloquence exceedingly splendid, what else could anyone think to be the cause, unless it be the really incredible vastness and difficulty of the subject? To begin with, a knowledge of very many matters must be grasped, without which oratory is but an empty and ridiculous swirl of verbiage: and the distinctive style has to be formed, not only by the choice of words, but also by the arrangement of the same; and all the mental emotions, with which nature has endowed the human race, are to be intimately understood, because it is in calming or kindling the feelings of the audience that the full power and science of oratory are to be brought into play. To this there should be added a certain humour, flashes of wit, the culture befitting a gentleman, and readiness and terseness alike in repelling and in delivering the attack, the whole being combined with a delicate charm and urbanity. Further, the complete history of the past and a store of precedents must be retained in the memory, nor may a knowledge of statute law and our national law in general be omitted. And why should I [Crassus] go on to describe the speaker's delivery? That needs to be controlled by bodily carriage, gesture, play of features and changing intonation of voice; and how important that is wholly by itself, the actor's trivial art and the stage proclaim; for there, although all are labouring to regulate the expression, the voice, and the movements of the body, everyone knows how few actors there are, or ever have been, whom we could bear to watch! What need to speak of that universal treasure-house the memory? Unless this faculty be placed in charge of the ideas and phrases which have been thought out and well weighed, even though as conceived by the orator they were of the highest excellence, we know that they will all be wasted.

Let us therefore cease to wonder what may be the cause of the rarity of orators, since oratory is the result of a whole number of things, in any one of which to succeed is a great achievement, and let us rather exhort our children, and the others whose fame and repute are dear to us, to form a true understanding of the greatness of their task, and not to believe that they can gain their coveted object by reliance on the rules or teachers or methods of practice employed by everybody, but to rest assured that they can do this by the help of certain other means.

VI. And indeed in my opinion, no man can be an orator complete in all points of merit, who has not attained a knowledge of all important subjects and arts. For it is from knowledge that oratory must derive its beauty and fullness, and unless there is such knowledge, well-grasped and comprehended by the speaker, there must be something empty and almost childish in the utterance. Not that I am going to lay so heavy a burden upon orators—least of all upon our own, amid all the distractions of life in Rome—as to hold that there is nothing of which it is permissible for them to be ignorant, although the significance of the term "orator," and the mere act of professing eloquence, seem to undertake and to promise that every subject whatsoever, proposed to an orator, will be treated by him with both distinction and knowledge. But being assured that to most men this appears a vast and indeed limitless enterprise, and perceiving that the Greeks, men not only abounding in genius and learning, but also amply endowed with leisure and the love of study, have already made a sort of division of the arts,—nor did every student of theirs work over the whole field by himself, but they separated from other uses of speech that portion of oratory which is concerned with the public discussions of the law-courts and of debate, and left that branch only to the orator—I shall not include in this work more than has been assigned to this type of oratory by the all but unanimous judgement of the most eminent men, after investigation and long argument of the matter; nor shall I recall, from the cradle of our boyish learning of days gone by, a long string of precepts, but I shall repeat the things I heard of as once handled in a discussion between men who were the most eloquent of our nation, and of the highest rank in distinction of every kind. Not that I despise what the Greek craftsmen and teachers of oratory have left us; but that is open to the view and ready to the hand of every man, nor could it be more happily set forth or more clearly expounded by any interpretations of my own, so that you will forgive me, brother mine, I do believe, if I prefer to Greek instruction the authoritative judgement of those to whom the highest honours in eloquence have been awarded by our own fellow-countrymen. . . .

XIV. Indeed in handling those causes which everybody acknowledges to be within the exclusive sphere of oratory, there is not seldom something to be brought forth and employed, not from practice in public speaking—the only thing you allow the orator—but from some more abstruse branch of knowledge. I ask, for instance, whether an advocate can either assail or defend a commander-in-chief without experience of the art of war, or sometimes too without knowledge of the various regions of land or sea? Whether he can address the popular assembly in favour of the passing or rejection of legislative proposals, or the Senate concerning any of the departments of State administration, if he lack consummate knowledge—practical as well as theoretical of political science? Whether a speech can be directed to inflaming or even repressing feeling and passion—a faculty of the first importance to the orator—unless the speaker has made a most careful search into all those theories respecting the natural characters and the habits of conduct of mankind, which are unfolded by the philosophers?

And I rather think I shall come short of convincing you on my next point—at all events I will not hesitate to speak my mind: your natural science itself, your mathematics, and other studies which just now you reckoned as belonging peculiarly to the rest of the arts, do indeed pertain to the knowledge of their professors, yet if anyone should wish by speaking to put these same arts in their full light, it is to oratorical skill that he must run for help. If, again, it is established that Philo, that master-builder who constructed an arsenal for the Athenians, described the plan of his work very eloquently to the people, his eloquence must be ascribed not to his architectural, but rather to his oratorical ability. So too, if Marcus Antonius here had had to speak on behalf of Hermodorus upon the construction of dockyards, having got up his case from his client, he would then have discoursed gracefully and copiously of an art to which he was not a stranger. Asclepiades also, he with whom we have been familiar both as physician and as friend, at the time when he was surpassing the rest of his profession in eloquence, was exhibiting, in such graceful speaking, the skill of an orator, not that of a physician. In fact that favourite assertion of Socrates—that every man was eloquent enough upon a subject that he knew—has in it some plausibility but no truth: it is nearer the truth to say that neither can anyone be eloquent upon a subject that is unknown to him, nor, if he knows it perfectly and yet does not know how to shape and polish his style, can he speak fluently even upon that which he does know.

XV. Accordingly, should anyone wish to define in a comprehensive manner the complete and special meaning of the word, he will be an orator, in my opinion worthy of so dignified a title, who, whatever the topic that crops up to be unfolded in discourse, will speak thereon with knowledge, method, charm and retentive memory, combining with these qualifications a certain distinction of bearing. If however someone considers my expression "whatever the topic" to be altogether too extensive, he may clip and prune it to his individual taste, but to this much I shall hold fast—though the orator be ignorant of what is to be found in all the other arts and branches of study, and know only what is dealt with in debate and the practice of public-speaking; none the less, if he should have to discourse even on these other subjects, then after learning the technicalities of each from those who know the same, the orator will speak about them far better than even the men who are masters of these arts. For example, should our friend Sulpicius here have to speak upon the art of war, he will inquire of our relative Gaius Marius, and when he has received his teachings, will deliver himself in such fashion as to seem even to Gaius Marius to be almost better informed on the subject than Gaius Marius himself; while if his topic is to be the law of private rights, he will consult yourself and, notwithstanding your consummate learning and skill in these very things which you have taught him, he will surpass you in the art of exposition. If again some matter should confront him wherein he must speak of human nature, human vices or the passions, of moderation or self-control, of sorrow or death, then perhaps if he thinks fit—although an orator must have knowledge of such things—he will have taken counsel with Sextus Pompeius, a man accomplished in moral science; so much he will assuredly achieve, that whatever his subject and whoever his instructor, on that subject he will express himself far more gracefully than his master himself. Nevertheless, if he will listen to me, since philosophy is divided into three branches, which respectively deal with the mysteries of nature, with the subtleties of dialectic, and with human life and conduct, let us quit claim to the first two, by way of concession to our indolence, but unless we keep our hold on the third, which has ever been the orator's province, we shall leave the orator no sphere wherein to attain greatness. For which reason this division of philosophy, concerned with human life and manners, must all of it be mastered by the orator; as for the other matters, even though he has not studied them, he will still be able, whenever the necessity arises, to beautify them by his eloquence, if only they are brought to his notice and described to him.

XVI. Indeed if it is agreed in learned circles that a man who knew no astronomy—Aratus to wit—has sung of the heavenly spaces and the stars in verse of a consummate finish and excellence, and that another who was a complete stranger to country life, Nicander of Colophon, has written with distinction on rural affairs, using something of a poet's skill and not that of a farmer, what reason is there why an orator should not discourse most eloquently concerning those subjects which he has conned for a specific argument and occasion? The truth is that the poet is a very near kinsman of the orator, rather more heavily fettered as regards rhythm, but with ampler freedom in his choice of words, while in the use of many sorts of ornament he is his ally and almost his counterpart; in one respect at all events something like identity exists, since he sets no boundaries or limits to his claims, such as would prevent him from ranging whither he will with the same freedom and licence as the other. For with regard to your remark, Scaevola, that, had you not been in my domain, you would not have endured my assertion that the orator must be accomplished in every kind of discourse and in every department of culture, I should certainly never have made that assertion, did I consider myself to be the man I am endeavouring to portray. But, as was often said by Gaius Lucilius—who was not altogether pleased with you, and for that very reason less intimate with myself than he wished, but for all that an instructed critic and thorough gentleman of the city—my opinion is this, that no one should be numbered with the orators who is not accomplished in all those arts that befit the well-bred; for though we do not actually parade these in our discourse, it is none the less made clear to demonstration whether we are strangers to them or have learned to know them. Just as ball-players do not in their game itself employ the characteristic dexterity of the gymnasium, and yet their very movements show whether they have had such training or know nothing of that art; and, just as, in the case of those who are portraying anything, even though at the moment they are making no use of the painter's art, there is none the less no difficulty in seeing whether or not they know how to paint; even so is it with these same speeches in the Courts, the popular assembly and the Senate-house—granting that the other arts may not be specially brought into play, still it is made easily discernible whether the speaker has merely floundered about in this declamatory business or whether, before approaching his task of oratory, he has been trained in all the liberal arts.

BOOK THREE

XIV. . . . For the genuine orator must have investigated and heard and read and discussed and handled and debated the whole of the contents of the life of mankind, inasmuch as that is the field of the orator's activity, the subject matter of his study. For eloquence is one of the supreme virtues—although all the virtues are equal and on a par, but nevertheless one has more beauty and distinction in outward appearance than another, as is the case with this faculty, which, after compassing a knowledge of facts, gives verbal expression to the thoughts and purposes of the mind in such a manner as to have the power of driving the hearers forward in any direction in which it has applied its weight; and the stronger this faculty is, the more necessary it is for it to be combined with integrity and supreme wisdom, and if we bestow fluency of speech on persons devoid of those virtues, we shall not have made orators of them but shall have put weapons into the hands of madmen.

XV. This method of attaining and of expressing thought, this faculty of speaking, was, I say, designated by the ancient Greeks wisdom; this was the source that produced men like Lycurgus and Pittacus and Solon of old, and after their likeness came the Coruncanii and Fabricii, the Catos and Scipios of Rome, not so much perhaps as the result of instruction but owing to a similarity of intention and of will. Others again with the same wisdom but a different principle as to life's purposes pursued tranquillity and leisure—for instance Pythagoras, Democritus and Anaxagoras, and these abandoned the sphere of government and gave themselves entirely to study; and owing to its tranquillity and to the intrinsic attractiveness of knowledge, which is the sweetest of human pleasures, this life of study laid its charm on a larger number of persons than was advantageous to the commonwealth. Consequently when men of outstanding intellectual ability devoted themselves to this pursuit, as a result of this unlimited command of unoccupied free time, persons of very great learning, being supplied with over-abundant leisure and extreme fertility of intellect, formed the opinion that it was their duty to devote themselves to the pursuit of far more numerous lines of investigation than was really necessary. For in old days at all events the same system of instruction seems to have imparted education both in right conduct and in good speech; nor were the professors in two separate groups, but the same masters gave instruction both in ethics and in rhetoric, for instance the great Phoenix in Homer, who says that he was assigned to the young Achilles by his father Peleus to accompany him to the wars in order to make him "an orator and man of action too." But just as persons usually engaged in constant daily employment, when debarred from work because of the weather, betake themselves to tennis or gambling or dicing or even devise for themselves some novel game to occupy their leisure, so when the persons in question have been debarred from their work of politics by the circumstances of the time or have chosen to take a vacation, some of them have devoted themselves entirely to poetry, others to mathematics and others to music, and others also have created for themselves a new interest and amusement as dialecticians, and have spent the whole of their time and their lives in the sciences that were invented for the purpose of moulding the minds of the young on the lines of culture and of virtue.

XVI. But as there have been certain persons and those a considerable number who either held a high position on account of their twofold wisdom, as men of action and as orators—two careers that are inseparable—, for instance Themistocles and Pericles and Theramenes, or other persons who were not themselves so much engaged in public life but were professional teachers of this same wisdom, for instance Gorgias, Thrasymachus, Isocrates, persons have been found who being themselves copiously furnished with learning and with talent, but yet shrinking on deliberate principle from politics and affairs, scouted and scorned this practice of oratory. The chief of these was Socrates, the person who on the evidence of all men of learning and the verdict of the whole of Greece, owing not only to his wisdom and penetration and charm and subtlety but also to his eloquence and variety and fertility easily came out top whatever side in a debate he took up; and whereas the persons engaged in handling and pursuing and teaching the subjects that we are now investigating were designated by a single title, the whole study and practice of the liberal sciences being entitled philosophy, Socrates robbed them of this general designation, and in his discussions separated the science of wise thinking from that of elegant speaking, though in reality they are closely linked together; and the genius and varied discourses of Socrates have been immortally enshrined in the compositions of Plato, Socrates himself not having left a single scrap of writing. This is the source from which has sprung the undoubtedly absurd and unprofitable and reprehensible severance between the tongue and the brain, leading to our having one set of professors to teach us to think and another to teach us to speak. For because of the plurality of schools that virtually sprang from Socrates, owing to the fact that out of his various and diverse discussions, ranging in every direction, one pupil had picked up one doctrine and another another, there were engendered families at discord with one another and widely separated and unlike, although all philosophers claimed and sincerely claimed the title of followers of Socrates.

XVII. And in the first place from Plato himself sprang Aristotle and Xenophon, on one of whom was bestowed the name of the Peripatetic School and on the other that of the Academy; and next from Antisthenes, who in the Socratic discourse had been captivated chiefly by the ideal of endurance and hardness, came first the Cynics and next the Stoics; and then from Aristippus, who had taken delight rather in the Socratic discussions on the subject of pleasure, was derived the Cyrenaic philosophy, which Aristippus and his successors maintained without modification, whereas the contemporary thinkers that make pleasure the sole standard of value, in doing so with greater modesty neither satisfy the claims of virtue, which they do not despise, nor successfully defend pleasure, which they wish to embrace. There have also been other groups of philosophers who almost all professed to be followers of Socrates, the Eretrians, the pupils of Erillus, the Megareans, the school of Pyrrho, but these have long ago been routed out of existence by the forceful arguments of the aforesaid schools. But from among the systems still surviving, the philosophy that has undertaken the championship of pleasure, although some may accept it as true, is nevertheless quite remote from the man whom we are seeking and whom we wish to be the political leader of the nation, guiding the government and pre-eminent for wisdom and eloquence in the Senate, in the assembly of the people and in public causes. And nevertheless no wrong will be done to that philosophy by us, for we shall not be debarring it from a position that it aspires to occupy, but it will be reposing where it wishes to be, in its own charming gardens, where moreover as it reclines it gently and tactfully appeals to us to abandon the platform and the courts and parliament,—perhaps a wise invitation, particularly in the present state of public affairs. However for my part my present inquiry is not which system of philosophy is the truest but which is the most fully akin to the orator. Consequently let us dismiss the masters in question, without any derogatory comment, as they are excellent fellows and happy in their belief in their own happiness, and only let us warn them to keep to themselves as a holy secret, though it may be extremely true, their doctrine that it is not the business of a wise man to take part in politics—for if they convince us and all our best men of the truth of this they themselves will not be able to live the life of leisure which is their ideal.

XVIII. Moreover, the Stoics, of whom I by no means disapprove, I nevertheless dismiss—and I do not fear their anger, because anger is quite unknown to them, and I am grateful to them for being the only one of all the schools that has pronounced eloquence to be a virtue and a form of wisdom. But clearly there is something in them that is quite out of keeping with the orator whom we are depicting: in the first place their assertion that all those who are not wise are slaves, brigands, enemies, madmen, and that all the same nobody is wise—yet it would be the height of folly to place a public meeting or the Senate or any assembly of people under the direction of a person who holds the view that not one of those present is sane, or a citizen, or a free man. There is the further point that even the style of their discourse, though possibly subtle and undoubtedly penetrating, yet for an orator is bald, unfamiliar, jarring on the ear of the public, devoid of clarity, fullness and spirit, while at the same time of a character that makes it quite impossible to employ it in public speaking; for the Stoics hold a different view of good and bad from all their fellow-citizens or rather from all other nations, and give a different meaning to "honour," "disgrace," "reward," "punishment"—whether correctly or otherwise does not concern us now, but if we were to adopt their terminology, we should never be able to express our meaning intelligibly about anything.

There remain the Peripatetics and the Academics, though the latter are really two schools of thought under one name. For Plato's nephew Speusippus and his Xenocrates and Xenocrates' pupils Polemo and Crantor did not seriously disagree on any point of opinion from Aristotle, their fellow-pupil under Plato, although possibly they were not his equals in fullness and variety of style; whereas Polemo's pupil Arcesilas, to begin with, selected for adoption from the various writings of Plato and the Socratic dialogues the dogma that nothing can be apprehended with certainty either by the senses or by the mind; and he is said to have employed a remarkably attractive style of discourse in reject-ing mental and sensory judgement entirely and to have initiated the practice—an entirely Socratic one it is true—of not stating his own opinion but arguing against the opinions put forward by everyone else. From this source descended the more recent Academy of our day, in which the almost inspired intellectual acumen and rhetorical fluency of Carneades have made him the leading figure; and though at Athens I got to know a number of his pupils, I myself nevertheless can recommend as entirely reliable authorities my father-in-law Scaevola, who in his youth heard Carneades at Rome, and my friend the distinguished Quintus Metellus, son of Lucius, who used to say that as a young man he heard him on many occasions at Athens when he was already showing signs of age.

XIX. However, the streams of learning flowing from the common watershed of wis-dom, as rivers do from the Apennines, divided in two, the philosophers flowing down into the entirely Greek waters of the Eastern Mediterranean with its plentiful supply of harbours, while the orators glided into the rocky and inhospitable Western seas of our outlandish Tuscany, where even Ulysses himself lost his bearings. Consequently if we are contented with this degree of eloquence, and with the orator who knows that one must either deny the charge brought against one, or if one cannot do that then prove that the action of the accused party was either a right action, or due to someone else's fault or transgression, or legal, or not illegal, or inadvertent, or inevitable, or incorrectly desig-nated in the charge, or that the proceedings being taken are irregular and illegal; and if you people think it sufficient to learn the instructions drawn up by your writers on the science of rhetoric, instructions nevertheless that have been expounded by Antonius in a much more graceful and more copious form than they are enunciated by the authors in question—well, if you are content with these rules and also the ones you have desired me to state, you are making the orator abandon a vast, immeasurable plain and confine himself to quite a narrow circle. If on the other hand you chose to follow the famous Pericles of old, or even our friend Demosthenes with whom his many writings have made us better acquainted, and if you have grown to love that glorious and supreme ideal, that thing of beauty, the perfect orator, you are bound to accept either the modern dialectic of Carneades or the earlier method of Aristotle. For, as I said before, the older masters down to Socrates used to combine with their theory of rhetoric the whole of the study and the science of everything that concerns morals and conduct and ethics and politics; it was subsequently, as I have explained, that the two groups of students were separated from one another, by Socrates and then by all the Socratic schools, and the philosophers, looked down on eloquence and the orators on wisdom, and never touched anything from the side of the other study except what this group borrowed from that one, or that one from this;

whereas they would have drawn from the common supply indifferently if they had been willing to remain in the partnership of early days. But just as the old pontiffs owing to the vast number of sacrifices decided to have a Banquet Committee of three members, though they had themselves been appointed by Numa for the purpose among others of holding the great Sacrificial Banquet of the Games, so the followers of Socrates cut connexion with the practising lawyers and detached these from the common title of philosophy, although the old masters had intended there to be a marvellously close alliance between oratory and philosophy.

XX. This being so, I will enter a brief plea on my own behalf, and will beg you to believe that what I say is not said about myself personally but about the orator as such. For I myself am a person who, having been given by my father an extremely careful education in my youth, and having brought into public life an amount of talent of which I am myself conscious, although not the amount with which you perhaps credit me, cannot assert that I pursued the studies with which I am now dealing exactly in the manner in which I am going to say they ought to be pursued: inasmuch as I came forward as a public advocate at an extremely early age, and when only one and twenty conducted the impeachment of a very eloquent and very distinguished man,—in fact public life was my education, and practical experience of the laws and institutions of the state and the custom of the country was my schoolmaster. Though thirsty for those accomplishments of yours of which I am speaking I had only a small taste of them, having during my quaestorship in Asia secured the services of a professor of rhetoric from the Academy, a person of about the same age as myself, the great Metrodorus whose memory Antonius recalled; and also on my way home from Asia, at Athens, where I should have made a longer stay if I had not been so angry with the authorities there for refusing to repeat the celebration of the mysteries, for which I had arrived two days late; and consequently the fact that I include in my treatment this extensive and important field of learning is not only not in my favour but rather tells against me—for my subject is not what I myself can achieve but what the orator as such can—and against these exponents of the science of rhetoric, who are exceedingly foolish persons, as they only write about the classification of cases and the elementary rules and the methods of stating the facts; whereas eloquence is so potent a force that it embraces the origin and operation and developments of all things, all the virtues and duties, all the natural principles governing the morals and minds and life of mankind, and also determines their customs and laws and rights, and controls the government of the state, and expresses everything that concerns whatever topic in a graceful and flowing style. In this field I for my part occupy myself to the best of my ability, and with such capacity as is supplied me by my natural talents, my limited studies and my practical experience; though all the same I really do not yield much ground in debate to those who have pitched their camp for their lifetime solely in this province of philosophy.

XXI. For what proof can our friend Gaius Velleius bring to show that pleasure is the chief good, which I on my side am not able with greater fertility either to maintain if I choose or to rebut, by drawing on the arguments set out by Antonius, thanks to this practice in oratory in which Velleius is a tiro but every one of us an expert? For what is there that can be said on the subject of virtue by Stoics such as Sextus Pompeius or the two Balbi or my friend Marcus Vigellius who lived with Panaetius, to make it necessary either for me or for any one of you, to give ground to them in debate? For philosophy does not resemble the other sciences—for what good will a man be in geometry if he has not studied it? or in music? he will either have to hold his tongue or be set down as a positive lunatic; whereas the contents of philosophy are discovered by intellects of the keenest acumen in eliciting the probable answer to every problem, and the results are elaborated with practised eloquence. In this situation our popular orator, though perhaps inadequately schooled, having nevertheless had experience in speaking, will anyway be enabled merely by that ordinary experience to give those persons a sound drubbing, and will not allow them to despise and look down on him; whereas if there has really ever been a person who was able in Aristotelian fashion to speak on both sides about every subject and by means of knowing Aristotle's rules to reel off two speeches on opposite sides on every case, or in the manner of Arcesilas and Carneades argue against every statement put forward, and who to that method adds the experience and practice in speaking indicated, he would be the one and only true and perfect orator. For an orator cannot have sufficient cogency and weight if he lacks the vigour that public speaking demands, and cannot be adequately polished and profound if he lacks width of culture. Consequently let us for our part allow your old Mr. Raven to hatch out his own chicks in the nest, so that they may fly abroad as annoying and tiresome bawlers, and permit some Pamphilus or other to sketch out a subject of this importance on his tapes, like a nursery game, and let us for our part within the narrow limits of the debate of yesterday and today unfold the function of the orator in its entirety, provided it be granted that the subject is so extensive that it might be supposed to fill all the volumes of the philosophers, books which none of those gentlemen have ever had in their hands. . . .

XXXI. For to us belong—assuming that we are really orators, that is, persons competent to be retained as leaders and principals in civil actions and criminal trials and public debates—to us, I say, belong the broad estates of wisdom and of learning, which having been allowed to lapse and become derelict during our absorption in affairs, have been invaded by persons too generously supplied with leisure, persons who actually either banter and ridicule the orator after the manner of Socrates in Plato's *Gorgias,* or else write a few little manuals of instruction in the art of oratory and label them with the title of *Rhetoric*—just as if the province of the rhetoricians did not include their pronouncements on the subjects of justice and duty and the constitution and government of states, in short, the entire field of practical philosophy. As we can now no longer obtain these principles from elsewhere, we have to take them from the very persons who plundered us: only provided that we carry them over into the field of political science to which they belong and with which they are concerned, and, as I said before, avoid spending an entire lifetime in acquiring them, but after we have beheld the fountain-heads, which one who does not get to know them quickly will never get to know at all, then draw from these sources, whenever necessary, as much as the subject demands—for mankind is not endowed by nature with such keenness of intellect that anyone can discern these great matters without having had them pointed out to him, nor all the same do they involve so much obscurity that a man of keen intelligence cannot see to the bottom of them, provided he has looked closely at them. Consequently as the orator has the liberty to roam freely in so wide and measureless a field and wherever he takes his stand to find himself on his own ground, all the resources and embellishments of oratory are readily available; for a full supply of facts begets a full supply of words, and if the subjects discussed are themselves of an elevated character this produces a spontaneous brilliance in the language. Only let the intending speaker or writer, thanks to the training given by a liberal education in boyhood, possess a glowing enthusiasm as well as the assistance of good natural endowments, and, having had practice in the abstract discussions of general principles, have selected the most accomplished writers and orators for study and imitation: then of a certainty such a one will not have to come to your professors to be shown how to put words together and how to invest them with brilliance of style; so easily will nature of herself, if only she has received training, given a plentiful supply of matter, find her way without any guidance to the adornments of oratory. . . .

XXXVI. . . . At this stage I give full leave to anybody who wishes, to apply the title of orator to a philosopher who imparts to us an abundant command of facts and of language, or alternatively I shall raise no obstacle if he prefers to designate as a philosopher the orator whom I on my side am now describing as possessing wisdom combined with eloquence: only provided it be agreed that neither the tongue-tied silence of the man who knows the facts but cannot explain them in language, nor the ignorance of the person who is deficient in facts but has no lack of words, is deserving of praise. And if one had to choose between them, for my own part I should prefer wisdom lacking power of expression to talkative folly; but if on the contrary we are trying to find the one thing that stands top of the whole list, the prize must go to the orator who possesses learning. And if they allow him also to be a philosopher, that is the end of the dispute; but if they keep the two separate, they will come off second best in this, that the consummate orator possesses all the knowledge of the philosophers, but the range of philosophers does not necessarily include eloquence; and although they look down on it, it cannot but be deemed to add a crowning embellishment to their sciences. . . .

from The Orator

. . . Let us assume, then, at the beginning what will become clearer hereafter, that philosophy is essential for the education of our ideal orator; not that philosophy is everything, but that it helps the orator as physical training helps the actor (for it is frequently illuminating to compare great things with small). For no one can discuss great and varied subjects in a copious and eloquent style without philosophy—as, for example, in Plato's *Phaedrus* Socrates says that Pericles surpassed other orators because he was a pupil of Anaxagoras, the natural philosopher. From him Socrates thinks that Pericles learned much that was splendid and sublime, and acquired copiousness and fertility, and—most important to eloquence—knowledge of the kind of speech which arouses each set of feelings. The same may be held true of Demosthenes, from whose *Epistles* one may learn how diligent a pupil he was of Plato. Surely without philosophical training we cannot distinguish the genus and species of anything, nor define it nor divide it into subordinate parts, nor separate truth from falsehood, nor recognize "consequents," distinguish "contradictories" or analyse "ambiguities." What am I to say about the study of natural philosophy, which affords the orator a wealth of material? Again, would you think one could speak or think about life or duty or virtue or morals without thorough training in these very subjects? To express these many important ideas one must use innumerable stylistic ornaments; which at that time comprised the sole instruction given by those accounted teachers of rhetoric. As a consequence no one attains to that true and perfect eloquence, because there is one course of training in thought, and another in expression; from one group of teachers we seek instruction in facts, from others instruction in language. This is the reason why Marcus Antonius, who was regarded by our fathers' generation as easily the first in eloquence, and was a man naturally keen and intelligent, says in his sole published work that he had seen many good speakers, but none who were eloquent. Obviously there was in his mind an ideal of eloquence which he apprehended by the intellect but had never actually seen. Being a man of subtle intellect—this description is certainly true—he found much to seek both in himself and in others, and saw no one at all who could rightly be called eloquent. But if he did not consider himself or Lucius Crassus eloquent, he certainly had a mental picture of eloquence, and as this was deficient in no respect, he could not identify with it those who were deficient in one or more points. Let us search, then, Brutus, if we can, for this man whom Antonius never saw, or who has never existed at all. If we cannot present an exact copy—he said this was scarcely within the power of a god—yet we may be able to say what he ought to be like. . . .

The man of perfect eloquence should, then, in my opinion possess not only the faculty of fluent and copious speech which is his proper province, but should also acquire that neighbouring borderland science of logic; although a speech is one thing and a debate another, and disputing is not the same as speaking, and yet both are concerned with discourse—debate and dispute are the function of the logicians; the orator's function is to speak ornately. Zeno, the founder of the Stoic school, used to give an object lesson of the difference between the two arts; clenching his fist he said logic was like that; relaxing and extending his hand, he said eloquence was like the open palm. Still earlier Aristotle in the opening chapter of his *Art of Rhetoric* said that rhetoric is the counterpart of logic, the difference obviously being that rhetoric was broader and logic narrower. I therefore expect this perfect orator of ours to be familiar with all the theory of disputation which can be applied to speaking; this subject, as you well know from your training along this line, has been taught in two different ways. Aristotle himself taught many principles of argumentation, and the later dialecticians, as they are called, produced many thorny speculations. For my part I advise one who is attracted by the glory of eloquence not to be entirely unacquainted with these latter authors, but to be thoroughly trained either in the older logic of Aristotle, or the newer of Chrysippus. He should know first the force, nature and classes of words, both singly and in the sentence; then the different modes of predication; the method of distinguishing truth from falsity; the proper deduction to be drawn from each, *i.e.* what is consequent and what is contrary; and since many ambiguous statements are made, he should know how these can be solved and explained. These are the things the orator must get,—for they are continually coming up—but because in themselves they are somewhat unattractive, a certain grace of style will have to be used in presenting them.

Furthermore, since in all subjects that are taught by systematic principles, we must first of all determine what each thing is—for unless the disputants are agreed as to what is the subject under debate there can be no proper discussion, nor can they arrive at any result—we must frequently give a verbal explanation of our ideas about each thing, and must make plain by definition the obscure concept of a subject, since definition is a statement giving the subject of discussion in the briefest possible form. Then, as you know, after explaining the genus of each thing we must consider what are the species or subdivisions of the genus in question, so that the whole speech may be divided between them. The man whom we wish to be eloquent will, then, possess the ability to define the subject, and will not do it so briefly and compactly as is the custom in the learned discussions of philosophers, but with greater clarity and at the same time with greater fullness, and in a way better adapted to the ordinary judgement and popular intelligence. He will likewise, when the subject demands this, divide a genus into definite species, so that no species may be left out or be superfluous. But when or how he may do this is immaterial at present, since, as I said above, I wish to be a critic, not a teacher.

He should not confine his study to logic, however, but have a theoretical acquaintance with all the topics of philosophy and practical training in debating them. For philosophy is essential to a full, copious and impressive discussion and exposition of the subjects which so often come up in speeches and are usually treated meagrely, whether they concern religion, death, piety, patriotism, good and evil, virtues and vices, duty, pain, pleasure, or mental disturbances and errors. I am speaking now of the raw material of the speech, not about its literary style. For it is desirable that the orator should have a subject worthy of a cultivated audience before he considers the language or style of expression. It is also desirable that he should not be ignorant of natural philosophy either, which will impart grandeur and loftiness, as I said above about Pericles. When he turns from a consideration of the heavens to human affairs, all his words and thoughts will assuredly be loftier and more magnificent.

Nor, while he is acquainted with the divine order of nature, would I have him ignorant of human affairs. He should understand the civil law, which is needed daily in practice in the courts of law. What is more disgraceful than to attempt to plead in legal and civil disputes when ignorant of the statutes and the civil law? He should also be acquainted with the history of the events of past ages, particularly, of course, of our state, but also of imperial nations and famous kings; here our task has been lightened by the labour of our friend Atticus, who has comprised in one book the record of seven hundred years, keeping the chronology definite and omitting no important event. To be ignorant of what occurred before you were born is to remain always a child. For what is the worth of human life, unless it is woven into the life of our ancestors by the records of history? Moreover, the mention of antiquity and the citation of examples give the speech authority and credibility as well as affording the highest pleasure to the audience.

from De Partitione Oratoria

. . . But as this topic of virtues and vices is of very wide extent, on this occasion it shall be summarized into a single limited and brief discourse in place of a number of different ones. Virtue has a twofold meaning, for it is exhibited either in knowledge or in conduct. The virtue that is designated prudence and intelligence and the most impressive name of all, wisdom, exercises its influence by knowledge alone; but the virtue applauded in moderating the desires and controlling the emotions has its function in action, and the name of this virtue is temperance. The virtue of prudence when displayed in a man's private affairs is usually termed personal sagacity and when in public affairs political wisdom. Similarly temperance is directed both to one's own affairs and those of the community, and is manifested in two ways in respect of profitable things—in not seeking those which one has not got and in refraining from using those which are in one's power. In respect of unprofitable things temperance is similarly twofold; that which withstands coming evils is named fortitude, and that which steadfastly endures present evil patience. But the virtue that embraces these qualities under a single head is called greatness of mind; this includes liberality in the use of money and also loftiness of mind in accepting unprofitable things and especially wrongs, and every quality of this kind, dignified and calm. The part of virtue displayed in society is called justice, and that manifested towards the gods religion, towards parents piety, or in general goodness, in matters of trust good faith, in moderating punishment mercy, in benevolence friendliness.

These virtues so far are displayed in action. But there are others which are so to speak the handmaidens and companions of wisdom; of these one is displayed in debate, distinguishing truth from falsehood and judging the logical consequence of given premisses—this virtue resides entirely in the method and science of debating; while the sphere of the other is oratory. For eloquence is nothing else but wisdom delivering copious utterance; and this, while derived from the same class as the virtue above that operates in debate, is more abundant and wider and more closely adapted to the emotions and to the feelings of the common herd. But the guardian of all the virtues, which shuns disgrace and attains praise in the greatest degree, is modesty. These then practically are as it were habits of mind that are so characterized and constituted as to be mutually distinct from each other and each in a class of virtue belonging to itself; and in proportion as a particular action is directed by them, so it must of necessity be morally good and supremely praiseworthy.

But there are certain other states of mind trained and prepared for virtue by proper studies and sciences, as for instance among personal matters the study of literature, rhythms and music, mensuration and astronomy, riding and hunting and fencing; and interests more important in the life of the community consisting in the special cultivation of some particular kind of virtue, or devotion to the service of religion, or outstanding and exceptional filial affection or friendship or hospitality. These are the classes of virtues. Those of the vices are their opposites; but careful attention must be given to them to save ourselves from being deceived by those vices which seem to imitate virtue. For cunning masquerades as prudence, boorish contempt for pleasure as temperance, pride in over-valuing honours and superciliousness in looking down on them as high-mindedness, profusion as liberality, audacity as bravery, savage hardness as endurance, harshness as justice, superstition as religion, softness as gentleness, timidity as modesty, verbal controversy and logic-chopping on the one hand as skilfulness in argument, and an empty flux of talk on the other as oratorical power. And again valuable studies are counterfeited by excesses in the same department. Consequently all the resources of panegyric and reprehension will be adopted from these divisions of the virtues and vices; but in the whole fabric of the speech the greatest attention is to be focussed on the quality of a person's breeding and upbringing and education and character; and on any important or startling occurrence that a man has encountered, especially if this can appear to be due to the intervention of providence; and then each individual's opinions and utterances and actions will be classified under the scheme of the virtues that has been propounded, and these same topics of research will be drawn on to supply the causes and results and consequences of things. Nor yet will it be proper to pass over in silence the death of those persons whose life is going to be praised, in case of there being something noticeable either in the nature of their death itself or in the events that follow after death. . . .

from De Officiis

My dear son, now that you have studied for a full year under Cratippus and in a city like Athens, you should be well equipped with the principles and doctrines of moral philosophy. A master of such power cannot fail to enrich your mind with ethical theories, while the cultured city in which you live will offer you many models for imitation. However, I have always found it best in my own case to combine the study of Latin and Greek in oratory as well as in philosophy, and I think it would be well for you to follow my example if you wish to be equally at home in the two languages. Here I flatter myself I have rendered good service to my countrymen, and it is gratifying to find that not only persons ignorant of Greek, but even educated men admit that I have done something towards developing their minds and forming their style. You should therefore continue your studies under the first thinker of the age, and that you will certainly desire to do, so long as you are not dissatisfied with your progress. But in reading the exposition of my theories which differ little from those of the Peripatetics (for we both claim to be followers of Socrates and Plato), whatever opinion you may form on the subject matter—and you are free to judge for yourself—I am confident you will improve your Latin style. Still I would not have you think I say this in arrogance. I profess no monopoly in philosophical science, but I fancy I am within my rights in claiming as peculiarly my own a happy, perspicuous, and ornate style—the proper field of the orator, which I have cultivated all my life. I urge you, therefore, my dear son, to read with care not only my orations but also my philosophical works which are now almost as numerous as the others. In the orations there is greater vigour, but the unimpassioned and temperate style of my essays is no less worthy of study.

I do not find that any Greek author has yet succeeded in elaborating at once the foren-sic and the calm philosophical style, with the possible exception of Demetrius of Phale-rum, a keen logician and an orator who, though he lacks force, has the charm that marks the disciple of Theophrastus. What degree of perfection I myself have attained in these two styles let others judge; if I have failed, it is not for want of effort. I indulge the fancy that Plato, had he chosen to practise oratory, would have made an impressive and eloquent pleader, and that if Demosthenes had followed up and published the doctrines he learned from Plato he would have been distinguished for the elegance and splendour of his dic-tion. I have the same opinion of Aristotle and Isocrates, but each of them took such delight in his own pursuit that he looked coldly on the pursuit of the other. . . .

Animals of every species are endowed with the instinct of self-preservation which leads them to preserve life and limb, to avoid what seems hurtful, and to seek and provide the necessaries of life, such as food and shelter. The reproductive instinct and the love of offspring are also universal. But there is a wide gulf between man and beast. Swayed by sense alone, the beast lives in the present, heedless of the past, or future. But man endowed with reason perceives the connection of things, marks their causes and effects, traces their analogies, links the future with the past, and, surveying without effort the whole course of life, prepares what is needful for the journey. Nature with the aid of reason likewise binds man to man, unites them by the bond of language and of social life, inspires them with a strong love of offspring, and impels them to multiply the occasions of meeting and consorting with their fellows. These are the motives that incite a man to procure a comfortable livelihood not only for himself but for his wife and children and all whom he cherishes and is bound to support; and this responsibility rouses his energies and braces him for work.

The distinctive faculty of man is his eager desire to investigate the truth. Thus, when free from pressing duties and cares, we are eager to see or hear, or learn something new, and we think our happiness incomplete unless we study the mysteries and the marvels of the universe. From this it is evident that what is true, simple, and pure, is most in harmony with human nature. With the instinct of curiosity is allied the desire of independence; a well-constituted character will bow to no authority but that of a master or a just and legitimate ruler who aims at the public good: hence arises fortitude or indifference to the accidents of fortune. How precious should we deem the gift of reason since man is the only living being that has a sense of order, decorum and moderation in word and deed. No other creature is touched by the beauty, grace and symmetry of visible objects; and the hu-man mind transferring these conceptions from the material to the moral world recognises that this beauty, harmony and order are still more to be maintained in the sphere of pur-pose and of action; reason shuns all that is unbecoming or unmanly, all that is wanton in thought or deed. These are the constituent elements of the conception of honour which is the subject of our inquiry: honour even when cast into the shade loses none of its beauty; honour, I say, though praised by no one, is praiseworthy in itself.

You have now before you, my dear Marcus, the very form, I may say, the face, of hon-our; and, as Plato says of Wisdom, could we but see it with our eyes, what a divine passion it would inspire! Honour springs from one of four sources. It consists in sagacity and the perception of the truth, or in the maintenance of human society, respect for the rights of others, and the faithful observance of contracts, or in the greatness and strength of a lofty and invincible spirit, or finally in that order and measure in word and deed which constitute temperance and self-command. The cardinal virtues are indeed inseparably connected, yet each of them is the source of definite classes of duties. Wisdom or prudence, for example, the first in our division, is concerned with the investigation and discovery of the truth; this is its peculiar function. He is justly considered the wisest and the most prudent of men who penetrates furthest into the truth of things and has the keenest and swiftest eye to see and unfold their principles. Truth is therefore the material on which this virtue works, the sphere in which it moves. The function of the other virtues is to provide and maintain all that is necessary for our daily life, to strengthen the bonds of human society, and to evoke that great and noble spirit which enlarges our resources and secures advantages for ourselves and our kin, but is even more conspicuous by its indifference to these objects. Order, consistency, moderation and similar qualities fall under this category and are not so much speculative as active virtues; for it is by applying measure and law to the affairs of life that we shall best observe honour and decorum.

Of the four parts into which we have divided the conception of honour, the first, consisting in the investigation of the truth, touches human nature most nearly. We are all carried away, by the passion for study and learning; here we think it noble to excel and count it an evil and a shame if we stumble or stray, if we are ignorant or credulous. In following this natural and noble instinct there are two errors to be avoided; in the first place we must not mistake the unknown for the known and blindly give it our assent; to escape this error, as all must wish to do, it is necessary to devote time and trouble to the consideration of every question. In the second place it is wrong to waste our energies on dark, thorny, and barren studies. If we avoid these errors and bestow our toil and care on subjects that are honourable and worthy of study, we shall deserve nothing but praise. Thus Sulpicius was once distinguished in astronomy as our contemporary Sextus Pompeius is in mathematics; many have made their name in logic, more in civil law; but though all these branches of knowledge are concerned with the investigation of the truth, it would be wrong to be diverted from active work by any such pursuit. The worth of virtue lies in action, yet we have many times of rest, permitting us to return to our favourite pursuits: and even without our effort, our beating, restless mind will keep us ever at study. Now every thought and operation of the mind is employed in deciding about things that concern our honour and happiness or in pursuing knowledge and learning. So much for the first source of duty. . . .

Vitruvius

C. 70–C. 25 B.C.

A liberal education forms, as it were, a single body made up of these members. Those, therefore, who from tender years receive instruction in the various forms of learning, recognize the same stamp on all the arts, and an intercourse between all the studies, and so they more readily comprehend them all.

—THE TEN BOOKS ON ARCHITECTURE

Few biographical details are known about the Roman architect and engineer Marcus Vitruvius Pollio. He may have worked for Julius Caesar, and Octavian (the emperor Augustus) employed him as a military engineer. Fragmentary information about his life can be gleaned from his treatise *De architectura libri decem* (The Ten Books on Architecture). This treatise was known throughout the Middle Ages, and illustrated editions of the work appeared in the sixteenth century. Vitruvius's principles of design influenced architects of the Renaissance and Baroque periods.

THE SELECTION

De architectura assumes a broad definition of architecture, offering practical advice on everything from the design of public buildings and private homes to building materials and methods, and from city planning to mechanical engineering. Book I includes Vitruvius's defense of the full circle of liberal education for the professional architect. He recommends that technical training be complemented by instruction in geometry, history, moral philosophy, physics, music, law, astronomy, and even medicine. He includes philosophy out of a concern for the future architect's moral character.

from The Ten Books on Architecture
Chapter I: The Education of the Architect

1. The architect should be equipped with knowledge of many branches of study and varied kinds of learning, for it is by his judgement that all work done by the other arts is put to test. This knowledge is the child of practice and theory. Practice is the continuous and regular exercise of employment where manual work is done with any necessary material according to the design of a drawing. Theory, on the other hand, is the ability to demonstrate and explain the productions of dexterity on the principles of proportion.

2. It follows, therefore, that architects who have aimed at acquiring manual skill without scholarship have never been able to reach a position of authority to correspond to their pains, while those who relied only upon theories and scholarship were obviously hunting the shadow, not the substance. But those who have a thorough knowledge of both, like men armed at all points, have the sooner attained their object and carried authority with them.

3. In all matters, but particularly in architecture, there are these two points:—the thing signified, and that which gives it its significance. That which is signified is the subject of which we may be speaking; and that which gives significance is a demonstration on scientific principles. It appears, then, that one who professes himself an architect should be well versed in both directions. He ought, therefore, to be both naturally gifted and amenable to instruction. Neither natural ability without instruction nor instruction without natural ability can make the perfect artist. Let him be educated, skilful with the pencil, instructed in geometry, know much history, have followed the philosophers with attention, understand music, have some knowledge of medicine, know the opinions of the jurists, and be acquainted with astronomy and the theory of the heavens.

4. The reasons for all this are as follows. An architect ought to be an educated man so as to leave a more lasting remembrance in his treatises. Secondly, he must have a knowledge of drawing so that he can readily make sketches to show the appearance of the work which he proposes. Geometry, also, is of much assistance in architecture, and in particular it teaches us the use of the rule and compasses, by which especially we acquire readiness in making plans for buildings in their grounds, and rightly apply the square, the level, and the plummet. By means of optics, again, the light in buildings can be drawn from fixed quarters of the sky. It is true that it is by arithmetic that the total cost of buildings is calculated and measurements are computed, but difficult questions involving symmetry are solved by means of geometrical theories and methods.

5. A wide knowledge of history is requisite because, among the ornamental parts of an architect's design for a work, there are many the underlying idea of whose employment he should be able to explain to inquirers. For instance, suppose him to set up the marble statues of women in long robes, called Caryatides, to take the place of columns, with the mutules and coronas placed directly above their heads, he will give the following explanation to his questioners. Caryae, a state in Peloponnesus, sided with the Persian enemies against Greece; later the Greeks, having gloriously won their freedom by victory in the war, made common cause and declared war against the people of Caryae. They took the town, killed the men, abandoned the State to desolation, and carried off their wives into slavery, without permitting them,

however, to lay aside the long robes and other marks of their rank as married women, so that they might be obliged not only to march in the triumph but to appear forever after as a type of slavery, burdened with the weight of their shame and so making atonement for their State. Hence, the architects of the time designed for public buildings statues of these women, placed so as to carry a load, in order that the sin and the punishment of the people of Caryae might be known and handed down even to posterity.

6. Likewise the Lacedaemonians under the leadership of Pausanias, son of Agesipolis, after conquering the Persian armies, infinite in number, with a small force at the battle of Plataea, celebrated a glorious triumph with the spoils and booty, and with the money obtained from the sale thereof built the Persian Porch, to be a monument to the renown and valour of the people and a trophy of victory for posterity. And there they set effigies of the prisoners arrayed in barbarian costume and holding up the roof, their pride punished by this deserved affront, that enemies might tremble for fear of the effects of their courage, and that their own people, looking upon this ensample of their valour and encouraged by the glory of it, might be ready to defend their independence. So from that time on, many have put up statues of Persians supporting entablatures and their ornaments, and thus from that motive have greatly enriched the diversity of their works. There are other stories of the same kind which architects ought to know.

7. As for philosophy, it makes an architect high-minded and not self-assuming, but rather renders him courteous, just, and honest without avariciousness. This is very important, for no work can be rightly done without honesty and incorruptibility. Let him not be grasping nor have his mind preoccupied with the idea of receiving perquisites, but let him with dignity keep up his position by cherishing a good reputation. These are among the precepts of philosophy. Furthermore philosophy treats of physics (in Greek φυσιολογία) where a more careful knowledge is required because the problems which come under this head are numerous and of very different kinds; as, for example, in the case of the conducting of water. For at points of intake and at curves, and at places where it is raised to a level, currents of air naturally form in one way or another; and nobody who has not learned the fundamental principles of physics from philosophy will be able to provide against the damage which they do. So the reader of Ctesibius or Archimedes and the other writers of treatises of the same class will not be able to appreciate them unless he has been trained in these subjects by the philosophers.

8. Music, also, the architect ought to understand so that he may have knowledge of the canonical and mathematical theory, and besides be able to tune ballistae, catapultae, and scorpiones to the proper key. For to the right and left in the beams are the holes in the frames through which the strings of twisted sinew are stretched by means of windlasses and bars, and these strings must not be clamped and made fast until they give the same correct note to the ear of the skilled workman. For the arms thrust through those stretched strings must, on being let go, strike their blow together at the same moment; but if they are not in unison, they will prevent the course of projectiles from being straight.

9. In theatres, likewise, there are the bronze vessels (in Greek ἠχεῖα) which are placed in niches under the seats in accordance with the musical intervals on mathematical principles. These vessels are arranged with a view to musical concords or harmony, and apportioned in the compass of the fourth, the fifth, and the octave, and so on up to the double octave, in such a way that when the voice of an actor falls in unison with any of them

its power is increased, and it reaches the ears of the audience with greater clearness and sweetness. Water organs, too, and the other instruments which resemble them cannot be made by one who is without the principles of music.

10. The architect should also have a knowledge of the study of medicine on account of the questions of climates (in Greek κλίματα), air, the healthiness and unhealthiness of sites, and the use of different waters. For without these considerations, the healthiness of a dwelling cannot be assured. And as for principles of law, he should know those which are necessary in the case of buildings having party walls, with regard to water dripping from the eaves, and also the laws about drains, windows, and water supply. And other things of this sort should be known to architects, so that, before they begin upon buildings, they may be careful not to leave disputed points for the householders to settle after the works are finished, and so that in drawing up contracts the interests of both employer and contractor may be wisely safe-guarded. For if a contract is skilfully drawn, each may obtain a release from the other without disadvantage. From astronomy we find the east, west, south, and north, as well as the theory of the heavens, the equinox, solstice, and courses of the stars. If one has no knowledge of these matters, he will not be able to have any comprehension of the theory of sundials.

11. Consequently, since this study is so vast in extent, embellished and enriched as it is with many different kinds of learning, I think that men have no right to profess themselves architects hastily, without having climbed from boyhood the steps of these studies and thus, nursed by the knowledge of many arts and sciences, having reached the heights of the holy ground of architecture.

12. But perhaps to the inexperienced it will seem a marvel that human nature can comprehend such a great number of studies and keep them in the memory. Still, the observation that all studies have a common bond of union and intercourse with one another, will lead to the belief that this can easily be realized. For a liberal education forms, as it were, a single body made up of these members. Those, therefore, who from tender years receive instruction in the various forms of learning, recognize the same stamp on all the arts, and an intercourse between all studies, and so they more readily comprehend them all. This is what led one of the ancient architects, Pytheos, the celebrated builder of the temple of Minerva at Priene, to say in his Commentaries that an architect ought to be able to accomplish much more in all the arts and sciences than the men who, by their own particular kinds of work and the practice of it, have brought each a single subject to the highest perfection. But this is in point of fact not realized.

13. For an architect ought not to be and cannot be such a philologian as was Aristarchus, although not illiterate; nor a musician like Aristoxenus, though not absolutely ignorant of music; nor a painter like Apelles, though not unskilful in drawing; nor a sculptor such as was Myron or Polyclitus, though not unacquainted with the plastic art; nor again a physician like Hippocrates, though not ignorant of medicine; nor in the other sciences need he excel in each, though he should not be unskilful in them. For, in the midst of all this great variety of subjects, an individual cannot attain to perfection in each, because it is scarcely in his power to take in and comprehend the general theories of them.

14. Still, it is not architects alone that cannot in all matters reach perfection, but even men who individually practise specialties in the arts do not all attain to the highest point of merit. Therefore, if among artists working each in a single field not all, but only a few in

an entire generation acquire fame, and that with difficulty, how can an architect, who has to be skilful in many arts, accomplish not merely the feat—in itself a great marvel—of being deficient in none of them, but also that of surpassing all those artists who have devoted themselves with unremitting industry to single fields?

15. It appears, then, that Pytheos made a mistake by not observing that the arts are each composed of two things, the actual work and the theory of it. One of these, the doing of the work, is proper to men trained in the individual subject, while the other, the theory, is common to all scholars: for example, to physicians and musicians the rhythmical beat of the pulse and its metrical movement. But if there is a wound to be healed or a sick man to be saved from danger, the musician will not call, for the business will be appropriate to the physician. So in the case of a musical instrument, not the physician but the musician will be the man to tune it so that the ears may find their due pleasure in its strains.

16. Astronomers likewise have a common ground for discussion with musicians in the harmony of the stars and musical concords in tetrads and triads of the fourth and the fifth, and with geometricians in the subject of vision; and in all other sciences many points, perhaps all, are common so far as the discussion of them is concerned. But the actual undertaking of works which are brought to perfection by the hand and its manipulation is the function of those who have been specially trained to deal with a single art. It appears, therefore, that he has done enough and to spare who in each subject possesses a fairly good knowledge of those parts, with their principles, which are indispensable for architecture, so that if he is required to pass judgment and to express approval in the case of those things or arts, he may not be found wanting. As for men upon whom nature has bestowed so much ingenuity, acuteness, and memory that they are able to have a thorough knowledge of geometry, astronomy, music, and the other arts, they go beyond the functions of architects and become pure mathematicians. Hence they can readily take up positions against those arts because many are the artistic weapons with which they are armed. Such men, however, are rarely found, but there have been such at times; for example, Aristarchus of Samos, Philolaus and Archytas of Tarentum, Apollonius of Perga, Eratosthenes of Cyrene, and among Syracusans Archimedes and Scopinas, who through mathematics and natural philosophy discovered, expounded, and left to posterity many things in connexion with mechanics and with sundials.

17. Since, therefore, the possession of such talents due to natural capacity is not vouchsafed at random to entire nations, but only to a few great men; since, moreover, the function of the architect requires a training in all the departments of learning; and finally, since reason, on account of the wide extent of the subject, concedes that he may possess not the highest but not even necessarily a moderate knowledge of the subjects of study, I request, Caesar, both of you and of those who may read the said books, that if anything is set forth with too little regard for grammatical rule, it may be pardoned. For it is not as a very great philosopher, nor as an eloquent rhetorician, nor as a grammarian trained in the highest principles of his art, that I have striven to write this work, but as an architect who has had only a dip into those studies. Still, as regards the efficacy of the art and the theories of it, I promise and expect that in these volumes I shall undoubtedly show myself of very considerable importance not only to builders but also to all scholars.

Seneca

c. 4 B.C.–A.D. 65

Wisdom is a large and spacious thing.

Lucius Annaeus Seneca, Roman senator, prolific essayist, playwright, and poet, was born in Spain and educated in the city of Rome in rhetoric and philosophy. He was a contemporary of Jesus and the Apostles. His brother Novatus (who later took the name Gallio) served as proconsul of Achaia at the time of St. Paul (Acts 18:12–17). He tutored the troubled young emperor Nero, for whom he wrote "On Mercy" *(De Clementia),* an essay admired in the Middle Ages, and later by Petrarch, Erasmus, and John Calvin. Seneca made his lasting mark as a moral philosopher who was committed to the practical ethics of Stoicism. Stoicism originated in Greece in the fourth century B.C. just after the humiliating collapse of Alexander the Great's empire. It sought peace in the human heart in the midst of the strife, pain, and futility of a troubled world. It flourished in Athens under the leadership of Zeno, Chrysippus, and Cleanthes. Along with Epicureanism, it continued for centuries as one of the two most influential schools of philosophy in the Roman world, one of the many ways in which "captive Greece took Rome captive," in the poet Horace's apt phrase. Implicated in a conspiracy against Nero, Seneca was ordered by the emperor to commit suicide.

THE SELECTIONS

The extended essay "On Anger" *(De ira)* includes a brief passage on the moral formation of children, particularly how to curb their anger without breaking their spirit.

"On the Private Life" *(De otio)* survives only as a fragment of a larger treatise; both its beginning and end are missing. In it, Seneca deftly parries the still-familiar accusation that the contemplative life can be of no real service to the community. Seneca refuses to choose between the extremes of the contemplative life and the active life. Instead, he desires to grasp truth through private contemplation and to render service to the community with that truth through public activity. Activity is not busy-ness. Busy-ness leads to the distracted life, a life "always on the go" with "no time to turn from things human to things divine." For the Stoics, contemplation is not a path to self-absorbed idleness; "it is an anchorage, not a harbor."

In his letter titled "On Liberal and Vocational Studies" (Epistle 88), Seneca dismisses education aimed at preparing students for "money-making" vocations and praises liberal learning. Unexpectedly, however, he reduces the conventional definition of "liberal studies" from the Greek's more complete *enkuklios paideia* (the circle of learning) of poetry, music, mathematics, and astronomy. "The arts which belong to the education of boys, and are somewhat similar to the liberal arts," he writes, "are those which the Greeks call the 'cycle of studies' *[enkuklios paideia]*, but which we Romans call the 'liberal.' However, those alone are really liberal—or rather, to give them a truer name, free—whose concern is virtue." It is important to keep in mind Seneca's distinction between the popularly accepted use of the phrase "liberal studies" and his more restricted, idealized use of it to mean the cultivation of wisdom and virtue. If this distinction is not kept in mind, Seneca may be taken as saying the opposite of his true position. Clearly, Seneca is preoccupied with the ethical purpose of literature and other studies—that is, with how they contribute to the examined life and to right conduct. He warns against the danger of misdirected, disordered, and disproportionate education, against the moral hazard of mere mastery and proficiency apart from ethics, and against the folly of being distracted by the *how* of the universe to the exclusion of the *why*—all warnings repeated centuries later by Augustine in his *Confessions*.

from "On Anger"

The period of education calls for the greatest, and what will also prove to be the most profitable, attention; for it is easy to train the mind while it is still tender, but it is a difficult matter to curb the vices that have grown up with us. . . .

It will be of the utmost profit, I say, to give children sound training from the very beginning; guidance, however, is difficult, because we ought to take pains neither to develop in them anger nor to blunt their native spirit. The matter requires careful watching; for both qualities—that which should be encouraged and that which should be checked—are fed by like things, and like things easily deceive even a close observer. By freedom the spirit grows, by servitude it is crushed; if it is commended and is led to expect good things of itself, it mounts up, but these same measures breed insolence and temper; therefore we must guide the child between the two extremes, using now the curb, now the spur. He should be subjected to nothing that is humiliating, nothing that is servile; it should never be necessary for him to beg submissively, nor should begging ever prove profitable—rather let his own desert and his past conduct and good promise of it in the future be rewarded. In struggles with his playmates we should not permit him either to be beaten or to get angry; we should take pains to see that he is friendly toward those with whom it is his practice to engage in order that in the struggle he may form the habit of wishing not to hurt his opponent but merely to win. Whenever he gets the upper hand and does something praiseworthy, we should allow him to be encouraged but not elated, for joy leads to exultation, exultation to over-conceit and a too high opinion of oneself. We shall grant him some relaxation, though we shall not let him lapse into sloth and ease, and we shall keep him far from all taint of pampering; for there is nothing that makes the child hot-tempered so much as a soft and coddling bringing up. Therefore the more an only child is indulged, and the more liberty a ward is allowed, the more will his disposition be spoiled. He will not withstand rebuffs who has never been denied anything, whose tears have always been wiped away by an anxious mother, who has been allowed to have his own way with his tutor. Do you not observe that with each advancing grade of fortune there goes the greater tendency to anger? It is especially apparent in the rich, in nobles, and in officials when all that was light and trivial in their mind soars aloft upon the breeze of good fortune. Prosperity fosters wrath when the crowd of flatterers, gathered around, whispers to the proud ear: "What, should that man answer *you* back? Your estimate of yourself does not correspond with your importance; you demean yourself"—these and other adulations, which even the sensible and originally well-poised mind resists with difficulty. Childhood, therefore, should be kept far from all contact with flattery; let a child hear the truth, sometimes even let him fear, let him be respectful always, let him rise before his elders. Let him gain no request by anger; when he is quiet let him be offered what was refused when he wept. Let him, moreover, have the sight but not the use of his parents' wealth. When he has done wrong, let him be reproved. It will work to the advantage of children to give them teachers and tutors of a quiet disposition. Every young thing attaches itself to what is nearest and grows to be like it; the character of their nurses and tutors is presently reproduced in that of the young men. There was a boy who had been brought up in the house of Plato, and when he had returned to his parents and saw his father in a blustering rage, his comment was: "I never saw this sort of thing at Plato's." I doubt not that he was quicker to copy his father than he was to copy Plato! Above all, let his food be simple, his clothing inexpensive, and his style of living like that of his companions. The boy will never be angry at some one being counted equal to himself, whom you have from the first treated as the equal of many.

from "On The Private Life"
Preface

. . . With great accord they urge vices upon us. Even if we do nothing else for our well-be-ing, our retreat will itself do us good; we shall be better on our own. And what if we retreat into the best company[1] and select a model there for our lives? That only happens in retire-ment. It is then that decisions once made can be realized, when no one intervenes with the help of the populace to deflect a judgment which is still weak. It is then that life, fragmented by an enormous variety of aims, can follow an even, unitary course. For the worst of our evils is that we vary our vices themselves. Thus we cannot even manage to persist in evil already familiar. One thing after another appeals to us, and we have the further vexation that our judgments are not only perverse but fickle. We fluctuate, and grasp one thing after another. We abandon what we sought and seek again what we abandoned. We alternate between desire and regret. We depend entirely on the judgments of others; what seems best to us is what the many pursue and praise, not that which deserves pursuit and praise; nor do we judge a path to be good or bad by itself, but by the number of footprints on it—and none of them coming back!

Can a Stoic choose the private life?

STOIC AND EPICUREAN ATTITUDES

You will say to me: "What do you mean, Seneca? Are you deserting your party? Surely your Stoics say: 'Till the final extremity of life we shall remain in action. We shall not cease to devote ourselves to the good of the community, to aid the individual, to raise an aged hand to assist even our enemies. We are the ones who grant no respite for age—as that excellent author puts it,

> we press the helmet to our grizzled hair.[2]

We are they for whom there is not a moment's inactivity till death—so much so that death itself, if we had our say, would not be inactive.' Why are you, in Zeno's own headquarters, uttering precepts of Epicurus? If you are displeased with your party, why not defect out-right, instead of betraying it?"

For the moment, I shall just answer: "Surely you can only want me to be like my lead-ers? Well then, I shall not go where they send me but where they lead."

DIVISION OF THE SUBJECT

Next, I shall prove to you that I am not abandoning the precepts of the Stoa. It is not even that the Stoics themselves have abandoned them, though I would have every excuse for

---

1. By "the best company" Seneca means the company of great writers, particularly of the leading Stoic philosophers.
2. Vergil, *Aeneid*, ix.612.

following not their precepts but their example. I will divide what I have to say into two parts. Firstly, that one can give oneself over entirely, even from earliest youth, to the contemplation of truth, seeking the principle of living and practising it in secret. Secondly, that one has every right to do this on completion of service, when the best of life is over, and to turn the mind to other activities, like the Vestal virgins whose years are allotted to different duties; they learn to perform the sacred rites and, having learned them, teach them.

I shall show that the Stoics too have this doctrine. It is not that I make it a rule not to do anything contrary to what Zeno or Chrysippus say. Rather, the facts themselves allow me to go along with their opinion. To follow one person all the time is to belong not to a court, but a clique. If only things were all fully grasped! If only truth were open and acknowledged, and we never changed our principles! As it is, we must search for the truth along with the very people who would teach it.

Two schools, on this point as on others, are particularly at variance, the Epicureans and the Stoics. But each of them directs you, by a different route, to the private life. Epicurus says: "The wise man will not go into public life, unless something interferes." Zeno says: "He will go into public life, unless something impedes." The former aims for a private life on principle, the latter on special grounds. But these grounds are wide in extent. If the public realm is too corrupt to be helped, if it has been taken over by the wicked, the wise man will not struggle pointlessly nor squander himself to no avail. If he has too little authority or strength, if the public realm will not accept him or his health impedes him, in the same way that he will not launch a battered ship onto the sea or register for military service if disabled, he will not embark on a course which he knows he cannot manage.

THE TWO COMMONWEALTHS

So it is possible even for one whose resources are still intact, before experiencing any storms, to settle in safety, apply himself thenceforth to liberal arts and demand uninterrupted retirement, a devotee of the virtues which even the quietest can exercise. What is required, you see, of any man is that he should be of use to other men—if possible, to many; failing that, to a few; failing that, to those nearest him; failing that, to himself. For when he makes himself useful to others, he busies himself for the community. In the same way that he who makes himself worse harms not himself alone but everyone whom he could have benefitted had he become better, so anyone who serves himself well is of use to others by the very fact of preparing what will be of use to them.

We must grasp that there are two public realms, two commonwealths. One is great and truly common to all, where gods as well as men are included, where we look not to this corner or that, but measure its bounds with the sun. The other is that in which we are enrolled by an accident of birth—I mean Athens or Carthage or some other city that belongs not to all men but only a limited number. Some devote themselves at the same time to both commonwealths, the greater and the lesser, some only to the one or the other. We can serve this greater commonwealth even in retirement—indeed better, I suspect, in retirement—by enquiring what virtue is, whether it is one or many, whether nature or art makes men good; whether this receptacle of earth and sea and of things attached to earth and sea is one, or whether God has strewn abroad a multitude of such bodies; whether the matter from which all things come to be is altogether continuous and a plenum, or dispersed, with an intermixture of void and solid bodies; where God resides, whether he views his handiwork in idleness or acts upon it, and whether he surrounds it from without or pervades its entirety; whether the world is immortal, or to be numbered among things that collapse and are temporal. What service to God is there in this contemplation? That the greatness of his work be not without witness.

NATURE, CONTEMPLATION AND ACTION

We [Stoics] regularly say that the highest good is to live according to nature; and Nature has begotten us for both—to contemplate reality and to act. Let me now prove what I just said. And yet, why should I? It will be proved, if each consults himself on the extent of his appetite for knowledge of the unknown and his excitement at any report of it. There are people who sail the seas and endure the toils of the longest journey for the sole reward of coming to know something hidden and far away. That is what packs the crowds into public spectacles, what compels people to pry into things barred to them, to search out things ever more hidden, to unravel antiquities and hear about the ways of barbarous nations. Nature has given us a mind full of curiosity. Aware of her own skill and beauty, she brought us into being to view the mighty spectacle. She would lose all satisfaction in herself, were she to display works so great and glorious, so delicately drawn, so bright and, in more ways than one, so beautiful, to a lonely solitude. You can realize that her wish was to be viewed, and not just seen, if you look at the place that we were given. We were established in her midst and given a commanding view of all things. Not only was man stood upright. To fit him for contemplation, enabling him to follow the stars from their rising as they glide to their fall and to turn his face with the turning world, she raised his head aloft and placed it upon a neck which he can move. Moreover, she caused six signs of the zodiac to rise by day and six by night, revealing every region of herself, so that through those things which she had made visible to iris eye she might arouse an appetite for the rest. We cannot cast our eyes upon all things or their true extent. But our perspicacity has uncovered a way of investigation and put down a basis for truth, allowing enquiry to proceed from the obvious to the obscure and discover things older than the world itself. What was the source of these stars? What was the condition of the universe before the different elements separated to form its parts? What is the principle which unfolded them while they were immersed and indistinct? Who put things in their place? Was it by their nature that heavy things fell and light things rose—or, quite apart from physical thrust and weight, did some higher power lay down the law for them? What is the truth of that argument for the divine spirit in men, that a part of it—sparks, as it were, from the stars—leaped down to earth and was caught in an alien environment?

Our speculation has burst through the ramparts of heaven, not content to know merely what is shown to it. "I investigate," it says, "what lies beyond the world. Is it a vast abyss or has it limits of its own to enclose it? And what is the condition of things outside? Are they shapeless and indistinct, taking up the same room in all directions? Or are they also arranged in some order? Are they contiguous with this world or withdrawn far from it, leaving it to turn in a vacuum? Is it out of indivisible bodies that anything which has been or will be born is constructed? Or is their matter a continuum, subject throughout to transformation? Are the elements contrary to one another—or is it that, rather than clashing, they work variously together?"

Man was born to ask such questions. Think how little time he has, even if he claims every moment for himself? Suppose that he allows nothing to escape him through self-indulgence, nothing to slip away through carelessness, that he hoards his hours with the utmost parsimony, that he reaches the ultimate limit of human life and that nothing in him decreed by nature is deranged by fortune—none the less, for knowledge of things immortal, man is all *too* mortal. So I live according to Nature if I devote myself wholly to her, if I marvel at her and worship her. Nature wished me to do both—to act and to be free for contemplation. I am doing both. Even contemplation involves action.

"But it matters," you may say, "whether you go to it just for pleasure. You could be seeking nothing besides uninterrupted contemplation without any outcome—contemplation is agreeable and has its attractions." To this my reply will be: it matters just as much what your attitude is in your political life. Are you always on the go, allowing yourself no time to turn from things human to things divine? To seek wealth, without any love of virtue and without mental cultivation, and merely to make exertions are not at all commendable (these all need to be combined with one another and intertwined). In the same way, virtue is an incomplete and feeble good when wasted on a retirement without activity, never displaying what it has learned. No one would deny that virtue should test its progress by action; that, instead of just pondering what should be done, it should at some stage put a hand to it and turn its ideas into reality. But suppose that the wise man himself is not the cause of delay, that there is nothing lacking in the agent, just a lack of things to do—you will surely allow him his own company then?

What is the wise man's attitude as he retreats into retirement? One of knowing that, even then, he will be doing things for the benefit of posterity. We are certainly ones to claim that Zeno and Chrysippus accomplished more than if they had commanded armies, held public office and passed laws—and they did pass laws, though not for just one state but for the entire human race! So why should such retirement be wrong for the good man, if it enables him to govern the centuries to come and address not just a few men but all men of all nations, present and future? In short, I put the question to you, did Cleanthes and Chrysippus and Zeno live by their teachings? You will certainly reply that they did live as they said one should live. Yet none of them administered the affairs of a commonwealth. "But they did not have the fortune or the standing that normally gets people into public administration." None the less, they did not lead idle lives. They found a way to make their very repose more profitable to men than the bustle and sweat of others. Hence they can be seen to have done much, though they did nothing in the public realm.

Moreover, there are three kinds of life, and it is regularly asked which is the best. One is given to pleasure, the other to contemplation, the third to action. If we first put aside all contentiousness and that implacable hatred which we declare on those who follow a different rule from ours, we can see that all three come to the same conclusion under one label or another. The man who favours pleasure has not dispensed with contemplation, nor the contemplative with pleasure; nor has he whose life is dedicated to action dispensed with contemplation. "But it makes a very great difference," you may say, "whether a thing is an objective or an accessory to some other objective." The difference, I grant you, is great. Yet you cannot have one without the other. The contemplative cannot contemplate without action, the man of action cannot act without contemplation; nor does that third character, of whom we have agreed to think ill, favour an idle pleasure but one which he has made stable by his reason. So this very school of voluptuaries is also committed to activity. Why should it not be? Epicurus himself says that he will sometimes withdraw from pleasure and even go for pain, if the pleasure is threatened by remorse, or a lesser pain is to take the place of one more serious. My point is that all schools approve of contemplation. Others make for it directly. We treat it as an anchorage, not a harbor.

IS ANY COMMONWEALTH FIT FOR THE WISE?

Note also that the law laid down by Chrysippus allows you to live in retirement—I do not mean just putting up with retirement, but choosing it. Our school says that the wise man will not attach himself to just any commonwealth. But what difference does it make how the wise man comes to retirement, whether it is that the right commonwealth is unavailable to him or that he himself is unavailable to the commonwealth, if no such commonwealth is going to be available to any wise man? But there will never be one available to the choosy. I ask you, what commonwealth is any wise man going to attach himself to? The Athenian? That was where Socrates was condemned, where Aristotle had to flee to avoid condemnation, where envy oppresses the excellent. You cannot be telling me that the wise man will attach himself to *that* commmonwealth! The Carthaginian, then? That seat of unremitting sedition, where the best men were menaced by liberty, where fairness and goodness were held in utter contempt, where inhuman cruelty towards enemies extended to enmity even towards its own citizens! He will flee that one as well. Were I to go through each commonwealth, I would not find one that could endure the wise man or be endured by him. But if no commonwealth is to be found of the kind that we imagine, retirement becomes a necessity for all wise men, because the one thing which could be preferred to retirement nowhere exists. If someone says that sailing is best and then says that you should not sail on a sea where shipwrecks regularly occur and there are often sudden storms to sweep the helmsman off course, he would be telling me, I think, not to weigh anchor, though speaking in praise of sailing. . . .

❦

"On Liberal and Vocational Studies"

Y<small>OU</small> have been wishing to know my views with regard to liberal studies. My answer is this: I respect no study, and deem no study good, which results in money-making. Such studies are profit-bringing occupations, useful only in so far as they give the mind a preparation and do not engage it permanently. One should linger upon them only so long as the mind can occupy itself with nothing greater; they are our apprenticeship, not our real work. Hence you see why "liberal studies" are so called; it is because they are studies worthy of a free-born gentleman. But there is only one really liberal study,—that which gives a man his liberty. It is the study of wisdom, and that is lofty, brave, and great-souled. All other studies are puny and puerile. You surely do not believe that there is good in any of the subjects whose teachers are, as you see, men of the most ignoble and base stamp? We ought not to be learning such things; we should have done with learning them.

Certain persons have made up their minds that the point at issue with regard to the liberal studies is whether they make men good; but they do not even profess or aim at a knowledge of this particular subject. The scholar busies himself with investigations into language, and if it be his desire to go farther afield, he works on history, or, if he would extend his range to the farthest limits, on poetry. But which of these paves the way to virtue? Pronouncing syllables, investigating words, memorizing plays, or making rules for the scansion of poetry,—what is there in all this that rids one of fear, roots out desire, or bridles the passions? The question is: do such men teach virtue, or not? If they do not teach it, then neither do they transmit it. If they do teach it, they are philosophers. Would you like to know how it happens that they have not taken the chair for the purpose of teaching virtue? See how unlike their subjects are; and yet their subjects would resemble each other if they taught the same thing.

It may be, perhaps, that they make you believe that Homer was a philosopher, although they disprove this by the very arguments through which they seek to prove it. For sometimes they make of him a Stoic, who approves nothing but virtue, avoids pleasures, and refuses to relinquish honour even at the price of immortality; sometimes they make him an Epicurean, praising the condition of a state in repose, which passes its days in feasting and song; sometimes a Peripatetic, classifying goodness in three ways; sometimes an Academic, holding that all things are uncertain. It is clear, however, that no one of these doctrines is to be fathered upon Homer, just because they are all there; for they are irreconcilable with one another. We may admit to these men, indeed, that Homer was a philosopher; yet surely he became a wise man before he had any knowledge of poetry. So let us learn the particular things that made Homer wise.

It is no more to the point, of course, for me to investigate whether Homer or Hesiod was the older poet, than to know why Hecuba, although younger than Helen, showed her years so lamentably. What, in your, opinion, I say, would be the point in trying to determine the respective ages of Achilles and Patroclus? Do you raise the question, "Through what regions did Ulysses stray?" instead of trying to prevent ourselves from going astray at all times? We have no leisure to hear lectures on the question whether he was sea-tost between Italy and Sicily, or outside our unknown world (indeed, so long a wandering could not possibly have taken place within its narrow bounds); we ourselves encounter storms of the spirit, which toss us daily, and our depravity drives us into all the ills which troubled Ulysses. For us there is never lacking the beauty to tempt our eyes, or the enemy to assail us; on this side are savage monsters that delight in human blood, on that side the treacherous allurements of the ear, and yonder is shipwreck and all the varied category of misfortunes. Show me rather, by the example of Ulysses, how I am to love my country, my wife, my father, and how, even after suffering shipwreck, I am to sail toward these ends, honourable as they are. Why try to discover whether Penelope was a pattern of purity, or whether she had the laugh on her contemporaries? Or whether she suspected that the man in her presence was Ulysses, before she knew it was he? Teach me rather what purity is, and how great a good we have in it, and whether it is situated in the body or in the soul.

Now I will transfer my attention to the musician. You, sir, are teaching me how the treble and the bass are in accord with one another, and how, though the strings produce different notes, the result is a harmony; rather bring my soul into harmony with itself, and let not my purposes be out of tune. You are showing me what the doleful keys are; show me rather how, in the midst of adversity, I may keep from uttering a doleful note. The mathematician teaches me how to lay out the dimensions of my estates; but I should rather be taught how to lay out what is enough for a man to own. He teaches me to count, and adapts my fingers to avarice; but I should prefer him to teach me that there is no point in such calculations, and that one is none the happier for tiring out the bookkeepers with his possessions—or rather, how useless property is to any man who would find it the greatest misfortune if he should be required to reckon out, by his own wits, the amount of his holdings. What good is there for me in knowing how to parcel out a piece of land, if I know not how to share it with my brother? What good is there in working out to a nicety the dimensions of an acre, and in detecting the error if a piece has so much as escaped my measuring-rod, if I am embittered when an ill-tempered neighbour merely scrapes off a bit of my land? The mathematician teaches me how I may lose none of my boundaries; I, however, seek to learn how to lose them all with a light heart. "But," comes the reply, "I am being driven from the farm which my father and grandfather owned!" Well? Who owned the land before your grandfather? Can you explain what people (I will not say what person) held it originally? You did not enter upon it as a master, but merely as a tenant. And whose tenant are you? If your claim is successful, you are tenant of the heir. The lawyers say that public property cannot be acquired privately by possession; what you hold and call your own is public property—indeed, it belongs to mankind at large. O what marvellous skill! You know how to measure the circle; you find the square of any shape which is set before you; you compute the distances between the stars; there is nothing which does not come within the scope of your calculations. But if you are a real master of your profession, measure me the mind of man! Tell me how great it is, or how puny! You know what a straight line is; but how does it benefit you if you do not know what is straight in this life of ours?

I come next to the person who boasts his knowledge of the heavenly bodies, who knows

> Whither the chilling star of Saturn hides,
> And through what orbit Mercury doth stray.[3]

Of what benefit will it be to know this? That I shall be disturbed because Saturn and Mars are in opposition, or when Mercury sets at eventide in plain view of Saturn, rather than learn that those stars, wherever they are, are propitious, and that they are not subject to change? They are driven along by an unending round of destiny, on a course from which they cannot swerve. They return at stated seasons; they either set in motion, or mark the intervals of the whole world's work. But if they are responsible for whatever happens, how will it help you to know the secrets of the immutable? Or if they merely give indications, what good is there in foreseeing what you cannot escape? Whether you know these things or not, they will take place.

---

3. Vergil, *Georgics*, i.336f.

Behold the fleeting sun,
The stars that follow in his train, and thou
Shalt never find the morrow play thee false,
Or be misled by nights without a cloud.[4]

It has, however, been sufficiently and fully ordained that I shall be safe from anything that may mislead me. "What," you say, "does the 'morrow never play me false'? Whatever happens without my knowledge plays me false." I, for my part, do not know what is to be, but I do know what may come to be. I shall have no misgivings in this matter; I await the future in its entirety; and if there is any abatement in its severity, make the most of it. If the morrow treats me kindly, it is a sort of deception; but it does not deceive me even at that. For just as I know that all things can happen, so I know, too, that they will not happen in every case. I am ready for favourable events in every case, but I am prepared for evil.

In this discussion you must bear with me if I do not follow the regular course. For I do not consent to admit painting into the list of liberal arts, any more than sculpture, marble-working, and other helps toward luxury. I also debar from the liberal studies wrestling and all knowledge that is compounded of oil and mud; otherwise, I should be compelled to admit perfumers also, and cooks, and all others who lend their wits to the service of our pleasures. For what "liberal" element is there in these ravenous takers of emetics, whose bodies are fed to fatness while their minds are thin and dull? Or do we really believe that the training which they give is "liberal" for the young men of Rome, who used to be taught by our ancestors to stand straight and hurl a spear, to wield a pike, to guide a horse, and to handle weapons? Our ancestors used to teach their children nothing that could be learned while lying down. But neither the new system nor the old teaches or nourishes virtue. For what good does it do us to guide a horse and control his speed with the curb, and then find that our own passions, utterly uncurbed, bolt with us? Or to beat many opponents in wrestling or boxing, and then to find that we ourselves are beaten by anger?

"What then," you say, "do the liberal studies contribute nothing to our welfare?" Very much in other respects, but nothing at all as regards virtue. For even these arts of which I have spoken, though admittedly of a low grade—depending as they do, upon handiwork—contribute greatly toward the equipment of life, but nevertheless have nothing to do with virtue. And if you inquire, "Why, then, do we educate our children in the liberal studies?" it is not because they can bestow virtue, but because they prepare the soul for the reception of virtue. Just as that "primary course," as the ancients called it, in grammar, which gave boys their elementary training, does not teach them the liberal arts, but prepares the ground for their early acquisition of these arts, so the liberal arts do not conduct the soul all the way to virtue, but merely set it going in that direction.

Posidonius divides the arts into four classes: first we have those which are common and low, then those which serve for amusement, then those which refer to the education of boys, and, finally, the liberal arts. The common sort belong to workmen and are mere hand-work; they are concerned with equipping life; there is in them no pretence to beauty or honour. The arts of amusement are those which aim to please the eye and the ear. To this class you may assign the stage-machinists, who invent scaffolding that goes aloft of

4. Vergil, *Georgics*, i.424ff.

its own accord, or floors that rise silently into the air, and many other surprising devices, as when objects that fit together then fall apart, or objects which are separate then join together automatically, or objects which stand erect then gradually collapse. The eye of the inexperienced is struck with amazement by these things; for such persons marvel at everything that takes place without warning, because they do not know the causes. The arts which belong to the education of boys, and are somewhat similar to the liberal arts, are those which the Greeks call the "cycle of studies," but which we Romans call the "liberal." However, those alone are really liberal—or rather, to give them a truer name, "free"—whose concern is virtue.

"But," one will say, "just as there is a part of philosophy which has to do with nature, and a part which has to do with ethics, and a part which has to do with reasoning, so this group of liberal arts also claims for itself a place in philosophy. When one approaches questions that deal with nature, a decision is reached by means of a word from the mathematician. Therefore mathematics is a department of that branch which it aids." But many things aid us and yet are not parts of ourselves. Nay, if they were, they would not aid us. Food is an aid to the body, but is not a part of it. We get some help from the service which mathematics renders; and mathematics is as indispensable to philosophy as the carpenter is to the mathematician. But carpentering is not a part of mathematics, nor is mathematics a part of philosophy. Moreover, each has its own limits; for the wise man investigates and learns the causes of natural phenomena, while the mathematician follows up and computes their numbers and their measurements. The wise man knows the laws by which the heavenly bodies persist, what powers belong to them, and what attributes; the astronomer merely notes their comings and goings, the rules which govern their settings and their risings, and the occasional periods during which they seem to stand still, although as a matter of fact no heavenly body can stand still. The wise man will know what causes the reflection in a mirror; but the mathematician can merely tell you how far the body should be from the reflection, and what shape of mirror will produce a given reflection. The philosopher will demonstrate that the sun is a large body, while the astronomer will compute just how large, progressing in knowledge by his method of trial and experiment; but in order to progress, he must summon to his aid certain principles. No art, however, is sufficient unto itself, if the foundation upon which it rests depends upon mere favour. Now philosophy asks no favours from any other source; it builds everything on its own soil; but the science of numbers is, so to speak, a structure built on another man's land—it builds on alien soil. It accepts first principles, and by their favour arrives at further conclusions. If it could march unassisted to the truth, if it were able to understand the nature of the universe, I should say that it would offer much assistance to our minds; for the mind grows by contact with things heavenly, and draws into itself something from on high. There is but one thing that brings the soul to perfection—the unalterable knowledge of good and evil. But there is no other art which investigates good and evil.

I should like to pass in review the several virtues. Bravery is a scorner of things which inspire fear; it looks down upon, challenges, and crushes the powers of terror and all that would drive our freedom under the yoke. But do "liberal studies" strengthen this virtue? Loyalty is the holiest good in the human heart; it is forced into betrayal by no constraint, and it is bribed by no rewards. Loyalty cries: "Burn me, slay me, kill me! I shall not betray my trust; and the more urgently torture shall seek to find my secret, the deeper in my heart will I bury it!" Can the "liberal arts" produce such a spirit within us? Temperance controls our desires; some it hates and routs, others it regulates and restores to a healthy measure, nor does it ever approach our desires for their own sake. Temperance knows that the best measure of the appetites is not what you want to take, but what you ought to take. Kindliness forbids you to be over-bearing towards your associates, and it forbids you to be grasping. In words and in deeds and in feelings it shows itself gentle and courteous to all men. It counts no evil as another's solely. And the reason why it loves its own good is chiefly because it will some day be the good of another. Do "liberal studies" teach a man such character as this? No; no more than they teach simplicity, moderation and self-restraint, thrift and economy, and that kindliness which spares a neighbour's life as if it were one's own and knows that it is not for man to make wasteful use of his fellow-man.

"But," one says, "since you declare that virtue cannot be attained without the 'liberal studies,' how is it that you deny that they offer any assistance to virtue?" Because you cannot attain virtue without food, either; and yet food has nothing to do with virtue. Wood does not offer assistance to a ship, although a ship cannot be built except of wood. There is no reason, I say, why you should think that anything is made by the assistance of that without which it cannot be made. We might even make the statement that it is possible to attain wisdom without the "liberal studies"; for although virtue is a thing that must be learned, yet it is not learned by means of these studies.

What reason have I, however, for supposing that one who is ignorant of letters will never be a wise man, since wisdom is not to be found in letters? Wisdom communicates facts and not words; and it may be true that the memory is more to be depended upon when it has no support outside itself. Wisdom is a large and spacious thing. It needs plenty of free room. One must learn about things divine and human, the past and the future, the ephemeral and the eternal; and one must learn about Time. See how many questions arise concerning time alone: in the first place, whether it is anything in and by itself; in the second place, whether anything exists prior to time and without time; and again, did time begin along with the universe, or, because there was something even before the universe began, did time also exist then? There are countless questions concerning the soul alone: whence it comes, what is its nature, when it begins to exist, and how long it exists; whether it passes from one place to another and changes its habitation, being transferred successively from one animal shape to another, or whether it is a slave but once, roaming the universe after it is set free; whether it is corporeal or not; what will become of it when it ceases to use us as its medium; how it will employ its freedom when it has escaped from this present prison; whether it will forget all its past, and at that moment begin to know itself when, released from the body, it has withdrawn to the skies.

Thus, whatever phase of things human and divine you have apprehended, you will be wearied by the vast number of things to be answered and things to be learned. And in order that these manifold and mighty subjects may have free entertainment in your soul, you must remove therefrom all superfluous things. Virtue will not surrender herself to these narrow bounds of ours; a great subject needs wide space in which to move. Let all other things be driven out, and let the breast be emptied to receive virtue.

"But it is a pleasure to be acquainted with many arts." Therefore let us keep only as much of them as is essential. Do you regard that man as blameworthy who puts superfluous things on the same footing with useful things, and in his house makes a lavish display of costly objects, but do not deem him blameworthy who has allowed himself to become engrossed with the useless furniture of learning? This desire to know more than is sufficient is a sort of intemperance. Why? Because this unseemly pursuit of the liberal arts makes men troublesome, wordy, tactless, self-satisfied bores; who fail to learn the essentials just because they have learned the non-essentials. Didymus the scholar wrote four thousand books. I should feel pity for him if he had only read the same number of superfluous volumes. In these books he investigates Homer's birthplace, who was really the mother of Aeneas, whether Anacreon was more of a rake or more of a drunkard, whether Sappho was a bad lot, and other problems the answers to which, if found, were forthwith to be forgotten. Come now, do not tell me that life is long! Nay, when you come to consider our own countrymen also, I can show you many works which ought to be cut down with the axe.

It is at the cost of a vast outlay of time and of vast discomfort to the ears of others that we win such praise as this: "What a learned man you are!" Let us be content with this recommendation, less citified though it be: "What a good man you are!" Do I mean this? Well, would you have me unroll the annals of the world's history and try to find out who first wrote poetry? Or, in the absence of written records, shall I make an estimate of the number of years which lie between Orpheus and Homer? Or shall I make a study of the absurd writings of Aristarchus, wherein he branded the text of other men's verses, and wear my life away upon syllables? Shall I then wallow in the geometrician's dust? Have I so far forgotten that useful saw "Save your time"? Must I know these things? And what may I choose not to know?

Apion, the scholar, who drew crowds to his lectures all over Greece in the days of Gaius Caesar and was acclaimed a Homerid by every state, used to maintain that Homer, when he had finished his two poems, the *Iliad* and the *Odyssey*, added a preliminary poem to his work, wherein he embraced the whole Trojan war. The argument which Apion adduced, to prove this statement was that Homer had purposely inserted in the opening line two letters which contained a key to the number of his books. A man who wishes to know many things must know such things as these, and must take no thought of all the time which one loses by ill-health, public duties, private duties, daily duties, and sleep. Apply the measure to the years of your life; they have no room for all these things.

I have been speaking so far of liberal studies; but think how much superfluous and un-practical matter the philosophers contain! Of their own accord they also have descended to establishing nice divisions of syllables, to determining the true meaning of conjunctions and prepositions; they have been envious of the scholars, envious of the mathematicians. They have taken over into their own art all the superfluities of these other arts; the result is that they know more about careful speaking than about careful living. Let me tell you what evils are due to over-nice exactness, and what an enemy it is of truth! Protagoras declares that one can take either side on any question and debate it with equal success—even on this very question, whether every subject can be debated from either point of view. Nausiphanes holds that in things which seem to exist, there is no difference between existence and non-existence. Parmenides maintains that nothing exists of all this which seems to exist, except the universe alone. Zeno of Elea removed all the difficulties by removing one; for he declares that nothing exists. The Pyrrhonean, Megarian, Eretrian, and Academic schools are all engaged in practically the same task; they have introduced a new knowledge, non-knowledge. You may sweep all these theories in with the superfluous troops of "liberal" studies; the one class of men give me a knowledge that will be of no use to me, the other class do away with any hope of attaining knowledge. It is better, of course, to know useless things than to know nothing. One set of philosophers offers no light by which I may direct my gaze toward the truth; the other digs out my very eyes and leaves me blind. If I cleave to Protagoras, there is nothing in the scheme of nature that is not doubtful; if I hold with Nausiphanes, I am sure only of this—that everything is unsure; if with Parmenides, there is nothing except the One; if with Zeno, there is not even the One.

What are we, then? What becomes of all these things that surround us, support us, sustain us? The whole universe is then a vain or deceptive shadow. I cannot readily say whether I am more vexed at those who would have it that we know nothing, or with those who would not leave us even this privilege. Farewell.

Quintilian

C. 35– C. 100

All previous ages have toiled that we might reap the fruit of wisdom.

INSTITUTES

Marcus Fabius Quintilianus was born in Spain about a generation after Seneca. He, too, studied in Rome. He was a teacher of Pliny the Younger and of the emperor Domitian's grand-nephews. He carried forward the Greek ideal of the *enkuklios paideia,* and his philosophy of education bears the stamp of Aristotle and Cicero. In Quintilian's estimation, Cicero "succeeded in reproducing the force of Demosthenes, the copious flow of Plato, and the charm of Isocrates." His recommended "Great Books" curriculum included Homer, Hesiod, Aeschylus, Sophocles, Herodotus, Thucydides, Demosthenes, Isocrates, Plato, Xenophon, Aristotle, Virgil, Horace, Sallust, Livy, and many other Greek and Roman authors from the ranks of the poets, historians, orators, and philosophers. Above all, his task was to form the ideal orator, whom Marcus Cato famously defined as "a good man skilled in speaking." "I hold that no one can be a true orator," Quintilian declared, "unless he is also a good man and, even if he could be, I would not have it so" (*Institutes,* I.ii.3).

THE SELECTION

The twelve books of the *Institutes (Institutio Oratoria)* comprise one of the greatest educational treatises ever written. It is a treasury of advice on reading, writing, rhetorical eloquence, and memory. It is as practical as penmanship, spelling, and discipline, and even weighs in on the debate between home schooling and public education. But Quintilian's advice is never merely practical; he maintains a clear moral vision for education. Not content with skills alone, he seeks above all to shape the character of his students. For a teacher of Quintilian's habit of mind, wisdom, virtue, and eloquence were inseparable. Orators are not to be sophists who separate skill from truth and character, nor are they to be abstract philosophers who never translate theoretical precepts into the day-to-day life of virtue. As was true for the ideal upheld by Cicero and soon by Tacitus, Quintilian's orator is more than an accomplished public speaker; he is an esteemed statesman, advocate, judge, or other civic leader. Quintilian directs the talented and trained orator's attention beyond a lucrative profession in the law courts to the enduring reward and delight of the inner man. His love for learning is evident in his tribute to the life of the mind that echoes Cicero's praise of his teacher Archias: "The study of literature is a necessity for boys and the delight of old age, the sweet companion of our privacy and the sole branch of study which has more solid substance than display."

from the Institutes
Book I

PREFACE

My aim, then, is the education of the perfect orator. The first essential for such an one is that he should be a good man, and consequently we demand of him not merely the possession of exceptional gifts of speech, but of all the excellences of character as well. For I will not admit that the principles of upright and honourable living should, as some have held, be regarded as the peculiar concern of philosophy. The man who can really play his part as a citizen and is capable of meeting the demands both of public and private business, the man who can guide a state by his counsels, give it a firm basis by his legislation and purge its vices by his decisions as a judge, is assuredly no other than the orator of our quest. Wherefore, although I admit I shall make use of certain of the principles laid down in philosophical textbooks, I would insist that such principles have a just claim to form part of the subject-matter of this work and do actually belong to the art of oratory. I shall frequently be compelled to speak of such virtues as courage, justice, self-control; in fact scarcely a case comes up in which some one of these virtues is not involved; every one of them requires illustration and consequently makes a demand on the imagination and eloquence of the pleader. I ask you then, can there be any doubt that, wherever imaginative power and amplitude of diction are required, the orator has a specially important part to play? These two branches of knowledge were, as Cicero has clearly shown, so closely united, not merely in theory but in practice, that the same men were regarded as uniting the qualifications of orator and philosopher. Subsequently this single branch of study split up into its component parts, and thanks to the indolence of its professors was regarded as consisting of several distinct subjects. As soon as speaking became a means of livelihood and the practice of making an evil use of the blessings of eloquence came into vogue, those who had a reputation for eloquence ceased to study moral philosophy, and ethics, thus abandoned by the orators, became the prey of weaker intellects. As a consequence certain persons, disdaining the toil of learning to speak well, returned to the task of forming character and establishing rules of life and kept to themselves what is, if we *must* make a division, the better part of philosophy, but presumptuously laid claim to the sole possession of the title of philosopher, a distinction which neither the greatest generals nor the most famous statesmen and administrators have ever dared to claim for themselves. For they preferred the performance to the promise of great deeds. I am ready to admit that many of the old philosophers inculcated the most excellent principles and practised what they preached. But in our own day the name of philosopher has too often been the mask for the worst vices. For their attempt has not been to win the name of philosopher by virtue and the earnest search for wisdom; instead they have sought to disguise the depravity of their characters by the assumption of a stern and austere mien accompanied by the wearing of a garb differing from that of their fellow men. Now as a matter of fact we all of us frequently handle those themes which philosophy claims for its own. Who, short of being an utter villain, does not speak of justice, equity and virtue? Who (and even common country-folk are no exception) does not make some inquiry into the causes of natural phenomena? As for the special uses and distinctions of words, they should be a subject of study common to all who give any thought to the meaning of language. But it is surely the orator who will have the greatest mastery of all such departments of knowledge and the greatest power to express it in words. And if ever he had reached perfection, there would be no need to go to the schools of philosophy for the precepts of virtue. As things stand, it is occasionally necessary to have recourse to those authors who have, as said above, usurped the better part of the art of oratory after its desertion by the orators and to demand back what is ours by right, not with a view to appropriating their discoveries, but to show them that they have appropriated what in truth belonged to others. Let our ideal orator then be such as to have a genuine title to the name of philosopher: it is not sufficient that he should be blameless in point of character (for I cannot agree with those who hold this opinion): he must also be a thorough master of the science and the art of speaking, to an extent that perhaps no orator has yet attained. Still we must none the less follow the ideal, as was done by not a few of the ancients, who, though they refused to admit that the perfect sage had yet been found, none the less handed down precepts of wisdom for the use of posterity. Perfect eloquence is assuredly a reality, which is not beyond the reach of human intellect. Even if we fail to reach it, those whose aspirations are highest, will attain to greater heights than those who abandon themselves to premature despair of ever reaching the goal and halt at the very foot of the ascent. . . .

I.

I would, therefore, have a father conceive the highest hopes of his son from the moment of his birth. If he does so, he will be more careful about the groundwork of his education. For there is absolutely no foundation for the complaint that but few men have the power to take in the knowledge that is imparted to them, and that the majority are so slow of understanding that education is a waste of time and labour. On the contrary you will find that most are quick to reason and ready to learn. Reasoning comes as naturally to man as flying to birds, speed to horses and ferocity to beasts of prey: our minds are endowed by nature with such activity and sagacity that the soul is believed to proceed from heaven. Those who are dull and unteachable are as abnormal as prodigious births and monstrosities, and are but few in number. A proof of what I say is to be found in the fact that boys commonly show promise of many accomplishments, and when such promise dies away as they grow up, this is plainly due not to the failure of natural gifts, but to lack of the requisite care. But, it will be urged, there are degrees of talent. Undoubtedly, I reply, and there will be a corresponding variation in actual accomplishment: but that there are any who gain nothing from education, I absolutely deny. The man who shares this conviction, must, as soon as he becomes a father, devote the utmost care to fostering big the promise shown by the son whom he destines to become an orator.

Above all see that the child's nurse speaks correctly. The ideal, according to Chrysippus, would be that she should be a philosopher: failing that he desired that the best should be chosen, as far as possible. No doubt the most important point is that they should be of good character: but they should speak correctly as well. It is the nurse that the child first hears, and her words that he will first attempt to imitate. And we are by nature most tenacious of childish impressions, just as the flavour first absorbed by vessels when new persists, and the colour imparted by dyes to the primitive whiteness of wool is indelible. Further it is the worst impressions that are most durable. For, while what is good readily deteriorates, you will never turn vice into virtue. Do not therefore allow the boy to become accustomed even in infancy to a style of speech which he will subsequently have to unlearn.

As regards parents, I should like to see them as highly educated as possible, and I do not restrict this remark to fathers alone. We are told that the eloquence of the Gracchi owed much to their mother Cornelia, whose letters even to-day testify to the cultivation of her style. Laelia, the daughter of Gaius Laelius, is said to have reproduced the elegance of her father's language in her own speech, while the oration delivered before the triumvirs by Hortensia, the daughter of Quintus Hortensius, is still read and not merely as a compliment to her sex. And even those who have not had the fortune to receive a good education should not for that reason devote less care to their son's education; but should on the contrary show all the greater diligence in other matters where they can be of service to their children.

As regards the boys in whose company our budding orator is to be brought up, I would repeat what I have said about nurses. As regards his *paedagogi*,[1] I would urge that they should have had a thorough education, or if they have not, that they should be aware of the fact. There are none worse than those, who as soon as they have progressed beyond a knowledge of the alphabet delude themselves into the belief that they are the possessors of real knowledge. For they disdain to stoop to the drudgery of teaching, and conceiving that they have acquired a certain title to authority—a frequent source of vanity in such persons—become imperious or even brutal in instilling a thorough dose of their own folly. Their misconduct is no less prejudicial to morals. We are, for instance, told by Diogenes of Babylon, that Leonides, Alexander's *paedagogus*, infected his pupil with certain faults, which as a result of his education as a boy clung to him even in his maturer years when he had become the greatest of kings.

---

1. There is no translation for *paedagogus*, the slave-tutor. "Tutor," "guardian," "governor," and similar terms are all misleading. He had the general supervision of the boy, escorted him to school and elsewhere, and saw that he did not get into mischief, but did not, as a rule, direct his studies.

If any of my readers regards me as somewhat exacting in my demands, I would ask him to reflect that it is no easy task to create an orator, even though his education be carried out under the most favourable circumstances, and that further and greater difficulties are still before us. For continuous application, the very best of teachers and a variety of exercises are necessary. Therefore the rules which we lay down for the education of our pupil must be of the best. If anyone refuses to be guided by them, the fault will lie not with the method, but with the individual. Still if it should prove impossible to secure the ideal nurse, the ideal companions, or the ideal *paedagogus*, I would insist that there should be one person at any rate attached to the boy who has some knowledge of speaking and who will, if any incorrect expression should be used by nurse or *paedagogus* in the presence of the child under their charge, at once correct the error and prevent its becoming a habit. But it must be clearly understood that this is only a remedy, and that the ideal course is that indicated above.

I prefer that a boy should begin with Greek, because Latin, being in general use, will be picked up by him whether we will or no; while the fact that Latin learning is derived from Greek is a further reason for his being first instructed in the latter. I do not however desire that this principle should be so superstitiously observed that he should for long speak and learn only Greek, as is done in the majority of cases. Such a course gives rise to many faults of language and accent; the latter tends to acquire a foreign intonation, while the former through force of habit becomes impregnated with Greek idioms, which persist with extreme obstinacy even when we are speaking another tongue. The study of Latin ought therefore to follow at no great distance and in a short time proceed side by side with Greek. The result will be that, as soon as we begin to give equal attention to both languages, neither will prove a hindrance to the other.

Some hold that boys should not be taught to read till they are seven years old, that being the earliest age at which they can derive profit from instruction and endure the strain of learning. Most of them attribute this view to Hesiod, at least such as lived before the time of Aristophanes the grammarian, who was the first to deny that the *Hypothecae*, in which this opinion is expressed, was the work of that poet. But other authorities, among them Eratosthenes, give the same advice. Those however who hold that a child's mind should not be allowed to lie fallow for a moment are wiser. Chrysippus, for instance, though he gives the nurses a three years' reign, still holds the formation of the child's mind on the best principles to be a part of their duties. Why, again, since children are capable of moral training, should they not be capable of literary education? I am well aware that during the whole period of which I am speaking we can expect scarcely the same amount of progress that one year will effect afterwards. Still those who disagree with me seem in taking this line to spare the teacher rather than the pupil. What better occupation can a child have so soon as he is able to speak? And he must be kept occupied somehow or other. Or why should we despise the profit to be derived before the age of seven, small though it be? For though the knowledge absorbed in the previous years may be but little, yet the boy will be learning something more advanced during that year, in which he would otherwise have been occupied with something more elementary. Such progress each successive year increases the total, and the time gained during childhood is clear profit to the period of youth. Further as regards the years which follow I must emphasise the importance of learning what has to be learnt in good time. Let us not therefore waste the earliest years:

there is all the less excuse for this, since the elements of literary training are solely a question of memory, which not only exists even in small children, but is specially retentive at that age.

I am not however so blind to differences of age as to think that the very young should be forced on prematurely or given real work to do. Above all things we must take care that the child, who is not yet old enough to love his studies, does not come to hate them and dread the bitterness which he has once tasted, even when the years of infancy are left behind. His studies must be made an amusement: he must be questioned and praised and taught to rejoice when he has done well; sometimes too, when he refuses instruction, it should be given to some other to excite his envy, at times also he must be engaged in competition and should be allowed to believe himself successful more often than not, while he should be encouraged to do his best by such rewards as may appeal to his tender years.

These instructions may seem but trivialities in view of the fact that I am professing to describe the education of an orator. But studies, like men, have their infancy, and as the training of the body which is destined to grow to the fulness of strength begins while the child is in his cradle and at his mother's breast, so even the man who is destined to rise to the heights of eloquence was once a squalling babe, tried to speak in stammering accents and was puzzled by the shapes of letters. Nor does the fact that capacity for learning is inadequate, prove that it is not necessary to learn anything. No one blames a father because he thinks that such details should on no account be neglected in the case of his own son. Why then should he be criticised who sets down for the benefit of the public what he would be right to put into practice in his own house? There is this further reason why he should not be blamed. Small children are better adapted for taking in small things, and just as the body can only be trained to certain flexions of the limbs while it is young and supple, so the acquisition of strength makes the mind offer greater resistance to the acquisition of most subjects of knowledge. Would Philip of Macedon have wished that his son Alexander should be taught the rudiments of letters by Aristotle, the greatest philosopher of that age, or would the latter have undertaken the task, if he had not thought that even the earliest instruction is best given by the most perfect teacher and has real reference to the whole of education? Let us assume therefore that Alexander has been confided to our charge and that the infant placed in our lap deserves no less attention than he—though for that matter every man's child deserves equal attention. Would you be ashamed even in teaching him the alphabet to point out some brief rules for his education?

At any rate I am not satisfied with the course (which I note is usually adopted) of teaching small children the names and order of the letters before their shapes. Such a practice makes them slow to recognise the letters, since they do not pay attention to their actual shape, preferring to be guided by what they have already learned by rote. It is for this reason that teachers, when they think they have sufficiently familiarised their young pupils with the letters written in their usual order, reverse that order or rearrange it in every kind of combination, until they learn to know the letters from their appearance and not from the order in which they occur. It will be best therefore for children to begin by learning their appearance and names just as they do with men. The method, however, to which we have objected in teaching the alphabet, is unobjectionable when applied to syllables. I quite approve on the other hand of a practice which has been devised to stimulate children to learn by giving them ivory letters to play with, as I do of anything else that may be discovered to delight the very young, the sight, handling and naming of which is a pleasure.

As soon as the child has begun to know the shapes of the various letters, it will be no bad thing to have them cut as accurately as possible upon a board, so that the pen may be guided along the grooves. Thus mistakes such as occur with wax tablets will be rendered impossible; for the pen will be confined between the edges of the letters and will be prevented from going astray. Further by increasing the frequency and speed with which they follow these fixed outlines we shall give steadiness to the fingers, and there will be no need to guide the child's hand with our own. The art of writing well and quickly is not unimportant for our purpose, though it is generally disregarded by persons of quality. Writing is of the utmost importance in the study which we have under consideration and by its means alone can true and deeply rooted proficiency be obtained. But a sluggish pen delays our thoughts, while an unformed and illiterate hand cannot be deciphered, a circumstance which necessitates another wearisome task, namely the dictation of what we have written to a copyist. We shall therefore at all times and in all places, and above all when we are writing private letters to our friends, find a gratification in the thought that we have not neglected even this accomplishment.

As regards syllables, no short cut is possible: they must all be learnt, and there is no good in putting off learning the most difficult; this is the general practice, but the sole result is bad spelling. Further we must beware of placing a blind confidence in a child's memory. It is better to repeat syllables and impress them on the memory and, when he is reading, not to press him to read continuously or with greater speed, unless indeed the clear and obvious sequence of letters can suggest itself without its being necessary for the child to stop to think. The syllables once learnt, let him begin to construct words with them and sentences with the words. You will hardly believe how much reading is delayed by undue haste. If the child attempts more than his powers allow, the inevitable result is hesitation, interruption and repetition, and the mistakes which he makes merely lead him to lose confidence in what he already knows. Reading must therefore first be sure, then connected, while it must be kept slow for a considerable time, until practice brings speed unaccompanied by error. For to look to the right, which is regularly taught, and to look ahead depends not so much on precept as on practice; since it is necessary to keep the eyes on what follows while reading out what precedes, with the resulting difficulty that the attention of the mind must be divided, the eyes and voice being differently engaged. It will be found worth while, when the boy begins to write out words in accordance with the usual practice, to see that he does not waste his labour in writing out common words of everyday occurrence. He can readily learn the explanations or *glosses*, as the Greeks call them, of the more obscure words by the way and, while he is still engaged on the first rudiments, acquire what would otherwise demand special time to be devoted to it. And as we are still discussing minor details, I would urge that the lines, which he is set to copy, should not express thoughts of no significance, but convey some sound moral lesson. He will remember such aphorisms even when he is an old man, and the impression made upon his unformed mind will contribute to the formation of his character. He may also be entertained by learning the sayings of famous men and above all selections from the poets, poetry being more attractive to children. For memory is most necessary to an orator, as I shall point out in its proper place, and there is nothing like practice for strengthening and developing it. And at the tender age of which we are now speaking, when originality is impossible, memory is almost the only faculty which can be developed by the teacher. It will be worth while, by way of improving the child's pronunciation and distinctness of utterance, to make him rattle off a selection of names and lines of studied difficulty: they should be formed of a number of syllables which go ill together and should be harsh and rugged in sound: the Greeks call them "gags." This sounds a trifling matter, but its omission will result in numerous faults of pronunciation, which, unless removed in early years, will become a perverse and incurable habit and persist through life. . . .

II.

But the time has come for the boy to grow up little by little, to leave the nursery and tackle his studies in good earnest. This therefore is the place to discuss the question as to whether it is better to have him educated privately at home or hand him over to some large school and those whom I may call public instructors. The latter course has, I know, won the approval of most eminent authorities and of those who have formed the national character of the most famous states. It would, however, be folly to shut our eyes to the fact that there are some who disagree with this preference for public education owing to a certain prejudice in favour of private tuition. These persons seem to be guided in the main by two principles. In the interests of morality they would avoid the society of a number of human beings at an age that is specially liable to acquire serious faults: I only wish I could deny the truth of the view that such education has often been the cause of the most discreditable actions. Secondly they hold that whoever is to be the boy's teacher, he will devote his time more generously to one pupil than if he has to divide it among several. The first reason certainly deserves serious consideration. If it were proved that schools, while advantageous to study, are prejudicial to morality, I should give my vote for virtuous living in preference to even supreme excellence of speaking. But in my opinion the two are inseparable. I hold that no one can be a true orator unless he is also a good man and, even if he could be, I would not have it so. I will therefore deal with this point first.

It is held that schools corrupt the morals. It is true that this is sometimes the case. But morals may be corrupted at home as well. There are numerous instances of both, as there are also of the preservation of a good reputation under either circumstance. The nature of the individual boy and the care devoted to his education make all the difference. Given a natural bent toward evil or negligence in developing and watching over modest behaviour in early years, privacy will provide equal opportunity for sin. The teacher employed at home may be of bad character, and there is just as much danger in associating with bad slaves as there is with immodest companions of good birth. On the other hand if the natural bent be towards virtue, and parents are not afflicted with a blind and torpid indifference, it is possible to choose a teacher of the highest character (and those who are wise will make this their first object), to adopt a method of education of the strictest kind and at the same time to attach some respectable man or faithful freedman to their son as his friend and guardian, that his unfailing companionship may improve the character even of those who gave rise to apprehension.

Yet how easy were the remedy for such fears. Would that we did not too often ruin our children's character ourselves! We spoil them from the cradle. That soft upbringing, which we call kindness, saps all the sinews both of mind and body. If the child crawls on purple, what will he not desire when he comes to manhood? Before he can talk he can distinguish scarlet and cries for the very best brand of purple. We train their palates before we teach their lips to speak. They grow up in litters: if they set foot to earth, they are supported by the hands of attendants on either side. We rejoice if they say something over-free, and words which we should not tolerate from the lips even of an Alexandrian page are greeted with laughter and a kiss. We have no right to be surprised. It was we that taught them: they hear us use such words, they see our mistresses and minions; every dinner party is loud with foul songs, and things are presented to their eyes of which we should blush to speak. Hence springs habit, and habit in time becomes second nature. The poor children learn these things before they know them to be wrong. They become luxurious and effeminate, and far from acquiring such vices at schools, introduce them themselves.

I now turn to the objection that one master can give more attention to one pupil. In the first place there is nothing to prevent the principle of "one teacher, one boy" being combined with school education. And even if such a combination should prove impossible, I should still prefer the broad daylight of a respectable school to the solitude and obscurity of a private education. For all the best teachers pride themselves on having a large number of pupils and think themselves worthy of a bigger audience. On the other hand in the case of inferior teachers a consciousness of their own defects not seldom reconciles them to being attached to a single pupil and playing the part—for it amounts to little more—of a mere *paedagogus*.

But let us assume that influence, money or friendship succeed in securing a paragon of learning to teach the boy at home. Will he be able to devote the whole day to one pupil? Or can we demand such continuous attention on the part of the learner? The mind is as easily tired as the eye, if given no relaxation. Moreover by far the larger proportion of the learner's time ought to be devoted to private study. The teacher does not stand over him while he is writing or thinking or learning by heart. While he is so occupied the intervention of anyone, be he who he may, is a hindrance. Further, not all reading requires to be first read aloud or interpreted by a master. If it did, how would the boy ever become acquainted with all the authors required of him? A small time only is required to give purpose and direction to the day's work, and consequently individual instruction can be given to more than one pupil. There are moreover a large number of subjects in which it is desirable that instruction should be given to all the pupils simultaneously. I say nothing of the analyses and declamations of the professors of rhetoric: in such cases there is no limit to the number of the audience, as each individual pupil will in any case receive full value. The voice of a lecturer is not like a dinner which will only suffice for a limited number; it is like the sun which distributes the same quantity of light and heat to all of us. So too with the teacher of literature. Whether he speak of style or expound disputed passages, explain stories or paraphrase poems, everyone who hears him will profit by his teaching. But, it will be urged, a large class is unsuitable for the correction of faults or for explanation. It may be inconvenient: one cannot hope for absolute perfection; but I shall shortly contrast the inconvenience with the obvious advantages.

Still I do not wish a boy to be sent where he will be neglected. But a good teacher will not burden himself with a larger number of pupils than he can manage, and it is further of the very first importance that he should be on friendly and intimate terms with us and make his teaching not a duty but a labour of love. Then there will never be any question of being swamped by the number of our fellow-learners. Moreover any teacher who has the least tincture of literary culture will devote special attention to any boy who shows signs of industry and talent; for such a pupil will redound to his own credit. But even if large schools are to be avoided, a proposition from which I must dissent if the size be due to the excellence of the teacher, it does not follow that all schools are to be avoided. It is one thing to avoid them, another to select the best.

Having refuted these objections, let me now explain my own views. It is above all things necessary that our future orator, who will have to live in the utmost publicity and in the broad daylight of public life, should become accustomed from his childhood to move in society without fear and habituated to a life far removed from that of the pale student, the solitary and recluse. His mind requires constant stimulus and excitement, whereas retirement such as has just been mentioned induces languor and the mind becomes mildewed like things that are left in the dark, or else flies to the opposite extreme and becomes puffed up with empty conceit; for he who has no standard of comparison by which to judge his own powers will necessarily rate them too high. Again when the fruits of his study have to be displayed to the public gaze, our recluse is blinded by the sun's glare, and finds everything new and unfamiliar, for though he has learnt what is required to be done in public, his learning is but the theory of a hermit. I say nothing of friendships which endure unbroken to old age having acquired the binding force of a sacred duty: for initiation in the same studies has all the sanctity of initiation in the same mysteries of religion. And where shall he acquire that instinct which we call common feeling, if he secludes himself from that intercourse which is natural not merely to mankind but even to dumb animals? Further, at home he can only learn what is taught to himself, while at school he will learn what is taught others as well. He will hear many merits praised and many faults corrected every day: he will derive equal profit from hearing the indolence of a comrade rebuked or his industry commended. Such praise will incite him to emulation, he will think it a disgrace to be outdone by his contemporaries and a distinction to surpass his seniors. All such incentives provide a valuable stimulus, and though ambition may be a fault in itself, it is often the mother of virtues. I remember that my own masters had a practice which was not without advantages. Having distributed the boys in classes, they made the order in which they were to speak depend on their ability, so that the boy who had made most progress in his studies had the privilege of declaiming first. The performances on these occasions were criticised. To win commendation was a tremendous honour, but the prize most eagerly coveted was to be the leader of the class. Such a position was not permanent. Once a month the defeated competitors were given a fresh opportunity of competing for the prize. Consequently success did not lead the victor to relax his efforts, while the vexation caused by defeat served as an incentive to wipe out the disgrace. I will venture to assert that to the best of my memory this practice did more to kindle our oratorical ambitions than all the exhortations of our instructors, the watchfulness of our *paedagogi* and the prayers of our parents. Further while emulation promotes progress in the more advanced pupils, beginners who are still of tender years derive greater pleasure from imitating their comrades than their masters, just because it is easier. For children still in the elementary stages of education can scarce dare hope to reach that complete eloquence which they understand to be their goal: their ambition will not soar so high, but they will imitate the vine which has to grasp the lower branches of the tree on which it is trained before it can reach the topmost boughs. So true is this that it is the master's duty as well, if he is engaged on the task of training unformed minds and prefers practical utility to a more ambitious programme, not to burden his pupils at once with tasks to which their strength is unequal, but to curb his energies and refrain from talking over the heads of his audience. Vessels with narrow mouths will not receive liquids if too much be poured into them at a time, but are easily filled if the liquid is admitted in a gentle stream or, it may be, drop by drop; similarly you must consider how much a child's mind is capable of receiving: the things which are beyond their grasp will not enter their minds, which have not opened out sufficiently to take them in. It is a good thing therefore that a boy should have companions whom he will desire first to imitate and then to surpass: thus he will be led to aspire to higher achievement. I would add that the instructors themselves cannot develop the same intelligence and energy before a single listener as they can when inspired by the presence of a numerous audience.

For eloquence depends in the main on the state of the mind, which must be moved, conceive images and adapt itself to suit the nature of the subject which is the theme of speech. Further the loftier and the more elevated the mind, the more powerful will be the forces which move it: consequently praise gives it growth and effort increase, and the thought that it is doing something great fills it with joy. The duty of stooping to expend that power of speaking which has been acquired at the cost of such effort upon an audience of one gives rise to a silent feeling of disdain, and the teacher is ashamed to raise his voice above the ordinary conversational level. Imagine the air of a declaimer, or the voice of an orator, his gait, his delivery, the movements of his body, the emotions of his mind, and, to go no further, the fatigue of his exertions, all for the sake of one listener! Would he not seem little less than a lunatic? No, there would be no such thing as eloquence, if we spoke only with one person at a time. . . .

III.

The skilful teacher will make it his first care, as soon as a boy is entrusted to him, to ascertain his ability and character. The surest indication in a child is his power of memory. The characteristics of a good memory are twofold: it must be quick to take in and faithful to retain impressions of what it receives. The indication of next importance is the power of imitation: for this is a sign that the child is teachable: but he must imitate merely what he is taught, and must not, for example, mimic someone's gait or bearing or defects. For I have no hope that a child will turn out well who loves imitation merely for the purpose of raising a laugh. He who is really gifted will also above all else be good. For the rest, I regard slowness of intellect as preferable to actual badness. But a good boy will be quite unlike the dullard and the sloth. My ideal pupil will absorb instruction with ease and will even ask some questions; but he will follow rather than anticipate his teacher. Precocious intellects rarely produce sound fruit. By the precocious I mean those who perform small tasks with ease and, thus emboldened, proceed to display all their little accomplishments without being asked: but their accomplishments are only of the most obvious kind: they string words together and trot them out boldly and undeterred by the slightest sense of modesty. Their actual achievement is small, but what they can do they perform with ease. They have no real power and what they have is but of shallow growth: it is as when we cast seed on the surface of the soil: it springs up too rapidly, the blade apes the loaded ear, and yellows ere harvest time, but bears no grain. Such tricks please us when we contrast them with the performer's age, but progress soon stops and our admiration withers away.

Such indications once noted, the teacher must next consider what treatment is to be applied to the mind of his pupil. There are some boys who are slack, unless pressed on; others again are impatient of control: some are amenable to fear, while others are paralysed by it: in some cases the mind requires continued application to form it, in others this result is best obtained by rapid concentration. Give me the boy who is spurred on by praise, delighted by success and ready to weep over failure. Such an one must be encouraged by appeals to his ambition; rebuke will bite him to the quick; honour will be a spur, and there is no fear of his proving indolent.

Still, all our pupils will require some relaxation, not merely because there is nothing in this world that can stand continued strain and even unthinking and inanimate objects are unable to maintain their strength, unless given intervals of rest, but because study depends on the good will of the student, a quality that cannot be secured by compulsion. Consequently if restored and refreshed by a holiday they will bring greater energy to their learning and approach their work with greater spirit of a kind that will not submit to be driven. I approve of play in the young; it is a sign of a lively disposition; nor will you ever lead me to believe that a boy who is gloomy and in a continual state of depression is ever likely to show alertness of mind in his work, lacking as he does the impulse most natural to boys of his age. Such relaxation must not however be unlimited: otherwise the refusal to give a holiday will make boys hate their work, while excessive indulgence will accustom them to idleness. There are moreover certain games which have an educational value for boys, as for instance when they compete in posing each other with all kinds of questions which they ask turn and turn about. Games too reveal character in the most natural way, at least that is so if the teacher will bear in mind that there is no child so young as to be unable to learn to distinguish between right and wrong, and that the character is best moulded, when it is still guiltless of deceit and most susceptible to instruction: for once a bad habit has become engrained, it is easier to break than bend. There must be no delay, then, in warning a boy that his actions must be unselfish, honest, self-controlled, and we must never forget the words of Virgil,

So strong is custom formed in early years.

I disapprove of flogging, although it is the regular custom and meets with the acquiescence of Chrysippus, because in the first place it is a disgraceful form of punishment and fit only for slaves, and is in any case an insult, as you will realise if you imagine its infliction at a later age. Secondly if a boy is so insensible to instruction that reproof is useless, he will, like the worst type of slave, merely become hardened to blows. Finally there will be absolutely no need of such punishment if the master is a thorough disciplinarian. As it is, we try to make amends for the negligence of the boy's *paedagogus*, not by forcing him to do what is right, but by punishing him for not doing what is right. And though you may compel a child with blows, what are you to do with him when he is a young man no longer amenable to such threats and confronted with tasks of far greater difficulty? Moreover when children are beaten, pain or fear frequently have results of which it is not pleasant to speak and which are likely subsequently to be a source of shame, a shame which unnerves and depresses the mind and leads the child to shun and loathe the light. Further if inadequate care is taken in the choices of respectable governors and instructors, I blush to mention the shameful abuse which scoundrels sometimes make of their right to administer corporal punishment or the opportunity not infrequently offered to others by the fear thus caused in the victims. I will not linger on this subject; it is more than enough if I have made my meaning clear. I will content myself with saying that children are helpless and easily victimised, and that therefore no one should be given unlimited power over them. . . .

IV.

. . . We need have no fear at any rate that boys will find their work too exhausting: there is no age more capable of enduring fatigue. The fact may be surprising, but it can be proved by experiment. For the mind is all the easier to teach before it is set. This may be clearly proved by the fact that within two years after a child has begun to form words correctly, he can speak practically all without any pressure from outside. On the other hand how many years it takes for our newly-imported slaves to become familiar with the Latin language. Try to teach an adult to read and you will soon appreciate the force of the saying applied to those who do everything connected with their art with the utmost skill "he started young!" Moreover boys stand the strain of work better than young men. Just as small children suffer less damage from their frequent falls, from their crawling on hands and knees and, a little later, from their incessant play and their running about from morn till eve, because they are so light in weight and have so little to carry, even so their minds are less susceptible of fatigue, because their activity calls for less effort and application to study demands no exertion of their own, since they are merely so much plastic material to be moulded by the teacher. And farther owing to the general pliability of childhood, they follow their instructors with greater simplicity and without attempting to measure their own progress: for as yet they do not even appreciate the nature of their work. Finally, as I have often noticed, the senses are less affected by mere hard work than they are by hard thinking.

Moreover there will never be more time for such studies, since at this age all progress is made through listening to the teacher. Later when the boy has to write by himself, or to produce and compose something out of his own head, he will neither have the time nor the inclination for the exercises which we have been discussing. Since, then, the teacher of literature neither can nor ought to occupy the whole day, for fear of giving his pupil a distaste for work, what are the studies to which the spare time should preferably be devoted? For I do not wish the student to wear himself out in such pursuits: I would not have him sing or learn to read music or dive deep into the minuter details of geometry, nor need he be a finished actor in his delivery or a dancer in his gesture: if I did demand all these accomplishments, there would yet be time for them; the period allotted to education is long, and I am not speaking of duller wits. Why did Plato bear away the palm in all these branches of knowledge which in my opinion the future orator should learn? I answer, because he was not merely content with the teaching which Athens was able to provide or even with that of the Pythagoreans whom he visited in Italy, but even approached the priests of Egypt and made himself thoroughly acquainted with all their secret lore.

The plea of the difficulty of the subject is put forward merely to cloak our indolence, because we do not love the work that lies before us nor seek to win eloquence for our own because it is a noble art and the fairest thing in all the world, but gird up our loins for mercenary ends and for the winning of filthy lucre. Without such accomplishments many may speak in the courts and make an income; but it is my prayer that every dealer in the vilest merchandise may be richer than they and that the public crier may find his voice a more lucrative possession. And I trust that there is not one even among my readers who would think of calculating the monetary value of such studies. But he that has enough of the divine spark to conceive the ideal eloquence, he who, as the great tragic poet says, regards "oratory" as "the queen of all the world" and seeks not the transitory gains of advocacy, but those stable and lasting rewards which his own soul and knowledge and contemplation can give, *he* will easily persuade himself to spend his time not, like so many, in the theatre or in the Campus Martius, in dicing or in idle talk, to say naught of the hours that are wasted in sleep or long drawn banqueting, but in listening rather to the geometrician and the teacher of music. For by this he will win a richer harvest of delight than can ever be gathered from the pleasures of the ignorant, since among the many gifts of providence to man not the least is this that the highest pleasure is the child of virtue. But the attractions of my theme have led me to say overmuch. Enough of those studies in which a boy must be instructed, while he is yet too young to proceed to greater things! My next book will start afresh and will pass to the consideration of the duties of the teacher of rhetoric.

Book II

II.

As soon therefore as a boy has made sufficient progress in his studies to be able to follow what I have styled the first stage of instruction in rhetoric, he should be placed under a rhetorician. Our first task must be to enquire whether the teacher is of good character. The reason which leads me to deal with this subject in this portion of my work is not that I regard character as a matter of indifference where other teachers are concerned, (I have already shown how important I think it in the preceding book), but that the age to which the pupil has now attained makes the mention of this point especially necessary. For as a rule boys are on the verge of manhood when transferred to the teacher of rhetoric and continue with him even when they are young men: consequently we must spare no effort to secure that the purity of the teacher's character should preserve those of tenderer years from corruption, while its authority should keep the bolder spirits from breaking out into licence. Nor is it sufficient that he should merely set an example of the highest personal self-control; he must also be able to govern the behaviour of his pupils by the strictness of his discipline.

Let him therefore adopt a parental attitude to his pupils, and regard himself as the representative of those who have committed their children to his charge. Let him be free from vice himself and refuse to tolerate it in others. Let him be strict but not austere, genial but not too familiar: for austerity will make him unpopular, while familiarity breeds contempt. Let his discourse continually turn on what is good and honourable; the more he admonishes, the less he will have to punish. He must control his temper without however shutting his eyes to faults requiring correction: his instruction must be free from affectation, his industry great, his demands on his class continuous, but not extravagant. He must be ready to answer questions and to put them unasked to those who sit silent. In praising the recitations of his pupils he must be neither grudging nor over-generous: the former quality will give them a distaste for work, while the latter will produce a complacent self-satisfaction. In correcting faults he must avoid sarcasm and above all abuse: for teachers whose rebukes seem to imply positive dislike discourage industry. He should declaim daily himself and, what is more, without stint, that his class may take his utterances home with them. For however many models for imitation he may give them from the authors they are reading, it will still be found that fuller nourishment is provided by the living voice, as we call it, more especially when it proceeds from the teacher himself, who, if his pupils are rightly instructed, should be the object of their affection and respect. And it is scarcely possible to say how much more readily we imitate those whom we like. . . .

IX.

Though I have spoken in some detail of the duties of the teacher, I shall for the moment confine my advice to the learners to one solitary admonition, that they should love their masters not less than their studies, and should regard them as the parents not indeed of their bodies but of their minds. Such attachments are of invaluable assistance to study. For under their influence they find it a pleasure to listen to their teachers, believe what they say and long to be like them, come cheerfully and gladly to school, are not angry when corrected, rejoice when praised, and seek to win their master's affection by the devotion with which they pursue their studies. For as it is the duty of the master to teach, so it is the duty of the pupil to show himself teachable. The two obligations are mutually indispensable. And just as it takes two parents to produce a human being, and as the seed is scattered in vain, if the ground is hard and there is no furrow to receive it and bring it to growth, even so eloquence can never come to maturity, unless teacher and taught are in perfect sympathy. . . .

Book XII

I.

The orator then, whom I am concerned to form, shall be the orator as defined by Marcus Cato, "a good man, skilled in speaking." But above all he must possess the quality which Cato places first and which is in the very nature of things the greatest and most important, that is, he must be a good man. This is essential not merely on account of the fact that, if the powers of eloquence serve only to lend arms to crime, there can be nothing more pernicious than eloquence to public and private welfare alike, while I myself, who have laboured to the best of my ability to contribute something of value to oratory, shall have rendered the worst of services to mankind, if I forge these weapons not for a soldier, but for a robber. But why speak of myself? Nature herself will have proved not a mother, but a stepmother with regard to what we deem her greatest gift to man, the gift that distinguishes us from other living things, if she devised the power of speech to be the accomplice of crime, the foe to innocency and the enemy of truth. For it had been better for men to be born dumb and devoid of reason than to turn the gifts of providence to their mutual destruction. But this conviction of mine goes further. For I do not merely assert that the ideal orator should be a good man, but I affirm that no man can be an orator unless he is a good man. For it is impossible to regard those men as gifted with intelligence who on being offered the choice between the two paths of virtue and of vice choose the latter, nor can we allow them prudence, when by the unforeseen issue of their own actions they render themselves liable not merely to the heaviest penalties of the laws, but to the inevitable torment of an evil conscience. But if the view that a bad man is necessarily a fool is not merely held by philosophers, but is the universal belief of ordinary men, the fool will most assuredly never become an orator. To this must be added the fact that the mind will not find leisure even for the study of the noblest of tasks, unless it first be free from vice. The reasons for this are, first, that vileness and virtue cannot jointly inhabit in the selfsame heart and that it is as impossible for one and the same mind to harbour good and evil thoughts as it is for one man to be at once both good and evil: and secondly, that if the intelligence is to be concentrated on such a vast subject as eloquence it must be free from all other distractions, among which must be included even those preoccupations which are free from blame. For it is only when it is free and self-possessed, with nothing to divert it or lure it elsewhere, that it will fix its attention solely on that goal, the attainment of which is the object of its preparations. If on the other hand inordinate care for the development of our estates, excess of anxiety over household affairs, passionate devotion to hunting or the sacrifice of whole days to the shows of the theatre, rob our studies of much of the time that is their due (for every moment that is given to other things involves a loss of time for study), what, think you, will be the results of desire, avarice, and envy, which waken such violent thoughts within our souls that they disturb our very slumbers and our dreams? There is nothing so preoccupied, so distracted, so rent and torn by so many and such varied passions as an evil mind. For when it cherishes some dark design, it is tormented with hope, care and anguish of spirit, and even when it has accomplished its criminal purpose, it is racked by anxiety, remorse and the fear of all manner of punishments. Amid such passions as these what room is there for literature or any virtuous pursuit? You might as well look for fruit in land that is choked with thorns and brambles. Well then, I ask you, is not simplicity of life essential if we are to be able to endure the toil entailed by study? What can we hope to get from lust or luxury? Is not the desire win praise one of the strongest stimulants to a passion for literature? But does that mean that we are to suppose that praise is an object of concern to bad men? Surely every one of my readers must by now have realised that oratory is in the main concerned with the treatment of what is just and honourable? Can a bad and unjust man speak on such themes as the dignity of the subject demands? Nay, even if we exclude the most important aspects of the question now before us, and make the impossible concession that the best and worst of men may have the same talent, industry and learning, we are still confronted by the question as to which of the two is entitled to be called the better orator. The answer is surely clear enough: it will be he who is the better man. Consequently, the bad man and the perfect orator can never be identical. For nothing is perfect, if there exists something else that is better. However, as I do not wish to appear to adopt the practice dear to the Socratics of framing answers to my own questions, let me assume the existence of a man so obstinately blind to the truth as to venture to maintain that a bad man equipped with the same talents, industry and learning will be not a whit inferior to the good man as an orator; and let me show that he too is mad. There is one point at any rate which no one will question, namely, that the aim of every speech is to convince the judge that the case which it puts forward is true and honourable. Well then, which will do this best, the good man or the bad? The good man will without doubt more often say what is true and honourable. But even supposing that his duty should, as I shall show may sometimes happen, lead him to make statements which are false, his words are still certain to carry greater weight with his audience. On the other hand bad men, in their contempt for public opinion and their ignorance of what is right, sometimes drop their mask unawares, and are impudent in the statement of their case and shameless in their assertions. Further, in their attempt to achieve the impossible they display an unseemly persistency and unavailing energy. For in lawsuits no less than in the ordinary paths of life, they cherish depraved expectations. But it often happens that even when they tell the truth they fail to win belief, and the mere fact that such a man is its advocate is regarded as an indication of the badness of the case. . . .

II.

Since then the orator is a good man, and such goodness cannot be conceived as existing apart from virtue, virtue, despite the fact that it is in part derived from certain natural impulses, will require to be perfected by instruction. The orator must above all things devote his attention to the formation of moral character and must acquire a complete knowledge of all that is just and honourable. For without this knowledge no one can be either a good man or skilled in speaking, unless indeed we agree with those who regard morality as intuitive and as owing nothing to instruction: indeed they go so far as to acknowledge that handicrafts, not excluding even those which are most despised among them, can only be acquired by the result of teaching, whereas virtue, which of all gifts to man is that which makes him most near akin to the immortal gods, comes to him without search or effort, as a natural concomitant of birth. But can the man who does not know what abstinence is, claim to be truly abstinent? or brave, if he has never purged his soul of the fears of pain, death and superstition? or just, if he has never, in language approaching that of philosophy, discussed the nature of virtue and justice, or of the laws that have been given to mankind by nature or established among individual peoples and nations? What a contempt it argues for such themes to regard them as being so easy of comprehension! However, I pass this by; for I am sure that no one with the least smattering of literary culture will have the slightest hesitation in agreeing with me. I will proceed to my next point, that no one will achieve sufficient skill even in speaking, unless he makes a thorough study of all the workings of nature and forms his character on the precepts of philosophy and the dictates of reason. For it is with good cause that Lucius Crassus, in the third book of the *de Oratore*, affirms that all that is said concerning equity, justice, truth and the good, and their opposites, forms part of the studies of an orator, and that the philosophers, when they exert their powers of speaking to defend these virtues, are using the weapons of rhetoric, not their own. But he also confesses that the knowledge of these subjects must be sought from the philosophers for the reason that, in his opinion, philosophy has more effective possession of them. And it is for the same reason that Cicero in several of his books and letters proclaims that eloquence has its fountain-head in the most secret springs of wisdom, and that consequently for a considerable time the instructors of morals and of eloquence were identical. Accordingly this exhortation of mine must not be taken to mean that I wish the orator to be a philosopher, since there is no other way of life that is further removed from the duties of a statesman and the tasks of an orator. For what philosopher has ever been a frequent speaker in the courts or won renown in public assemblies? Nay, what philosopher has ever taken a prominent part in the government of the state, which forms the most frequent theme of their instructions? None the less I desire that he, whose character I am seeking to mould, should be a "wise man" in the Roman sense, that is, one who reveals himself as a true statesman, not in the discussions of the study, but in the actual practice and experience of life. But inasmuch as the study of philosophy has been deserted by those who have turned to the pursuit of eloquence, and since philosophy no longer moves in true sphere of action and in the broad daylight of the forum, but has retired first to porches and gymnasia and finally to the gatherings of the schools, all that is essential for an orator, and yet is not taught by the professors of eloquence, must undoubtedly be sought from those persons in whose possession it has remained. The authors who have discoursed on the nature of virtue must be read through and through, that the life of the orator may be wedded to the knowledge of things human and divine. But how much greater and fairer would such subjects appear if those who taught them were also those who could give them most eloquent expression! O that the day may dawn when the perfect orator of our heart's desire shall claim for his own possession that science that has lost the affection of mankind through the arrogance of its claims and the vices of some that have brought disgrace upon its virtues, and shall restore it to its place in the domain of eloquence, as though he had been victorious in a trial for the restoration of stolen goods! And since philosophy falls into three divisions, physics, ethics and dialectic, which, I ask you, of these departments is not closely connected with the task of the orator? . . .

On the other hand, there is no need for an orator to swear allegiance to any one philosophic code. For he has a greater and nobler aim, to which he directs all his efforts with as much zeal as if he were a candidate for office, since he is to be made perfect not only in the glory of a virtuous life, but in that of eloquence as well. He will consequently select as his models of eloquence all the greatest masters of oratory, and will choose the noblest precepts and the most direct road to virtue as the means for the formation of an upright character. He will neglect no form of exercise, but will devote special attention to those which are of the highest and fairest nature. For what subject can be found more fully adapted to a rich and weighty eloquence than the topics of virtue, politics, providence, the origin of the soul and friendship? The themes which tend to elevate mind and language alike are questions such as what things are truly good, what means there are of assuaging fear, restraining the passions and lifting us and the soul that came from heaven clear of the delusions of the common herd.

But it is desirable that we should not restrict our study to the precepts of philosophy alone. It is still more important that we should know and ponder continually all the noblest sayings and deeds that have been handed down to us from ancient times. And assuredly we shall nowhere find a larger or more remarkable store of these than in the records of our own country. Who will teach courage, justice, loyalty, self-control, simplicity, and contempt of grief and pain better than men like Fabricius, Curius, Regulus, Decius, Mucius and countless others? For if the Greeks bear away the palm for moral precepts, Rome can produce more striking examples of moral performance, which is a far greater thing. But the man who does not believe that it is enough to fix his eyes merely on his own age and his own transitory life, but regards the space allotted for an honourable life and the course in which glory's race is run as conditioned solely by the memory of posterity, will not rest content with a mere knowledge of the events of history. No, it is from the thought of posterity that he must inspire his soul with justice and derive that freedom of spirit which it is his duty to display when he pleads in the courts or gives counsel in the senate. No man will ever be the consummate orator of whom we are in quest unless he has both the knowledge and the courage to speak in accordance with the promptings of honour. . . .

I fear, however, that I may be regarded as setting too lofty an ideal for the orator by insisting that he should be a good man skilled in speaking, or as imposing too many subjects of study on the learner. For in addition to the many branches of knowledge which have to be studied in boyhood and the traditional rules of eloquence, I have enjoined the study of morals and of civil law, so that I am afraid that even those who have regarded these things as essential to my theme, may be appalled at the delay which they impose and abandon all hope of achievement before they have put my precepts to the test. I would ask them to consider how great are the powers of the mind of man and how astonishing its capacity for carrying its desires into execution: for has not man succeeded in crossing the high seas, in learning the number and the courses of the stars, and almost measuring the universe itself, all of them accomplishments of less importance than oratory, but of far greater difficulty? And then let them reflect on the greatness of their aims and on the fact that no labour should be too huge for those that are beckoned by the hope of such reward. If they can only rise to the height of this conception, they will find it easier to enter on this portion of their task, and will cease to regard the road as impassable or even hard. For the first and greatest of the aims we set before us, namely that we shall be good men, depends for its achievement mainly on the will to succeed: and he that truly and sincerely forms such resolve, will easily acquire those forms of knowledge that teach the way to virtue. For the precepts that are enjoined upon us are not so complex or so numerous that they may be acquired by little more than a few years' study. It is repugnance to learn that makes such labour long. For if you will only believe it, you will quickly learn the principles that shall lead you to a life of virtue and happiness. For nature brought us into the world that we might attain to all excellence of mind, and so easy is it for those to learn who seek for better things, that he who directs his gaze aright will rather marvel that the bad should be so many. For as water is the natural element of fish, dry land for creatures of the earth and the circumambient atmosphere for winged things, even so it should be easier to live according to nature than counter to her will. As regards other accomplishments, there are plenty of years available for their acquisition, even though we measure the life of man not by the span of age, but by the period of youth. For in every case order and method and a sense of proportion will shorten our labour. But the chief fault lies with our teachers, in that they love to keep back the pupils they have managed to lay their hands on, partly from the desire to draw their miserable fees for as long as possible, partly out of ostentation, to enhance the difficulty of acquiring the knowledge which they promise to impart, and to some extent owing to their ignorance or carelessness in teaching. The next most serious fault lies in ourselves, who think it better to linger over what we have learned than to learn what we do not yet know. For example, to restrict my remarks mainly to the study of rhetoric, what is the use of spending so many years, after the fashion now so prevalent (for I say nothing of those who spend almost their whole lives), in declaiming in the schools and devoting so much labour to the treatment of fictitious themes, when it would be possible with but slight expenditure of time to form some idea of what the true conflicts are in which the orator must engage, and of the laws of speaking which he ought to follow? In saying this, I do not for a moment mean to suggest that we should ever omit to exercise ourselves in speaking. I merely urge that we should not grow old over one special form of exercise. We have been in a position to acquire varied knowledge, to familiarise ourselves with the principles that should guide our life, and to try our strength in the courts, while we were still attending the schools. The theory of speaking is of such a nature that it does not demand many years for its acquisition. For any one of the various branches of knowledge which I have mentioned will, as a rule, be found to be comprised in a few volumes, a fact which shows that instruction does not require an indefinite amount of time to be devoted to it. The rest depends entirely on practice, which at once develops our powers and maintains them, once developed. Knowledge increases day by day, and yet how many books is it absolutely necessary to read in our search for its attainment, for examples of facts from the historians or of eloquence from the orators, or, again, for the opinions of the philosophers and the lawyers, that is to say, if we are content to read merely what is useful without attempting the impossible task of reading everything? But it is ourselves that make the time for study short: for how little time we allot to it! Some hours are passed in the futile labour of ceremonial calls, others in idle chatter, others in staring at the shows of the theatre, and others again in feasting. To this add all the various forms of amusement, the insane attention devoted to the cultivation of the body, journeys abroad, visits to the country, anxious calculation of loss and gain, the allurements of lust, wine-bibbing and those remaining hours which are all too few to gratify our souls on fire with passion for every kind of pleasure. If all this time were spent on study, life would seem long enough and there would be plenty of time for learning, even though we should take the hours of daylight only into our account, without asking any assistance from the night, of which no little space is superfluous even for the heaviest sleeper. As it is, we count not the years which we have given to study, but the years we have lived. And indeed even although geometricians, musicians and grammarians, together with the professors of every other branch of knowledge, spend all their lives, however long, in the study of one single science, it does not therefore follow that we require several lives more if we are to learn more. For they do not spend all their days even to old age in learning these things, but being content to have learned these things and nothing more, exhaust their length of years not in acquiring, but in imparting knowledge.

However, to say nothing of Homer, in whom we may find either the perfect achievements, or at any rate clear signs of the knowledge of every art, and to pass by Hippias of Elis, who not merely boasted his knowledge of the liberal arts, but wore a robe, a ring and shoes, all of which he had made with his own hands, and had trained himself to be independent of external assistance, we accept the universal tradition of Greece to the effect that Gorgias, triumphant over all the countless ills incident to extreme old age, would bid his hearers propound any questions they pleased for him to answer. Again in what branch of knowledge worthy of literary expression was Plato deficient? How many generations' study did Aristotle require to embrace not merely the whole range of philosophical and rhetorical knowledge, but to investigate the nature of every beast and plant. And yet they had to discover all these things which we only have to learn. Antiquity has given us all these teachers and all these patterns for our imitation, that there might be no greater happiness conceivable than to be born in this age above all others, since all previous ages have toiled that we might reap the fruit of their wisdom. Marcus Cato was at once a great general, a philosopher, orator, historian, and an expert both in law and agriculture, and despite his military labours abroad and the distractions of political struggles at home, and despite the rudeness of the age in which he lived, he none the less learned Greek, when far advanced in years, that he might prove to mankind that even old men are capable of learning that on which they have set their hearts. How wide, almost universal, was the knowledge that Varro communicated to the world! What of all that goes to make up the equipment of an orator was lacking to Cicero? Why should I say more, since even Cornelius Celsus, a man of very ordinary ability, not merely wrote about rhetoric in all its departments, but left treatises on the art of war, agriculture and medicine as well. Indeed the high ambition revealed by his design gives him the right to ask us to believe that he was acquainted with all these subjects.

But, it will be urged, to carry out such a task is difficult and has never been accomplished. To which I reply that sufficient encouragement for study may be found in the fact, firstly, that nature does not forbid such achievement and it does not follow that, because a thing never has been done, it therefore never can be done, and secondly, that all great achievements have required time for their first accomplishment. Poetry has risen to the heights of glory, thanks to the efforts of poets so far apart as Homer and Virgil, and oratory owes its position to the genius of Demosthenes and Cicero. Finally, whatever is best in its own sphere must at some previous time have been non-existent. But even if a man despair of reaching supreme excellence (and why should he despair, if he have talents, health, capacity and teachers to aid him?), it is none the less a fine achievement, as Cicero says, to win the rank of second or even third. For even if a soldier cannot achieve the glory of Achilles in war, he will not despise fame such as fell to the lot of Ajax and Diomede, while those who cannot be Homers may be content to reach the level of Tyrtaeus. Nay, if men had been obsessed by the conviction that it was impossible to surpass the man who had so far shown himself best, those whom we now regard as best would never have reached such distinction, Lucretius and Macer would never have been succeeded by Virgil, nor Crassus and Hortensius by Cicero, nor they in their turn by those who flourished after them. But even though we cannot hope to surpass the great, it is still a high honour to follow in their footsteps. Did Pollio and Messala, who began to plead when Cicero held the citadel of eloquence, fail to obtain sufficient honour in their lifetime or to hand down a fair name to posterity? The arts which have been developed to the highest pitch of excellence would deserve but ill of mankind if that which was best had also been the last of its line. Add to this the further consideration that even moderate eloquence is often productive of great results and, if such studies are to be measured solely by their utility, is almost equal to the perfect eloquence for which we seek. Nor would it be difficult to produce either ancient or recent examples to show that there is no other source from which men have reaped such a harvest of wealth, honour, friendship and glory, both present and to come. But it would be a disgrace to learning to follow the fashion of those who say that they pursue not virtue, but only the pleasure derived from virtue, and to demand this meaner recompense from the noblest of all arts, whose practice and even whose possession is ample reward for all our labours. Wherefore let us seek with all our hearts that true majesty of oratory, the fairest gift of god to man, without which all things are stricken dumb and robbed alike of present glory and the immortal record of posterity; and let us press forward to whatsoever is best, since, if we do this, we shall either reach the summit or at least see many others far beneath us.

Such, Marcellus Victorius, were the views by the expression of which it seemed to me that I might, as far as in me lay, help to advance the teaching of oratory. If the knowledge of these principles proves to be of small practical utility to the young student, it should at least produce what I value more,—the will to do well.

Tacitus

c. 55–c.117

Breadth of culture is an ornament that tells of itself even when one is not making a point of it: it comes prominently into view where you would least expect it.

A DIALOGUE ON ORATORY

Publius Cornelius Tacitus, Roman historian and orator, may have been born in southern Gaul. Little is known about his family or early life. He moved to Rome as a young man and may have studied with Quintilian. He became a lawyer and a senator, and late in life served for a time as proconsul of the province of Asia. He was a critic of imperial decadence who longed for the old virtues of the Republic. His most lasting achievements came not through politics but through scholarship. He wrote a biography of his father-in-law Agricola, governor of Britain, and *Germania,* a history of the German tribes on the frontier. Other important works include two histories of Imperial Rome: the *Histories* and the *Annals,* the latter of which includes the famous account of Nero's treacherous persecution of the Christians for his own amusement.

THE SELECTION

Written sometime after A.D. 101, *A Dialogue on Oratory* shows Tacitus's obvious debt to Cicero. The speaker in this short selection is Messalla, who laments the decline of education in modern Rome and upholds the ideal of "liberal culture" belonging to the broadly educated statesman.

from A Dialogue on Oratory

. . . Everybody is aware that it is not for lack of votaries that eloquence and the other arts as well have fallen from their former high estate, but because of the laziness of our young men, the carelessness of parents, the ignorance of teachers, and the decay of the old-fashioned virtue. It was at Rome that this backsliding first began, but afterwards it permeated Italy and now it is making its way abroad. You know provincial conditions, however, better than I do; I am going to speak of the capital and of our home-grown Roman vices, which catch on to us as soon as we are born, and increase with each successive stage of our development. But first I must say a word or two about the rigorous system which our forefathers followed in the matter of the upbringing and training of their children.

In the good old days, every man's son, born in wedlock, was brought up not in the chamber of some hireling nurse, but in his mother's lap, and at her knee. And that mother could have no higher praise than that she managed the house and gave herself to her children. Again, some elderly relative would be selected in order that to her, as a person who had been tried and never found wanting, might be entrusted the care of all the youthful scions of the same house; in the presence of such an one no base word could be uttered without grave offence, and no wrong deed done. Religiously and with the utmost delicacy she regulated not only the serious tasks of her youthful charges, but their recreations also and their games. It was in this spirit, we are told, that Cornelia, the mother of the Gracchi, directed their upbringing, Aurelia that of Caesar, Atia of Augustus : thus it was that these mothers trained their princely children. The object of this rigorous system was that the natural disposition of every child, while still sound at the core and untainted, not warped as yet by any vicious tendencies, might at once lay hold with heart and soul on virtuous accomplishments, and whether its bent was towards the army, or the law, or the pursuit of eloquence, might make that its sole aim and its all-absorbing interest.

Nowadays, on the other hand, our children are handed over at their birth to some silly little Greek serving-maid, with a male slave, who may be anyone, to help her—quite frequently the most worthless member of the whole establishment, incompetent for any serious service. It is from the foolish tittle-tattle of such persons that the children receive their earliest impressions, while their minds are still green and unformed; and there is not a soul in the whole house who cares a jot what he says or does in the presence of his baby master. Yes, and the parents themselves make no effort to train their little ones in goodness and self-control; they grow up in an atmosphere of laxity and pertness, in which they come gradually to lose all sense of shame, and all respect both for themselves and for other people. Again, there are the peculiar and characteristic vices of this metropolis of ours, taken on, as it seems to me, almost in the mother's womb—the passion for play actors, and the mania for gladiatorial shows and horse-racing; and when the mind is engrossed in such occupations, what room is left over for higher pursuits? How few are to be found whose home-talk runs to any other subjects than these? What else do we overhear our younger men talking about whenever we enter their lecture-halls? And the teachers are just as bad. With them, too, such topics supply material for gossip with their classes more frequently than any others; for it is not by the strict administration of discipline, or by giving proof of their ability to teach that they get pupils together, but by pushing themselves into notice at morning calls and by the tricks of toadyism.

I pass by the first rudiments of education, though even these are taken too lightly: it is in the reading of authors, and in gaining a knowledge of the past, and in making acquaintance with things and persons and occasions that too little solid work is done. Recourse is had instead to the so-called rhetoricians. As I mean to speak in the immediate sequel of the period at which this vocation first made its way to Rome, and of the small esteem in which it was held by our ancestors, I must advert to the system which we are told was followed by those orators whose unremitting industry and daily preparation and continuous practice in every department of study, are referred to in their own published works. You are of course familiar with Cicero's "Brutus," in the concluding portion of which treatise—the first part contains a review of the speakers of former days—he gives an account of his own first beginnings, his gradual progress, and what I may call his evolution as an orator. He tells us how he studied civil law with Q. Mucius, and thoroughly absorbed philosophy in all its departments as a pupil of Philo the Academic and Diodotus the Stoic; and not being satisfied with the teachers who had been accessible to him at Rome, he went to Greece, and travelled also through Asia Minor, in order to acquire a comprehensive training in every variety of knowledge. Hence it comes that in Cicero's works one may detect the fact that he was not lacking in a knowledge of mathematics, of music, of linguistics—in short, of any department of the higher learning. Yes, Cicero was quite at home in the subtleties of dialectic, in the practical lessons of ethical philosophy, in the changes and origins of natural phenomena. Yes, my good friends, that is the fact: it is only from a wealth of learning, and a multitude of accomplishments, and a knowledge that is universal that his marvellous eloquence wells forth like a mighty stream. The orator's function and activity is not, as is the case with other pursuits, hemmed in all round within narrow boundaries. He only deserves the name who has the ability to speak on any and every topic with grace and distinction of style, in a manner fitted to win conviction, appropriately to the dignity of his subject-matter, suitably to the case in hand, and with resulting gratification to his audience.

This was fully understood by the men of former days. They were well aware that, in order to attain the end in view, the practice of declamation in the schools of rhetoric was not the essential matter—the training merely of tongue and voice in imaginary debates which had no point of contact with real life. No, for them the one thing needful was to stock the mind with those accomplishments which deal with good and evil, virtue and vice, justice and injustice. It is this that forms the subject-matter of oratory. Speaking broadly, in judicial oratory our argument turns upon fair dealing, in the oratory of debate upon advantage, in eulogies upon moral character, though these topics quite frequently overlap. Now it is impossible for any speaker to treat them with fullness, and variety, and elegance, unless he has made a study of human nature, of the meaning of goodness and the wickedness of vice, and unless he has learnt to appreciate the significance of what ranks neither on the side of virtue nor on that of vice. This is the source from which other qualifications also are derived. The man who knows what anger is will be better able either to work on or to mollify the resentment of a judge, just as he who understands compassion, and the emotions by which it is aroused, will find it easier to move him to pity. If your orator has made himself familiar with these branches by study and practice, whether he has to address himself to a hostile or a prejudiced or a grudging audience, whether his hearers are ill-humoured or apprehensive, he will feel their pulse, and will handle them in every case as their character requires, and will give the right tone to what he has to say, keeping the various implements of his craft lying ready to hand for any and every purpose. There are some with whom a concise, succinct style carries most conviction, one that makes the several lines of proof yield a rapid conclusion: with such it will be an advantage to have paid attention to dialectic. Others are more taken with a smooth and steady flow of speech, drawn from the fountain-head of universal experience: in order to make an impression upon these we shall borrow from the Peripatetics their stock arguments, suited and ready in advance for either side of any discussion. Combativeness will be the contribution of the Academics, sublimity that of Plato, and charm that of Xenophon; nay, there will be nothing amiss in a speaker taking over even some of the excellent aphorisms of Epicurus and Metrodorus, and applying them as the case may demand. It is not a professional philosopher that we are delineating, nor a hanger-on of the Stoics, but the man who, while he ought to drink deeply at certain springs of knowledge, should also wet his lips at them all. That is the reason why the orators, of former days made a point of acquiring a knowledge of civil law, while they received a tincture also of literature, music, and mathematics. In the cases that come one's way, what is essential in most instances, indeed almost invariably, is legal knowledge, but there are often others in which you are expected to be well versed also in the subjects just mentioned.

Do not let anyone argue in reply that it is enough for us to be coached in some straightforward and clearly defined issue in order to meet the case immediately before us. To begin with, the use we make of what belongs to ourselves is quite different from our use of what we take on loan: there is obviously a wide gulf between owning what we give out and borrowing it from others. In the next place, breadth of culture is an ornament that tells of itself even when one is not making a point of it: it comes prominently into view where you would least expect it. This fact is fully appreciated not only by the learned and scholarly portion of the audience, but also by the rank and file. They cheer the speaker from the start, protesting that he has been properly trained, that he has gone through all the points of good oratory, and that he is, in short, an orator in the true sense of the word: and such an one cannot be, as I maintain, and never was any other than he who enters the lists of debate with all the equipment of a man of learning, like a warrior taking the field in full armour. Our clever speakers of today, however, lose sight of this ideal to such an extent that one can detect in their pleadings the shameful and discreditable blemishes even of our everyday speech. They know nothing of statute-law, they have no hold of the decrees of the senate, they go out of their way to show contempt for the law of the constitution, and as for the pursuit of philosophy and the sages' saws they regard them with downright dismay. Eloquence is by them degraded, like a discrowned queen, to a few commonplaces and cramped conceits. She who in days of yore reigned in the hearts of men as the mistress of all the arts, encircled by a brilliant retinue, is now curtailed and mutilated, shorn of all her state, all her distinction, I had almost said all her freedom, and is learnt like any vulgar handicraft.

This then I take to be the first and foremost reason why we have degenerated to such an extent from the eloquence of the orators of old. If you want witnesses, what weightier evidence can I produce than Demosthenes among the Greeks, who is said to have been one of Plato's most enthusiastic students? Our own Cicero tells us too—I think in so many words—that anything he accomplished as an orator he owed not to the workshops of the rhetoricians, but to the spacious precincts of the Academy. There are other reasons, important and weighty, which ought in all fairness to be unfolded by you, since I have now done my part and have as usual run up against quite a number of people who will be sure to say, if my words chance to reach their ears, that it is only in order to cry up my own pet vanities that I have been extolling a knowledge of law and philosophy as indispensable to the orator. . . .

Plutarch

c. 46–c. 120

The one and essential thing, the first, middle, and last, is a sound upbringing and right education.

"On Bringing up a Boy"

❧

The Greek biographer and essayist Mestrius Plutarchus was born in Chaeronea, Boeotia, studied in Athens, visited and lectured in Rome, and served as a priest at Delphi. He is probably best remembered for his celebrated *Parallel Lives,* paired biographies of eminent Greeks and Romans. His *Moralia* (or "Ethical Essays"), however, provide dozens of reflections on life, including education. His works were rendered into Latin and most European languages in the Renaissance by such eminent scholars as Leonardo Bruni, Erasmus, and Thomas Elyot. Plutarch's *Lives* influenced Montaigne, and Shakespeare adapted them for several of his plays, including *Julius Caesar* and *Antony and Cleopatra.*

THE SELECTIONS

Many recent scholars have come to doubt that Plutarch wrote the essay "On Bringing up a Boy," but it was popularly attributed to him for centuries and inspired imitations by early Christian authors and directly influenced later Renaissance treatises. Plutarch (or Pseudo-Plutarch) gives first place in the curriculum to the study of philosophy, narrowly conceived as instruction in right conduct. He praises the classical virtues over the transient vanities of status, wealth, beauty, and bodily strength and health. Echoing Cicero and Quintilian, Plutarch affirms both "the life of public utility as men of affairs, and the calm and tranquil

133

life as students of philosophy." Echoing Seneca, he seeks the mixed life of activity, contemplation, and pleasure in due proportion as checks upon one another.

"On the Student at Lectures," reproduced here in full, is set apart by its attention not to subject matter, technique, or the teacher, but to the student. Plutarch recognizes the student as an active participant in learning, a moral agent who must attentively receive instruction with humility, self-control, and reflection. The student is as accountable as the lecturer for the quality of instruction. As with so many great teachers before and since, Plutarch's goal is not to impart mere skills or to produce that pompous creature, the "well-informed man." Rather, he strives for virtue. His last word on the subject is emphatic: "Right listening will be for us the introduction to right living."

Plutarch's other educational essays include "How the Young Man Should Study Poetry," in which he presents poetry as preparatory to the study of philosophy.

from "On Bringing up a Boy"

. . . When children reach the age to be put under a mentor, it becomes especially necessary to take pains in the appointment of such a person. Otherwise we shall have them entrusted to some uncivilized or rascally fellow. What actually happens is often in the highest degree absurd. Respectable slaves are made into farmers, skippers, traders, stewards, or money-lenders, while any low specimen who is found to be a glutton and a tippler and of no use in any kind of business is taken and put in charge of the sons. A fit and proper attendant should possess the same qualities of mind as Phoenix, the attendant of Achilles.

We now reach a topic more important and vital than any yet treated—that of the right teachers for our children. The kind to be sought for are those whose lives are irreproachable, whose characters are unimpugned, and whose skill and experience are of the best. The root or fountain-head of character as a man and a gentleman lies in receiving the proper education. As farmers put stakes beside their plants, so the right kind of teacher provides firm support for the young in the shape of lessons and admonitions, carefully chosen so as to produce an upright growth of character.

As things are, the behaviour of some fathers is contemptible. Before making inquiry as to the proposed teachers, they put their children into the hands of frauds and charlatans, without knowing what they are about, or, maybe, because they are not competent to judge. In the latter case their behaviour is not so ridiculous, but there is another case in which it is in the last degree absurd. I mean, when they know, either from their own observation or from the accounts of others, how ignorant and bad certain educators are, and yet entrust their children to them. Sometimes this is because they cannot resist the fawning of some obsequious flatterer; sometimes it is done to gratify the whim of a friend. It would be just as reasonable for a sick man to gratify a friend by rejecting the doctor whose science could save him, and preferring the ignoramus who will kill him; or for a man to dismiss the best ship's-captain and appoint the worst, because a friend asked for it. In the name of all that is sacred, can any one called a "father" set the pleasing of somebody who asks a favour above the education of his children? There was good sense in a frequent saying of famous old Socrates, "If it could be done, one ought to mount the loftiest part of the city and shout: *Good people, what are you after? Why in such deadly earnest about making money, while troubling so little about the sons to whom you are to leave it?"* We may add that the conduct of such fathers is like that of a man who is anxious as to his shoe, while his foot may look after itself. Many fathers go to such lengths in the way of fondness for their money and want of fondness for their children, that, to avoid paying a larger fee, they choose utterly worthless persons to educate their sons, their object being an inexpensive ignorance. This reminds one of Aristippus and his neat and witty repartee to a foolish father. Questioned as to what fee he asked for educating the child, he replied, "Forty pounds." "Good heavens!" said the father: What an extravagant demand! For forty pounds I can buy a slave." "Very well," was the answer: "then you will have two slaves—your son, and the one you buy."

To put it shortly, it is surely absurd to train little children to receive their food with the right hand, and to scold them if they put out the left, and yet to take no precautions that they shall be taught moral lessons of a sound and proper kind.

What the consequence is to these admirable fathers, when they bring up their sons badly and educate them badly, is soon told. On coming of age and taking rank as men, the sons show an utter disregard of a wholesome and orderly life, and throw themselves headlong into low and irregular pleasures. Then at last, when it is of no use, and when their wrongdoing has brought him to his wits' end, the father repents of having sacrificed his children's education. Some of them take up with toadies and parasites, wretched nondescripts who are the ruin and bane of youth; others with haughty and expensive mistresses and strumpets, whom they ransom from their employers. Some spend recklessly on gormandizing; some are wrecked upon dice and carousals; some go so far as to venture on the more daring vices—they commit adultery, and think death not too much to pay for a single pleasure. Had these last studied philosophy, they would in all probability not have succumbed to temptation of this kind. They would have been told of the advice of Diogenes—who, however coarse in his language, is right in his facts—"Go to a brothel, my boy, and you will find that the expensive article is not a bit better than the cheap one."

In brief, then, I assert—and it would be fairer to regard me as repeating an oracle than as giving advice—that in these matters the one and essential thing, the first, middle, and last, is a sound upbringing and right education. It is this, I say, which leads to virtue and happiness.

Other blessings are on the human plane; they are slight and not worth serious pursuit. Good birth is a distinction, but the boon depends on one's ancestors. Wealth is a prize, but its possession depends on fortune, which often carries it off from those who have it and bestows it on those who never hoped for it. Moreover, great wealth is a target exposed to any rogue of a servant or blackmailer who is minded to "aim a purse" at it. And, worst of all, even the basest of men have their share of it. Fame, again, is imposing, but uncertain. Beauty, though greatly courted, is short-lived; health, though highly prized, is unstable; strength is a thing to be envied, but it falls an easy prey to disease and age. Let us tell any one who prides himself on his bodily strength that he is manifestly under a delusion. How small a fraction is human strength of the might of other animals, such as the elephant, the bull, and the lion!

Meanwhile culture is the only thing in us that is immortal and divine. In the nature of man there are two sovereign elements—understanding and reason. It is the place of the understanding to direct the reason and of the reason to serve the understanding. Fortune cannot overcome them, calumny cannot rob us of them, disease cannot corrupt them, old age cannot impair them. The understanding is the only thing that renews its youth as it grows old, and, while time carries off everything else, it brings old age one gift—that of knowledge. When, again, war comes like a torrent, tearing and sweeping everything away, it is of our mental culture alone that it cannot rob us. Stilpo, the Megarian philosopher, made what seems a memorable answer when Demetrius, after enslaving the city and razing it to the ground, asked him if he had lost anything. "O no!" said he, "for virtue is not made spoil of war." The reply of Socrates is evidently to the same tune and purpose. It was Gorgias, I believe, who asked him his opinion of the Great King, and whether he considered him happy. "I have no knowledge," said Socrates, "as to the state of his character and culture." He assumed that happiness depended upon these, and not upon the gifts of fortune.

Not only should the education of our children be treated as of the very first importance, but I once more urge that we should insist upon its being of the sound and genuine kind.

From pretentious nonsense our sons should be kept as far aloof as possible. To please the many is to displease the wise, an assertion in which I have the support of Euripides:

> I am not deft of words before the crowd,
> More skilled when with my compeers and the few.
> 'Tis compensation: they who 'mid the wise
> Are naught, surpass in gift of speech to mobs.

My own observation tells me that persons who make a business of speaking in a way to please and curry favour with the rabble, generally prove correspondingly dissolute and pleasure-loving in their lives. Nor, indeed, should we expect anything else; for if they have no regard to propriety when catering for the gratification of other people, it is not likely that they will permit right and sound principles to have the upper hand of their own voluptuous self-indulgence, nor that they will cultivate self-control rather than enjoyment.

And how can children learn from them anything admirable? Among admirable things is the practice of neither saying nor doing anything at random; and, as the proverb goes, "admirable things are difficult." Meanwhile, speeches made offhand are a mass of reckless slovenliness, without a notion where to begin or where to end.

Apart from other faults, extempore speakers drop into a terrible prolixity and verbiage, whereas premeditation keeps a speech safe within the lines of due proportion. When Pericles, "as tradition informs us," was called upon by the assembly, he frequently refused the call, on the ground that his thoughts were "not arranged." Demosthenes, who took him for his own political model, acted in the same way. If the Athenians called upon him to address them, he would resist, with the words, "I have not arranged my thoughts." This, it is true, may be unauthentic and a fabrication; but in the speech against Meidias we have an explicit statement as to the advantage of preparation. His words are: *"I admit, gentlemen, that I come prepared; and I have no wish to deny it. I have even conned over my speech to the best of my poor ability. It would have been insane conduct, if, after and amid such harsh treatment, I had paid no regard to what I meant to say to you on the subject."*

That impromptu speaking should be rejected altogether, or, failing this, that it should be practised only on unimportant subjects, I do not say. I am recommending a tonic regimen. Before manhood, I claim that there should be no speaking on the spur of the moment. But when the ability has taken firm root, it is only right for speech to enjoy free play as occasion invites. Though persons who have been in prison for a long time may subsequently be liberated, they are unsteady on their feet, a protracted habit of wearing chains making them unable to step out. Similarly if those who have for a long time kept their speaking under close constraint some day find it necessary to speak offhand, they nevertheless retain the same style of expression. But to let mere children make extempore speeches is to become responsible for the worst of twaddle and futility. There is a story of a wretched painter who showed Apelles a picture, with the remark, "I have just painted this at one sitting." "I can see," said Apelles, "without your telling me, that it has been quick work. But my wonder is that you haven't painted more than one as good."

While (to return to the original matter in hand) we must be careful to avoid a style which is theatrical and bombastic, we must be equally on our guard against one which is low and trivial. If the turgid style is unbusinesslike, too thin a style is ineffective. Just as the body should be not only healthy but also in good condition, so language must be full of strength and not simply free from disease. Keep on the safe side, and you are merely commended: face some risk, and you are admired. I take the same view of the mental disposition also. One should neither be over-bold, and so become brazen, nor yet timid and bashful, and so become mean-spirited. The rule of art and taste is *The middle course in all things*.

While I am still upon the subject of this part of education there is an opinion which I desire to express. A style consisting of single clauses I regard in the first instance as no slight evidence of poor taste, and, in the next, as too finical a thing ever to be maintained in practice. Here, as in everything else that caters for ear or eye, monotony is as cloying and irksome as variety is delightful.

There is no subject in the "regular curriculum" of which the eye or ear of a freeborn boy should be permitted to remain uninformed. But while he receives a cursory education in those subjects in order to taste their quality, the most important place—complete all-round proficiency being impossible—must belong to philosophy. We may explain by a comparison with travel, in which it is an excellent thing to visit a large number of cities, but good policy to settle in the best. As the philosopher Bion wittily remarked, when the suitors could obtain no access to Penelope they satisfied themselves with her handmaids, and when a man is unable to get hold of philosophy he makes dry bones of himself upon the remaining subjects, which are of no account.

Philosophy, then, should be put at the head of all mental culture. The services which have been invented for the care of the body are two—medicine and gymnastics—the one imparting health, the other good condition. But for the weaknesses and ailments of the soul philosophy is the only thing to be prescribed. It is from and with philosophy that we can tell what is becoming or disgraceful, what is just or unjust, what course, in short, is to be chosen or shunned. It teaches us how to behave towards the Gods, our parents, our elders, the laws, our rulers, friends, wives, children, and servants: that we should worship the Gods, honour our parents, respect our elders, obey the laws, give way to our rulers, love our friends, be continent towards our wives, show affection to our children, and abstain from cruelty to our slaves. Above all, it warns us against excess of joy when prosperous and excess of grief when unfortunate; against dissoluteness in our pleasures, or fury and brutality in our anger. These I judge to be chief among the blessings conferred by philosophy. To bear adversity nobly is to act the brave man, to bear prosperity unassumingly, the modest mortal. To get the better of pleasures by reason needs wisdom; to master anger requires no ordinary character.

Perfect men I take to be those who can blend practical ability with philosophy, and who can achieve both of two best and greatest ends—the life of public utility as men of affairs, and the calm and tranquil life as students of philosophy. For there are three kinds of life: the life of action, the life of thought, and the life of enjoyment. When life is dissolute and enslaved to pleasure, it is mean and animal; when it is all thought and fails to act, it is futile; when it is all action and destitute of philosophy, it is crude and blundering. We should therefore do our best to engage both in public business and in the pursuit of philosophy, as occasion offers. Of this kind was the public career of Pericles, of Archytas of Tarentum, of Dion of Syracuse, and of Epaminondas of Thebes. Of these Dion actually attached himself to Plato as his pupil.

There is no need, I think, to deal at any greater length with mental cultivation. It is, however, further desirable—or rather it is essential—that we should not neglect to possess the standard treatises, but should collect a stock of them, with the result of keeping our knowledge from starvation. Farmers stock [their fertilizers], and the employment of books is instrumental to culture in the same way.

Meanwhile we must not omit to exercise the body also. Our boys must be sent to the teacher of gymnastics and receive a sufficient amount of physical training, both to secure a good carriage and also to develop strength. Good condition is the foundation laid in childhood for a hale old age, and, just as our preparations for wintry weather should be made while it is fine, so we should store up provision for age in the shape of regular and temperate behaviour in youth. Physical exertion should, however, be so regulated that a boy does not become too exhausted to devote himself sufficiently to mental culture. As Plato observes, sleep and weariness are the enemies of study.

Upon this topic I need not dwell, but will pass on at once to the most important consideration of all—the necessity of training a boy for service as a fighting-man. For this he must go through hard drill in hurling the javelin, in shooting with the bow, and in hunting. "The goods of the vanquished," it has been said, "are prizes offered to the victor." There is no place in war for the physical condition of the cloister, and a lean soldier accustomed to warlike exercises will break through a phalanx of fleshy prize-fighters.

"Well but," some one may urge, "while you promised us a set of rules for the upbringing of free men, it turns out that you have nothing to say concerning that of poor and common people, but are satisfied to confine your suggestions to the rich." There is a ready reply to the objection. If possible, I should desire the proposed education to be applicable to all alike. But if there are cases in which limited private circumstances make it impossible to carry my rules into practice, the blame should be laid upon fortune, not upon him who offers the advice. Though a man is poor, he should make every possible effort to bring up his children in the ideal way. Failing this, he must come as near to it as he can.

After thus encumbering our discussion with this side-issue, I will now proceed with the connected account of such other matters as contribute to the right upbringing of the young.

And first, children should be led into right practices of persuasion and reasoning: flogging and bodily injury should be out of the question. Such treatment is surely more fit for slaves than for the free, whom the smart, or even the humiliation, of a beating deprives of all life and spirit, making their tasks a horror to them. The freeborn find praise a more effective stimulus to the right conduct, and blame a more effective deterrent from the wrong, than any kind of bodily assault. In the use of such praise and reprimand there should be a subtle alternation. When a child is too bold, it should first be shamed by reproof and then encouraged by a word of praise. We may take a pattern by nurses, who may have to make an infant cry, but who afterwards comfort it by offering it the breast. We must, however, avoid puffing children up with eulogies, the consequence of excessive praise being vanity and conceit.

I have noticed more than one instance in which the over-fondness of a father has proved to be a lack of fondness. To make my meaning clear, I will use an illustration. Being in too great haste for their children to take first place in everything, they impose extravagant tasks, which prove too great for their strength and end in failure, besides causing them such weariness and distress that they refuse to submit patiently to instruction. Water in moderation will make a plant grow, while a flood of water will choke it. In the same way the mind will thrive under reasonably hard work, but will drown if the work is excessive. We must therefore allow children breathing-time from perpetual tasks, and remember that all our life there is a division of relaxation and effort. Hence the existence of sleep as well as waking, of peace as well as war, of fine weather as well as bad, of holidays as well as business. In a word, it is rest that seasons toil. The fact is obvious, not merely in the case of living things, but in that of the inanimate world. We loosen a bow or a lyre, so that we may be able to tighten it. In fine, the body is kept sound by want and its satisfaction, the mind by relaxation and labour.

There are some fathers who have a culpable way of entrusting their sons to attendants and teachers, and then entirely omitting to keep the instruction of such persons under their own eye or ear. This is a most serious failure in their duty. Every few days they should personally examine their children, instead of confiding in the character of a hireling, whose attention to his pupils will be more conscientious if he is to be brought continually to book. In this connexion there is aptness in the groom's dictum that *nothing is so fattening to a horse as the eye of the king.*

Above all things one should train and exercise a child's memory. Memory serves as the storehouse of culture, and hence the fable that Recollection is the mother of the Muses— an indirect way of saying that memory is the best thing in the world to beget and foster wisdom. Whether children are naturally gifted with a good memory, or, on the contrary, are naturally forgetful, the memory should be trained in either case. The natural advantage will be strengthened, or the natural shortcoming made up. The former class will excel others, the latter will excel themselves. As Hesiod well puts it:

> If to the thing that is little you further add but a little,
> And do the same oft and, again, full soon it becometh a great thing.

This, then, is another fact for fathers to recognize—that the mnemonic element in education plays a most important part, not only in culture, but also in the business of life, inasmuch as the recollection of past experience serves as a guide to wise policy for the future.

Our sons must also be kept from the use of foul language. "The word," says Democritus, "is the shadow of the deed." More than that, we must render them polite and courteous, for there is nothing so detestable as a boorish character. One way in which children may avoid becoming disagreeable to their company is by refraining from absolute stubbornness in discussion. Credit is to be gained not merely by victory, but also by knowing how to accept defeat where victory is harmful. There is unquestionably such a thing as a "Cadmean victory." *À propos* I may quote the testimony of that wise poet Euripides:

> When two men speak, and one is full of anger,
> Wiser the one who strives not to reply.

This is the time to remember certain other habits quite as necessary—and more so—for the young to cultivate as any yet mentioned. These are modesty of behaviour, restraint of the tongue, mastery of the temper, and control of the hands. Let us see how important each of them is. We may take an illustration to bring home the notion more clearly. And, we will begin with the last. There have been those who, by lowering their hands to ill-gotten gains, have thrown away all the reputation won by their previous career. This was the case with the Lacedaemonian, Gylippus, who was driven into exile from Sparta for secretly broaching the money-bags. Absence of anger, again, is a quality of wisdom. Socrates once received a kick from a very impudent and gross young buffoon, but on seeing that his own friends were in such a violent state of indignation that they wanted to prosecute him, he remarked: "If a donkey had kicked me, would you have condescended to kick him back?" The fellow did not, however, get off scot-free, but finding himself universally reproached and nicknamed "Kicker," he hanged himself. When Aristophanes brought out the *Clouds*, and poured all manner of abuse upon Socrates, one of those present asked: "Pray, are you not indignant at his ridiculing you in this manner?" "Not I, indeed," replied Socrates; "this banter in the theatre is only in a big convivial party." A close counterpart of this attitude will be found in the behaviour of Plato and of Archytas of Tarentum. When the latter, on his return from the war in which he had held command, found that his land had gone out of cultivation, he summoned his manager and remarked: "You would have suffered for this, if I had not been too angry." When Plato, again, was once worked into a passion with a greedy and impudent slave, he called his sister's son Speusippus and said, "Go and give this fellow a thrashing: I am myself in a great passion."

But, it may be argued, it is difficult to reach so high a standard as this. I am well aware of it. We can therefore only do our best to take a pattern by such conduct, and minimize any tendency to ungovernable rage. As in other matters, we are no match for either the moral mastery or the finished character of those great models. Nevertheless we may act towards them as we might towards the Gods, serving as hierophants and torchbearers of their wisdom and endeavouring to imitate in our nibbling way as much as lies in our power.

As for the control of the tongue—the remaining point to be considered according to our promise—any one who regards it as of trivial moment is very much in the wrong. In a timely silence there is a wisdom superior to any speech. It is apparently for this reason that men in old times invented our mystic rites and ceremonies. The notion was that, through being trained to silence in connexion with these, we should secure the keeping of human secrets by carrying into them the same religious fear. Moreover, though multitudes have repented of talking, no man has repented of silence, and while it is easy to utter what has been kept back, it is impossible to recall what has been uttered.

My own reading affords countless instances of the greatest disasters resulting from an ungoverned tongue. I will content myself with mentioning one or two typical examples. When, upon the marriage of Philadelphus with his sister, Sotades composed a scurrilous verse, he paid ample atonement for talking out of season by rotting for a long time in prison. He thus purchased a laugh in others by long weeping of his own. The story is closely matched by that of the sophist Theocritus, who endured similar, but much more terrible, consequences for a similar remark. Alexander had ordered the Greeks to provide a stock of purple garments, with a view to the thanksgiving sacrifice on his return from his Persian victories, and the various peoples were contributing at so much per head. Hereupon Theocritus observed: "I have now become clear upon a point which used to puzzle me. This is what is meant by Homer's 'purple death'"—words which earned him the enmity of Alexander. Antigonus, the Macedonian king, had but one eye, and Theocritus made him excessively angry by a taunt at this disfigurement. Eutropion, the chief cook, who had become a person of importance, was sent to him by the king with a request that he would come to court and engage him in argument. On receiving repeated visits from Eutropion with this message, he remarked, "I am well aware that you want to dish me up raw to the Cyclops," thus twitting the one with being disfigured, the other with being a cook. "Then," replied Eutropion, "it will be without your head, for you shall be punished for such mad and reckless language." Thereupon he reported the words to the king, who sent and put Theocritus to death.

The last and most sacred requirement is that children should be trained to speak the truth. Lying is a servile habit; it deserves universal detestation and is unpardonable even in a decent slave. . . .

Above all things a father should set an example to his children in his own person, by avoiding all faults of commission or omission. His life should be the glass by which they form themselves and are put out of conceit with all ugliness of act or speech. For him to rebuke his erring sons when guilty of the same errors himself, is to become his own accuser while ostensibly theirs. Indeed, if his life is bad, he is disqualified from reproving even a slave, much more his son. Moreover, he will naturally become their guide and teacher in wrongdoing. Where there are old men without shame, inevitably there are quite shameless young ones also. To obtain good behaviour from our children we should therefore strive to carry out every moral duty. An example to follow is that of Eurydice, who, though belonging to a thoroughly barbarous country like Illyria, nevertheless took to study and self-improvement late in life for the sake of her children's education. Her maternal affection finds apt expression in the lines inscribed upon her offering to the Muses:

> In that, when mother to grown boys, she won
> Her soul's well-known desire—the skill to use
> The lore of letters—this Eurydice
> From Hierapolis sends to each Muse

To compass the whole of the foregoing elements of success is perhaps visionary—a counsel of perfection. But to cultivate the majority of them, though itself requiring good fortune as well as much care, is at any rate a thing within the reach of a human being.

⚒

"On the Student at Lectures"

My Dear Nicander,

This is an article upon "The Attitude of the Student," which I have written and am sending to you. Its purpose is to teach you the right attitude towards your philosophic teacher, now that you are a grown-up man and are no longer obliged merely to obey orders.

Some young men are so ill-informed as to suppose that absence of restraint is the same thing as freedom, whereas, by unchaining the passions, it makes them slaves to a set of masters more tyrannical than all the teachers and mentors of childhood. Herodotus says that when women take off the tunic they also take off shame. It is the same with some young men. In laying aside the garb of childhood they also lay aside shame and fear. No sooner do they unloose the cloak which controlled their conduct than they indulge in the utmost misbehaviour. With you it should be otherwise. You have been told over and over again that to "follow God" and to "obey reason" are the same thing. Understand, therefore, that with right-minded persons a coming of age does not mean rejection of rule, but change of ruler. For the hired or purchased[1] director of conduct they substitute one that is divine—namely, reason. Only those who follow reason deserve to be considered free; for they alone live as they choose, because they alone have learned to make the right choice, whereas ignorant and irrational desires and actions give small and paltry scope to the will, but great scope to repentance.

Note what happens in the case of naturalized citizens. Entire foreigners from another country will often grumble irritably at their experiences, whereas those who have previously been denizens of the state, and have therefore lived in intimate touch with the laws, will accept their obligations with cheerful readiness. So with yourself. For a long time you have been growing up in the company of philosophy. From the first you have been accustomed to a taste of philosophic reason in everything that you have been taught or told as a child. It should therefore be in a well-disposed and congenial spirit that you come to Philosophy, who alone can adorn a youth with that finish of manhood which genuinely and rationally deserves the name.

You will not, I believe, object to a prefatory remark upon the sense of hearing. Theophrastus asserts that it is the most susceptible of all the senses, inasmuch as nothing that can be seen, tasted, or touched, is the cause of such strong emotional disturbance and

---

1. The *paedagogus*, an attendant slave, who accompanied the boy and watched over his conduct.

excitement as takes hold upon the mind when certain sounds of beating, clashing, or ring-ing fall upon the ear. It is, however, more rational, rather than more emotional, than the other senses. Vice can find many places and parts of the body open for it to enter and seize upon the soul. But the only hold that virtue can take is upon pure young ears which have at all times been protected from the corruptions of flattery or the touch of low commu-nications. Hence the advice of Xenocrates, that ear-guards should be worn by boys more than by athletes, inasmuch as the latter merely have their ears disfigured by blows, while the former have their characters disfigured by words. Not that he would wed us to inatten-tion or deafness. It is but a warning to beware of wrong communications, and to see that others of the right nature have first been fostered in our character by philosophy and have mounted guard in that quarter which is most open to influence and persuasion.

Bias, the ancient sage, was once bidden by Amasis to send him that piece of meat from a sacrificial victim which was at the same time the best and the worst. He replied by tak-ing out and sending the tongue, on the ground that speech can do both the greatest harm and the greatest good. It is a general practice in fondling little children to take them by the ears, and to bid them do the same to us—an indirect and playful way of suggesting that we should be especially fond of those who make our ears the instruments to our advantage.

It is, of course, obvious that a youth cannot be debarred from any or every kind of hearing, or from tasting any discourse at all. Otherwise not only will he remain entirely without fruit or growth in the way of virtue; he will actually be perverted in the direc-tion of vice, his mind being an idle and uncultivated patch producing a plentiful crop of weeds. Propensity to pleasure and dislike of labour—the springs of innumerable forms of trouble and disease—are not of external origin, nor imported from teaching, but they well up naturally from the soil. If therefore they are left free to take their natural course; if they are not done away with, or turned aside, by sound instruction; if nature is not thus brought under control, man will prove more unreclaimed than any brute beast.

The hearing of lectures, then, may be of great profit, but at the same time of great danger, to a young man. This being so, I believe it a good thing to make the matter one of constant discussion, both with oneself and with others. In most cases we may notice a false procedure—that of cultivating the art of speaking before being trained to the art of listening. It is thought that, while speaking requires instruction and practice, any kind of listening is attended with profit. But not so. Whereas in ball-play one learns simultane-ously how to throw and how to catch, in the business of speech the right taking in is prior to the giving out, just as conception is prior to parturition. We are told that in the case of a hen laying a wind-egg her labour and travail end in nothing but an abortive and lifeless piece of refuse. So when a young man lacks the ability to listen, or the training to gather profit through the ear, the speech which he lets fall is wind-begotten indeed:

Sans all regard and sans note it is lost in the clouds and dispersed.

He will take a vessel and tilt it in the right direction for receiving anything to be poured into it, and so ensure a real "in-pouring" instead of a pouring to waste. But he does not learn to lend his own attention to a speaker and meet the lecture half-way, so as to miss no valuable point. On the contrary, his behaviour is in the last degree ridiculous. If he happens upon a person describing a dinner, a procession, a dream, or a brawling-match in which he has been engaged, he listens in silence and is eager for more. But if a teacher to whom he has attached himself tries to impart something useful, or to urge him to some duty, to admonish him when wrong, or to soothe him when angry, he is out of all patience. If possible, he shows fight, and is ambitious to get the best of the argument. Otherwise he is off and away to discourses of a different and a rubbishy kind, filling his ears—the poor leaky vessels—with anything rather than the thing they need.

From the right kind of breeder a horse obtains a good mouth for the bit, and a lad a good ear for reason. He is taught to do much listening, but to avoid much speaking. We may quote the remark of Spintharus in praise of Epaminondas, that he had scarcely ever met with any man either of greater judgement or of fewer words. Moreover, we are told, the reason why nature gave each of us two ears, but only one tongue, was that we should do less speaking than hearing.

A youth is at all times sure to find silence a credit to him; but in one case it is especially so—when he can listen to another without becoming excited and continually yelping; when, even if what is being said is little to his liking, he waits patiently for the speaker to finish; when, at the close, he does not immediately come to the attack with his contradiction, but (to quote Aeschines) waits a while, in case the speaker might wish to supplement his remarks, or perhaps to adjust or qualify his position. To take instant objection, neither party listening to the other but both talking at once, is an unseemly performance. On the other hand, those who have been trained to listen with modest self-control will accept a valuable argument and make it their own, while they will be in a better position to see through a worthless or false one and to expose it, thereby showing that they are lovers of truth, and not merely contentious, headstrong, or quarrelsome persons. It is, therefore not a bad remark of some, that there is more need to expel the wind of vanity and self-conceit from the young, than to expel the air from a skin, when you wish to pour in anything of value: otherwise they are too swollen and flatulent to receive it.

The presence of envious and malicious jealousy is, of course, never to good purpose, but always an impediment to proper action. In the case of a student at lectures it is the most perverse of prompters. Words which ought to do him good are rendered vexing, distasteful, and unwelcome by the fact that there is nothing which an envious man likes so little as an excellent piece of reasoning. And note that, when a man is piqued by fame or beauty belonging to others, he is envious and nothing more; what annoys him is another's good fortune. But when he is irritated by admirable argument, his vexation is at his own good, since reason—if he has a mind to accept it—is as much to the good of one who hears as light is to the good of one who sees.

Envy in other matters is the result of various coarse or low attitudes of mind; envy of a speaker is born of inordinate love of glory and unfair ambition. A person so disposed is prevented from listening to reason. His mind is perturbed and distracted. At one and the same time it is looking at its own endowments, to see if they are inferior to those of the speaker, and at the rest of the company, to see if they are wondering and admiring. It is disgusted at their applause, and exasperated at their approval. The previous portions of the speech it forgets and ignores, because the recollection is irksome. The parts yet to come it awaits with trembling anxiety, for fear they may prove better still. When the speaker is at his best, it is most eager for him to stop. When the lecture is over, it thinks of nothing that was said, but takes count of the expressions and attitudes of the audience. From those who give praise it dances away in a frenzy; and to those who carp and distort it runs to form one of the herd. If there is nothing to distort, it makes comparisons with others who have spoken "better and more eloquently to the same purpose." In the end our friend has so cruelly mishandled the lecture that he has made it of no use or profit to himself.

Let the love of glory, then, be brought to terms with the love of learning. Let us listen to a speaker with friendly courtesy, regarding ourselves as guests at a sacred banquet or sacrificial offering. Let us praise his ability when he makes a hit, or be satisfied with the mere goodwill of a man who is making the public a present of his views and endeavouring to convince others by means of the arguments which have convinced himself. When he goes right, let us consider that his rightness is due not to chance or accident, but to painstaking effort and learning. Let us take a pattern by it, and not only admire it, but emulate it. When he is at fault, let us stop and think for what reasons he is so, and at what point he began to go astray. Xenophon observes that good managers derive profit from their enemies as well as from their friends. In the same way those who are attentive and alert derive benefit from a speaker not only when he is in the right, but also when he is in the wrong. Paltry thought, empty phrase, affected bearing, vulgar, delight and excitement at applause, and the like, are more palpable to a listener in another's case than to a speaker in his own. It is well, therefore, to take the criticism which we apply to him, and apply it to ourselves, asking whether we commit any mistake of the kind without being aware of it. It is the easiest thing in the world to find fault with our neighbour, but it is a futile and meaningless proceeding, unless made to bear in some way upon the correction or prevention of similar faults. When lapses are committed, let us always be prompt to exclaim to ourselves in the phrase of Plato, "Am I, perhaps, as bad?" As, in the eyes of our neighbour we see the reflection of our own, so we should find a picture of our own speech in that of another. In that way we shall avoid treating others with overconfident contempt, and shall also look more carefully to our own deliverances.

There is another way in which comparison serves this useful purpose. I mean if, when we get by ourselves after the lecture, we take some point which appears to have been wrongly or unsatisfactorily treated, and attack the same theme, doing our best to fill in, to correct, to re-word, or to attempt an entirely original contribution to the subject, as the case may be—doing, in fact, as Plato did with the speech of Lysias. While to argue against a certain deliverance is not difficult, but, on the contrary, very easy, to set up a better in its stead is an extremely hard matter. As the Lacedaemonian said on hearing that Philip had razed Olynthus to the ground: "Yes, but to create a city as good is beyond the man's power." Accordingly, when we find that in dealing with the same subject we can do but little better than the speaker in the case, we make a large reduction in our contempt and speedily prune down that self-satisfied conceit which has been exposed during such process of comparison.

Nevertheless, though admiration, as opposed to contempt, certainly betokens a fairer and gentler nature, it is a thing which, in its own turn, requires no little—perhaps greater—caution. For while a contemptuous and over-confident person derives too little benefit from a speaker, an enthusiastic and guileless admirer derives too much injury. He forms no exception to the rule of Heracleitus that *"Any dictim will flutter a fool."* One should be frank in yielding praise to the speaker, but cautious in yielding belief to the assertion; a kindly and candid observer of the diction and delivery of the arguer, but a sharp and exacting critic of the truth and value of his argument. While we thus escape dislike from the speaker, we escape harm from the speech. How many false and pernicious doctrines we unawares accept through esteeming and trusting their exponent! The Lacedaemonian authorities, after examining a measure suggested by a man of evil life, instructed another person, famous for his conduct and character, to move it—a very proper and statesman-like encouragement to the people to be led more by the character of an adviser than by his speech. But in philosophy we must put aside the reputation of the speaker and examine the speech in and by itself. In lecturing, as in war, there is much that is mere show. The speaker's grey hairs, his vocal affectations, his supercilious airs, his self-glorification; above all, the shouting, applauding, and dancing of the audience overwhelm the young and inexperienced student and sweep him along with the current. There is deception in the language also, when it streams upon the question in a delightful flood, and when it contains a measure of studied art and the grandiose. As, in singing to the accompaniment of the flageolet, mistakes are generally undetected by an audience, so an elaborate and pretentious diction dazzles the hearer and blinds him to the sense. I believe it was Melanthius who, when asked about Diogenes' tragedy, replied: "I could not get a sight of it; it was hidden behind the words." But with the discourses and declamations of the majority of our professors it is not merely a case of using the words to screen the thoughts. They also dulcify the voice—modulating, smoothing, and intoning—till the hearer is carried away with a perfect intoxication. They give an empty pleasure, and are paid with an emptier fame. Their case, in fact, is one for the quip given by Dionysius. It was he, I think, who, during the performance of a distinguished harp-player, promised him a liberal reward, but subsequently gave him nothing, on the ground that he had made a sufficient return. "For as long a time as I was enjoying your singing," said he, "you were enjoying your expectations." The deliverer of the lectures in question finds that they represent a joint contribution of the same kind. He receives admiration as long as his entertainment lasts. As soon as no more pleasure is forthcoming for the ear, there is no more glory left for him. The one party has wasted his time, the other his professional life.

Let us, then, strip aside all this empty show of language, and make for the actual fruit. It is better to imitate the bee than the garland-maker. The latter looks for the bright-coloured fragrant petals, and, by twining and plaiting them together, produces an object which is pleasant enough, but short-lived and fruitless. Bees, on the contrary, frequently skim through meadows of violets, roses, or hyacinths, to settle upon the coarsest and bitterest thyme. To this they devote themselves

> Contriving yellow honey,

and then fly home to their proper business with something worth the getting. So a student who takes his work in real earnest will pay no regard to dainty flowery words nor to showy theatrical matter. These he will consider as fodder for drones who play the sophist. For his own part he will probe with keen attention into the sense of a speech and the quality of the speaker. Therefrom he will suck such part as will be of service and profit. He will remember that he has not come to a theatre or concert-hall, but to a classroom in the schools, and that his object is to get his life corrected by means of reason. Hence he should form a critical judgement of the lecture from his own case, that is to say, from a calculation of its effect upon himself. Has it been the chastening of a passion, the lightening of a grief? Has it been courage, firmness of spirit, enthusiasm for excellence and virtue? Upon rising from the barber's chair he will stand at the glass and put his hands to his head, inspecting the trim and arrangement of the hair. No less should he, immediately on leaving a lecture in the philosophic school, look at himself and examine his own mind, to see if it has got rid of any useless and uncomfortable growth and become lighter and more at ease. "There is no use," says Aristo, "in either a bath or a speech, unless it cleanses."

By all means let a young man, while profiting from a discourse, find pleasure in the process. But he must not treat the pleasure of the lecture as its end, nor expect to come out of the philosopher's school with a beaming face and humming a tune. He must not ask for scented unguents when what he needs is a lotion or a poultice. On the contrary, he should be grateful if a pungent argument acts upon his mind like smoke upon a hive, and clears out all the darkness and mistiness that fill it. Though it is quite right for a speaker not to be altogether without concern for an attractive and persuasive style of language, that should be a matter least regarded by the young student, at any rate in the first instance. Later, no doubt, the case may be different. It is when they are no longer thirsty that persons engaged in drinking will turn a cup about and inspect the chasing upon it. Similarly during a breathing-time, after taking our fill of the lesson, we may be permitted to examine any uncommon elegance in the language. But if from the very first, instead of taking a grip upon the substance, you insist upon "good pure Attic" expression, you are like a person who refuses to take an antidote unless the vessel is made of the best Attic earthenware; or who declines to put on a thick cloak in winter unless the wool is from Attic sheep, preferring to sit, stubborn and impracticable, in the thin napless mantle of the "style of Lysias." Perversities of this kind are responsible for a plentiful lack of good sense and an abundance of loquacious claptrap in the schools. Young fellows keep no watch upon the life, the practical action, or the public services of a philosopher, but make a great merit of diction, phrase, and fine method of statement, while they possess neither the ability nor the desire to find out whether the statement is valuable or worthless, whether it is vital or a mere futility.

The next rule concerns the propounding of difficulties. A guest at a dinner is bound to accept what is put upon the table, and neither to ask for anything else nor to find fault. When the feast consists of a discourse, any one who comes to it should listen and say nothing, if there is an understanding to that effect. Persons who cannot listen in a pleasant and sociable manner, but keep drawing the speaker off to other topics, interposing questions and mooting side-issues, get no benefit themselves and confuse both the speaker and the speech. When, however, he invites the audience to ask questions and advance difficulties, any that are proposed should prove to be useful and important. Odysseus, when in the suitors' company, incurs ridicule through

> Begging for morsels and scraps, and not for a sword or a cauldron.

They regard it as a sign of lofty-mindedness not only to give, but to ask for, something of value. It is, however, more a case for ridicule when a hearer poses a speaker with petty little problems of the kind often propounded by young men, when they are talking claptrap in order to make a show of attainments in logic or mathematics—for example, concerning "division of the indeterminate" and the nature of "lateral" or "diagonal" motion. The proper answer to such persons is the remark of Philotimus to a man who was suffering with abscesses and consumption, but who had been talking to him for some time about requiring "some little thing to cure a whitlow." Perceiving the man's condition from his complexion and breathing, Philotimus observed: "My good sir, a whitlow is not the question with you." Nor in your case, young sir, is it worth while to be discussing such questions as yours, but how you are to get rid of conceit, swaggering about love-affairs, and such-like nonsense, and how you are to plant your feet on the way to a healthy and sober-minded life.

Especially are you bound, in putting your questions, to accommodate yourself to a speaker's range of knowledge or natural ability—to his special *forte*. A philosopher who is more concerned with ethics should not be attacked with difficulties in natural science or mathematics, nor should one who prides himself upon his scientific knowledge be dragged into determining hypothetical syllogisms or solving fallacies. If you attempted to chop your wood with the key and to open your door with the axe, it would not be thought that you were making sport of these implements, but that you were depriving yourself of their respective powers and uses. In the same way, if you ask of a speaker a thing for which he has no gift or training, while you make no harvest of what he possesses and offers, you not only do yourself harm to that extent, but you incur condemnation for malicious ill-nature.

Be careful also not to propound difficulties yourself in too great numbers or too frequently. This is, in a sense, another way of showing off. Meanwhile, to listen equably when some one else is mooting them, shows that you are a clubbable person and a student. This is assuming you have no harassing and urgent trouble of your own, no mental disturbance to be controlled or malady to be comforted. It may not, after all, be (as Heracleitus says) "better to conceal ignorance," but to bring it into the open and cure it. If your mind is upset by a fit of anger, an attack of superstition, a violent quarrel with your friends, or a mad amorous passion which

> Stirreth the heart-strings that should rest unstirred,

you must not run away from a discourse which searches it home, and fly to others of a different nature. On the contrary, these are the very topics to which you should listen, both at lectures and also by privately approaching the lecturer afterwards and asking for further light.

The opposite course is the one too generally followed. So long as the philosopher is dealing with other persons, his hearers are all delight and admiration. But when he leaves those others alone and frankly administers some important reminder to themselves personally, they are disgusted with him for not minding his own business. Generally speaking, they think a philosopher is entitled to a hearing inside his school, as the tragedian is in the theatre; but in matters beyond it they do not consider him in any way superior to themselves. Towards a sophist their attitude is natural enough; for when he rises from his chair, lays aside his books and his introductory manuals, and makes his appearance in the practical departments of life, he ranks in the popular mind as an unimportant and inferior person. But towards a philosopher in the real sense their attitude is wrong. They do not recognize that a tone of earnestness or jest, a sign of approval or disapproval, a smile or a frown, on his part—and, above all, his direct handling of their individual cases—are fruitful in good to those who have learned the art of listening with submission.

Applause, again, has its duties, which call for a certain caution and moderation. A gentleman bestows neither too little nor too much of it. A hearer shows churlishly bad taste when nothing whatever in a lecture will make him thaw or unbend; when he is diseased with festering conceit and chronic self-complacency, and is all the time thinking he could improve upon the deliverance; when he neither makes any appropriate movement of the brow nor utters any sound to prove that he is a considerate and willing listener; when he is seeking a reputation for solidity and depth by means of silence, an affected gravity, and attitudes of pose, under the notion that applause is like money, and that whatever amount you give to another you take from yourself. The fact is that there are many who take up the well-known saying of Pythagoras and sing it to a false tune. His own gain from philosophy, he said, was to *"wonder at nothing"*; whereas theirs is to "praise nothing" or to "honour nothing." With them wisdom lies in contempt, and the way to be dignified is to be disdainful. While, by means of knowledge and the ascertainment of the cause in a given case, philosophic reason does away with the wonder and awe due to unenlightenment and ignorance, it does not destroy a generous appreciation. Those whose excellence is genuine and firmly seated find it the highest honour to bestow honour, the highest distinction to bestow distinction, where honour and distinction are due. Such conduct implies that they have fame enough and to spare, and are free from jealousy, whereas those who are niggards of praise to others are in all probability pinched and hungry for praise of their own.

On the other hand, the opposite type of hearer is the fluttering feather-head who uses no discrimination, but punctuates with loud cheers at every word and syllable. While he is frequently obnoxious to the disputant himself, he is invariably a nuisance to the hearers. He worries them on to their feet against their judgement, and drags them willy-nilly to join in the chorus because they are ashamed to refuse. Thanks to his applause deranging the lecture and making an imbroglio of it, he gets no good from it, but goes home with one of three descriptions to his credit—fleerer, sycophant, or ignoramus.

It is true that, when hearing a case in court, we must lean neither towards hostility nor towards favor, but towards justice as we best understand it. But at a lecture on a subject of learning there is neither law nor oath to debar us from granting the speaker an indulgent reception. The reason why the ancients placed the statue of Hermes in the company of the Graces was that speaking has a special claim to a gracious friendliness. It is impossible for any one to be so complete a failure or so utterly astray as to offer us nothing deserving of a cheer, in the shape of a thought, a reference to others, the mere choice of theme or purpose, or, possibly, in the wording or arrangement of the matter,

> As among urchin foot or mid coarse broom
> The tender snowflake springeth into bloom.

There are persons who, for exhibition purposes, can lend a fair measure of plausibility to a panegyric upon vomiting or fever, or even a pot; and surely a deliverance by a man who has some sort of claim to be thought, or to call himself, a philosopher cannot absolutely fail to afford a well-disposed or courteous audience some opportunity of finding relief in applause.

According to Plato young persons in the bloom of life can always manage somehow to excite a lover's passion. If they are white he calls them "saint-like"; if swarthy, "virile." A hook-nose is "regal," a snub nose "piquant"; a sallow skin is a "complexion of honey." He uses these pretty names, and is pleased and satisfied. Love has, indeed, an ivy-like gift for clinging to any pretext. Much less will an eager and earnest student of letters ever fail in inventiveness. In every speaker he will discover some grounds for reasonable applause. In the speech of Lysias, though Plato objects to its want of arrangement, and though he has no praise for its inventiveness, he nevertheless commends him for his manner of statement, and because there is "a clear round finish in the chiselling of every word." We might find fault with Archilochus for his subject-matter, Parmenides for his versification, Phocylides for his commonplaceness, Euripides for his garrulity, Sophocles for his inequality. Similarly one of the orators has no characterization, another exerts no passion, a third is lacking in grace and charm. Nevertheless each wins praise for a power to move and sway us in his own peculiar way.

The hearer, then, has ample scope for showing good feeling to a speaker. In some instances it is sufficient if, without further declaration by word of mouth, we contribute a kindly eye, a genial expression, a friendly and agreeable mood. There are certain things for which even the man who is a total failure may look, and which are but ordinary items of common etiquette for any and every audience. I mean an upright posture in our chairs, with no lolling or lounging; eyes kept directly upon the speaker; an air of businesslike attention; composure of countenance, with no sign, I need not say of insolence or peevishness, but of being taken up with other thoughts.

If in every exacting task beauty is made up of a number of factors happily combined in a due proportion and harmony, ugliness is the prompt and immediate outcome of the faulty omission or addition of this or that one element. And in this particular matter of listening, not only is there impropriety in a scowling brow, a disagreeable expression, a roving glance, a twisting of the body, and a crossing of the legs; but nodding or whispering to a neighbour, smiling, yawning sleepily, looking at the ground, and actions of a similar nature, are censurable and should be studiously avoided.

There are some who think that, though the speaker has a duty, the hearer has none. They expect the former to present himself with his thoughts studiously prepared; yet, without a thought or care for their own obligations, they drop casually in and take their seats, for all the world as if they had come to a dinner to enjoy themselves while others are doing the work. Yet even a polite table-companion has his part to play, much more a polite hearer. He is a partner in the speech and a coadjutor of the speaker; and he has no right to be sharply criticizing the mistakes, and taking every phrase and fact to task, while himself free from responsibility for the impropriety and the frequent solecisms which he commits as a hearer. In ball-play the catcher has to regulate his movements according to those of the thrower. So, in the case of a speech, there is a certain consonance of action in which both speaker and listener are concerned, if each is to sustain his proper part.

Our expressions in applauding must not, however, be used without discrimination. It is an unpleasing phrase of Epicurus when, in speaking of the little epistles from his friends, he says, "We give them a rattling clapping." But what of those who nowadays introduce such *outré* expressions into our lecture-rooms? The *Capital! Well said!* and *Very true!* which were the terms of commendation used by the hearers of Plato, Socrates, and Hypereides, are not enough for these persons. With their exclamations *Divine! An inspiration!* or *Unapproachable!* they commit a gross impropriety, libellously making out that the speaker requires far-fetched eulogies of an outrageous kind. Highly obnoxious also are those who accompany their attestations with an oath, as if they were in a court of law. And equally so those who blunder in their descriptive terms; for instance, when the lecturer is a philosopher and they call out, *A shrewd hit!,* or an old man and they exclaim *Cleverly put!* or *Brilliant!,* thus misapplying to a philosopher the expressions used at academic exercises, where the speaking is not serious but merely an exhibition of adroitness. To offer to a sober discourse such meretricious praise is like crowning an athlete with a wreath of lilies or roses instead of laurel or wild olive. Once when the poet Euripides was going over a song with an original setting for the benefit of the members of his chorus, and one of them happened to laugh, he observed: "If you had not been an ignorant dolt, you could not have laughed while I was teaching you a mixolydian[2] piece." So, I take it, a serious and practical philosopher might very well make short work of the airs and affectations of a hearer by saying, "I presume your case is one of foolishness or ill breeding; otherwise you would not have been piping out and jigging about at my remarks, when I was teaching, or admonishing, or arguing concerning religion, statesmanship, or the duties of office." Just frankly consider what it means, when a philosopher is speaking, and the shouting and hurrahing inside the building make people outside wonder whether it is a flute-player, a harpist, or a dancer who is being applauded.

Meanwhile, in listening to admonition and reproof, the pupil must be neither insensible nor unmanly. There are some who bear the philosopher's reproaches with an easy-going indifference, laughing under the correction and applauding the corrector, just as parasites applaud in sheer impudence and recklessness when they are abused by those who keep them. The shamelessness which such persons display is no proper or genuine proof of courage. When a jibe containing no insult, and uttered in a playful and tactful way, is borne cheerfully and without annoyance, it shows neither a want of spirit nor a want of breeding. On the contrary, it is exactly what a gentleman of the true Spartan style would do. But it is different when admonition takes in hand the correction of character by means of a stinging remedy in the shape of rational reproof. If a young man does not cower under the lesson and feel his soul burning with shame, till he breaks into a sweat and is ready to faint; if, on the contrary, he is unperturbed, gives a broad grin of self-depreciation, and refuses to take the matter seriously, then he is an extremely vulgar creature beyond all sense of shame, a constant habituation to misconduct having made his soul no more capable of a bruise than a thick callus in the flesh.

These form the one class. Youths of the opposite disposition, if a single hard word is said to them, turn deserters from philosophy and run away without a glance behind them. While nature has given them, in the shape of modesty, an excellent start towards moral salvation, they are so squeamish and timid that they throw their chance away. Unable to put up with reproof or to accept correction with spirit, they turn away to listen to the soft and agreeable utterances of some time-server or sophist, who charms them with melodi-

---

2. I.e., in the mixolydian mode, which was of a sad and dirgelike character.

ous phrases as useless and futile as they are pleasing. If a man runs away from the surgeon after the operation and objects to be bandaged, he is submitting to the pain of the treatment but refusing to put up with its benefit. So when a lesson has lanced and probed his folly, if he will not permit it to close and dress the wound, he is abandoning philosophy after feeling the sting and the pain but before deriving any advantage therefrom.

Euripides says that the wound of Telephus was

> Soothed by the filings ground from the same spear.

It is no less true that the sting implanted by philosophy in a youth of parts is cured by the same reasoning that caused the wound. While, therefore, it is right that the subject of reproof should feel some pain from the sting, he must not be crushed or dispirited, but, after undergoing the first discomposing rites of purification, he should look for some sweet and splendid revelation to follow the distress and confusion of the moment. For though the reproof may appear to be unjust, the proper course is to endure it with all patience until the speaker concludes. Then he may be met by a plea in self-defence, and by a request to reserve for some real fault all the vigorous candour which he has shown in the present instance.

To proceed to the next consideration. In reading and writing, playing the lyre, or wrestling, the first lessons are very harassing, laborious, and unsure; but, as we advance step by step, it is much as in dealing with mankind. By dint of frequent and familiar acquaintance we find that it all becomes pleasant and manageable, and every word or action easy. It is the same with philosophy. No doubt the language and matter, as first met with, contain something both hard and strange. But we must not take fright at the rudiments and prove so timid and spiritless as to abandon the study. On the contrary, our duty is to grapple with every question, to persevere, to be resolved on making progress, and then to wait for that familiarity which converts all right action into a pleasure. It will not be long before it arrives, casting upon the study a flood of light, and inspiring an ardent passion for excellence. To be without such passion and to put up with the ordinary type of life because one is driven from philosophy by a lack of mettle, is to be a miserable or cowardly creature.

We may also expect that at first the argumentation will prove somewhat difficult for young and inexperienced students to understand. For the most part, however, the obscurity and want of comprehension are due to themselves. Opposite dispositions lead to the same mistake. Thus one class, through bashfulness and a desire to spare the teacher, will shrink from putting questions and making sure of the argument, and will ostensibly assent as if they quite understood. The others, led by misplaced ambition and meaningless rivalry to make a show of cleverness and quickness, pretend to have mastered a thing before they take it in, and so will not take it in at all. The consequence is that when the former—the modest, and silent kind—go home, they will worry themselves with their perplexities, and in the end they will be driven perforce to trouble the speaker by harking back with their questions at a later date, when they will feel still more ashamed. Meanwhile the bold and ambitious kind will be perpetually cloaking their ignorance and hiding the fact that it haunts them.

Let us then thrust aside all this pretentious silliness, and march on towards learning. Let our business be to get an intelligent grasp upon valuable instruction. And let us put up with the laughter of those who are thought to be clever. Remember how Cleanthes and Xenocrates, though to all appearance slower than their fellow-pupils, refused to give up or run away from their studies. On the contrary, they were the first to joke at their own expense, comparing themselves to a narrow-necked bottle or a brass tablet, inasmuch as, though slow at taking their instruction in, they were safe, and sure at retaining it. Not only must we, as Phocylides puts it,

> Oft-times be baulked of our hope while seeking to come unto goodness;

we must also "oft-times" be laughed at, and bear with scoffing and jeering, meanwhile putting all our heart and energy into winning the struggle against our ignorance.

We must, however, be quite as careful not to err in the opposite direction. Some do so from sloth, which makes them a wearisome infliction. Unwilling to trouble themselves when alone, they keep troubling the teacher by repeatedly asking for information on the same questions. Like unfledged birds in the nest, they are perpetually agape to be fed from another's mouth, and expect to receive everything ready masticated by someone else.

Another kind, in the misplaced quest of a reputation for alertness and acumen, worry the lecturer with their fussy garrulity, perpetually mooting some unimportant difficulty or demanding some unnecessary demonstration,

> Till a short journey so becometh long

—as Sophocles says—not only to themselves but to every one else. By continually arresting the teacher with superfluous and futile questions, as if they were merely chatting with a companion, they interfere with the continuity of the lesson by a series of checks and delays. Persons of this class are (to quote Hieronymus) like wretched cowardly puppies, who bite the skins and tear the odds and ends of wild animals at home, but who never touch the animals themselves.

As for the former and lazy class, let us give them this advice. When they have managed to comprehend the main points, let them piece the rest together for themselves, using their memory as a guide to independent thought. And let them take the reasoning they hear from another as a beginning—a seed which they are to make grow and thrive.

The mind is not a vessel which calls for filling. It is a pile, which simply requires kindling-wood to start the flame of eagerness for original thought and ardor for truth. Suppose someone goes to borrow from his neighbour's fire, and then, on finding a large bright blaze, persists in staying and basking on the spot. It is the same when a man comes to another to borrow reason, and does not realize that he must kindle a light of his own in the shape of thinking for himself, but sits enchanted with enjoyment of the lecture. He derives from the lesson a ruddy glow or outward brilliance, but he fails to drive out the mould and darkness from within by the warming power of philosophy.

If therefore any advice is needed for the hearing of lectures, it is to remember the rule just given—to practise independent thought along with learning. We shall, thus attain, not to the ability of a sophist or the "well-informed" man, but to a deep-seated philosophic power. Right listening will be for us the introduction to right living.

Philo

C. 20 B.C.–C. A.D. 50

*The greatest of all propositions is virtue, for it is conversant about
the most important of all materials, namely, about the universal
life of man.*

"On Mating with the Preliminary Studies"

Though a near contemporary of Seneca, Philo (or Philo Judaeus) belongs geographically, religiously, and philosophically with the Alexandrian school that bridged the Hellenistic and Christian worlds in the eastern Mediterranean. Alexandria, founded in northern Egypt by Alexander the Great in the fourth century B.C., thrived as a center for commerce, culture, and scholarship. It was home to one of the finest universities and libraries in the world. In the third century B.C., Jewish scholars convened in Alexandria to produce the Greek translation of the Hebrew scriptures that we know as the Septuagint. Philo came from a prominent, politically connected family in the city's Jewish community, one of the largest outside Palestine. He was called upon for public service from time to time, and some of his extended family held high office in the Roman administration. He once represented his Jewish community as an envoy to Rome to plead that they not be penalized for refusing to worship the emperor Caligula. His heart, however, belonged to philosophy. Highly regarded among the emerging Neoplatonists, he wrote numerous treatises in Greek that attempted to synthesize Hebrew scriptures with Platonic philosophy, often spinning elaborate allegorical interpretations to do so. His extended metaphors startle the modern reader, but were commonplace both in literary studies prior to his time and in biblical interpretation for centuries afterward. Alexandria soon became known for the distinctively Platonic approach to Christian doctrine and life elaborated by Clement, Origen, and Gregory Thaumaturgus.

The Selections

Philo opens Book III of *On the Special Laws* with a brief meditation on the consolations of philosophy and the familiar conflict between the calling to wisdom and the demands of public duties.

"On Mating with the Preliminary Studies," the opening part of which is included here, develops a lengthy allegory on the liberal arts using the Patriarch Abraham, his wife Sarah, and her handmaiden Hagar. Like Seneca, Philo argues on behalf of the liberal arts as a preparation, or "handmaiden," for leading the soul to wisdom and virtue. This treatise shows the durability of the whole circle of the liberal arts curriculum, a legacy from the declining Greek world inherited by Christianity and solidified into the seven liberal arts of the Middle Ages.

"On the Life of Moses" fills in the biblical narrative in the book of Exodus by imagining what sort of education Moses received in Pharaoh's household in Egypt.

from On the Special Laws
Book III

There was once a time when, devoting my leisure to philosophy and to the contemplation of the world and the things in it, I reaped the fruit of excellent, and desirable, and blessed intellectual feelings, being always living among the divine oracles and doctrines, on which I fed incessantly and insatiably, to my great delight, never entertaining any low or grovelling thoughts, nor ever wallowing in the pursuit of glory or wealth, or the delights of the body, but I appeared to be raised on high and borne aloft by a certain inspiration of the soul, and to dwell in the regions of the sun and moon, and to associate with the whole heaven, and the whole universal world.

At that time, therefore, looking down from above, from the air, and straining the eye of my mind as from a watch-tower, I surveyed the unspeakable contemplation of all the things on the earth, and looked upon myself as happy as having forcibly escaped from all the evil fates that can attack human life. Nevertheless, the most grievous of all evils was lying in wait for me, namely, envy, that hates every thing that is good, and which, suddenly attacking me, did not cease from dragging me after it by force till it had taken me and thrown me into the vast sea of the cares of public politics, in which I was and still am tossed about without being able to keep myself swimming at the top. But though I groan at my fate, I still hold out and resist, retaining in my soul that desire of instruction which has been implanted in it from my earliest youth, and this desire taking pity and compassion on me continually raises me up and alleviates my sorrow. And it is through this fondness for learning that I at times lift up my head, and with the eyes of my soul, which are indeed dim (for the mist of affairs, wholly inconsistent with their proper objects, has overshadowed their acute clear-sightedness), still, as well as I may, I survey all the things around me, being eager to imbibe something of a life which shall be pure and unalloyed by evils.

And if at any time unexpectedly there shall arise a brief period of tranquillity, and a short calm and respite from the troubles which arise from state affairs, I then rise aloft and float above the troubled waves, soaring as it were in the air, and being, I may almost say, blown forward by the breezes of knowledge, which often persuades me to flee away, and to pass all my days with her, escaping as it were from my pitiless masters, not men only, but also affairs which pour upon me from all quarters and at all times like a torrent. But even in these circumstances I ought to give thanks to God, that though I am so overwhelmed by this flood, I am not wholly sunk and swallowed up in the depths. But I open the eyes of my soul, which from an utter despair of any good hope had been believed to have been before now wholly darkened, and I am irradiated with the light of wisdom, since I am not given up for the whole of my life to darkness. . . .

⌒∞⌒

from On Mating with the Preliminary Studies

I.

"But Sarah the wife of Abraham had not borne him any child. And she had an Egyptian handmaiden, who name was Hagar. And Sarah said unto Abraham, Behold, the Lord has closed me up, so that I should not bear children; go in unto my handmaiden that thou mayest have children by her." The name Sarah, being interpreted, means "my princedom." And the wisdom which is in me, and the temperance which is in me, and the particular justice, and each of the other virtues which belong to be alone, are the princedom of me alone. For such virtue, being a queen from its birth, rules over and governs me who have determined on obeying it.

Now this virtue, Moses (making a most paradoxical assertion) reports, as being both barren and also most prolific, since he affirms that the most populous of all nations is sprung from it. For, in real truth, virtue is barren with respect to all things which are evil, but is so exceedingly prolific of good things, that it stands in no need of the art of the midwife, for it anticipates it by bringing forth before its arrival. Therefore animals and plants, after considerable intervals and interruptions, bring forth their appropriate fruits, once, or at most twice a year; according to the number of times which nature has appointed each of them, and which is properly adapted to the seasons of the year. But virtue without any interruption, without any interval or any cessation, is continually bringing forth at all times and on all occasions, not indeed children, but virtuous reasonings, and irreproachable counsels, and praiseworthy actions.

II.

But neither is wealth, which it is not possible to employ, of any advantage to its possessors, nor is the fertility of wisdom of any service to us, unless it also brings forth such things as are serviceable to us. For some persons it judges to be in every respect worthy of living in its company; but others appear to have not yet arrived at such an age, as to be able to support so highly praised and well regulated a charge; whom, however, it permits to enter upon the preliminaries of marriage, holding out to them a hope that they may hereafter consummate the wedlock. Sarah therefore, the virtue which rules over my soul, has brought forth, but, she has not brought forth for me (for I should never as yet have been able, since I am quite young, to receive her offspring); she has brought forth, I say, wisdom, and the doing of just actions, and piety, by reason of the multitude of illegitimate children whom the vain opinions have brought forth to me. For the education of the offspring, and the constant superintendence and incessant care which they require, have compelled me to neglect the legitimate children, who are really citizens. It is well, therefore, to pray that virtue may not only bring forth, since she is prolific even without a prayer, but that she may bring for us; in order that we, receiving a share of her seed and of her offspring, may be happy. For she is accustomed to bring forth children to God alone, restoring with burning gratitude the first fruits of all the blessings which she has received, to him, who, as Moses says, "opened her womb," which was at all times virgin. For he also says that the lamp, that archetypal model after which the copy is made, shines in one part, that is to say, in the part which is turned towards God. For since that completes the number of seven, and stands in the middle of the six branches, which are divided into two lots of three each, acting as body-guards to it on either side, it sends its rays upwards toward that one being, namely God, thinking its light too brilliant for mortal sight to be able to stand its proximity.

III.

On this account he does not say that Sarah did not bring forth at all, but only that she did not bring forth for him, for Abraham. For we are not as yet capable of becoming the fathers of offspring of virtue, unless we first of all have a connection with her handmaiden; and the handmaiden of wisdom is the encyclical knowledge of music and logic, arrived at by previous instruction. For as in houses there are vestibules placed in front of staircases, and as in cities there are suburbs, through which one must pass in order to enter into the cities; so also the encyclical branches of instruction are placed in front of virtue, for they are the road which conducts to her. And as you must know that it is common for there to be great preludes to great propositions, and the greatest of all propositions is virtue, for it is conversant about the most important of all materials, namely, about the universal life of man; very naturally, therefore, that will not employ any short preface, but rather it will use as such, grammar, geometry, astronomy, rhetoric, music, and all the other sorts of contemplation which proceed in accordance with reason; of which Hagar, the handmaid of Sarah, is an emblem, as we will proceed to show.

"For Sarah," says Moses, "said unto Abraham, Behold, the Lord has closed me up, so that I may not bear children. Go in unto my handmaiden, that thou mayest have children by her." Now, we must take out of the present discussion those conjunctions and connections of body with body which have pleasure for their end. For this is the connection of the mind with virtue, which is desirous to have children by her, and which, if it cannot do so at once, is at all events taught to espouse her handmaid, namely, intermediate instruction.

IV.

And here it is worth while to admire wisdom, by reason of its modesty, which has not thought fit to reproach us with the slowness of our generation, or our absolute barrenness. And this, too, though the oracle says truly that she brought forth no child, not out of envy, but because of the unsuitableness of our own selves. For, says she, "The Lord has closed me up so, that I may not bear children." And she no longer adds the words, "to you," that she may not appear to mention the misfortunes of others, or to reproach them with theirs. "Therefore," says she, "go thou in to my handmaiden," that is to say, to the intermediate instruction of the intermediate and encyclical branches of knowledge, "that you may first have children by her"; for hereafter you shall be able to enjoy a connection with her mistress, tending to the procreation of legitimate children. For grammar, by teaching you the histories which are to be found in the works of poets and historians, will give you intelligence and abundant learning; and, moreover, will teach you to look with contempt on all the vain fables which erroneous opinions invent, on account of the ill success which history tells us that the heroes and demigods who are celebrated among those writers, meet with.

And music will teach what is harmonious in the way of rhythm, and what is ill arranged in harmony, and, rejecting all that is out of tune and all that is inconsistent with melody, will guide what was previously discordant to concord. And geometry, sowing the seeds of equality and just proportion in the soul, which is fond of learning, will, by means of the beauty of continued contemplation, implant in you an admiration of justice. And rhetoric, having sharpened the mind for contemplation in general, and having exercised and trained the faculties of speech in interpretations and explanations, will make man really rational, taking care of that peculiar and especial duty which nature has bestowed upon it, but upon no other animal whatever. And dialectic science, which is the sister, the twin sister of rhetoric, as some persons have called it, separating true from false arguments, and refuting the plausibilities of sophistical arguments, will cure the great disease of the soul, deceit.

It is profitable, therefore, to aide among these and other sciences resembling them, and to devote one's especial attention to them. For perhaps, I say, as has happened to many, we shall become known to the queenly virtues by means of their subjects and handmaidens. Do you not see that our bodies do not use solid and costly food before they have first, in their age of infancy, used such as had no variety, and consisted merely of milk? And, in the same way, think also that infantine food is prepared for the soul, namely the encyclical sciences, and the contemplations which are directed to each of them; but that the more perfect and becoming food, namely the virtues, is prepared for those who are really full-grown men.

V.

Now the first characteristics of the intermediate instruction are represented by two symbols, the race and the name. As to race, the handmaiden is an Egyptian, and her name is Hagar; and this name, being interpreted, means "emigration." For it follows of necessity that the man who delights in the encyclical contemplations, and who joins himself as a companion to varied learning, is as such enrolled under the banners of the earthly and

Egyptian body; and that he stands in need of eyes in order to see and to read, and of ears in order to attend and to hear, and of his other external senses, in such a manner as to be able to unfold each of the objects of the external sense. For it is not natural to suppose that the subject of judgment can possibly be comprehended without some power which is to judge; and the power which judges of the objects of the external sense is the external sense, so that without the external sense it would not be possible for any thing in that world which is perceptible by the external sense to be accurately known, though those are the matters which are the principal field for philosophical speculation.

But the external sense, being that portion of the soul which most resembles the body, is deeply rooted in the entire vessel of the soul; and the vessel of the soul is, by a figurative way of speaking, called Egypt. And there is one characteristic derived from her race, which the handmaiden of virtue possesses. But what or what kind of characteristic that is which is derived from the name, we must now proceed to consider.

The intermediate instruction has the same rank and classification as a sojourner. For all knowledge, and wisdom, and virtue, are the only real native and original inhabitants and citizens of the universe. And all the other kinds of instruction, which obtain the second, and third, and lowest honours, are on the confines, between foreigners and citizens. For they are not connected with either race without some alloy, and yet again they are not connected with both according to a certain community and participation. For they are sojourners from the fact of their passing their time among citizens; but from the fact of their not being settled inhabitants, they also resemble foreigners. In the same manner, according to my idea, as adopted children, inasmuch as they inherit the property of those who have adopted them, resemble real legitimate children; but inasmuch as they were not begotten by them, they resemble strangers. The same relation, then, that a mistress has to her handmaidens, or a wife, who is a citizen, to a concubine, that same relation has virtue, that is Sarah, to education, that is Hagar. So that very naturally, since the husband, by name Abraham, is one who has an admiration for contemplation and knowledge; virtue, that is Sarah, would be his wife, and Hagar, that is all kinds of encyclical accomplishments, would be his concubine. Whoever, therefore, has acquired wisdom from his teachers, would never reject Hagar. For the acquisition of all the preliminary branches of education is wholly necessary. . . .

❦

from On the Life of Moses
Book I

V.

But when the child began to grow and increase, he was weaned, not in accordance with the time of his age, but earlier than usual; and then his mother, who was also his nurse, came to bring him back to the princess who had given him to her, inasmuch as he no longer required to be fed on milk, and as he was now a fine and noble child to look upon. And when the king's daughter saw that he was more perfect than could have been expected at his age, and when from his appearance she conceived greater good will than ever towards him, she adopted him as her son, having first put in practice all sorts of contrivances to increase the apparent bulk of her belly, so that he might be looked upon as her own genuine child, and not as a supposititious one; but God easily brings to pass whatever he is inclined to effect, however difficult it may be to bring to a successful issue.

Therefore the child being now thought worthy of a royal education and a royal attendance, was not, like a mere child, long delighted with toys and objects of laughter and amusement, even though those who had undertaken the care of him allowed him holidays and times for relaxation, and never behaved in any stern or morose way to him; but he himself exhibited a modest and dignified deportment in all his words and gestures, attending diligently to every lesson of every kind which could tend to the improvement of his mind. And immediately he had all kinds of masters, one after another, some coming of their own accord from the neighbouring countries and the different districts of Egypt, and some being even procured from Greece by the temptation of large presents. But in a short time he surpassed all their knowledge, anticipating all their lessons by the excellent natural endowments of his own genius; so that everything in his case appeared to be a recollecting rather than a learning, while he himself also, without any teacher, comprehended by his instinctive genius many difficult subjects; for great abilities cut out for themselves many new roads to knowledge. And just as vigorous and healthy bodies which are active and quick in motion in all their parts, release their trainers from much care, giving them little or no trouble and anxiety, and as trees which are of a good sort, and which have a natural good growth, give no trouble to their cultivators, but grow finely and improve of themselves, so in the same manner the well disposed soul, going forward to meet the lessons which are imparted to it, is improved in reality by itself rather than by its teachers, and taking hold of some beginning or principle of knowledge, bounds, as the proverb has it, like a horse over the plain.

Accordingly he speedily learnt arithmetic, and geometry, and the whole science of rhythm and harmony and metre, and the whole of music, by means of the use of musical instruments, and by lectures on the different arts, and by explanations of each topic; and lessons on these subjects were given him by Egyptian philosophers, who also taught him the philosophy which is contained in symbols, which they exhibit in those sacred characters of hieroglyphics, as they are called, and also that philosophy which is conversant about that respect which they pay to animals which they invest with the honours due to God.

And all the other branches of the encyclical education he learnt from Greeks; and the philosophers from the adjacent countries taught him Assyrian literature and the knowledge of the heavenly bodies so much studied by the Chaldaeans. And this knowledge he derived also from the Egyptians, who study mathematics above all things, and he learnt with great accuracy the state of that art among both the Chaldaeans and Egyptians, making himself acquainted with the points in which they agree with and differ from each other—making himself master of all their disputes without encouraging any disputatious disposition in himself—but seeking the plain truth, since his mind was unable to admit any falsehood, as those are accustomed to do who contend violently for one particular side of a question; and who advocate any doctrine which is set before them, whatever it may be, not inquiring whether it deserves to be supported, but acting in the same manner as those lawyers who defend a cause for pay, and are wholly indifferent to the justice of their cause.

VI.

And when he had passed the boundaries of the age of infancy he began to exercise his intellect; not, as some people do, letting his youthful passions roam at large without restraint, although in him they had ten thousand incentives by reason of the abundant means for the gratification of them which royal places supply; but he behaved with temperance and fortitude, as though he had bound them with reins, and thus he restrained their onward impetuosity by force. And he tamed, and appeased, and brought under due command every one of the other passions which are naturally and as far as they are themselves concerned frantic, and violent, and unmanageable. And if any one of them at all excited itself and endeavoured to get free from restraint he administered severe punishment to it, reproving it with severity of language; and, in short, he repressed all the principal impulses and most violent affections of the soul, and kept guard over them as over a restive horse, fearing lest they might break all bounds and get beyond the power of reason which ought to be their guide to restrain them, and so throw everything everywhere into confusion.

For these passions are the causes of all good and of all evil; of good when they submit to the authority of dominant reason, and of evil when they break out of bounds and scorn all government and restraint.

Very naturally, therefore, those who associated with him and every one who was acquainted with him marvelled at him, being astonished as at a novel spectacle, and inquiring what kind of mind it was that had its abode in his body, and that was set up in it like an image in a shrine; whether it was a human mind or a divine intellect, or something combined of the two; because he had nothing in him resembling the many, but had gone beyond them all and was elevated to a more sublime height. For he never provided his stomach with any luxuries beyond those necessary tributes which nature has appointed to be paid to it, and as to the pleasures of the organs below the stomach he paid no attention to them at all, except as far as the object of having legitimate children was concerned.

And being in a most eminent degree a practiser of abstinence and self-denial, and being above all men inclined to ridicule a life of effeminacy and luxury (for he desired to live for his soul alone, and not for his body), he exhibited the doctrines of philosophy in all his daily actions, saying precisely what he thought, and performing such actions only as were consistent with his words, so as to exhibit a perfect harmony between his language and his life, so that as his words were such also was his life, and as his life was such likewise was his language, like people who are playing together in tune on a musical instrument.

Therefore men in general, even if the slightest breeze of prosperity does only blow their way for a moment, become puffed up and give themselves great airs, becoming insolent to all those who are in a lower condition than themselves, and calling them dregs of the earth, and annoyances, and sources of trouble, and burdens of the earth, and all sorts of names of that kind, as if they had been thoroughly able to establish the undeviating character of their prosperity on a solid foundation, though, very likely, they will not remain in the same condition even till tomorrow, for there is nothing more inconstant than fortune, which tosses human affairs up and down like dice. Often has a single day thrown down the man who was previously placed on an eminence, and raised the lowly man on high. And while men see these events continually taking place, and though they are well assured of the fact, still they overlook their relations and friends, and transgress the laws according to which they were born and brought up; and they overturn their national hereditary customs to which no just blame whatever is attached; dwelling in a foreign land, and by reason of their cordial reception of the customs among which they are living, no longer remembering a single one of their ancient usages.

Clement of Alexandria

c. 150–215

But our Educator is the holy God, Jesus, the Word guiding all mankind.

CHRIST THE EDUCATOR

ↄ◈ↄ

Few details are known about the life and career of Titus Flavius Clement. He may have been born in Athens and raised a pagan. He came to Alexandria in 180 and studied under the Christian Stoic Pantaenus. Famous for its library and university, and as home to the astronomer Ptolemy, Alexandria flourished as an intellectual center for Platonists, Aristotelians, Stoics, and later Christians and Gnostics. Philo of Alexandria's own attempt to synthesize Judaism and Platonism may have served as a model for the later project to reconcile Christianity and the wisdom of the Greeks. Clement headed the city's famous catechetical school, which prepared men and women for church membership, among them his brightest student, Origen. In his fifties, Clement left Alexandria (perhaps fleeing local persecution during the reign of Emperor Septimius Severus) and reportedly traveled to Jerusalem and Antioch, where he earned the respect of church leaders.

Clement promoted an early Christian humanism that married Christianity and liberal education. The Church historian Eusebius records that "Clement was noted in Alexandria for his patient study of Holy Scriptures."[1] But Clement also read widely in the poets and philosophers. In fact, his writings cite hundreds of classical authors. He marked out what could be called a "maximalist" position for the integration of Christian faith and

---

1. *Ecclesiastical History*, V.1, 1..

pagan knowledge; he saw all truth as one regardless of its source. But the proper limits of this compatibility continued (and continue) to be controversial. Christians debated whether their children ought to attend pagan schools for a classical humanist education; whether Christian adults ought to teach in these schools; whether the Church ought to found its own academies; and whether pagan poets and philosophers could possibly be "baptized" for the church's use. Tertullian, the fiery apologist of the Western church, had famously asked, "What has Athens to do with Jerusalem?" And the early *Didascalia Apostolorum* directed the faithful to "abstain from all the heathen books" and look only to Scripture for instruction in history, literature, and law. Clement, though, placed so much emphasis on enlightenment and secret knowledge that he veered dangerously close to the Gnostics, heretics whom he in fact rebuked. He remained a troubling figure for the early church as it struggled to embrace his contributions while guarding itself against the excesses of his enthusiasm for worldly learning.

THE SELECTIONS

In the three books of *Christ the Educator (The Pedagogue)*, Clement uses the metaphor of the pedagogue as a powerful image for Christ. In Clement's hands, the humble Greek or Roman pedagogue—a slave hired to conduct a child safely to school each day and guard his morals—is transformed into a master teacher. The apostle Paul provided the precedent for this adaptation; he spoke of children's "*paideia* in the Lord" (Ephesians 6:4), of God's word as a "*paideia* in righteousness" (II Timothy 3:16), and of the Old Testament law as a faithful *paidagogos* leading men to Christ (Galatians 3:24). Clement of Rome, a church leader of the late first century, also referred to "*paideia* in Christ" in his letter to the Corinthian church.[2] Similarly, for Clement of Alexandria, Christianity is the true *paedeia*, and Christ is the ultimate Pedagogue. In the selection that follows, the Greek word *paidagogos* is translated as "educator," but it is helpful to keep in mind the fuller image of leading, shepherding, and conducting from one place to another.

The three books of the *Stromateis* (or *Miscellanies*) are a patchwork of reflections on the right relationship between Christianity and Greek culture. Clement argues that philosophy was a preparation for the Gospel in the way that the law of God had been a preparation for Christ (Galatians 3:24).

from Christ the Educator
Book One

CHAPTER 1

O you who are children! An indestructible corner stone of knowledge, holy temple of the great God, has been hewn out especially for us as a foundation for the truth. This corner

---

2. See Arthur F. Holmes, *Building the Christian Academy* (Grand Rapids, MI: William B. Eerdmans, 2001), 16.

stone is noble persuasion, or the desire for eternal life aroused by an intelligent response to it, laid in the ground of our minds.

For, be it noted, there are these three things in man: habits, deeds, and passions. Of these, habits come under the influence of the word of persuasion, the guide to godliness. This is the word that underlies and supports, like the keel of a ship, the whole structure of the faith. Under its spell, we surrender, even cheerfully, our old ideas, become young again to gain salvation, and sing in the inspired words of the psalm: "How good is God to Israel, to those who are upright of heart." As for deeds, they are affected by the word of counsel, and passions are healed by that of consolation.

These three words, however, are but one: the self-same Word who forcibly draws men from their natural, worldly way of life and educates them to the only true salvation: faith in God. That is to say, the heavenly Guide, the Word, once He begins to call men to salvation, takes to Himself the name of persuasion (this sort of appeal, although only one type, is properly given the name of the whole, that is, word, since the whole service of God has a persuasive appeal, instilling in a receptive mind the desire for life now and for the life to come); but the Word also heals and counsels, all at the same time. In fact, He follows up His own activity by encouraging the one He has already persuaded, and particularly by offering a cure for his passions.

Let us call Him, then, by the one title: Educator of little ones, an Educator who does not simply follow behind, but who leads the way, for His aim is to improve the soul, not just to instruct it; to guide to a life of virtue, not merely to one of knowledge. Yet, that same Word does teach. It is simply that in this work we are not considering Him in that light. As Teacher, He explains and reveals through instruction, but as Educator He is practical. First He persuades men to form habits of life, then He encourages them to fulfill their duties by laying down clear-cut counsels and by holding up, for us who follow, examples of those who have erred in the past. Both are most useful: the advice, that it may be obeyed; the other, given in the form of example, has a twofold object—either that we may choose the good and imitate it or condemn and avoid the bad.

Healing of the passions follows as a consequence. The Educator strengthens souls with the persuasion implied in these examples, and then He gives the nourishing, mild medicine, so to speak, of His loving counsels to the sick man that he may come to a full knowledge of the truth. Health and knowledge are not the same; one is a result of study, the other of healing. In fact, if a person is sick, he cannot master any of the things taught him until he is first completely cured. We give instructions to someone who is sick for an entirely different reason than we do to someone who is learning; the latter, we instruct that he may acquire knowledge, the first, that he may regain health. Just as our body needs a physician when it is sick, so, too, when we are weak, our soul needs the Educator to cure its ills. Only then does it need the Teacher to guide it and develop its capacity to know, once it is made pure and capable of retaining the revelation of the Word.

Therefore, the all-loving Word, anxious to perfect us in a way that leads progressively to salvation, makes effective use of an order well adapted to our development; at first, He persuades, then He educates, and after all this He teaches.

CHAPTER 7

We have now shown that not only does Scripture call all of us children, but also it figuratively calls us who follow Christ, little ones, and that the only perfect being is the Father of all (in fact, the Son is in Him, and the Father is in the Son). If we would follow right order, we should now speak of the Educator of little ones and explain who He is.

He is called Jesus. On occasion, He speaks of Himself as a Shepherd, as when He says: "I am the Good Shepherd." In keeping with this metaphor of shepherds leading their sheep, He leads His children, the Shepherd with the care of His little ones. The little ones, in their simplicity, are given the figurative name of sheep; "And there shall be one sheepfold," He says, "and one Shepherd."

Therefore, the Word who leads us His children to salvation is unquestionably an Educator of little ones. In fact, through Osee [Hosea], the Word says plainly of Himself: "I am your Educator." The material He educates us in is fear of God, for this fear instructs us in the service of God, educates to the knowledge of truth, and guides by a path leading straight up to heaven.

Education is a word used in many different senses: There is education in the sense of the one who is being led and instructed; there is that of the one who leads and gives instruction; and thirdly, there is education in the sense of the guidance itself; and finally, the things that are taught, such as precepts. The education that God gives is the imparting of the truth that will guide us correctly to the contemplation of God, and a description of holy deeds that endure forever. Just as the general directs a line of battle with the safety of his soldiers in mind, and as the helmsman pilots his ship conscious of his responsibility for the lives of his passengers, so the Educator, in his concern for us, leads His children along a way of life that ensures salvation. In brief, all that we could reasonably ask God to do for us is within the reach of those who trust in the Educator of little ones. Again, just as the helmsman does not always sail with the wind, but sometimes when there is a squall, sets his prow head on against it, so, too, the Educator never falls in with the winds sweeping through this world, nor does He suffer His children to be driven like a ship into a wild and unregulated course of life. Rather, assisted only by the favorable breeze of the Spirit of truth, He holds steadfastly to the rudder, that is, the hearing of His children, until He brings them safely to anchor in the port of heaven.

The habits that men speak of as hereditary, for the most part pass away, but the education God gives is a possession that endures forever. It is related how Phenix was the pedagogue of Achilles; Adrastrus, of the sons of Croesus; Leonides, of Alexander; and Nausithoon, of Philip. Yet one of them, Phenix, was mad with lust; another, Adrastrus, was a fugitive; Leonides did not rid his Macedonian pupil of his vanity, and Nausithoon did not cure the Pellean of his drunkenness. Again, the Thracian Zoporus was unable to restrain Alcibiades from immorality, and, besides, he was a bought slave. The pedagogue of the children of Themistocles, Sicinnos, was a spineless menial. The story goes that he used to dance and invented the dance step called the Sicinnis. We must not forget, either, the so-called royal pedagogues of the Persian court, four in number, whom the Persian kings chose from all the Persians according to merit and set over their children; but the children learned only how to use the bow and arrow, and once they come of age begin to have intercourse with sister and mother, with married women and others without number, like wild boars well-practised in sexual indulgence.

But our Educator is the holy God, Jesus, the Word guiding all mankind. God Himself, in His love for men, is our Educator. The Holy Spirit says about Him somewhere in a canticle: "He founded the people in a desert land, in a drought of burning heat, in a place without water: He encircled him and taught him: and He kept him as the apple of His eye. As an eagle might shelter its brood, and yearn after its young, and having flown about, show them its wings and take them upon its shoulders. The Lord alone was their leader, and there was no strange god with them." As far as I can see, Scripture is undoubtedly presenting a picture of the Educator of children, and describing the guidance He imparts. When He speaks in His own person, He also confesses Himself to be the Educator: "I am the Lord thy God, who brought thee out of the land of Egypt." But who has the authority to lead in or out? Is it not the Educator? It is He who appeared to Abraham and said to him: "I am your God: be pleasing before Me." He fashioned Moses by a gradual process into a worthy child, truly as an educator would, commanding him: "Be without blame. And I will establish My covenant between Me and your descendants." Here is a share, indeed, in friendship that is undying.

He manifests Himself plainly as the Educator of Jacob, too. For example, He said to him: "I will be with you and protect you wherever you go. I will bring you back to this land; indeed I will not forsake you till I fulfill My promise" to you. He is also said to have wrestled with him: "Jacob remained behind, all alone. Someone wrestled with him," that is, the Educator, "until the break of dawn." This is the Man who leads and who carries, He who wrestled with Jacob and anointed him for his toil as an athlete. But because the Word was not only the wrestling Master of Jacob, but also the Educator of all mankind, when Jacob asked, as Scripture says, "What is your name?" He answered: "Why do you ask My name?" He was saving His new name for His new people, the little ones. The Lord God still remained without a name, since He had not yet become man. However, "Jacob named the place Phanuel, saying: I have seen a heavenly being face to face, yet my life has been saved." The face of God is the Word, for God is revealed by Him and made known. Jacob also received the name Israel from the time that he had seen the Lord. It was God the Word, the Educator, who said to him on another occasion: "Do not fear to go down to Egypt." See how the Educator follows a just man, anoints the athlete, and teaches him how to overcome his adversary.

It was He who taught Moses also to act the part of educator. For the Lord said: "He that hath sinned against Me, him will I strike out of My book: but go there, and lead the people whither I have told thee." In this passage, He teaches him the art of educating. And well He might, for it was through Moses, in fact, that the Lord of the ancient people was the Educator of His children. It is in His own person, however, face to face, that He is the guide of the new people.

He said to Moses: "Behold, My angel shall go before thee," to establish the Gospel and the authority of the Word to guide; and then, adhering to His own divine decree, He adds: "On the day I shall visit, I shall bring down on them their sin," that is, on the day I shall sit as Judge, I shall mete out the punishments due to sin. He passes sentence on those who disobey Him, both as Educator and as Judge; the Word, with all His love for man, does not pass over their sin in silence, but punishes that they may repent. "The Lord, indeed, desires the conversion of the sinner more than his death." Let us little ones, then, attending to the story of the sins of others, refrain from like offenses, from fear of the threat of suffering like punishment. What sin did they commit? "In their fury, they slew men, and in their willfulness, they hamstrung oxen. Cursed be their fury."

Who could teach with greater love for men than He? In other times, the older people had an old Covenant: as law, it guided them through fear; as word, it was a messenger. But the new and young people have received a new and young Covenant: the Word has become flesh, fear has been turned into love, and the mystic messenger of old has been born, Jesus. Of old, this same Educator proclaimed: "Thou shalt fear the Lord, thy God." But to us He appeals: "Thou shalt love the Lord thy God." And so He gives command: "Cease from thy deeds," that is, your old sins, "and learn to do well; turn away from evil and do good. Thou hast loved justice and hated iniquity." This is My new Covenant, written with the letters of the old.

But the newness of the Word does not at all lessen respect due Him. The Lord says through Jeremias: "Say not, I am a child. Before I formed thee in the bowel of thy mother, I knew thee: and before thou camest forth out of the womb, I sanctified thee." In this passage, possibly the inspired Word refers to us who before the foundation of the world have been destined by God for the faith, and now, by the will of God just being fulfilled, are little ones, in that we have become newborn into the calling and into salvation. For that reason, Scripture adds these words: "I have made thee a prophet unto the nations," meaning that he must needs begin to prophesy and that the name "young" ought not to seem a reproach to those who are called little ones.

The Law is the old gift bestowed by the Word through Moses. So Scripture says: "The law has been given through Moses" (not by Moses, but by the Word through Moses His servant; and at that, given only for a time), "but everlasting grace and truth was through Jesus Christ." Notice the wording of Scripture: in speaking of the Law, it says it was only given, but the truth, being the gift of the Father, is the eternal achievement of the Word, and so is no longer said to be given, but rather "was, through Jesus Christ, without whom was made nothing."

For his part, Moses made way for the perfect Educator, the Word, prophesying both His name and His method of educating, and placed Him in charge of the people with the command to obey Him. He said: "God will raise up to thee a prophet of thy brethren like unto me," meaning Jesus, son of Naim, but implying Jesus, the Son of God. That name, Jesus, already predicted in the law, described the Lord, for Moses, taking thought for the best interests of the people, said: "Him thou shalt hear: and he that will not hear this prophet, him He threatens." The name that He has tells us by divine inspiration that the Educator will save. It is for this reason that the Scripture associates Him with a rod that suggests correction, government and sovereignty. Scripture seems to be suggesting that those whom the Word does not heal through persuasion He will heal with threats; and those whom threats do not heal the rod will; and those whom the rod does not heal fire will consume. "And there shall come forth," it is said, "a rod out of the root of Jesse."

Consider the carefulness and the wisdom and the power of this Educator: "He shall not judge according to appearance, nor reprove according to gossip, but He shall judge judgment with humility, and shall reprove the sinners of the earth." And through the lips of David, He says: "The Lord chastising has chastised me, but He hath not delivered me over to death." Indeed, the very act of being chastised, and being educated by the Lord as a child, means deliverance from death. Again, He says through the same Psalmist: "Thou shalt rule them with a rod of iron." Similarly, the Apostle exclaimed when he was aroused by the Corinthians: "What is your wish? Shall I come to you with a rod, or in love and in the spirit of meekness?" By another Psalmist, the Lord says again: "The Lord will send forth the rod of power out of Sion." This "rod and staff of Thine," bespeaking education, "they have comforted me," another says.

Such, then, is the authority wielded by the Educator of children, awe-inspiring, consoling, leading us to salvation.

from the Stromateis
Book One

5. Philosophy, a Preparatory Science for Christianity

So, before the Lord's coming, philosophy was an essential guide to righteousness for the Greeks. At the present time, it is a useful guide towards reverence for God. It is a kind of preliminary education for those who are trying to gather faith through demonstration. "Your foot will not stumble," says Scripture, if you attribute good things, whether Greek or Christian, to Providence. God is responsible for all good things: of some, like the blessings of the Old and New Covenants, directly; of others, like the riches of philosophy, indirectly. Perhaps philosophy too was a direct gift of God to the Greeks before the Lord extended his appeal to the Greeks. For philosophy was to the Greek world what the Law was to the Hebrews, a tutor escorting them to Christ. So philosophy is a preparatory process; it opens the road for the person whom Christ brings to his final goal. Solomon says, "Surround Wisdom with a stockade, and she will exalt you; she will shield you with a rich crown," since once you have fortified her with a fence by means of the true riches of philosophy, you will keep her inaccessible to the sophists. . . .

6. Philosophy Is Excellent Training

Our readiness to see what we ought to see is largely due to this preliminary training. This training must be in perceiving intelligible objects with the mind. Their nature is of three kinds, considered in number, size, and definition. Definition on the basis of demonstrations implants in the soul of one who follows the argument a faith which is precise and incapable of coming to any other conclusion about the subject of the demonstration; such a definition does not allow us to succumb to those who seek to deceive and undermine us. In the course of these studies, the soul is purified from its sense perceptions and rekindled with the power of discerning the truth. "For the preservation of a good diet of education forms virtuous natures, and those naturally excellent latch on to education of this sort and grow even better than they were before, particularly in the production of offspring, as with the rest of the animal creation." That is why Scripture says, "Go to the ant, you sluggard, and become wiser than he." The ant at the time of harvest lays up an ample and varied store of food against the threat of winter. "Or go to the bee and learn her diligence." For she feeds over the whole meadow to produce a single honeycomb.

If you pray in your inner room, as the Lord taught, in a spirit of adoration, then your domestic economy would no longer be confined to your domicile, but would extend to your soul. What should it feed on? How? In what quantity? What should we store in its treasury? When should these treasures be produced? For whom? Those who live by virtue emerge, not naturally but by education, like doctors or pilots. We all alike can see a vine or a horse. Only the cultivator will know whether the vine is good for bearing grapes or not; only the groom will readily distinguish a sluggish from a speedy horse. Admittedly some people are naturally more inclined to virtue than others; this is shown by the practices of those so endowed compared with the rest. But this by no means proves perfection in virtue on the part of those better endowed, since those less inclined to virtue by nature have been known through the enjoyment of appropriate education to achieve personal excellence in every regard, and again by contrast, those favorably endowed become wicked through neglect. God has created us sociable and righteous by nature.

It follows that we may not say that righteousness appears simply by a divine dispensation. We are to understand that the good of creation is rekindled by the commandment, when the soul learns by instruction to be willing to choose the highest. But just as we say that it is possible to have faith without being literate, so we assert that it is not possible to understand the statements contained in the faith without study. To assimilate the right affirmations and reject the rest is not the product of simple faith, but of faith engaged in learning. Ignorance involves a lack of education and learning. It is teaching which implants in us the scientific knowledge of things divine and human. It is possible to live uprightly in poverty. It is also possible in wealth. We admit that it is easier and quicker to track down virtue if we have a preliminary education. It can be hunted down without these aids, although even then those with learning, "with their faculties trained by practice," have an advantage. "Hatred," says Solomon, "stirs up strife, but education guards the paths of life." There is no possibility of being deceived or kidnapped by those who engage in evil artifices to injure their listeners. "Education without refutation goes astray," he says. We must claim our share in the pattern of refutation in order to repress the false views of the sophists.

Anaxarchus the Eudaemonist wrote well in his book *On Sovereignty*: "Wide learning is both of great advantage and great disadvantage to its possessor. It benefits the person of skill, it damages the person who lightly says anything in any company. You must know the limits of the appropriate moment. That is the definition of wisdom. Those who make speeches at the wrong moment, even if they are full of sense, are not counted wise and have a reputation for folly." Hesiod too says,

> The Muses who make one rich in thoughts,
> inspired, vocal.

By "rich in thoughts" he means one who is fluent in the use of words; by "inspired" and "vocal" he means one who is skilled, wise, and knowing of truth.

9. Faith Grounded in Reason Is Preferable to Simple Faith

There are some people who imagine they are fully equipped by nature, and do not consider it right to have anything to do with philosophy or dialectic—more, they refuse to engage in the consideration of the natural world at all. All they ask for is simply and solely faith. It is as if they expected to gather grapes from the very first without taking any care of the vine. The vine is allegorically the Lord. From him, with care and an agricultural skill that follows the Word, we can harvest the fruit. We have to prune, dig, fasten, and all the rest. We need the pruning-knife, the mattock, and all the other tools of agriculture for the care of the vine, if we want it to produce edible fruit for us. In farming or medicine, the expert is the person who has grasped a wide variety of lessons to enable him to become a better farmer or doctor. So here I affirm that the expert is the one who brings everything to bear on the truth. He culls whatever is useful from mathematics, the fine arts, literary studies, and, of course, philosophy, and protects the faith from all attacks. No one bothers about the athlete whose only contribution to the community is his physical strength.

We approve of the sea-captain who has had plenty of experience and has visited "the cities of many peoples," and the doctor who has treated many patients. This is how some people form the idea of "the empirical doctor." Anyone who brings every experience to bear on right action, taking models from Greeks and non-Greeks alike, is a highly skilled hunter of truth. He really is "many-wiled." Like the testing stone (a stone from Lydia that was believed to distinguish genuine from false gold), our "man of many skills," our Christian Gnostic, is also competent to distinguish sophistry from philosophy, superficial adornment from athletics, cookery from pharmacy, rhetoric from dialectic, and then in Christian thought, heresies from the actual truth. The person who yearns to touch the fringes of God's power must of necessity become a philosopher to have a proper conception about intellectual objects. He must be able also to distinguish the ambiguities and nominally similar terms in the two Testaments. It is in fact by an ambiguity that the Lord outwits the devil at the time of the temptation, and I no longer understand how the inventor of philosophy and dialectic can be deceived by the method of ambiguity and led astray, as some people suppose.

Admittedly the prophets and apostles had no knowledge of the techniques which clarify philosophical exercises. The intelligence of the Spirit of prophecy and instruction speaks obscurely because everyone does not have the capacity to listen with understanding; for clarity it demands the techniques of teaching. The prophets and the Spirit's disciples have learned to know this intelligence without stumbling. For by faith they realized that the Spirit did not speak simply and that it was impossible to receive its words in their true sense without a period of learning. Scripture says, "Write my commandments twice, according to your wishes and your true knowledge, so as to answer words of truth to those who pose you questions." What is the true knowledge of answering questions? The same as the true knowledge of asking questions. This is of course dialectic. Well then. Is not speech an action? Does action not arise from speech? If we are not acting according to the rational Word, we would be acting irrationally. The action in accordance with the rational Word is brought to fulfillment in accord with God. "And nothing came into being without him," says Scripture of the Word of God. Did the Lord not do everything by his Word? Animals work when they are driven by pressure of fear. Are we not to say that the so-called orthodox are drawn to good works without knowing what they are doing?

13. GREEK AND NON-GREEK PHILOSOPHIES CONTAIN GERMS OF THE TRUTH

Truth is one. Error has countless ways of going astray. The philosophic sects, whether Greek or not, are like the Maenads scattering the limbs of Pentheus, each boasting their own limited claim as the whole truth. Everything is illuminated when the true light rises. So all who stretched out towards the truth, Greeks and non-Greeks alike, could be shown to possess some portion of the Word of Truth—some a considerable part, others a fraction, as it falls out. Eternity holds together in a single moment the whole of time: future, present, and past as well. But truth is far more potent than eternity in bringing together its own seeds, even if they have fallen into alien soil. We could discover that very many of the opinions voiced among the sects (those that have not been rendered totally deafened or cut off from following nature, so that they cut off Christ's head as the pack of women did with the man), even if they seem mutually inconsistent, do in fact accord with their own kind and with truth in general. They follow one another to make a whole, like members of a body, parts of a total, species, or genus. The high note is opposed to the low note, but both form a single chord. In numbers, odd and even are different, but both form an integral part of arithmetic, just as circle, triangle, rectangle, and other figures differ from one another in form. In the universe too, all the parts, even if they differ from one another, preserve a family relationship to the whole. So in the same way, philosophy, Greek and non-Greek, has made of eternal truth a kind of dismembering, not in the legends of Dionysus but in the theological understanding of the eternal Word. If anyone brings together the scattered limbs into a unity, you can be quite sure without risk of error that he will gaze on the Word in his fullness, the Truth.

It is written in Ecclesiastes: "I have wisdom above all those who were in Jerusalem before me, and my heart has had great experience of wisdom and revealed knowledge. I have come to know allegorical and scientific knowledge. This is the choice of the Spirit, since in copious wisdom there is copious true knowledge." Anyone skilled in all aspects of wisdom is a Christian Gnostic in the full sense of the word. Again it is written: "The advantage of the knowledge of wisdom is that it gives life to the person who has it." Again, here is a quotation to give clearer confirmation to my words: "All this is accessible to those who have intelligence" ("all" means both Greek and non-Greek, since one without the other would no longer be all), "as is clear to those who are willing to acquire perceptivity. Prefer my instruction to silver, and revealed knowledge to tested gold; prefer perceptivity to pure gold. For Wisdom is better than precious stones; all the objects you value cannot compare with her."

19. THE GREEK PHILOSOPHERS ATTAINED PARTIAL TRUTH

So there is evidence that the Greeks too hold some true doctrines. There are other grounds too from which this can be seen. Paul in the *Acts of the Apostles* is recorded as addressing the people on the Areopagus: "I observe that you are somewhat religious. As I passed through investigating your objects of worship, I found an altar on which was inscribed TO AN UNKNOWN GOD. I am proclaiming to you the god you worship in ignorance. The god who made the world and everything in it is Lord of heaven and earth, and does not live in temples built by human hands. He does not need anything, to be served by human hands. He gives to all life, breath, and all else. He has made every race of human beings to live on all the face of the earth. He has set prescribed times and boundaries to their lives, for them to seek the divine in the hope of feeling for him or finding him. And yet he is not far from each one of us. We live and move and exist in him, as some of your own poets have said: 'For we are in fact his family.'" From this it is clear that by using poetic examples from the *Phaenomena* of Aratus he approves the best statements of the Greeks. Besides, he refers to the fact that in the person of the unknown god the Greeks are indirectly honoring God the creator, and need to receive him and learn about him with full knowledge through the Son.

"I sent you to the gentiles for this purpose," says Scripture, "to open their eyes, for them to turn from darkness to light and from the power of Satan to God, for them to receive release from sins and an inheritance among those who are sanctified by faith in me." So these are "the opened eyes of the blind," which means the clear knowledge of the Father through the Son, the direct grasp of the thing to which the Greeks indirectly allude. "To turn from the power of Satan" means to go right away from sin, the source of their slavery. However, we do not accept every form of philosophy without qualification, only that about which Socrates speaks in the pages of Plato: "As they say in the mysteries, 'Many carry the thyrsus, few become Bacchants,'" alluding to the fact that many are called but few chosen. Anyway, he makes it clear when he adds, "These last are to my way of thinking simply those who have practiced philosophy properly. So far as I could in my whole life, I never neglected these people, but made every effort to be of their number. Whether I really did make an effort and achieved something, I shall know for sure a little later, when I reach my destination, God willing."

Do you not think that he has been convinced out of the Hebrew Scriptures to show this clear hope in justice after death? Again in the *Demodocus* (if it is an authentic work of Plato) he says, "Do not imagine philosophy is spending one's life stooped over practical skills or in the pursuit of wide erudition. No; that is in my view a scandal." I suppose he knew with Heraclitus the truth: "Much learning does not teach intelligence." In the fifth book of the *Republic* he says,—"'Are we to rank as philosophers all these and others engaged in similar studies and those concerned with minor practical skills?' 'No,' I replied, 'only caricatures of philosophers.' 'Whom do you call the true philosophers?' he asked. 'Those whose joy is in the contemplation of truth,' I responded." For philosophy does not consist in geometry with its postulates and hypotheses, or in music, which operates by approximation, or in astronomy which is stuffed full of arguments which have to do with physical nature, arguments which are fluid and depend on probability. Philosophy operates through knowledge of the Good in its own being, and through the truth, which are not identical with the Good, but more like paths to it. Socrates does not grant that the educational curriculum finds its outcome in the Good either; it rather contributes to the soul's awakening and its practice in the direction of intelligible objects.

So if people say that it was by accident that the Greeks delivered a slice of true philosophy, the accident was a part of the divine dispensation (no one is going to deify Spontaneity out of regard for us); but if it was by coincidence, the coincidence was governed by Providence. Again, if anyone were to say that the Greeks have grasped an innate notion of nature, nature is the work of a single creator, as we know, just as we have declared righteousness natural. If it is said that they possess only the common human mind, let us consider who is the father of that common human mind and of the righteousness that accords with its widespread existence. If anyone speaks of a gift of prediction or lays the responsibility on telepathy, he is talking about forms of prophecy. Yes, and others claim that the philosophers made some statements to reflect the truth. The divine Apostle writes of us: "At present we see as in a mirror." We know ourselves by reflection from it. We contemplate, so far as we may, the creative cause on the basis of the divine element in us. It is written: "You have seen your brother; you have seen your God." I think it is the Savior who has now at last been named to us as God. But after we have got rid of our flesh it will be "face to face," definitively, with a firm grasp, once our heart is pure. Those among the Greeks with the most precise grasp of philosophy discern God through a reflection or through a transparent medium. Such are the images of truth our weakness admits, like an image perceived in water or seen through transparent or translucent bodies. . . .

20. PHILOSOPHY'S CONTRIBUTION TO THE ATTAINMENT OF TRUTH

When a crew of men haul on their boat, we do not say that they constitute a large number of causes. There is one cause comprising several elements. Each individual is not the cause of the boat's being hauled except in cooperation with the others. In the same way, philosophy makes a contribution to grasping the truth—it is a search for truth. It is not of itself the cause of the grasp. It is a contributory cause together with the others, though perhaps a contributory cause is a cause of sorts. Blessedness is a single thing; its causes, the virtues, are multiple. Warmth is produced by sun, fire, baths, clothes. In the same way, truth is one; there are many contributory factors to its investigation; its discovery depends on the Son. Consider this: virtue is single in power, but the fact is that when it is realized in one form of action it is called practical wisdom, in another, disciplined moderation, in others, courage or justice. So by analogy, truth is one, but there is a truth of geometry found in geometry, of music in music; there is no reason why there should not be a Greek truth in the best philosophy. But it is only this unreachable sovereign truth in which we are educated by God's Son.

It is in this way that when one and the same coin is given to a sea-captain we speak of money to pay for passage, to a tax-collector, tax, to the property owner, rent, to the teacher, tuition, to the salesperson, deposit. Each virtue, each truth, while carrying a common name, is responsible solely for the result that accords with its character. A life of blessedness results from a blend of these (Do not imagine that blessedness depends on words!), when we apply the word "blessed" to an upright life and to the person who has ordered his soul in accordance with virtue. Even if philosophy contributes from a distance to the discovery of truth, as it reaches out with different efforts towards a knowledge that is closely linked to such truth as lies in our scope, still it is a genuine contribution for the person who is committed to the effort to grasp true knowledge with the help of the Logos. The truth vouchsafed to the Greeks is not the same as ours, even if it does share the same name; it is separated by the grandeur of revealed knowledge, by more authoritative demonstration, by divine power, and so on. We are "Godtaught." We have been educated in a course which is really holy by God's Son. The Greeks do not develop their souls in the same way at all; their process of learning is different.

Captiousness may require us to go on making distinctions. In saying that philosophy is a joint and contributory cause to the grasp of truth, because it is a search for truth, we shall be accepting it as a kind of preparatory education for the Christian Gnostic. We do not regard a joint cause as a simple cause or a contributory cause as having a comprehensive grasp of its object. We do not regard philosophy as a *sine qua non*. Almost all of us, without going through the full curriculum of Greek philosophy, sometimes even without literacy, under the impulse of non-Greek philosophy coming from God, have "in power" grasped through faith the teaching about God. Our education was under the sole charge of Wisdom. Anything which operates in conjunction with something else and is incapable of achieving results on its own, is termed a conjoint and contributory cause from the fact that its causality is shared with another cause, or because it receives the name of cause only when it comes together with something else, and of itself is incapable of producing results which accord with truth. And yet philosophy on its own did bring the Greeks to righteousness, though not to perfect righteousness (we have seen it as a contributor to this, rather as the first two steps make a contribution to a prospective ascent to the loft or the elementary teacher to the prospective philosopher). It does not mean that its removal entails any elimination or destruction of the truth for the universal Word, since sight, hearing, and speech contribute to truth, but it is mind alone that recognizes it. The contributory causes vary in their efficacity. Clarity contributes to the transmission of truth, dialectic to escaping from the attacks of the heresies.

The Savior's teaching is sufficient without additional help, for it is "the power and wisdom of God." The addition of Greek philosophy does not add more power to the truth; it reduces the power of the sophistic attack on it. It turns aside the treacherous assaults on truth, and is rightly called the wall of defense for the vine. Truth following faith is as essential to life as bread. The preliminary education is like a savory accompaniment or dessert.

> At the end of a meal a rich dessert,

says the Theban poet Pindar. Scripture declares outright: "The innocent man will be more ready for anything if he keeps me company; the wise man will receive knowledge." Also the Lord says, "Anyone who speaks on his own authority is seeking his own glory. Anyone who is seeking the glory of the one who sent him is true; there is no unrighteousness in him." Once again, it is dishonest to appropriate ideas from foreign people and proudly put them forward as one's own, puffing up one's own reputation and playing false with the truth. This is the person whom Scripture calls "robber." At least it is said, "My son, do not tell lies; lies lead to theft." The robber really does hold what he holds as a result of theft, whether it be gold, or silver, or ideas, or doctrines. There is partial truth within their stolen material, but their knowledge of it is guesswork, entangled in chains of logic. It follows that with proper instruction they will have a firm grasp of knowledge.

Origen

c. 185–250

*Extract from the philosophy of the Greeks what may serve as a
course of study or a preparation for Christianity.*

"A Letter from Origen to Gregory, Bishop of Caesarea"

Origen was raised by Christian parents in Alexandria and educated by his father and Clement of Alexandria. He studied the Scriptures along with Greek literature and philosophy. His father was killed during the persecution of the church under the emperor Severus, and the young Origen longed for his own martyrdom. A brilliant young scholar, Origen was appointed to be head of the celebrated catechetical school when he was only seventeen or eighteen. He led an ascetic life of severe self-denial, dedicating himself to his studies and to his students. From an early age, he was drawn to an allegorical interpretation of Scripture and wrote numerous commentaries and apologetical works. After a dispute with the bishop of Alexandria, he was banished from Alexandria and departed to found a school at Caesarea in Palestine. Gregory Thaumaturgus (c. 205–c. 270) was converted by Origen and studied with him there in Caesarea. Origen suffered imprisonment and torture under the persecution of the emperor Decius and died within a few years of his release. His unorthodox views of creation, the human soul, and redemption led several synods and a church council to condemn him as a heretic. The historian Eusebius gives a detailed account of Origen's life in his *Ecclesiatical History* (Book VI).

The Selections

"A Letter from Origen to Gregory, Bishop of Caesarea" returns to the prominent interpretation of Greek philosophy as preparation for the gospel. Origen uses the metaphor of "plundering the Egyptians" to justify Christianity's appropriation of the classical tradition. In their flight from Egypt, the Israelites were laden with gold and silver treasure that they later used to make the Tabernacle and its furnishings. After Solomon's reign, and the division of Israel and Judah, King Jeroboam made two golden calves, saying, "Behold your gods, O Israel, that brought you up from the land of Egypt" (I Kings 12:28). Despite his odd confusion of Hadad the Edomite (I Kings 11:14) with Jeroboam, Origen's obvious point, later repeated by Augustine in his *On Christian Doctrine*, is that God's good gifts and skills can be used or abused, directed toward God's service or perverted toward sin and rebellion and the love of self. Promoting the benefits of a liberal education, Origen also acknowledges the spiritual and moral hazards of "worldly" learning.

The clearest picture we have of Origen the teacher comes from his student Gregory Thaumaturgus. In his *Oration and Panegyric Addressed to Origen*, Gregory provides a moving and impassioned tribute to his teacher's gifts. Under his teacher's guidance, Gregory studied a range of disciplines, including physics, geometry, astronomy, and logic, and culminating in philosophy. Gregory recalled that Origen enticed him to study as "he lauded the lovers of philosophy with large laudations and many noble utterances, declaring that those only live a life truly worthy of reasonable creatures who aim at living an upright life, and who seek to know first of all themselves, what manner of persons they are, and then the things that are truly good, which men ought to strive after, and then the things that are really evil, from which man ought to flee" (VI). Origin reaffirmed the Delphic injunction to "know thyself." The connection in Gregory's mind between wisdom and virtue could not be clearer.

A Letter from Origen to Gregory, Bishop of Caesarea

Greeting in God, my most excellent sir, and venerable son Gregory, from Origen. A natural readiness of comprehension, as you well know, may, if practice be added, contribute somewhat to the contingent end, if I may so call it, of that which any one wishes to practice. Thus, your natural good parts might make of you a finished Roman lawyer or a Greek philosopher, so to speak, of one of the schools in high reputation. But I am anxious that you should devote all the strength of your natural good parts to Christianity for your end; and in order to [do] this, I wish to ask you to extract from the philosophy of the Greeks what may serve as a course of study or a preparation for Christianity, and from geometry and astronomy what will serve to explain the sacred Scriptures, in order that all that the sons of the philosophers are wont to say about geometry and music, grammar, rhetoric, and astronomy, as fellow-helpers to philosophy, we may say about philosophy itself, in relation to Christianity.

Perhaps something of this kind is shadowed forth in what is written in Exodus from the mouth of God, that the children of Israel were commanded to ask from their neighbours, and those who dwelt with them, vessels of silver and gold, and raiment, in order that, by spoiling the Egyptians, they might have material for the preparation of the things which pertained to the service of God. For from the things which the children of Israel took from the Egyptians the vessels in the holy of holies were made,—the ark with its lid, and the Cherubim, and the mercy-seat, and the golden coffer, where was the manna, the angels' bread. These things were probably made from the best of the Egyptian gold. An inferior kind would be used for the solid golden candlestick near the inner veil, and its branches, and the golden table on which were the pieces of shewbread, and the golden censer between them. And if there was a third and fourth quality of gold, from it would be made the holy vessels; and the other things would be made of Egyptian silver. For when the children of Israel dwelt in Egypt, they gained this from their dwelling there, that they had no lack of such precious material for the utensils of the service of God. And of the Egyptian raiment were probably made all those things which, as the Scripture mentions, needed sewed and embroidered work, sewed with the wisdom of God, the one to the other, that the veils might be made, and the inner and the outer courts. And why should I go on, in this untimely digression, to set forth how useful to the children of Israel were the things brought from Egypt, which the Egyptians had not put to a proper use, but which the Hebrews, guided by the wisdom of God, used for God's service? Now the sacred Scripture is wont to represent as an evil the going down from the land of the children of Israel into Egypt, indicating that certain persons get harm from sojourning among the Egyptians, that is to say, from meddling with the knowledge of this world, after they have subscribed to the law of God, and the Israelitish service of Him. Ader [Hadad] at least, the Idumaean, so long as he was in the land of Israel, and had not tasted the bread of the Egyptians, made no idols. It was when he fled from the wise Solomon, and went down into Egypt, as it were flying from the wisdom of God, and was made a kinsman of Pharaoh by marrying his wife's sister, and begetting a child, who was brought up with the children of Pharaoh, that he did this. Wherefore, although he did return to the land of Israel, he returned only to divide the people of God, and to make them say to the golden calf, "These be thy gods, O Israel, which brought thee up from the land of Egypt." And I may tell you from my experience, that not many take from Egypt only the useful, and go away and use it for the service of God; while Ader the Idumaean has many brethren. These are they who, from their Greek studies, produce heretical notions, and set them up, like the golden calf, in Bethel, which signifies "God's house." In these words also there seems to me an indication that they have set up their own imaginations in the Scriptures, where the word of God dwells, which is called in a figure Bethel. The other figure, the word says, was set up in Dan. Now the borders of Dan are the most extreme, and nearest the borders of the Gentiles, as is clear from what is written in Joshua, the son of Nun. Now some of the devices of these brethren of Ader, as we call them, are also very near the borders of the Gentiles.

Do you then, my son, diligently apply yourself to the reading of the sacred Scriptures. Apply yourself, I say. For we who read the things of God need much application, lest we should say or think anything too rashly about them. And applying yourself thus to the study of the things of God, with faithful prejudgments such as are well pleasing to God, knock at its locked door, and it will be opened to you by the porter, of whom Jesus says, "To him the porter opens." And applying yourself thus to the divine study, seek aright, and with unwavering trust in God, the meaning of the holy Scriptures, which so many have missed. Be not satisfied with knocking and seeking; for prayer is of all things indispensable to the knowledge of the things of God. For to this the Saviour exhorted, and said not only, "Knock, and it shall be opened to you; and seek, and ye shall find," but also, "Ask, and it shall be given unto you." My fatherly love to you has made me thus bold; but whether my boldness be good, God will know, and His Christ, and all partakers of the Spirit of God and the Spirit of Christ. May you also be a partaker, and be ever increasing your inheritance, that you may say not only, "We are become partakers of Christ," but also partakers of God.

Gregory Thaumaturgus,
"Oration and Panegyric Addressed to Origen"

ARGUMENT XI: ORIGEN IS THE FIRST AND THE ONLY ONE THAT EXHORTS GREGORY TO ADD TO HIS ACQUIREMENTS THE STUDY OF PHILOSOPHY, AND OFFERS HIM IN A CERTAIN MANNER AN EXAMPLE IN HIMSELF. OF JUSTICE, PRUDENCE, TEMPERANCE, AND FORTITUDE. THE MAXIM, KNOW THYSELF.

He [Origen] was also the first and only man that urged me to study the philosophy of the Greeks, and persuaded me by his own moral example both to hear and to hold by the doctrine of morals, while as yet I had by no means been won over to that, so far as other philosophers were concerned (I again acknowledge it),—not rightly so, indeed, but unhappily, as I may say without exaggeration, for me. I did not, however, associate with many at first, but only with some few who professed to be teachers, though, in good sooth, they all established their philosophy only so far as words went. This man, however, was the first that induced me to philosophize by his words, as he pointed the exhortation by deeds before he gave it in words, and did not merely recite well-studied sentences; nay, he did not deem it right to speak on the subject at all, but with a sincere mind, and one bent on striving ardently after the practical accomplishment of the things expressed, and he endeavoured all the while to show himself in character like the man whom he describes in his discourses as the person who shall lead a noble life, and he ever exhibited (in himself), I would say, the pattern of the wise man. But as our discourse at the outset proposed to deal with the truth, and not with vain-glorious language, I shall not speak of him now as the exemplar of the wise man. And yet, if I chose to speak thus of him, I should not be far astray from the truth. Nevertheless, I pass that by at present. I shall not speak of him as a perfect pattern, but as one who vehemently desires to imitate the perfect pattern, and strives after it with zeal and earnestness, even beyond the capacity of men, if I may so express myself; and who labours, moreover, also to make us, who are so different, of like character with himself, not mere masters and apprehenders of the bald doctrines concerning the impulses of the soul, but masters and apprehenders of these impulses themselves.

For he pressed us on both to deed and to doctrine, and carried us along by that same view and method, not merely into a small section of each virtue, but rather into the whole, if mayhap we were able to take it in. And he constrained us also, if I may so speak, to practice righteousness on the ground of the personal action of the soul itself, which he persuaded us to study, drawing us off from the officious anxieties of life, and from the turbulence of the forum, and raising us to the nobler vocation of looking into ourselves, and dealing with the things that concern ourselves in truth. Now, that this is to practice righteousness, and that this is the true righteousness, some also of our ancient philosophers have asserted (expressing it as the *personal action*, I think), and have affirmed that this is more profitable for blessedness, both to the men themselves and to those who are with them, if indeed it belongs to this virtue to recompense according to desert, and to assign to each his own. For what else could be supposed to be so proper to the soul? Or what could be so worthy of it, as to exercise a care over itself, not gazing outwards, or busying itself with alien matters, or, to speak shortly, doing the worst injustice to itself, but turning its attention inwardly upon itself, rendering its own due to itself, and acting thereby righteously? To practice righteousness after this fashion, therefore, he impressed upon us, if I may so speak, by a sort of force. And he educated us to prudence none the less,—teaching [us] to be at home with ourselves, and to desire and endeavour to know ourselves, which indeed is the most excellent achievement of philosophy, the thing that is ascribed also to the most prophetic of spirits as the highest argument of wisdom—the precept, *Know thyself.* And that this is the genuine function of prudence, and that such is the heavenly prudence, is affirmed well by the ancients; for in this there is one virtue common to God and to man; while the soul is exercised in beholding itself as in a mirror, and reflects the divine mind in itself, if it is worthy of such a relation, and traces out a certain inexpressible method for the attaining of a kind of apotheosis. And in correspondence with this come also the virtues of temperance and fortitude: temperance, indeed, in conserving this very prudence which must be in the soul that knows itself, if that is ever its lot (for this temperance, again, surely means just a sound prudence): and fortitude, in keeping stedfastly by all the duties which have been spoken of, without falling away from them, either voluntarily or under any force, and in keeping and holding by all that has been laid down. For he teaches that this virtue acts also as a kind of preserver, maintainer, and guardian.

Basil the Great

c. 329–79

So we also must consider that a contest, the greatest of all contests, lies before us, for which we must do all things, and, in preparation for it, must strive to the best of our power, and must associate with poets and writers of prose and orators and with all men from whom there is any prospect of benefit with reference to the care of our soul.

"To Young Men, on How They Might
Derive Profit from Pagan Literature"

Basil of Caesarea, bishop, scholar, and teacher, came from Cappadocia in Asia Minor and studied at Caesarea, Constantinople, and Athens. His literary education steeped him in Greek epic and lyric poetry, plays, histories, and Platonic philosophy. His theological education introduced him to Origen's work. Together with his brother Gregory of Nyssa and their mutual friend Gregory of Nazianzus—the three "Cappadocian Fathers" of the church—he provided intellectual leadership for the Eastern church in the critical fourth century, when it was beset by the Arian heresy. His rules for monastic living are still fundamental to communities of the Orthodox Church and influenced Cassian and Benedict in the formation of their monastic movements in the West.

THE SELECTIONS

Basil's sermon "To Young Men, On How They Might Derive Profit from Pagan Literature" became an admired and frequently quoted exposition on Christian education, establishing itself as one of the definitive statements on Christianity's response to pagan culture. Popular during the Renaissance, it was translated into Latin by Petrarch's friend Leonardo Bruni, cited by Aeneas Sylvius, recommended in the Jesuits' *Ratio Studioruin,* and published in many editions from the late fifteenth through the twentieth centuries, often paired with (Pseudo-) Plutarch. The sixteenth-century reformer John Calvin used Basil to defend a broad appropriation of the wisdom of the ancients (see his commentary on Titus, excerpted later in this anthology).

Basil's intimate knowledge of classical authors is evident throughout his treatise. He quotes freely and with approval from Hesiod, Homer, Plutarch, and others. For Basil, Christianity was still engaged in a fruitful conversation with the ancients. In his defense, he cites the biblical precedents of Moses and Daniel, both of whom mastered the learning of pagan cultures as they prepared themselves for God's work. Basil is not naïve, however. He counsels selective and discriminating use of the Greek poets, orators, historians, and philosophers. Imitation of some model or other is unavoidable; the challenge is judiciously to imitate what is skillful, right, and good among the pagans. Basil's spirit is generous, and he welcomes compatibility wherever he finds it. His eye is on the permanent things and the "care of our souls." Of perhaps more importance than the actual sources he cites in the following selection is the example Basil sets by how he handles Greek literature.

Gregory Nazianzus's funeral oration pays tribute to Basil's philosophy of education. In the excerpt below, Gregory defends the usefulness of pagan learning in terms similar to the selective synthesis encouraged by Clement, Origen, and Basil. He cites Paul's urging of the Corinthian church to take every thought captive to the obedience of Christ (II Corinthians 10:5). He praises Basil's natural gifts, diligence, wisdom, prudence, and encyclopedic learning: "his galleon was laden with all the learning attainable by the nature of man." Gregory's eulogy provides a glimpse of the liberal arts curriculum of the early church, consisting at least of rhetoric, grammar, philosophy, astronomy, and geometry.

"To Young Men, on How They Might Derive Profit from Pagan Literature"

I. There are many considerations which urge me to counsel you, my children, on what things I judge to be best and on those which I am confident, if you accept them, will be to your advantage. For the fact that I have reached this age, and have already been trained through many experiences, and indeed also have shared sufficiently in the all-teaching vicissitude of both good and evil fortune, has made me conversant with human affairs, so that I can indicate the safest road, as it were, to those who are just entering upon life. Moreover, I come immediately after your parents in natural relationship to you, so that I myself entertain for you no less good-will than do your fathers; and I am sure, unless I am somewhat wrong in my judgment of you, that you do not long for your parents when your eyes rest upon me. If, then, you should receive my words with eagerness, you will belong to the second class of those praised by Hesiod; but should you not do so, I indeed should not like to say anything unpleasant, but do you of yourselves remember the verses in which he says: "Best is the man who sees of himself at once what must be done, and excellent is he too who follows what is well indicated by others, but he who is suited for neither is useless in all respects."

Do not think it strange, then, if I say to you, who each day resort to teachers and hold converse with the famous men of the ancients through the words which they have left behind them, that I myself have discovered something of especial advantage to you. This it is, and naught else, that I have come to offer you as my counsel—that you should not surrender to these men once for all the rudders of your mind, as if of a ship, and follow them whithersoever they lead; rather, accepting from them only that which is useful, you should know that which ought to be overlooked. What, therefore, these things are, and how we shall distinguish between them, is the lesson which I shall teach you from this point on.

II. We, my children, in no wise conceive this human life of ours to be an object of value in any respect, nor do we consider anything good at all, or so designate it, which makes its contribution to this life of ours only. Therefore neither renown of ancestry, nor strength of body, nor beauty, nor stature, nor honours bestowed by all mankind, nor kingship itself, nor other human attribute that one might mention, do we judge great, nay, we do not even consider them worth praying for, nor do we look with admiration upon those who possess them, but our hopes lead us forward to a more distant time, and everything we do is by way of preparation for the other life. Whatever, therefore, contributes to that life, we say must be loved and pursued with all our strength; but what does not conduce to that must be passed over as of no account. Now just what this life is, and how and in what manner we shall live it, would take too long to discuss in view of our present purpose, and would be for the more mature to hear than for hearers of your age. After saying this much at least, I may perhaps be able to show you that if one sums up all the happiness together from the time men have first existed and collects it into one whole, he will find that it is equivalent not even to a trivial part of those other goods, but that the total of the goods of the present life is more removed in value from the least among the former goods of the other life than shadows and dreams fall short of reality. Nay, rather—that I may use a more suitable illustration—to the degree that the soul is more precious than the body in all respects, so great is the difference between the two lives. Now to that other life the Holy Scriptures lead the way, teaching us through mysteries. Yet so long as, by reason of your age, it is impossible for you to understand the depth of the meaning of these, in the meantime, by means of other analogies which are not entirely different, we give, as it were in shadows and reflections, a preliminary training to the eye of the soul, imitating those who perform their drills in military tactics, who, after they have gained experience by means of gymnastic exercises for the arms and dance-steps for the feet, enjoy when it comes to the combat the profit derived from what was done in sport. So we also must consider that a contest, the greatest of all contests, lies before us, for which we must do all things, and, in preparation for it, must strive to the best of our power, and must associate with poets and writers of prose and orators and with all men from whom there is any prospect of benefit with reference to the care of our soul. Therefore, just as dyers first prepare by certain treatments whatever material is to receive the dye, and then apply the colour, whether it be purple or some other hue, so we also in the same manner must first, if the glory of the good is to abide with us indelible for all time, be instructed by these outside means, and then shall understand the sacred and mystical teachings; and like those who have become accustomed to seeing the reflection of the sun in water, so we shall then direct our eyes to the light itself.

III. Now if there is some affinity between the two bodies of teachings, knowledge of them should be useful to us; but if not, at least the fact that by setting them side by side we can discover the difference between them, is of no small importance for strengthening the position of the better. And yet with what can you compare the two systems of education and hit upon the true similitude? Perhaps, just as it is the proper virtue of a tree to be laden with beautiful fruit, although it also wears like a fair raiment leaves that wave about its branches, so likewise the fruit of the soul, the truth is primarily its fruitage, yet it is clad in the certainly not unlovely raiment even of the wisdom drawn from the outside,[1] which we may liken to foliage that furnishes both protection to the fruit and an aspect not devoid of beauty. Now it is said that even Moses, that illustrious man whose name for wisdom is greatest among all mankind, first trained his mind in the learning of the Egyptians, and then proceeded to the contemplation of Him who is. And like him, although in later times, they say that the wise Daniel at Babylon first learned the wisdom of the Chaldaeans and then applied himself to the divine teachings.

IV. But that this pagan learning is not without usefulness for the soul has been sufficiently affirmed; yet just how you should participate in it would be the next topic to be discussed.

First, then, as to the learning to be derived from the poets, that I may begin with them, inasmuch as the subjects they deal with are of every kind, you ought not to give your attention to all they write without exception; but whenever they recount for you the deeds or words of good men, you ought to cherish and emulate these and try to be as far as possible like them; but when they treat of wicked men, you ought to avoid such imitation, stopping your ears no less than Odysseus did, according to what those same poets say, when he avoided the songs of the Sirens. For familiarity with evil words is, as it were, a road leading to evil deeds. On this account, then, the soul must be watched over with all vigilance, lest through the pleasure the poets' words give we may unwittingly accept something of the more evil sort, like those who take poisons along with honey. We shall not, therefore, praise the poets when they revile or mock, or when they depict men engaged in amours or drunken, or when they define happiness in terms of an over-abundant table or dissolute songs. But least of all shall we give attention to them when they narrate anything about the gods, and especially when they speak of them as being many, and these too not even in accord with one another. For in their poems brother is at feud with brother, and father with children, and the latter in turn are engaged in truceless war with their parents. But the adulteries of gods and their amours and their sexual acts in public, and especially those of Zeus, the chief and highest of all, as they themselves describe him, actions which one would blush to mention of even brute beasts—all these we shall leave to the stage-folk.

These same observations I must make concerning the writers of prose also, and especially when they fabricate tales for the entertainment of their hearers. And we shall certainly not imitate the orators in their art of lying. For neither in courts of law nor in other affairs is lying befitting to us, who have chosen the right and true way of life, and to whom refraining from litigation has been ordained in commandment. But we shall take rather those passages of theirs in which they have praised virtue or condemned vice. For just as in the case of other beings enjoyment of flowers is limited to their fragrance and colour, but the bees, as we see, possess the power to get honey from them as well, so it is possible here also for those who are pursuing not merely what is sweet and pleasant in such writings to store away from them some benefit also for their souls. It is, therefore, in

---

1. I.e., from the pagan literature of the Greeks.

accordance with the whole similitude of the bees, that we should participate in the pagan literature. For these neither approach all flowers equally, nor in truth do they attempt to carry off entire those upon which they alight, but taking only so much of them as is suitable for their work, they suffer the rest to go untouched. We ourselves too, if we are wise, having appropriated from this literature what is suitable to us and akin to the truth, will pass over the remainder. And just as in plucking the blooms from a rose-bed we avoid the thorns, so also in garnering from such writings whatever is useful, let us guard ourselves against what is harmful. At the very outset, therefore, we should, examine each of the branches of knowledge and adapt it to our end, according to the Doric proverb, "bringing the stone to the line."

V. And since it is through virtue that we must enter upon this life of ours, and since much has been uttered in praise of virtue by poets, much by historians, and much more still by philosophers, we ought especially to apply ourselves to such literature. For it is no small advantage that a certain intimacy and familiarity with virtue should be engendered in the souls of the young, seeing that the lessons learned by such are likely, in the nature of the case, to be indelible, having been deeply impressed in them by reason of the tenderness of their souls. Or what else are we to suppose Hesiod had in mind when he composed these verses which are on everybody's lips, if he were not exhorting young men to virtue?—that "rough at first and hard to travel, and full of abundant sweat and toil, is the road which leads to virtue, and steep withal." Therefore it is not given to everyone to climb this road, so steep it is, nor, if one essays to climb it, easily to reach the summit. But when once one has come to the top he is able to see how smooth and beautiful, how easy and pleasant to travel it is, and more agreeable than that other road which leads to vice, which it is possible to take all at once from near at hand, as this same poet has said. For to me it seems that he has narrated these things for no other reason than to urge us on to virtue and to exhort all men to be good, and to keep us from becoming weak and cowardly in the face of the toils and desisting before reaching the end. And assuredly, if anyone else has sung the praise of virtue in terms like Hesiod's, let us welcome his words as leading to the same end as our own.

Moreover, as I myself have heard a man say who is clever at understanding a poet's mind, all Homer's poetry is an encomium of virtue, and all he wrote, save what is accessory, bears to this end, and not least in those verses in which he has portrayed the leader of the Cephallenians, after being saved from shipwreck, as naked, and the princess as having first shown him reverence at the mere sight of him (so far was he from incurring shame through merely being seen naked, since the poet has portrayed him as clothed with virtue in place of garments), and then, furthermore, Odysseus as having been considered worthy of such high honour by the rest of the Phaeacians likewise that, disregarding the luxury in which they lived, they one and all admired and envied the hero, and none of the Phaeacians at the moment would have desired anything else more than to become Odysseus, and that too just saved from a shipwreck. For in these passages, the interpreter of the poet's mind was wont to declare that Homer says in a voice that all but shouts: "You must give heed unto virtue, O men, which swims forth even with a man who has suffered shipwreck, and, on his coming naked to land, will render him more honoured than the happy Phaeacians." And truly this is so. Other possessions, in fact, no more belong to their possessors than to any chance corner whatever, quickly shifting now here, now there, as in a game of dice; but virtue alone of possessions cannot be taken away, as it remains with a man whether he be living or dead. It was for this reason indeed, as it seems to me, that Solon said this with respect to the rich: "But we will not exchange with them our virtue for their wealth, since the one abides always, while riches change their owners every day." And similar to these words are those of Theognis also in which he says that God, whomsoever he means indeed by this term, inclines the scale for men at one time this way, at another that way, now to be rich, but now to have nothing.

And furthermore, the sophist from Ceos, Prodicus, somewhere in his writings uttered a doctrine kindred to these others regarding virtue and vice; therefore we must apply our minds to him also, for he is not a man to be rejected. His narrative runs something like this, so far as I recall the man's thought, since I do not know the exact words, but only that he spoke in general to the following effect, not employing metre. When Heracles was quite a young man and was nearly of the age at which you yourselves are now, while he was deliberating which of the two roads he should take, the one leading through toils to virtue, or the easiest, two women approached him, and these were Virtue and Vice. Now at once, although they were silent, the difference between them was evident from their appearance. For the one had been decked out for beauty through the art of toiletry, and was overflowing with voluptuousness, and she was leading a whole swarm of pleasures in her train; now these things she displayed, and promising still more than these she tried to draw Heracles to her. But the other was withered and squalid, and had an intense look, and spoke quite differently; for she promised nothing dissolute or pleasant, but countless sweating toils and labours and dangers through every land and sea. But the prize to be won by these was to become a god, as the narrative of Prodicus expressed it; and it was this second woman that Heracles in the end followed.

VI. And almost all the writers who have some reputation for wisdom have, to a greater or less degree, each to the best of his power, discoursed in their works in praise of virtue. To these men we must hearken and we must try to show forth their words in our lives; for he in truth who confirms by act his devotion to wisdom, which among others is confined to words, "He alone has understanding, but the others flit about as shadows."

It seems to me that such harmony between profession and life is very much as if a painter had made a likeness of a man of quite wondrous beauty, and this same man should be such in reality as the painter had portrayed him on his panels. For brilliantly to praise virtue in public, and to make long speeches about it, but in private to rate pleasure before temperance, and self-interest before justice, resembles, as I would assert, these stage-folk who bring out plays and often appear as kings and potentates, although they are neither kings nor potentates, and perhaps not even free men at all. Again, a musician would not willingly consent that his lyre should be out of tune, nor a leader of a chorus that his chorus should not sing in the strictest possible harmony; but shall each individual person be at variance with himself, and shall he exhibit a life not at all in agreement with his words? But one will say, quoting Euripides, "the tongue has sworn, but the mind is unsworn," and the appearance of being good will be his aim instead of being good. Yet this is the last extreme of injustice, if we are to hearken to the words of Plato—"to appear to be just without being so."

VII. As to the passages in literature, then, which contain admonitions of excellent things, let us accept this procedure. And since the virtuous deeds, likewise, of the men of old have been preserved for us, either through an unbroken oral tradition or through being preserved in the words of poets or writers of prose, let us not fail to derive advantage from this source also. For example, a certain fellow, a market-lounger, kept railing at Pericles, but he paid no attention; and he kept it up all day long, he giving Pericles a merciless dressing of abuse, but he taking no heed of it. Then, when it was already evening and dark, though the man was scarcely desisting, Pericles escorted him home with a light, lest his own schooling in philosophy be utterly brought to naught. Again, a certain man, having become enraged against Eucleides of Megara, threatened him with death and took oath upon it; but Eucleides took a counter-oath, to the effect that verily he would appease the man and make him put aside his wrath against him. How very valuable it is that an example of this kind should be recalled to memory by a man who is on the point of being held in the grip of a fit of passion! For one must not put a simple-minded trust in the tragedy when it says "Against enemies anger arms the hand," but, on the contrary, we should not permit ourselves to be aroused to anger at all; but if this is not easy to achieve, we should at least apply reason to our anger as a sort of curb and not allow it to be carried too far beyond the bounds.

But let us bring our discussion back again to the examples of virtuous deeds. A certain man kept striking Socrates, son of Sophroniscus, full in the face, falling upon him unmercifully; yet he did not oppose, but permitted the wine-mad fellow to satiate his rage, so that his face was presently swollen and bruised from the blows. Now when the man ceased striking him, Socrates, it is said, did nothing except inscribe on his own forehead, like the name of the sculptor on a statue, "So-and-so (naming the man) made this," and only to that extent avenged himself. Since these examples tend to nearly the same end as our own precepts, I maintain that it is of great value for those of your age to imitate them. For this example of Socrates is akin to that precept of ours—that to him who strikes us on the cheek, so far from avenging ourselves upon him we should offer the other cheek also. And the example of Pericles or Eucleides is akin to the precept that we should submit to those who persecute us and gently suffer their anger; and this other one—that we should pray for blessings for our enemies instead of cursing them. For whoever has been instructed in these examples beforehand cannot after that distrust those precepts as utterly impossible to obey. I should not pass over the example of Alexander, who, when he had taken prisoner the daughters of Darius, although it had been testified to him that they possessed a marvellous beauty, did not think it fitting even to look upon them, judging it to be disgraceful for one who had captured men to be vanquished by women. Indeed, this example tends to the same purport as that well-known precept of ours—that he who looks upon a woman to enjoy her, although he does not commit adultery in act, yet in truth, because he has received the desire into his soul, is not free of guilt. But as for the action of Cleinias, one of the disciples of Pythagoras, it is difficult to believe that it is by mere chance that it coincides with our own principles, and not through its imitating them designedly. What was it, then, that Cleinias did? Although it was possible by taking oath to escape a fine of three talents, he paid rather than swear, and that too though it would have been a true oath that he would have taken. He must have heard, it seems to me, our commandment forbidding the taking of an oath. . . .

X. But although we Christians shall doubtless learn all these things more thoroughly in our own literature, yet for the present, at least, let us trace out a kind of rough sketch, as it were, of what virtue is according to the teaching of the pagans. For by those who make it their business to gather the benefit to be derived from each source many accretions from many sides are wont to be received, as happens to mighty rivers. Indeed we are entitled to consider that the poet's saying about "adding little to little" holds good no more for increment of money than it does for increment in respect of knowledge of any kind whatever. Bias, for instance, when he was asked by his son, who was about to depart for Egypt, what he could do that would gratify him most, replied: "By acquiring travel-supplies for your old age," meaning by "travel-supplies" virtue, no doubt, though the terms in which he defined it were too narrow, seeing that he limited to human life the benefit to be derived from virtue. But as for me, if anyone should mention the old age of Tithonus, or that of Arganthonius, or of Mathusala, whose life was the longest of any man's (for he is said to have lived a thousand years lacking thirty), or if anyone reckons up all the time which has elapsed since men have existed, I shall laugh thereat as at a childish idea when I gaze towards that long and ageless eternity whose limit the mind can in no wise grasp any more than it can conceive an end for the immortal soul. It is for this eternity that I would exhort you to acquire travel-supplies, leaving no stone unturned, as the proverb has it, wherever any benefit towards that end is likely to accrue to you. And because this is difficult and calls for toil, let us not on this account draw back, but recalling the words of him who urged that every man should choose the life which is in itself best, in the expectation that through habit it will prove agreeable, we should attempt the best things. For it would be disgraceful that we, having thrown away the present opportunity, should at some later time attempt to summon back the past when all our vexation will gain us nothing.

Accordingly, of the things which in my judgment are best, some I have told you at this time, while others I shall continue to recommend to you throughout my whole life: but as for you, remembering that there are three infirmities, pray do not seem to resemble the one which is incurable, nor to exhibit the disease of the mind, which resembles that which those endure who are afflicted in body. For whereas those who suffer from slight ailments go of themselves to physicians, and those who are attacked by more serious diseases summon to their homes those who will treat them; yet those who have reached the stage of melancholy that is absolutely beyond remedy do not even admit physicians when they call. Pray do you not become afflicted in this last-named manner, characteristic of the men of the present time, by avoiding those whose reasoning faculties are sound.

❧

Gregory Nazianzen, "Funeral Oration on the Great St. Basil,
Bishop of Caesarea in Cappadocia.

I take it as admitted by men of sense, that the first of our advantages is education; and not only this our more noble form of it, which disregards rhetorical ornaments and glory, and holds to salvation, and beauty in the objects of our contemplation: but even that external culture which many Christians ill-judgingly abhor, as treacherous and dangerous, and keeping us afar from God. For as we ought not to neglect the heavens, and earth, and air, and all such things, because some have wrongly seized upon them, and honour God's works instead of God: but to reap what advantage we can from them for our life and enjoyment, while we avoid their dangers; not raising creation, as foolish men do, in revolt against the Creator, but from the works of nature apprehending the Worker, and, as the divine apostle says, bringing into captivity every thought to Christ: and again, as we know that neither fire, nor food, nor iron, nor any other of the elements, is of itself most useful, or most harmful, except according to the will of those who use it; and as we have compounded healthful drugs from certain of the reptiles, so from secular literature we have received principles of enquiry and speculation, while we have rejected their idolatry, terror, and pit of destruction. Nay, even these have aided us in our religion, by our perception of the contrast between what is worse and what is better, and by gaining strength for our doctrine from the weakness of theirs. We must not then dishonour education, because some men are pleased to do so, but rather suppose such men to be boorish and uneducated, desiring all men to be as they themselves are, in order to hide themselves in the general, and escape the detection of their want of culture. But come now, and, after this sketch of our subject and these admissions, let us contemplate the life of Basil. . . .

Who possessed such a degree of the prudence of old age, even before his hair was gray? since it is by this that Solomon defines old age. Who was so respectful to both old and young, not only of our contemporaries, but even of those who long preceded him? Who, owing to his character, was less in need of education? Yet who, even with his character, was so imbued with learning? What branch of learning did he not traverse; and that with unexampled success, passing through all, as no one else passed through any one of them: and attaining such eminence in each, as if it had been his sole study? The two great sources of power in the arts and sciences, ability and application, were in him equally combined. For, because of the pains he took, he had but little need of natural quickness, and his natural quickness made it unnecessary for him to take pains; and such was the cooperation and unity of both, that it was hard to see for which of the two he was more remarkable. Who had such power in Rhetoric, which breathes with the might of fire, different as his disposition was from that of rhetoricians? Who in Grammar, which perfects our tongues in Greek and compiles history, and presides over metres and legislates for poems? Who in Philosophy, that really lofty and high reaching science, whether practical and speculative, or in that part of it whose oppositions and struggles are concerned with logical demonstrations, which is called Dialectic, and in which it was more difficult to elude his verbal toils, if need required, than to escape from the Labyrinths? Of Astronomy, Geometry, and numerical proportion he had such a grasp, that he could not be baffled by those who are clever in such sciences: excessive application to them he despised, as useless to those whose desire is godliness: so that it is possible to admire what he chose more than what he neglected, or what he neglected more than what he chose. Medicine, the result of philosophy and laboriousness, was rendered necessary for him by his physical delicacy, and his care of the sick. From these beginnings he attained to a mastery of the art, not only in its empirical and practical branches, but also in its theory and principles. But what are these, illustrious though they be, compared with the moral discipline of the man? To those who have had experience of him, Minos and

Rhadamanthus[2] were mere trifles, whom the Greeks thought worthy of the meadows of Asphodel and the Elysian plains, which are their representations of our Paradise, derived from those books of Moses which are also ours, for though their temis are different, this is what they refer to under other names.

Such was the case, and his galleon was laden with all the learning attainable by the nature of man; for beyond Cadiz[3] there is no passage.

---

2. Kings of Crete and Lycia, fabled to have been made judges in the lower world because of their justice when on earth.

3. The Atlantic Ocean beyond Cadiz was reputed impassable by the ancients.

John Chrysostom

c. 345–407

Let us then implant in him this wisdom and let us exercise him therein, that he may know the meaning of human desires, wealth, reputation, power, and may distain these and strive after the highest.

"Address on Vainglory"

John Chrysostom came from the same remarkable generation that produced the Cappadocian Fathers, Jerome, and Augustine. He was born in Antioch, studied rhetoric, and trained for a career in law, but after his baptism he became a monk and then a priest. He learned theology at the important school at Antioch, which was more Aristotelian in its approach than was the Platonic Alexandria. The title "Chrysostom" means "golden-mouthed"; his sermons were models of eloquence. He became bishop of Constantinople, and in that office he actively promoted evangelization among the pagans and preached against luxury and excess. He was exiled from Constantinople for siding with Origen's defenders. His views on education are contained in the selection below and in his treatise "Against the Detractors of Monastic Life."

THE SELECTION

Chrysostom's advice in "The Right Way for Parents to Bring Up Their Children" is an appendage to his "Address on Vainglory." The relationship of the two parts remains a bit of a puzzle. Chrysostom sees the soul as a precious work of art that must be guarded and labored over, carefully fashioned into a thing of beauty. His primary concern is with the molding, forming, and training of the soul. He seeks to inculcate a philosophical habit of

191

mind along with self-restraint and wisdom. In this process, imitation is inevitable. Something or someone will be the child's pattern. He must, therefore, be taught to emulate the good and reject the bad. Chrysostom compares the soul to an athlete, a statue, and a city. The metaphor of the statue was common in antiquity, appearing in Plato's *Phaedrus* and in Plotinus's *Ennius*. Plotinus urged his students to "be always at work carving your own statue" (1.6, 9). Much more extended, however, is Chyrostom's metaphor of the city of the soul, with its five gates: the mouth, the ear, the nose, the eye, and the sense of touch. All of these entrances to the city of the soul must be guarded and the city itself must be ruled well.

Chrysostom's continuity with the classical tradition is obvious. M. L. W. Laistner writes, "his main point, in which he is merely repeating with a Christian slant what the greatest of the pagan educators, from Plato and Isocrates to Quintilian, had stated emphatically long before, is that the moral purpose of education is more important than anything else."[1]

from the "Address on Vainglory and the Right Way for Parents to Bring Up Their Children"

. . . The man-child has lately been born. His father thinks of every means, not whereby he may direct the child's life wisely, but whereby he may adorn it and clothe it in fine raiment and golden ornaments. Why dost thou this, O man? Granted that thou dost thyself wear these, why dost thou rear in this luxury thy son who is as yet still ignorant of this folly? For what purpose dost thou put a necklet about his throat? There is need for a strict tutor to direct the boy, no need for gold. And thou lettest his hair hang down behind, thereby at once making him look effeminate and like a girl and softening the ruggedness of his sex. Implanting in him from the first an excessive love of wealth and teaching him to be excited by things of no profit, why dost thou plot even greater treachery against him? Why dost thou excite him with the pleasures of the body? "If a man have long hair," Paul says (1 Corinthians 11:14), "it is a shame unto him." Nature disallows it, God has not sanctioned it, the thing is forbidden. It is an act of pagan superstition. Many also hang golden earrings on their children. Would that not even girls took pleasure in these; but you inflict this outrage on boys.

Many may laugh at what I am saying on the ground that these things are trifles. They are not trifles but of the first importance. The girl who has been reared in her mother's quarters to be excited by female ornaments, when she leaves her father's house will be a sore vexation to her bridegroom and a greater burden to him than the tax collectors. I have told you already that vice is hard to drive away for this reason, that no one takes thought for his children, no one discourses to them about virginity and sobriety or about contempt of wealth and fame, or of the precepts laid down in the Scriptures.

What will become of boys when from earliest youth they are without teachers? If grown men, after being nurtured from the womb and continuing their education to old age, still

---

1. *Christianity and Pagan Culture in the Later Roman Empire* (Ithaca, NY: Cornell University Press, 1951), 53.

do not live righteously, what wrong will not children, accustomed from the threshold of life to empty words, commit? In our own day every man takes the greatest pains to train his boy in the arts and in literature and speech. But to exercise this child's soul in virtue, to that no man any longer pays heed.

I shall not cease exhorting and begging and supplicating you before all else to discipline your sons from the first. If thou dost care for thy son, show it thus, and in other ways too thou wilt have thy reward. Hearken to the words of Paul, "if they continue in faith and charity and holiness with sobriety" (1 Timothy 2:15). And even if thou art conscious of a myriad vices within thyself, nevertheless devise some compensation for thy vices. Raise up an athlete for Christ! I do not mean by this, hold him back from wedlock and send him to desert regions and prepare him to assume the monastic life. It is not this that I mean. I wish for this and used to pray that all might embrace it; but as it seems to be too heavy a burden, I do not insist upon it. Raise up an athlete for Christ and teach him though he is living in the world to be reverent from his earliest youth.

If good precepts are impressed on the soul while it is yet tender, no man will be able to destroy them when they have set firm, even as does a waxen seal. The child is still trembling and fearful and afraid in look and speech and in all else. Make use of the beginning of his life as thou shouldst. Thou wilt be the first to benefit, if thou hast a good son, and then God. Thou dost labor for thyself.

They say that pearls when first they are collected are but water. But if he that receives them is skilled in his craft, he places the drop on his hand; and, moving it with a gentle rotating movement as it lies on the palm of his upturned hand, he shapes it skillfully and renders it perfectly round. Then, when it has received its form, he can no longer mold it; for that which is soft and with its proper shape not yet set firm is in every way adaptable and therefore is easily suited to every purpose. But that which is hard, having acquired a certain material outline, can be deprived of its hardness only with difficulty and is not changed into another shape.

To each of you fathers and mothers I say, just as we see artists fashioning their paintings and statues with great precision, so we must care for these wondrous statues of ours. Painters when they have set the canvas on the easel paint on it day by day to accomplish their purpose. Sculptors, too, working in marble, proceed in a similar manner; they remove what is superfluous and add what is lacking. Even so must you proceed. Like the creators of statues do you give all your leisure to fashioning these wondrous statues for God. And, as you remove what is superfluous and add what is lacking, inspect them day by day, to see what good qualities nature has supplied so that you will increase them, and what faults so that you will eradicate them. And, first of all, take the greatest care to banish licentious speech; for love of this above all frets the souls of the young. Before he is of an age to try it, teach thy son to be sober and vigilant and to shorten sleep for the sake of prayer, and with every word and deed to set upon himself the seal of the faith.

Regard thyself as a king ruling over a city which is the soul of thy son; for the soul is in truth a city. And, even as in a city some are thieves and some are honest men, some work steadily and some transact their business fitfully, so it is with the thoughts and reasoning in the soul. Some make war on wrongdoers, like soldiers in a city; others take thought for everything, both the welfare of the body and of the home, like those who carry on the government in cities. Some give orders, like the magistrates, some again counsel lewdness, like profligates, others reverence, like the virtuous. And some are effeminate, even as are women among us; others speak folly, like children. And some again receive orders as slaves, like servants in the city, while others are wellborn, like free men.

Hence we need laws to banish evildoers and admit the good and prevent the evildoers from rising up against the good. And, just as in a city, if laws are passed which permit thieves great license, the general welfare is undermined, and if the soldiers do not devote their ardor to its proper use, they ruin the body politic, and if each citizen abandons his own household affairs and busies himself with another's, he destroys good order by his greed and ambition—so it is also in the case of the child.

The child's soul then is a city, a city but lately founded and built, a city containing citizens who are strangers with no experience as yet, such as it is very easy to direct; for men who have been reared and have grown old under a bad constitution it would be difficult to reform, though not impossible. Even they can be reformed if they be willing. But those who are quite without experience would readily accept the laws that thou givest them.

Draw up laws then for this city and its citizens, laws that inspire fear and are strong, and uphold them if they are being transgressed; for it is useless to draw up laws, if their enforcement does not follow.

Draw up laws, and do you pay close attention; for our legislation is for the world and today we are founding a city. Suppose that the outer walls and four gates, the senses, are built. The whole body shall be the wall, as it were, the gates are the eyes, the tongue, the hearing, the sense of smell, and, if you will, the sense of touch. It is through these gates that the citizens of the city go in and out; that is to say, it is through these gates that thoughts are corrupted or rightly guided.

Well now, let us first of all approach the gate of the tongue, seeing that this is the busiest of all; and let us, to begin with and before all the other gates, provide this one with doors and bolts, not of wood or iron but of gold. Verily the city that is thus equipped is golden; for it is not any mortal but the King of the universe who intends to dwell in this city, if it has been well built. And, as our discourse proceeds, you shall see where we set up His palace. So let us build for the city gates and bolts of gold, that is, the words of God, even as the prophet says (Psalms 119:103; 19:10): "The words of God are sweeter than honey and honeycomb to my mouth, more precious than gold and a stone of great price." Let us teach the child so that the words revolve on his lips all the time, even on his walks abroad, not lightly nor incidentally nor at rare intervals, but without ceasing. It is not enough merely to cover the gates with gold leaf. They must be fashioned of gold thick and solid through and through, and they must have precious stones set well in instead of merely laid on the surface. The bolt of these gates shall be the Cross of the Lord fashioned through and through of precious gems and set athwart the middle of the gates. But when we have fashioned the gates massive and golden and have fixed on the bolt, we must fashion the citizens also to be worthy of the city. Of what character shall these citizens be? We must train the child to utter grave and reverent words. We must drive many strangers away, so that no corrupt men may also find their way in to mingle with these citizens. Words that are insolent and slanderous, foolish, shameful, common, and worldly, all these we must expel. And no one save only the King must pass through these gates (cf. Ezekiel 44:2). For Him and all that are His this gate shall be open so that one may say of it (Psalms 118:20): "This is the gate of the Lord into which the righteous shall enter," and, as the blessed Paul says (Ephesians 4:29), "speech that is good for edifying, that it may minister grace unto the hearers." Let their words be giving thanks, solemn hymns; let their discourse ever be about God, about heavenly philosophy.

How shall this be? And in what manner shall we train them? If we are zealous critics of those that are growing. The boy is very easily guided. He does not fight for wealth or glory—he is still a small boy—nor on behalf of wife or children or home. What reason for insolence or evil-speaking should he have? He contends only with companions of his own age.

Make a law straightway that he use no one in despite, that he speak ill of no man, that he swear not, that he be not contentious. If thou shouldst see him transgressing this law, punish him, now with a stern look, now with incisive, now with reproachful, words; at other times win him with gentleness and promises. Have not recourse to blows constantly and accustom him not to be trained by the rod; for if he feel it constantly as he is being trained, he will learn to despise it. And when he has learnt to despise it, he has reduced thy system to nought. Let him rather at all times fear blows but not receive them. Threaten him with the tawse, but do not lay it on and do not let thy threats proceed to action. Do not let it appear that thy words do not pass the stage of threats; for a threat is only of use when attended by the belief that it will be put into effect. If the offender learn your intention, he will despise it. So let him expect chastisement but not receive it, so that his fear may not be quenched but may endure, like a raging fire drawing thorny brushwood from every side or like a sharp and searching pick digging to the very depths. Yet when thou dost see that he has profited by fear, forbear, seeing that our human nature has need of some forbearance.

Teach him to be fair and courteous. If thou dost see a servant ill-used by him, do not overlook it, but punish him who is free; for if he knows that he may not ill use even a slave, he will abstain all the more from insulting or slandering one who is free and of his class. Stop his mouth from speaking evil. If thou dost see him traducing another, curb him and direct his tongue toward his own faults.

Exhort his mother, too, to converse with the child thus, and his tutor and his servant, so all of them together may be his guardians and on the watch that none of those evil thoughts spring out from the boy and from that mouth and from the golden gates.

And do not, I pray, think that this takes a long time. If from the first thou dost firmly lay on thy behests and threats and dost appoint so many guardians, two months suffice, and all is in good order and the habit is firmly established as his second nature.

Thus this gate will have been made worthy of the Lord, when no word that is shameful or flippant or foolish or the like is spoken, but all beseems the Master. If those who give military training teach their sons from the first to be soldiers and to shoot and to put on military dress and to ride, and their tender years are no hindrance, how much more should those who are soldiers of God assume all this royal discipline. So let him learn to sing hymns to God that he may not spend his leisure on shameful songs and ill-timed tales.

Let this gate thus be made secure and let these be the citizens that are enrolled. But the others within the city let us put to death, as bees kill drones, and let us not allow them to sally forth or buzz.

Now let us pass to another gate. Which is that? One that lies close by the first and resembles it greatly, I mean, the sense of hearing. The first gate has citizens that go forth from within, and none that enter in by it; but this second gate has only those that enter in from outside, none that pass out through it. The second then much resembles the first. If it be agreed that none that is pernicious and corrupt may tread upon its threshold, the mouth experiences but little trouble; for he that hears no base or wicked words does not utter base words either. But if this gate stands wide open to all, the other will suffer harm and all those within will be thrown into confusion. And it was needful to speak fully about the former gate and first to block up its entrance.

Let children then hear nothing harmful from servants or tutor or nurses. But, even as plants need the greatest amount of care when they are tender shoots, so also do children; and so let us take thought for good nurses that a fair foundation from the ground up be laid for the young and that from the beginning they may receive nought that is evil.

Therefore let them not hear frivolous and old wives' tales: "This youth kissed that maiden. The king's son and the younger daughter have done this." Do not let them hear these stories, but let them hear others simply told with no elaboration. They can hear such from slaves but not from all. They must not be allowed to consort with all the servants, but rather let those who are participating with us in training stand out clearly, as though they were approaching a holy statue. If we were builders and were erecting a house for the ruler, we should not permit one and all of the servants to approach the building. Would it not then be absurd, when we are establishing a city and citizens for the heavenly King, to entrust the task indiscriminately to all? Let those of the servants who are well fitted take part. If there be none, then hire someone who is free, a virtuous man, and entrust the task especially to him, so that he may have a full share in the undertaking.

Let them not hear such tales. But when the boy takes relaxation from his studies—for the soul delights to dwell on stories of old—speak to him, drawing him away from all childish folly; for thou art raising a philosopher and athlete and citizen of heaven. Speak to him and tell him this story: "Once upon a time there were two sons of one father, even two brothers." Then after a pause continue: "And they were the children of the same mother, one being the elder, the other the younger son. The elder was a tiller of the ground, the younger a shepherd; and he led out his flocks to woodland and lake." Make thy stories agreeable that they may give the child pleasure and his soul may not grow weary. "The other son sowed and planted. And it came to pass that both wished to do honor to God. And the shepherd took the firstlings of his flocks and offered them to God." Is it not a far better thing to relate this than fairy tales about sheep with golden fleeces? Then arouse him—for not a little depends on the telling of the story—introducing nothing that is un-true but only what is related in the Scriptures: "Now when he offered the firstlings to God, straightway fire came down from heaven and bore them off to the altar aloft. But the elder son did not so but went away and, after storing up for himself the first fruits from his toil, brought the second-best to God. And God paid no heed to them but turned away and let them lie on the ground. But the other offering he received for himself in heaven. Even so it happens with earthly rulers. The master honors one who brings gifts and receives him in his house; another he suffers to stand outside. Even so it was in this story. And then what happened? The elder brother was very wroth as having been dishonored and passed over for another, and his countenance fell. God said unto him: 'Why art thou wroth? Didst thou not know that thou madest an offering to God? Why hast thou insulted me? What grievance hast thou? Why didst thou offer me the second-best?'" If it seems well to use simpler language, thou wilt say: "The elder brother had nothing to say and kept quiet," or better, "was silent. And thereafter, seeing his younger brother, he said to him: 'Let us go to the field.' And the elder caught the younger unawares and slew him. And he thought that God saw him not. But God came to him and said to him: 'Where is thy brother?' He replied: 'I know not. Am I my brother's keeper?' And God said unto him: 'the voice of thy brother's blood crieth unto me from the ground.'"

And let the child's mother sit by while his soul is being formed thus by such tales, so that she too may take part and praise the story. "What happened next? God received the younger son into heaven; having died he is up above." The child also learns the story of raising from the dead. If in pagan legend such marvels are told, one says: "He made the soul the soul of a hero." And the child believes and, while he does not know what a hero is, he knows that it is something greater than a man. And as soon as he hears, he marvels. Much more will he do so when he hears of raising from the dead and that the younger brother's soul went up to heaven. "And so God received the one straightway; but the other, the slayer, lived for many years continuously in misfortune, with fear and trembling as his companions, and suffered ten thousand ills and was punished every day." And do thou relate the punishment with much intensity and not simply that he heard God say: "Groaning and trembling thou shalt be on the earth"; for the child does not understand this yet. But say: "Just as thou, when thou art standing before thy teacher and art in an agony of doubt whether thou art to receive a whipping, thou tremblest and art afraid, even so did he live all his days, because he had given offense to God."

So far is enough for the child. Tell him this story one evening at supper. Let his mother repeat the same tale; then, when he has heard it often, ask him too, saying: "Tell me the story," so that he may be eager to imitate you. And when he has memorized it thou wilt also tell him how it profits him. The soul indeed, as it receives the story within itself before thou bast elaborated it, is aware that it will benefit. Nevertheless, do thou say hereafter: "Thou dost see how great a sin is greed, how great a sin it is to envy a brother. Thou dost see how great a sin it is to think that thou canst hide aught from God; for He sees all things, even those that are done in secret." If only thou sowest the seed of this teaching in the child, he will not need his tutor, since this fear that comes from God, this complete fear has possessed the boy instead and shakes his soul.

This is not all. Go leading him by the hand in church and pay heed particularly when this tale is read aloud. Thou wilt see him rejoice and leap with pleasure because he knows what the other children do not know, as he anticipates the story, recognizes it, and derives great gain from it. And hereafter the episode is fixed in his memory.

He can profit in other ways from the story. So let him learn from thee: "There is no reason for grief in adversity. God shows this from the very first in the example of this boy, seeing that He received one who was righteous through death into heaven."

When this story is firmly planted in the child's understanding, introduce another, again about two brothers, and speak thus: "Again there were two brothers, an elder and a younger. The elder was a hunter, the younger dwelt at home." Now this story, insofar as the reversal of fortune is greater and the brothers are older, gives more pleasure than the former one. "Now these two brothers were also twins. And after their birth the mother loved the younger, the father the elder son. Now the elder passed much of his time out of doors in the fields, but the younger indoors. And it came to pass when his father was old, that he said to the son whom he loved: 'My son, I am old. Go thou and prepare me some game, capture a roe or a hare and bring it and cook it that I may eat and bless thee.' But to the younger son he spoke no such words. But his mother heard what the father had said and called her younger son and said unto him: 'Child, thy father has bidden thy brother bring to him game that he may eat and bless him. Hearken to me and go to the flock and fetch me fair and tender kids, and I will prepare them as thy father loveth, and thou shalt carry them to him that he may eat and bless thee.' Now the father's eyes were dim from old age. And so when the younger son brought the kids, his mother seethed them, and placing the viands on the dish gave it to her son, and he bore it in. And she put the skin of the goats upon him that he might not be found out, since his skin was smooth but his brother was hairy, so that the younger might escape detection and his father perceive it not. And so she sent him in. But the father, thinking that it was in truth his elder son, ate and gave him his blessing. But then, as soon as the father had made an end of the blessing, the elder son came bringing game; and when he saw what had happened, he lifted up his voice and wept."

See how many fair lessons this story begets, and do not follow it right through to the end, but rather see how many lessons this part begets. First, children learn to reverence and honor their fathers, when they see so keen a rivalry for the father's blessing. And they will sooner suffer a myriad stripes than to hear their parents curse them. If a story can so master the children's soul that it is thought worthy of belief, the veritable truth, it will surely enthrall them and fill them with great awe. Again, they must learn to despise the belly; for the story must also show them that he gained nothing by being first-born and the elder. Because of the greed of his belly he betrayed the advantage of his birthright.

Then, when the boy has grasped this fully, thou wilt say to him again on another evening: "Tell me the story of those two brothers." And if he begins to relate the story of Cain and Abel, stop him and say: "It is not that one that I want, but the one of the other brothers, in which the father gave his blessing." Give him hints but do not as yet tell him their names. When he has told you all, spin the sequel of the yarn, and say:

"Hear what occurred afterwards. Once again the elder brother, like the brother in the former story, was minded to slay his brother, and he was awaiting his father's death. But their mother hearing him and being fearful sent the younger into exile." Then, as the inward sense transcends the child's intelligence, it can be simplified to his level of understanding and implanted in this tender childish intelligence, if we adapt the tale. And we shall speak to him thus: "This brother went away and came to a certain place. And he had no one with him, no slave or nurse or tutor or anyone else. And having come to a certain place he prayed, saying: 'Lord, give me bread and raiment and preserve me.' And then, when he had spoken thus, he fell asleep from sorrow. And in a dream he saw a ladder reaching from the earth to heaven and the angels of God ascending and descending on it and God Himself standing above at the head of the ladder; and he said, 'Give me Thy blessing.' And He blessed him and named him Israel."

I have remembered opportunely, and the name suggests another notion to my mind. What is this? Let us afford our children from the first an incentive to goodness from the name that we give them. Let none of us hasten to call his child after his forebears, his father and mother and grandsire and great-grandsire, but rather after the righteous—martyrs, bishops, apostles. Let this be an incentive to the children. Let one be called Peter, another John, another bear the name of one of the saints.

And do not, I pray, follow Greek customs. It is a great disgrace and laughable when in a Christian household some Greek pagan customs are observed; and they kindle lamps and sit watching to see which is the first to be extinguished and consumed, and other such customs which bring certain destruction to those who practice them. Do not regard such doings as paltry and trivial.

And so I urge this on you too, to call your children by the names of the righteous. In early times these other customs were reasonable, and men used to call their children by the names of their forebears. It was a consolation for death that the departed should seem to live through his name. But this is so no longer. We see at least that the righteous did not name their children in this wise. Abraham begat Isaac. Jacob and Moses were not called after their forebears, and we shall not find a single one of the righteous who was named so. How great is the virtue of which this is a token, this naming and calling by name, seeing that we shall find no other reason for the change of name save that it brings virtue to mind. "Thou shalt be called Cephas," says Christ (John 1:42), "which is by interpretation Peter." Why? Because thou didst acknowledge me. And thou shalt be called Abraham. Why? Because thou shalt be the father of nations (Genesis 17:4). And Israel, because he saw God (cf. Genesis 35:9–10). And so let us begin the care and training of our children from that point.

But as I was relating: "He saw a ladder extended and reaching up to heaven." So let the name of the saints enter our homes through the naming of our children, to train not only the child but the father, when he reflects that he is the father of John or Elijah or James; for, if the name be given with forethought to pay honor to those that have departed, and we grasp at our kinship with the righteous rather than with our forebears, this too will greatly help us and our children. Do not because it is a small thing regard it as small; its purpose is to succour us.

But as I was saying, let us return to the sequel of the story: "He saw a ladder firmly planted. He craved a blessing. God blessed him. He departed to his kinsmen. He was a shepherd." Relate further the story of his bride and his return home, and the boy will profit much therefrom. Consider how many things he will learn. He will be trained to trust in God, to despise no one though the son of one who is wellborn, to feel no shame at simple thrift, to bear misfortune nobly, and all the rest.

Next, when he has grown older, tell him also more fearful tales; for thou shouldst not impose so great a burden on his understanding while he is still tender, lest thou dismay him. But when he is fifteen years old or more, let him hear of Hell. Nay, when he is ten or eight or even younger, let him hear in full detail the story of the flood, the destruction of Sodom, the descent into Egypt—whatever stories are full of divine punishment. When he is older let him hear also the deeds of the New Testament—deeds of grace and deeds of hell. With these stories and ten thousand others fortify his hearing, as thou dost offer him also examples drawn from his home.

But if any man would relate what is base, let us not, as I have said, suffer him to come near the boy. If thou dost see a slave in his presence speaking lewdly, punish him straightway and inquire zealously and sharply into the offense committed. If thou dost see a girl—but better by far that no woman, save it be some time an old woman with no charms to captivate a youth, come near him and the flame of desire be not kindled. But from a young woman shield him as from fire. In this way then he will speak no foolish word, if he hears nought that is foolish but is brought up on those stories that we have told.

Let us pass on, if thou wilt, to another gate, the sense of smell. This gate too admits much that is harmful if it be not kept barred—I mean fragrant scents and herbs. Nothing weakens, nothing relaxes the right tension of the soul as a pleasure in sweet odors. "How then," says some one, must one take pleasure in filth?" That is not my meaning, but that one should not take pleasure either in the one or in the other. Let no one bring him perfume; for, as soon as it penetrates to the brain, the whole body is relaxed. Thereby pleasures are fanned into flame and great schemes for their attainment. So bar this gate, for its function is to breathe the air, not to receive sweet odors. It may be that some laugh at us for troubling about trifles, if we discourse about such a commonwealth. These are no trifles; nay, if we carry out our plan, our concern is with the origin and rhythmical education of the world.

Then there is yet another gate, fairer than those others but difficult to guard, the gate of the eyes; difficult for this reason, that it lies high up and open and is beautiful. It has many little postern gates and not only sees but is seen if well fashioned.

Here strict laws are needed, the first being: Never send thy son to the theater that he may not suffer utter corruption through his ears and eyes. And when he is abroad in the open squares, his attendant must be especially watchful as he passes through the alleys and must warn the boy of this, so that he may never suffer this corruption.

That he may not suffer it by his own appearance must have our careful thought. We must remove the chief part of his physical charm by clipping the locks on his head all round to attain severe simplicity. If the boy complain because he is being deprived of this charm, let him learn first of all that the greatest charm is simplicity.

That he may avoid seeing what he should not, those tales are sufficient protection which tell of "the sons of God that lapsed by coming in unto the daughters of men" (Genesis 6:4), and of the people of Sodom, of Gehenna, and the rest.

In this matter the tutor and attendant must exercise the greatest care. Show the boy other fair sights, and thou wilt steer his eyes away from those others. Show him the sky, the sun, the flowers of the earth, meadows, and fair books. Let these give pleasure to his eyes; and there are many others that are harmless.

This gate is difficult to guard, since there burns a fire within and, so to speak, a natural compulsion. Let him learn hymns. If he is not inwardly aroused, he will not wish to see outwardly. Let him not bathe in company with women—such familiarity is evil—and let him not be sent into a crowd of women.

Let him hear the whole story of Joseph continually. Furthermore, let him learn of the kingdom of Heaven and the great reward that awaits those who live sober lives. Promise him also that thou wilt lead to him a fair maid and tell him that thou hast made him the heir of thy property. Do not spare thy threats, if thou dost see the contrary disposition in him, and say to him: "My son, we shall not light upon a virtuous woman unless thou hast shown great watchfulness and devotion to virtue. And that thou mayest be steadfast, I shall soon guide thee to marriage."

Above all, if he is trained to speak no shameful word, he has a firm foundation of reverence derived from above. Speak to him of the beauty of the soul, instil into him a resolute spirit against womankind. Say that to be despised by the slave woman is meet only for a slave, and that a young man has the greatest need of earnestness. He who speaks will be conspicuous, he who sees will not be conspicuous; for this sense is swift and, as he sits among many, he can pick what maid he wishes with quick glances. Let him have no converse with any woman save only his mother. Let him see no woman. Do not give him money, let nothing shameful come in his way. Let him despise luxury and everything of that kind.

There is yet another gateway, unlike the others because it extends through the whole body. We call it touch. It appears to be closed, yet it is, as it were, open and sends within whatever comes. Let us not allow it to have any truck with soft raiment or bodies. Let us make it austere. We are raising an athlete, let us concentrate our thought on that. And so let him not use soft couches or raiment. Let these be our ordinances.

Come now, when we have entered this city, let us write down and ordain laws, seeing that our arrangement of the gates is so fair. First, let us thoroughly inform ourselves about the houses and chambers of the citizens that we may know where dwell the zealous and where the effete.

The seat and habitation of spirit, we are told, are the breast and the heart within the breast; of the appetitive part of the soul, the liver; of the reasoning part, the brain. Spirit produces both good and bad qualities; the good are sobriety and equability, the bad, rashness and ill temper. So, too, with the appetitive part; the good it causes is sobriety, the evil, licentiousness. And with the rational part the good is understanding, the bad, folly. Let us then have a care that the good qualities come to birth in these places and that they bear citizens of like character and not evil. These properties of the soul have been established to be like the mothers of our rational thoughts.

Let us pass to the despotic part of the soul, spirit. We must not eliminate it utterly from the youth nor yet allow him to use it all the time. Let us train boys from earliest childhood to be patient when they suffer wrongs themselves, but, if they see another being wronged, to sally forth courageously and aid the sufferer in fitting measure.

How shall we attain this? If they practice themselves among their own slaves and are patient when slighted and refrain from anger when they are disobeyed, but narrowly examine the faults that they themselves have committed against others. The father is arbiter at all times in such matters. If the laws are transgressed, he will be stern and unyielding; if they are observed, he will be gracious and kind and will bestow many rewards on the boy. Even so God rules the world with the fear of Hell and the promise of His Kingdom. So must we too rule our children.

And let there be many on all sides to spur the boy on, so that he may be exercised and practiced in controlling his passions among the members of the household. And, just as athletes in the wrestling school train with their friends before the contest, so that when they have succeeded against these they may be invincible against their opponents, even so the boy must be trained in the home. Let his father or brother oftentimes play the chief part in treating him with despite. And let them all strive their hardest to overcome him. Or let someone in wrestling stand up to him and defend himself so that the boy may try his strength against him. So, too, let the slaves provoke him often rightly or wrongly, so that he may learn on every occasion to control his passion. If his father provoke him, it is no great test; for the name of father, taking first possession of his soul, does not permit him to rebel. But let his companions in age, whether slave or free, do this, that he may learn equability amongst them.

There is still another method. What is that? When he becomes angry, remind him of the lessons that he has learned at home. When he is wroth with his slave, if he himself has not committed a fault, remind him that he should behave as he would have done on those former occasions. If thou dost see him striking the slave, demand satisfaction for this, and do likewise if thou dost see him using the slave ill. Let him be neither indulgent nor harsh, that he may be both a man and equable. Oftentimes he needs the help that spirit can give, as would be the case if at some time he himself have children or be the master of slaves. At all times the faculty of spirit is serviceable; it is only unprofitable when we defend ourselves. For this reason also Paul never made use of it for himself but only for others who had suffered wrong. And Moses, seeing his brother wronged, was wroth, and that right nobly, although he was "the meekest of men" (Exodus 2:11 ff.). But when he was used despitefully, he no longer defended himself but fled. Let the boy hear these tales. When we are still engaged in ordering the gates, we need the more artless stories; when we have entered in and are training the citizens, then is the time for those of a loftier kind. And so, let this be his first law, never to defend himself when ill used or suffering misfortune, and never to allow another to undergo this.

The father, if he discipline himself also, will be far better in teaching the boy these precepts; for, if for no other reason, he will improve himself so as not to spoil the example that he sets. Let the boy be taught to suffer despite and contumely. Let him not demand from the servants such services as a free man demands, but for the most part let him minister to his own needs. Let the slaves only render such services as he cannot do for himself. A free man, for example, cannot do his own cooking; for he must not devote himself to such pursuits at the cost of neglecting the labors befitting a free man. If, however, the boy would wash his feet, never let a slave do this, but let him do it for himself. Thus thou wilt render the free man considerate toward his slaves and greatly beloved by them. Do not let a slave hand him his cloak, and do not let him expect another to serve him in the bath, but let him do all these things for himself. This will make him strong and simple and courteous.

Teach him the facts of natural society and the difference between slave and free man. Say to him: "My son, there were no slaves of old in the time of our forebears, but sin brought slavery in its train; for when one insulted his father, he paid this penalty, to become his brothers' bondsman (Genesis 9:21–25). Beware lest thou be the slave of thy slaves. If thou art wroth and thy conduct is the same as theirs and thou art no whit more virtuous than they, thou wilt earn no greater respect than they. Strive therefore to be their master and become so, not by doing as they do, but by thy habits, so that being a free man thou art never a slave of these. Dost thou not see how many fathers have renounced their sons and have introduced slaves in their place? Look then that no such thing happens to you. Truly I neither wish nor desire it, but the choice lies with you."

In this way dispose his spirit to gentleness and bid him treat his servants like brothers, and teach him the facts of natural society, quoting to him the words of Job (31:13–15): "If I did despise the cause of my manservant or of my maidservant, when they contended with me; what shall I do when God afflicteth me and when he visiteth, what shall I answer him? Did not he that made me in the womb make them? Were we not fashioned in the same womb?" And again: "If my maidservants said often, 'who would give us of his flesh to be satisfied,' since I am too kindly."

Or dost thou think Paul a simpleton for saying that one who knows not how to rule his own house cannot superintend the church either (I Timothy 3:5)? So say to the boy: "If thou dost see that thy servant has destroyed one of thy pencils or broken a pen, be not angry or abusive but forgiving and placable. Thus taught by small losses thou wilt learn to bear the greater. Or it might be the strap about your writing tablets or the bronze chain that is broken." Children are made fractious by the loss of such articles and incline rather to lose their soul than to let the culprit go unpunished. There then one must soften the asperity of his anger. Believe me, the boy who is indifferent to such things and placable will endure every loss when he becomes a man. So if the boy has tablets fashioned of fine wood, clean and without stain, held together by bronze chains, and silver pencils and other like boyish possessions, and his servant lose or break them, and then the boy refrain from anger, he has displayed already all the marks of a philosophic mind. Do not straightway buy him others, lest you abate his sufferings; but when you see that he no longer misses his loss or is distressed by it, then heal his misfortune.

I am not speaking of trifles, we are discussing the governance of the world. Train the boy also, if he has a younger brother, to let him take precedence or, if not, his servant; for this also involves a philosophical disposition.

Mold his spirit so that it begets rational thoughts that are friendly to us. When he is dependent on no one, when he suffers loss, when he needs no service, when he does not resent honor paid to another, what source will there be left for anger?

It is now time to pass to desire. Both the self-restraint and the harm involved are twofold, that he may not himself suffer outrage nor yet himself do outrage to girls. The medical guild tell us that this desire attacks with violence after the fifteenth year. How shall we tie down this wild beast? What shall we contrive? How shall we place a bridle on it? I know none, save only the restraint of hell-fire.

First then let us guide it away from shameful spectacles and songs. Never let a freeborn boy enter the theater. If he yearn after the pleasure to be found there, let us point out any of his companions who are holding back from this, so that he may be held fast in the grip of emulation. Nothing, yea nothing, is so effective as emulation. Let us act thus in every instance, especially if he be emulous; for this is a more potent instrument than fear or promises or ought else.

Next, let us devise for him other harmless pleasures. Let us lead him to saintly men, let us give him recreation, let us show our regard for him by many gifts, so that his soul may patiently bear our rejection of the theater. In place of those spectacles introduce pleasing stories, flowery meadows, and fair buildings. And thereafter let us overthrow those spectacles by our argument, as we say to him: "My child, spectacles such as those, the sight of naked women uttering shameful words, are for slaves. Promise me not to listen to or speak any unseemly word and go thy way. There it is impossible not to hear what is base; what goes on is unworthy of thy eyes." As we speak to him, let us kiss him and put our arms about him, and press him to us to show our affection. By all these means let us mold him.

Well then, as I said before, never allow any maid to approach him or to serve him, save it be a slave of advancing years, an old woman. And let us guide the conversation to the kingdom of heaven and to those men of old, pagan or Christian, who were illustrious for their self-restraint. Let us constantly flood his ears with talk of them. If we should also have servants of sober conduct, let us draw comparisons also from them, saying how absurd to have so sober a servant, while the free man is inferior to him in conduct. There is another remedy yet. Which is that? Let him also learn to fast, not indeed all the while, but on two days of the week, on Wednesday and Friday. Let him visit the church. And let the father take the boy in the evening when the theater is ended and point to the spectators coming out and make fun of the older men because they have less sense than the young and the young men because they are inflamed with desire. And let him ask the boy: "What have all these people gained? Nothing but shame, reproach, and damnation." Abstention from all these spectacles and songs conduces not a little to virtue.

Furthermore, let him learn to pray with great fervor and contrition; and do not tell me that a lad would never conform to these practices. Certainly the lad would conform to them if he were keen-eyed and wide-awake. We see many examples of it among the men of old, for instance, Daniel or Joseph. And do not speak to me of Joseph's seventeen years and consider first why he won his father's love, and that more than the older sons. Was not Jacob younger than he? or Jeremiah? Was not Daniel twelve years of age? Was not Solomon himself but twelve when he prayed that wondrous prayer (I Kings 3:6–9)? Did not Samuel when still young instruct his own teacher (I Samuel 3:17)? So let us not despair; for one who is too immature in soul does not conform even when he is an adult. Let the boy be trained to pray with much contrition and to keep vigils as much as he is able, and let the stamp of a saintly man be impressed on the boy in every way. If he refrains from oaths, and from insults when he is insulted, and from slander and hatred, and if he fasts and prays, all this is a sufficient guide to virtue.

If thou dost bring him up to the secular life, introduce his bride to him straightway and do not wait for him to be a soldier or engage in political life before you do so. First train his soul and then take thought for his reputation in the world. Or dost thou think the fact of a virgin youth and a virgin maid being united is a trifling contribution to their marriage? It is no trifle, not only for the virtue of the youth but for the maiden's also. Will not then the charm of their love be wholly pure? Above all, will not God then be the more gracious and fill that marriage with countless blessings, when they come together according to His ordinances? And He makes the youth remember his love always. And if he is held fast in this affection, he will spurn every other woman.

If thou dost sing the maiden's praise for her beauty and her comeliness and all the rest, adding that "she will not endure to be thy mate if she learns that thou art slothful," he will reflect deeply, seeing that his ultimate happiness is imperiled. If love of the betrothed induced the holy patriarch after he had been deceived to serve for a second term of seven years, to serve for fourteen in all (Genesis 29:20–30), how much more must we. Say to him: "All that know thy bride—her father and mother, her servants and neighbors and friends—are deeply concerned for thee and thy way of life, and all will report to her." Bind him then with this fetter, the fetter that makes virtue secure. Then, even if he cannot have a wife from his earliest manhood, let him have a betrothed from the first and let him strive to show himself a good man. This is enough safeguard to ward off every evil.

There is yet another protection of virtue. Let him often see the head of his church and let him hear many words of praise from the bishop's lips; and let his father pride himself on this before all the hearers. Let the maidens as they see him be filled with awe; and so the tales and the fear of his father and his promises; and with these the reward laid up for him from God, even the numerous blessings which the virtuous shall enjoy—all this will afford him great security.

Refer also to distinctions—won in the army and in political life; and, besides, at all times express contempt for lewdness and give abundant praise for self-restraint. All these things serve to restrain the boy's soul; and so we shall find them giving birth to serious reflections.

There is something more. Let us go to the master principle which keeps everything under control. To what do I allude? I mean wisdom. Here great labor is needed to render him sagacious and to banish all folly. This is the great and wondrous function of philosophy, that he may know God and all the treasure laid up in Heaven, and Hell and the kingdom of the other world. "Fear of the Lord is the beginning of wisdom" (Proverbs 1:7).

Let us then implant in him this wisdom and let us exercise him therein, that he may know the meaning of human desires, wealth, reputation, power, and may disdain these and strive after the highest. And let us bring words of exhortation to his mind: "My child, fear God alone and fear none other but Him."

By this means he will be a man of good understanding and charm; for nothing is as productive of folly as those passions. The fear of God and the power of forming such a judgment of human affairs as it behooves us to have are sufficient for wisdom. The summit of wisdom is refusal to be excited at childish things. So let him be taught to think nothing of wealth or worldly reputation or power or death or the present life on earth. So will he be sagacious. If we lead him to the bridal chamber with a training such as this, consider how great a gift he will be to the bride.

Let us celebrate the marriage without flutes or harp or dancing; for a groom like ours is ashamed of such absurd customs. Nay, let us invite Christ there, for the bridegroom is worthy of Him. Let us invite His disciples; all things shall be of the best for the groom. And he himself will learn to train his own sons in this way, and they theirs in turn, and the result will be a golden cord.

Let us teach him to attend to political affairs, such as are within his capacity and free from sin. If he serve as a soldier, let him learn to shun base gain; and so too, if he defend the cause of those who have suffered wrong, or in any other circumstance.

Let his mother learn to train her daughter by these precepts, to guide her away from extravagance and personal adornment and all other such vanities that are the mark of harlots. Let the mother act by this ordinance at all times and guide the youth and the maiden away from luxury and drunkenness. This also contributes greatly to virtue. Young men are troubled by desire, women by love of finery and excitement. Let us therefore repress all these tendencies. Thus we shall be able to please God by rearing such athletes for Him, that we and our children may light on the blessings that are promised to them that love Him (cf. I Corinthians 2:9), by the grace and mercy of our Lord Jesus Christ, to Whom with the Father and the Holy Spirit be ascribed glory, power, and honor, now and for evermore. Amen.

Jerome

c. 342–420

*Is it surprising that I too, admiring the fairness of her form and the
grace of her eloquence, desire to make that secular wisdom which
is my captive and my handmaid, a matron of the true Israel?*

LETTER TO MAGNUS

Eusebius Hieronimus Sophronius, known to history as Jerome, was raised by Christian parents in a town on the Adriatic Sea. He studied in Rome and became conversant with Greek and Latin literature, philosophy, and rhetoric, indebted mostly to Cicero. He served for two years as papal secretary, and may have aspired to be pope himself. He traveled extensively to Antioch, Palestine, and Constantinople, and for a time lived as a desert ascetic. During his short stay in Constantinople in 381, he studied with Gregory of Nazianzus and knew Gregory of Nyssa. In 386, he established a monastery in Bethlehem. He labored as a translator, preacher, apologist, and opponent of Pelagianism. His substantial scholarly legacy includes the Vulgate translation of the Bible from the original Hebrew and Greek into Latin, his translations of works of Origen and the Church historian Eusebius into Latin, his commentaries on Scripture, and sermons. His more than one hundred letters were admired by Renaissance humanists, including Erasmus.

THE SELECTIONS

Many of Jerome's letters contain at least passing references to education and to the proper use of Greek and Roman culture. The first letter excerpted below is to Eustochium (384), one of two women (the other was Paula) who had followed him to Bethlehem and established a convent there not far from his monastery. Jerome never underestimates the reality of spiritual warfare, the dangers of infatuation with the distractions of the world, and the need for renunciation. He quotes the Apostle Paul's emphatic instruction to Christians not to be bound together with unbelievers (II Corinthians 6:14–15). He distances the "books of God" from the "books of men," fearing that immature Christians might be led astray by others' fondness for secular poets, orators, and philosophers. This letter includes Jerome's famous account of his frightening vision of Christ in judgment who accused him of being a Ciceronian and not a Christian.

His letter to Magnus (397) adds an important counterbalance to his stern advice to Eustochium. Jerome here defends the proper use of secular writers, appealing to the precedent of the apostles and Church fathers. He mentions the Apostle Paul, Pantaenus, Clement, Origen, Basil, Gregory Nazianzus, Tertullian, and many other Greek and Latin leaders. The letter is included in its entirety.

Jerome's letter to Laeta (403) offers advice for the education of her daughter Paula, the elder Paula's granddaughter. The young Paula had been set apart for a life devoted to the Church, and she came to Bethlehem where she eventually served as head of the convent founded by her grandmother and Eustochium. Jerome's debt to Quintilian's *Institutes* is heavy (to the point of reproducing parts of Book I verbatim).

Letter to Eustochium

. . . Do not seek to appear over-eloquent, nor trifle with verse, nor make yourself gay with lyric songs. And do not, out of affectation, follow the sickly taste of married ladies who, now pressing their teeth together, now keeping their lips wide apart, speak with a lisp, and purposely clip their words, because they fancy that to pronounce them naturally is a mark of country breeding. Accordingly they find pleasure in what I may call an adultery of the tongue. For "what communion hath light with darkness? And what concord hath Christ with Belial?" How can Horace go with the psalter, Virgil with the gospels, Cicero with the apostle? Is not a brother made to stumble if he sees you sitting at meat in an idol's temple? Although "unto the pure all things are pure," and "nothing is to be refused if it be received with thanksgiving," still we ought not to drink the cup of Christ, and, at the same time, the cup of devils. Let me relate to you the story of my own miserable experience.

Many years ago, when for the kingdom of heaven's sake I had cut myself off from home, parents, sister, relations, and—harder still—from the dainty food to which I had been accustomed; and when I was on my way to Jerusalem to wage my warfare, I still could not bring myself to forego the library which I had formed for myself at Rome with great care and toil. And so, miserable man that I was, I would fast only that I might afterwards read Cicero. After many nights spent in vigil, after floods of tears called from my inmost heart, after the recollection of my past sins, I would once more take up Plautus. And when at times I returned to my right mind, and began to read the prophets, their style seemed rude and repellent. I failed to see the light with my blinded eyes; but I attributed the fault not to them, but to the sun. While the old serpent was thus making me his plaything, about the middle of Lent a deep-seated fever fell upon my weakened body, and while it destroyed my rest completely—the story seems hardly credible—it so wasted my unhappy frame that scarcely anything was left of me but skin and bone. Meantime preparations for my funeral went on; my body grew gradually colder, and the warmth of life lingered only in my throbbing breast. Suddenly I was caught up in the spirit and dragged before the judgment seat of the Judge; and here the light was so bright, and those who stood around were so radiant, that I cast myself upon the ground and did not dare to look up. Asked who and what I was I replied: "I am a Christian." But He who presided said: "Thou liest, thou art a follower of Cicero and not of Christ. For 'where thy treasure is, there will thy heart be also.'" Instantly I became dumb, and amid the strokes of the lash—for He had ordered me to be scourged—I was tortured more severely still by the fire of conscience, considering with myself that verse, "In the grave who shall give thee thanks?" Yet for all that I began to cry and to bewail myself, saying: "Have mercy upon me, O Lord: have mercy upon me." Amid the sound of the scourges this cry still made itself heard. At last the bystanders, falling down before the knees of Him who presided, prayed that He would have pity on my youth, and that He would give me space to repent of my error. He might still, they urged, inflict torture on me, should I ever again read the works of the Gentiles. Under the stress of that awful moment I should have been ready to make even still larger promises than these. Accordingly I made oath and called upon His name, saying: "Lord, if ever again I possess worldly books, or if ever again I read such, I have denied Thee." Dismissed, then, on taking this oath, I returned to the upper world, and, to the surprise of all, I opened upon them eyes so drenched with tears that my distress served to convince even the incredulous. And that this was no sleep nor idle dream, such as those by which we are often mocked, I call to witness the tribunal before which I lay, and the terrible judgment which I feared. May it never, hereafter, be my lot to fall under such an inquisition! I profess that my shoulders were black and blue, that I felt the bruises long after I awoke from my sleep, and that thenceforth I read the books of God with a zeal greater than I had previously given to the books of men.

Letter to Magnus, an Orator of Rome

That our friend Sebesius has profited by your advice I have learned less from your letter than from his own penitence. And strange to say the pleasure which he has given me since his rebuke is greater than the pain he caused me from his previous waywardness. There has been indeed a conflict between indulgence in the father, and affection in the son; while the former is anxious to forget the past, the latter is eager to promise dutiful behaviour in the future. Accordingly you and I must equally rejoice, you because you have successfully put a pupil to the test, I because I have received a son again.

You ask me at the close of your letter why it is that sometimes in my writings I quote examples from secular literature and thus defile the whiteness of the church with the foulness of heathenism. I will now briefly answer your question. You would never have asked it, had not your mind been wholly taken up with Tully [Cicero]; you would never have asked it had you made it a practice instead of studying Volcatius to read the holy scriptures and the commentators upon them. For who is there who does not know that both in Moses and in the prophets there are passages cited from Gentile books and that Solomon proposed questions to the philosophers of Tyre and answered others put to him by them. In the commencement of the book of Proverbs he charges us to understand prudent maxims and shrewd adages, parables and obscure discourse, the words of the wise and their dark sayings; all of which belong by right to the sphere of the dialectician and the philosopher. The Apostle Paul also, in writing to Titus, has used a line of the poet Epimenides: "The Cretians are always liars, evil beasts, slow bellies." Half of which line was afterwards adopted by Callimachus. It is not surprising that a literal rendering of the words into Latin should fail to preserve the metre, seeing that Homer when translated into the same language is scarcely intelligible even in prose. In another epistle Paul quotes a line of Menander: "Evil communications corrupt good manners." And when he is arguing with the Athenians upon the Areopagus he calls Aratus as a witness citing from him the words "For we are also his offspring," . . . the close of a heroic verse. And as if this were not enough, that leader of the Christian army, that unvanquished pleader for the cause of Christ, skilfully turns a chance inscription into a proof of the faith. For he had learned from the true David to wrench the sword of the enemy out of his hand and with his own blade to cut off the head of the arrogant Goliath. He had read in Deuteronomy the command given by the voice of the Lord that when a captive woman had had her head shaved, her eyebrows and all her hair cut off, and her nails pared, she might then be taken to wife. Is it surprising that I too, admiring the fairness of her form and the grace of her eloquence, desire to make that secular wisdom which is my captive and my handmaid, a matron of the true Israel? Or that shaving off and cutting away all in her that is dead whether this be idolatry, pleasure, error, or lust, I take her to myself clean and pure and beget by her servants for the Lord of Sabaoth? My efforts promote the advantage of Christ's family, my so-called defilement with an alien increases the number of my fellow-servants. Hosea took a wife of whoredoms, Gomer the daughter of Diblaim, and this harlot bore him a son called Jezreel or the seed of God. Isaiah speaks of a sharp razor which shaves "the head of sinners and the hair of their feet"; and Ezekiel shaves his head as a type of that Jerusalem which has been an harlot, in sign that whatever in her is devoid of sense and life must be removed.

Cyprian, a man renowned both for his eloquence and for his martyr's death, was assailed—so Firmian tells us—for having used in his treatise against Demetrius passages from the Prophets and the Apostles which the latter declared to be fabricated and made up, instead of passages from the philosophers and poets whose authority he, as a heathen, could not well gainsay. Celsus and Porphyry have written against us and have been ably answered, the former by Origen, the latter by Methodius, Eusebius, and Apollinaris. Origen wrote a treatise in eight books, the work of Methodius extended to ten thousand lines while Eusebius and Apollinaris composed twenty-five and thirty volumes respectively. Read these and you will find that compared with them I am a mere tyro in learning, and that, as my wits have long lain fallow, I can barely recall as in a dream what I have learned as a boy. The emperor Julian found time during his Parthian campaign to vomit forth seven books against Christ and, as so often happens in poetic legends, only wounded himself with his own sword. Were I to try to confute him with the doctrines of philosophers and stoics you would doubtless forbid me to strike a mad dog with the club of Hercules. It is true that he presently felt in battle the hand of our Nazarene or, as he used to call him, the Galilaean, and that a spear-thrust in the vitals paid him due recompense for his foul calumnies. To prove the antiquity of the Jewish people Josephus has written two books against Appio a grammarian of Alexandria; and in these he brings forward so many quotations from secular writers as to make me marvel how a Hebrew brought up from his childhood to read the sacred scriptures could also have perused the whole library of the Greeks. Need I speak of Philo whom critics call the second or the Jewish Plato?

Let me now run through the list of our own writers. Did not Quadratus a disciple of the apostles and bishop of the Athenian church deliver to the Emperor Hadrian (on the occasion of his visit to the Eleusinian mysteries) a treatise in defence of our religion. And so great was the admiration caused in everyone by his eminent ability that it stilled a most severe persecution. The philosopher Aristides, a man of great eloquence, presented to the same Emperor an apology for the Christians composed of extracts from philosophic writers. His example was afterwards followed by Justin, another philosopher who delivered to Antoninus Pius and his sons and to the senate a treatise *Against the Gentiles*, in which he defended the ignominy of the cross and preached the resurrection of Christ with all freedom. Need I speak of Melito bishop of Sardis, of Apollinaris chief-priest of the Church of Hierapolis, of Dionysius bishop of the Corinthians, of Tatian, of Bardesanes, of Irenaeus successor to the martyr Pothinus; all of whom have in many volumes explained the uprisings of the several heresies and tracked them back, each to the philosophic source from which it flows. Pantaenus, a philosopher of the Stoic school, was on account of his great reputation for learning sent by Demetrius bishop of Alexandria to India, to preach Christ to the Brahmans and philosophers there. Clement, a presbyter of Alexandria, in my judgment the most learned of men, wrote eight books of *Miscellanies* [*Stromateis*] and as many of *Outline Sketches*, a treatise against the Gentiles, and three volumes called the *Pedagogue*. Is there any want of learning in these, or are they not rather drawn from the very heart of philosophy? Imitating his example Origen wrote ten books of *Miscellanies*, in which he compares together the opinions held respectively by Christians and by philosophers, and confirms all the dogmas of our religion by quotations from Plato and Aristotle, from Numenius and Cornutus. Miltiades also wrote an excellent treatise against the Gentiles. Moreover Hippolytus and a Roman senator named Apollonius have each compiled apologetic works. The books of Julius Africanus who wrote a history of his own times are still extant, as also are those of Theodore who was afterwards called Gregory, a man endowed with apostolic miracles as well as with apostolic virtues. We still have the works of Dionysius bishop of Alexandria, of Anatolius chief priest of the church of Laodicea, of the presbyters Pamphilus, Pierius, Lucian, Malchion; of Eusebius bishop of Caesarea, Eustathius of Antioch and Athanasius of Alexandria; of Eusebius of Emisa, of Triphyllius of Cyprus, of Asterius of Scythopolis, of the confessor Serapion, of Titus bishop of Bostra; and of the Cappadocians Basil, Gregory [Nazianzus], and Amphilochius. All these writers so frequently interweave in their books the doctrines and maxims of the philosophers that you might easily be at a loss which to admire most, their secular erudition or their knowledge of the scriptures.

I will pass on to Latin writers. Can anything be more learned or more pointed than the style of Tertullian? His *Apology* and his books *Against the Gentiles* contain all the wisdom of the world. Minucius Felix a pleader in the Roman courts has ransacked all heathen literature to adorn the pages of his *Octavius* and of his treatise *Against the Astrologers* (unless indeed this latter is falsely ascribed to him). Arnobius has published seven books against the Gentiles, and his pupil Lactantius as many, besides two volumes, one *On Anger* and the other *On the Creative Activity of God.* If you read any of these you will find in them an epitome of Cicero's dialogues. The Martyr Victorinus though as a writer deficient in learning is not deficient in the wish to use what learning he has. Then there is Cyprian. With what terseness, with what knowledge of all history, with what splendid rhetoric and argument has he touched the theme that idols are no Gods! Hilary too, a confessor and bishop of my own day, has imitated Quintilian's twelve books both in number and in style, and has also shewn his ability as a writer in his short treatise against Dioscorus the physician. In the reign of Constantine the presbyter Juvencus set forth in verse the story of our Lord and Saviour, and did not shrink from forcing into metre the majestic phrases of the Gospel. Of other writers dead and living I say nothing. Their aim and their ability are evident to all who read them.

You must not adopt the mistaken opinion, that while in dealing with the Gentiles one may appeal to their literature in all other discussions one ought to ignore it; for almost all the books of all these writers—except those who like Epicurus are no scholars—are extremely full of erudition and philosophy. I incline indeed to fancy—the thought comes into my head as I dictate—that you yourself know quite well what has always been the practice of the learned in this matter. I believe that in putting this question to me you are only the mouthpiece of another who by reason of his love for the histories of Sallust might well be called Calpurnius Lanarius. Please beg of him not to envy eaters their teeth because he is toothless himself, and not to make light of the eyes of gazelles because he is himself a mole. Here as you see there is abundant material for discussion, but I have already filled the limits at my disposal.

Letter to Laeta

For, in answer to your prayers and those of the saintly Marcella, I wish to address you as a mother and to instruct you how to bring up our dear Paula, who has been consecrated to Christ before her birth and vowed to His service before her conception. . . .

Thus must a soul be educated which is to be a temple of God. It must learn to hear nothing and to say nothing but what belongs to the fear of God. It must have no understanding of unclean words, and no knowledge of the world's songs. Its tongue must be steeped while still tender in the sweetness of the psalms. Boys with their wanton thoughts must be kept from Paula: even her maids and female attendants must be separated from worldly associates. For if they have learned some mischief they may teach more. Get for her a set of letters made of boxwood or of ivory and called each by its proper name. Let her play with these, so that even her play may teach her something. And not only make her grasp the right order of the letters and see that she forms their names into a rhyme, but constantly disarrange their order and put the last letters in the middle and the middle ones at the beginning that she may know them all by sight as well as by sound. Moreover, so soon as she begins to use the style upon the wax, and her hand is still faltering, either guide her soft fingers by laying your hand upon hers, or else have simple copies cut upon a tablet; so that her efforts confined within these limits may keep to the lines traced out for her and not stray outside of these. Offer prizes for good spelling and draw her onwards with little gifts such as children of her age delight in. And let her have companions in her lessons to excite emulation in her, that she may be stimulated when she sees them praised. You must not scold her if she is slow to learn but must employ praise to excite her mind, so that she may be glad when she excels others and sorry when she is excelled by them. Above all you must take care not to make her lessons distasteful to her lest a dislike for them conceived in childhood may continue into her maturer years. The very words which she tries bit by bit to put together and to pronounce ought not to be chance ones, but names specially fixed upon and heaped together for the purpose, those for example of the prophets or the apostles or the list of patriarchs from Adam downwards as it is given by Matthew and Luke. In this way while her tongue will be well-trained, her memory will be likewise developed. Again, you must choose for her a master of approved years, life, and learning. A man of culture will not, I think, blush to do for a kinswoman or a highborn virgin what Aristotle did for Philip's son when, descending to the level of an usher, he consented to teach him his letters. Things must not be despised as of small account in the absence of which great results cannot be achieved. The very rudiments and first beginnings of knowledge sound differently in the mouth of an educated man and of an uneducated. Accordingly you must see that the child is not led away by the silly coaxing of women to form a habit of shortening long words or of decking herself with gold and purple. Of these habits one will spoil her conversation and the other her character. She must not therefore learn as a child what afterwards she will have to unlearn. The eloquence of the Gracchi is said to have been largely due to the way in which from their earliest years their mother spoke to them. Hortensius became an orator while still on his father's lap. Early impressions are hard to eradicate from the mind. When once wool has been dyed purple who can restore it to its previous whiteness? An unused jar long retains the taste and smell of that with which it is first filled. Grecian history tells us that the imperious Alexander who was lord of the whole world could not rid himself of the tricks of manner and gait which in his childhood he had caught from his governor Leonides. We are always ready to imitate what is evil; and faults are quickly copied where virtues appear inattainable. Paula's nurse must not be intemperate, or loose, or given to gossip. Her bearer must be respectable, and her foster-father of grave demeanour. When she sees her grandfather, she must leap upon his breast, put her arms round his neck, and, whether he likes it or not, sing Alleluia in his ears. She may be fondled by her grandmother, may smile at her father to shew that she recognizes him, and may so endear herself to everyone, as to make the whole family rejoice in the possession of such a rosebud. She should be told at once whom she has for her other grandmother and whom for her aunt; and she ought also to learn in what army it is that she is enrolled as a recruit, and what Captain it is under whose banner she is called to serve. Let her long to be with the absent ones and encourage her to make playful threats of leaving you for them.

. . . Moreover, if you will only send Paula, I promise to be myself both a tutor and a foster father to her. Old as I am I will carry her on my shoulders and train her stammering lips; and my charge will be a far grander one than that of the worldly philosopher [Aristotle]; for while he only taught a King of Macedon who was one day to die of Babylonian poison, I shall instruct the handmaid and spouse of Christ who must one day be offered to her Lord in heaven.

Augustine

354–430

For lo, O Lord, my King and my God, for Thy service be whatever useful thing my childhood learned; for Thy service, that I speak— write—read—reckon.

CONFESSIONS

Augustine, one of the greatest Christian theologians of the West, was born in the north-African town of Thagaste, an outpost of the Roman Empire not too far from Carthage. His pagan father and devout Christian mother envisioned a successful career in rhetoric for their brilliant son. His Roman liberal arts education immersed him in Virgil and Cicero and offered some study of the Greek language and literature, through which he came to know the work of Plato, Aristotle, Seneca, the Neoplatonist philosopher Plotinus, and some Scripture. For about ten years Augustine adhered enthusiastically to the gnostic sect of the Manicheans, but he eventually became disillusioned with their doctrines and superficial celebrity leaders.

Augustine taught rhetoric in Thagaste, Carthage, Rome, and finally in Milan, where he held a coveted imperial appointment. There he heard the preaching of Bishop Ambrose, and in a wrenching spiritual crisis vividly portrayed in his *Confessions,* he converted to Christianity and was baptized. He returned to Africa, became a priest and a reluctant church administrator, founded a monastery, and rose to become bishop of Hippo. The scholar who had craved a scholarly life of uninterrupted contemplation found himself battling Donatist schismatics and Pelagian heretics, and leading the church during the violent collapse of the Roman Empire in the West. Late in his life he recalled his efforts as a young Christian to write treatises on all of the liberal arts (numbering seven, but excluding astronomy). He completed a book on grammar (lost within his lifetime and never recovered) and a large part of a treatise on music. He never returned to his work on the five other arts: dialectic, rhetoric, geometry, arithmetic, and philosophy (see Augustine's *Retractions*, 1.5.3). His monumental legacy, however, includes hundreds of surviving letters, sermons, commentaries, numerous treatises on theology and philosophy, a spiritual autobiography, and his massive theology of history, *The City of God*.

THE SELECTIONS

Augustine's *Confessions* (written between 397 and 400) has endured for sixteen hundred years as the greatest Christian autobiography. Unsparing in its self-examination yet abounding in hope and joy, the *Confessions* testifies to Augustine's pride and God's mercy. For Augustine, the task of education is inseparable from its moral context; it requires humility, sacrifice, gratitude, love, and true delight. Apart from God, human learning and skill impede our knowledge of God and knowledge of self. Knowledge of the natural world, pursued for human power and glory, will "eclipse" our knowledge of God. Preoccupation with the countable, measurable, weighable objects of the visible world will distract us from the knowledge of self. Only the humble and poor in spirit will know as they are known. The *Confessions* embodies an entire theology of education—education as worship. Augustine's recollections of his childhood education are painful, however, and it is only in hindsight that he begins to grasp God's work of grace.

In the centuries after Augustine's death, *On Christian Doctrine* became one of the most influential educational treatises in all of medieval Christendom. Throughout its four concise books, Augustine addresses timeless questions of the proper handling of Christian Scripture and the necessary intellectual and spiritual preparation for a minister of the gospel. At its core in Book II stands a spirited defense of "pagan" rhetorical skills and their usefulness to the educated Christian. Having established earlier in Book II the practicality to the church of the various branches of secular learning (whether history, natural science, mechanical arts, logic, rhetoric, or mathematics), Augustine proceeds to caution his reader against the vanity of a great deal of human knowledge. Nevertheless, he ends by encouraging the "plundering of the Egyptians" in words that echo Origen's.

Augustine's theology of education is further developed in his dialogue *On the Teacher* and in his treatise *On Order*.

from the Confessions
Book I

[IX] 14

O God my God, what miseries and mockeries did I now experience, when obedience to my teachers was proposed to me, as proper in a boy, in order that in this world I might prosper, and excel in tongue-science, which should serve to the "praise of men," and to deceitful riches. Next I was put to school to get learning, in which I (poor wretch) knew not what use there was; and yet, if idle in learning, I was beaten. For this was judged right by our fore-fathers; and many, passing the same course before us, framed for us weary paths, through which we were fain to pass; multiplying toil and grief upon the sons of Adam. But, Lord, we found that men called upon Thee, and we learnt from them to think of Thee (according to our powers) as of some great One, who, though hidden from our senses, couldest hear and help us. For so I began, as a boy, to pray to Thee, my aid and refuge; and broke the fetters of my tongue to call on Thee, praying Thee, though small, yet with no small earnestness, that I might not be beaten at school. And when Thou heardest me not, (not thereby giving me over to folly,) my elders, yea my very parents, who yet wished me no ill, mocked my stripes, my then great and grievous ill.

[IX] 15

Is there, Lord, any of soul so great, and cleaving to Thee with so intense affection, (for a sort of stupidity will in a way do it); but is there anyone, who, from cleaving devoutly to Thee, is endued with so great a spirit, that he can think as lightly of the racks and hooks and other torments, (against which, throughout all lands, men call on Thee with extreme dread,) mocking at those by whom they are feared most bitterly, as our parents mocked the torments which we suffered in boyhood from our masters? For we feared not our torments less; nor prayed we less to Thee to escape them. And yet we sinned, in writing or reading or studying less than was exacted of us. For we wanted not, O Lord, memory or capacity, whereof Thy will gave enough for our age; but our sole delight was play; and for this we were punished by those who yet themselves were doing the like. But elder folks' idleness is called "business"; that of boys, being really the same, is punished by those elders; and none commiserates either boys or men. For will any of sound discretion approve of my being beaten as a boy, because, by playing at ball, I made less progress in studies which I was to learn, only that, as a man, I might play more unbeseemingly? And what else did he, who beat me? who, if worsted in some trifling discussion with his fellow-tutor, was more embittered and jealous than I, when beaten at ball by a playfellow?

[XII] 19

In boyhood itself, however, (so much less dreaded for me than youth,) I loved not study, and hated to be forced to it. Yet I was forced; and this was well done towards me, but I did not well; for, unless forced, I had not learnt. But no one doth well against his will, even though what he doth, be well. Yet neither did they well who forced me, but what was well came to me from Thee, my God. For they were regardless how I should employ what they forced me to learn, except to satiate the insatiate desires of a wealthy beggary, and a shameful glory. But Thou, *by whom the very hairs of our head are numbered,* didst use for my good the error of all who urged me to learn; and my own, who would not learn, Thou didst use for my punishment—a fit penalty for one, so small a boy and so great a sinner. So by those who did not well, Thou didst well for me; and by my own sin Thou didst justly punish me. For Thou hast commanded, and so it is, that every inordinate affection should be its own punishment.

[XIII] 20

But why did I so much hate the Greek, which I studied as a boy? I do not yet fully know. For the Latin I loved; not what my first masters, but what the so-called grammarians taught me. For those first lessons, reading, writing and arithmetic, I thought as great a burden and penalty as any Greek. And yet whence was this too, but from the sin and vanity of this life, because *I was flesh, and a breath that passeth away and cometh not again?* For those first lessons were better certainly, because more certain; by them I obtained, and still retain, the power of reading what I find written, and myself writing what I will; whereas in the others, I was forced to learn the wanderings of one Aeneas, forgetful of my own, and to weep for dead Dido, because she killed herself for love; the while, with dry eyes, I endured my miserable self dying among these things, far from Thee, O God my life.

[XIII] 21

For what more miserable than a miserable being who commiserates not himself; weeping the death of Dido for love to Aeneas, but weeping not his own death for want of love to Thee, O God. Thou light of my heart, Thou bread of my inmost soul, Thou Power who givest vigour to my mind, who quickenest my thoughts. I loved Thee not. I committed fornication against Thee, and all around me thus fornicating there echoed "Well done! well done!" *for the friendship of this world is fornication against Thee;* and "Well done! well done!" echoes on till one is ashamed not to be thus a man. And all this I wept not, I who wept for Dido slain, and "seeking by the sword a stroke and wound extreme," myself seeking the while a worse extreme, the extremest and lowest of Thy creatures, having forsaken Thee, earth passing into the earth. And if forbid to read all this, I was grieved that I might not read what grieved me. Madness like this is thought a higher and a richer learning, than that by which I learned to read and write.

[XIII] 22

But now, my God, cry Thou aloud in my soul; and let Thy truth tell me, "Not so, not so. Far better was that first study." For, lo, I would readily forget the wanderings of Aeneas and all the rest, rather than how to read and write. But over the entrance of the Grammar School is a vail drawn! true; yet is this not so much an emblem of aught recondite, as a cloak of error. Let not those, whom I no longer fear, cry out against me, while I confess to Thee, my God, whatever my soul will, and acquiesce in the condemnation of my evil ways, that I may love Thy good ways. Let not either buyers or sellers of grammar-learning cry out against me. For if I question them whether it be true, that Aeneas came on a time to Carthage, as the Poet tells, the less learned will reply that they know not, the more learned that he never did. But should I ask with what letters the name "Aeneas" is written, every one who has learnt this will answer me aright, as to the signs which men have convention-ally settled. If again, I should ask, which might be forgotten with least detriment to the concerns of life, reading and writing or these poetic fictions? who does not foresee, what all must answer who have not wholly forgotten themselves? I sinned, then, when as a boy I preferred those empty to those more profitable studies, or rather loved the one and hated the other. "One and one, two;" "two and two, four;" this was to me a hateful sing-song: "the wooden horse lined with armed men," and "the burning of Troy," and "Creusa's shade and sad similitude," were the choice spectacle of my vanity.

[XIV] 23

Why then did I hate the Greek classics, which have the like tales? For Homer also curi-
ously wove the like fictions, and is most sweetly-vain, yet was he bitter to my boyish taste.
And so I suppose would Virgil be to Grecian children, when forced to learn him as I was
Homer. Difficulty, in truth, the difficulty of a foreign tongue, dashed, as it were, with gall
all the sweetness of Grecian fable. For not one word of it did I understand, and to make
me understand I was urged vehemently with cruel threats and punishments. Time was
also, (as an infant,) I knew no Latin; but this I learned without fear or suffering, by mere
observation, amid the caresses of my nursery and jests of friends, smiling and sportively
encouraging me. This I learned without any pressure of punishment to urge me on, for
my heart urged me to give birth to its conceptions, which I could only do by learning
words not of those who taught, but of those who talked with me; in whose ears also I gave
birth to the thoughts, whatever I conceived. No doubt then, that a free curiosity has more
force in our learning these things, than a frightful enforcement. Only this enforcement
restrains the rovings of that freedom, through Thy laws, O my God, Thy laws, from the
master's cane to the martyr's trials, being able to temper for us a wholesome bitter, recalling us to Thyself from that deadly pleasure which lures us from Thee.

[XV] 24

Hear, Lord, my prayer; let not my soul faint under Thy discipline, nor let me faint in con-
fessing unto Thee all Thy mercies, whereby Thou hast drawn me out of all my most evil
ways, that Thou mightest become a delight to me above all the allurements which I once
pursued; that I may most entirely love Thee, and clasp Thy hand with all my affections,
and Thou mayest yet rescue me from every temptation, even unto the end. For, lo, O Lord,
my King and my God, for Thy service be whatever useful thing my childhood learned;
for Thy service, that I speak—write—read—reckon. For Thou didst grant me Thy discipline, while I was learning vanities; and my sin of delighting in those vanities Thou hast
forgiven. In them, indeed, I learnt many a useful word, but these may as well be learned in
things not vain; and that is the safe path for the steps of youth.

[XVI] 25

But woe is thee, thou torrent of human custom! Who shall stand against thee? How long
shalt thou not be dried up? How long roll the sons of Eve into that huge and hideous ocean,
which even they scarcely overpass who climb the cross? Did not I read in thee of Jove the
thunderer and the adulterer? Both, doubtless, he could not be; but so the feigned thunder
might countenance and pander to real adultery. And now which of our gowned masters,
lends a sober ear to one who from their own school cries out, "These were Homer's fictions, transferring thing human to the gods; would he had brought down things divine
to us!" Yet more truly had he said, "These are indeed his fictions; but attributing a divine
nature to wicked men, that crimes might be no longer crimes, and whoso commits them
might seem to imitate not abandoned men, but the celestial gods."

[XVI] 26

And yet, thou hellish torrent, into thee are cast the sons of men with rich rewards, for
compassing such learning; and a great solemnity is made of it, when this is going on in the

forum, within sight of laws appointing a salary beside the scholar's payments; and thou lashest thy rocks and roarest, "Hence words are learnt; hence eloquence; most necessary to gain your ends, or maintain opinions." As if we should have never known such words as "golden shower," "lap," "beguile," "temples of the heavens," or others in that passage, unless Terence had brought a lewd youth upon the stage, setting up Jupiter as his example of seduction.

> Viewing a picture, where the tale was drawn,
> Of Jove's descending in a golden shower
> To Danae's lap a woman to beguile.

And then mark how he excites himself to lust as by celestial authority:

> And what God? Great Jove,
> Who shakes heav'n's highest temples with his thunder,
> And I, poor mortal man, not do the same!
> I did it, and with all my heart I did it.

Not one whit more easily are the words learnt for all this vileness; but by their means the vileness is committed with less shame. Not that I blame the words, being, as it were, choice and precious vessels; but that wine of error which is drunk to us in them by intoxicated teachers; and if we, too, drink not, we are beaten, and have no sober judge to whom we may appeal. Yet, O my God, (in whose presence I now without hurt may remember this,) all this unhappily I learnt willingly with great delight, and for this was pronounced a hopeful boy.

[XVII] 27

Bear with me, my God, while I say somewhat of my wit, Thy gift, and on what dotages I wasted it. For a task was set me, troublesome enough to my soul, upon terms of praise or shame, and fear of stripes, to speak the words of Juno, as she raged and mourned that she could not

> This Trojan prince from Latinum turn.

Which words I had heard that Juno never uttered; but we were forced to go astray in the footsteps of these poetic fictions, and to say in prose much what he expressed in verse. And his speaking was most applauded, in whom the passions of rage and grief were most pre-eminent, and clothed in the most fitting language, maintaining the dignity of the character. What is it to me, O my true life, my God, that my declamation was applauded above so many of my own age and class? Is not all this smoke and wind? And was there nothing else whereon to exercise my wit and tongue? Thy praises, Lord, Thy praises might have stayed the yet tender shoot of my heart by the prop of Thy Scriptures; so had it not trailed away amid these empty trifles, a defiled prey for the fowls of the air. For in more ways than one do men sacrifice to the rebellious angels.

[XVIII] 28

But what marvel that I was thus carried away to vanities, and went out from Thy presence, O my God, when men were set before me as models, who, if in relating some action of theirs, in itself not ill, they committed some barbarism or solecism, being censured, were abashed; but when in rich and adorned and well-ordered discourse they related their own disordered life, being be-praised, they gloried? These things Thou seest, Lord, and holdest Thy peace; *long-suffering, and plenteous in mercy and truth*. Wilt Thou hold Thy peace for ever? And even now Thou drawest out of this horrible gulf the soul that seeketh Thee, that thirsteth for Thy pleasures, *whose heart saith unto Thee, I have sought Thy face; Thy face, Lord, will I seek*. For *darkened* affections is removal from Thee. For it is not by our feet, or change of place, that men leave Thee, or return unto Thee. Or did that Thy younger son look out for horses or chariots, or ships, fly with visible wings, or journey by the motion of his limbs, that he might in a far country waste in riotous living all Thou gavest at his departure? A loving Father, when Thou gavest, and more loving unto him, when he returned empty. So then in lustful, that is, in darkened affections, is the true distance from Thy face.

[XVIII] 29

Behold, O Lord God, yea, behold patiently as Thou art wont, how carefully the sons of men observe the covenanted rules of letters and syllables received from those who spake before them, neglecting the eternal covenant of everlasting salvation received from Thee. Insomuch, that a teacher or learner of the hereditary laws of pronunciation will more offend men, by speaking without the aspirate, of a "uman being," in despite of the laws of grammar, than if he, a "human being," hate a "human being" in despite of Thine. As if any enemy could be more hurtful than the hatred with which he is incensed against him; or could wound more deeply him whom he persecutes, than he wounds his own soul by his enmity. Assuredly no science of letters can be so innate as the record of conscience, "that he is doing to another what from another he would be loth to suffer." How deep are Thy ways, O God, Thou only great, *that sittest* silent *on high* and by an unwearied law dispensing penal blindness to lawless desires. In quest of the fame of eloquence, a man standing before a human judge, surrounded by a human throng, declaiming against his enemy with fiercest hatred, will take heed most watchfully, lest, by an error of the tongue, he murder the word "human being"; but takes no heed, lest, through the fury of his spirit, he murder the real human being.

Book III

[IV] 7

Among such as these, in that unsettled age of mine, learned I books of eloquence, wherein I desired to be eminent, out of a damnable and vainglorious end, a joy in human vanity. In the ordinary course of study, I fell upon a certain book of Cicero, whose speech almost all admire, not so his heart. This book of his contains an exhortation to philosophy, and is called "Hortensius." But this book altered my affections, and turned my prayers to Thyself, O Lord; and made me have other purposes and desires. Every vain hope at once became worthless to me; and I longed with an incredibly burning desire for an immortality of wisdom, and began now to arise, that I might return to Thee. For not to sharpen my tongue, (which thing I seemed to be purchasing with my mother's allowances, in that my nineteenth year, my father being dead two years before,) not to sharpen my tongue did I employ that book; nor did it infuse into me its style, but its matter.

[IV] 8

How did I burn then, my God, how did I burn to re-mount from earthly things to Thee, nor knew I what Thou wouldest do with me? For with Thee is wisdom. But the love of wisdom is in Greek called "philosophy," with which that book inflamed me. Some there be that seduce through philosophy, under a great, and smooth, and honourable name coloring and disguising their own errors: and almost all who in that and former ages were such, are in that book censured and set forth: there also is made plain that wholesome advice of Thy Spirit, by Thy good and devout servant; *Beware lest any man spoil you through philosophy and vain deceit, after the tradition of men, after the rudiments of the world, and not after Christ. For in Him dwelleth all the fullness of the Godhead bodily.* And since at that time (Thou, O light of my heart, knowest) Apostolic Scripture was not known to me, I was delighted with that exhortation, so far only, that I was thereby strongly roused, and kindled, and inflamed to love, and seek, and obtain, and hold, and embrace not this or that sect, but wisdom itself whatever it were; and this alone checked me thus enkindled, that the name of Christ was not in it. For this name, according to Thy mercy, O Lord, this name of my Saviour Thy Son, had my tender heart, even with my mother's milk, devoutly drunk in and deeply treasured; and whatsoever was without that name, though never so learned, polished, or true, took not entire hold of me.

[V] 9

I resolved then to bend my mind to the holy Scriptures, that I might see what they were. But behold, I see a thing not understood by the proud, nor laid open to children, lowly in access, in its recesses lofty, and veiled with mysteries; and I was not such as could enter into it, or stoop my neck to follow its steps. For not as I now speak, did I feel when I turned to those Scriptures; but they seemed to me unworthy to be compared to the stateliness of Tully [Cicero]: for my swelling pride shrunk from their lowliness, nor could my sharp wit pierce the interior thereof. Yet were they such as would grow up in a little one. But I disdained to be a little one; and, swollen with pride, took myself to be a great one.

Book IV

[XVI] 28

And what did it profit me, that scarce twenty years old, a book of Aristotle, which they call the ten Predicaments, falling into my hands, (on whose very name I hung, as on something great and divine, so often as my rhetoric master of Carthage, and others, accounted learned, mouthed it with cheeks bursting with pride,) I read and understood it unaided? And on my conferring with others, who said that they scarcely understood it with very able tutors, not only orally explaining it, but drawing many things in sand, they could tell me no more of it than I had learned, reading it by myself. And the book appeared to me to speak very clearly of substances, such as "man," and of their qualities, as the figure of a man, of what sort it is; and stature, how many feet high; and his relationship, whose brother he is; or where placed; or when born; or whether he stands or sits; or be shod or armed; or does, or suffers anything; and all the innumerable things which might be ranged under these nine Predicaments, of which I have given some specimens, or under that chief Predicament of Substance.

[XVI] 29

What did all this further me, seeing it even hindered me? when, imagining whatever was, was comprehended under those ten Predicaments, I essayed in such wise to understand, O my God, Thy wonderful and unchangeable Unity also, as if Thou also hadst been subjected to Thine own greatness or beauty; so that (as in bodies) they should exist in Thee, as their subject: whereas Thou Thyself art Thy greatness and beauty; but a body is not great or fair in that it is a body, seeing that, though it were less great or fair, it should notwithstanding be a body. But it was falsehood which of Thee I conceived, not truth; fictions of my misery, not the realities of Thy Blessedness. For Thou hadst commanded, and it was done in me, that the *earth should bring forth briars and thorns to me,* and that *in the sweat of my brows I should eat my bread.*

[XVI] 30

And what did it profit me, that all the books I could procure of the so-called liberal arts, I, the vile slave of vile affections, read by myself, and understood? And I delighted in them, but knew not whence came all, that therein was true or certain. For I had my back to the light, and my face to the things enlightened; whence my face, with which I discerned the things enlightened, itself was not enlightened. Whatever was written, either on rhetoric, or logic, geometry, music, and arithmetic, by myself without much difficulty or any instructor, I understood, Thou knowest, O Lord my God; because both quickness of understanding, and acuteness in discerning, is Thy gift: yet did I not thence sacrifice to Thee. So then it served not to my use, but rather to my perdition, since I went about to get so good a *portion of my substance* into my own keeping; and I *kept not my strength for Thee,* but wandered from Thee *into a far country, to spend it upon harlotries.* For what profited me good abilities, not employed to good uses? For I felt not that those arts were attained with great difficulty, even by the studious and talented, until I attempted to explain them to such; when he most excelled in them, who followed me not altogether slowly.

[XVI] 31

But what did this further me, imagining that Thou, O Lord God, the Truth, wert a vast and bright body, and I a fragment of that body? Perverseness too great! But such was I.

Nor do I blush, O my God, to *confess to Thee Thy mercies towards me,* and to call upon Thee, who blushed not then to profess to men my blasphemies, and to bark against Thee.

What profited me then my nimble wit in those sciences and all those most knotty volumes, unravelled by me, without aid from human instruction; seeing I erred so foully, and with such sacrilegious shamefulness, in the doctrine of piety? Or what hindrance was a far slower wit to Thy little ones, since they departed not far from Thee, that in the nest of Thy Church they might securely be fledged, and nourish the wings of charity, by the food of a sound faith. O Lord our God, *under the shadow of Thy wings let us hope;* protect us, and carry us. Thou wilt carry us both when little, and *even to hoar hairs wilt Thou carry us;* for our firmness, when it is Thou, then is it firmness; but when our own, it is infirmity. Our good ever lives with Thee; from which when we turn away, we are turned aside. Let us now, O Lord, return, that we may not be overturned, because with Thee our good lives without any decay, which good art Thou; nor need we fear, lest there be no place whither to return, because we fell from it: for through our absence, our mansion fell not—Thy eternity.

Book V

[III] 3

I would lay open before my God that nine and twentieth year of mine age. There had then come to Carthage, a certain Bishop of the Manichees, Faustus by name, a great snare of the Devil, and many were entangled by him through that lure of his smooth language: which though I did commend, yet could I separate from the truth of the things which I was earnest to learn: nor did I so much regard the service of oratory as the science which this Faustus, so praised among them, set before me to feed upon. Fame had before bespoken him most knowing in all valuable learning, and exquisitely skilled in the liberal sciences. And since I had read and well remembered much of the philosophers, I compared some things of theirs with those long fables of the Manichees, and found the former the more probable; even although they *could only prevail so far as to make judgment of this lower world, the Lord of it they could by no means find out. For Thou art great, O Lord, and hast respect unto the humble, but the proud Thou beholdest afar off.* Nor dost Thou *draw near,* but to *the contrite in heart,* nor art found by the proud, no, not though by curious skill they could number the stars and the sand, and measure the starry heavens, and track the courses of the planets.

[III] 4

For with their understanding and wit, which Thou bestowest on them, they search out these things; and much have they found out; and foretold, many years before, eclipses of those luminaries, the sun and moon,—what day and hour, and how many digits,—nor did their calculation fail; and it came to pass as they foretold; and they wrote down the rules they had found out, and these are read at this day, and out of them do others foretell in what year and month of the year, and what day of the month, and what hour of the day, and what part of its light, moon or sun is to be eclipsed, and so it shall be, as it is foreshewed. At these things men, that know not this art, marvel and are astonished, and they that know it, exult, and are puffed up; and by an ungodly pride departing from Thee, and failing of Thy light, they foresee a failure of the sun's light, which shall be, so long before, but see not their own, which is. For they search not religiously whence they have the wit, wherewith they search out this. And finding that Thou madest them, they give not themselves up to Thee, to preserve what Thou madest, nor sacrifice to Thee, what they have made themselves; nor slay their own soaring imaginations, as *fowls of the air,* nor their own diving curiosities, (wherewith, like the *fishes of the sea,* they wander over the unknown paths of the abyss,) nor their own luxuriousness, as *beasts of the field,* that *Thou, Lord, a consuming fire,* mayest burn up those dead cares of theirs, and re-create themselves immortally.

[III] 5

But they knew not the way, Thy Word, by Whom Thou madest these things which they number, and themselves who number, and the sense whereby they perceive what they number, and the understanding, out of which they number; or that *of Thy wisdom there is no number.* But the Only Begotten is Himself *made unto us wisdom, and righteousness, and sanctification,* and was numbered among us, and *paid tribute unto Caesar.* They knew not this Way whereby to descend to Him from themselves, and by Him ascend unto Him. They knew not this way, and deemed themselves exalted amongst the stars and shining; and behold, they *fell upon the earth, and their foolish heart was darkened.* They discourse many things truly concerning the creature; but Truth, Artificer of the creature, they seek not piously, and therefore find Him not; or if they find Him, *knowing Him to be God, they glorify Him not as God, neither are thankful, but become vain in their imaginations,* and *profess themselves to be wise,* attributing to themselves what is Thine; and thereby with most perverse blindness, study to impute to Thee what is their own, forging lies of Thee who art the Truth, and *changing the glory of uncorruptible God, into an image made like corruptible man, and to birds, and four-footed beasts, and creeping things, changing Thy truth into a lie, and worshipping and serving the creature more than the Creator.*

[III] 6

Yet many truths concerning the creature retained I from these men, and saw the reason thereof from calculations, the succession of times, and the visible testimonies of the stars; and compared them with the saying of Manichaeus, which in his frenzy he had written most largely on these subjects; but discovered not any account of the solstices, or equinoxes, or the eclipses of the greater lights, nor whatever of this sort I had learned in the books of secular philosophy. But I was commanded to believe; and yet it corresponded not with what had been established by calculations and my own sight, but was quite contrary.

[IV] 7

Doth then, O Lord God of truth, whoso knoweth these things, therefore please Thee? Surely unhappy is he who knoweth all these, and knoweth not Thee: but happy whoso knoweth Thee, though he know not these. And whoso knoweth both Thee and them is not the happier for them, but for Thee only, if, *knowing Thee, he glorifies Thee as God, and is thankful, and becomes not vain in his imaginations.* For as he is better off who knows how to possess a tree, and return thanks to Thee for the use thereof, although he know not how many cubits high it is, or how wide it spreads, than he that can measure it, and count all its boughs, and neither owns it, nor knows or loves its Creator: so a believer, whose all this world of wealth is, and *who having nothing, yet possesseth all things,* by cleaving unto Thee, whom all things serve, though he know not even the circles of the Great Bear, yet is it folly to doubt but he is in a better state than one who can measure the heavens, and number the stars, and poise the elements, yet neglecteth Thee *who halt made all things in number, weight, and measure.*

Book X

[VIII] 15

Great is this force of memory, excessive great, O my God; a large and boundless chamber! who ever sounded the bottom thereof? yet is this a power of mine, and belongs unto my nature; nor do I myself comprehend all that I am. Therefore is the mind too strait to contain itself. And where should that be, which it containeth not of itself? Is it without it, and not within? how then doth it not comprehend itself? A wonderful admiration surprises me, amazement seizes me upon this. And men go abroad to admire the heights of mountains, the mighty billows of the sea, the broad tides of rivers, the compass of the ocean, and the circuits of the stars, and pass themselves by; nor wonder, that when I spake of all these things, I did not see them with mine eyes, yet could not have spoken of them, unless I then actually saw the mountains, billows, rivers, stars which I had seen, and that ocean which I believe to be, inwardly in my memory, and that, with the same vast spaces between, as if I saw them abroad. Yet did not I by seeing draw them into myself, when with mine eyes I beheld them; nor are they themselves with me, but their images only. And I know by what sense of the body each was impressed upon me.

from On Christian Doctrine
Book II

CHAPTER 39: TO WHICH OF THE ABOVE-MENTIONED STUDIES ATTENTION SHOULD BE GIVEN, AND IN WHAT SPIRIT

Accordingly, I think that it is well to warn studious and able young men, who fear God and are seeking for happiness of life, not to venture heedlessly upon the pursuit of the branches of learning that are in vogue beyond the pale of the Church of Christ, as if these could secure for them the happiness they seek; but soberly and carefully to discriminate among them. And if they find any of those which have been instituted by men varying by reason of the varying pleasure of their founders, and unknown by reason of erroneous conjectures, especially if they involve entering into fellowship with devils by means of leagues and covenants about signs, let these be utterly rejected and held in detestation. Let the young men also withdraw their attention from such institutions of men as are unnecessary and luxurious. But for the sake of the necessities of this life we must not neglect the arrangements of men that enable us to carry on intercourse with those around us. I think, however, there is nothing useful in the other branches of learning that are found among the heathen, except information about objects, either past or present, that relate to the bodily senses, in which are included also the experiments and conclusions of the useful mechanical arts, except also the sciences of reasoning and of number. And in regard to all these we must hold by the maxim, "Not too much of anything"; especially in the case of those which, pertaining as they do to the senses, are subject to the relations of space and time.

What, then, some men have done in regard to all words and names found in Scripture, in the Hebrew, and Syrian, and Egyptian, and other tongues, taking up and interpreting separately such as were left in Scripture without interpretation; and what Eusebius has done in regard to the history of the past with a view to the questions arising in Scripture that require a knowledge of history for their solution;—what, I say, these men have done in regard to matters of this kind, making it unnecessary for the Christian to spend his strength on many subjects for the sake of a few items of knowledge, the same, I think, might be done in regard to other matters, if any competent man were willing in a spirit of benevolence to undertake the labour for the advantage of his brethren. In this way he might arrange in their several classes, and give an account of the unknown places, and animals, and plants, and trees, and stones, and metals, and other species of things that are mentioned in Scripture, taking up these only, and committing his account to writing. This might also be done in relation to numbers, so that the theory of those numbers, and those only, which are mentioned in Holy Scripture, might be explained and written down. And it may happen that some or all of these things have been done already (as I have found that many things I had no notion of have been worked out and committed to writing by good and learned Christians), but are either lost amid the crowds of the careless, or are kept out of sight by the envious. And I am not sure whether the same thing can be done in regard to the theory of reasoning; but it seems to me it cannot, because this runs like a system of nerves through the whole structure of Scripture, and on that account is of more service to the reader in disentangling and explaining ambiguous passages, of which I shall speak hereafter, than in ascertaining the meaning of unknown signs, the topic I am now discussing.

CHAPTER 40: WHATEVER HAS BEEN RIGHTLY SAID BY THE HEATHEN, WE MUST APPROPRIATE TO OUR USES

Moreover, if those who are called philosophers, and especially the Platonists, have said aught that is true and in harmony with our faith, we are not only not to shrink from it, but to claim it for our own use from those who have unlawful possession of it. For, as the Egyptians had not only the idols and heavy burdens which the people of Israel hated and fled from, but also vessels and ornaments of gold and silver, and garments, which the same people when going out of Egypt appropriated to themselves, designing them for a better use, not doing this on their own authority, but by the command of God, the Egyptians themselves, in their ignorance, providing them with things which they themselves, were not making a good use of; in the same way all branches of heathen learning have not only false and superstitious fancies and heavy burdens of unnecessary toil, which every one of us, when going out under the leadership of Christ from the fellowship of the heathen, ought to abhor and avoid; but they contain also liberal instruction which is better adapted to the use of the truth, and some most excellent precepts of morality; and some truths in regard even to the worship of the One God are found among them. Now these are, so to speak, their gold and silver, which they did not create themselves, but dug out of the mines of God's providence which are everywhere scattered abroad, and are perversely and unlawfully prostituting to the worship of devils. These, therefore, the Christian, when he separates himself in spirit from the miserable fellowship of these men, ought to take away from them, and to devote to their proper use in preaching the gospel. Their garments, also,—that is, human institutions such as are adapted to that intercourse with men which is indispensable in this life,—we must take and turn to a Christian use.

And what else have many good and faithful men among our brethren done? Do we not see with what a quantity of gold and silver and garments Cyprian, that most persuasive teacher and most blessed martyr, was loaded when he came out of Egypt? How much Lactantius brought with him? And Victorinus, and Optatus, and Hilary, not to speak of living men! How much Greeks out of number have borrowed! And prior to all these, that most faithful servant of God, Moses, had done the same thing; for of him it is written that he was learned in all the wisdom of the Egyptians. And to none of all these would heathen superstition (especially in those times when, kicking against the yoke of Christ, it was persecuting the Christians) have ever furnished branches of knowledge it held useful, if it had suspected they were about to turn them to the use of worshipping the One God, and thereby overturning the vain worship of idols. But they gave their gold and their silver and their garments to the people of God as they were going out of Egypt, not knowing how the things they gave would be turned to the service of Christ. For what was done at the time of the exodus was no doubt a type prefiguring what happens now. And this I say without prejudice to any other interpretation that may be as good, or better.

CHAPTER 41: WHAT KIND OF SPIRIT IS REQUIRED FOR THE STUDY OF HOLY SCRIPTURE

But when the student of the Holy Scriptures, prepared in the way I have indicated, shall enter upon his investigations, let him constantly meditate upon that saying of the apostle's, "Knowledge puffeth up, but charity edifieth." For so he will feel that, whatever may be the riches he brings with him out of Egypt, yet unless he has kept the Passover, he cannot be safe. Now Christ is our Passover sacrificed for us, and there is nothing the sacrifice of Christ more clearly teaches us than the call which He himself addresses to those whom He sees toiling in Egypt under Pharaoh: "Come unto me, all ye that labour and are heavy laden, and I will give you rest. Take my yoke upon you, and learn of me; for I am meek and lowly in heart: and ye shall find rest unto your souls. For my yoke is easy, and my burden is light." To whom is it light but to the meek and lowly in heart, whom knowledge does not puff up, but charity edifieth? Let them remember, then, that those who celebrated the Passover at that time in type and shadow, when they were ordered to mark their door-posts with the blood of the lamb, used hyssop to mark them with. Now this is a meek and lowly herb, and yet nothing is stronger and more penetrating than its roots; that being rooted and grounded in love, we may be able to comprehend with all saints what is the breadth, and length, and depth, and height,—that is, to comprehend the cross of our Lord, the breadth of which is indicated by the transverse wood on which the hands are stretched, its length by the part from the ground up to the crossbar on which the whole body from the head downwards is fixed, its height by the part from the crossbar to the top on which the head lies, and its depth by the part which is hidden, being fixed in the earth. And by this sign of the cross all Christian action is symbolized, viz., to do good works in Christ, to cling with constancy to Him, to hope for heaven, and not to desecrate the sacraments. And purified by this Christian action, we shall be able to know even "the love of Christ which passeth knowledge," who is equal to the Father, by whom all things, were made, "that we may be filled with all the fullness of God." There is besides in hyssop a purgative virtue, that the breast may not be swollen with that knowledge which puffeth up, nor boast vainly of the riches brought out from Egypt. "Purge me with hyssop," the psalmist says, "and I shall be clean; wash me, and I shall be whiter than snow. Make me to hear joy and gladness." Then he immediately adds, to show that it is purifying from pride that is indicated by hyssop, "that the bones which Thou hast broken may rejoice."

CHAPTER 42: SACRED SCRIPTURE COMPARED WITH PROFANE AUTHORS.

But just as poor as the store of gold and silver and garments which the people of Israel brought with them out of Egypt was in comparison with the riches which they afterwards attained at Jerusalem, and which reached their height in the reign of King Solomon, so poor is all the useful knowledge which is gathered from the books of the heathen when compared with the knowledge of Holy Scripture. For whatever man may have learnt from other sources, if it is hurtful, it is there condemned; if it is useful, it is therein contained.

And while every man may find there all that he has learnt of useful elsewhere, he will find there in much greater abundance things that are to be found nowhere else, but can be learnt only in the wonderful sublimity and wonderful simplicity of the Scriptures. When, then, the reader is possessed of the instruction here pointed out, so that unknown signs have ceased to be a hindrance to him; when he is meek and lowly of heart, subject to the easy yoke of Christ, and loaded with His light burden, rooted and grounded and built up in faith, so that knowledge cannot puff him up, let him then approach the consideration and discussion of ambiguous signs in Scripture. And about these I shall now, in a third book, endeavour to say what the Lord shall be pleased to vouchsafe.

Cassiodorus

c. 485–c. 585

*For learning taken from the ancients in the midst of praising the
Lord is not considered tasteless boasting.*

INSTITUTIONS OF DIVINE AND SECULAR LEARNING

Born to a distinguished noble family shortly after the fall of the city of Rome, Cassiodorus (Flavius Magnus Aurelius Cassiodorus Senator) witnessed at firsthand the tumultuous years of those early Germanic kingdoms whose conquests fragmented the empire in the West. He also lived through the Eastern Roman Empire's reconquest of Italy under the emperor Justinian. He was appointed to the office of consul and held various positions of trust close to the Ostrogothic king Theodoric. He was a contemporary of Boethius, author of the celebrated treatise *The Consolation of Philosophy,* who also served Theodoric until he was accused of treason, imprisoned, and executed. Cassiodorus left the imperial capital at Ravenna and settled for a time in Constantinople and then at a monastery in the East. Returning to Italy, he founded a monastery on his estate at Vivarium, modeled perhaps on Benedict's community at Monte Cassino. Recognizing himself as a remnant of a dying civilization, he hoped to preserve the legacy of literate Greco-Roman culture. At Vivarium, monks labored to learn Scripture, the Church Fathers, and the liberal arts; meticulously and prayerfully copied the books of the Bible and Latin authors; translated Greek texts; and organized a treasured library. Above all, these efforts served to promote the study of Scripture. In historian Peter Brown's apt simile, "Like a newly formed planetary system, Latin culture as a whole was supposed to spin in orbit around the vast sun of the Word of God."[1] Despite Cassiodorus's noble intentions, however, his monastery only briefly survived his death, and his library was scattered.

THE SELECTION

Cassiodorus's *Institutions of Divine and Secular Learning*, completed sometime in the 550s, provided practical instruction and inspiration for the capable (and less capable) monks at Vivarium. He sees their labors as worship. His pastoral concern for his community of learning is clear: "Quickly now, O dear brothers, hasten to advance in Sacred Scripture, since you know that I have gathered so many great and varied works for you to increase your learning with the aid of the Lord's grace" (I.xxxiii). The treatise is divided into two books. The first deals with the canon of Scripture and the Church Fathers; the second deals with each of the seven liberal arts. The two passages included here orient learning toward the glory of God, defend the use of secular studies, warn against distraction, acknowledge the need for humble recognition of the limits of human understanding, and express gratitude to God for his gift of knowledge.

from Institutions of Divine and Secular Learning
Book I

PREFACE

1. When I realized that there was such a zealous and eager pursuit of secular learning, by which the majority of mankind hopes to obtain knowledge of this world, I was deeply grieved, I admit, that Holy Scripture should so lack public teachers, whereas secular authors certainly flourish in widespread teaching. Together with blessed Pope Agapetus of Rome, I made efforts to collect money so that it should rather be the Christian schools in the city of Rome that could employ learned teachers—the money having been collected—from whom the faithful might gain eternal salvation for their souls and the adornment of sober and pure eloquence for their speech. They say that such a system existed for a long time at Alexandria and that the Hebrews are now using it enthusiastically in Nisibis, a city of Syria. But since I could not accomplish this task because of raging wars and violent struggles in the Kingdom of Italy—for a peaceful endeavour has no place in a time of unrest—I was moved by divine love to devise for you, with God's help, these introductory books to take the place of a teacher. Through them I believe that both the textual sequence of Holy Scripture and also a compact account of secular letters may, with God's grace, be revealed: These works may seem rather plain in style since they offer not polished eloquence but basic description. But they are of great use as an introduction to the source both of knowledge of this world and of the salvation of the soul. I commend in them not my own teaching, but the words of earlier writers that we justly praise and gloriously her-

---

1. *The Rise of Western Christendom: Triumph and Diversity,* A.D. *200–1000* (Malden, MA: Blackwell, 1997), 150.

ald to later generations. For learning taken from the ancients in the midst of praising the Lord is not considered tasteless boasting. Furthermore, you make a serious teacher angry if you question him often; but however often you want to return to these books, you will not be rebuked with any severity.

2. Therefore, beloved brothers, let us ascend without hesitation to Holy Scripture through the excellent commentaries of the Fathers, as if on the ladder of Jacob's vision so that, lifted by their thoughts, we are worthy to arrive at full contemplation of the Lord. For commentary on Scripture is, as it were, Jacob's ladder, by which the angels ascend and descend [Gen. 28:12]; on which the Lord leans, stretching out his hand to those who are weary, and supports the tired steps of those ascending by granting them contemplation of Him. So in this matter, if it is approved, we ought to keep this sequence [cf. the ladder] of reading, so that the recruits of Christ, after they have learned the Psalms, should study the divine text in corrected books until, by continuous practice, with God's help, it is well known to them. The books should be corrected to prevent scribal errors from being fixed in untrained minds, because what is fixed and rooted in the depths of memory is hard to remove. Happy indeed is the mind that has stored such a mysterious treasure in the depths of memory [cf. Virgil *Georgics* 2.490ff.], with God's help; but much happier the mind that knows the ways of understanding from its energetic investigation. As a result, such a mind vigorously expels human thoughts and is occupied to its salvation with divine utterances. I recall that I have seen many men with powerful memories who, asked about the most obscure passages, have solved the questions put to them by examples drawn only from divine authority, for a matter stated obscurely in one place is set down more clearly in another book. An example of this is the Apostle Paul who to a large extent in the letter written to the Hebrews elucidates the writings of the Old Testament by their fulfilment in the new times.

3. Therefore, dearest brothers, after the soldiers of Christ have filled themselves with divine study and, grown strong by regular reading, have begun to recognize passages cited as circumstances indicate, then they may profit from going through this guide. It is divided into two books, briefly indicating the works to be read and the proper order for reading them; thus, the student can learn where Latin commentators explain a given passage. But if he finds something in these writers discussed in a cursory fashion, then those who know the language should seek from Greek expositors helpful interpretations. In this way indifference and negligence may be removed and vital knowledge sought by minds set aflame in the training school of Christ.

4. They say that the Divine Scriptures of the Old and New Testament from the beginning to the end were elucidated in Greek by Clement of Alexandria surnamed "Stromateus," by Cyril, bishop of the same city, by John Chrysostom, Gregory, and Basil as well as other scholarly men whom eloquent Greece praises. But we, with the Lord's aid, rather seek Latin writers. Since I am writing for Italians so it has seemed most appropriate to point out Roman commentators, for everyone accepts more easily what is reported in his native language. Hence it can happen that something is treated by ancient teachers that could not be provided by modern ones. Therefore it will be enough to point out to you the most learned commentators; when you are sent to such writers you find the proper and full measure of teaching. It will also be better for you not to be drinking in striking novelty but to satisfy yourself at the spring of the ancients. Consequently I may teach at

my leisure and instruct you without blameworthy presumption; and I think that this type of instruction is profitable even to us, teaching others in such a way that we most suitably avoid the snares of those who misrepresent us.

5. So in the first book you have teachers of a former age always available and prepared to teach you, not so much by their speech as through your eyes. Therefore, brothers eager for learning, wisely moderate your desires, and in imitation of those who desire to gain health of the body, let us learn what is to be read in proper order. For those who want to be cured ask the doctors what foods they should take first, what refreshment they should take next, so that an indiscriminate appetite does not tax rather than restore the failing strength of their weakened limbs.

6. In the second book on the arts and disciplines of liberal studies a few things need to be imbibed; and yet in this setting there is little harm to the person who slips, if he errs while keeping his faith firm. Whatever has been found in Divine Scripture on such matters will be better understood if one has prior acquaintance with them. It is well-known that, at the beginning of spiritual wisdom, information on these subjects was sowed, as it were, that secular teachers afterwards wisely transferred to their own rules as I have perhaps shown at suitable places in my *Psalm Commentary*.

7. Therefore, pray to God, the source of all that is useful; read, I pray, constantly; go over the material diligently; for frequent and intense meditation is the mother of understanding. I have not forgotten that the most eloquent commentator Cassian in his *Conversations* Book 5 related that a certain old and simple man had been asked about a most obscure passage of Divine Scripture and that he, after long prayer, by the light from above understood and explained the most difficult matters to his questioners. He had suddenly been filled by divine inspiration with what he had not learned before from human teachers. St Augustine tells a similar story in his *Christian Learning* of an illiterate foreign servant who through constant prayer suddenly read a book that was handed to him as though he had been taught by long practice in school. Concerning this matter Augustine himself spoke later as follows: although these miracles are surprising, and there is the statement that "all things are possible to those who believe" [Mark 9:22], we ought not to pray for such things often, but rather stick to the practice of ordinary teaching so that we do not rashly seek after those things that are beyond us and risk testing the precept of the Lord who says in Deuteronomy: "You shall not put the Lord your God to the test" [Deut. 6:16], and again says in the Gospel, "an evil and adulterous generation demands a sign," and so forth [Matthew 12:39]. Therefore let us pray that those things that are now closed be opened to us and that we never be cut off from our zeal for reading; even David when he was constantly occupied with the law of the Lord nevertheless cried out to the Lord saying, "give me discernment that I may learn your commands" [Psalms 118:73]. Such is the sweet gift of this pursuit that the more one understands the more one seeks.

8. Although all Divine Scripture shines with heavenly brilliance and the excellence of the Holy Spirit appears clearly in it, I have dedicated my efforts to the Psalter, the Prophets, and the Apostolic Letters, since they seem to me to stir deeper profundities, and to contain, as it were, the glorious citadel and summit of the whole Divine Scripture. I have read over carefully all nine sections containing the divine authority as best as an old man could. I carefully collated against older books as my friends read aloud to me from these.

In this pursuit I claim that I have struggled, God willing, to achieve a harmonious eloquence without mutilating the sacred books by taking undue liberties.

9. I believe this also ought to be noted: St Jerome, led by consideration for the simple brothers, said in his preface to the Prophets that he had marked his translation as it is now read today, by *cola* and *commata*,[2] for the sake of those who had not learned punctuation from the teachers in the schools of secular learning. Guided by the authority of this great man, I have judged it right to follow to the extent that other books be supplied with punctuation marks. But for very elementary reading, let those parts of the text that, as I have said, Jerome set out by *cola* and *commata* in lieu of punctuation, be enough so that I do not seem to have presumptuously gone beyond the judgment of such a great man. The rest of the volumes that were not marked with such punctuation I have left to be examined and corrected by scribes who are specially precise and attentive. Although they cannot altogether maintain the fine points of orthography, they will, I think, hasten to complete at least the correction of the ancient books in every way. They understand their own critical marks that by and large refer and call attention to this skill. To eliminate ingrained error to some extent from their midst, I have set down in a following book on the rules of proper spelling a summary that is suited to their understanding so that crude conjectures of hasty correctors should not be passed on for posterity to complain of. I have tried to locate as many of the earlier writers on orthography as I could for use by the scribes, who can be if not corrected in every respect, at least greatly improved. Correct spelling is usually set out without ambiguity by the Greeks; among the Latin writers it has obviously been neglected because of its difficulty and hence also it now requires the serious attention of the reader.

CHAPTER 28: READING FOR THOSE WHO CANNOT ATTEMPT ADVANCED STUDY

1. But if some simple brothers cannot learn what has been anthologized in the following book because almost all brevity is obscure, let it suffice for them to consider the basic divisions of these matters, their uses and their excellences, so that they may be drawn to the knowledge of divine law by strong motivation. They will find in the various holy Fathers the source from which they can fulfil their desires with the greatest richness, provided they have a sincere desire for reading and a firm commitment to understand. Then a blessed perseverance may make scholars of those at first frightened off by profound study.

2. Still, let us learn that knowledge is not found in letters alone, but that God gives complete wisdom "to everyone according as he will" [1 Corinthians 12:11]. For if the knowledge of good things were only in letters, those who do not know letters obviously would not have righteous wisdom. But since many illiterate men come to true knowledge and perceive the right faith by heavenly inspiration, God surely gives pure and devout minds what he judges to be useful to them. For it is written: "Happy the man whom You instruct, O Lord, whom by your law You teach" [Psalms 93:12]. We should, therefore, seek in good actions and continual prayer to reach, in the companionship of the Lord, true faith and holy works in which our life is eternal. For it is written: "Unless the Lord build the house, they labour in vain who build it" [Psalms 126:1].

---

2. *Cola et commata*: a method of punctuation by phrases, devised by St. Jerome for parts of his translation of the Bible.

3. On the other hand, the holy Fathers have not decreed that the study of secular letters should be rejected either, since to a considerable degree it is by this that our minds are equipped to understand Sacred Scripture. But if, with the support of divine grace, we seek knowledge of these matters seriously and reasonably, not in order to find in secular letters hope of advancement, but so that passing through them we should be eager to deserve useful and redemptive wisdom from the "Father of Lights" [James 1:17]. For how many great philosophers choosing only this knowledge were unable to reach the source of wisdom and without the true light have been submerged in the blindness of ignorance. As someone has said, whatever is not sought for in its own way cannot be completely tracked down.

4. Many of our Fathers, schooled in secular learning and abiding in the law of the Lord, reached true wisdom, as blessed Augustine recalls in his book *Christian Learning* with the words "haven't we seen Cyprian that sweet teacher and holy martyr come out of Egypt heavily laden with gold and silver and clothing, and with similar burdens Lactantius, Victorinus, Optatus, and Hilary?" I add Ambrose, Augustine himself, Jerome and many others "of the innumerable Greeks." And "the very faithful servant of God, Moses himself, also did this of whom it is written that he was 'learned in all the wisdoms of the Egyptians'" [Acts 7:22]. Let us imitate these men and let us carefully but without hesitation, hasten to read both kinds of teaching if we can—for who would dare to hesitate with the example of so many such men before us?—with the full knowledge, as has often been said already, that the Lord can give good and true wisdom. As the Book of Wisdom says: "Wisdom comes from the Lord and with Him it remains forever" [Ecclesiasticus 1:1].

5. Therefore with all effort, with all toil, and with every desire, let us seek to deserve the attainment of such a great gift with the Lord's blessing. For this is a salutary, profitable, glorious, and eternal attainment for us from which death, inconstancy, and forgetfulness cannot separate us but will make us rejoice in that sweet land, our home, with the Lord in eternal exultation. But if in some of the brothers, as Virgil reminds us, "cold blood stands like a barrier around their hearts" [Virgil, *Georgics* 2.484] so that they cannot be completely educated in either human or divine letters, let them be supported by a certain elementary kind of knowledge and choose clearly what follows: "Let the countryside and running streams please me in the vales" [Virgil, *Georgics* 2.485]. It is quite appropriate for monks to cultivate gardens, to plough fields, and to rejoice in the harvest of fruits. For it says in Psalm 127: "You will eat hard-earned bread, you are blessed and it will be well for you" [Psalms 127:2].

6. If you are looking for authors on this subject, Gargilius Martialis has written most beautifully on gardens and also carefully described fertilizers for vegetables and their properties. By reading from his commentary, everyone with the Lord's aid can be fed and kept healthy. I have left this book to you among others. Columella and Aemilianus among others are equally praiseworthy writers on the cultivation of fields, the raising of bees, doves, and fish. But Columella, an eloquent and charming writer, discusses various types of agriculture in sixteen books, more suitable for the learned than for the untaught; scholars of this work are treated not only to ordinary produce, but also to a most satisfying banquet. Aemilianus, an eloquent commentator, has discussed gardens and flocks and other matters in twelve clear and explanatory books. I have left these with the Lord's aid among others to you to be read.

7. When these things are prepared for pilgrims and for the sick they become heavenly although they appear to be earthly. What a wonderful thing it is to refresh the weary either with sweet fruit or nourish them with baby dove eggs or to feed them with fish or soothe them with sweet honey. Since the Lord commanded us to give "even cold water in His name" [Matthew 10:42; Mark 9:40] to the poor man, how much more pleasing will it be to give the sweetest food to all the needy in return for which you can receive on the day of judgment the resultant reward multiplied. One must not neglect whatever activities can profitably aid man.

Book II

CONCLUSION

1. I believe that with the Lord's aid we have fulfilled our promises to the best of our ability. Let us consider why this arrangement of the disciplines led up to the stars. The obvious purpose was to direct our mind, which has been dedicated to secular wisdom and cleansed by the exercise of the disciplines, from earthly things and to place it in a praiseworthy fashion in the divine structure.

2. Some have been led astray by the beauty and brilliance of the shining stars, and eagerly seek reasons for their own destruction. In their mental blindness they tripped over the motions of the stars and through dangerous calculations that are called astrology (*mathesis*) they were sure that they could foresee the course of events. Not only men of our own language, but also Plato, Aristotle, and other men of high intelligence, who are motivated by the truth of the facts, condemned, in full agreement, astrologers, saying that the only result of such a belief would be confusion. If the human race were forced by the inevitability of its birth to various actions, why would good behaviour gain praise or evil behaviour come under the punishment of laws? And although these men were not dedicated to heavenly wisdom, they nevertheless, to bear witness to the truth, rightly attacked the errors of those of whom the Apostle says: "You are observing days and months; I fear for you lest perhaps I have laboured among you in vain" [Galatians 4:10–11].

The Lord gives fuller command on this subject in Deuteronomy: "let there not be found among you anyone who purifies his son or daughter; divining by means of fire or observing the flight of birds, soothsayer, charmer, diviner, or caster of spells, nor one who consults marvels or questions the dead. Anyone who does such things is an abomination to the Lord your God" [Deuteronomy 18:10–12].

3. Let us who truly desire to reach the heavens by the use of our mental faculties believe that God has arranged everything according to his will. Let us reject and condemn the vanities of this world. Let us, as we stated in the first book, look through the books of Divine Scripture, keeping a strict order. For by referring everything to the glory of the Creator, we may usefully bring to the mysteries on high that understanding those men have vainly sought in trying to gain human praise. As blessed Augustine and other most learned Fathers say, secular writings should not be rejected. It is right, however, as Divine Scripture says, to "meditate on the law day and night" [Psalms 1:2; cf. Joshua 1:8], because

from time to time we gain from secular letters commendable knowledge of some matters, but from divine law we gain eternal life.

4. Anyone fired with love for heaven and stripped of earthly desires, who wishes to look at the excellences on high should read the Apocalypse of St John. Fixed in contemplation of it, he will know the Lord Christ who by his providence conceived so many marvellous works, arranged them rationally, completed them with his excellence, and supports them now with the divine spirit, frightens them by his power, controls them by his faithfulness; incomprehensible, ineffable, and known more fully to no one else than to himself. He will also recognize that the Lord sits on his majestic throne, advises the churches through his holy angels, threatens the evil with punishment, promises rewards to the good, and is reverently worshipped with the greatest awe by all the elders, the archangels and the army of the entire heavenly host; and it is their particular and specific duty to sing in harmony with eternal unwearied reverence the glory of the holy Trinity. He also knows this world is ruled by the Lord's sway, and, at the end of the world, when the Lord wishes, it will be changed for the better. The dead will rise when the angels sound their trumpets, and the human race that had been buried in long infirmity will be restored in a new life. After destroying the son of iniquity he will come, terrible and fearsome, with thunder and lightning before him to judge the world. He will reveal his powers that in his first coming he did not show everywhere because of his provident plan. The reader will know afterwards how the Church, freed from such great labours and calamities, will rejoice forever with the Lord, and with what justice those who follow the orders of the devil will perish with him. Truly he will be filled with great exultation since he will be perfected by a vision of these things. After these events there will be, as is written, "a new heaven and a new earth" [Revelation 21:1]; if only we believe this firmly and securely, we will arrive at the sight of that glory by the grace of Christ.

5. But if in this world we wish to be filled with a greater light so that even while we are here we can taste the sweetness of the life to come, let us consider, with as much awe and admiration as human mind temperately is capable of, how the holy Trinity distinct in persons but inseparably connected and consubstantial in nature operates within the universe its creation and is everywhere entire; second, how it does not cease to be present although it is absent in evil; third, that the divine substance is beyond all light and its brightness is unique and cannot as it now is be fully grasped by any of its creations. As the Apostle says, "We shall see him just as he is" [1 John 3:2]; fourth, the nature of compassion that is in Christ the king; that the Lord of angels did not disdain to assume the human condition, but, the life of all, chose to undergo the punishment of the cross. To enable the human race to conquer death, he, who cannot die, deigned to die in the flesh he had assumed—there are other things that various Fathers, filled with divine spirit, have written truly on this subject.

6. On these and like matters indeed all wonder fails, all human investigation surrenders. These are the delights of Christians; this is the great consolation of the sorrowful, since we drive from us the devil and his works by the single-minded consideration of these matters with the Lord's aid. Nevertheless, these things must be regarded with such awe that they are believed continually and without doubt; we must admit that these matters are beyond us, so that in every way they remain fixed in our minds. For although our senses may give way before such considerations, our Father must not in any way stumble.

When in his generosity we shall see him, we shall be granted what we cannot achieve here. We shall know without doubt to the best of our ability; we shall see by his kindness insofar as he has granted us the capacity. As the Apostle says: "We now see through a mirror in an obscure manner, but then face to face" [1 Corinthians 13:12].

7. What is the meaning of this statement that the face of God is promised to the blessed, although He is shaped by no difference in parts? Certainly the face of God is the knowledge of his excellence that we must adore, the holy statement of the divine light, the outstanding greatness of his omnipotence, such great purity of justice, that all other, justice compared to his is trivial, the unchangeable strength of truth, the balanced harmony of patience, the unfailing fullness of goodness, the amazing order of his plan, his marvellous glory and exceptional mercy. O great joy of the faithful, to whom it is promised to see the Lord "as he is" [1 John 3:2]; since they believe most reverently in him, they are already filled with the great hope of blessedness. What will the sight we believe in add when he has already given such great things? Indeed it is a gift beyond value to see the Creator, from whom everything that has life gains its life, from whom everything that exists has its knowledge, from whom everything that has been created is directed, from whom whatever has been restored to the better rises and is repaired, from whom whatever is sought for salvation comes, from whom the virtues proceed by which the world itself is overcome. Although he sustains all things, and as pious judge governs all things in a way we cannot tell of, these will be the sweetest gifts when the merciful Redeemer deigns to appear to us. Such things as these that can be thought about that majesty are what the Apostle calls the face of God.

8. Grant we ask, O Lord, the most glorious holiness of this vision, so that you do not allow those in whom you have stirred up such great desire to be deprived of this goodness. Grant us sight of you who live forever, who deigned to die for us; let us see the glory of your majesty, you who wished to appear humble in our flesh. For even to this world it was granted that you look kindly on your servants; but this world did not receive the ability for your servants to look fully and clearly on your countenance. Be sure, Lord, to confer these things on those who believe in you, on whom you have bestowed all benefits.

9. On this subject, most beloved brothers, Father Augustine is as usual helpful to the faithful. He presented a full and wonderful discussion of it in the book that he wrote to Paulina *On Seeing God*. At the end of it he discussed clearly and briefly how God is seen. Let us not, therefore, trust in our merits but in the grace of the Lord, and continually ask that sight of him be given to us. He generously made a threefold promise to his people when he says: "Ask, and it shall be given you; seek, and you shall find; knock, and it shall be opened to you" [Matthew 7:7; Luke 11:9]. From that, most dear brothers, it turns out that we truly deserve to come to heaven rather by the Lord's generosity than by the way in which the pagans falsely believed they could raise themselves to the structure on high. We may perhaps seem to have exceeded the measure of the book; but in comparison with Genesis and Exodus and other books, these books, which we consider long, begin to be short.

Gregory the Great

c. 540–604

*And indeed exceedingly lovely is the sweetness of the contemplative
life which carries the soul above itself, opens the heavens, shows
that earthly cares should be scorned, discloses spiritual truths to
the eyes of the mind, and hides those of the body.*

HOMILIES ON THE BOOK OF EZEKIEL

Gregory was born into a pious, noble Roman family. He received a classical education in the liberal arts, excelling in the trivium, but never learned Greek. He was a
gifted administrator and served the municipal government as prefect of Rome. After his
father's death, he founded six Benedictine monasteries on family property in Sicily, and
a seventh, St. Andrew's, on his estate in central Rome. He gave away the rest of his wealth
to the poor. Pope Benedict I ordained him as a deacon, and Gregory served his successor for six years as a papal emissary to the imperial court at Constantinople. Upon his
return to Rome, Gregory became the abbot of St. Andrew's but was soon elected pope (in
590). For the next fourteen years he led the Western church through a time of invasion,
plague, flood, and famine as Rome's administration and buildings crumbled. Gregory
sent Augustine of Canterbury to evangelize the Anglo-Saxons in England and reformed
the church's liturgy and music. He became a great preacher and theologian and is considered one of the four "doctors of the Latin Church," along with Ambrose, Jerome, and Augustine of Hippo. His writings include the *Dialogues*, the second book of which comprises
the *Life and Miracles of St. Benedict* (594).

THE SELECTION

In this excerpt from the second of his *Homilies on the Book of Ezekiel*, Gregory ponders the symbolic meaning of the prophet's measuring rod being "six cubits and a hand-breath" in length (Ezekiel 40:5). In his vision, Ezekiel uses this reed to measure the Temple, and Gregory interprets it as a symbolic representation of the active and the contemplative life. Gregory affirms the goodness of both lives, seeing the two embodied in the New Testament in Mary and Martha (Luke 10:38–42). The sisters chose two good things, but Jesus says that Mary chose the best. Martha's activity is good but temporal; Mary's contemplation is good and eternal. Properly directed, both ways of life, Gregory says, can be motivated by love of God and love of neighbor. Action that ministers in mercy to a neighbor is not restless and distracted activity. (The contrast is striking between Gregory's definition of the active life and modernity's endless striving after productivity and the conquest of nature.) Thomas Aquinas drew inspiration from Gregory's homilies centuries later in his treatise *On the Teacher,* excerpted later in this anthology.

from Homilies on the Book of Ezekiel

. . . There are two ways of life whereby Almighty God instructs [the hearers] through Holy Writ, viz. the active and the contemplative. And what is expressed by six cubits if not the active life, because God completed all His works on the sixth day. Truly the handbreadth, which is said to be in addition to the six cubits, is from the seventh, but still falls short of a cubit. Therefore the active life is signified by the six cubits and the contemplative by the handbreadth because we complete the former by works, but even when we strive concerning the latter we hardly avail to attain too little.

So the active life is to give bread to the hungry, to teach the ignorant with the word of wisdom, to set aright the lost, to recall a proud neighbor to the life of humility, to care for the weak, which services each of us should perform, and provide the wherewithal of subsistence for those entrusted to us. Truly the contemplative life is to hold fast with the whole mind, at least to the charity of God, our neighbor but to abstain from external action; to cleave to the sole desire for the Creator, so that the only recourse for the spirit is, scorning all cares, to burn to see the face of its Creator, so that it now understands how to bear the weight of corruptible flesh with grief; to seek with all its desires to be among those hymn-singing choirs of Angels, to mingle with the citizens of Heaven, to rejoice at the eternal incorruption in the presence of God. Then the hand and the fingers are stretched in the handbreadth. But too little of the measurement of the cubit is covered by the handbreadth, because however great the love with which the spirit burns, however great the virtue with which it has mentally reached toward God, it still does not perfectly see that which it should love, but yet begins to see what it loves because as that most powerful preacher says: "For now we see through a glass darkly; but then face to face" (1 Cor. 13:12). And: "Now I know in part; but then shall I know even as also I am known." Therefore we touch the handbreadth from the seventh cubit because, placed in this life, we taste the mere beginnings of inward contemplation. But because the active life can be perfectly led, and man, who should do good works, was created on the sixth day, the reed is six cubits long.

Those two women well signify these two ways of life, viz. Martha and Mary, one of whom was cumbered about much serving but the other sat at the Lord's feet and heard His words. But when Martha complained against her sister because she neglected to help her the Lord replied saying: "Martha, thou art careful and art troubled about many things; But one thing is necessary. Mary hath chosen the best part which shall not be taken away from her" (Lk.12:41–42). Behold Martha's part is not censured but Mary's is praised. Nor does He say that Mary has chosen a good part but the best, so that Martha's too was shown to be good. But why Mary's is the best is implied when it says: "Which shall not be taken away from her." The active life indeed fails with the body. For who will offer bread to the hungry in the Eternal Kingdom where none goes hungry? Who will give drink to the thirsty where none thirsts? Who will bury the dead where none dies? Therefore the active life is taken away with this present age but the contemplative is begun here that it may be perfected in the Heavenly Kingdom, because the fire of love, which begins to glow here, when it has seen Him Whom it loves, will burn the more brightly in His love. So the contemplative life is not taken away, because it is perfected when removed from the light of the present age.

These two ways of life were, as was also said before us, symbolized by Blessed Jacob's two wives, viz. Leah and Rachel. For Leah is interpreted as meaning laborious and Rachel truly as a sheep, or a manifest beginning. Then the active life is laborious because it is fatiguing in work, but the simple contemplative strives also to see its beginning, viz. Him Who said: "I am the beginning, for which reason I speak to you" (Jh. 8:25). Then Blessed Jacob had indeed desired Rachel but in the night accepted Leah because all who are turned to the Lord have desired the contemplative life and seek the quiet of the Eternal Kingdom, but must first in the night of this present life perform the works which they can, sweat with effort, i.e. accept Leah in order that they afterward rest in the arms of Rachel, in order to see the beginning. Then Rachel was a seer, and sterile, Leah truly purblind, but fertile, Rachel beautiful and barren, because the contemplative life is splendid in the spirit but, whereas it seeks to rest in silence, it does not produce sons from preaching. It sees and does not bring forth, because in zeal for its quiet it is less kindled in the collection of others, and does not suffice to reveal to others by preaching how much it inwardly perceives. Leah truly is purblind and fertile because the active life, while it is engaged in labor, sees less but when, now by word now by example, it kindles its neighbors to follow suit, it produces many sons in the good work. And if it does not avail to stretch its mind in contemplation yet it is able to beget followers from that which it does outwardly. Therefore the reed is rightly said to measure first six cubits and then a handbreadth because it first leads an active life in order to come later to contemplation.

But it must be understood that just as a good order of life is to strive from the active to the contemplative, so the spirit frequently reverts from the contemplative to the active, so that the active life may be lived the more perfectly because the contemplative has kindled the mind. Therefore we must pass from the active to the contemplative, yet sometimes because of what we have perceived inwardly in the mind it is better to withdraw from the contemplative to the active. Thus that same Jacob returned after Rachel's embrace to Leah's because even after the beginning is glimpsed, the laborious life of good works is not to be wholly abandoned.

Then there is in the contemplative life much mental struggle, when it rises toward the heavenly, when it stretches the spirit in spiritual things, when it strives to transcend everything which is bodily seen, when it narrows in order to extend. And sometimes indeed it conquers and overcomes the resistant shadows of its blindness so that lightly and stealthily it touches the hem of the uncircumscribed light, but repelled forthwith it turns back to itself and from that light to which it passed with inspiration it returns with a sigh to the darkness of its blindness. This is well portrayed in the sacred narrative which tells of Blessed Jacob wrestling with the Angel. For when Jacob was returning to his proper parents he met an Angel along the way with whom he wrestled in a great struggle. But he who wrestles in a match sometimes finds he is superior and sometimes he with whom he fights is inferior. Therefore the Angel stands for God, and Jacob, who fights with the Angel, symbolizes the soul of each perfect man who is placed in contemplation. Because plainly the soul, when it strives to contemplate God, as if engaged in a struggle now conquers, as it were, because by understanding and perceiving it grazes the hem of the uncircumscribed light, but now succumbs because even in touching it falls once more. Therefore the Angel is, so to speak, conquered when God is seized by the inward understanding.

But it is to be noted that this same conquered Angel grasped the tendon of Jacob's thigh and immediately rendered him powerless, and from that time Jacob was lame in one foot, plainly because when Almighty God is already recognized through yearning and the understanding He withers every carnal desire in us. And we who, as it were, standing once on two feet were seen to seek God and to own the world, after the recognition of the sweetness of God, have one sound foot and limp with the other, because it is needful that the love of this world be weakened and only the love of God grow strong within us. If, therefore, we hold the Angel we limp on one foot, because when the strength of inward love increases in us the strength of the flesh undoubtedly declines. Then everyone who is lame in one leg is supported on the one foot which is sound, because his earthly desire is sustained with total virtue on the single foot of God's love. And he stands thereon because he has already lifted from the earth the foot of worldly love which he was wont to place on the ground. Therefore, if we return to our proper parents, i.e. to our spiritual fathers, let us too hold fast to the Angel on the way so that we may lay hold on God in inward sweetness. And indeed exceedingly lovely is the sweetness of the contemplative life which carries the soul above itself, opens the heavens, shows that earthly cares should be scorned, discloses spiritual truths to the eyes of the mind, and hides those of the body. Thus it is well said of the Church in the Song of Solomon: "I sleep, and my heart watcheth" (Cant. 5:2). Truly he sleeps with watchful heart because insofar as he progresses by contemplation inwardly he refrains from restless action outwardly.

But amid these things it must be realized that as long as life continues in this mortal flesh none can advance so far in the virtue of contemplation as to fix the eyes of his mind on the uncircumscribed ray of light itself. Nor is Almighty God seen in His splendor, but the soul glimpses something short of it and progresses refreshed thereby, and afterward attains to the glory of His image. For thus Esaias, when he acknowledged that he had seen the Lord, saying: "In the year that King Uzziah died I saw the Lord sitting upon a throne, high and lifted up," immediately added: "and His train filled the Temple" (Es. 6:1). When King Uzziah, a haughty, presumptuous man, dies the Lord is seen, because when the elation of this world is destroyed by the mind's yearning, then the mind itself contemplates the glory of God. And it is to be noted that the Lord is seated upon a throne, high and lifted up. For what is His throne if not the human or angelic creature over which He presides through the understanding which He gave? Obviously this throne is said to be high and lifted up because human nature when uplifted progresses to heavenly glory, and an angelic creature, despite the fall of many spirits, once established in Heaven, lest it fall, is uplifted thither whence it is confirmed. Truly His Temple is this throne because the Eternal King dwells where He sits. Therefore His Temple are we, in whose minds He deigns to dwell. But His train filled the Temple because whatever is seen of Him momentarily is still not He Himself but from beneath Him. Thus Jacob saw the Angel and says that he had seen the Lord, because when we see His ministers we are already uplifted far above ourselves. Truly it is to be noted that it says: "filled the Temple," since even if an Angel appears it nevertheless satisfies the yearning of an infirm mind so that if it cannot do more yet it wonders at the little it sees. Therefore His train filled the Temple because, as was said, when the mind has progressed in contemplation it contemplates not yet what He Himself is but what is beneath Him. Evidently in this contemplation a foretaste of inward peace is already attained. Since this foretaste is, as it were, a part and cannot now be perfect, it is rightly written in the Apocalypse: "There was silence in Heaven, as it were for half an hour" (Apc. 8:1). Surely Heaven is the soul of a righteous man, as the Lord says through the Prophet: "Heaven is my throne" (Es. 66:1). And: "The Heavens declare the glory of God" (Ps. 18:1). Therefore, when the quiet of the contemplative life prevails in the mind there is silence in Heaven because the noise of actions dies away from thought so that the spirit inclines to the secret inner ear. But because this mental quiet cannot be perfect in this life, the silence in Heaven is said to be not a whole hour but as it were half an hour so that the very half hour is not fully perceived either since "as it were" is added, because as soon as the spirit has begun to sustain itself and be perfused with the light of inward quiet, with the swift return of the noise of thoughts it is confused about itself and by its confusion blinded. Then the contemplative life, which is there said to be as it were half an hour, is in Ezekiel the Prophet called not a cubit but a handbreadth. Behold, dearest brothers, when we desired to express the causes of each life we spoke a little too widely through aberration. But for good minds, to whom either life is lovely for the living, it should not be burdensome for the hearing. Then follows: "And He measured the breadth of the building one reed and the height one reed" (40:5).

Almighty God, Who is neither stretched by the great nor narrowed by the least, thus speaks of the whole Church at the same time as He speaks of a single soul. And often there is no reason why what He says of a single soul should not be understood as referring at the same time to the whole Church. Therefore the breadth of the building pertains to charity, of which the Psalmist said: "Thy commandment is exceeding broad" (Ps. 118:96). For nothing is broader than to receive all men in the bosom of love and sustain no straits of hatred. Surely charity is so broad that it can capture even enemies in the breadth of its love. Hence also the injunction: "Love your enemies, do good to them which hate you" (Lk. 6:27). We must also consider that the breadth extends in equality but the height in sublimity. Therefore the breadth pertains to charity for our neighbor, and the height to understanding of our Maker. But the breadth and the height of the building measure one reed because each soul will be as wide in love for its neighbor as it is high in knowledge of God. For while it spreads out through love it exalts itself above through knowledge, and the more it is uplifted the further it extends abroad in love of neighbor. And because the building in which God dwells is made from both angelic and human nature, insofar as an angelic creature is above and a human still below, each can be symbolized by the breadth and the height of the building, because the one still lives in the depths but the other remains in the heights. But each is measured by one reed, because the humility of men is sometimes led through to equality with the Angels. Thus it is written: "They shall neither marry nor be married, but shall be as the angels of God in heaven" (Mt. 22:30). Moreover it is said through John: "the measure of a man, which is of an angel" (Apc. 22:17). Because man is led even to that height of glory in which the Angels rejoice that they are established. Therefore the breadth of the building is as great as the height because all the elect who now labor in the depths will sometime be equal to those most blessed spirits. But amid this let us return to the mind and let us love God and our neighbor with all our hearts. Let us be spread in the affection of charity that we may be exalted in the glory of the highness. Let us through love have compassion on our neighbor that we may be joined together through knowledge of God. Let us stoop to the least of our brothers on earth, and let us be made equal to the Angels in Heaven, because a Man who signifies the Savior with His image measured the breadth of the building with one reed and the height too with one reed. But now He measures conduct, He weighs works, He considers thoughts, so that retribution will later be rendered by Jesus Christ the Only-Begotten of the Father, Who lives and reigns with Him in the Unity of the Holy Spirit through all ages of ages. Amen.

Alcuin

c. 735–804

Wisdom is the chief adornment, and this I urge you to seek above all things.

ON GRAMMAR

⟪❧⟫

T he Saxon teacher Alcuin was educated in York by Albert (or Aelbert), a student of the Venerable Bede, renowned author of the *Ecclesiastical History of the English Nation*. Alcuin became master of the school in York. He later served as bishop of York until called to the continent to direct the emperor Charlemagne's educational reforms. Alcuin had met Charlemagne in Italy in 781 after a visit to Rome. The emperor appointed him to be "Master of the Palace School," in which position he was charged with supervising the education of the sons of Frankish nobility. From this position of influence, Alcuin led a remarkable revival of learning. One of Charlemagne's biographers called Alcuin "the most learned man anywhere to be found." Another biographer boasted that under this schoolmaster "the modern Gauls or Franks came to equal the Romans and the Athenians." Alcuin himself envisioned a greater Athens with a greater Academy elevated above their ancient models by the Holy Spirit.[1] Modern critics may fault Alcuin for his lack of originality, but the breadth of his accomplishments is remarkable by any standard: he wrote commentaries on Scripture, narrative poems, moral treatises, biographies, and textbooks on grammar and other subjects. He also produced a corrected edition of Jerome's Latin Bible and helped reform local liturgy to bring it into conformity and unity with Rome. In general, Europe's Christian schools trace their heritage to this scholar. His dialogue *On*

---

1. See Christopher Dawson, *Religion and the Rise of Western Culture* (New York: Sheed and Ward, 1950), 71.

Grammar (not included here) captures Alcuin's love of liberal learning: "It is easy indeed to point out to you the path of wisdom, if only ye love it for the sake of God, for knowledge, for purity of heart, for understanding the truth, yea, and for itself. Seek it not to gain the praise of men or the honors of this world, nor yet for the deceitful pleasures of riches, for the more these are loved, so much the farther do they cause those who seek them to depart from the light of truth and knowledge."[2]

THE SELECTIONS

The first selection is not actually from Alcuin's hand. It is a letter dispatched from Charlemagne urging the abbot of Fulda to implement the emperor's educational reforms (which were the reforms of Alcuin) with diligence. Charlemagne's insistence on piety, wisdom, and eloquence restates three themes that endure in the Great Tradition for the next thousand years.

A prose translation of a poem by Alcuin and excerpts from two of his letters follow. The poem pays tribute to his beloved teacher Albert. Alcuin praises him for striving to "irrigate their lands with learning" and repeats the images of thirst and rain. Similar themes continue in the two letters, and the second also includes a poignant reminder to teachers: "As a careful shepherd provides the best pasture for his flock, so a good teacher should with all his zeal provide for his subjects the pasture of eternal life."

from Charlemagne's "Capitulary of 787"

Charles, by the grace of God, King of the Franks and of the Lombards, and Patrician of the Romans, to Baugulfus, abbot, and to his whole congregation and the faithful committed to his charge:

Be it known to your devotion, pleasing to God, that in conjunction with our faithful we have judged it to be of utility that, in the bishoprics and monasteries committed by Christ's favor to our charge, care should be taken that there shall be not only a regular manner of life and one conformable to holy religion, but also the study of letters, each to teach and learn them according to his ability and the divine assistance. For even as due observance of the rule of the house tends to good morals, so zeal on the part of the teacher and the taught imparts order and grace to sentences; and those who seek to please God by living aright should also not neglect to please him by right speaking. It is written, "By thine own words shalt thou be justified or condemned"; and although right doing be preferable to right speaking, yet must the knowledge of what is right precede right action. Every one, therefore, should strive to understand what it is he would fain accomplish; and this right understanding will be the sooner gained according as the utterances of the tongue are free from error. And if false speaking is to be shunned by all men, especially should it be shunned by those who have elected to be the servants of the truth.

---

2. From Andrew Fleming West, *Alcuin and the Rise of the Christian Schools* (London: Heinemann, 1893), 94.

During past years we have often received letters from different monasteries, inform-ing us that at their sacred services the brethren offered up prayers on our behalf; and we have observed that the thoughts contained in these letters, though in themselves most just, were expressed in uncouth language, and while pious devotion dictated the senti-ments, the unlettered tongue was unable to express them aright. Hence there has arisen in our minds the fear lest, if the skill to write rightly were thus lacking, so too would the power of rightly comprehending the sacred Scriptures be far less than was fitting; and we all know that though verbal errors be dangerous, errors of the understanding are yet more so. We exhort you, therefore, not only not to neglect the study of letters, but to ap-ply yourselves thereto with perseverance and with that humility which is well pleasing to God; so that you may be able to penetrate with greater ease and certainty the mysteries of the Holy Scriptures. For as these contain images, tropes, and similar figures, it is impos-sible to doubt that the reader will arrive far more readily at the spiritual sense according as he is the better instructed in learning. Let there, therefore, be chosen for this work men who are both able and willing to learn, and also desirous of instructing others; and let them apply themselves to the work with a zeal equaling the earnestness with which we recommend it to them. It is our wish that you may be what it behooves the soldiers of the Church to be—religious in heart, learned in discourse, pure in act, eloquent in speech; so that all who approach your house, in order to invoke the Divine Master or to behold the excellence of the religious life, may be edified in beholding you, and instructed in hearing you discourse or chant, and may return home rendering thanks to God most high.

Fail not, as thou regardest our favor, to send a copy of this letter to all thy suffragans and to all the monasteries; and let no monk go beyond his monastery to administer jus-tice, or to enter the assemblies and the voting-places, Adieu.

⌘

Alcuin on St Peter's School, York, 732–86

Of whom [Archbishop Egbert] the Muse forbids me to say more, passing on to the end of the poem, and to the deeds of my own master, Albert [Aethelbert] the wise, who took the insignia of the venerable see after Egbert.

A good man and just, broad, pious and kind; supporter, teacher and lover of the Catho-lic faith; ruler, doctor, defender, and pupil of the Church.

Bide with me for a while, I pray ye, youth of York, while I proceed with poetic steps to treat of him, because here he often drenched your senses with nectar, pouring forth sweet juices from his honey-flowing bosom. Fairest Philosophy took him from his very cradle and bore him to the topmost towers of learning, opening to him the hidden things of wisdom. He was born of ancestors of sufficient note, by whose care he was soon sent to kindly school, and entered at the Minster in his early years, that his tender age might grow up with holy understanding. Nor was his parents' hope in vain; even as a boy as he grew in body so he became proficient in the understanding of books.

Then pious and wise, teacher at once and priest, he was made a colleague of Bishop Egbert, to whom he was nearly allied by right of blood. By him he is made advocate of the clergy, and at the same time is preferred as master in the city of York.

There he moistened thirsty hearts with diverse streams of teaching and the varied dews of learning, giving to these the art of the science of grammar, pouring on those the rivers of rhetoric. Some he polished on the whetstone of law, some he taught to sing together in Aeonian chant, making others play on the flute of Castaly, and run with the feet of lyric poets over the hills of Parnassus. Others the said master made to know the harmony of heaven, the labours of sun and moon, the five belts of the sky, the seven planets, the laws of the fixed stars, their rising and setting, the movements of the air, the quaking of sea and earth, the nature of men, cattle, birds and beasts, the divers kinds of numbers and various shapes. He gave certainty to the solemnity of Easter's return; above all, opening the mysteries of holy writ and disclosing the abysses of the rude and ancient law. Whatever youths he saw of conspicuous intelligence, those he joined to himself, he taught, he fed, he loved; and so the teacher had many disciples in the sacred volumes, advanced in various arts. Soon he went in triumph abroad, led by the love of wisdom, to see if he could find in other lands anything novel in books or schools, which he could bring home with him. He went also devoutly to the city of Romulus, rich in God's love, wandering far and wide through the holy places. Then returning home, he was received everywhere by kings and princes as a prince of doctors, whom great kings tried to keep that he might irrigate their lands with learning. But the master hurrying to his appointed works returned home to his fatherland by God's ordinance. For no sooner had he been borne to his own shores, than he was compelled to take on him the pastoral care, and made high priest at the people's demand.

But his old fervent industry for reading the Scriptures was not diminished by the weight of his cares, and he was made both a wise doctor and a pious priest.

As prelate he built a great altar where king Edwin had received baptism, covered it in all parts with silver, gold and precious stones and dedicated it to Paul, the doctor of the world, whom, as a doctor he especially loved.

Then the illustrious minister in holy orders, the prelate perfect in good works and full of days, gladly handed over to his beloved disciple Eanbald the episcopal ornaments, while he sought for himself a sequestered cloister in which to devote himself wholly to God's service. But he gave the dearer treasures of his books to the other son, who was always close to his father's side, thirsting to drink the floods of learning. His name, if you care to know it, these verses on the face of them will at once betray. Between them he divided his wealth of different kinds: to the one, the rule of the church, the ornaments, the lands, the money; to the other, the sphere of wisdom, the school, the master's chair, the books, which the illustrious master had collected from all sides, piling up glorious treasures under one roof.

There you will find the footsteps of the old fathers, whatever the Roman has of himself in the sphere of Latin, or which famous Greece passed on to the Latins, or which the Hebrew race drinks from the showers above, or Africa has spread abroad with light-giving lamp.

What father Jerome, what Hilarius, bishop Ambrose, Augustine, Saint Athanasius felt, what old Orosius published, whatever the chief doctor Gregory teaches and Pope Leo, what Basil and Fulgentius, while Cassiodorus, Chrysostom and John also shine. Whatever Aldhelm taught and Bede the Master, what Victorinus and Boethius wrote; the ancient historians, Pompeius, Pliny, keen Aristotle himself and the mighty orator Tully [Cicero]. What also Sedulius, and Juvencus himself sings, Alcimus and Clemens, Prosper, Paulinus, Arator; what Fortunatus and Lactantius produce; what Virgilius Maro, Statius and Lucan the historian, what too the masters of the art of grammar have written, Probus and Phocas, Donatus, Priscian, Servius, Euticius, Yomperus, Comminianus. You will find there, reader, many other masters eminent in the schools, in art, and in oratory, who have written many a volume of sound sense, the writing of whose names in verse would take longer than the usage of the bow allows.

⸎

Letters

EX-SCHOOLMASTER ALCUIN RECOMMENDS EANBALD II, ARCHBISHOP OF YORK, TO SEPARATE THE GRAMMAR, SONG, AND WRITING SCHOOLS, 796

To his most beloved son in Christ, Archbishop Eanbald, his devoted father Albinus, greeting.

Praise and glory to the Lord God Almighty who has preserved my days in good prosperity, so that I might rejoice in the elevation of my dearest son, and that I, the lowest slave of the church, should have educated one of my sons, who, by the grace of Him who is the giver of all good, is thought worthy to be the dispenser of the mysteries of Christ and to labour in my stead in the church where I was brought up and taught, and to preside over the treasures of wisdom, the inheritance of which my beloved master Archbishop Albert left to me.

Your holy wisdom should provide masters for the boys, and the clerks. Let there be separate spheres for those who read books, who serve singing, who are assigned to the writing school. Have special masters for each of these classes, lest having leisure time they wander about the place and practice empty games or be employed in other futilities. Let your most wise prudence, my most beloved son, consider all this, so that a well of all goodness and learning may be found in the principal seat of our nation, from which the thirsty traveller or the lover of church learning, may draw whatever his soul desires.

Let your most diligent piety also consider where to order inns, that is hospitals, to be erected in which the poor and the traveller may be received daily and be relieved at your expense.

ALCUIN ON HEXHAM SCHOOL, C. 797

To the pastor of chief dignity, Ethelbert bishop, and all the congregation serving God in the church of St Andrew, Alcuin, client of your love, greeting in Christ. . . .

May the light of learning remain among you. . . . Teach the boys and young men diligently the learning of books in the way of God, that they may become worthy successors in your honours and intercessors for you. . . . He who does not sow neither shall he reap, and he who does not learn cannot teach. And such a place without teachers shall not, or hardly, be saved. It is a great work of charity to feed the poor with food for the body, but a greater to fill the hungry soul with spiritual learning. As a careful shepherd provides the best pasture for his flock, so a good teacher should with all his zeal provide for his subjects the pasture of eternal life. For the increase of the flock is the glory of the shepherd, and the multitude of learned men is the safety of the world. I know that you, most holy fathers, know this well and will willingly carry it out.

Rhabanus Maurus

c. 776–856

Above all it is necessary that he, who aims to attain the summit of wisdom, should be converted to the fear of the Lord, in order to know what the divine will bids us strive for and shun.

"EDUCATION OF THE CLERGY"

Rhabanus was born in Mainz, Germany, and studied first at the monastic school at Fulda and then with Alcuin at Tours. Alcuin honored him with the name "Maurus," one of St. Benedict's disciples. A lifelong servant of the Church, Maurus became a Benedictine monk, schoolmaster, deacon, priest, abbot of the monastery at Fulda, and finally archbishop of Mainz. Deeply learned, he mastered Scripture and the Church Fathers, knew Greek and Roman literature, wrote commentaries on most of the Bible, and produced several textbooks on the liberal arts. He also composed many hymns, some of which are included in modern Lutheran hymnals.

THE SELECTION

Maurus's "Education of the Clergy" places education in the service of the church, the institution that painstakingly preserved the learning of antiquity against great odds in the Dark Ages and that required a literate clergy to fulfill its ongoing mission of prayer, study, evangelism, and worship. Believing that the only possible source of truth and wisdom is God, Maurus embraces truth and wisdom wherever they are found—a generous view of secular learning characteristic also of many of the Church Fathers. And like so many before him in the Great Tradition, Maurus never separates knowledge from right conduct.

True education presupposes humility and the fear of the Lord. From this foundation, Maurus describes in detail the trivium and quadrivium of the seven liberal arts as they became standardized in the Middle Ages.

"Education of the Clergy"

1. An ecclesiastical education should qualify the sacred office of the ministry for divine service. It is fitting that those who from an exalted station undertake the direction of the life of the Church, should acquire fulness of knowledge, and that they further should strive after rectitude of life and perfection of development. They should not be allowed to remain in ignorance about anything that appears beneficial for their own information or for the instruction of those entrusted to their care. Therefore they should endeavor to grasp and include in their knowledge the following things: An acquaintance with Holy Scripture, the unadulterated truth of history, the derivative modes of speech, the mystical sense of words, the advantages growing out of the separate branches of knowledge, the integrity of life that manifests itself in good morals, delicacy and good taste in oral discourse, penetration in the explanation of doctrine, the different kinds of medicine, and the various forms of disease. Any one to whom all this remains unknown, is not able to care for his own welfare, let alone that of others.

2. The foundation, the content, and the perfection of all wisdom is Holy Scripture, which has taken its origin from that unchangeable and eternal Wisdom, which streams from the mouth of the Most High, which was begotten before every other creature through the Holy Spirit, which is a light incessantly beaming from the words of Holy Scripture. And when anything else deserves the name of wisdom, it goes back in its origin to this one source of the wisdom of the Church. Every truth, which is discovered by any one, is recognized as true by the truth itself through the mediation of the truth; every good thing, which is in any way traced out, is recognized and determined as good by the good itself; all wisdom, which is brought to light by any one, is found to be wisdom by wisdom itself. And all that is found of truth and wisdom in the books of the philosophers of this world, dare be ascribed to nothing else than just to truth and wisdom; for it was not originally invented by those among whose utterances it is found; it has much rather been recognized as something present from eternity, so far as wisdom and truth, which bring illumination to all with their instruction, have granted the possibility of such-recognition.

3. Now the Holy Scriptures, which come to the aid of the weakness of the human will, have, in dependence upon the one perfect language in which under favorable circumstances they might have spread over the whole globe, been widely circulated in the different languages of the translators, in order that they might be known to the nations unto salvation. Those who read them strive for nothing else than to grasp the thought and meaning of those who wrote them, in order thereby to fathom the will of God, at whose bidding and under whose direction, as we believe, they were written. But those who read superficially allow themselves to be deceived through the manifold recurring passages, the sense of which is obscure, and the meaning of which is doubtful; they assign to what is read a meaning that does not belong to it; they seek errors where no errors are to be

found; they surround themselves with an obscurity, in which they can not find the right path. I have no doubt that this has been so ordered by God's providence that the pride of man may be restrained through spiritual labor; in order that the knowledge of man may be divorced from pride, to which it easily falls a prey, and then loses its value entirely.

4. Above all it is necessary that he, who aims to attain the summit of wisdom, should be converted to the fear of the Lord, in order to know what the divine will bids us strive for and shun. The fear of the Lord fills us with the thought of our mortality and future death. With mortification of the flesh it nails, as it were, the movements of pride to the martyr cross of Christ. Then it is enjoined to be lowly in piety. Therefore we are not to raise any objection to the Holy Scriptures, either when we understand them and feel ourselves smitten by their words, or when we do not understand them, and give ourselves up to the thought that we can understand and grasp something better out of our own minds. We should remember that it is better and more comfortable to truth, to believe what is written, even if the sense remains concealed from us, than to hold that for true which we are able to recognize by our own strength.

5. The first of the liberal arts is grammar, the second rhetoric, the third dialectic, the fourth arithmetic, the fifth geometry, the sixth music, the seventh astronomy.

Grammar takes its name from the written character, as the derivation of the word indicates. The definition of grammar is this: Grammar is the science which teaches us to explain the poets and historians; it is the art which qualifies us to write and speak correctly. Grammar is the source and foundation of the liberal arts. It should be taught in every Christian school, since the art of writing and speaking correctly is attained through it. How could one understand the sense of the spoken word or the meaning of letters and syllables, if one had not learned this before from grammar? How could one know about metrical feet, accent, and verses, if grammar had not given one knowledge of them? How should one learn to know the articulation of discourse, the advantages of figurative language, the laws of word formation, and the correct forms of words, if one had not familiarized himself with the art of grammar?

All the forms of speech, of which secular science makes use in its writings, are found repeatedly employed in the Holy Scriptures. Every one, who reads the sacred Scriptures with care, will discover that our (biblical) authors have used derivative forms of speech in greater and more manifold abundance than would have been supposed and believed. There are in the Scriptures not only examples of all kinds of figurative expressions, but the designations of some of them by name; as, allegory, riddle, parable. A knowledge of these things is proved to be necessary in relation to the interpretation of those passages of Holy Scripture which admit of a twofold sense; an interpretation strictly literal would lead to absurdities. Everywhere we are to consider whether that, which we do not at once understand, is to be apprehended as a figurative expression in some sense. A knowledge of prosody, which is offered in grammar, is not dishonorable, since among the Jews, as St. Jerome testifies, the Psalter resounds sometimes with iambics, sometimes with Alcaics, sometimes chooses sonorous Sapphics, and sometimes even does not disdain catalectic feet. But in Deuteronomy and Isaiah, as in Solomon and Job, as Josephus and Origen have pointed out, there are hexameters and pentameters. Hence this art, though it may be secular, has nothing unworthy in itself; it should rather be learned as thoroughly as possible.

6. According to the statements of teachers, rhetoric is the art of using secular discourse effectively in the circumstances of daily life. From this definition rhetoric seems indeed to have reference merely to secular wisdom. Yet it is not foreign to ecclesiastical instruction. Whatever the preacher and herald of the divine law, in his instruction, brings forward in an eloquent and becoming manner; whatever in his written exposition he knows how to clothe in adequate and impressive language, he owes to his acquaintance with this art. Whoever at the proper time makes himself familiar with this art, and faithfully follows its rules in speaking and writing, needs not count it as something blameworthy. On the contrary, whoever thoroughly learns it so that he acquires the ability to proclaim God's word, performs a good work. Through rhetoric anything is proved true or false. Who would have the courage to maintain that the defenders of truth should stand weaponless in the presence of falsehood, so that those, who dare to represent the false, should know how by their discourse to win the favor and sympathy of the hearers, and that, on the other hand, the friends of truth should not be able to do this; that those should know how to present falsehood briefly, clearly, and with the semblance of truth, and that the latter, on the contrary, should clothe the truth in such an exposition, that listening would become a burden, apprehension of the truth a weariness, and faith in the truth an impossibility?

7. Dialectic is the science of the understanding, which fits us for investigations and definitions, for explanations, and for distinguishing the true from the false. It is the science of sciences. It teaches how to teach others; it teaches learning itself; in it the reason marks and manifests itself according to its nature, efforts, and activities; it alone is capable of knowing; it not only will, but can lead others to knowledge; its conclusions lead us to an apprehension of our being and of our origin; through it we apprehend the origin and activity of the good, of Creator and creature; it teaches us to discover the truth and to unmask falsehood; it teaches us to draw conclusions; it shows us what is valid in argument and what is not; it teaches us to recognize what is contrary to the nature of things; it teaches us to distinguish in controversy the true, the probable, and the wholly false; by means of this science we are able to investigate everything with penetration, to determine its nature with certainty, and to discuss it with circumspection.

Therefore the clergy must understand this excellent art and constantly reflect upon its laws, in order that they may be able keenly to pierce the craftiness of errorists, and to refute their fatal fallacies.

8. Arithmetic is the science of pure extension determinable by number; it is the science of numbers. Writers on secular science assign it, under the head of mathematics, to the first place, because it does not presuppose any of the other departments. Music, geometry, and astronomy, on the contrary, need the help of arithmetic; without it they cannot arise or exist. We should know, however, that the learned Hebrew Josephus, in his work on Antiquities, Chapter VIII of Book I, makes the statement that Abraham brought arithmetic and astronomy to the Egyptians; but that they as a people of penetrating mind, extensively developed from these germs the other sciences. The holy Fathers were right in advising those eager for knowledge to cultivate arithmetic, because in large measure it turns the mind from fleshly desires, and furthermore awakens the wish to comprehend what with God's help we can merely receive with the heart. Therefore the significance of number is not to be underestimated. Its very great value for an interpretation of many passages of Holy Scripture is manifest to all who exhibit zeal in their investigations. Not without good

reason is it said in praise of God, "Thou hast ordained all things by measure, number, and weight" (Book of Wisdom 11:21).

But every number, through its peculiar qualities, is so definite that none of the others can be like it. They are all unequal and different. The single numbers are different; the single numbers are limited; but all are infinite.

Those with whom Plato stands in especial honor will not make bold to esteem numbers lightly, as if they were of no consequence for the knowledge of God. He teaches that God made the world out of numbers. And among us the prophet says of God, "He forms the world by number." And in the Gospel the Savior says, "The very hairs of your head are all numbered." . . . Ignorance of numbers leaves many things unintelligible that are expressed in the Holy Scripture in a derivative sense or with a mystical meaning.

9. We now come to the discussion of geometry. It is an exposition of form proceeding from observation; it is also a very common means of demonstration among philosophers, who, to adduce at once the most full-toned evidence, declare that their Jupiter made use of geometry in his works. I do not know indeed whether I should find praise or censure in this declaration of the philosophers, that Jupiter engraved upon the vault of the skies precisely what they themselves draw in the sand of the earth.

When this in a proper manner is transferred to God, the Almighty Creator, this assumption may perhaps come near the truth. If this statement seems admissible, the Holy Trinity makes use of geometry in so far as it bestows manifold forms and images upon the creatures which up to the present day it has called into being, as in its adorable omnipotence it further determines the course of the stars, as it prescribes their course to the planets, and as it assigns to the fixed stars their unalterable position. For every, excellent and well-ordered arrangement can be reduced to the special requirements of this science. . . .

This science found realization also at the building of the tabernacle and temple; the same measuring rod, circles, spheres, hemispheres, quadrangles, and other figures were employed. The knowledge of all this brings to him, who is occupied with it, no small gain for his spiritual culture.

10. Music is the science of time intervals as they are perceived in tones. This science is as eminent as it is useful. He who is a stranger to it is not able to fulfil the duties of an ecclesiastical office in a suitable manner. A proper delivery in reading and a lovely rendering of the Psalms in the church are regulated by a knowledge of this science. Yet it is not only good reading and beautiful psalmody that we owe to music; through it alone do we become capable of celebrating in the most solemn manner every divine service. Music penetrates all the activities of our life, in this sense namely, that we above all carry out the commands of the Creator and bow with a pure heart to his commands; all that we speak, all that makes our hearts beat faster, is shown through the rhythm of music united with the excellence of harmony; for music is the science which teaches us agreeably to change tones in duration and pitch. When we employ ourselves with good pursuits in life, we show ourselves thereby disciples of this art; so long as we do what is wrong, we do not feel ourselves drawn to music. Even heaven and earth, as everything that happens here through the arrangement of the Most High, is nothing but music, as Pythagoras testifies that this world was created by music and can be ruled by it. Even with the Christian religion music is most intimately united; thus it is possible that to him, who does not know even a little music, many things remain closed and hidden.

11. There remains yet astronomy which, as some one has said, is a weighty means of demonstration to the pious, and to the curious a grievous torment. If we seek to investigate it with a pure heart and an ample mind, then it fills us, as the ancients said, with great love for it. For what will it not signify, that we soar in spirit to the sky, that with penetration of mind we analyze that sublime structure, that we, in part at least, fathom with the keenness of our logical faculties what mighty space has enveloped in mystery! The world itself, according to the assumption of some, is said to have the shape of a sphere, in order that in its circumference it may be able to contain the different forms of things. Thus Seneca, in agreement with the philosophers of ancient times, composed a work under the title "The Shape of the Earth."

Astronomy, of which we now speak, teaches the laws of the stellar world. The stars can take their place or carry out their motion only in the manner established by the Creator, unless by the will of the Creator a miraculous change takes place. Thus we read that Joshua commanded the sun to stand still in Gibeon, that in the days of King Josiah the sun went backward ten degrees, and that at the death of the Lord the sun was darkened for three hours. We call such occurrences miracles (*Wunder*), because they contradict the usual course of things, and therefore excite wonder. . . .

That part of astronomy, which is built up on the investigation of natural phenomena, in order to determine the course of the sun, of the moon, and stars, and to effect a proper reckoning of time, the Christian clergy should seek to learn with the utmost diligence, in order through the knowledge of laws brought to light and through the valid and convincing proof of the given means of evidence, to place themselves in a position, not only to determine the course of past years according to truth and reality, but also for further times to draw confident conclusions, and to fix the time of Easter and all other festivals and holy days, and to announce to the congregation the proper celebration of them.

12. The seven liberal arts of the philosophers, which Christians should learn for their utility and advantage, we have, as I think, sufficiently discussed. We have this yet to add. When those, who are called philosophers, have in their expositions or in their writings, uttered perchance some truth, which agrees with our faith, we should not handle it timidly, but rather take it as from its unlawful possessors and apply it to our own use.

Hugh of St. Victor

1096–1141

*Of all things to be sought, the first is that Wisdom in which the
Form of the Perfect Good stands fixed.*

Didascalicon

〰️

F ew details of Hugh's early life are known with certainty. He was educated at a monastic school in Saxony, and in his *Didascalicon* he recalls his childhood love of liberal learning. Against his parents' wishes, he became an Augustinian monk, and while still a young man he made his way to the Augustinian Abbey of St. Victor in Paris. The Victorines were leaders in scholastic theology, and here on the banks of the Seine, Huge spent the rest of his life as scholar, author, benefactor of the abbey, teacher of the liberal arts, and eventually master of the school. Hugh wrote commentaries on Scripture and treatises on mysticism and theology, including *De Sacramentis*. Though possessing one of the greatest minds of the twelfth century, he was admired for his self-effacing humility.

The opening of *De Sacramentis* (not included here) captures his understanding of the union of the liberal arts with Scripture and of the ultimate aim of all learning: "All the arts of the natural world subserve our knowledge of God, and the lower wisdom—rightly ordered—leads to the higher. The trivium serves the literal meaning, the quadrivium the figurative meaning. Above and before all these is that divine being to whom Scripture leads by faith and works; in the knowledge of whose truth and the love of whose excellence man is restored to his true [nature]."[1]

---

1. Quoted in Margaret T. Gibson, "*De doctrina christiana* in the School of St. Victor," in Edward D. English, ed., *Reading and Wisdom: the* de doctrina christiana *of Augustine in the Middle Ages* (Notre Dame, IN: University of Notre Dame Press, 1995), 43.

THE SELECTION

Hugh's *Didascalicon* is a rewarding educational handbook and ought to be read in its entirety. Written sometime in the 1120s, the book outlines the "what" and "how" of education. Book I cites the familiar Delphic injunction to "know thyself," connecting Hugh to an unbroken tradition reaching back through Augustine to the ancients. Hugh's primary concern is reading, and he offers wise and gentle instruction on developing sound habits of mind and heart—advice as pertinent today as it was nine hundred years ago. He also discourses on the benefits of the liberal arts, and his pages brim with references to Homer, Socrates, Plato, Aristotle, Cicero, Vitruvius, and Quintilian. Hugh also quotes freely from Scripture and the Church Fathers.

from the Didascalicon
Preface

There are many persons whose nature has left them so poor in ability that they can hardly grasp with their intellect even easy things, and of these persons I believe there are two kinds. There are those who, while they are not unaware of their own dullness, nonetheless struggle after knowledge with all the effort they can put forth and who, by tirelessly keeping up their pursuit, deserve to obtain as a result of their will power what they by no means possess as a result of their work. Others, however, because they know that they are in no way able to compass the highest things, neglect even the least, and, as it were, carelessly at rest in their own sluggishness, they all the more lose the light of truth in the greatest matters for their refusal to learn those smallest of which they are capable. It is of such that the Psalmist declares, "They were unwilling to understand how they might do well." Not knowing and not wishing to know are far different things. Not knowing, to be sure, springs from weakness; but contempt of knowledge springs from a wicked will.

There is another sort of man whom nature has enriched with the full measure of ability and to whom she shows an easy way to come at truth. Among these, even granting inequality in the strength of their ability, there is nevertheless not the same virtue or will in all for the cultivation of their natural sense through practice and learning. Many of this sort, caught up in the affairs and cares of this world beyond what is needful or given over to the vices and sensual indulgences of the body, bury the talent of God in earth, seeking from it neither the fruit of wisdom nor the profit of good work. These, assuredly, are completely detestable. Again, for others of them, lack of family wealth and a slender income decrease the opportunity of learning. Yet, we decidedly do not believe that these can be altogether excused by this circumstance, since we see many laboring in hunger, thirst, and nakedness attain to the fruit of knowledge. And still it is one thing when one is not able, or to speak more truly, when one is not easily able to learn, and another when one is able but unwilling to learn. Just as it is more glorious to lay hold upon wisdom by sheer exertion, even though no resources support one, so, to be sure, it is more loathsome to enjoy natural ability and to have plenty of wealth, yet to grow dull in idleness.

The things by which every man advances in knowledge are principally two—namely, reading and meditation. Of these, reading holds first place in instruction, and it is of reading that this book treats, setting forth rules for it. For there are three things particularly necessary to learn for reading: first, each man should know what he ought to read; second, in what order he ought to read, that is, what first and what afterwards; and third, in what manner he ought to read. These three points are handled one by one in this book. . . .

Book One

CHAPTER ONE: CONCERNING THE ORIGIN OF THE ARTS

Of all things to be sought, the first is that Wisdom in which the Form of the Perfect Good stands fixed. Wisdom illuminates man so that he may recognize himself; for man was like all the other animals when he did not understand that he had been created of a higher order than they. But his immortal mind, illuminated by Wisdom, beholds its own principle and recognizes how unfitting it is for it to seek anything outside itself when what it is in itself can be enough for it. It is written on the tripod of Apollo: "Know thyself," for surely, if man had not forgotten his origin, he would recognize that everything subject to change is nothing. . . .

CHAPTER THREE: WHICH ARTS ARE PRINCIPALLY TO BE READ

Out of all the sciences above named, however, the ancients, in their studies, especially selected seven to be mastered by those who were to be educated. These seven they considered so to excel all the rest in usefulness that anyone who had been thoroughly schooled in them might afterward come to a knowledge of the others by his own inquiry and effort rather than by listening to a teacher. For these, one might say, constitute the best instruments, the best rudiments, by which the way is prepared for the mind's complete knowledge of philosophic truth. Therefore they are called by the name tri*vium* and quadri*vium*, because by them, as by certain *ways (viae)*, a quick mind enters into the secret places of wisdom.

In those days, no one was thought worthy the name of master who was unable to claim knowledge of these seven. Pythagoras, too, is said to have maintained the following practice as a teacher for seven years, according to the number of the seven liberal arts, no one of his pupils dared ask the reason behind statements made by him; instead, he was to give credence to the words of the master until he had heard him out, and then, having done this, he would be able to come at the reason of those things himself. We read that some men studied these seven with such zeal that they had them completely in memory, so that whatever writings they subsequently took in hand or whatever questions they proposed for solution or proof, they did not thumb the pages of books to hunt for rules and reasons which the liberal arts might afford for the resolution of a doubtful matter, but at once had the particulars ready by heart. Hence, it is a fact that in that time there were so many learned men that they alone wrote more than we are able to read. But the students of our day, whether from ignorance or from unwillingness, fail to hold to a fit method of study, and therefore we find many who study but few who are wise. Yet it seems to me that the student should take no less care not to expend his effort in useless studies than he should to avoid a lukewarm pursuit of good and useful ones. It is bad to pursue something good negligently; it is worse to expend many labors on an empty thing. But because not everyone is mature enough to know what is of advantage to him, I shall briefly indicate to the student which writings seem to me more useful than others; and then I shall add a few words on the method of study.

CHAPTER FOUR: CONCERNING THE TWO KINDS OF WRITINGS

There are two kinds of writings. The first kind comprises what are properly called the arts; the second, those writings which are appendages of the arts. The arts are included in philosophy: they have, that is, some definite and established part of philosophy for their subject matter—as do grammar, dialectic, and others of this sort. The appendages of the arts, however, are only tangential to philosophy. What they treat is some extra-philosophical matter. Occasionally, it is true, they touch in a scattered and confused fashion upon some topics lifted out of the arts, or, if their narrative presentation is simple, they prepare the way for philosophy. Of this sort are all the songs of the poets—tragedies, comedies, satires, heroic verse and lyric, iambics, certain didactic poems, fables and histories, and also the writings of those fellows whom today we commonly call "philosophers" and who are always taking some small matter and dragging it out through long verbal detours, obscuring a simple meaning in confused discourses—who, lumping even dissimilar things together, make, as it were, a single "picture" from a multitude of "colors" and forms. Keep in mind the two things I have distinguished for you—the arts and the appendages of the arts.

Between these two, however, there is in my view such distance as the poet describes when he says:

> As much as the wiry willow cedes to the pale olive,
> Or the wild nard to roses of Punic red.

It is a distance such that the man wishing to attain knowledge, yet who willingly deserts truth in order to entangle himself in these mere by-products of the arts, will find, I shall not say infinite, but exceedingly great pains and meagre fruit. Finally, the arts themselves, without these things that border on them, are able to make the student perfect, while the latter things, without the arts, are capable of conferring no perfection: and this the more especially since the latter have nothing desirable with which to tempt the student except what they have taken over and adapted from the arts; and no one should seek in them anything but what is of the arts. For this reason it appears to me that our effort should first be given to the arts, in which are the foundation stones of all things and in which pure and simple truth is revealed—and especially to the seven already mentioned, which comprise the tools of all philosophy; afterwards, if time affords, let these other things be read, for sometimes we are better pleased when entertaining reading is mixed with serious, and rarity makes what is good seem precious. Thus, we sometimes more eagerly take up a thought we come upon in the midst of a story.

It is in the seven liberal arts, however, that the foundation of all learning is to be found. Before all others these ought to be had at hand, because without them the philosophical discipline does not and cannot explain and define anything. These, indeed, so hang together and so depend upon one another in their ideas that if only one of the arts be lacking, all the rest cannot make a man into a philosopher. Therefore, those persons seem to me to be in error who, not appreciating the coherence among the arts, select certain of them for study, and, leaving the rest untouched, think they can become perfect in these alone.

CHAPTER FIVE: THAT TO EACH ART SHOULD BE GIVEN WHAT BELONGS TO IT

There is still another error, hardly less serious than that just mentioned, and it must be avoided with the greatest care: certain persons, while they omit nothing which ought to be read, nonetheless do not know how to give each art what belongs to it, but, while treating one, lecture on them all. In grammar they discourse about the theory of syllogisms; in dialectic they inquire into inflectional cases; and what is still more ridiculous, in discussing the title of a book they practically cover the whole work, and, by their third lecture, they have hardly finished with the incipit. It is not the teaching of others that they accomplish in this way, but the showing off of their own knowledge. Would that they seemed to everyone as they seem to me! Only consider how perverse this practice is. Surely the more you collect superfluous details the less you are able to grasp or to retain useful matters.

Two separate concerns, then, are to be recognized and distinguished in every art: first, how one ought to treat of the art itself, and second, how one ought to apply the principles of that art in all other matters whatever. Two distinct things are involved here: treating *of* the art and treating *by means of* the art. Treating of an art is treating, for instance, of grammar; but treating by means of that art is treating some matter grammatically. Note the difference between these two—treating of grammar, and treating some matter grammatically. We treat of grammar when we set forth the rules given for words and the various precepts proper to this art; we treat grammatically when we speak or write according to rule. To treat of grammar, then, belongs only to certain books, like Priscian, Donatus, or Servius; but to treat grammatically belongs to all books.

When, therefore, we treat of any art—and especially in teaching it, when everything must be reduced to outline and presented for easy understanding—we should be content to set forth the matter in hand as briefly and as clearly as possible, lest by excessively piling up extraneous considerations we distract the student more than we instruct him. We must not say everything we can, lest we say with less effect such things as need saying. Seek, therefore, in every art what stands established as belonging specifically to it. Later, when you have studied the arts and come to know by disputation and comparison what the proper concern of each of them is, then, at this stage, it will be fitting for you to bring the principles of each to bear upon all the others, and, by a comparative and back-and-forth examination of the arts, to investigate the things in them which you did not well understand before. Do not strike into a lot of by-ways until you know the main roads: you will go along securely when you are not under the fear of going astray.

CHAPTER SIX: WHAT IS NECESSARY FOR STUDY

Three things are necessary for those who study: natural endowment, practice, and discipline. By natural endowment is meant that they must be able to grasp easily what they hear and to retain firmly what they grasp; by practice is meant that they must cultivate by assiduous effort the natural endowment they have; and by discipline is meant that, by leading a praiseworthy life, they must combine moral behavior with their knowledge. Of these three in turn we shall now set forth a few remarks by way of introduction.

CHAPTER SEVEN: CONCERNING APTITUDE AS RELATED TO NATURAL ENDOWMENT

Those who work at learning must be equipped at the same time with aptitude and with memory, for these two are so closely tied together in every study and discipline that if one of them is lacking, the other alone cannot lead anyone to perfection—just as earnings are useless if there is no saving of them, and storage equipment is useless if there is nothing to preserve. Aptitude gathers wisdom, memory preserves it.

Aptitude is a certain faculty naturally rooted in the mind and empowered from within. It arises from nature, is improved by use, is blunted by excessive work, and is sharpened by temperate practice. As someone has very nicely said:

> Please! Spare yourself for my sake—there's only drudgery in those papers! Go run
> in the open air!

Aptitude gets practice from two things—reading and meditation. Reading consists of forming our minds upon rules and precepts taken from books, and it is of three types: the teacher's, the learner's, and the independent reader's. For we say, "I am reading the book *to* him," "I am reading the book *under* him," and "I am reading the book." Order and method are what especially deserve attention in the matter of reading.

CHAPTER EIGHT: CONCERNING ORDER IN EXPOUNDING A TEXT

One kind of order is observed in the disciplines, when I say, for instance, that grammar is more ancient than dialectic, or arithmetic comes before music; another kind in codices or anthologies, when I declare, for instance, that the Catilinarian orations are ahead of the *Jugurtha*; another kind in narration, which moves in continuous series; and another kind in the exposition of a text.

Order in the disciplines is arranged to follow nature. In books it is arranged according to the person of the author or the nature of the subject matter. In narration it follows an arrangement which is of two kinds—either natural, as when deeds are recounted in the order of their occurrence, or artificial, as when a subsequent event is related first and a prior event is told after it. In the exposition of a text, the order followed is adapted to inquiry.

Exposition includes three things: the letter, the sense, and the inner meaning. The letter is the fit arrangement of words, which we also call construction; the sense is a certain ready and obvious meaning which the letter presents on the surface; the inner meaning is the deeper understanding which can be found only through interpretation and commentary. Among these, the order of inquiry is first the letter, then the sense, and finally the inner meaning. And when this is done, the exposition is complete.

CHAPTER NINE: CONCERNING THE METHOD OF EXPOUNDING A TEXT

The method of expounding a text consists in analysis. Every analysis begins from things which are finite, or defined, and proceeds in the direction of things which are infinite, or undefined. Now every finite or defined matter is better known and able to be grasped by our knowledge; teaching, moreover, begins with those things which are better known and, by acquainting us with these, works its way to matters which lie hidden. Furthermore, we investigate with our reason (the proper function of which is to analyze) when, by analysis and investigation of the natures of individual things, we descend from universals to particulars. For every universal is more fully defined than its particulars : when we learn, therefore, we ought to begin with universals, which are better known and determined and inclusive; and then, by descending little by little from them and by distinguishing individuals through analysis, we ought to investigate the nature of the things those universals contain.

CHAPTER TEN: CONCERNING MEDITATION

Meditation is sustained thought along planned lines: it prudently investigates the cause and the source, the manner and the utility of each thing. Meditation takes its start from reading but is bound by none of reading's rules or precepts. For it delights to range along open ground, where it fixes its free gaze upon the contemplation of truth, drawing together now these, now those causes of things, or now penetrating into profundities, leaving nothing doubtful, nothing obscure. The start of learning, thus, lies in reading, but its consummation lies in meditation; which, if any man will learn to love it very intimately and will desire to be engaged very frequently upon it, renders his life pleasant indeed, and provides the greatest consolation to him in his trials. This especially it is which takes the soul away from the noise of earthly business and makes it have even in this life a kind of foretaste of the sweetness of the eternal quiet. And when, through the things which God has made, a man has learned to seek out and to understand him who has made them all, then does he equally instruct his mind with knowledge and fill it with joy. From this it follows that in meditation is to be found the greatest delight.

There are three kinds of meditation: one consists in a consideration of morals, the second in a scrutiny of the commandments, and the third in an investigation of the divine works. Morals are found in virtues and vices. The divine command either orders, or promises, or threatens. The work of God comprises what his power creates, what his wisdom disposes, and what his grace co-effects. And the more a man knows how great is the admiration which all these things deserve, the more intently does he give himself to continual meditation upon the wonders of God.

CHAPTER ELEVEN: CONCERNING MEMORY

Concerning memory I do not think one should fail to say here that just as aptitude investigates and discovers through analysis, so memory retains through gathering. The things which we have analyzed in the course of learning and which we must commit to memory we ought, therefore, to gather. Now "gathering" is reducing to a brief and compendious outline things which have been written or discussed at some length. The ancients called such an outline an "epilogue," that is, a short restatement, by headings, of things already said. Now every exposition has some principle upon which the entire truth of the matter and the force of its thought rest, and to this principle everything else is traced back. To look for and consider this principle is to "gather."

The fountainhead is one, but its derivative streams are many: why follow the windings of the latter? Lay hold upon the source and you have the whole thing. I say this because the memory of man is dull and likes brevity, and, if it is dissipated upon many things, it has less to bestow upon each of them. We ought, therefore, in all that we learn, to gather brief and dependable abstracts to be stored in the little chest of the memory, so that later on, when need arises, we can derive everything else from them. These one must often turn over in the mind and regurgitate from the stomach of one's memory to taste them, lest by long inattention to them, they disappear.

I charge you, then, my student, not to rejoice a great deal because you may have read many things, but because you have been able to retain them. Otherwise there is no profit in having read or understood much. And for this reason I call to mind again what I said earlier: those who devote themselves to study require both aptitude and memory.

CHAPTER TWELVE: CONCERNING DISCIPLINE

A certain wise man, when asked concerning the method and form of study, declared:

> A humble mind, eagerness to inquire, a quiet life,
> Silent scrutiny, poverty, a foreign soil.
> These, for many, unlock the hidden places of learning.

He had heard, I should judge, the saying, "Morals equip learning." Therefore he joined rules for living to rules for study, in order that the student might know both the standard of his life and the nature of his study. Unpraiseworthy is learning stained by a shameless life. Therefore, let him who would seek learning take care above all that he not neglect discipline.

CHAPTER THIRTEEN: CONCERNING HUMILITY

Now the beginning of discipline is humility. Although the lessons of humility are many, the three which follow are of especial importance for the student: first, that he hold no knowledge and no writing in contempt; second, that he blush to learn from no man; and third, that when he has attained learning himself, he not look down upon everyone else.

Many are deceived by the desire to appear wise before their time. They therefore break out in a certain swollen importance and begin to simulate what they are not and to be ashamed of what they are; and they slip all the farther from wisdom in proportion as they think, not of being wise, but of being thought so. I have known many of this sort who, although they still lacked the very rudiments of learning, yet deigned to concern themselves only with the highest problems, and they supposed that they themselves were well on the road to greatness simply because they had read the writings or heard the words of great and wise men. "We," they say, "have seen them. We have studied under them. They often used to talk to us. Those great ones, those famous men, they know us." Ah, would that no one knew me and that I but knew all things! You glory in having seen, not in having understood, Plato. As a matter of fact, I should think it not good enough for you to listen to me. I am not Plato. I have not deserved to see him. Good for you! You have drunk at the very fount of philosophy—but would that you thirsted still! "The king, having drunk from a goblet of gold, drinks next from a cup of clay!" Why are you blushing? You have heard Plato !—may you hear Chrysippus too! The proverb says, "What you do not know, maybe Ofellus knows." There is no one to whom it is given to know all things, no one who has not received his special gift from nature. The wise student, therefore, gladly hears all, reads all, and looks down upon no writing, no person, no teaching. From all indifferently he seeks what he sees he lacks, and he considers not how much he knows, but of how much he is ignorant. For this reason men repeat Plato's saying: "I would rather learn with modesty what another man says than shamelessly push forward my own ideas." Why do you blush to be taught, and yet not blush at your ignorance? The latter is a greater shame than the former. Or why should you affect the heights when you are still lying in the depths? Consider, rather, what your powers will at present permit: the man who proceeds stage by stage moves along best. Certain fellows, wishing to make a great leap of progress, sprawl headlong. Do not hurry too much, therefore; in this way you will come more quickly to wisdom. Gladly learn from all what you do not know, for humility can make you a sharer in the special gift which natural endowment has given to every man. You will be wiser than all if you are willing to learn from all.

Finally, hold no learning in contempt, for all learning is good. Do not scorn at least to read a book, if you have the time. If you gain nothing from it, neither do you lose anything; especially since there is, in my judgment, no book which does not set forth something worth looking for, if that book is taken up at the right place and time; or which does not possess something even special to itself which the diligent scrutinizer of its contents, having found it nowhere else, seizes upon gladly in proportion as it is the more rare.

Nothing, however, is good if it eliminates a better thing. If you are not able to read everything, read those things which are more useful. Even if you should be able to read them all, however, you should not expend the same labor upon all. Some things are to be read that we may know them, but others that we may at least have heard of them, for sometimes we think that things of which we have not heard are of greater worth than they are, and we estimate more readily a thing whose fruit is known to us.

You can now see how necessary to you is that humility which will prompt you to hold no knowledge in contempt and to learn gladly from all. Similarly, it is fitting for you that when you have begun to know something, you not look down upon everyone else. For the vice of an inflated ego attacks some men because they pay too much fond attention to their own knowledge, and when they seem to themselves to have become something, they think that others whom they do not even know can neither be nor become as great. So it is that in our days certain peddlers of trifles come fuming forth; glorying in I know not what, they accuse our forefathers of simplicity and suppose that wisdom, having been born with themselves, with themselves will die. They say that the divine utterances have such a simple way of speaking that no one has to study them under masters, but can sufficiently penetrate to the hidden treasures of Truth by his own mental acumen. They wrinkle their noses and purse their lips at lecturers in divinity and do not understand that they themselves give offense to God, whose words they preach—words simple to be sure in their verbal beauty, but lacking savor when given a distorted sense. It is not my advice that you imitate men of this kind.

The good student, then, ought to be humble and docile, free alike from vain cares and from sensual indulgences, diligent and zealous to learn willingly from all, to presume never upon his own knowledge, to shun the authors of perverse doctrine as if they were poison, to consider a matter thoroughly and at length before judging of it, to seek to *be* learned rather than merely to seem so, to love such words of the wise as he has grasped, and ever to hold those words before his gaze as the very mirror of his countenance. And if some things, by chance rather obscure, have not allowed him to understand them, let him not at once break out in angry condemnation and think that nothing is good but what he himself can understand. This is the humility proper to a student's discipline.

CHAPTER FOURTEEN: CONCERNING EAGERNESS TO INQUIRE

Eagerness to inquire relates to practice and in it the student needs encouragement rather than instruction. Whoever wishes to inspect earnestly what the ancients in their love of wisdom have handed down to us, and how deserving of posterity's remembrance are the monuments which they left of their virtue, will see how inferior his own earnestness is to theirs. Some of them scorned honors, others cast aside riches, others rejoiced in injuries received, others despised hardships, and still others, deserting the meeting places of men for the farthest withdrawn spots and secret haunts of solitude, gave themselves over to philosophy alone, that they might have greater freedom for undisturbed contemplation insofar as they subjected their minds to none of the desires which usually obstruct the path of virtue. We read that the philosopher Parmenides dwelt on a rock in Egypt for fifteen years. And Prometheus, for his unrestrained love of thinking, is recorded to have been exposed to the attacks of a vulture on Mount Caucasus. For they knew that the true good lies not in the esteem of men but is hidden in a pure conscience and that those are not truly men who, clinging to things destined to perish, do not recognize their own good. Therefore, seeing that they differed in mind and understanding from all the rest of men, they displayed this fact in the very far-removal of their dwelling places, so that one community might not hold men not associated by the same objectives. A certain man retorted to a philosopher, saying, "Do you not see that men are laughing at you?" To which the philosopher replied, "They laugh at me, and the asses bray at them." Think if you can how much he valued the praise of those men whose vituperation, even, he did not fear. Of another man we read that after studying all the disciplines and attaining the very peaks of all the arts he turned to the potter's trade. Again, the disciples of a certain other man, when they exalted their master with praises, gloried in the fact that among all his other accomplishments he even possessed that of being a shoemaker.

I could wish that our students possessed such earnestness that wisdom would never grow old in them. None but Abisag the Sunamitess warmed the aged David, because the love of wisdom, though the body decay, will not desert her lover. "Almost all the powers of the body are changed in aged men; while wisdom alone increases, all the rest fade away." "The old age of those who have formed their youth upon creditable pursuits becomes wiser with the years, acquires greater polish through experience, greater wisdom with the passage of time, and reaps the sweetest fruits of former studies. That wise and well-known man of Greece, Themistocles, when he had lived a full one-hundred seven years and saw that he was about to die, is said to have declared that he was sad to depart this life when he had just begun to be wise. Plato died writing in his eighty-first year. Socrates filled ninety-nine years with the pain and labor of teaching and writing. I pass over in silence all the other philosophers—Pythagoras, Democritus, Xenocrates, Zeno, and the Elean (Parmenides)—who flourished throughout a long life spent in the pursuit of wisdom. I come now to the poets—Homer, Hesiod, Simonides, and Tersichorus, who, when advanced in years, sang, with the approach of death—how shall I say it ?—a swan-song sweeter than even their former wont. When Sophocles, after an exceedingly old age and a long neglect of his family affairs, was accused by his sons of madness, he declaimed to the judge the story of Oedipus which he had only recently composed, and gave such a specimen of his wisdom in these already broken years that he moved the austere dignity of the courtroom to the applause of the theatre. Nor is this a matter for wonder, when even Cato the censor, most erudite of the Romans, neither blushed nor despaired to learn Greek when he was already an old man. And, indeed, Homer reports that from the tongue of Nestor, who was already stooped with age and nearly decrepit, flowed speech "sweeter than honey." Consider, then, how much these men loved wisdom when not even decrepit age could call them away from its quest.

The greatness of that love of wisdom, therefore, and the abundance of judgment in elderly men is aptly inferred from the interpretation of that very name "Abisag" which I mentioned above. "For 'Abisag' means 'father mine, superabounding' or again 'my father's deep-voiced cry,' whence it is most abundantly shown that, with the aged, the thunder of divine discourse tarries beyond human speech. For the word 'superabounding' here signifies fulness, not redundance. And indeed, 'Sunamitess' in our language means 'scarlet woman,'" an expression which can aptly enough signify zeal for wisdom.

Chapter Fifteen: Concerning the Four Remaining Precepts

The four following precepts are so arranged that they alternately refer first to discipline and next to practice.

Chapter Sixteen: On Quiet

Quiet of life—whether interior, so that the mind is not distracted with illicit desires, or exterior, so that leisure and opportunity are provided for creditable and useful studies—is in both senses important to discipline.

Chapter Seventeen: On Scrutiny

Now, scrutiny, that is, meditation, has to do with practice. Yet it seems that scrutiny belongs under eagerness to inquire, and if this is true, we are here repeating ourselves needlessly, since we mentioned the latter above. It should, however, be recognized that there is a difference between these two. Eagerness to inquire means insistent application to one's work; scrutiny means earnestness in considering things. Hard work and love make you carry out a task; concern and alertness make you well-advised. Through hard work you keep matters going; through love you bring them to perfection. Through concern you look ahead; through alertness you pay close attention. These are the four footmen who carry the chair of Philology, for they give practice to the mind over which Wisdom sits ruler. The chair of Philology is the throne of Wisdom, and it is said to be carried by these bearers because it is carried forward when one practices these things. Therefore, the two front bearers, because of their power, are neatly designated as the youths Philos and Kophos, that is Love and Hard Work, because they bring a task to external perfection; the two rear bearers are with equal neatness designated as the maidens Philemia and Agrimnia (Epimeleia and Agrypnia), that is Concern and Alertness, because they inspire interior and secret reflection. There are some who suppose that by the Chair of Philology is meant the human body, over which the rational soul presides, and which four footmen carry—that is, the four elements of which the two upper ones, namely fire and air, are masculine in function and in gender, and the two lower, earth and water, feminine.

CHAPTER EIGHTEEN: ON PARSIMONY

Men have wished to persuade students to be content with slender means, that is, not to hanker after superfluities. This is a matter of especial importance for their discipline. "A fat belly," as the saying goes, "does not produce a fine perception." But what will the students of our time be able to say for themselves on this point? Not only do they despise frugality in the course of their studies, but they even labor to appear rich beyond what they are. Each one boasts not of what he has learned but of what he has spent. But perhaps the explanation of this lies in their wish to imitate their masters, concerning whom I can find nothing worthy enough to say!

CHAPTER NINETEEN: ON A FOREIGN SOIL

Finally, a foreign soil is proposed, since it too gives a man practice. All the world is a foreign soil to those who philosophize. However, as a certain poet says:

> I know not by what sweetness native soil attracts a man
> And suffers not that he should e'er forget.

It is, therefore, a great source of virtue for the practiced mind to learn, bit by bit, first to change about in visible and transitory things, so that afterwards it may be able to leave them behind altogether. The man who finds his homeland sweet is still a tender beginner; he to whom every soil is as his native one is already strong; but he is perfect to whom the entire world is as a foreign land. The tender soul has fixed his love on one spot in the world; the strong man has extended his love to all places; the perfect man has extinguished his. From boyhood I have dwelt on foreign soil, and I know with what grief sometimes the mind takes leave of the narrow hearth of a peasant's hut, and I know, too, how frankly it afterwards disdains marble firesides and panelled halls.

John of Salisbury

c. 1115–80

The first task of man aspiring to wisdom is the contemplation of what he himself is: what is within him, what without, what below, what above, what opposite, what before, and what after.

POLICRATICUS

J ohn of Salisbury stood at the transition in medieval philosophy between the Christianized Platonism of Augustine and the Christianized Aristotelianism of Thomas Aquinas. Indeed, he was an early witness to the West's gradual and fragmentary recovery of Aristotle. John was born at Old Sarum, near Salisbury, England, sometime between 1115 and 1120. He studied under Abelard in Paris and then under William of Conches at Chartres, where he occupied himself with theology, grammar, logic, and rhetoric. The influence of the rhetorical tradition on John, especially Cicero and Quintilian, is evident in his copious writings. Though a profoundly learned man, he did not lead a cloistered life. Instead, he worked in many capacities in the church's administrative bureaucracy. He served as secretary to two archbishops of Canterbury, the second of whom was Thomas à Becket, later murdered by knights loyal to England's Henry II. John's career of service to the church culminated in his appointment by the king of France to the archbishopric of Chartres.

THE SELECTION

John presented a beautifully illuminated manuscript copy of his *Policraticus* (1159) to Thomas à Becket. Intended mostly as a treatise on the idea of the good ruler, the *Policrati-*

cus is also a meditation on the delights and consolations of books and reading, on human frailty, on memory, on the seven liberal arts, and on the proper relationship between sacred and secular texts and learning. Once again we encounter the injunction to "know thyself." In harmony with St. Augustine, "whom no one keeps in mind as much as he should," John urges that learning never be separated from the two divine prerequisites of grace and humility, and never cease to aim at love. Education is primarily about the formation of the soul, about the cultivation of the inner man and the contemplative path to piety, wisdom, and virtue.

The *Metalogicon* (also 1159) ought to be compared with Hugh of St. Victor's *Didascalicon*. Primarily a treatise on the *trivium*, it reinforces the proper method of study found in Book III of Hugh's *Didascalicon*. It also repeats the themes of humilty, grace, and love from the *Policraticus*. Worth noting, especially in contrast to modern education's preoccupation with originality and autonomy, is John's emphasis on the imitation of models and on the unbroken chain of giving and receiving between teacher and student. The famous image of dwarfs standing on the shoulders of giants as a picture of this indebtedness to predecessors appears here in the context of John's tribute to his own teacher, Bernard of Chartres. Centuries later, Isaac Newton applied this well-known metaphor to advancement of science.

from the Policraticus
Book I

INTRODUCTION

The pleasure of letters, agreeable in many respects, is especially so for the reason that all inconvenience due to interval of time or space is banished, friends are brought into the presence of one another, and matters worth knowing do not remain unknown because of their separation. For arts as well had inevitably perished, law disappeared, fidelity and religion itself crumbled, and even the proper use of language been lost, had not divine commiseration, to offset human frailty, provided mortals with the knowledge of letters.

The experiences of our ancestors, ever incentives and aids to virtue, would never have inspired or saved a single soul, had not the loyalty, zeal, and diligence of writers triumphing over sloth transmitted them to posterity.

Even as it is, the shortness of life, our obtuseness, our careless indifference, and our sterile activities permit us to know but little; and even this little is straightway driven from our minds by forgetfulness, that betrayer of knowledge, that ever hostile and faithless counterpart of memory. Who would ever have heard of an Alexander or a Caesar? Who would ever have felt admiration for the Stoics or Peripatetics, had not the testimony of writers given them their distinction? Who would ever have followed in the footsteps, so revered, of the apostles and prophets, had not Holy Scripture consecrated them to the service of posterity?

Triumphal arches add to the glory of illustrious men only when the writing upon them informs in whose honor they have been reared, and why. It is the inscription that tells the spectator that the triumphal arch is that of our own Constantine,[1] liberator of his country and promoter of peace. Indeed no one has ever gained permanent fame except as the result of what he has written or of what others have written of him. The memory of fool or emperor is, after a brief lapse of time, the same unless it be prolonged by courtesy of writers. How many great kings do you imagine there have been, with regard to whom there is nowhere in the world a thought given or a word uttered? Therefore there is no wiser policy for those who crave glory than to cultivate sedulously the favor of scholars and writers; for their own achievements, doomed to utter darkness unless illumined by the lamp of letters, avail them naught. Whatever popularity and renown are derived from other sources are as when Echo, of whom we read in fable, catches up the applause of the theater, no sooner begun than done.

In addition we can with utmost confidence draw upon letters for solace in sorrow, rest in labor, cheerfulness in poverty, self-restraint in pleasure and in wealth. When an active intellect devotes itself to reading and writing what is really worth while, the soul is purged of its defects and is revivified even in adversity by a mysterious and serene cheerfulness. One will find no human activity more agreeable or more profitable unless it be divinely inspired piety, which by prayer converses with Deity, or, with heart full of love, takes God into the soul and fondly meditates upon his wondrous ways. Believe me as one who knows, that all the sweetness of the world is as wormwood when compared with such experience, and all the more in proportion to the normality of one's senses and the keenness and unimpaired vigor of his mind. . . .

Book III

CHAPTER TWO: MAN'S FIRST CONTEMPLATION IN HIS ASPIRATION FOR WISDOM; THE FRUITS OF SUCH CONTEMPLATION

The first task of man aspiring to wisdom is the consideration of what he himself is: what is within him, what without, what below, what above, what opposite, what before, and what after.

Next perhaps comes that which those whose task it was to hand down to posterity the first principles of philosophy thought ought to be investigated; that is to say the substance, quantity, relation, quality, position, place, time, state, activity, and passivity of individual things; the peculiar properties in all of these; whether they admit of increase, can tolerate contraries, and whether anything is found opposed to them.

So far they displayed wisdom and zeal, and yet they were somewhat careless in that, amid such light cast upon things, they attained to no knowledge of themselves and lost the knowledge of the light inaccessible; being vain in their thoughts and professing themselves to be wise, they became fools, and their foolish heart was darkened. This is proved by the fact that, giving themselves up to dishonorable passions, they would do that which was seemly neither to their sex, age, nor fortune, nor even to nature, and they degraded

---

1. There was a belief, unfounded, that Britain was the birthplace of Constantine.

the persons of all by the testimony of their works. They were given over to a reprobate sense, and this is clear to those who are more fully acquainted with the Apostle. The strongest proof of all, however, is this: that credence is granted each on the basis of his faith and sincerity. For the works that each does offer testimony concerning himself, while he who does not know himself, what of profit does he know? "If thou knowest not thyself, O fairest among women, go forth and follow after the steps of the flocks."

There is an oracle of Apollo which is thought to have come down from the skies; *Noti seliton*, that is, Know thyself. With this in mind, the moralist writes:

> Learn, puny beings, to know the cause of things;
> Why we are born and what our lives should be;
> What course we have to run in life;
> How just to miss the danger of the turn;
> What limit should be placed upon our wealth;
> What prayer we may address to God above;
> What use to make of gold acquired in mart;
> How much to spend on country and on kin;
> What role has been assigned to you by God,
> For you to play upon the stage of life.

Such contemplation bears fourfold fruit: benefit to self, affection for neighbor, scorn for the world, and love of God. Is not that a good tree which bringeth forth such sweet fruit and produces such advantages? Surely he will not vaunt himself who is a little one in his own eyes. Who will not blush at his own poverty as he thinks over the number of desirable things that he has or has not? But if he recount the number of his undesirable possessions he finds abundant cause for reasonable grief and humility.

Who seeks comfort from God is thrown back upon himself wherever he turns, saying "I have been humbled, O Lord, exceedingly; quicken thou me according to thy word." Or again, he says "For I am ready for scourges and my sorrow is continually before me." . . .

Book VII

CHAPTER NINE: SPIRIT IN WHICH TO READ
THE POTENTIALLY HELPFUL AND HARMFUL

. . . At any rate he who makes a wide survey in order to select his specialty displays discretion and is the more devoted to his choice after having weighed the value of others. Perhaps that is the intention of the moralist who enjoins the reading of books. In the primer of precepts also, in which little children receive their first lessons in order that the instruction and practice of virtue which their tender minds have absorbed may not readily be forgotten (since the jar as well long retains the odor of

That which it once when new absorbed),[2]

Cato or someone else (for the author is uncertain) said

Read much but having read keep reading much.

I am inclined to think that there is nothing more helpful than this for one aspiring to knowledge, except keeping the commandments of God, which is undoubtedly the one and only way of progress in philosophy.

All reading should be done in such a way that some of it when finished should be disregarded, some condemned, and some viewed *en passant*, that the subject matter be not entirely unknown; but above all careful attention should be given to those matters which lay the foundation of the life of the state, be it by the law of the state or else by ethical principles, or which have in view the health of body and soul. Since then the chief branch among the liberal arts, without which no one can teach or be taught properly, is to be merely greeted *en passant* and as it were from the door, who can imagine that time should be devoted to other branches which being difficult to understand or impractical and harmful do not conduce to the betterment of man? For even those things that are required for man's use prove very harmful if they occupy his attention to the exclusion of all others.

Does anyone doubt the desirability of reading the historians, the orators, and the authorities on approved mathematics, since without a knowledge of them men cannot be, or at least usually are not, liberally educated? Indeed those who are ignorant of those writers are termed illiterate even if they can read and write. But when such writers lay claim to the mind as though it belonged exclusively to them, although they praise learning they do not teach; rather they hinder the cultivation of virtue. This is the reason that Cicero when dealing with the poets, to make his remarks more effective, burst out "The shout of approbation of the populace, as though it were some great and wise teacher qualified to recommend, puts the stamp of genius upon whom it wishes. But they who are so lauded, what darkness do they spread, what fears engender, and what passions inflame!" It is they who commend debauchery and adultery, foster arts of deception, teach theft, rapine, incendiarism, and set before the eyes of an untutored people all the examples of evil that are, have been, or can be imagined. What conflagration kindled in the sky, inundation of the sea, or quaking of the earth works such havoc with the nations as do those writers with our morals?

The most popular of the comic writers, in the *Eunuch*, records how a young man's lust flares up as he gazes upon a painting on the wall representing how the god shakes the dome of heaven with his thunder, rains a shower of gold through the sky-light, and seduces Danaë shut up with her seven guards. The populace sees, marvels, and praises similar scenes in each and every painting. It is the rare spectator that pays any attention to edifying themes.

A thing, Sir, lacking rime and reason too
Cannot be guided straight by reason. Hence
The curses that love brings with it, abuse

---

2. Horace, *Epistles*, I.ii.69–70.

And jealousy and quarrels, reconcilement,
War; then peace again. Should you desire
To make these insecurities secure
By sense, you'll do about as much as if
You set yourself the task of being
Sensibly insane. And now you say
In anger to yourself, "What! I return
To her who treats me so; another man
As well and how much more? Not I!
To die were better; she shall perceive that I
Am more a man." One tiny tear squeezed out
By rubbing hard her eyes will quench the flame
Of your indignant words. She'll turn the trick;
And you will be the one upon the rack.[3]

It is evident that the reasoning of the slave is employed to anticipate the reproaches of the harlot; but whatever is said to this effect is received as if the slave were calling back the infatuated lover to his mistress.

Elsewhere however Cicero highly commends writers. He says

> He alone who fears no contempt himself casts contempt upon poets and writers in other branches of artistic literature, as well as upon the historians. They know what virtue is and offer the material for philosophic study, for they brand vices; they do not teach them. Their works are attractive too on account of the help and pleasure they give to the reader. They make their way amid dangers which threaten character, with the intention of securing a foothold for virtue.
>
> Amid weapons, fires, through storms at sea, and despite so many disturbances, such sedition and plots on the part of nations, Ulysses experienced Scylla and Charybdis in order to make his way back finally in his old age to his native land. He lost his men as the result of the various vicissitudes of exile, but it was their own weakness and their love of pleasure that destroyed them. Yet the narrative of all this is interesting, for the mischance even of a friend, though bitter, serves as a warning; and the closer the intimacy with the unfortunate one the greater the force of the warning, so true it is that example is often more effective than precept. Evils are more easily avoided the more clearly they are foreseen. With difficulty and, so to speak, alone Ulysses escaped; but then too there are few who surmount their difficulties and attain the enjoyment of philosophy and their hereditary delights, if we may use the expression.

Quite in harmony with Cicero, if you deign to listen to the lyric poet although his lyre is silent, is Flaccus (perhaps you prefer to call him Horace), who congratulates himself that he had found in Maeonia's son more that was honorable and helpful than had been formulated on the precepts of many Stoics.

---

3. Terence, *Eun.* 57–70.

While you declaim at Rome, my Maximus,
Out in Praeneste I have read again
The works of him who teaches us what is
The beautiful, the base, the wise to do,
And what is not, with greater grace and truth
Than Cantor or Chrysippus; for the tale
In which because of Paris' love the Greeks
And Trojans clashed in long protracted war,
Contains the passions wild of foolish kings
And peoples. Antenor moves to cut away
The causes of the war. And Paris what?
To reign in peace and live in bliss, no one
Can force him to it!
Within, without the walls of Troy we see
The sins of faction, craft, and crime and lust
And wrath. The kings commit their folly,
Achaeans pay the price.

I myself am of the opinion of those who believe that a man cannot be literate without a knowledge of the authors. Copious reading however by no means makes the philosopher, since it is grace alone that leads to wisdom. Hence Augustine, that teacher of the Church whom no one keeps in mind as much as he should, criticized Varro, and yet in order to show that he was a very scholarly man he added, after other remarks in which he gives him unique praise,

> Finally, Cicero himself in the book entitled *Academica* testifies to his merits in the statement that he himself engaged in the argument that took place there with Varro, a man (mark his words) easily surpassing all in keenness and, undoubtedly, in knowledge. He does not say "most fluent" or "most eloquent" since he was in that line deficient, but says "easily surpassing all in keenness and undoubtedly in knowledge."
>
> Moreover, in the first book, while praising Varro's literary output, he says "When I found myself a stranger and a wanderer in my native city, your books like welcoming friends led me home, as it were, so that at length I was able to recognize who and where I was. It has been you who have spread before us the pages of our country's past, you who have described the law of our ritual and our priests, our public and domestic life, and the names, types, and significance of our habitations, regions, and places and of all else human and divine." Yet this man so distinguished and of such outstanding knowledge, who read so much that we marvel that he had any time to write and who wrote more than we believe any human being could have read—this man, I repeat, of such great talent and such learning, had he been the assailant and destroyer of divine matters on which he wrote and had he stated that they belonged to the domain not of religion but of superstition, would not I imagine have written more that deserved ridicule, scorn, and execration.

If therefore a man, as Cicero testifies, most keen and undoubtedly of great learning, may be charged with superstition and convicted on the evidence of his own writings, and if it be conceded that superstition by reason of its falsehood is opposed to virtue, which consists of truth alone, and that wisdom cannot exist without virtue, who can believe that from reading alone, without the presence of grace which illumines, creates, and gives life to the virtues, man can attain wisdom?

CHAPTER ELEVEN: WHAT CONSTITUTES TRUE PHILOSOPHY; THE AIM OF ALL WRITING

Herin lies true philosophy, and it is the most pleasant and salutary advantage that wide reading confers. Wisdom itself embraces a knowledge of all things, directs all things, and itself fixes the proper limit of deeds, words, and thoughts everywhere in the life of man. There is however that for which even she knows not how to fix a boundary; there is that for which she establishes a mode in the fact that it has no limit. Whatever wisdom does and whatever she says leads to the truth, that with true philosophers she has no limit; for her substance is of that which nowhere has an end. If indeed, according to Plato, the philosopher is he who loves God, what else is philosophy if not the love of the divine? This is something that brooks no limit, otherwise philosophy herself would be restricted, and this is inexpedient; for that which is restricted also ceases to be, and if God's love be extinguished the word philosophy vanishes into thin air.

So also the Incarnate Wisdom of God, though He limits many things, enjoins that love for God be limitless; except that this mode is prescribed for charity, that God be loved with love that has no limits; for Jesus said "Thou shalt love thy neighbor as thyself." He likewise had said before "Thou shalt love the Lord thy God with thy whole heart and with thy whole soul and with thy whole mind and with thy whole strength." He also added "On these two words dependeth the whole law and the prophets." If therefore all that has been written attends on the prophets and the law, that is to say, if all teaching has the aim of subjecting man to the law of God, who doubts that all things are accredited to the law of God; who doubts that all things are accredited to the realm of charity? Whoever then by the agency of philosophy acquires or spreads charity has attained his aim as a philosopher. Consequently this is the true and unvarying rule of philosophers, that each one busy himself in all that he reads or learns, does, or abstains from doing, with advancing the cause of charity. Charity is never meaningless and apart; it conducts honor, self-control, and sobriety, modesty, and the whole army of venerable virtues to man as to the temple of the Lord and dedicates him to piety.

All that has not this aim in the arts and in literature is not philosophic doctrine but the idle fable and pretext of those over whose impiety the wrath of God is revealed from heaven. All their chattering seems flat, silly, and senseless to the true philosopher. Listen not to me but to the prophet speaking of such things: "The wicked have told me fables but not as thy law." Therefore to give expression to truth and justice is common both to those who are philosophers and to those who are not; to tell the truth and lies, to teach good and evil, is not a characteristic of philosophers. It is only at times that the mere imitator of the philosopher teaches righteousness, but he who practices the righteousness which he teaches really is a philosopher.

CHAPTER TWELVE: THE ABSURDITY OF THE FRIVOLOUS
WHO DEEM WISDOM BUT WORDS; INSPIRED BOOKS
SHOULD BE READ IN ONE WAY AND SECULAR IN ANOTHER

Those who suppose that philosophy consists of words alone are subject to an especial and shameless form of error; they are in error in thinking virtue but words, in regarding a consecrated wood nothing but firewood. For virtue is esteemed for its works, and virtue is the inseparable companion of wisdom. Consequently it is a fact that they who cling to words prefer to seem rather than to be wise. They wander around the streets; they tread the thresholds of the learned; they raise trivial questions; their words are involved to obscure their own meaning and that of others; they are more eager to argue than to weigh, if a difficult point comes up. Vaunting rather than loving wisdom, they fear to betray their own ignorance, and with false modesty they prefer to remain in ignorance rather than to search and learn, especially if others are present who, they imagine, know what they do not.

One cannot put up with their airs. They talk offhand on any subject; they pass judgment on everybody; they blame others; praise themselves; boast that they have discovered again that which is in reality commonplace, having come down to our times through the ages from the ancients and on the evidence of books. They multiply their words so that often they are harder to understand by reason of the weight and multitude of words than because of the difficulty of the theme. When one of them has succeeded in making himself incomprehensible, he thinks that he has won the right of being regarded as a philosopher superior to others.

Often one who knows very little propounds much that even Pythagoras himself would not be able to clarify. At times he goes over and over the same subjects, and because he does not know where to turn he flounders pitifully; he wears bare the same theme and circles around the same point. Hearing him at a distance you marvel that a third Cato has descended from the sky. He will seem a jack-of-all trades; if you ask his profession or trade, he is

> A teacher, rhetorician, geometrician,
> Painter, trainer, augur, tight-rope walker,
> Doctor, or astrologer; he knows
> It all.[4]

He far outstrips your hungry mountebank the Greek. Should you command he'll even fly the skies, and with greater skill than Daedalus he'll conduct you where you will through empty space. If you come to him for instruction, if you inquire carefully into the meaning of what authors have written, or if you examine the written word, straightway he will upbraid your insensibility and call you dumber than an Arcadian ass. As long as you ask the meaning embedded in the written word your wits are heavier than lead; the written word is useless and you must not worry about what it has to say. If you insist, you are warned to avoid it as dangerous, for the letter killeth. Be careful not to be the serpent, which eats earth all the days of its life.

---

4. Juvenal, *Sat.*, iii.76–77.

What you must do is to disport yourself, chat, or argue, for he who uses the most words is regarded as the greatest scholar. No attention need be given to the source or subject of the opinions that anyone expresses, provided he keeps talking. It makes not the slightest difference on what reasoning anyone relies, provided he succeed in giving not its reality but its shadow. What is true or false, probable or improbable, are idle questions, seeing that the semblance of probabilities is preferred to all else. Whatever your decision, some analogy will immediately nullify it; for what applies in one example will, despite all, apply in another. None the less it is a fact that what is plausible is not for that reason true, and what seems false is not always false. If you endeavor to demonstrate the dissimilarity of similar propositions, you are undertaking a thankless task. Your opponent will either shout you down or will mock your superfluous effort, since there must be some dissimilarity in all similar things; otherwise they would not be called similar rather than more properly identical. To teach why this is not so is judged not only stupid but worthy of derision.

You are immediately asked whether you wish to harangue the meeting. They say that they had agreed to listen to a Peripatetic [logician] not to a Hermagoras [philosopher]; though as a matter of fact in their rambling and wandering about, rather than in the careful investigation of truth, they imitate the Peripatetics. If however this discussion is carried on and similarities and dissimilarities are sought with the aim of acquiring fluency in delivery, the practice is indeed praiseworthy. I am inclined to think that nothing else is more beneficial for youth, provided they do not allow their eyes to be blinded in a thick cloud of deception. For nothing is more useful, nothing more conducive to the attainment of fame and wealth by the young man, than fluency of speech, which is the result of the possession of an abundance of facts in the mind and an abundance of words in the mouth.

To pour out a flood of words without mastery of the subject is the trait of a fool, not of a teacher or a student. You will see many of this type dragging out the day with a long discourse but saying very little or nothing at all. You are worn out with listening; he, were he not an unusually verbose man, might well be thoroughly exhausted with his talking. You have not yet caught the drift of his remarks or what he means; you are expecting the end; he has hardly completed his introduction. Endure to the end however and see at what he is aiming. Finally sum up what he has strung together; there will rise before your mind

> Dreams as it were of sick man conjuring up
> Deceptive shapes that neither head or foot
> Can be allotted to a single form.[5]

One would imagine him a man with clouded brain who in default of reason cannot control his tongue; one would believe him passing sleepless nights, and that his reason put to sleep, derangement alone were awake in him. Should one moved to pity advise him to be sparing of himself he flies into a rage, devises all sorts of abuse, and wrangles alike with those who pity and those who sneer; he spews upon friend and foe alike.

---

5. Horace, *A.P.* 7–9.

If once you have started you must put up with him or suffer the abuse of a violent tongue. Therefore stop unless you prefer to be smirched with a foul tongue; for filth too, the more it is stirred up, the worse it smells. You recall the words of a man of sound sense:

> The crazy bard they fear to touch, and flee
> If they be wise; the children chase and dare
> To follow him.[6]

Although in private life among the seriously minded a man of this type seems with good reason useless, he is however acceptable to the populace, which takes delight in matters that provide it with cause for gaiety and jocularity; for he is the best medium of arousing mirth, is more effective than any mimic. To avoid his enmity you must bear patiently what he has to say and humor the madman who spares no one. If perchance you desire to check him, in the kindest manner beg him to put more thought into his instruction and argument and keep the balance by subtracting words. For he who regulates language according to the requirement of the theme and makes the theme appropriate to the occasion is following the most effective rule governing the whole of oratory. Such eloquence gives rise to praise with which truth, the friend of virtue and all the moral duties, is in accord.

To be verbose and misleading in speech is characteristic of a counter-hopper, of one who disregards reputation entirely and who arouses the hate and contempt of men of character. The Spirit of wisdom is authority for the saying, "He that speaketh sophistically is hateful." Yet the ability to detect the sophistries of false reasoners is of no slight advantage; without the ability to detect these, whoever advances to the examination of truth and to the discussion of facts is comparable to the useless soldier who marches unarmed against a well trained and well equipped foe. It is therefore permitted that one debating for purposes of training practice deception in his turn and, as in an officers' training camp in the midst of civilians, play at campaigning; but when the debater's attention is directed to the serious side of philosophy, sophisms are not in evidence. If per chance they should come to view on either side they are to be rebuked by men of wisdom, just as in the state the deception of the wicked in business transactions is held in check. To make language harmonize with facts and facts with the times and to censure wisely intruding fallacies is not a matter of a few days nor an easy task. As a result many advancing to the fray turn back and, making a display of a portion of the wardrobe of philosophy, vaunt themselves in the presence of the uninformed as if philosophy had fallen completely under their jurisdiction. For as someone has remarked (I remember the lines but the author's name escapes me),

> The lad that can combine two halves in one
> Thus poses and thus talks, as if he had
> Now mastered all the arts.

---

6. Horace, *A.P.* 455–56.

With regard to genera and species such an imposter offers a new theory that had escaped Boethius and was unknown to Plato, one that he had lately by happy chance found in abstruse writings of Aristotle. He is prepared to solve the ancient question, laboring with which the world has already grown old and on which more time has been spent than the line of the Caesars has consumed in subduing and ruling the world, more money squandered than Croesus possessed with all his wealth. For this has engaged the attention of many so long that at length, since they spend their whole life in search of it alone, they have discovered neither this nor anything else; possibly for the reason that what alone could be discovered did not suffice for the curiosity in them.

Just as in the shadow cast by any body it is vain to seek a firm foundation of substance, so in those matters which are intelligible only and can be universally conceived but cannot universally be, nowhere can the substance of a more tangible existence be detected. To spend one's life on these points is equivalent to accomplishing nothing and to wasting one's efforts; they are but the mist of fleeting things, and the more eagerly they are sought the more quickly they fade away.

Authorities explain this problem in many ways and in various terms, and since they employ words without discrimination they appear to have upheld various views and have left for disputatious individuals much controversial matter. Hence it is that our disputant having grasped sensible and other individual things, since these are said to be the sole realities, divides them into various states, and according to this classification he establishes in the individual things themselves the explicitly specific and the explicitly general.

There are some who adopt forms in the fashions of the mathematicians and refer to them all that is said with regard to universals; others banish concepts and maintain that they come under the names of universals. There were those also who said that even words were genera and species; but their view has already been exploded and has readily disappeared along with its exponent. However there are still found those following in their footsteps, although they blush to acknowledge either the originator or the view, clinging merely to names; they attribute to words what they deny to objects and concepts.

> Each one possesses mighty influence
> In his support,[7]

and from the words of authorities who have indiscriminately employed names for things and things for names, he contributes his own theory or, if you will, error.

From such sources a luxuriant growth of discussion springs up, and each one gathers that from which he may be able to support his own heresy. There is no escaping from genera and species, and you may put into this harbor from whatsoever place the discussion sets out. Suddenly you will be surprised to discover in yourself that painter described by the poet, who for all requirements knew how to paint only a cypress tree. Thus Rufus is crazy over Naevia, from whom, on the testimony of Coquus, no plight can estrange him, for

---

7. Lucan, *Phars.* i.127.

Whatever Rufus does, for Rufus there
Is only Naevia; in joy, in grief,
When silent, he talks alone of her.
He dines, he toasts, he asks, denies or nods,
But Naevia is all. No Naevia suppose,
He will be dumb.[8]

That subject seems best suited for philosophical discussion in which there is a some-what free scope for assuming what you wish and less certainty, owing to the difficulty of the subject or the lack of skill of your disputant. Very often just as the soldier has his eyes open for rough and narrow places on the route, to impede more easily the progress of the foe, so one will raise difficult questions suggested by books or arguments or, if another subject is brought forward, will purposely slip off into these side tracks as if by accident. If you fail to satisfy him (for there is no one who has the ability to explain all that even fools can ask) straightway, what knowing winks, grimaces, waving of arms, shouting, jumping about, and gestures that would seem grotesque in any actor or mimic! Especially unsatisfactory will you prove unless you reply in his own words and say only what he is accustomed to hear.

Yet he himself with all his hair-splitting is absolutely ignorant of the solution. In one point however he has perhaps been somewhat careful of his own interest, in that he has pocketed all the proceeds of his bombast. None the less quite easily, like a bladder pricked by a needle, all the loquacity that was resounding in the bellows of his ignorant throat dies away at times if a man of sense inject a single remark.

I cannot imagine that those are more fitted for philosophic discussion who meet every remark with a long formal speech, as if in reply to every question they had to deliver a public address. A rule has been handed down that he who says more or less than has been asked him is ignorant of the proper line to be followed in debate. Besides, when anyone is to be instructed, that only should be stated which aids in solving the question. Conse-quently it is evident that they who read everything in connection with every question, and while investigating one point strive to settle all, do not possess the correct technique of teaching, for they are either ignorant of the proper method or by disguising their calling are possibly making a display of their own endowments, and, as Cicero puts it, they show what they themselves, rather than what their profession, can accomplish.

Therefore they who fill their elementary Porphyry with all the divisions of philosophy, blunt the keenness of mind and the memory of those who are to be introduced to the subject. They disconcert the prospective student with their solemnity to such a degree that he feels he has undertaken a burden too heavy for his strength. I would perhaps concede that the Holy Scriptures whose every tittle is filled with holy signs, should be read with such solem-nity for the reason that the treasure of the Holy Ghost by whose hand they have been written cannot be entirely plumbed. For although on the face of it the written word lends itself to one meaning only, manifold mysteries lie hidden within, and from the same source allegory often edifies faith and character in various ways. Mystical interpretation leads upward in manifold ways, so that it provides the letter not only with words but with reality itself.

---

8. Martial, *Epigr.* 1.68.1–4.

But in liberal studies where not things but words merely have meaning, he who is not content with the first meaning of the letter seems to me to lose himself, or to be desirous of leading his auditors away from an understanding of truth that they may be held by him for a longer period. I really think our poor Porphyry foolish if he wrote in such a manner that his meaning can be understood only by those who have previously read Aristotle, Plato, and Plotinus. For myself I take leave of anyone who presumes to introduce me to any study by such a short cut, since I shall indeed follow the one who expounds the letter and by opening up the surface, so to say, imparts the historical meaning.

CHAPTER FOURTEEN: THE PUPIL'S SEVENTH KEY

In Quintilian's work on the education of the orator love for his teacher is laid down as the pupil's seventh key, and accordingly instructors are to be loved and respected as parents are; for as the latter are creators of the bodies, so the former are the creators of the souls of their listeners (not generating of themselves the substance of spirit but engendering as it were wisdom in the minds of their listeners by making over their nature for the better). Such attachments are of great assistance to study, for pupils are glad to listen to those whom they love; they believe what they are told by them, desire to be like them; under the impulse of loyalty and affection they are eager and glad to form those throngs of pupils; do not become angry when rebuked; are not confused when praised, and will themselves well deserve to be held very dear because of their devotion to study. For as the function of teachers is to teach, so that of auditors to show themselves teachable; otherwise neither without the help of the other avails. Just as man owes his origin to each of two progenitors and as you labor in vain if you scatter seed on ground that has not been broken and softened by the furrow, so eloquence cannot mature unless there be a spirit of harmony between the teacher and the taught.

So states Quintilian in his rules governing eloquence, but what he says applies as well to instruction in wisdom. Assuredly eloquence is not attained without rules for wisdom, and he is not merely ridiculous but somewhat lacking in sense who, though not instructed by philosophy how to speak with a degree of accuracy, forces his way into the forum of those who have ears to hear.

The book entitled *Christian Teaching* sets forth several other keys for the understanding of the Scriptures, and these Tichonius has enumerated. They by no means clash with those just mentioned; rather they all depend upon one, for zeal in investigation embraces all of them. As for the rest, language was established by the teaching of the gentiles, with the intention that it be explicitly applied to the instruction of the faithful. However the one unique key of keys, as it were, is that that openeth and no man shutteth, locketh and no man openeth, without which no man attains the understanding of truth; and whoever does not grasp it and does not hold tight to it, him I deem a madman, not a sage.

from the Metalogicon
Book I

CHAPTER 23: THE CHIEF AIDS TO PHILOSOPHICAL INQUIRY
AND THE PRACTICE OF VIRTUE; AS WELL AS HOW GRAMMAR
IS THE FOUNDATION OF BOTH PHILOSOPHY AND VIRTUE

The chief aids to philosophical inquiry and the practice of virtue are reading, learning, meditation, and assiduous application. Reading scrutinizes the written subject matter immediately before it. Learning likewise generally studies what is written, but also sometimes moves on to what is preserved in the archives of the memory and is not in the writing, or to those things that become evident when one understands the given subject. Meditation, however, reaches out farther to what is unknown, and often even rises to the incomprehensible by penetrating, not merely the apparent aspects, but even the hidden recesses of questions. The fourth is assiduous application. The latter, although it owes its form to previous cognition, and requires scientific knowledge, still smooths the way for understanding, since, in itself, it constitutes "a good understanding for all who do it." The heralds of the truth, it is written, "have proclaimed the works of God, and have understood His doings." Scientific knowledge, by the nature of things, must precede the practice and cultivation of virtue, which does not "run without knowing where it is going," and does not merely "beat the air" in its battle against vice. Rather "it sees its goal, and the target at which it aims." It does not haphazardly chase ravens with a piece of pottery and a bit of mud. But scientific knowledge is the product of reading, learning, and meditation. It is accordingly evident that grammar, which is the basis and root of scientific knowledge, implants, as it were, the seed [of virtue] in nature's furrow after grace has readied the ground. This seed, provided again that cooperating grace is present, increases in substance and strength until it becomes solid virtue, and it grows in manifold respects until it fructifies in good works, wherefore men are called and actually are "good." At the same time, it is grace alone which makes a man good. For grace brings about both the willing and the doing of good. Furthermore, grace, more than anything else, imparts the faculty of writing and speaking correctly to those to whom it is given, and supplies them with the various arts. Grace should not be scorned when it generously offers itself to the needy, for if despised, it rightly departs, leaving the one who has spurned it no excuse for complaint.

CHAPTER 24: PRACTICAL OBSERVATIONS ON READING
AND LECTURING, TOGETHER WITH [AN ACCOUNT OF] THE
METHOD EMPLOYED BY BERNARD OF CHARTRES AND HIS FOLLOWERS

One who aspires to become a philosopher should therefore apply himself to reading, learning, and meditation, as well as the performance of good works, lest the Lord become angry and take away what he seems to possess. The word "reading" is equivocal. It may refer either to the activity of teaching and being taught, or to the occupation of studying written things by oneself. Consequently, the former, the intercommunication between teacher and learner, may be termed (to use Quintilian's word) the "lecture"; the latter, or the scrutiny by the student, the "reading," simply so called. On the authority of the same Quintilian, "the teacher of grammar should, in lecturing, take care of such details as to have his students analyze verses into their parts of speech, and point out the nature of the metrical feet which are to be noted in poems. He should, furthermore, indicate and condemn whatever is barbarous, incongruous, or otherwise against the rules of composition." He should not, however, be overcritical of the poets, in whose case, because of the requirements of rhythm, so much is overlooked that their very faults are termed virtues. A departure from the rule that is excused by necessity, is often praised as a virtue, when observance of the rule would be detrimental. The grammarian should also point out metaplasms, schematisms, and oratorical tropes, as well as various other forms of expression that may be present. He should further suggest the various possible ways of saying things, and impress them on the memory of his listeners by repeated reminders. Let him "shake out" the authors, and, without exciting ridicule, despoil them of their feathers, which (crow fashion) they have borrowed from the several branches of learning in order to bedeck their works and make them more colorful. One will more fully perceive and more lucidly explain the charming elegance of the authors in proportion to the breadth and thoroughness of his knowledge of various disciplines. The authors by *diacrisis*, which we may translate as "vivid representation" or "graphic imagery," when they would take the crude materials of history, arguments, narratives, and other topics, would so copiously embellish them by the various branches of knowledge, in such charming style, with such pleasing ornament, that their finished masterpiece would seem to image all the arts. Grammar and Poetry are poured without stint over the length and breadth of their works. Across this field, as it is commonly called, Logic, which contributes plausibility by its proofs, weaves the golden lightening of its reasons; while Rhetoric, where persuasion is in order, supplies the silvery luster of its resplendent eloquence. Following in the path of the foregoing, Mathematics rides [proudly] along on the four-wheel chariot of its Quadrivium, intermingling its fascinating demonstration in manifold variety. Physical philosophy, which explores the secret depths of nature, also brings forth from her [copious] stores numerous lovely ornaments of diverse hue. Of all branches of learning, that which confers the greatest beauty is Ethics, the most excellent part of philosophy, without which the latter would not even deserve its name. Carefully examine the works of Vergil or Lucan, and no matter what your philosophy, you will find therein its seed or seasoning. The fruit of the lecture on the authors is proportionate both to the capacity of the students and to the industrious diligence of the teacher. Bernard of Chartres, the greatest font of literary learning in Gaul in recent times, used to teach grammar in the following way. He would point out, in reading the authors, what was simple and according to rule. On the other hand, he would explain grammatical figures, rhetorical embellishment, and sophistical quibbling, as well as the relation of given passages to other studies. He would do so, however, without trying to teach everything at one time. On the contrary, he would dispense his instruction to his hearers gradually, in a manner commensurate with their powers of assimilation. And since, diction is lustrous either because the words are well chosen, and the adjectives and verbs admirably suited to the nouns with which they are used, or because of the employment of metaphors, whereby speech is transferred to some beyond-the-ordinary meaning for sufficient reason, Bernard used to inculcate this in the minds of his hearers whenever he had the opportunity. In view of the fact that exercise both strengthens and sharpens our mind, Bernard would bend every effort to bring his students to imitate what they were hearing. In some cases he would rely on exhortation, in others he would resort to punishments, such as flogging. Each student was daily required to recite part of what he had heard on the previous day. Some would recite more, others less. Each succeeding day thus became the disciple of its predecessor. The evening exercise, known as the "declination," was so replete with grammatical instruction that if anyone were to take part in it for an entire year, provided he were not a dullard, he would become thoroughly familiar with the [correct] method of speaking and writing, and would not be at a loss to comprehend expressions in general use. Since, however, it is not right to allow any school or day to be without religion, subject matter was presented to foster faith, to build up morals, and to inspire those present at this quasicollation to perform good works. This [evening] "declination," or philosophical collation, closed with the pious commendation of the souls of the departed to their Redeemer, by the devout recitation of the Sixth Penetential Psalm and the Lord's Prayer. He [Bernard] would also explain the poets and orators who were to serve as models for the boys in their introductory exercises in imitating prose and poetry. Pointing out how the diction of the authors was so skillfully connected, and what they had to say was so elegantly concluded, he would admonish his students to follow their example. And if, to embellish his work, someone had sewed on a patch of cloth filched from an external source, Bernard, on discovering this, would rebuke him for his plagiary, but would generally refrain from punishing him. After he had reproved the student, if an unsuitable theme had invited this, he would, with modest indulgence, bid the boy to rise to real imitation of the [classical authors], and would bring about that he who had imitated his predecessors would come to be deserving of imitation by his successors. He would also inculcate as fundamental, and impress on the minds of his listeners, what virtue exists in economy; what things are to be commended by facts and what ones by choice of words, where concise and, so to speak, frugal speech is in order, and where fuller, more copious expression is appropriate; as well as where speech is excessive, and wherein consists just measure in all cases. Bernard used also to admonish his students that stories and poems should be read thoroughly, and not as though the reader were being precipitated to flight by spurs. Wherefore he diligently and insistently demanded from each, as a daily debt, something committed to memory. At the same time, he said that we should shun what is superfluous. According to him, the works of distinguished authors suffice. As a matter of fact, to study everything that everyone, no matter how insignificant, has ever said, is either to be excessively humble and cautious, or overly vain and ostentatious. It also deters and stifles minds that would better be freed to go on to other things. That which preempts the place of something that is better is, for this reason, disadvantageous, and does not deserve to be called "good." To examine and pore over everything that has been written, regardless of whether it is worth reading, is as pointless as to fritter away one's time with old wives' tales. As Augustine says in his book *On Order*: "Who is there who will bear that a man who has never heard that Daedalus flew should [therefore] be considered unlearned? And, on the contrary, who will not agree that one who says that Daedalus did fly should be branded a liar; one who believes it, a fool; and one who questions [anyone] about it, impudent? I am wont to have profound pity for those of my associates who are accused of ignorance because they do not know the name of the mother of Euryalus, yet who dare not call those who ask such questions 'conceited and pedantic busy-bodies.'" Augustine summarizes the matter aptly and with truth. The ancients correctly reckoned that to ignore certain things constituted one of the marks of a good grammarian. A further feature of Bernard's method was to have his disciples compose prose and poetry every day, and exercise their faculties in mutual conferences, for nothing is more useful in introductory training than actually to accustom one's students to practice the art they are studying. Nothing serves better to foster the acquisition of eloquence and the attainment of knowledge than such conferences, which also have a salutary influence on practical conduct, provided that charity moderates enthusiasm, and that humility is not lost during progress in learning. A man cannot be the servant of both learning and carnal vice. My own instructors in grammar, William of Conches, and Richard, who is known as "the Bishop," a good man both in life and conversation, who now holds the office of archdeacon of Coutances, formerly used Bernard's method in training their disciples. But later, when popular opinion veered away from the truth, when men preferred to seem, rather than to be philosophers, and when professors of the arts were promising to impart the whole of philosophy in less than three or even two years, William and Richard were overwhelmed by the onslaught of the ignorant mob, and retired. Since then, less time and attention have been given to the study of grammar. As a result, we find men who profess all the arts, liberal and mechanical, but who are ignorant of this very first one [i.e., grammar], without which it is futile to attempt to go on to the others. But while other studies may also contribute to "letters," grammar alone has the unique privilege of making one "lettered." Romulus, in fact, refers to grammar as "letters," Varro calls it "making lettered," one who teaches or professes grammar is spoken of as "lettered." In times past, the teacher of grammar was styled a "teacher of letters." Thus Catullus says: "Silla, the 'teacher of letters,' gives thee a present." Hence it is probable that anyone who spurns grammar, is not only not a "teacher of letters," but does not even deserve to be called "lettered."

CHAPTER 25: A SHORT CONCLUSION CONCERNING THE VALUE OF GRAMMAR

Those who only yesterday were mere boys, being flogged by the rod, yet who today are [grave] masters, ensconced in the [doctor's] chair and invested with the [official] stole, claim that those who praise grammar do so out of ignorance of other studies. Let such patiently heed the commendation of grammar found in the book, *On the Education of an Orator.* If the latter is acceptable to them, then let them [condescend to] spare innocent grammarians. In the aforesaid work we find this statement: "Let no one despise the principles of grammar as of small account. Not that it is a great thing to distinguish between consonants and vowels, and subdivide the latter into semivowels and mutes. But, as one penetrates farther into this (so to speak) sanctuary, he becomes conscious of the great intricacy of grammatical questions. The latter are not only well calculated to sharpen the wits of boys, but also constitute fit subject matter to exercise the most profound erudition and scientific knowledge." [Quintilian also says:] "Those who deride this art [of grammar] as petty and thin, deserve even less toleration. For if grammar does not lay beforehand a firm foundation for the orator, the [whole] structure will collapse. Grammar is accordingly first among the liberal arts. Necessary for the young, gratifying to the old, and an agreeable solace in solitude, it alone, of all branches of learning, has more utility than show."

Book III

. . . Our own generation enjoys the legacy bequeathed to it by that which preceded it. We frequently know more, not because we have moved ahead by our own natural ability, but because we are supported by the [mental] strength of others, and possess riches that we have in inherited from our forefathers. Bernard of Chartres used to compare us to [puny] dwarfs perched on the shoulders of giants. He pointed out that we see more and farther than our predecessors, not because we have keener vision or greater height, but because we are lifted up and borne aloft on their gigantic stature. I readily agree with the foregoing.

Thomas Aquinas

c. 1225–74

For the end of the contemplative life . . . is the seeing of truth.

On the Teacher

Thomas was born into a large noble family on an estate near Aquino, Italy. He was educated in the liberal arts at the Benedictine monastery at Monte Cassino, the very heart of the monastic tradition in the West. At the University of Naples, Thomas was first introduced to the expanding corpus of Aristotle's works. He then decided to join the new order of lowly Dominican friars, thwarting his father's ambition to see the talented youth become abbot of Monte Cassino. Angered, his family took him captive and spent the next year trying to talk him out of his decision before they relented. He continued his study of Aristotle under Albert the Great, first in Paris and then in Cologne, encountering the commentaries on Aristotle written by the Islamic scholars Averroes and Avicenna. With the reappearance of works by Aristotle that the West had not seen for hundreds of years, the central theological and philosophical question of the thirteenth century became, in effect, "What has Aristotle to do with Christ?" Thomas labored to reconcile much of Aristotle with the teaching of the church. In G. K. Chesterton's helpful formulation, "St. Thomas did not reconcile Christ to Aristotle; he reconciled Aristotle to Christ."[1] Nevertheless, his handling of Aristotle was controversial in his own day and for some fifty years after his death. Thomas devoted his life to teaching and writing, producing a formidable number of works, including commentaries on Aristotle and the multivolume theological

---

1. *Saint Thomas Aquinas* (New York: Doubleday, 1956), 10.

treatises *Summa Contra Gentiles* and *Summa Theologica*. He taught at the University of Paris at the same time as Bonaventure, and he figures prominently in Dante's *Paradiso*.

THE SELECTIONS

Thomas's "Letter to Brother John" offers advice to an inquiring young friar. In contrast to the analytical treatise it is paired with here, the gentle letter shows a less daunting side of the famous scholar. In the aftermath of the First World War, French scholar A. G. Sertillanges was inspired by the principles in this letter to write his own reflections on the calling of the life of the mind (*The Intellectual Life*), a portion of which is included later in this anthology.

On the Teacher, the eleventh question from Thomas's *Disputed Questions on Truth* (1256–59), engages with Augustine's dialogue by the same title and with Pope Gregory's homilies on Ezekiel. The word translated here as "science" does not mean the modern empiricism of the natural sciences but rather knowledge broadly conceived. Article Four, on the active and contemplative life, ought to be compared with Seneca's *De Otio*.

Letter to Brother John

Since you have asked me, my very dear John in Christ, how you should apply yourself in order to gain something from the treasure-house of knowledge, let this be the advice handed down to you by me on this subject.

Make up your mind to start on small streams rather than to plunge into the sea; for one should progress from easier matters to those that are more difficult. This is, then, my advice and instruction for you. I counsel you to be slow to speak and slow to take the speaker's stand. Embrace purity of mind; do not neglect prayer; cherish your cell most of the time, if you wish to be admitted to the vintage-room [of knowledge]. Be friendly to all men; do not be curious about the private activities of other people; do not try to be overfamiliar with anyone, for too much familiarity breeds contempt and provides an opportunity for neglecting one's studies.

Do not get interested in any way in worldly talk or deeds. Avoid idle talk on all matters; do not fail to imitate the example of holy and good men; do not be concerned about what speaker you are listening to; instead, when something good is said, commit it to memory. Be sure that you understand whatever you read. Make certain that you know the difficulties and store up whatever you can in the treasure-house of the mind; keep as busy as a person who seeks to fill a vessel.

Do not seek higher positions. Follow in the footsteps of Blessed Dominic who brought forth and increased the buds, the flowers and the fruits that were useful and wonderful in the vineyard of the Lord of Hosts, as long as he lived.

If you follow these words of advice, you will be able to attain your every desire.

⤳⊗⤸

from On the Teacher
Article 1: Can a man teach and be called a master or God alone?

It seems that only God can teach and be called a teacher.

1. Matthew 23.8 says, "You have but one master," and earlier, "Do not be called Rabbi," on which the Gloss comments, "Lest you attribute to men divine honour or usurp what is God's." Therefore, to be a master and to teach seem to belong to God alone.

2. Moreover, if a man teaches it is only through signs, because if he seems also to teach something through the things themselves, as for example by walking when asked what walking is, this does not suffice for teaching, unless some sign be added, as Augustine proves in *On the Teacher* 1.3. The reason is that there are many aspects of a single thing and it is unclear which is relevant when it is pointed at, whether its substance or some accident of it. But we cannot come to knowledge of things through signs, because knowledge of things is more powerful than knowledge of signs, since knowledge of signs is ordered to knowledge of things as to its end, and the effect cannot be more potent than its cause. Thus no one can pass on knowledge of things to another and thus he cannot teach him.

3. Moreover, if signs of certain things be proposed one man to another, either the one to whom they are proposed knows the things of which they are the signs or he doesn't. If he knows them, he is not taught concerning the things. If he does not know them but is ignorant of the things, the meanings of the signs cannot be known by him. For if someone does not know the thing that is a stone, he cannot know what is meant by the word "stone." Not knowing the meaning of the signs, he cannot learn anything through the signs. Therefore if all a man does in teaching is to propose signs, it seems that one man cannot be taught by another man.

4. Moreover, teaching is nothing other than causing knowledge in another in some way. But the subject of knowledge is intellect, and the sensible signs by which alone a man seems to teach do not reach to the intellective part but remain in the sensitive part. Therefore, a man cannot be taught by a man.

5. Moreover, if science is caused in one man by another, either the knowledge was in the learner or it was not. If it was not in him and is caused in the man by another, the latter created knowledge in the former, which is impossible. If it was in him, either it was in him in complete actuality, and thus is not caused, because what is does not come to be, or it was in him as a kind of rational seed [*ratio seminalis*], but rational seeds cannot be brought to actuality by any created power, but are inserted in nature by God alone, as Augustine says in the literal commentary on Genesis. It remains then that one man cannot be taught by another.

6. Moreover, science is a kind of accident, but an accident cannot pass from its subject. Therefore, since teaching seems to be the transfer of the master's knowledge to the student, one man cannot be taught by another.

7. Moreover, on the remark in Romans 10:17, "Faith comes from hearing," the Gloss says, "Although God teaches within, an outward herald proclaims. But science is caused in the interior of the mind and not outside in the senses." Therefore, a man is taught by God alone, not by another man.

8. Moreover, Augustine says in *On the Teacher*, "God alone has a chair in the heavens and on it he teaches truth; a man is so related to that chair as the farmer to the tree, which he does not make but cultivates." Therefore, no man can be called a teacher of science, but rather disposes for science.

9. Moreover, if man were a true teacher, he would have to teach truth. But whoever teaches truth, illumines the mind, since truth is the light of the mind. Therefore, a man would illumine the mind if he taught. But this is false, since it is God who illumines every man coming into this World (John 1:9). Therefore, one man cannot truly teach another.

10. Moreover, if one man teaches another, he would have to bring someone who knows potentially to the state of actually knowing, so that his knowledge is brought from potency to act. But what is brought from potency to act is necessarily changed. Therefore, science or wisdom will be changed, which is in conflict with Augustine in *Eighty-three Questions*, where he says that when wisdom comes to man, it is the man who changes, not wisdom.

11. Moreover, science seems to be nothing else than the inscription of things in the soul, since science is said to be the assimilation of the knower to the known. But a man cannot inscribe in another's soul the likenesses of things, for then he would work within him, but that belongs to God alone. Therefore, one man cannot teach another.

12. Moreover, Boethius says in the *Consolation of Philosophy* 5.5 that through teaching the mind of man is summoned to know, but one who summons the intellect to know does not cause it to know, any more than he who summons another to bodily seeing causes him to see. Therefore, one man does not cause another to know, and thus is not properly said to teach him.

13. Moreover, certainty of knowledge is required for science, otherwise it is not science, but opinion or belief as Augustine says in *On the Teacher*. But one man cannot cause certainty in another through the sensible signs that he proposes, for what is in the senses is always oblique to what is in intellect, whereas certainty rather comes about through something direct. Therefore, one man cannot teach another.

14. Moreover, an intelligible light and species are required for science, but neither can be caused in a man by another man, because then a man would have to create something, since such simple forms seem to be produced only through creation. Therefore, a man cannot cause science in another and thus cannot teach.

15. Moreover, only God can form the mind of man, as Augustine says in *On Free Will* 1.17. But science is a kind of form of mind. Therefore God alone causes science in the soul.

16. Moreover, ignorance like guilt is in the mind, but only God purges the mind of guilt. Isaiah 43:25: "I am, I am he that blots out thy iniquities for my own sake: and I will not remember thy sins." Therefore, God alone purges the mind of ignorance, and thus he alone teaches.

17. Moreover, since science is certain knowledge, one receives science from another through whose speech he is made certain. But one is not made certain because he hears a man speaking, otherwise, whatever is said to him by a man would hold as certain for him,

He is only made certain by hearing the truth speak within, which he consults concerning what he hears a man say in order that he might become certain. Therefore, a man does not teach, but truth speaks within and that is God.

18. Moreover, no one learns, through the speech of another, things which he would have been able to respond if asked before the speech. But the pupil, before the master speaks to him, would if asked respond concerning the things the master proposes. For he is only taught by the master when he knows that things are as the master proposes. Therefore, one man is not taught by another's speaking.

ON THE CONTRARY:

1. There is what is said in 2 Timothy 1:11: ". . . of which I have been appointed a preacher . . . and a teacher of the Gentiles." Therefore a man can be, and be called, a teacher.

2. Moreover, see 2 Timothy 3:14: "But do thou continue in the things thou hast learned, and that have been entrusted to thee," and the Gloss on this passage: "From me, as from a true teacher." Thus, concluding as before.

3. Moreover, Matthew 23:8 and 9 both say that your master is one and your father is one. But the fact that God is the father of all does not prevent a man too from truly being called a father. So this too excludes the claim that a man cannot truly be called a master.

4. Moreover, on Romans 10:15, "How beautiful are the feet of those who preach," the Gloss says, "These are the feet that illumine the Church," speaking of the apostles. Since, to illumine is the act of the teacher, it seems that teaching pertains to men.

5. Moreover, it is said in *Meteorology* 4 that anything is perfect when it can generate something like itself. But science is perfect knowledge. Therefore, a man who has science, can teach another.

6. Moreover, Augustine, in *Against the Manicheans* 2.4, says that earth, which before sin was watered by a spring, after sin needed rain descending from the clouds. So the human mind, which is signified by earth, was made fruitful by the spring of truth, but after sin needed the teaching of others, like rain descending from the clouds. Therefore, at least after sin, a man can be taught by another man.

RESPONSE:

It should be said that there is the same diversity of opinion in three matters, namely, in bringing forms into existence, in the acquisition of virtue and in the acquisition of knowledge.

For some said that all sensible forms are from an external agent which is a substance or a separate form which they called the giver of forms or agent intellect, and that all lesser natural agents only prepare matter for the reception of form. So too Avicenna says in his *Metaphysics* the cause of the worthy habit is not our action but action rather adapts to it and prevents the contrary, such that habit comes from a substance perfecting the souls of men, which is the agent intelligence or a substance similar to it.

Likewise they hold that science is effected in us only by a separate agent. Hence Avicenna said in *On Natural Things* 6, 4.2 that intelligible forms flow into our mind from the agent intelligence.

Others thought the opposite, namely that whatever is inserted in things has its cause not in an external agent but is only brought to light by the external action. For some held that all natural forms are actually latent in matter and that the natural agent does nothing other than to bring them from a hidden to a manifest condition.

Similarly, some held that all the habits of virtue are implanted in us by nature and that actions make these habits emerge from obscurity just as rubbing removes rust from steel and reveals its brightness.

So too some said that knowledge of all things is created along with the soul and that through teaching and the external aids of teaching nothing else happens than that the soul is led to the remembrance or consideration of what it previously knew. Hence they say that learning is nothing but remembering.

But these opinions are without foundation. For the first opinion excludes proximate causes by attributing to first causes alone all effects coming about in inferior things, which derogates from the order of the universe, which consists of the order and connection of causes. The first cause out of the eminence of his goodness not only makes things to be but also to be causes.

The second opinion comes to the same absurdity. Since the removal of an impediment is only to cause accidentally, as is said in *Physics* 8, if inferior agents did nothing but make the hidden manifest by removing impediments whereby forms and the habits of virtue and sciences were obscured, it would follow that all inferior agents accidentally.

Therefore, following the teaching of Aristotle, the middle way between these two extremes is to be held in all these matters. For natural forms do indeed pre-exist in matter, but not actually, as these said, but only potentially, from which they are brought into act by the proximate external agent, not only the first cause, as the other opinion would have it.

Similarly, according to this teaching in *Ethics* 6, the habits of the virtues before their perfection pre-exist in us in certain natural inclinations which are, as it were, the beginnings of virtue, but afterwards, by the doing of works they are brought to their fitting completion.

And we ought to say the same about the acquisition of sciences: certain seeds of the sciences pre-exist us, namely, the first conceptions of the intellect which are known right away by the light of the agent intellect through species abstracted from sensible things, whether these be complex, like axioms, or incomplex like the notions of being and one, and the like, which the intellect apprehends straightaway. Everything that follows is included in these universal principles as in certain seminal reasons. Therefore when the mind led from this universal knowledge to the actual knowing of particulars, which it previously knew in the universal and as it were potentially, then someone is said to acquire science.

But it should be noted that in natural things something is said to pre-exist potentially in two ways. In one way, in complete active potency, namely, when an intrinsic principle is sufficient to bring about a perfect act, as is evident in healing, for from the natural power which is in him the sick person is brought to health.

In another way, in passive potency, namely, when the intrinsic principle does not suffice for bringing to actuality, as is clear when fire is made from air, for this could not come to be through any power existing in the air.

Therefore when something pre-exists in complete active potency, the extrinsic agent only acts by aiding the intrinsic agent and supplying it with the things by which it comes forth to actuality, as the physician in healing is the minister of nature which principally acts by aiding nature and providing medicine which nature uses as instruments in healing.

But when something pre-exists only in passive potency, then it is the extrinsic agent that principally leads from potency to act, as fire makes of air, which is potentially fire, actual fire.

Therefore, science pre-exists in the learner in active and not purely passive potency, otherwise a man could not acquire science on his own.

Therefore, just as there are two ways to be cured, one by the operation of nature alone, the other by nature as aided by medicine, so too there are two ways of acquiring science, one, when natural reason by itself comes to knowledge of the unknown, and this way is called *discovery*, another when someone outside aids natural reason, and this way is called *learning*.

In things that come about both by nature and by art, art acts in the same way and through the same means as nature. For just as nature restores health to one suffering a chill by heating, so too the physician, which is why art is said to imitate nature. It happens similarly in the acquisition of science, because the teacher leads another in the same way to knowledge of the unknown as one by discovery brings himself to knowledge of the unknown.

But the process of coming to knowledge of the unknown by discovery is to apply the common self-evident principles to determinate matters and then to proceed to particular conclusions, and from those to others. So one man is said to teach another following this same discourse of reason which natural reason executes, showing signs to another so that the natural reason of the pupil, through what is proposed, as through certain instruments, comes to knowledge of the unknown.

Therefore, just as the physician is said to cause health in the infirm by acting with nature, so too a man is said to cause science in another by the activity of his natural reason, and this is to teach. Hence one man is said to teach another and to be his master. And thus the Philosopher says in *Posterior Analytics* 1 that demonstration is syllogism that causes one to know.

If however someone proposed to another what is not included in self-evident principles or is not shown to be included, he will not cause knowledge, but perhaps opinion or belief, though these two are also in a way caused by innate principles. From these self-evident principles, one considers that those things which necessarily follow are to be held as certain and what is contrary to them to be repudiated, whereas to others he can give or withhold assent.

The light of reason by which principles of this kind are known is placed in us by God, bringing about in us a kind of likeness of uncreated truth. Hence, since all human teaching is only efficacious because of the power of this light, it follows that it is God alone who teaches within and principally, just as nature principally and within heals. Nevertheless, man can be properly said both to heal and to teach in the way explained.

Ad 1. It should be said that because the Lord commanded his disciples not to be called masters, lest this be taken to be absolutely forbidden, the Gloss explains how this prohibition should be understood. We are forbidden to call a man master in this sense that we attribute to him the principal role in teaching, which belongs to God, as if placing our hope in the wisdom of men rather than in what we hear from a man, consulting the divine truth, which speaks in us through the impress of his likeness, thanks to which we can judge all things.

Ad 2. It should be said that knowledge of things is not effected in us by knowledge of signs, but through knowledge of other more certain things, namely principles, which are proposed to us through signs and are applied to what previously was absolutely unknown although known by us in a certain respect, as has been said. For the knowledge of principles not knowledge of signs, causes in us knowledge of conclusions.

Ad 3. It should be said that the things of which we are taught by means of signs we indeed know in one respect but do not know in another. If we are taught what a man is we must know something of him beforehand, such as the notion of animal or of substance or at least of being itself, which cannot be unknown to us, and likewise if we are taught some conclusion, we must previously know what the predicate and subject are as also the previously known principles through which the conclusion is taught. For all learning comes from previously existing knowledge, as is said at the beginning of the *Posterior Analytics*, so the argument does not work.

Ad 4. It should be said that from sensible signs, which are received in the sense power, the intellect receives intelligible intentions, which it uses for bringing about science in itself. Signs are not the proximate cause of science, but reason, moving discursively from principles to conclusions, as has been said.

Ad 5. It should be said science previously existed in the one taught, not in complete act, but as it were in seminal reasons, according to universal concepts, knowledge of which is naturally put in us, which are like seeds of all the knowledge that follows. However, although through a created power the seminal reasons are not actualized as if they were infused by some created power, none the less what is in them originally and virtually can be brought to actuality by the act of a created power.

Ad 6. It should be said that the teacher does not transfer knowledge into the learner as numerically the same knowledge which was in the master comes to be in the pupil, but because through teaching there comes to be in the pupil knowledge similar to that which is in the master, brought forth from potency to act, as has been said.

Ad 7. It should be said that just as the physician, although he acts externally—nature alone acting internally—is said to cause health, so a man is said to teach truth although he states it externally, God teaching within.

Ad 8. It should be said that Augustine in *On the Teacher* does not mean to deny that a man teaches from without when he proves that God alone teaches, because God alone teaches within.

Ad 9. It should be said that man can truly be called a true teacher and a teacher of the truth and enlightener of the mind, not as if he were infusing light to reason, but as it were aiding the light of reason to the perfection of science through what he externally proposes. It is in this sense that it is said in Ephesians 3:8–9, "To me the least of all the saints is given this grace . . . to enlighten all men."

Ad 10. It should be said that wisdom is twofold, created and uncreated, and both are said to be infused in man and by this infusion a man is changed for the better. But uncreated wisdom is in no way mutable, though created wisdom is mutable accidentally, not as such. For it can be considered in two ways. In one way, with respect to the eternal things with which it is concerned and thus it is wholly immutable; in another way, according to the existence it has in the subject, and thus it is changed accidentally, when the subject is changed from having it potentially to having it actually. For the intelligible forms in which wisdom consists, are both likenesses of things and forms perfecting the intellect.

Ad 11. It should be said that intelligible forms are inscribed in the learner and through them the knowledge acquired through teaching is constituted, immediately by the agent intellect, but mediately by him who teaches. For the teacher proposes signs of intelligible things from which the agent intellect receives intelligible intentions and inscribes them in the possible intellect. Hence the teacher's words being heard or seen in writing, are related to causing science in the intellect just as things outside the soul are, because the agent intellect receives intelligible intentions from both, although the words of the teacher are more closely related to causing science than sensible things existing outside the soul, insofar as they are signs of intelligible intentions.

Ad 12. It should be said that intellect and bodily sight are not wholly alike, for bodily sight is not a collating power, such that from some of its objects it goes on to others, but all its objects are visible to it as soon as it turns to them. One having sight is related to intuiting all visible things as one who has a habit is to considering the things he knows habitually, and thus the one seeing does not need to be incited by anything else in order to see, except insofar as his sight is directed by another to the visible, as by pointing or the like. The intellectual power, since it is collative, goes from some things to others, and thus is not related equally to all intelligible things to be considered. Some it sees straightaway because they are self-evident and in them are implicitly contained other things which it cannot understand save through the office of reason by explicating. In order to know such things, before it has the habit, it is not only in accidental potency but also in essential potency, for it needs a mover which actualizes it by way of teaching, as is said in *Physics* 8. He who already knows things habitually does not need this. Therefore the teacher stirs the intellect to knowing what he teaches, as an essential mover bringing actuality from potency. But the one showing something to bodily sight, stirs it like an accidental mover, as one having the habit of science can be stirred to consider something.

Ad 13. It should be said that all the certainty of science derives from the certainty of the principles, for conclusions are known with certainty when they are resolved into the principles. Something is known with certainty in the light of reason divinely inserted within, whereby God speaks in us; but not by the man teaching without, save insofar as he in teaching us resolves conclusions into principles. We would not receive the certainty of science if there was not in us the certainty of the principles into which the conclusions are resolved.

Ad 14. It should be said that the man teaching externally does not infuse the intelligible light, but is in some way the cause of the intelligible species, insofar as he proposes to us certain signs of intelligible intentions, which our intellect receives from the signs and stores in itself.

Ad 15. It should be replied that when it is said that only God can form the mind, this should be understood of its ultimate form, without which it would be regarded as un-formed, however many other forms it has. But this is the form by which it is turned to the word and inheres in it, by which alone the rational nature is called formed, as is clear from Augustine in the literal commentary on Genesis.

Ad 16. It should be said that fault is in the affection, in which God alone can make an impression, as will be clear in the following article; but ignorance is in the intellect, on which a created power too can make an impression, as the agent intellect impresses intelligible species on the possible intellect; by the mediation of which, from sensible things and from the teaching of men, science is caused in our soul, as has been said.

Ad 17. It should be said that, as has been remarked, the certainty of science is in God alone, who instils in us the light of reason, through which we know the principles from which the certainty of science derives; yet science is caused in us in some way by man as well, as has been said.

Ad 18. It should be said that the learner interrogated before the teacher speaks would respond about the principles through which he will be taught, but not about the conclusions which someone would teach him: hence he does not learn principles from the master, but only conclusions.

Article 2: Can someone be called his own teacher?

It seems not.

1. Because an action ought to be attributed to the principal cause rather than to the instrumental; but what functions as the principal cause of the science caused in us is the agent intellect. But the man who teaches outside is an instrumental cause proposing to the agent intellect instruments by which it can attain to science. Therefore, the agent intellect is more of a teacher than the man outside. If because of exterior speech, the one speaking is said to be the master of him who hears, so much the more so should the one who hears be called his own teacher, because of the light of the agent intellect.

2. Someone learns only insofar as he arrives at certainty of knowledge; but certainty of knowledge comes about in us through principles naturally known in the light of the agent intellect: Therefore, it belongs chiefly to the agent intellect to teach, with the same conclusion as above.

3. Moreover, teaching belongs more properly to God than to man; hence Matthew 23:8: "You have but one teacher." But God teaches us insofar as he gives us the light of reason by which we can judge all things. Therefore, the act of teaching ought chiefly to be attributed to that with the same conclusion as before.

4. Moreover, to know something by way of discovery is more perfect than to learn from another, as is evident in *Ethics* 1.4. Therefore, if the term "teacher" is taken from that mode of acquiring science whereby one learns from another, so that one is the teacher of the other in a much fuller sense the term "teacher" should be taken from the mode of receiving science by way of discovery, so that someone can be called his own teacher.

5. Moreover, just as someone is led to virtue by another or by himself, so one is led to knowledge both by discovering on his own and by learning from another. Those who come to the works of virtue without an external instructor or legislator are said to be a law unto themselves; Romans 2:14: "Since gentiles who have not the law naturally do what is of the law, they are a law unto themselves." Therefore, one who acquires knowledge by himself ought to be called his own teacher.

6. Moreover, the teacher is the cause of knowledge as the physician is of health, as has been said. But the physician heals himself. Therefore, one is able to teach himself.

ON THE CONTRARY:

1. The Philosopher says in *Physics* 8 that it is impossible that the one teaching learns, because the teacher must have knowledge where the learner does not. Therefore, no one can teach himself or be called his own teacher.

2. Moreover, master, like lord, implies a relation of being placed above. But relations of this kind cannot obtain between a thing and itself. No one is his own father or lord. Therefore, no one can be called his own teacher.

RESPONSE:

It should be said that without any doubt one can, through the light of natural reason placed within him and without any external aid, come to knowledge of many unknown things, as is evident in all who acquired science by way of discovery. And thus in a certain way one can be the cause of his own knowing, but he cannot properly be called his own teacher or be said to teach himself.

For we find two kinds of agent principles in natural things, as the Philosopher makes clear in *Metaphysics* 8.

There is a kind of agent that has within itself everything that it causes in the effect, whether in the same manner, as with univocal agents, or in a more eminent way, as in equivocal agents. But there are some agents in which there exists only partially within them what they bring, as motion causes heat, and heat causes medicine, in which heat is found either actually or virtually, but heat is not the whole of health but a part of it. In the primary agents there is action in the fullest sense, but not in agents of the secondary sort, because a thing acts insofar as it is actual. Hence, since it is not actually or more than partially what is brought about in the effect, it is not a perfect agent.

But teaching implies the perfect act of knowing in the teacher or master; hence it is required that he who teaches or is a master should have the science he causes in another, explicitly and perfectly, as it is acquired in the learning through teaching.

When someone acquires knowledge by himself through an intrinsic principle, what is the agent cause of science does not possess the science to be acquired, save in part, namely with respect to the seminal reasons of science, which are common principles. Therefore, from such causality the name teacher or doctor cannot be derived, properly speaking.

Ad 1. It should be said of the agent intellect that, though in a certain respect it is a more principal cause than the man teaching outside, science does not completely exist beforehand in it, as in the teacher. Hence the argument does not work.

Ad 2 The answer is similar to the first.

Ad 3. It should be said that God explicitly knows all things that man is taught by him, so the notion of teacher can fittingly be attributed to him; not so the agent intellect, for the reason given.

Ad 4. It should be said that the manner of acquiring science through discovery is more perfect on the part of the one receiving science, insofar as he is shown to be more equipped to know, yet on the part of the one causing science teaching is more perfect. The one teaching, who explicitly knows the whole science, can lead us to science more expeditiously than anyone can be brought to it on his own because he foreknows the principles of the science in some generality.

Ad 5. It should be said that law functions in practical matters as principle does in speculative matters, but not as the master; hence it doesn't follow from the fact that one can be a law unto himself that he can be his own teacher.

Ad 6. It should be said that the physician heals insofar as he has health, not actually, but in the knowledge of art; but the master teaches insofar as he actually has science. Hence he who actually has health, in the sense that he has knowledge of it by art, can cause health in himself. But it is not possible that someone actually have the science and yet not have it and thus be able to be taught by himself.

Article 4: Is teaching an act of the active or contemplative life?

It seems that it is an act of the contemplative.

1. The active life fails when the body does, as Gregory teaches in commenting on Ezekiel. But to teach does not fail with the body, because the angels too, who lack body, teach, as has been said. Therefore it seems that teaching pertains to the contemplative life.

2. Moreover, as Gregory also says, the active life is first engaged in so that afterwards we might come to the contemplative. But teaching follows and does not precede contemplation. Therefore, to teach does not pertain to the active life.

3. Moreover, as Gregory says in the same place, since the active life is occupied with work it sees less, but it is necessary that one who teaches sees more than one who simply contemplates. Therefore teaching pertains rather to the contemplative than to the active.

4. Moreover, a thing is perfect in itself and passes on a like perfection to others for the same reason, just through the same heat fire is hot and heats. But for one to be perfect in himself in the consideration of divine things pertains to the contemplative life. Therefore teaching too, which is the transmission of the same perfection to another, pertains to the contemplative life.

5. Moreover, the active life turns on temporal things but teaching turns rather on the eternal, teaching about that which is more excellent and perfect. Therefore, teaching does not pertain to the active life, but to the contemplative.

ON THE CONTRARY:

1. In the same homily, Gregory says, "The active life is to give bread to the hungry and to teach the word of wisdom to those who do not know it."

2. Moreover, the works of mercy pertain to the active life, and teaching is numbered among spiritual alms. Therefore teaching is of the active life.

RESPONSE:

It should be said that the contemplative and active lives are distinguished from one another by end and by matter.

Temporal things, on which human acts bear, are the matter of the active life, whereas the matter of the contemplative is the notions of knowable things on which the contemplator dwells. This diversity of matter comes from the diversity of ends, just as in everything else the matter is determined according to the requirements of the end.

For the end of the contemplative life, as we now speak of it, is the seeing of truth; I mean uncreated truth to the degree possible for the one contemplating. Which in this life is imperfectly seen, but in the future life will be seen perfectly. Hence Gregory also says that the contemplative life begins here, that it might be perfected in the heavenly fatherland.

But the end of the active life is action, which is aimed at for its usefulness to neighbours.

We find a twofold matter in the act of teaching, a sign of which is that there is a double object conjoined to the act of teaching. One matter of it is the thing itself that is taught, another the one to whom the science is passed on. By reason of the first matter, the act of teaching pertains to the contemplative life, but by reason of the second to the active.

From the point of view of its end, teaching is seen to pertain to the active life alone, because its ultimate matter, in which it achieves the intended end, is the matter of the active life. Hence it pertains rather to the active than to the contemplative life, although it also in a certain way pertains to the contemplative, as is clear from what has been said.

Ad 1. It should be said that the active life in this respect fails with the body it is engaged in with labour and with which it supplies the infirmities of neighbours, in keeping with what Gregory says, that the active life is laborious, because it involves sweaty work, neither of which will obtain in the future life. Nevertheless, there is hierarchical action in the celestial spirits, as Dionysius says, and that action is of a higher mode than the active life of which we are treating. Hence the teaching there will also be far different from this teaching.

Ad 2. It should be said that Gregory in the same place writes that the well-ordered living is to move on to the contemplative from the active; but often the soul usefully applies to the active what is drawn from the contemplative, such that when the mind is kindled by the contemplative the active is more perfectly lived. It should be noted, however, that the active precedes the contemplative with respect to those acts in which it in no way is like the contemplative, but with respect to those acts which take their matter from the contemplative the active life must follow the contemplative.

Ad 3. It should be said that the vision of the teacher is the beginning of teaching, but the teaching itself consists rather in the transmission of knowledge of the things seen than in the vision of them. Hence the vision of the teacher pertains to the contemplative rather than to the active.

Ad 4. It should be said that that argument proves that the contemplative life is the principle of teaching; just as heat is not the heating but the principle of heating, so the contemplative life is found to be the principle of the active insofar as it directs it, just as conversely the active life disposes for the contemplative.

Ad 5. The solution is obvious from what has been said, because with respect to the first matter, teaching belongs to the contemplative, as has been said.

Bonaventure

1221-74

It is to groans of prayer through Christ Crucified, in Whose blood we are cleansed from the filth of vices, that I first of all invite the reader.

THE JOURNEY OF THE MIND TO GOD

B onaventure was born in Bagnorea, Italy, where he was educated by the Franciscans, a new order founded by the Christian mystic Francis of Assisi (1181–1226). Bonaventure continued his studies in the liberal arts at the University of Paris and then taught for twelve years as a professor there. He and Thomas Aquinas were granted their doctoral degrees by the University of Paris on the same day in 1267. Even after he became head of the Franciscan order, Bonaventure continued to lecture and preach from time to time at the university. His several volumes of writings include the standard life of Francis, commentaries on Scripture, sermons, and spiritual meditations. Among his finest works is a guide for leaders of religious communities, *De sex alis seraphim* (The Six Wings of the Seraph). A worthy leader, according to Bonaventure, must possess a zeal for justice and display kindness, patience, an exemplary life, discernment, and devotion to God. Intellectually and spiritually, Bonaventure continues in the line of Plato, Augustine, Anselm, Bernard of Clairvaux, and the Victorines. Compared with his contemporary Thomas Aquinas, the Franciscan's mysticism and devotional style stand out in sharp contrast to the Dominican's systematic academic arguments. Bonaventure was appointed a cardinal in 1273, using the position to seek the reconciliation of the Roman and Orthodox churches.

The Selection

Bonaventure's *Journey of the Mind to God (Itinerarium)* was written in 1259, when he was head of the Franciscans and during a time of conflict over the order's identity and commitment to poverty. In general, it is a guide to the spiritual life for students at the university. Themes that permeated medieval education appear with vigor here: wisdom, peace, love, the centrality of Christ, and the need for prayer and grace and safeguards against human vanity. Bonaventure begins with a benediction of peace and an account of his own search for peace and the beginning of his journey toward the contemplative life. His symbolic interpretation of Scripture and his mysticism may sound foreign to modern ears, but his advice regarding the necessary preconditions of learning is timeless. Certainly, Bonaventure's ideal standard is a reminder that the "integration of faith and learning" has behind it a long history of careful reflection. Bonaventure could not have imagined a university ever wanting to separate faith from learning.

from The Journey of the Mind to God

Prologue

1. In the beginning I call upon the very first Beginning from Whom all enlightenment flows, the *Father of Lights,* from Whom is *every best and perfect gift,* that is upon the Eternal Father, through His Son, our Lord Jesus Christ, that, through the intercession of the most Blessed Virgin Mary, Mother of that same God and our Lord Jesus Christ, and through that of blessed Francis, our guide and father, *He may enlighten the eyes of our mind to guide our feet into the way of* that *peace which surpasses all understanding,* that peace which our Lord Jesus Christ preached to us and which He gave to us. His message of peace our father Francis ever repeated, announcing "Peace" at the beginning and at the end of all his sermons, making every greeting a wish for peace, making every prayer a sigh for ecstatic peace, like a citizen of that Jerusalem, about which the Man of Peace, *who was peaceable with those that hated peace,* exhorts us concerning it: *Pray for the things that are to the peace of Jerusalem.* For He knew indeed that only in peace was the throne of Solomon established, as it is written: *In peace is his place and his abode is in Zion.*

2. Inspired by the example of our blessed father, Francis, I wanted to seek after this peace with yearning soul, sinner that I am and all unworthy, yet seventh successor as Minister to all the brethren in the place of the blessed father after his death; it happened that, thirty-three years after the death of the Saint, about the time of his passing, moved by a divine impulse, I withdrew to Mount Alverno, as to a place of quiet, there to satisfy the yearning of my soul for peace. While I dwelt there, pondering on certain spiritual ascents to God, I was struck, among other things, by that miracle which in this very place had happened to the blessed Francis, that is, the vision he received of the winged seraph in the form of the Crucified. As I reflected on this marvel, it immediately seemed to me that this vision might suggest the rising of Saint Francis into contemplation and point out the way by which that state of contemplation may be reached.

3. The six wings of the seraph can be rightly understood as signifying the six progressive illuminations by which the soul is disposed, as by certain grades or steps, to pass over to peace through the ecstatic transports of Christian wisdom. The road to this peace is through nothing else than a most ardent love of the Crucified, which so transformed Paul into Christ when he *was rapt to the third heaven* that he declared: *With Christ I am nailed to the Cross; it is now no longer I that live, but Christ lives in me.* This love so absorbed the soul of Francis too that his spirit shone through his flesh the last two years of his life, when he bore the most holy marks of the Passion in his body!

The figure of the six wings of the Seraph, therefore, brings to mind the six stages of illumination, which begin with creatures and lead up to God, into union with Whom no one rightly enters save through the Crucified. For *he who enters not by the door, but climbs up another way, is a thief and a robber. But if anyone enter* by this door, *he shall go in and out and shall find pastures.* For this reason Saint John writes in the Apocalypse: *Blessed are they who wash their robes in the blood of the Lamb, that they may have the right to the tree of life, and that by the gates they may enter into the city*; that is to say, no one can enter by contemplation into the heavenly Jerusalem unless he enters through the blood of the Lamb as through a door. For no one is in any way disposed for divine contemplations that lead to spiritual transports unless, like Daniel, he is also *a man of desires!* Now, such desires are enkindled in us in two ways, to wit, through *the outcry of prayer,* which makes one sigh *from anguish of heart,* and through *the refulgence of speculation* by which the mind most directly and intensely turns itself toward the rays of light.

4. Wherefore, it is to groans of prayer through Christ Crucified, in Whose blood we are cleansed from the filth of vices, that I first of all invite the reader. Otherwise he may come to think that mere reading will suffice without fervor, speculation without devotion, investigation without admiration, observation without exultation, industry without piety, knowledge without love, understanding without humility, study without divine grace, the mirror without divinely inspired wisdom. To those, therefore, who are already disposed by divine grace, to the humble and pious, to the contrite and devout, to those who are anointed *with the oil of gladness,* to the lovers of divine wisdom and to those inflamed with a desire for it, to those who wish to give themselves to glorifying, admiring, and even savoring God, to those I propose the following considerations, wishing at the same time to warn them that the mirror of the external world put before them is of little or no avail unless the mirror of our soul has been cleansed and polished. First, then, O man of God, arouse in yourself remorse of conscience before you raise your eyes to the rays of Wisdom reflected in its mirrors, lest perchance from the very beholding of these rays you fall into a more perilous pit of darkness.

5. I have thought it well to divide this tract into seven chapters, prefixing titles for the easier understanding of the matters about which we must speak. I entreat the reader to consider the intention of the writer more than the work, the sense of the words more than the uncultivated style, the truth more than the adornment, and the exercise of the affections more than the instruction of the mind. He who would achieve this ought not to run perfunctorily through these considerations, but rather take his time and mull them over.

CHAPTER ONE

. . . 15. Therefore, whoever is not enlightened by such great splendor in created things is blind; whoever remains unheedful of such great outcries is deaf; whoever does not praise God in all these effects is dumb; whoever does not turn to the First Principle after so many signs is a fool. So, open your eyes, alert the ears of your spirit, unlock your lips, and apply your heart that you may see, hear, praise, love, and adore, magnify, and honor your God in every creature, lest perchance the entire universe rise against you. For because of this, *the whole world shall fight against the unwise.* But on the other hand, it will be a matter of glory for the wise, who can say with the prophet: *For you have given me, O Lord, a delight in your doings, and in the work of your hands I shall rejoice. How great are your works, O Lord! You have made all things in wisdom; the earth is filled with your riches.*

CHAPTER SEVEN

. . . 6. If you wish to know how these things may come about, ask grace, not learning; desire, not understanding; the groaning of prayer, not diligence in reading; the Bridegroom, not the teacher; God, not man; darkness, not clarity; not light, but the fire that wholly inflames and carries one into God through transporting unctions and consuming affections. God Himself is this fire, and *His furnace is in Jerusalem* and it is Christ who enkindles it in the white flame of His most burning Passion. This fire he alone truly perceives who says: *My soul chooses hanging, and my bones, death.* He who loves this death can see God, for it is absolutely true that *Man shall not see me and live.*

Let us, then, die and enter into this darkness. Let us silence all our cares, our desires, and our imaginings. With Christ crucified, let us pass *out of this world to the Father,* so that, when the Father is shown to us, we may say with Philip: *It is enough for us.* Let us hear with Paul: *My grace is sufficient for you,* and rejoice with David, saying: *My flesh and my heart have fainted away: You are the God of my heart, and the God that is my portion forever. Blessed be the Lord forever, and let all the people say: so be it, so be it.* Amen.

Petrarch

1304-74

Believe me, many things are attributed to gravity and wisdom which are really due to incapacity and sloth.

LETTER TO BOCCACCIO, MAY 28, 1362

Francesco Petrarca (Petrarch), historian, poet, and man of letters, was born in Arezzo, Italy, near Florence. His family wandered for a time but then settled in Carpentras, near Avignon, France, seat of the papacy during the so-called "Babylonian Captivity" of the church. His scholarly father introduced him to Cicero and Virgil, the beginning of a lifelong obsession, yet insisted that he pursue the more practical study of the law. Reluctantly, Petrarch studied civil law for seven years ("lost years," he recalled) at the University of Montpellier and then at Bologna. The Black Death claimed many of Petrarch's friends and family, including his son; his poems and letters reflect a poignant sense of exile, loss, and the transience and fragility of life. As a young man, the first book he purchased was Augustine's *City of God*. For many years he carried a treasured copy of Augustine's *Confessions* with him as he traveled around Europe. "I carried the book through most of Italy and through France and Germany," he wrote, "because I was delighted with its substance, with its author, and with its handy pocket size. Thus by constant use hand and book became so inseparable that they seemed to grow together." Alongside the Church Fathers, he knew the works of Homer, Plato, and Aristotle in translation, and he immersed himself in the Latin of Cicero, Virgil, Horace, Seneca, Quintilian, and the historians Sallust and Livy. He scoured the monastic libraries of Europe in search of neglected Latin texts, uncovering parts of Quintilian and some of Cicero's missing letters and orations, including letters to Brutus and the speech *Pro Archia Poeta*. In the very act of recovery, however, he was aware of how many more treasures had been forever lost through violence, ignorance, and carelessness.

Along with other Italian classical scholars, Petrarch is credited with rejuvenating the ancient model of liberal education, the *studia humanitatis* of Renaissance humanism. His insistence on the centrality of self-knowledge in education connects him with a long tradition. He is often praised for being the first "modern," or at least the key transitional figure between the medieval and modern worldviews. But this dubious compliment obscures how far his imagination reached back into Christian thought. He was indeed a humanist man of letters, but he was also an Augustinian man of faith. Petrarch's extensive writings include an epic poem *(Africa),* a treatise on the religious life *(De otio religiosorum),* sonnets to his beloved Laura, the letter known as "The Ascent of Mt. Ventoux," correspondence with Boccaccio and other friends, and a few highly imaginative letters to dead authors, including Homer and Cicero. He died at his home in Arqua, studying a copy of Homer's *Odyssey.*

The Selections

Petrarch was one of the greatest epistolary writers of his or any age. His letters exude warmth and wit and anxiety over the culture of learning and civilization in general. It is hard to imagine that Petrarch thought of himself as living on the eve of a cultural rebirth. Four of his letters from the 1350s and '60s are included here (only the one to Francesco Nelli in its entirety). The letter to Lapo Castiglionchio reminds us how rare, precious, and labor-intensive were books before the mass production made possible by the printing press. A fuller view of Petrarch's complex understanding of education should include his dialogue, *My Secret,* especially Book II.

To Lapo da Castiglionchio, 1355

Your Cicero has been in my possession four years and more. There is a good reason, though, for so long a delay; namely, the great scarcity of copyists who understand such work. It is a state of affairs that has resulted in an incredible loss to scholarship. Books that by their nature are a little hard to understand are no longer multiplied, and have ceased to be generally intelligible, and so have sunk into utter neglect, and in the end have perished. This age of ours consequently has let fall, bit by bit, some of the richest and sweetest fruits that the tree of knowledge has yielded; has thrown away the results of the vigils and labours of the most illustrious men of genius, things of more value, I am almost tempted to say, than anything else in the whole world. . . .

But I must return to your Cicero. I could not do without it, and the incompetence of the copyists would not let me possess it. What was left for me but to rely upon my own resources, and press these weary fingers and this worn and ragged pen into the service? The plan that I followed was this. I want you to know it, in case you should ever have to grapple with a similar task. Not a single word did I read except as I wrote. But how is that,

I hear someone say; did you write without knowing what it was that you were writing? Ah! but from the very first it was enough for me to know that it was a work of Tullius, and an extremely rare one too. And then as soon as I was fairly started I found at every step so much sweetness and charm, and felt so strong a desire to advance, that the only difficulty which I experienced in reading and writing at the same time came from the fact that my pen could not cover the ground so rapidly as I wanted it to, whereas my expectation had been rather that it would outstrip my eyes, and that my ardour for writing would be chilled by the slowness of my reading. So the pen held back the eye, and the eye drove on the pen, and I covered page after page, delighting in my task, and committing many and many a passage to memory as I wrote. For just in proportion as the writing is slower than the reading does the passage make a deep impression and cling to the mind.

And yet I must confess that I did finally reach a point in my copying where I was overcome by weariness; not mental, for how unlikely that would be where Cicero was concerned, but the sort of fatigue that springs from excessive manual labour. I began to feel doubtful about this plan that I was following, and to regret having undertaken a task for which I had not been trained; when suddenly I came across a place where Cicero tells how he himself copied the orations of—someone or other; just who it was I do not know, but certainly no Tullius, for there is but one such man, one such voice, one such mind. These are his words: "You say that you have been in the habit of reading the orations of Cassius in your idle moments. But I," he jestingly adds, with his customary disregard of his adversary's feelings, "have made a practice of *copying* them, so that I might *have* no idle moments." As I read this passage I grew hot with shame, like a modest young soldier who hears the voice of his beloved leader rebuking him. I said to myself, "So Cicero copied orations that another wrote, and you are not ready to copy his? What ardour! what scholarly devotion! what reverence for a man of godlike genius!" These thoughts were a spur to me, and I pushed on, with all my doubts dispelled. If ever from my darkness there shall come a single ray that can enhance the splendour of the reputation which his heavenly eloquence has won for him, it will proceed in no slight measure from the fact that I was so captivated by his ineffable sweetness that I did a thing in itself most irksome with such delight and eagerness that I scarcely knew I was doing it at all.

So then at last your Cicero has the happiness of returning to you, bearing you my thanks. And yet he also stays, very willingly, with me; a dear friend, to whom I give the credit of being almost the only man of letters for whose sake I would go to the length of spending my time, when the difficulties of life are pressing on me so sharply and inexorably and the cares pertaining to my literary labours make the longest life seem far too short, in transcribing compositions not my own. I may have done such things in former days, when I thought myself rich in time, and had not learned how stealthily it slips away: but I now know that this is of all our riches the most uncertain and fleeting; the years are closing in upon me now, and there is no longer any room for deviation from the beaten path. I am forced to practice strict economy; I only hope that I have not begun too late. But Cicero! he assuredly is worthy of a part of even the little that I still have left. Farewell.

To Francesco Nelli, September 18, probably 1360

I noticed in a letter of yours that you were pleased at my mixture of sacred and secular themes, and that you thought Saint Jerome would have been likewise pleased. You mention the charm of variety, the beauty of structure, the force of association. What can I reply? You must make your own judgments, and certainly you are not easily or commonly deceived, except that well-wishers readily err, and often are eager to do so.

But putting all this to one side, let me speak of myself and of my new but serious enthusiasm, which turns my thoughts and my writings to sacred literature. Let the supercilious laugh, who are revolted by the austerity of holy words, as the modest garb of a chaste matron repels those who are used to the flaunting colors of light women. I think that the Muses and Apollo will not merely grant me permission, they will applaud, that after giving my youth to studies proper to that age, I should devote my riper years to more important matters. Nor am I to be criticized, if I, who so often used to rouse by night to work for empty fame and celebrate the futile lauds of men, should now arise at midnight to recite the lauds of my creator, and devote the hours proper to quiet and repose to him who shall neither slumber nor sleep while he keepeth Israel; nor is he content with universal custodianship, but he watches over me personally and is solicitous for my welfare. I am clearly conscious of this, and all men capable of gratitude must feel the same. He cares for each individual as if he were forgetful of mankind *en masse;* and so he rules the mass as if he were careless of each individual. Thus I have it firmly fixed in mind that if it be heaven's will I shall spend the rest of my life in these studies and occupations. In what state could I better die than in loving, remembering, and praising him, without whose constant love I should be nothing, or damned, which is less than nothing? And if his love for me should cease, my damnation would have no end.

I loved Cicero, I admit, and I loved Virgil. I delighted in their thought and expression so far that I thought nothing could surpass them. I loved many others also of the troop of great writers, but I loved Cicero as if he were my father, Virgil as my brother. My admiration, my familiarity with their genius, contracted in long study, inspired in me such love for their persons that you may think it hardly possible to feel a like affection for living men. Similarly I loved, of the Greeks, Plato and Homer. When I compared their genius with that of our own masters I was often in despair of sound judgment.

But now I must think of more serious matters. My care is more for my salvation than for noble language. I used to read what gave me pleasure, now I read what may be profitable. This is my state of mind, and it has been so for some time. I am not just beginning this practice, and my white hair warns me that I began none too soon. Now my orators shall be Ambrose, Augustine, Jerome, Gregory; my philosopher shall be Paul, my poet David. You remember that years ago, in the first eclogue of my *Bucolicum carmen* I contrasted him with Homer and Virgil, and I left the victory among them undecided. But now, in spite of my old deep-rooted habit, experience and the shining revelation of truth leave me in no doubt as to the victor. But although I put the Christian writers first, I do not reject the others. (Jerome said that he did so, but it seems to me from the imitative style of his writing that he actually approved them.) I seem able to love both groups at once, provided that I consciously distinguish between those I prefer for style and those I prefer for substance. Why should I not act the prudent householder, who assigns part of his furniture for use and another for ornament, who appoints some of his slaves to guard his son, and others to provide the son with sport? Both gold and silver are kinds of money, and you must know their value and not confound them. Especially since those ancient writers demand nothing of me except that I do not let them fall into oblivion. Happy that I have spent upon them my early studies, they now let me give all my time to more important matters.

Since I had already come of myself to this conclusion, I shall now so act the more confidently thanks to your encouragement. If circumstances require, I shall practice, for style, Virgil and Cicero, and I shall not hesitate to draw from Greece whatever Rome may seem to lack. But for the direction of life, though I know much that is useful in the classics, I shall still use those counselors and guides to salvation, in whose faith and doctrine there can be no suspicion of error. First among them in point of merit will David always be to me, the more beautiful for his naivety, the more profound, the more vigorous, for his purity. I want to have his Psalter always at hand during my waking hours where I may steal a glance at it; and I want to have it beneath my pillow when I sleep and when I come to die. I think that such an outcome will be no less glorious for me than was the act of Plato, greatest of philosophers, in keeping the *Mimes* of Sophron under his pillow.

Farewell, and remember me.

To Boccaccio, May 28, 1362

. . . Believe me, many things are attributed to gravity and wisdom which are really due to incapacity and sloth. Men often despise what they despair of obtaining. It is in the very nature of ignorance to scorn what it cannot understand, and to desire to keep others from attaining what it cannot reach. Hence the false judgments upon matters of which we know nothing, by which we evince our envy quite as clearly as our stupidity.

Neither exhortations to virtue nor the argument of approaching death should divert us from literature; for in a good mind it excites the love of virtue, and dissipates, or at least diminishes, the fear of death. To desert our studies shows want of self-confidence rather than wisdom, for letters do not hinder but aid the properly constituted mind which possesses them; they facilitate our life, they do not retard it. Just as many kinds of food which lie heavy on an enfeebled and nauseated stomach furnish excellent nourishment for one who is well but famishing, so in our studies many things which are deadly to the weak mind may prove most salutary to an acute and healthy intellect, especially if in our use of both food and learning we exercise proper discretion. If it were otherwise, surely the zeal of certain persons who persevered to the end could not have roused such admiration. Cato, I never forget, acquainted himself with Latin literature as he was growing old, and Greek when he had really become an old man. Varro, who reached his hundredth year still reading and writing, parted from life sooner than from his love of study. Livius Drusus, although weakened by age and afflicted with blindness, did not give up his interpretation of the civil law, which he carried on to the great advantage of the state. . .

Besides these and innumerable others like them, have not all those of our own religion whom we should wish most to imitate devoted their whole lives to literature, and grown old and died in the same pursuit? Some, indeed, were overtaken by death while still at work reading or writing. To none of them, so far as I know, did it prove a disadvantage to be noted for secular learning, except to Jerome, whom I mentioned above; while to many, and Jerome himself not least, it was a source of glory. I do not forget that Benedict was praised by Gregory for deserting the studies which he had begun, to devote himself to a solitary and ascetic mode of life. Benedict, however, had renounced, not the poets especially, but literature altogether. Moreover, I very much doubt if his admirer would have been himself admired had he proceeded to adopt the same plan. It is one thing to have learned, another to be in the process of learning. It is only the hope of acquisition which the boy renounces,—quite a different thing from the learning itself, which an older person gives up; the former but turns away from an obstacle, while the latter sacrifices an ornament. The trials and uncertainties of acquisition are alone surrendered in one case; in the other the man sacrifices the sure and sweet fruit of long, laborious years, and turns his back upon the precious treasure of learning which he has gathered together with great effort.

While I know that many have become famous for piety without learning, at the same time I know of no one who has been prevented by literature from following the path of holiness. The apostle Paul was, to be sure, accused of having his head turned by study, but the world has long ago passed its verdict upon this accusation. If I may be allowed to speak for myself, it seems to me that, although the path to virtue by the way of ignorance may be plain, it fosters sloth. The goal of all good people is the same, but the ways of reaching it are many and various. Some advance slowly, others with more spirit; some obscurely, others again conspicuously. One takes a lower, another a higher path. Although all alike are on the road to happiness, certainly the more elevated path is the more glorious. Hence ignorance, however devout, is by no means to be put on a plane with the enlightened devoutness of one familiar with literature. Nor can you pick me out from the whole array of unlettered saints, an example so holy that I cannot match it with a still holier one from the other group.

But I will trouble you no longer with these matters, as I have already been led by the nature of the subject to discuss them often. I will add only this: if you persist in your resolution to give up those studies which I turned my back upon so long ago, as well as literature in general, and, by scattering your books, to rid yourself of the very means of study,—if this is your firm intention, I am glad indeed that you have decided to give me the preference before everyone else in this sale. As you say, I am most covetous of books. I could hardly venture to deny that without being refuted by my works. Although I might seem in a sense to be purchasing what is already my own, I should not like to see the books of such a distinguished man scattered here and there, or falling, as will often happen, into profane hands. In this way, just as we have been of one mind, although separated in the flesh, I trust that our instruments of study may, if God will grant my prayer, be deposited all together in some sacred spot where they may remain a perpetual memorial to us both. I came to this decision upon the day on which he died who I hoped might succeed me in my studies. I cannot, however, fix the prices of the books, as you most kindly would have me do. I do not know their titles and number, or their value. You can arrange this by letter, and on the understanding that if it should ever occur to you to spend with me the little time which remains to us, as I have always wished, and you at one time seemed to promise, you will find the books you send with those that I have recently gathered together here, all of them equally yours, so that you will seem to have lost nothing, but rather gained, by the transaction.

Lastly, you assert that you owe money to many, to me among others. I deny that it is true in my case. I am surprised at so unfounded and even absurd a scruple of conscience on your part. I might apply Terence's saying, that you seem "to be looking for a joint in a reed." You owe me nothing but love, and not even that, since you long ago paid me in full,—unless it be that you always are owing, because you are always receiving. Still, one who pays back so promptly cannot properly be said ever to owe.

As to the complaint of poverty, which I have frequently heard from you before, I will not attempt to furnish any consolation or to cite any illustrious examples of indigence. You know them already. I will only say plainly what I have always said: I congratulate you for preferring liberty of mind and tranquil poverty to the opulence which I might have procured for you, even though tardily. But I cannot praise you for scorning the oft-repeated invitation of a friend. I am not in a position to endow you. If I were, I should not confine myself to pen or words; but should address you with the thing itself. But I am amply supplied with all that two would need, if, with a single heart, they dwelt beneath a single roof. You insult me if you scorn my offers, still more so, if you are suspicious of their sincerity.

To Boccaccio, August 28, 1364

. . . There has arisen of late a set of dialecticians, who are not only ignorant but demented. Like a black army of ants from some old rotten oak, they swarm forth from their hiding-places and devastate the fields of sound learning. They condemn Plato and Aristotle, and laugh at Socrates and Pythagoras. And, good God! under what silly and incompetent leaders these opinions are put forth! I should prefer not to give a name to this group of men. They have done nothing to merit one, though their folly has made them famous. I do not wish to place among the greatest of mankind those whom I see consorting with the most abject. These fellows have deserted all trustworthy leaders, and glory in the name of those who, whatever they may learn after death, exhibited in this world no trace of power, or knowledge, or reputation for knowledge. What shall we say of men who scorn Marcus Tullius Cicero, the bright sun of eloquence? Of those who scoff at Varro and Seneca, and are scandalised at what they choose to call the crude, unfinished style of Livy and Sallust? And all this in obedience to leaders of whom no one has ever heard, and for whom their followers ought to blush! Once I happened to be present when Virgil's style was the subject of their scornful criticism. Astonished at their crazy out break, I turned to a person of some cultivation and asked what he had detected in this famous man to rouse such a storm of reproach. Listen to the reply he gave me, with a contemptuous shrug of the shoulders: "He is too fond of conjunctions." Arise, O Virgil, and polish the verses that, with the aid of the Muses, thou didst snatch from heaven, in order that they may be fit to deliver into hands like these!

How shall I deal with that other monstrous kind of pedant, who wears a religious garb, but is most profane in heart and conduct; who would have us believe that Ambrose, Augustine, and Jerome were ignoramuses, for all their elaborate treatises? I do not know the origin of these new theologians, who do not spare the great teachers, and will not much longer spare the Apostles and the Gospel itself. They will soon turn their impudent tongues even against Christ, unless he, whose cause is at stake, interferes and curbs the raging beasts. It has already become a well-established habit with these fellows to express their scorn by a mute gesture or by some impious observation, whenever revered and sacred names are mentioned. "Augustine," they will say, "saw much, but understood little." Nor do they speak less insultingly of other great men.

Recently one of these philosophers of the modern stamp happened to be in my library. He did not, like the others, wear a religious habit, but, after all, Christianity is not a matter of clothes. He was one of those who think they live in vain unless they are constantly snarling at Christ or his divine teachings. When I cited some passage or other from the Holy Scriptures, he exploded with wrath, and with his face, naturally ugly, still further disfigured by anger and contempt, he exclaimed : "You are welcome to your two-penny church fathers; as for me, I know the man for me to follow, *for I know him whom I have believed*." "You," I replied, "use the words of the Apostle. I would that you would take them to heart!" "Your Apostle," he answered, "was a sower of words and a lunatic." "You reply like a good philosopher," I said. "The first of your accusations was brought against him by other philosophers, and the second to his face by Festus, Governor of Syria. He did indeed sow the word, and with such success that, cultivated by the beneficent plough of his successors and watered by the holy blood of the martyrs, it has borne such an abundant harvest of faith as we all behold." At this he burst forth into a sickening roar of laughter. "Well, be a 'good Christian'! As for me, I put no faith in all that stuff. Your Paul and your Augustine and all the rest of the crowd you preach about were a set of babblers. If you could but stomach Averroes you would quickly see how much superior he was to these empty-headed fellows of yours." I was very angry, I must confess, and could scarcely keep from striking his filthy, blasphemous mouth. "It is the old feud between me and other heretics of your class. You can go," I cried, "you and your heresy, and never return." With this I plucked him by the gown, and, with a want of ceremony less consonant with my habits than his own, hustled him out of the house.

There are thousands of instances of this kind, where nothing will prevail,—not even the majesty of the Christian name nor reverence for Christ himself (whom the angels fall down and worship, though weak and depraved mortals may insult him), nor yet the fear of punishment or the armed inquisitors of heresy. The prison and stake are alike impotent to restrain the impudence of ignorance or the audacity of heresy.

Such are the times, my friend, upon which we have fallen; such is the period in which we live and are growing old. Such are the critics of today, as I so often have occasion to lament and complain,—men who are innocent of knowledge or virtue, and yet harbour the most exalted opinion of themselves. Not content with losing the words of the ancients, they must attack their genius and their ashes. They rejoice in their ignorance, as if what they did not know were not worth knowing. They give full rein to their licence and conceit, and freely introduce among us new authors and outlandish teachings.

If you, having no other means of defence, have resorted to the fire to save your works from the criticism of such despotic judges, I cannot disapprove the act and must commend your motives. I have done the same with many of my own productions, and almost repent me that I did not include all while it was yet in my power; for we have no prospect of fairer judges, while the number and audacity of the existing ones grow from day to day. They are no longer confined to the schools, but fill the largest towns, choking up the streets and public squares. We are come to such a pass that I am sometimes angry at myself for having been so vexed by the recent warlike and destructive years, and having bemoaned the depopulation of the earth. It is perhaps depopulated of true men, but was never more densely crowded with vices and the creatures of vice. In short, had I been among the Aediles, and felt as I do now, I should have acquitted the daughter of Appius Claudius.—But now farewell, as I have nothing more to write to you at present.

Pier Paolo Vergerio

1370–1444

What way of life . . . can be more delightful, or indeed more beneficial, than to read and write all the time: for moderns to understand things ancient; for present generations to converse with their posterity; and thus to make every time our own, both past and future?

CHARACTER AND STUDIES BEFITTING A FREE-BORN YOUTH

Pier Paolo Vergerio was born at Capodistria, Italy. He studied and taught at Florence, Bologna, and Padua in fields as diverse as rhetoric, canon law, logic, and medicine. The University of Padua ranked with the most important centers for learning in Italy at the time (Petrarch had lived near Padua and knew the university faculty). A lifelong student, Vergerio left teaching for a while to study Greek in Florence under Manuel Chrysoloras, who had come from Constantinople to be the first professor of Greek the West had seen for many centuries. (Later, after the fall of Constantinople to Muslim armies in 1453, a flood of refugee Greek scholars came to Italy to teach.) Vergerio distinguished himself as among the first scholars in the West able again to translate directly from Greek texts. Vergerio also wrote an introduction to Quintilian, a life of Seneca, studies of Jerome, a life of Petrarch, and various treatises, histories, and plays. He served as secretary to two popes, attended the Council of Constance, and debated Hussites. He spent the last decades of his remarkable life as secretary to the Holy Roman Emperor Sigismund, and he died in Budapest.

THE SELECTION

Vergerio probably wrote his *Character and Studies Befitting a Free-Born Youth (De ingenuis moribus)* around 1402–3. It is addressed to his young charge Ubertino da Carrara, a prince at the court of Padua. It was copied and widely distributed throughout Europe, and was still in use as a textbook in the 1500s. Vergerio's ambitious curriculum links all of the disciplines and includes physical training and recreation. In the section on liberal studies included here, he repeatedly urges Ubertino to strive for wisdom and virtue, not material profit or idle pleasure. The one is fit for free men, the other for slaves. Vergerio also writes passionately about the present generation's moral obligation to preserve and pass on to posterity the legacy of the past.

from The Character and Studies Befitting a Free-Born Youth

WHAT LIBERAL STUDIES ARE: A GENERAL TREATMENT

We call those studies liberal, then, which are worthy of a free [*liber*] man: they are those through which virtue and wisdom are either practiced or sought, and by which the body or mind is disposed towards all the best things. From this source people customarily seek honor and glory, which for the wise man are the principal rewards of virtue. Just as profit and pleasure are laid down as ends for illiberal intellects, so virtue and glory are goals for the noble.

It is therefore fitting to aim for these from the start of infancy and to strive for wisdom with all one's zeal. For if no one can achieve excellence in any of the private arts, even those that require less intellectual ability, without applying one's self to them from earliest youth, what shall we conclude in the case of wisdom, which is relevant to so many great issues and contains the precepts and guiding principles of our entire life? For without question we will not be—insofar as we wish both to be wise and to be regarded as such—we will not be, I say, wise in old age unless we have first begun to be wise in youth. Nor indeed should we accept the common opinion which everybody repeats, and believe that those who are intelligent beyond their years in their youth eventually tend to lose their mental edge after they have become older. In certain respects, to be sure, this is not incompatible with our understanding of the human body: the senses flourish in childhood, then wither with advancing age. In this regard there is good reason for a certain old man to have been silenced by a young man—the name of each, however, is unknown. For when the young man was considered wise and virtuous beyond his years and was shown to the old man as a prodigy, the old man said, "one who is so wise in his youth will inevitably be senile in his old age"—saying this with his voice raised so that the young man might hear. But the young man forgot none of his inborn shrewdness and immediately turned toward him, saying, "So you must have been remarkably wise in your youth"—running him through with his own weapons, as they say.

Indeed, there is also by nature in many young men such quickness of understanding and such shrewdness in inquiry that, even without much formal learning, they are able to speak about the most important subjects and utter the weightiest opinions. And if their inborn power is strengthened by knowledge and aided by learning, this education will generally produce the greatest men. So we must take diligent care of men like these, but not neglect those of average intellect; rather we must help them the more in that their natural ability falls short. Nevertheless all of them are to be bound over to their studies and labors from childhood,

> while young minds are malleable, while they are young enough to change,

as Vergil's verse goes.

We must, then, press onwards the more as that time of life is better suited to learning than other times, yet we should learn at every age—unless there is a time when learning is more shameful than ignorance! The contrary judgment was expressed by Cato, the head of the Porcius family, who learned Latin letters on the threshold of old age and Greek when he was quite old; he did not believe it degrading for an old man to learn what is fine for any man to know. Even so great a philosopher as Socrates applied himself to the lyre when he was already advanced in years and turned over his fingers to a teacher for guidance. Meanwhile, our young people, for God's sake, are too lazy and soft to learn, and feel ashamed to be subject to a teacher though they have scarcely been weaned! But they are not to be left to their own judgment; they must be induced through various devices to undertake a good and principled course of studies.

Some must be snared by praise and the attractions of honor; others by little gifts and compliments; still others must be compelled by threats and floggings. And indeed all these arts must be so correctly weighed and reasonably controlled that teachers may vary their use even in the case of the selfsame mind, and care must be taken that they be neither too indulgent toward their students nor too harsh. For just as excessive freedom unhinges innate good qualities, so harsh, unrelenting criticism saps intellectual energies and quenches the little fires that nature lights in children. Boys who fear everything will dare nothing, and it is the case that boys who are afraid of making mistakes in every single thing will make mistakes always. Above all, those who abound in black bile should be controlled more loosely, and it is a good idea to give them their head to enjoy freedom and fun. Not all (as Aristotle would have it), but certainly a great many clever people have this sort of complexion.

But it happens that a great many of those endowed with a noble intellect, while they are striving to follow the right course of studies, are called back under compulsion; or as a result of certain bars, as it were, set across their path, they are forced to stop in mid-course or are sidetracked into another one. For a great many students, limited family resources have been the impediment which constrained a noble mind, born for better things, to enslave itself to the pursuit of gain. Yet a noble nature generally rises above the greatest difficulties, and great material wealth usually injures good minds more than the most abject poverty. Of such men it is generally said, not without some resentment: "O how great this man would have been, if he had been born in lesser circumstances!" For some, the authority of parents and childhood habits stand in the way, for we follow seamlessly as adults the habits we have formed as children, and boys willingly let themselves be shaped by the desires of the parents who have given them birth and brought them up. But we also generally follow the customary practices of our cities, as though what others approve of and do is necessarily the best course [for us]. So this kind of decision is the most difficult of all, for either it is not a free decision, or we come to it only after being steeped in false opinions derived from bad customs and the corrupt conversation of mankind.

Nevertheless there are some to whom the ability has been given as a singular gift of God to enter and stick to the right way by themselves, without any guide—"to those few," and the ones "whom" (as the poet says) "favoring Jove loved," or even begat, to give mythology its due. We understand that Hercules in particular was like this, as the Greeks relate and the Romans after them recalled. He saw before him two paths, one of virtue and the other of pleasure, and being, as it happened, at the age when one must choose one's way for all of life, he withdrew into a solitary place. There, by himself, he thought long and hard (judgment and discernment being weak at that age), and after rejecting pleasure, he at last embraced virtue. From that time forth he made a path to heaven for himself via many formidable labors, according to human belief. So much, then, for him. For ourselves it is a good outcome whether we are led to virtue by the hand of precept or compelled thereto by force and necessity; and fortunate indeed is the necessity that drives one to the good.

THE FINEST STUDIES: ARMS AND LETTERS

To be sure, I see that this has happened in some measure to you, Ubertino, as well. For among the studies and liberal arts of mankind are two in particular that have the greatest affinity with cultivating virtue and obtaining glory, namely, instruction in letters and arms. And although through the indulgence of your father you were allowed to pursue only the latter, which is almost the private preserve of your family, you have embraced both with such tenacious diligence and zeal that you have left your contemporaries far behind and are able to compete with your elders in both species of renown. You therefore do well in not neglecting the art of war, in which your ancestors have always excelled, and in attempting to add new renown in letters to your family's old glory in arms.

For you are not eager to imitate those (of whom there is a large crowd in our times) who shrink from the reputation of being learned, as though it were something shameful, nor do you approve of the opinion of Licinius, the old Roman emperor, who used to call letters a poison and a public plague. States would be far more blessed, Plato says, if philosophers ruled or if their rulers happened to be philosophers. To be sure, it is true that the disciplines of letters take away neither madness nor wickedness. But they are a great help to those who were born for virtue and wisdom, and they often provide the means for uncovering stupidity or more destructive kinds of wrongdoing. For we know that Claudius (to stick with Roman emperors) was quite learned, and it is an established fact that Nero, his stepson and successor as emperor, was particularly well-educated; of these two, the former was notoriously deranged and the latter was steeped in cruelty and all the vices. Nevertheless, Nero once said, on the pretext of showing mercy, that he wished he were unlettered. But if he could have been merciful in some other way besides illiteracy, surely he would have wished for that! But in my view, if he had been allowed to cast letters aside, which were ill-suited to his character, he would have done so with the same readiness and enthusiasm with which he stripped away that feigned and temporary clemency, so as to leave no room in himself for any of the virtues or liberal arts. By way of contrast, Giacomo da Carrara, your ancestor, a prudent man and a generous prince but not himself very learned, nevertheless cultivated learned men wondrously, and held that this one thing had been lacking to his good fortune, that he was not educated to the extent that a modest man might wish to be.

One may wish to be learned in old age, but it is not easy to achieve this unless we have nurtured learning in ourselves from our earliest years with zealous effort. So we need to prepare in youth those consolations which can bring delight in honorable old age; studies which are burdensome to youth will be pleasant relaxations to age. In this sense they are truly great bulwarks, whether we seek a remedy against sloth or solace in the face of worry and care. For there are two kinds of life befitting a free man, one consisting entirely in leisure and contemplation, the other in action and business. It can escape no one that the knowledge and use of writing is very necessary to the former kind of life; and in the latter their utility can easily be discerned from the following argument. To say nothing of how much wiser they can become from the precepts of literary authorities as well as from the example of those about whom books are written, men of action can have no more pleasant relaxation when they are tired, whether they engage in affairs of state or foreign wars or whether they busy themselves with their own affairs and those of their friends. Also, when times and moments arise when it is necessary to withdraw from the active life—for we are often unwillingly prevented from participating in affairs of state, and wars are not always being waged, and particular days and nights offer occasions when it is fitting to stay at home and be by one's self—at such times, then, when we may not take part in outdoor diversions, reading and books will come to our assistance. That is, unless we want to indulge ourselves utterly with sleep and rot with indolence, or imitate the custom of the emperor Domitian, who every day at a fixed time went off by himself and chased flies with an iron stylus. He was the son of Vespasian and the younger brother of Titus, but without question he was far from being their equal. Indeed, he was considered the most repulsive of the emperors as Titus is thought to be the most virtuous of all (Titus being he whom the histories call the "darling of humankind"). Thus the reputation of Titus is as celebrated as that of Domitian is detested.

The fact is that posterity is free in its judgment of the lives and affairs of mankind; it does not shrink from condemning the wicked, nor does it begrudge praise to those who deserve it. In this respect it is, as we see, a great prerogative of princes—indeed, I might almost say it is a necessity set before them—to act well if they value the judgment of mankind and a lasting reputation among posterity. Other, more humble men need great energy and strength of character to emerge into the light [of fame], and their sins are hidden by the obscurity of their lot. In princes and great men, however, virtue—either because it is rare amidst good fortune and therefore more greatly admired, or because it gleams more brightly from fortune's splendor—virtue, even modest virtue, is considered remarkable and renowned; whereas evil deeds cannot remain hidden, even secret ones, nor can silence be long preserved once they become known. For the very men who minister to their pleasures, the very companions and witnesses of their crimes, bring them into the open and are the first to condemn them. An example is the witty jest one of Domitian's intimate servants used to censure the emperor's lunatic behavior, for when he was once asked whether anyone was inside with Domitian, he answered, "not even a fly," as though the emperor had wiped them all out with his stylus.

One might perhaps forgive Domitian for this indecorous form of hunting if only it were established what he got up to when alone during the winter, or if he had not deserved hatred for his foul crimes much more than mockery for his repulsive fly-hunts. For what Scipio used to say about himself—that he was never less alone or at leisure than when he seemed to be so—cannot happen to just anyone, but only to those endowed with great intellects and outstanding virtue. Even though that man seems to me in no way inferior who is able to preserve his solitude even in a crowd and his tranquillity in the midst of business affairs. This was in fact written of Cato, who, while the senate was being called into session, used to pore over books in the senate-house. No doubt this was why he habitually offered highly beneficial advice to his country concerning both current affairs and matters of permanent importance.

Yet if literary study offered no other reward—and its rewards are certainly numerous and great—the distraction it offers from the many things we cannot bring to mind without disgracing ourselves or remember without causing ourselves pain ought in any case to make it quite valuable enough. For if there is anything either in ourselves or our fortune that causes us discomfort, we are easily relieved of it for this reason: that the pursuit of knowledge gives birth to wondrous pleasures in the human mind and in due course bears the richest fruits, whenever a seed of this kind falls into a good mind that is suited to nurture it. Therefore when we are alone and free from all our other cares, what better thing can we do than resort to our books, where everything is either most agreeable for learning or most conducive to living a good, holy life?

For although written records are very valuable indeed for other purposes, they are especially valuable for preserving the memory of the past, as they contain the deeds of mankind, the unhoped-for turns of fortune, the unusual works of nature, and (more important than all these things) the guiding principles of historical periods. For human memory and objects passed from hand to hand gradually decay and scarcely survive the lifetime of one person, but what has been skillfully entrusted to books endures forever. Perhaps a picture or carven marble or cast metal can excel even a well-written book, but such objects do not describe the times, nor do they readily disclose motivation in all its variety; they only express exterior states and fall easily into ruin. What is preserved in literary form, however, not only renders speech but also distinguishes styles of speaking and represents people's thoughts. And if it has been published in numerous copies, it cannot easily perish, provided its diction is distinguished. For whatever is written in an undistinguished way is not given credibility and cannot long endure.

What way of life, then, can be more delightful, or indeed more beneficial, than to read and write all the time: for moderns to understand things ancient; for present generations to converse with their posterity; and thus to make every time our own, both past and future? What excellent furniture books make! as we say; and as Cicero says, What a happy family books make! Absolutely honest and well-behaved! A family that does not fuss or shout, that is neither rapacious, voracious or contumacious, that speaks or remains silent as it is bidden, that always stands ready to execute your every command, and that you never hear saying anything you don't want to hear, and that only says as much as you want to hear.

So, since our memory cannot hold everything and indeed retains very little, scarcely enough for particular purposes, books, in my view, should be acquired and preserved as a kind of second memory. For letters and books constitute a fixed record of things and are the communal repository of all things knowable. If by chance we are not able to create anything ourselves, we ought at least to pass on carefully the books we have received from those who have come before us to those who will come after, keeping them whole and uncorrupted, and in this manner we will usefully serve the interests of posterity and give past generations at least this one recompense for their labors. In this respect we can perhaps find fault with a certain age and the ages that followed them; we may even become aggrieved, though profitlessly, that they allowed so many remarkable works of famous authors to perish. Of some of these we have the names alone (though embellished with high praises); in the case of other authors, parts and fragments have come down to us. That is why we long so for their works: from the famous names and the renown they have won. The excellence and value of what yet survives makes the loss of the rest hard to endure, even though we have received much of their surviving works in such a badly corrupted, mutilated and mangled state that it would almost have been better if nothing of them had survived.

But not the least part of this great loss must seem the many things worthy of note that have been done in Italy, now largely hidden from us, knowledge of which has perished with the books and records of them. Thus we know the deeds of the barbarians, but are ignorant of much of our own history thanks to the plight of books. And so it has come about that we seek reliable knowledge even of Roman history from Greek authors, for a great many things but sparingly recorded in Latin writers, or completely unknown to them, are found widely diffused in Greek authors, although the [ancient] Greek language, which at one time our ancestors used to speak as though it was their mother tongue, has almost died out among its own people, and among us Latin-speakers is thoroughly extinct, except for a certain few people who in this age have applied themselves to it, and now are bringing it from the tomb back to life.

But I return to history, whose loss is the more serious in that knowledge of it is more useful and pleasant. For to the truly noble mind, and to those who are obligated to involve themselves in public affairs and human communities, knowledge of history and the study of moral philosophy are the more suitable subjects. The rest of the arts are called liberal because they befit free men, but philosophy is liberal because its study makes men free. Thus in philosophy we find rules explaining what one may profitably do or shun, but in history we find [moral] examples; in the former the duties of all mankind may be found and what it is fitting for each person to do, but in the latter what has been done or said in every age. Unless I am mistaken, a third study should be added to these [in the case of the public man]: eloquence, which is a distinct part of civics. Through philosophy we can acquire correct views, which is of first importance in everything; through eloquence we can speak with weight and polish, which is the one skill that most effectively wins over the minds of the masses; but history helps us with both. For if we consider old people wiser and listen to them gladly because they have found out many things in the course of their long lives both through their own experience and through the other people they have seen and heard, how much ought we to esteem those who have memorized things worth knowing from many centuries and are able to produce an example to illuminate every situation? The outcome of these studies is to enable anyone to speak well and to inspire him to act as well as possible; this is the mark of the greatest men and the absolutely finest characters.

There were four things which the Greeks used to teach their boys: letters, wrestling, music, and drawing, which some call sketching. We shall speak of wrestling and music later. Drawing as it is now practiced is not worthy of a free man, except perhaps insofar as it pertains to writing (for penmanship is actually a form of drawing and sketching); for the rest, it is the business of painters. However, among the Greeks, Aristotle tells us, this kind of business was not only useful, but also honorable. For skill in design helped in the purchase of vases, paintings, and statues, which the Greeks took much pleasure in, and prevented their being deceived about price, and it gave them great appreciation for the beauty and charm of things both natural and artificial. Great men need to be able to talk among themselves and make judgements about matters of this kind.

The fruits of literature, on the other hand, are always great, for the whole of life and for every kind of person, but it is particularly beneficial to the studious for forming habits [of virtue] and strengthening the memory of times past as well as for the acquisition of learning. From the beginning, therefore, if we want some profit from our studies, we must practice appropriate patterns of speech, and take care that we are not found making embarrassing small slips while pursuing great effects. Next, we must take up the practice of disputation, through which, by supple argument, we seek what is true or false in each and every subject. Disputation is the science of learning and the learning of science, and so opens with ease the way to every kind of knowledge. Rhetoric is third among the rational disciplines; through it one seeks the art of eloquence, which we have also placed third among the principal parts of civics. But although in times gone by it used to be widely studied as part of a nobleman's education, rhetoric has now fallen almost totally into disuse. It has been completely exiled from legal proceedings, where contending parties no longer use long speeches, but rather adduce laws against each other dialectically in support of their cases. In judicial rhetoric many young Romans once achieved great glory, either by denouncing the guilty or defending the innocent. For deliberative rhetoric as well there has been no room among princes and lords for a long time, since they want an opinion explained in few words and arguments brought nakedly into council; while in popular regimes the most brilliant speakers are thought to be those who speak artlessly and at great length. There remains only the demonstrative genus, which, though it has never fallen out of use, is scarcely ever used correctly today. For in making speeches, nearly everyone uses those arts which may be more properly described as contrary to art. In this state of affairs, the one whom we wish to be well educated must nevertheless work at rhetoric, so that in situations appropriate to each genus of rhetoric he can use his art to speak with polish and elaboration.

Next comes poetics, which, even if it contributes a great deal to the life and speech of those who study it, nevertheless seems more suited to pleasure. Indeed the art of music, which also delights the listener, was once held in great honor among the Greeks, nor was anyone considered liberally educated unless he knew how to sing and play the lyre. Socrates himself learned these skills as an old man, and enjoined noble youths to acquire them, not to stimulate licentious behavior but to moderate the movements of soul under the rule of reason. For just as not every voice makes a melodious sound, but only one that harmonizes well, so also not all movements of the soul, but only those which accord with reason, contribute to a harmonious life. But inasmuch as the use of musical modes is highly effective in relaxing the mind and calming the passions, knowledge of this subject is indeed worthy of a free mind and provides the principles according to which we theorize concerning the various natures and properties of sounds and their mutual proportions, from which are produced consonances and dissonances.

The discipline concerning numbers, called arithmetic, and the one concerning magnitudes, called geometry, are similar. In these disciplines the different species of numbers and magnitudes are established and their many properties are demonstrated in accordance, respectively, with the various relationships among equals and unequals, and among lines, surfaces, and bodies. Knowledge of this sort is most pleasant and contains within itself a high degree of certainty. Another very fine discipline is the one that treats the motions, magnitudes, and distances of the heavenly bodies, for it calls us away from the shadows and murkiness down here and leads the eyes and the mind to that shining home above, adorned with so many lights. As we gaze upwards, it is pleasant to pick out the constellations of the fixed stars and to note the locations and names of the planets and their conjunctions, and likewise to foresee and foretell far in advance the eclipses of the sun and moon. Indeed, knowledge about nature is especially appropriate to and in conformity with the human intellect, for through this knowledge we understand the principles and processes of natural things, both animate and inanimate, as well as the causes and effects of the motions and transformations of those things which are contained in heaven and on earth, and we are able to explain many things that generally seem miraculous to the vulgar. There is nothing that is not pleasant to understand, but it is especially pleasant to concern ourselves with those things which cause sensible effects in the air and round about the earth. The studies closely related to them, like perspective and systems of weights and measures, are equally attractive subjects for investigation.

Since I have advanced so far in my discourse, let me touch also on the remaining disciplines. Medicine is a very fine thing to know about and very useful for bodily health, but its practice contains very little that is suitable for the noble mind. Skill in the law is useful, both to the community and to the individual, and is held in great honor everywhere; indeed, it is derived from moral philosophy, just as medicine is from natural philosophy. But while it is honorable to explain the law to students, or to be consulted on points of law by litigants, it is unseemly for those who handle cases to try to sell their efforts for a fee or settlement. Divine science concerns the loftiest causes and matters remote from our senses that only intelligence can reach.

We have enumerated almost all the chief disciplines, not in order that each person need necessarily understand all of them to the point of being learned, or being considered learned—indeed each discipline could absorb all a man's efforts, and the capacity to be content with modest learning is a virtue just like being content with modest wealth. We have done this rather so that everyone might embrace the study most suitable to himself—although all studies are so linked together that no one of them can be well understood if the others are completely unknown.

However, intellects do differ. Some find readily in any given subject the argument and the middle term to prove their own assertions, while others are slow to find arguments but distinguish judiciously among them. Intellects of the former kind are better at posing arguments, while the latter excel as respondents. Likewise, the former type is suited to poetry and the theoretical sciences, the latter to the empirical sciences. Some are quick-witted, but slow of speech and tongue; such persons seem to be best at prepared speeches and artful orations. On the other hand those who are ready both of mind and speech are excellently suited to dialectical disputations. Those whose speech is quicker than their wit—that is, those who have a ready tongue but a dull mind—excel at neither kind of speaking. Furthermore, in certain people the power of memory is very strong, and these are good at historical investigation and at taking in large law books. In this regard we should know that memory apart from intellect is not worth much, but intellect without memory is worth almost nothing, at least as far as learning disciplines is concerned. Yet such a mind can have value in matters of action, since it is possible to write down things that have been done or must be done to compensate for poor memory. Nevertheless, in the case of book-learning, whatever we do not have by heart or cannot easily recall we seem not to know at all.

There are, beyond these, people whose psychic powers are abstracted from sensible and material things, and more suited to understanding immaterial substances and universals; others, by contrast, are prone to run off and busy themselves with particulars. The latter are suited to practical wisdom and natural science, the former to mathematics and to the divine science called metaphysics. For the rest, people should follow the studies appropriate to their natural bent, as the intellect may be speculative or practical. In addition, there are certain limited intellects, the cloddish sort, as the lawyers say, which although they are feeble-minded in everything else, nevertheless have one or another outstanding talent. They should be allowed to do only what they are judged most capable of doing. Aristotle, indeed, being concerned with the active, civic life, believed one should not over-indulge in the liberal arts nor linger over them in pursuit of perfection. For someone who dedicates himself completely to theory and the delights of literature perchance becomes dear to himself, but whether a prince or a private citizen, he is surely of little use to his city.

Such are the definitions we need to make concerning disciplines and intellectual abilities and the genera of both. In this respect it must be observed, to begin with, that it is beneficial to learn from the best masters not only the more important rules that are taught to advanced students, but the first elements of the arts as well. Nor should we spend our time dipping into just any authors; we should read the best. For this reason even Philip, king of Macedon, wanted Alexander to learn his first lessons from Aristotle, and the old Romans took care that when they turned their children over to a school, they were first educated in Vergil. Both had the best of reasons. For what has been sown in young minds puts down deep roots and there is no force that can afterwards pull it up again. Hence, if they become accustomed to the best [teachers and authors] from the beginning, they will use and possess them always as their paramount authorities and guides. But if they imbibe any errors, twice as much time will be needed: to shake out errors, and then to inculcate true precepts. That is why Timotheus, a famous musician of his time, who was exiled from Sparta because he had increased the number of strings on the lyre and invented new musical modes, required a fixed fee from students who had not begun their studies under other teachers, but demanded double from those who had learned something from others.

In the process of learning, the very thing that ought to be a great help, namely, a great desire to learn, often becomes for many people an impediment. They want to take in everything at the same time, and are able to retain nothing as a result. For as excess food does not nourish, but disgusts the stomach, weighing down and weakening the rest of the body, so a great abundance of things ingested all at once into the memory slips away heedlessly now and weakens the memory for the future. So always let those who are eager to learn read widely, but let them select a few things each day that their memory can digest, and in this way let them store away three or four things or more, as each one's ability or leisure will allow, as the special profit of that day. By reading other things, they will succeed in preserving by meditation what they have already learned and daily reading will make more familiar to them what they have yet to master.

What is more, this excessive desire to know and learn is generally joined with a certain disorderly curiosity to investigate. For when people like this are eager to take up many things one by one, they fall upon the various disciplines all at once, going back now to this one, now to that; now they embrace one subject with all their strength, then, having cast that aside, they embrace another for a bit, then another. This is not only completely useless, but even very damaging, for there is truth in the proverb which says: wines turn sour when they are rebottled too often. So it is better to devote oneself to one thing and to pursue it with all one's zeal, and to try to grasp the disciplines in the order they were transmitted by their authors. For those who read books in a disorderly way, now beginning from the end, now dipping into the middle, learning second what they should have learned first—the only profit such people take from their reckless reading is the appearance of having read nothing at all. And we should familiarize ourselves with the numerous books within the same discipline so as always to have the better ones foremost.

Not everyone should undertake the same amount of labor, but each according to his turn of mind. For some minds penetrate like lead (so to speak), others like iron. Leaden minds that are blunt are not much good for learning, while those whose mental edge is sharp but soft and easily bent require frequent breaks in their studying. If they do not penetrate through to their goal with the first blow, they grow blunter the more they try. But nothing is impervious to those who been allotted an intellect of iron, if it is also sharp, unless they want to penetrate an unbreakable barrier. If they have blunt iron minds, they can still prevail over all difficulties through diligent effort. Hence if they do not understand something, they do not spit it out immediately like the proud, nor do they fall into despair, like the weak of will; they simply persevere the more in their intention. But it is also very true that those who are keener in mind are less strong in memory, and those who grasp things quickly retain fewer of them. So in order to preserve and strengthen memory, the plan Cato said he used is especially germane: he used to call to mind in the evening whatever he had done, seen, or read during the day, as though demanding an account of the day's business from himself, like someone who wanted to take account not only of his business activities, but also of his leisure. So we shall therefore, if we are able, take care to remember everything. If we cannot, let us at least cling tenaciously to the things we have chosen for ourselves as especially important.

It will moreover be profitable to confer often with our classmates about our common studies, for disputation sharpens the mind, educates the tongue, and strengthens the memory, and not only do we learn numerous things through disputation, but we also understand better, express more aptly, and remember more firmly the things we learn this way. But also, by teaching others what we learn, we will be of no small help to ourselves; teaching what you have learned is the best way to improve. However it happens to almost all learners, when they make good progress in something at first, that they immediately think they have achieved great things in the disciplines and would dispute already as though they were learned men and would defend their own opinions strenuously, which is a great obstacle to them. For the first step in learning is the capacity to doubt, nor is there anything so inimical to learning as the presumption of one's own erudition or excessive reliance upon one's own wits: the one takes away our interest in learning, while the other diminishes it, and in this way students unnecessarily deceive themselves. The easiest person to deceive is one's self, and there is no one our deceit damages more than ourselves. This comes about because inexperienced students have not yet been permitted to assess the byways, bends and precipices which lie hidden in the sciences; hence they either mistakenly correct many things in books which they are unable to understand well on their own, or they blame the ignorance and carelessness of scribes, passing deliberately over the numerous things they do not understand. Effort and perseverance will shrug off such attitudes, however.

Everything will happen satisfactorily if time will be apportioned suitably, if every day we allot fixed times to letters and are not distracted by affairs of any kind from reading something every day. For if Alexander used to read a great deal while campaigning, if Caesar used to write books even while marching with his army, and Augustus, after having undertaken so great an affair as the Modenese war, nevertheless always read or wrote in camp and declaimed every day, what activity is there that could interrupt our citified leisure hours and summon us for so long from our literary studies? Moreover it is useful to regard the loss of even the least bit of time as significant and to account for our time like our life and our health, so that we do not lose anything needlessly, just as when we allot our moments of inactivity, which others use for leisure, to less strenuous studies or pass such times in pleasant reading. And indeed there is good reason also to assemble those good moments that others usually neglect, as when someone reads at table and falls asleep (or escapes sleep) reading. True, doctors claim these things harm the vision and the eyes, but this is only the case if one reads excessively, that is, either too intently or after a heavy meal. But this, too, would be of no small profit: if inside our libraries we should set up right before our eyes those devices which are used to measure the hours and times, so that we may see time glide away, as it were; and if we should use those places for no other purpose than that for which they have been established, and allow there no extraneous thoughts or activities.

On Physical Exercises and Military Pursuits

... for those who take pleasure in literary studies, a variety of reading brings comfort and new readings relieve the boredom of old ones. From time to time, however, one needs to do absolutely nothing and be entirely free from work, so as to meet once again the demands of work and toil. For the muscle which is always stretched taut usually breaks if it is not sometimes relaxed—though for the wise man there is no time more toilsome than when he is doing nothing—assuming the wise man could do nothing. We have heard that certain people are accustomed to apportion their time as follows: that over a day and a night they allow a third of their time to sleep, a third to recoup their strength and find respite from work, and they give the rest to liberal studies. For my part, I am not ready to condemn this plan, but I cannot entirely commend it, either. This, however, I can affirm and affirm boldly: that the less of our life that slips away from us, and the longer we live on this account, the more of our time we should liberate for good letters.

Christine de Pizan

c. 1363–c.1430

I dare say there is no treasure the like of understanding. Who would not undertake any labor, you champions of wisdom, to acquire it?

THE BOOK OF THE BODY POLITIC

Italian by birth, Christine de Pizan lived in France from the time she was a small child. Her father had moved the family from Venice to Paris, where he served as court astrologer, physician, and secretary to France's king Charles V. Christine grew up at court and received an excellent classical education. She married quite young, but after the death of the king, her father, and then her husband, she was left to support herself and her small children. She turned to writing, producing dozens of important works of biography, history, educational theory, and poetry. She lived through part of the Hundred Years' War, and one of her poems took Joan of Arc as its theme. She spent the last dozen years of her life at a convent at Poissy, outside of Paris.

THE SELECTION

The first part included here of *The Book of the Body Politic* (c. 1407) differs little from classical treatments of the education of the sons of nobility. It is similar to its contemporaries as well, but originality was not the goal for any of these authors. Christine de Pizan holds up a "mirror" to the young prince, helping him to examine himself against the standard set by the heroes of antiquity. The second excerpt, however, is more distinctive. It recognizes differences in society and considers the sort of education appropriate to the "estate" of the clergy. She encourages university students by way of a beautiful testimony to the love of learning. Following the example of the Stoics, she maintains the connection between wisdom and virtue.

from The Book of the Body Politic
"On Princes"

CHAPTER 2: WHICH DESCRIBES HOW VIRTUOUS FELICITY IS SYMBOLIZED

First we have to discuss virtue, to the benefit of the rule of life for the three different estates. Virtue must regulate human life in all its works. Without it, no one can have honor. Whatever the degree of honor, Valerius says, honor is the plentiful food of virtue. And on this subject, Aristotle said, "Reverence is due to honor as a testimony of virtue," which means that honor must not be attributed but to a virtuous person, because he is not speaking about the powerful nor about the rich, but the virtuous. According to him, only the good are honored. Nothing is more desired by noble hearts than honor. As he says himself in the fourth book of the *Ethics*, neither power nor riches is without honor. Now it is true that kings and powerful princes are especially invested with honor, and as a consequence, virtue, so it is appropriate to distinguish the aspects of virtue. In chapter 20 of his book, *The City of God*, St. Augustine says that the philosophers say that virtue is the objective of all human good and evil. That is, human happiness comes from being virtuous.

Now it is fitting that there is great delight in happiness, otherwise it would not be happiness, and this joy and happiness ancient philosophers described and symbolized in this manner: Felicity is a very beautiful and refined queen seated on a royal throne, and the virtues are seated around her and look at her, waiting to hear her commands, to serve her, and to obey. She commands Prudence to inquire how she can stay healthy and in good condition so that she can reign a long time. And she commands Justice to do everything that she should and keep the laws so that there will be peace. And she commands Courage that if any pain should come to her body, to moderate it by resisting it with virtuous thought. She commands Temperance to take wine, food and other delectable things in moderation so that anything she takes is for a reason and not to her detriment. This description allows one to understand that to be virtuous is nothing more than to have in one everything that attracts good and which pushes away evil and vice. Thus, in order to govern the body of the public polity well, it is necessary for the head to be healthy, that is, virtuous. Because if it is ill, the whole body will feel it. Therefore we begin by speaking of medicine for the head, that is, for the king or princes, and, since this is a work beginning with the head, we will take first the "head" of age, that is the childhood of the prince who is brought up on the responsibility of his parents.

Chapter 3: This tells how one ought to bring up the children of princes

Because we are expressly commanded to love God, the first thing is to introduce the child of the prince to this love very early and to teach him simple little prayers appropriate to the understanding of the child.

For things taught early in childhood are lost with difficulty. Such things are agreeable God; the Psalmist says "The Lord has perfect praise in the mouth of children and sucklings," that is, He approves of it. As he gets older he should learn his letters and to follow the religious service. God be praised, to teach their children to hear Mass and to say their Hours has been the praiseworthy custom of the princes of France more than in other places.

Also one ought to provide a tutor who is wise and prudent more in morals than in lofty learning, despite the fact that in ancient times, the children of princes were taught by philosophers. For example, Philip, king of Macedon and father of the great Alexander, wrote to Aristotle that while he had had great joy when a male infant was born to him, he had a greater joy yet that he was born at this time so that he could be instructed and taught by Aristotle who eventually was the teacher of Alexander the Great. Nevertheless, because at present princes do not desire to be educated in the sciences as they used to be and as I would wish it pleased God that they were, I believe that it would be better to have a very discrete and wise tutor, who had good morals and loved God, rather than the most excellent and subtle philosopher. Yet it would be much more praiseworthy to find a perfect one who was a notable scholar as well.

And so princes ought to carefully search for one because the good morals that the child sees in his tutor, and the wise words and countenance he experiences provide both an education and a mirror for him. So the wise tutor ought to conduct himself with great prudence in such an office, because despite the fact that it is a child's nature not to learn except out of fear of punishment, nevertheless, it is good that the child of the prince be brought to fear in other ways than severe beatings. For too strict a correction in a child that is brought up in pleasures and who already senses the power of authority because of the honor that others pay him could lead, instead of to correction, to indignation towards learning as well as towards his tutor, which would undermine his discipline, to the detriment of the tutor and, perhaps, of the health of the delicately raised child. But what should the wise tutor do? He ought to follow the example of the lion, because it is the custom to raise the children of princes with other children, sons of barons, who are all his pupils. He ought to be severe with them when they misbehave and beat them as is customary but threaten them more by severe expression than by beatings, and likewise to use threats on the prince's son if he does not correct himself. At some point, let him feel the rod, and by this see to it that he is ashamed of his misdeed, fearful, and obedient.

The wise tutor ought not to be too familiar with or too close to his pupils because they will fear him less, and the child should not see him play games, laugh, or speak foolishly, but, instead that he is not too familiar with anyone but is half school master to everyone. And his countenance should be dignified and firm, and his dress be clean and honorable. In front of his pupil, he should not speak empty words but profitable ones, and give good examples; however, he should not always have a sour face and proud words. He ought to welcome him with gentle words when he does well which will reward him if he does something good. The master shall give him these little things that delight children, or sometimes tell him childish stories or something that makes them laugh. The purpose of all that is that he love his tutor as well as his studies. The master should regulate the day well, and arrange time and rules for the child to begin and end school, and then give him some time to play before his dinner, which should be orderly, and not too rich or delicate in meats and wines, which to some degree can cause corruption or illness. And when the child comes to learn his grammar then the tutor should begin to use a bit more subtle words and teaching, according to how he sees what the child is able to understand, and thus, little by little, teach more and more, just as a nurse increases the food of the child according to his growth.

Truly, I believe that the prince would want to have his child to be introduced to learning so that he knows the rules of grammar and understands Latin, which if pleased God, I would wish were generally the custom for all children of princes at present and for the future, because I believe that the greater good would ensue and virtue would increase for them and their subjects. So they should have their children learn as much as possible, to advance as far as Logic, and then have them continue if they can. So the very wise prince, the duke of Orleans, did and used to do for his children, as he was asked by the very wise, good, and virtuous duchess, his wife, who values and honors education and knowledge, and like a prudent mother is careful that letters and all the virtues are being learned by her children.

With the wise tutor described above, when the understanding of the child begins to grow and to understand better, then he ought to feed him more advanced learning and manners by giving him examples or having him read in books. And he ought to make him understand the difference between good and evil, and teach and show him the path to follow in good morals, manners, and virtue as the valiant and renowned princes, his predecessors, and others did, and show him the great good which comes from being good and governing oneself well, and also the opposite; the evil which comes to the bad or vicious. And if he seems at all inclined or talented in learning, he ought to encourage him through pleasant words and reasons, so that he will understand the great happiness to be found in learning, opening up for him the path to philosophy, and making him appreciate and understand it. And if he has such a tutor at the beginning, if he continues with such learning when he comes of age the son of the prince will have excellence in virtue and great fame.

CHAPTER 4: ON THE SORT OF PERSON TO BE ENTRUSTED WITH THE GOVERNING OF THE CHILDREN OF PRINCES

When the son of the prince has grown older, then he ought to be separated from the women who have cared for him and his care ought to be entrusted principally to one older knight of great authority, and one ought to carefully look to see that he is wise, loyal, prudent, and of good manner of life, and that he have similar persons around him. This knight must take as much or more diligent care of the habits of the child as he does of his body. So he ought to take care that he rises early; that he hears Mass, says his Hours, has a pleasant and confident expression, speaks well to people, greets them kindly, gives to everyone the honor due to his position. This knight ought often to show him what the honor and valor of knighthood is, and tell him the great deeds of many worthy knights.

He ought to make him recognize who is good and who is the better in his father's household and who he ought to honor the most. And he ought to show him and teach him the emblems of arms and order of battles and chivalry, how to fight, to attack, to defend, and for what quarrels one must take arms and fight, what armor is the best, strongest, and most sure, and most comfortable, and he ought to explain to him why it is so and how one should arm according to the kind of battle, what arms one would use, how one fought in times past and how now, how to determine who is good and worthy, and to attract them to oneself, to honor them, and to love them.

The knight ought to take care that there be neither great nor humble tellers of dishonest or evil ideas around the son of the prince when he has grown older, and that they not introduce the prince to folly. And he ought to take care that the children who are around him are well brought up, so that he is not induced to do wrong or to childish folly. If the child of the prince does wrong he should correct him, saying that it is not appropriate to his rank for the prince to do this, and that if he does not change he will encounter shame and blame, and that a prince without honor is worth nothing, and that if he does not desire to be governed this way, that he will have to leave. And thus he ought to counsel, tell, and admonish him often, and in this way the sons of princes and lords ought to be governed if they desire to be honorable in the future. Valerius affirms this for us in his book which speaks of how the ancients introduced the young to good manners, to withstand hardship, and to be honorable and brave. He told of the chivalry and bravery of the good, and gave good examples, telling them that nothing leads to honor as well as virtue.

At meals, he has songs sung about the deeds of the noble dead and the good deeds of their ancestors so that the will of the young person is made courageous. Valerius says that the ancients taught bravery, chivalry and good manners this way in their schools. These schools, he says, resulted in the Caesars and the noble families, renowned for accomplishments and bravery. And there is no doubt that good example and wise advice often heard and seen in childhood can cause a man to grow up excellent in all virtue, and similarly, by evil teaching one can be brought to the way of perdition. As Averroes says in the second book of *Physics,* one can acquire a second nature by long habit of good or evil, and that is why parents ought to keep children from bad habits in youth as much as they can, for, says Orosius, an earthenware pot keeps the odor of what it contained for a long time. It is because of this that the ancient Greeks who governed themselves with great learning and cleverness, took great pains to ensure that the people whom they hated delighted in evil habits, and this gave them the means to be avenged on them.

"On the Common People"

CHAPTER 4: HERE WE BEGIN TO DISCUSS THE THIRD ESTATE OF THE PEOPLE, AND FIRST, CLERICS STUDYING THE BRANCHES OF KNOWLEDGE

In the community of people are found three estates, which means, especially in the city of Paris and other cities, the clergy, the burghers and merchants, and the common people, such as artisans and laborers. Now it is suitable to consider the things to say that are beneficial as examples of good living for each of the distinct estates since they are different. And because the clerical class is high, noble, and worthy of honor amongst the others, I will address it first, that is, the students, whether at the University of Paris or elsewhere.

Oh well advised, oh happy people! I speak to you, the disciples of the study of wisdom, who, by the grace of God and good fortune or nature apply yourselves to seek out the heights of the clear rejoicing star, that is, knowledge, do take diligently from this treasure, drink from this clear and healthy fountain. Fill yourself from this pleasant repast, which can so benefit and elevate you! For what is more worthy for a person than knowledge and the highest learning? Certainly, you who desire it and employ yourself with it, you have chosen the glorious life! For by it, you can understand the choice of virtue and the avoidance of vice as it counsels the one and forbids the other.

There is nothing more perfect than the truth and clarity of things which knowledge demonstrates how to know and understand. There is no treasure of the goods of fortune that he who has tasted of the highest knowledge would exchange for a drop of the dregs of wisdom. And truly, no matter what others say, I dare say there is no treasure the like of understanding. Who would not undertake any labor, you champions of wisdom, to acquire it? For if you have it and use it well, you are noble, you are rich, you are all perfect! And this is plain in the teachings of the philosophers, who teach and instruct the way to come through wisdom to the treasure of pure and perfect sufficiency.

The very worthy philosopher Cleanthes, having already experienced the true desire to taste wisdom, had so much love for it that because he was too poor to buy books or even something to live on, he drew water all night for the needs of students in order to have enough to live on. By day, he listened to the study and the lessons of Chryssipus, who was a very fine philosopher, so that his learning would be complete. Thus by industry and long patience he became a very noble man, who was worthy of the highest praise as much for the constancy of his labor as the knowledge he acquired. Thus, in a letter, Seneca said that Cleanthes, by the labor he had undertaken, helped himself to come to the perfection of knowledge.

On the subject of the love of knowledge and the diligence and care needed to learn, in order to have the great good that comes to those who acquire it, we will tell a little of other philosophers to whet the appetite of those who study.

The philosopher Plato loved knowledge so much that by the hard work of acquiring it, he filled himself with wisdom and learning. This Plato was Aristotle's teacher and lived during the time of Socrates the philosopher. He benefited so much from learning that because of the nobility of his mind he was reputed to be the wisest of all mortal men. And he showed that he was fond of knowledge, for he went everywhere looking for books, even to Italy. About this, Valerius says that his great diligence and desire for learning took him to consult books everywhere, and so, by him, knowledge was expanded and dispersed around the world.

This eminent man died at the age of eighty-one. His death showed the love he had for all kinds of books, for found near him were the books of a woman poet, named Sappho, who wrote about love in joyous and graceful verses, so Orosius says. And so, perhaps he looked at them to take pleasure in her pleasant poems.

Valerius' book tells of the philosopher Democritus, who, according to what Aristotle says in the first book of *On Generation and Corruption,* was concerned about everything, that is, that he wanted to talk and debate about everything that was said. Therefore, Aristotle recommended his natural philosophy and his opinions in many places. He is praised and recommended so much by Valerius because, first, he despised riches, which many times are an impediment to the acquisition of philosophy, and also he tells how Democritus was able to abandon his riches, which were so great that his father could give food to Xerxes' entire army. Nonetheless, so that he could retire to study, he threw aside the concerns and occupations that come to those with wealth; he distributed all that he had and retained scarcely what he needed to live on.

Secondly, Valerius recommends him because he did not seek worldly honors, which are an impediment to the conquest of wisdom. And because he lived for a long time in Athens, employing all his time in educating himself, and he lived unknown in the city. As he testifies in one of his volumes, he chose the solitary life to be outside the tumult that impedes thought. So it appears that he had a great desire for wisdom, for he avoided with all his power anything which could hinder his acquisition of it.

On the subject of the love of knowledge and study, Valerius says of the philosopher Carneades, that he was the upright, hardworking knight of wisdom, because, for eighty years he lived as a philosopher. So amazing was his concentration on works of learning that he often forgot to take his meal at table. He was so abstracted that his loyal servant, Meleisa, would put his food in his hand. This philosopher cared for nothing in the world but virtue.

I could speak of other noble philosophers and seekers of wisdom, but will not, for the sake of brevity. I tell the above stories to bring them to the memory of good students so that they see that books of such topics can teach them knowledge in order that they may increase in goodness and virtue. For there is no doubt that the sciences perfect the habits. If people are so perverse that it suffices them that others think that they know the sciences, and they do not use their wisdom for themselves, but only teach it to others, then they resemble people who die of hunger with food near them. And no doubt, such people are more to blame when they are mistaken than are others.

CHAPTER 5: MORE ON THE SAME SUBJECT

Because it is an important subject and appropriate to know, and because not everyone has the book by Valerius to study at his pleasure the subjects of which he speaks, it pleases me to speak about study.

As I said before, the student ought to have great diligence in order to acquire wisdom. Valerius teaches how one ought to have moderate diligence and not be too excessive in this exercise. He says that Scaevola, who was an excellent jurist and expert in common law in Rome and who composed many laws, after his arduous work and study, took recreation in a variety of games. And Valerius explained and approved of it, saying that the nature of things does not allow a person to work continually, but that it is necessary to rest and stay sometimes at leisure. Leisure does not mean to do nothing physical, but means any joyful work or sport that will refresh his understanding, because the sensitive qualities of the soul become weak from long attention to study, and they would not be refreshed by complete cessation of all activity. If they give themselves no recreation, those whose work is study become melancholy because the mind is overworked, and if they go to sleep they will suffer from bad dreams. And so the remedy for such labor is to rejoice the spirit in games and play. Just as rich food pleases us more when alternated with plain food, so the work of study is best nourished when one sometimes plays, and so Cato says, "vary your work with diversions." In Book 4 of *Ethics*, Aristotle says "one should exercise the virtue of temperance and moderation in work and play"; to which Seneca, in his book *On Tranquility of Mind*, adds "fertile fields are soon exhausted by continual and uninterrupted cultivation." So continual mental work destroys the strength and leads to frenzy, and so nature gives humans an inclination to play and relax from time to time. It is for this reason that there are laws establishing certain holidays so that people come together in public to bring joy and a cessation of work. On this, it is said of Socrates, from whom no part of wisdom was hidden, that he was not ashamed when Alcibiades mocked him for playing with little children, because it was an account of this recreation that his understanding was clearer and more lively at study. This is why in his old age he learned to play the harp.

Leonardo Bruni

c. 1370–1444

We must not forget that true distinction is to be gained by a wide and varied range of such studies as conduce to the profitable enjoyment of life.

ON THE STUDY OF LITERATURE

Leonardo Bruni was born in Arezzo, Italy, the birthplace of Petrarch. He initially studied law at the University of Florence, but falling under the spell of the classics, he studied under Petrarch's disciple Coluccio Salutati and then, like his friend Vergerio, under the Greek scholar Chrysoloras. He served as apostolic secretary to four popes and attended the Council of Constance. Under the patronage of the Medici family, he became chancellor of the Republic of Florence. His scholarship focused on reviving the classical world on its own terms, and he became a champion of the *studia humanitatis*. He produced important translations directly from Greek into Latin, including works by Aristotle, Plato, Xenophon, Aristophanes, Plutarch, and Basil's *Address to Young Men*. He wrote biographies of Aristotle, Cicero, Dante, and Petrarch, dialogues modeled on Cicero, and a history of Florence that champions political liberty. He is buried at the Church of Sante Croce in Florence.

THE SELECTION

On the Study of Literature (De studiis et literis) is written in the form of a letter to Battista Malatesta, daughter of the Count of Urbino. It was probably written in the 1420s. Battista loved classical literature, was a scholar in her own right, and wrote poetry and an admired oration to the Holy Roman Emperor Sigismund. After a brief and unhappy marriage, she lived as a sister of the Franciscan Order of Santa Chiara. Bruni directs Battista away from preparation for the public life that is not open to her and urges her instead to study "the whole field of religion and morals." Her study of the Church Fathers and of the poets, historians, and orators of antiquity will endow her with breadth, nobility, and grace. Bruni closes with an important reminder that appears throughout the letter: the inseparability of style and content, "the two sides of learning." The influence of Cicero and Quintilian is evident.

On the Study of Literature

I feel myself constrained, dear lady, by many successive reports of your wonderful virtues to write to you in commendation of the perfect development of those innate powers of which I have heard so much that is excellent, or, if that is too much, at least to urge you, through these literary efforts of mine, to bring them to such a perfection. There is, indeed, no lack of examples of women renowned for their letters and their eloquence that I could mention to exhort you to excellence. Cornelia, the daughter of Scipio, wrote letters in the most elegant of styles, which letters survived for many centuries after her death. The poetical works of Sappho were held in the highest honor among the Greeks for their unique eloquence and literary skill. Then, too, there was Aspasia, a learned lady of the time of Socrates, who was outstanding in eloquence and literature, and from whom even so great a philosopher as Socrates did not blush to admit he had learned certain things. I could mention still others, but let these three stand sufficient as examples of the most renowned women. Be encouraged and elevated by their excellence! It is not fitting that such understanding and intellectual power as you possess were given you in vain, not fitting that you should be satisfied with mediocrity; such gifts expect and encourage the highest excellence. And your glory will be all the brighter, for those other women flourished in ages when there was an abundance of learned persons whose very number decreases the estimation in which we must hold them, while you live in these times when learning has so far decayed that it is regarded as positively miraculous to meet a learned man, let alone a woman. By learning, however, I do not mean that confused and vulgar sort such as is possessed by those who nowadays profess theology, but a legitimate and liberal kind which joins literary skill with factual knowledge, a learning Lactantius possessed, and Augustine, and Jerome, all of whom were finished men of letters as well as great theologians. It is shameful, by contrast, how very little modern theologians know of letters.

But I digress. Let me rather pursue our discourse, not for you to be instructed by me (for of that I imagine you have no need), but simply for you to understand my views, on the subject of literary study.

The person aiming at the kind of excellence which I am calling you to needs first, I think, to acquire no slender or common, but a wide and exact, even *recherché* familiarity with literature. Without this basis, no one can build himself any high or splendid thing. The one who lacks knowledge of literature will neither understand sufficiently the writings of the learned, nor will he be able, if he should himself attempt to write, to avoid making a laughingstock of himself. To attain this knowledge, elementary instruction has its place, but much more important is our own effort and study. Elementary instruction, indeed, need hardly detain us. Everyone knows that, in the first instance the mind needs an instructor to train and as it were initiate it so that it can recognize not only the parts of speech and their function, but also those smaller details and elements of speech. But these we absorb in childhood as though dreaming; afterwards when we have moved on to greater things, they somehow come back to our lips, and it is only then that we taste their sweetness and true flavor. There is another more robust kind of elementary instruction, useful more to adults than children: the instruction, I mean, of those who are called grammarians, those who have thoroughly investigated every detail in our books, and in so doing have created a kind of literary discipline. Servius and Priscian are grammarians of this sort. But believe me, our own study is far more important. Study reveals and explains to us not only the words and syllables but also the tropes and figures of speech in all their beauty and polish. Through study we receive our literary formation, and, as it were, our teaching; through it, indeed, we learn much that a teacher could never teach us: vocalic melody, elegance, concinnity, charm. The most important rule of study is to see to it that we study only those works that are written by the best and most approved authors, and avoid the crude and ignorant writings which only ruin and degrade our natural abilities. The reading of clumsy and corrupt writers imbues the reader with their own vices, and infests his mind with a similar corruption. Study is, so to speak, the pabulum of the mind by which the intellect is trained and nourished. For this reason, just as gastronomes are careful in the choice of what they put in their stomachs, so those who wish to preserve purity of taste will only allow certain reading to enter their minds.

This then will be our first study: to read only the best and most approved authors. Our second will be to bring to this reading a keen critical sense. The reader must study the reasons why the words are placed as they are, and the meaning and force of each element of the sentence, the smaller as well as the larger; he must thoroughly understand the force of the several particles whose idiom and usage he will copy from the authors he reads.

Hence a woman who enjoys sacred literature and who wished to observe stylistic propriety will take up Augustine and Jerome and any authors she finds similar to them, such as Ambrose and Cyprian. But the greatest of all those who have ever written of the Christian religion, the one who excels them all with his brilliance and richness of expression, is Lactantius Firmianus, without doubt the most eloquent of all Christian authors, and the one whose eloquence and technique are best able to nourish and educate the type of ability I am considering. I recommend most of all his volumes *Against False Religion*, and also *On the Wrath of God*, and *The Creation of Man*. Please do read them if you love literature, and you will enjoy a pleasure like ambrosia and nectar. If you have any translations by you of Gregory Nazianzen, John Chrysostom, or St. Basil the Great, the Greek Doctors of the Church, I would advise you to read them, too—so long as you read them in good Latin translations, not perversions. A woman, on the other hand, who enjoys secular literature will choose Cicero, a man—Good God!—so eloquent! so rich in expression! so polished! so unique in every *genus* of glory! Next will be Vergil, the delight and ornament of our literature, then Livy and Sallust and the other poets and writers in their order. With them she will train and strengthen her taste, and she will be careful, when she is obliged to say or write something, to use no word she has not first met in one of these authors.

It will moreover be profitable for her from time to time to make an effort to read well aloud. For in prose, as well as in verse, there are certain rhythms, inflexions, and pacings, an orchestration, as it were, recognized and measured by the sense of hearing, which causes the voice at one moment to drop and at another to rise, and to create beautifully ordered connections between the cola, commata, and periods. This will be readily apparent in every good writer. She will clearly grasp this when she reads aloud and she will fill her ears with it as with a harmony, and will hear it also afterwards when she writes, and will imitate it. Another result of her reading will be to have each word drop in place at its proper time, so that there is never haste when there should be emphasis, nor emphasis when haste is called for.

Again, I would not have her ignorant of writing. I do not now speak of calligraphy (although I commend whoever possesses that skill), but the formation of phonemes and syllables. She should understand how each is to be written, the nature of the letters and word division, which abbreviations may be employed and which should be avoided. This is a small matter, of course, but it is a mark of our education, to lack which betrays manifest ignorance. She ought also to know and memorize the quantity of every syllable, that is, whether it is long, short, or common. This knowledge is necessary to understand many passages which would otherwise be unintelligible, such as that of Vergil,

> *Omnibus in morem tonsâ coma pressa coronâ,*
> Each with his hair bound by a trimmed garland in
>   the traditional manner

and a thousand other examples. It is likewise unseemly for one who fancies oneself a *littérateur* to misunderstand so basic a thing as the quantity of syllables, especially since verse is universally held to be no contemptible part of literature; but verses are made up of feet; and feet are constituted by the quantity of their syllables. What a person has to offer who does not understand quantity, what poetical taste he can possibly have, is something I do not for my part clearly understand.

This knowledge is likewise necessary, I believe, in composing and writing prose. Metre is not absent from prose simply because the multitude do not perceive it; it is in fact the source of aural sweetness and pleasure. It makes a great difference, according to Aristotle, which metres are used at the beginning and end of a sentence, and even in the middle there are certain metres which are preferable and others which should be avoided. He himself particularly approved the paean, which has two forms: a long followed by three short beats, or three shorts followed by a long. He thought the latter suitable for *clausulae*, and the former for the beginnings of sentences and perfectly appropriate in the middle as well. He disapproved of the dactyl and the iamb: the former he thought too elevated, and the latter too low. Cicero's favorite metres in *clausulae* were the dichoreus, which is made up of two trochees, the cretic, which is long-short-long, and the aforementioned paean. He held the iamb to be the most appropriate in the middle of the period when we are employing a low or ordinary style, and when a fuller style is being employed, the dactyl, the paean, or the dochimius (a five-syllable foot: a short, two long, a short, and a long), which latter rhythm he considered to be suitable in all parts of the sentence. Moreover, it is clear that argument, narration, and lamentation all have their several rhythms appropriate to them. Anger and mental excitation will not accept the spondee, requiring as they do a quick and hasty rhythm; narration and instruction, on the contrary, demand deliberate and stable rhythms, and so are averse to "headlong" feet. Thus, every variety of communication has its appropriate rhythm. Any writer who ignores this fact will be writing as chance directs, like a man stumbling in the dark.

There will, perhaps, be many who think exaggerated my attention to this point. They must remember, however, that I am speaking of persons of great abilities and promise. Mediocrities may go, or rather crawl, as they can. It is sure that no one reaches the pinnacle of literary skill except by knowledge of and practice in all these things. Then, too, the purpose of my treatise is to cover the whole field of literature: not only normal practice, but also the glories, the elegancies, and the finer charms of discourse. I would have our writer possess a rhetorical *garniture de toilette*, a fine wardrobe, an abundant stock of domestic furniture, if I may call it that, which she can produce and display as the need arises.

Having said that genuine learning was a combination of literary skill and factual knowledge, we have set forth our view of what literary skill is. Let us now, therefore, say something about knowledge. Here again I have in mind someone whose intellect shows the greatest promise, who despises no branch of learning, who holds all the world as her province, who, in a word, burns marvellously with a desire for knowledge and understanding. An ardent and well-motivated person like this needs, I think, to be applauded and spurred on in some directions, while in others she must be discouraged and held back. Disciplines there are, of whose rudiments some knowledge is fitting, yet whereof to obtain the mastery is a thing by no means glorious. In geometry and arithmetic, for example, if she waste a great deal of time worrying their subtle obscurities, I should seize her and tear her away from them. I should do the same in astrology, and even, perhaps, in the art of rhetoric. I say this with some hesitation, since if any living men have labored in this art, I would profess myself to be of their number. But there are many things here to be taken into account, the first of which is the person whom I am addressing. For why should the subtleties of the *status*, the *epicheiremata*, the *krinomena*, and a thousand other rhetorical conundrums consume the powers of a woman, who never sees the forum? That art of delivery, which the Greeks call *hypocrisis* and we *pronunciatio*, and which Demosthenes said was the first, the second, and the third most important acquirement of the orator, so far is that from being the concern of a woman that if she should gesture energetically with her arms as she spoke and shout with violent emphasis, she would probably be thought mad and put under restraint. The contests of the forum, like those of warfare and battle, are the sphere of men. Hers is not the task of learning to speak for and against witnesses, for and against torture, for and against reputation; she will not practice the commonplaces, the syllogisms, the sly anticipation of an opponent's arguments. She will, in a word, leave the rough-and-tumble of the forum entirely to men.

When, then, do I encourage her, when do I spur her on? Just when she devotes herself to divinity and moral philosophy. It is there I would beg her to spread her wings, there apply her mind, there spend her vigils. It will be worth our while to dwell on this in some detail. First, let the Christian woman desire for herself a knowledge of sacred letters. What better advice could I give? Let her search much, weigh much, acquire much in this branch of study. But let her fondness be for the older authors. The moderns, if they are good men, she will honor and revere, but she should pay scant attention to their writings. A woman of literature will find no instruction in them that is not in St. Augustine, and St. Augustine, moreover, unlike them, has the diction of an educated person, and one well worth attending to.

Nor would I have her rest content with a knowledge of sacred literature; let her broaden her interests into the secular studies as well. Let her know what the most excellent minds among the philosophers have taught about moral philosophy, what their doctrines are concerning continence, temperance, modesty, justice, courage, liberality. She should understand their beliefs about happiness: whether virtue is in itself sufficient for happiness, or whether torture, poverty, exile, or prison can affect it. Whether, when such misfortunes befall the blessed, they are made miserable thereby, or whether they simply take away happiness without inducing actual misery. Whether human felicity consists in pleasure and the absence of pain, as Epicurus would have it, or in moral worth, as Zeno believed, or in the exercise of virtue, which was Aristotle's view. Believe me, such subjects as these are beautiful and intellectually rewarding. They are valuable not only for the guidance they give in life, but they also supply us with a marvelous stock of knowledge which can be used in every variety of oral and written expression.

These two subjects, then, divinity and moral philosophy, will be her most important goals, the *raisons d'être* of her studies. Other subjects will be related to them in proportion as they contribute to them or to their embellishment. It is true that the marvel of human excellence, that excellence which raises a name to genuine celebrity, is a direct result of a wide and various knowledge; and it is true, too, that we should read much and learn much, selecting, acquiring, weighing, and examining all things from all points of view, from which process we derive great benefit for our studies. Yet at the same time we should choose carefully and consider thoughtfully the time at our disposal in order to give first place to those things that are most important and most useful.

To the aforesaid subjects there should first be joined, in my view, a knowledge of history, which is a subject no scholar should neglect. It is a fit and seemly thing to be familiar with the origins and progress of one's own nation, and with the deeds in peace and in war of great kings and free peoples. Knowledge of the past gives guidance to our counsels and our practical judgment, and the consequences of similar undertakings [in the past] will encourage or deter us according to our circumstances in the present. History, moreover, is the most commodious source of that stock of examples of outstanding conduct with which it is fitting frequently to embellish our conversation. Then, too, some of the outstanding historians are distinguished and polished writers as well, and so make valuable reading for literary purposes: Livy, I mean, and Sallust and Tacitus and Curtius, and especially Julius Caesar, who described his own deeds with the greatest ease and elegance in his *Commentaries*. These, then, the woman of high promise will go on to acquire, the more so as they make pleasant reading. For here there are no subtleties to be unravelled, no knotty *quaestiones* to be untied; only narrations of facts that are easy to grasp, and, once grasped (at least by an outstanding mind such as I am considering), will never be forgotten.

I would further urge her not to neglect the orators. Where else is virtue praised with such passion, and vice condemned with such ferocity? It is the orators who teach us to praise the good deed and to hate the bad; it is they who teach us how to soothe, encourage, stimulate, or deter. All these things the philosophers do, it is true, but in some special way anger, mercy and the arousal and pacification of the mind are completely within the power of the orator. Then, too, those figures of speech and thought, which like stars or torches illuminate our diction and give it distinction, are the proper tools of the orator which we borrow from them when we speak or write, and turn to our use as the occasion demands. In sum, all the richness, power, and polish in our expression, its lifeblood, as it were, we derive from the orators.

The poets, too, I would have her read and understand. This is a knowledge which all great men have possessed. Aristotle, at least, frequently cites passages of Homer, Hesiod, Pindar, Euripides, and the other poets, showing by his familiar knowledge and ready quotation of them that he was no less a student of the poets than of the philosophers. Plato as well makes frequent use of the poets, bringing them in freely, even gratuitously; indeed, he often uses their authority to confirm his own. So much for the Greeks; what of the Latin writers? Is Cicero to be thought too little versed in poetical knowledge when, not content with Ennius, Pacuvius, Accius, and the other Latin poets, he fills his works with his own renderings from the Greek poets? What of the austere and hard-boiled Seneca: did not even he write poems and entire works in verse? I pass over Augustine, Jerome, Lactantius and Boethius, whose writings show a great knowledge of poetry. In my view, the man who has not read the poets is, as it were, maimed as regards literature. The poets have many wise and useful things to say about life and how it should be lived; in them are to be found the principles and causes of nature and birth—the seeds, as it were, of all teachings—by their antiquity and their reputation for wisdom they possess a high authority, by their elegance they have acquired a splendor and a distinction, by their nobility and liberality they have so far made themselves a worthy study for free men, that he who knows them not seems to be something of a rustic. Does Homer lack any sort of wisdom that we should refuse him the repute of being most wise? Some say that his poetry provides a complete doctrine of life, divided into periods of peace and war. And indeed in the affairs of war, what has he not told us of the prudence of the general, of the cunning and bravery of the soldier, of the kinds of trickery to be allowed or omitted, of advice, of counsel? Aeneas, being in a certain battle the leader of the Trojans, has driven the Greeks with great force of arms back to their lines, and is recklessly urging his men on, when, just as he is about to throw his entire force against the Greeks, Hector speeds to him and advises him to act with caution and prudence, saying that a man who leads an army needs caution more than reckless bravery. How valuable a precept, by the immortal God, especially coming from the brave Hector! Nowadays our generals, ignoring this counsel and using rashness instead of caution, have brought ruin and slaughter upon themselves and their men. In the same author, we see Iris, having been sent to Agamemnon and found him asleep, rouse him and reprove him for sleeping when so great a responsibility was his and the safety of his people had been committed to his care. Here again, how wise this is!—whether you want to call it a doctrine or a counsel or an admonition. Did Socrates or Plato or Pythagoras ever give better or holier advice to a general? And he has ten thousand more such counsels which I would gladly speak of, did I not fear being too prolix. And again in the affairs of peace his precepts are as many and as excellent.

But come, lest we attribute all to Homer and the Greeks, let us consider the great value of our Vergil's wisdom when he reveals, as from an oracle or from the secret places of nature:

> Know first, the heav'ns, and earth's broad glist'ning fields,
> Fair Cynthia's seat, and far, the starry seas,
> An inward spirit feeds; and through each joint,
> Throughout the shapeless mass infused, doth stir
> A Mind that mingles with the mighty whole.
> Thence man- and cattle-kind, thence soar th'aerial
> Beasts, and thence from 'neath the flashing waves
> Doth Ocean's shudd'ring prodigies come forth;
> Fire throughout each vein doth lively surge
> And every seed tells of its heav'nly birth.

And so on. Can we esteem the philosophers at such a rate when we read passages such as this? Which of them ever laid bare the nature and essence of soul with such knowledge? What about when the same poet, as though divinely inspired, prophesied just before Our Lord's birth in the words:

> Now comes the earth's last age, now in full Time
> Springs th'order new: thus spake the Cumaean rhyme.
> Now comes the Virgin, now Saturnian states
> Return anew, and now from Heaven's gate
> Comes down Heav'n's offspring, Earth's renewed race.

The wisest of the ancients tell us that the divine mind dwells in the poets, and that they are called *vates* because they speak not so much of their own accord as through a divine inspiration, in a kind of higher mental state. Though here Vergil appeals to the authority of the Cumaean Sibyl, who, as Lactantius shows, had predicted the advent of Christ. The Sibyl then did prophesy Christ's coming, but did not clearly reveal the time when He would come; but Vergil, born many ages after the Sibyl, recognized that that time was now come and announced in wonder and amazement "the new offspring sent from Heaven." And still some say we should not read the poets, that we should never taste a branch of literature that I might with exact truth pronounce divine! Such persons are most often those who, having no training in polite learning themselves, in consequence neither understand nor value in literature any excellent thing. My view of the matter is that poetical knowledge is of primary importance in our education, alike for its utility, as aforesaid—that wide and various acquaintance we get with facts—and for the brilliance of its language. Moreover, it is the *quickest* of our studies: we learn it while young when we can concentrate on practically nothing else; its rounded rhythms make it easy to retain; it accompanies us everywhere, and comes back to us spontaneously without need for books so that it can be done even when doing something else. And the degree to which poetry accords with nature may, I think, be seen from the fact that common, uneducated persons without any knowledge of letters or learning, if they have the wit, enjoy the employment of their crude powers in making certain sounds and rhythms. Even when their sense would be better and more easily expressed in prose, they think they have made something worth hearing only when they have stuck it into verse. Again, when Mass is being said in church, we sometimes yawn and fall asleep even when it is being done very beautifully, but when once that poetical refrain breaks out, the *Primo dierum omnium,* or the *Iste Confessor,* or the *Ut queant laxis resonare fibris,* which of us is so earthbound as not to feel some lifting up of the soul, some inspired feeling? It is for this reason that certain of the ancients believed the soul to be a number and a harmony. It was certain (they thought) that all things in accordance with nature enjoyed that which was most similar and related to themselves, and there was nothing which so softened and delighted our souls as harmony and number. But this is another and greater subject. For the moment, this only would I have be understood: that it is to poetry, more than to any other branch of letters, that nature attracts us; that it possesses utility, pleasure, and nobility; and that that man who has no knowledge of it can by no means be said to be liberally educated.

I have, I realize, gone on about poetry rather more than I had at first intended; once started, it is more difficult to control the multitude of ideas that seem to come thronging around of their own accord than to mind what it is one should be saying. But I was the more inclined to do so as I am aware that a prince of your house, if he should happen to hear of this discourse of mine, will be the first to object to it. He is, to be sure, a man of the noblest birth and outstanding for the number and greatness of his virtues, but a stubborn fellow in debate, who is reluctant to abandon a position once taken. So having sometime declared that we should not read the poets, he pursues his error even unto death. But I want no quarrel with him, especially in writing, for though far removed, I owe him the deepest reverence; but I am perfectly willing to ask of a certain other person among those who attack the poets why it is we should not read them. Having no clear case against them, he charges the poets with containing tales of love affairs and unnatural vice. But I would dare affirm that in no other writers can be found so many examples of womanly modesty and goodness: Penelope's chastity and faithfulness to Ulysses, Alcestis' wonderful modesty towards Admetus, the marvelous constancy of both in the face of calamities and long separation from their husbands. Many such instances can be read in the poets, the finest patterns of the wifely arts. Yes; *amours* are sometimes described, such as the tale of Phoebus and Daphne, and of Vulcan and Venus, but who is so doltish as not to understand that such things are fictional and allegorical? The things to be condemned, moreover, are very few, while many are the things that are good and well worth the knowing, as I showed above with Homer and Vergil. It is the height of injustice to forget about the things that truly deserve praise, and to remember only those things that suit one's own argument. "I would be pure," says my austere critic; "I would rather abandon the good in fear of the evil than run the risk of evil in hope of something good; hence I may neither read the poets myself nor allow others to do so." But Plato and Aristotle studied them, and I refuse to allow that they yield to you either in moral seriousness or in practical understanding. Or do you think you see farther than they? "I am a Christian," my critic says; "their mores are not mine." As though honor and moral seriousness were something different then from what they are now! As though the same and even worse cannot be found in the Holy Scriptures! Do we not find there depicted Samson's wild lusts, when he put his mighty head in a wench's lap and was shorn of his strength-giving hair? Is this not poetical? And is this not shameful? I pass over in silence the shocking crime of Lot's daughters, the detestable filthiness of the Sodomites, two circumstances that I, praiser of poets though I be, can hardly suffer myself to relate. Why speak of David's passion for Bathsheba, his crime against Uriah, Solomon's fratricide and his flock of concubines? All of these stories are wicked, obscene, and disgusting, yet do we say that the Bible is not therefore to be read? Surely not. Then neither are the poets to be rejected because of the occasional reference to human pleasures. For my part, whenever I read Vergil's account of the *affaire* of Dido and Aeneas, I am so lost in admiration of his poetical genius that I scarcely attend to the thing itself, knowing it to be a fiction. Other poetical fictions affect me the same way. My concupiscence is not aroused, since I know the circumstances to be fictional and allegorical in intent. When I read the Scriptures, on the contrary, knowing the facts to be true, I suffer temptation. But I don't insist; I am perfectly willing to abandon a little of my ground, especially given that I am addressing a woman. I admit that, just as there are distinctions between nobles and commoners, so too among the poets there are certain grades of respectability. If somewhere a comic poet has made his theme too explicit, if a satirist excoriates vice a little too frankly, let her avert her gaze and not read them. For these are the plebian poets. The aristocrats of poesy, Vergil, I mean, and Seneca and Statius and the others of their sort, must be read if she is not to do without the greatest ornaments of literature. And without them, she may not hope for glory.

In sum, then, the excellence I speak of comes only from a wide and various knowledge. It is needful to read and comprehend a great deal, and to bestow great pains on the philosophers, the poets, the orators and historians and all the other writers. For thus comes that full and sufficient knowledge we need to appear eloquent, well-rounded, refined, and widely cultivated. Needed too is a well-developed and respectable literary skill of our own. For the two together reinforce each other and are mutually beneficial. Literary skill without knowledge is useless and sterile; and knowledge, however extensive, fades into the shadows without the glorious lamp of literature. Of what advantage is it to know many fine things if one has neither the ability to talk of them with distinction or write of them with praise? And so, literary skill and factual knowledge are in a manner of speaking wedded to each other. It was the two joined together that advanced the glory and fame of those ancients whose memory we venerate: Plato, Democritus, Aristotle, Theophrastus, Varro, Cicero, Seneca, Augustine, Lactantius, Jerome, with all of whom we can scarce decide whether it is their knowledge or their literary power that is the greater.

To conclude: the intellect that aspires to the best, I maintain, must be in this way doubly educated, and it is for the sake of acquiring these two knowledges that we mass up our reading; yet we must also take stock of the time at our disposal, devoting ourselves only to the most important and the most useful subjects, and not wasting time with the obscure and profitless. It is religion and moral philosophy that ought to be our particular studies, I think, and the rest studied in relation to them as their handmaids, in proportion as they aid or illustrate their meaning; and it is with this in mind that we must fix upon the poets, orators and other writers. In literary study care should be taken to employ noble precepts and long and perceptive observation, and never to read any but the best and most approved books.

Such are my opinions about the study of literature, though if you hold different views, I shall willingly yield to you. For I do not write as master to pupil (I should not presume so much), but simply as one of the crowd of your admirers, who want to unite my convictions with yours and, as they say, cheer the runner on to victory. Farewell.

Aeneas Silvius

1405–64

And is it not fitting that the king should have a liberal education, that he may garner truth for himself in the books of the philosophers?

THE EDUCATION OF BOYS

Aeneas Silvius Piccolomini (born Enea Silvio de' Piccolomini) was the eldest son of a large noble family in Corsignano, Italy, a town not too far from Siena. He was taught Latin grammar and poetry by a local priest before attending the University of Siena. On his own initiative he read Cicero, Horace, Virgil, and Livy. He studied classics for two years in Florence before returning to Siena, where his family hoped he would practice law. By his own account, he was a wild youth with a zest for life and travel (indeed, he fathered an illegitimate son). He attended the Council of Basel as secretary to a cardinal, wrote a celebrated commentary on the proceedings, and skillfully made his way through the contending factions of bishops. All of this quickly earned him a reputation as a gifted historian and orator

Aeneas Silvius served as secretary to the Holy Roman Emperor Frederick III, who appointed him imperial poet. While at court, he wrote plays, novels, poems, and dialogues, collected a personal library, studied diligently, and promoted classical humanism in letters to his friends and to the nobility. From this point, his rise was meteoric. Soon after his ordination to the priesthood, he was made Bishop of Trieste, and in fairly short order he became bishop of Siena, cardinal, and finally pope (1458–64), adopting the name Pius II. As pope, he continued to write and edit. He dreamed of a new crusade to conquer Constantinople, which had fallen to the Turks in 1453, and died as he headed off to lead the troops.

THE SELECTION

The Education of Boys (De liberorum educatione) was written in 1450. It is a lengthy treatise addressed to Ladislaus, king of Bohemia and Hungary and prince of Austria. The young king was only nine or ten years old at the time (and he ended up dying at the age of eighteen). The treatise borrows extensively from Leonardo Bruni's translation of Basil's *Address to Young Men,* Quintilian's *Institutes,* (Pseudo-)Plutarch's *On Bringing Up a Boy,* and John of Salisbury's *Policraticus,* often using long passages verbatim. Aeneas also relies throughout on Plato, Cicero, the Bible, Jerome, Augustine, and many others, combining seamlessly the classical and Christian traditions. After a long salutation to the young king, Aeneas describes the benefits of physical training and health and then proceeds to discuss liberal learning in detail. In the sections included here, Aeneas extols the blessings of liberal education, recalls to the king's attention the eternal value of religious instruction, recommends the best Latin authors and works (for Aeneas did not read Greek), defends secular learning, urges him to form his character, and finally anticipates a future treatise on ethics better suited to the king's maturity.

from The Education of Boys

. . . After this brief statement of what we think had to be said on the care of the body, we now hasten to the education of the mind. In this matter we desire you to be convinced that there is nothing that men possess on earth more precious than intellect, and that other goods of human life which we pursue are truly insignificant and unworthy. "Nobility is beautiful but it is a good not one's own; riches are precious but they are the possession of fortune; glory is pleasant but it is inconstant; beauty is becoming but it is fleeting and ephemeral; health is desirable but indeed subject to change; you desire strength but it easily declines in sickness or old age." Nothing is more excellent than intellect and reason. "These no attack of fortune may take away, no calumny may tear asunder. And although all the others are lessened by time, yet age increases knowledge and reason. War, carrying away each possession and bearing all along, is unable to uproot doctrine. When Demetrius had levelled conquered Megara to the ground, he asked Stilpo, a philosopher coming from this place, whether he had lost anything that belonged to him. Stilpo replied, 'No indeed, for war takes no spoils from virtue.' But when Gorgias inquired of Socrates whether the king of the Persians was happy, Socrates replied: 'I do not know how much virtue and knowledge he has.' Accordingly, happiness endures because of these two and not because of the goods of fortune." Take this maxim, and entrust it to your memory, King Ladislaus, destined to be most rich: "Although extensive realms await you, still you cannot be called happy unless, endowed with virtue, you abound in the goods of the mind more than in those of fortune." For kingdoms and the wealth of the world are no more the property of their possessors than of anyone else, but, "as in the game of dice, now they pass here, now they are returned hither. The firm possession of virtue is alone unchangeable for the living and the dead, and Solon rightly said concerning riches, 'we shall not exchange riches for virtue.'" Therefore while riches flow upon you take care lest virtue be wanting, without which no one merits the name either of king or of man. As in the winter it is fitting to endure hardships with tranquillity, "so in boyhood good morals ought to be assumed as the best provision for an old age of virtue." Who knows the changeable fortunes of life? There is nothing fixed under the sun; now men are rich, now they are poor, now they rule, again they serve; now they rejoice in health, again they are sick. "No one knows in the morning how evening will turn out." No one has so many protecting deities that he can promise himself the morrow. "Wherefore Theseus," as Cicero says is related in Euripides, "was accustomed to say, 'For since I remembered what I had heard from a seer, I was contemplating my future miseries. I was always planning either bitter death or sad flight of exile or some other weight of evil, that if any misfortune should chance to happen, no sudden care might tear me unprepared.'" But nothing offers a surer refuge against the attacks of unpropitious fortune than philosophy. "Hence when Dionysius the Younger, expelled from power and driven into exile, was asked what profit to him were Plato and philosophy, he replied: 'That I might hear with tranquil and calm spirit just such a change of fortune.'" Therefore whether circumstances be unpropitious or propitious to us we ought to have recourse to philosophy, which is the study of virtue, and of which kings especially should be lovers. Many things are necessary for the king, who as Aristotle judged, is a kind of living law. The burden of government is great, for a king must strive not only to save himself but also in accordance with justice to lead the multitude entrusted to him unto the way of salvation and peace. For it is written: "An unwise king will be the ruin of his people, but a wise one will enrich his cities." Truly also Vegetius says: "No one ought to know more or better than a ruler whose prudence should profit all his subjects." And so when Solomon felt the burden of great responsibility and had the choice of requesting whatsoever he wished from the Lord, he begged: "Give to your servant a docile heart that can judge your people and decide between good and evil." When Philip of Macedon was advising his son Alexander, he ordered him to heed Aristotle and to pursue philosophy, and he added: "May you not do many things of such a nature which I regret to have done."

Wherefore we think that you ought to be convinced as a boy destined to rule that the study of philosophy is necessary; "but philosophy, the mother of all arts," which "Plato thinks the gift," and Cicero "the invention of the gods," cannot easily be comprehended without learning. "This will lead you first to divine worship, then to justice which arises from the human race being formed into a society, then to modesty and greatness of soul, and will remove from your soul the darkness as if from your eyes," that you may see "all that is above or below, the beginning, end, and middle of everything." Who therefore would be unwilling to toil over learning when such great fruit is perceived from it, in which there is knowledge of good and evil, which refers to our past, regulates the present, and foretells the future? Every age without learning is dark; and an illiterate ruler cannot do without another's guidance. And since the courts of kings are filled with flatterers, who will speak the truth to the ruler? And is it not fitting that the king should have a liberal education, that he may garner truth for himself in the books of the philosophers? "Indeed Demetrius of Phalerum advised king Ptolemy to procure books dealing with kingdoms and empires and to read them thoroughly; for what friends do not dare to advise kings, these matters are found written in books."

Therefore greatest attention and zeal must be given to letters. It was once asked at what age boys ought to be assigned to learning. Hesiod thought not before the age of seven, since "that seemed the earliest age" capable of instruction and susceptible of labor; Eratosthenes likewise enjoined the same. But "Aristophanes and Chrysippus," with whom Quintilian agrees, held that "no time should be free from care." Therefore, training should have begun from the very cradle so that nurses might have contributed something to you. "These nurses Chrysippus would have wise, if possible," that no contagion might be contracted from them, for the worse things cling more tenaciously and "good things are easily changed into worse." "The words of a mother" seasoned with patience and elegance have often been profitable to sons, as many write concerning "Cornelia the mother of the Gracchi," whose eloquence redounded upon her sons. It makes a great deal of difference whether mothers or anyone else who rear boys be polished or coarse, prudent or foolish. But you have now escaped from the yoke of a nurse; you lost your mother, very brilliant and eloquent beyond measure, before you could know her. But let us dismiss the past, more to be lamented than reformed. Let us turn to your present age.

We believe that you were instructed as is befitting a Christian, that you know the Lord's Prayer, the Salutation of the Blessed Virgin, the Gospel of John, the Creed, some prayers, what sins are mortal, the Gifts of the Holy Ghost, the Commandments of Almighty God, the Works of Mercy, and finally the way of saving the soul and leading it to heaven. We do not doubt that you are convinced that after this life another exists, which will be joyful and sweet for the good, bitter and irksome to the evil. For not only the Sacred Books but also pagan literature show this. "Socrates," as is found in Cicero, "argued that there is a twofold path, and two courses for souls departing from the body; for those who have polluted themselves with human vices and shameful deeds and have surrendered themselves wholly to unlawful pleasures or in offending the state have committed outrages, there is a certain road removed from the assembly of the gods; but for those who have kept themselves pure and chaste and were imitators of the life of the gods in human body, there lies open an easy return to them from whom they set out." What shall we say, we to whom the Gospels have been preached, and who can seem to know rather than to believe the incarnation of our Saviour, confirmed by so many miracles? We, indeed, if we have the right attitude, shall judge "that this life of man is of no value at all," and we shall decide that nothing must be considered good which is not useful for the next life. And so in this life nothing can be called excellent: "dignity, a long line of ancestors, strength of body, beauty, stature, honors received from all men, royal power. But our hopes will have to pass beyond these and plan everything with a view to preparation for the other life." But to point out what this life is, "or how it will be lived, is more of a task than we have undertaken for the present. Besides, this matter requires older scholars than you to be fully comprehended." But let it suffice to have said this: "If anyone should imagine all the happiness since the creation of men and should gather it into one whole, truly he will find it to equal but a small part of those goods; and that all human joys collected together are further removed from the least good of that life than a shadow and dream from reality. The Sacred Books lead directly to this life, instructing us in secrets to whose profound sense, because of your age, you may not yet penetrate," but it is to your advantage to be trained in other books of learned men. For as Basil says: "We must apply ourselves to poets, orators, and other writers, and to all men from whom some profit may come to us for training our intellect." But since literature continually cries out that God must be worshipped beyond all else, you will first of all give yourself and entrust yourself to Him; He is your Creator, your Father, and your Master; you owe everything to Him. And since all men ought to give thanks to God, do you especially continue to be very grateful and serve Him through whose bounty you have been born a king. You could have been born one of the common people or one of the peasants, but the inscrutable judgment of God has placed you upon a lofty throne. You should not be elated, nor swollen with pride, nor lord it over others, because what has been given to you might have been given to another. The greater you were born, the more humbly you ought to conduct yourself, to bow before religion, to be present at the divine offices. All else easily serves him to whom divine worship is dear. "Seek ye first the kingdom of God," says Holy Scripture, "and after this all things shall be added unto you." Although "the Romans" were pagans, "they considered that all things must be placed second to religion; even in those affairs in which they wished the glory of the greatest majesty to be observed, the imperial powers did not hesitate to help the state carry out religious rites, thus thinking that they would be the rulers of human affairs if they had well and faithfully served the divine power." What ought we to do who have a knowledge of the true God? Do not think that religion is subject to you, even though you rejoice in the name of a great ruler. Not the master, but the son of the Church, you are subject to the authority of the priests in the things that are of God. Although emperor Theodosius was very powerful and governed the Roman empire, still he bent his neck before Ambrose, bishop of the Church of Milan, and humbly performed the penance imposed. Constantine always displayed the greatest reverence for the priesthood and did not wish to pronounce judgment over the bishops in the Council of Nicaea, saying that gods should not be judged by men. Nor is this strange; for Clement, who succeeded Peter in the apostolic office, said that all the rulers of the earth and all men ought to be obedient and bow their heads before priests; but that the latter should be judged by the Lord alone, for they are His and not another's. And who is he who would judge the servant of another? Now if men do not permit this, neither shall the God of gods and the Lord of lords allow this in any manner. So that most holy bishop says that Peter, the keeper of the keys of eternal life, preached. You therefore will honor priests, who are the servants of God; and will not allow them to be oppressed, burdened, nor afflicted with any injuries. You will not say that a priest is foolish, unworthy, impure; this is nothing to you; he has his judge; whatever crime he commits will not be unavenged. You will not listen to dissolute and immoderate youths who through flattery endeavor to persuade you otherwise. . . .

The disciplines are interconnected and a person cannot gain one unless he acquires the light of another. For who has the art of correct speaking unless he has seen the poets, and read the historians and orators? Whence, except from these, is whatever there is of reason, of antiquity, of authority, and of custom in grammar? Wherefore, the second part of grammar requires not only that the aforementioned authors be read and understood, "but that every class of writers" who have been tried, approved, and discussed, should be read and understood, "not only because of their contents but also because of their words which frequently receive their authority from writers." Therefore it is advantageous and necessary that your teachers be very industrious in collecting, investigating, and explaining them to you. The ancients decreed "that reading should commence with Homer and Vergil, although there is need of mature judgment to comprehend their virtues. But for the acquisition of this judgment, there is abundance of time nor will they be read but once. In the meantime, the mind of the boy will be exalted by the sublimity of the heroic verse, and will conceive ardor from the magnitude of affairs and be endowed with the noblest sentiments," as Augustine also approves in his first book of the *City of God*. But I do not see how Greek can be given to you, as a teacher of this subject is lacking. But I would say that you should acquire it, if you have the opportunity; for a knowledge of Greek, which not a few of the Latin emperors learned, would help not a little to direct the kingdom of Hungary, in which there are many Greeks, and would contribute much light to your Latin speech. For with me the authority of great Cato, who as an old man gave his attention to Greek letters, prevails more than that of Gaius Marius, who thought it disgraceful to learn this language whose teachers were slaves. We have the desire to learn this language but the opportunity is lacking; hence let us speak of Latin authors, of whom there is not such a great lack that with them we cannot acquire a fuller and more elegant Latin speech.

Soon the throng of those who wish to seem more theologians than they really are will revile me because I am about to speak of the poets and to urge the reading of them. "Why do you bring poets from Italy to us," they will say, "and why do you hasten to corrupt the holy morals of Germany with the effeminate licentiousness of the poets? Was not 'Marcus Noblior branded as shameful by your Romans for bringing the poet Ennius into Aetolia?' Did not your Cicero whom you follow, whom you admire, say in his *Tusculan Disputations* that the poets were rightly banished by Plato from that state which he founded, since he required the best morals and the best conditions for his state? What about Boethius? Did he not call the muses of the poets 'prostitute actresses?' What about St. Jerome? Did he not relate that he was beaten by an angel because he was eagerly pursuing profane learning? Depart from us and take your poets with you." And likewise certain lawyers, whose doctrine is contained not in texts but in glosses, and who think that nothing in civil law can be preferable to the books of the *authenticum*.

We shall reply to these objectors in a few words: if all the men of Germany should think as they, we shall depart most willingly rather than remain with so much ignorance or blindness. But there are also learned men in these regions who greatly cherish the poets and orators and who are not moved by the arguments of their adversaries. For although Noblior had his detractors, still he did not yield to the multitude disparaging him; and Africanus the Elder imitated him, since not content with having loved the poet, he commanded that his statue be placed on the tomb of his own ancestors, so that if there should be a question of authority, I would say that Africanus and Nobilior carry greater weight than the rest of the multitude could have. The authority of Plato, cited by Cicero, can be refuted without difficulty. Hear what Cicero added; these are his words: "But why are we angry with the poets? Some philosophers may be found who said that pain was the greatest of evils." And then he cites examples of philosophers who introduced a pernicous doctrine. Wherefore the philosophers ought to be expelled on the same grounds on which Plato excluded the poets. But what should I say concerning theologians? What error against faith has not arisen from theologians? Who introduced the Arian madness, separated the Greeks from the Church, seduced the Bohemians, except theologians? Formerly the Romans drove the whole class of physicians from the city because many crimes were found among them, but afterwards, when the guilty were punished, they received back the innocent. What about the orators? Did not Cicero say that many cities were utterly destroyed because of the eloquence of wicked persons? As not all orators, doctors, theologians, philosophers ought to be rejected because of some evil among them, similarly not all poets should be shunned because of the vices of some. Otherwise Plato himself ought to have been driven from that state which he formed, since he was devoted to tragedy; and in Macrobius are found his poems from which it is assumed that he was a poet; nor would Cicero have remained in that state, since not only was he a very great admirer of the poets but he also wrote three books on his times in a poetic way and in verse. That Boethius seems to reprove, demands not so much explanation as laughter. For who would refrain from laughing when it is reported that a poet is condemned by a poet? For is not Boethius poetical everywhere? When philosophy itself converses with him, it does so very frequently in verses and imaginative passages. How many stories are there not in his works, and how many kinds of metre? Boethius seems to be similar to him who swore that we ought not to swear. But we do not impute to Boethius, a great philosopher and poet, what these think, but we judge that he was of another mind, concerning which it would now be tedious to speak.

I come now to Jerome, whose footsteps I should like all living to follow. For so we should all be endowed with eloquence and holiness of life. What need is there to censure him, who, after he had pursued all profane studies, then said he was beaten with blows. I am inclined to think in regard to this affair as the familiar proverb of the Florentines has it. For they say, "When you have completely filled your home in every quarter, then be mindful that you live rightly." He abounds plentifully in poetic words and there is never a line of his which is not redolent with Tullian eloquence, although he rejected Cicero and all pagan books. So I would say of the other doctors of the Church, whose fluency, which would otherwise be silent, the poets adorned. And it is not strange when the leader of the Christian army and the invincible orator, the Apostle Paul, very frequently read the rolls of the poets, whose verses are found incorporated throughout his Epistles. For, as Jerome remarks, "what he wrote to Titus, 'The Cretans are always liars, evil beasts, slothful bellies,' is a verse of the poet Epimenides. In another place he employs a line of Menander: 'Evil morals corrupt good manners.'" It is not strange if the translation in Latin does not preserve the metre word for word, since the Homeric verse in the same tongue scarcely does. There is a wide field and rich material for disputation. An almost infinite number can be added who assert that profane literature and especially the poets should be read; indeed, Cyprian, a man distinguished for eloquence, was attacked, as the martyr Firmian relates, because in writing against Demetrius he employed the testimony of prophets and apostles, which Demetrius had said were imaginary and invented, and not rather that of philosophers and poets whose authority as a pagan he could not contradict." But why cite other witnesses after Paul? Or to whom will he give credance who does not believe Paul? Let whoever wishes follow his own error; we with Paul and the other saints and the most learned men shall not only not avoid the reading of the poets but we shall urge that it be embraced in every way and by rule.

We do not lay it down as a principle that "all that poets write should be read without exception," and that boys "should study them excessively." For since there are many erotic and vicious things in them, the mind must not be applied to all that is said by them, just as not all theologians nor philosophers must be heard. "But whenever they recount the words or deeds of good men," then the reader "ought to be incited and inflamed with his whole mind, and should strive to be as far as possible like them. But when they treat of wicked men, the reader ought to avoid such imitation." Listen to Basil, that holy and learned man: "We," he said, "praise the poets, but not when they relate contentions, nor when they portray buffoons, lovers, drunkards, or sarcastic people, nor when they define happiness as consisting in a rich table and dissolute song; and not at all when they say anything about the gods, and especially when they so describe them as if they were many and discordant." And a little later he says, "The same must be said of the other writers and especially when they are being read for pleasure." And again, "But then we embrace the orators, especially when they either extol virtues or attack vices. Therefore in the reading of poets and other writers it will be proper to imitate the bees. For as others indeed take nothing from the flowers beyond the fragrance and color, the bees know whence to draw the honey; likewise those who follow not the pleasantness of words alone are able to take some fruit. Moreover, the bees do not approach all flowers equally, and if they approach any, they do not drain them all, but that having been taken which is suitable for their work, they suffer the rest to flourish."

I am not able to refrain from again employing the testimony of St. Jerome, that we may teach how to supply a remedy to the place whence a wound was inflicted. When he, in a letter written to an orator of the city, pointed out that Paul was not ignorant of profane literature and that he had made uses of the verses of the poets, he added that he had read "in Deuteronomy the precept of the Lord, that the head of a captive woman should be shaven, her eyebrows and all the hair and nails of her body should be removed and then she might be married." To this he added of himself: "What is strange if I wish to change pagan learning because of the charm of eloquence and the beauty of its parts from a hand-maid and captive to an Israelite? For whatever idolatry was in it is dead, whatever pleasure, error, or licentiousness is either cut off or shaven." Now you have a scheme for reading the poets and other authors. "Far when you have received from them whatever is in accordance with truth, you will pass over all the rest as you avoid the thorns in gathering roses. So accepting as much as has been usefully written, you will decline the rest which can do much harm. For in the beginning of any discipline, no matter what it may be, you should consider and direct it towards the end. And since we ascend from this life to a better one by virtue, and virtue has been praised much by the poets, much by the historians, and much more by the philosophers, we ought to attend especially to their words. A certain habit of virtue and a familiarity with it, instilled in the minds and youthful souls of boys, has no little usefulness, since they are generally very attentive, and whatever is learned at this tender age is almost indelible"; whence Horace says: "An earthen pot, once it has been stained, will preserve the odor fresh." So from the reading of ancient and modern authors who have written prudently, a twofold advantage will attend you. For by the study of virtue you will make your life better, and you will acquire grammar and skill in the usage of the best and most elegant words and a great store of maxims.

Receive this further instruction and learn what authors you should read while you are a boy. They are poets, historians, philosophers, and orators. For we shall reserve the theologians for another time, although some of those included under the name of philosophers might be given to a boy without danger as we shall afterwards indicate. For there is nothing which philosophy may ignore. Let the discernment of your teacher assist you in choosing the poets who may be entrusted to you. Among the epic poets let him prefer before all Vergil, whose eloquence, whose reputation, is so great that it can be augmented by no praise, diminished by no censure. In him the careful reader will discover the different

kinds of style, which are thought to "be four: brevity, fullness, simplicity, and elegance."
Lucan, a distinguished author of history, and Statius, who is quite polished, should not
be neglected. Ovid is everywhere concise, everywhere delightful, but in many places too
wanton; yet his most famous work, to which he gave the name *Metamorphoses*, ought in
no wise to be cast aside, as the knowledge of this on account of the skill displayed in the
stories is of no small profit. Others who write in heroic verse are far inferior to these and
ought to be called versifiers rather than poets; I would consider that Claudian and the
author of the *Argonauts* least contemptible. Only three satirists are found among us today:
Horace, Juvenal, and Persius. Martialis also perhaps may seem a satirist, but his verse has
not observed the laws of satire. Horace, a little younger than Vergil, was a man of much
learning; he is useful everywhere whether you read his *odes*, his *epodes*, his *satires*, or his
Epistles. Still, there are certain things in him which I would not wish to read nor explain
to you while you are still a boy. Juvenal, a poet of great genius, has said many things too
indiscreetly, yet in some satires he has shown himself so religious that he seems to yield to
no teacher of our faith. Persius is too obscure but is useful. Martial is harmful; although
flowery and elegant, he is packed with thorns, so that he does not permit the roses to be
plucked without pricking. All those who write elegies should be withheld from a boy. For
such as Tibullus, Propertius, Catullus, and whatever of Sappho has been translated among
us, are very effeminate. For they continuously describe erotic things and lovers complain
that they are deserted. Therefore, let them be put aside or let them be reserved for a more
mature age. The writers of comedy can contribute much to eloquence, since they extend
to all persons and affections. Of these we have only two, Plautus and Terence. The writers
of tragedy are also very useful for boys, but besides Seneca, the nephew of the great Seneca, we have no Latin tragedian except Gregory Corario Venetu, who, when I was a youth,
turned into tragedy the story of Tereus as found in Ovid. And since gravity and elegance
are desired in speech, you will find the former in tragedy and the latter in comedy. But
your teacher ought to take care that he may not seem to urge anything vicious while he
selects comedies and tragedies. But let him order that the characters who speak and the
emotions which follow be considered and meditated upon.

Indeed there is a galaxy of orators who can be read, but Cicero is the most brilliant
of all and sufficiently pleasant and clear to beginners. He can not only be profitable but
also loved, and I think that his books *de officiis*, are not only useful but even necessary for
you. Ambrose also wrote, in imitation of Cicero, a *de officiis*, a work not to be despised
which I should think ought to be read most suitably with his, so that what of Cicero is not
in harmony with our faith may be corrected from Ambrose. The works of Lactantius are
elegant; there is nothing crude in Jerome; the books of Augustine are faultless; you can
make use of Gregory with no small advantage. In our day the volumes of Leonardo Bruni,
Guarino of Verona, Poggio of Florence, Ambrose the monk of Camaldoli, are concise and
fruitful for readers. Boys ought to read historians also, such as Livy and Sallust, although
to understand them, there is need of maturity. Then we have Justin and Quintus Curtius
and Arrian, whom Petrus Paulus translated, in all of whom we find truth and not fables.
The History of Alexander ought to be run through. And to these men Valerius, the historian and philosopher, is not unworthy to be added. Suetonius should not be entrusted to
a boy. Also stories from Genesis, the Books of Kings, the Book of Macchabees, the Books
of Judith, Esdras, Esther, the Gospels, the Acts of the Apostles will be taken up with great

profit. "For," as Cicero says, "history is the witness of time, the light of truth, the teacher of life, the messenger of antiquity." Therefore it is advantageous to know as many histories as possible and to train yourself in them, so that, by the example of others, you may know how to follow what is useful and to avoid what is harmful. Still we do not wish you to be engaged in superfluous work, and it is sufficient to have learned what is taken from or related by noted authors. But I would not permit in any manner the histories of the Bohemians or of the Hungarians to be given to a boy, if I had any authority. For they are written by the ignorant, containing many foolish things, many lies, no maxims, no ornaments of style. As Pliny says, no book is so bad that nothing useful can be taken from it, and therefore it may seem proper to entrust every sort of writer to the reader; yet they ought not to be given to boys but to men already learned. For unless boys be steeped in the best things, their intellects are depraved and they can acquire no discernment. And now, concerning the second part of grammar, you shall consider sufficient has been said. But we should, however, make one last observation, that these authors ought not to be approached all at the same time, and that we do not think that you must study them all necessarily and with great zeal, lest the enormity of the task should render literature hateful to you. . . .

Perhaps some one might ask how "these things are to be learned or whether they can be transmitted and learned. Some deny this because the mind is confused and wearied by so many studies of such diversity. But these do not understand sufficiently how great is the power of the human mind, which is so busy, so active and which directs attention in every corner, so to say, that it can not even do only one thing but it expends all its power on many things, not only on the same day but even at the same moment of time. Who would not become dulled if he were to endure for a whole day one teacher of one art? The spirit will be refreshed by a change as the stomach is invigorated by a moderate variety of food. Farmers cultivate at the same time their fields, their vineyards, their olive trees, and their groves; they care for their meadows, their herds, their flocks, and their bees." Why may not boys, whose dispositions are much more docile than those of young men, pursue the various disciplines, I would not say at the same moment but at the same time? Therefore those who direct you as a boy will take care that throughout the day, you listen to different teachers, that you devote yourself now to grammar, now to dialectic, and now to another study, and they will not refuse a proper time for play and a proper time for bodily training.

But although the intellect is especially enlightened by studies of this kind, it is not immediately shown what is honorable, what is disgraceful, what is just, what must be chosen and what avoided. The known marks of virtue are not too deeply hidden in the poets, orators, and historians; from these things you must rise higher with all your affection; you must pass over to philosophy itself concerning which we made mention in the beginning. But here perhaps one of your companions will say: "What are you doing, Aeneas? While the boy is sweating over the arts, seven of which you mentioned before, shall he pursue philosophy? Why do we return to this subject?" But such a one does not know what the name of philosopher connotes, the inventor of which name, it is agreed, was Pythagoras. For formerly when good and learned men were called wise he fled pride and wished to be called a philosopher, that is a lover of wisdom, not a wise man. Wisdom embraces not only the seven arts mentioned above but professes the knowledge of all things and of the causes by which these things exist. Wherefore one will not be called a philosopher because he has pursued the seven arts, but because he has acquired a part of philosophy. Philosophers at the beginning regarded natural causes alone and followed Thales, the Milesian, who is said to have first disputed concerning them. Then came Socrates who called moral philosophy out of the heavens. Thereupon it came about that philosophy was divided into two parts: one is called natural and the other, moral. But through the intervention of Plato's divine genius, it was decided to add a third member, which is called rational.

But up to this point we have said little about the morals which should be learned from philosophy. Wherefore at the conclusion of the book but not at the conclusion of study we again send the boy to moral philosophy. "For this will point out with certain reason, what worship must be paid to the Divine Majesty, how we should act toward parents, nobles, foreigners, officials, soldiers, friends, wives, citizens, peasants, and slaves." This will teach you, O illustrious king, to despise avarice, a too great love of money, which as Sallust says no wise man ever desires. "This will advise you to observe modesty towards women, to hold your children and your neighbors dear, not to serve with the servants, to respect your elders, to obey the laws, to repress your anger, to despise pleasures, to pity the oppressed, to assist with your wealth, to confer worthy rewards, to grant justice to each and every one," to punish the guilty and, what is most important, "it will not allow you to be puffed up with joy at the favorable turns of fortune nor to be cast down with sadness at adverse misfortunes," and will offer you a way by which you can live rightly and usefully command your subjects. For all these things should not to be withheld from a boy, provided that a choice of books be made. Pleasing, clear and open, elegant and polished books should be given to him, as we said above. To the books mentioned can be added Cicero's *Tusculan disputations, de senectute, de anticitia,* and whatever he has written concerning morals. Seneca is to be received as useful and also Pliny in his Letters, and Boethius in his *de consolatione.* And I would not deny that more books of learned men than these exist which can safely be given to boys. But I demand discernment on the part of the teacher, that he be acquainted with books which are elegant and concise and acknowledged as authorities. But since that part of philosophy which is called ethics leaves no part of the human life untouched, but governs youths, young men and old, we believe that for the present we have pointed out sufficiently how much should be given to the boy and from what sources they should be learned. We shall have to speak more in detail in other books as the periods of your life will require if God, the Creator of the world, and the Author of your soul will prolong our life—unless after we have said that you ought to read so many distinguished authors we shall judge it more modest to be silent than to speak anything further. But do you meanwhile so endeavor to practice and learn what you have been taught is proper for a boy, that you may be most eager for the other parts of this work. Farewell.

Erasmus

c. 1469–1536

Children owe little gratitude to parents who are their parents only in the physical sense of the word, but have failed to provide them with the proper upbringing.

ON EDUCATION FOR CHILDREN

⚜

A native of Rotterdam in the Netherlands, Desiderius Erasmus attended schools in Gouda, Utrecht, and Deventer. He became a leading humanist scholar and prolific author, famous throughout Europe for his edition of the Greek New Testament, translations of classical texts, brilliant satires, letters, and countless treatises. He angered many in the Catholic Church, however, with his biting accusations of worldliness, doctrinal confusion, and corruption. Nevertheless, he also opposed Luther and the Protestant movement for dividing Christendom. He traveled throughout Europe, was the toast of royal courts, and taught in Paris. He was a close friend of Sir Thomas More's, spending many happy and productive years in his home. Erasmus lived for a time in Oxford, and lectured at Cambridge University in 1511–14. At Oxford he began a long friendship with John Colet, an important educational reformer who later refounded St. Paul's school in London. He also admired the work of another Oxford professor, the Spanish scholar Juan Luis Vives. Regarding Erasmus's contribution to educational thought, Craig R. Thompson writes that "in his lifetime no one did more to advance the intelligent study of classical languages and literature and to explain their value for Christians."[1] His educational treatises bear the imprint of Plato, Isocrates, Xenophon, Cicero, Seneca, Quintilian, Plutarch, Augustine, and Jerome. He is buried in the Minster overlooking the Rhine River in Basel, Switzerland.

---

1. *Collected Works of Erasmus*, Vol. 23, xxvi.

THE SELECTIONS

Erasmus's dialogues *Antibarbari (The Antibarbarians)* were begun in the late 1480s and the first edition appeared in 1500. These dialogues defend humanist education, particularly the use of Greek and Latin classics. All things can and must be brought into subjection to Christ, Erasmus argues, and literature helps bring us to our full humanity. Included here is a fine discussion of Augustine and his use of the classical past, including the important metaphor of the Israelites "spoiling" the Egyptians. In these excerpts, the character Jacob Batt is speaking.

   On Education for Children (De pueris ac liberaliter instituendis declamatio) was written about 1509 but not published until 1529. Erasmus relies on Quintilian and (Pseudo-) Petrarch, and writes angrily against prosperous parents who neglect the proper education of their children and fail to distinguish between doing well and being good.

   The Education of a Christian Prince (1516) bears obvious similarities to the two other works excerpted here. Erasmus returned often to the same authors and anecdotes. This treatise is of particular note because it is addressed to the young Prince Charles, soon to become the Holy Roman Emperor Charles V, heir to the Austrian and Spanish thrones and monarch over the largest empire the world had ever known. The entire work has some bearing on education broadly defined, but the brief section included here concerns the scope of the work as a whole and offers advice on the choice of a proper tutor for the prince.

from The Antibarbarians

THE PAGANS PERFECTED SYSTEMS OF KNOWLEDGE ACCORDING TO THE DIVINE PLAN, NOT FOR US TO SCORN THEM, BUT FOR OUR USE

When I look a little more closely at the wonderful arrangement, the harmony as they call it, of things, it always seems to me—and not to me only: many of the weightiest authors have thought the same—that it was not without divine guidance that the business of discovering systems of knowledge was given to the pagans. For the great and eternal Disposer, who is wisdom itself, establishes all things with consummate skill, differentiates them with beautiful play of interchange, and orders them with perfect rightness, so that each balances another in a marvellous way; nor does he allow anything to move at random in all the immense variety of the world. It was he who willed that the Golden Age in which he had chosen to be born was to be sovereign over all epochs which came before or followed after; it pleased him that whatever existed in nature should be put to use for increasing the happiness and glory of that time. He himself promised that this should be done: "I, if I be lifted up from the earth," he says, "will draw all unto me." Here it seems to me that he most aptly uses the word *traho*, "I draw," so that one may understand that all things, whether hostile or heathen or in any other way far removed from him, must be drawn, even if they do not follow, even against their will, to the service of Christ. What of that great universal harmony, which in the eyes of St Augustine meant that not even bad things were created without intention? All those allegories, signs, and mysteries existing from the beginning of the world—in which direction did they point? Why, to the century of Christ. What about the whole Mosaic law, all those rites and ceremonies, those forms of worship, those promises and prophecies? Is not Paul the witness that all these things happened to them for examples? Not to speak of the transfer of empires, what was the purpose of "founding the Roman nation with such vast effort," and through such great disasters and bloodstained victories subjugating the entire world to the City which held sway? Was it not according to the divine plan, so that when the Christian religion was born, it might spread abroad the more easily into different parts of the world, diffused as it were from one head into the separate members? And again, what was his intention in allowing almost the whole earth to be entangled with such lunatic, scandalous religions? Why, so that when the One arose, it would overturn all the others with the utmost glory. Nothing fine is ever done without struggle.

It was Greece, devoted to study, which discovered the arts; then Latium entered into rivalry with her, and was the victor as far as concerns war, but barely equalled her achievements in literature and oratory. Some concerned themselves with searching out the hidden causes of things; others, bound by the fetters of Prometheus, observed the regular revolutions of the heavenly lights. There were those who tried to explore divine mysteries; one discovered methods of argument and another laws of oratory; some portrayed the customs of men with great sagacity, and for some their great concern was to hand on to posterity the memory of past deeds. In law, in philosophy, how the ancients laboured! Why did all this happen? So that we on our arrival could hold them in contempt? Was it not rather that the best religion should be adorned and supported by the finest studies?

Everything in the pagan world that was valiantly done, brilliantly said, ingeniously thought, diligently transmitted, had been prepared by Christ for his society. He it was who supplied the intellect, who added the zest for inquiry, and it was through him alone that they found what they sought. Their age produced this harvest of creative work, not so much for them as for us; just as every region cannot supply every commodity, nor (as Virgil says) does every land grow everything, so it seems to me that every century is allotted its own gifts. Many of the philosophers wore out their lives and their brains in seeking the highest good; but the real highest good, the perfect gift, was reserved by Christ for his own time. However he did not intend all the rest to be useless and done to no purpose. We see with our own eyes how in material things nature takes care that no portion of time shall slip away uselessly. Look at the trees (the sight of them suggests this example to me): in early spring they supply sap to nourish the leaves, and now you see the leaves are joined by flowers, and how much pleasure it gives us to look at them. As summer comes, these little flowers swell out gradually into the pulp of the fruit; in autumn, the trees will stand weighed down with ripe apples, and, as soon as they let them fall, once again that season which passes from autumn into winter is spent in making new shoots for the coming summer. Even winter itself is not idle, but reestablishes things in an interval of quiet; the same effect is produced by the revolving of the heavenly bodies, disposed in such varying ways. There is a great discord in nature which is the completest concord. All things, both particular and universal, are carried in the same direction; they all face the same way, tend towards one thing. So while Christ, the greatest and best of disposers, allocated to his own century in a special way the recognition of the highest good, he gave the centuries immediately preceding a privilege of their own: they were to reach the thing nearest to the highest good, that is, the summit of learning. What could man acquire, by virtuous striving, that is more valuable than knowledge? Indeed, on this point God was willing to consult the laziness or the leisure of the Christians, by taking away a great deal of the hard work from us, who were likely to have much to do elsewhere. It is much easier to master a thing which is already worked out to the last detail than to invent it. If they had not sown the seed of letters, perhaps we should have had nothing to reap; what should we have discovered by ourselves, we who have never added anything to their inventions, but have damaged many of them and thrown them all into confusion? This makes it all the more ungracious, in fact spiteful, that we should not be willing to accept things freely offered, which were to be of so much use to us, and which cost them so dearly; and we not only refuse a splendid gift, but treat the giver of the gift with contempt, instead of the gratitude we owe him.

IT IS IGNORANCE RATHER THAN ERUDITION WHICH MAKES MEN INSOLENT

. . . Now let us imagine two other people, both worthy men, one, uncouth, the other educated: which is to be preferred to the other? (They shuffle and stammer: just find a man, they say, who has both worth and learning.) I admit that there is a great scarcity of this kind of person, for there are plenty of unlearned and unworthy people everywhere. But why should they stammer when Jerome never did? He freely and at the top of his voice, as they say, put saintly learning above saintly simplicity. "Daniel," he says, "at the end of his most holy vision, says that the righteous shall shine like stars, and the wise"—that is the learned—"like the firmament." Do you see what difference there is between righteous simplicity and learned righteousness? The first is compared to stars, the last to heaven. A little before this he says: "Holy simplicity is profitable only to itself, and however much it builds up the church by the merit of the life lived, it does an equal amount of harm if it does not resist the destroyers." Jerome is right here as in everything; for the more widely a good thing is known, the more influential for good it must be. The man who lives an upright life is indeed doing a great thing, but it is useful only to himself, or at most to the few with whom he passes his days. If learning is added to his upright life, how much the power of his virtue will be increased, more brilliantly and more widely known as if a torch had been set before it! And if he is one of those who can put down in writing the most beautiful meditations of his heart, that is if he is eloquent as well as learned, the usefulness of this man must necessarily be widespread and pervasive, not only among his friends, his equals, his neighbours, but for strangers, for posterity, for the people at the uttermost ends of the earth. Worth without learning will die with its possessor, unless it be commended to posterity in written works. But where there is learned scholarship, nothing stops it from spreading out to all humanity, neither land nor sea nor the long succession of the centuries. I would not like here to bring up an invidious comparison as to which has been of most value to our religion, the blood of the martyrs or the pens of the learned writers. I am not disparaging the glory of the martyrs, which a man could not attain to even by unlimited eloquence; but to speak simply of usefulness to us, we owe more to some heretics than to some martyrs. There was indeed a plentiful supply of martyrs, but very few doctors. The martyrs died, and so diminished the number of Christians; the scholars persuaded others and so increased it. In short, the martyrs would have shed their blood in vain for the teaching of Christ unless the others had defended it against the heretics by their writings. The Christian religion found Good Letters a valuable safeguard in times of stress, and it will not be so ungrateful now, when it has peace and prosperity, as to thrust them into exile—for it was through them that it attained peace and happiness.

I cannot help being amazed at some people who quite deliberately admit that they shun literature; we have already shown how idiotic it is to say they are abstaining from the inventions of the heathen. Is there anything in what they say about wishing to avoid pride? Surely it is not so much because their weak minds tremble as because they want a cover for their indolence that they invent a sin where no sin is. I could believe these people were simply mistaken if they altered their ways when admonished and rebuked; but what kind of religion will that be which for fear of some trifling trouble falls into utter ruin? So while these silly fools, trembling like women, do their stupid best to flee from naughty curiosity, they fall into a different but much more dangerous vice. "It is in vain that you have avoided one vice, if you have been turned to wrong ways by another," says Horace. You have escaped from Scylla to no purpose if you fall into Charybdis; it is no good avoiding the storm only to break up your ship on the rocks. The childish, not to say perverse, timorousness of these people is what David was talking about (that holiest of kings and prophets): "They were afraid where no fear was." For the man who, superstitiously observes the wind will never trust himself to the sea; and one who anxiously watches the clouds will never reap. What could be more disastrous than to raise up imaginary fears where the most distinguished work is to be done, and snore idly away where there is acute and certain danger? With their idiotic solicitude they want to remove the mote of curiosity from our eyes, and do not feel the beam of laziness in theirs. They reproach us with always wanting to learn more when we know more than enough already; but they take no interest in learning the things without which we are not human, or even alive. Supposing we have overstepped the limits, which is the way of honour where honourable things are concerned—to go too far or not far enough? Is it better to exceed or fall short? They are afraid that somewhere in the pagan books they might find something that sounded not quite strict enough to crabbed ears, but they are not afraid of that terrifying word of the Lord, "Thou wicked servant, wherefore gavest thou not my money into the bank, that at my coming I might have required mine own with usury?" So true it is that there is nothing so unpleasing to God as sloth! The prodigal son, who had spent all his substance on harlots, pimps, and cookshops, he joyfully welcomed back; but the servant who returned to him even an undiminished talent was bitterly reproached. God, our parent, imparted to us, as seeds of fine skills, intellect, understanding, memory, and other gifts of the mind, which are talents put out to usury, and if we double them by practice and study, our Lord on his return will praise us as industrious servants and give them to us for our inheritance; but if we bury the talent we have received in the ground, how shall we bear the eyes, the face, the voice of our returning Lord, when others are counting out the profit they have made from what they were given, and we in our indolence present our useless talents? This is where these timorous people should rightly be afraid, not where there is so much profit and so little danger.

AUTHORITIES CONFUTED BY AUTHORITIES

. . . We will hasten on to the rest of the subject when we have quoted one other testimony. I have decided now to be content with two, but they are both weighty. Augustine, a man who was equally outstanding in erudition and holiness, and also of such a strict conscience—not to say hypercritical—that he often seems to me (I say it with apologies to so great a man) to tremble without cause, a thing which is easy to deduce from his life and from his *Confessions* and *Retractations*—Augustine, I say, being the great man he was, would certainly have dissuaded people from secular literature, as they call it, if he had thought it harmful, or useless, or suspect. It is he who, in those books he entitles *On Christian Doctrine*, suggests two kinds of teaching, "which are practised even in Gentile, that is to say pagan, morals," he says (or secular as those people call it). "Of these kinds of teaching, one is concerned with those principles which have been instituted by men, the other with those which have come to their notice either as already established or as divinely instituted. That one," he goes on, "which is established by men is partly a matter of superstition and partly not." To avoid repeating the whole argument, which is a most prolix one, I will omit his actual words and sum up the whole thing briefly.

In the last category, which he calls superstitious, he includes sorcery, incantations, enchantments, spells, divination by sacrifices or bird-flight, soothsaying, necromancy, pyromancy, alphitomancy, hydromancy, geomancy, chiromancy, and other things of the same kind. These belong to the soothsayers and wizards and can only be practised by the aid of wicked spirits, and so he rightly judges them to be what the Christian should shun. Certain types of observations he also assigns to this category because they are most productive of worry and futility: for instance, the interpretation of visions and dreams, inspection of entrails, the flight and song of birds, observation of monsters, thunderstorms, lightning, stars, casting lots, sneezing, weasels or mice running to meet one or squeaking or nibbling at anything, ears ringing or eyes popping, leaves rustling, names and apparitions, and suchlike rubbish.

Under the other heading, of things instituted by men and yet free from superstition, he ranges these: writing, names of things, manner of speech, laws, public decrees, and many other things of this nature. These he not only does not reprove, but thinks they closely concern a Christian man, and he should do his best to learn them.

In the first class, that of notation, he places almost all the liberal disciplines, logic, rhetoric, physics, arithmetic, geometry, music, finally histories and the knowledge of antiquity. I should even be ready to cite the opinion of St Augustine about each one of these, but you must also be willing to hear. On grammar his views are plain enough not to need discussion, and, as to what pertains to dialectic, he argues lengthily and meticulously as usual about dialectical methods, truth and falsity of connections, the consequent and the inconsequent, opposition and definition and partition. He even goes to St Paul for the forms of connections, as he puts it, so that he seems to have wished to teach us if we are ignorant of dialectic. This discipline is commended by him in that same chapter of the treatise (I think I can give the wording, since I have just read it): "But in all kinds of questions which must be examined and solved in theological study, the skilled knowledge of disputation is of the greatest value, so essential is it here to avoid the inclination to quarrel." A little further on: "There are steps in the reasoning process," he says, "carrying with them false opinions, which follow on the error of the person engaged in debate, and may be used as inferences by a learned and good man, so that the one who has produced them will be covered with confusion and abandon his error, because if he insisted on retaining it he would be obliged to stick to the very things he condemns."

So much for dialectics. As for the poets and orators, on whom he has said a great deal, I am purposely omitting them here, intending to return to them in the right place. The other arts, less important certainly, but exacting, Augustine thought likely to be of no little advantage to a theologian, as Quintilian thought they were to an orator; and on the subject of music we have this: "We find metre and music honourably mentioned in many places in Scripture. The errors of Gentile superstition, however, are not to be listened to: they said the nine Muses were the daughters of Jove and Memory." Then, quoting Varro, he explains how the fable began, adding: "But whether it was as Varro narrated or not, we have no need to abandon music because of the superstitions of the unenlightened, if there is anything useful we can take from it for the understanding of Scripture."

The discussion on arithmetic opens as follows: "Even the ignorance of numbers results in inability to understand many things which are symbolically and mystically expressed in the Scriptures." All the complications of the discussions he enters into in the same way about geometry and astronomy it is scarcely profitable to recall. Again he judges the knowledge of natural history particularly necessary to the study of Holy Scripture, because it is scattered all over with the names of animals, plants, stones, and unless you have some idea of the importance and nature of these from the instruction of natural history, you will look pretty rash if you try to explain them. Here is the important point of this passage: "Ignorance of objects makes figurative expressions obscure when we do not know the nature of animals, plants, or stones or other things which occur in Scripture and are used for the sake of some similitude." He continues the subject with pertinence and erudition.

When it comes to the philosophers, who particularly profess to teach the way to happiness, what does he say? It will be a marvel if he does not forbid them to be read. They have dared to proclaim themselves masters of truth, full of universal knowledge, and have thus shown themselves to be the originators of universal error, whose teachings produced almost all our heresies, whose intricate deductions, like so many battering-rams, have been used to beat against the walls of Christian faith. Listen to what this justest of men says about them: "If those who are called philosophers, especially the Platonists, have chanced to say things that are true, and in agreement with our faith, far from fearing these utterances we should claim them for our own, taking them over from their unlawful possessors." I wish I could give you the exact words of what follows, a charming passage about the household goods of the Egyptians, but nevertheless I will give a faithful account of it: we read in Exodus, he says, that when the Hebrews were secretly preparing to fly under their leader Moses from their servitude in Egypt, each took from his obliging neighbour all sorts of household goods, an immense amount of rings, clothes, and vessels, and, having spoiled the Egyptians, they departed secretly. As we know that this flight, this theft, was done with the sanction of God, we may take it that there is a significance here: that divine providence was acting in consideration for the timidity of some people who would have been frightened to spoil the Egyptians, that is to take over the wisdom of the heathen, unless they had such an example of this very thing, such a commander, such a leader.

To come out of Egypt is to leave behind heathen superstition and be converted to the Christian religion. To take away the wealth of Egypt is to transfer heathen literature to the adornment and use of our faith. The barbarians will perhaps make fun of the interpreter, and they would be right, if I were not putting forward Augustine's interpretation, not mine. For just as the Hebrews, he says, in old days seized whatever they judged would be useful to them, leaving behind what they thought harmful, or useless, or unhallowed, so it behooves us to leave to the heathen their vices, superstitions, lusts, desires—these, I say, are to be left to their owners. But if there is among them any gold of wisdom, any silver of speech, any furniture of good learning, we should pack up all that baggage and turn it to our own use, never fearing to be accused of thieving, but rather venturing to hope for reward and praise for the finest of deeds. Here again we must avoid the imputation of making difficulties on the question of what is to be left to the heathen as pernicious or adopted as useful; Augustine excepts nothing from his classification but those things he names as superstitious. Otherwise he does not withdraw from that arrangement of his, and this is characteristic of him: he wrote that those disciplines which were discovered by human minds, like dialectic, rhetoric, natural science, history, and so on, seemed to him marked out with gold and silver, because men themselves did not produce them but dug them out like gold and silver from what might be called the ore of divine providence, which runs through all things. By the clothes of the Egyptians he understands disciplines which were certainly instituted by mortal men, but fitted like garments to human society, such as the rules of oratory, ordinances of the people, pontifical decrees, which indeed are all of the greatest use and in his opinion should by all means be snatched from the heathen. Lastly he confirms and enriches the statement with a happy illustration: "This was done by many of our good and faithful people. Do we not see how Cyprian came out of Egypt with his bags stuffed with silver and clothing, sweetest of scholars and blessed martyr as he was? How much did Lactantius bring? and Victorinus, Optatus, Hilary? To say nothing of the living, how much more was brought by innumerable Greeks? Moses himself had done this first, that most faithful servant of God, of whom it is written that he was learned in all the wisdom of the Egyptians. The prevailing heathen superstition would never have allowed such men as these to take over the disciplines it considered useful (especially in times when it was trying to shake off the yoke of Christ and persecuting the Christians) if it had ever suspected that these studies would be used for worshipping the one God, in order that the false cult of idols might be destroyed. . . .

⟨✖⟩

from On Education for Children

Nature, the mother of all things, has equipped brute animals with more means to fulfil the functions of their species; but to man alone she has given the faculty of reason, and so she has thrown the burden of human growth upon education. Therefore it is right to say that the beginning and the end, indeed the total sum of man's happiness, are founded upon a good upbringing and education. Demosthenes used these terms in speaking about correct pronunciation. He is right of course, but a sound education contributes much more to human wisdom than mere pronunciation can enrich eloquence. A proper and conscientious instruction is the well-spring of all moral goodness. By contrast, the doors are flung wide open to folly and evil when education becomes corrupted and careless. Education is that special task which has been entrusted to us. This is why to other creatures nature has given swiftness of foot or wing, keenness of sight, strength or massiveness of body, coverings of wool or fur, or the protection of scales, plates, horns, claws, or poisons, and has so enabled them to protect themselves, hunt for food, and rear their young. Man alone she has created weak, naked, and defenseless. But as compensation, she has given him a mind equipped for knowledge, for this one capacity, if properly exploited, embraces all others. Animals are less easily taught than humans, but their instincts are more highly developed. Bees, for example, do not have to be taught how to construct cells, gather nectar, or make honey. Ants are not trained to store up their winter supplies during the summer in a hole in the ground, because they are guided by instinct. But man cannot even eat, walk, or speak without instruction. Trees, as you well know, do not grow any fruit, or only inferior fruit, unless they are properly grafted, and animals are of no use to man if they are left to their own capacities. A hound is not prepared by nature for the hunt, nor a horse for the saddle, nor an ox for the plough, unless we apply our efforts to their training. So what then are we to expect of man? He will most certainly turn out to be an unproductive brute unless at once and without delay he is subjected to a process of intensive instruction. Here I do not need to remind you of the well-known anecdote told of Lycurgus, who produced two dogs, the first pure-bred, the other a mongrel. The pure-bred dog, however, had been poorly trained and so went straight for the food placed in front of him, whereas the mongrel, who had been well drilled, abandoned his meal and rushed after game. This story demonstrates that while nature is strong, education is more powerful still. Men will do everything to have dogs that will serve them well in the hunt or to have horses that are full of stamina for travel, and any care they devote to these ends seems to be perfectly in order. But they neglect altogether or postpone until it is too late any thought of raising a son who will be a source of pride and well-being to his parents, to whom they can safely entrust a good share of responsibility in the administration of the family estate, and whose affection will comfort and sustain them under the growing burden of old age, a son who will be a faithful protector of his family, a good husband to his wife, and a solid and useful citizen of his country.

For whom do men plough, sow, and build? For whom do they ransack land and sea for wealth? Do they not do it all for their children? But what advantage or honour lies in these things if the beneficiaries are unable to make proper use of them? It is strange that so much energy should be expended on amassing property, while the owner as such receives no attention at all. Who would buy a lyre for an unmusical person or present an illiterate with a library? Why then all this accumulation of wealth for the benefit of someone who has not been taught how to make use of it? If you give wealth to a person who has been properly educated, you are handing him the tools for doing good; if you give the same to a person whose nature is savage and uncultivated, however, you are only providing him with the resources for living a wicked and irresponsible life. Can anything represent greater heights of madness than a father who acts in this manner? Such a father may ensure that his son suffers no physical harm and can perform his ordinary functions; yet at the same time he neglects the spirit, which is the driving force of all moral action.

I hardly need to add that nothing is more conducive to wealth, social status, influence, and even good health, all blessings which parents earnestly desire their children to enjoy, than moral and intellectual excellence. Parents wish for their children to be successful in the hunt yet give them no hunting-spear to make the catch possible. You cannot bestow upon your son the supreme good, but at least you can equip him with the means to win its sublime treasures. You have surely fallen to the depths of absurdity when you possess a dog that has been carefully trained or a horse that has been painstakingly broken and schooled, but at the same time have a son who lacks moral and intellectual instruction. So it is possible that you may own land that is beautifully cultivated but a son whose culture has been shamefully neglected, or a mansion filled with exquisite works of art but a son whose soul has no beauty at all.

And then there are parents, parents often widely praised for their practical wisdom, who postpone any thought of educating their child until he is already at an age when results are less easily obtained; or indeed they never entertain the thought at all. All their concern is for his material and external well-being, even before the heir to their wealth is born. So the parents take every precaution. While the woman is still with child, a reader of horoscopes is summoned to determine whether the infant will be male or female. He is also asked what the child's career will be; and so he may predict, "He will be successful as a soldier," and the parents will say, "We will enter him for service at court"; or he may predict, "He will occupy a high position in the church," and they will say, "We must find him a prosperous diocese or abbey somewhere and make him a provost or dean." If this kind of foresight, which extends even into the period before birth, is not considered premature, is it too early to take thought for a child's education? Why all this early concern that your son should be a general or a magistrate, but no reflection at all on the fact that he should serve the state well in these positions? Well in advance you arrange for your son to become bishop or abbot, but you fail to give him an upbringing that would enable him to discharge these offices well. You set him, as it were, on a chariot, but fail to teach him the art of driving; or you post him at a ship's tiller, but neglect to teach him what every captain ought to know. Thus the most precious of all your possessions, for whose sake all the rest is gathered, is the most neglected. Your lands, mansions, utensils, clothing, and furnishings gleam with prosperity; your horses have been splendidly schooled and your servants superbly trained; your son's mind alone presents a bleak picture of waste and neglect. Suppose you buy a slave, "just off the block," as the saying goes, a rough and uncivilized creature. If he is still young, however, you will determine what occupation would be suitable for him and you will soon begin to train him in a particular skill such as cooking, medicine, farming, or household administration. Yet you would neglect your son as though he were born for a life of idleness. You may object that your son has the necessary means to live his life. True, but he does not have the means to live a good life.

It seems to be customary that the wealthier a person is, the less he cares for the education of his children. "What need," our magnate says, "do my children have of philosophy? They will have plenty of everything." Yes, but the greater your wealth the more you need the guidance of philosophy. The larger a ship and the bulkier its cargo, the more it needs a skilful steersman. What single-mindedness marks the actions of princes, who strive to bequeath such huge domains to their sons! Yet these same persons could not care less to have their children educated in the skills which are so essential for good government.

How much more does he give who gives the means for living well than he who merely gives life. Children owe little gratitude to parents who are their parents only in the physical sense of the word, but have failed to provide them with the proper upbringing. There is a well-known saying attributed to Alexander the Great: "Were I not Alexander, I should want to be Diogenes." Plutarch is right to criticize Alexander for this remark: the more he expanded his empire, the more Alexander should also have wished for the wisdom of Diogenes.

But it is even more disgraceful if parents not only neglect their children's education but also corrupt them into following evil habits. The famous philosopher Crates of Thebes saw this perversity in human character, and was fully justified in threatening that he would climb to the highest point in the city and there cry out at the top of his voice, denouncing the folly of mankind, "What kind of insanity has beset you, wretched people? Why all this anxious care to gather wealth and possessions, while you give no attention to your children, for whom you are accumulating all these things?" Women who only give birth to their children but are not concerned to raise them are hardly even half-mothers; so also fathers who supply all their children's physical wants to the point of spoiling them but totally neglect their upbringing are not even fathers in half the sense of the word. Trees perhaps come into existence as trees once and for all, even if they turn out wild and barren; and horses are born as horses, even if they prove to be useless. But man certainly is not born, but made man. Primitive man, living a lawless, unschooled, promiscuous life in the woods, was not human, but rather a wild animal. It is reason which defines our humanity; and where everything is done at the whim of physical desire, reason does not hold its rightful place. If physical shape constituted man's true nature, then statues would have to be included among the human race.

Aristippus once gave a witty answer to a wealthy but dull-witted citizen who had asked what benefits a young man would derive from education: "Well, he will at least have this advantage, that in the theatre he won't sit down as one lump of stone upon another." Another philosopher, Diogenes if I am not mistaken, showed an equally delightful sense of humour. In full daylight he used to make his way through the crowded market-place, carrying a lamp; when asked what he was looking for, he replied, "I am looking for a man." He was aware, of course, of the crowd around him, but to him it was nothing more than a herd of animals, not a gathering of human beings. Another day the same philosopher stationed himself in a prominent place and summoned a throng of people, shouting, "Let all men come here." A large number of people assembled but he kept on shouting, "Let all men come here," so that some became rather annoyed and shouted back, "Here we are, the men you are looking for; tell us what you have to say." To which he replied, "I want men, not you; you are not human," and he drove them away with his stick.

It is beyond argument that a man who has never been instructed in philosophy or in any branch of learning is a creature quite inferior to the brute animals. Animals only follow their natural instincts; but man, unless he has experienced the influence of learning and philosophy, is at the mercy of impulses that are worse than those of a wild beast. There is no beast more savage and dangerous than a human being who is swept along by the passions of ambition, greed, anger, envy, extravagance, and sensuality. Therefore, a father who does not arrange for his son to receive the best education at the earliest age is neither a man himself nor has any fellowship with human nature.

Would a human soul imprisoned inside an animal body not be considered a hideous prodigy? We have all read the story of Circe who with her sorcery transformed men into lions, bears, or swine and so encased their souls inside animal bodies. Apuleius relates how such a fate once befell him. St Augustine, too, believes that men can be changed into werewolves. Who could bear to be the father of such a monstrosity? However, a bestial mind inhabiting a human body represents an even greater outrage. Yet the majority of parents, wise though they may appear to themselves and to others, are content to raise such offspring. She-bears, we are told, give birth to unrecognizable lumps, which they must patiently lick into shape; but no bear-cub is as raw and ill-defined a mass of material as the human mind at the time of birth. Unless you mould and shape the mind of your child, you will be the father of a monster, not of a human being. If your child were born with some physical defect, with, for instance, a cone-shaped head, a humpback, a club-foot, or six fingers on each hand, how upset you would be and how ashamed to be called the father of a freak rather than of a human being. Can you remain insensitive, then, when your child's mind is deformed? It is a heart-breaking experience for parents when their recently born child proves to be an idiot or an imbecile. It is as though they have brought a monstrosity and not a human child into the world; and were it not for the restraining force of the law, they would destroy the creature. Would you blame nature for having denied intelligence to your child, while you cause this to happen through your own negligence? In fact, an imbecile mind is better than an evil mind; or to put it differently, it is better to be a swine than to be a man who has neither culture nor moral sense. The child that nature has given you is nothing but a shapeless lump, but the material is still pliable, capable of assuming any form, and you must so mould it that it takes on the best possible character. If you are negligent, you will rear an animal; but if you apply yourself, you will fashion, if I may use such a bold term, a godlike creature.

from The Education of a Christian Prince

TO THE MOST ILLUSTRIOUS PRINCE CHARLES, GRANDSON OF THE INVINCIBLE EMPEROR MAXIMILIAN, FROM DESIDERIUS ERASMUS OF ROTTERDAM

Wisdom in itself is a wonderful thing, Charles greatest of princes, and no kind of wisdom is rated more excellent by Aristotle than that which teaches how to be a beneficent prince; for Xenophon in his *Oeconomicus* rightly considers that there is something beyond human nature, something wholly divine, in absolute rule over free and willing subjects. This naturally is the wisdom so much to be desired by princes, the one gift which the young Solomon, highly intelligent as he was, prayed for, despising all else, and wished to have seated continually beside his royal throne. This is that virtuous and beautiful Shunamite, in whose embraces David, wise father of a wise son, took his sole delight. She it is who says in Proverbs: "By me princes rule and nobles dispense justice." Whenever kings invite her to their councils and cast out those evil counsellors—ambition, anger, greed, and flattery—the commonwealth flourishes in every way and, knowing that it owes its felicity to the wisdom of its prince, says with well-earned satisfaction: "All good things together came to me with her." And so Plato is nowhere more meticulous than in the education of the guardians of his republic, whom he would have surpass all the rest not in riches and jewels and dress and ancestry and retainers, but in wisdom only, maintaining that no commonwealth can be happy unless either philosophers are put at the helm, or those to whose lot the rule happens to have fallen embrace philosophy—not that philosophy, I mean, which argues about elements and primal matter and motion and the infinite, but that which frees the mind from the false opinions of the multitude and from wrong desires and demonstrates the principles of right government by reference to the example set by the eternal powers. Something of the sort must have been, I think, in Homer's mind, when Mercury arms Ulysses against Circe's witchcraft with the herb called moly. And Plutarch has good reason for thinking that no man does the state a greater service than he who equips a prince's mind, which must consider all men's interests, with the highest principles, worthy of a prince; and that no one, on the other hand, brings such appalling disaster upon the affairs of mortal men as he who corrupts the prince's heart with wrongful opinions or desires, just as a man might put deadly poison in the public spring from which all men draw water. A very famous remark of Alexander the Great points usefully in the same direction; he came away from talking with Diogenes the Cynic full of admiration for his lofty philosophic mind, unshakeable, invincible, and superior to all mortal things, and said: "If I were not Alexander, I should desire to be Diogenes"; in fact, the more severe the storms that must be faced by great power, the more he well might wish for the mind of a Diogenes, which might be equal to the immense burden of events.

But you, noble Prince Charles, are more blessed than Alexander, and will, we hope, surpass him equally in wisdom too. He for his part had seized an immense empire, but not without bloodshed, nor was it destined to endure. You were born to a splendid empire and are destined to inherit one still greater, so that, while he had to expend great efforts on invasion, you will have perhaps to work to ensure that you can voluntarily hand over part of your dominions rather than seize more. You owe it to heaven that your empire came to you without the shedding of blood, and no one suffered for it; your wisdom must now ensure that you preserve it without bloodshed and at peace. And such is your good nature, your honesty of mind, and your ability, such the upbringing you have had under the most high-minded teachers, and above all so many are the examples which you see around you from among your ancestors, that we all expect with confidence to see Charles one day perform what the world lately looked for from your father Philip; nor would he have disappointed public expectation had not death carried him off before his time. And so, although I knew that your Highness had no need of any man's advice, least of all mine, I had the idea of setting forth the ideal of a perfect prince for the general good, but under your name, so that those who are brought up to rule great empires may learn the principles of government through you and take from you their example. This serves a double purpose: under your name this useful work will penetrate everywhere, and by these first fruits I, who am already your servant, can give some kind of witness to my devotion to you.

I have taken Isocrates' work on the principles of government and translated it into Latin, and in competition with him I have added my own, arranged as it were in aphorisms for the reader's convenience, but with considerable differences from what he laid down. For he was a sophist, instructing some petty king or rather tyrant, and both were pagans; I am a theologian addressing a renowned and upright prince, Christians both of us. Were I writing for an older prince, I might perhaps be suspected by some people of adulation or impertinence. As it is, this small book is dedicated to one who, great as are the hopes he inspires, is still very young and recently invested with government, and so has not yet had the opportunity to do very much that in other princes is matter for praise or blame. Consequently, I am free of both suspicions, and cannot be thought to have had any purpose but the common good, which should be the sole aim both of kings and of their friends and servants. Among the countless distinctions which under God your merit will win for you, it will be no small part of your reputation that Charles was a prince to whom a man need not hesitate to offer the picture of a true and upright Christian prince without any flattery, knowing that he would either gladly accept it as an excellent prince already, or wisely imitate it as a young man always in search of self-improvement. Farewell. [Basel, about March 1516]

THE BIRTH AND UPBRINGING OF A CHRISTIAN PRINCE

. . . The good and wise prince should always bear in mind, in attending to his children's upbringing, that those who are born to the state must be brought up for the state, and not to suit his own feelings; what is to the public advantage always takes precedence over the private feelings of a parent.

However many statues he may set up and however much he may toil over the constructions he erects, the prince can leave no finer monument to his good qualities than a son who is in every way of the same stock and who recreates his father's excellence in his own excellent actions. He does not die who leaves a living likeness of himself.

For this task, therefore, he should pick out from the whole range of his subjects (or indeed recruit from anywhere else) men of integrity, purity, and dignity; men who have been taught by long practical experience and not just by petty maxims; men whose age will win them respect, whose unblemished lives will earn them obedience, and whose pleasant and friendly manner will bring them affection and good will. This is so that the tender young mind may neither take hurt from the harshness of its teachers and thus begin to hate virtue before he understands it, nor on the other hand degenerate in a way it ought not after being spoiled by a tutor's over-indulgence.

As in all education, so indeed especially in that of the prince, moderation is to be exercised in such a way that while the tutor sternly restrains the frivolity of youth nevertheless the friendly manner in which he does so tempers and mollifies the severity of his control.

The future prince's educator must, as Seneca elegantly puts it, be a man who knows how to reprimand without giving way to abuse and how to praise without giving way to flattery; let the prince at once respect him for his disciplined life and like him for his agreeable manner.

Some princes investigate very carefully who should be entrusted with the care of a special horse or bird or hound but think it of no importance to whose care they commit the training of a son, and he is very often put in the hands of the sort of teachers whom no ordinary citizen with a little intelligence would want for his children. But what was the point of begetting a son to govern if you do not take care over training him for government?

The child born to the throne is not to be entrusted to just anyone you please even in the case of his nurses, but to women of blameless character who have been prepared and instructed for the task; nor should he associate with unselected companions, but with boys of good and respectable character who have been brought up and trained in the ways of courtesy and decency. You will have to keep at a distance from his sight and hearing the usual crowd of pleasure-seeking youngsters, drunkards, foul-mouthed people, and especially the flatterers, as long as his moral development is not yet firmly established.

Since for the most part the nature of man inclines towards evil, and furthermore no nature is so blessed at birth that it cannot be corrupted by perverse training, how can you expect anything but evil from a prince who, whatever his nature at birth (and a good lineage does not guarantee a mind as it does a kingdom), is subjected from the very cradle to the most stupid ideas and spends his boyhood among silly women and his youth among whores, degenerate comrades, the most shameless flatterers, buffoons, street-players, drinkers, gamblers, and pleasure-mongers as foolish as they are worthless. In this company he hears nothing, learns nothing, and takes in nothing except pleasure, amusement, pride, arrogance, greed, irascibility, and bullying; and from this schooling he is soon installed at the helm of the kingdom.

Since in all skills the highest are the most difficult, none is finer or more difficult than to rule well; why is it then that for this one skill alone we do not see the need for training but think a birthright is enough?

If as boys they did nothing but play at tyrants, what (I ask you) are they to work at as adults except tyranny?

It is scarcely possible even to hope that all men should be good; but it is not hard to pick out from so many thousands of them one or two who stand out in virtue and wisdom, through whom in a short while a great many others could be made good. In his youth the prince should for quite some time be distrustful of his years, partly because of his inexperience and partly because of his impetuous spirit, and he should beware of tackling anything of great importance except with the advice of wise counsellors, especially that of the older ones, whose company he must cultivate so that the impetuosity of youth may be tempered by respect for his elders.

Let whoever takes on the office of educating a prince reflect time and again on this, that the job he is doing is in no way an ordinary one: it is both by far the greatest and by far the most hazardous of all. And let him first of all approach it in a spirit worthy of the task, considering not how many benefices he can get out of it but in what way he can give back to the country, which is entrusting its hopes to his good faith, a beneficent prince.

Bear in mind, you who are the tutor, how much you owe to your country, which has entrusted to you the consummation of its happiness. It is in your hands whether you prefer to provide your country with someone who will be a benign influence or to visit it with the destruction of a deadly plague.

Therefore the man into whose arms the state has put its son would be wise to take notice in the first place of what inclinations the boy already has at the time, because even at this age it is possible to recognise by certain signs whether he is more prone to arrogance and fits of temper, or to ambition and a thirst for fame, or to pleasures of the flesh, gambling, and the pursuit of wealth, or to revenge and war, or to impulsiveness and tyranny. Then at those points where he feels the boy is inclined to go wrong let him especially fortify the young mind with healthy precepts and relevant principles and try to guide its nature, while still responsive, in a different direction. Again, where his nature is found to be rightly disposed, or at any rate to have only such faults as are easily turned to a good use (ambition and prodigality are perhaps examples of this), let him concentrate all the more on these positive qualities and actively cultivate them.

But it is not enough just to hand out the sort of maxims which warn him off evil things and summon him to the good. No, they must be fixed in his mind, pressed in, and rammed home. And they must be kept fresh in the memory in all sorts of ways: sometimes in a moral maxim, sometimes in a parable, sometimes by an analogy, sometimes by a live example, an epigram, or a proverb; they must be carved on rings, painted in pictures, inscribed on prizes, and presented in any other way that a child of his age enjoys, so that they are always before his mind even when he is doing something else.

The examples set by famous men vividly inspire a noble youth's imagination, but the ideas with which it is imbued are of much the greatest importance, for they are the source from which the whole character of his life develops. Consequently, if it is an untutored boy we have in our charge, we must make every effort to have him drink, from the start, from the purest and healthiest sources and to protect him in advance, as if by an antidote, against the poison of what the common people think. But if it turns out that he has already been somewhat contaminated by popular opinions, then we shall have to take the greatest care to release him from them gradually and to implant wholesome ones in place of the diseased ones that have been eradicated. For, as Aristo puts it in Seneca, it is fruitless to show a madman how he ought to speak, or go about things, or conduct himself in company and in private, unless you have first rid him of the underlying disease. It is similarly fruitless to give advice on the principles of government without previously setting a prince's mind free from those popular opinions which are at once most widely held and yet most fallacious.

There is no reason for the tutor to withdraw or lose confidence if he happens to encounter a rather wild and intractable spirit in his pupil. For, given that there is no wild animal so fierce and savage that it cannot be controlled by the persistent attention of a trainer, why should he think that any human spirit is so hopelessly crude that it will not respond to painstaking education? Equally, he has no reason to think of letting up if his pupil presents a more fortunate nature. For the richer the soil is by nature, the more readily the ground is invaded and taken over by useless grasses and weeds unless the farmer is on the alert. So it is with a man's character: the more promising, the more noble, the more upright it is, the more it is at the mercy of many shameful vices unless it is nourished by wholesome teachings.

We usually take the most care in reinforcing those shores most severely pounded by the waves. Now there are innumerable things which can distract a prince's mind from its proper course: great good fortune, abundant material wealth, the pleasures of extravagant luxury, freedom to do as he likes, the precedents of famous but foolish rulers, the very tides and tempest of human affairs, and (above all else) flattery disguised as sincerity and frankness. For this reason, the prince must be carefully prepared against all these by the best principles and by taking praiseworthy princes as his models.

Just as someone who poisons the public fountain from which everybody drinks deserves the severest punishment, so someone who implants in a prince's mind perverted ideas, which will eventually be the ruin of a great many people, is the most vicious of men.

Given that anyone who debases the prince's coinage is punished with death, how much more deserving of that punishment is someone who corrupts his mind?

The teacher should make a start on his duties at once so as to sow the seeds of right conduct while the prince's understanding is still sensitive, while his mind is furthest removed from all vices and plastic enough to take on any form from the hand that moulds it. Wisdom has its period of infancy, as does piety. The teacher's objective is always the same, but he must use different methods at different times. While his pupil is still a little child, he can introduce into entertaining stories, amusing fables, and clever parables the things he will teach directly when the boy is older.

When the little pupil has enjoyed hearing Aesop's fable of the lion being saved in his turn by the good offices of the mouse, or of the dove protected by the industry of the ant, and when he has had a good laugh, then the teacher should spell it out: the fable applies to the prince, telling him never to look down on anybody but to try assiduously to win over by kindness the heart of even the humblest of the common people, for no one is so weak but that he may at some time be a friend who can help you or an enemy who can harm you, however powerful you may be yourself.

When he has had his fun out of the eagle, queen of the birds, who was almost totally destroyed by that very lowliest of insects the beetle, the teacher should again point out the meaning: not even the most powerful prince can afford to provoke or disregard even the humblest enemy. Often those who can do no harm physically can do so by guile.

When he has learned with pleasure the story of Phaethon, the teacher should show that he represents a prince who seized the reins of government in the headstrong enthusiasm of youth but with no supporting wisdom and brought ruin upon himself and the entire world.

When he has recounted the story of Cyclops, whose eye was put out by Ulysses, the teacher should say in conclusion that the prince who has great physical, but not mental, strength is like Polyphemus.

Who has not been glad to hear about how the bees and ants govern themselves? When the prince's childish mind has digested these tasty morsels, then his tutor should bring out whatever feature is educationally relevant, such as that the king never flies far afield since his wings are too small in proportion to his body, and that he alone has no sting. From this the lesson is drawn that it is the part of a good prince always to confine his activities within the limits of his realm and that clemency should be the quality for which he is particularly praised. The same procedure should be carried on throughout. This treatise is not concerned to provide a long list of examples, but merely to point out the principles and the general direction.

Where the material seems rather harsh, the tutor should smooth and soften it with an agreeable style of speech. The teacher should give his praise in the presence of others, but with sincerity and on valid grounds. His rebukes should be delivered in private and in such a way that the severity of his admonition is toned down by a touch of pleasantness in manner. This should be particularly observed when the prince is a little older.

What must be implanted deeply and before all else in the mind of the prince is the best possible understanding of Christ; he should be constantly absorbing his teachings, gathered together in some convenient form drawn from the original sources themselves, from which the teaching is imbibed not only more purely but also more effectively. Let him become convinced of this, that what Christ teaches applies to no one more than to the prince.

A large section of the masses are swayed by false opinions, just like those people trussed up in Plato's cave, who regarded the empty shadows of things as the things themselves. But it is the role of the good prince not to be impressed by the things that the common people consider of great consequence, but to weigh all things, considering whether they are really good or bad. But nothing is truly bad unless it is bound up with depravity, and nothing really good unless associated with moral worth.

Therefore the tutor should first see that his pupil loves and honours virtue as the most beautiful thing of all, the greatest source of happiness, and especially fitting for a prince, and that he loathes and shrinks from depravity as being the most appalling and wretched of things.

Martin Luther

1483–1546

Now that God has today so graciously bestowed upon us an abundance of arts, scholars, and books, it is time to reap and gather in the best as well as we can, and lay up treasure in order to preserve for the future something from these years of jubilee, and not lose this bountiful harvest.

To the Councilmen of All Cities in Germany

Martin Luther was born in the small village of Eisleben, Saxony, the son of a peasant miner who wanted better things for his eldest child. Educated for a year by the Brethren of the Common Life and then for four years at a school in Eisenach, the talented scholar entered the University of Erfurt, quickly earning bachelor's and master's degrees. Heeding his father's wishes, he continued on at Erfurt to study law, but soon entered the city's Augustinian monastery to become a monk. He lived a life of extreme self-denial and devotion to his order, but was tormented by doubts about his soul's salvation. He continued to study theology and lectured at the recently founded University of Wittenberg and at Erfurt. His primary influences included Augustine, Anselm, Bernard of Clairvaux, and Jean Gerson.

In 1511 Luther was appointed full time to the University of Wittenberg, where he earned his Doctor of Theology degree, preached, and lectured, principally on the Psalms, Romans, and Galatians. At this point he began developing his theology of justification by faith alone. He also became close friends with the humanist professor of Greek, Philip Melanchthon. Some humanists, like Melanchthon, were won over by his theology; others, like Erasmus, remained loyal to the Catholic Church. Luther himself, however, was not a humanist. In 1517 he protested the abuse of the sale of indulgences and posted his *Ninety-five Theses,* unexpectedly opening a series of ever-widening attacks on Catholic practice, theology, and governance. After several high-profile debates with leading theologians, he was excommunicated by Pope Leo X and tried by the Holy Roman Emperor Charles V at Worms.

Luther's sweeping reforms of church and society included a call for reform of Europe's universities. His theology focused on points of tension between the world's culture and the claims of Christ, including a radical division between ancient philosophy and the Bible. In particular, he angrily denounced Aristotle's grip on the university curriculum. Nevertheless, Luther was not among the radical educational reformers who rejected outright all secular learning. For all of his bulldog polemics, Luther remained a defender of scholarship in the service of church, state, and community.

THE SELECTION

Luther's three most important statements on education are included in addresses to the nobility, city councilmen, and parents: *An Appeal to the Christian Nobility* (1520); *To the Councilmen of All Cities in Germany That They Establish and Maintain Christian Schools* (1524); and *A Sermon on Keeping Children in School* (1530). Only part of the 1524 address to the councilmen of Germany is included here. In it, Luther reminds the community of its urgent duty to educate its children, a responsibility shared by parents and the government. Luther also offers a spirited defense of the study of Hebrew, Greek, and Latin, ties education to leadership, and finally recommends the provision of well-stocked libraries.

from To the Councilmen of All Cities in Germany

. . . It is a sin and a shame that matters have come to such a pass that we have to urge and be urged to educate our children and young people and to seek their best interests, when nature itself should drive us to do this and even the heathen afford us abundant examples of it. There is not a dumb animal which fails to care for its young and teach them what they need to know; the only exception is the ostrich, of which God says in Job 31 [39:16, 14] that she deals cruelly with her young as if they were not hers, and leaves her eggs upon the ground. What would it profit us to possess and perform everything else and be like pure saints, if we meanwhile neglected our chief purpose in life, namely, the care of the young? I also think that in the sight of God none among the outward sins so heavily burdens the world and merits such severe punishment as this very sin which we commit against the children by not educating them.

When I was a lad they had this maxim in school: *"Non minus est negligere scholarem, quam corrumpere virginem"*; "It is just as bad to neglect a pupil as to despoil a virgin." The purpose of this maxim was to keep the schoolmasters on their toes, for in those days no greater sin was known that that of despoiling a virgin. But, dear Lord God, how light a sin it is to despoil virgins or wives (which, being a bodily and recognized sin, may be atoned for) in comparison with this sin of neglecting and despoiling precious souls, for the latter sin is not even recognized or acknowledged and is never atoned for. O woe unto the world for ever and ever! Children are born every day and grow up in our midst, but, alas! there is no one to take charge of the youngsters and direct them. We just let matters take their own course. The monasteries and foundations should have seen to it; therefore, they are the very ones of whom Christ says, "Woe unto the world because of offenses! Whoever causes one of these little ones who believe in me to sin, it would be better for him to have a millstone fastened round his neck, and to be drowned in the depth of the sea" (Matt. 18:7, 6). They are nothing but devourers and destroyers of children.

Ah, you say, but all that is spoken to the parents; what business is it of councilmen and the authorities? Yes, that is true; but what if the parents fail to do their duty? Who then is to do it? Is it for this reason to be left undone, and the children neglected? How will the authorities and council then justify their position, that such matters are not their responsibility?

There are various reasons why parents neglect this duty. In the first place, there are some who lack the goodness and decency to do it, even if they had the ability. Instead, like the ostrich [Job 39:14–16], they deal cruelly with their young. They are content to have laid the eggs and brought children into the world; beyond this they will do nothing more. But these children are supposed to live among us and with us in the community. How then can reason, and especially Christian charity, allow that they grow up uneducated, to poison and pollute the other children until at last the whole city is mined, as happened in Sodom and Gomorrah [Gen. 19:1–25], and Gibeah [Judges 19–20], and a number of other cities?

In the second place, the great majority of parents unfortunately are wholly unfitted for this task. They do not know how children should be brought up and taught, for they themselves have learned nothing but how to care for their bellies. It takes extraordinary people to bring children up right and teach them well.

In the third place, even if parents had the ability and desire to do it themselves, they have neither the time nor the opportunity for it, what with their other duties and the care of the household. Necessity compels us, therefore, to engage public schoolteachers for the children—unless each one were willing to engage his own private tutor. But that would be too heavy a burden for the common man, and many a promising boy would again be neglected on account of poverty. Besides, many parents die, leaving orphans, and if we do not know from experience how they are cared for by their guardians it should be quite clear from the fact that God calls himself Father of the fatherless [Ps. 68:5], of those who are neglected by everyone else. Then too there are others who have no children of their own, and therefore take no interest in the training of children.

It therefore behooves the council and the authorities to devote the greatest care and attention to the young. Since the property, honor, and life of the whole city have been committed to their faithful keeping, they would be remiss in their duty before God and man if they did not seek its welfare and improvement day and night with all the means at their command. Now the welfare of a city does not consist solely in accumulating vast treasures, building mighty walls and magnificent buildings, and producing a goodly supply of guns and armor. Indeed, where such things are plentiful, and reckless fools get control of them, it is so much the worse and the city suffers even greater loss. A city's best and greatest welfare, safety, and strength consist rather in its having many able, learned, wise, honorable, and well-educated citizens. They can then readily gather, protect, and properly use treasure and all manner of property.

So it was done in ancient Rome. There boys were so taught that by the time they reached their fifteenth, eighteenth, or twentieth year they were well versed in Latin, Greek, and all the liberal arts (as they are called), and then immediately entered upon a political or military career. Their system produced intelligent, wise, and competent men, so skilled in every art and rich in experience that if all the bishops, priests, and monks in the whole of Germany today were rolled into one, you would not have the equal of a single Roman soldier. As a result their country prospered; they had capable and trained men for every position. So at all times throughout the world simple necessity has forced men, even among the heathen, to maintain pedagogues and schoolmasters if their nation was to be brought to a high standard. Hence, the word "schoolmaster" is used by Paul in Galatians 4 as a word taken from the common usage and practice of mankind, where he says, "The law was our schoolmaster."

Since a city should and must have [educated] people, and since there is a universal dearth of them and complaint that they are nowhere to be found, we dare not wait until they grow up of themselves; neither can we carve them out of stone nor hew them out of wood. Nor will God perform miracles as long as men can solve their problems by means of the other gifts he has already granted them. Therefore, we must do our part and spare no labor or expense to produce and train such people ourselves. For whose fault is it that today our cities have so few capable people? Whose fault, if not that of authorities, who have left the young people to grow up like saplings in the forest, and have given no thought to their instruction and training? This is also why they have grown to maturity so misshapen that they cannot be used for building purposes, but are mere brushwood, fit only for kindling fires.

After all, temporal government has to continue. Are we then to permit none but louts and boors to rule, when we can do better than that? That would certainly be a crude and senseless policy. We might as well make lords out of swine and wolves, and set them to rule over those who refuse to give any thought to how they are ruled by men. Moreover, it is barbarous wickedness to think no further than this: We will rule now; what concern is it of ours how they will fare who come after us? Not over human beings, but over swine and dogs should such persons rule who in ruling seek only their own profit or glory. Even if we took the utmost pains to develop a group of able, learned, and skilled people for positions in government, there would still be plenty of labor and anxious care involved in seeing that things went well. What then is to happen if we take no pains at all?

"All right," you say again, "suppose we do have to have schools; what is the use of teaching Latin, Greek, and Hebrew, and the other liberal arts? We could just as well use German for teaching the Bible and God's word, which is enough for our salvation." I reply: Alas! I am only too well aware that we Germans must always be and remain brutes and stupid beasts, as the neighboring nations call us, epithets which we richly deserve. But I wonder why we never ask, "What is the use of silks, wine, spices, and other strange foreign wares when we ourselves have in Germany wine, grain, wool, flax, wood, and stone not only in quantities sufficient for our needs, but also of the best and choicest quality for our glory and ornament?" Languages and the arts, which can do us no harm, but are actually a greater ornament, profit, glory, and benefit, both for the understanding of Holy Scripture and the conduct of temporal government—these we despise. But foreign wares, which are neither necessary nor useful, and in addition strip us down to a mere skeleton—these we cannot do without. Are not we Catalans justly dubbed fools and beasts?

Truly, if there were no other benefit connected with the languages, this should be enough to delight and inspire us, namely, that they are so fine and noble a gift of God, with which he is now so richly visiting and blessing us Germans above all other lands. We do not see many instances where the devil has allowed them to flourish by means of the universities and monasteries; indeed, these have always raged against languages and are even now raging. For the devil smelled a rat, and perceived that if the languages were revived a hole would be knocked in his kingdom which he could not easily stop up again. Since he found he could not prevent their revival, he now aims to keep them on such slender rations that they will of themselves decline and pass away. They are not a welcome guest in his house, so he plans to offer them such meager entertainment that they will not prolong their stay. Very few of us, my dear sirs, see through this evil design of the devil.

Therefore, my beloved Germans, let us get our eyes open, thank God for this precious treasure, and guard it well, lest the devil vent his spite and it be taken away from us again. Although the gospel came and still comes to us through the Holy Spirit alone, we cannot deny that it came through the medium of languages, was spread abroad by that means, and must be preserved by the same means. For just when God wanted to spread the gospel throughout the world by means of the apostles he gave the tongues for that purpose [Acts 2:1–11]. Even before that, by means of the Roman Empire he had spread the Latin and Greek languages widely in every land in order that his gospel might the more speedily bear fruit far and wide. He has done the same thing now as well. Formerly no one knew why God had the languages revived, but now for the first time we see that it was done for the sake of the gospel, which he intended to bring to light and use in exposing and destroying the kingdom of Antichrist. To this end he gave over Greece to the Turk in order that the Greeks, driven out and scattered, might disseminate their language and provide an incentive to the study of other languages as well.

In proportion then as we value the gospel, let us zealously hold to the languages. For it was not without purpose that God caused his Scriptures to be set down in these two languages alone—the Old Testament in Hebrew, the New in Greek. Now if God did not despise them but chose them above all others for his word, then we too ought to honor them above all others. St. Paul declared it to be the peculiar glory and distinction of Hebrew that God's word was given in that language, when he said in Romans 3[:1–2], "What advantage or profit have those who are circumcised? Much indeed. To begin with, God's speech is entrusted to them." King David too boasts in Psalm 147[:19–20], "He declares his word to Jacob, his statutes and ordinances to Israel. He has not dealt thus with any other nation or revealed to them his ordinances." Hence, too, the Hebrew language is called sacred. And St. Paul, in Romans 1[:2], calls it "the holy scriptures," doubtless on account of the holy word of God which is comprehended [*verfasset*] therein. Similarly, the Greek language too may be called sacred, because it was chosen above all others as the language in which the New Testament was to be written, and because by it other languages too have been sanctified as it spilled over into them like a fountain through the medium of translation.

And let us be sure of this: we will not long preserve the gospel without the languages. The languages are the sheath in which this sword of the Spirit [Eph. 6:17] is contained;

they are the casket in which this jewel is enshrined; they are the vessel in which this wine is held; they are the larder in which this food is stored; and, as the gospel itself points out [Matt. 14:20], they are the baskets in which are kept these loaves and fishes and fragments. If through our neglect we let the languages go (which God forbid!), we shall not only lose the gospel, but the time will come when we shall be unable either to speak or write a correct Latin or German. As proof and warning of this, let us take the deplorable and dreadful example of the universities and monasteries, in which men have not only unlearned the gospel, but have in addition so corrupted the Latin and German languages that the miserable folk have been fairly turned into beasts, unable to speak or write a correct German or Latin, and have well-nigh lost their natural reason to boot.

For this reason even the apostles themselves considered it necessary to set down the New Testament and hold it fast in the Greek language, doubtless in order to preserve it for us there safe and sound as in a sacred ark. For they foresaw all that was to come, and now has come to pass; they knew that if it was left exclusively to men's memory, wild and fearful disorder and confusion and a host of varied interpretations, fancies, and doctrines would arise in the Christian church, and that this could not be prevented and the simple folk protected unless the New Testament were set down with certainty in written language. Hence, it is inevitable that unless the languages remain, the gospel must finally perish.

Experience too has proved this and still gives evidence of it. For as soon as the languages declined to the vanishing point, after the apostolic age, the gospel and faith and Christianity itself declined more and more until under the pope they disappeared entirely. After the decline of the languages Christianity witnessed little that was worth anything; instead, a great many dreadful abominations arose because of ignorance of the languages. On the other hand, now that the languages have been revived, they are bringing with them so bright a light and accomplishing such great things that the whole world stands amazed and has to acknowledge that we have the gospel just as pure and undefiled as the apostles had it, that it has been wholly restored to its original purity, far beyond what it was in the days of St. Jerome and St. Augustine. In short, the Holy Spirit is no fool. He does not busy himself with inconsequential or useless matters. He regarded the languages as so useful and necessary to Christianity that he ofttimes brought them down with him from heaven. This alone should be a sufficient motive for us to pursue them with diligence and reverence and not to despise them, for he himself has now revived them again upon the earth. . . .

It is not necessary to repeat here that the temporal government is a divinely ordained estate (I have elsewhere treated this subject so fully that I trust no one has any doubt about it). The question is rather: How are we to get good and capable men into it? Here we are excelled and put to shame by the pagans of old, especially the Romans and the Greeks. Although they had no idea of whether this estate were pleasing to God or not, they were so earnest and diligent in educating and training their young boys and girls to fit them for the task, that when I call it to mind I am forced to blush for us Christians, and especially for us Germans. We are such utter blockheads and beasts that we dare to say, "Pray, why have schools for people who are not going to become spiritual?" Yet we know, or at least we ought to know, how essential and beneficial it is—and pleasing to God—that a prince, lord, councilman, or other person in a position of authority be educated and qualified to perform the functions of his office as a Christian should.

Now if (as we have assumed) there were no souls, and there were no need at all of schools and languages for the sake of the Scriptures and of God, this one consideration alone would be sufficient to justify the establishment everywhere of the very best schools for both boys and girls, namely, that in order to maintain its temporal estate outwardly the world must have good and capable men and women, men able to rule well over land and people, women able to manage the household and train children and servants aright. Now such men must come from our boys, and such women from our girls. Therefore, it is a matter of properly educating and training our boys and girls to that end. I have pointed out above that the common man is doing nothing about it; he is incapable of it, unwilling, and ignorant of what to do. Princes and lords ought to be doing it, but they must needs be sleigh riding, drinking, and parading about in masquerades. They are burdened with high and important functions in cellar, kitchen, and bedroom. And the few who might want to do it must stand in fear of the rest lest they be taken for fools or heretics. Therefore, dear councilmen, it rests with you alone; you have a better authority and occasion to do it than princes and lords.

But, you say, everyone may teach his sons and daughters himself, or at least train them in proper discipline. Answer: Yes, we can readily see what such teaching and training amount to, even when the training is done to perfection and succeeds, the net result is little more than a certain enforced outward respectability; underneath, they are nothing but the same old blockheads, unable to converse intelligently on any subject, or to assist or counsel anyone. But if children were instructed and trained in schools, or wherever learned and well-trained schoolmasters and schoolmistresses were available to teach the languages, the other arts, and history, they would then hear of the doings and sayings of the entire world, and how things went with various cities, kingdoms, princes, men, and women. Thus, they could in a short time set before themselves as in a mirror the character, life, counsels, and purposes—successful and unsuccessful—of the whole world from the beginning; on the basis of which they could then draw the proper inferences and in the fear of God take their own place in the stream of human events. In addition, they could gain from history the knowledge and understanding of what to seek and what to avoid in this outward life, and be able to advise and direct others accordingly. The training we undertake at home, apart from such schools, is intended to make us wise through our own experience. Before that can be accomplished we will be dead a hundred times over, and will have acted rashly throughout our mortal life, for it takes a long time to acquire personal experience.

Now since the young must always be hopping and skipping, or at least doing something that they enjoy, and since one cannot very well forbid this—nor would it be wise to forbid them everything—why then should we not set up such schools for them and introduce them to such studies? By the grace of God it is now possible for children to study with pleasure and in play languages, or other arts, or history. Today, schools are not what they once were, a hell and purgatory in which we were tormented with *casualibus* and *temporalibus*, and yet learned less than nothing despite all the flogging, trembling, anguish, and misery. If we take so much time and trouble to teach children card-playing, singing, and dancing, why do we not take as much time to teach them reading and other disciplines while they are young and have the time, and are apt and eager to learn? For my part, if I had children and could manage it, I would have them study not only languages and history, but also singing and music together with the whole of mathematics. For what is all this but mere child's play? The ancient Greeks trained their children in these disciplines; yet they grew up to be people of wondrous ability, subsequently fit for everything. How I regret now that I did not read more poets and historians, and that no one taught me them! Instead, I was obliged to read at great cost, toil, and detriment to myself, that devil's dung, the philosophers and sophists, from which I have all I can do to purge myself.

So you say, "But who can thus spare his children and train them all to be young gentlemen? There is work for them to do at home," etc. Answer: It is not my intention either to have such schools established as we have had heretofore, where a boy slaved away at his Donatus and Alexander for twenty or thirty years and still learned nothing. Today we are living in a different world, and things are being done differently. My idea is to have the boys attend such a school for one or two hours during the day, and spend the remainder of the time working at home, learning a trade, or doing whatever is expected of them. In this way, study and work will go hand-in-hand while the boys are young and able to do both. Otherwise, they spend at least ten times as much time anyway with their pea shooters, ballplaying, racing, and tussling.

In like manner, a girl can surely find time enough to attend school for an hour a day, and still take care of her duties at home. She spends much more time than that anyway in sleeping, dancing, and playing. Only one thing is lacking, the earnest desire to train the young and to benefit and serve the world with able men and women. The devil very much prefers coarse blockheads and ne'er-do-wells, lest men get along too well on earth. The exceptional pupils, who give promise of becoming skilled teachers, preachers, or holders of other ecclesiastical positions, should be allowed to continue in school longer, or even be dedicated to a life of study, as we read of [those who trained] the holy martyrs SS. Agnes, Agatha, Lucy, and others. That is how the monasteries and foundations originated; they have since been wholly perverted to a different and damnable use. There is great need of such advanced study, for the tonsured crowd is fast dwindling. Besides, most of them are unfit to teach or to rule, for all they know is to care for their bellies, which is indeed all they have been taught. We must certainly have men to administer God's word and sacraments and to be shepherds of souls. But where shall we get them if we let our schools go by the board, and fail to replace them with others that are Christian? The schools that have been maintained hitherto, even though they do not die out entirely, can produce nothing but lost and pernicious deceivers. . . .

. . . [N]o effort or expense should be spared to provide good libraries or book repositories, especially in the larger cities which can well afford it. For if the gospel and all the arts are to be preserved, they must be set down and held fast in books and writings (as was done by the prophets and apostles themselves, as I have said above). This is essential, not only that those who are to be our spiritual and temporal leaders may have books to read and study, but also that the good books may be preserved and not lost, together with the arts and languages which we now have by the grace of God. St. Paul too was concerned about this when he charged Timothy to give attention to reading [I Tim. 4:13], and bade him bring with him the parchments from Troas [II Tim. 4:13].

Indeed, all the kingdoms which ever amounted to anything gave careful attention to this matter. This is especially true of the people of Israel, among whom Moses was the first to begin the practice when he had the book of the law kept in the ark of God [Deut.

31:25–26]. He put it in charge of the Levites so that whoever needed a copy might obtain one from them. He even commanded the king to procure from them a copy of this book [Deut. 17:18]. Thus, we see how God directed the Levitical priesthood, among its other duties, to watch over and care for the books. Later this library was added to and improved by Joshua, then by Samuel, David, Solomon, Isaiah, and by many other kings and prophets. Thence have come the Holy Scriptures of the Old Testament, which would never have been collected or preserved had God not required such care to be bestowed upon them.

Following this example, the monasteries and foundations of old also established libraries, although there were few good books among them. What a loss it was that they neglected to acquire books and good libraries at that time, when the books and men for it were available, became painfully evident later when, as time went on, unfortunately all the arts and languages declined. Instead of worthwhile books, the stupid, useless, and harmful books of the monks, such as *Catholicon, Florista, Grecista, Labyrinthus, Dormi secure*, and the like asses' dung were introduced by the devil. Because of such books the Latin language was ruined, and there remained nowhere a decent school, course of instruction, or method of study. This situation lasted until, as we have experienced and observed, the languages and arts were laboriously recovered—although imperfectly—from bits and fragments of old books hidden among dust and worms. Men are still painfully searching for them every day, just as people poke through the ashes of a ruined city seeking the treasures and jewels.

This served us right; God has properly repaid us for our ingratitude in not considering his kindness toward us and failing to provide for a constant supply of good books and learned men while we had the time and opportunity. When we neglected this, as though it were no concern of ours, he in turn did the same; instead of Holy Scripture and good books, he suffered Aristotle to come in, together with countless harmful books which drew us farther from the Bible. In addition to these he let in those devil's masks, the monks, and those phantoms which are the universities, which we endowed with vast properties. We have taken upon ourselves the support of a host of doctors, preaching friars, masters, priests, and monks; that is to say, great, coarse, fat asses decked out in red and brown birettas, looking like a sow bedecked with a gold chain and jewels. They taught us nothing good, but only made us all the more blind and stupid. In return, they devoured all our goods and filled every monastery, indeed every nook and cranny, with the filth and dung of their foul and poisonous books, until it is appalling to think of it.

Isn't it a crying shame that heretofore a boy was obliged to study for twenty years or even longer merely to learn enough bad Latin to become a priest and mumble through the mass? Whoever got that far was accounted blessed, and blessed was the mother who bore such a child! And yet he remained all his life a poor ignoramus, unable either to cackle or to lay an egg. Everywhere we were obliged to put up with teachers and masters who knew nothing themselves, and were incapable of teaching anything good or worthwhile. In fact, they did not even know how to study or teach. Where does the fault lie? There were no other books available than the stupid books of the monks and the sophists. What else could come out of them but pupils and teachers as stupid as the books they used? A jackdaw hatches no doves, and a fool cannot produce a sage. That is the reward of our ingratitude, that men failed to found libraries but let the good books perish and kept the poor ones.

My advice is not to heap together all manner of books indiscriminately and think only of the number and size of the collection. I would make a judicious selection, for it is not necessary to have all the commentaries of the jurists, all the sentences of the theologians, all the *quaestiones* of the philosophers, and all the sermons of the monks. Indeed, I would discard all such dung, and furnish my library with the right sort of books, consulting with scholars as to my choice.

First of all, there would be the Holy Scriptures, in Latin, Greek, Hebrew, and German, and any other language in which they might be found. Next, the best commentaries, and, if I could find them, the most ancient, in Greek, Hebrew, and Latin. Then, books that would be helpful in learning the languages, such as the poets and orators, regardless of whether they were pagan or Christian, Greek or Latin, for it is from such books that one must learn grammar. After that would come books on the liberal arts, and all the other arts. Finally, there would be books of law and medicine; here too there should be careful choice among commentaries.

Among the foremost would be the chronicles and histories, in whatever languages they are to be had. For they are a wonderful help in understanding and guiding the course of events, and especially for observing the marvelous works of God. How many fine tales and sayings we should have today of things that took place and were current in German lands, not one of which is known to us, simply because there was no one to write them down, and no one to preserve the books had they been written. That is why nothing is known in other lands about us Germans, and we must be content to have the rest of the world refer to us as German beasts who know only how to fight, gorge, and guzzle. The Greeks and Latins, however, and even the Hebrews, wrote their things down, so accurately and diligently that if even a woman or a child said or did something out of the ordinary the whole world must read of it and know it. Meanwhile, we Germans are nothing but Germans, and will remain Germans.

Now that God has today so graciously bestowed upon us an abundance of arts, scholars, and books, it is time to reap and gather in the best as well as we can, and lay up treasure in order to preserve for the future something from these years of jubilee, and not lose this bountiful harvest. For it is to be feared—and the beginning of it is already apparent—that men will go on writing new and different books until finally, because of the devil's activity; we will come to the point where the good books which are now being produced and printed will again be suppressed, and the worthless and harmful books with their useless and senseless rubbish will swarm back and litter every nook and corner. The devil certainly intends that we shall again be burdened and plagued as before with nothing but *Catholicons, Floristae*, Modernists, and the accursed dung of monks and sophists, forever studying but never learning anything.

Therefore, I beseech you, my dear sirs, to let this sincere effort of mine bear fruit among you. Should there be any who think me too insignificant to profit by my advice, or who despise me as one condemned by the tyrants, I pray them to consider that I am not seeking my own advantage, but the welfare and salvation of all Germany. Even if I were a fool and had hit upon a good idea, surely no wise man would think it a disgrace to follow me. And if I were a very Turk or a heathen, and my plan were nevertheless seen to benefit not myself but the Christians, they ought not in fairness to spurn my offer. It has happened before that a fool gave better advice than a whole council of wise men. Moses was obliged to take advice from Jethro [Exod. 18:17–24].

Herewith I commend all of you to the grace of God. May he soften and kindle your hearts that they may be deeply concerned for the poor, miserable, and neglected youth, and with the help of God aid and assist them, to the end that there may be a blessed and Christian government in the German lands with respect to both body and soul, with all plenty and abundance, to the glory and honor of God the Father, through our Savior Jesus Christ. Amen.

Ulrich Zwingli

1484–1531

"Rank, beauty and wealth are not genuine riches, for they are subject to chance. The only true adornments are virtue and honour."

Of the Upbringing and Education of Youth

Ulrich Zwingli was a native of Switzerland and a contemporary of Martin Luther and Erasmus. He entered the priesthood and served as an army chaplain and then at the Minster in Zurich. He was influenced by Luther, but his theology, politics, and path to reform were distinctly his own. He was also more truly a Christian humanist than Luther, having been shaped by the writings of Pico della Mirandola and Erasmus. Zwingli collected a large, comprehensive library, including many classical texts and Erasmus's recently published Greek New Testament. Like Luther, but unlike Erasmus, Zwingli rejected papal authority, preached salvation by faith alone, and sought to adhere to Scripture alone as the source for doctrine, worship, and governance. In the 1520s, the citizens of the canton of Zurich defied the jurisdiction of the bishop of Constance and reorganized their church, changing doctrine and stripping down the liturgy. Zwingli moved even farther than Luther had toward a purely symbolic understanding of the Eucharist, and Philip Melanchthon's efforts to mediate between these reformers' views could not achieve reconciliation and build unity within emerging Protestantism. The patriotic Zwingli died bearing arms in the second battle of Kappel in 1531 during the civil war between the Protestant and Catholic cantons.

The Selection

Zwingli addressed *Of the Upbringing and Education of Youth* (1523) to the young noble-man Gerold Meyer von Knonau. By his own admission, the treatise is haphazard, but he feared that if he waited he would never complete a full and careful treatment of education. Zwingli does not map out a curriculum much beyond mastery of Latin, Greek, and He-brew. Instead, he focuses on character. The properly educated youth will manifest modesty, moderation, self-control, simple tastes, obedience, nobility, service to his neighbor, and hard work.

Of the Upbringing and Education of Youth in Good Manners and Christian Discipline

To the noble and pious youth Gerold Meyer, I, Ulrich Zwingli, wish grace and peace from God and our Lord Jesus Christ. On your return from the baths at Baden you have been received everywhere with presents, some honouring you in one way and some in another. It would therefore be regarded as most discourteous on my part, my dear Gerold, if I too did not welcome you with a gift: the more so as it is the usual custom amongst friends to honour in that way those who return from or are still at the baths. I number you amongst my friends for two reasons: first, because you are seriously and (as I hope) not unprofit-ably devoted to learning; and second, because you are one of those who serve under our Glareanus. I have considered at length what gift would be most acceptable to you, and I have reached the conclusion that that which will serve you best must be either religious or literary in character, or perhaps both. For by nature you are born to divine favour and virtue, and already you reveal the acceptable fruits of discipline and culture. However, no matter how diligently I applied myself to the task I could never achieve anything of literary merit. Therefore I thought it might be profitable both for yourself and others if I fulfilled my obligation towards you by setting out certain precepts which would be wholesome and helpful for both body and soul and which would serve to the advancement of virtue and piety. For some time I have been planning a book on the right upbringing and education of youth, but my plans were hindered by the many distracting matters which came up (as things then were). But as I have considered what gift I should make, my earlier project has taken shape again. I notice that many writers, when they have finished their work, are anx-ious to dedicate it to someone who is truly worthy of it. But with us the very opposite is the case. For the one to whom this book will be dedicated is already found, but I myself lack the time and leisure, the nine years which a workman should spend upon his work. Being in a strait between the two demands, the first, that I must have something to give you, and the second, that I have had neither the time nor the leisure to fulfil the task properly, I have found, I think, a way to satisfy both of us. I have stolen sufficient time hurriedly to gather together some precepts and admonitions—but not too many, and all carefully selected so as not to drive away, for it is often the case that when little is poured out, the desire to drink is all the greater. You must not weigh and judge these counsels according to their outward form, but according to their content, and the spirit which has given them birth. For anyone who is not ungodly can promise a godly work: but even the most learned would be ashamed to promise a work of art. These precepts of mine fall into three parts:

The first tells how the tender mind of youth is to be instructed in the things of God;

The second, how it is to be instructed in the things which concern itself;

And the third, how it is to be instructed in conduct towards others.

It is not my purpose to set out the directions which ought to be given from the cradle or during the earliest years at school, but those which are suitable for young men who have already attained to discretion and can stand on their own feet. I count you amongst this number. You will, I hope, diligently read these directions and so model yourself upon them that you will be a living example to others. May God himself do this work in you. Amen.

PART I

First and chiefly, it is beyond our human capacity to bring the hearts of men to faith in the one God even though we had an eloquence surpassing that of Pericles. For that is something which only our heavenly Father can do as he draws us to himself. Yet it is still the case, in the words of St. Paul, that "faith cometh by hearing, and hearing by the Word of God," though this does not mean that very much can be accomplished by the preaching of the external word apart from the internal address and compulsion of the Spirit. Therefore it is necessary not merely to instil faith into the young by the pure words which proceed from the mouth of God, but to pray that he who alone can give faith will illuminate by his Spirit those whom we instruct in his Word.

It seems to me to be quite in keeping with Christ's own teaching to bring young people to a knowledge of God in and through external phenomena. For as we bring before them the fair structure of the universe, pointing them to each part in particular, we learn that all these things are changing and destructible, but that he who conjoined them (and many other things besides) in so lasting and marvellous a whole is necessarily unchanging and immutable. Again, we learn that he who has so skilfully ordered all these things need never be suspected of forgetting or disregarding his handiwork, for even with men it is counted a reproach if the head of the household does not keep a careful watch over all domestic matters.

Thus the young man is taught that all things are ordained by the providence of God: for of the two sparrows sold for a farthing not one can fall to the ground except by decision of the divine providence (which has also numbered the very hairs of our head), nothing being too insignificant for its care.

Hence it is clear that the divine providence appoints the things necessary for the body as well as the soul. We see that by it the ravens are liberally fed and the lilies gloriously arrayed. By such forms of the divine providence the spirit of man is taught that it ought never to give way either to anxiety or to ignoble greed. And if the temptation to greed or anxiety is hewn down and uprooted as soon as it begins to spring up, we shall keep our soul from a harmful poison.

For we shall then know in our heart that God is not only the Lord but also the Father of all those who trust in him. We shall know that men ought to run to him for help no less than they do to an earthly father. We shall know that in his words he has promised us that help, indeed he wills that we should make our prayer to him. If, then, we are afflicted by sickness of mind or body, we are taught to look only to him for healing. If we are oppressed by enemies or harassed by envy and hatred, we learn to flee only to him. If we desire wisdom or learning, we are taught to ask it of him alone. Indeed, it is from him that we are to seek even our wife and children, and if riches and honour are showered liberally upon us, we ought to pray to him that our heart may be kept from corruption or from turning aside from him.

I need not say more. Instructed in this way, the soul knows that it ought to ask all things from God. And it knows how shameful it is to ask anything which God cannot fittingly give. In fact, it will be ashamed either to ask or to have anything that it cannot fittingly receive from God. It will keep before it and lay up for itself only the things which are a true source of blessing.

The young man whom we teach will know and understand the mystery of the Gospel as follows. First, he must know the original estate of man, how he transgressed the commandment of God and became a prey to death, how by his transgression he infected and corrupted his offspring—the whole human race—for the dead cannot give birth to the living and we do not find Moors born in Britain. From this the young man will learn and acknowledge his own sickness. And he will see that sickness, too, when he realizes that everything that we do has its origin in frailty, lust and temptation, but God himself is far above all such temptation, for in him is no temptation. Hence it follows that if we would dwell with God, we must be set free from all temptations. There can be no fellowship between the godly and the wicked, nor can the wicked bear with the godly (for the Neros order the Senecas to be punished, and the Ennii and the Scipios are covered by the same tomb). Similarly, only those can dwell with God who are holy (as God himself is holy), whose lives are without blemish and whose hearts are pure: "Blessed are the pure in heart, for they shall see God."

But beset on every hand by gross temptations, how can we attain to such purity? for we are set between the hammer and the anvil, half beast and half angel. God requires of us a perfect righteousness, but we are corrupted and full of sin and whether we will or no we can do nothing but evil. Therefore we have no choice but to give up ourselves into the hand of God, to abandon ourselves entirely to his grace. And here it is that there breaks forth the light of the Gospel, the good news proclaimed to us that Christ releases us from the desperate plight in which we were held. And Christ redeems us far better than any Saviour Jupiter. First he restores the conscience, which is reduced almost to despair. He unites it with himself in an unshakable hope, thus setting it at rest. For he himself is free from all the pollutions and onslaughts of sin, being conceived of the Holy Ghost and born of a pure Virgin. And first he puts forth his righteousness for us, bearing our griefs and sicknesses: then he redeems all those who steadfastly believe. For those who believe in the bountiful gift which God has made our poor race in Christ are saved and made co-heirs with Christ, to enjoy eternal felicity with the Father: for he wills that where he is, there his servants may be also.

The righteousness of Christ, put forth for us who are sinful and lost, releases us from sin and the guilt and suffering of sin and makes us worthy before God. And it does so for this reason, that Christ is able to attain the standard of divine righteousness, being free from all corrupt affections. And he, the righteous and more than righteous, that is, God himself, was made like one of us. Hence it follows that his righteousness (which lacked in us) was made ours: "for of God he is made unto us wisdom, righteousness, sanctification and redemption." Now therefore we have access by him to God, for he is ours, a sure token of divine grace, an advocate, a pledge, a security, an intercessor, a mediator, the first and the last, the alpha and omega, our all.

Those who understand and believe the mystery of the Gospel thus far are born of God: for blinded by human folly the mind cannot of itself attain to the deep counsel of divine grace. By this we learn that those who are born again of the Gospel do not sin: for "whosoever is born of God sinneth not," and whosoever believes the Gospel is born of God. Hence it follows that those who are born again of the Gospel do not sin, that is, sin is not imputed to them to death and perdition, for Christ has redeemed them at the price of his death.

As long as we are absent from the Lord in this mortal body we cannot be free from temptations. Therefore we cannot be entirely without sin. But Christ himself is ours and makes good all our deficiencies. For he is an eternal God and Spirit. And that means that he is of sufficient value to redeem the offences of all men, more so indeed than the offences themselves can possibly require.

But such confidence in Christ does not make us idle. On the contrary it equips and constrains us to do good and to live rightly, for such confidence is not of man. For in most things the human mind depends upon the external senses. But how can it come to put its confidence in something which none of the senses can perceive? In view of this, we can very well see that such faith and confidence in Christ can derive only from God. Now where God works, you need have no fear that things will not be done rightly.

For God is an entelechy, that is, a perfect and immutable force which moves all things and itself remains unmoved. And as such, he will never allow the heart which he has drawn to himself to be unmoved or static. This statement has to be confirmed, not by proofs but by practice. For only believers know and experience the fact that Christ will not let his people be idle. They alone know how joyful and pleasant a thing it is to engage in his service.

Therefore those who have rightly understood the mystery of the Gospel will exert themselves to live rightly. As far as possible, then, we should learn the Gospel with all exactness and diligence. And as occasion offers we should study what services will be most pleasing to God: and undoubtedly these are the very ones which he himself renders to us, righteousness, fidelity and mercy. For God is a Spirit, and he can be truly worshipped only with the sacrifice of a consecrated spirit. The young man should see to it, then, that he studies to grow up a man of God, righteous in life and as nearly like God as possible. For God does good to all and is profitable to all. He does hurt only to those who first do hurt to him. So, too, the man who is most like God is the one who studies to be profitable to all, to be all things to all men, and to keep himself from all forms of evil. When we consider our own powers, these things are very difficult, but "to him that believeth all things are possible."

PART II

Once a young man is instructed in the solid virtue which is formed by faith, it follows that he will regulate himself and richly adorn himself from within: for only he whose whole life is ordered finds it easy to give help and counsel to others.

But a man cannot rightly order his own soul unless he exercises himself day and night in the Word of God. He can do that most readily if he is well versed in such languages as Hebrew and Greek, for a right understanding of the Old Testament is difficult without the one, and a right understanding of the New is equally difficult without the other.

But we are instructing those who have already learned the rudiments, and everywhere Latin has the priority. In these circumstances I do not think that Latin should be altogether neglected. For an understanding of Holy Scripture it is of less value than Hebrew and Greek, but for other purposes it is just as useful. And it often happens that we have to do the business of Christ amongst those who speak Latin. No Christian should use these languages simply for his own profit or pleasure: for languages are gifts of the Holy Ghost.

After Latin we should apply ourselves to Greek. We should do this for the sake of the New Testament, as I have said already. And if I may say so, to the best of my knowledge the Greeks have always handled the doctrine of Christ better than the Latins. For that reason we should always direct our young men to this source. But in respect of Greek as well as Latin we should take care to garrison our souls with innocence and faith, for in these tongues there are many things which we learn only to our hurt: wantonness, ambition, violence, cunning, vain philosophy and the like. But the soul, like Ulysses, can steer safely past all these if it is only forewarned, that is, if at the first sound of the voices it pays heed to the warning: Hear this in order to shun and not to receive.

I put Hebrew last because Latin is in general use and Greek follows most conveniently. Otherwise I would willingly have given Hebrew the precedence, for in many places even amongst the Greeks those who are ignorant of Hebrew forms of speech have great difficulty in attempting to draw out the true sense of Scripture. But it is not my purpose to speak exhaustively of these languages.

If a man would penetrate to the heavenly wisdom, with which no earthly wisdom ought rightly to be considered, let alone compared, it is with such arms that he must be equipped. And even then he must still approach with a humble and thirsting spirit.

If he does come, however, he will everywhere find patterns of right conduct, that is, he will find Christ himself, the perfect exemplar of all virtues. And if he knows Christ fully both in his words and deeds, he will know that in all his acts and counsels, so far as human frailty allows, he must venture to manifest some part of the virtues of Christ.

He will learn of Christ both in speech and in silence, each at the proper time. In early youth, he will be ashamed to speak those things which are more fitting in adults, for he will note that Christ did not begin to preach until about his thirtieth year. It is true that when he was only twelve he attracted the attention of the doctors of the law, but from this instance we do not learn to rush in hastily, but from early youth to exert ourselves in the high matters which are worthy of God.

For as silence is always the greatest adornment of a wife, so nothing is more becoming to youth than to try to be silent for a time, so that mind and tongue may be instructed both individually and together, and thus learn to co-operate with each other. It is not my intention to enforce a five years' silence, like that which Pythagoras demanded of his disciples, but to warn against a too great readiness in speech. And I forbid a young man to speak at all unless he has something useful and necessary to say.

Quite naturally, a young man acquires the manner of speech of his teacher. He must be careful, then, not to follow him in what is bad, for even in speech there is sure to be some defect. And this warning must not be treated too lightly, for amongst the ancients it is recorded that some imitated their masters' defects not only in speech but in life. To recognize deficiency in language is easy, but in expression and enunciation (we are not speaking technically, for which this is not the place) the common faults are these: the rate of speaking is either too fast or too slow; the tone is either too low and weak or too high and strong, irrespective of the subject matter; the style is monotonous: and the accompanying gestures are hackneyed, or perhaps the gesticulation is not appropriate to what is being said.

It has been observed that when elephants are alone they anxiously apply themselves to learn things for which they are beaten. In the same way the young man should constantly practise how to compose his mouth and features, and also how to use his hands, so that he may rightly indicate whatever is required and not merely beat the air.

And in all these things he must study moderation, that what he does may serve the truth and not merely please men: for how can the Christian soul countenance such meretricious devices? So then, when I ask that the young man should practise, I mean only that each one should learn privately to master or to eliminate his external faults, which are always the sure marks of an undeveloped or defective spirit.

Above all else, the spirit itself must be sound and ordered. Where such is the case, it is easy to control the external movement of the features, so that instead of knitting our brows or twisting our mouths or shaking our heads or tossing our hands hither and thither we direct all our gestures with the simple and unaffected moderation of the peasant. Thus far concerning speech and silence.

Superfluity of wine is something which the young man must avoid like poison. In the young its effect is to inflame the body, which by nature is already prone to violence and lust. It also brings to premature age. And from the very outset it so corrupts the body that instead of finding in age the peace which we supposed we meet with nothing but trouble. For those who are accustomed to excess of wine will inevitably succumb at length to some dangerous sickness, epilepsy, paralysis, dropsy, elephantiasis and the like. Therefore if you would be old long, be old betimes.

Other foods ought to be plain, for in youth the stomach is naturally designed to be fit, and what need is there of partridge, thrush, titlark, goat, roebuck and other delicacies? Much better to leave such things until old age, when the teeth and jaws are worn out and the throat has hardened with long use and the stomach has grown cold and the body is half-dead; it is then that these things are needed. For how shall we nourish our old age if for lack of self-control wanton youth has grown weary of the very things which age desires and in which it delights?

Hunger we should stay by eating but not banish completely. For it is written that Galenus lived for a hundred and twenty years because he was never satisfied when he left the table. I do not mean that you should starve yourself to death, but that you should not give rein to a voracious appetite (beyond what is necessary for life). I know quite well that in this matter there are faults on both sides. On the one hand there is the man who is wolf-like in his voracity: and on the other hand the man who makes himself useless for lack of sustenance.

I can think of nothing more foolish than to seek fame by way of expensive apparel. If we are to judge only according to outward appearance, we shall have to ascribe glory and honour to the papal mules, which are so strong that they can carry more gold and silver and precious stones than any Milo. But who will not be ashamed of such costly attire when he hears of the Son of God and of the Virgin crying in the manger, with no more clothes in which to be swaddled than those which the Virgin Mary had taken with her (not yet expecting his birth).

Those who make daily display of new clothes give sure evidence of an inconstant, or (if that is too strong) an effeminate or childish turn of mind. They are not Christians. For while they array themselves after this fashion they allow the destitute to perish with cold and hunger. So then the Christian must guard against excessive and wanton apparel as against any other form of evil.

It is when the young man begins to fall in love that he must show true nobility of spirit. And as in war others exercise their arms with weapons and feats of strength, so the young man must now apply all his forces in defence against senseless passion. That he should fall in love is inevitable. But let him be careful not to give way to despairing passion, but to single out as the object of his affection someone whose ways he can always bear with in lawful wedlock. Let him approach that one, but let his union with her be so pure and undefiled that apart from her he knows no other.

What need is there to forbid the Christian youth all desire for fame or wealth when such evils are castigated even by pagan writers? He is no Christian who gives way to covetous ambition, the ambition which not only engulfs ones and twos and threes but overthrows flourishing kingdoms, devastates powerful cities and attacks and overturns the very foundations of government. Once this evil takes hold of the spirit, right conduct becomes impossible. Ambition is a deadly poison. And today it has gained the mastery and is rampant everywhere. Only through Christ can we destroy this evil, by seeking diligently to follow him: for what was Christ's work except to destroy this evil?

I advise the young man not to despise mathematics (with which we may also reckon music), but he ought not to devote too much time to this subject. It is useful to those who know it and an obstacle to those who do not. But it does not yield any great profit to those who grow old in its service, and they are reduced to wandering from place to place in order not to perish for lack of activity.

I do not blame anyone for learning the art of war, but I should judge differently if I did not see other kingdoms fleeing the pursuits which are beneficial to the life of the community. A Christian should avoid the weapons of war as far as the security and peace of the state allow. For God made David to triumph when he was unskilled in arms and went against Goliath with a sling. And he protected the unarmed Israelites against the invading enemy. Undoubtedly, then, he will help and protect us—or if he sees fit he will put weapons in our hands. For "he teaches our hands to fight." But if the young man does undergo military training, he must see to it that his only purpose is to protect his own country and those whom God approves.

It is my wish that all men (and especially those who are commanded to preach the Word of God) should make it their aim to be able to emulate the ancient city of Marseilles, which numbered amongst its citizens only those who were masters of a trade and could support themselves. If that were so with us, then idleness, which is the root and seed of all forms of wantonness, would be excluded, and our bodies would be healthier and stronger and would live longer.

PART III

The noble spirit must first consider the fact that Christ gave himself up to death on our behalf and became ours: therefore we ought to give up ourselves for the good of all men, not thinking that we are our own, but that we belong to others. For we are not born to live to ourselves, but to become all things to all men.

From early boyhood, then, the young man ought to exercise himself only in righteousness, fidelity and constancy: for with virtues such as these he may serve the Christian community, the common good, the state and individuals. Only the weak are concerned to find a quiet life: the most like to God are those who study to be of profit to all even to their own hurt.

In this connection, however, we must be careful to see that the things undertaken for God's honour or the state or the common good are not corrupted by the devil or by self-pleasing, so that in the long run we turn to our own interest that which we want to be regarded as undertaken in the interests of others. For many begin well at the first, but they are quickly perverted and turned aside from all that is good by that vainglory which is the bane of all good counsels.

As regards the good or evil fortunes of others, a Christian spirit will conduct itself as if they were his own. When fortune comes to another he will think of it as coming to himself, and similarly with adversity. For he will look upon the whole fellowship only as one household or family, indeed as one body, in which all the members rejoice and suffer together and help one another, so that whatever happens to one happens to all.

So then he will "rejoice with them that do rejoice and weep with them that weep," looking upon the fortunes of others as his own; for as Seneca says, What happens to one can happen to everyone.

Yet the Christian ought not to show joy or grief after the common manner, being carried away by good fortune and plunged into despair by evil. On the contrary, seeing we must always be affected either by the one emotion or the other, we ought so to moderate them (if we are wise) that we never trespass the bounds of due decorum. And that is how we are to rejoice at the prosperity of others as at our own, and that is how we are also to weep, bearing all things with moderation and self-control.

I do not believe that a young man should be debarred from seemly pleasures, for instance at those times when the sexes are accustomed to come together publicly, the marriage of relatives, annual games, carnivals and festivals: for I note that Christ himself did not despise the wedding feast. Seeing such things are necessary, I am better pleased if they are done publicly and not in corners or secretly, for the multitude of witnesses is more frightening to some than their own conscience, and if there are any who are shameless enough to conduct themselves indecorously in public, no good can be expected of them.

When communal gatherings of this kind do take place, the young man ought always to study to profit by them, so that he will not return home any the worse (which was the complaint of Socrates). To that end he should mark those who are behaving honourably and decorously, that he may be able to follow them, and also those who are behaving scandalously and dishonourably, that he may avoid them.

But these things are not suitable for adults. For that reason it is my advice that the young ought to be allowed to attend such gatherings as infrequently as possible. Inevitably there is an almost frantic enthusiasm for associating with others in this way, but recovery from this enthusiasm should be swift. To help toward recovery, reasons can be offered which will satisfy those who realize that we are intent always upon better things.

When a neighbour is in trouble, we ought not to allow anything to hinder us from going. We should be the first there and the last away, and we must exert ourselves, to weigh the hurt, treating it and removing it and proffering counsel.

Next to immortal God our parents ought to be held in highest esteem, as is customary even amongst pagans and unbelievers. To our parents we ought always to yield. And though at times they may not act according to the mind of Christ (which is our mind), we must not oppose them violently, but tell them as gently as possible what they ought to say and do. And if they will not listen, it is better to leave them than to insult or reproach them.

Anger (as the natural scientists tell us) is a product of heat; and as youth is the time of heat, the young man ought to keep a careful watch against anger, that his words and actions may not be impelled by it. Since anger continues with us, we ought to mistrust anything that might give rise to it.

If an insult is offered which we cannot swallow because it is too bitter, it is better to bring the matter before a magistrate or to take it to court. For if we give back word for word or reproach those who reproach us, we only make ourselves like those whom we reproach.

At the proper time there is no reason why you should not play games with your equals, but they ought to be useful either educationally or as bodily exercise. Games with educational value are those which involve numbers (from which we learn arithmetic), or strategy, as for example chess, which teaches how to advance and retreat, and how to keep careful watch behind and before; for the main lesson we learn from this game is not to assume anything rashly. But even in this moderation is to be observed, for there are some who push aside the serious affairs of life and give themselves to this one thing alone. For my part, I would allow such recreations only occasionally and as a pastime. Dicing and card-games I condemn absolutely.

The games which exercise the body are running, jumping, throwing, fighting and wrestling, but the latter only in moderation, for it often takes on a serious character. Such sports are common to almost all peoples, but especially amongst the Swiss, who find them useful in many different circumstances. I do not find the same value in swimming, though at the proper time it is pleasurable to stretch one's limbs in water and imitate the fish. And on occasion swimming has also proved useful, as with the man who swam from the Capitol and told Camillus of the pitiable state to which the city had been reduced by covetousness. Chloelia too escaped to her own people by swimming.

Our conversation and speech should all be of a kind to profit those with whom we live. If we have to reprove or punish, we ought to do it wisely and wittily, and so good humouredly and considerately that we not only drive away the offence but win over the offender, binding him more closely to us.

We ought to follow after truth with such consistency and single-heartedness that we weigh not only our own speech but that of others, lest it contain any deceit or falsehood. A man of noble spirit is never more perturbed than when he involuntarily lets slip an untruth—not to mention his shame and horror when he lets out a flood of idle and empty gossip invented by himself or repeated from others. The Christian is commanded to speak truth with his neighbour. Christ himself is the truth. Therefore the Christian must cleave steadfastly to the truth. "A double-minded man is unstable in all his ways." A man who is inconsistent in his speech cannot be trusted. The heart declares itself in speech. If the speech be empty and untruthful and inconsistent, it is a sure sign that things are far worse inwardly. At the same time, lies cannot be concealed indefinitely, although they may be for a long time. For that reason it is foolish to cherish or mitigate a secret evil by hoping that it will remain secret.

But we must study to be truthful not only in our words but in all our actions. We must never do anything which is manifestly false. The face and hands and all the external features must not pretend to be other than the heart, which is the source of all our actions. If someone enters in a way quite different from that which his nature demands, his affected walk is quite enough to show us what manner of man he is, frivolous, and of a dissolute spirit.

But what need I say more? The young man ought to fix his whole attention upon the fullest possible absorbing of Christ himself. Where that is done, he will be a rule to himself. And acting rightly, he will never be lifted up or cast down. He will increase daily, but he will see to it that he himself decreases. He will progress, but he will always reckon himself the least of all. He will do good to others, but he will never hold it against them, for that was the way of Christ. And to be perfect, we must set ourselves to follow Christ alone.

These then, my dear Gerold, are what appear to me to be the essentials in the instruction of a young nobleman. I need not draw attention to the disjointedness of their presentation, for that is easily perceived. It is for you to ponder them in your mind and then to express in your conduct that which I have roughly sketched out on paper. In so doing, you will give order to that which is scattered and disorderly, and you will be a living example of the rule which I have written out for you. Indeed, if you apply yourself to them, may it not be that you will attain a greater completeness and perfection than I have been able to show in words. But you will have to stretch every nerve, which will have the useful result of banishing indolence, the mother of all mischief, to which so many are of evil custom shamefully addicted, as though their only ambition were to live upon others and to fulfil all manner of wickedness. But turn your own youth to good account, as the poet said, for the time passes quickly and the latter days are seldom better than the former.

The true Christian is not the one who merely speaks about the laws of God, but the one who with God's help attempts great things. And for that reason, noble youth, see to it that you adorn more illustriously and with true adornment the fair gifts of race, physique and patrimony with which you have been endowed. I say less than I ought? Rank, beauty and wealth are not genuine riches, for they are subject to chance. The only true adornments are virtue and honour. May God so lead you through the things of this world that you may never be separated from him. Amen.

Juan Luis Vives

1492–1540

This then is the fruit of all studies; this is the goal. Having acquired our knowledge, we must turn it to usefulness, and employ it for the common good.

THE TRANSMISSION OF KNOWLEDGE

Juan Luis Vives was born in Valencia, Spain, in the year of Columbus's first voyage to the New World and under the rule of an empire newly unified by Isabella and Ferdinand. He was educated at an academy in Valencia and then at the College of Beauvais, Paris. He turned away, however, from the extreme dialectical method he learned at Valencia and Paris and supported instead the grammarians and rhetoricians of the humanist revival. He lived and taught in Leuven and studied there for a short time under Erasmus, who welcomed Vives enthusiastically as an ally in the spread of humanism. At Leuven he lectured on Cicero and Pliny and formed a friendship with the distinguished Greek scholar Guillaume Budé. In 1522, Vives published his commentaries on Augustine's *City of God,* dedicating the work to King Henry VIII. He also dedicated *De Institutione Feminae Christianae* (1523) to Queen Catherine.

With the encouragement of Thomas More, Cardinal Wolsey invited Vives to Oxford, where Vives divided his time between his rooms at Corpus Christi College and Henry's turbulent court. He supervised the education of Princess Mary and wrote *De ratione studii puerilis* (1523) for her instruction. Vives sided with the Spanish Catherine of Aragon in Henry's attempted divorce, but urged her, unsuccessfully, not to cooperate with the sham trial. Henry asked him to leave the household, and Vives lost his royal patronage. In 1528 he returned to Bruges, where he had lived off and on for many years. He met Ignatius Loyola there, possibly influencing the Jesuits' educational reforms. Vives died in Bruges at the age of 48. Among Vives's many other works are *An Introduction to Wisdom* (1524) and translations into Latin of Isocrates' *Areopagitica* and *Nicocles.*

Thomas More praised the young Vives's work as "elegant and learned." More asked, "Who surpasses Vives in the number and quality of his studies?" "Who instructs with more clearness, with more pleasure, or with more success than Vives?"[1] Despite this high praise, Vives nearly vanished from memory when utilitarianism swept through educational theory in the nineteenth century. Still, John Henry Newman included long passages from Vives's *Causes of the Corruption of the Arts and Sciences* in the appendix to the first edition of *The Idea of a University.* And Foster Watson, who translated a few of Vives's educational treatises into English in the early twentieth century and tried to claim him (unconvincingly) as a precursor of the Baconians, suggested that he could be considered "emphatically the greatest European educational leader of the first half of the sixteenth century."[2]

THE SELECTION

Vives's *The Transmission of Knowledge (De tradendis disciplinis)* was published in Latin in Antwerp in 1531 and not translated into English until 1913. Two chapters from the book's appendix are included here, "The Aim of Studies" and "The Scholar and the World." Like Augustine, Vives is keenly interested in what could be called the "moral framework" of education, or the prerequisites of character necessary to true education. Education requires humility, not boastfulness; gratitude to God, not grasping ambition; and a generous spirit of mutual service to the truth, not competition. Vives insists that education must aim at usefulness, but this standard of judgment is not the utilitarian dream of power and mastery over the material world. Rather, education must be useful in cultivating wisdom and in serving the wider community.

from The Transmission of Knowledge
"The Aim of Studies"

Now that we have finished the consideration of the humanistic arts, let us state what the man thus cultured should do, how he should spend the rest of his life, whether separately by himself or with others, in the employment and practice of the knowledge he has acquired, and in its dissemination; how he should bear himself towards his colleagues who are similarly equipped with knowledge and training; how he should receive their opinions and judgments concerning himself; and how he should consign his contributions to literature, so as to transmit them to posterity.

He will not necessarily follow the details one by one, in the order in which we have dealt with them. He will not think it wrong to glance back again at what has been dis-

---

1. Foster Watson, *On Education: A Translation of the* De tradendis disciplinis *of Juan Luis Vives* (Cambridge: Cambridge University Press, 1913), xxiii.
2. Ibid., vii.

cussed earlier, even when he has reached a later stage. He will mix his studies and consult again the first part when he has reached the third, and the third when he is studying, say, the sixth. For all studies have a connexion with one another, and a certain affinity. One may be taken in hand because it is necessary for present usefulness; another because it is an alleviation from present labour. The student will be always desirous of learning, and will never suppose that he has already reached the highest point of learning. Seneca has said very incisively: That many men would attain to true learning, if they did not believe that they had already attained to it. So Lucilius said: A man must go on learning, as long as he is ignorant of anything, and if we credit the proverb, "as long as he lives," since there is no subject in the whole of nature so manifest and easy, which might not occupy the whole age of man's life. The man really desirous of learning will not blush to learn from any man whatsoever, who can teach him anything. Why should one man be ashamed to learn from another man, when the whole human race is not ashamed to learn many things from beasts. But a man must so study as not to shatter his mind by overwork. Especially one must have due regard to sound health, and the health of those committed to our care. When learned men realise that they excel the rest of mankind in mind, judgment, knowledge of things, or that at least others regard them as if they did so excel, they then entertain haughty spirits, as if the men amongst whom they lived, were cattle—whence is developed an incredibly great arrogance. That is a holy saying of the Apostle Paul: That men are puffed up by knowledge whilst they are edified by love. The follower of wisdom may turn his eyes on himself, nor does he need any other testimony than that in which his own conscience reposes. He will weigh in his mind how many things there are which he is conscious that he does not know, yet which others never doubt he does know; how often he wanders in mind, how often he slips, how often he is deceived, and how far he departs from the truth, so that not without the greatest reason and cause, Socrates, who was called by the consent of Greece, the wisest of men, confessed that "neither he nor any other man knew anything." This great saying has constantly possessed the minds of the philosophers. And certainly if anyone rightly weighs the matter, and counts it out, he will find that "there is nothing we know more certainly than the duties of religion." But rightly the opinion of Theophrastus is praised, "that even the knowledge possessed by all men, is a very small portion compared with the amount of that, of which all men are ignorant." To follow this aspect at further length is apart from our purpose. What if anyone would examine things one by one, and bring them to a close testing, would not those magnificent titles to knowledge begin to appear paltry? What are languages other than words? Or what importance is it to know Latin, Greek, Spanish and French, if the knowledge contained in those languages were taken away from them? Dialectic and Rhetoric are the means of knowledge, not knowledge itself, and are better taught us by Nature, than by a master.

All philosophy has depended upon opinions and conclusions from probability. But this is not the place for expounding this question in detail. Well, then, we will grant that you know something sure and ascertained. Do you not recognise that you have had that benefit of knowledge conferred on you by another? Why should another's garment fitted on you make your mind arrogant? If you have got something good, it is another's; if it is bad, it is your own alone. For if you learn well, then it is God's gift, and you will displease Him, if you do not ascribe to Him all the glory which accrues to you through your learning. I have nothing to say against a learned man perceiving that he is learned and esteeming himself as wiser than other men, for he would neither be learned nor wise, unless he saw this clearly. But I wish him to remember from Whom he received that wisdom, and having received it, to ascribe it to Him alone, from Whom he possesses it, even as if it were a mortgage. If he sees that he is admired by men, let him not be self-satisfied, which is a dangerous thing, nor let his eyes settle on the ground, so that honour should be offered him by men, and applaud himself as if he had performed his work by his own merit. This, as Job says, is to kiss one's own hand, the greatest of iniquities, and the greatest denial of God.

Erudition involves four factors: natural capacity, judgment, memory, application. Pray tell me, whence the first three of these come: whence except from God? If praise is to be given to learned man, it must be sought in the last-named element. And this element is the lowest and least of all, and even for that how greatly is a man helped by having a bodily frame, not heavy, nor stupefied, but of sound health. And are not these states of the body the gift of God? What then remains in himself for the learned man to boast about? Well, do you say; He has willed to work? But how many others would will, if it were, through the goodness of God, permitted to them to do what it is permitted to you? Amid the praises given to himself, the wise man directs himself to the contemplation of that holy and divine wisdom, in comparison with the lowest part of which, as Paul says, all human wisdom is mere foolishness. Let it come into a man's mind, that, if men are stirred so greatly by the sight of a single little drop, how would they bear themselves, if there were vouchsafed to them the sight of that full and eternal spring, whence the whole current of wisdom flows? Then will he adore, with humble mind, the Giver of all good gifts, and return thanks that He has held him worthy of gifts in richer proportion than He has imparted to others; and that He has willed him to be the instrument of any part of His counsel and His work. For all of us are the instruments of His will. Therefore no man has so great an erudition, or is so endowed with so much practical wisdom, that he should suppose that God has need of him for the working out of His plans. For firstly it is a most thorough piece of presumption to suppose that you can excel in something, in which no other could excel if he applied his mind to it. For God needs no human instruments for carrying out His plans. With clay he can open the eyes of the blind. "From stones he can raise up sons to Abraham, and he has chosen the weaklings of the world to confound the strong." If you then have become so wise and distinguished a man, by the goodness of God, then also those others to whom He has vouchsafed a similar blessing will also be as wise and distinguished as you.

We must therefore pray to Him, Who gives us everything, and Who works through us, what seems good to Him, that our learning be turned to our good, lest He make us an instrument to the good of others, whilst it becomes an injury to ourselves; so that it may not happen to us, as is the case sometimes with bad doctors, who cure others, but cannot heal themselves; or as with the trumpeters who incite others on to battle, whilst they themselves take no part in the fight; or as with candles, which afford light to others, whilst they themselves are burnt out. And so, as often as we proceed to study, let us begin by prayer, as is recorded of Thomas Aquinas and many other holy men. Certainly we ought to pray that our studies may be sound, of no harm to anybody, and that we may be sources of sound health to ourselves and the community at large.

If now we must propose some end to each of the actions of our life, so much the more must this be the case with studies, so that it may be settled whither our labour tends.

We must not always be studying so that we do nothing but study, nor must the mind, bound by no law and with no useful aim, delight itself in any inane sort of contemplation and knowledge of things. Socrates said that he had no time to busy himself with poetic fables, since he did not as yet know himself, and that it was ridiculous that he who did not know himself should closely investigate other people's concerns. Much less is the fruit of studies to be estimated by their return in money. Such an opinion has only been held by debased natures, who are far removed from any true idea of studies. For nothing is so distant from literature as either the desire or the anxiety for money; so that wherever this desire settles in a man of studies, forthwith it drives away the zeal for intellectual research, because study does not commit itself with full confidence to any souls, except those free and loosed from that disease. People say: "First get rich; then become philosophical." Nay, rather it should be said: "We must first philosophise, and afterwards get rich." For if we first get rich we shall soon no longer wish to busy ourselves with philosophy, and, made anxious by the possession of wealth, snatched away to a thousand vices, ignorant of philosophy, we shall be ignorant of the true use of riches. But if once we become philosophers, then it will be easy, afterwards, to get as rich as it is at all necessary to be. One can suggest no case in which anyone applying industry to the study of philosophy would not be impelled to the pursuit of practical wisdom. A poor man must study philosophy, because he has nothing, so that the sense of his poverty may be alleviated. The rich man must study philosophy, because he has possessions, so that he may use them more wisely. The happy man will be a philosopher so that he may turn his happiness into a rightful channel. The unhappy man will be a philosopher, so that he may bear his misfortunes the more lightly. To be sure, every kind of knowledge is sold, but with the greater proportion of men, only to their injury; but at any rate the professions should not be practised merely for gain, e.g. law, medicine, theology. The learned man should not press forward to the undertaking of state affairs, although he ought to desire to be of use to as wide a circle as possible. He should not think that he is born for himself alone, as the old philosopher admonished Plato. On this point we have that saying of the Apostle: He who seeks a bishopric seeks a good work. Further, let a good man take possession of the place which previously was held by a bad man. But he who has pressed himself forward has not so much charm and strength as he who is chosen by others. If he be invited, let him first observe diligently the minds of his fellow citizens whether they are sound or curable, so that if by any means he may be able to be of use, he must not refuse to undertake the labour, but if it would only be to take up a useless and irritating work, let him altogether decline. This, Plato is said to have done, because he despaired that he could ever bring the minds of the people into any soundness of health. Princes are, for the most part, of hearts so corrupt, and so intoxicated by the magnitude of their good fortune, that by no art can they be reformed for the better, since they show themselves harsh and insensate to those who would heal them. Those blind men and leaders of the blind, as the Lord calls them, must be left alone. We must transfer our solicitude to the people, who are more tractable, for they offer themselves more easily to be dealt with and are more responsive to one caring for them. This also did Christ, with Whom a Prince is not valued more highly than anyone of the people.

Nothing has so sullied the glory of all kinds of knowledge and of all learning, and debased it, as the frivolity of some smatterers who constantly flatter any people whatsoever especially princes, being particularly drawn to some new rather than some longer-known person. But this is precisely what truly learned men will not do. The mass of the people, it is true, do not understand the difference. They suppose that every one is a learned man, who writes or speaks the Latin tongue in some form or other. Yet those who thus act defend themselves by the specious argument that they did not praise the pseudo-learned men for such, as they really were, but for the qualities which they ought to have shown. This gives but a very slight "colour" to their praise, and one which others do not recognise. Hence they accuse the learned man of sycophancy, and attach the stigma to the profession of literature itself and detest it, as if it commended a wicked Prince, and made him out to be a very good Prince. Nay even the Prince himself, imbued with the depraved opinion, believes that he is estimated as his flatterers describe him. Hence he becomes from day to day more and more arrogant and intolerable. When he has begun this kind of life he gets confirmed in it, since he finds he obtains so much praise from it, and seeing that it has all been handed down to posterity in the works of the learned, he thinks it must therefore be fixed for certain. If the learned men had not been accustomed to flatter princes, then the latter would, on the one hand, have esteemed learning higher, and, on the other, they would rejoice immeasurably to be praised by them, i.e. according to the saying of the ancient poet *a laudatis viris*. Then, too, the learned man's upbraiding would have had great weight. Nor, then, would the approval of a learned man be otherwise than the weightiest testimony of a most conscientious authority. So, too, a prince not less than any others would regard it as the amplest reward of his virtue in this life, to receive the approval of the learned man. But now princes do not value it at a hair, since they see they can buy it for a farthing or two, nay even for a bit of bread. When circumstances justify the praise of princes, let the praise be somewhat sparing, and in such a manner, that they feel that they would rather be admonished and stimulated in their actions than have their praises sung, as if their course of life were already ended. If you may hope for any good from it, vices ought to be freely condemned, only let there be no bitterness nor rage. But if you are only causing hatred, and you can do no good, then it is better to abstain from the useless task. Nor ought the faults of the powerful, nor indeed of any man, to be covered over, on the ground of expectation of a reward, or for the sake of any gain, for this is particularly shameful. For it has the effect that the bad go on the more boldly in their wickedness, and moreover, with the consent of learned men, others are encouraged to follow their example.

There are others who do not seek from their studies to obtain money, but glory. This is a little better I confess, but only if in youth and in the young man, it may supply very great goads to noble actions. But when this motive appears later in life, it is the ground and source of many evils, as I have elsewhere shown, because we set all our store on being seen by those looking on, nothing on our conscience, which will judge us, in our actions, more justly than any fellow-man possibly can. And thus we often fall by the hope of glory which we have seized, because he who gave us false credit afterwards perceives his error, or he who judged rightly begins himself to be deceived, although it happens more frequently that mistaken estimates are turned to what is sounder, since time confirms what is true and solid, but shatters and removes false and empty judgments. Therefore let no one have confidence that he will secure glory with posterity through the empty favour of the living and by pretence of noble work. For so soon as the passions which have been stirred up have subsided, judgment enters in their place, and this puts things in more exact proportions. Thus, there are many who were honoured in their lifetime, who, after their death, have been accounted ignoble and contemptible. Hence it happens, as I have already said, that time destroys the falsity of opinions, whilst it strengthens right judgments. How uncertain is fame! how slippery! Many have promised immortality to themselves, and have not been able to retain fame for their lifetime, as e.g. Apion, the grammarian, who, as we read in Pliny, said, That he had endowed with immortality those to whom he had addressed some of his works, yet of his own books, not even a single letter is extant. Nay, also, how unfortunate is the fame of those who have done deserving work! The works of Ovid remain, but not those of Chrysippus or Crantor. The works of Vincent of Beauvais have come to us complete; but not so those of Titus Livius, not those of Polybius, not those of Marcus Varro, not even those of Marcus Tullius Cicero! As Martial not inaptly said, "If a book is going to have a long life, it must have a (protecting) genius." We must add, how changeful a book's fame is! The same book seems beautiful at one time and in certain places, and at another time and in other places, detestable. Many splendid discoveries become obscure by the natural powers and diligence of posterity, so that the later books block up by their size many of the earlier books, just as lights are darkened by the heights of surrounding buildings. But, put the case that you have obtained renown, praise, glory; what good will it be to you when you come to die? For then you will perceive none of these things, which are happening here, no more than the horse, when he is proclaimed victor in the Olympian games, or the picture of Apelles, which we study closely with admiration. What is all the renown of his name, to Cicero? or to Aristotle? So with others, how does their glory now affect them though they were once illustrious in arms or in letters? Or in life itself, if out of public view, what glory does a man feel? What glory affects him when he is asleep? If you are present when you are praised then it necessarily follows that those who praise you to your face, are vain; or else that you willingly listen to words of praise said in your presence. What can in that case be said with propriety? O learned, O eloquent man (nay, rather, O light and empty-minded man!),—not even if you consider a slight meed of praise the due reward of your literary labour. But if you take no note of the praise of men, and desire to obey faithfully your own conscience, and through it, to serve God, how much more lasting and solid glory will be yours, if the living God praises you in your life, if the Ever-Present praises the man before Him; the Immortal God, the mortal man. He who ever looks on thee, He who will pronounce no false judgment, but who will judge you from your own evidence! "Not he that commendeth himself is approved," says Paul, "but whom the Lord commendeth."

A learned man must often reflect on the migration of our temporal life, and on the eternal life, and by meditating often and deeply, make the thought of death familiar, so as not to be terrified by the mention of it. Then will come into his mind, that Judge, the Rewarder of his actions, one by one, before Whom, in a short time, he must appear when he has left the stage and the hypocrisy of life. To be approved of God will then become the sole aim of his life. For to whom else would the accused person or the patron desire to vindicate himself, if he were wise, but to his Judge? To whom else, the athlete, to whom the pugilist, to whom, everyone who does anything which has to receive a judgment upon it? When that old Greek poet had recited his poem, and all men had abandoned him, Plato was worth the whole of the people of Athens to him. Will not Christ be the same to us, by the wisdom of God? "It is a great thing," says an old proverb, "for an athlete to have pleased Hercules." How much more then for us to have pleased God? by Whom we are praised so often as we have done anything pleasing to Him. Certainly there can be nothing more pleasant to Him, than that we offer our erudition and whatsoever of His gifts we possess to the use of our fellow men, i.e. of His children, for whom God has imparted those great goods that to whomsoever they are allotted, they should be of use to the community at large. God wishes us to give freely of that which we have freely received—although for giving up those things which He has so richly bestowed on us, He most abundantly recompenses us. O wonderful kindness of God! For what He gives us freely, He most amply rewards us, if we bestow it on others.

This then is the fruit of all studies; this is the goal. Having acquired our knowledge, we must turn it to usefulness, and employ it for the common good. Whence follows immortal reward not in money, not in present favour, or pleasures, which are fleeting and momentary. Do we then live rightly and teach rightly, if we do it for the sake of money? Would we exchange the rich gift of God for so vile and contemptible a reward? Would we exchange it for glory? Wretch that I should be, if I were to chase so eagerly after that which, in spite of such labours and pains, cannot be preserved, and which is so uncertain and fleeting, that no servitude can be compared with it; more wretched still, if I were to buy people's good word in exchange for such an excellent and holy reward, and prefer to be praised by mortal men rather than by the immortal God; by fools, rather than by Wisdom Itself. O how we fish with a golden hook, for merely foul eels!

With bold confidence, therefore, we must study all branches of knowledge for that use, for which they were appointed by God. We ought therefore, not always to be studying, but our study must be attuned to practical usefulness in life. Every study is unlimited in itself, but at some stage we ought to begin to turn it to the use and advantage of other people. For this purpose, practical wisdom is necessary; because practice leads us to the consideration of subjects separate from one another, and practical wisdom rules as the valuer and judge of the circumstances considered as a whole.

"The Scholar and the World"

If the learned man intends to go into the sight and haunts of men, then should he have thought over his preparation for this purpose, as if he were in training for a fight, so that he should not be taken possession of by any of those debased passions which attack and beset us on every side. For he who is often listened to by others will sometimes listen to himself. Let him strengthen his mind at home, with great and strong thoughts, tending to the disdain of honours and dignities. Let him think of those words which he has heard from God: That they are the salt of the earth, the light of the world. It is little fitting that the salt become savourless, or the light become darkness. For then what are we to think will happen to those things which are salted with such salt, or lighted by such light? Let him then go forth furnished and armed with reasons by which he may successfully resist any attack of his enemy. Let him, in very deed, preserve that "salt" and "light" in the whole framing of his mind, and in the restraint of all emotions; let him use the wisest and most opportune words—so that he be not importunate even in his wisdom, for in that case he will make his wisdom offensive and hateful. But as often as opportunity serves, and wherever he betakes himself, let him show himself to those in his presence, as if he brought health to the assembly. Let him adorn his own bodily bearing with modesty and self-control. In all his words and deeds let there be gravity and consistency, so that he may be an example to others for a like rationality of life. He will indeed convince greatly by his rhetoric, but most of all by his blamelessness of life. So that all which proceeds from him may be the more exact and pure, let him constantly take thought that he says and does nothing which has not got good ground for it, and which may not be followed as an example by right-minded men. For they should be able to think that what he does is a law for their life. But to the evil-minded and envious he should serve as a suggestion to inquiry and an example against false judgments. He must therefore be somewhat cautious in action, slow in judgment, and particularly circumspect in his speech. Through him literature and knowledge will gain a respectful hearing, and many men through their desire for such excellence which they observe in him, will give themselves up to the study of knowledge, because they see such delightful and splendid results in him.

How ashamed must learned men be, that often uneducated men have better control of their passions than they themselves, steeped as they are in the precepts of wisdom. It is for this reason there is often a great outcry by many against the pursuit of learning, and it becomes hated by many, who think they will have more practical wisdom if they have nothing whatever to do with it. For those advantages which learned men bring to the sight of men should in truth excel in their inner worth, not in mere display. A hypocritical mind betrays itself at length, and is so much the more hateful and detestable, the longer and the more prominently it has maintained its false position. Moreover, the roots of truth are great and solid. However much it may be hidden, light will send forth its splendour eventually. Wisely says Epictetus: "The sheep boast not in the presence of the shepherd how much they have eaten on any day, but they show it through its effects, by their milk, wool, and offspring." The mass of studious people call that age happy, in which there is a great amount of learning. But much more is that period of time fortunate in which the learned men show themselves so in very deed, because they have read what will be of advantage to know, and have suggested it to others, who when they hear and see it, are compelled to cry out: Here are those who speak as they live, and live as they speak. This is what the philosopher Adamantius is said to have pronounced on Origen as Eusebius tells us. Do not blush if you do not achieve success in something which you have done as well as you possibly could. Blush to do badly what you could do well. Learned men should show themselves gentle, affable, self-controlled, unvanquished by depraved desires, and should demonstrate how much wisdom can accomplish in the human mind, when it has the sovereignty; and what a great distance there is between the wise man and the fool. It will be sufficient for them if they can be strong and efficacious in the really great and noble matters; not to desire to be esteemed highly in all sorts of occupations, in war, in horsemanship, hunting, fishing, dancing, games, in impudent trifling and raillery. All this is the part of busy-bodies, not of wise men, and learned men become ridiculous who are as zealous in such pursuits, as in that of forming wise judgments. For in the same manner as we perceive nothing clearly if we come out of the light into darkness, nor in going from the dark into the light, so it is not surprising that the learned man talks idly when he is brought in to the discussion of foolish matters, in the same way that triflers are blind in questions of practical wisdom.

It is the work of a learned man to pass on that same learning to others; and, as it were, from his own light to kindle light in the minds of others; like as it is said in the vision of Daniel: That those who have brought many to righteousness "shall shine as the stars for ever and ever," and our Lord said that that man would be called great in the Kingdom of Heaven who himself had fulfilled the precepts of righteousness and taught them to others. And in teaching, what master shall we rather imitate than Christ Himself Whom the Father sent from Heaven to teach the human race. After Him, though at a great distance, come those who have been His followers. He indeed, since He was the Divine Wisdom, only put forward those teachings which would be of service to his listeners, not those which would show how great He Himself was. For if he had sought to declare His glory, or to disclose Himself, what was there He could not do, and what marvels could He not have disclosed! Yet He would have gone beyond all power of comprehension, even of angels. Yet all that He said was for our service, not for His own ostentation. We must seek neither luxuriousness nor delight. Pliny is of opinion that there is an especial ground for studies in the case of those who, unconquered by difficulties, have undertaken, as their own pleasure, to be helpful to others. The Lord was content to have only a few disciples to whom He showed the wisdom of God and the way of eternal salvation. Who can now bewail the fewness of his scholars, when the Creator of the human race was satisfied with a school of twelve men? A large class-room rather serves the object of ambition than that of serious education. Moreover, we ought to take to heart those sayings of the ancients concerning the school: That we must teach without envy, learn without shame, always acknowledging our thanks to the teacher, and not ascribe to ourselves the credit of what has really been discovered by others.

The wise man will reflect that this world is, as it were, a certain State, of which he is a citizen, or as a certain great house, of which he is one of the family, and that it is not matter of consequence by whom anything good is said, as long as it is said truly; that further, here in this State those treasures which are collected together are to be applied to public use; it is of no consequence by whom they were collected, the main point is, they are provided and they should be distributed. Therefore each man, for his part, to the utmost of his strength, will himself contribute, and will freely help others to contribute. Since he is conscious of and alive to his weakness (otherwise he cannot be called a wise or a learned man), let him call to mind how much injury he would inflict on the human race, if he should wish that nobody should be either better or more learned than himself. Moreover, as to the course of instruction, Cicero quotes a passage from Plato, expressing the opinion of Socrates. He writes that the latter was accustomed to state, that his work would be completed, if everyone was sufficiently aroused by his exhortation, to work zealously to see and know the truth. But we will use a better known analogy; a student needs a leader just so long as he does not know the road; but when he is able to proceed along the road alone, he has more need of courage than of a master.

Learned men should live in unity with one another and deal with everyone courteously. For it is very disgraceful in us, that robbers and lions live in greater harmony amongst themselves than do the learned. Neither unanimity nor benevolence will be lacking in the learned, if they have pursued their studies whole-heartedly and religiously; not for glory or reward, for where the desire of these things prevails it is difficult to preserve the sanctity of society. When a comparison of studies is made, then the name of "vanquished" should not be given to the man, who allows that another has argued better than he. For that word "vanquished" signifies something very different from the fact to which it is in this case applied. For in this sort of battle, those who differ are not enemies. This is a very bitter and inimical word applied to what is a very pleasant contest, one in its nature full of good-will between the opponents. For what greater or closer union can we find than that of the mind of one man who is helped by another man's mind towards practical wisdom or virtue. It is a similar relation to that of the husbandman to his field, so that not undeservedly those who train the minds of others may be termed their parents. As is sight to the eyes, so is insight to the mind. Those who cannot see sufficiently clearly through their eyes, yield their judgment to those who have more distinct vision, and do so ungrudgingly. That man possesses sharper and sounder eyes; this man has a mind of clearer insight by nature, or is better trained by experience, age, and industry. Though, of course, sight-observation receives greater praise than mental vision, according to circumstances, as e.g. when a coin is lost, plenty are to be found able to join in the search.

When a man has come to a mature age, we may describe his speeches by such terms as contests, struggles, fights, victories. Let everyone, I beg, consider how great a benefit it is to be freed from the tyranny of ignorance, which is the heaviest and most shameful of all servitudes. Plato says wisely: That it is as much preferable to be beaten in a disputation than to beat, as it is better to be freed from a great evil than to be the one who liberates. For what more deadly thing can happen to men than to form a false opinion? Though in some cases it may be more glorious to be a liberator, it is certainly more useful to be made free. But we should all gladly be delivered from this great evil of ignorance, if disputations were less theatrical, and there were not so much deference shown to the listeners who surround the disputants. The disputation ought to be rather a friendly discussion than a hostile fight for victory. This, should be the case in all kinds of discussions, but particularly in theology, in which subject, impious attacks are made on holy truth, and doubts are started in the minds of listeners, about things which ought to be held as certain, fixed and unshakable. The Demon-Enemy then stirs up these scattered doubts and increases them. Men set their hands to the same work, whilst each one exerts himself for the glory of his intellect, rather than for the assertion of truth. We ought to yield to every truth, not only that which concerns pious and sacred matters, but also in secular affairs, and we ought to obey the precept of the wise man: "In no circumstances, to contradict the word of truth."

Clear and wise judgments are of the greatest use in all studies, when, as Tacitus says, "critics have pronounced their judgments without inflicting injury." For there is nothing more harmful than to confuse the standard of judgments, as in the course of volitions, that a man should not clearly know what sort of actions he approves and what he disapproves. This is an especial danger of our times, when it is most dangerous to speak on almost any subject. So stirred are all men's minds to contentions, and prepared for wordy fighting, that it is not safe to offer observations on any matters even if one is looking at them from another standpoint than that in debate. The tender and weak self-consciousness believes itself to be attacked, as horses afflicted with ulcers instantly are aroused in action, when they hear the scraper or *strigilis*. Nevertheless, very many have offered incitement to the increase of this vice (whilst they bitterly blamed others), not so as to advance the truth, but only for insulting and bringing shame on another's name, either drawn on by hatred or allured by the hope of a false glory, under the impression that by this means they would be regarded as splendid and excellent, just so far as they should manage to show others to be disgraceful. It has happened to them quite otherwise than they expected. For whilst all men praise the intellect of the learned man, when it is pure there is sure blame for the malice of even the most erudite scholar. But, further consider how great a blow all this hatred brings on knowledge. The influence of those men thus hatefully wrangling and, as it were, at enmity to the death, steadily is lost; men of distinguished ability lose courage, and after being made disgusted with all this bitterness, and these perpetual gladiatorial displays, they recoil and shrink from studies. All progress in studies is ruined, and truth is obscured whilst some scholars prefer that letters should remain corrupt rather than be restored to soundness by those men to whom they are unfriendly. How great a crime it is when eloquence, wit and other marvellous gifts of God, given to men by God, for the good of mankind, are converted to its injury, by wrong employment of what is good. Such courses of conduct are not fit for beasts, let alone men. Quintilian, though a heathen, had more religion in him than we Christians. For he said: "It would have been better for us to have been born mutes and to lack all reason, than to convert the gifts of Providence into the injury of men to one another." Of what consequence is it how one person attacks another, whether it is with the sword or with the pen, when the intention is just the same? For the most part, you injure more keenly with speech or with the pen, than with the sword; for you only severely wound the body with the sword, but with language you pierce even the soul. The branches of learning are called humanistic, since they make us human. They have their source in God, to make us good men. He who looks in jealousy on another, in regard to anything with which God has endowed him, does he not impugn the sacred judgment of God and condemn the distribution of His gifts? And yet what ground is there for complaining of God? Has He not dealt profusely in His gifts to you? You see some placed above you, but how many more are there placed less favourably than you? The scholar should be slow in imposing limits, and be far from making rash assertions. When he is going to reprehend anything in others, let him read it over and over again, turn it over in his mind, closely examine it, lest in his condemnation, he affirm anything rashly. If he is commending anything, I would be willing for him to be less circumspect. Let him take care lest he does not sufficiently reflect on what he condemns, so that it shall not happen that the man, to whom he attributes a fault, has greater reason for his view, than he, as a critic, has against him. It would be better to say nothing than that the condemnation should recoil on the judge. But if I expect this practical wisdom, or courtesy, in the learned man, how can I adequately express my feelings with regard to those who twist and distort what has been rightly said, so that they may be thought to be clever controversialists. For if to alter any statement to make it better for some pious and very useful purpose is unlawful in the eyes of many people, it is certainly a great crime to twist it into something worse.

When the Florentine Hadrian (who afterwards was Pope) was yet dean at Leuven, he was often present at the public disputations. If any expressions were brought forward which had been borrowed from authors, he would explain them sympathetically, but never would he speak deprecatingly of any of them, even if some of those quoted were still living, e.g. James Faber and Erasmus of Rotterdam. We ought to speak guardedly of the living, of the dead reverently; for the latter are now exempt from envy and have returned to their Judge, and have undergone of that judgment which remains for all, particularly with regard to their life and moral conduct. It is indeed permissible to speak with somewhat more freedom of their learning. Those authors by whose writings a scholar has made progress should be quoted with gratitude. "Nor should he wish," says Pliny, "rather to be caught in a theft than in paying back a loan, especially when personal advantage has accrued from the borrowing." Formerly men were so just and generous in rendering everyone his own that not a single word would they snatch from another author. This is evident in Plato, Aristotle, Cicero, Seneca, Plutarch and others. Now, words, meanings, and even whole arguments, sometimes discoveries, and works, are appropriated stealthily. This is absolutely a slavish practice and is the source of many animosities in the learned world. For to whom would it not be a serious matter to have his slaves, not to say his sons, led away from him? Would that against this sort of kidnapping there might be the protection of a *lex Fannia*. Nor is it pleasant to find disputes as to the fatherland of a writer, the school of thought, or the date to which he belongs, like that foolish person, whom Horace so wisely censures:

> qui redit in fastos et virtutem aestimat annis.[3]

Not that it is a matter of indifference, for books deserve more respect, when they have satisfied thinkers for many ages, and the consensus of so many minds for so long a period has confirmed the judgment so that there is only substantially one opinion offered concerning the writers. Here, every new opinion only is a hindrance, because it has not yet been thoroughly known and tested. If anyone has corrected another writer in a word or two, or in many words, he should not demand to be constantly considered more learned on that account, or to have it thought that he has therefore rendered greater service to that particular subject. Many men foolishly make this claim for themselves. If they make an emendation in any great author, they think that they must immediately be held superior to that author, as e.g. if a great man makes a slip through lapse of memory or through thoughtlessness (for Horace declares that Homer sometimes is caught napping). Then, too, sometimes knowledge of the (learned) language falls short, and then those semi-learned men seize hold of any mistake in Latin or Greek, as if it were a very great iniquity. They demand from us a knowledge of Latin and Greek speech, i.e. of foreign and unknown languages, such as scarcely is shown in Cicero or Demosthenes, or in any of those writers, who sucked in their language with their mother's milk, and who had the whole of the people as it were for their schoolmaster, and in those points of usage in their language as to which they were in any doubt, they could consult a neighbouring cobbler or a smith. But if those same keen critics were to offer themselves and their works for judgment, they would, I believe, soon become more gentle in their charges against others. We have not a few examples of this most ungracious severity of judgment, not only in ancient times, but in this latest age, e.g. in Laurentius Valla, Politian, Beroaldus, Mancinellus. Nor has our own time produced a smaller number, even if I now pass by the calumnies of this nature, in those writers of

---

3. "He calculates the date and estimates its value according to the number of years it has been written" (*Epistles* II, 1.48).

whom I have spoken when I was dealing with the corruptions of grammar. I should not, indeed, deny that it is in the interest of knowledge that great writers should be criticised adversely, if necessary. But the critic does not instantly contribute more or even as much to the subject by his notes as he who composed the work itself. In the writer on any one branch of learning, you should interpret favourably his mistakes in speaking of another branch, e.g. the mistakes made in theology by the writer of history; the mistakes made in history by the metaphysician; as long as he is satisfactory in his own subject. You should still more leniently excuse any errors of language. We ought to welcome a good sentence expressed in French or Spanish, whilst we should not countenance corrupt Latin. I maintain with Marcus Tullius Cicero himself, that I should prefer the words of wisdom, inelegantly expressed, rather than foolish fluency. Augustine rightly observes, that men are injured by solecisms and barbarisms in proportion to their own weakness of knowledge. The weaker they are, the keener their wish to seem more learned, not in the knowledge of the things which build up their wisdom, but through the signs of outward knowledge, which make it easy to become inflated with arrogance, since even material knowledge often raises a man's neck, if it is not bowed under the yoke of the Lord.

But I would not have the inexperienced and base writers boast as if they had the knowledge of things, because they lack power of expression. On the contrary, such writers deserve double condemnation, first because they are lacking in real knowledge and secondly because they have abandoned all grace and eloquence of words. If indeed the investigation into the subject-matter of knowledge were in their hands, it would be an ignorant and unsuitable demand to begin a controversy with them concerning the words they used, and to start a quarrel with them on that point. For example, it is clear that many words were poured forth, to no purpose, by John Pico in his well-known letter to Hermolaus. For the subject-matter complained of is not to be found in Averroes and Scotus, as he assumes it is, and these writers are not so much to be blamed by us as being base, as for their emptiness.

In the schools and in all life wherever anyone receives praise for his native ability, judgment, study, manifold learning, and knowledge widely spread over various subjects, a man ought certainly never to be extolled in his presence for his virtue and piety, lest he become puffed up by this breeze of praise, and lose the very good itself for which we are praising him, by the fact of his being praised. Nor should he receive other than well-weighed praise, in his absence, and that only for works which we have read. Paul does not wish any man to be the judge of what he has done, or to notice what other men see in him, or what he hears of himself. And the wise man says: "A man does not know if he is worthy of hatred or of love, i.e. we must wait for the end of every man, for man is an animal exceedingly susceptible to change. Learned men should so treat one another that, according to the doctrine of Paul, they should neither judge one another, nor hear unwillingly a judgment passed on themselves, but await patiently that tribunal, and holy and just Court, of God. He judges dementedly and acts shamelessly, who anticipates the judgment of his own fellow servants, which is in the hands of our common Lord. He who has fallen under the judgment of men, let him bear in mind what Paul counselled: "I esteem it as nothing that I am condemned by you or by any human court. The Lord lives. He will truly and justly pass His sentence on me. His examination of me I fear. For that I will prepare myself as far as I am able."

Thomas Elyot

c. 1490–1546

*Verily there may no man be an excellent poet nor orator unless he
have part of all other doctrine, specially of noble philosophy.*

<space style="display: block; text-align: right; margin-right: 20%;">The Book Named the Governor</space>

Sir Thomas Elyot was probably born in Wiltshire, England. His father was a justice and provided an excellent education for Thomas, first at home and then in law at the Middle Temple and Oxford University. Thomas Elyot moved in the highest circles of power during the turmoil of Henry VIII's break from Rome. He knew Thomas More, who introduced him to the humanist education of the "New Learning." More's home opened a world of celebrated international scholars to Elyot. More hosted Erasmus, Vives, William Lily, and John Colet. Through Cardinal Wolsey's influence, Elyot became chief clerk of the King's Council. Following publication of *The Book Named the Governor* in 1531, which he dedicated to King Henry, Elyot served as ambassador to the court of the emperor Charles V in the midst of Henry's attempted divorce from Catherine of Aragon, Charles's aunt. Later, Elyot retired to his estate at Carlton, near Cambridge, and devoted himself to his books. He prepared a Latin-English dictionary and translated Isocrates' *To Nicocles* (under the title *Doctrinal of Princes)* and (Pseudo-)Plutarch's "On Bringing Up a Boy" (under the title *The Education of Children, Translated Out of Plutarch).*

THE SELECTION

Renaissance authors produced a stream of advice books to princes, most of them forgotten. But among the enduring ones were Machiavelli's *The Prince,* Erasmus's *The Education of a Christian Prince,* and Elyot's *The Book Named the Governor.* This last book, published in 1531, defends monarchy, provides a detailed system of classical education for future leaders, and lays out other qualifications for magistrates (such as wisdom, understanding, and experience). In his description of the ideal education for the sons of nobility, Elyot discusses physical exercise, recreation, hunting, and the arts. But at the heart lies an extensive curriculum for students, spanning ages seven to twenty-one, of Greek and Roman authors and the Bible. Elyot moves quickly beyond rudimentary instruction in skills and maps out a broad reading program in literature, rhetoric, history, geography, and philosophy, including a few modern authors among the ancients. While he might seem at times to reduce classical literature to a series of morality tales, his primary intention is to mold character. He seeks to instill in youth a wholesome appetite for honorable conduct and an admiration for what is truly praiseworthy. For Elyot, education means knowledge joined to wisdom, judgment, eloquence, delight and wonder, and virtue. His plan is daunting and inspiring. The twentieth-century American humanist Paul Elmer More described Elyot's book as "the first treatise on education in the English tongue and still, after all these years, one of the wisest."

from The Book Named the Governor

X. WHAT ORDER SHOULD BE IN LEARNING AND WHICH AUTHORS SHOULD BE FIRST READ

Now let us return to the order of learning apt for a gentleman. Wherein I am of the opinion of Quintilian that I would have him learn Greek and Latin authors both at one time; or else to begin with Greek, forasmuch as that it is hardest to come by, by reason of the diversity of tongues, which be five in number, and all must be known, or else scarcely any poet can be well understood. And if a child do begin therein at seven years of age, he may continually learn Greek authors three years, and in the meantime use the Latin tongue as a familiar language; which in a nobleman's son may well come to pass, having none other persons to serve him or keeping him company but such as can speak Latin elegantly. And what doubt is there but so may he as soon speak good Latin as he may do pure French, which now is brought into as many rules and figures and as long a grammar as is Latin or Greek. I will not contend who among them that do write grammars of Greek (which now almost be innumerable) is the best, but that I refer to the discretion of a wise master. Anyway I would advise him not to detain the child too long in that tedious labour, either in the Greek or Latin grammar. For a gentle wit is therewith soon fatigued.

Grammar being but an introduction to the understanding of authors, if it be made too long or exquisite to the learner, it in a manner mortifieth his courage. And by that time he cometh to the most sweet and pleasant reading of old authors, the sparks of fervent desire of learning is extinct with the burden of grammar, like as a little fire is soon quenched with a great heap of small sticks, so that it can never come to the principal logs where it should long burn in a great pleasant fire.

Now to follow my purpose: after a few and quick rules of grammar, immediately, or interlacing it therewith, would be read to the child Aesop's fables in Greek, in which argument children much do delight. And surely it is a much pleasant lesson and also profitable, as well for that it is elegant and brief (and notwithstanding it hath much variety in words, and therewith much helpeth to the understanding of Greek) as also in those fables is included much moral and politic wisdom. Wherefore, in the teaching of them, the master diligently must gather together those fables which may be most accommodate to the advancement of some virtue whereto he perceiveth the child inclined, or to the rebuke of some vice whereto he findeth his nature disposed. And therein the master ought to exercise his wit, as well to make the child plainly to understand the fable as also declaring the signification thereof compendiously and to the purpose, foreseen alway that as well this lesson as all other authors which the child shall learn, either Greek or Latin, verse or prose, be perfectly had without the book: whereby he shall not only attain plenty of the tongues called *Copia*,[1] but also increase and nourish remembrance wonderfully.

The next lesson would be some quick and merry dialogues elect out of Lucian, which be without ribaldry or too much scorning, for either of them is exactly to be eschewed, specially for a nobleman, the one annoying the soul, the other his estimation concerning his gravity. The comedies of Aristophanes may be in the place of Lucian, and by reason that they be in metre they be the sooner learned by heart. I dare make none other comparison between them for offending the friends of them both, but this much dare I say, that it were better that a child should never read any part of Lucian than all Lucian.

I could rehearse divers other poets which for matter and eloquence be very necessary, but I fear me to be too long from noble Homer, from whom as from a fountain proceeded all eloquence and learning. For in his books be contained and most perfectly expressed, not only the documents martial and discipline of arms, but also incomparable wisdom, and instructions for politic governance of people, with the worthy commendation and laud of noble princes; wherewith the readers shall be so all inflamed that they most fervently shall desire and covet, by the imitation of their virtues, to acquire semblable glory. For the which occasion, Aristotle, most sharpest witted and excellent learned philosopher, as soon as he had received Alexander from King Philip his father, he before any other thing taught him the most noble works of Homer; wherein Alexander found such sweetness and fruit that ever after he had Homer not only with him in all his journeys but also laid him under his pillow when he went to rest, and often times would purposely wake some hours of the night to take as it were his pastime with that most noble poet.

For by the reading of his work called *Iliad*, where the assembly of the most noble Greeks against Troy is recited with their affairs, he gathered courage and strength against his enemies, wisdom, and eloquence for consultation and persuasions to his people and army. And by the other work called *Odyssey*, which recounteth the sundry adventures of the wise Ulysses, he by the example of Ulysses apprehended many noble virtues, and also learned to escape the fraud and deceitful imaginations of sundry and subtle crafty wits. Also there

---

1. Abundance. Elyot alludes to Erasmus's *De copia verborum*; he means that the child will learn the elegance of variety in expression.

shall he learn to ensearch and perceive the manners and conditions of them that be his familiars, sifting out (as I might say) the best from the worst, whereby he may surely commit his affairs, and trust to every person after his virtues. Therefore I now conclude that there is no lesson for a young gentleman to be compared with Homer, if he be plainly and substantially expounded and declared by the master.

Notwithstanding, forasmuch as the said works be very long, and do require therefore a great time to be all learned and conned, some Latin author would be therewith mixed, and specially Virgil; which, in his work called *Aeneid*, is most like to Homer and almost the same Homer in Latin. Also, by the joining together of those authors, the one shall be the better understood by the other. And verily (as I before said) none one author serveth to so divers wits as doth Virgil. For there is not that affect or desire whereto any child's fantasy is disposed, but in some of Virgil's works may be found matter thereto apt and propise.[2]

For what thing can be more familiar than his *Bucolics*? Nor no work so nigh approacheth to the common dalliance and manners of children, and the pretty controversies of the simple shepherds therein contained wonderfully rejoiceth the child that heareth it well declared, as I know by mine own experience. In his *Georgics*, Lord, what pleasant variety there is; the divers grains, herbs, and flowers that be there described, that, reading therein, it seemeth to a man to be in a delectable garden or paradise. What ploughman knoweth so much of husbandry as there is expressed? Who, delighting in good horses, shall not be thereto more inflamed, reading there of the breeding, choosing, and keeping of them? In the declaration whereof Virgil leaveth far behind him all breeders, hackneymen, and skosers.[3]

Is there any astronomer that more exactly setteth out the order and course of the celestial bodies, or that more truly doth divine in his prognostications of the times of the year, in their qualities, with the future estate of all things provided by husbandry, than Virgil doth recite in that work?

If the child have a delight in hunting, what pleasure shall he take of the fable of Aristeus; semblably in the hunting of Dido and Aeneas, which is described most elegantly in his book of *Aeneid*. If he have pleasure in wrestling, running, or other like exercise, where shall he see any more pleasant esbatements[4] than that which was done by Eurealus and other Trojans, which accompanied Aeneas? If he take solace in hearing minstrels, what minstrel may be compared to Jopas, which sang before Dido and Aeneas, or to blind Demodocus, that played and sang most sweetly at the dinner that the King Alcinous made to Ulysses, whose ditties and melody excelled as far the songs of our minstrels as Homer and Virgil excel all other poets?

If he be more desirous (as the most part of children be) to hear things marvellous and exquisite, which hath in it a visage of some things incredible, whereat shall he more wonder than when he shall behold Aeneas follow Sibyl into Hell? What shall he more dread than the terrible visages of Cerberus, Gorgon, Megera, and other furies and monsters? How shall he abhor tyranny, fraud, and avarice, when he doth see the pains of Duke Theseus, Prometheus, Sisyphus, and such other tormented for their dissolute and vicious liv-

2. Suitable.
3. Horse dealers.
4. Amusements.

ing? How glad soon after shall he be when he shall behold in the pleasant fields of Elysium the souls of noble princes and captains which, for their virtue and labours in advancing the public weals of their countries, do live eternally in pleasure inexplicable? And in the last books of *Aeneid* shall he find matter to minister to him audacity, valiant courage, and policy, to take and sustain noble enterprises, if any shall be needful for the assailing of his enemies.

Finally (as I have said) this noble Virgil, like to a good nurse, giveth to a child, if he will take it, everything apt for his wit and capacity; wherefore he is in the order of learning to be preferred before any other author Latin. I would set next unto him two books of Ovid, the one called *Metamorphosis*, which is as much to say as changing of men into other figure or form; the other is entitled *De fastis*, where the ceremonies of the Gentiles, and specially the Romans, be expressed: both right necessary for the understanding of other poets. But because there is little other learning in them concerning either virtuous manners or policy, I suppose it were better that as fables and ceremonies happen to come in a lesson, it were declared abundantly by the master than that in the said two books a long time should be spent and almost lost: which might be better employed on such authors that do minister both eloquence, civil policy, and exhortation to virtue. Wherefore in his place let us bring in Horace, in whom is contained much variety of learning and quickness of sentence.

This poet may be interlaced with the lesson of the *Odyssey* of Homer, wherein is declared the wonderful prudence and fortitude of Ulysses in his passage from Troy. And if the child were induced to make verses by the imitation of Virgil and Homer, it should minister to him much delectation and courage to study; the making of verses is not discommended in a nobleman, since the noble Augustus and almost all the old emperors made books in verses.

The two noble poets Silius and Lucan be very expedient to be learned; for the one setteth out the emulation in qualities and prowess of two noble and valiant captains, one enemy to the other, that is to say, Silius writeth of Scipio the Roman, and Hannibal Duke of Carthage; Lucan declareth a semblable matter, but much more lamentable: forasmuch as the wars were civil, and, as it were, in the bowels of the Romans, that is to say, under the standards of Julius Caesar and Pompey.

Hesiod, in Greek, is more brief than Virgil, where he writeth of husbandry, and doth not rise so high in philosophy, but is fuller of fables: and therefore is more illecebrous.[5]

And here I conclude to speak any more of poets, necessary for the childhood of a gentleman; for as much as these I doubt not will suffice until he pass the age of thirteen years. In which time childhood declineth, and reason waxeth ripe, and deprehendeth[6] things with a more constant judgment. Here I would should be remembered that I require not that all these works should be thoroughly read of a child in this time, which were almost impossible. But I only desire that they have, in every of the said books, so much instruction that they may take thereby some profit.

Then the child's courage, inflamed by the frequent reading of noble poets, daily more and more desireth to have experience in those things that they so vehemently do commend in them that they write of.

---

5. Alluring.
6. Understands.

Leonidas, the noble King of Sparta, being once demanded of what estimation in poetry Tirtaeus (as he supposed) was, it is written that he answering said that for stirring the minds of young men he was excellent, forasmuch as they, being moved with his verses, do run into the battle, regarding no peril, as men all inflamed in martial courage.

And when a man is come to mature years, and that reason in him is confirmed with serious learning and long experience, then shall he, in reading tragedies, execrate and abhor the intolerable life of tyrants, and shall contemn the folly and dotage expressed by poets lascivious.

Here will I leave to speak of the first part of a nobleman's study; and now will I write of the second part, which is more serious, and containeth in it sundry manners of learning.

XI. The Most Commodious and Necessary Studies Succeeding Ordinately the Lesson of Poets

After that fourteen years be passed of a child's age, his master if he can, or some other studiously exercised in the art of an orator, shall first read to him somewhat of that part of logic that is called *Topica*, either of Cicero, or else of that noble clerk of Almaine,[7] which late flowered, called Agricola: whose work prepareth invention, telling the places from whence an argument for the proof of any matter may be taken with little study; and that lesson, with much and diligent learning, having mixed therewith none other exercise, will in the space of half a year be perfectly conned. Immediately after that, the art of rhetoric would be semblably taught, either in Greek, out of Hermogines, or of Quintilian in Latin, beginning at the third book, and instructing diligently the child in that part of rhetoric principally which concerneth persuasion, forasmuch as it is most apt for consultations. There can be no shorter instruction of rhetoric than the treatise that Tully[8] wrote into his son, which book is named the partition of rhetoric. And in good faith, to speak boldly that I think, for him that needeth not or doth not desire to be an exquisite orator, the little book made by the famous Erasmus (whom all gentle wits are bound to thank and support), which he calleth *Copiam Verborum et Rerum*, that is to say, plenty of words and matters, shall be sufficient.

Isocrates, concerning the lesson of orators, is everywhere wonderful profitable, having almost as many wise sentences as he hath words, and with that is so sweet and delectable to read that, after him, almost all other seem unsavoury and tedious; and in persuading as well a prince as a private person to virtue, in two very little and compendious works, whereof he made the one to King Nicocles, the other to his friend Demonicus, would be perfectly conned and had in continual memory.

Demosthenes and Tully by the consent of all learned men have pre-eminence and sovereignty over all orators, the one reigning in wonderful eloquence in the public weal of the Romans, who had the empire and dominion of all the world, the other, of no less estimation, in the city of Athens, which of long time was accounted the mother of Sapience, and the palace of Muses and all liberal sciences. Of which two orators may be attained not only eloquence, excellent and perfect, but also precepts of wisdom, and gentle manners, with most commodious examples of all noble virtues and policy. Wherefore the master

---

7. Germany.
8. Cicero.

in reading them must well observe and express the parts and colours of rhetoric in them contained, according to the precepts of that art before learned.

The utility that a nobleman shall have by reading these orators is that when he shall hap to reason in counsel, or shall speak in a great audience or to strange ambassadors of great princes, he shall not be constrained to speak words sudden and disordered, but shall bestow them aptly and in their places. Wherefore the most noble Emperor Octavius is highly commended, for that he never spake in the Senate, or to the people of Rome, but in an oration prepared and purposely made.

Also to prepare the child to understanding of histories, which, being replenished with the names of countries and towns unknown to the reader, do make the history tedious or else the less pleasant, so if they be in any wise known, it increaseth an inexplicable delectation. It shall be therefore, and also for refreshing the wit, a convenient lesson to behold the old tables of Ptolemy, wherein all the world is painted, having first some introduction into the sphere, whereof now of late be made very good treatises, and more plain and easy to learn than was wont to be.

Albeit there is none so good learning as the demonstration of cosmography of material figures and instruments, having a good instructor. And surely this lesson is both pleasant and necessary. For what pleasure is it in one hour to behold those realms, cities, seas, rivers, and mountains, that unneth[9] in an old man's life cannot be journeyed and pursued; what incredible delight is taken in beholding the diversities of people, beasts, fowls, fishes, trees, fruits, and herbs: to know the sundry manners and conditions of people, and the variety of their natures, and that in a warm study or parlour, without peril of the sea or danger of long and painful journeys: I cannot tell what more pleasure should happen to a gentle wit, than to behold in his own house everything that within all the world is contained. The commodity thereof knew the great King Alexander, as some writers do remember. For he caused the countries whereunto he purposed any enterprise diligently and cunningly to be described and painted, that beholding the picture, he might perceive which places were most dangerous, and where he and his host might have most easy and covenable[10] passage.

Semblable did the Romans in the rebellion of France and the insurrection of their confederates, setting up a table openly, wherein Italy was painted, to the intent that the people looking in it should reason and consult in which places it were best to resist or invade their enemies.

I omit, for length of the matter, to write of Cyrus, the great King of Persia, Crassus the Roman, and divers other valiant and expert captains, which have lost themselves and all their army by ignorance of this doctrine.

Wherefore it may not be of any wise man denied but that cosmography is to all noblemen, not only pleasant, but profitable also, and wonderful necessary.

In the part of cosmography wherewith history is mingled Strabo reigneth, which took his argument of the divine poet Homer. Also Strabo himself (as he saith) laboured a great part of Africa and Egypt, where undountedly be many things to be marvelled at. Solinus writeth almost in like form, and is more brief, and hath much more variety of things and matters, and is therefore marvellous delectable; yet Mela is much shorter, and his style

---

9. Scarcely.
10. Convenient.

(by reason that it is of a more antiquity) is also more clean and facile. Wherefore he, or Dionysius, shall be sufficient.

Cosmography being substantially perceived, it is then time to induce a child to the reading of histories: but first to set him in a fervent courage, the master in the most pleasant and elegant wise expressing what incomparable delectation, utility, and commodity shall happen to emperors, kings, princes, and all other gentlemen by reading of histories, showing to him that Demetrius Phalareus, a man of excellent wisdom and learning, and which in Athens had been long exercised in the public weal, exhorted Ptolemy, King of Egypt, chiefly above all other studies to haunt and embrace histories, and such other books wherein were contained precepts made to kings and princes: saying that in them he should read those things which no man durst report unto his person. Also Cicero, father of the Latin eloquence, calleth an history the witness of times, mistress of life, the life of remembrance, of truth the light, and messenger of antiquity.

Moreover, the sweet Isocrates exhorteth the King Nicocles, whom he instructeth, to leave behind him statues and images that shall represent rather the figure and similitude of his mind than the features of his body, signifying thereby the remembrance of his acts written in histories.

By semblable advertisements shall a noble heart be trained to delight in histories. And then, according to the counsel of Quintilian, it is best that he begin with Titus Livius, not only for his elegancy of writing, which floweth in him like a fountain of sweet milk, but also forasmuch as by reading that author he may know how the most noble city of Rome, of a small and poor beginning, by prowess and virtue little and little came to the empire and dominion of all the world.

Also in that city he may behold the form of a public weal: which, if the insolency and pride of Tarquin had not excluded kings out of the city, it had been the most noble and perfect of all other.

Xenophon, being both a philosopher and an excellent captain, so invented and ordered his work named *Paedia Cyri*, which may be interpreted *The Childhood* or *Discipline of Cyrus*, that he leaveth to the readers thereof an incomparable sweetness and example of living, specially for the conducting and well ordering of hosts or armies. And therefore the noble Scipio, who was called Africanus, as well in peace as in war was never seen without this book of Xenophon.

With him may be joined Quintus Curtius, who writeth the life of King Alexander elegantly and sweetly. In whom may be found the figure of an excellent prince, as he that incomparably excelled all other kings and emperors in wisdom, hardiness, strength, policy, agility, valiant courage, nobility, liberality, and courtesy, wherein he was a spectacle or mark for all princes to look on. Contrariwise when he was once vanquished with volupty[11] and pride his tyranny and beastly cruelty abhorreth all readers. The comparison of the virtues of these two noble princes, equally described by two excellent writers, well expressed, shall provoke a gentle courage to contend to follow their virtues.

Julius Caesar and Salust for their compendious writing, to the understanding whereof is required an exact and perfect judgment, and also for the exquisite order of battle and continuing of the history without any variety, whereby the pain of study should be allevi-

---

11. Voluptuousness.

ate: they two would be reserved until he that shall read them shall see some experience in semblable matters. And then shall he find in them such pleasure and commodity as therewith a noble and gentle heart ought to be satisfied. For in them both it shall seem to a man that he is present and heareth the counsels and exhortations of captains, which be called *Conciones*, and that he seeth the order of hosts when they be embattled, the fierce assaults and encounterings of both armies, the furious rage of that monster called war. And he shall wene[12] that he heareth the terrible dints of sundry weapons and ordnance of battle, the conduct and policies of wise and expert captains, specially in the commentaries of Julius Caesar, which he made of his exploiture in France and Britain and other countries now reckoned among the provinces of Germany; which book is studiously to be read of the princes of this realm of England and their counsellors, considering that thereof may be taken necessary instructions concerning the wars against Irishmen or Scots, who be of the same rudeness and wild disposition that the Swiss and Britons were in the time of Caesar. Semblable utility shall be found in the history of Titus Livius, in his third Decades, where he writeth of the battles that the Romans had with Hannibal and the Carthaginians.

Also there be divers orations, as well in all the books of the said authors as in the history of Cornelius Tacitus, which be very delectable, and for counsels very expedient to be had in memory. And in good faith I have often thought that the consultations and orations written by Tacitus do import a majesty with a compendious eloquence therein contained.

In the learning of these authors a young gentleman shall be taught to note and mark, not only the order and elegancy in declaration of the history, but also the occasion of the wars, the counsels and preparations on either part, the estimation of the captains, the manner and form of their governance, the continuance of the battle, the fortune and success of the whole affairs. Semblably out of the wars in other daily affairs, the estate of the public weal, if it be prosperous or in decay, what is the very occasion of the one or of the other, the form and manner of the governance thereof, the good and evil qualities of them that be rulers, the commodities and good sequel of virtue, the discommodities and evil conclusion of vicious license.

Surely if a nobleman do thus seriously, and diligently read histories, I dare affirm there is no study or science for him of equal commodity and pleasure, having regard to every time and age.

By the time that the child do come to seventeen years of age, to the intent his courage be bridled with reason, it were needful to read unto him some works of philosophy; specially that part that may inform him unto virtuous manners, which part of philosophy is called moral. Wherefore there would be read to him, for an introduction, two the first books of the work of Aristotle called *Ethicae*, wherein is contained the definitions and proper significations of every virtue; and that to be learned in Greek; for the translations that we yet have be but a rude and gross shadow of the eloquence and wisdom of Aristotle. Forthwith would follow the work of Cicero, called in Latin *De officiis*, whereunto yet is no proper English word to be given; but to provide for it some manner of exposition, it may be said in this form: "Of the duties and manners appertaining to men." But above all other, the works of Plato would be most studiously read when the judgment of a man

12. Think.

is come to perfection, and by the other studies is instructed in the form of speaking that philosophers used. Lord God, what incomparable sweetness of words and matter shall he find in the said works of Plato and Cicero; wherein is joined gravity with delectation, excellent wisdom with divine eloquence, absolute virtue with pleasure incredible, and every place is so enfarced[13] with profitable counsel joined with honesty, that those three books be almost sufficient to make a perfect and excellent governor. The proverbs of Solomon with the books of Ecclesiastes and Ecclesiasticus be very good lessons. All the historical parts of the Bible be right necessary for to be read of a nobleman, after that he is mature in years. And the residue (with the New Testament) is to be reverently touched, as a celestial jewel or relic, having the chief interpreter of those books true and constant faith, and dreadfully to set hands thereon, remembering that Uzza, for putting his hand to the holy shrine that was called *Archa federis*, when it was brought by King David from the city of Gaba, though it were wavering and in danger to fall, yet was he stricken of God, and fell dead immediately. It would not be forgotten that the little book of the most excellent doctor Erasmus Roterodamus (which he wrote to Charles, now being Emperor and then Prince of Castile), which book is entitled *The Institution of a Christian Prince*, would be as familiar alway with gentlemen at all times and in every age as was Homer with the great King Alexander, or Xenophon with Scipio; for as all men may judge that have read that work of Erasmus, that there was never book written in Latin that in so little a portion contained of sentence, eloquence, and virtuous exhortation, a more compendious abundance. And here I make an end of the learning and study whereby noblemen may attain to be worthy to have authority in a public weal. Alway I shall exhort tutors and governors of noble children, that they suffer them not to use ingurgitations of meat or drink, nor to sleep much, that is to say, above eight hours at the most. For undoubtedly both repletion and superfluous sleep be capital enemies to study, as they be semblably to health of body and soul. Aulus Gellius saith that children, if they use of meat and sleep over much, be made therewith dull to learn, and we see that thereof slowness is taken, and the children's personages do wax uncomely, and less grow in stature. Galen will not permit that pure wine, without allay of water, should in any wise be given to children, forasmuch as it humecteth[14] the body, or maketh it moister and hotter than is convenient, also it filleth the head with fume, in them specially, which be like as children of hot and moist temperature. These be well nigh the words of the noble Galen. . . .

XII. WHY GENTLEMEN IN THIS PRESENT TIME BE NOT EQUAL IN DOCTRINE TO THE ANCIENT NOBLEMEN

. . . Now some man will require me to show mine opinion if it be necessary that gentlemen should after the age of fourteen years continue in study. And to be plain and true therein, I dare affirm that, if the elegant speaking of Latin be not added to other doctrine, little fruit may come of the tongue; since Latin is but a natural speech, and the fruit of speech is wise sentence, which is gathered and made of sundry learning.

And who that hath nothing but language only may be no more praised than a popinjay, a pie, or a starling, when they speak fitly. There be many nowadays in famous schools and universities which be so much given to the study of tongues only, that when they write

13. Stuffed, filled.
14. Moistens.

epistles, they seem to the reader that, like to a trumpet, they make a sound without any purpose, whereunto men do hearken more for the noise than for any delectation that thereby is moved. Wherefore they be much abused that suppose eloquence to be only in words or colours of rhetoric, for, as Tully saith, what is so furious or mad a thing as a vain sound of words of the best sort and most ornate, containing neither cunning nor sentence? Undoubtedly very eloquence is in every tongue where any matter or act done or to be done is expressed in words clean, proper, ornate, and comely: whereof sentences be so aptly compact that they by a virtue inexplicable do draw unto them the minds and consent of the hearers, they being therewith either persuaded, moved, or to delectation induced. Also every man is not an orator that can write an epistle or a flattering oration in Latin; whereof the last (as God help me) is too much used. For a right orator may not be without a much better furniture, Tully saying that to him belongeth the explicating or un-folding of sentence, with a great estimation in giving counsel concerning matters of great importance, also to him appertaineth the steering and quickening of people languishing or despairing, and to moderate them that be rash and unbridled. Wherefore noble authors do affirm that, in the first infancy of the world, men wandering like beasts in woods and on mountains, regarding neither the religion due unto God, nor the office pertaining unto man, ordered all thing by bodily strength: until Mercurius (as Plato supposeth) or some other man helped by sapience and eloquence, by some apt or proper oration, assembled them together and persuaded to them what commodity was in mutual conversation and honest manners. But yet Cornelius Tacitus describeth an orator to be of more excellent qualities, saying that an orator is he that can or may speak or reason in every question sufficiently elegantly: and to persuade properly, according to the dignity of the thing that is spoken of, the opportunity of time, and pleasure of them that be hearers. Tully before him affirmed that a man may not be an orator heaped with praise, but if he have gotten the knowledge of all things and arts of greatest importance. And how shall an orator speak of that thing that he hath not learned? And because there may be nothing but it may happen to come in praise or dispraise, in consultation or judgment, in accusation or defence; therefore an orator, by other instruction perfectly furnished, may, in every mat-ter and learning, commend or dispraise, exhort or dissuade, accuse or defend eloquently, as occasion happeneth. Wherefore inasmuch as in an orator is required to be a heap of all manner of learning, which of some is called the world of science, of other the circle of doctrine, which is in one word of Greek *Encyclopedia*; therefore at this day may be found but a very few orators. For they that come in message from princes be, for honour, named now orators, if they be in any degree of worship; only poor men having equal or more of learning being called messengers. Also they which do only teach rhetoric, which is the science whereby is taught an artificial form of speaking, wherein is the power to persuade, move, and delight, or by that science only do speak or write, without any adminiculation of other sciences, ought to be named rhetoricians, declamators, artificial speakers (named in Greek *Logodedali*), or any other name than orators. Semblably they that make verses expressing thereby none other learning but the craft of versifying be not of ancient writers named poets, but only called versifiers. For the name of a poet, whereat now (specially in this realm) men have such indignation that they use only poets and poetry in the con-tempt of eloquence, was in ancient time in high estimation: insomuch that all wisdom was supposed to be therein included, and poetry was the first philosophy that ever was known:

whereby men from their childhood were brought to the reason how to live well, learning thereby not only manners and natural affections, but also the wonderful works of nature, mixing serious matter with things that were pleasant; as it shall be manifest to them that shall be so fortunate to read the noble works of Plato and Aristotle, wherein he shall find the authority of poets frequently alleged: yea and that more is, in poets was supposed to be science mystical and inspired, and therefore in Latin they were called *Vates*, which word signifieth as much as prophets. And therefore Tully in his *Tusculan Questions* supposeth that a poet cannot abundantly express verses sufficient and complete, or that his eloquence may flow without labour words well sounding and plenteous, without celestial instinction, which is also by Plato ratified. . . .

XIII. The Second and Third Decay of Learning among Gentlemen

. . . Verily there may no man be an excellent poet nor orator unless he have part of all other doctrine, specially of noble philosophy. And to say the truth, no man can apprehend the very delectation that is in the lesson of noble poets unless he have read very much and in divers authors of divers learning. Wherefore, as I late said, to the augmentation of understanding, called in Latin *intellectus et mens*, is required to be much reading and vigilant study in every science, specially of that part of philosophy named moral, which instructeth men in virtue and politic governance. Also no noble author, specially of them that wrote in Greek or Latin before twelve hundred years passed, is not for any cause to be omitted. For therein I am of Quintilian's opinion, that there is few or none ancient work that yieldeth not some fruit or commodity to the diligent readers. And it is a very gross or obstinate wit that by reading much is not somewhat amended.

Concerning the election of other authors to be read I have (as I trust) declared sufficiently my concept and opinion in the tenth and eleventh chapters of this little treatise.

Finally, like as a delicate tree that cometh of a kernel, which, as soon as it burgeoneth out leaves, if it be plucked up or it be sufficiently rooted, and laid in a corner, it becometh dry or rotten and no fruit cometh of it, if it be removed and set in another air or earth, which is of contrary qualities where it was before, it either semblably dieth or beareth no fruit, or else the fruit that cometh of it loseth his verdure and taste, and finally his estimation. So the pure and excellent learning whereof I have spoken, though it be sown in a child never so timely, and springeth and burgeoneth never so pleasantly, if, before it take a deep root in the mind of the child, it be laid aside, either by too much solace or continual attendance in service, or else is translated to another study which is of a more gross or unpleasant quality before it be confirmed or stablished by often reading or diligent exercise, in conclusion it vanisheth and cometh to nothing. . . .

Philip Melanchthon

1497–1560

There is in that work a perfect and absolute image of human wisdom, as much as can ever exist and be imagined altogether, and in every kind of teaching there is nothing sweeter, nothing more splendid and nothing in which greater splendour of eloquence shines forth.

"Preface to Homer"

Philip Melanchthon (a Greek form of Philip Schwarzerdt) was born in Bretten in southwest Germany. He was the grandnephew of Johannes Reuchlin, the distinguished Hebrew and Greek scholar, who encouraged Melanchthon's gifts for classical studies. Melanchthon earned his bachelor of arts degree from the University of Heidelberg in 1511 and his master of arts from the University of Tübingen in 1514, where he was lecturing by the age of twenty. He admired Erasmus's scholarship and corresponded with him for many years, although the two humanists ended up on opposing sides during the Reformation.

In 1518, Frederick the Wise appointed Melanchthon as professor of Greek at the University of Wittenberg. Greek had been part of the university's curriculum since its founding in 1502–3. Melanchthon lectured on Homer, Paul's epistles, and the Psalms. He became a star of the faculty, and his lectures drew students from across Germany. Generations of future teachers and scholars owed their inspiration to this devoted university professor. Melanchthon reformed Wittenberg's arts curriculum to emphasize rhetoric and philosophy, edited classical texts, wrote prefaces to the works of Homer, Aristotle, and Cicero (including *On Duties*), wrote orations on Plato, Aristotle, Galen, and Erasmus, and authored numerous textbooks on Greek, rhetoric, dialectics, and natural philosophy. He helped reform the curricula at other German universities as well, and his contemporaries honored him with the title "Praeceptor Germaniae"—the Teacher of Germany.

Melanchthon's arrival at Wittenberg coincided with Luther's early quarrel with the Catholic Church. Melanchthon was persuaded by Luther's views of Scripture, salvation, and the church, and became Luther's close ally, advising him on his translation of the Greek New Testament and drafting important statements of Lutheran doctrine, including the Augsburg Confession of 1530. He also maintained a long friendship with John Calvin. Melanchthon tried to mediate among the splintering factions of Protestantism, between humanists and Reformers, and even between Catholics and Protestants.

THE SELECTION

The "Preface to Homer" (delivered perhaps in 1538) is one of a number of orations Melanchthon gave at Wittenberg over his long career. Taken together, they express Melanchthon's philosophy of Christian humanist education.[1] The "Preface to Homer" is a spirited and witty defense of the classics as a whole and of Homer in particular. Homer's enduring value, according to Melanchthon, lies not only in his ability to delight his reader or to shape his taste and judgment, but also and especially in the poet's ability to cultivate and enrich our higher natures. Melanchthon draws from Homer a moral lesson: "Those who consider everything in relation to its usefulness for them, and who measure happiness by the possession of the goods of fortune, should remember that they are grasping fragile and most unstable goods that are often destructive for those who own them, and that by the movement of one moment their entire happiness and they themselves can be completely overturned."

Further study of Melanchthon's philosophy of education should include his "Reply to Pico," an imaginative treatise in which the Wittenberg professor responds to a letter written by the Italian philosopher Pico della Mirandola, who died before Melanchthon was born. In his reply, Melanchthon argues that rhetoric and philosophy are both gifts from God and that neither eloquence nor wisdom can survive without the other. Philosophy must know how to express itself clearly, and oratory must have something worth saying.[2]

"Preface to Homer"

Since I am about to enter upon the interpretation of the Homeric poem in a few days, it has seemed right that I commend, as I can, that lecture and these studies to the young by an oration in this place. I believe I can do so quite rightly, given that the matter is most worthy of commendation, and also much needed in these present times and amidst such corrupt judgements of men. I consider in my mind these admirable gifts of God, namely the study of literature and of the humanities—and apart from the Gospel of Christ this world holds nothing more splendid nor more divine and I also consider, on the other hand, by what

---

1. A good collection of Melanchthon's orations is available in *Orations on Philosophy and Education,* ed. by Sachiko Kusukawa and trans. by Christine F. Salazar (Cambridge: Cambridge University Press, 1999).

2. Melanchthon's reply and Pico's original letter can be found in Quirinus Breen, *Christianity and Humanism: Studies in the History of Ideas* (Grand Rapids, MI: Eerdmans, 1968), 52–68 and 15–25.

blindness the minds of men are enveloped in unnatural and Cimmerian darkness; they spurn these true and greatest gifts, and with great effort they pursue means for their wishes and desires that are not only inferior but also ruinous and destructive to themselves. When I weigh these things in my heart, I am violently moved, for it comes to my mind by what dense darkness and, so to speak, black night the hearts of men are surrounded. I am not further astonished, if men are blind in things that are divine and beyond human understanding, when I see them thus treading under foot these their own and personal goods for which they are intended by divine providence, and which they could have comprehended and cherished.

We disdain, and make the butt of our jokes, the study of classics, by which that part of us that alone deserves the name "man," that is made in the image of God and for the possession of true and everlasting happiness, was meant to be refined and roused. Instead of these, we pursue with mad and blind effort I know not what illusions held out by Satan, and worthless shadows, and hitherto have not had the reverence to look at that sun. That unceasing enemy of humankind leads our minds away from admiration and love for what is true and good by whatever kind of deceit he can, and he blinds our eyes by false appearances and obscures them to such an extent that we see and cherish anything rather than that which we should have seen and cherished most.

What happens to the Muses and the study of them now is the same as Strabo reports as having once happened in Iassus to a singer accompanying himself on the cithara. When he was singing learnedly and sweetly in the theatre there and the Iassians were listening to him, as soon as a bell rang (which was the sign of the sale of fish on offer), immediately all left the singer behind and scattered to buy fish, with the exception of one somewhat deaf man who alone remained, not having heard the sound of the bell. The singer thereupon turned to him and said: "I am immensely grateful to you—because of the enthusiasm for music as well as because of the honour to me—for not dashing out immediately at the ringing of the bell, like all the others, in order to buy fish." The man said: "What do you say? Has the bell rung yet then?" When the singer confirmed this, he said: "Good luck to you," rose and forthwith he, too, ran out to buy fish. The singer was abandoned alone, and in a city of that size he did not find anyone who cared more for music than for rotten fish.

In such a way these studies and writings are neglected in our times. Each one rushes towards the mean and gainful arts, they are slaves to their detestable desires and to their stomachs, and they know no god besides these. Only very few take care to refine and honour their minds, the better and more divine part of them. Just as in a noisy and drunken banquet men talk nonsense, laugh, bawl and make loud noise while some famous musician is playing, and they neither pay attention nor receive in their ears and hearts the sweetness of the music, nor enjoy it thoroughly, so our times, as if intoxicated and frantic with their desires, neither listen to the voices of the Muses nor pay attention to them. Those who by their authority and efforts should have eminently fostered and honoured these studies, the majority being barbarians and without education, greatly desire rather to see them oppressed and annihilated. When Herod, the king of the Jewish people, was raised to royal honours from humble and obscure origins, he ordered all books containing genealogies to be burnt and destroyed so that, the distinction between nobility and obscurity being removed, the obscurity of his own origins would be less disreputable. In just the same way uneducated men hate literature and want it destroyed, hoping that thereby they can hide their own ignorance better.

So it happens that literature is attacked by some and abandoned by others; blind desire carries away each one in a different way, and we admire anything rather than the true good, and we do not even recognise it. So Satan holds human minds shackled by his fetters, and he leads them astray to whatever place he wants, and indeed now the disgrace of ignorance is considered the least of ills; if we were not insane and enslaved in our minds, we would not consider anything sadder or more worth fleeing. In the mean time some pursue honours, others the basest pleasures and the majority riches and money. They value these possessions alone at an enormous price, selling their life and soul at a profit, as one says. The wretched people measure happiness by these things, not considering how often that unhappy happiness is not merely interrupted by a slight change, but truly and absolutely turned upside down. Many have learnt this lesson from experience, the teacher of the foolish.

But what shall I say? We can see that it happens generally that the best things are held in utmost contempt and, on the other hand, that the worst things are made great. Therefore, if the same happens to literature and the teaching of classics, this must not appear to us as something new or excessively astonishing, nor is it fitting for us to be alienated from loving and cherishing these studies by the exceedingly bad judgement and error of the crowds. The matter itself and indignation move me to say this beforehand, as I am about to speak of Homer and of these our studies. For who would not be moved, seeing such extraordinary contempt for the best things? In your kindness, bear with me in this complaint that my distress and the indignity of the matter have wrung out of me.

But to get down to our actual topic, I have, as I said, decided to expound—with the help of the gods—Homer's poem; I chose to speak briefly about it first on this occasion. I do so also in order to be able to commend it to the young by this oration; and to honour it with worthy praise, although it can never be honoured as it deserves, and Homer's splendour surpasses any oration. But just as great deities are sometimes worshipped with sacrifices of coarse grain and salt, so we bestow upon the praise of such a great writer what little we can in our insignificance. We shall not be talking here about the birth, country and life of Homer, for this has been expounded with sufficient accuracy and at length by others; we shall discuss, briefly and as well as the short time will allow, the poem itself and the usefulness that scholars can derive from it. For those who read Homer in such a way that they derive nothing but pleasure from it, and aphorisms collected like little flowers, act like someone who tends a very fertile field only for the sake of their mind, so that he may occasionally crown himself with flowers growing there, neglecting care for the produce that he could reap in great abundance. Someone said, correctly, I believe, that such a man is not a sufficiently judicious steward. Even though one can obtain such pleasure from reading Homer as from hardly any other author—and it is entirely so arranged by nature that the highest true pleasure is matched with the highest usefulness—this must nevertheless not be the foremost object of attention. There is another one that is greater and preferable, beyond question; just as the heads of families are usually circumspect in what concerns their family; so immediately in the beginning we should devise a method in our minds if we are to attach any value to the task of reading this or that author. If we do this in studying Homer, then immediately the endless multitude of benefits becomes clear to us, as a throng of good things (*myrmēkia agathōn*), which we can demand from that text abundantly and to our fill, as they say. If anyone were to include and enumerate them all in a single oration, it would be as Virgil said [*Georgics* 2.105–8]: "We who would have knowledge of this world would likewise fain to learn how many grains of sand on the Lybian plain are stirred by the Westwind, or when the East falls in unwonted fury on the ships, would know how many billows of the Ionian Sea roll shoreward." To speak the truth, although I have not so completely forgotten who I am as to dare claim that I could perceive and know all those prodigious and countless riches of the Homeric poem, of which no doubt only the smallest part is known, nevertheless I feel that it is clearly happening to me that, as one says, the abundance is making me needy. For when I contemplate this work, manifold things, appearing from every side like divine miracles, leave me stupefied and anxious, so that it is difficult to judge where I should begin and where I should stop. For I fear that I should fare like those who, having deliberated greatly and at length, have to choose from an enormous heap of precious things certain treasures (*keimēlia*) and sometimes err through excessive care and doubt, and, leaving the best behind, set apart the less precious. In the same way I, too, fear that, passing by the better things which others perhaps admire more, I may choose the inferior ones; but whether this is noticed I do not regard it as being of great moment. For it does not escape me that the keenness of people's minds is usually blunted by the splendour of the Homeric song, just as the eyes' keenness and faculty are overpowered by the rays of the sun. We shall therefore assemble a few examples out of an infinite variety—a task like enclosing the sea in narrow water-pipes—and enumerate summarily and briefly those which have seemed to us the most admirable in that poem.

First I declare that no work has been brought forth by any human mind since the beginning of the world, in any language or nation—with the exception of the holy writings—in which there is such a wealth of teaching or of elegance and pleasantness. I am not unaware that this is a daring statement and one that excites ill will, but at the same time I do not doubt that nobly educated minds, who have tasted Homer only lightly and, as they say, with the foremost part of the lips, will agree ardently with me on this. But now I shall not talk about that teaching which contains the nature of things, which transmits the positions of the celestial circles and the stars and their rising and setting, which shows the harmony of the temperature of the human body, the symmetry (*symmetrian*) of its members and their various conditions. I shall not speak about the hidden learning with which the Homeric poem is filled and crowded throughout, for the short time does not allow us to enumerate the individual examples; let us come to our better-known ones. What moral injunction will you give me for ordering one's life well and happily, that has ever been uttered by wise men, for which there is not some splendid and distinguished example in Homer? What duty is there in life or what matter is there altogether of which there is not a likeness portrayed in it? They are the most refined, the sweetest and at the same time the wisest thoughts about all things and matters that can be conceived by any human mind. For what is sweeter or more ethical (*ēthikon*) to think, what can one be admonished more seriously for, than that which Homer repeats in several passages of his poem to those who are angry for a not unreasonable cause—*ameinō d'aisima panta*—that is, nothing is better in all things than moderation, readiness to be appeased and forbearance? What is more just and human than the utterance of Diomedes in book nine of the *Iliad* to decree, as the first law in the assembly, freedom for those who speak and patience for those who listen? Do we not see how our century is afflicted more than anything else by the fact that the mighty cannot bear free speech, and not even any thought of freedom? What is more heroic than Hector saying: "There is one perfect omen, to defend one's country" [*Iliad* xii.243]—that there is one most auspicious sign, and that is to fight bravely and to die nobly for one's country? If the princes of our times had this sentence before their eyes and inscribed in their hearts, we would not see the Turks attack Germany and the Christian world again and again with impunity, nor would we fear their arrival quite so much. What is more divine than when he writes that he who has not rendered thanks to his parents for his nursing dies a premature death, among the first. Likewise, he says: "Ill deeds do not attain to virtue, and even a slow man catches up with a fast one" [*Odyssey* viii.329]—that evil deeds do not lead to success or have a good outcome, and that the wicked man, however fast he may be and however versed in deceit, is nevertheless caught, and even by one who is lame. There is no doubt that this kind of saying was first uttered by the holy fathers and transmitted to posterity. Then they were passed on from one to the other, one could say from hand to hand, and finally extended to the men by whom they were included in these written monuments, so that, put in an illustrious and perspicuous place, they could be kept in the memory of all posterity and beheld with admiration.

Homer's poem is full of such sentences that have almost the weight and authority of laws, and which had to be by right respected with extraordinary scrupulousness, like oracles or divine responses, and committed to memory and always kept before one's eyes. And it seems that what Cicero said of Euripides—that he believed his individual verses to be separate testimonies—can be said much more truly of Homer, since Euripides and the other poets gush forth from Homer like rivulets from a never-failing source.

In any kind of art some principles and common notions are passed on, to which those who occupy themselves with those arts turn their thoughts as by the Lesbian rule. You will remember, young men, that Boethius in his dialectics calls common preconceptions (*prolēpseis*) of that kind maxims. I should say that the entire Homeric poem consists of such maxims, that is of common and most useful rules and precepts for morals, life and civil duties, for which there is widespread use in every life and in all its actions. He teaches many things, admonishes wisely on many, and instils in the young the most honourable and agreeable notions of modesty, respect and the other virtues. No one is a better teacher of the habits of pleasantness and humanity than he; he demonstrates and accomplishes a certain experience of life in the young, which is otherwise held in highest praise, but is attributed only to old age. The passage from the Latin poet is well known: ". . . older age does not have only what we flee; experience comes with advanced years" [Ovid, *Metamorphoses*, vi.28f]. Indeed, reading Homer performs this divine service, namely to impress the prudence of the old upon the youthful mind, for they can obtain and draw from this poem, by a short-cut, as from a treasure or a spring those things which old people usually learn from long experience, and which numerous years, the variety of things and the experiences of human life teach them. For the teaching of how to live rightly and happily is not delivered less successfully there than in any writings of the philosophers, as Horace said truthfully of Homer [*Letters* i.2.4]: "What could there be that is ugly, that is beautiful and that is useful, that he did not teach more clearly and better than Chrysippus or Crantor?" Indeed, he envelops the most serious and holy tenets in the sweetest and most pleasant poetic images, so that noble and inquiring (*syzētika*) minds are educated with, as Plutarch says, a sense of beauty.

Nor is ethics (*to ēthikon*), that is the grace and gentleness of manners, and the moderation and humanity of the mind, expressed in any writings as it is in Homer's poem. Therefore, if it is true that, as they say, studies are transformed into manners, there can be no anger, but rather, by contact with the most humane and delightful poet, minds also grow gentle and become more humane and peaceful. I believe that great men endowed with outstanding intellects have noticed this, and some call the Homeric poem the workshop of humanity, others the fountain of all pleasantness and beauty. Pliny calls Homer the most eminent father of higher teaching and of antiquity, while Plato calls him the best teacher for life [*Laches* 201b1]. In order to understand that these magnificent titles have been rightly attributed to Homer, and to understand his poem, let us display to ourselves the entire body of the work, so that we do not have to conjecture, as with a ruined statue, from the mutilated parts and limbs.

The Homeric poem has two themes; one is entitled *Iliad*, the other *Odyssey*. Plutarch judges that in the *Iliad* Homer celebrates physical strength, in the *Odyssey* the powers of the intellect [*Fortune of Alexander* 327f.]. In the *Iliad* he describes, according to tradition, the most noble and therefore the honourable and pious war which the Greeks waged against the barbarians in defence of conjugal virtue, in order to avenge adultery and the violation of hospitality. The *Odyssey* contains the wanderings of Ulysses by whose image the poet wanted to describe a wise and civil man cast about by varied storms of fortune, who knew how to sway and temper fortune by judgement.

I believe that there is only little for me to say here about that part [i.e. *the Odyssey*], as we have decided to expound it first. There is no doubt that in the *Iliad* the poet wanted to describe the arts of the military and of war, in the *Odyssey* those of peace; and so in the entire poem he meant to form, educate and prepare the kind of intellect that one day must rule the state by either kind of art. Accordingly, in the *Odyssey* he paints a picture of civil and peaceful life, but in the *Iliad* he sets out military examples; for by these arts states and kingdoms are acquired, held and ruled, and whoever will some day lead the state must be instructed in these arts. Homer's verse to that effect is well known, of which they say that Alexander the Great was so pleased by it that he always kept quoting it: "Both a good king and a strong fighter" [*Iliad* iii.179].

But let us see what Homer assigns to that man whom he conceives as a civil man, a prince in the state and endowed with such gifts of the intellect and such arts and virtues. First of all he assigns to him a great love for his country, and we know that after the love for God this is the highest degree of piety and justice. As Herodotus reports, Solon, when staying with Croesus, ascribes the highest degree of happiness to him who dies for his country, and the next degree to him who fulfils his duty towards his parents [*Histories*, i.3of.]. In order that Ulysses be filled with this love for his country and that he be made more distinguished, the poet conceives many opportunities and various obstacles by which his return to his country is hindered, against all of which he struggles with counsel, reason and the powers of the mind, and all of which he surmounts in the end. And what is the country that he holds so dear? To be sure, a barren, narrow island, attached to the roughest rocks like a bird's nest, as Cicero says [*On the Orator* i.xliv.196]. He has such longing and love for it that he would not hesitate to prefer the smoke coming from there to immortality.

And we can see that this fondness has been extraordinary in all great and distinguished men. Demosthenes writes [*Letters* ii.20] that when he was in exile in Calauria, he used to climb every day to the top of the sanctuary where he had taken refuge, and, measuring the distance with his eyes, gazed in the direction of Athens with great longing and love; although his country had been ungrateful and wicked towards him, it was still dearer to him than his life or his soul.

The next degree of virtue, to return to our topic and children, and, for the prince, especially towards his citizens and subjects, which Homer attributes to Ulysses to the highest degree. How piously does he cherish and revere his parents! With what love does he embrace his son or his wife, from whom he would not suffer himself to be torn away, not even by familiarity with immortal goddesses! With what care and solicitude does he protect the life of his companions, even though they do not deserve it! How he keeps watch for them and does not decline any kind of trouble or toil when considering their safety!

Because the poet makes him a most wise and constant man, he contrives various opportunities in which these virtues can be seen, and he exposes him to various misfortunes and dangers in which his fortitude is shown and his ready power of judgement shines forth. For we know that adverse fortune is like a practice-field and a gymnasium, where strength of the mind and uncommon virtue are exercised and seen. It is also remarkable that he makes him most wise and most eloquent, and attributes to him speech flowing like rivers swollen with the snows of winter, and he opposes and compares two completely perfect ways of speaking in Menelaus and Ulysses. Moreover, he pretends that Ulysses is ruled and protected by Minerva, in order to show that great men are dear to God and that, supported by His help, they can accomplish great things.

Then he makes him fight with the Cyclops and with the suitors, that is with tyrants and with quarrelsome and vicious men occupying the bed and possessions of others, because for heroic and distinguished men there have always been struggles and contests with these two types of men. And, what needs to be observed in particular, Homer conceives him as being most patient and persevering in what he has determined. In order to keep his course and to achieve what he wants, he does not let himself be defeated or broken by any trouble or toil or by any abuse. When he already seems to have done with dangers and ills, even in his own house he endures much that is unbearable, he withstands being torn and needy, being made sport of, being beaten, having bones thrown at him by the suitors and being mocked by his household. He conceals everything for a time, waiting for the opportunity to regain his house, take possession of his things and take revenge. That virtue is unique in distinguished men—not only to achieve great and memorable things for the good of their country and of many men at risk of their life, but also to withstand and endure injustice, disgrace, abuse and disrepute, and persevere on their determined course, aiming for and following only what is honourable and beneficial. The phrase by Ennius about Fabius is well known: "For he did not put reputation above safety." It is clearly Ulysses' kind of wisdom, by which unfortunate and miserable facts are sustained and endured. I shall desist from talking about Ulysses, whom Philostratus [*Lives of the Sophists* 1.8.3] calls Homer's delight (*athyrma*), since I would run out of time more quickly than of things to say. For in Homer there are countless passages intended and devised as if by divine providence (and Horace has said not rashly that they are wonderful), and throughout they are all created with incredible elegance and pleasantness, diversified by various moods, chiefly the dispositions (*ēthesi*), however, and by many splendid and pleasant accidents—indeed arranged with such order and economy (*oikonomiai*) of things that I would consider anyone who is not charmed by reading Homer lacking in any sense of humanity: an animal, not a man.

There is in that work a perfect and absolute image of human wisdom, as much as can ever exist and be imagined altogether, and in every kind of teaching there is nothing sweeter, nothing more splendid and nothing in which greater splendour of eloquence shines forth. It was rightly said by Fabius[3] that just as the courses of all streams and springs take their origin from the ocean, Homer had given a model and origin to all parts of eloquence. For he did not collect rainwater, as Pindar says, but he rushes forth in a living river, created by the gift of divine providence so that he might thereby test all his strength by eloquence.

Although after his age there flourished a considerable number of poets, he himself nevertheless always kept his, that is the highest and noblest, place, and he alone snatches away the palm of victory from all poets that any age has brought forth, and he leaves them all far behind. He achieved this, namely that it requires a great nature and a great mind to follow his virtues, not by emulation, which is impossible, but at least with the intellect. Manilius sings of him, splendidly as well as truthfully:

> Yet all posterity has for its verse drawn on the rich
> stream issuing from his lips and, daring to
> channel his river into slender rills, has
> become fertile by the wealth of One. [*Astronomica* II.8–11]

And Theocritus says that if the birds of the Muses, that is the other poets, dared compete with Homer, they would toil in vain and it would be like the cry of the cuckoo compared to the sweet song of the nightingale. Philostratus, too, declares that Homer is not like the sculptor Euphranor, who excelled among the others in his art by certain virtues, but is most distinguished in all of them, any of which would be highly praised in one person. He records an agreeable story about Homer which I thought was not inappropriate to relate briefly here.

He says that, as a youth, Achilles was stirred with astonishing enthusiasm and love for music and poetry, so that he entreated the Muses every day with prayers to be made into an outstanding musician with their help. When he would not stop pleading, finally the Muse Calliope appeared to him and warned him not to fight against destiny, for it pleased the gods otherwise, to make him not a singer but an outstanding warrior, who would perform such deeds that poets would take them as a subject for their writings. Indeed, after a hundred years there would be a bard by the name of Homer, who would celebrate his exploits and brave deeds in an immortal song. This is what Philostratus says of Homer. Without doubt he means that Homer was roused by divine power and sang his song inspired by divine virtue.

It can be seen in many passages that he sang as if from the innermost part of the temple or from the tripod of Apollo, higher and more divine than human understanding. This is

---

3. Quintilian, *Education of the Orator* x.1.46.

shown by a few oracles scattered in his poem, which could not have been conceived by the human mind without the inspiration of a god—such as the one about the descendants of Aeneas and the everlasting existence of the future Roman empire, which is rendered by Virgil in the following verse: "And the sons of your sons, and those who are born from them" [*Aeneid* 3.98]. Therefore Democritus says, not without reason, that Homer had been assigned a soul with the gift of divination [*Fragment* 21.1].

However, this is neither the place nor the time to pursue this argument. Let us therefore return to our subject and to what is more befitting our studies and manners. At the present occasion I have no leisure to consider these hidden topics of philosophy (*ta philosophoumena*) concerning the origins of things, the motion of the celestial bodies and stars, the elements, the earth and counter-earth, the constitution of man, the soul and its parts, the seat of the faculties of the soul, the single faculties, the emotions (praiseworthy and corrupt ones), then reason and intellect, and sensation and appetite which are locked in constant struggle with the former, the more divine part of man and his dumb part. Even if, as I say, I am not at liberty to consider these, the students should nevertheless know that the seeds and origins of all these things are in Homer. And there has been no better or more outstanding painter of our nobler and more divine part than Homer.

Therefore, in Silius [*Punica* xiii. 778–97], Scipio lauds Homer's shade, that he has seen in the netherworld, with great but not false praise, and, in a passage of great skill, he wishes for such a poet for his own times. For the sake of the young men here it is not troublesome to quote the passage; this is what he says:

> And he saw, walking along the boundaries of Elysium,
> the figure of a youth, his hair bound by a purple fillet
> and flowing over his shining neck.
> "Tell me, young maid," he said, "who is he? For with a light beyond compare
> shines the man's venerable brow, and many souls
> follow him in admiration, surrounding him with joyous cries.
> That countenance, were it not in the Stygian shadows,
> I would easily believe to be a god." "You would not be wrong," said
> the wise handmaid of Trivia, "he is worthy of being held to be a god,
> and a great genius dwells in his mighty mind.
> He described the Earth, the sea and the stars,
> and he matched the Muses in song, Phoebus in honour.
> Before he ever saw it, all this region, he revealed in order to the world,
> and he raised fame of your Troy up to the stars."
> Scipio gazed with joyful eyes at the ghost of Homer, and said:
> "If Fate would suffer such a poet to sing the deeds of Rome
> for all the world to hear, how much greater impression the same
> deeds would make upon posterity, if Homer testified to them!
> How fortunate was Aeacid [Achilles], whose lot it was to be made known to all
> by such a voice. The hew was made greater by the poet's verse."

So much about Scipio's praise of Homer in Silius.

However, we meet with an objection, and indeed from that most distinguished and learned man, Plato, who, condemning Homer as for a capital crime, excludes him from his Republic, and thrusts him out and despatches him into exile. I can echo the words of Chrysostom on this accusation: it is difficult to judge between such great men, just as it is difficult to utter a verdict when two men, both good, both eminent and honourable, both friends, disagree in their judgements on some serious and weighty matter, so that one does not appear to condemn the judgement of one of them by one's speech. But let us see what moved Plato to expel Homer from the city created by him [*Republic* iii.9.39[8a]]. For one must not think that he is doing so rashly, especially when he himself called him the best and most divine of poets (*ariston kai theiotaton tōn poiētōn*).

So what has that innocent nightingale done to deserve being banished from the Platonic fields? It can be objected that he had related some ridiculous and absurd things about the immortal gods and about religion. I agree, a great and capital crime. But let Plato or another champion of his judgement tell me what else Homer could have related about the gods or about religion, as it was then in Greece, and whether Plato himself knew and recounted anything much better. Homer himself followed what was then customary regarding religion or the immortal gods, and in those times there was no other form of religion among these people than the one Homer describes. I shall not discuss here whether it was true or false. Certainly Homer agrees in this with Plato and some most distinguished men, that there is a God and that He cares for human affairs; therefore he assembles so many counsels of the gods, in order to show that human affairs do not arise fortuitously or by chance, but are arranged and ruled by the immortal gods. He makes God loving of humans (*philanthropon*), and therefore Jupiter is shown by him lamenting that he is affected by human vicissitudes, and that he grieves about the ills and miseries of mankind; he declares that the good are protected and showered with good things, the wicked punished by divine power. Minerva commends Ulysses in the first book of the *Odyssey*, first of all for his virtue and nobility, and then also because of his zeal for piety and religion, or the worship of the gods. If human nature strives by its own powers, what better or more sublime can it imagine about the will of God than that He loves, protects and helps the good, hates the impious and the wicked and afflicts them with punishment, and attends to and rules human affairs?

As for what allegorical themes other than these he has added, it can easily be understood that he pursued another objective, and that he alluded to the manners of men and to the nature of things, and that he concealed serious and ponderous tenets in these poetic images, as was the custom in those times. Since Plato, too, sometimes sports in that way with the immortal gods, in order to demonstrate something else, he who wants to be such a strict judge of others can be convicted of just the same crime. Furthermore, one can also retort what Chrysostom says, namely that Homer described "some things according to belief, others according to truth" (*ta men kata doxan, tade kat' alētheian*) [*Orations*, liii.4.6]. And that is sufficient for me to say about the first issue.

The second objection made is that he attributed tears to great and heroic men; I do not see why this should merit rebuke. On the contrary, it seems praiseworthy to me that he did not think idly of the stupid and imaginary Stoic freedom from passions (*apatheia*), but presented such images of affairs and men as they are in the nature of things and in life; he did not invent marvellous opinions remote from human common sense, but expressed in his song the things that are most usual in life and consistent with common sense. He intended to show how great men are faced with very serious and sad vicissitudes, and are overcome by great emotions of the soul—as the Roman poet says of his Aeneas: "he feigns hope on his face and deep in his heart stifles anguish" [Virgil, *Aeneid* i.209]. And elsewhere: "he rages with the mighty fire of anger" [ibid. iv.532]. For the poets described the heroes as they were, without doubt also exposed to human vicissitudes and moved by them. They set before us familiar images of emotions, actions and duties in life, and of men, and they did not follow the strange paradoxes (*atopōtata paradoxa*) which some of the philosophers greatly enjoy.

Furthermore, the third crime held against Homer by Plato, I believe, was that he invented the underworld, for he is thought to inspire in men the fear of death, when they imagine for themselves after this life the horrors of what he depicts in the underworld, and thus the reading of Homer's poem appears to sap the strength of the mind. We shall reply to this briefly that Homer intended to celebrate the tenet of the immortality of the soul, to which the more sagacious and noble men of all centuries have adhered. He wanted to show that there was some place and abode after this life, where the souls of the good and the wicked live, and where there is some honour for the good and the wicked are punished. Furthermore he followed the familiar opinion that men then had of the netherworld. He did not contrive anything new or unheard of, or alien to the common judgement of that age, as the philosophers did.

These are the capital crimes for which Homer is punished with exile by Plato, and is relegated from the Platonic city to I know not what lonely lands, to the Scythians, I believe, or the Garamantes. Nor is this done at random, for Chrysostom is witness [*Orations* xxxvi.9.7] that even those who were barbarians and unacquainted with Greek learning, softened by the sweetness of the Homeric song, began, for that one reason, to make themselves acquainted with Greek writing, so that they could learn that poem by heart, and it was even repeated among the Indians. So, to whatever people Plato banished Homer from his Greece, he made it immediately more cultivated and more human by acquaintance and contact with him, as by the arrival of a god.

To Plato's stance in this matter we can also oppose the unanimity of all the best and wisest men who have flourished in all the centuries since Homer through the praise of their intellect, teaching, virtue or wisdom. For there was no one among them who did not praise Homer's poem with a loud voice or did not cherish him and worship him like a god. Archelaus, the best and wisest king of the Spartans, never used to go to bed, nor go out when he had arisen from his bed, without first reading with attention, almost solemnly, something from Homer; whenever he had some time free from his duties, he immediately rushed to his Homer, saying that he went to his lover and darling.

Nor is it unknown how much Alexander of Macedon relished Homer's poem. Whether he dealt with serious things or jests, even when he armed himself for war, he used to repeat Homer's songs. When a casket from the spoils of Babylon, made of gold and gems, of enormous value, was brought to him and the others assigned it to various uses for the keeping of precious things, Alexander replied that there was nothing for which the box was more appropriate than for keeping the Homeric poem; for the most noble treasure a no less noble vessel in which to preserve it was proper. We, however, young men, who do not possess golden vessels or ones adorned with jewels, let us nevertheless emulate Alexander the

Great and store this valuable treasure in a no less noble casket, namely in our hearts, and adorn and enrich the more excellent and divine part of ourselves by it.

"What are you telling me about treasures and riches?" some may ask, and indeed we can see that Homer, in his lifetime, was destitute, and that so far none of his disciples has become rich. We know that this is true, and that it is all too true in these our times; but we have to remember that it is certain and evident proof of public misfortune that we see these studies despised. But these ignoble thoughts and most sordid words should not concern us. Those who spurn those far more excellent goods for the sake of sordid gain are not worth being initiated into these sacred rites of the Muses, or admitted to this sanctuary of humanity and virtue. Homer does not swell the purse with gold or silver, nor the stomach with fat, nor does he encircle the fingers with rings adorned with jewels; but he certainly fills the mind with treasure, which is the more excellent and immortal part of ourselves, and adorns and enriches it. It should not deter us that Homer was destitute and despised in his lifetime, and that those who cherish studies of this kind are destitute. It is a condition universal to all the best things that they are despised in this miserable life full of errors and blindness. In what way have those who proclaim the word of God, the preachers of eternal salvation, who announce liberation from death, from sin and from eternal torment in the underworld, always been received and treated by the ungrateful world, and how are they treated today? It must not appear greatly surprising or new to us that the good things are neglected and the lesser ones, by contrast, become great; this is not a new situation in the world, and it is already beginning to be almost customary from a depraved habit. Let us, on the other hand, consider it thus that Homer does not serve gain, but that he is better than that; for virtue and the Muses refuse to prostitute themselves and, as the saying goes, to sit in the place of the harlots [Ovid, *Letters from Pontus* ii.iii.20]. Those who consider everything in relation to its usefulness for them, and who measure happiness by the possession of the goods of fortune, should remember that they are grasping fragile and most unstable goods that are often destructive for those who own them, and that by the movement of one moment their entire happiness and they themselves can be completely overturned. If these studies are prevented because of indigence and contempt then, by the same move, humanity, virtue and nobility are excluded, the disciples of the Muses, to whom Homer is father and tutor, and all that is truly good, holy and pious in the world is excluded. On to all this one can inscribe the epigram (*epigramma*) that someone set up on his dwellings: "This is not a large house, what of it? Often virtue gifted with genius is hidden under a poor roof." I have spoken.

Johann Sturm

1507–89

No one can either write or speak excellently who has acquired the
arts and methods but has no understanding of the subject matter.

<small>LETTER TO ROGER ASCHAM, SEPTEMBER 9, 1550</small>

Johann (or Johannes) Sturm, among the most significant educators of the sixteenth century, was born in Luxembourg and educated by the Brethren of the Common Life, the religious community that had produced Thomas à Kempis and educated the young Erasmus. Sturm studied the classics at the universities of Liege and Louvain and translated Aristotle into Latin. He mastered Cicero's style, edited a nine-volume edition of Cicero's works, and earned the title the "German Cicero." An early convert to Lutheranism, he was influenced by Philip Melanchthon. After a brief time studying and lecturing in Paris, he was called to Strasbourg in 1536 to help with educational reforms there. Swept by Lutheranism, Strasbourg had exploded into violence and provoked Erasmus's bitter condemnation. Yet it managed to become a publishing and education center for the Reformation and was home for a time to Martin Bucer (the Protestant reformer who tried to reconcile the followers of Zwingli and Luther) and John Calvin. Sturm served for more than forty years as head of the Protestant academy in Strasbourg, striving to fulfill his motto of *sapiens et eloquens pietas*—wise and eloquent piety. In the next century, his academy developed under royal patronage into the celebrated University of Strasbourg.

Sturm proposed a system of public education that assisted home and church in cultivating leaders who desired virtue more than glory or money. Education in the service of the community required devoted teachers who loved learning, virtue, and teaching. Although he was an educational innovator, Sturm's conception of learning echoed classical models more than it anticipated modern egalitarian and democratized mass education. Clearly, he valued quality more than quantity, and his system discriminated among the more and less able students. His carefully graded and sequential curriculum chose the best and most difficult authors among the classics, leaving other good books for leisure hours at home. He weighted his booklist heavily with Plato, Virgil, and Cicero. Indeed, Cicero's style set the standard of excellence: "Boys must keep in mind that nothing not used by Cicero or not permitted by the teacher is true oratory." For Sturm, Plato and Cicero served as peerless models of the union of philosophy and oratory. Sturm himself refused to separate wisdom from eloquence, style from content.[1]

THE SELECTION

Between 1550 and 1568, Sturm exchanged a number of letters in Latin with his close friend Roger Ascham. These letters are filled with warmth, good humor, a shared love of learning, and news of politics and diplomacy. At the time of their first letters in 1550, Sturm was laboring at his reforms in Strasbourg and continuing to translate and edit Greek and Latin classics, while Ascham was teaching at Cambridge and tutoring the princess Elizabeth during King Edward's brief reign. The first excerpt included here begins with Ascham's admiration for the royal household, in particular Elizabeth's dazzling intellectual achievements. Sturm replies with his own observations on Elizabeth and in typical fashion ponders the relationship between wisdom and eloquence.

from The Latin Letters of Roger Ascham and Johann Sturm

ROGER ASCHAM TO JOHANN STURM, APRIL 4, 1550

I have determined to ask you to do something for literature, for the sake of your own name and for my own use, unless this seem to be too much of self-love on my part. In the reading of the Scriptures, in which I have resolved to build the strongest tabernacle of my life and studies in preference to anything else, with the favor of Christ, I have in mind to join Plato, Aristotle, Demosthenes, and Marcus Cicero to the rest of my labors. I am not so exactly pleased or slothfully content with that kind of study that I either contemn altogether the doctors' and jurisconsults' books or never touch them at all. For these contain the arts and excellent learning, and have much importance to all the use and splendor of mortal life. But in such variety of the most proper study, let everyone go, as far as I am concerned, somewhat like Atilius the poet, as Cicero says, the hard way: "To each one his bride, to me my own."

Aristotle in learning and judgment not only surpasses all the others, but in my opinion even himself, in those books where he explains the art of eloquence with a most beautiful doctrine. A divine discipline of reason, nature, and custom he buries with a divine talent

---

1. See his 138 oration, "The Correct Opening of Elementary Schools of Letters," in Lewis W. Spitz and Barbara Sher Tinsley, eds., *Johann Sturm on Education* (St. Louis, MO: Concordia, 1995).

in the rest of his books. Here he presents and explains almost nothing which is not for popular habit and the daily use of human life.

And the more I wonder at these books above the rest, the more I pay respect to Daniel Barber and P. Victor, who have truly with great diligence written commentaries on them. Although I desire earnestly to, I cannot find out what Gregory Nazianzen has to say about these Greek commentaries in those books which Erasmus testifies to have read over at the Aldines with a "slow haste." For I do not believe that these are those anonymous commentaries printed in France. Of all these I willingly recognize the diligence and vehemently approve the good intentions. But when from your works, which I know from frequent reading and by the words of many men whom I meet often, I see clearly that you are versed in these books on rhetoric with such great talent and common sense, I have resolved not to explain the literature either in respect to what they proclaim or what I feel about it myself, but to leave it to rest upon your opinion.

And it is this, most human Sturm, that I seek so eagerly from you: that by your own excellent art you bring out into the light and clearly explain the supreme art of the greatest artist of all.

Now truly, if I had any aptitude for persuasion or power of compulsion, I would use it entire to urge you to do this, and not I alone, but many others demand this from you. Since their wishes are involved with the greatest profit to literature and the tremendous praise of your name, how much your humanity should incline you to gratify them, consider again and again. We do not seek to have you burden yourself with new labors; we long for the old ones, that they may spread abroad most diffusely the mature fruit of your studies. For we have seen and read a great part of those labors which you undertook in explaining those books of rhetoric, and so much ardor have you excited in us for seeing the rest of them, that it can in no wise be satisfied unless by the light of your talent. Therefore, best Sturm, hurry and proceed to do good to everyone at the prayer of one man.

The nobility in England was never more literate. Our most illustrious King Edward, by his talent, industry, constancy, and learning far surpasses his own age and the [religious] faith of other men. For not influenced by the reports of others, but many times an eye-witness myself, occasions which I consider blessings to me, have I seen the choir of all the virtues that have marched into his spirit. France I doubt not will find the highest excellence of learning in the famous Duke of Suffolk and in the remainder of that legation of young nobles educated in Latin and Greek along with our King, who have, on this very day when I write to you, set out for France.

There are now many honorable ladies who surpass the daughters of Thomas More in all kinds of learning; but among them all the most shining star, not so much for the clarity of her mind as for the splendor of her virtue and her letters, is my mistress, Elizabeth, sister of our King. She so shines forth that, in justly commending her great versatility, my task is not to find something to praise but to find limits to my praising. But I shall write nothing to which I have not been an eye-witness. She had me for a tutor in the Latin and Greek languages for two years. Now freed from the turbulence of the court and restored to the pleasantness of my former literary leisure, I have by her royal beneficence an honorable place and condition in this University.

The ornaments of nature and of fortune, gathered together in my most illustrious mistress, are difficult to judge; I hardly know which is to be estimated the higher. Aristotle's excellence is wholly transfused into her. For in her are contained all beauty, stature, prudence, and industry. She has just passed her sixteenth birthday, and is so grave in age and so gentle in her rank to a degree unheard of. Her study of the true faith and of learning is most energetic. She has talent without a woman's weakness, industry with a man's perseverance, and a memory than which I know none quicker to perceive or longer to retain. She speaks in French and Italian as well as she speaks in English; in Latin easily, correctly, and thoughtfully; and she has even spoken with me in Greek tolerably well, frequently, and voluntarily. When she writes in Greek or Latin, nothing is more beautiful than her handwriting. She is as skilled in music as she is delighted by it. In adornment she is elegant rather than showy, and seems by her contempt of gold and headdresses to represent by all her plan of life not Phaedra, but Hippolyta.

She has read almost all of Cicero with me and the largest part of Titus Livy. For from these two authors alone she drew her knowledge of the Latin tongue. The beginning of the day she always gives to the New Testament in Greek, and later reads selected orations of Isocrates and the tragedies of Sophocles. For I believed that from these she would derive purity of speech, the most suitable teaching of the mind, and a subsequent manner of living fit for her high position and for all contingencies of chance. To teach her religion, she added Cyprian and the *Commonplaces* of P. Melanchthon, next the fountains of the Scripture, and others of a similar nature, from whom she could taste the purity of learning in conjunction with elegance of speech.

In every style of writing she readily notices any word of curious, far-fetched, or doubtful use. Those foolish imitators of Erasmus, who have bound the Latin tongue in wretched fetters of proverbs, she cannot endure. She approves a style born from the subject, chaste from its suitability, and beautiful from its perspicuity. She admires uniquely modest metaphors and comparisons well collated and contrasting felicitously with one another. Her ears are sharpened so by the careful notice of these matters, nay, have been made so discriminating and so exact in judgment, that nothing occurs in Greek, Latin, or English composition, either loose and wandering on the one hand, or tight and well-defined on the other, or too diffuse or justly tempered, that she does not so scrupulously notice while reading as to reject it at once with great disgust or receive it with the greatest pleasure.

I do not deceive you, Sturm, nor is there need to; but I wish to sketch out for you so much of on outline of her excellent talent and intellect, and while my mind has been so totally fixed, I have enjoyed writing to you of my most dear remembrances of my most illustrious mistress. If you should write anything to this most noble princess, most learned Sturm, it would be most gratefully received and most discreetly read through. But I fear that delighted by the pleasure of recording these things about her or by the joy of writing to you, I may have become somewhat prolix in my long letter.

Johann Sturm to Roger Ascham, September 9, 1550

See, my Ascham, what your letter has brought about. In my little book written about changing the species of composition of the orators, I addressed your Elizabeth, in order that, since she can unravel the most artificial speech and the most involved patterns, she can judge also this little work, which has been composed in a light and compact style at night. For I believe that the web of Penelope in Homer can justly be compared with the verses of the poets and the periods of the orators. Both these things ought not only be compared, but ripped apart and altered and even destroyed as often as they seem to stand emending. And certainly, in the juvenile state and in the feminine sex, especially little girls, what occupation could be more honorable? What exercise more liberal? What habit more pleasant than that of the pen, of composition, of pure, splendid, perfect, and consummate speech, toward which we all struggle and contend?

Since you are a literate man, and a good one, and worthy of that glorious name of evangelist, all these points do not appear merely, but even shine forth in your letter: there was, I believe, nothing in your letter untrue to the virtues end praises of the Prince's sister, of that royal stock.

But what in our times more desirable can befall mortal men that that from the families of the rulers and the nobility there arise genius in both sexes who are charmed by the study of literature, who cultivate letters, who study and follow out the teaching of the arts and worldly affairs in their own characters? Therefore are the English more blest in this kind of good people than the Germans, among whom of the nobility there are very few who think that distinction in literature pertains to their own rank. Since in your country the greater part of the nobles strive to become educated—or if they realize this too late, nevertheless they think that this thing now concerns themselves and their people—therefore do we now take hope that the praise which Italy once claimed always as her own, and later France and Germany tried to assume, emulous of Italy, England can appropriate finally and completely to herself. And may such a dwelling as the masters of eloquence and learning once had at Athens and at Rome, the two cities which you mentioned, be established for them now in England, so that your people, who strive to copy classic virtues, may equal classic glory and achievement.

But when I come to you, my Ascham, I know not whether to congratulate you the more to whom the Lord has given such a pupil, or Princess Elizabeth, to whom such a highly trained master; to make sure, I congratulate you both, and rejoice, concluding that the two years in which you taught and she learned were happy ones. I am happy also to hear of your leisure, that Edward the King made you his benign concession both largely and liberally. Indeed the designs of our studies demand busy leisure and leisurely business, for to the people generally we seem to rest in our labors and to labor in ease. When the rest of men are at hunting or a-fishing or a-building, they are considered occupied with labors. When educated men read, write, annotate, they are considered idlers, when as a matter of fact they are tossed about in a life vexed and troubled by the labors of their genius, by the fear of danger, not by the hardship of their toil, but by the undertaking and the cogitation of the greatest and immortal thoughts. But since that greatest leisure is given to you, the most abundant and pleasant fruits of it will come also to me. For you promised to me in your letter many more and frequent letters, which I await most avidly, not only because of that friendship of yours toward me, which I observe in your letters, but also especially because of the learning and the two arts in which I have these many years been engaged, dialectic and eloquence. For we both wish to be dialecticians and rhetoricians. But you are, and I fervently hope to be, elegant in style and polished: and assuredly the profession of dialectic today, obscure and abject, is separated from that wealth of eloquence, and this very eloquence separated from the teaching of dialectic swells up, puffs out, and wanders in error, and brings us to naught by any road or reason, to naught by craftsmanship. And so your judgment and mine are the same: we desire the same, follow and strive for the same. They all undertake the same study who aspire to live in literature and to reach fame through literature.

Now indeed to return to your letter, I enjoyed it immensely, first because it demonstrated your friendship toward me and then because it told me much about your kingdom, which we consider most noble and fortified by the strength of many ages; about your king, for whom a certain and excellent hope is received as to his wisdom, clemency, and religion; and finally about Elizabeth, your princess. In proportion as this passage was more detailed, I wished in reading that it were still longer.

These matters, I repeat, were all thoroughly enjoyable. But when you credit me with so much, more than I can acknowledge by any means, then you strike me with shame, to quote Horace, because I cannot demonstrate the teaching and good judgment which you so ascribe to me. But indeed, when you ask me to translate and edit the *Phaedo* of Plato and the books *de Anima* of Aristotle, and his works on rhetoric, and to translate the orations of Demosthenes and Aeschines against each other, and to publish the books I promised, *The Methods of Speaking Latin*, well, I do not try to escape the toil so much, which might be undertaken, as I do the audacity in undertaking and the suspicion of temerity and presumption in publishing, which recalled me, as it were, when last year I entered the editorial arena. For I had resolved to edit Aristotle's books on rhetoric with the entire works of the commentators; a part of this I had already given to the copyist. But I changed my mind, first because of the reasons I spoke of; then because certain other matters intervened which deterred me from the undertaking. But I propose to resume my work on them this winter and complete what I have begun, if God grant me the life and strength.

The orations of Demosthenes and Aeschines I am interpreting for my students; but in this way, that I shall be engaged more in explaining them than in translating them. For I deem it enough if I explain the thought and the force and power of the individual words; what remains of the labor is spent in pointing out the art; so that they understand the gathering and analysis of subject matter, consider the logical divisions and parts; the composition as a whole; the methods of argument; the forms of syllogistic summary; the wit of the apothegms; the embellishment of indefinite and the logical conclusions of definite issues; the amplifications in each; the kinds of repetition in all; the connections and rhythms of passages, clauses, and sentences.

Both of you must be content with this my wintry labor; you my dear Ascham, who ask, and Bucer, who seems to have urged you on; as for the *Phaedo* and Aristotle's books *de Anima*, at another time, when I have time, if life is present and I can. Just because I have observed in the *Gorgias* certain elements which pertain to the function of dialectic, I cannot therefore elaborate somewhat on the *Phaedo*, which is a perpetual classic, and which will not offend the ears and the minds of literate men; and even if I comprehend the rhetoric, and can in some way draw it into the light, I cannot therefore sustain by argument and writing that most noble disputation concerning life, death, and the immortality of the soul, about the passing of good men from life; about the rewards of the most honorable; and about the eternity of all things.

But you discourage me in asking for the books about the Latin language; for I promised them some years before this. I can only confess openly that even if I had the talent, I have not the resources, as I have often told Bucer. For what a task it is to compose a work of such a kind, from which in brief you can attain such ability and ease after the observance of the precepts, that whatsoever you embrace in thought you can also express in Latin; not only will it be pure, but also elegant, ornate, and graceful; and that you shall have examples in readiness which must augment and complete the design of your words and your thoughts; and you shall have these not all collected but also distinctly and properly arranged in their most profitable places. Such a work, when I have begun it with thought, tried and proved it by careful deliberation, I suffer to fall imperfect with others as long as I am constrained by my resources, although our gymnasium constrains me enough: however, because it constrains me, it does not force me. I think that I can do enough for men if I am not indolent in the rest of my duties.

Now, concerning what you wrote of Augustine, I praise your judgment, and I am delighted in that section of your letter by your humanity and friendliness. To this theologian I concede much without hesitation on account of his learning, for he teaches all things, makes shrewd conclusions, and refutes craftily, erring not at all in proposition, division, argument, or development. But when I urge my students to the cultivation of eloquence, not only do I consider the subject matter, but also the adornment and the treatment, so that I think them superior in speaking, but Augustine in learning, notwithstanding they are erudite and well-read, and so must be preferred in the first place. For the teacher must ever and ever beware, in teaching the Latin and Greek languages, lest authors inferior in rhetoric be preferred, because of their handling of material, to Cicero, Demosthenes, and the other better writers. For name of wisdom and knowledge is pleasing to everyone; and knowledge itself, indeed not only much desired but very healthful also. For no one can either write or speak excellently who has acquired the arts and methods but has no understanding of the subject matter. . . .

This must be considered first of all: whether the student may be permitted to read at random from all periods, or whether there should be some discrimination in times, periods, and materials.

The Greeks set up Homer to be learned by heart for their young people; that could be done without trouble because the children had imbibed the words of their fathers along with the milk of their mothers. The Roman grammarians taught Vergil in their schools; there was no danger from that source. Those same Romans interpreted Homer from the first; the alien tongue was no hindrance although the Romans spoke Latin, and the Greeks could do the same if they liked the language. But what useful information could a lad pick up toward the shaping and purity of his style from Cato's distichs, from Aquinas, Gerso, or Cocca? I have named a few: from these very many others can be considered of the same herd. I do not mean to be nasty, but they are simply not suitable for our purpose.

But even to these let us add that barbarous welter of grammarians, dialecticians, physicians, theologians, and philosophers who have caught at sordid things more readily than at pure, at utilitarian values rather than thorny studies. A great number of these quacks guard themselves even today in our colleges of sophistry and fight viciously about their own barbarousness as though it were another Palladium. Oh delightful flock! oh holy conspiracy! In which it is glorious to be conquered and shameful to conquer: What can the condition of literature be, the condition of religion, in such a foulness of speech, language, and eloquence? For who would not spurn them, if he but saw the empty sounds from their mouths, the deformity of their words, the stupidity of their sentences, the weakness of their judgments, the stubbornness of their spirits, the vulgarity of their habits, and the wandering of their standards? Who have displaced liberality with license, who have corrupted the arts and sciences, who have dishonored and defiled history, religion, and ceremony, not only by a rotten kind of style, but also by ignorant opinions; remote from every consensus of learning, who have obscured the matter by their bickering and have polluted it by their defenses. Are such to be set up in our cities as instructors of children and to imbue the minds of young people with their writings, so that corruption is uttered for purity, barbarisms for good Latin, the meaningless for the clear-cut, and the chaotic for the well-ordered? Why shall we not retain the same judgment in things less perfect and consummate which we employ against things wholly evil?

But the study of matter always has been considered more important than the study of words. It is plainly the duty of eloquence first to consider matter, then words. For it is faulty to speak what is inane or stupid. Nevertheless, since we require not only wisdom from the orator but also the embellishment of words, let us separate the two, which cling together in other respects by nature. Wisdom demands that you question what you speak: that it be true, probable, certain, intelligent, instructive, and refined. What does embellishment demand? That it be expressive, meaningful, sonorous, full, harmonious, ornate, and elegant. But if wisdom should demand of me to drop my system of adornment, I must be content with purity, I must not affect the rest of the decoration, I must suffer myself to be freed from great labors, extreme cares, and daily vigils.

If however I should neglect that purity, surely I shall not conform to that wisdom, however circumspect it may be. But if it reply that to be gifted with learning is great, but that it is excellent to join eloquence to that same system of oratory and to learn both from the best rather than from the worst rank of authors, and that labors are best expended upon the most perfect writers, then I shall follow the advice of wisdom as though given by a divinely appointed oracle.

Therefore I wish those authors to be explained to the children in the beginning, and these to be read first in the training of habits who have adjoined eloquence to learning; not who, content with learning, have either contemned eloquence or could not even aspire to it. . . . This reason prompted me to place Chrysostom before Augustine, not because Augustine is not wiser or is not fluent, but because he is less fluent than Chrysostom, who is yet erudite and scholarly. I award to Chrysostom the first place in respect to his language and his age, but not in learning and talent, since in these I put many others before Chrysostom himself. For by the study of eloquence one learns the importance of avoiding not only barbarisms, but also of preferring always the better before the good. But perhaps I shall seem to confide too little in your candor, I who excuse these matters so carefully; therefore since I think it makes a very great difference, as to the order in which they are read, it has seemed good to explain to you my feeling. I do not think that you will receive it as strange.

But I have spoken freely because you say in your letter that the name of peace is sweet, and peace itself salutary. I know the exact place in which Cicero says the same thing and gives his opinion in the same words, whose form of argument I have tried to express here, that I may play the rhetorician with you. And unless you keep watch, not far hence I shall sport again, having set the example, after I ask once more about your mistress Elizabeth what I want and how I want it. For I cannot forget that she joins to the training of the great matters about which you write the art of eloquence and loves that exercise, which, although it gently becomes her sex, yet lies spurned by almost all. But she thinks rightly with herself: for if the form of body in young ladies is pleasing, why not also the form of modest, chaste, pure, and beautiful speech? Thence the other exercises of young ladies are common to the nobility and common stock—spinning, weaving, and embroidery; and often we see lowborn women working more skillfully than the nobility. However, elegance of speech apparently prefers to dwell in the houses of the nobility and in the distinguished families, so that the nobility differ as much from the vulgar by suavity of speech as by dress and accomplishment.

Moreover, it is true that these very elements are the precious furniture of high-born ladies: gems, bracelets, and other adornments; and they are usually baubles of fortune and often in rather bad natures abundant. But elegance of speech and beauty of voice cannot be separated from beauty of mind, and are the mark of excellent talent and noble nature. And while the titles and ornaments of riches are celebrated only at home, the artful utterance is noticed at once and often wings its way to foreign nations and peoples, who consider it admirable.

The more do I approve Mistress Elizabeth's industry. It will have such effect that the nobility of young girls, maidens, and mature women shall be judged, not only by the antiquity of their families, but also by the elegance of their learning and speech. Therefore it is most fit that I send her this little book [*de periodis unus*]. For in the publication of books it is foolish to address them to those who are ignorant of the matters which are propounded, or who do not greatly love those same matters. Thus since my book cannot speak for itself, for it is not fluent, you may deprecate it as far as it sins, and commend it where it sins not, and in both respects act as its patron, especially to King Edward, to whom I also send a copy, so that it may be defended by a tri-partite patronage: first by you to Princess Elizabeth, then by her brother, King Edward; and if he wishes to be the highest patron by virtue of his royalty, what greater blessing could my little book ask for?

John Calvin

1509–64

*For since all truth is of God, if any ungodly man has said anything
true, we should not reject it, for it also has come from God.*

COMMENTARY ON TITUS 1:12

⟨∞⟩

John Calvin, Christian humanist and leading theologian of the Reformed church, was born in Noyon, France, and reared in aristocratic circles. His father was employed by the local cathedral and hoped to see his son ordained to the priesthood. To that end, young Calvin entered the University of Paris, then dominated by the humanist spirit of Erasmus, Jacques Lefevre, and Guillaume Budé. He attended the university at the same time as the future Jesuits Francis Xavier and Ignatius Loyola. Calvin earned a bachelor's degree and an M.A. but at his father's urging turned his attention to the more lucrative profession of law, continuing his studies at Orleans and Bourges. Influenced at many points by the humanist revival, he avidly learned Latin, Greek, and Hebrew, and imbibed Cicero and Quintilian. In 1532, Calvin published his first scholarly treatise, a commentary on Seneca's *De clementia* (On Mercy). Within two years, however, this promising classicist experienced, in his words, a "sudden conversion" from Catholicism and was forced to flee Paris. In Basel, Calvin completed and published his monumental *Institutes of the Christian Religion,* a comprehensive statement of Reformed theology. Calvin was soon called to Geneva to help lead the Reformation movement that had recently swept the Swiss canton. He labored to reorganize the church, but he was banished after a conflict with civil authorities and fled to Strasbourg. Despite his banishment from Geneva, Calvin wrote the important reply to Jacopo Sadoleto's appeal to Geneva to return to the Catholic faith, after which Calvin's friends in Geneva's government brought him back to the canton to continue his reforms.

For the next two decades, Calvin influenced a generation of reformers from all over Europe. The academy in Geneva, founded by Calvin about the year 1558, educated leaders for church and state, was modeled on Sturm's successes in Strasbourg, and grew into the University of Geneva. Calvin was about a generation younger than Luther and Zwingli and never met the German and Swiss reformers, though he knew their work well. He formed a friendship and corresponded for many years with Philip Melanchthon.

THE SELECTIONS

Calvin's first edition of his *Institutes of the Christian Religion* appeared in Latin in 1536 and was soon translated into French and several other languages. A final expanded edition appeared in 1559. A work of systematic theology, it quickly established its place as one of the most important theological treatises of the Reformation. Admirers have even ranked it with Aquinas's *Summa*. As a manual or handbook of theology it explores every doctrine of the Apostles' Creed. Each page reveals Calvin's mastery of classical literature, Scripture, and the theology of Saint Augustine. Included here is a short section from Book II on the knowledge of God, primarily as it is affected by the frailty and fallen condition of man's reason and will. Calvin points to the goodness of God's gifts and urges humility and gratitude as man's proper response to divine blessing.

In addition to the *Institutes,* Calvin wrote commentaries on many of the books of the Bible and innumerable sermons. In his commentary on Titus 1:12, Calvin uses the opportunity presented by the Apostle Paul's reference to the Greek poet Epimenides to defend the Christian's use of classical learning, citing the authority of Basil of Caesarea.

from Institutes of the Christian Religion

12. SUPERNATURAL GIFTS DESTROYED; NATURAL GIFTS CORRUPTED; BUT ENOUGH OF REASON REMAINS TO DISTINGUISH MAN FROM BRUTE BEASTS

And, indeed, that common opinion which they have taken from Augustine pleases me: that the natural gifts were corrupted in man through sin, but that his supernatural gifts were stripped from him. For by the latter clause they understand the light of faith as well as righteousness, which would be sufficient to attain heavenly life and eternal bliss. Therefore, withdrawing from the Kingdom of God, he is at the same time deprived of spiritual gifts, with which he had been furnished for the hope of eternal salvation. From this it follows that he is so banished from the Kingdom of God that all qualities belonging to the blessed life of the soul have been extinguished in him, until he recovers them through the grace of regeneration. Among these are faith, love of God, charity toward neighbor, zeal for holiness and for righteousness. All these, since Christ restores them in us, are considered adventitious, and beyond nature: and for this reason we infer that they were taken away. On the other hand, soundness of mind and uprightness of heart were withdrawn at the same time. This is the corruption of the natural gifts. For even though something of understanding and judgment remains as a residue along with the will, yet we shall not call a mind whole and sound that is both weak and plunged into deep darkness. And depravity of the will is all too well known.

Since reason, therefore, by which man distinguishes between good and evil, and by which he understands and judges, is a natural gift, it could not be completely wiped out; but it was partly weakened and partly corrupted, so that its misshapen ruins appear. John speaks in this sense: "The light still shines in the darkness, but the darkness comprehends it not" [John 1:5]. In these words both facts are clearly expressed. First, in man's perverted and degenerate nature some sparks still gleam. These show him to be a rational being, differing from brute beasts, because he is endowed with understanding. Yet, secondly, they show this light choked with dense ignorance, so that it cannot come forth effectively.

Similarly the will, because it is inseparable from man's nature, did not perish, but was so bound to wicked desires that it cannot strive after the right. This is, indeed, a complete definition, but one needing a fuller explanation.

Therefore, so that the order of discussion may proceed according to our original division of man's soul into understanding and will, let us first of all examine the power of the understanding.

When we so condemn human understanding for its perpetual blindness as to leave it no perception of any object whatever, we not only go against God's Word, but also run counter to the experience of common sense. For we see implanted in human nature some sort of desire to search out the truth to which man would not at all aspire if he had not already savored it. Human understanding then possesses some power of perception, since it is by nature captivated by love of truth. The lack of this endowment in brute animals proves their nature gross and irrational. Yet this longing for truth, such as it is, languishes before it enters upon its race because it soon falls into vanity. Indeed, man's mind, because of its dullness, cannot hold to the right path, but wanders through various errors and stumbles repeatedly, as if it were groping in darkness, until it strays away and finally disappears. Thus it betrays how incapable it is of seeking and finding truth.

Then it grievously labors under another sort of vanity: often it cannot discern those things which it ought to exert itself to know. For this reason, in investigating empty and worthless things, it torments itself in its absurd curiosity, while it carelessly pays little or no attention to matters that it should particularly understand. Indeed, it scarcely ever seriously applies itself to the study of them. Secular writers habitually complain of this perversity, yet they are almost all found to have entangled themselves in it. For this reason, Solomon, through the whole of his Ecclesiastes, after recounting all those studies in which men seem to themselves to be very wise, declares them to be vain and trifling [chs. 1:2, 14; 2:11; etc.].

13. THE POWER OF THE UNDERSTANDING WITH RESPECT TO EARTHLY THINGS AND THE FORM OF THE HUMAN COMMUNITY

Yet its efforts do not always become so worthless as to have no effect, especially when it turns its attention to things below. On the contrary, it is intelligent enough to taste something of things above, although it is more careless about investigating these. Nor does it carry on this latter activity with equal skill. For when the mind is borne above the level of the present life, it is especially convinced of its own frailty. Therefore, to perceive more clearly how far the mind can proceed in any matter according to the degree of its ability, we must here set forth a distinction. This, then, is the distinction: that there is one kind of understanding of earthly things; another of heavenly. I call "earthly things" those which do not pertain to God or his Kingdom, to true justice, or to the blessedness of the future life; but which have their significance and relationship with regard to the present life and are, in a sense, confined within its bounds. I call "heavenly things" the pure knowledge of God, the nature of true righteousness, and the mysteries of the Heavenly Kingdom. The first class includes government, household management, all mechanical skills, and the liberal arts. In the second are the knowledge of God and of his will, and the rule by which we conform our lives to it.

Of the first class the following ought to be said: since man is by nature a social animal, he tends through natural instinct to foster and preserve society. Consequently, we observe that there exist in all men's minds universal impressions of a certain civic fair dealing and order. Hence no man is to be found who does not understand that every sort of human organization must be regulated by laws, and who does not comprehend the principles of those laws. Hence arises that unvarying consent of all nations and of individual mortals with regard to laws. For their seeds have, without teacher or lawgiver, been implanted in all men.

I do not dwell upon the dissension and conflicts that immediately spring up. Some, like thieves and robbers, desire to overturn all law and right, to break all legal restraints, to let their lust alone masquerade as law. Others think unjust what some have sanctioned as just (an even commoner fault), and contend that what some have forbidden is praiseworthy. Such persons hate laws not because they do not know them to be good and holy; but raging with headlong lust, they fight against manifest reason. What they approve of in their understanding they hate on account of their lust. Quarrels of this latter sort do not nullify the original conception of equity. For, while men dispute among themselves about individual sections of the law, they agree on the general conception of equity. In this respect the frailty of the human mind is surely proved: even when it seems to follow the way, it limps and staggers. Yet the fact remains that some seed of political order has been implanted in all men. And this is ample proof that in the arrangement of this life no man is without the light of reason.

14. UNDERSTANDING AS REGARDS ART AND SCIENCE

Then follow the arts, both liberal and manual. The power of human acuteness also appears in learning these because all of us have a certain aptitude. But although not all the arts are suitable for everyone to learn, yet it is a certain enough indication of the common energy that hardly anyone is to be found who does not manifest talent in some art. There are at hand energy and ability not only to learn but also to devise something new in each art or to perfect and polish what one has learned from a predecessor. This prompted Plato to teach wrongly that such apprehension is nothing but recollection. Hence, with good reason we are compelled to confess that its beginning is inborn in human nature. Therefore this evidence clearly testifies to a universal apprehension of reason and understanding by nature implanted in men. Yet so universal is this good that every man ought to recognize for himself in it the peculiar grace of God. The Creator of nature himself abundantly arouses this gratitude in us when he creates imbeciles. Through them he shows the endowments that the human soul would enjoy unpervaded by his light, a light so natural to all that it is certainly a free gift of his beneficence to each! Now the discovery or systematic transmission of the arts, or the inner and more excellent knowledge of them, which is characteristic of few, is not a sufficient proof of common discernment. Yet because it is bestowed indiscriminately upon pious and impious, it is rightly counted among natural gifts.

15. SCIENCE AS GOD'S GIFT

Whenever we come upon these matters in secular writers, let that admirable light of truth shining in them teach us that the mind of man, though fallen and perverted from its wholeness, is nevertheless clothed and ornamented with God's excellent gifts. If we regard the Spirit of God as the sole fountain of truth, we shall neither reject the truth itself, nor despise it wherever it shall appear, unless we wish to dishonor the Spirit of God. For by holding the gifts of the Spirit in slight esteem, we contemn and reproach the Spirit himself. What then? Shall we deny that the truth shone upon the ancient jurists who established civic order and discipline with such great equity? Shall we say that the philosophers were blind in their fine observation and artful description of nature? Shall we say that those men were devoid of understanding who conceived the art of disputation and taught us to speak reasonably? Shall we say that they are insane who developed medicine, devoting their labor to our benefit? What shall we say of all the mathematical sciences? Shall we consider them the ravings of madmen? No we cannot read the writings of the ancients on these subjects without great admiration. We marvel at them because we are compelled to recognize how preeminent they are. But shall we count anything praiseworthy or noble without recognizing at the same time that it comes from God? Let us be ashamed of such ingratitude, into which not even the pagan poets fell, for they confessed that the gods had invented philosophy, laws, and all useful arts. Those men whom Scripture[I Cor. 2:14] calls "natural men" were, indeed, sharp and penetrating in their investigation of inferior things. Let us, accordingly, learn by their example how many gifts the Lord left to human nature even after it was despoiled of its true good.

16. HUMAN COMPETENCE IN ART AND SCIENCE ALSO DERIVES FROM THE SPIRIT OF GOD

Meanwhile, we ought not to forget those most excellent benefits of the divine Spirit, which he distributes to whomever he wills, for the common good of mankind. The understanding and knowledge of Bezalel and Oholiab, needed to construct the Tabernacle, had to be instilled in them by the Spirit of God [Ex. 31:2-11; 35:30-35]. It is no wonder, then, that the knowledge of all that is most excellent in human life is said to be communicated to us through the Spirit of God. Nor is there reason for anyone to ask, What have the impious, who are utterly estranged from God, to do with his Spirit? We ought to understand the statement that the Spirit of God dwells only in believers [Rom. 8:9] as referring to the Spirit of sanctification through whom we are consecrated as temples to God [I Cor. 3:16]. Nonetheless he fills, moves, and quickens all things by the power of the same Spirit, and does so according to the character that he bestowed upon each kind by the law of creation. But if the Lord has willed that we be helped in physics, dialectic, mathematics, and other like disciplines, by the work and ministry of the ungodly, let us use this assistance. For if we neglect God's gift freely offered in these arts, we ought to suffer just punishment for our sloths. But lest anyone think a man truly blessed when he is credited with possessing great power to comprehend truth under the elements of this world [cf. Col. 2:8], we should at once add that all this capacity to understand, with the understanding that follows upon it, is an unstable and transitory thing in God's sight, when a solid foundation of truth does not underlie it. For with the greatest truth Augustine teaches that as the free gifts were withdrawn from man after the Fall, so the natural ones remaining were corrupted. On this, the Master of the Sentences and the Schoolmen, as we have said, are compelled to agree with him. Not that the gifts could become defiled by themselves, seeing that they came from God. But to defiled man these gifts were no longer pure, and from them he could derive no praise at all.

⸎

Commentary on Titus 1:12

12. *One of themselves, who was a prophet of their own.* I have no doubt that he who is here spoken of is Epimenides, who was a native of Crete; for, when the Apostle says that this author was "one of themselves," and was "a prophet of their own," he undoubtedly means that he belonged to the nation of the Cretans. Why he calls him a Prophet—is doubtful. Some think that the reason is, that the book from which Paul borrowed this passage bears the title "concerning oracles." Others are of opinion that Paul speaks ironically, by saying that they have such a Prophet—a Prophet worthy of a nation which refuses to listen to the servants of God. But as poets are sometimes called by the Greeks "prophets," and as the Latin authors call them *Vates*, I consider it to denote simply a teacher. The reason why they were so called appears to have been, that they were always reckoned to be "a divine race and moved by divine inspiration." Thus also Adimantus, in the Second Book of Plato's treatise *Peri Politeias* [*The Republic*] after having called the poets "sons of the gods," adds, that they also became their prophets. For this reason I think that Paul accommodates his style to the ordinary practice. Nor is it of any importance to inquire on what occasion Epimenides calls his countrymen liars, namely, because they boast of having the sepulcher of Jupiter; but seeing that the poet takes it from an ancient and well-known report, the Apostle quotes it as a proverbial saying.

From this passage we may infer that those persons are superstitious, who do not venture to borrow anything from heathen authors. All truth is from God; and consequently, if wicked men have said anything that is true and just, we ought not to reject it; for it has come from God. Besides, all things are of God; and, therefore, why should it not be lawful to dedicate to his glory everything that can properly be employed for such a purpose? But on this subject the reader may consult Basil's discourse *pros tous neous* [*To Young Men, On How They Might Derive Profit from Pagan Literature*].

Roger Ascham

1515–68

In the end, the good or ill bringing up of children doth as much serve to the good or ill service of God, our Prince, and our whole country, as any one thing doth beside.

THE SCHOOLMASTER

❦

Roger Ascham, Greek and Latin scholar and tutor to the children of Henry VIII, was born in Kirby Wiske in Yorkshire. For his early education, he was taken into the household and patronage of Antony Wingfield. His patron then sent him St. John's College, Cambridge, where he studied Greek, a rare opportunity that had only recently become possible in England. Cambridge at the time was under the influence of Renaissance humanism and Lutheranism, and Ascham embraced both. In the eighteenth century, Samuel Johnson connected the two influences in his *Life of Ascham*: "Those who were zealous for the new learning, were often no great friends to the old religion; and Ascham, as he became a Grecian, became a protestant." Upon earning his B.A. at the age of eighteen, Ascham was elected to a fellowship at St. John's, where he lectured in Greek and mathematics and was awarded an M.A. in 1537. While he continued to perfect his knowledge of Greek and Latin, he also read widely in the works of his contemporaries, including Erasmus, his friend Johann Sturm, Philip Melanchthon, Machiavelli, Castiglione, and Sadoleto. He was summoned to court to teach Greek to the princess Elizabeth, served as secretary for a diplomatic mission to the court of Charles V, and traveled extensively in Germany and briefly in Italy. Somehow he was able to navigate England's turbulent religious and political waters during the Reformation and Counter-Reformation as Latin secretary in turn to Edward, Queen Mary, and Queen Elizabeth. His most important book, *The Schoolmaster,* was written at the request of Sir Edward Sackville and published posthumously by Ascham's widow in 1570.

THE SELECTION

Ascham wrote *The Schoolmaster* in English, aiming his treatise at a wide audience and at the same time shaping modern English prose style (the spelling and punctuation have been updated for clarity in the edition used here). He draws from a familiar list of Greek and Latin philosophers, orators, and poets, as well as the Church Fathers. This list includes Plato, Isocrates, Xenophon, Demosthenes, Aristotle, Cicero, Horace, Plutarch, Quintilian, and Chrysostom. Ascham praises Erasmus and repeatedly recommends Sturm's edition of Cicero's letters, holding up Cicero as the model of eloquence and pure Latin. *The Schoolmaster* shows Ascham's gentle spirit and love of learning, a love that he is eager to instill in teachers and students. The section excerpted here conveys an experienced teacher's alertness to varying abilities among students, preferring the steady, hardworking scholar to the quick but superficial star performer. In the section immediately following this one, Ascham balances his criticism of too much severity in a teacher with warnings against the more common fault of too much leniency. When he speaks of a "fond schoolmaster," he means a foolish or silly one. At the point where this section picks up, Ascham has just finished explaining six principles of translation and analysis.

from The Schoolmaster

If your scholar do miss sometimes in marking rightly the aforesaid six things, chide not hastily, for that shall both dull his wit and discourage his diligence, but monish him gently, which shall make him both willing to amend, and glad to go forward in love and hope of learning.

I have now wished, twice or thrice, this gentle nature to be in a schoolmaster: and, that I have done so, neither by chance, nor without some reason, I will now declare at large why, in mine opinion, love is fitter than fear, gentleness better than beating, to bring up a child rightly in learning.

With the common use of teaching and beating in common schools of England, I will not greatly contend, which if I did, it were but a small grammatical controversy, neither belonging to heresy nor treason, nor greatly touching God nor the Prince: although in very deed, in the end, the good or ill bringing up of children doth as much serve to the good or ill service of God, our Prince, and our whole country, as any one thing doth beside.

I do gladly agree with all good schoolmasters in these points: to have children brought to good perfectness in learning; to all honesty in manners; to have all faults rightly amended; to have every vice severely corrected; but for the order and way that leadeth rightly to these points we somewhat differ. For commonly, many schoolmasters—some, as I have seen, more, as I have heard tell—be of so crooked a nature, as, when they meet with a hard-witted scholar, they rather break him than bow him, rather mar him than mend him. For when the schoolmaster is angry with some other matter, then will he soonest fall to beat his scholar; and though he himself should be punished for his folly, yet must he beat some scholar for his pleasure, though there be no cause for him to do so, nor yet fault in the scholar to deserve so. These, you will say, be fond schoolmasters, and few they be that be found to be such. They be fond, indeed, but surely over many such be found everywhere. But this will I say, that even the wisest of your great beaters do as oft punish nature as they do correct faults. Yea, many times the better nature is sorely punished; for, if one, by quickness of wit, take his lesson readily, another, by hardness of wit, taketh it not so speedily, the first is always commended, the other is commonly punished; when a wise schoolmaster should rather discreetly consider the right disposition of both their natures, and not so much way what either of them is able to do now, as what either of them is likely to do hereafter. For this I know, not only by reading of books in my study, but also by experience of life abroad in the world, that those which be commonly the wisest, the best learned, and best men also, when they be old, were never commonly the quickest of wit when they were young. The causes why, amongst other, which be many, that move me thus to think, be these few, which I will reckon. Quick wits commonly be apt to take, unapt to keep; soon hot and desirous of this and that; as cold and soon weary of the same again; more quick to enter speedily than able to pierce far: even like over sharp tools, whose edges be very soon turned. Such wits delight themselves in easy and pleasant studies, and never pass far forward in high and hard sciences. And therefore the quickest wits commonly may prove the best poets, but not the wisest orators: ready of tongue to speak boldly, not deep of judgment, either for good counsel or wise writing. Also, for manners and life, quick wits commonly be, in desire, newfangle, in purpose, unconstant, light to promise anything, ready to forget everything, both benefit and injury; and thereby neither fast to friend nor fearful to foe; inquisitive of every trifle; not secret in greatest affairs; bold with any person; busy in every matter; soothing such as be present, nipping any that is absent; of nature also, always, flattering their betters, envying their equals, despising their inferiors; and, by quickness of wit, very quick and ready, to like none so well as 'themselves.

Moreover commonly, men, very quick of wit, be also very light of conditions, and thereby very ready of disposition, to be carried over quickly, by any light company, to any riot and unthriftiness when they be young; and therefore seldom either honest of life or rich in living when they be old. For, quick in wit and light in manners be either seldom troubled, or very soon weary, in carrying a very heavy purse. Quick wits also be, in most part of all their doings, overquick, hasty, rash, heady, and brainsick. These two last words, heady and brainsick, be fit and proper words, rising naturally of the matter, and termed aptly by the condition of overmuch quickness of wit. In youth also they be ready scoffers, privy mockers, and ever over light and merry. In age, soon testy, very waspish, and always over miserable; and yet few of them come to any great age by reason of their misordered life when they were young; but a great deal fewer of them come to show any great countenance, or bear any great authority abroad in the world, but either live obscurely, men know not how, or die obscurely, men mark not when. They be like trees that show forth fair blossoms and broad leaves in spring time; but bring out small and not long lasting fruit in harvest time; and that only such as fall and rot before they be ripe, and so never, or seldom, come to any good at all. For this ye shall find most true by experience, that

amongst a number of quick wits in youth, few be found, in the end, either very fortunate
for themselves or very profitable to serve the common wealth, but decay and vanish, men
know not which way; except a very few, to whom peradventure blood and happy parent-
age may perchance purchase a long standing upon the stage. The which felicity, because
it cometh by others procuring, not by their own deserving, and stand by other men's feet,
and not by their own, what outward brag so ever is borne by them, is indeed, of itself, and
in wise men's eyes, of no great estimation.

Some wits, moderate enough by nature, be many times marred by overmuch study
and use of some sciences, namely, Music, Arithmetic, and Geometry. These sciences, as
they sharpen men's wits overmuch, so they change men's manners oversore, if they be not
moderately mingled, and wisely applied to some good use of life. Mark all mathematical
heads, which be only and wholly bent to those sciences, how solitary they be themselves,
how unfit to live with others, and how unapt to serve in the world. This is not only known
now by common experience, but uttered long before by wise men's judgment and sentence. Galene saith much music marreth men's manners; and Plato hath a notable place of
the same thing in his books *de Rep.* well marked also, and excellently translated by Tully
himself. Of this matter, I wrote once more at large, twenty years ago, in my book of shooting: now I thought but to touch it, to prove that overmuch quickness of wit, either given
by nature or sharpened by study, doth not commonly bring forth either greatest learning,
best manners, or happiest life in the end.

Contrarywise, a wit in youth, that is not over dull, heavy, knotty, and lumpish, but
hard, rough, and though somewhat staffish, as Tully wisheth, *otium, quietum, non langui-
dum*; and *negotium cum labore, non cum perieulo*, such a wit I say, if it be at the first well
handled by the mother, and rightly smoothed and wrought as it should, not over thwartly,
and against the wood, by the schoolmaster, both for learning and whole course of living,
proveth always the best. In wood and stone, not the softest, but hardest, be always aptest
for portraiture, both fairest for pleasure, and most durable for profit. Hard wits be hard to
receive, but sure to keep; painful without weariness, heedful without wavering, constant
without newfangleness; bearing heavy things, though not lightly, yet willingly; entering
hard things, though not easily, yet deeply, and so come to that perfectness of learning in
the end that quick wits seem in hope, but do not in deed, or else very seldom, ever attain
unto. Also, for manners and life, hard wits commonly are hardly carried, either to desire
every new thing, or else to marvel at every strange thing; and therefore they be careful
and diligent in their own matters, not curious and busy in other men's affairs and so they
become wise themselves, and also are counted honest by others. They be grave, steadfast,
silent of tongue, secret of heart. Not hasty in making, but constant in keeping any promise. Not rash in uttering, but wary in considering every matter and, thereby, not quick in
speaking, but deep of judgment, whether they write, or give counsel in all weighty affairs.
And these be the men that become in the end both most happy for themselves, and always
best esteemed abroad in the world.

I have been longer in describing the nature, the good or ill success, of the quick and
hard wit, than perchance some will think this place and matter doth require. But my
purpose was hereby plainly to utter what injury is offered to all learning, and to the commonwealth also, first, by the fond father in choosing, but chiefly by the lewd schoolmaster
in beating and driving away the best natures from learning. A child that is still, silent,

constant, and somewhat hard of wit, is either never chosen by the father to be made a scholar, or else, when he cometh to the school, he is smally regarded, little looked unto, he lacketh teaching, he lacketh couraging, he lacketh all things, only he never lacketh beating, nor any word that may move him to hate learning, nor any deed that may drive him from learning to any other kind of living.

And when this sad-natured and hard-witted child is beat from his book, and becometh after either student of the common law, or page in the court, or servingman, or bound apprentice to a merchant, or to some handicraft, he proveth in the end wiser, happier, and many times honester too, than many of these quick wits do by their learning.

Learning is both hindered and injured too by the ill choice of them that send young scholars to the universities, of whom must needs come all our divines, lawyers, and physicians.

These young scholars be chosen commonly, as young apples be chosen by children, in a fair garden about St. Jamestide: a child will choose a sweeting, because it is presently fair and pleasant, and refuse a runnet, because it is then green, hard, and sour, when the one, if it be eaten, doth breed both worms and ill-humours; the other, if it stand his time, be ordered and kept as it should, is wholesome of itself, and helpeth to the good digestion of other meats. Sweetings will receive worms, rot, and die on the tree, and never or seldom come to the gathering for good and lasting store.

For very grief of heart I will not apply the similitude: but hereby is plainly seen how learning is robbed of her best wits, first by the great beating, and after by the ill choosing of scholars, to go to the universities. Whereof cometh partly that lewd and spiteful proverb, sounding to the great hurt of learning and shame of learned men, that the greatest clerks be not the wisest men.

And though I, in all this discourse, seem plainly to prefer hard and rough wits before quick and light wits both for learning and manners, yet am I not ignorant that some quickness of wit is a singular gift of God, and so most rare amongst men, and namely such a wit as is quick without lightness, sharp without brittleness, desirous of good things without newfangleness, diligent in painful things without wearisomeness, and constant in good will to do all things well, as I know was in Sir John Cheke, and is in some that yet live, in whom all these fair qualities of wit are fully met together.

But it is notable and true that Socrates saith in Plato to his friend Crito:—That that number of men is fewest which far exceed, either in good or ill, in wisdom or folly, but the mean betwixt both, be the greatest number, which he proveth true in divers other things, as in greyhounds, amongst which few are found exceeding great or exceeding little, exceeding swift or exceeding slow; and therefore, I speaking of quick and hard wits, I meant the common number of quick and hard wits amongst the which, for the most part, the hard wit proveth many times the better learned, wiser, and honester man; and therefore do I the more lament that such wits commonly be either kept from learning by fond fathers, or beat from learning by lewd schoolmasters.

And speaking thus much of the wits of children for learning, the opportunity of the place, and goodness of the matter might require to have here declared the most special notes of a good wit for learning in a child, after the manner and custom a good horseman, who is skilful to know, and able to tell others, how by certain sure signs a man may choose a colt, that is like to prove another day excellent for the saddle. And it is pity that commonly more care is had, yea, and that amongst very wise men, to find out rather a cunning man for their horse than a cunning man for their children. They say nay in word, but they do so in deed. For, to the one, they will gladly give a stipend of 200 crowns by year, and loth to offer to the other 200 shillings. God, that sitteth in heaven, laugheth their choice to scorn, and rewardeth their liberality as it should; for He suffereth them to have tame and well ordered horse, but wild and unfortunate children, and, therefore, in the end they find more pleasure in their horse than comfort in their children.

But concerning the true notes of the best wits for learning in a child, I will report, not mine own opinion, but the very judgment of him that was counted the best teacher and wisest man that learning maketh mention of, and that is Socrates in Plato, who expresseth orderly these seven plain notes to choose a good wit in a child for learning:

1. Euphues.
2. Mnemon.
3. Philomathes.
4. Philoponos.
5. Philekoos.
6. Zetetikos.
7. Philepainos.

And because I write English, and to Englishmen, I will plainly declare in English both what these words of Plato mean, and how aptly they be linked, and how orderly they follow one another.

1. EUPHUES.

Is he that is apt by goodness of wit, and appliable by readiness of will, to learning, having all other qualities of the mind and parts of the body, that must another day serve learning, not troubled, mangled, and halved, but found whole, full, and able to do their office; as a tongue, not stammering, or ever hardly drawing forth words, but plain and ready to deliver the meaning of the mind; a voice, not soft, weak, piping, womanish, but audible, strong, and manlike; a countenance, not wearish and crabbed, but fair and comely; a personage, not wretched and deformed, but tall and goodly; for surely a comely countenance, with a goodly stature, giveth credit to learning and authority to the person; otherwise commonly, either open contempt, or privy disfavour doth hurt, or hinder, both person and learning. And, even as a fair stone requireth to be set in the finest gold, with the best workmanship, or else it loseth much of the grace and price, even so, excellency in learning, and namely divinity, joined with a comely personage, is a marvellous jewel in the world. And how can a comely body be better employed than to serve the fairest exercise of God's greatest gift, and that is learning? But commonly, the fairest bodies are bestowed on the foulest purposes. I would it were not so, and with examples herein I will not meddle; yet I wish, that those should both mind it, and meddle with it, which have most occasion to look to it, as good and wise fathers should do, and greatest authority to amend it, as good and wise magistrates ought to do; and yet I will not let openly to lament the unfortunate case of learning herein.

For, if a father have four sons, three fair and well formed both mind and body, the fourth, wretched, lame, and deformed, his choice shall be, to put the worst to learning, as one good enough to become a scholar. I have spent the most part of my life in the university, and therefore I can bear good witness that many fathers commonly do thus; whereof, I have heard many wise, learned, and as good men as ever I knew, make great, and oft complain: a good horseman will choose no such colt, neither for his own, nor yet for his master's saddle. And thus much of the first note.

2. MNEMON.

Good of memory: a special part of the first note [*Euphues*], and a mere benefit of nature; yet it is so necessary for learning, as Plato maketh it a separate and perfect note of itself, and that so principal a note, as without it, all other gifts of nature do small service to learning. Afranius, that old Latin poet, maketh memory the mother of learning and wisdom, saying thus:—

Usus me genuit, Mater peperit memoria, and though it be the mere gift of nature, yet is memory well preserved by use, and much increased by order, as our scholar must learn another day in the university; but in a child, a good memory is well known, by three properties: that is, if it be quick in receiving, sure in keeping, and ready in delivering forth again.

3. PHILOMATHES.

Given to love learning: for though a child have all the gifts of nature at wish, and perfection of memory at will, yet if he have not a special love to learning, he shall never attain to much learning. And therefore Isocrates, one of the noblest schoolmasters that is in memory of learning, who taught kings and princes, as Halicarnassaeus writeth, and out of whose school, as Tully saith, came forth more noble captains, more wise counsellors, than did out of Epeius' horse at Troy. This Isocrates, I say, did cause to be written, at the entry of his school, in golden letters, this golden sentence, *ean es philomathes, ese polymathes*, which excellently said in Greek, is thus rudely in English, if thou lovest learning, thou shalt attain to much learning.

4. PHILOPONOS.

Is he that hath a lust to labour, and a will to take pains. For, if a child have all the benefits of nature, with perfection of memory, love, like, and praise learning ever so much, yet if he be not of himself painful, he shall never attain unto it. And yet where love is present, labour is seldom absent, and namely in study of learning, and matters of the mind; and therefore did Isocrates rightly judge, that if his scholar were *philomathes*, he cared for no more. Aristotle, varying from Isocrates in private affairs of life, but agreeing with Isocrates in common judgment of learning, for love and labour in learning is of the same opinion, uttered in these words, in his rhetoric *ad Theodecten*. Liberty kindleth love; love refuseth no labour; and labour obtaineth whatsoever it seeketh. And yet nevertheless, goodness of nature may do little good; perfection of memory may serve to small use; all love may be employed in vain; any labour may be soon gravelled, if a man trust always to his own singular wit, and will not be glad sometime to hear, take advice, and learn of another; and therefore doth Socrates very notably add the fifth note.

5. Philekoos.

He that is glad to hear and learn of another. For otherwise, he shall stick with great trouble, where he might go easily forward; and also catch hardly a very little by his own toil, when he might gather quickly a good deal by another man's teaching. But now there be some that have great love to learning, good lust to labour, be willing to learn of others, yet, either of a fond shamefastness, or else of a proud folly, they dare not, or will not, go to learn of another; and therefore doth Socrates wisely add the sixth note of a good wit in a child for learning, and that is:

6. Zetetikos.

He that is naturally bold to ask any question, desirous to search out any doubt, not ashamed to learn of the meanest, not afraid to go to the greatest, until he be perfectly taught, and fully satisfied. The seventh and last point is:

7. Philepainos.

He that loveth to be praised for well doing, at his father or master's hand. A child of this nature will earnestly love learning, gladly labour for learning, willingly learn of another, boldly ask any doubt. And thus, by Socrates' judgment, a good father, and a wise schoolmaster, should choose a child to make a scholar of that hath by nature the foresaid perfect qualities, and comely furniture, both of mind and body; hath memory, quick to receive, sure to keep, and ready to deliver; hath love to learning; hath lust to labour; hath desire to learn of others; hath boldness to ask any question; hath mind holy bent, to win praise by well doing.

   The two first points be special benefits of nature: which nevertheless be well preserved, and much increased by good order. But as for the five last, love, labour, gladness to learn of others, boldness to ask doubts, and will to win praise, be won and maintained by the only wisdom and discretion of the schoolmaster. Which five points, whether a schoolmaster shall work sooner in a child, by fearful beating, or courteous handling, you that be wise, judge.

   Yet some men, wise in deed, but in this matter, more by severity of nature than any wisdom at all, do laugh at us when we thus wish and reason, that young children should rather be allured to learning by gentleness and love than compelled to learning by beating and fear. They say our reasons serve only to breed forth talk and pass away time, but we never saw a good schoolmaster do so, nor never read of a wise man that thought so.

   Yes, forsooth, as wise as they be, either in other men's opinion or in their own conceit, I will bring the contrary judgment of him who, they themselves shall confess, was as wise as they are, or else they may be justly thought to have small wit at all; and that is Socrates, whose judgment in Plato is plainly this in these words; which, because they be very notable, I will recite them in his own tongue: *ouden mathema meta douleias chre manthanein: oi men gar tou somatos ponoi bia ponoumenoi cheiron ouden to soma apergazontai; psyche de, biaion ouden emmonon mathema*; in English thus, no learning ought to be learned with bondage; for bodily labours, wrought by compulsion, hurt not the body, but any learning learned by compulsion tarrieth not long in the mind. And why? For whatsoever the mind doth learn unwillingly with fear, the same it doth quickly forget without care. And lest proud wits, that love not to be contraried, but have lust to wrangle or trifle away truth, will say that Socrates meaneth not this of children's teaching but of some other higher learning. Hear what Socrates in the same place doth more plainly say: *me toinyn bia, o ariste, tous paidas en tois mathemasin, alla paizontas trephe*; that is to say, and therefore, my dear friend, bring not up your children in learning by compulsion and fear, but by playing and pleasure. And you, that do read Plato, as you should, do well perceive that these be no questions asked by Socrates as doubts, but they be sentences first affirmed by Socrates as mere truths, and after given forth by Socrates as right rules most necessary to be marked, and fit to be followed of all them that would have children taught as they should. And in this council, judgment, and authority of Socrates I will repose myself until I meet with a man of the contrary mind whom I may justly take to be wiser than I think Socrates was. Fond schoolmasters neither can understand nor will follow this good counsel of Socrates, but wise riders, in their office, can and will do both; which is the only cause that commonly the young gentlemen of England, go so unwillingly to school, and run so fast to the stable. For in very deed fond schoolmasters, by fear, do beat into them the hatred of learning, and wise riders, by gentle allurements, do breed up in them the love of riding. They find fear and bondage in schools, they feel liberty and freedom in stables; which causeth them utterly to abhor the one and most gladly to haunt the other. And I do not write this that in exhorting to the one I would dissuade young gentlemen from the other: yea, I am sorry, with all my heart, that they be given no more to riding than they be; for of all outward qualities, to ride fair is most comely for himself, most necessary for his country, and the greater he is in blood, the greater is his praise, the more he doth exceed all other therein. It was one of the three excellent praises amongst the noble gentlemen of the old Persians always to say truth, to ride fair, and shoot well; and so it was engraven upon Darius's tomb, as Strabo beareth witness:

> Darius the king, lieth buried here,
>   Who in riding and shooting had never peer.

But, to our purpose, young men, by any means losing the love of learning, when by time they come to their own rule, they carry commonly from the school with them a perpetual hatred of their master, and a continual contempt of learning. If ten gentlemen be asked, why they forget so soon in court that which they were learning so long in school, eight of them, or let me be blamed, will lay the fault on their ill handling by their schoolmasters.

Cuspinian doth report that that noble Emperor Maximilian would lament very oft his misfortune herein.

Yet, some will say that children of nature love pastime and mislike learning, because, in their kind, the one is easy and pleasant, the other hard and wearisome, which is an opinion not so true as some men ween; for the matter lieth not so much in the disposition of them that be young, as in the order and manner of bringing up by them that be old, nor yet in the difference of learning and pastime. For, beat a child if he dance not well, and cherish him though he learn not well, ye shall have him unwilling to go to dance, and glad to go to his book. Knock him always when he draweth his shaft ill, and favour him again though he fault at his book, ye shall have him very loth to be in the field and very willing to be in the school. Yea, I say more, and not of myself, but by the judgment of those from whom few wise men will gladly dissent, that if ever the nature of man be given at any time more than other to receive goodness, it is in innocence of young years, before that experience of evil have taken root in him. For the pure clean wit of a sweet young babe is like the newest wax, most able to receive the best and fairest printing, and like a new bright silver dish never occupied to receive and keep clean any good thing that is put into it.

And thus, will in children, wisely wrought withal, may easily be won to be very well willing to learn. And wit in children, by nature, namely memory, the only key and keeper of all learning, is readiest to receive and surest to keep any manner of thing that is learned in youth. This, lewd and learned, by common experience, know to be most true. For we remember nothing so well when we be old as those things which we learned when we were young; and this is not strange, but common in all nature's works. Every man sees, as I said before, new wax is best for printing, new clay fittest for working, new shorn wool aptest for soon and surest dyeing, new fresh flesh for good and durable salting. And this similitude is not rude, nor borrowed of the larder house, but out of his schoolhouse, of whom the wisest of England need not be ashamed to learn. Young grafts grow not only soonest but also fairest, and bring always forth the best and sweetest fruit; young whelps learn easily to carry; young popinjays learn quickly to speak. And so, to be short, if in all other things, though they lack reason, sense, and life, the similitude of youth is fittest to all goodness, surely nature, in mankind, is most beneficial and effectual in this behalf.

Therefore, if to the goodness of nature be joined the wisdom of the teacher in leading young wits into a right and plain way of learning, surely children, kept up in God's fear, and governed by His grace, may most easily be brought well to serve God and country both by virtue and wisdom.

But if will and wit, by farther age, be once allured from innocency, delighted in vain sights, filled with foul talk, crooked with wilfulness, hardened with stubbornness, and let loose to disobedience, surely it is hard with gentleness, but impossible with severe cruelty, to call them back to good frame again. For, where the one perchance may bend it, the other shall surely break it; and so, instead of some hope, leave an assured desperation and shameless contempt of all goodness, the farthest point in all mischief, as Xenophon doth most truly and most wittily mark.

Therefore, to love or to hate, to like or contemn, to ply this way or that way to good or to bad, ye shall have as ye use a child in his youth.

And one example, whether love or fear doth work more in a child for virtue and learning, I will gladly report: which may be heard with some pleasure, and followed with more profit. Before I went into Germany I came to Broadgate, in Leicestershire, to take my leave of that noble Lady Jane Grey, to whom I was exceeding much beholding. Her parents, the duke and the duchess, with all the household, gentlemen, and gentlewomen, were hunting in the park. I found her, in her chamber reading "Phaedon Platonis" in Greek, and that with as much delight as some gentlemen would read a merry tale in Bocase [Boccaccio]. After salutation and duty done, with some other talk, I asked her why she would lose such pastime in the park? Smiling, she answered me, "I wist all their sport in the park is but a shadow to that pleasure that I find in Plato. Alas! good folk, they never felt what true pleasure meant." "And how came you, madam," quoth I, "to this deep knowledge of pleasure, and what did chiefly allure you unto it, seeing, not many women, but very few men, have attained thereunto?" "I will tell you," quoth she; "and tell you a truth which, perchance, ye will marvel at. One of the greatest benefits that ever God gave me is that He sent me so sharp and severe parents and so gentle a schoolmaster. For when I am in presence either of father or mother, whether I speak, keep silence, sit, stand, or go, eat, drink, be merry or sad, be sewing, playing, dancing, or doing anything else; I must do it, as it were, in such weight, measure, and number, even so perfectly as God made the world, or else I am so sharply taunted, so cruelly threatened, yea, presently sometimes with pinches, nips, and bobs, and other ways which I will not name for the honour I bear them, so without measure misordered, that I think myself in hell till time come that I must go to M. Elmer, who teacheth me so gently, so pleasantly, with such fair allurements to learning, that I think all the time nothing whilst I am with him. And when I am called from him I fall on weeping, because whatsoever I do else but learning is full of grief, trouble, fear, and whole misliking unto me. And thus my book hath been so much my pleasure, and bringeth daily to me more pleasure and more, that in respect of it, all other pleasures, in very deed, be but trifles and troubles unto me." I remember this talk gladly, both because it is so worthy of memory, and because also it was the last talk that ever I had and the last time that ever I saw that noble and worthy lady.

I could be over long, both in showing just causes and in reciting true examples why learning should be taught; rather by love than fear. He that would see a perfect discourse of it, let him read that learned treatise which my friend Joan. Sturmius wrote, *"De Institutione Principis,"* to the Duke of Cleves.

The godly counsels of Solomon and Jesus, the son of Sirach, for sharp keeping in and bridling of youth, are meant rather for fatherly correction than masterly beating, rather for manners than for learning, for other places than for schools. For God forbid, but all evil touches wantonness, lying, picking, sloth, will, stubbornness, and disobedience should be with sharp chastisement daily cut away.

This discipline was well known and diligently used among the Grecians and old Romans, as doth appear in Aristophanes, Isocrates, and Plato, and also in the comedies of Plautus, where we see that children were under the rule of three persons—preceptor, pedagogue, parent. The schoolmaster taught him learning with all gentleness, the governor corrected his manners with much sharpness, the father held the stern of his whole obedience; and so he that used to teach did not commonly use to beat, but remitted that over to another man's charge. But what shall we say when now in our days the schoolmaster is used both for preceptor in learning and pedagogue in manners? Surely I would he should not confound their offices, but discreetly use the duty of both, so that neither ill touches should be left unpunished nor gentleness in teaching anywise omitted. And he shall well do both if wisely he do appoint diversity of time and separate place for either purpose; using always such discreet moderation as the school-house should be counted a sanctuary against fear, and very well learning a common pardon for ill doing if the fault of itself be not over heinous.

And thus the children, kept up in God's fear and preserved by His grace, finding pain in ill doing, and pleasure in well studying, should easily be brought to honesty of life and perfectness of learning, the only mark that good and wise fathers do wish and labour that their children should most busily and carefully shoot at.

Society of Jesus's Ratio Studiorum

1599

*Let our Scholastics strive especially to preserve purity of mind and
right intention in their studies: seeking nothing further in these
than Divine glory and the profit of souls.*

RATIO STUDIORUM

Not the product of any one author, the *Ratio Studiorum* of 1599 is the foundation of
the Jesuit system of education. The Jesuit order, also known as the Company or
Society of Jesus, was founded by Ignatius of Loyola (1491–1556), author of the influential
Spiritual Exercises and primary author of the society's *Constitutions*. The order was formally approved by the pope in 1540 and quickly became an agent of the Counter-Reformation's efforts to combat the advance of Protestantism. Its primary role was educational,
however, and its mission extended internationally in the era of European discovery and
colonization. The Jesuits were suppressed in 1773 but refounded in 1814, after which a
revised edition of the *Ratio* was issued.

The *Ratio* reflects the humanist education of its time. Cicero seems to dominate the
curriculum, and his speech *Pro Archia Poeta* is included in the humanities curriculum.
Primarily, the *Ratio* provides not a required curriculum but a detailed system of instruction, covering administration, the school calendar, classes, the library, and examinations.
The guiding inspiration of the Jesuit system is its vision of education as an extension of
the command that we glorify God and love our neighbor. The Jesuits founded many colleges, beginning with Messina in 1548 and then elsewhere in Italy, Spain, Portugal, France,
Catholic Germany, and beyond. The number of institutions and students grew rapidly.

THE SELECTIONS

The *Ratio* is not a long work; a clear sense of its structure and spirit can be gained from a few short selections. The rules for teachers of rhetoric and the humanities explain two parts of the curriculum and daily routine. The last excerpt describes the qualities of good students (or "scholastics").

from Ratio Studiorum

RULES FOR PROFESSORS OF RHETORIC

1. *Grade.*—The grade of this class cannot be easily assigned to certain definite ends: for it instructs to perfect eloquence, which embraces the two highest faculties, oratory and poetry (of these two, however, the preference is always given to oratory); nor does it serve only for usefulness, but also nourishes culture.

Nevertheless it can be said in general that it is confined to three great fields, the precepts of oratory, style, and erudition.

As to the precepts, Quintilian and Aristotle may be added to Cicero. Although precepts may be looked for and noted in other sources, still in the daily prelections nothing is to be explained except the rhetorical books of Cicero and the rhetoric of Aristotle, and, if he likes, the poetics of Aristotle. Style is to be learned only from Cicero (although the most approved historians and poets may be tasted); all of his books are well adapted for the study of style; but let only the orations be given as prelections, so that the principles of the art may be seen as practiced in the speeches.

Let erudition be derived from history and the customs of tribes, from Scriptural authority, and from all doctrine, but in small quantity as benefits the capacity of the students. In Greek the following belong to rhetoric especially the quantity of syllables and the fuller knowledge of authors and of dialects.

2. *Division of Time.*—This will be the division of time in the first hour: In the morning the memory will be exercised, the Preceptor will correct the written work which was corrected by the Decurions, meantime giving to the pupils various exercises which will be mentioned below in Rule 5; and finally the last prelection will be gone over.

The second hour of the morning will be devoted to the prelection either of the precepts if the oration is explained after dinner, or of the oration if the precepts are explained after dinner, provided there is consistency in the order which is begun at the opening of the year; the repetition follows this, and when it is necessary a subject is given for writing an oration or a poem; if there is any time left over, let it be given either to concertatio, or to going over what they have written during the first hour.

In the first hour of the afternoon after the repetition of the last prelection, let there be had a new prelection either of an oration if in the morning the precepts have been explained, or of the precepts if the oration has been explained in the morning. This is followed by repetition as usual.

During the second hour of the afternoon after repeating the last lesson of the Greek author, let a new lesson be begun and recited. The remaining time shall be reserved sometimes for correcting the Greek written work, sometimes for Greek syntax and versification, and sometimes for Greek concertatio.

On a weekly holiday let a historian, or something pertaining to erudition, be explained and reviewed.

On Saturday, after a short review of the whole week, let a historian or a poet be explained during the first hour of the morning. During the last hour, there should be held a declamation or prelection by one of the students, or they should go to hear some lecture, or there should be a concertatio. After lunch let a poet be explained and Greek be reviewed. But if at any place besides the two hours in the morning and two in the afternoon, a half-hour is added, that will be devoted to a historical writer or to a poet; and if this occurs, the prelections on Saturday will either not differ from the other days, or omitting them altogether, a fuller repetition will be held and a concertatio.

3. Memory Exercise.—Since daily exercise of the memory is necessary for a rhetorician, and in this class the prelections are often longer than can well be committed to memory, let the Preceptor himself decide how much is to be learned and how much is to be memorized, in case he should call for it. Let it be according to custom that from time to time someone should recite from the platform what he has learned from the best authors, in order to exercise the memory and connect the gestures with the words.

4. Method of Correcting Written Work.—In correcting papers, let him show whether the error is in oratorical or poetic skill, in elegance, in polished writing, in connected prose, in the arrangement of numbers, in spelling, or some other fault; if any part is done falsely, obscurely, or inelegantly; if taste has been ill preserved; if any digression is too long, or other errors of this nature. Finally when the paper is completed let each hand to the Prefect, either entirely copied or at least corrected, his own paper which before he had presented in parts, so that it may be evident that they have been corrected by all.

5. Exercises in Class.—Exercises for the scholars while the master is correcting the written work will be, for example, to imitate some passage of a poet or an orator; to write a description, for instance, of gardens or temples or a storm, or some such thing; to practice changing expressions in various ways; to translate a Greek oration into Latin, or vice versa; to express in prose style the verses of some poet, either Latin or Greek; to change one kind of poem into another; to write epigrams, inscriptions, and epitaphs; to collect Greek or Latin phrases from good orators and poets; to accommodate the figures of rhetoric to certain subjects; to find arguments on a certain subject from the loci, and topics of rhetoric and other things of the same kind.

6 Prelection.—The prelection is of a double nature; in the one, which pertains to art, precepts are explained; in the other, which pertains to style, orations are explained. In each, however, two things must be considered: first, what authors are to be used for the prelection; then what method of interpretation shall be maintained.

Authors: Concerning this first part, enough was said in Rule I: For only Cicero may be employed for orations, while Quintilian and Aristotle as well as Cicero may be employed for fundamental precepts. Oratory should never be neglected, and even the precepts should be explained during almost the entire year (for great indeed is the force of the oratorical precepts); but instead of this, where it is the custom, the study of some other author who has more erudition or variety is not forbidden at the end of the year. But some prelection on a poet can sometimes be brought in the explanation of the precepts or the prelection of an oration.

7. Explanation of the Precepts.—As regards the manner of interpreting, the precepts are to be explained as follows: In the first place, the meaning of the precept is to be made clear, comparing the opinions of the interpreters if the precept is an obscure one, and the interpreters do not agree. Second, other orators must be cited, if they teach the same, or the same author, if he teaches the same elsewhere. Third, some reason for the precept itself must be presented. Fourth, there should be brought forth some similar examples of orators and poets, most illustrative of it, in which the same precept is used. Fifth, if anything of erudition from various sources or from history is pertinent, let it be added. At least, it must be shown how the precept can be applied to our own needs; and in addition how very much it can be applied in choice and elegant words.

8. Interpretation of an Orator.—If an oration or poem is being explained, first its meaning must be explained, if it is obscure, and the various interpretations considered. Second, the whole method of the workmanship, whether invention, disposition, or delivery is to be considered, also how aptly the author ingratiates himself, how appropriately he speaks, or from what topics he takes his material for persuading, for ornament, or for moving his audience; how many precepts he unites in one and the same place, by what method he includes with the figures of thought the means of instilling belief, and again the figures of thought which he weaves into the figures of words. Third, some passages similar in subject matter and expression are to be adduced and other orators or poets who have used the same precept for the sake of proving or narrating something similar are to be cited. Fourth, let the facts be confirmed by the statements of authorities, if opportunity offers. Fifth, let statements from history, from mythology, and from all erudition be sought which illustrate the passage. At last, let the words be considered carefully, and their fitness, their elegance, their number, and their rhythm noted. However, let these things be considered, not that the master may always discuss everything, but that from them he may select those which are more fitting.

9. A Topic for the Writing of an Oration.—A topic must be dictated for an oration, either in entirety at the beginning of the month, or by parts each week (for an oration is to be finished completely every month). But let it be a short speech which contains all parts of the oration; let him point out places for strengthening and amplification, special figures which may be introduced, and some places where good authors may be imitated. Occasionally, when the author in imitation of whom they are writing the oration has been designated, let only the subject be given verbally.

10. A Topic for Poetry.—A topic for a poem may be given either in writing or orally, by assigning only a title, or else certain added thoughts; it may be short, such as an epigram, an ode, an elegy, or an epistle, which can be finished on one occasion, or longer, so that they may construct a whole poem, like an oration, on many occasions.

11. The Greek Theme.—The same practice is to be followed in regard to the Greek theme unless it is thought that for a certain time everything should be dictated word for word, at least once every week either in prose or in verse.

12. Concertatio.—Let there be established a concertatio, or exercise, first in correcting those points which one of the rivals finds in the oration of the other; then in those things with which they were occupied during the first hour, each making the other a proposition in turn; then in distinguishing and forming figures; then in reciting and applying the precepts of rhetoric, or letters, or poetry, or history; then in setting forth the more difficult parts in authors and in explaining the difficulties; then in investigating the customs of the ancients and matters of erudition. Also in hieroglyphics, Pythagorean symbols, apothegms, adages, emblems and enigmas, or both a poem and an oration suitable to the students of humanities should be recited from the pulpit every other Saturday by one or another student in the last half-hour of the afternoon.

13. Greek Prelection.—The prelection of Greek, whether of orators, historians, or poets, should be only from the ancient and classical writers, Demosthenes, Plato, Thucydides, Homer, Hesiod, Pindar, and others of this nature (provided they are expurgated), among whom should be preserved, by every right, SS. Nazianzen, Basil, and Chrysostom.

14. Greek Grammar.—At the beginning of the year Greek syntax and prosody, if necessary, are to be explained on alternate days. Syntax shall be reviewed briefly and only its principal points shall be considered.

15. Prelection on the Weekly Holiday.—For the sake of erudition other and more learned subjects are taken on recreation days in place of the historian, for example, hieroglyphics, heraldry, questions of poetical technique, epigrams, epitaphs, odes, elegies, epics, tragedies, the Roman Senate, the Greek Senate, the warfare of Greeks and Romans, gardening, clothing, meals, triumphs, the Sibyls, and other kindred subjects, but in moderation.

16. Private Declamation.—Declamation or prelection of a poem or a Greek oration or both a speech and a poem should be given from the platform by one or other of the pupils before the class of humanities on alternate Saturdays the last half-hour in the morning.

17. Public Declamation.—In the hall or chapel let there be given every month a rather serious oration or poem, or both, now in Latin, now in Greek, now in the vernacular, or a debate, with arguments on both sides, and a decision; but not, however, unless it is known and approved by the Prefect of Higher Studies.

18. Affixing Poems.—Let choice poems written by the pupils be affixed to the walls of the classroom nearly every other month, to celebrate any rather famous day, or the announcement of a magistracy, or some other occasion. Moreover, according to the custom of the region, there may be short prose selections, such as inscriptions for coats of arms, churches, sepulchres, gardens, or statues; or descriptions, as of a city, a harbor, or an army; or narratives, as of some deed of one of the Saints, and there may be added, but not without the consent of the Rector, drawings which represent some motto or some proposed subject.

19. Private Drama.—Occasionally the master is allowed to propose to the scholars, for a subject, some short action as of an eclogue, drama, or dialogue; so that those which have been written the best of all may be presented within the class, parts being assigned to the student, but without any elaborate staging.

20. Exercises of our Own People.—Ours shall perform in common all the exercises which we have mentioned in the method of teaching: but these shall be particular to them that at home, three or four times a week, for an hour which seems the most convenient to the Rector, they shall have repetitions in the presence of the master or someone else whom the Rector himself shall appoint; in these they shall review the prelections of Latin and Greek, and papers shall be corrected; let them be ordered to cultivate the memory by daily learning, and to read much attentively. For nothing fertilizes the mind so much as does the frequent testing of each other in speaking from a platform in the courtyard, in the church, in the school, and even in the refectory in connection with fellow students. To the same end let their poems, approved by the Preceptor, with their names subscribed, be posted publicly, but always in a suitable place.

RULES FOR THE PROFESSOR OF HUMANITIES

I. Grade.—In the first rule, for such knowledge of language as consists especially in propriety and copiousness, let there be explained in the daily prelections Cicero alone of the orators in those books of his which contain his philosophy or morals; of the historians, Caesar, Sallust, Livy, Curtius, and others of the same kind; of the poets, especially Virgil, excepting some of the eclogues and the fourth book of the Aeneid.

Let a brief summary of the precepts of rhetoric from Cyprian be given in the second semester; during which time omitting the philosophic writings of Cicero. Some of his easier orations as the *Pro lege Manilea, Pro archia, Pro Marcello,* and others addressed to Caesar can be taken. Of the Greek language, that part belongs to this class which is properly called syntax, taking care in the meantime that they understand the Greek writers fairly well, and know how to write Greek somewhat.

2. *Division of Time.*—The division of time will be this: The first hour in the morning Cicero and the art of versification will be recited by heart to the Decurions; the Preceptor will correct the written work which he receives from the Decurions, assigning in the meanwhile to the students various exercises mentioned below in Rule 4; at the end of the hour some will recite aloud, and the master will examine the marks given by the Decurions. In the second hour of the morning the last prelection will be repeated briefly, and a new one will be explained for a half an hour, or a little more, and will immediately be recited, and if there is any time left, it will be taken up in concertatio among the students. In the final half-hour at the beginning of the first semester, a historian and the art of versification will be taken on alternate days; but when the art of versification is finished, the historian will be taken briefly; then in the second semester every day the rhetoric of Cyprian will be either explained or repeated or disputation will be held on it.

In the first afternoon hour a poet and a Greek author will be recited from memory, the master looking over the marks given by the Decurions, and correcting the written work which had been assigned in the morning or which remained over from the written work done at home. At the end of the hour a theme will be dictated. The following hour and a half will be divided equally between reviewing and explaining some poet and in a Greek prelection and writing.

On a holiday let the matter of the prelection on the last holiday be recited from memory; and let the papers which remain be corrected, according to custom. Let the second hour be used for some epigram, ode, or elegy, or something about metaphors, figures, and especially metrics, according to the custom from the beginning of the year; or let some theme or essay be explained and reviewed, or let there be a concertatio.

On Saturday let the prelections of the entire week be recited from memory during the first hour; let them be reviewed the second hour. During the last half-hour let either a declamation or prelection by one of the pupils be held, or let them go to hear a lecture, or let there be a concertatio.

During the first half-hour after lunch let a poet and the catechism be recited from memory while the master examines papers, if any remain from that week, and looks over the marks of the Decurions.

Let the following hour and a half be divided equally between the review of a poet, or the explanation and consideration of some short poem, and a study of Greek in the same way.

Let the last half-hour be occupied in an explanation of the catechism or in a pious exhortation unless this was held on Friday: but if it was, let the time be occupied by that subject in whose place the catechism had been substituted.

3. *Method of Correcting a Paper.*—In correcting a paper, let him show if it is too little pertinent, or elegant, or metrical; if the passage assigned for imitation is too little followed; if there is a fault in spelling or something else, let him order these to be expressed in various ways, so that the pupils may obtain a variety of expressions from this exercise.

4. *Exercises while Written Work Is Being Corrected.*—The exercises while the master is correcting the written work, will be, for example, to collect phrases from the prelections and to vary them in different ways, to put together some sentences of Cicero which have been broken up, to make phrases, to change a poem of one kind into another, to imitate some passage, to write in Greek, and other things of this kind.

5. *Prelection.*—Let the prelection be lightly sprinkled with ornaments of erudition at times, and as far as the explanation of the passage requires; the master should himself rather completely occupy himself in observations on the Latin language in the force and etiology of words which he chooses from approved authors, especially from the ancients in the use and variety of forms of expression in imitation of some author, and let him not think it foreign to his purpose to bring in at times something in the vernacular if it is especially helpful for the interpretation, or if it contains something especially excellent. When he has explained an oration, let him investigate the precepts of the art. At last it will be permitted, if it seems good, to turn everything into the vernacular, but as elegantly as possible.

6. *Subject for Written Work.*—The subject-matter for written work is to be dictated. In the first semester, generally in the form of a letter, word for word, in the vernacular language, and it often is profitable to compose it in such a way that the whole of it is taken here and there from the prelections already explained; but generally once a week let them write without any help, having first explained some form of epistle, and having pointed out some epistles of Cicero or Pliny belonging to that class. Then in the second semester let their talent be called forth, and first let chrias be written, then introductions, narrations, and elegant compositions, the subjects of which have been given at some length. Let him dictate the subject of the poem with a large variety of expressions. The method of the Greek theme will be the same as that of the Latin prose, except that generally it is to be taken from the author himself, and the rules of syntax are to be explained beforehand.

7. *Concertatio.*—The concertatio or exercise will be concerned with both those things which one rival has found fault with in another's written work, and in proposing those things in which they have exercised themselves during the first hour, and in reciting by heart phrases given by the Preceptor, or in varying these phrases, and in reciting and applying the precepts of letter writing and rhetoric, and in asking about the quantity of syllables, citing from memory the rule or the line from the poet, or in investigating the

propriety or etiology of some word, and in interpreting some passage of a Greek or Latin author, and in inflecting and forming the more difficult and irregular Greek verbs, and in other things of like kind, according to the judgment of the Preceptor.

8. *Metric and Rhetorical Art.*—Let the metric art be quickly reviewed, only dwelling on those parts which seem to need it more, and applying rather than explaining it. Let the precepts of rhetoric be briefly illustrated, and with added examples from the book of precepts and, if the matter permits, from the daily prelections.

9. *Greek Prelection.*—In the Greek prelection on alternate days grammar and author will be explained, and as regards the grammar, after briefly going through what has been given in the first class, syntax and the rules of accent will be given. But the author in the first semester for prose will be taken from some of the easier ones as some orations of Isocrates and Sts. Chrysostom and Basil, or from the epistles of Plato and Synesius, or something selected from Plutarch; in the second semester some poem will be explained, for example, something from Phocyllis, Theognis, St. Gregory Nazianzen, Synesius, and other like writers.

The explanation, however, as suits the grade of this school, will concern rather the knowledge of the language than erudition.

But towards the end of the year the rules of Greek syllabification can be given along with an author on alternate days, and sometimes also phrases which have been disarranged can be put together.

10. *Affixing Poems.*—Let choice poems written by the pupils be affixed to the walls of the schoolroom, nearly every other month, to celebrate any rather famous day or the announcing of a magistracy, or some other occasion; moreover, according to the custom of the region, there may be short prose selections, such as inscriptions for coats of arms, churches, sepulchres, gardens, or statues; or descriptions, as of a city, a harbor, or an army; or narrative, as of some deed of one of the Saints, and there may be added, but not without the consent of the Rector, drawings which represent some motto or some proposed subject.

RULES FOR THE SCHOLASTICS OF OUR SOCIETY

1. *Purity of Mind and Intention.*—Let our Scholastics strive especially to preserve purity of mind and right intention in their studies: seeking nothing further in these than Divine glory and the profit of souls; in their prayers let them frequently ask for grace that they may progress in doctrine and that they may at length become suitable, as the Society expects of them, to cultivate the vineyard of Christ our Lord by their example and their learning.

2. *Joining Solid Virtues with Their Studies.*—Let them resolve to apply their minds seriously and constantly to their studies; and as they realize that they must take care lest in their love of studies, their love of solid virtues and a religious life grow lukewarm in fervor; so let them each persuade himself that he can do nothing in college more pleasing to God than to apply himself diligently to his studies with that intention of which we have spoken; and although they never arrive at the practice, of what they shall have learned, let them decide for themselves that the labor of studies which they have undertaken out of obedience and charity, as is suitable, is a work of great value in the sight of the Divine and Highest Majesty.

3. Studying According to the Direction of the Superior.—Let them apply themselves to those subjects and hear those Preceptors whom the Superior shall assign; let all diligently observe the division of time and the method of study prescribed by the Prefect or the master, and let them not use any other books than those given them by the Prefect.

4. Diligence.—Let them be constant in attending lectures and diligent in studying them beforehand and reviewing them after they have been heard; in asking those things which they do not understand; in taking notes on those things which are important, to which they can refer later on when their memory fails them.

5. Public Disputations.—Let them be present at the ordinary disputations of the classes which they attend; and let them take care to offer, but modestly, a good example of their learning.

6. Private Disputations.—Let all be present, besides, at daily private disputations and reviews; and let those who partake obey strictly him who presides.

7. Moderation.—When they shall go to public schools, let the associates go and return with that inward moderation which is fitting to their own edification and that of others.

8. Speech with Outsiders.—Let the speech of those who have the right of speaking with outside Scholastics be only about matters pertaining to literature or to the advantage of the spirit, according as it seems to all to be advantageous to the greater glory of God.

9. Use of the Latin Language.—Let all of these, but especially the students of the liberal arts, converse among themselves in Latin; and let them commit to memory whatever is prescribed by their masters; and let them diligently practice style in composition.

10. Time of Study.—Let no one apply himself to the toil of reading or writing for more than two hours, but let his study be interrupted by a short interval of time.

11. Method of Private Study.—In the hours assigned for private study, let those who are working in the higher faculties review at home the things which they have heard or written in class, and learn them thoroughly; let them examine their knowledge by proposing objections to themselves and answering them; if they cannot answer some, let them take note of them for inquiry or disputation.

John Milton

1608–74

The end then of learning is to repair the ruins of our first parents by regaining to know God aright, and out of that knowledge to love him, to imitate him, to be like him, as we may the nearest by possessing our souls of true virtue, which being united to the heavenly grace of faith, makes up the highest perfection.

OF EDUCATION

John Milton, one of the greatest poets in English literature, was born in London in Bread Street, a short walk from St. Paul's Cathedral. (His childhood home and the old St. Paul's were consumed in the Great Fire of 1666.) His father hired a private tutor for young Milton before he was sent to neighboring St. Paul's School, which had been refounded the previous century by the humanist scholar John Colet. Milton entered Christ's College, Cambridge, in 1625, earning his B.A. and M.A. He became proficient in several languages and wrote poetry in Latin, Italian, and English. For several years after leaving Cambridge, he read voraciously in Greek and Latin authors. He then toured Europe for more than a year, visiting France, Italy, and Geneva. In Florence he met the aging Galileo, who was then under house arrest. Upon returning to England, Milton ran a small school in London for his two nephews and a handful of other boys. He married three times and fathered three children. During the English Civil War he allied himself with the Puritans and wrote political and religious tracts favoring republicanism and the anti-episcopacy cause. He served the Commonwealth government as Latin secretary to Olive Cromwell. His greatest work, the epic poem *Paradise Lost,* first appeared in 1667 and in its final form in 1674, the year of Milton's death.

467

THE SELECTION

Milton's *Of Education* was published in 1644, the same year as *Areopagitica,* his famous defense of freedom of the press. It proposes a daunting program of study for future leaders of the church and state, so rigorous in fact as to be beyond the reach of any one student and even the most liberally educated teachers. Milton offers his curriculum as an ideal. As he indicates in the opening section, he wrote *Of Education* at the request of Samuel Hartlib. Hartlib was a German educational reformer and promoter of modern science who emigrated to London and spent a short time at Cambridge. He championed the writings of several modern educational theorists, including Jacob Comenius, an enthusiastic Baconian. Milton's affiliation with Hartlib's progressive educational movement makes his place in the Great Tradition ambiguous. Milton has often been identified in hindsight as an innovator and harbinger of the utilitarian educational philosophies to come. Some claim to hear in his desire to "repair the ruin of our first parents" an echo of the Baconian intention to "reverse the Fall." The treatise itself, however, seems only to hint in this direction. Rather, it connects itself to the Greek and Latin tradition and directs education primarily toward knowledge of God, wisdom, and virtue.

Nevertheless, Samuel Johnson's concern that the Baconian study of nature distracts us from the weightier matters of life must be taken into consideration when evaluating Milton. In his *Life of Milton,* Johnson writes "that the knowledge of external nature, and the sciences which that knowledge requires or includes, are not the great or the frequent business of the human mind." Consequently, "Those authors . . . are to be read at schools that supply most axioms of prudence, most principles of moral truth, and most materials for conversation; and these purposes are best served by poets, orators, and historians." Johnson numbers Milton among those modern "innovators" who "are turning off attention from life to nature. They seem to think that we are placed here to watch the growth of plants, or the motions of the stars. Socrates was rather of opinion that what we had to learn was, how to do good and avoid evil."

from Of Education

Master Hartlib, I am long since persuaded, that to say or do aught worth memory and imitation, no purpose or respect should sooner move us than simply the love of God, and of mankind. Nevertheless, to write now the reforming of education, though it be one of the greatest and noblest designs that can be thought on, and for the want whereof this nation perishes; I had not yet at this time been induced, but by your earnest entreaties and serious conjurements; as having my mind for the present half diverted in the pursuance of some other assertions, the knowledge and the use of which cannot but be a great furtherance both to the enlargement of truth, and honest living with much more peace. Nor should the laws of any private friendship have prevailed with me to divide thus, or transpose my former thoughts, but that I see those aims, those actions, which have won you with me the esteem of a person sent hither by some good providence from a far country to be the occasion and incitement of great good to this island. And, as I hear, you have obtained the same repute with men of most approved wisdom, and some of the highest authority among us; not to mention the learned correspondence which you hold in foreign parts, and the extraordinary pains and diligence, which you have used in this matter both here and beyond the seas; either by the definite will of God so ruling, or the peculiar sway of nature, which also is God's working. Neither can I think that so reputed and so valued as you are, you would to the forfeit of your own discerning ability, impose upon me an unfit and overponderous argument; but that the satisfaction, which you profess to have received from those incidental discourses which we have wandered into, hath pressed and almost constrained you into a persuasion, that what you require from me in this point, I neither ought nor can in conscience defer beyond this time both of so much need at once, and so much opportunity to try what God hath determined. I will not resist therefore whatever it is, either of divine or human obligement, that you lay upon me; but will forthwith set down in writing, as you request me, that voluntary idea, which hath long in silence presented itself to me, of a better education, in extent and comprehension far more large, and yet of time far shorter, and of attainment far more certain, than hath been yet in practice. Brief I shall endeavour to be; for that which I have to say, assuredly this nation hath extreme need should be done sooner than spoken. To tell you therefore what I have benefited herein among old renowned authors, I shall spare; and to search what many modern Januas and Didactics, more than ever I shall read, have projected, my inclination leads me not. But if you can accept of these few observations which have flowered off, and are as it were the burnishing of many studious and contemplative years altogether spent in the search of religious and civil knowledge, and such as pleased you so well in the relating, I here give you them to dispose of.

The end then of learning is to repair the ruins of our first parents by regaining to know God aright, and out of that knowledge to love him, to imitate him, to be like him, as we may the nearest by possessing our souls of true virtue, which being united to the heavenly grace of faith, makes up the highest perfection. But because our understanding cannot in this body found itself but on sensible things, nor arrive so clearly to the knowledge of God and things invisible, as by orderly conning over the visible and inferior creature, the same method is necessarily to be followed in all discreet teaching. And seeing every nation affords not experience and tradition enough for all kind of learning, therefore we are chiefly taught the languages of those people who have at any time been most industrious after wisdom; so that language is but the instrument conveying to us things useful to be known. And though a linguist should pride himself to have all the tongues that Babel cleft the world into, yet if he have not studied the solid things in them as well as the words and lexicons, he were nothing so much to be esteemed a learned man, as any yeoman or tradesman competently wise in his mother dialect only. Hence appear the many mistakes which have made learning generally so unpleasing and so unsuccessful; first, we do amiss to spend seven or eight years merely in scraping together so much miserable Latin and Greek, as might be learned otherwise easily and delightfully in one year. And that which casts our proficiency therein so much behind, is our time lost partly in too oft idle vacancies given both to schools and universities; partly in a preposterous exaction, forcing the empty wits of children to compose themes, verses, and orations, which are the acts of ripest judgment, and the final work of a head filled by long reading and observing, with elegant maxims and copious invention. These are not matters to be wrung from poor striplings, like blood out of the nose, or the plucking of untimely fruit; besides the ill habit which they get of wretched barbarizing against the Latin and Greek idiom, with their untutored Anglicisms, odious to be read, yet not to be avoided without a well-continued and judicious conversing among pure authors digested, which they scarce taste: whereas, if after some preparatory grounds of speech by their certain forms got into memory, they were led to the praxis thereof in some chosen short book lessoned thoroughly to them, they might then forthwith proceed to learn the substance of good things, and arts in due order, which would bring the whole language quickly into their power. This I take to be the most rational and most profitable way of learning languages, and whereby we may best hope to give account to God of our youth spent herein. And for the usual method of teaching arts, I deem it to be an old error of universities, not yet well recovered from the scholastic grossness of barbarous ages, that instead of beginning with arts most easy, (and those be such as are most obvious to the sense,) they present their young unmatriculated novices at first coming with the most intellective abstractions of logic and metaphysics; so that they having but newly left those grammatic flats and shallows where they stuck unreasonably to learn a few words with lamentable construction, and now on the sudden transported under another climate to be tossed and turmoiled with their unballasted wits in fathomless and unquiet deeps of controversy, do for the most part grow into hatred and contempt of learning, mocked and deluded all this while with ragged notions and babblements, while they expected worthy and delightful knowledge; till poverty or youthful years call them importunately their several ways, and hasten them with the sway of friends either to an ambitious and mercenary, or ignorantly zealous divinity; some allured to the trade of law, grounding their purposes not on the prudent and heavenly contemplation of justice and equity, which was never taught them, but on the promising and pleasing thoughts of litigious terms, fat contentions, and flowing fees; others betake them to state affairs, with souls so unprincipled in virtue and true generous breeding, that flattery and courtshifts and tyrannous aphorisms appear to them the highest points of wisdom; instilling their barren hearts with a conscientious slavery; if, as I rather think, it be not feigned. Others, lastly, of a more delicious and airy spirit, retire themselves (knowing no better) to the enjoyments of ease and luxury, living out their days in feast and jollity; which indeed is the wisest and the safest course of all these, unless they were with more integrity undertaken. And these are the errors, and these are the fruits of mispending our prime youth at the schools and universities as we do, either in learning mere words, or such things chiefly as were better unlearned.

I shall detain you now no longer in the demonstration of what we should not do, but straight conduct you to a hill-side, where I will point you out the right path of a virtuous and noble education; laborious indeed at the first ascent, but else so smooth, so green, so full of goodly prospect, and melodious sounds on every side, that the harp of Orpheus was not more charming. I doubt not but ye shall have more ado to drive our dullest and laziest youth, our stocks and stubs, from the infinite desire of such a happy nurture, than we have now to hale and drag our choicest and hopefullest wits to that asinine feast of sowthistles and brambles, which is commonly set before them as all the food and entertainment of their tenderest and most docible age. I call therefore a complete and generous education, that which fits a man to perform justly, skilfully, and magnanimously all the offices, both private and public, of peace and war. And how all this may be done between twelve and one-and-twenty, less time than is now bestowed in pure trifling at grammar and sophistry, is to be thus ordered.

First, to find out a spacious house and ground about it fit for an academy, and big enough to lodge a hundred and fifty persons, whereof twenty or thereabout may be attendants, all under the government of one, who shall be thought of desert sufficient, and ability either to do all, or wisely to direct and oversee it done. This place should be at once both school and university, not needing a remove to any other house of scholarship, except it be some peculiar college of law, or physic, where they mean to be practitioners; but as for those general studies which take up all our time from Lilly to commencing, as they term it, master of art, it should be absolute. After this pattern, as many edifices may be converted to this use as shall be needful in every city throughout this land, which would tend much to the increase of learning and civility every where. This number, less or more thus collected, to the convenience of a foot company, or interchangeably two troops of cavalry, should divide their day's work into three parts as it lies orderly; their studies, their exercise, and their diet.

For their studies; first, they should begin with the chief and necessary rules of some good grammar, either that now used, or any better; and while this is doing, their speech is to be fashioned to a distinct and clear pronunciation, as near as may be to the Italian, especially in the vowels. For we Englishmen being far northerly, do not open our mouths in the cold air wide enough to grace a southern tongue; but are observed by all other nations to speak exceeding close and inward; so that to smatter Latin with an English mouth, is as ill a hearing as law French. Next, to make them expert in the usefullest points of grammar; and withal to season them and win them early to the love of virtue and true labour, ere any flattering seducement or vain principle seize them wandering, some easy and delightful book of education would be read to them; whereof the Greeks have store, as Cebes, Plutarch, and other Socratic discourses. But in Latin we have none of classic authority extant, except the two or three first books of Quintilian, and some select pieces elsewhere. But here the main skill and groundwork will be, to temper them such lectures and explanations upon every opportunity, as may lead and draw them in willing obedience, enflamed with the study of learning, and the admiration of virtue; stirred up with high hopes of living to be brave men, and worthy patriots, dear to God, and famous to all ages. That they may despise and scorn all their childish and ill-taught qualities, to delight in manly and liberal exercises; which he who hath the art and proper eloquence to catch them with, what with mild and effectual persuasions, and what with the intimation of some fear, if need be, but chiefly by his own example, might in a short space gain them to an incredible diligence and courage; infusing into their young breasts such an ingenuous and noble ardor, as would not fail to make many of them renowned and matchless men. At the same time, some other hour of the day, might be taught them the rules of arithmetic, and soon after the elements of geometry, even playing, as the old manner was. After evening repast, till bedtime, their thoughts would be best taken up in the easy grounds of religion, and the story of Scripture. The next step would be to the authors of agriculture, Cato, Varro, and Columella, for the matter is most easy; and if the language be difficult, so much the better, it is not a difficulty above their years. And here will be an occasion of inciting, and enabling them hereafter to improve the tillage of their country, to recover the bad soil, and to remedy the waste that is made of good; for this was one of Hercules's praises. Ere half these authors be read (which will soon be with plying hard and daily) they cannot choose but be masters of any ordinary prose. So that it will be then seasonable for them to learn in any modern author the use of the globes, and all the maps; first with the old names, and then with the new; or they might be then capable to read any compendious method of natural philosophy. And at the same time might be entering into the Greek tongue, after the same manner as was before prescribed in the Latin; whereby the difficulties of grammar being soon overcome, all the historical physiology of Aristotle and Theophrastus are open before them, and, as I may say, under contribution. The like access will be to Vitruvius, to Seneca's natural questions, to Mela, Celsus, Pliny, or Solinus. And having thus passed the principles of arithmetic, geometry, astronomy, and geography, with a general compact of physics, they may descend in mathematics to the instrumental science of trigonometry, and from thence to fortification, architecture, enginery, or navigation. And in natural philosophy they may proceed leisurely from the history of meteors, minerals, plants, and living creatures, as far as anatomy. Then also in course might be read to them out of some not tedious writer the institution of physic; that they may know the tempers, the humours, the seasons, and how to manage a crudity; which he who can wisely and timely do, is not only a great physician to himself and to his friends, but also may at some time or other save an army by this frugal and expenseless means only; and not let the healthy and stout bodies of young men rot away under him for want of this discipline; which is a great pity, and no less a shame to the commander. To set forward all these proceedings in nature and mathematics, what hinders but that they may procure, as oft as shall be needful, the helpful experiences of hunters, fowlers, fishermen, shepherds, gardeners, apothecaries; and in the other sciences, architects, engineers, mariners, anatomists; who doubtless would be ready, some for reward, and some to favour such a hopeful seminary. And this will give them such a real tincture of natural knowledge, as they shall never forget, but daily augment with delight. Then also those poets which are now counted most hard, will be both facile and pleasant, Orpheus, Hesiod, Theocritus, Aratus, Nicander, Oppian, Dionysius, and in Latin, Lucretius, Manilius, and the rural part of Virgil.

By this time, years, and good general precepts, will have furnished them more distinctly with that act of reason which in ethics is called Proairesis; that they may with some judgment contemplate upon moral good and evil. Then will be required a special reinforcement of constant and sound indoctrinating to set them right and firm, instructing them more amply in the knowledge of virtue and the hatred of vice; while their young and pliant affections are led through all the moral works of Plato, Xenophon, Cicero, Plutarch, Laertius, and those Locrian remnants; but still to be reduced in their nightward studies wherewith they close the day's work, under the determinate sentence of David or Solomon, or the evangels and apostolic Scriptures. Being perfect in the knowledge of personal duty, they may then begin the study of oeconomics. And either now or before this, they may have easily learned at any odd hour the Italian tongue. And soon after, but with wariness and good antidote, it would be wholesome enough to let them taste some choice comedies, Greek, Latin or Italian; those tragedies also, that treat of household matters, as Trachiniae, Alcestis, and the like. The next removal must be to the study of politics; to know the beginning, end, and reasons of political societies; that they may not in a dangerous fit of the commonwealth be such poor, shaken, uncertain reeds, of such a tottering conscience, as many of our great counsellors have lately shown themselves, but stedfast pillars of the state. After this, they are to dive into the grounds of law, and legal justice; delivered first and with best warrant by Moses; and as far as human prudence can be trusted, in those extolled remains of Grecian law-givers, Lycurgus, Solon, Zaleucus, Charondas, and thence to all the Roman edicts and tables with their Justinian; and so down to the Saxon and common laws of England, and the statutes. Sundays also and every evening may be now understandingly spent in the highest matters of theology, and church-history ancient and modern; and ere this time the Hebrew tongue at a set hour might have been gained, that the Scriptures may be now read in their own original; whereto it would be no impossibility to add the Chaldee, and the Syrian dialect. When all these employments are well conquered, then will the choice histories, heroic poems, and attic tragedies of stateliest and most regal argument, with all the famous political orations, offer themselves; which if they were not only read, but some of them got by memory, and solemnly pronounced with right accent and grace, as might be taught, would endue them even with the spirit and vigour of Demosthenes or Cicero, Euripides or Sophocles. And now lastly will be the time to read them with those organic arts, which enable men to discourse and write perspicuously, elegantly, and according to the fitted style of lofty, mean, or lowly. Logic, therefore, so much as is useful, is to be referred to this due place with all her well-couched heads and topics, until it be time to open her contracted palm into a graceful and ornate rhetoric taught out of the rule of Plato, Aristotle, Phalereus, Cicero, Hermogenes, Longinus. To which poetry would be made subsequent, or indeed rather precedent, as being less subtile and fine, but more simple, sensuous, and passionate. I mean not here the prosody of a verse, which they could not but have hit on before among the rudiments of grammar; but that sublime art which in Aristotle's poetics, in Horace, and the Italian commentaries of Castlevetro, Tasso, Mazzoni, and others, teaches what the laws are of a true epic poem, what of a dramatic, what of a lyric, what decorum is, which is the grand masterpiece to observe. This would make them soon perceive what despicable creatures our common rhymers and play-writers be; and show them what religious, what glorious and magnificent use might be made of poetry, both in divine and human things. From hence, and not till now, will be the right season of forming them to be able writers and composers in every excellent matter, when they shall be thus fraught with an universal insight into things. Or whether they be to speak in parliament or council, honour and attention would be waiting on their lips. There would then also appear in pulpits other visages, other gestures, and stuff otherwise wrought than what we now sit under, ofttimes to as great a trial of our patience as any other that they preach to us. These are the studies wherein our noble and our gentle youth ought to bestow their time in a disciplinary way from twelve to one-and-twenty; unless they rely more upon their ancestors dead than upon themselves living. In which methodical course it is so supposed they must proceed by the steady pace of learning onward, as at convenient times, for memory's sake, to retire back into the middleward, and sometimes into the rear of what they have been taught, until they have confirmed and solidly united the whole body of their perfected knowledge, like the last embattling of a Roman legion. Now will be worth the seeing, what exercises and recreations may best agree, and become these studies.

THEIR EXERCISE

The course of study hitherto briefly described is, what I can guess by reading, likest to those ancient and famous schools of Pythagoras, Plato, Isocrates, Aristotle, and such others, out of which were bred such a number of renowned philosophers, orators, historians, poets, and princes all over Greece, Italy, and Asia, besides the flourishing studies of Cyrene and Alexandria. But herein it shall exceed them, and supply a defect as great as that which Plato noted in the commonwealth of Sparta; whereas that city trained up their youth most for war, and these in their academies and Lycaeum all for the gown, this institution of breeding which I here delineate shall be equally good both for peace and war. Therefore about an hour and a half ere they eat at noon should be allowed them for exercise, and due rest afterwards; but the time for this may be enlarged at pleasure, according as their rising in the morning shall be early. The exercise which I commend first, is the exact use of their weapon, to guard, and to strike safely with edge or point; this will keep them healthy, nimble, strong, and well in breath, is also the likeliest means to make them grow large and tall, and to inspire them with a gallant and fearless courage, which being tempered with seasonable lectures and precepts to them of true fortitude and patience, will turn into a native and heroic valour, and make them hate the cowardice of doing wrong. They must be also practised in all the locks and gripes of wrestling, wherein Englishmen were wont to excel, as need may often be in fight to tug, to grapple, and to close. And this perhaps will be enough, wherein to prove and heat their single strengh. The interim of unsweating themselves regularly, and convenient rest before meat, may both with profit and delight be taken up in recreating and composing their travailed spirits with the solemn and divine harmonies of music heard or learned; either whilst the skilful organist plies his grave and fancied descant in lofty fugues, or the whole symphony with artful and unimaginable touches adorn and grace the well-studied chords of some choice composer; sometimes the lute or soft organ stop waiting on elegant voices, either to religious, martial, or civil ditties; which, if wise men and prophets be not extremely out, have a great power over dispositions and manners, to smooth and make them gentle from rustic harshness and distempered passions. The like also would not be unexpedient after meat, to assist and cherish nature in her first concoction, and send their minds back to study in good tune and satisfaction. Where having followed it close under vigilant eyes, till about two hours before supper, they are by a sudden alarum or watchword, to be called out to their military motions, under sky or covert, according to the season, as was the Roman wont; first on foot, then as their age permits, on horseback, to all the art of cavalry; that having in sport, but with much exactness and daily muster, served out the rudiments of their soldiership, in all the skill of embattling, marching, encamping, fortifying, besieging, and battering with all the helps of ancient and modern stratagems, tactics, and warlike maxims, they may as it were out of a long war come forth renowned and perfect commanders in the service of their country. They would not then, if they were trusted with fair and hopeful armies, suffer them for want of just and wise discipline to shed away from about them like sick feathers, though they be never so oft supplied; they would not suffer their empty and unrecruitable colonels of twenty men in a company, to quaff out, or convey into secret hoards, the wages of a delusive list, and a miserable remnant; yet in the mean while to be overmastered with a score or two of drunkards, the only soldiery left about them, or else to comply with all rapines and violences. No certainly, if they knew aught of that knowledge that belongs to good men or good governors, they would not suffer these things. But to return to our own institute; besides these constant exercises at home, there is another opportunity of gaining experience to be won from pleasure itself abroad; in those vernal seasons of the year when the air is calm and pleasant, it were an injury and sullenness against nature, not to go out and see her riches, and partake in her rejoicing with heaven and earth. I should not therefore be a persuader to them of studying much then, after two or three years that they have well laid their grounds, but to ride out in companies with prudent and staid guides to all the quarters of the land; learning and observing all places of strength, all commodities of building and of soil, for towns and tillage, harbours and ports for trade. Sometimes taking sea as far as to our navy, to learn there also what they can in the practical knowledge of sailing and of sea-fight. These ways would try all their peculiar gifts of nature, and if there were any secret excellence among them would fetch it out, and give it fair opportunities to advance itself by, which could not but mightily redound to the good of this nation, and bring into fashion again those old admired virtues and excellencies with far more advantage now in this purity of Christian knowledge. Nor shall we then need the monsieurs of Paris to take our hopeful youth into their slight and prodigal custodies, and send them over back again transformed into mimics, apes, and kickshows. But if they desire to see other countries at three or four and twenty years of age, not to learn principles, but to enlarge experience, and make wise observation, they will by that time be such as shall deserve the regard and honour of all men where they pass, and the society and friendship of those in all places who are best and most eminent. And perhaps, then other nations will be glad to visit us for their breeding, or else to imitate us in their own country.

Now lastly for their diet there cannot be much to say, save only that it would be best in the same house; for much time else would be lost abroad, and many ill habits got; and that it should be plain, healthful, and moderate, I suppose is out of controversy. Thus, Mr. Hartlib, you have a general view in writing, as your desire was, of that, which at several times I had discoursed with you concerning the best and noblest way of education; not beginning as some have done from the cradle, which yet might be worth many considerations, if brevity had not been my scope; many other circumstances also I could have mentioned, but this, to such as have the worth in them to make trial, for light and direction may be enough. Only I believe that this is not a bow for every man to shoot in, that counts himself a teacher; but will require sinews almost equal to those which Homer gave Ulysses; yet I am withal persuaded that it may prove much more easy in the assay, than it now seems at distance, and much more illustrious; howbeit, not more difficult than I imagine, and that imagination presents me with nothing but very happy, and very possible according to best wishes; if God have so decreed, and this age have spirit and capacity enough to apprehend.

Giambattista Vico

1668–1744

*Let our efforts not be directed towards achieving superiority over
the Ancients merely in the field of science, while they surpass us
in wisdom; let us not be merely more exact and more true than the
Ancients, while allowing them to be more eloquent than we are;
let us equal the Ancients in the fields of wisdom and eloquence as
we excel them in the domain of science.*

ON THE STUDY METHODS OF OUR TIME

Giambattista Vico, Italian humanist, philosopher, and historian, was born in humble circumstances in Naples. His father was a bookseller, and with his father's encouragement he read widely in the classics and largely educated himself. He also attended the local grammar school and was educated sporadically by the Jesuits. Aside from the nine years he served as tutor to the sons of Domenica Rocca, he lived and worked his entire life in Naples. He earned a law degree from the University of Naples in 1694. He aspired to teach jurisprudence there, but instead he labored for more than forty years as a professor of rhetoric, specializing in Latin authors. Vico published poetry, treatises on metaphysics, history, rhetoric, philology, and law, and an autobiography. Despite his brilliance and originality, his books were virtually unknown in his own time, and he died in poverty and obscurity. His work was not appreciated until his "discovery" by the Romantic movement in the nineteenth century. His admirers included Goethe, Coleridge, Dostoevsky, and Croce. Vico's *New Science,* first published in 1725, has received the most scholarly attention, but his early works on education, especially his orations, deserve to be better known. Vico opposed Descartes' ahistorical path to certainty and tried to remind proponents of the scientific revolution that precision, objectivity, clarity, and certainty are not the same thing as Truth. He valued what John Henry Newman later (and Plato long before) called "seeing things whole." Vico tried to hold on to imagination and memory in a world increasingly preoccupied with truncated reason.

THE SELECTIONS

Vico presented his six "Inaugural Orations" at the University of Naples between 1699 and 1707. Each of these orations on humanistic education merits careful attention. The first places Vico within the long line of teachers who have understood self-knowledge (leading ultimately to knowledge of God) as the primary end of education. As a whole, the orations show Vico's debt to the Greek, Roman, and Renaissance humanists. Only the sixth oration, however, is included here. Vico writes within a theological framework. His philosophy of education acknowledges God as man's creator, man as God's image-bearer, and the Fall as corrupting human will and capacity. In part, we need education because we are finite and fallen. Man's pride confuses his mind, corrupts and divides his language, and disorders his passions. To address this threefold penalty, education seeks wisdom; and wisdom in its fullest meaning embraces knowledge, eloquence, and prudence. True education is not a matter of raw intelligence or accumulated data; it is knowledge joined to eloquence joined to prudence.

Vico continues with the threads of wisdom, eloquence, and prudence in his treatise *On the Study Methods of Our Time*, which followed the orations in 1709. Vico's concern here is that modernity's preoccupation with the rational investigation of nature has substituted for the once-predominant study of man (the same warning raised by Samuel Johnson later in the century). He warns against the risks posed to civilization by this dangerous distraction. Scientific knowledge by itself is not, and cannot be, wisdom.

Late in his career, Vico delivered an address at the yearly opening of the Academy of Oziosi, founded in the early eighteenth century and revived briefly in the 1730s. The Academy took its inspiration from ancient Athens and provided a forum for scholars to discuss their interests and research. "The Academies and the Relation between Philosophy and Eloquence" (1737) reaches back to Demosthenes, Cicero, and Horace to argue in defense of rhetoric.

"On the Proper Order of Studies"
Oration VI

[I] The situation of adolescents who have to be educated in the liberal arts and sciences most certainly seems difficult to me, given that their parents, who neither have knowledge of such things nor even inquire of those who do have such knowledge, without exploring the inherent constitution of their children and without discerning their native talents, push the youth to study one or another of the arts and sciences, most often contrary to their inclination, on the grounds of their own desires or to satisfy family needs. Or if naturally inclined to these studies they are often pushed into them without adequate preparation in related studies.

"Here there are tears, here there is misery," when, deprived of those studies which are necessary for the discipline to which they are applying themselves, they advance not at all or only a little and then with great difficulty. Attributing it to a fault in their own character, when it is rather a mistake of the parents, they lose all hope of acquiring that discipline. Even if they succeed in becoming more learned whether or not they share the goals of their parents, the parents force them into the study of jurisprudence to bring honor to the family. But because they are of a timid and shy nature they care little for clients, or high offices, or public responsibilities. Parents, desiring great financial gain, push their sons into the medical arts, but because of their higher aspirations they instead behold with admiration those most respected gentlemen who occupy and serve in the various offices of the commonwealth. Hence it happens that as long as the respect due to their fathers binds them, they continue to pursue those studies unwillingly and with disdain and do not cultivate them either seriously or with enthusiasm. At the first opportunity to be free from the bond of filial devotion, having abandoned entirely and put behind them the study of the liberal arts, they pass their lives in idleness and some even in immoral conduct. But if there is someone, as becomes a courageous man, who will persist on the road he has entered, and under the unwise pressure of his parents having learned nothing methodically and all against his natural disposition, now at a difficult age when he may have family as well as public responsibilities, he must learn the same things by himself. In this process so many and so formidable difficulties stand in his way that most men would be left with nothing more than a bitter longing for a sounder education.

[2] Meanwhile, I have often myself thought about this inconvenience or, rather, misfortune. I have accused nature by which it has been arranged that man must choose his vocation in life at an age when he knows nothing about anything and has no basis for choosing. While I was investigating the reasons for this, I recalled to myself that the beginning and source of all evils is the sin of Adam and the original corruption. However, when I thought about this more deeply, I saw myself to be unjust. Indeed, if we ourselves contemplate our own corrupted human nature we will discover that it not only points out to us those studies which we must cultivate but will also clearly disclose the order and path by which we shall approach them. These are the two most important topics that we shall now consider.

[3] And if I say that each of you must search within himself in order to consider carefully his human nature, he will in truth see himself to be nothing but mind, spirit, and capacity for language. Indeed, when he analyzes his body and its functions he will judge it to be either that of a brute or in common with the brutish. From this he will note that man is thoroughly corrupted, first by the inadequacy of language, then by a mind cluttered with opinions, and finally a spirit polluted by vices He will observe that these are the divine punishments by which the Supreme Will punished the sin of the first parent so that humankind who descended from him will become separated, scattered, and dispersed. For having introduced so many families of languages as a punishment to the impious Nimrod and having spread them throughout all the world, he caused nations to be separated from nations. With the flow and flux of time which changes every language, he also willed that within those nations the language of the fathers become unknown to their descendants. Moreover, having introduced opinions in which there is only a semblance of truth, passion, according to the inclination of each person, will lay hold of it as a truth. And, therefore, to each his own opinion and as it is commonly said—as many heads, so many opinions. Finally, so great is the baseness of vice that those who are vicious make every effort not to look upon their own. They detest those of others, and the same vices which are in us are those we reproach in others. Thus the miserly wants nothing to

do with the miserly and the unjust man complains of being wronged by another unjust man. God does not will that any society be founded upon vice, not even one of the vicious among themselves.

[4] Even more to the point, because of the fault of the original parent, as I have said before, the Supreme Will inflicted the same punishments in an unfortunate manner on each and every man as he did in scattering mankind. Hence, since man's language in almost all situations is inadequate, it does not come to the aid of the mind and even fails it when the mind seeks its help in expressing itself. Because speech is awkward and uncultivated, it corrupts the meaning of the mind with words that are without merit. With words that are obscure, it betrays it, or with words that are ambiguous what we say is misunderstood or stumbles over itself by the very words which are spoken. To these deficiencies of language are added those of the mind. Dullness constantly grips the mind. False images of things toy with it and very often deceive it. Rash judgments cause the mind to form hasty conclusions. Faulty reasoning lays hold of it, and finally this confusion of things baffles and bewilders it. But, by Hercules, how much more grave are the shortcomings of the soul which are churned up by every storm and flux of the passions more turbulent than those of the straits! Thus it burns with desire and trembles in fear! It becomes dissipated in pleasures and is given to weakness in pain! It desires all things but never finds delight in any choice! What it once disapproved it now approves, what it now disapproves it once approved! It is constantly unhappy with itself, always running away from itself and yet seeking itself! Moreover, self-love, as its own tormentor, makes use of these wicked plagues and tortures. Because basic human nature has been changed by original sin, assemblies of men may appear to be societies, but the truth is that isolation of spirits is greatest where many bodies come together. Even more is it like the crowded inmates of a prison where the spirits that I have mentioned above endure punishments, each in the cell to which it is assigned.

[5] I have enumerated as the punishments for corrupted human nature the inadequacy of language, the opinions of the mind, and the passions of the soul. Therefore, the remedies are eloquence, knowledge, and virtue. These three are like the three points around which all the orb of the arts and sciences encircles. All wisdom is contained in these three most excellent things—to know with certainty, to act rightly, and to speak with dignity. Such a man as that would never be ashamed of his errors, never repentant for having acted viciously, never regretful of having spoken without propriety and decorum. He is without doubt a true man whom the Terentian character describes neatly, "I am a man, and nothing human is foreign to me." Chremes—not for hope of gain, not out of necessity, not out of indebtedness, but simply in a neighborly spirit—asks Menedemus, who plays the part of the fool, tormenting and punishing himself, the reasons why he does this: "Don't cry! Help me to understand what bothers you! Don't conceal it! Don't be afraid!" And he promises him the following: "Trust me, I say! I will help by comforting and advising you and will support you!"

[6] Three are the very duties of wisdom—with eloquence to tame the impetuousness of the fools, with prudence to lead them out of error, with virtue toward them to earn their goodwill, and in these ways, each according to his ability, to foster with zeal the society of men. Those who do these things are indeed men much above the rest of mankind, and, if I may say, only a little less than the gods. A glory neither counterfeit nor transitory but solid and true follows such men. Certainly a fame based on merits so great

which others cannot reach will be known far and wide. For no other reason, the very wise poets created their poetic fables of Orpheus with his lyre taming the wild animals and Amphion with his song able to move the stones, which arranged themselves of their own accord by his music, thus erecting the walls of Thebes. For their feats, the lyre of the one and the dolphin of the other have been hurled into the heavens and are seen among the stars. Those rocks, those oaken planks, those wild animals are the fools among men. Orpheus and Amphion are the wise who have brought together by means of their eloquence the knowledge of things divine and human and have led isolated man into union, that is, from love of self to the fostering of human community, from sluggishness to purposeful activity, from unrestrained license to compliance with law and by conferring equal rights united those unbridled in their strength with the weak.

[7] This is always the truest, greatest, and most excellent goal of these studies. Many choose not to pursue them but are rather moved by the false, the base, and the abject, and because they are moved by the false, the base, and the abject it follows necessarily that they apply themselves to these studies falsely, basely, and abjectly. Here I could easily account for such people, but for reasons of honor, I will not mention them. However, on this subject I should give you a brief comment. He who in these studies is not seeking wisdom, that is, who does not cultivate these studies in order to improve his character and inform his mind with truth, his spirit with virtue, and his speech with eloquence so that he becomes constant with himself as a man and, as much as possible, able to help human society, is often other than what he professes to be. He is frequently speechless about much that is necessary to the very art which he professes. He often loathes, and neglects, and corrupts the very art which he professes. But in truth, he who in wisdom applies himself to correct his corrupted nature always acts with all the techniques of his art in which he has been instructed, he always acts with zeal and seriousness, he always acts in accord with the proper purpose of his own art. And in the community where those who profess their arts for the sake of the truth only, and only for the well-being of humanity, how flourishing are its citizens, how fortunate the commonwealth, I shall, to be brief, leave for you yourselves to think about!

[8] Having established that the same consideration of corrupted humanity has admonished us to embrace the whole sphere of human arts and sciences, let us now see in what order it dictates to us that we should learn them (which will be the other part of my argument). And so that you can more easily understand it, I should at the beginning explain what constitutes wisdom and the means toward its end.

[9] Wisdom, as is frequently said, consists in the knowledge of things divine and prudent judgment in human affairs and speech that is true and proper. But even before true and effective principles concerning language, it is necessary that we first have speech that is grammatically correct. What then follows is knowledge of the divine, which here I understand and speak of as, first, those things for whom nature is God and are called natural things, and, second, those things for whom God is the nature and are properly called divine things. We consider among natural things those which have been already fully accepted by man, namely geometric figures and numbers from which mathematics constructs its own demonstrations, and also causes which are most frequently debated among the learned doctors and are investigated by physics. Under physics I include anatomy, which is the study of the fabric of the human body, and that part of medicine which in-

quires into the causes of illness and which is nothing else than the physics of illnesses is indeed properly called the art of medicine and is an effective corollary of the integration of physics and anatomy, such as mechanics is the practical application of the integration of physics and mathematics. Divine things, however, are the human mind and God. Metaphysics studies both in order to contribute to science, while theology studies them in order to contribute to religion. Therefore, with these doctrines the knowledge of all things both natural and divine is completed. Wise judgment in human affairs requires that each perform his duties as man and as citizen. Moral doctrine renders man virtuous, civil doctrine makes of him a wise citizen, and both, when adjusted to our own religion, form that theology which is called moral theology. These three doctrines come together and unite in jurisprudence. Jurisprudence is indeed almost exclusively composed of moral doctrine because it is neither a science nor an art but is the knowledge of right, and its intent is justice; of civil doctrine, because it is concerned with advantages to the public; and of moral theology, because we are interpreting the right within a Christian commonwealth. Hence about things divine and human, we either debate among the learned or converse among the common man, and with the former it is necessary that we discourse in truth, and with the latter it is necessary that we use a speech that is appealing. Truth is the purpose and goal of logic in speech, while rhetoric teaches an appealing way of speaking free from meter, and an appealing speech in verse is the purpose and goal of the art of poetry.

[10] Now it is necessary that you know that almost all of the arts and sciences which I have mentioned have their own written histories, and as methodologies provide the general principles of things, the several histories authenticate them with specific examples. The most able writers in each language make up the history of languages. From these writers the best examples to establish how this or that people spoke have been transmitted, and the most famous orators and poets are the exemplars in the art of oratory and poetry. Concerning physical phenomena, histories have been written and continue to be written every day. And what about the observation and the recording of illnesses and the devising of certain pharmaceuticals which the common man refers to as some specific medication? Are they not commentaries on physics and the art of medicine? And does not mechanics write of the histories of new inventions of war, navigation, and architecture? By no means would you be wrong in calling histories of dogmatic and moral theology those which transmit the dogmas of faith revealed by the supreme God and the regulations of customs which are prescribed from one time to another. Certainly theologians counted the sacred books for the most part as historical. And is not the ecclesiastical tradition an uninterrupted and continuous succession of ecclesiastical doctrine and discipline? Commentaries, annals, records of the lives of famous men and of public affairs—are they not parts of the moral and civil doctrines so that they can properly be called by a most precise term, history? Truly, the histories of jurisprudence encompass those laws which have been promulgated within the commonwealth from time to time, and the interpretations given to them by the jurisconsults and the examples of legal decisions which have been rendered. Pure mathematics, by contrast, has no history because specific examples are unnecessary, and neither does logic because it uses examples from other disciplines. When examples are lacking, it constructs them. Even less does metaphysics have a history because it studies the human mind and God as the purest and simplest of natures and nothing else.

[11] At this point I derive from the Greeks that division by which all disciplines separate the esoteric from the exoteric, but I understand them differently. The esoteric disciplines are those which must be heard from teachers in order to be more easily acquired, and I understand them as the methods and principles of study of the arts and sciences. The exoteric, which truly each of us is capable of learning by himself, are those disciplines which are derived from the recorded histories of the arts and sciences.

[12] Therefore, all the store of the human arts and sciences having been made accessible so that we may learn them to attain wisdom, we must follow our own corrupted nature as a guide. There is no doubt that childhood is an age when reason is much weaker while memory is so much stronger. In fact, children of three years of age already have all the words and all the expressions necessary for everyday life which a voluminous dictionary would hardly be able to contain. There is no discipline which needs reason so much less and memory so much more than language. In fact, language is based on the common agreement and usage of the people, "among whom there is the choice of the rules and norms of speech."

Therefore, there is no other age better than childhood for learning languages. And here one of you will ask, Which languages are the best to devote ourselves to learning? That same knowledge of our corrupted nature will answer this question. In fact, among the particular punishments which I have identified, I list the roughness, the diversity, and the obscurity of languages which have torn apart human society. These defects have to be remedied by the teaching of languages, which as far as possible should be polished, unambiguous, and communal so that by this human society may again be embraced. Of these languages, there are two. One is Greek and the other Latin. Both are unambiguous, but Greek is the more learned while in these days Latin is the more widespread. Therefore, youths must apply themselves to these two, and beyond this, so that they better understand the meaning of the sacred books which are the principal instruments of Christian theology, it would be helpful to them also to master the sacred language.

[13] Having left childhood behind, the human mind, which is reason, begins to emerge from the mire of matter. Moreover, we say that opinions are punishments inflicted on the mind because of original sin. Therefore, corrupted nature demands that opinions from these early years must be overcome. And yet phantasy in youth is most vigorous. Proof of this would be that when we are young we make up opinions of distant cities and regions which are later difficult to dispel and replace with other images. So deeply are they engraved that it would hardly be possible to erase them completely and build others in their place. Nothing is more adverse to reason than phantasy. (We experience this in women, in whom phantasy prevails and reason is used less. Because of this they are plagued more than men with violent and confused emotions.) This being the case with phantasy, it is necessary that we imitate the medical doctors who use dangerous poisons in proper dosages for illness and in this manner heal. Phantasy must shrink so that reason will be strengthened. Adolescents, therefore, must apply themselves to mathematics, which is a discipline still very much aided by the ability to construct images. Often, for example, it is necessary to picture in the mind a very long series of forms or numbers in order to construct a proof and arrive at the truth of the conclusion. By doing this the human mind cleanses and purifies itself when it considers points and lines which have neither thickness nor body. And in this way, youths become accustomed to derive from those things

which have been agreed upon among men a truth from a given truth so that in physics, which is the most debated of the disciplines, they can apply a similar method. Advancing in maturity and in the use of mathematics, the human mind becomes progressively more free from the body and acts in a rational manner, and from things which are perceived by the senses it is able to gather together those things which escape all sensations even though they are still substances. And so we move from mathematics to physics, which considers those substances that are not perceived by the senses and their figure and motion, which are not perceptible but are the principles and causes of natural phenomena. And so the human mind is purified by means of mathematics and physics from grossness and denseness of thinking so that it gradually reaches the contemplation of incorporeal realities and with an uncontaminated and pure intellect comprehends itself and through itself Almighty God. The human mind will be led from the known facts of mathematics to the doubtful in physics to metaphysics, which seeks out those realities which are true, certain, and thoroughly known. Having then reached metaphysics and having acquired possession of the rules concerning the false, the probable, and the true, at this point the very art of oratory is appropriate for the purpose of interpretation. Then having known Almighty God, whom nature discloses, may you seek to reach that level of the knowledge of Him which our religion teaches and may you turn your mind to Christian theology.

[14] Wise judgment concerning human affairs follows the acquisition of the perfect knowledge of things divine. In the ordering of these disciplines we must imitate those who plot the course of ships, and as they observe the heavens, the pole star, and other stars so as to hold to a steady course through the oceans and steer safely to their harbors, so we contemplate divine things, the human mind, and the supreme God, and we use the knowledge of them as the Ursa Minor so that we may steer the course of human life cautiously and securely through the shoals of opinion, the shallows of doubt, and the hidden rocks of error. Since fools do not have the skill of knowing the true, they are ignorant of the true limits that set apart good from evil, which is the knowledge of the source of all human practical wisdom. There are many evil things that appear to be good. In contrast, there are many good things that give the appearance of evil, and those who are imprudent in these things follow the pleasures of the body and abhor work, poverty, and the death of an honest man. Consequently, they afflict themselves with their own vices and corrupt the society of men. For this reason, corrupted human nature longs to know because it longs to be happy. Those who have not ordered their literary studies for the gaining of wisdom as the source of human happiness may cast off the punishments inflicted on language or mind but still have not freed the spirit from those punishments. For this same reason, there are indeed most learned men who, however, are driven around in circles by ambition, anxiously living for the fleeting glory of their erudition and burning with jealousy for those who are more learned than they. And so it happens that they propose for themselves as goals those studies which are the means to achieving wisdom. The true function of the disciplines which I have previously proposed is to accustom the mind to true things, so that as soon as it is so accustomed, it may enjoy them. And thus, because man desires the true, he can do the good easily, and when he is in the habit of doing it, he chooses over all else the true goals of all good things in the conduct of his life, that is, the virtues and the good arts of the spirit, and through them he cultivates the divinity of the mind, and by means of the mind, reaches God. Therefore, having been imbued with the

knowledge of divine things, may you learn prudence in human affairs, first, the moral, which forms man, then the civil, which forms the citizen. In this way, having expertise in them, you will easily apply yourselves to moral theology so that in the future you will be able to guide princes as their advisers in ordering and administering public affairs with the wisest of counsel. Consequently, you will act in a most expedient manner in learning jurisprudence, which almost all would derive from moral and civil doctrines and from the dogmas and customs of the Christians. Finally, you have been instructed in these studies of wisdom so that each of you may earn merit far and wide from human society and be of help, not only to yourselves or to a few, but to as many as possible, and to this end you should join with these studies those of eloquence. Indeed, let none of you fear, when all of these studies for the cultivation of wisdom have been pursued, that he will grow old in learning them from the learned teachers. He will become old, most certainly he will become old, if he cultivates them without the proper instruction, if he cultivates them not in accord with their purpose, and if he cultivates them in an inappropriate sequence. Fabius Quintilian eloquently refers to this as wasting time by taking shortcuts. More acutely and no less true, if I am not mistaken, you might have said, They stand still because they rush ahead. And how is it that there are so many obstacles to no one more than to the one who hurries? Those who follow a confused order of studies move as though in a labyrinth and fail to progress. The shortest way of all is the direct way and the advantage of having an order is to complete the most in the shortest period of time. Because these studies, which are joined by nature and which we have arranged in the order that I have explained, have been split up and confused by the foibles of men, they appear to be many, but in reality they are not many but are one and the same perceived in many different lights. All the principles of the arts and the doctrines of the sciences which we have judged to be esoteric and to be learned from the teachers, if nothing foreign from other disciplines is added to them, are all very short. (What need is there to introduce anything if all else has been taught in its proper sequence?) We have judged that the histories of the sciences and the arts are exoteric and so it is possible that you can learn them by yourselves.

[15] Moreover, O youth of great hope, the counsel which I give you is to follow the most excellent goal and method of studies. In fact, if you consider this by the light of honesty, you will find it the most excellent, if by the light of utility, the best, and if for ease of learning, the most expedient. This is the advice which I am not ashamed to have given, because, though I be not wise, I have followed those who are. If they always act because they have the ability to act, I, for my part, have said those things because of the prodding of my corrupted nature. I have done that in this oration because it is as much as I may seriously and diligently do for you according to the proper object of my profession and according to my part as a man in serving human society.

On the Study Methods of Our Time

VII

But the greatest drawback of our educational methods is that we pay an excessive amount of attention to the natural sciences and not enough to ethics. Our chief fault is that we disregard that part of ethics which treats of human character, of its dispositions, its passions, and of the manner of adjusting these factors to public life and eloquence. We neglect that discipline which deals with the differential features of the virtues and vices, with good and bad behavior-patterns, with the typical characteristics of the various ages of man, of the two sexes, of social and economic class, race and nation, and with the art of seemly conduct in life, the most difficult of all arts. As a consequence of this neglect, a noble and important branch of studies, i.e., the science of politics, lies almost abandoned and untended.

Since, in our time, the only target of our intellectual endeavors is truth, we devote all our efforts to the investigation of physical phenomena, because their nature seems unambiguous; but we fail to inquire into human nature which, because of the freedom of man's will, is difficult to determine. A serious drawback arises from the uncontrasted preponderance of our interest in the natural sciences.

Our young men, because of their training, which is focused on these studies, are unable to engage in the life of the community, to conduct themselves with sufficient wisdom and prudence; nor can they infuse into their speech a familiarity with human psychology or permeate their utterances with passion. When it comes to the matter of prudential behavior in life, it is well for us to keep in mind that human events are dominated by Chance and Choice, which are extremely subject to change and which are strongly influenced by simulation and dissimulation (both pre-eminently deceptive things). As a consequence, those whose only concern is abstract truth experience great difficulty in achieving their means, and greater difficulty, in attaining their ends. Frustrated in their own plans, deceived by the plans of others, they often throw up the game. Since, then, the course of action in life must consider the importance of the single events and their circumstances, it may happen that many of these circumstances are extraneous and trivial, some of them bad, some even contrary to one's goal. It is therefore impossible to assess human affairs by the inflexible standard of abstract right; we must rather gauge them by the pliant Lesbic rule, which does not conform bodies to itself, but adjusts itself to their contours.

The difference, therefore, between abstract knowledge and prudence is this: in science, the outstanding intellect is that which succeeds in reducing a large multitude of physical effects to a single cause; in the domain of prudence, excellence is accorded to those who ferret out the greatest possible number of causes which may have produced a single event, and who are able to conjecture which of all these causes is the true one. Abstract knowledge—science—is concerned with the highest verity; common sense, instead, with the lowliest. On the basis of this, the distinguished features of the various types of men should be marked out: the fool, the astute ignoramus, the learned man destitute of prudence, and the sage. In the conduct of life the fool, for instance, pays no attention to the highest or the meanest truths; the astute ignoramus notices the meanest but is unable to perceive the highest; the man who is learned but destitute of prudence, deduces the lowest truths from the highest; the sage, instead, derives the highest truths from the unimportant ones. Abstract, or general truths are eternal; concrete or specific ones change momentarily from truths to untruths. Eternal truths stand above nature; in nature, instead, everything is unstable, mutable. But congruity exists between goodness and truth; they partake of the same essence, of the same qualities. Accordingly, the fool, who is ignorant of both general and particular truths, constantly suffers prompt penalties for his arrogance. The astute ignoramus, who is able to grasp particular truths but incapable of conceiving a general truth, finds that cleverness, which is useful to him today, may be harmful to him tomorrow. The learned but imprudent individual, traveling in a straight line from general truths to particular ones, bulls his way through the tortuous paths of life. But the sage who, through all the obliquities and uncertainties of human actions and events, keeps his eye steadily focused on eternal truth, manages to follow a roundabout way whenever he cannot travel in a straight line, and makes decisions, in the field of action, which, in the course of time, prove to be as profitable as the nature of things permits.

Therefore, it is an error to apply to the prudent conduct of life the abstract criterion of reasoning that obtains in the domain of science. A correct judgment deems that men—who are, for the most part, but fools—are ruled, not by forethought, but by whim or chance. The doctrinaires judge human actions as they *ought* to be, not as they actually are (i.e., performed more or less at random). Satisfied with abstract truth alone, and not being gifted with common sense, unused to following probability, those doctrinaires do not bother to find out whether their opinion is held by the generality and whether the things that are truths to them are also such to other people. This failure to concern themselves with the opinions of others has not only been a source of blame, but has proved to be extremely prejudicial, not only to private persons but to eminent leaders and great rulers as well. Let an example which is right to the point be quoted here: While the assembly of the French Estates was in session, Henry III, King of France, ordered Duke Henry de Guise, a very popular member of the French aristocracy, to be put to death, in spite of the fact that the Duke was under the protection of a safe conduct. Although just cause underlay that order of the king, such cause was not made manifest. The case having been brought up in Rome, Cardinal Ludovico Madruzzi, a man of great judgment in public affairs, commented: "Rulers should see to it not only that their actions are true and in conformity with justice, but that they also *seem* to be so."

Madruzzi's statement was proved true by the calamities which overtook France shortly after.

The Romans, who were great experts in political matters, paid particular attention to appearances. Both their judges and their senators, on giving out an opinion, were always wont to say: "It seems."

To summarize: It was because of their knowledge of the greatest affairs that philosophers were, by the Greeks, called "politici," i.e., experts in matters bearing on the total life of the body politic. Subsequently, philosophers were called Peripatetics and Academics, these names being derived from two small sections of the town of Athens, where their schools stood. Among the Ancients, the teaching of rational, physical, and ethical doctrines was entrusted to philosophers who took good care to adjust those doctrines to the practical common sense that should govern human behavior.

Today, on the contrary, we seem to have reverted to the type of physical research which was typical of pre-Socratic times.

There was an epoch when the "fourfold philosophy" i.e., logic, physics, metaphysics, and ethics was handed down by its teachers in a manner fitted to foster eloquence: i.e., the attempt was made to fuse philosophy with eloquence. Demosthenes was a product of the Lyceum; Cicero, of the Academy: there is no doubt that they were the two foremost speakers of the two most splendid of languages. Today, those branches of philosophical theory are taught by such a method as to dry up every fount of convincing expression, of copious, penetrating, embellished, lucid, developed, psychologically effective, and impassionate utterance. The listeners' minds undergo a process of constriction, so as to assume the shape of those young virgins,

> ... whom their mothers compel to bend their
> shoulders, to stoop, to bind their bosom
> in order to achieve slimness;
> if one of the girls is fleshier, they call her "the boxer"
> and stint her on food;
> if by nature she is healthy, they reduce her, by a special cure,
> to the slenderness of a reed.
> (Terence, *The Eunuch* II.iii.23–26)

Here some learned pundit might object that, in the conduct of life, I would have our young students become courtiers, and not philosophers; pay little attention to truth and follow not reality but appearances; and cast down morality and put on a deceitful "front" of virtue.

I have no such intention. Instead, I should like to have them act as philosophers, even at court; to care for truth that both is and has the appearance of truth, and to follow that which is morally good and which everybody approves.

As for eloquence, the same men assert that the modern study methods, far from being detrimental, are most useful to it. "How much preferable it is," they say, "to induce persuasion by solid arguments based on truth, to produce such an effect on the mind that, once that truth coalesces with reason, it can never again be separated from it, rather than to coerce the listener's soul by meretriciously eloquent allurements, by blazes of oratorical fire which, as soon as they are extinguished, cause him to revert to his original disposition!"

The answer is that eloquence does not address itself to the rational part of our nature, but almost entirely to our passions. The rational part in us may be taken captive by a net woven of purely intellectual reasonings, but the passional side of our nature can never be swayed and overcome unless this is done by more sensuous and materialistic means. The role of eloquence is to persuade; an orator is persuasive when he calls forth in his hearers the mood which he desires. Wise men induce this condition in themselves by an act of volition. This volition, in perfect obedience, follows the dictates of their intellect; consequently, it is enough for the speaker to point their duty to such wise men, and they do it. But the multitude, the *vulgus*, are overpowered and carried along by their appetite, which is tumultuous and turbulent; their soul is tainted, having contracted a contagion from the body, so that it follows the nature of the body, and is not moved except by bodily things. Therefore, the soul must be enticed by corporeal images and impelled to love; for once it loves, it is easily taught to believe; once it believes and loves, the fire of passion must be infused into it so as to break its inertia and force it to *will*. Unless the speaker can compass these three things, he has not achieved the effect of persuasion; he has been powerless to convince.

Two things only are capable of turning to good use the agitations of the soul, those evils of the inward man which spring from a single source: desire. One is philosophy, which acts to mitigate passions in the soul of the sage, so that those passions are transformed into virtues; the other is eloquence, which kindles these passions in the common sort, so that they perform the duties of virtue.

It may be objected that the form of government under which we live at present no longer allows eloquence to exercise its control over free peoples. To which I answer that we ought to be thankful to our monarchs for governing us not by fist but by laws. However, even under the republican form of government, orators have gained distinction by their fluent, broad, impassioned style of delivery in the law courts, the assemblies, and the religious convocations, to the greatest advantage of the state, and to the signal enrichment of our language. . . .

In conclusion: whosoever intends to devote his efforts, not to physics or mechanics, but to a political career, whether as a civil servant or as a member of the legal profession or of the judiciary, a political speaker or a pulpit orator, should not waste too much time, in his adolescence, on those subjects which are taught by abstract geometry. Let him, instead, cultivate his mind with an ingenious method; let him study topics, and defend both sides of a controversy, be it on nature, man, or politics, in a freer and brighter style of expression. Let him not spurn reasons that wear a semblance of probability and verisimilitude. Let our efforts not be directed towards achieving superiority over the Ancients merely in the field of science, while they surpass us in wisdom; let us not be merely more exact and more true than the Ancients, while allowing them to be more eloquent than we are; let us equal the Ancients in the fields of wisdom and eloquence as we excel them in the domain of science.

⸎

"The Academies and the Relation between Philosophy and Eloquence"

This name, "Academy," which we have taken from the Greeks to signify a community of scholars joined together for the purpose of exercising their powers of thought in works of erudition and learning, seems in regard to its origin to be suited to this most noble gathering more than to any other. Other academies have been instituted either for delivering discourses on special problems weighed in terms of an acute balancing of positions and counterpositions, or for considering particular topics of languages or scrutinizing particular experiments. But the Academy established by Socrates was a place where he, with elegance, copiousness, and ornament, reasoned about all parts of human and divine knowing; for this reason it is declared that the members of this Academy should, with cultivated, abundant, and ornate dissertations, course throughout all of the ample field of knowledge. Thus this Academy can rightfully call itself the one where Socrates reasoned.

This way of proceeding, above all, has the very great advantage that, although the noble spirits who gather here have applied themselves either for pleasure or for profession to a particular study of letters, thanks to such gatherings they succeed with time in acquiring all the cognitions necessary for an accomplished and wise thinker. Furthermore, and this is of very great importance, heart and language are here reunited in their natural bond, which Socrates, "full of philosophy in language and breast," had firmly brought together. For beyond his school a violent divorce existed: the sophists exercised a vain art of speaking and the philosophers a dry and unadorned manner of understanding. Still other Greek "philosophizers," although of a nation as refined and noble as one could ever name or imagine, wrote in a language that was stretched like a very fine and pure veil of soft wax over the abstract forms of thought they conceived; and yet, although they had renounced ornament and copiousness in their philosophical argumentation, still they preserved elegance.

But when in the midst of the most robust barbarism there was a return to cultivating the ancient philosophies, which was given a beginning by Averroes' commentaries on the works of Aristotle, a kind of blind speaking was introduced, bereft of light, lacking in any softness of color, a cloying manner of reasoning, always in the same syllogistic form and quite spiritless gait, enumerating each order of discourse—*praemitto primo, praemitto secundo, obiicies primo, obiicies secundo.* Moreover, if I am not mistaken, I hold the opinion that if eloquence does not regain the luster of the Latins and Greeks in our time, when our sciences have made progress equal to and perhaps even greater than theirs, it will be because the sciences are taught completely stripped of every badge of eloquence. And, for all that Cartesian philosophy would claim to have corrected of the erroneous order of thought of which the Scholastics were guilty, placing the total force of its proofs in the geometric method, such a method is so subtle and drawn out that if by chance, attention to one proposition is broken, it is completely lost to whoever is listening to comprehend anything of the whole of what is being said.

Yet Demosthenes came forth from the Platonic Academy where he had listened for a good eight years, and he came armed with his invincible enthymeme, which he formed by means of a very well regulated excess, going outside his case into quite distant things with which he tempered the lightning flashes of his arguments, which, when striking, amazed the listeners so much the more by how much he had diverted them. From the same Academy Cicero professed himself to be endowed with the felicity of his copiousness, which, like a great winter torrent, overflows banks, floods countrysides, crashes down over cliffs and hillsides, rolling before it heavy stones and ancient oaks; and triumphant over all that had given him resistance, he returns to the proper riverbed of his case.

It is of no use to defend our own small spirit (on account of which we pretend to be wholly spirit) by saying that Demosthenes and Cicero flourished in popular republics in which, as Tacitus says, eloquence and liberty are on a par. In fact, the eloquence that Cicero had used in liberty was later employed before Caesar, ruler of Rome, on behalf of

Quintus Ligarius. In this case Cicero absolutely took the accused from Caesar's hands, he whom the dictator, on entering the Council, had himself openly professed to condemn, [later] saying these words: "Had Cicero not spoken so well today, Ligarius would not flee from our hands." In the sixteenth century, in which a well-spoken wisdom was celebrated, Giulio Camillo Delminio made tears come to the eyes of Francis I, King of France, with the oration he delivered for the liberation of his brother, just as Monsignor Giovanni della Casa moved the Emperor Charles V with what he said to him for the return of Piacenza. The oration on behalf of Ligarius is still the most glorious of all those of Cicero. He triumphed with language over him who with arms had triumphed over the whole world. Of the other two orations (the one delivered to a very great king, the other to a renowned emperor), the former is a queen and the latter is the empress of Tuscan orations.

Now to bring together in brief what has been said, you, *signori*, with masterful awareness, endeavor to employ in practice that precept of Horace which, condensed in three lines, contains all the art of using language well in prose as in verse. "Right thinking is the first principle and source of writing," because there is no eloquence without truth and dignity; of these two parts wisdom is composed. "Socratic writings will direct you in the choice of subjects," that is, the study of morals, which principally informs the wisdom of man, to which more than in the other parts of philosophy Socrates divinely applied himself, whence of him it was said: "Socrates recalled moral philosophy from the heavens." And "when the subject is well conceived, words will follow on spontaneously," because of the natural bond by which we claim language and heart to be held fast together, for to every idea its proper voice stands naturally attached. Thus, eloquence is none other than wisdom speaking.

A good three years have now passed since this noble Academy, honorably received in this worthy place by Signor Don Niccolò Salerni, was founded; and with the same fervor with which it commenced, it happily continues against the malign course of foolish Fortune who cuts across beautiful enterprises and, being envious, she frequently overwhelms them in their earliest magnanimous efforts. Now, in this year you, in your generosity, beyond any I merit, wished and commanded me *custode* and colleague of Signor de Canosa (with whose most noble personage this community is adorned), having appointed Signor Don Paolo Doria censor, a mind of rare and sublime intelligence and most celebrated for many works of philosophy and mathematics among the learned of his age. And, by way of overwhelming me with highest and sovereign honor, he commanded that I make the annual opening address.

Therefore, having collected all my powers in a thought of highest reverence, the formula being dictated to me by the great Father Augustine, under whose protection this Academy stands resigned, I conceived this prayer with these solemn and consecrated words—Hear, humbly I pray you, hear, not fabulous Minerva, but Eternal Wisdom, generated from the divine head of the true Jove, the omnipotent Your Father. Today in Your praise, in Your honor, in Your glory is reopened this fourth Academy year, that it might be for the perfection of these well-born intelligences, because wisdom, which is mind and language, is the perfecter of man in his properly being man.

Edmund Burke

1729–97

If education takes in vice as any part of its system, there is no doubt but that it will operate with abundant energy, and to an extent indefinite.

Letter to a Member of the National Assembly

Edmund Burke, Whig statesman and conservative opponent of the French Revolution, was born in Dublin, Ireland. His father was an attorney, and Edmund was educated at Trinity College, Dublin, where he too took up the study of law, later serving as a member of Parliament from 1765 to 1794. Burke defended the American colonists' resistance to Parliament's taxation and imperial management, seeing their fight as a genuine effort to preserve the inherited constitutional rights of English subjects. He opposed the French Revolution, however, as a reckless war against history and prescription, propelled by a zeal for doctrinaire innovation at the expense of gradual, moderate reform. His *Reflections on the Revolution in France* (1790) articulated the conservative case for attending to time, circumstance, convention, experience, and practical wisdom in matters of reform. He opposed the abstractions of France's theorists, who attempted to reconstruct politics, society, and even the constitution of human nature on an allegedly rational basis. Burke launched a lonely crusade against the excesses of the Revolution, issuing unheeded warnings that in the early days before the Terror seemed shrill and exaggerated, and which cost him the support of the Whig leadership.

THE SELECTION

In one section of his *Letter to a Member of the National Assembly* (1791), Burke addresses the implications of Rousseau's ethics for education. He considers what sort of mind and character would be formed by a system based on Rousseau's teachings and what that innovation portended for France's future. Burke was alarmed by Rousseau's "philosophy of vanity," seeing it as a new morality destined to replace Christian humility with ethical egotism. He criticizes Rousseau's *Confessions* and *Nouvelle Eloise* for promoting a generalized humanitarian benevolence in place of the hard work of self-control and duty. A free government, Burke believed, was possible only through the effort of "much thought, deep reflection, a sagacious, powerful, and combining mind."[1]

Oriel College's John Davidson later wrote of Burke's example, "If any mind improved like his, is to be our instructor, we must go to the fountain head of things as he did, and study not his works but his method; by the one we may become feeble imitators, by the other arrive at some ability of our own. But, as all biography assures us, he, and every other able thinker, has been formed, not by a parsimonious admeasurement of studies to some definite future object . . . , but by taking a wide and liberal compass, and thinking a great deal on many subjects with no better end in view than because the exercise was one which made them more rational and intelligent beings."[2]

from Letter to a Member of the National Assembly

Besides the sure tokens which are given by the spirit of their particular arrangements, there are some characteristic lineaments in the general policy of your tumultuous despotism, which, in my opinion, indicate, beyond a doubt, that no revolution whatsoever in their disposition is to be expected. I mean their scheme of educating the rising generation, the principles which they intend to instil, and the sympathies which they wish to form in the mind at the season in which it is the most susceptible. Instead of forming their young minds to that docility, to that modesty, which are the grace and charm of youth, to an admiration of famous examples, and to an averseness to anything which approaches to pride, petulance, and self-conceit (distempers to which that time of life is of itself sufficiently liable), they artificially foment these evil dispositions, and even form them into springs of action. Nothing ought to be more weighed than the nature of books recommended by public authority. So recommended, they soon form the character of the age. Uncertain indeed is the efficacy, limited indeed is the extent of a virtuous institution. But if education takes in vice as any part of its system, there is no doubt but that it will operate with abundant energy, and to an extent indefinite. The magistrate, who in favour of freedom thinks himself obliged to suffer all sorts of publications, is under a stricter duty than any other well to consider what sort of writers he shall authorize, and shall recommend by the strongest of all sanctions, that is, by public honours and rewards. He ought to be cautioned how he recommends authors of mixed or ambiguous morality. He ought to be fearful of putting into the hands of youth writers indul-

---

1. *Reflections on the Revolution in France*, ed. by L. G. Mitchell (Oxford: Oxford University Press, 1993), 247.

2. Quoted by John Henry Newman in *The Idea of a University*, Discourse VII.

gent to the peculiarities of their own complexion, lest they should teach the humours of the professor, rather than the principles of the science. He ought, above all, to be cautious in recommending any writer who has carried marks of a deranged understanding; for where there is no sound reason there can be no real virtue; and madness is ever vicious and malignant.

The assembly proceeds on maxims the very reverse of these. The assembly recommends to its youth a study of the bold experimenters in morality. Everybody knows that there is a great dispute amongst their leaders, which of them is the best resemblance of Rousseau. In truth, they all resemble him. His blood they transfuse into their minds and into their manners. Him they study; him they meditate; him they turn over in all the time they can spare from the laborious mischief of the day, or the debauches of the night. Rousseau is their canon of holy writ; in his life he is their canon of *Polycletus*; he is their standard figure of perfection. To this man and this writer, as a pattern to authors and to Frenchmen, the foundries of Paris are now running for statues, with the kettles of their poor and the bells of their churches. If an author had written like a great genius on geometry, though his practical and speculative morals were vicious in the extreme, it might appear, that in voting the statue, they honoured only the geometrician. But Rousseau is a moralist, or he is nothing. It is impossible, therefore, putting the circumstances together, to mistake their design in choosing the author with whom they have begun to recommend a course of studies.

Their great problem is to find a substitute for all the principles which hitherto have been employed to regulate the human will and action. They find dispositions in the mind of such force and quality as may fit men, far better than the old morality, for the purposes of such a state as theirs, and may go much further in supporting their power, and destroying their enemies. They have therefore chosen a selfish, flattering, seductive, ostentatious vice, in the place of plain duty. The true basis of the Christian system, humility, is the low, but deep and firm foundation of all real virtue. But this, as very painful in the practice, and little imposing in the appearance, they have totally discarded. Their object is to merge all natural and all social sentiment in inordinate vanity. In a small degree, and conversant in little things, vanity is of little moment. When full grown, it is the worst of vices, and the occasional mimic of them all. It makes the whole man false. It leaves nothing sincere or trustworthy about him. His best qualities are poisoned and perverted by it, and operate exactly as the worst. When your lords had many writers as immoral as the object of their statue (such as Voltaire and others) they chose Rousseau; because in him that peculiar vice, which they wished to erect into ruling virtue, was by far the most conspicuous.

We have had the great professor and founder of *the philosophy of vanity* in England. As I had good opportunities of knowing his proceedings almost from day to day, he left no doubt on my mind that he entertained no principle either to influence his heart, or to guide his understanding but *vanity*. With this vice he was possessed to a degree little short of madness. It is from the same deranged, eccentric vanity, that this, the insane *Socrates* of the National Assembly, was impelled to publish a mad confession of his mad faults, and to attempt a new sort of glory from bringing hardily to light the obscure and vulgar vices, which we know may sometimes be blended with eminent talents. He has not observed on the nature of vanity who does not know that it is omnivorous; that it has no choice in its food; that it is fond to talk even of its own faults and vices, as what will excite surprise and draw attention, and what will pass at worst for openness and candour.

It was this abuse and perversion, which vanity makes even of hypocrisy, that has driven Rousseau to record a life not so much as chequered, or spotted here and there, with virtues, or even distinguished by a single good action. It is such a life he chooses to offer to the attention of mankind. It is such a life that, with a wild defiance, he flings in the face of his Creator, whom he acknowledges only to brave. Your assembly, knowing how much more powerful example is found than precept, has chosen this man (by his own account without a single virtue) for a model. To him they erect their first statue. From him they commence their series of honours and distinctions.

It is that new invented virtue, which your masters canonize, that led their moral hero constantly to exhaust the stores of his powerful rhetoric in the expression of universal benevolence; whilst his heart was incapable of harbouring one spark of common parental affection. Benevolence to the whole species, and want of feeling for every individual with whom the professors come in contact, form the character of the new philosophy. Setting up for an unsocial independence, this their hero of vanity refuses the just price of common labour, as well as the tribute which opulence owes to genius, and which, when paid, honours the giver and the receiver; and then he pleads his beggary as an excuse for his crimes. He melts with tenderness for those only who touch him by the remotest relation, and then, without one natural pang, casts away, as a sort of offal and excrement, the spawn of his disgustful amours, and sends his children to the hospital of foundlings.

The bear loves, licks, and forms her young; but bears are not philosophers. Vanity, however, finds its account in reversing the train of our natural feelings. Thousands admire the sentimental writer; the affectionate father is hardly known in his parish.

Under this philosophic instructor in the *ethics of vanity*, they have attempted in France a regeneration of the moral constitution of man. Statesmen, like your present rulers, exist by everything which is spurious, fictitious, and false; by everything which takes the man from his house, and sets him on a stage—which makes him up an artificial creature, with painted, theatric sentiments, fit to be seen by the glare of candlelight, and formed to be contemplated at a due distance. Vanity is too apt to prevail in all of us, and in all countries. To the improvement of Frenchmen it seems not absolutely necessary that it should be taught upon system. But it is plain that the present rebellion was its legitimate offspring, and it is piously fed by that rebellion with a daily dole.

If the system of instruction recommended by the assembly be false and theatric, it is because their system of government is of the same character. To that, and to that alone, it is strictly conformable. To understand either, we must connect the morals with the politics of the legislators. Your practical philosophers, systematic in everything, have wisely begun at the source. As the relation between parents and children is the first amongst the elements of vulgar, natural morality, they erect statues to a wild, ferocious, low-minded, hard-hearted father, of fine general feelings: a lover of his kind, but a hater of his kindred. Your masters reject the duties of his vulgar relation, as contrary to liberty; as not founded in the social compact; and not binding according to the rights of men; because the relation is not, of course, the result of *free election;* never so on the side of the children, not always on the part of the parents.

The next relation which they regenerate by their statues to Rousseau is that which is next in sanctity to that of a father. They differ from those old-fashioned thinkers, who considered pedagogues as sober and venerable characters, and allied to the parental. The moralists of the dark times, *preceptorem Sancti voluere parentis esse loco.* In this age of light, they teach the people that preceptors ought to be in the place of gallants. They systematically corrupt a very corruptible race (for some time a growing nuisance amongst you), a set of pert, petulant literators, to whom instead of their proper, but severe unostentatious duties, they assign the brilliant part of men of wit and pleasure, of gay, young, military sparks, and danglers at toilets. They call on the rising generation in France to take a sympathy in the adventures and fortunes, and they endeavour to engage their sensibility on the side of pedagogues who betray the most awful family trusts, and vitiate their female pupils. They teach the people that the debauchers of virgins, almost in the arms of their parents, may be safe inmates in their houses, and even fit guardians of the honour of those husbands who succeed legally to the office which the young literators had pre-occupied, without asking leave of law or conscience.

Thus they dispose of all the family relations of parents and children, husbands and wives. Through this same instructor, by whom they corrupt the morals, they corrupt the taste. Taste and elegance, though they are reckoned only among the smaller and secondary morals, yet are of no mean importance in the regulation of life. A moral taste is not of force to turn vice into virtue; but it recommends virtue with something like the blandishments of pleasure; and it infinitely abates the evils of vice. Rousseau, a writer of great force and vivacity, is totally destitute of taste in any sense of the word. Your masters, who are his scholars, conceive that all refinement has an aristocratic character. The last age had exhausted all its powers in giving a grace and nobleness to our mutual appetites, and in raising them into a higher class and order than seemed justly to belong to them. Through Rousseau, your masters are resolved to destroy these aristocratic prejudices. The passion called love has so general and powerful an influence; it makes so much of the entertainment, and indeed so much of the occupation of that part of life which decides the character for ever, that the mode and the principles on which it engages the sympathy, and strikes the imagination, become of the utmost importance to the morals and manners of every society. Your rulers are well aware of this; and in their system of changing your manners to accommodate them to their politics, they found nothing so convenient as Rousseau. Through him they teach men to love after the fashion of philosophers; that is, they teach to men, to Frenchmen, a love without gallantry; a love without anything of that fine flower of youthfulness and gentility, which places it, if not among the virtues, among the ornaments of life. Instead of this passion, naturally allied to grace and manners, they infuse into their youth an unfashioned, indelicate, sour, gloomy, ferocious medley of pedantry and lewdness; of metaphysical speculations blended with the coarsest sensuality. Such is the general morality of the passions to be found in their famous philosopher, in his famous work of philosophic gallantry the *Nouvelle Eloise.*

When the fence from the gallantry of preceptors is broken down, and your families are no longer protected by decent pride, and salutary domestic prejudice, there is but one step to a frightful corruption. The rulers in the National Assembly are in good hopes that the females of the first families in France may become an easy prey to dancing-masters, fiddlers, pattern-drawers, friseurs, and valets de chambre, and other active citizens of that description, who having the entry into your houses, and being half domesticated by their situation, may be blended with you by regular and irregular relations. By a law they have made these people their equals. By adopting the sentiments of Rousseau they have made them your rivals. In this manner these great legislators complete their plan of levelling, and establish their rights of men on a sure foundation.

I am certain that the writings of Rousseau lead directly to this kind of shameful evil. I have often wondered how he comes to be so much more admired and followed on the Continent than he is here. Perhaps a secret charm in the language may have its share in this extraordinary difference. We certainly perceive, and to a degree we feel, in this writer, a style glowing, animated, enthusiastic; at the same time that we find it lax, diffuse, and not in the best taste of composition; all the members of the piece being pretty equally laboured and expanded, without any due selection or subordination of parts. He is generally too much on the stretch, and his manner has little variety. We cannot rest upon any of his works, though they contain observations which occasionally discover a considerable insight into human nature. But his doctrines, on the whole, are so inapplicable to real life and manners, that we never dream of drawing from them any rule for laws or conduct, or for fortifying or illustrating anything by a reference to his opinions. They have with us the fate of older paradoxes,

Cum ventum ad *verum est sensus moresque* repugnant,
Atque ipsa utilitas justi prope mater et aequi.[3]

Perhaps bold speculations are more acceptable because more new to you than to us, who have been long since satiated with them. We continue, as in the two last ages to read, more generally than I believe is now done on the Continent, the authors of sound antiquity. These occupy our minds. They give us another taste and turn; and will not suffer us to be more than transiently amused with paradoxical morality. It is not that I consider this writer as wholly destitute of just notions. Amongst his irregularities, it must be reckoned that he is sometimes moral, and moral in a very sublime strain. But the *general spirit and tendency* of his works is mischievous; and the more mischievous for this mixture: for perfect depravity of sentiment is not reconcilable with eloquence; and the mind (though corruptible, not complexionally vicious) would reject, and throw off with disgust, a lesson of pure and unmixed evil. These writers make even virtue a pander to vice.

However, I less consider the author than the system of the assembly in perverting morality through his means. This I confess makes me nearly despair of any attempt upon the minds of their followers, through reason, honour, or conscience. The great object of your tyrants is to destroy the gentlemen of France; and for that purpose they destroy, to the best of their power, all the effect of those relations which may render considerable men powerful or even safe. To destroy that order, they vitiate the whole community. That no means may exist of confederating against their tyranny, by the false sympathies of the *Nouvelle Eloise* they endeavour to subvert those principles of domestic trust and fidelity, which form the discipline of social life. They propagate principles by which every servant may think it, if not his duty, at least his privilege to betray his master. By these principles every considerable father of a family loses the sanctuary of his house. *Debet sua cuique domus esse perfugium tutissimum,*[4] says the law, which your legislators have taken so much pains first to

---

3. "When it comes to the truth, one's character revolts, and expediency itself is the motherr of justice and equity" (Horace, *Satires*, I.iii.98–99).
4. "Home ought to be a refuge where you are safest" (Cicero, *In Catilinam*, iv.2).

decry, then to repeal. They destroy all the tranquillity and security of domestic life; turning the asylum of the house into a gloomy prison, where the father of the family must drag out a miserable existence, endangered in proportion to the apparent means of his safety; where he is worse than solitary in a crowd of domestics, and more apprehensive from his servants and inmates, than from the hired, bloodthirsty mob without doors, who are ready to pull him to the lanterne.

It is thus, and for the same end, that they endeavour to destroy that tribunal of conscience which exists independently of edicts and decrees. Your despots govern by terror. They know that he who fears God fears nothing else: and therefore they eradicate from the mind, through their Voltaire, their Helvetius, and the rest of that infamous gang, that only sort of fear which generates true courage. Their object is, that their fellow-citizens may be under the dominion of no awe, but that of their committee of research, and of their lanterne.

Edward Copleston

1776–1849

There must be surely a cultivation of mind, which is itself good: a good of the highest order; without any immediate reference to bodily appetites, or wants of any kind.

"A Reply to the Calumnies"

Edward Copleston, provost of Oriel College, Oxford, was born at the rectory of St. Mary's church in the village of Offwell, Devon. He was elected a fellow of Oriel College in 1795, and taught for ten years there as professor of poetry. Under his leadership as Provost from 1814 to 1828, Oriel reached the height of its prestige and seemed to define the academic life of Oxford. Copleston was a member of the Noetics, a group of liberal Anglicans at Oxford. His students recalled him as a gifted teacher and lecturer, and he left a legacy of distinguished fellows and a reformed tutorial system. John Henry Newman became a fellow of Oriel during Copleston's tenure. Newman admired Copleston's chivalric battle against the rising utilitarianism in education. He later said in *The Idea of a University* (Discourse VI) that Copleston's "name lives, and ever will live, for the distinction which his talents bestowed on [Oriel], for the academical importance to which he raised it, for the generosity of spirit, the liberality of sentiment, and the kindness of heart, with which he adorned it, and which even those who had least sympathy with some aspects of his mind and character could not but admire and love." After Oriel, Copleston spent the last two decades of his life as Bishop of Llandaff and Dean of St. Paul's, London.

THE SELECTION

A series of book reviews appeared in the *Edinburgh Review* between 1808 and 1810 that sharply criticized Cambridge and Oxford for the quality of their instruction in mathematics and science. The utilitarians at the *Edinburgh Review* charged Cambridge and Oxford with keeping these subjects in their "infancy" and Oxford with producing pedantic and inept classical scholars. The education offered there was simply "useless." Universities should be research institutions and add to the storehouse of useful knowledge demanded by modern industrial society. Copleston, professor of poetry at the time, launched three "replies" to these "calumnies" against Oxford. The first reply, from 1810, is the most extensive, and Newman quotes from it in Discourse VII of his *Idea of a University*. Most of chapter 3 and part of chapter 5 are included here. In the debate over the usefulness of education, Copleston focuses on the more fundamental question of education's usefulness *to what end*. The real contested ground is the *telos* of education.

from "Reply to the Calumnies of the Edinburgh Review Against Oxford,
Containing an Account of Studies Pursued in That University"

CHAPTER 3

Much has been said, and well said, on this subject: but I have not yet seen the question argued exactly on its right grounds. Neither do I propose in the present treatise to supply all the deficiencies which I speak of in its advocates, but rather to point out two or three leading principles, which have not been made sufficiently prominent in these discussions, if they have been noticed at all.

Some, who dispute the utility of Classical learning, have joined issue on this ground: What remuneration does a boy receive for the time and money expended in this pursuit? For what employment does it fit him? or how does it enable him to improve his fortunes?

To this I answer, that the object of Classical education is not to fit him for any *specific* employment, or to increase his fortune. Such, I admit, is the object of most parents when educating their children; but it is an object not only different from that of true philosophy or enlightened policy, but even frequently at variance with it. The peculiar interest of the individual is not always the same, is seldom precisely the same, with the interest of the public. And he who serves the one most faithfully, always forgets, and often injures, the other. The true principles of educating a gentleman cannot be better sketched than they are by Locke, although his language already sounds rather quaintly.

> The great work of a Governor is to fashion the carriage and form the mind; to settle in his pupil good habits, and the principles of virtue and wisdom; to give him, by little and little, a view of mankind; and work him into a love and imitation of what is excellent and praise-worthy; and, in the prosecution of it, to give him vigour, activity, and industry. The studies which he sets him upon are but, as it were, the exercise of his faculties, and employment of his time, to keep him from sauntering and idleness,

to teach him application, and accustom him to take pains, and to give him some little
taste of what his own industry must perfect. For who expects that, under a tutor, a
young gentleman should be an accomplished critic, orator, or logician; go to the bottom of metaphysics, natural philosophy, or mathematics; or be a master in history or
chronology? Though something of each of these is to be taught him: but it is only to
open the door, that he may look in, and, as it were, begin an acquaintance, but not
to dwell there.

It is remarkable, however, that Locke, like most other writers on education, occasionally confounds two things which ought to be kept perfectly distinct, viz. that mode of
education which would be most beneficial, as a system, to society at large, with that which
would contribute most to the advantage and prosperity of an individual. These things are
often at variance with each other. The former is that alone which deserves the attention of
a philosopher; the latter is narrow, selfish, and mercenary. It is this last indeed, on which
the world are most eager to inform themselves: but the persons, who instruct them, however they may deserve the thanks and esteem of those whom they benefit, do no service to
mankind. There are but so many good places in the theatre of life; and he who puts us in
the way of procuring one of them, does to *us* indeed a great favour, but none to the whole
assembly.

It is again sometimes asked, with an air of triumph, what is the *utility* of these studies? and *utility* is vauntingly pronounced to be the sole standard, by which all systems of
education must be tried.

If in our turn we were to ask what utility is, we should, I believe, have many answers
not quite consistent with each other. And the best of them perhaps would only give us
other words equally loose and indefinite; such as *wiser, better, happier*; none of which can
serve to untie a knotty question, and all of which lead us into a wider field of doubt and
enquiry, than the subject which originally produced them. Before I attempt to show what
the utility of Classical learning is, in my own sense of the word, let it be permitted me to
explain what it is not; and to take up the enquiry a little farther back than writers on this
subject commonly go.

It is an undisputed maxim in political economy, that the separation of professions, and
the division of labour, tend to the perfection of every art—to the wealth of nations—to
the general comfort and well-being of the community. This principle of division is in
some instances pursued so far, as to excite the wonder of people, to whose notice it is for
the first time pointed out. There is no saying to what extent it may not be carried; and the
more the powers of each individual are concentrated in one employment, the greater skill
and quickness will he naturally display in performing it. But while he thus contributes
more effectually to the accumulation of national wealth, he becomes himself more and
more degraded as a rational being. In proportion as his sphere of action is narrowed, his
mental powers and habits become contracted; and he resembles a subordinate part of
some powerful machinery, useful in its place, but insignificant and worthless out of it.

So sensible is the great and enlightened Adam Smith of the force of this objection,
that he endeavours to meet it by suggesting, that the means of intellectual improvement
multiply rapidly with the increasing wealth of society; that the facility therefore of acquiring these means may increase in the same ratio with the injurious tendency of that

system we have been just considering; and thus counteract or compensate all its evil. An answer, which affords a much stronger proof of the candour of the philosopher, than it is a satisfactory defense of his system against the supposed objection. The evil of that system is certain, and almost demonstrable; the remedy suggested is doubtful, and even conjectural. It would have been better to alter the shape of the whole question, and remove at once the ground-work of the objection, by guarding his theory against that extreme in which it takes its rise.

If indeed national wealth were the sole object of national institutions, there can be no doubt but that the method demonstrated by Dr. Smith, being the surest means of attaining that end, would be the great leading principle of political philosophy. In his own work *it is* the great and sole end of his enquiry: and no one can blame him for confining himself to that single consideration. His undertaking required no more, and he has performed his part well. But, in truth, national wealth is not the ultimatum of human society; and although we must forbear entering on the boundless enquiry, *what is the chief good*, yet all reflecting minds will admit that it is not wealth. If it be necessary, as it is beyond all question necessary, that society should be split into divisions and subdivisions, in order that its several duties may be well performed, yet we must be careful not to yield up ourselves wholly and exclusively to the guidance of this system: we must observe what its evils are, and we should modify and restrain it, by bringing into action other principles, which may serve as a check and counterpoise to the main force.

One of the greatest faults in all moral and political reasoning is an excessive and immoderate application of one principle, to the exclusion of others, with which it ought in reason to be combined; and whose relative force should always vary with the circumstances of the case.

There can be no doubt that every art is improved by confining the professor of it to that single study. There are emergencies, which call for his *whole mind and faculties* to be absorbed in it, which require him to forget every other relation of life, however sacred or natural, except that artificial one in which he is then placed. Times will occur when a Surgeon or a General must dismiss the common feelings of human nature, and, in order to do his task well, must look upon himself as engaged in working out one problem, and upon all around him as instruments subservient merely to the acquisition of some one distinct purpose, without regard to their bearings on anything besides.

But although the Art itself is advanced, by this concentration of mind in its service, the individual who is confined to it goes back. The advantage of the community is nearly in an inverse ratio with his own. Reason and common sense require that neither object should be exclusively regarded. And if, as in the cases above mentioned, an *entire* sacrifice of the individual is demanded, in all other cases that sacrifice can be required only in proportion as they approximate to this extreme. And thus a wide space is left to the discretion of the individual, where the claims of the community are either not pressing, or are wholly silent.

Of course it will be understood, that in this statement I consider the intellectual enjoyment of the individual merely, when speaking of his *advantage*, and that I do not lose sight of that enjoyment, which even the most confined exercise of the intellect imparts: I consider it as abridged only in proportion to the contracted sphere of action in which he is doomed to move.

Indeed, when the emergency is past, society itself requires some other contribution from each individual, besides the particular duties of his profession. And if no such liberal intercourse be established, it is the common failing of human nature, to be engrossed with petty views and interests, to under-rate the importance of all in which we are not concerned, to carry our partial notions into cases where they are inapplicable, to act, in short, as so many unconnected units, displacing and repelling one another.

In the cultivation of literature is found that common link, which, among the higher and middling departments of life, unites the jarring sects and subdivisions in one interest, which supplies common topics, and kindles common feelings, unmixed with those narrow prejudices with which all professions are more or less infected. The knowledge too, which is thus acquired, expands and enlarges the mind, excites its faculties, and calls those limbs and muscles into freer exercise, which, by too constant use in one direction, not only acquire an illiberal air, but are apt also to lose somewhat of their native play and energy. And thus, without directly qualifying a man for any of the employments of life, it enriches and ennobles all. Without teaching him the peculiar business of any one office or calling, it enables him to act his part in each of them with better grace and more elevated carriage; and, if happily planned and conducted, is a main ingredient in that complete and generous education, which fits a man "to perform justly, skilfully, and magnanimously, all the offices, both private and public, of peace and war."

Thus far then we have considered the utility of those liberal pursuits, which in a refined state of society engage the attention of the higher orders, and which, by common consent, impart a dignity to the several professions of life, and to mercantile adventure.

It still remains to prove, that what is called *Classical literature* answers this purpose most effectually.

And here, if the question is to be compendiously treated, it must be allowed me to take for granted many points, which a captious adversary might dispute, but which the authority of the greatest names, and the general experience of educated men concur in establishing. That the relics of Grecian and Roman literature contain some of the choicest fruits of human genius; that the poets, the historians, the orators, and the philosophers, of Greece especially, have each in their several lines brought home, and laid at our feet, the richest treasures of invention; that the history of those early times presents us with a view of things "nobly done and worthily spoken"; that the mind and spirit which breathed then, lives still, and will for ever live in the writings which remain to us; that, according as taste, and genius, and learning, have been valued among men, those precious remains have been held still dearer and more sacred; are all positions which it is better to assume as indisputable, than to embarrass the present argument with any new attempt to prove them.

Neither is it necessary to say much in order to silence the feeble and querulous cry, that all the good which those works contain may be had through the medium of *translation*. To demonstrate, indeed, how, from the very nature of language, translation cannot adequately perform this office, would require an extended argument. I would rather appeal to the reflection and experience of every man who is acquainted with more than one language, whether he has not often felt a translated thought, even when best executed, to be rather a cold inanimate bust, than a living counterpart of the original: whether he has not been affected by sentiments or descriptions in one language, in a degree which no power or skill can equal in another. Even the rudest languages have in some words and phrases, or some peculiarity of construction, their characteristic advantage; and the more copious and perfect a language is, the more must these advantages be multiplied. A bare chronicle of facts indeed, or a rigid demonstration in science, may perhaps be transferred from one to the other without loss or injury. For where the ideas are few, simple, and determinate, they readily find in all languages an adequate expression. But how shall the inspirations of genius and fancy be packed up, lettered, and consigned over, from hand to hand, in this literary traffic? How shall even the ordinary phraseology of moral reasoning, of sentiment, of opinion, preserve its native colouring, and exact features? How shall the language of varied passion, of tender feeling, of glowing description, find, in the distant region to which it is transported, the precise measure of its value? How, after this change of place and manners, where all is so new and so different, how shall it suit itself with the commodities adapted to its former wants and habits? Mere subsistence, it is true, the bread of life may be obtained every where. The great truths of religion, the bare theorems of science, whatever is addressed to the understanding strictly, may perhaps pass unimpaired. But all that constitutes the grace, the beauty, the charm, the dignity of composition, all that tends to awaken the fancy, or to affect the heart, like the finer and more volatile parts of substances, is lost during the experiment; or if these qualities be partially retained, they are in a manner the invention of the translator; and serve rather to tell us, that the original was excellent, than to present us with a view of that excellence itself.

The writer of an Article in the Edinburgh Review, on "Edgeworth's Professional Education," whose petulant sarcasms alternately provoke our spleen and our laughter, endeavours to convince the world, that, notwithstanding the advantage of Classical learning, the ascendancy it has acquired in English Education is preposterous, and the mode of teaching it in English Schools, and Universities, utterly absurd. I confess it was the reading of that article, which drew forth the present remarks, and I had designed a formal discussion of the false opinions and accusations contained in it. The bulk of this volume, however, swelling imperceptibly far beyond my first intention, induces me to contract the plan; and the truly meagre and flimsy texture of the article itself is hardly deserving of any solid criticism. There is a sprightliness, however, and vivacity, which takes with the world at first reading, and raises a transient admiration, which perhaps was the sole ambition of the writer: for, upon comparing one page with another, he seems wholly regardless of the dull virtue of consistency, and, like some popular divines, thinks only how he may keep up the requisite smartness for his fifteen minutes to amuse his audience.

He may think it injustice to compress his airy satire; but there is really not time for quoting him always in his own words. I could wish the reader of this chapter first to give an attentive perusal to the Reviewer, while I endeavour to exhibit his impeachment in distinct charges.

1st. That Classical learning forms the *sole* business of English Education.

2dly. That hence the taste and imagination only of the student are cultivated.

3dly. That the instruction of public schools and universities, even in Classical literature, is of a limited and mistaken kind.

4thly. That in Oxford particularly, every manly exercise of the reasoning powers is discouraged.

The first charge, besides being spun and twisted into the materials of every page, is also distinctly laid before us in the following terms.

> A young Englishman goes to school at six or seven years old: and he remains in a
> course of education till twenty-three or twenty-four years of age. In all that time, his
> sole and exclusive occupation is learning Latin and Greek.

From the manner in which the phrase *learning Latin and Greek* is used, one might be led to suppose that the Grammar and the Lexicon were the sole companions of the Student; that Latin and Greek were a sort of *black art*, something wholly unconnected with the system of nature and of human affairs; that the languages were learnt for the sake of the sound or form of the letters; not for the stores of taste and knowledge which they contain. What else is the Reviewer's notion of learning Greek? Can we be said to learn Greek, without making ourselves acquainted with the authors who wrote in Greek? A modern language may perhaps be learned without much of its literature: but how is it possible to separate the study of an ancient language from the study of those works in which it has been preserved? Of all known languages, the Greek perhaps is the most copious and extensive; and no one can pretend to call himself a master of it, who has not studied the several classes of authors in which its compass and variety is displayed. The language of Aristotle is as different from that of Homer, Sophocles, or Pindar, as these again are from Thucydides, Xenophon, or Demosthenes. It would be useless to pursue the topic through all its branches. Those who are acquainted with the subject will admit the statement as soon as it is made and those who are not, will hardly, I presume, apply to the Edinburgh Review for information about the Classics.

How idle then, how perfectly senseless, all this declamation about Latin and Greek! unless the study of Bacon, of Locke, of Milton, of Addison, and all our greatest moralists, historians, and poets, be rightly called *learning English*. What is to hinder the student from deriving all the benefit which the reading of valuable authors is supposed to impart? or rather, if these works are studied, how can he avoid deriving it?

Yet even Mr. Edgeworth, the author of the book which gives occasion to the Review, (although a writer not of the same empty class with the Reviewer, but one who to great ingenuity and vivacity adds much good sense, and gives many proofs of a good heart), even he is weak enough to say, "that young men intended for Clergymen should not go to any University, till they are *thoroughly masters of the learned languages, particularly of Greek.*" I am at a loss to conceive what so intelligent a writer could mean by this passage. The absurdity of teaching Greek, without teaching the best authors who have written in that language, appears to me so striking, that no words can make it more evident; and to suppose that these authors can be *thoroughly studied* before a young man goes to the University, or even during the whole time he stays there, is equally against reason and common sense.

The first charge then of this Reviewer, as far as it implies a study of language merely, is already answered. . . .

The second charge also requires no separate notice. If the Poets alone were selected by us out of the great mass of ancient learning, some ground might appear to exist for this complaint. But the fact is far otherwise: and facts are stubborn things.

The third charge is worked up with all the smirking pleasantry and pert playfulness peculiar to a certain school, whether consisting of Divines, or Lecturers, or Letter-writers, or Reviewers, whose main object seems to be, to have their laugh out, whatever truth or justice or decency or right reason may say to the contrary. And perhaps the wisest way is to let them have their laugh out. It is a miserable ambition, and its success need not be envied; provided the world are disposed to listen afterwards to plain sense and unvarnished truth. The whole system is ridiculed, by which the Classics are usually taught. It is not merely insinuated, but asserted, that the knowledge of minute points of Grammar and the mechanism of Latin verse are deemed the highest accomplishments of a Scholar—and that "his object is not to reason, *to imagine*, and to invent; but to conjugate, decline, and derive."

> The great system of facts with which he is most perfectly acquainted, are the intrigues of the Heathen Gods: with whom Pan slept?—with whom Jupiter?—whom Apollo ravished? These facts the English youth get by heart the moment they quit the nursery; and are most sedulously and industriously instructed in them till the best and most active part of life is passed away.

I have copied the very words of this filthy ribaldry, in order that the reader may judge of the pure virtuous indignation which glowed in the breast of the satirist who wrote it. The description is applied to the whole course of English Education, even to the advanced period of twenty-four. Now it is difficult to say how such an adversary is to be treated. To contradict him flatly, might be thought unmannerly; and yet that is the only treatment he properly deserves, who with wanton levity perverts the truth. If the passage had occurred in a farce, or burlesque comedy, we should forgive the falsehood for the sake of the humour; and because the writer himself does not expect to be believed. But this we are told by a person who affects in other passages the grave censor and indignant moralist, and who with a magisterial air, forsooth, after his play is over, vouchsafes his serious advice on the subject of Education. . . .

Let us now proceed to more important matters.

Upon the subject of school exercises scarcely any thing can be said, which has not been said long ago by writers of great authority. The opinions of *this* writer are of no value. In fact, it may be said of him, as of some late publishers of Sermons, that he has no opinions. One while he tells us, that the "imagination is too much cultivated"; at another, that the student's great object is not to *imagine*, but to learn the technical rules of grammar. In one page he objects to the study of ancient Metaphysics, Morals, and Politics, *"that the Greek alone is study enough without them"*; and in the next, that *"all the solid and masculine parts of the understanding are left wholly without cultivation."*

It may be curious however to see the real opinions of two illustrious writers on this point of school compositions. Milton rejects the practice altogether, and calls it "forcing the empty wits of children to compose themes, verses, and orations, which are the acts of ripest judgment, and the final work of a head filled, by long reading and observing, with elegant maxims and copious inventions. These are not matters," he continues, "to be wrung from poor striplings, like blood out of the nose, or the plucking of untimely fruit." He makes no difference between compositions, in Latin and English, in verse and prose: he equally proscribes them all.

Locke is just as adverse to the practice, and much more diffuse in his reasoning against it. "By all means," says he, "obtain, if you can, that your son be not employed in making

Latin themes and declamations, and, least of all, verses of any kind." He then proceeds to inveigh against all such exercises, especially in Latin; and condemns verses of every kind, chiefly for this reason. "If he has no genius to poetry, it is the most unreasonable thing in the world to torment a child, and waste his time about that which can never succeed; and if he have a poetic vein, it is to me the strangest thing in the world, that the father should desire or suffer it to be cherished or improved"; adding, in substance, "that it is not likely to promote his fortunes, but rather to make him poor and idle."

The sketch of "a complete and generous education" drawn by the first of these great masters, is magnificent indeed and imposing, but has never been thought reducible to practice, even by his fondest admirers. It is read, and will continue to be read, for its bold and large conceptions, and the majestic eloquence of its style—for that heavenly fancy, and that mighty soul which breathes through all his works, and which makes even his prejudices and his errors awful.

For the memory of the other I also feel sincere reverence, although his own opinions would have been entitled to greater respect, if he had himself treated with more deference the opinions of others who had gone before him, and the practice of sensible men of his own time, whose judgment was worth more, in proportion as it was confirmed by experience. The light freedom indeed, and the confidence with which this philosopher attacks all established notions, is one of the principal blemishes in his character. Intrepid and sagacious he certainly is; but these are not the only qualities requisite in a discoverer of truth; especially if the enquiry be of such a nature as to draw after it important practical consequences. Caution and respect for the opinions of others, in all cases, but more particularly in matters incapable of demonstration, are virtues not of the lowest order.

To these authorities, as in a matter of judgment and experience, we may surely oppose that of Cicero and Quintilian. Locke pronounces, that writing does not help towards good speaking. Cicero says, it is the best and most efficient preparation for it. Quintilian recommends it as a main part of the education of an Orator; and describes, with his usual candour and good sense, his own method in examining the compositions of his pupils So much for authority in this matter. The thing itself strikes every one at first sight as reasonable: and the experience of most persons concerned in education bears testimony to its use. Without some exercise in composition, the student, who has read even the best authors, feels a difficulty and embarrassment in arranging his thoughts on any given subject, in connecting, illustrating, and adorning them. Just as in the conduct of life, if he has never been accustomed to think or act for himself, although he may have lived among the purest examples, yet when called upon to act or reason, he is apt to be disconcerted, diffident, and confused. In fact, the utility, and almost necessity, of *practice* is so received a maxim, that we may fairly demand the strongest proof against it, before we give way. Milton's reason does not meet the question. It is not for the value *to us* of what the boy writes, that we impose the task, but for the benefit of the exercise to himself.

To write well is, as he justly calls it, "the act of ripest judgment"; it is the last best fruit of an educated mind: but without previous effort and training, it is idle to expect that these manly virtues will ever arrive at maturity. That finished offspring of genius starts not, like Minerva from the head of Jupiter, perfect at once in stature, and clad in complete armour: but is the produce of slow birth, and often of a hard delivery; the tender nursing of many an infant year—the pupil of a severe school, formed and chastened by a persevering discipline.

The same reply may be made to the objection against verses. It is not that we seek to stock the world with new poems, but to give play in the most effectual manner to the *poetic faculty*, which exists, to a certain degree in all minds, and which, like every other faculty, ought to lie wholly uncultivated in none. At least it is an irreparable injury to young minds, if it be entirely neglected. They may still be useful members in the mechanism of society, if the powers of reasoning and calculation only be encouraged: but they lose that intellectual charm, from which life borrows its loveliest graces; they lose, in a refined age, the means of recommending Virtue herself, if taste and elegance be not found in her train. The reasoning of Locke on this subject does, I confess, appear to me sordid and illiberal. He says, indeed, in a phrase not very intelligible, that we must be careful how we "make anything a boy's business but downright virtue." But the improvement of the faculties which God has implanted in us, is surely itself a virtue. Our attention may be given in undue measure to one, and may violate that just harmony, without which nothing is virtuous, nothing lovely. But the faculty itself, which he condemns, was one of the kindest gifts of heaven. And why then should man be niggardly where Providence has been bountiful? Why should he think scorn of that pleasant land, and undervalue those fair possessions, which were not thought beneath the care even of the Almighty? In the garden of Eden, we read, was made to grow, not only what was good for food, but every tree also that was pleasant to the sight: and in that garden man was placed, to keep it, and to dress it.

That in some schools too much stress is laid upon this accomplishment, I will not take upon me to deny. Let the excess, where it is an excess, be blamed and corrected. The reproach of the Reviewer, however, extends equally to the Universities: and here I can undertake to affirm, the charge is false. If any thing, the fault lies on the other side. Verses, especially Latin verses, are looked upon as a boyish exercise; and although it is the practice not to call for this exercise, except from those who are known to excel in it, yet even this limited demand is seldom satisfied. So prevalent is the conviction, that the highest excellence alone can give it dignity; and that other roads to distinction are open, in which every degree of merit will command respect. Its utility, however, even in the lower department of elegiac verse, is not generally understood. It imparts a habit of compression without obscurity; a habit of selecting the fittest materials, and of setting them in the nicest order; and a command of pure, terse, and polished diction, which cannot long be practised without imparting a salutary tincture to all other kinds of composition. Still, I admit, it is not a principal, but a subordinate feature, in every sound plan of education; and the farther we advance in life, the more urgently do other claims press upon us.

It is time however to notice the fourth charge of the Reviewer, the substance of which is, "that in Oxford particularly, every manly exercise of the reasoning powers is discouraged."

The best answer to this will be given in the account of our studies; and something, I trust, has been already said in refutation of it, when the false estimate made of the nature of Classical learning was exposed. The student undergoes a close examination in the *subject matter* of all he reads, and some of the works most read are no light exercise of the understanding. Strict Logic, Divinity, and Mathematical theorems, whether pure or mixed, cannot fail to discipline the reasoning powers; and these form a part of the studies in every College. There are lectures read in Experimental Philosophy, in Astronomy, in Chemistry, in Mineralogy, and in Botany: how far these pursuits *exercise* the student's mind, can only be collected from the general tendency of such studies. They do not enter (except the two first, and these at the option of the candidate) into the examination for degrees; and as they are taught not by Tutors, but by public Professors, it cannot well be ascertained what impression they make on each individual.

In reply however to the frivolous impertinence about checking the progress of science, and keeping us back to the measure of the ancients, let it suffice to state, that a rank fallacy runs through the whole argument. The writer confounds the *cultivation of literature* with the *acquisition of science*. In the former, unless our models be defective, which is not attempted to be shewn, the study of those models must be as beneficial now as ever. In the latter, the ancients are not made our guides. We study them for the facts, the reasonings, the descriptions, the characters and the sentiments, for the principles and the examples of pure taste, which they contain. These must ever be what they once were, and their relative importance must ever remain the same. It is not the discovery of neutral salts, or the decomposition of alkalis, that can alter the value of ancient literature—that can make eloquence less powerful, poetry less charming, historical example less forcible, or moral and political reflections less instructive. Where then is the wisdom of bringing into comparison things which have no common points of relation; which are in fact heterogeneous, and incommensurate with each other? Whatever may be the advancement later ages have made in the knowledge of the properties of bodies, the temper and constitution of the human mind cannot have changed; and the writers best adapted to make impression there, if we turn not stupidly and sullenly away, will perform their office now as heretofore.

Never let us believe that the improvement of chemical arts, however much it may tend to the augmentation of national riches, can supersede the use of that intellectual laboratory, where the sages of Greece explored the hidden elements of which man consists, and faithfully recorded all their discoveries. Never let us permit the volumes which inclose these early records, which present us with a distinct view, not only of the results, but of each varied process in all its stages; never let us permit them to moulder and perish as they lie, insensible of that kind Providence which preserved them through their long and dark voyage, and of those heroic efforts which baffled all the fury of ignorance, and enabled them to ride out the storm in safety. Some indeed have unhappily foundered in their course; but even of these, the scattered wreck has been washed in by the waves, and proves to us, while we gather along the shore its glittering fragments, how precious the lading was which has been cast away.

If, in the search for these dismembered parts, something more than sober reason would dictate has been felt, some devotional passion, as for "the torn body of a martyred saint," why should we scoff at the honest toil, and not rather admire and applaud the zeal which sustains it? As the feigned wandering of that Egyptian Queen for her lost Osiris, or, as the nobler fable tells, though born in later days, of the Virgin Truth, whose lovely form, once so perfect and glorious to look upon, was by a race of wicked deceivers hewn into a thousand pieces, and scattered to the four winds; so has it been with the body of ancient learning, mangled and dispersed as it was throughout the world. And it is only by long search and painful diligence, that limb after limb has been found, and restored in some measure to that form of perfect beauty which it once had. The service surely is entitled to our thanks and praise: and that enthusiasm, which magnifies the value even of the minutest relic, will meet with respect and forgiveness among liberal minds. Mockery we know will always be the engine of vulgar malice, to undermine that which overtops itself; and envy will affect to despise what it does not and cannot possess. But from the more enlightened class, especially from those who hold up the torch of criticism, and pour its useful beams to the remote corners of our island, it is not too much to expect that the peaceful and inoffensive pursuits of learning may be shielded from scorn and calumny—that they will not at least themselves wantonly attack them with rude clamour or insulting sarcasm, and least of all *fabricate* abuses for the sake of venting their spleen, or displaying the vain talent of wit and raillery.

CHAPTER V

. . . Upon this subject I have already treated at some length in the third Chapter. But the fallacy is of such perpetual recurrence, that I must request a little farther attention while the solidity of this pretension is accurately examined. *Utility,* if it means any thing, means that which is conducive to some good end. Thus a thing may be useful which is not good in itself, provided it lead to what is good. It is the value of the end, which must determine the value of the means. And if a question arise concerning the comparative utility of two things, it can only be determined by considering the nature of the ends to which they respectively lead.

Now all those arts and studies which relate to the improvement of manufactures, and to the raising or multiplying the means of subsistence, terminate merely in the bodily wants of man. Our houses are better furnished, our table may be better supplied, our travelling more commodious; and all these are very desirable ends. But will any man who aspires to the name of philosopher maintain, that these are the principal ends of human life—that a rational being is most nobly occupied in supplying his bodily wants—in ministering to the caprices of fashion in dress, in building, in equipage, or in diet? There surely is some object paramount to all these, for which his faculties are fitted, and towards which they receive from nature some secret impulse and bias; an impulse which he is enabled to obey, in proportion as the pressure of those other motives is lessened, which are inferior in dignity, although prior in necessity. To make *necessity* the standard of what is praiseworthy or honourable, is against the uniform judgment of mankind. If that position were admitted, the lowest employments of life are unjustly depressed: for what services are more necessary than those which provide us with food and raiment? If the other wants and pleasures of life could not be consulted, without a sacrifice of these, no man could hesitate to which to give the preference. It is only on the presumption that these can be supplied by ordinary hands, and that there is time and labour enough at the disposal of society for other purposes, that we can at all justify those less necessary pursuits, which engage the attention of the higher departments in civilized life. This universal testimony of mankind, uncalled for and undesigned, appears to me the strongest evidence for the reasonableness of that distinction which every where prevails, and which admits only of such variations as local and accidental peculiarities naturally cause. The main principle is not only observable, but is prominent under all these variations, and has been so in all ages of the world.

Still we are continually reminded, that solid and useful attainments are preferable to those which are less necessary, and which adorn rather than support life. I readily grant that they are so: but only when brought into *competition* with each other. It is only when we are called upon to *make a choice between two*—when we cannot *have both*. We must build our house before we furnish it: but he who supplies the library and the pictures may surely be allowed to rank above the artificer that raised the walls and framed the roof.

Neither can any distinction be justly made between the case of *manual* and *intellectual* labour. They cannot indeed be altogether separated, even in the lowest occupations. And where the labour is purely intellectual, I do not see how its dignity can be measured by the tendency it has to satisfy the bodily wants of men. It is not, at least, a self-evident proposition; which this Reviewer presumes it to be. And if it be true, much more reason does there seem for measuring the mechanical and corporeal employments of life by that standard. But it is *not true*, and never will be *established* in the opinions of men. It may be brought forward upon occasion, like many other plausible deceptions, to serve a temporary purpose, to excite odium against one party, or to acquire popular favour for another; and the mischief may be great for a time, although the delusion cannot be lasting.

There must be surely a cultivation of mind, which is itself a good: a good of the highest order; without any immediate reference to bodily appetites, or wants of any kind. Of this cultivation I should say, as of many professions and trades, that it must not be allowed to *interfere* with duties of a plainer kind. If they cannot *both* be allowed in the same society, that which is least necessary must give way. But in the present case, such is not the question. No pretence is set up, that an undue proportion is withdrawn from the general population, and employed in these studies; but that the *studies themselves* are frivolous, because they do not immediately tend to what is called *practical* good.

There are, it is true, emergencies of so imperious a nature, that they seem, while they last, to exalt the merit of him who relieves them, above that of every other service. An emergency of this kind is war. But no one surely can desire war on its own account. No sincere Christian, or friend to mankind, can wish the profession of arms to be extended beyond the necessity of the case. The necessity may be lamented, but, after the unvarying experience the world has had, it is the weak and visionary theorist only that can expect to see it altogether removed. And having this experience before us, any system of national education would be *wrong*, which unfitted men for that state of things—any system would be *imperfect*, which had not some tendency, direct or indirect, to fit them for it. And if Classical education be regarded in this light, there is none in which it will be found more faultless. A high sense of honour, a disdain of death in a good cause, a passionate devotion to the welfare of one's country, a love of enterprise, and a love of glory, are among the first sentiments, which those studies communicate to the mind. And as their efficacy is undoubted in correcting the narrow habits and prejudices to which the separation of the professions gives birth; so in the rough school of war is it more especially exemplified, in mitigating the tone of that severe instructor, and in softening some of his hardest features.

But I will not return, however attractive the theme, to a consideration of the merits of the best Classic writers. The praises we bestow upon them will be regarded by our adversaries, not as *proofs*, but as *encomiums*; and if what has been said is not sufficient, there is nothing, I believe, that can be said, to convince a hesitating and candid enquirer, how naturally they tend to inspire just and elevated thoughts; thoughts not merely adapted to solitude and contemplation, but to the intercourse of social life, and to the discharge of its most active duties.

Let me be permitted however, before I quit the subject, to transcribe a passage from the same Review; written at a time when candour and liberal sentiment towards English Universities were not unknown to it.

> It is the respect which men of rank in England usually pay to a Classical education, that drew from our Author the following compliment, in which we heartily join, in favour of our southern neighbours, and which is valuable, as coming from a man little accustomed to the complimentary style. "We ought to judge in matters of education, rather from experience than from mere reasoning. We should enquire what nation has produced the most active, and the greatest men; not indeed the greatest number of compilers and of book makers, but of the most intrepid, the most acute, accomplished, and magnanimous characters? This is very probably the English nation."

If such be the advantages of a system founded in the study of ancient literature, it cannot be an object of indifference with the nation, to see it firmly established and well endowed. To preserve and uphold with due care this venerable edifice, a large appropriation both of the men and of the property of the country may well be made. Many there certainly ought to be, whose peculiar office should lead them to examine diligently all its parts, to bring together such materials as are necessary to counteract decay, to maintain its solidity, to cleanse, to improve and embellish it. But it is the *free communication of its use to the public*, which is their leading purpose; and, according as that duty is well or ill performed, the judgment of the public should be pronounced.

That some of its apartments might not be arranged more commodiously, or furnished better, is more than I would presume to say. But on the subject of Political Economy, of which we now hear so much, I will venture a few observations in our defense.

This is, beyond a doubt, of all sciences relating to human interests, that in which the greatest progress has been made in modern times; and much honour is due to those writers who have let in light upon this hitherto obscure and unfrequented track. But the effect of novelty and discovery is to attract for a season an undue proportion of public favour. Such appears to me to have been the mistake with regard to Political Economy: and, in many instances, it has been a dangerous, if not a mischievous mistake: for the attainment of this science seems almost to have supplanted all the other branches of knowledge requisite for a statesman; to have often narrowed his views, and to have made him regard every public measure simply in the relation it bears to national wealth. But this object, as I have already contended, and ever will contend, against the clamorous sciolists of the day, is not the prime business of true policy. However important and even necessary it may be, it is a subordinate and not a predominant concern in public affairs—not less than the management and improvement of an estate in private life is an inferior duty to the education of children, the maintenance of character, and the guidance of a house.

Still it cannot be disputed, that the science has a tendency, if rightly studied, to enlarge the mind, and that it will enable a man to perform many of the relative duties of life, both public and private, more correctly. On this account the introduction of it into the Lectures on Modern History has always appeared to me a great improvement; and the still farther extension of the same enquiry would, I am persuaded, be much approved.

Its great leading principles however are soon acquired: the ordinary reading of the day supplies them. And with the majority of students, the more accurate study and investigation of its theorems may well be reserved for those situations and occasions, in which many of them will be placed at some future season, and which afford ample time for the completion of such enquiries. When combined with practical exertions, and called forth by particular occasions, these studies gain a firmer hold, and are pursued with more eager interest. The mind should indeed be early disciplined and fitted for that work: but the work itself may be done when the time comes.

It is a folly to think that every thing which a man is to know must be taught him while young; as if he were to spring at once from College, and be intrusted with the immediate management of the world; as if life had no intervals for extending knowledge: as if intellectual exercise and the act of learning were unbecoming the state of manhood.

With regard to this science in particular, there are many points in it, which make me think it a fitter employment for the mind in an advanced period of life, than when the affections are young and growing, and liable to be cramped and stunted by the views of human nature which it continually presents. There is perhaps something in all theoretical views of society, which tends to harden the feelings, and to represent man as a blind part of a blind machine. The frame-work of that great structure must, we know, be put together upon such principles. And the more enlarged our sphere of action is, the more correct and luminous ought our notions to be of their relative power and importance. But by far the greater part of those who are educated for active professions have less occasion for contemplating these abstract notions, than for adapting themselves promptly to the limited relations of life in which they are placed; and in which the remedy of evils caused by the friction of the machine and by external accident, requires not that comprehensive view of its whole construction to be for ever present to the mind. It is not then that I would keep these truths out of sight; it is not that I would deny the utility of them in every sphere and condition; but where a choice is left us among many pursuits, all of which are in their several degrees beneficial, I would be very cautious how that was singled out and made predominant, which is so prone to usurp over the rest, and the abuse of which is not a laughable, but a serious evil.

Much we are told from day to day of the folly of pedantry. The folly is indeed ridiculous, and it is seldom spared. But the pedant in chemistry, or in physics, is at least as disagreeable an animal as the pedant in classical learning; and the pedant in political economy is not disagreeable only, but dangerous. And if a prospect were open to a young man of a period of leisure after his term of college-study should be expired, it seems more advisable to lay the foundation for this science by exercising his mind in sound Logic and in Mathematical reasoning, upon which any other system of close and severe reasoning may soon be built, than to run the risk of sacrificing that more generous discipline, which, if not imparted at an early period of life, is seldom acquired afterwards.

Never, while the world lasts, will it be wholly disabused of that specious error, that the more there is crammed into a young man's mind, whether it stays there or not, whether it is digested or not, still the wiser he is. And writings such as those which I have been examining, smart, witty, and confident, tend to confirm this diseased habit of thinking, and to spread the contagion. A half educated father hears that lectures are read in Chemistry, Botany, Mineralogy, &c. &c. at one place, and his son is learning nothing of this sort at school. Incapable of judging how mental powers are improved by continual exercise, and how the moral character is in a great measure formed by the study of good authors, he fancies that when the grammar of a language is learnt, all farther attention to that language is lost time—that there is nothing new gained, because there is no new name. If the boy is captivated by the novelty and variety of the studies which are presented to him, he seldom returns with any relish to philological pursuits. He may become a skilful agriculturist, an improver of manufactures, a useful inspector of roads, mines, and canals: but all that distinguishing grace, which a liberal education imparts, he foregoes for ever. It cannot be acquired in a later period of life, if the morning of his days have been occupied with other cares, and the intellectual habits already settled in different forms and postures. If, as too often happens, these matters are received into the ears, but take no possession of the mind, there is not only a moral blank, but an intellectual barrenness—a poverty of fancy and invention, a dearth of historical and poetical illustration, a want of all those ideas which decorate and enliven truth, which enable us to live over again the times that are past, to combine the produce of widely distant ages, and to multiply into one another the component parts of each. The experiment is a cruel one. I have seen it tried; and have witnessed the melancholy and irreparable result.

On the contrary, if this liberal instruction be first provided, and if the intellect be duly prepared by correct Logic, and pure Mathematical science, there is no analysis, which the business of life may afterwards call upon him to investigate, beyond the reach of a moderate understanding. The habit of discrimination, the power of stating a question distinctly, and of arguing with perspicuity, are of much greater importance than the hasty acquisition of miscellaneous knowledge. Not that I would be understood to exclude the study of those matters from a University. They are taught, and esteemed and encouraged here: but we do not deny that they are the subordinate, and not the leading, business of education: and (what I think should never be forgotten) they are much more easily attained by a well disciplined mind, after he enters into life, than the other studies upon which we lay the greatest stress.

If it be seriously complained of as a defect, that scepticism either in philosophy or religion is discountenanced, I can only pity the folly of the writer who could advance so untenable a position. If indeed the object of education be to distract the mind of the student, to make his opinions loose, wavering, and inconstant, instead of guiding his choice, assessing his judgment, and concentrating his powers, then we must admit that we are altogether under a mistake. If he was sent here, not to be fed with what we believed to be the most wholesome diet, but to be turned adrift amongst a medley of all sorts of food and all sorts of poison, and left to choose for himself, then indeed have we to learn our duty, and to begin at that point where we have hitherto fancied education ought to end. But the wretched absurdity of this doctrine is too manifest to bear a question. It must seem like trifling to attempt its refutation. . . .

Thomas Arnold

1795–1842

It is no wisdom to make boys prodigies of information; but it is our wisdom and our duty to cultivate their faculties each in its season, first the memory and imagination, and then the judgment; to furnish them with the means, and to excite the desire, of improving themselves, and to wait with confidence for God's blessing on the result.

USE OF THE CLASSICS

Thomas Arnold, headmaster of Rugby boys' school, was born in East Cowes on the Isle of Wight off the south coast of England. He was educated at Winchester and at Corpus Christi College, Oxford. For about four years he was a fellow of Oriel College, Oxford, while Edward Copleston was provost there. An ordained deacon in the Church of England, Arnold involved himself in pressing questions of church reform, church establishment, and Catholic emancipation, and was considered for a bishopric. Politically he was a Whig, favoring a range of political and social reforms, but remaining pessimistic about the future. He founded a school at Laleham and then became the famous headmaster of Rugby, transforming the school into a peer of Eton and a model for school reform throughout England.

Arnold focused on Christian piety, character formation, and intellectual development. He preached weekly sermons (considered by some to be the finest of the age), encouraged team sports, and expanded the curriculum to include mathematics, French, and modern history. Classics, however, continued to constitute about half the curriculum. Arnold's Rugby was immortalized in his student Thomas Hughes's *Tom Brown's Schooldays* (1857).

Arnold distinguished himself as a scholar with a three-volume edition of Thucydides (1830–35), a three-volume *History of Rome* (1838–43), and numerous shorter works. He was appointed Regius Professor of Modern History at Oxford the year before his death.

His son Thomas was a professor of English literature under John Henry Newman at the Catholic University of Ireland. His son Matthew, author of *Culture and Anarchy* (1869), became one of the most celebrated men of letters in Victorian England.

THE SELECTION

Arnold's article, "Rugby School—Use of the Classics," appeared in the *Quarterly Journal of Education* in 1834. The first part of the article (omitted here) briefly describes Rugby's system of education at the time, including a chart of the distribution of the curriculum among the "forms" (the school grades). In the section reproduced here, Arnold defends the "usefulness" of the Greek and Latin languages and authors in a modern, practical age. At the very least, these classical authors are the foundation of the Western mind.

from "Rugby School—Use of the Classics"

In any statement of the business of a school, such as has been given above, there will be an unintentional exaggeration, unless the reader makes due allowance for the difference between the theory of any institution and its practical working. But on the other hand, a reader unacquainted with the real nature of a classical education, will be in danger of undervaluing it, when he sees that so large a portion of time at so important a period of human life is devoted to the study of a few ancient writers, whose works seem to have no direct bearing on the studies and duties of our own generation. For instance, although some provision is undoubtedly made at Rugby for acquiring a knowledge of modern history, yet the History of Greece and Rome is more studied than that of France and England; and Homer and Virgil are certainly much more attended to than Shakespeare and Milton. This appears to many persons a great absurdity; while others who are so far swayed by authority as to believe the system to be right, are yet unable to understand how it can be so. A journal of education may not be an unfit place for a few remarks on this subject.

It may freely be confessed that the first origin of classical education affords in itself no reasons for its being continued now. When Latin and Greek were almost the only written languages of civilized man, it is manifest that they must have furnished the subjects of all liberal education. The question therefore is wholly changed, since the growth of a complete literature in other languages; since France, and Italy, and Germany, and England, have each produced their philosophers, their poets, and their historians, worthy to be placed on the same level with those of Greece and Rome.

But although there is not the *same* reason now which existed three or four centuries ago for the study of Greek and Roman literature, yet there is another no less substantial. Expel Greek and Latin from your schools, and you confine the views of the existing generation to themselves and their immediate predecessors: you will cut off so many centuries of the world's experience, and place us in the same state as if the human race had first come into existence in the year 1500. For it is nothing to say that a few learned individuals might still study classical literature; the effect produced on the public mind would be no greater than that which has resulted from the labours of our oriental scholars; it would not spread beyond themselves, and men in general after a few generations would know as little of Greece and Rome, as they do actually of China and Hindostan. But such an ignorance would be incalculably more to be regretted. With the Asiatic mind, we have no nearer connexion or sympathy than that which is derived from our common humanity. But the mind of the Greek and of the Roman is in all the essential points of its constitution our own; and not only so, but it is our own mind developed to an extraordinary degree of perfection. Wide as is the difference between us with respect to those physical instruments which minister to our uses or our pleasures; although the Greeks and Romans had no steam-engines, no printing-presses, no mariner's compass, no telescopes, no microscopes, no gunpowder; yet in our moral and political views, in those matters which most determine human character, there is a perfect resemblance in these respects. Aristotle, and Plato, and Thucydides, and Cicero, and Tacitus, are most untruly called ancient writers; they are virtually our own countrymen and contemporaries, but have the advantage which is enjoyed by intelligent travellers, that their observation has been exercised in a field out of the reach of common men; and that having thus seen in a manner with our eyes what we cannot see for ourselves, their conclusions are such as bear upon our own circumstances, while their information has all the charm of novelty, and all the value of a mass of new and pertinent facts, illustrative of the great science of the nature of civilized man.

Now when it is said, that men in manhood so often throw their Greek and Latin aside, and that this very fact shows the uselessness of their early studies, it is much more true to say that it shows how completely the literature of Greece and Rome would be forgotten, if our system of education did not keep up the knowledge of it. But it by no means shows that system to be useless, unless it followed that when a man laid aside his Greek and Latin books, he forgot also all that he had ever gained from them. This, however, is so far from being the case, that even where the results of a classical education are least tangible, and least appreciated even by the individual himself, still the mind often retains much of the effect of its early studies in the general liberality of its tastes and comparative comprehensiveness of its views and notions.

All this supposes, indeed, that classical instruction should be sensibly conducted; it requires that a classical teacher should be fully acquainted with modern history and modern literature, no less than with those of Greece and Rome. What is, or perhaps what used to be, called a mere scholar, cannot possibly communicate to his pupils the main advantages of a classical education. The knowledge of the past is valuable, because without it our knowledge of the present and of the future must be scanty; but if the knowledge of the past be confined wholly to itself, if, instead of being made to bear upon things around us, it be totally isolated from them, and so disguised by vagueness and misapprehension as to appear incapable of illustrating them, then indeed it becomes little better than laborious trifling, and they who declaim against it may be fully forgiven. . . .

In the statement of the business of Rugby School which has been given above, one part of it will be found to consist of works of modern history. An undue importance is attached by some persons to this circumstance, and those who would care little to have their sons familiar with the history of the Peloponnesian war are delighted that they should study the Campaigns of Frederic the Great or of Napoleon. Information about modern events is more useful, they think, than that which relates to antiquity; and such information they wish to be given to their children.

This favourite notion of filling boys with useful information is likely, we think, to be productive of some mischief. It is a caricature of the principles of inductive philosophy, which, while it taught the importance of a knowledge of facts, never imagined that this knowledge was of itself equivalent to wisdom. Now it is not so much our object to give boys "useful information," as to facilitate their gaining it hereafter for themselves, and to enable them to turn it to account when gained. The first is to be effected by supplying them on any subject with a skeleton which they may fill up hereafter. For instance, a real knowledge of history in after life is highly desirable; let us see how education can best facilitate the gaining of it. It should begin by impressing on a boy's mind the names of the greatest men of different periods, and by giving him a notion of their order in point of time, and the part of the earth on which they lived. This is best done by a set of pictures bound up together in a volume, such, for instance, as those which illustrated Mrs. Trimmer's little histories, and to which the writer of this article is glad to acknowledge his own early obligations. Nor could better service be rendered to the cause of historical instruction than by publishing a volume of prints of universal history, accompanied with a very short description of each. Correctness of costume in such prints, or good taste in the drawing, however desirable if they can be easily obtained, are of very subordinate importance: the great matter is that the print should be striking, and full enough to excite and to gratify curiosity. By these means a lasting association is obtained with the greatest names in history, and the most remarkable actions of their lives: while their chronological arrangement is learnt at the same time from the order of the pictures; a boy's memory being very apt to recollect the place which a favourite print holds in a volume, whether it comes towards the beginning, middle, or end, what picture comes before it, and what follows it. Such pictures should contain as much as possible the poetry of history: the most striking characters, and most heroic actions, whether of doing or of suffering; but they should not embarrass themselves with its philosophy, with the causes of revolutions, the progress of society, or the merits of great political questions. Their use is of another kind, to make some great name, and great action of every period, familiar to the mind; that so in taking up any more detailed history or biography, (and education should never forget the importance of preparing a boy to derive benefit from his accidental reading,) he may have some association with the subject of it, and may not feel himself to be on ground wholly unknown to him. He may thus be led to open volumes into which he would otherwise have never thought of looking: he need not read them through—indeed it is sad folly to require either man or boy to read through every book they look at, but he will see what is said about such and such persons or actions; and then he will learn by the way something about other persons and other actions; and will have his stock of associations increased, so as to render more and more information acceptable to him.

After this foundation, the object still being rather to create an appetite for knowledge than to satisfy it, it would be desirable to furnish a boy with histories of one or two particular countries, Greece, Rome, and England, for instance, written at no great length, and these also written poetically much more than philosophically, with much liveliness of style, and force of painting, so as to excite an interest about the persons and things spoken of. The absence of all instruction in politics or political economy, nay even an absolute erroneousness of judgment on such matters, provided always that it involves no wrong principle in morality, are comparatively of slight importance. Let the boy gain, if possible, a strong appetite for knowledge to begin with; it is a later part of education which should enable him to pursue it sensibly, and to make it, when obtained, wisdom.

But should his education, as is often the case, be cut short by circumstances, so that he never receives its finishing lessons, will he not feel the want of more direct information and instruction in its earlier stages? The answer is, that every thing has its proper season, and if summer be cut out of the year, it is vain to suppose that the work of summer can be forestalled in spring. Undoubtedly, much is lost by this abridgment of the term of education, and it is well to insist strongly upon the evil, as it might, in many instances, be easily avoided. But if it is unavoidable, the evil consequences arising from it cannot be prevented. Fulness of knowledge and sagacity of judgment are fruits not to be looked for in early youth; and he who endeavours to force them does but interfere with the natural growth of the plant, and prematurely exhaust its vigour.

In the common course of things, however, where a young person's education is not interrupted, the later process is one of exceeding importance and interest. Supposing a boy to possess that outline of general history which his prints and his abridgments will have given him, with his associations, so far as they go, strong and lively, and his desire of increased knowledge keen, the next thing to be done is to set him to read some first-rate historian, whose mind was formed in, and bears the stamp of, some period of advanced civilization, analogous to that in which we now live. In other words, he should read Thucydides or Tacitus, or any writer equal to them, if such can be found, belonging to the third period of full civilization, that of modern Europe since the middle ages. The particular subject of the history is of little moment, so long as it be taken neither from the barbarian, nor from the romantic, but from the philosophical or civilized stage of human society; and so long as the writer be a man of commanding mind, who has fully imbibed the influences of his age, yet without bearing its exclusive impress. And the study of such a work under an intelligent teacher becomes indeed the key of knowledge and of wisdom: first it affords an example of good historical evidence, and hence the pupil may be taught to notice from time to time the various criteria of a credible narrative, and by the rule of contraries to observe what are the indications of a testimony questionable, suspicious, or worthless. Undue scepticism may be repressed by showing how generally truth has been attained when it has been honestly and judiciously sought; while credulity may be checked by pointing out, on the other hand, how manifold are the errors into which those are betrayed whose intellect or whose principles have been found wanting. Now too the time is come when the pupil may be introduced to that high philosophy which unfolds "the causes of things." The history with which he is engaged presents a view of society in its most advanced state, when the human mind is highly developed, and the various crises which affect the growth of the political fabric are all overpast. Let him be taught to analyze the subject thus presented to him; to trace back institutions, civil and religious, to their origin; to explore the elements of the national character, as now exhibited in maturity, in the vicissitudes of the nation's fortune, and the moral and physical qualities of its race; to observe how the morals and the mind of the people have been subject to a succession of influences, some accidental, others regular; to see and remember what critical seasons of improvement have been neglected, what besetting evils have been wantonly aggravated by wickedness or folly. In short, the pupil may be furnished as it were with certain formulae, which shall enable him to read all history beneficially; which shall teach him what to look for in it, how to judge of it, and how to apply it.

Education will thus fulfil its great business, as far as regards the intellect, to inspire it with a desire of knowledge, and to furnish it with power to obtain and to profit by what it seeks for. And a man thus educated, even though he knows no history in detail but that which is called ancient, will be far better fitted to enter on public life than he who could tell the circumstances and the date of every battle and every debate throughout the last century; whose information in the common sense of the term, about modern history, might be twenty times more minute. The fault of systems of classical education in some instances has been, not that they did not teach modern history, but that they did not prepare and dispose their pupils to acquaint themselves with it afterwards; not that they did not attempt to raise an impossible superstructure, but that they did not prepare the ground for the foundation, and put the materials within reach of the builder.

That impatience, which is one of the diseases of the age, is in great danger of possessing the public mind on the subject of education; an unhealthy restlessness may succeed to lethargy. Men are not contented with sowing the seed unless they can also reap the fruit; forgetting how often it is the law of our condition, that "one soweth and another reapeth." It is no wisdom to make boys prodigies of information; but it is our wisdom and our duty to cultivate their faculties each in its season, first the memory and imagination, and then the judgment; to furnish them with the means, and to excite the desire, of improving themselves, and to wait with confidence for God's blessing on the result.

John Henry Newman

1801–90

*You see, then, gentlemen, here are two methods of Education;
the one aspires to be philosophical, the other to be mechanical;
the one rises toward ideas, the other is exhausted upon what is
particular and external.*

IDEA OF A UNIVERSITY, DISCOURSE V

John Henry Newman, liberal learning's preeminent defender, was born in London and
reared in the Anglican Church by pious parents, who introduced him to Calvinist theology and British evangelicalism. From ages seven to fifteen, Newman attended boarding
school at the respectable Great Ealing School near London. There he studied Latin authors, Greek, French, music, and mathematics, and acted in school plays. He then went to
Oxford, where he continued his intense study of the classics and mathematics, earning his
B.A. from Trinity College in 1820. In 1822, Newman was elected to a fellowship at Oriel
College, the center of Oxford's intellectual life at the time. Within the next few years, he
was ordained in the Church of England, became a tutor at Oriel, and began his long service
as vicar of St. Mary's University Church, an appointment he held until 1843. At Oriel,
Newman's outlook on education was influenced by Provost Edward Copleston and by the
lingering spirit of John Davison and Thomas Arnold.

Copleston and Davison's battle with utilitarian education formed Newman's own conception and rhetorical defense of liberal education. His systematic study of the Church
Fathers led him to embrace high-church Anglicanism and to publish, in 1833, his first
book, *The Arians of the Fourth Century*. His preaching and writing established his reputation as a master of English oratory and prose. 1833 also marked the beginning of the Oxford Movement (or Tractarianism), in which Newman played a leading role. The Oxford
Movement stirred controversy by fighting against state interference in church affairs and

520

advocating the restoration of Anglo-Catholicism within the Church of England. In 1845, at the midpoint of his life, Newman converted to Roman Catholicism, and two years later he was ordained a Catholic priest.

In 1851, Newman was asked by Catholic bishops in Ireland to advise them on the estab-lishment of a Catholic university in Dublin. Newman became the university's first president that same year. The public lectures he delivered on education in 1852 were published as the *Discourses on the Scope and Nature of University Education,* and later expanded with the ad-dition of other lectures into the landmark book *The Idea of a University* (1873 and sub-sequent revised editions). Achieving mixed success as an administrator, Newman left Dublin in 1858. He wrote a classic spiritual autobiography, the *Apologia pro Vita Sua* (1864 and 1865), and was later elected an honorary fellow of Trinity College (1877) and appointed a cardinal by Pope Leo XIII (1879).

THE SELECTIONS

In *The Idea of a University,* Newman attempts to define the university according to its end or purpose. The university is not a church, or seminary, or scientific academy, he writes. Rather, it is a place that teaches universal knowledge (see Discourse II). Its range of subjects provides students with an enlarged and connected view of knowledge. It offers not exhaustive knowledge of detail and data, but a complete education that connects the circle of learning, that compares truth with truth, and maintains due proportion among the parts. At least eight times in *The Idea of the University,* Newman speaks of the desire to "see things as they are" (or some variation on this goal). These words echo Matthew Arnold's poetic praise of Sophocles, who, says Arnold, "saw life steadily, and saw it whole" (from his poem, "To a Friend"). This is liberal learning's noble telos. Modern education's deadening tendency, in contrast, is to focus increasingly on the temporal, earthly, tan-gible, fragmented, and abstract. Newman rejects an encroaching philosophy of education driven by Enlightenment secularism, imperialistic Baconianism, and Lockean utilitarian-ism.

The Idea of a University is one of the greatest English prose works of the nineteenth cen-tury, and justice to its structure and content demands that it be read in its entirety. It should also be supplemented by *University Sketches* (1856), Newman's observations on education from Greek and Roman antiquity through the Middle Ages and into the nineteenth century. Newman's philosophy of education ought to be regarded as part of a continuously devel-oping idea passed on in the West since the time of Homer. As Newman biographer A. Dwight Culler wrote, "The ideal ruler of Plato, the ideal orator of Aristotle and Cicero, the medieval saint, the perfect prince and poet of the Renaissance—these are the figures from which Newman's ideal of the perfect student is descended. . . ."[1]

Discourse V (originally number VI in the 1852 edition) defends knowledge as an end in itself against the demands of Bacon's utilitarian descendants that knowledge justify itself by its power and instrumental application. Newman's definition of education is anchored in Aristotle and Cicero, and his vision of the unity of knowledge, the "whole circle" of

---

1. *The Imperial Intellect: A Study in Newman's Educational Ideal* (New Haven, CT: Yale University Press, 1955), 189.

learning, echoes the Greeks' *enkuklios paideia*. Newman also includes a sane reminder of knowledge's inability in and of itself to make students virtuous.

"Christianity and Letters" was delivered to the faculty of the Catholic University of Dublin in November 1854. Newman considers the arts curriculum from a Christian perspective. Following a broad preliminary discussion of civilization and Christianity, he shows how Jerusalem and Athens, the sacred and secular, have been reconciled in the Christian civilization of the West.

from The Idea of a University
Discourse V. Knowledge Its Own End

A university may be considered with reference either to its Students or to its Studies; and the principle, that all Knowledge is a whole and the separate Sciences parts of one, which I have hitherto been using in behalf of its studies, is equally important when we direct our attention to its students. Now, then, I turn to the students, and shall consider the education which, by virtue of this principle, a University will give them; and thus I shall be introduced, Gentlemen, to the second question, which I proposed to discuss, viz, whether and in what sense its teaching, viewed relatively to the taught, carries the attribute of Utility along with it.

I.

I have said that all branches of knowledge are connected together, because the subject-matter of knowledge is intimately united in itself, as being the acts and the work of the Creator. Hence it is that the Sciences, into which our knowledge may be said to be cast, have multiplied bearings one on another, and an internal sympathy, and admit, or rather demand, comparison and adjustment. They complete, correct, balance each other. This consideration, if well-founded, must be taken into account, not only as regards the attainment of truth, which is their common end, but as regards the influence which they exercise upon those whose education consists in the study of them. I have said already, that to give undue prominence to one is to be unjust to another; to neglect or supersede these is to divert those from their proper object. It is to unsettle the boundary lines between science and science, to disturb their action, to destroy the harmony which binds them together. Such a proceeding will have a corresponding effect when introduced into a place of education. There is no science but tells a different tale, when viewed as a portion of a whole, from what it is likely to suggest when taken by itself, without the safeguard, as I may call it, of others.

Let me make use of an illustration. In the combination of colours, very different effects are produced by a difference in their selection and juxta-position; red, green, and white, change their shades, according to the contrast to which they are submitted. And, in like manner, the drift and meaning of a branch of knowledge varies with the company in which it is introduced to the student. If his reading is confined simply to one subject, however such division of labour may favour the advancement of a particular pursuit, a point into which I do not here enter, certainly it has a tendency to contract his mind. If it is incorporated with others, it depends on those others as to the kind of influence which it exerts upon him. Thus the Classics, which in England are the means of refining the taste, have in France subserved the spread of revolutionary and deistical doctrines. In Metaphysics, again, Butler's Analogy of Religion, which has had so much to do with the conversion to the Catholic faith of members of the University of Oxford, appeared to Pitt and others, who had received a different training, to operate only in the direction of infidelity. And so again, Watson, Bishop of Llandaff, as I think he tells us in the narrative of his life, felt the science of Mathematics to indispose the mind to religious belief, while others see in its investigations the best parallel, and thereby defence, of the Christian Mysteries. In like manner, I suppose, Arcesilas would not have handled logic as Aristotle, nor Aristotle have criticized poets as Plato; yet reasoning and poetry are subject to scientific rules.

It is a great point then to enlarge the range of studies which a University professes, even for the sake of the students; and, though they cannot pursue every subject which is open to them, they will be the gainers by living among those and under those who represent the whole circle. This I conceive to be the advantage of a seat of universal learning, considered as a place of education. An assemblage of learned men, zealous for their own sciences, and rivals of each other, are brought, by familiar intercourse and for the sake of intellectual peace, to adjust together the claims and relations of their respective subjects of investigation. They learn to respect, to consult, to aid each other. Thus is created a pure and clear atmosphere of thought, which the student also breathes, though in his own case he only pursues a few sciences out of the multitude. He profits by an intellectual tradition, which is independent of particular teachers, which guides him in his choice of subjects, and duly interprets for him those which he chooses. He apprehends the great outlines of knowledge, the principles on which it rests, the scale of its parts, its lights and its shades, its great points and its little, as he otherwise cannot apprehend them. Hence it is that his education is called "Liberal." A habit of mind is formed which lasts through life, of which the attributes are, freedom, equitableness, calmness, moderation, and wisdom; or what in a former Discourse I have ventured to call a philosophical habit. This then I would assign as the special fruit of the education furnished at a University, as contrasted with other places of teaching or modes of teaching. This is the main purpose of a University in its treatment of its students.

And now the question is asked me, What is the *use* of it? and my answer will constitute the main subject of the Discourses which are to follow.

2.

Cautious and practical thinkers, I say, will ask of me, what, after all, is the gain of this Philosophy, of which I make such account, and from which I promise so much. Even supposing it to enable us to exercise the degree of trust exactly due to every science respectively, and to estimate precisely the value of every truth which is anywhere to be found, how are we better for this master view of things, which I have been extolling? Does it not reverse the principle of the division of labour? will practical objects be obtained better or worse by its cultivation? to what then does it lead? where does it end? what does it do? how does it profit? what does it promise? Particular sciences are respectively the basis of definite arts, which carry on to results tangible and beneficial the truths which are the subjects of the knowledge attained; what is the Art of this science of sciences? what is the fruit of such a Philosophy? what are we proposing to effect, what inducements do we hold out to the Catholic community, when we set about the enterprise of founding a University?

I am asked what is the end of University Education, and of the Liberal or Philosophical Knowledge which I conceive it to impart: I answer, that what I have already said has been sufficient to show that it has a very tangible, real, and sufficient end, though the end cannot be divided from that knowledge itself. Knowledge is capable of being its own end. Such is the constitution of the human mind, that any kind of knowledge, if it be really such, is its own reward. And if this is true of all knowledge, it is true also of that special Philosophy, which I have made to consist in a comprehensive view of truth in all its branches, of the relations of science to science, of their mutual bearings, and their respective values. What the worth of such an acquirement is, compared with other objects which we seek,— wealth or power or honour or the conveniences and comforts of life, I do not profess here to discuss; but I would maintain, and mean to show, that it is an object, in its own nature so really and undeniably good, as to be the compensation of a great deal of thought in the compassing, and a great deal of trouble in the attaining.

Now, when I say that Knowledge is, not merely a means to something beyond it, or the preliminary of certain arts into which it naturally resolves, but an end sufficient to rest in and to pursue for its own sake, surely I am uttering no paradox, for I am stating what is both intelligible in itself, and has ever been the common judgment of philosophers and the ordinary feeling of mankind. I am saying what at least the public opinion of this day ought to be slow to deny, considering how much we have heard of late years, in opposition to Religion, of entertaining, curious, and various knowledge. I am but saying what whole volumes have been written to illustrate, viz., by a "selection from the records of Philosophy, Literature, and Art, in all ages and countries, of a body of examples, to show how the most unpropitious circumstances have been unable to conquer an ardent desire for the acquisition of knowledge." That further advantages accrue to us and redound to others by its possession, over and above what it is in itself, I am very far indeed from denying; but, independent of these, we are satisfying a direct need of our nature in its very acquisition; and, whereas our nature, unlike that of the inferior creation, does not at once reach its perfection, but depends, in order to it, on a number of external aids and appliances, Knowledge, as one of the principal of these, is valuable for what its very presence in us does for us after the manner of a habit, even though it be turned to no further account, nor subserve any direct end.

3.

Hence it is that Cicero, in enumerating the various heads of mental excellence, lays down the pursuit of Knowledge for its own sake, as the first of them. "This pertains most of all to human nature," he says, "for we are all of us drawn to the pursuit of Knowledge; in which to excel we consider excellent, whereas to mistake, to err, to be ignorant, to be deceived, is both an evil and a disgrace." And he considers Knowledge the very first object to which we are attracted, after the supply of our physical wants. After the calls and duties of our animal existence, as they may be termed, as regards ourselves, our family, and our neighbours, follows, he tells us, "the search after truth. Accordingly, as soon as we escape from the pressure of necessary cares, forthwith we desire to see, to hear, and to learn; and consider the knowledge of what is hidden or is wonderful a condition of our happiness."

This passage, though it is but one of many similar passages in a multitude of authors, I take for the very reason that it is so familiarly known to us; and I wish you to observe, Gentlemen, how distinctly it separates the pursuit of Knowledge from those ulterior objects to which certainly it can be made to conduce, and which are, I suppose, solely contemplated by the persons who would ask of me the use of a University or Liberal Education. So far from dreaming of the cultivation of Knowledge directly and mainly in order to our physical comfort and enjoyment, for the sake of life and person, of health, of the conjugal and family union, of the social tie and civil security, the great Orator implies, that it is only after our physical and political needs are supplied, and when we are "free from necessary duties and cares," that we are in a condition for "desiring to see, to hear, and to learn." Nor does he contemplate in the least degree the reflex or subsequent action of Knowledge, when acquired, upon those material goods which we set out by securing before we seek it; on the contrary, he expressly denies its bearing upon social life altogether, strange as such a procedure is to those who live after the rise of the Baconian philosophy, and he cautions us against such a cultivation of it as will interfere with our duties to our fellow-creatures. "All these methods," he says, "are engaged in the investigation of truth; by the pursuit of which to be carried off from public occupations is a transgression of duty. For the praise of virtue lies altogether in action; yet intermissions often occur, and then we recur to such pursuits; not to say that the incessant activity of the mind is vigorous enough to carry us on in the pursuit of knowledge, even without any exertion of our own." The idea of benefiting society by means of "the pursuit of science and knowledge" did not enter at all into the motives which he would assign for their cultivation.

This was the ground of the opposition which the elder Cato made to the introduction of Greek Philosophy among his countrymen, when Carneades and his companions, on occasion of their embassy, were charming the Roman youth with their eloquent expositions of it. The fit representative of a practical people, Cato estimated every thing by what it produced; whereas the Pursuit of Knowledge promised nothing beyond Knowledge itself. He despised that refinement or enlargement of mind of which he had no experience.

4.

Things, which can bear to be cut off from every thing else and yet persist in living, must have life in themselves; pursuits, which issue in nothing, and still maintain their ground for ages, which are regarded as admirable, though they have not as yet proved themselves to be useful, must have their sufficient end in themselves, whatever it turn out to be. And we are brought to the same conclusion by considering the force of the epithet, by which the knowledge under consideration is popularly designated. It is common to speak of "*liberal* knowledge," of the "*liberal* arts and studies," and of a "*liberal* education," as the especial characteristic or property of a University and of a gentleman; what is really meant by the word? Now, first, in its grammatical sense it is opposed to *servile*; and by "servile work" is understood, as our catechisms inform us, bodily labour, mechanical employment, and the like, in which the mind has little or no part. Parallel to such servile works are those arts, if they deserve the name, of which the poet speaks, which owe their origin and their method to hazard, not to skill; as, for instance, the practice and operations of an empiric. As far as this contrast may be considered as a guide into the meaning of the word, liberal education and liberal pursuits are exercises of mind, of reason, of reflection.

But we want something more for its explanation, for there are bodily exercises which are liberal, and mental exercises which are not so. For instance, in ancient times the practitioners in medicine were commonly slaves; yet it was an art as intellectual in its nature, in spite of the pretence, fraud, and quackery with which it might then, as now, be debased, as it was heavenly in its aim. And so in like manner, we contrast a liberal education with a commercial education or a professional; yet no one can deny that commerce and the professions afford scope for the highest and most diversified powers of mind. There is then a great variety of intellectual exercises, which are not technically called "liberal;" on the other hand, I say, there are exercises of the body which do receive that appellation. Such, for instance, was the palæstra, in ancient times; such the Olympic games, in which strength and dexterity of body as well as of mind gained the prize. In Xenophon we read of the young Persian nobility being taught to ride on horseback and to speak the truth; both being among the accomplishments of a gentleman. War, too, however rough a profession, has ever been accounted liberal, unless in cases when it becomes heroic, which would introduce us to another subject.

Now comparing these instances together, we shall have no difficulty in determining the principle of this apparent variation in the application of the term which I am examining. Manly games, or games of skill, or military prowess, though bodily, are, it seems, accounted liberal; on the other hand, what is merely professional, though highly intellectual, nay, though liberal in comparison of trade and manual labour, is not simply called liberal, and mercantile occupations are not liberal at all. Why this distinction? because that alone is liberal knowledge, which stands on its own pretensions, which is independent of sequel, expects no complement, refuses to be informed (as it is called) by any end, or absorbed into any art, in order duly to present itself to our contemplation. The most ordinary pursuits have this specific character, if they are self-sufficient and complete; the highest lose it, when they minister to something beyond them. It is absurd to balance, in point of worth and importance, a treatise on reducing fractures with a game of cricket or a fox-chase; yet of the two the bodily exercise has that quality which we call "liberal," and the intellectual has it not. And so of the learned professions altogether, considered merely as professions; although one of them be the most popularly beneficial, and another the most politically important, and the third the most intimately divine of all human pursuits, yet the very greatness of their end, the health of the body, or of the commonwealth, or of the soul, diminishes, not increases, their claim to the appellation "liberal," and that still more, if they are cut down to the strict exigencies of that end. If, for instance, Theology, instead of being cultivated as a contemplation, be limited to the purposes of the pulpit or be represented by the catechism, it loses,—not its usefulness, not its divine character, not its meritoriousness (rather it gains a claim upon these titles by such charitable condescension),—but it does lose the particular attribute which I am illustrating; just as a face worn by tears and fasting loses its beauty, or a labourer's hand loses its delicateness;—for Theology thus exercised is not simple knowledge, but rather is an art or a business making use of Theology. And thus it appears that even what is supernatural need not be liberal, nor need a hero be a gentleman, for the plain reason that one idea is not another idea. And in like manner the Baconian Philosophy, by using its physical sciences in the service of man, does thereby transfer them from the order of Liberal Pursuits to, I do not say the inferior, but the distinct class of the Useful. And, to take a different instance, hence again, as is evident, whenever personal gain is the motive, still more distinctive an effect has it upon the character of a given pursuit; thus racing, which was a liberal exercise in Greece, forfeits its rank in times like these, so far as it is made the occasion of gambling.

All that I have been now saying is summed up in a few characteristic words of the great Philosopher. "Of possessions," he says, "those rather are useful, which bear fruit; those *liberal, which tend to enjoyment.* By fruitful, I mean, which yield revenue; by enjoyable, *where nothing accrues of consequence beyond the using."*

5.

Do not suppose, that in thus appealing to the ancients, I am throwing back the world two thousand years, and fettering Philosophy with the reasonings of paganism. While the world lasts, will Aristotle's doctrine on these matters last, for he is the oracle of nature and of truth. While we are men, we cannot help, to a great extent, being Aristotelians, for the great Master does but analyze the thoughts, feelings, views, and opinions of human kind. He has told us the meaning of our own words and ideas, before we were born. In many subject-matters, to think correctly, is to think like Aristotle; and we are his disciples whether we will or no, though we may not know it. Now, as to the particular instance before us, the word "liberal" as applied to Knowledge and Education, expresses a specific idea, which ever has been, and ever will be, while the nature of man is the same, just as the idea of the Beautiful is specific, or of the Sublime, or of the Ridiculous, or of the Sordid. It is in the world now, it was in the world then; and, as in the case of the dogmas of faith, it is illustrated by a continuous historical tradition, and never was out of the world, from the time it came into it. There have indeed been differences of opinion from time to time, as to what pursuits and what arts came under that idea, but such differences are but an additional evidence of its reality. That idea must have a substance in it, which has maintained its ground amid these conflicts and changes, which has ever served as a standard to measure things withal, which has passed from mind to mind unchanged, when there was so much to colour, so much to influence any notion or thought whatever, which was not founded in our very nature. Were it a mere generalization, it would have varied with the subjects from which it was generalized; but though its subjects vary with the age, it varies not itself. The palæstra may seem a liberal exercise to Lycurgus, and illiberal to Seneca; coach-driving and prize-fighting may be recognized in Elis, and be condemned in England; music may be despicable in the eyes of certain moderns, and be in the highest place with Aristotle and Plato,—(and the case is the same in the particular application of the idea of Beauty, or of Goodness, or of Moral Virtue, there is a difference of tastes, a difference of judgments)—still these variations imply, instead of discrediting, the archetypal idea, which is but a previous hypothesis or condition, by means of which issue is joined between contending opinions, and without which there would be nothing to dispute about.

I consider, then, that I am chargeable with no paradox, when I speak of a Knowledge which is its own end, when I call it liberal knowledge, or a gentleman's knowledge, when I educate for it, and make it the scope of a University. And still less am I incurring such a charge, when I make this acquisition consist, not in Knowledge in a vague and ordinary sense, but in that Knowledge which I have especially called Philosophy or, in an extended sense of the word, Science; for whatever claims Knowledge has to be considered as a good, these it has in a higher degree when it is viewed not vaguely, not popularly, but precisely and transcendently as Philosophy. Knowledge, I say, is then especially liberal, or sufficient for itself, apart from every external and ulterior object, when and so far as it is philosophical, and this I proceed to show.

6.

Now bear with me, Gentlemen, if what I am about to say, has at first sight a fanciful appearance. Philosophy, then, or Science, is related to Knowledge in this way:—Knowledge is called by the name of Science or Philosophy, when it is acted upon, informed, or if I may use a strong figure, impregnated by Reason. Reason is the principle of that intrinsic fecundity of Knowledge, which, to those who possess it, is its especial value, and which dispenses with the necessity of their looking abroad for any end to rest upon external to itself. Knowledge, indeed, when thus exalted into a scientific form, is also power; not only is it excellent in itself, but whatever such excellence may be, it is something more, it has a result beyond itself. Doubtless; but that is a further consideration, with which I am not concerned. I only say that, prior to its being a power, it is a good; that it is, not only an instrument, but an end. I know well it may resolve itself into an art, and terminate in a mechanical process, and in tangible fruit; but it also may fall back upon that Reason which informs it, and resolve itself into Philosophy. In one case it is called Useful Knowledge, in the other Liberal. The same person may cultivate it in both ways at once; but this again is a matter foreign to my subject; here I do but say that there are two ways of using Knowledge, and in matter of fact those who use it in one way are not likely to use it in the other, or at least in a very limited measure. You see, then, here are two methods of Education; the end of the one is to be philosophical, of the other to be mechanical; the one rises towards general ideas, the other is exhausted upon what is particular and external. Let me not be thought to deny the necessity, or to decry the benefit, of such attention to what is particular and practical, as belongs to the useful or mechanical arts; life could not go on without them; we owe our daily welfare to them; their exercise is the duty of the many, and we owe to the many a debt of gratitude for fulfilling that duty. I only say that Knowledge, in proportion as it tends more and more to be particular, ceases to be Knowledge. It is a question whether Knowledge can in any proper sense be predicated of the brute creation; without pretending to metaphysical exactness of phraseology, which would be unsuitable to an occasion like this, I say, it seems to me improper to call that passive sensation, or perception of things, which brutes seem to possess, by the name of Knowledge. When I speak of Knowledge, I mean something intellectual, something which grasps what it perceives through the senses; something which takes a view of things; which sees more than the senses convey; which reasons upon what it sees, and while it sees; which invests it with an idea. It expresses itself, not in a mere enunciation, but by an enthymeme: it is of the nature of science from the first, and in this consists its dignity. The principle of real dignity in Knowledge, its worth, its desirableness, considered irrespectively of its results, is this germ within it of a scientific or a philosophical process. This is how it comes to be an end in itself; this is why it admits of being called Liberal. Not to know the relative disposition of things is the state of slaves or children; to have mapped out the Universe is the boast, or at least the ambition, of Philosophy.

Moreover, such knowledge is not a mere extrinsic or accidental advantage, which is ours today and another's tomorrow, which may be got up from a book, and easily forgotten again, which we can command or communicate at our pleasure, which we can borrow for the occasion, carry about in our hand, and take into the market; it is an acquired illumination, it is a habit, a personal possession, and an inward endowment. And this is the reason, why it is more correct, as well as more usual, to speak of a University as a place of education, than of instruction, though, when knowledge is concerned, instruction would at first sight have seemed the more appropriate word. We are instructed, for instance, in manual exercises, in the fine and useful arts, in trades, and in ways of business; for these are methods, which have little or no effect upon the mind itself, are contained in rules committed to memory, to tradition, or to use, and bear upon an end external to themselves. But education is a higher word; it implies an action upon our mental nature, and the formation of a character; it is something individual and permanent, and is commonly spoken of in connexion with religion and virtue. When, then, we speak of the communication of Knowledge as being Education, we thereby really imply that that Knowledge is a state or condition of mind; and since cultivation of mind is surely worth seeking for its own sake, we are thus brought once more to the conclusion, which the word "Liberal" and the word "Philosophy" have already suggested, that there is a Knowledge, which is desirable, though nothing come of it, as being of itself a treasure, and a sufficient remuneration of years of labour.

7.

This, then, is the answer which I am prepared to give to the question with which I opened this Discourse. Before going on to speak of the object of the Church in taking up Philosophy, and the uses to which she puts it, I am prepared to maintain that Philosophy is its own end, and, as I conceive, I have now begun the proof of it. I am prepared to maintain that there is a knowledge worth possessing for what it is, and not merely for what it does; and what minutes remain to me today I shall devote to the removal of some portion of the indistinctness and confusion with which the subject may in some minds be surrounded.

It may be objected then, that, when we profess to seek Knowledge for some end or other beyond itself, whatever it be, we speak intelligibly; but that, whatever men may have said, however obstinately the idea may have kept its ground from age to age, still it is simply unmeaning to say that we seek Knowledge for its own sake, and for nothing else; for that it ever leads to something beyond itself, which therefore is its end, and the cause why it is desirable;—moreover, that this end is twofold, either of this world or of the next; that all knowledge is cultivated either for secular objects or for eternal; that if it is directed to secular objects, it is called Useful Knowledge, if to eternal, Religious or Christian Knowledge;—in consequence, that if, as I have allowed, this Liberal Knowledge does not benefit the body or estate, it ought to benefit the soul; but if the fact be really so, that it is neither a physical or a secular good on the one hand, nor a moral good on the other, it cannot be a good at all, and is not worth the trouble which is necessary for its acquisition.

And then I may be reminded that the professors of this Liberal or Philosophical Knowledge have themselves, in every age, recognized this exposition of the matter, and have submitted to the issue in which it terminates; for they have ever been attempting to make men virtuous; or, if not, at least have assured that refinement of mind was virtue, and, that they themselves were the virtuous portion of mankind. This they have professed on the one hand; and on the other, they have utterly failed in their professions, so as ever to make themselves a proverb among men, and a laughing-stock both to the grave and the dissipated portion of mankind, in consequence of them. Thus they have furnished against themselves both the ground and the means of their own exposure, without any trouble at all to any one else. In a word, from the time that Athens was the University of the world, what has Philosophy taught men, but to promise without practising, and to aspire without attaining? What has the deep and lofty thought of its disciples ended in but eloquent words? Nay, what has its teaching ever meditated, when it was boldest in its remedies for human ill, beyond charming us to sleep by its lessons, that we might feel nothing at all? like some melodious air, or rather like those strong and transporting perfumes, which at first spread their sweetness over every thing they touch, but in a little while do but offend in proportion as they once pleased us. Did Philosophy support Cicero under the disfavour of the fickle populace, or nerve Seneca to oppose an imperial tyrant? It abandoned Brutus, as he sorrowfully confessed, in his greatest need, and it forced Cato, as his panegyrist strangely boasts, into the false position of defying heaven. How few can be counted among its professors, who, like Polemo, were thereby converted from a profligate course, or like Anaxagoras, thought the world well lost in exchange for its possession? The philosopher in Rasselas taught a superhuman doctrine, and then succumbed without an effort to a trial of human affection.

"He discoursed," we are told, "with great energy on the government of the passions. His look was venerable, his action graceful, his pronunciation clear, and his diction elegant. He showed, with great strength of sentiment and variety of illustration, that human nature is degraded and debased, when the lower faculties predominate over the higher. He communicated the various precepts given, from time to time, for the conquest of passion, and displayed the happiness of those who had obtained the important victory, after which man is no longer the slave of fear, nor the fool of hope. . . . He enumerated many examples of heroes immoveable by pain or pleasure, who looked with indifference on those modes or accidents to which the vulgar give the names of good and evil."

Rasselas in a few days found the philosopher in a room half darkened, with his eyes misty, and his face pale. "Sir," said he, "you have come at a time when all human friendship is useless; what I suffer cannot be remedied, what I have lost cannot be supplied. My daughter, my only daughter, from whose tenderness I expected all the comforts of my age, died last night of a fever." "Sir," said the prince, "mortality is an event by which a wise man can never be surprised; we know that death is always near, and it should therefore always be expected." "Young man," answered the philosopher, "you speak like one who has never felt the pangs of separation." "Have you, then, forgot the precept," said Rasselas, "which you so powerfully enforced? . . . consider that external things are naturally variable, but truth and reason are always the same." "What comfort," said the mourner, "can truth and reason afford me? Of what effect are they now, but to tell me that my daughter will not be restored?"

8.

Better, far better, to make no professions, you will say, than to cheat others with what we are not, and to scandalize them with what we are. The sensualist, or the man of the world, at any rate is not the victim of fine words, but pursues a reality and gains it. The Philosophy of Utility, you will say, Gentlemen, has at least done its work; and I grant it,—it aimed low, but it has fulfilled its aim. If that man of great intellect [Francis Bacon] who has been its Prophet in the conduct of life played false to his own professions, he was not bound by his philosophy to be true to his friend or faithful in his trust. Moral virtue was not the line in which he undertook to instruct men; and though, as the poet calls him, he were the "meanest" of mankind, he was so in what may be called his private capacity and without any prejudice to the theory of induction. He had a right to be so, if he chose, for any thing that the Idols of the den or the theatre had to say to the contrary. His mission was the increase of physical enjoyment and social comfort; and most wonderfully, most awfully has he fulfilled his conception and his design. Almost day by day have we fresh and fresh shoots, and buds, and blossoms, which are to ripen into fruit, on that magical tree of Knowledge which he planted, and to which none of us perhaps, except the very poor, but owes, if not his present life, at least his daily food, his health, and general well-being. He was the divinely provided minister of temporal benefits to all of us so great, that, whatever I am forced to think of him as a man, I have not the heart, from mere gratitude, to speak of him severely. And, in spite of the tendencies of his philosophy, which are, as we see at this day, to depreciate, or to trample on Theology, he has himself, in his writings, gone out of his way, as if with a prophetic misgiving of those tendencies, to insist on it as the instrument of that beneficent Father, who, when He came on earth in visible form, took on Him first and most prominently the office of assuaging the bodily wounds of human nature. And truly, like the old mediciner in the tale, "he sat diligently at his work, and hummed, with cheerful countenance, a pious song"; and then in turn "went out singing into the meadows so gaily, that those who had seen him from afar might well have thought it was a youth gathering flowers for his beloved, instead of an old physician gathering healing herbs in the morning dew."[2]

Alas, that men, in the action of life or in their heart of hearts, are not what they seem to be in their moments of excitement, or in their trances or intoxications of genius,—so good, so noble, so serene! Alas, that Bacon too in his own way should after all be but the fellow of those heathen philosophers who in their disadvantages had some excuse for their inconsistency, and who surprise us rather in what they did say than in what they did not do! Alas, that he too, like Socrates or Seneca, must be stripped of his holy-day coat, which looks so fair, and should be but a mockery amid his most majestic gravity of phrase; and, for all his vast abilities, should, in the littleness of his own moral being, but typify the intellectual narrowness of his school! However, granting all this, heroism after all was not his philosophy:—I cannot deny he has abundantly achieved what he proposed. His is simply a Method whereby bodily discomforts and temporal wants are to be most effectually removed from the greatest number; and already, before it has shown any signs of exhaustion, the gifts of nature, in their most artificial shapes and luxurious profusion and diversity, from all quarters of the earth, are, it is undeniable, by its means brought even to our doors, and we rejoice in them.

---

2. Fouqué's *Unknown Patient.*

9.

Useful Knowledge then, I grant, has done its work; and Liberal Knowledge as certainly has not done its work,—that is, supposing, as the objectors assume, its direct end, like Religious Knowledge, is to make men better; but this I will not for an instant allow, and, unless I allow it, those objectors have said nothing to the purpose. I admit, rather I maintain, what they have been urging, for I consider Knowledge to have its end in itself. For all its friends, or its enemies, may say, I insist upon it, that it is as real a mistake to burden it with virtue or religion as with the mechanical arts. Its direct business is not to steel the soul against temptation or to console it in affliction, any more than to set the loom in motion, or to direct the steam carriage; be it ever so much the means or the condition of both material and moral advancement, still, taken by and in itself, it as little mends our hearts as it improves our temporal circumstances. And if its eulogists claim for it such a power, they commit the very same kind of encroachment on a province not their own as the political economist who should maintain that his science educated him for casuistry or diplomacy. Knowledge is one thing, virtue is another; good sense is not conscience, refinement is not humility, nor is largeness and justness of view faith. Philosophy, however enlightened, however profound, gives no command over the passions, no influential motives, no vivifying principles. Liberal Education makes not the Christian, not the Catholic, but the gentleman. It is well to be a gentlemen, it is well to have a cultivated intellect, a delicate taste, a candid, equitable, dispassionate mind, a noble and courteous bearing in the conduct of life;—these are the qualities of a large knowledge; they are the objects of a University; I am advocating, I shall illustrate and insist upon them; but still, I repeat, they are no guarantee for sanctity or even for conscientiousness, they may attach to the man of the world, to the profligate, to the heartless,—pleasant, alas, and attractive as he shows when decked out in them. Taken by themselves, they do but seem to be what they are not; they look like virtue at a distance, but they are detected by close observers, and on the long run; and hence it is that they are popularly accused of pretence and hypocrisy, not, I repeat, from their own fault, but because their professors and their admirers persist in taking them for what they are not, and are officious in arrogating for them a praise to which they have no claim. Quarry the granite rock with razors, or moor the vessel with a thread of silk; then may you hope with such keen and delicate instruments as human knowledge and human reason to contend against those giants, the passion and the pride of man.

Surely we are not driven to theories of this kind, in order to vindicate the value and dignity of Liberal Knowledge. Surely the real grounds on which its pretensions rest are not so very subtle or abstruse, so very strange or improbable. Surely it is very intelligible to say, and that is what I say here, that Liberal Education, viewed in itself, is simply the cultivation of the intellect, as such, and its object is nothing more or less than intellectual excellence. Every thing has its own perfection, be it higher or lower in the scale of things; and the perfection of one is not the perfection of another. Things animate, inanimate, visible, invisible, all are good in their kind, and have a *best* of themselves, which is an object of pursuit. Why do you take such pains with your garden or your park? You see to your walks and turf and shrubberies; to your trees and drives; not as if you meant to make an orchard of the one, or corn or pasture land of the other, but because there is a special beauty in all that is goodly in wood, water, plain, and slope, brought all together by art into one shape, and grouped into one whole. Your cities are beautiful, your palaces, your public buildings, your territorial mansions, your churches; and their beauty leads to nothing beyond itself. There is a physical beauty and a moral: there is a beauty of person, there is a beauty of our moral being, which is natural virtue; and in like manner there is a beauty, there is a perfection, of the intellect. There is an ideal perfection in these various subject-matters, towards which individual instances are seen to rise, and which are the standards for all instances whatever. The Greek divinities and demigods, as the statuary has moulded them, with their symmetry of figure, and their high forehead and their regular features, are the perfection of physical beauty. The heroes, of whom history tells, Alexander, or Cæsar, or Scipio, or Saladin, are the representatives of that magnanimity or self-mastery which is the greatness of human nature. Christianity too has its heroes, and in the supernatural order, and we call them Saints. The artist puts before him beauty of feature and form; the poet, beauty of mind; the preacher, the beauty of grace: then intellect too, I repeat, has its beauty, and it has those who aim at it. To open the mind, to correct it, to refine it, to enable it to know, and to digest, master, rule, and use its knowledge, to give it power over its own faculties, application, flexibility, method, critical exactness, sagacity, resource, address, eloquent expression, is an object as intelligible (for, here we are inquiring, not what the object of a Liberal Education is worth, nor what use the Church makes of it, but what it is in itself), I say, an object as intelligible as the cultivation of virtue, while, at the same time, it is absolutely distinct from it.

10.

This indeed is but a temporal object, and a transitory possession; but so are other things in themselves which we make much of and pursue. The moralist will tell us that man, in all his functions, is but a flower which blossoms and fades, except so far as a higher principle breathes upon him, and makes him and what he is immortal. Body and mind are carried on into an eternal state of being by the gifts of Divine Munificence; but at first they do but fail in a failing world; and if the powers of intellect decay, the powers of the body have decayed before them, and, as an Hospital or an Almshouse, though its end be ephemeral, may be sanctified to the service of religion, so surely may a University, even were it nothing more than I have as yet described it. We attain to heaven by using this world well, though it is to pass away; we perfect our nature, not by undoing it, but by adding to it what is more than nature, and directing it towards aims higher than its own.

from The Idea of a University
"Christianity and Letters"

4.

In the country which has been the fountain head of intellectual gifts, in the age which preceded or introduced the first formations of Human Society, in an era scarcely historical, we may dimly discern an almost mythical personage, who, putting out of consideration the actors in Old Testament history, may be called the first Apostle of Civilization. Like an Apostle in a higher order of things, he was poor and a wanderer, and feeble in the flesh, though he was to do such great things, and to live in the mouths of a hundred generations and a thousand tribes. A blind old man; whose wanderings were such that, when he became famous, his birth-place could not be ascertained, so that it was said,—

> Seven famous towns contend for Homer dead,
> Through which the living Homer begged his bread.

Yet he had a name in his day; and, little guessing in what vast measures his wish would be answered, he supplicated, with a tender human sentiment, as he wandered over the islands of the Ægean and the Asian coasts, that those who had known and loved him would cherish his memory when he was away. Unlike the proud boast of the Roman poet, if he spoke it in earnest, "Exegi monumentum ære perennius," he did but indulge the hope that one, whose coming had been expected with pleasure, might excite regret when he had departed, and be rewarded by the sympathy and praise of his friends even in the presence of other minstrels. A set of verses remains, which is ascribed to him, in which he addresses the Delian women in the tone of feeling which I have described. "Farewell to you all," he says, "and remember me in time to come, and when any one of men on earth, a stranger from far, shall inquire of you, O maidens, who is the sweetest of minstrels here about, and in whom do you most delight? then make answer modestly, It is a blind man, and he lives in steep Chios."

The great poet remained unknown for some centuries,—that is, unknown to what we call fame. His verses were cherished by his countrymen, they might be the secret delight of thousands, but they were not collected into a volume, nor viewed as a whole, nor made a subject of criticism. At length an Athenian Prince took upon him the task of gathering together the scattered fragments of a genius which had not aspired to immortality, of reducing them to writing, and of fitting them to be the text-book of ancient education. Henceforth the vagrant ballad-singer, as he might be thought, was submitted, to his surprise, to a sort of literary canonization, and was invested with the office of forming the young mind of Greece to noble thoughts and bold deeds. To be read in Homer soon became the education of a gentleman; and a rule, recognized in her free age, remained as a tradition even in the times of her degradation. Xenophon introduces to us a youth who knew both Iliad and Odyssey by heart; Dio witnesses that they were some of the first books put into the hands of boys; and Horace decided that they taught the science of life better than Stoic or Academic. Alexander the Great nourished his imagination by the scenes of the Iliad. As time went on, other poets were associated with Homer in the work of education, such as Hesiod and the Tragedians. The majestic lessons concerning duty and religion, justice and providence, which occur in Æschylus and Sophocles, belong to a higher school than that of Homer; and the verses of Euripides, even in his lifetime, were so familiar to Athenian lips and so dear to foreign ears, that, as is reported, the captives of Syracuse gained their freedom at the price of reciting them to their conquerors.

Such poetry may be considered oratory also, since it has so great a power of persuasion; and the alliance between these two gifts had existed from the time that the verses of Orpheus had, according to the fable, made woods and streams and wild animals to follow him about. Soon, however, Oratory became the subject of a separate art, which was called Rhetoric, and of which the Sophists were the chief masters. Moreover, as Rhetoric was especially political in its nature, it presupposed or introduced the cultivation of History;

and thus the pages of Thucydides became one of the special studies by which Demosthenes rose to be the first orator of Greece.

But it is needless to trace out further the formation of the course of liberal education; it is sufficient to have given some specimens in illustration of it. The studies, which it was found to involve, were four principal ones, Grammar, Rhetoric, Logic, and Mathematics; and the science of Mathematics, again, was divided into four, Geometry, Arithmetic, Astronomy, and Music; making in all seven, which are known by the name of the Seven Liberal Arts. And thus a definite school of intellect was formed, founded on ideas and methods of a distinctive character, and (as we may say) of the highest and truest character, as far as they went, and which gradually associated in one, and assimilated, and took possession of, that multitude of nations which I have considered to represent mankind, and to possess the *orbis terrarum*.

When we pass from Greece to Rome, we are met with the common remark, that Rome produced little that was original, but borrowed from Greece. It is true; Terence copied from Menander, Virgil from Homer, Hesiod, and Theocritus; and Cicero professed merely to reproduce the philosophy of Greece. But, granting its truth ever so far, I do but take it as a proof of the sort of instinct which has guided the course of Civilization. The world was to have certain intellectual teachers; and no others; Homer and Aristotle, with the poets and philosophers who circle round them, were to be the schoolmasters of all generations, and therefore the Latins, falling into the law on which the world's education was to be carried on, so added to the classical library as not to reverse or interfere with what had already been determined. And there was the more meaning in this arrangement, when it is considered that Greek was to be forgotten during many centuries, and the tradition of intellectual training to be conveyed through Latin; for thus the world was secured against the consequences of a loss which would have changed the character of its civilization. I think it very remarkable, too, how soon the Latin writers became text-books in the boys' schools. Even to this day Shakespeare and Milton are not studied in our course of education; but the poems of Virgil and Horace, as those of Homer and the Greek authors in an earlier age, were in schoolboys' satchels not much more than a hundred years after they were written.

I need not go on to show at length that they have preserved their place in the system of education in the *orbis terrarum*, and the Greek writers with them or through them, down to this day. The induction of centuries has often been made. Even in the lowest state of learning the tradition was kept up. St. Gregory the Great, whose era, not to say whose influence, is often considered especially unfavourable to the old literature, was himself well versed in it, encouraged purity of Latinity in his court, and is said figuratively by the contemporary historian of his life to have supported the hall of the Apostolic See upon the columns of the Seven Liberal Arts. In the ninth century, when the dark age was close at hand, we still hear of the cultivation, with whatever success (according of course to the opportunities of the times, but I am speaking of the nature of the studies, not of the proficiency of the students), the cultivation of Music, Dialectics, Rhetoric, Grammar, Mathematics, Astronomy, Physics, and Geometry; of the supremacy of Horace in the schools, "and the great Virgil, Sallust, and Statius." In the thirteenth or following centuries, of "Virgil, Lucian, Statius, Ovid, Livy, Sallust, Cicero, and Quintilian;" and after the revival of literature in the commencement of the modern era, we find. St. Carlo Borromeo enjoining the use of works of Cicero, Ovid, Virgil, and Horace.

5.

I pass thus cursorily over the series of informations which history gives us on the subject, merely with a view of recalling to your memory, Gentlemen, and impressing upon you the fact, that the literature of Greece, continued into, and enriched by, the literature of Rome, together with the studies which it involves, has been the instrument of education, and the food of civilization, from the first times of the world down to this day;—and now we are in a condition to answer the question which thereupon arises; when we turn to consider, by way of contrast, the teaching which is characteristic of Universities. How has it come to pass that, although the genius of Universities is so different from that of the schools which preceded them, nevertheless the course of study pursued in those schools was not superseded in the middle ages by those more brilliant sciences which Universities introduced? It might have seemed as if Scholastic Theology, Law, and Medicine, would have thrown the Seven Liberal Arts into the shade, but in the event they failed to do so. I consider the reason to be, that the authority and function of the monastic and secular schools, as supplying to the young the means of education, lay deeper than in any appointment of Charlemagne, who was their nominal founder, and were based in the special character of that civilization which is so intimately associated with Christianity, that it may even be called the soil out of which Christianity grew. The medieval sciences, great as is their dignity and utility, were never intended to supersede that more real and proper cultivation of the mind which is effected by the study of the liberal Arts; and, when certain of these sciences did in fact go out of their province and did attempt to prejudice the traditional course of education, the encroachment was in matter of fact resisted. There were those in the middle age, as John of Salisbury, who vigorously protested against the extravagances and usurpations which ever attend the introduction of any great good whatever, and which attended the rise of the peculiar sciences of which Universities were the seat; and, though there were times when the old traditions seemed to be on the point of failing, somehow it has happened that they have never failed; for the instinct of Civilization and the common sense of Society prevailed, and the danger passed away, and the studies which seemed to be going out gained their ancient place, and were acknowledged, as before, to be the best instruments of mental cultivation, and the best guarantees for intellectual progress.

And this experience of the past we may apply to circumstances in which we find ourselves at present; for, as there was a movement against the Classics in the middle age, so has there been now. The truth of the Baconian method for the purposes for which it was created, and its inestimable services and inexhaustible applications in the interests of our material well-being, have dazzled the imaginations of men, somewhat in the same way as certain new sciences carried them away in the age of Abelard; and since that method does such wonders in its own province, it is not unfrequently supposed that it can do as much in any other province also. Now, Bacon himself never would have so argued; he would not have needed to be reminded that to advance the useful arts is one thing, and to cultivate the mind another. The simple question to be considered is, how best to strengthen, refine, and enrich the intellectual powers; the perusal of the poets, historians, and philosophers of Greece and Rome will accomplish this purpose, as long experience has shown; but that the study of the experimental sciences will do the like, is proved to us as yet by no experience whatever.

Far indeed am I from denying the extreme attractiveness, as well as the practical benefit to the world at large, of the sciences of Chemistry, Electricity, and Geology; but the question is not what department of study contains the more wonderful facts, or promises the more brilliant discoveries, and which is in the higher and which in an inferior rank; but simply which out of all provides the most robust and invigorating discipline for the unformed mind. And I conceive it is as little disrespectful to Lord Bacon to prefer the Classics in this point of view to the sciences which have grown out of his philosophy as it would be disrespectful to St. Thomas in the middle ages to have hindered the study of the Summa from doing prejudice to the Faculty of Arts. Accordingly, I anticipate that, as in the middle ages both the teaching and the government of the University remained in the Faculty of Arts, in spite of the genius which created or illustrated Theology and Law, so now too, whatever be the splendour of the modern philosophy, the marvellousness of its disclosures, the utility of its acquisitions, and the talent of its masters, still it will not avail in the event, to detrude classical literature and the studies connected with it from the place which they have held in all ages in education.

Such, then, is the course of reflection obviously suggested by the act in which we have been lately engaged, and which we are now celebrating. In the nineteenth century, in a country which looks out upon a new world, and anticipates a coming age, we have been engaged in opening the Schools dedicated to the studies of polite literature and liberal science, or what are called the Arts, as a first step towards the establishment on Catholic ground of a Catholic University. And while we thus recur to Greece and Athens with pleasure and affection, and recognize in that famous land the source and the school of intellectual culture, it would be strange indeed if we forgot to look further south also, and there to bow before a more glorious luminary, and a more sacred oracle of truth, and the source of another sort of knowledge, high and supernatural, which is seated in Palestine. Jerusalem is the fountain-head of religious knowledge, as Athens is of secular. In the ancient world we see two centres of illumination, acting independently of each other, each with its own movement, and at first apparently without any promise of convergence. Greek civilization spreads over the East, conquering in the conquests of Alexander, and, when carried captive into the West, subdues the conquerors who brought it thither. Religion, on the other hand, is driven from its own aboriginal home to the North and West by reason of the sins of the people who were in charge of it, in a long course of judgments and plagues and persecutions. Each by itself pursues its career and fulfils its mission; neither of them recognizes, nor is recognized by the other. At length the Temple of Jerusalem is rooted up by the armies of Titus, and the effete schools of Athens are stifled by the edict of Justinian. So pass away the ancient Voices of religion and learning; but they are silenced only to revive more gloriously and perfectly elsewhere. Hitherto they came from separate sources, and performed separate works. Each leaves an heir and successor in the West, and that heir and successor is one and the same. The grace stored in Jerusalem, and the gifts which radiate from Athens, are made over and concentrated in Rome. This is true as a matter of history. Rome has inherited both sacred and profane learning; she has perpetuated and dispensed the traditions of Moses and David in the supernatural order, and of Homer and Aristotle in the natural. To separate those distinct teachings, human and divine, which meet in Rome, is to retrograde; it is to rebuild the Jewish Temple and to plant anew the groves of Academus.

Irving Babbitt

1865–1933

Cosmopolitan breadth of knowledge and sympathy do not by themselves suffice; to be humanized these qualities need to be tempered by discipline and selection.

LITERATURE AND THE AMERICAN COLLEGE

⚛

Irving Babbitt, founder of the American "New Humanism" movement, was born in Dayton, Ohio, in the last year of the Civil War. Descended from early Puritan settlers and a line of Congregationalist ministers, Babbitt attended Harvard, where he studied ancient and modern languages—including Greek, Latin, French, German, and Italian—and took his degree in classics in 1889. He then removed to Paris, where for two years he taught classics and studied Sanskrit and Pali. After returning to earn an M.A. at Harvard, he taught briefly at Williams College before coming back to Harvard yet again, teaching there for nearly forty years (from 1894 until his death in 1933). Despite his training in the classics, he taught French literature at his alma mater.

Babbitt married in 1900, formed a close professional and personal relationship with Princeton's Paul Elmer More, and built an international reputation as a distinguished literary and cultural critic. His students at Harvard included T. S. Eliot. With More, Babbitt founded the movement known as the New Humanism, based on a Socratic concern for carefully defined terms, clear principles of discernment of that which is worthy of our love, and a belief that the individual will and appetite must be always restrained. The New Humanism (as distinguished from John Dewey's secular humanism) rejected both Baconian power over nature and Romantic sentimental humanitarianism as proper goals for education. Bacon and Rousseau were twin manifestations of the modern expansive, imperial self, the New Humanists believed, as opposed to the disciplined self essential to true humanism. At some personal risk, Babbitt also attacked President Charles Eliot's reforms at Harvard, including his innovative elective system that dismantled the college's unifying prescriptive core. Several of his articles for the *Nation,* the *Atlantic Monthly,* and other publications were collected in 1908 as his first book, *Literature and the American College: Essays in Defense of the Humanities.* Other major works include *Rousseau and Romanticism* (1919) and *Democracy and Leadership* (1924).

THE SELECTIONS

Chapters 1 and 6 from *Literature and the American College* are included here. Babbitt first defines humanism, carefully distinguishing it from humanitarianism. True humanism is both a "doctrine and a discipline," that is to say, not only a dominant set of ideas about truth and value but also a principle of selection that shapes our judgment of excellence and an ethic of self-control. Ideas and character cannot be separated. Classical literature possesses a proven and unequalled formative power to shape the intellect, will, and imagination. Babbitt calls for connecting the classics to modern life and citizenship rather than indulging in their study merely as an antiquarian exercise. He calls for "a type of scholar intermediary between the high school pedagogue and the university specialist, who can interpret the classics in a large and liberal spirit to American undergraduates, carrying with him into his task the consciousness that he is forming the minds and characters of future citizens of a republic."

Babbitt's careful attempt to define (or to recover a proper definition of) humanism begins with the ancient Roman scholar Aulus Gellius. Gellius's comments about *humanitas* provide a fuller context for Babbitt's analysis:

> Those who have spoken Latin and have used the language correctly do not give to the word *humanitas* the meaning which it is commonly thought to have, namely, what the Greeks call [philanthropy], signifying a kind of friendly spirit and good-feeling towards all men without distinction; but they give to *humanitas* about the force of the Greek [*paideia*]; that is, what we call *eruditionem institutionemque in bonas artes,* or "education and training in the liberal arts." Those who earnestly desire and seek after these are the most highly humanized. For the pursuit of that kind of knowledge, and the training given by it, have been granted to man alone of all the animals, and for that reason it is termed *humanitas,* or "humanity."
>
> That it is in this sense that our earliest writers have used the word, and in particular Marcus Varro and Marcus Tullius [Cicero], almost all the literature shows.

From Literature and the American College
Chapter 1: What Is Humanism?

One of our Federal Judges said, not long ago, that what the American people need is ten per cent of thought and ninety per cent of action. In that case we ought all to be happy, for that is about what we have already. One is reminded by contrast of an accusation brought by a recent historian of Greek philosophy against Socrates, who, according to this historian, exaggerates the reasonableness of human nature. Only think rightly, Socrates seems to say, and right acting may be counted on to follow. The English and American temper is in this respect almost the reverse of Socratic. Act strenuously, would appear to be our faith, and right thinking will take care of itself. We feel that we can afford to "muddle along" in theory if only we attain to practical efficiency.

This comparative indifference to clearness and consistency of thought is visible even in that chief object of our national concern, education. The firmness of the American's faith in the blessings of education is equalled only by the vagueness of his ideas as to the kind of education to which these blessings are annexed. One can scarcely consider the tremendous stir we have been making for the past thirty years or more about education, the time and energy and enthusiasm we are ready to lavish on educational undertakings, the libraries and laboratories and endowments, without being reminded of the words of Sir Joshua Reynolds: "A provision of endless apparatus, a bustle of infinite inquiry and research, may be employed to evade and shuffle off real labor—the real labor of thinking." We live so fast, as the saying is, that we have no time to think. The task of organizing and operating a huge and complex educational machinery has left us scant leisure for calm reflection. Evidently a little less eagerness for action and a little more of the Socratic spirit would do no harm. We are likely, however, to be arrested at the very outset of any attempt to clarify our notions about education, as Socrates was in dealing with the problems of his own time, by the need of accurate definition. The Socratic method is, indeed, in its very essence a process of right defining. It divides and subdivides and distinguishes between the diverse and sometimes contradictory concepts that lurk beneath one word; it is a per-petual protest, in short, against the confusion that arises from the careless use of general terms, especially when they have become popular catchwords. If Socrates were here today, we can picture to ourselves how he would go around "cross-examining" those of us (there are some college presidents in the number) who repeat so glibly the current platitudes about liberty and progress, democracy, service, and the like; and he would no doubt get himself set down as a public nuisance for his pains, as he was by his fellow Athenians.

A good example of the confusion rising from general terms is the term that is more im-portant than any other, perhaps, for our present argument. To make a plea for humanism without explaining the word would give rise to endless misunderstanding. It is equally on the lips of the socialistic dreamer and the exponent of the latest philosophical fad. In an age of happy liberty like the present, when any one can employ almost any general term very much as he pleases, it is perhaps inevitable that the term humanism, which still has certain gracious associations lingering about it, should be appropriated by various theo-rists, in the hope, apparently, that the benefit of the associations may accrue to an entirely different order of ideas. Thus the Oxford philosopher, Mr. F. C. S. Schiller, claims to be a humanist, and in the name of humanism threatens to "do strange deeds upon the clouds." Renan says that the religion of the future will be a "true humanism." The utopists who have described their vision of the future as "humanism" or the "new humanism" are too numerous to mention. Gladstone speaks of the humanism of Auguste Comte, Professor Herford of the humanism of Rousseau, and the Germans in general of the humanism of Herder; whereas Comte, Rousseau, and Herder were all three not humanists, but humanitarian enthusiasts. A prominent periodical, on the other hand, laments the decay of the "humanitarian spirit" at Harvard, meaning no doubt humanistic. We evidently need a working definition not only of humanism, but of the words with which it is related or confused,—humane, humanistic, humanitarian, humanitarianism. And these words, if successfully defined, will help us to a further necessary definition,—that of the college. For any discussion of the place of literature in the college is conditioned by a previous question: whether there will be any college for literature to have a place in. The college has been brought to this predicament not so much perhaps by its avowed enemies as by those who profess to be its friends. Under these circumstances our prayer, like that of Ajax, should be to fight in the light.

I

The first step in our quest would seem to be to go back to the Latin words (*humanus, humanitas*) from which all the words of our group are derived. Most of the material we need will be found in a recent and excellent study by M. Gaston Boissier of the ancient meanings of *humanitas*. From M. Boissier's paper it would appear that *humanitas* was from the start a fairly elastic virtue with the Romans, and that the word came to be used rather loosely, so that in a late Latin writer, Aulus Gellius, we find a complaint that it had been turned aside from its true meaning. *Humanitas,* says Gellius, is incorrectly used to denote a "promiscuous benevolence, what the Greeks call philanthropy," whereas the word really implies doctrine and discipline, and is applicable not to men in general but only to a select few,—it is, in short, aristocratic and not democratic in its implication.[1]

The confusion that Gellius complains of is not only interesting in itself, but closely akin to one that we need to be on guard against today. If we are to believe Gellius, the Roman decadence was like our own age in that it tended to make love for one's fellow men, or altruism, as we call it, do duty for most of the other virtues. It confused humanism with philanthropy. Only our philanthropy has been profoundly modified, as we shall see more fully later, by becoming associated with an idea of which only the barest beginnings can be found in antiquity—the idea of progress.

It was some inkling of the difference between a universal philanthropy and the indoctrinating and disciplining of the individual that led Aulus Gellius to make his protest. Two words were probably needed in his time; they are certainly needed today. A person who has sympathy for mankind in the lump, faith in its future progress, and desire to serve the great cause of this progress, should be called not a humanist, but a humanitarian, and his creed may be designated as humanitarianism. From the present tendency to regard humanism as an abbreviated and convenient form for humanitarianism there must arise every manner of confusion. The humanitarian lays stress almost solely upon breadth of

---

1. See *Noctes Atticae*, xiii, 17.

knowledge and sympathy. The poet Schiller, for instance, speaks as a humanitarian and not as a humanist when he would "clasp the millions to his bosom," and bestow "a kiss upon the whole world." The humanist is more selective in his caresses. Aulus Gellius, who was a man of somewhat crabbed and pedantic temper, would apparently exclude sympathy almost entirely from his conception of *humanitas* and confine the meaning to what he calls *cura et discipline*; and he cites the authority of Cicero. Cicero, however, seems to have avoided any such one-sided view. Like the admirable humanist that he was, he no doubt knew that what is wanted is not sympathy alone, nor again discipline and selection alone, but a disciplined and selective sympathy. Sympathy without selection becomes flabby, and a selection which is unsympathetic tends to grow disdainful.

The humanist, then, as opposed to the humanitarian, is interested in the perfecting of the individual rather than in schemes for the elevation of mankind as a whole; and although he allows largely for sympathy, he insists that it be disciplined and tempered by judgment. One of the most recent attempts to define humanism, that of Brunetière,[2] who was supposed to be out of touch with his own time, suffers, nevertheless, from our present failure to see in the term anything more than the fullness of knowlege and sympathy. Brunetière thinks he has discovered a complete definition of humanism in the celebrated line of Terence: "Humani nihil a me alienum puto." This line expresses very well a universal concern for one's fellow creatures, but fails to define the humanist because of the entire absence of the idea of selection. It is spoken in the play as an excuse for meddling; and might serve appropriately enough as a motto for the humanitarian busybody with whom we are all so familiar nowadays, who goes around with schemes for reforming almost everything—except himself. As applied to literature, the line might be cited as a justification for reading anything, from Plato to the Sunday supplement. Cosmopolitan breadth of knowledge and sympathy do not by themselves suffice; to be humanized these qualities need to be tempered by discipline and selection. From this point of view the Latin *litteræ humaniores* is a happier phrase than our English "humane letters," because of the greater emphasis the Latin comparative puts on the need of selection.

The true humanist maintains a just balance between sympathy and selection. We moderns, even a champion of the past like Brunetière, tend to lay an undue stress on the element of sympathy. On the other hand, the ancients in general, both Greek and Roman, inclined to sacrifice sympathy to selection. Gellius's protest against confusing *humanitas* with a promiscuous philanthropy instead of reserving it for doctrine and discipline would by itself be entirely misleading. Ancient humanism is as a whole intensely aristocratic in temper; its sympathies run in what would seem to us narrow channels; it is naturally disdainful of the humble and lowly who have not been indoctrinated and disciplined. Indeed, an unselective and universal sympathy, the sense of the brotherhood of man, as we term it, is usually supposed to have come into the world only with Christianity. We may go farther and say that the exaltation of love and sympathy as supreme and all-sufficing principles that do not need to be supplemented by doctrine and discipline is largely peculiar to our modern and humanitarian era. Historically, Christians have always inclined to reserve their sympathies for those who had the same doctrine and discipline as themselves, and only too often have joined to a sympathy for their own kind a fanatical hatred for

2. *Histoire de la Littérature francaise classique*, t. i, p. 28.

everybody else. One whole side of Christianity has put a tremendous emphasis on selection—even to the point of conceiving of God Himself as selective rather than sympathetic ("Many are called, few are chosen," etc.). We may be sure that stalwart believers like St. Paul or St. Augustine or Pascal would look upon our modern humanitarians with their talk of social problems and their tendency to reduce religion to a phase of the tenement-house question as weaklings and degenerates. Humanitarianism, however, and the place it accords to sympathy is so important for our subject that we shall have to revert to it later. For the present, it is enough to oppose the democratic inclusiveness of our modern sympathies to the aristocratic aloofness of the ancient humanist and his disdain of the profane vulgar (*Odi profanum vulgus et arceo*). This aloofness and disdain are reflected and in some ways intensified in the humanism of the Renaissance. The man of the Renaissance felt himself doubly set above the "raskall many," first by his doctrine and discipline and then by the learned medium through which the doctrine and discipline were conveyed. The echo of this haughty humanism is heard in the lines of Milton:—

> Nor do I name of men the common rout,
> That wandering loose about,
> Grow up and perish as the summer fly,
> Heads without name, no more remembered.

Later on this humanistic ideal became more and more conventionalized and associated with a hierarchy of rank and privilege. The sense of intellectual superiority was reinforced by the sense of social superiority. The consequent narrowing of sympathy is what Amiel objects to in the English gentleman: "Between gentlemen, courtesy, equality, social proprieties; below that level, haughtiness, disdain, coldness, indifference. . . . The politeness of a gentleman is not human and general, but quite individual and personal." It is a pity, no doubt, that the Englishman is thus narrow in his sympathies; but it will be a greater pity, if, in enlarging his sympathies, he allows his traditional disciplines, humanistic and religious, to be relaxed and enervated. The English humanist is not entirely untrue to his ancient prototype even in the faults of which Amiel complains. There is a real relation, as Professor Butcher points out, between the English idea of the gentleman and scholar and the view of the cultivated man that was once held in the intensely aristocratic democracy of Athens.

II

We should of course remember that though we have been talking of ancient humanism and humanists, the word humanist was not used until the Renaissance and the word humanism not until a still later period. In studying the humanism of the Renaissance the significant contrast that we need to note is the one commonly made at this time between humanity and divinity. In its essence the Renaissance is a protest against the time when there was too much divinity and not enough humanity, against the starving and stunting of certain sides of man by mediaeval theology, against a vision of the supernatural that imposed a mortal constraint upon his more purely human and natural faculties. The models of a full and free play of these faculties were sought in the ancient classics, but the cult of the ancients soon became itself a superstition, so that a man was called a humanist from the mere fact of having received an initiation into the ancient languages, even though he had little or nothing of the doctrine and discipline that the term should imply. Very few of the early Italian humanists were really humane. For many of them humanism, so far from being a doctrine and discipline, was a revolt from all discipline, a wild rebound from the mediaeval extreme into an opposite excess. What predominates in the first part of the Renaissance is a movement of emancipation—emancipation of the senses, of the intellect, and in the northern countries of the conscience. It was the first great modern era of expansion, the first forward push of individualism. As in all such periods, the chief stress is on the broadening of knowledge, and, so far as was compatible with the humanistic exclusiveness, of sympathy. The men of that time had what Emerson calls a canine appetite for knowledge. The ardor with which they broke away from the bonds and leading-strings of mediaeval tradition, the exuberance with which they celebrated the healing of the long feud between nature and human nature, obscured for a time the need of decorum and selection. A writer like Rabelais, for instance, is neither decorous nor select; and so in spite of his great genius would probably have seemed to a cultivated ancient barbaric rather than humane. Such a disorderly and undisciplined unfolding of the faculties of the individual, such an overemphasis on the benefits of liberty as compared with the benefits of restraint, brought in its train the evils that are peculiar to periods of expansion. There was an increase in anarchical self-assertion and self-indulgence that seemed a menace to the very existence of society; and so society reacted against the individual and an era of expansion was followed by an era of concentration. This change took place at different times, and under different circumstances, in different countries. In Italy the change coincides roughly with the sack of Rome (1527) and the Council of Trent; in France it follows the frightful anarchy of the wars of religion and finds political expression in Henry IV, and literary expression in Malherbe. Of course in so complex a period as the Renaissance we must allow for innumerable eddies and crosscurrents and for almost any number of individual exceptions. In an age as well as in an individual there are generally elements, often important elements, that run counter to the main tendency. But if one is not a German doctor who has to prove his "originality," or a lover of paradox for its own sake, it is usually possible to discern the main drift in spite of the eddies and counter-currents.

We may affirm, then, that the main drift of the later Renaissance was away from a humanism that favored a free expansion toward a humanism that was in the highest degree disciplinary and selective. The whole movement was complicated by what is at bottom a different problem, the need that was felt in France and Italy, at least, of protecting society against the individual. One can insist on selection and discipline without at the same time being so distrustful of individualism. Many of the humanists of this period fell into hardness and narrowness (in other words, ceased to be humane) from overemphasis on a discipline that was to be imposed from without and from above, and on a doctrine that was to be codified in a multitude of minute prescriptions. The essence of art, according to that highly astringent genius, Scaliger, who had a European influence on the literary criticism of this age, is *electio et fastidium sui*—selection and fastidiousness toward one's self (in practice Scaliger reserved his fastidiousness for other people). This spirit of fastidious selection gained ground until instead of the expansive Rabelais we have the exclusive Malherbe, until a purism grew up that threatened to impoverish men's ideas and emotions as well as their vocabulary. Castiglione had said in his treatise on the Courtier that there should enter into the make-up of the gentleman an element of aloofness and disdain (*sprezzatura*), a saying that, properly interpreted, contains a profound truth. Unfortunately, aristocratic aloofness, coupled with fastidious selection and unleavened by broad and sympathetic knowledge, leads straight to the attitude that Voltaire has hit off in his sketch of the noble Venetian lord Pococurante,—to the type of scholar who would be esteemed, not like the man of today by the inclusiveness of his sympathies, but by the number of things he had rejected. Pococurante had cultivated *sprezzatura* with a vengeance, and rejected almost everything except a few verses of Virgil and Horace. "What a great man is this Pococurante!" says the awe-stricken Candide; "nothing can please him."

The contrast between the disciplinary and selective humanism of the later Renaissance and the earlier period of expansion should not blind us to the underlying unity of aim. Like the ancient humanists whom they took as their guides, the men of both periods aimed at forming the complete man (*totus, teres atque rotundus*). But the men of the later period and the neo-classicists in general hoped to attain this completeness not so much by the virtues of expansion as by the virtues of concentration. It seemed to them that the men of the earlier period had left too much opening for the whims and vagaries of the individual; and so they were chiefly concerned with making a selection of subjects and establishing a doctrine and discipline that should be universal and human. To this end the classical doctrine and discipline were to be put into the service of the doctrine and discipline of Christianity. This attempt at a compromise between the pagan and Christian traditions is visible both in Catholic countries in the Jesuit schools, and in Protestant countries in the selection of studies that took shape in the old college curriculum. No doubt the selection of both divinity and humanity that was intended to be representative was inadequate; and no doubt the whole compromise between doctrines and disciplines, that were in many respects divergent and in some respects hostile, laid itself open to the charge of being superficial. The men of the early Renaissance had felt more acutely the antagonism between divinity as then understood and humanity, and had often taken sides uncompromisingly for one or the other. Machiavelli accused Christianity of having made the world effeminate, whereas Luther looked on the study of the pagan classics, except within the narrowest bounds, as pernicious. Calvin execrated Rabelais, and Rabelais denounced Calvin as an impostor. Yet, after all, the effort to make the ancient humanities and arts of expression tributary to Christianity was in many respects admirable, and the motto that summed it up, *sapiens atque eloquens pietas*, might still, if properly interpreted, be used to define the purpose of the college.

A desideratum of scholarship at present is a study of the way certain subjects came to be selected as representative and united into one discipline with elements that were drawn from religion; we need, in short, a more careful history than has yet been written of the old college curriculum. Closely connected with this and equally needful is a history of the development of the gentleman, going back to the work of Castiglione and other Italian treatises on manners in the sixteenth century, and making clear especially how the conception of the gentleman came to unite with that of the scholar so as to form an ideal of which something still survives in England. A Castiglione in Italy and a Sir Philip Sidney in England already realize the ideal of the gentleman and scholar, and that with the splendid vitality of the Renaissance. But a Scaliger, for all his fastidious selection, remains a colossal pedant. In general, it is only under French influence that scholarship gets itself disengaged from pedantry and acquires urbanity and polish, that the standards of the humanist coalesce with those of the man of the world. But it is likewise under French influence that the ideal of the gentleman and scholar is externalized and conventionalized, until in some of the later neo-classic Pococurantes it has degenerated into a mixture of snobbishness and superficiality, until what had once been a profound insight becomes a mere polite prejudice. We must not, however, be like the leaders of the great romantic revolt who, in their eagerness to get rid of the husk of convention, disregarded also the humane aspiration. Even in his worst artificiality, the neo-classicist is still related to the ancient humanist by his horror of one-sidedness, of all that tends to the atrophy of certain faculties and the hypertrophy of others, by his avoidance of everything that is excessive and over-emphatic; and, inasmuch as it is hard to be an enthusiast and at the same time moderate, by his distrust of enthusiasm. He cultivates detachment and freedom from affectation (*sprezzatura*) and wonders at nothing (*nil admirari*); whereas the romanticist, as all the world knows, is prone to wonder at everything—especially at himself and his own genius. In his appearance and behavior, the neo-classicist would be true to the general traits of human nature, and is even careful to avoid technical and professional terms in his writing and conversation. "Perfected good breeding," says Dr. Johnson, "consists in having no particular mark of any profession, but a general elegance of manners." (A standard that Dr. Johnson himself did not entirely attain.) At the bottom of the whole point of view is the fear of specialization. "The true gentleman and scholar" (*honnête homme*), says La Rochefoucauld, "is he who does not pride himself on anything." We may contrast this with a maxim that is sometimes heard in the American business world: A man who knows two things is damned. In other words, the man of that time would rather have been thought superficial than one-sided, the man of today would rather be thought one-sided than superficial.

III

We may perhaps venture to sum up the results of our search for a definition of humanism. We have seen that the humanist, as we know him historically, moved between an extreme of sympathy and an extreme of discipline and selection, and became humane in proportion as he mediated between these extremes. To state this truth more generally, the true mark of excellence in a man, as Pascal puts it, is his power to harmonize in himself opposite virtues and to occupy all the space between them (*tout l'entredeux*). By his ability thus to unite in himself opposite qualities man shows his humanity, his superiority of essence over other animals. Thus Saint Francois de Sales, we are told, united in himself the qualities of the eagle and the dove—he was an eagle of gentleness. The historian of Greek philosophy we have already quoted remarks on the perfect harmony that Socrates had attained between thought and feeling. If we compare Socrates in this respect with Rousseau, who said that "his heart and his head did not seem to belong to the same individual," we shall perceive the difference between a sage and a sophist. Man is a creature who is foredoomed to one-sidedness, yet who becomes humane only in proportion as he triumphs over this fatality of his nature, only as he arrives at that measure which comes from tempering his virtues, each by its opposite. The aim, as Matthew Arnold has said in the most admirable of his critical phrases, is to see life steadily and see it whole; but this is an aim, alas, that no one has ever attained completely—not even Sophocles, to whom

Arnold applies it. After man has made the simpler adjustments, there are other and more difficult adjustments awaiting him beyond, and the goal is, in a sense, infinitely remote.

For most practical purposes, the law of measure is the supreme law of life because it bounds and includes all other laws. It was doubtless the perception of this fact that led the most eminent personality of the Far East, Gotama Buddha, to proclaim in the opening sentence of his first sermon that extremes are barbarous. But India as a whole failed to learn the lesson. Greece is perhaps the most humane of countries, because it not only formulated clearly the law of measure ("nothing too much"), but also perceived the avenging nemesis that overtakes every form of insolent excess (ὕβρις) or violation of this law.

Of course, even in Greece any effective insight into the law of measure was confined to a minority, though at times a large minority. The majority at any particular instant in Greece or elsewhere is almost sure to be unsound, and unsound because it is one-sided. We may borrow a homely illustration from the theory of commercial crises. A minority of men may be prudent and temper their enterprise with discretion, but the majority is sure to over-trade, and so unless restrained by the prudent few will finally bring on themselves the nemesis of a panic. The excess from which Greek civilization suffered should be of special interest, because it is plain that so humane a people could not have failed to make any of the ordinary adjustments. Without attempting to treat fully so difficult a topic, we may say that Greece, having lost its traditional standards through the growth of intellectual skepticism, fell into a dangerous and excessive mobility of mind because of its failure to develop new standards that would unify its life and impose a discipline upon the individual. It failed, in short, to mediate between unity and diversity, or, as the philosophers express it, between the absolute and the relative. The wisest Greek thinkers, notably Socrates and Plato, saw the problem and sought a solution; but by putting Socrates to death Athens made plain that it was unable to distinguish between its sages and its sophists.

There is the One, says Plato, and there is the Many. "Show me the man who can combine the One with the Many and I will follow in his footsteps, even as in those of a God."[3] To harmonize the One with the Many, this is indeed a difficult adjustment, perhaps the most difficult of all, and so important, withal, that nations have perished from their failure to achieve it. Ancient India was devoured by a too overpowering sense of the One. The failure of Greece, on the other hand, to attain to this restraining sense of unity led at last to the pernicious pliancy of the "hungry Greekling," whose picture Juvenal has drawn.

The present time in its loss of traditional standards is not without analogy to the Athens of the Periclean age; and so it is not surprising, perhaps, that we should see a refurbishing of the old sophistries. The so-called humanism of a writer like Mr. F. C. S. Schiller has in it something of the intellectual impressionism of a Protagoras.[4] Like the ancient sophist,

---

3. *Phaedrus*, 266b. The Greeks in general did not associate the law of measure with the problem of the One and the Many. Aristotle, who was in this respect a more representative Greek than Plato, can scarcely be said to have connected his theory of the contemplative life or attainment to a sense of the divine unity, with his theory of virtue as a mediating between extremes.

4. Mr. Schiller himself points out this connection (see *Humanism*, p. xvii). As will appear clearly from a later passage, I do not quarrel with the pragmatists for their appeal to experience and practical results, but for their failure, because of an insufficient feeling for the One, to arrive at real criteria for testing experience and discriminating between judgments and mere passing impressions.

the pragmatist would forego the discipline of a central standard, and make of individual man and his thoughts and feelings the measure of all things. "Why may not the advancing front of experience," says Professor James, "carrying its imminent satisfaction and dissatisfaction, cut against the black inane, as the luminous orb of the moon cuts against the black abyss?"[5] But the sun and moon and stars have their preordained courses, and do not dare, as the old Pythagoreans said, to transgress their numbers. To make Professor James's metaphor just, the moon would need to deny its allegiance to the central unity, and wander off by itself on an impressionistic journey of exploration through space. It is doubtless better to be a pragmatist than to devote one's self to embracing the cloud Junos of Hegelian metaphysics. But that persons who have developed such an extreme sense of the otherwiseness of things as Professor James and his school should be called humanists—this we may seriously doubt. There would seem to be nothing less humane—or humanistic—than pluralism pushed to this excess, unless it be monism pushed to a similar extremity.

The human mind, if it is to keep its sanity, must maintain the nicest balance between unity and plurality. There are moments when it should have the sense of communion with absolute being, and of the obligation to higher standards that this insight brings; other moments when it should see itself as but a passing phase of the everlasting flux and relativity of nature; moments when, with Emerson, it should feel itself "alone with the gods alone"; and moments when, with Sainte-Beuve, it should look upon itself as only the "most fugitive of illusions in the bosom of the infinite illusion." If man's nobility lies in his kinship to the One, he is at the same time a phenomenon among other phenomena, and only at his risk and peril neglects his phenomenal self. The humane poise of his faculties suffers equally from an excess of naturalism and an excess of supernaturalism. We have seen how the Renaissance protested against the supernaturalist excess of the Middle Ages, against a one-sidedness that widened unduly the gap between nature and human nature. Since that time the world has been tending to the opposite extreme; not content with establishing a better harmony between nature and human nature, it would close up the gap entirely. Man, according to the celebrated dictum of Spinoza, is not in nature as one empire in another empire, but as a part in a whole. Important faculties that the supernaturalist allowed to decay the naturalist has cultivated, but other faculties, especially those relating to the contemplative life, are becoming atrophied through long disuse. Man has gained immensely in his grasp on facts, but in the meanwhile has become so immersed in their multiplicity as to lose that vision of the One by which his lower self was once overawed and restrained. "There are two laws discrete," as Emerson says in his memorable lines; and since we cannot reconcile the "Law for man" and the "Law for thing," he would have us preserve our sense for each separately, and maintain a sort of "double consciousness," a "public" and a "private" nature; and he adds in a curious image that a man must ride alternately on the horses of these two natures, "as the equestrians in the circus throw themselves nimbly from horse to horse, or plant one foot on the back of one and the other foot on the back of the other."

There is, perhaps, too much of this spiritual circus-riding in Emerson. Unity and plurality appear too often in his work, not as reconciled opposites, but as clashing antino-

---

5. *Humanism and Truth*, p. 16.

mies. He is too satisfied with saying about half the time that everything is like everything else, and the rest of the time that everything is different from everything else. And so his genius has elevation and serenity, indeed, but at the same time a disquieting vagueness and lack of grip in dealing with particulars. Yet Emerson remains an important witness to certain truths of the spirit in an age of scientific materialism. His judgment of his own time is likely to be definitive:—

> Things are in the saddle
> And ride mankind.

Man himself and the products of his spirit, language, and literature, are treated not as having a law of their own, but as things; as entirely subject to the same methods that have won for science such triumphs over phenomenal nature. The president of a congress of anthropologists recently chose as a motto for his annual address the humanistic maxim: "The proper study of mankind is man"; and no one, probably, was conscious of any incongruity. At this rate, we may soon see set up as a type of the true humanist the Chicago professor who recently spent a year in collecting cats'-cradles on the Congo.

The humanities need to be defended today against the encroachments of physical science, as they once needed to be against the encroachment of theology. . . .

Chapter 6: The Rational Study of the Classics[6]

Dean Swift, in his description of the battle between the ancient and modern books in the king's library, has very wisely refrained from telling the outcome of the encounter. The conflict is not even yet fought to a finish, but the advantage is more and more on the side of the moderns. By its unconscious drift not less than by its conscious choice of direction, the world seems to be moving away from the classics. The modern mind, as the number of subjects that solicit attention increases, tends, by an instinct of self-preservation, to reject everything that has even the appearance of being non-essential.

If, then, the teacher of the classics is thus put on the defensive, the question arises how far his position is inevitable, and how far it springs from a failure to conform his methods to existing needs. Present methods of classical teaching reflect the change that has taken place during the past thirty years in our whole higher education. This period has seen the rise of graduate schools organized with a view to the training of specialists on the German plan, and superimposed on undergraduate systems belonging to an entirely different tradition. The establishment of the first of these graduate schools, that of the Johns Hopkins University, and the impulse there given to work of the type leading to the German doctor's degree, is an event of capital importance in American educational history. President Gilman contemplated with something akin to enthusiasm the introduction of the German scientific spirit, of *strengwissenschaftliche Methode*, the instinct for research and original work, into the intellectual life of the American student. The results have

---

6. It might be well to point out that this essay was written in 1896, from six to eleven years before the other essays in the volume, and refers in places to conditions that have since undergone some change.

more than justified his expectations. In all that relates to accurate grasp of the subject in hand, to strenuous application and mastery of detail, the standard of American scholarship has risen immensely during the last few years, and will continue to rise. Our universities are turning out a race of patient and laborious investigators, who may claim to have rivaled the Germans on their own ground, as Horace said the Romans had come to rival the Greeks:—

> Venimus ad summum fortunae; pingimus atque Psallimus et luctamur Achivis doctius unctis.

There are, however, even among those who recognize the benefits of the German scientific spirit, many who feel at the same time its dangers and drawbacks. A reaction is beginning against a too crude application of German methods to American educational needs. There are persons at present who do not believe that a man is fitted to fill a chair of French literature in an American college simply because he has made a critical study of the text of a dozen mediaeval beast fables and written a thesis on the Picard dialect, and who deny that a man is necessarily qualified to interpret the humanities to American undergraduates because he has composed a dissertation on the use of the present participle in Ammianus Marcellinus. It is held by others, who put the matter on broader grounds, that German science is beginning to show signs of a decadence similar to the decadence that overtook Greek science in the schools of Alexandria. Matthew Arnold declares the great Anglo-Saxon failing during the present century to have been an excessive faith in machinery and material appliances. May we not with equal truth say that the great German failing during the same period has been an excessive faith in intellectual machinery and intellectual appliances? What else but intellectual machinery is that immense mass of partial results which has grown out of the tendency of modern science to an ever minuter subdivision and analysis? The heaping up of volumes of special research and of investigations of infinitesimal detail has kept pace in Germany with the multiplication of mechanical contrivances in the Anglo-Saxon world. One sometimes asks in moments of despondency whether the main achievement of the nineteenth century will not have been to accumulate a mass of machinery that will break the twentieth century's back. The Cornell University library already contains, for the special study of Dante alone, over seven thousand volumes; about three fourths of which, it may be remarked in passing, are nearly or quite worthless, and only tend to the confusion of good counsel. Merely to master the special apparatus for the study of Dante and his times, the student, if he conforms to the standard set for the modern specialist, will run the risk of losing his intellectual symmetry and sense of proportion, precisely the qualities of which he will stand most in need for the higher interpretation of Dante.

Nowhere, perhaps, is this disposition to forget the end of knowledge in the pursuit of its means and appliances more apparent than in the study of the classics. There is no intention, in saying this, to underrate the services that nineteenth-century scholars, especially those of Germany, have rendered the cause of classical learning. In their philological research and minute criticism of texts they are only following a method which, though first formulated and systematically applied by Bentley, goes back in its main features to the great scholars of the Renaissance. Is there not, however, a fallacy in assuming that material so strictly limited in amount as that remaining to us from classical antiquity is forever to be primarily the subject of scientific investigation? The feudal institutions which saved France from anarchy during the Middle Ages had come, in the eighteenth century, to be the worst of anachronisms; and in like manner the type of scholarship which was needed at the beginning of the Renaissance to rescue and restore the texts of the classical writers will come to be a no less flagrant anachronism if persisted in after that work has been thoroughly done. The method which in the sixteenth century produced a Stephanus or a Casaubon will only give us today the spectacle of the "German doctor desperate with the task of saying something where everything has been said, and eager to apply his new theory of fog as an illuminating medium." As the field of ancient literature is more and more completely covered, the vision of the special investigator must become more and more microscopic. The present generation of classical philologists, indeed, reminds one of a certain sect of Japanese Buddhists which believes that salvation is to be attained by arriving at a knowledge of the infinitely small. Men have recently shown their fitness for teaching the humanities by writing theses on the ancient horse-bridle and the Roman doorknob.

Doubtless the time has not yet come for what may be called the age of research in the ancient languages to be finally brought to a close. Of Greek literature especially, we may say, in the words of La Fontaine, "That is a field which cannot be so harvested that there will not be something left for the latest comer to glean." But while there may still be subjects of research in the classics that will reward the advanced student, it is doubtful whether there are many such whose study the beginner may profitably undertake as a part of his preparation in his specialty. In doing the work necessary under existing conditions to obtain the doctor's degree in the classics, it may be questioned whether a man has chosen the best means of getting at the spirit, or even the letter, of ancient literature or of qualifying himself to become an exponent of that literature to others. It is claimed by the advocates of research that the training the student gets in his investigation, even though he fail to arrive at any important result, is in itself valuable and formative to a high degree. He is at least initiated into that *strengwissenschaftliche Methode* on which President Gilman lays such particular stress. We must recognize a large measure of truth in the claims thus put forward by the advocates of research. It is by his power to gather himself together, to work within limits, as Goethe has told us in a well-known phrase, that the master is first revealed. In so far, then, as the German scientific method forces us to gather ourselves together and to work within limits, thereby increasing our power of concentration, our ability to lay firm hold upon the specific fact, we cannot esteem it too highly. There can be no more salutary discipline for a person who is afflicted with what may be termed a loose literary habit of mind than to be put through a course of exact research. The lack of the power to work within limits, to lay firm hold upon the specific fact, is a fault of the gravest character, even when it appears in a mind like that of Emerson.

The question arises, however, whether an unduly high price has not been paid for accuracy and scientific method when these qualities have been obtained at the sacrifice of breadth. Would it not be possible to devise a series of examinations, somewhat similar in character, perhaps, to those now held for honors at Oxford and Cambridge—examinations which would touch upon ancient life and literature at the largest possible number of points, and which might serve to reveal, as the writings of a doctor's thesis does not, the range as well as the exactness of a student's knowledge? Some test is certainly needed which shall go to show, the general culture of a candidate as well as his special proficiency, his familiarity with ideas as well as with words, and his mastery of the spirit, as well as of the mechanism, of the ancient languages.

It is precisely in the failure to distinguish between the spirit and the mechanism of languages, in the unwillingness to recognize literature as having claims apart from philology, that the danger of the present tendency chiefly consists. The opinion seems to be gaining ground that the study of literature by itself is unprofitable, hard to disassociate from dilettanteism, and not likely to lead to much except a lavish outlay of elegant epithets of admiration. A professor of Greek in one of the Eastern colleges is reported to have said that the literary teaching of the classics would reduce itself in practice to ringing the changes on the adjective "beautiful!" It is rigorous scientific method, we are told, that needs to be painfully acquired. If a man has a certain right native instinct, his appreciation of the literature will take care of itself; and if this native instinct is lacking, it is something that no pressure from without will avail to produce. It is, then, *strengwissenschaftliche Methode* with its talismanic virtues that our every effort should be directed to impart, whereas the taste for literature is to be reckoned in with Dogberry's list of things that come by nature. It is in virtue of some such sentiments as this that the study of philology seems at present to be driving the study of literature more and more from our Eastern universities. Do not the holders of this view, we may ask, emphasize unduly the influence their method will have upon individuals, and at the same time fail to consider the effect it may have in the formation of a tendency? In the long run the gradual working of any given ideal upon the large body of average men, who simply take on the color of their environment, will produce a well-nigh irresistible movement in the direction of that ideal. If the minutiae rather than the larger aspects of the classics are insisted upon, the taste for small things will spread like a contagion among the rank and file of classical scholars, and we shall soon be threatened with an epidemic of pedantry. A particular type of school is as much in need of a congenial atmosphere in which to flourish as a plant is in need of a congenial soil and climate in which to flower and bring forth fruit. We cannot readily imagine a Professor Jowett appearing under existing conditions at the University of Berlin. Besides, the danger is to be taken into account that if present methods are pushed much further, the young men with the right native instinct for literature are likely to be driven out of the classics entirely. Young men of this type may not all care to be educated as though they were to be "editors, and not lovers of polite literature"; they may not feel the fascination of spending months in a classical seminary, learning how to torment the text and the meaning of a few odes of Horace,—

> And torture one poor word ten thousand ways.

There is, to be sure, a very real danger in some subjects, especially in English literature, that the instruction may take too belletristic a turn. The term "culture course" has come to mean, among the undergraduates of one of our Eastern colleges, a course in which the students are not required to do any work. It is one of the main advantages of Latin and Greek over modern languages that the mere mastering of an ancient author's meaning will give to a course enough bone and sinew of solid intellectual effort to justify the teacher in adding thereto the flesh and blood of a literary interpretation. In a civilization so hard and positive in temper as our own, it is not the instinct for philology, but rather the instinct for literature and the things of the imagination, which is likely to remain latent if left to itself. A certain dry, lexicographical habit of mind is said by Europeans to be the distinctive mark of American scholarship. Instead of fostering this habit of mind in the study of the classics by an undue insistence on philology, it should be our endeavor to counteract it by giving abundant stimulus and encouragement to the study of them as literature. In the classics more than in other subjects, the fact should never be forgotten that the aim proposed is the assimilation, and not the accumulation, of knowledge. In the classics, if nowhere else, mere erudition should be held in comparatively little account except in so far as it has been converted into culture; and culture itself should not be regarded as complete until it has so penetrated its possessor as to become a part of his character. Montaigne has said somewhere in his essays that he loved to forge his mind rather than to furnish it. The metaphor of Montaigne's phrase is somewhat mixed, but the idea it embodies is one that men born into a late age of scholarship cannot ponder too carefully. As the body of learning transmitted from the past increases in volume, it becomes constantly more difficult to maintain the exact relation between the receipt and the assimilation of knowledge which has been declared by the greatest of the Hindu sages to be the root of all wisdom. "Without knowledge," says Buddha, "there is no reflection, without reflection there is no knowledge; he who has both knowledge and reflection is close upon Nirvâna."

The risk we run nowadays is that of having our minds buried beneath a dead-weight of information which we have no inner energy, no power of reflection, to appropriate to our own uses and convert into vital nutriment. We need to be on our guard against allowing the mere collector of information to gain an undue advantage over the man who would maintain some balance between his knowledge and reflection. We are, for instance, putting a premium on pedantry, if we set up as the sole test of proficiency in the classics the degree of familiarity shown with that immense machinery of minute learning that has grown up about them. This is to exalt that mere passive intellectual feeding which is the bane of modern scholarship. It is to encourage the man who is willing to abandon all attempt at native and spontaneous thought and become a mere register and repertory of other men's ideas in some small department of knowledge. The man who is willing to reduce his mind to a purely mechanical function may often thereby gain a mastery of facts that will enable him to intimidate the man who would make a larger use of his knowledge; for there are among scholars, as Holmes says there are in society, "fellows," who have a number of "ill-conditioned facts which they lead after them into decent company, ready to let them slip, like so many bulldogs, at every ingenious suggestion or convenient generalization or pleasant fancy." There has always existed between the man of the literal fact and the man of the general law, between the man of cold understanding and the man of thought and imagination, an instinctive aversion. We can trace the feud that has divided the two classes of minds throughout history. They were arrayed against each other in fierce debate for centuries during the Middle Ages under the name of Realists and Nominalists. The author of one of the oldest of the Hindu sacred books pronounces an anathema on two classes of people, the grammarian and the man who is over-fond of a good dinner, and debars them both from the hope of final salvation.

The remark has frequently been made that quarrels would not last long if the fault were on one side only. We may apply this truth to the debate in question, which considered in its essence, springs from the opposition between the lovers of synthesis and the lovers of analysis. Now, Emerson has profoundly said, in his essay on Plato, that the main merit of the Greeks was to have found and occupied the right middle ground between synthesis and analysis; and this will continue to be the aim of the true scholar.

The old humanism, such as it still survives at Oxford, has in it much that is admirable; but it has become, in some respects at least, antiquated and inadequate. It would sometimes seem to lead, as it did in the case of Walter Pater, to an ultra-aesthetic and epicurean attitude toward life—to a disposition to retire into one's ivory tower, and seek in ancient literature merely a source of exquisite solace. The main fault of this English humanism, however, is that it treats the classical writers too much as isolated phenomena; it fails to relate them in a broad and vital way to modern life. It would seem, then, that new life and interest are to be infused into the classics not so much by a restoration of the old humanism as by a larger application to them of the comparative and historical methods. These methods, we hasten to add, should be informed with ideas and reinforced by a sense of absolute values. Especially in the case of a language like Latin, whose literature is so purely derivative, and which has in turn radiated its influence along so many different lines to the modern world, any mere disconnected treatment of individual authors is entirely insufficient. The works of each author, indeed, should first be considered by themselves and on their own merits, but they should also be studied as links in that unbroken chain of literary and intellectual tradition which extends from the ancient to the modern world.

It is by bringing home to the mind of the American student the continuity of this tradition that one is likely to implant in him, more effectually, perhaps, than in any other way, that right feeling and respect for the past which he so signally lacks. For if the fault of other countries and other times has been an excess of reverence for the past, the danger of this country today would seem rather to be an undue absorption in the present. No great monument of a former age, no Pantheon or Notre Dame, rises in the midst of our American cities to make a silent plea for the past against the cheap and noisy tendencies of the passing hour. From various elements working together obscurely in his consciousness—from the theory of human perfectibility inherited from the eighteenth century, from the more recent doctrine of evolution, above all from the object lesson of his own national life—the average American has come to have an instinctive belief that each decade is a gain over the last decade, and that each century is an improvement on its predecessor; the first step he has to take in the path of culture is to realize that movement is not necessarily progress, and that the advance in civilization cannot be measured by the increase in the number of eighteen-story buildings. The emancipation from this servitude to the present may be reckoned as one of the chief benefits to be derived from classical study. Unfortunately this superficial modernism turns many away from the study of the classics altogether, and tends to diminish, even in those who do study them, that faith and enthusiasm so necessary to overcome the initial difficulties.

The American, it is true, is often haunted, in the midst of all his surface activity, with a vague sense that, after all, his life may be deficient in depth and dignity; it is not so often, however, that he succeeds in tracing this defect in his life to its lack of background and perspective, to the absence in himself of a right feeling for the past—that feeling which, as has been truly said, distinguishes more than any other the civilized man from the barbarian. As has already been remarked, this feeling is to be gained, in the case of the classics, not so much by treating them as isolated phenomena as by making clear the manifold ways in which they are related to the present, by leaving no chasm between ancient and modern life over which the mind is unable to pass. One of the important functions, then, of the classical teacher should be to bridge over the gap between the Greek and Roman world and the world of today. No preparation can be too broad, no culture too comprehensive, for the man who would fit himself for the adequate performance of such a task. His knowledge of modern life and literature needs to be almost as wide as his knowledge of the life and literature of antiquity. The ideal student of the classics should not rest satisfied until he is able to follow out in all its ramifications that Greek and Latin thought which, as Max Müller says, runs like fire in the veins of modern literature. In the case of an author like Virgil, for instance, he should be familiar not only with the classical Virgil, but also with the Virgil of after-centuries,—with Virgil the magician and enchanter who haunted the imagination of the Middle Ages, with Virgil the guide of Dante, and so on, down to the splendid ode of Tennyson. If he is dealing with Aristotle, he should be able to show the immense influence exercised by Aristotle over the mediaeval and modern European mind, both directly through the Latin tradition and indirectly through Averrhoës and the Arabs. If his author is Euripides, he should know in what way Euripides has affected modern dramatic art; he should be capable of making a comparison between the "Hippolytus" and the "Phèdre" of Racine. If he is studying Stoicism, he should be able to contrast the stoical ideal of perfection with the Christian ideal of the perfect life as elaborated by writers like St. Bonaventura and St. Thomas Aquinas. He should neglect far less than has been done heretofore the great patristic literature in Greek and Latin, as giving evidence of the process by which ancient thought passed over into thought of the mediaeval and modern types. These are only a few examples, chosen almost at random, of the wide and fruitful application that may be made of the comparative method.

How much, again, might be done to enhance the value of classical study by a freer use than has hitherto been made of the historical method! The word "historical" is intended to be taken in a large sense; what is meant is not so much a mere cataloguing of the events of ancient civilization as an investigation of the various causes that led to the greatness or decline of ancient societies. The last word on the reasons for the rise and fall of the Romans has not been spoken by Montesquieu. An investigation of the kind referred to would allow the application of many of the theories of modern science, but its results would have far more than an abstract scientific interest; they would provide us with instruction and examples to meet the problems of our own times. From the merest inattention to the teachings of the past, we are likely, in our national life, to proceed cheerfully to

> Commit the oldest sins the newest kind of ways.

A sober reflection on the history of the ancient republics might put us on our guard against many of the dangers to which we ourselves are exposed. It might cure us in part of our cheap optimism. It might, in any case, make us conscious of that tendency of which Macchiavelli had so clear a vision,—the tendency of a state to slip down an easy slope of prosperity into vice:—

Et in vitium fortuna labier aequa.

How much light must be shed—to give but a single illustration of what is meant—on contemporary as well as on Roman politics by a course, properly conducted, on the correspondence of Cicero!

The method just suggested of studying the classics might possibly render them less liable to the complaint now made that they are entirely remote from the interests and needs of the present. It is this feeling of the obsoleteness of the classics, joined to the utilitarian instinct so deeply imbedded in the American character, that is creating such a wide-spread sentiment in favor of giving the place they now hold to modern languages. The American student of the future is evidently going to have a chance to follow in the footsteps of that remarkable young woman, Miss Blanche Amory of "Pendennis," who, it will be remembered, "improved her mind by a sedulous study of the novels of the great modern authors of the French language." It would appear, from a comparison of the catalogues of one of our Eastern universities, that its undergraduates now have an opportunity to read "La Débâcle" of Emile Zola, where twenty years ago they would have been required to read the "Antigone" of Sophocles.

We will not attempt for the present a full discussion of this important question as to the relative educational value of ancient and modern languages, but a few reasons may be given briefly in support of the view that modern languages, however valuable as a study supplementary to the classics, are quite inadequate to take their place.

M. Paul Bourget, in a recent autobiographical sketch, tells us that, as a young man, he steeped his mind in the works of Stendhal and Baudelaire and other modern literature of the same type. He fails to explain, either to himself or others, the fact that these modern books, though written, as he says, in all truth and sincerity, should yet have given him a view of life which later led only to bitter disappointment and disillusion. M. Bourget's difficulty might have been less if he had taken into account that the authors of whom he speaks, so far from serving as a stimulus to his will and reason, merely invited him to retire into a corner and try strange experiments on his own emotional nature, and draw new and novel effects from his own capacity for sensation; that they held out to him, in short, the promise of a purely personal and sensuous satisfaction from life,—a promise which life itself may be counted upon not to keep. Now modern authors are not all, like Baudelaire, of the violently subjective type, but the intrusion of the author and his foibles into his work, the distortion of the objective reality of life by its passage through the personal medium, is much more frequent in modern than in ancient literature. Much of modern literature merely encourages to sentimental and romantic revery rather than to a resolute and manly grappling with the plain facts of existence. Romanticism may not mean the Commune, as Thiers said it did, but we may at least say that literature of the romantic type, compared with that in the classical tradition, is so deficient in certain qualities of sobriety and discipline as to make us doubt its value as a formative influence upon the minds of the young. Classical literature, at its best, does not so much tend to induce in us a certain state of feelings, much less a certain state of the nerves; it appeals rather to our higher reason and imagination—to those faculties which afford us an avenue of escape from ourselves, and enable us to become participants in the universal life. It is thus truly educative in that it leads him who studies it out and away from himself. The classical spirit, in its purest form, feels itself consecrated to the service of a high, impersonal reason. Hence its sentiment of restraint and discipline, its sense of proportion and pervading law. By bringing our acts into an ever closer conformity with this high, impersonal reason, it would lead us, although along a different path, to the same goal as religion, to a union ever more intimate with

> our only true, deep-buried selves,
> Being one with which we are one with the whole world.

By a complete and harmonious development of all our faculties under the guidance and control of this right reason, it would raise us above the possibility of ever again falling away

> Into some bondage of the flesh or mind,
> Some slough of sense, or some fantastic maze
> Forged by the imperious, lonely thinking power.

This high message contained in classical literature calls for the active exercise of our own best faculties, of our intellect and imagination, in order to be understood. It may be because of this purely intellectual appeal of the classics that there is so much initial inertia to overcome in awakening an interest in them. Indeed, to transform into a Greek scholar the average young man of today, whose power of attention has been dissipated in the pages of the American newspaper, whose mind has been relaxed by reading the modern erotic novel,—this, to borrow one of Phillips Brooks's phrases, would sometimes seem about as promising an enterprise as to make a lancehead out of putty. The number of those who can receive the higher lessons of Greek culture is always likely to be small. The classical spirit, however, is salutary and formative wherever it occurs, and if a man is not able to appreciate it in Pindar, he may in Horace; and if not in Horace, then in Molière. French literature of the seventeenth century is, as a whole, the most brilliant manifestation of the classical spirit in modern times, and one might teach French with considerable conviction, were it not for the propensity of the American student to confine his reading in French to inferior modern authors, and often, indeed, to novels of the decadence.

Decadent novels and other fungous growths of a similar nature are not peculiar to French, but are multiplying with alarming rapidity in all the great European literatures. Modern literature has been more or less sentimental since Petrarch, and a morbidly subjective strain has existed in it since Rousseau, while of late a quality is beginning to appear which we cannot better describe than as neurotic. We may say, to paraphrase an utterance of Chamfort's, that the success of some contemporary books is due to the correspondence that exists between the state of the author's nerves and the state of the nerves of his public. Spiritual despondency, which under the name of *acedia* was accounted one of the seven deadly sins during the Middle Ages, has come in these later days to be one of the main resources of literature. Life itself has recently been defined by one of the lights of the French deliquescent school as "an epileptic fit between two nothings." It is no small resource to be able to escape from these miasmatic exhalations of contemporary literature into the bracing atmosphere of the classics; to be able to rise into that purer ether

> where those immortal shapes
> Of bright aerial spirits live insphered
> In regions mild of calm and serene air.

We can, then, by no means allow the claims of those who find in modern languages an adequate substitute for the classics. However, we agree with those who assert that if the classics are to maintain their traditional place, they should be related more largely to the needs and aspirations of modern life. With this end in view, classical study must take a new direction; we need to emulate the spirit of the great scholars of the Renaissance, but to modify their methods. As to the present excess of German tendency in American classical scholarship, it may be left to remedy itself. The German research method appeals, indeed, to certain hard, positive qualities in the American mind, but other sides of the German ideal the American will find distasteful, on closer acquaintance; above all, he will prove incapable, in the long run, of the sublime disinterestedness of the German specialist, who, so far from asking himself whether his work will ever serve any practical purpose, never stops to inquire whether it will serve any purpose at all. A reaction, then, against the exaggerations of German method and of the scientific spirit will do no harm, though the classics need to benefit by a full application of the historical and comparative methods. There is needed in the classics today a man who can understand the past with the result, not of loosening, but of strengthening his grasp upon the present. There is needed a type of scholar intermediary between the high school pedagogue and the university specialist, who can interpret the classics in a large and liberal spirit to American undergraduates, carrying with him into his task the consciousness that he is forming the minds and characters of future citizens of a republic. The teaching of the classics thus understood could be made one of the best preparations for practical life, and less might be heard of the stock complaint about wasting time in the study of the dead languages. As to this last charge, we may quote from the most eloquent appeal that has been made of late years for a more liberal study of the classics,—that of Lowell in his Harvard Anniversary address. If the language of the Greeks is dead, he there says, "yet the literature it enshrines is rammed with life as perhaps no other writing, except Shakespeare's, ever was or will be. It is as contemporary with today as with the ears it first enraptured, for it appeals not to the man of then or now, but to the entire round of human nature itself. Men are ephemeral or evanescent, but whatever page the authentic soul of man has touched with her immortalizing finger, no matter how long ago, is still young and fair as it was to the world's gray fathers. Oblivion looks in the face of the Grecian Muse only to forget her errand. . . . We know not whither other studies will lead us, especially if dissociated from this; we do know to what summits, far above our lower region of turmoil, this has led, and what the many-sided outlook thence."

There was never greater need of the Hellenic spirit than there is today, and especially in this country, if that charge of lack of measure and sense of proportion which foreigners bring against Americans is founded in fact. As Matthew Arnold has admirably said, it is the Greek writers who best show the modern mind the path that it needs to take; for the modern man cannot, like the man of the Middle Ages, live by the imagination and religious faculty alone; on the other hand, he cannot live solely by the exercise of his reason and understanding. It is only by the union of these two elements of his nature that he can hope to attain a balanced growth, and this fusion of the reason and the imagination is found realized more perfectly than elsewhere in the Greek classics of the great age. Those who can receive the higher initiation into the Hellenic spirit will doubtless remain few in number, but these few will wield a potent influence for good, each in his own circle, if only from the ability they will thereby have acquired to escape from contemporary illusions. For of him who has caught the profounder teachings of Greek literature we may say, in the words of the "Imitation," that he is released from a multitude of opinions.

Paul Elmer More

1864–1937

Other men are creatures of the visible moment; [the aristocrat of the mind] is a citizen of the past and of the future. And such a charter of citizenship it is the first duty of the college to provide.

"ACADEMIC LEADERSHIP"

Paul Elmer More, American scholar, essayist, and Christian Platonist, was born in St. Louis, Missouri, and educated at Washington University and Harvard. He briefly taught Sanskrit at Harvard and Bryn Mawr before beginning his career as a distinguished editor for the *Independent* (1901–3), the *New York Evening Post* (1903–9), and finally the *Nation* (1909–14). After 1914, he continued to write and lecture on behalf of the classical tradition, standards of taste and literary judgment, and the ethic of self-restraint. Allied with Irving Babbitt, he promoted the principles of the New Humanism in the face of naturalism's assault on human nature. Modernity's blind faith in evolution and progress had led to the "collapse of reason," he feared. The doctrine of evolution, he wrote in 1915, is "a faith in drifting; a belief that things of themselves, by a kind of natural gravity of goodness in them, move always on and on in the right direction; a confident trust in human nature as needing no restraint and compression, but rather full liberty to follow its own impulsive desires to expand; and inclination to take sides with the emotions in their rebellion against the inhibitions of judgment."[1] This failure of judgment and loss of restraint, he believed, had contributed to the catastrophe of the Great War. More's works include the collected *Shelburne Essays* (eleven volumes), *On Being Human, The Greek Tradition* (five volumes), the *New Shelburne Essays* (three volumes), and his poignant late work, *Pages from an Oxford Diary.*

---

1. *Aristocracy and Justice*, Shelburne Essays, Ninth Series (Boston: Houghton Mifflin, 1915), viii–ix.

THE SELECTION

"Academic Leadership" was written before the outbreak of the First World War but published in 1915 as part of *Aristocracy and Justice (Shelburne Essays,* ninth series). In this essay, More ponders what sort of education is most likely to yield a disciplined mind. He quickly arrives at a core curriculum consisting of instruction in Greek and Latin, philosophy, and mathematics. Such humanistic studies, rather than utilitarian training, truly develop orderly thought, imagination, and concentration. His philosophy of education is anchored in Homer, the English humanist Thomas Elyot, Shakespeare, and Burke. Rather than shrink at charges of elitism in such a curriculum, More defends the "aristocracy of the mind" that civilization has always required and that the modern West urgently needs in order to correct its cultural drift.

"Academic Leadership"

Any one who has traveled much about the country of recent years must have been impressed by the growing uneasiness of mind among thoughtful men.[2] Whether in the smoking-car, or the hotel corridor, or the college hall, everywhere, if you meet them off their guard and stripped of the optimism which we wear as a public convention, you will hear them saying in a kind of amazement, "What is to be the end of it all?" They are alarmed at the unsettlement of property and the difficulties that harass the man of moderate means in making provision for the future; they are uneasy over the breaking up of the old laws of decorum, if not of decency, and over the unrestrained pursuit of excitement at any cost; they feel vaguely that in the decay of religion the bases of society have been somehow weakened. Now, much of this sort of talk is as old as history, and has no special significance. We are prone to forget that civilization has always been a *tour de force,* so to speak, a little hard-won area of order and self-subordination amidst a vast wilderness of anarchy and barbarism that are continually threatening to overrun their bounds. But that is equally no reason for over-confidence. Civilization is like a ship traversing an untamed sea. It is a more complex machine in our day, with command of greater forces, and might seem correspondingly safer than in the era of sails. But fresh catastrophes have shown that the ancient perils of navigation still confront the largest vessel, when the crew loses its discipline or the officers neglect their duty; and the analogy is not without its warning.

Only a year after the sinking of the *Titanic* I was crossing the ocean, and it befell by chance that on the anniversary of that disaster we passed not very far from the spot where the proud ship lay buried beneath the waves. The evening was calm, and on the lee deck a dance had been hastily organized to take advantage of the benign weather. Almost alone I stood for hours at the railing on the windward side, looking out over the rippling water where the moon had laid upon it a broad street of gold. Nothing could have been more peaceful; it was as if Nature were smiling upon earth in sympathy with the strains of music and the sound of laughter that reached me at intervals from the revelling on the other

---

2. Written, all this, before the European war.

deck. Yet I could not put out of my heart an apprehension of some luring treachery in this scene of beauty—and certainly the world can offer nothing more wonderfully beautiful than the moon shining from the far East over a smooth expanse of water. Was it not in such a calm as this that the unsuspecting vessel, with its gay freight of human lives, had shuddered, and gone down, forever? I seemed to behold a symbol; and there came into my mind the words we used to repeat at school, but are, I do not know just why, a little ashamed of today:

> Thou, too, sail on, O Ship of State!
> Sail on, O Union, strong and great!
> Humanity with all its fears,
> With all its hopes of future years,
> Is hanging breathless on thy fate!

Something like this, perhaps, is the feeling of many men—men by no means given to morbid gusts of panic—amid a society that laughs over much in its amusement and exults in the very lust of change. Nor is their anxiety quite the same as that which has always disturbed the reflecting spectator. At other times the apprehension has been lest the combined forces of order might not be strong enough to withstand the ever-threatening inroads of those who envy barbarously and desire recklessly; whereas today the doubt is whether the natural champions of order themselves shall be found loyal to their trust, for they seem no longer to remember clearly the word of command that should unite them in leadership. Until they can rediscover some common ground of strength and purpose in the first principles of education and law and property and religion, we are in danger of falling a prey to the disorganizing and vulgarizing domination of ambitions which should be the servants and not the masters of society.

Certainly, in the sphere of education there is a growing belief that some radical reform is needed; and this dissatisfaction is in itself wholesome. Boys come into college with no reading and with minds unused to the very practice of study; and they leave college, too, often, in the same state of nature. There are even those, inside and outside of academic halls, who protest that our higher institutions of learning simply fail to educate at all. That is slander; but in sober earnest, you will find few experienced college professors, apart from those engaged in teaching purely utilitarian or practical subjects, who are not convinced that the general relaxation is greater now than it was twenty years ago. It is of considerable significance that the two student essays which took the prizes offered by the Harvard *Advocate* in 1913 were both on this theme. The first of them posed the question: "How can the leadership of the intellectual rather than the athletic student be fostered?" and was virtually a sermon on a text of President Lowell's: "No one in close touch with American education has failed to notice the lack among the mass of undergraduates of keen interest in their studies, and the small regard for scholarly attainment."

Now, the *Advocate* prizeman has his specific remedy, and President Lowell has his, and other men propose other systems and restrictions; but the evil is too deep-seated to be reached by any superficial scheme of honours or to be charmed away by insinuating appeals. The other day Mr. William F. McCombs, chairman of the National Committee which engineered a college president into the White House, gave this advice to our academic youth: "The college man must forget—or never let it creep into his head—that he's a highbrow. If it does creep in, he's out of politics." To which one might reply in Mr. McCombs's own dialect, that unless a man can make himself a force in politics (or at least in the larger life of the State) precisely by virtue of being a "highbrow," he had better spend his four golden years other-where than in college. There it is: the destiny of education is intimately bound up with the question of social leadership, and unless the college, as it used to be in the days when the religious hierarchy it created was a real power, can be made once more a breeding place for a natural aristocracy, it will inevitably degenerate into a school for mechanical apprentices or into a pleasure resort for the *jeunesse dorée* (*sc.* the "gold coasters"). We must get back to a common understanding of the office of education in the construction of society and must discriminate among the subjects that may enter into the curriculum by their relative value towards this end.

A manifest condition is that education should embrace the means of discipline, for without discipline the mind will remain inefficient just as surely as the muscles of the body, without exercise, will be left flaccid. That should seem to be a self-evident truth. Now it may be possible to derive a certain amount of discipline out of any study, but it is a fact, nevertheless, which cannot be gainsaid, that some studies lend themselves to this use more readily and effectively than others. You may, for instance, if by extraordinary luck you get the perfect teacher, make English literature disciplinary by the hard manipulation of ideas; but in practice it almost inevitably happens that a course in English literature either degenerates into the dull memorizing of dates and names or, rising into the O Altitudo, evaporates in romantic gush over beautiful passages. This does not mean, of course, that no benefit may be obtained from such a study, but it does preclude English literature generally from being made the backbone, so to speak, of a sound curriculum. The same may be said of French and German. The difficulties of these tongues in themselves and the effort required of us to enter into their spirit imply some degree of intellectual gymnastics, but scarcely enough for our purpose. Of the sciences it behooves one to speak circumspectly; undoubtedly mathematics and physics, at least, demand such close attention and such firm reasoning as to render them properly a part of any disciplinary education. But there are good grounds for being sceptical of the effect of the non-mathematical sciences on the immature mind. Any one who has spent a considerable portion of his undergraduate time in a chemical laboratory, for example, as the present writer has done, and has the means of comparing the results of such elementary and pottering experimentation with the mental grip required in the humanistic courses, must feel that the real training obtained therein was almost negligible. If I may draw further from my own observation I must say frankly that, after dealing for a number of years with manuscripts prepared for publication by college professors of the various faculties, I have been forced to the conclusion that science, in itself, is likely to leave the mind in a state of relative imbecility. It is not that the writing of men who got their early drill too exclusively, or even predominantly, in the sciences lacks the graces of rhetoric—that would be comparatively a small matter—but such men in the majority of cases, even when treating subjects within their own field, show a singular inability to think clearly and consecutively, so soon as they are freed from the restraint of merely describing the process of an experiment. On the contrary, the manuscript of a classical scholar, despite the present dry-rot of philology, almost invariably gives signs of a habit of orderly and well-governed cerebration.

Here, whatever else may be lacking, is discipline. The sheer difficulty of Latin and Greek, the highly organized structure of these languages, the need of scrupulous search to find the nearest equivalents for words that differ widely in their scope of meaning from their derivatives in any modern vocabulary, the effort of lifting one's self out of the familiar rut of ideas into so foreign a world, all these things act as a tonic exercise to the brain. And it is a demonstrable fact that students of the classics do actually surpass their unclassical rivals in any field where a fair test can be made. At Princeton, for instance, Professor West has shown this superiority by tables of achievements and grades, which he has published in the *Educational Review* for March, 1913; and a number of letters from various parts of the country, printed in the *Nation*, tell the same story in striking fashion. Thus, a letter from Wesleyan (September 7, 1911) gives statistics to prove that the classical students in that university outstrip the others in obtaining all sorts of honours, commonly even honours in the sciences. Another letter (May 8, 1913) shows that in the first semester in English at the University of Nebraska the percentage of delinquents among those who entered with four years of Latin was below 7; among those who had three years of Latin and one or two of a modern language the percentage rose to 15; two years of Latin and two years of a modern language, 30 per cent; one year or less of Latin and from two to four years of a modern language, 35 per cent. And in the *Nation* of April 23, 1914, Professor Arthur Gordon Webster, the eminent physicist of Clark University, after speaking of the late B. O. Peirce's early drill and life-long interest in Greek and Latin, adds these significant words: "Many of us still believe that such a training makes the best possible foundation for a scientist." There is reason to think that this opinion is daily gaining ground among those who are zealous that the prestige of science should be maintained by men of the best calibre.

The disagreement in this matter would no doubt be less, were it not for an ambiguity in the meaning of the word "efficient" itself. There is a kind of efficiency in managing men, and there also is an intellectual efficiency, properly speaking, which is quite a different faculty. The former is more likely to be found in the successful engineer or business man than in the scholar of secluded habits, and because often such men of affairs received no discipline at college in the classics the argument runs that utilitarian studies are as disciplinary as the humanistic. But efficiency of this kind is not an academic product at all, and is commonly developed, and should be developed, in the school of the world. It comes from dealing with men in matters of large physical moment, and may exist with a mind utterly undisciplined in the stricter sense of the word. We have had more than one illustrious example in recent years of men capable of dominating their fellows, let us say in financial transactions, who yet, in the grasp of first principles and in the analysis of consequences, have shown themselves to be as inefficient as children.

Probably, however, few men who have had experience in education will deny the value of discipline to the classics, even though they hold that other studies, less costly from the utilitarian point of view, are equally educative in this respect. But it is further of prime importance, even if such an equality, or approach to equality, were granted, that we should select one group of studies and unite in making it the core of the curriculum for the great mass of undergraduates. It is true in education as in other matters that strength comes from union and weakness from division, and if educated men are to work together for a common end they must have a common range of ideas, with a certain solidarity in their way of looking at things. As matters actually are, the educated man feels terribly his isolation under the scattering of intellectual pursuits, yet too often lacks the courage to deny the strange popular fallacy that there is virtue in sheer variety and that somehow well-being is to be struck out from the clashing of miscellaneous interests rather than from concentration. In one of his annual reports some years ago President Eliot, of Harvard, observed from the figures of registration that the majority of students still at that time believed the best form of education for them was in the old humanistic courses, and *therefore*, he argued, the other courses should be fostered. There was never perhaps a more extraordinary syllogism since the *argal* of Shakespeare's grave-digger. I quote from memory, and may slightly misrepresent the actual statement of the influential "educationalist," but the spirit of his words, as indeed of his practice, is surely as I give it. And the working of this spirit is one of the main causes of the curious fact that scarcely any other class of men in social intercourse feel themselves, in their deeper concerns, more severed one from another than those very college professors who ought to be united in the battle for educational leadership. This estrangement is sometimes carried to an extreme almost ludicrous. I remember once in a small but advanced college the consternation that was awakened when an instructor in philosophy went to a colleague—both of them now associates in a large university—for information in a question of biology. "What business has he with such matters," said the irate biologist: "let him stick to his last, and teach philosophy if he can!" That was a polite jest, you will say. Perhaps; but not entirely. Philosophy is indeed taught in one lecture hall, and biology in another, but of conscious effort to make of education an harmonious driving force there is next to nothing. And as the teachers, so are the taught.

Such criticism does not imply that advanced work in any of the branches of human knowledge should be curtailed; but it does demand that, as a background to the professional pursuits, there should be a common intellectual training through which all students should pass, acquiring thus a single body of ideas and images in which they could always meet as brother initiates.

We shall, then, make a long step forward when we determine that in the college, as distinguished from the university, it is better to have the great mass of men, whatever may be the waste in a few unmalleable minds, go through the discipline of a single group of studies—with, of course, a considerable freedom of choice in the outlying field. And it will probably appear in experience that the only practicable group to select is the classics, with the accompaniment of philosophy and the mathematical sciences. Latin and Greek are, at least, as disciplinary as any other subjects; and if it can be further shown that they possess a specific power of correction for the more disintegrating tendencies of the age, it ought to be clear that their value as instruments of education outweighs the service of certain other studies which may seem to be more immediately serviceable.

For it will be pretty generally agreed that efficiency of the individual scholar and unity of the scholarly class are, properly, only the means to obtain the real end of education, which is social efficiency. The only way, in fact, to make the discipline demanded by a severe curriculum and the sacrifice of particular tastes required for unity seem worth the cost, is to persuade men that the resulting form of education both meets a present and serious need of society and promises to serve those individuals who desire to obtain society's fairer honours. Mr. McCombs, speaking for the "practical" man, declares that there is no place in politics for the intellectual aristocrat. A good many of us believe that unless the very reverse of this is true, unless the educated man can somehow, by virtue of his education, make of himself a governor of the people in the larger sense, and even to some extent in the narrow political sense, unless the college can produce a hierarchy of character and intelligence which shall in due measure perform the office of the discredited oligarchy of birth, we had better make haste to divert our enormous collegiate endowments into more useful channels.

And here I am glad to find confirmation of my belief in the stalwart old *Boke Named the Governour*, published by Sir Thomas Elyot in 1531, the first treatise on education in the English tongue and still, after all these years, one of the wisest. It is no waste of time to take account of the theory held by the humanists when study at Oxford and Cambridge was shaping itself for its long service in giving to the oligarchic government of Great Britain whatever elements it possessed of true aristocracy. Elyot's book is equally a treatise on the education of a gentleman and on the ordinance of government, for, as he says elsewhere, he wrote "to instruct men in such virtues as shall be expedient for them which shall have authority in a weal public." I quote from various parts of his work with some abridgment, retaining the quaint spelling of the original, and I beg the reader not to skip, however long the citation may appear:

> Beholde also the ordre that god hath put generally in al his creatures, begynning at the moste inferiour or base, and assendynge upwarde; so that in euery thyng is ordre, and without ordre may be nothing stable or permanent; and it may nat be called ordre, excepte it do contayne in it degrees, high and base, accordynge to the merite or estimation of the thyng that is ordred. And therfore hit appereth that god gyueth nat to euery man like gyftes of grace, or of nature, but to some more, some lesse, as it liketh his diuine maiestie. For as moche as understandying is the most excellent gyfte that man can receiue in his creation, it is therfore congruent, and accordynge that as one excelleth an other in that influence, as therby beinge next to the similitude of his maker, so shulde the astate of his persone be auanced in degree or place where understandynge may profite. Suche oughte to be set in a more highe place than the residue where they may se and also be sene; that by the beames of theyr excellent witte, shewed throughe the glasse of auctorite, other of inferiour understandynge may be directed to the way of vertue and commodious liuynge. . . .
>
> Thus I conclude that nobilitie is nat after the vulgare opinion of men, but is only the prayse and surname of vertue; whiche the lenger it continueth in a name or lignage, the more is nobilitie extolled and meruailed at. . . .
>
> If thou be a gouernour, or haste ouer other soueraygntie, knowe thy selfe. Knowe that the name of a soueraigne or ruler without actuall gouernaunce is but a shadowe, that gouernaunce standeth nat by wordes onely, but principally by acte and example; that by example of gouernours men do rise or falle in vertue or vice. Ye shall knowe all way your selfe, if for affection or motion ye do speke or do nothing unworthy the immortalitie and moste precious nature of your soule. . . .
>
> In semblable maner the inferior persone or subiecte aught to consider, that all be it he in the substaunce of soule and body be equall with his superior, yet for als moche as the powars and qualities of the soule and body, with the disposition of

reason, be nat in euery man equall, therfore god ordayned a diuersitie or preeminence in degrees to be amonge men for the necessary derection and preseruation of them in conformitie of lyuinge. . . .

Where all thynge is commune, there lacketh ordre; and where ordre lacketh, there all thynge is odiouse and uncomly.

Such is the goal which the grave Sir Thomas pointed out to the noble youth of his land at the beginning of England's greatness, and such, within the bounds of human frailty, has been the ideal even until now which the two universities have held before them. Naturally the method of training prescribed in the sixteenth century for the attainment of this goal is antiquated in some of its details, but it is no exaggeration, nevertheless, to speak of the *Boke Named the Governour* as the very Magna Charta of our education. The scheme of the humanist might be described in a word as a disciplining of the higher faculty of the imagination to the end that the student may behold, as it were in one sublime vision, the whole scale of being in its range from the lowest to the highest under the divine decree of order and subordination, without losing sight of the immutable veracity at the heart of all development, which "is only the praise and surname of virtue." This was no new vision, nor has it ever been quite forgotten. It was the whole meaning of religion to Hooker, from whom it passed into all that is best and least ephemeral in the Anglican Church. It was the basis, more modestly expressed, of Blackstone's conception of the British Constitution and of liberty under law. It was the kernel of Burke's theory of statecraft. It is the inspiration of the sublimer science, which accepts the hypothesis of evolution as taught by Darwin and Spencer, yet bows in reverence before the unnamed and incommensurable force lodged as a mystical purpose within the unfolding universe. It was the wisdom of that child of Stratford who, building better than he knew, gave to our literature its deepest and most persistent note. If anywhere Shakespeare seems to speak from his heart and to utter his own philosophy, it is in the person of Ulysses in that strange satire of life as "still wars and lechery" which forms the theme of *Troilus and Cressida*. Twice in the course of the play Ulysses moralizes on the causes of human evil. Once it is in an outburst against the devastations of disorder:

> Take but degree away, untune that string,
> And, hark, what discord follows! each thing meets
> In mere oppugnancy: the bounded waters
> Should lift their bosoms higher than the shores,
> And make a sop of all this solid globe:
> Strength should be lord of imbecility,
> And the rude son should strike his father dead:
> Force should be right; or rather, right and wrong,
> Between whose endless jar justice resides,
> Should lose their names, and so should justice too.
> Then every thing includes itself in power,
> Power into will, will into appetite.

And, in the same spirit, the second tirade of Ulysses is charged with mockery at the vanity of the present and at man's usurpation of time as the destroyer instead of the preserver of continuity:

> For time is like a fashionable host
> That slightly shakes his parting guest by the hand,
> And with his arms outstretch'd, as he would fly,
> Grasps in the corner: welcome ever smiles,
> And farewell goes out sighing. O, let not virtue seek
> Remuneration for the thing it was;
> For beauty, wit,
> High birth, vigour of bone, desert in service,
> Love, friendship, charity, are subjects all
> To envious and calumniating time.

To have made this vision of the higher imagination a true part of our self-knowledge, in such fashion that the soul is purged of envy for what is distinguished and we feel ourselves fellows with the preserving, rather than the destroying, forces of time, is to be raised into the nobility of the intellect. To hold this knowledge in a mind trained to fine efficiency and confirmed by faithful comradeship is to take one's place with the rightful governors of the people. Nor is there any narrow or invidious exclusiveness in such an aristocracy, which differs in this free hospitality from an oligarchy of artificial prescription. The more its membership is enlarged, the greater is its power and the more secure are the privileges of each individual. Yet, if not exclusive, an academic aristocracy must by its very nature be exceedingly jealous of any levelling process which would shape education to the needs of the intellectual proletariat and so diminish its own ranks. It cannot admit that, if education is once levelled downwards, the whole body of men will of themselves gradually raise the level to the higher range; for its creed declares that elevation must come from leadership rather than from self-motion of the mass. It will therefore be opposed to any scheme of studies which relaxes discipline or destroys intellectual solidarity. It will look with suspicion on any system which turns out half-educated men with the same diplomas as the fully educated, thinking that such methods of slurring differences are likely to do more harm by discouraging the ambition to attain what is distinguished than good by spreading wide a thin veneer of culture. In particular it will distrust the present huge overgrowth of courses in government and sociology, which send men into the world skilled in the machinery of statecraft and with minds sharpened to the immediate demands of special groups, but with no genuine training of the imagination and no understanding of the longer problems of humanity. It will think that the dominance of such studies is one of the causes that men leave our colleges with no hold on the past, with nothing, as Burke said, "amidst so vast a fluctuation of passions and opinions, to concentrate their thoughts, to ballast their conduct, to preserve them from being blown about by every wind of fashionable doctrine." It will set itself against any regular subjection of the "fierce spirit of liberty," which is the breath of distinction and the very charter of aristocracy, to the sullen spirit of equality, which proceeds from envy in the baser sort of democracy. It will regard the character of education and the disposition of the curriculum as a question of supreme importance; for its motto is always, *abeunt studia in mores.*

Now this aristocratic principle has, so to speak, its everlasting embodiment in Greek literature, from whence it was taken over into Latin and transmitted, with much mingling of foreign and even contradictory ideas, to the modern world. From Homer to the last runnings of the Hellenic spirit you will find it taught by every kind of precept and enforced by every kind of example; nor was Shakespeare writing at hazard, but under the instinctive guidance of genius, when he put his aristocratic creed into the mouth of the hero who to the end remained for the Greeks the personification of their peculiar wisdom. In no other poetry of the world is the law of distinction, as springing from a man's perception of his place in the great hierarchy of privilege and obligation from the lowest human being up to the Olympian gods, so copiously and magnificently set forth as in Pindar's Odes of Victory. And Æschylus was the first dramatist to see with clear vision the primacy of the intellect in the law of orderly development, seemingly at variance with the divine immutable will of Fate, yet finally in mysterious accord with it. When the philosophers of the later period came to the creation of systematic ethics they had only the task of formulating what was already latent in the poets and historians of their land; and it was the recollection of the fulness of such instruction in the *Nicomachean Ethics* and the Platonic Dialogues, with their echo in the *Officia* of Cicero, as if in them were stored up all the treasures of antiquity, that raised our Sir Thomas into wondering admiration:

> Lorde god, what incomparable swetnesse of wordes and mater shall he finde in the saide warkes of Plato and Cicero; wherin is ioyned grauitie with dilectation, excellent wysedome with diuine eloquence, absolute vertue with pleasure incredible, and euery place is so farced [crowded] with profitable counsaile, ioyned with honestie, that those thre bokes be almoste sufficient to make a perfecte and excellent gouernour.

There is no need to dwell on this aspect of the classics. He who cares to follow their full working in this direction, as did our English humanist, may find it exhibited in Plato's political and ethical scheme of self-development, or in Aristotle's ideal of the Golden Mean which combines magnanimity with moderation, and elevation with self-knowledge. If a single word were used to describe the character and state of life upheld by Plato and Aristotle, as spokesmen of their people, it would be *eleutheria*, liberty: the freedom to cultivate the higher part of a man's nature—his intellectual prerogative, his desire of truth, his refinements of taste—and to hold the baser part of himself in subjection; the freedom also, for its own perfection, and indeed for its very existence, to impose an outer conformity to, or at least respect for, the laws of this inner government on others who are of themselves ungoverned. Such liberty is the ground of true distinction; it implies the opposite of an equalitarianism which reserves its honours and rewards for those who attain a bastard kind of distinction by the cunning of leadership without departing from common standards, for the demagogues, that is, who rise by flattery. But this liberty is by no means dependent on the artificial distinctions of privilege; on the contrary, it is peculiarly adapted to an age whose appointed task must be to create a natural aristocracy as a *via media* between an equalitarian democracy and a prescriptive oligarchy or a plutocracy. The fact is notable that, as the real hostility to the classics in the present day arises from an instinctive suspicion of them as standing in the way of a downward-levelling mediocrity, so, at other times, they have fallen under displeasure for their veto on a contrary excess. Thus, in his savage attack on the Commonwealth, to which he gave the significant title *Behemoth*, Hobbes lists the reading of classical history among the chief causes of the rebellion. "There were," he says, "an exceeding great number of men of the better sort, that had been so educated as that in their youth, having read the books written by famous men of the ancient Grecian and Roman commonwealths concerning their polity and great actions, in which books the popular government was extolled by that glorious name of liberty, and monarchy disgraced by the name of tyranny, they became thereby in love with their forms of government; and out of these men were chosen the greatest part of the House of Commons; or if they were not the greatest part, yet by advantage of their eloquence were always able to sway the rest." To this charge Hobbes returns again and again, even declaring that "the universities have been to this nation as the Wooden Horse was to the Trojans." And the uncompromising monarchist of the *Leviathan*, himself a classicist of no mean attainments, as may be known by his translation of Thucydides, was not deceived in his accusation. The tyrannicides of Athens and Rome, the Aristogeitons and Brutuses and others, were the heroes by whose example the leaders of the French Revolution were continually justifying their acts.

> There Brutus starts and stares by midnight taper.
> Who all the day enacts—a woollen-draper.

And again, in the years of the Risorgimento, more than one of the champions of Italian liberty went to death with those great names on their lips.

So runs the law of order and right subordination. But if the classics offer the best service to education by inculcating an aristocracy of intellectual distinction, they are equally effective in enforcing the similar lesson of time. It is a true saying of our ancient humanist that "the longer it continueth in a name or lineage, the more is nobility extolled and marvelled at." It is true because in this way our imagination is working with the great conservative law of growth. Whatever may be in theory our democratic distaste for the insignia of birth, we cannot get away from the fact that there is a certain honour of inheritance and that we instinctively pay homage to one who represents a noble name. There is nothing really illogical in this, for, as an English statesman has put it, "the past is one of the elements of our power." He is the wise democrat who, with no opposition to such a decree of Nature, endeavours to control its operation by expecting noble service where the memory of nobility abides. When, recently, Oxford bestowed its highest honour on an American, distinguished not only for his own public acts but for the great tradition embodied in his name, the Orator of the University did not omit this legitimate appeal to the imagination, singularly appropriate in its academic Latin:

> . . . Statim succurrit animo antiqua illa Romae condicio, cum non tam propter singulos cives quam propter singulas gentes nomen Romanum floreret. Cum enim civic alicujus et avum et proavum principes civitatis esse creatos, cum patrem legationis munus apud aulam Britannicam summa cum laude esse exsecutum cognovimus; cum denique ipsum per totum bellum stipendia equo meritum, summa pericula "Pulcra pro Libertate" ausum, . . . Romanae alicujus gentis—Brutorum vel Decio-

rum—annales evolvere videmur, qui testimonium adhibent "fortes creari fortibus," et majorum exemplis et imaginibus nepotes ad virtutem accendi.[3]

Is there any man so dull of soul as not to be stirred by that enumeration of civic services zealously inherited; or is there any one so envious of the past as not to believe that such memories should be honoured in the present as an incentive to noble emulation?

Well, we cannot all of us count Presidents and Ambassadors among our ancestors, but we can, if we will, in the genealogy of the inner life enroll ourselves among the adopted sons of a family in comparison with which the Bruti and Decii of old and the Adamses of today are veritable *new men*. We can see what defence against the meaner depredations of the world may be drawn from the pride of birth, when, as it sometimes happens, the obligation of a great past is kept as a contract with the present; shall we forget to measure the enlargement and elevation of mind which ought to come to a man who has made himself the heir of the ancient Lords of Wisdom? "To one small people," as Sir Henry Maine has said, in words often quoted, "it was given to create the principle of Progress. That people was the Greek. Except the blind forces of Nature, nothing moves in this world which is not Greek in its origin." That is a hard saying, but scarcely exaggerated. Examine the records of our art and our science, our philosophy and the enduring element of our faith, our statecraft and our notion of liberty, and you will find that they all go back for their inspiration to that one small people, and strike their roots into the soil of Greece. What we have added, it is well to know; but he is the aristocrat of the mind who can display a diploma from the schools of the Academy and Lyceum and from the Theatre of Dionysus. What tradition of ancestral achievement in the Senate or on the field of battle shall broaden a man's outlook and elevate his will equally with the consciousness that his way of thinking and feeling has come down to him by so long and honourable a descent, or shall so confirm him in his better judgment against the ephemeral and vulgarizing solicitations of the hour? Other men are creatures of the visible moment; he is a citizen of the past and of the future. And such a charter of citizenship it is the first duty of the college to provide.

I have limited myself in these pages to a discussion of what may be called the public side of education, considering the classics in their power to mould character and to foster sound leadership in a society much given to drifting. Of the inexhaustible joy and consolation they afford to the individual, only he can have full knowledge who has made the writers of Greece and Rome his friends and counsellors through many vicissitudes of life. It is related of Sainte-Beuve, who, according to Renan, read everything and remembered everything, that one could observe a peculiar serenity on his face whenever he came down from his study after reading a book of Homer. The cost of learning the language of Homer is not small; but so are all fair things difficult, as the Greek proverb runs, and the reward in this case is precious beyond estimation.

---

3. "One's mind reverts inevitably to that ancient state of affairs in Rome, when the Roman name was illustrious not only through individual citizens, but also through particular families. For when we consider that a man's grandfather and great-grandfather held the highest office in a State, and that his father represented his country with the highest distinction at the court of Great Britain, and when we remember, finally, that the man himself gave all his strength to military service throughout a war, incurring extreme perils 'For the sake of Sweet Liberty.' . . . In these recollections we seem to be unrolling the annals of some Roman family,—of the Bruti or the Decii,—annals bearing witness to the fact that 'the strong are born to be strong,' and that by the examples and traditions of their ancestors the descendants are incited to distinguished achievement."—The honour was bestowed on the late Charles Francis Adams.

A. G. Sertillanges

1863–1948

Let us not be like those people who always seem to be pallbearers at the funeral of the dead. Let us utilize, by living, the qualities of the dead. Truth is ever new.

THE INTELLECTUAL LIFE

Antonin Gilbert Sertillanges, French theologian and neo-Thomist philosopher, entered the Dominican order in Belmont, Spain, in 1883 and was ordained to the priesthood in 1888. A distinguished and prolific scholar, he taught theology in Corsica, served as secretary to the *Revue thomiste* and on the editorial board of the *Revue Benedictine,* and was appointed professor of moral philosophy at the Catholic Institute in Paris. In 1918 he became a philosopher in the Academy of Moral and Political Science in Paris. During World War I, he preached a series of patriotic sermons published as *The Heroic Life.* He taught in Jerusalem, Holland, and Belgium before returning to France in 1939. He produced over seven hundred publications, including books, journal articles, sermons, and spiritual meditations.

THE SELECTION

First published in 1920, *The Intellectual Life* is a quiet reflection on the virtues of the life of the mind. It was inspired by Thomas Aquinas's "Letter to Brother John." In the first chapter, included here, Sertillanges explores the Christian scholar's calling. Writing in the immediate aftermath of the First World War, Sertillanges encourages scholars to satisfy their troubled century's longing for truth. The serious call to the intellectual life requires obedience, persistent effort, self-discipline, "long self-examination," and a devotion to truth.

from The Intellectual Life
Chapter 1: The Intellectual Vocation

I. THE INTELLECTUAL HAS A SACRED CALL

When we speak of vocation, we refer to those who intend to make intellectual work their life, whether they are entirely free to give themselves up to study, or whether, though engaged in some calling, they hold happily in reserve, as a supplement of their activity and as a reward, the development and deepening of their mind.

I say the deepening, in order to set aside the idea of a superficial tincture of knowledge. A vocation is not fulfilled by vague reading and a few scattered writings. It requires penetration and continuity and methodical effort, so as to attain a fulness of development which will correspond to the call of the Spirit, and to the resources that it has pleased Him to bestow on us.

This call is not to be taken for granted. To start precipitately on a road which one could not tread with a firm step would be merely to prepare the way for disillusionment. Everyone has the duty to work; and after a first early and toilsome training no one acts wisely if he lets his mind fall gradually back into its primitive ignorance; but the effortless maintenance of what one has acquired is one thing, and it is quite another to consolidate from the foundations upwards a sum of knowledge recognized as merely provisional, seen to be simply and solely a starting-point.

This second state of mind is that of one who has the vocation. It implies a serious resolution. The life of study is austere and imposes grave obligations. It pays, it pays richly; but it exacts an initial outlay that few are capable of. The athletes of the mind, like those of the playing field, must be prepared for privations, long training, a sometimes superhuman tenacity. We must give ourselves from the heart, if truth is to give itself to us. Truth serves only its slaves.

This way of life must not be entered on without long self-examination. The intellectual vocation is like every other: it is written in our instincts, in our powers, in a sort of inner impulse of which reason must judge. Our dispositions are like the chemical properties which determine, for every body, the combinations into which that body can enter. A vocation is something that cannot be had for the asking. It comes from heaven and from our first nature. The whole point is to be docile to God and to oneself as soon as they have spoken.

Understood in this sense, Disraeli's saying that you may do what you please, provided it really pleases you, contains a great meaning. Our liking, if correlated to our fundamental tendencies and to our aptitudes, is an excellent judge. If St. Thomas could say that pleasure characterizes functions and may serve to classify men, he must be led to conclude that pleasure can also reveal our vocation. Only we must search down into the depths where liking and the spontaneous impulse are linked up with the gifts of God and His providence.

Besides the immense interest of realizing oneself in one's fulness, the investigation into an intellectual vocation has a more general interest which no one may disregard.

Christianized humanity is made up of various personalities, no one of which can refuse to function without impoverishing the group and without depriving the eternal Christ of a part of His kingdom. Christ reigns by unfolding Himself in men. Every life of one of His members is a characteristic moment of His duration; every individual man and Christian is an instance, incommunicable, unique, and therefore necessary, of the extension of the "spiritual body." If you are designated as a light bearer, do not go and hide under the bushel the gleam or the flame expected from you in the house of the Father of all. Love truth and its fruits of life, for yourself and for others; devote to study and to the profitable use of study the best part of your time and your heart.

All roads but one are bad roads for you, since they diverge from the direction in which your action is expected and required. Do not prove faithless to God, to your brethren and to yourself by rejecting a sacred call.

That presupposes you to come to the intellectual life with unselfish motives, not through ambition or foolish vanity. The jingling bells of publicity tempt only frivolous minds. Ambition offends eternal truth by subordinating truth to itself. Is it not a sacrilege to play with the questions that dominate life and death, with mysterious nature, with God—to achieve some literary or philosophical celebrity at the expense of the true and independently of the true? Such aims, and especially the first mentioned, would not sustain the seeker; his effort would speedily be seen to slacken, his vanity to fall back on some empty satisfaction, with no care for the reality of things.

But it presupposes also that to the acceptance of the end you add the acceptance of the means; otherwise there would be no real obedience to your vocation. Many people would like to possess knowledge! A vague aspiration turns the eyes of the multitude towards horizons that the greater number admire from afar off, as the victim of gout or asthma looks up to the eternal snows. To get something without paying for it is the universal desire; but it is the desire of cowardly hearts and weak brains. The universe does not respond to the first murmured request, and the light of God does not shine under your study lamp unless your soul asks for it with persistent effort.

You are consecrated by your vocation. Will what truth wills; consent for the sake of truth to bestir yourself, to take up your abode within its proper realm, to organize your life, and, realizing your inexperience, to learn from the experience of others.

"If youth but knew!" The young, above all, need this warning. Science in the broad meaning of the word, *scientia*, is knowledge through causes; but actively, as to its attainment, it is a creation by causes. We must recognize and adopt the causes of knowledge, then provide them, and not defer attention to the foundations of our building until the moment of putting up the roof.

In the first free years after early studies, when the ground of our intelligence has been newly turned-up, and the seed sown, what splendid tillage could be undertaken! That is the time that will never come again, the time that we shall have to live on by and by. What it is, we shall be; for we can hardly put down new roots. The future is always the heir of the past; the penalty for neglecting, at the right time, to prepare it, is to live on the surface of things. Let each one think of that, while thinking may be of some avail.

How many young people, with the pretension to become workers, miserably waste their days, their strength, the vigor of their intelligence, their ideal! Either they do not work—there is time enough!—or they work badly, capriciously, without knowing what they are nor where they want to go nor how to get there. Lectures, reading, choice of companions, the proper proportion of work and rest, of solitude and activity, of general culture and specialization, the spirit of study, the art of picking out and utilizing data gained, some provisional output which will give an idea of what the future work is to be, the virtues to be acquired and developed,—nothing of all that is thought out and no satisfactory fulfillment will follow.

What a difference, supposing equal resources, between the man who understands and looks ahead, and the man who proceeds at haphazard! "Genius is long patience," but it must be organized and intelligent patience. One does not need extraordinary gifts to carry some work through; average superiority suffices; the rest depends on energy and wise application of energy. It is as with a conscientious workman, careful and steady at his task: he gets somewhere, while an inventive genius is often merely an embittered failure.

What I have just said is true of everyone. But I apply it especially to those who know that they have at their disposal only a part of their life, the least part, in which to give themselves to the labors of the mind. They, more than others, must be men consecrated by their vocation. What they cannot spread out over all their years, they must concentrate in a small space. The special asceticism and the heroic virtue of the intellectual worker must be their daily portion. But if they consent to this double self-offering, I tell them in the name of the God of truth not to lose courage.

If genius is not necessary for production, still less is it necessary to have entire liberty. What is more, liberty presents pitfalls that rigorous obligations may help us to avoid. A stream narrowly hemmed in by its banks will flow more impetuously. The discipline of some occupation is an excellent school; it bears fruit in the hours of studious leisure. The very constraint will make you concentrate better, you will learn the value of time, you will take eager refuge in those rare hours during which, the claims of duty satisfied, you can turn to your ideal and enjoy the relaxation of some chosen activity after the labor imposed by the hard necessity of getting a livelihood.

The worker who thus finds in a fresh effort the reward of previous effort, who prizes it as a miser prizes his hoard, is usually passionately devoted to his ideal; he cannot be turned aside from a purpose thus consecrated by sacrifice. If his progress seems slower, he is capable of getting farther. Like the poor drudging tortoise, he does not dawdle, he persists, and in a few years' time he will have outstripped the indolent hare whose agile movements were the envy of his own lumbering gait.

The same is true of the isolated worker, deprived of intellectual resources and stimulating society, buried in some little provincial spot, where he seems condemned to stagnate, exiled far from rich libraries, brilliant lectures, an eagerly responsive public, possessing only himself and obliged to draw solely on that inalienable capital.

He must not lose courage either. Though he have everything against him, let him but keep possession of himself and be content with that. An ardent heart has more chance of achieving something than a crammed head abusing the opportunities of great cities. Here again strength may spring from difficulty. It is in the steep mountain passes that one bends and strains; level paths allow one to relax, and a state of uncontrolled relaxation quickly becomes fatal.

The most valuable thing of all is will, a deeply rooted will; to will to be somebody, to achieve something; to be even now in desire that somebody, recognizable by his ideal. Everything else always settles itself. There are books everywhere and only a few are necessary. Society, stimulation, one finds these in spirit in one's solitude: the great are there, present to those who call on them, and the great ages behind impel the ardent thinker forward. As to lectures, those who can have them do not follow them or follow them but ill, if they have not in themselves, at need, the wherewithal to do without such fortunate help. As to the public, if it sometimes stimulates, it often disturbs, scatters the mind; and by going to pick up two pennies in the street, you may lose a fortune. An impassioned solitude is better, for there every seed produces a hundredfold, and every ray of sunlight suffuses the whole landscape with autumnal gold.

St. Thomas of Aquin, as he was coming to settle in Paris and descried the great city in the distance, said to the brother who was with him: "Brother, I would give all that for the commentary of Chrysostom on St. Matthew." When one feels like that, it does not matter where one is nor what resources one has, one is stamped with the seal; one is of the elect of the Spirit; one has only to persevere, and to trust life, as it is ruled for us by God.

You, young man who understand this language and to whom the heroes of the mind seem mysteriously to beckon, but who fear to lack the necessary means, listen to me. Have you two hours a day? Can you undertake to keep them jealously, to use them ardently, and then, being of those who have authority in the Kingdom of God, can you drink the chalice of which these pages would wish to make you savor the exquisite and bitter taste? If so, have confidence. Nay, rest in quiet certainty.

If you are compelled to earn your living, at least you will earn it without sacrificing, as so many do, the liberty of your soul. If you are alone, you will but be more violently thrown back on your noble purposes. Most great men followed some calling. Many have declared that the two hours I postulate suffice for an intellectual career. Learn to make the best use of that limited time; plunge every day of your life into the spring which quenches and yet ever renews your thirst.

Do you want to have a humble share in perpetuating wisdom among men, in gathering up the inheritance of the ages, in formulating the rules of the mind for the present time, in discovering facts and causes, in turning men's wandering eyes towards first causes and their hearts towards supreme ends, in reviving if necessary some dying flame, in organizing the propaganda of truth and goodness? That is the lot reserved for you. It is surely worth a little extra sacrifice; it is worth steadily pursuing with jealous passion.

The study and practice of what Pére Gratry calls Living Logic, that is, the development of our mind, the human word, by contact direct or indirect with the Spirit and the Divine Word—that serious study and persevering practice will give you entry into the wondrous sanctuary. You will be of those who grow, who enrich themselves, and who make ready to receive magnificent gifts. You too, one day, if God so wills, will have a place in the assembly of noble minds.

II. THE INTELLECTUAL DOES NOT STAND ALONE

It is another characteristic of the intellectual vocation that the Christian worker who is consecrated by his call must not be an isolated unit. Whatever be his position, however alone or hidden we suppose him to be materially, he must not yield to the lure of individualism, which is a distorted image of Christian personality.

As life-giving as is solitude, so paralyzing and sterilizing is isolation.

By being only a soul, one ceases to be a man, Victor Hugo would say. Isolation is inhuman; for to work in human fashion is to work with the feeling for man, his needs, his greatness, and the solidarity which binds us closely together in a common life.

A Christian worker should live constantly in the universal, in history. Since he lives with Jesus Christ he cannot separate times, nor men, from Him. Real life is a life in common, an immense family life with charity for its law; if study is to be an act of life, not an art pursued for art's sake and an appropriation of mere abstractions, it must submit to be governed by this law of oneness of heart. "We pray before the crucifix," says Gratry—we must also work before the crucifix—"but the true cross is not isolated from the earth."

A true Christian will have ever before his eyes the image of this globe, on which the Cross is planted, on which needy men wander and suffer, all over which the redeeming Blood, in numberless streams, flows to meet them. The light that he has confers on him a priesthood; the light that he seeks to acquire supposes an implicit promise that he will share it. Every truth is practical; the most apparently abstract, the loftiest, is also the most practical. Every truth is life, direction, a way leading to the end of man. And therefore Jesus Christ made this unique assertion: "I am the Way, the Truth, and the Life."

Work always then with the idea of some utilization, as the Gospel speaks. Listen to the murmur of the human race all about you; pick out certain individuals of certain groups whose need you know, find out what may bring them out of their night and ennoble them; what in any measure may save them. The only holy truths are redeeming truths; and was it not in view of our work as of everything else that the Apostle said: "This is the will of God, your sanctification?"

Jesus Christ needs our minds for His work, as on earth He needed His own human mind. He has gone, but we continue Him; we have that measureless honor. We are His members, therefore have a share in His spirit, are therefore His cooperators. He acts outwardly through us, and inwardly through the inspirations of His Spirit, as in His lifetime He acted outwardly by His voice, inwardly by His grace. Our work being a necessary part of that action, let us work as Jesus meditated—as He drew on the life-springs of the Father to pour them out on the world.

III. The Intellectual Belongs to His Time

And then reflect that if all times are equal before God, if His eternity is a radiant center from which all points on the circumference of time are at an equal distance, it is not the same with the ages and with us, who dwell on the circumference. We are here at a given point on the mighty wheel, not elsewhere. If we are here, it is because God has placed us here. Every moment of duration concerns us, and every age is our neighbor, as well as every man; but the word "neighbor" is a relative word to which the wisdom of Providence attaches a precise meaning for each of us, and to which each of us, in submissive wisdom, must also attach a precise meaning.

Here I am, a man of the twentieth century, living in a time of permanent drama, witnessing upheavals such as perhaps the globe never before saw since the mountains rose and the seas were driven into their caverns. What have I to do for this panting, palpitating century? More than ever before thought is waiting for men, and men for thought. The world is in danger for lack of life-giving maxims. We are in a train rushing ahead at top speed, no signals visible. The planet is going it knows not where, its law has failed it: who will give it back its sun?

All this is not intended to narrow down the field of intellectual research and to confine it to exclusively religious study. That will be evident. I have already said that every truth is practical, that every truth has a saving power. But I am indicating a spirit, and this spirit, both in general and because of what is opportune at the present time, excludes mere dilettantism.

It also excludes a certain archaeological tendency, a love of the past which turns away from present suffering, an esteem for the past which seems not to recognize the universal presence of God. Every age is not as good as every other, but all ages are Christian ages, and there is one which for us, and in practice, surpasses them all: our own. In view of it are our inborn resources, our graces of today and tomorrow, and consequently the efforts that we must make in order to correspond with them.

Let us not be like those people who always seem to be pallbearers at the funeral of the past. Let us utilize, by living, the qualities of the dead. Truth is ever new. Like the grass of morning, moist with glistening dew, all the old virtues are waiting to spring up afresh. God does not grow old. We must help our God to renew, not the buried past and the chronicles of a vanished world, but the eternal face of the earth.

Albert Jay Nock

1870–1945

We can do nothing for the Great Tradition; our fidelity to it can do everything for us.

THE THEORY OF EDUCATION IN THE UNITED STATES

Albert Jay Nock, American individualist and man of letters, was born in Scranton, Pennsylvania, but raised in Brooklyn, New York, and in rural Michigan. His father was a minister in the Protestant Episcopal Church, and Nock himself prepared for the ministry and served for about a dozen years as an Episcopal priest. He was at first largely self-educated, but later attended a prep school and then Bard College. He married and had two sons, but under mysterious circumstances abandoned his family and his calling to the ministry. His writing career began in 1908, and for nearly forty years he worked as an editor and author. He worked for the *American Magazine,* the *Nation,* and the *Freeman*; contributed to the *Atlantic Monthly,* the *American Mercury,* and *Harper's*; and wrote a biography of Thomas Jefferson, two books on Rabelais, the libertarian polemic *Our Enemy, The State,* several collections of literary and social criticism, and a classic autobiography, *The Memoirs of a Superfluous Man.* Nock was a Jeffersonian individualist who defended political, economic, and intellectual freedom while at the same time mercilessly exposing and condemning vulgar materialism and the false promises of mass democracy.

THE SELECTION

Nock believed that he had the misfortune of living "after the deluge" in American education, the flood that had swept away the old order of the Great Tradition. From his first
published essay through the publication of his autobiography some thirty-five years later,
Nock discriminated carefully between formative and instrumental knowledge, between
education and training, between wisdom and mere cleverness. His *Theory of Education
in the United States* (1932) was first delivered as a series of lectures at Jefferson's University of Virginia. He anchored true education in Plato's effort to "see things as they are."
Nock believed that about the year 1900 a revolution had swept away traditional humanistic
learning in America. Instrumental learning, with its love of relevance, preparation for the
"real world," and vocational practicality, had carried the day. Formative education could
not withstand the appeal of technical proficiency and the illusion that the "machinery" of
education provided the key to the quality of education. Chapters 6 and 7 are included here
and give a good sense of the whole, but the entire book deserves careful consideration.[1]

from The Theory of Education in the United States
Chapter 6

Traditionally, an educational system was conceived of as an organic whole, with distinct
lines fixed between its units; and each unit was supposed to exercise its function with strict
reference to the units preceding and succeeding it. When we organised our system, this was
also our general plan. Our units were the primary and secondary schools, the undergraduate college, the university and the technical school. The intention was that a person should
proceed directly through the primary school into the secondary school, and through that
into the undergraduate college. On leaving college, he was prepared to enter the university,
if he was looking forward to one of the four so-called "learned" professions. Otherwise, if he
proposed to occupy himself with one of the sciences, or with some pursuit like agriculture,
architecture, engineering, for which a considerable technical training is necessary, he was
also prepared to begin that; he was qualified to enter the institute of science or the technical school. I do not say that this intention was always and everywhere carried out; at the
University of Paris, in the sixteenth century, students entered under the Faculty of Law with
very little preparation, sometimes with none. In a new civilisation like ours, local poverty,
poor equipment, the scarcity of teachers, and other difficult obstacles stood in the way of
orderly consecutive progress through all these grades. Nevertheless, this was the intention;
and in general, probably, it was as well kept to as circumstances permitted.

    The intention was, moreover—and this is most important—that the character of this
progress through the schools and the undergraduate college, right up to the doors of the
university or technical school, should be purely disciplinary. The curricula of the primary
and secondary school and of the college should be fixed, invariable, the same for all par-

---

1. For further reading, see "The Value to the Clergyman of Training in the Classics" *(School Review,* June 1908),
"American Education" *(Atlantic Monthly,* May 1931), "The Disadvantages of Being Educated"*(Harper's,* September
1932), and various sections of his *Memoirs of a Superfluous Man* (1943).

ticipants. There should be no elective studies. The student took what was deemed best for him, or left the place; he had no choice. Hence there was no overlapping or reduplication of function anywhere along the line. The college, for example, did not reach back into the work of the secondary school to fill up any holes or take up any slack in the student's career there. If the student came to college unprepared in any particular, he was unprepared, and there was nothing to do about it but to remand him. No more did the college reach forward into the purview of the university or the technical school with any pre-vocational or pre-professional exercises. Each institution kept strictly to the doings in its own bailiwick, as a unit in a general system.

Such, I say, is the traditional way in which the mechanism of an educational system is supposed to work; and such, speaking broadly and with regard to the force of circumstances, was the way that our mechanism was set up to work. The progress through school and college did, in fact, remain quite strictly disciplinary up to the revolutionary period which set in, as well as one can put a date to it, about thirty-five years ago. Now, it was of the very essence of this disciplinary character—the very fifth essence, as a mediaevalist might say—that all the knowledge canvassed in these fixed curricula should be of the order known as formative. Instrumental knowledge, knowledge of the sort which bears directly on doing something or getting something, should have no place there; it should have as strict an institutional quarantine raised against it as cities raise against a plague. This discrimination was quite carefully regarded in our institutions until the revolution of thirty-five years ago broke it down. I suggest that we look for a moment at the disciplinary fixed curricula made up of purely formative studies, to see what it actually came to in practice.

Let us look at it in this way: let us suppose that an educable person found good schools and a good college, where all circumstances were favourable—there were such—what would he do, and what might be expected of him? After the three Rs, or rather for a time in company with them, his staples were Latin, Greek and mathematics. He took up the elements of these two languages very early, and continued at them, with arithmetic and algebra, nearly all the way through the primary, and all the way through the secondary schools. Whatever else he did, if anything, was inconsiderable except as related to these major subjects; usually some readings in classical history, geography and mythology. When he reached the undergraduate college at the age of sixteen or so, all his language-difficulties with Greek and Latin were forever behind him; he could read anything in either tongue, and write in either, and he was thus prepared to deal with both literatures purely as literature, to bestow on them a purely literary interest. He had also in hand arithmetic, and algebra as far as quadratics. Then in four years at college he covered practically the whole range of Greek and Latin literature; mathematics as far as the differential calculus, and including the mathematics of elementary physics and astronomy; a brief course, covering about six weeks, in formal logic; and one as brief in the bare history of the formation and growth of the English language.

What was the purpose of this? We may admit, I presume, the disciplinary value of these studies, since that has never been seriously disputed, so far as I know, but we may say a word, perhaps, about their formative character. The literatures of Greece and Rome comprise the longest and fullest continuous record available to us, of what the human mind has been busy about in practically every department of spiritual and social activity;

every department, I think, except one—music. This record covers twenty-five hundred consecutive years of the human mind's operations in poetry, drama, law, agriculture, philosophy, architecture, natural history, philology, rhetoric, astronomy, politics, medicine, theology, geography, everything. Hence the mind that has attentively canvassed this record is not only a disciplined mind but an *experienced* mind; a mind that instinctively views any contemporary phenomenon from the vantage-point of an immensely long perspective attained through this profound and weighty experience of the human spirit's operations. If I may paraphrase the words of Emerson, this discipline brings us into the feeling of an immense longevity, and maintains us in it. You may perceive at once, I think, how different would be the view of contemporary men and things, how different the appraisal of them, the scale of values employed in their measurement, on the part of one who has undergone this discipline and on the part of one who has not. These studies, then, in a word, were regarded as formative because they are *maturing*, because they powerfully inculcate the views of life and the demands on life that are appropriate to maturity and that are indeed the specific marks, the outward and visible signs, of the inward and spiritual grace of maturity. And now we are in a position to observe that the establishment of these views and the direction of these demands is what is traditionally meant, and what we citizens of the republic of letters now mean, by the word *education*; and the constant aim at inculcation of these views and demands is what we know under the name of the Great Tradition of our republic.

An educational system was set up in our country, and lavishly endowed in response to the noble sentiment of parents for the advancement of their children. It was to be equalitarian, as the average man understood equality; that is to say, everybody should be regarded as able to take in its benefits. It should be democratic, as the average man understood democracy; that is to say, no one had any natural right to anything that everybody could not get. Very well, then, we said, education, traditionally, is the establishment of certain views of life and the direction of certain demands on life, views and demands which take proper account of the fundamental instincts of mankind, all in due measure and balance; the instinct of workmanship, the instinct of intellect and knowledge, of religion and morals, of beauty and poetry, of social life and manners. The aim at an inculcation of these views and demands is the Great Tradition of a truly civilised society. The traditional discipline, the process which has been found most competent to the purpose, is that chiefly of scrutinising the longest available continuous record of what the human mind has hitherto done with those instincts; what it has made out of them; what its successes and failures have been; and what is to be learned from both. Bring on your children, and we will put them through this process under the sanction of an equalitarian and democratic theory.

It did not work. We discovered almost at once that it did not work, and that apparently there was no way of making it work. The reason it did not work was that this process postulated an educable person, and everybody is not educable. Far from it, we discovered that relatively very few are educable, very few indeed. There became evident an irreconcilable disagreement between our equalitarian theory and the fact of experience. Our theory assumed that all persons are educable; our practical application of it simply showed that the Creator, in His wisdom and in His loving-kindness, had for some unsearchable reason not quite seen His way to fall in with our theory, for He had not made all persons educable. We found to our discomfiture that the vast majority of mankind have neither the force of intellect to apprehend the processes of education, nor the force of character to make an educational discipline prevail in their lives.

Thus we were faced with a serious dilemma. On the one side was our equalitarian theory, with all the power of a strong sentiment behind it, pushing it on into the test of practice. On the other side was the fact that an inscrutable Providence had most signally failed to do its part towards enabling our theory to stand this test. We had, then, the choice of revising our theory, or of letting it stand and sophisticating our practice into some sort of correspondence with it. If we let go of the equalitarian idea in our theory, the democratic idea would disappear with it; for if all persons are not educable, then some persons may pretend to a distinction to which all others may not pretend, whereby education becomes a kind of class-prerogative; and this is undemocratic.

We made our choice, leaving our theory unrevised and unexamined; it remains today the theory upon which our system undertakes to operate. I repeat for the sake of emphasis, that as far as I know, this theory has never been formally brought before the bar of letters for examination and critical judgment. Then, having made our choice, we set out at once on the business of overhauling, recasting, readjusting and tinkering the mechanics of our system; and this has gone on without cessation for thirty-five years, and so energetically as to degenerate at last into a mere panicky license of innovation. Plan after plan, method after method, programme after programme has been hailed and touted as the one thing needful, put into effect, carried on for a while, and then become outmoded in favour of some other; our shores are strewn with their wreckage—

Que regio in terris nostri non plena laboris?

Chapter 7

In the course of this procedure there came to pass the complete obliteration of a most important distinction which several writers have of late tried to revive, myself among them—I dealt with it in a brief essay published three years ago—the distinction between training and education. As we have observed, very few people are educable. The great majority remain, we may say, in respect of mind and spirit, structurally immature; therefore no amount of exposure to the force of any kind of instruction or example can ever determine in them the views of life or establish in them the demands on life, that are characteristic of maturity. You may recall the findings of the army tests; they created considerable comment when they were published. I dare say these tests are rough and superficial, but under any discount you think proper, the results in this case are significant. I do not remember the exact figures, but they are unimportant; the tests showed that an enormous number of persons of military age had no hope of ever getting beyond the average fourteen-year-old stage of development. When we consider what that average is, we are quite free to say that the vast majority of mankind cannot possibly be educated. They can, however, be trained; anybody can be trained. Practically any kind of mentality is capable of making some kind of response to some kind of training; and here was the salvation of our system's theory. If all hands would simply agree to call training education, to regard a trained person as an educated person and a training-school as an educational institution, we need not trouble ourselves about our theory; it was safe. Since everybody is trainable, the equalitarian side of our theory was safe. Since training in anything for anybody is a mere matter of money, equipment, and specific instruction, the democratic side of our theory was safe. Since a trained citizenry is equivalent to an educated citizenry, the patriotic aspect of our theory might have as much made of it as ever. Since, finally, opportunities for every conceivable kind of training might become abundant and cheap, in innumerable cases to be enjoyed for nothing, or nearly nothing, the parental sentiment in behalf of posterity was satisfied.

What we did, then, actually, was to make just this identification of training with education, and to reconstruct our system accordingly; and this was the revolution of thirty-five years ago. I do not say that at every step we were fully conscious of what we were doing, or of its implications and probable consequences; we proceeded, rather, as most revolutionists do, by a series of improvisations. We have been proceeding in that way ever since, and this too is characteristic of periods of attempted consolidation after a revolution. But that is what we actually did. The revolutionary principle was the identification of training with education; the revolutionary process was the summary sweeping away of the discipline set by the Great Tradition, and the construction of another procedure to replace it.

It may be remarked here that with the disappearance of the distinction between training and education, another distinction of great importance also disappeared, necessarily disappeared. I refer to the distinction between formative knowledge and instrumental knowledge. The discipline set by the Great Tradition concerned itself exclusively with formative knowledge. To justify replacing this discipline with another procedure which concerned itself chiefly with instrumental knowledge, as the procedure of training must obviously do, it became convenient to maintain that the distinction between these two orders of knowledge was quite artificial, that instrumental studies were in themselves formative, as much so as any, and altogether to be preferred on this account as well as on all others. Nothing worth having was to be gained by the intensive study of Greek and Roman literature, classical history, mathematics and formal logic, that could not be gained to better purpose by the study, say, of modern languages, English and the sciences. The revolutionary spirit had its way so completely that this distinction at once faded out of sight, and at present, probably, most of the younger spirits among us are quite unaware that it was ever drawn.

As is the case with all revolutions, great general dissatisfaction put a powerful weapon in the hands of the revolutionists. The product of our system was poor, as a rule, and, as again is always the case in such circumstances, nobody was much interested in getting at the real reasons why it was poor, but rather to pitch upon the first thing in sight and take it as a ground of complaint. The great question thus became, What is the use of sheer mathematics, of sheer Greek and Latin? The question, too, was put with an animus that precluded anything like reasonable consideration, because collisions of opinion occurred and people became ruffled. The fact of the matter was that we had been trying to make a great many persons bear a discipline that they were distinctly unable to bear; the discipline was appropriate only to educable persons, and they were ineducable. Our educational theory required us to attempt this impossibility, and the results were what might be expected even if we had been administering that discipline to the best advantage, which for reasons that I have already cited, we were not always able to do. But all this did not count. Dissatisfaction pitched upon the first thing in sight, the discipline itself, declared it worthless and insisted on its being done away.

In making up a procedure to replace the discipline of the Great Tradition, we were accidentally affected by certain social phenomena appearing at this time, which struck us with all the force of novelty. One was the general preoccupation with natural science, brought about by an unprecedented irruption of invention and discovery. Science touched the popular sense of awe and wonder. In a memorable conflict with many of the dogmatic constructions of organised Christianity, it had come off easily first best; and this had immense popular significance, such significance as is hard for us now even to imagine. Men's minds were full of the marvels of science; their imaginations were busy with its alluring prospect of further marvels. Here, then, was something out of which to construct a procedure. Children should not grow up ignorant of these matters, they should be taught "something about" the natural sciences. This idea was plausible, none could have been more so, and considering the great general preoccupation with the wonders of invention and discovery, none could have been more acceptable.

Accepted it accordingly was, and our institutions began at once to deal in dilutions of various sciences. Our secondary schools and colleges began to deal in diluted chemistry, diluted botany, diluted biology, and so on; the sum coming to a quite impressive list. Now, the point worth remarking here is that this fell in extremely well with the conditions imposed by our theory, because everybody can do anything with these dilutions of science that anybody can do, and nobody can get anything more out of them than everybody can get. Regarded as educational pursuits, they thus amply satisfy the requirements of an equalitarian and democratic theory. They do so because they rest wholly upon evidence of the senses. I do not say that all science rests upon evidence of the senses—there is no need to raise that point—but only that these dilutions do, and that therefore they are accessible to an extremely low order of intelligence, and are easily taught. This feature of our curricula is that upon which Matthew Arnold showered such exquisite raillery in his description of the Lycurgus House Academy and its guiding spirit, Archimedes Silverpump, Ph.D.; and in the summary of the Lycurgus House curriculum as drawn up by the hand of Silverpump's old pupil, Mr. Bottles. In that half-page you will miss hardly a single stock phrase of the eager innovator of yesterday; and probably no better criticism on the worth of his endeavours was ever formulated than the one that is implicit in the words of Mr. Bottles:

> "That will do for land and the Church," said Arminius. "And now let us hear about commerce." "You mean how was Bottles educated?" answered I. "Here we get into another line altogether, but a very good line in its way, too. Mr. Bottles was brought up at the Lycurgus House Academy, Peckham. You are not to suppose from the name of Lycurgus that any Latin and Greek was taught in the establishment; the name only indicates the moral discipline and the strenuous earnest character imparted there. As to the instruction, the thoughtful educator who was principal of the Lycurgus House Academy—Archimedes Silverpump, Ph.D., you must have heard of him in Germany—had modern views. 'We must be men of our age,' he used to say. 'Useful knowledge, living languages, and the forming of the mind through observation and

experiment, these are the fundamental articles of my educational creed.' Or, as I have heard his pupil Bottles put it in his expansive moments after dinner (Bottles used to ask me to dinner till that affair of yours with him in the Reigate train): 'Original man, Silverpump! fine mind! fine system! None of your antiquated rubbish—all practical work—latest discoveries in science—mind kept constantly excited—lots of interesting experiments—lights of all colours—fizz! fizz! bang! bang! That's what I call forming a man!'"

Interest in vocationalism also affected the content of our new procedure. The teaching of science answered the innovator's demand that our system should be modern and up to date, that we should be "men of our time." Vocationalism answered his demand that education should be "a preparation for life." These two demands were the revolution's main fulcrum for ousting the earlier discipline. It was easy to say that the earlier discipline is medieval and out of relation to modern life, for in a sense that is true; but it is true in a sense easily misunderstood and distorted. It was easy to say that this discipline sends out its votaries quite unprepared to meet the actual conditions of present-day living, for that also is true in a sense; it did not send them out with any direct, specific preparation for getting anything or for doing anything. This it never did, never pretended to do. A general preparation it did give an educable person, first by inculcating habits of orderly, profound and disinterested thought; and second, by giving him an immense amount of experienced acquaintance with the way the human mind had worked in all departments of its activity. But this benefit, besides being communicable only to a few, could easily be made to seem vague and illusory in competition with those held out by a programme of vocationalism. Moreover, the economic circumstances of the country threw a halo of great seriousness around vocationalism's programme. With the closing of the frontier in 1890 and the subsequent centralisation of economic control, the opportunities for individual initiative rapidly dwindled. The stratification of our society into a small owning and exploiting class and a propertyless labouring class became more clearly apparent than ever before, and this gave rise to a sense that time was pressing. It was borne in upon our public that if a person wished to get on in the world, he had to hurry up about it. Not only were his chances of getting into the owning and exploiting class becoming few and small, but his prospective hold on even a middle-class position was becoming most uncertain; and on the other hand, the likelihood of his sinking into the exploited and propertyless labouring class was increasing at an alarming rate. He had no time for more than a vocational training. The ensuing mass-movement towards our technical and vocational schools and the vocational departments of our universities confirmed us in our theory, and set us to work even harder at making our general system correspond as closely to our theory as ever we could. Our institutions became more than ever equalitarian in the popular sense, more than ever democratic; more faithfully than ever did they try "to give the people what they want." The result is seen in the impressive nationwide exhibit of what Mr. Flexner calls "bargain-counter education" that is spread before us at the present time, not only by our universities, which were the special subject of Mr. Flexner's examination, but by our secondary schools, which were the subject of Mr. Learned's examination, and by our colleges.

Another matter is worth our notice as bearing upon this situation; that is, the curious popular veneration for mere size and numbers, and the resulting persuasion that bigness is the same thing as greatness. The United States has made itself known as the land where "big things are done in a big way," and has not much troubled itself, as a rule, by the question whether they were always worth doing. The sanction of bigness was sufficient. By force of this persuasion, a big school is a great school. The first question asked about an educational institution is, How many students has it? Here we see our theory again emerging. An institution pretending really to educate people who are really educable would have relatively few students, not only because there are relatively few educable persons, but because of what is known in economics as the law of diminishing returns. If it had a relatively large number of students, the fact would in itself be enough to raise the suspicion that it was not doing its work well. The presence of large numbers is in the nature of things a pretty fair measure of an institution's equalitarian and democratic character, in the popular sense of those terms, and of its concern with "bargain-counter education," which with equal justice and perhaps no less elegance, Mr. Flexner might have styled grab-bag education.

In one of Mr. Hoover's campaign-speeches, according to the newspapers, he congratulated the country on having ten times as many students as any other country, in what he called "its institutions of higher learning." His congratulations were accepted without thought or question; their hollowness was not exposed, so far as I know, by a single editorial article; even the opposition newspapers said nothing about it. Probably campaign-speeches are not taken very seriously; we have learned to judge them rather by their sound than by their sense. Yet my impression is that this incident tends somewhat to show how devoutly incurious our public is about its fetish of size and number. Otherwise surely it would have occurred to some one to say, "But this may not be at all a matter for congratulation. Perhaps it is quite the opposite. In itself, the fact of our having so large an institutional population means nothing either way. Everything surely depends on what the students are like, and what the institutions are like, and what the students do in the institutions, and what sort of folk they are when they come out. Tell us about these matters, and then we will say whether we are to be congratulated or not." Quite possibly indeed, for anything that Mr. Hoover's speech implied to the contrary, the other nations may be the ones to be congratulated, not ourselves. Mr. Hoover was, in short, making an interested appeal to an undiscriminating and irrational popular sentiment of veneration for sheer size, sheer number; and this is clap-trap.

Simone Weil

1909–43

*Academic work is one of those fields containing a pearl so precious
that it is worthwhile to sell all our possessions, keeping nothing for
ourselves, in order to be able to acquire it.*

"Reflections on the Right Use of School Studies
with a View to the Love of God"

Simone Weil was born in Paris to Jewish parents. Her father served in the French
army during World War I. She attended schools in Paris, studied philosophy, and
trained to become a teacher. Her intellectual and spiritual eclecticism led her to Plato,
Indian literature and philosophy, Christian mysticism, and quantum physics. She taught
at several girls' schools around France, but during the Great Depression supported radical
labor movements and even worked for a time as a machinist in a Renault factory in order
to understand labor conditions. She served briefly in the anarchist cause in the Spanish
Civil War. After several mystical experiences, she converted to Roman Catholicism, but
she was never quite orthodox in her theology or her view of Scripture.

In the dark days after Paris fell to Hitler, Weil fled with her family first to the south
of France and then to New York. Eager to assist the French Resistance, however, she
moved to London to work at the French headquarters there. At the request of the Resistance, she wrote what was later published as *The Need for Roots,* a vision of order intended
to form the philosophical foundations for France's recovery after the war. No less an admirer than T. S. Eliot called Weil "a woman of genius, of a kind of genius akin to that of
the saints." Though frustrated by Weil's "errors and exaggerations," Eliot included Weil
in the modern canon of authors of the first importance, calling *The Need for Roots* "one
of those books which ought to be studied by the young before their leisure has been lost
and their capacity for thought destroyed in the life of the hustings and the legislative as-

sembly; books the effect of which, we can only hope, will become apparent in the attitude of another generation."[1] Exhausted by her work and refusing to eat more than the wartime diet of the average citizen in occupied France, Weil died from tuberculosis at a sanatorium in Kent, England, at the age of thirty-four. Her voluminous writings were all published posthumously.

THE SELECTION

Weil's "Reflections on the Right Use of School Studies with a View to the Love of God," first published in *Waiting for God*, is an essay to be meditated upon rather than dissected and analyzed. It is a gentle call to the contemplative life in the midst of the busy, distracted, and violent twentieth century. In such a world, Weil resurrects an earlier Christianity's "habit of attention" and its tireless yearning for truth, delight in learning, and humility. Of humility she writes, it is "a far more precious treasure than all academic progress."

"Reflections on the Right Use of School Studies with a View to the Love of God"

The key to a Christian conception of studies is the realization that prayer consists of attention. It is the orientation of all the attention of which the soul is capable toward God. The quality of the attention counts for much in the quality of the prayer. Warmth of heart cannot make up for it.

The highest part of the attention only makes contact with God, when prayer is intense and pure enough for such a contact to be established; but the whole attention is turned toward God.

Of course school exercises only develop a lower kind of attention. Nevertheless, they are extremely effective in increasing the power of attention that will be available at the time of prayer, on condition that they are carried out with a view to this purpose and this purpose alone.

Although people seem to be unaware of it today, the development of the faculty of attention forms the real object and almost the sole interest of studies. Most school tasks have a certain intrinsic interest as well, but such an interest is secondary. All tasks that really call upon the power of attention are interesting for the same reason and to an almost equal degree.

School children and students who love God should never say: "For my part I like mathematics"; "I like French"; "I like Greek." They should learn to like all these subjects, because all of them develop that faculty of attention which, directed toward God, is the very substance of prayer.

If we have no aptitude or natural taste for geometry, this does not mean that our faculty for attention will not be developed by wrestling with a problem or studying a theorem. On the contrary it is almost an advantage.

---

1. Preface to Simone Weil, *The Need for Roots: Prelude to a Declaration of Duties toward Mankind,* trans. by Arthur Wills (New York: G. P. Putnam's Sons, 1952), vi, xii.

It does not even matter much whether we succeed in finding the solution or understanding the proof, although it is important to try really hard to do so. Never in any case whatever is a genuine effort of the attention wasted. It always has its effect on the spiritual plane and in consequence on the lower one of the intelligence, for all spiritual light lightens the mind.

If we concentrate our attention on trying to solve a problem of geometry, and if at the end of an hour we are no nearer to doing so than at the beginning, we have nevertheless been making progress each minute of that hour in another more mysterious dimension. Without our knowing or feeling it, this apparently barren effort has brought more light into the soul. The result will one day be discovered in prayer. Moreover, it may very likely be felt in some department of the intelligence in no way connected with mathematics. Perhaps he who made the unsuccessful effort will one day be able to grasp the beauty of a line of Racine more vividly on account of it. But it is certain that this effort will bear its fruit in prayer. There is no doubt whatever about that.

Certainties of this kind are experimental. But if we do not believe in them before experiencing them, if at least we do not behave as though we believed in them, we shall never have the experience that leads to such certainties. There is a kind of contradiction here. Above a given level this is the case with all useful knowledge concerning spiritual progress. If we do not regulate our conduct by it before having proved it, if we do not hold on to it for a long time by faith alone, a faith at first stormy and without light, we shall never transform it into certainty. Faith is the indispensable condition.

The best support for faith is the guarantee that if we ask our Father for bread, he does not give us a stone. Quite apart from explicit religious belief, every time that a human being succeeds in making an effort of attention with the sole idea of increasing his grasp of truth, he acquires a greater aptitude for grasping it, even if his effort produces no visible fruit. An Eskimo story explains the origin of light as follows: "In the eternal darkness, the crow, unable to find any food, longed for light, and the earth was illumined." If there is a real desire, if the thing desired is really light, the desire for light produces it. There is a real desire when there is an effort of attention. It is really light that is desired if all other incentives are absent. Even if our efforts of attention seem for years to be producing no result, one day a light that is in exact proportion to them will flood the soul. Every effort adds a little gold to a treasure no power on earth can take away. The useless efforts made by the Curé d'Ars, for long and painful years, in his attempt to learn Latin bore fruit in the marvelous discernment that enabled him to see the very soul of his penitents behind their words and even their silences.

Students must therefore work without any wish to gain good marks, to pass examinations, to win school successes; without any reference to their natural abilities and tastes; applying themselves equally to all their tasks, with the idea that each one will help to form in them the habit of that attention which is the substance of prayer. When we set out to do a piece of work, it is necessary to wish to do it correctly, because such a wish is indispensable in any true effort. Underlying this immediate objective, however, our deep purpose should aim solely at increasing the power of attention with a view to prayer; as, when we write, we draw the shape of the letter on paper, not with a view to the shape, but with a view to the idea we want to express. To make this the sole and exclusive purpose of our studies is the first condition to be observed if we are to put them to the right use.

The second condition is to take great pains to examine squarely and to contemplate attentively and slowly each school task in which we have failed, seeing how unpleasing and second rate it is, without seeking any excuse or overlooking any mistake or any of our tutor's corrections, trying to get down to the origin of each fault. There is a great temptation to do the opposite, to give a sideways glance at the corrected exercise if it is bad and to hide it forthwith. Most of us do this nearly always. We have to withstand this temptation. Incidentally, moreover, nothing is more necessary for academic success, because, despite all our efforts, we work without making much progress when we refuse to give our attention to the faults we have made and our tutor's corrections.

Above all it is thus that we can acquire the virtue of humility, and that is a far more precious treasure than all academic progress. From this point of view it is perhaps even more useful to contemplate our stupidity than our sin. Consciousness of sin gives us the feeling that we are evil, and a kind of pride sometimes finds a place in it. When we force ourselves to fix the gaze, not only of our eyes but of our souls, upon a school exercise in which we have failed through sheer stupidity, a sense of our mediocrity is borne in upon us with irresistible evidence. No knowledge is more to be desired. If we can arrive at knowing this truth with all our souls we shall be well established on the right foundation.

If these two conditions are perfectly carried out there is no doubt that school studies are quite as good a road to sanctity as any other.

To carry out the second, it is enough to wish to do so. This is not the case with the first. In order really to pay attention, it is necessary to know how to set about it.

Most often attention is confused with a kind of muscular effort. If one says to one's pupils: "Now you must pay attention," one sees them contracting their brows, holding their breath, stiffening their muscles. If after two minutes they are asked what they have been paying attention to, they cannot reply. They have been concentrating on nothing. They have not been paying attention. They have been contracting their muscles.

We often expend this kind of muscular effort on our studies. As it ends by making us tired, we have the impression that we have been working. That is an illusion. Tiredness has nothing to do with work. Work itself is the useful effort, whether it is tiring or not. This kind of muscular effort in work is entirely barren, even if it is made with the best of intentions. Good intentions in such cases are among those that pave the way to hell. Studies conducted in such a way can sometimes succeed academically from the point of view of gaining marks and passing examinations, but that is in spite of the effort and thanks to natural gifts; moreover such studies are never of any use.

Will power, the kind that, if need be, makes us set our teeth and endure suffering, is the principal weapon of the apprentice engaged in manual work. But, contrary to the usual belief, it has practically no place in study. The intelligence can only be led by desire. For there to be desire, there must be pleasure and joy in the work. The intelligence only grows and bears fruit in joy. The joy of learning is as indispensable in study as breathing is in running. Where it is lacking there are no real students, but only poor caricatures of apprentices who, at the end of their apprenticeship, will not even have a trade.

It is the part played by joy in our studies that makes of them a preparation for spiritual life, for desire directed toward God is the only power capable of raising the soul. Or rather, it is God alone who comes down and possesses the soul, but desire alone draws God down. He only comes to those who ask him to come; and he cannot refuse to come to those who implore him long, often, and ardently.

Attention is an effort, the greatest of all efforts perhaps, but it is a negative effort. Of itself, it does not involve tiredness. When we become tired, attention is scarcely possible any more, unless we have already had a good deal of practice. It is better to stop working altogether, to seek some relaxation, and then a little later to return to the task; we have to press on and loosen up alternately, just as we breathe in and out.

Twenty minutes of concentrated, untired attention is infinitely better than three hours of the kind of frowning application that leads us to say with a sense of duty done: "I have worked well!"

But, in spite of all appearances, it is also far more difficult. Something in our soul has a far more violent repugnance for true attention than the flesh has for bodily fatigue. This something is much more closely connected with evil than is the flesh. That is why every time that we really concentrate our attention, we destroy the evil in ourselves. If we concentrate with this intention, a quarter of an hour of attention is better than a great many good works.

Attention consists of suspending our thought, leaving it detached, empty, and ready to be penetrated by the object; it means holding in our minds, within reach of this thought, but on a lower level and not in contact with it, the diverse knowledge we have acquired which we are forced to make use of. Our thought should be in relation to all particular and already formulated thoughts, as a man on a mountain who, as he looks forward, sees also below him, without actually looking at them, a great many forests and plains. Above all our thought should be empty, waiting, not seeking anything, but ready to receive in its naked truth the object that is to penetrate it.

All wrong translations, all absurdities in geometry problems, all clumsiness of style, and all faulty connection of ideas in compositions and essays, all such things are due to the fact that thought has seized upon some idea too hastily, and being thus prematurely blocked, is not open to the truth. The cause is always that we have wanted to be too active; we have wanted to carry out a search. This can be proved every time, for every fault, if we trace it to its root. There is no better exercise than such a tracing down of our faults, for this truth is one to be believed only when we have experienced it hundreds and thousands of times. This is the way with all essential truths.

We do not obtain the most precious gifts by going in search of them but by waiting for them. Man cannot discover them by his own powers, and if he sets out to seek for them he will find in their place counterfeits of which he will be unable to discern the falsity.

The solution of a geometry problem does not in itself constitute a precious gift, but the same law applies to it because it is the image of something precious. Being a little fragment of particular truth, it is a pure image of the unique, eternal, and living Truth, the very Truth that once in a human voice declared: "I am the Truth."

Every school exercise, thought of in this way, is like a sacrament.

In every school exercise there is a special way of waiting upon truth, setting our hearts upon it, yet not allowing ourselves to go out in search of it. There is a way of giving our attention to the data of a problem in geometry without trying to find the solution or to the words of a Latin or Greek text without trying to arrive at the meaning, a way of waiting, when we are writing, for the right word to come of itself at the end of our pen, while we merely reject all inadequate words.

Our first duty toward school children and students is to make known this method to them, not only in a general way but in the particular form that bears on each exercise. It is not only the duty of those who teach them but also of their spiritual guides. Moreover the latter should bring out in a brilliantly clear light the correspondence between the attitude of the intelligence in each one of these exercises and the position of the soul, which, with its lamp well filled with oil, awaits the Bridegroom's coming with confidence and desire. May each loving adolescent, as he works at his Latin prose, hope through this prose to come a little nearer to the instant when he will really be the slave—faithfully waiting while the master is absent, watching and listening—ready to open the door to him as soon as he knocks. The master will then make his slave sit down and himself serve him with meat.

Only this waiting, this attention, can move the master to treat his slave with such amazing tenderness. When the slave has worn himself out in the fields, his master says on his return, "Prepare my meal, and wait upon me." And he considers the servant who only does what he is told to do to be unprofitable. To be sure in the realm of action we have to do all that is demanded of us, no matter what effort, weariness, and suffering it may cost, for he who disobeys does not love; but after that we are only unprofitable servants. Such service is a condition of love, but it is not enough. What forces the master to make himself the slave of his slave, and to love him, has nothing to do with all that. Still less is it the result of a search the servant might have been bold enough to undertake on his own initiative. It is only watching, waiting attention.

Happy then are those who pass their adolescence and youth in developing this power of attention. No doubt they are no nearer to goodness than their brothers working in fields and factories. They are near in a different way. Peasants and workmen possess a nearness to God of incomparable savor which is found in the depths of poverty, in the absence of social consideration and in the endurance of long drawn-out sufferings. If, however, we consider the occupations in themselves, studies are nearer to God because of the attention which is their soul. Whoever goes through years of study without developing this attention within himself has lost a great treasure.

Not only does the love of God have attention for its substance; the love of our neighbor, which we know to be the same love, is made of this same substance. Those who are unhappy have no need for anything in this world but people capable of giving them their attention. The capacity to give one's attention to a sufferer is a very rare and difficult thing; it is almost a miracle; it is a miracle. Nearly all those who think they have this capacity do not possess it. Warmth of heart, impulsiveness, pity are not enough.

In the first legend of the Grail, it is said that the Grail (the miraculous vessel that satisfies all hunger by virtue of the consecrated Host) belongs to the first comer who asks the guardian of the vessel, a king three-quarters paralyzed by the most painful wound, "What are you going through?"

The love of our neighbor in all its fullness simply means being able to say to him: "What are you going through?" It is a recognition that the sufferer exists, not only as a unit in a collection, or a specimen from the social category labeled "unfortunate," but as a man, exactly like us, who was one day stamped with a special mark by affliction. For this reason it is enough, but it is indispensable, to know how to look at him in a certain way.

This way of looking is first of all attentive. The soul empties itself of all its own contents in order to receive into itself the being it is looking at, just as he is, in all his truth.

Only he who is capable of attention can do this.

So it comes about that, paradoxical as it may seem, a Latin prose or a geometry problem, even though they are done wrong, may be of great service one day, provided we devote the right kind of effort to them. Should the occasion arise, they can one day make us better able to give someone in affliction exactly the help required to save him, at the supreme moment of his need.

For an adolescent, capable of grasping this truth and generous enough to desire this fruit above all others, studies could have their fullest spiritual effect, quite apart from any particular religious belief.

Academic work is one of those fields containing a pearl so precious that it is worth while to sell all our possessions, keeping nothing for ourselves, in order to be able to acquire it.

C. S. Lewis

1898–1963

It is a good rule, after reading a new book, never to allow yourself another new one till you have read an old one in between. If that is too much for you, you should at least read one old one to every three new ones.

"ON THE READING OF OLD BOOKS"

Clive Staples Lewis was born in Belfast, Northern Ireland. He was educated at boarding schools in England and Ireland and by a private tutor before entering University College, Oxford, in 1917. His university education was interrupted when he joined the British army during World War I. He fought in the trenches of the Somme Valley, was wounded in 1918, but returned to active service until he was discharged in 1919. Lewis thereupon resumed his work at Oxford, completing his studies in classics, philosophy, history, and English. He began his academic career as a tutor in philosophy but soon became a fellow and tutor in English literature at Magdalen College, Oxford, a decision that shaped the course of the rest of his life. He remained at Magdalen for twenty-nine years before heading to Magdalene College, Cambridge, in 1954.

A stubborn atheist for many years, Lewis converted to Christianity in 1931, in part through the influence of his Oxford friend J. R. R. Tolkien. His companions at Oxford also included Dorothy Sayers, Charles Williams, Owen Barfield, and his beloved brother, Warren ("Warnie") Lewis. During the Second World War, Lewis achieved international acclaim as an apologist for the Christian faith. In 1956, he married Joy Davidman, who died from cancer four years later. His popular books include *The Problem of Pain, The Screwtape Letters, Mere Christianity, The Abolition of Man, The Four Loves,* a science fiction trilogy, the classic children's series *Chronicles of Narnia,* and an autobiography titled *Surprised by Joy.*

THE SELECTION

Lewis's finest book on education is *The Abolition of Man,* a set of lectures that should be read alongside the last volume of his science fiction trilogy, *That Hideous Strength.* In non-fiction and fiction, these two books capture Lewis's horror at the dehumanizing effect of modern education, which abolishes man by making him "all head" (at the hands of the Baconians) or "all belly" (at the hands of the Rousseauists), negating the mediation of the heart. These books, however, do not lend themselves well to anthologizing; they need to be read and appreciated as complete works. Included here, then, is a lesser-known essay by Lewis titled "On the Reading of Old Books" (published in *God in the Dock* and in *The Grand Miracle).* With his customary clarity, Lewis achieves the kind of simplicity that lies on the far side of much thought and labor. He recommends the "old books" for their power to draw the modern reader into a conversation that has been going on for centuries; these books offer the long view, a wider perspective, and they often sit in judgment on us if we but listen. Lewis invites us to open the windows and "keep the clean sea breeze of the centuries blowing through our minds." Above all, he encourages us to stand "against the world" in a worthy cause. "On the Reading of Old Books" was originally written during World War II as an introduction to a new translation of St. Athanasius's *The Incarnation of the Word of God* (1944).

Elsewhere, Lewis wrote the following about the power of good books:

> Those of us who have been true readers all our life seldom realise the enormous exten-
> sion of our being which we owe to authors. We realise it best when we talk with an
> unliterary friend. He may be full of goodness and good sense but he inhabits a tiny
> world. In it, we should be suffocated. The man who is contented to be only himself,
> and therefore less a self, is in prison. My own eyes are not enough for me, I will see
> through those of others.[1]

"On the Reading of Old Books"

There is a strange idea abroad that in every subject the ancient books should be read only by the professionals, and that the amateur should content himself with the modern books. Thus I have found as a tutor in English literature that if the average student wants to find out something about Platonism, the very last thing he thinks of doing is to take a translation of Plato off the library shelf and read the *Symposium.* He would rather read some dreary modern book ten times as long, all about "isms" and influences and only once in twelve pages telling him what Plato actually said. The error is rather an amiable one, for it springs from humility. The student is half afraid to meet one of the great philosophers face to face. He feels himself inadequate and thinks he will not understand him. But if he only knew, the great man, just because of his greatness, is much more intelligible than his modern com-

---

1. *An Experiment in Criticism* (Cambridge: Cambridge University Press, 1961), 140.

mentator. The simplest student will be able to understand, if not all, yet a very great deal of what Plato said; but hardly anyone can understand some modern books on Platonism. It has always therefore been one of my main endeavors as a teacher to persuade the young that firsthand knowledge is not only more worth acquiring then secondhand knowledge, but is usually much easier and more delightful to acquire.

This mistaken preference for the modern books and this shyness of the old ones is nowhere more rampant than in theology. Wherever you find a little study circle of Christian laity you can be almost certain that they are studying not St. Luke or St. Paul or St. Augustine or Thomas Aquinas or Hooker or Butler, but M. Berdyaev or M. Maritain or Mr. Niebuhr or Miss Sayers or even myself.

Now this seems to me topsy-turvy. Naturally, since I myself am a writer, I do not wish the ordinary reader to read no modern books. But if he must read only the new or only the old, I would advise him to read the old. And I would give him this advice precisely because he is an amateur and therefore much less protected than the expert against the dangers of an exclusive contemporary diet. A new book is still on its trial and the amateur is not in a position to judge it. It has to be tested against the great body of Christian thought down the ages, and all its hidden implications (often unsuspected by the author himself) have to be brought to light. Often it cannot be fully understood without the knowledge of a good many other modern books. If you join at eleven o'clock a conversation which began at eight you will often not see the real bearing of what is said. Remarks which seem to you very ordinary will produce laughter or irritation and you will not see why—the reason, of course, being that the earlier stages of the conversation have given them a special point. In the same way sentences in a modern book which look quite ordinary may be directed "at" some other book; in this way you may be led to accept what you would have indignantly rejected if you knew its real significance. The only safety is to have a standard of plain, central Christianity ("mere Christianity" as Baxter called it) which puts the controversies of the moment in their proper perspective. Such a standard can be acquired only from the old books. It is a good rule, after reading a new book, never to allow yourself another new one till you have read an old one in between. If that is too much for you, you should at least read one old one to every three new ones.

Every age has its own outlook. It is specially good at seeing certain truths and specially liable to make certain mistakes. We all, therefore, need the books that will correct the characteristic mistakes of our own period. And that means the old books. All contemporary writers share to some extent the contemporary outlook—even those, like myself, who seem most opposed to it. Nothing strikes me more when I read the controversies of past ages than the fact that both sides were usually assuming without question a good deal which we should now absolutely deny. They thought that they were as completely opposed as two sides could be, but in fact they were all the time secretly united—united *with* each other and *against* earlier and later ages—by a great mass of common assumptions. We may be sure that the characteristic blindness of the twentieth century—the blindness about which posterity will ask, "But how *could* they have thought that?"—lies where we have never suspected it, and concerns something about which there is untroubled agreement between Hitler and President Roosevelt or between Mr. H. G. Wells and Karl Barth. None of us can fully escape this blindness, but we shall certainly increase it, and weaken our guard against it, if we read only modern books. Where they are true they will give us truths which we half knew already. Where they are false they will aggravate the error with which we are already dangerously ill. The only palliative is to keep the clean sea breeze of the centuries blowing through our minds, and this can be done only by reading old books. Not, of course, that there is any magic about the past. People were no cleverer then than they are now; they made as many mistakes as we. But not the *same* mistakes. They will not flatter us in the errors we are already committing; and their own errors, being now open and palpable, will not endanger us. Two heads are better than one, not because either is infallible, but because they are unlikely to go wrong in the same direction. To be sure, the books of the future would be just as good a corrective as the books of the past, but unfortunately we cannot get at them.

I myself was first led into reading the Christian classics, almost accidentally, as a result of my English studies. Some, such as Hooker, Herbert, Traherne, Taylor and Bunyan, I read because they are themselves great English writers: others, such as Boethius, St. Augustine, Thomas Aquinas, and Dante, because they were "influences." George MacDonald I had found for myself at the age of sixteen and never wavered in my allegiance, though I tried for a long time to ignore his Christianity. They are, you will note, a mixed bag, representative of many churches, climates and ages. And that brings me to yet another reason for reading them. The divisions of Christendom are undeniable and are by some of these writers most fiercely expressed. But if any man is tempted to think—as one might be tempted who read only contemporaries—that "Christianity" is a word of so many meanings that it means nothing at all, he can learn beyond all doubt, by stepping out of his own century, that this is not so. Measured against the ages "mere Christianity" turns out to be no insipid interdenominational transparency, but something positive, self-consistent, and inexhaustible. I know it, indeed, to my cost. In the days when I still hated Christianity, I learned to recognize, like some all too familiar smell, that almost unvarying *something* which met me, now in Puritan Bunyan, now in Anglican Hooker, now in Thomist Dante. It was there (honeyed and floral) in Francis de Sales; it was there (grave and homely) in Spenser and Walton; it was there (grim but manful) in Pascal and Johnson; there again, with a mild, frightening, paradisial flavor, in Vaughan and Boehme and Traherne. In the urban sobriety of the eighteenth century one was not safe—Law and Butler were two lions in the path. The supposed "paganism" of the Elizabethans could not keep it out; it lay in wait where a man might have supposed himself safest, in the very center of *The Faerie Queene* and the *Arcadia*. It was, of course, varied; and yet—after all—so unmistakably the same; recognizable, not to be evaded, the odor which is death to us until we allow it to become life:

> an air that kills
> From yon far country blows.

We are all rightly distressed, and ashamed also, at the divisions of Christendom. But those who have always lived within the Christian fold may be too easily dispirited by them. They are bad, but such people do not know what it looks like from without. Seen from there, what is left intact, despite all the divisions, still appears (as it truly is) an immensely formidable unity. I know, for I saw it; and well our enemies know it. That unity any of us can find by going out of his own age. It is not enough, but it is more than you had thought till then. Once you are well soaked in it, if you then venture to speak, you will have an amusing experience. You will be thought a Papist when you are actually reproducing Bunyan, a pantheist when you are quoting Aquinas, and so forth. For you have now got on to the great level viaduct which crosses the ages and which looks so high from the valleys, so low from the mountains, so narrow compared with the swamps, and so broad compared with the sheep tracks.

The present book is something of an experiment. The translation is intended for the world at large, not only for theological students. If it succeeds, other translations of other great Christian books will presumably follow. In one sense, of course, it is not the first in the field. Translations of the *Theologia Germanica*, the *Imitation*, the *Scale of Perfection*, and the *Revelations* of Lady Julian of Norwich are already on the market, and are very valuable, though some of them are not very scholarly. But it will be noticed that these are all books of devotion rather than of doctrine. Now the layman or amateur needs to be instructed as well as to be exhorted. In this age his need for knowledge is particularly pressing. Nor would I admit any sharp division between the two kinds of book. For my own part, I tend to find the doctrinal books often more helpful in devotion than the devotional books, and I rather suspect that the same experience may await many others. I believe that many who find that "nothing happens" when they sit down, or kneel down, to a book of devotion, would find that the heart sings unbidden while they are working their way through a tough bit of theology with a pipe in their teeth and a pencil in their hand.

This is a good translation of a very great book. St. Athanasius has suffered in popular estimation from a certain sentence in the "Athanasian Creed." I will not labor the point that that work is not exactly a creed and was not by St. Athanasius, for I think it is a very fine piece of writing. The words "Which Faith except every one do keep whole and undefiled, without doubt he shall perish everlastingly" are the offense. They are commonly misunderstood. The operative word is *keep*; not *acquire*, or even *believe*, but *keep*. The author, in fact, is not talking about unbelievers; but about deserters, not about those who have never heard of Christ, nor even those who have misunderstood and refused to accept Him, but of those who having really understood and really believed, then allow themselves, under the sway of sloth or of fashion or any other invited confusion to be drawn away into sub-Christian modes of thought. They are a warning against the curious modern assumption that all changes of belief, however brought about, are necessarily exempt from blame. But this is not my immediate concern. I mention "the Creed (commonly called) of St. Athanasius" only to get out of the reader's way what may have been a bogey and to put the true Athanasius in its place. His epitaph is *Athanasius contra mundum*, "Anthanasius against the world." We are proud that our country has more than once stood against the world. Athanasius did the same. He stood for the Trinitarian doctrine, "whole and undefiled," when it looked as if all the civilized world was slipping back from Christianity into the religion of Arius—into one of those "sensible" synthetic religions which are so strongly recommended today and which, then as now, included among their devotees many highly cultivated clergymen. It is his glory that he did not move with the times; it is his reward that he now remains when those times, as all times do, have moved away.

When I first opened his *De Incarnatione* I soon discovered by a very simple test that I was reading a masterpiece. I knew very little Christian Greek except that of the New Testament and I had expected difficulties. To my astonishment I found it almost as easy as

Xenophon; and only a mastermind could, in the fourth century, have written so deeply on such a subject with such classical simplicity. Every page I read confirmed this impression. His approach to the miracles is badly needed today, for it is the final answer to those who object to them as "arbitrary and meaningless violations of the Laws of Nature." They are here shown to be rather the retelling in capital letters of the same message which Nature writes in her crabbed cursive hand; the very operations one would expect of Him who was so full of life that when He wished to die He had to "borrow death from others." The whole book, indeed, is a picture of the Tree of Life—a sappy and golden book, full of buoyancy and confidence. We cannot, I admit, appropriate all its confidence today. We cannot point to the high virtue of Christian living and the gay, almost mocking courage of Christian martyrdom, as a proof of our doctrines with quite that assurance which Athanasius takes as a matter of course. But whoever may be to blame for that it is not Athanasius.

Dorothy Sayers

1893–1957

However firmly a tradition is rooted, if it is never watered, though it dies hard, yet in the end it dies.

"THE LOST TOOLS OF LEARNING"

❧

D orothy L. Sayers, novelist, playwright, and translator, was born in Oxford, England. Her father was headmaster of the Christ Church Cathedral Choir School, and she was educated first in Salisbury and then at Somerville College, Oxford. Among the first women to graduate from Oxford, she earned a first-class honors degree in medieval literature in 1915. She left academia, however, to work in the publishing and advertising industries. Sayers soon turned to writing detective fiction, and in 1923 published the first of her many novels about Lord Peter Wimsey and Harriet Vane. Her circle of friends included G. K. Chesterton, T. S. Eliot, C. S. Lewis, and Charles Williams. She married in 1926 and settled in Essex, where she lived and worked for the next thirty years. Aside from her many popular novels, she wrote a defense of religious orthodoxy (*Creed or Chaos*), an enduring book on the task of the Christian artist (*The Mind of the Maker*), and a distinguished translation of Dante's *Divine Comedy,* which is still in print.

THE SELECTION

Sayers delivered "The Lost Tools of Learning" as a lecture at Oxford in 1947. Like Eliot and Lewis, she opposed the programs for educational reform circulating in Britain after World War II. In this lecture she claims to enter the debate merely as a concerned amateur, but her sly and witty contribution turns the tables on modernity by suggesting that some of the very things modern man cherishes most can only be salvaged by recovering the wisdom of the Middle Ages. "If we are to produce a society of educated people, fitted to preserve their intellectual freedom amid the complex pressures of our modern society," she warns, "we must turn back the wheel of progress some four or five hundred years, to the point at which education began to lose sight of its true object. . . ." Her program for reform (if "program" is not too rigid a word) seeks to recover the "lost tools" of medieval Scholasticism—namely, the grammar, dialectic, and rhetoric of the Trivium. In Sayers's view, the Trivium develops a disciplined mind prepared to master any subject. All subjects, in fact, such as history and mathematics, have their respective "grammars" of rudimentary knowledge. Any teacher who has faced a classroom filled with bright students who seem to lack all background knowledge, to lack any foundation on which to build, will appreciate Sayers's recommendations. Her exclusive emphasis on technique may seem to put her at odds with most of the other authors in this anthology. Indeed, she has little to say here about wisdom and virtue. But kept within the boundaries and the aims she describes, her advice harmonizes well with the Great Tradition. Sayers calls us to retrace our steps to where we dropped the thread and take it up again.

"The Lost Tools of Learning"

That I, whose experience of teaching is extremely limited, should presume to discuss education is a matter, surely, that calls for no apology. It is a kind of behavior to which the present climate of opinion is wholly favorable. Bishops air their opinions about economics; biologists, about metaphysics; inorganic chemists, about theology; the most irrelevant people are appointed to highly technical ministries; and plain, blunt men write to the papers to say that Epstein and Picasso do not know how to draw. Up to a certain point, and provided the criticisms are made with a reasonable modesty, these activities are commendable. Too much specialization is not a good thing. There is also one excellent reason why the veriest amateur may feel entitled to have an opinion about education. For if we are not all professional teachers, we have all, at some time or another, been taught. Even if we learnt nothing—perhaps in particular if we learnt nothing—our contribution to the discussion may have a potential value.

I propose to deal with the subject of teaching, properly so-called. It is in the highest degree improbable that the reforms I propose will ever be carried into effect. Neither the parents, nor the training colleges, nor the examination boards, nor the boards of governors, nor the ministries of education, would countenance them for a moment. For they amount to this: that if we are to produce a society of educated people, fitted to preserve their intellectual freedom amid the complex pressures of our modern society, we must turn back the wheel of progress some four or five hundred years, to the point at which education began to lose sight of its true object, towards the end of the Middle Ages.

Before you dismiss me with the appropriate phrase—reactionary, romantic, mediaevalist, *laudator temporis acti* [praiser of times past], or whatever tag comes first to hand—I will ask you to consider one or two miscellaneous questions that hang about at the back, perhaps, of all our minds, and occasionally pop out to worry us.

When we think about the remarkably early age at which the young men went up to university in, let us say, Tudor times, and thereafter were held fit to assume responsibility for the conduct of their own affairs, are we altogether comfortable about that artificial prolongation of intellectual childhood and adolescence into the years of physical maturity which is so marked in our own day? To postpone the acceptance of responsibility to a late date brings with it a number of psychological complications which, while they may interest the psychiatrist, are scarcely beneficial either to the individual or to society. The stock argument in favor of postponing the school-leaving age and prolonging the period of education generally is there is now so much more to learn than there was in the Middle Ages. This is partly true, but not wholly. The modern boy and girl are certainly taught more subjects—but does that always mean that they actually know more?

Has it ever struck you as odd, or unfortunate, that today, when the proportion of literacy throughout Western Europe is higher than it has ever been, people should have become susceptible to the influence of advertisement and mass propaganda to an extent hitherto unheard of and unimagined? Do you put this down to the mere mechanical fact that the press and the radio and so on have made propaganda much easier to distribute over a wide area? Or do you sometimes have an uneasy suspicion that the product of modern educational methods is less good than he or she might be at disentangling fact from opinion and the proven from the plausible?

Have you ever, in listening to a debate among adult and presumably responsible people, been fretted by the extraordinary inability of the average debater to speak to the question, or to meet and refute the arguments of speakers on the other side? Or have you ever pondered upon the extremely high incidence of irrelevant matter which crops up at committee meetings, and upon the very great rarity of persons capable of acting as chairmen of committees? And when you think of this, and think that most of our public affairs are settled by debates and committees, have you ever felt a certain sinking of the heart?

Have you ever followed a discussion in the newspapers or elsewhere and noticed how frequently writers fail to define the terms they use? Or how often, if one man does define his terms, another will assume in his reply that he was using the terms in precisely the opposite sense to that in which he has already defined them? Have you ever been faintly troubled by the amount of slipshod syntax going about? And, if so, are you troubled because it is inelegant or because it may lead to dangerous misunderstanding?

Do you ever find that young people, when they have left school, not only forget most of what they have learnt (that is only to be expected), but forget also, or betray that they have never really known, how to tackle a new subject for themselves? Are you often bothered by coming across grown-up men and women who seem unable to distinguish between a book that is sound, scholarly, and properly documented, and one that is, to any trained eye, very conspicuously none of these things? Or who cannot handle a library catalogue? Or who, when faced with a book of reference, betray a curious inability to extract from it the passages relevant to the particular question which interests them?

Do you often come across people for whom, all their lives, a "subject" remains a "subject," divided by watertight bulkheads from all other "subjects," so that they experience very great difficulty in making an immediate mental connection between let us say, algebra and detective fiction, sewage disposal and the price of salmon—or, more generally, between such spheres of knowledge as philosophy and economics, or chemistry and art?

Are you occasionally perturbed by the things written by adult men and women for adult men and women to read? We find a well-known biologist writing in a weekly paper to the effect that: "It is an argument against the existence of a Creator" (I think he put it more strongly; but since I have, most unfortunately, mislaid the reference, I will put his claim at its lowest)—"an argument against the existence of a Creator that the same kind of variations which are produced by natural selection can be produced at will by stock breeders." One might feel tempted to say that it is rather an argument *for* the existence of a Creator. Actually, of course, it is neither; all it proves is that the same material causes (recombination of the chromosomes, by crossbreeding, and so forth) are sufficient to account for all observed variations—just as the various combinations of the same dozen tones are materially sufficient to account for Beethoven's Moonlight Sonata and the noise the cat makes by walking on the keys. But the cat's performance neither proves nor disproves the existence of Beethoven; and all that is proved by the biologist's argument is that he was unable to distinguish between a material and a final cause.

Here is a sentence from no less academic a source than a front-page article in the *Times Literary Supplement*: "The Frenchman, Alfred Epinas, pointed out that certain species (e.g., ants and wasps) can only face the horrors of life and death in association." I do not know what the Frenchman actually did say; what the Englishman says he said is patently meaningless. We cannot know whether life holds any horror for the ant, nor in what sense the isolated wasp which you kill upon the window-pane can be said to "face" or not to "face" the horrors of death. The subject of the article is mass behavior in *man*; and the human motives have been unobtrusively transferred from the main proposition to the supporting instance. Thus the argument, in effect, assumes what it set out to prove—a fact which would become immediately apparent if it were presented in a formal syllogism. This is only a small and haphazard example of a vice which pervades whole books—particularly books written by men of science on metaphysical subjects.

Another quotation from the same issue of the *TLS* comes in fittingly here to wind up this random collection of disquieting thoughts—this time from a review of Sir Richard Livingstone's *Some Tasks for Education*: "More than once the reader is reminded of the value of an intensive study of at least one subject, so as to learn the meaning of knowledge and what precision and persistence is needed to attain it. Yet there is elsewhere full recognition of the distressing fact that a man may be master in one field and show no better judgement than his neighbor anywhere else; he remembers what he has learnt, but forgets altogether how he learned it."

I would draw your attention particularly to that last sentence, which offers an explanation of what the writer rightly calls the "distressing fact" that the intellectual skills bestowed upon us by our education are not readily transferable to subjects other than those in which we acquired them: "he remembers what he has learnt, but forgets altogether how he learned it."

Is not the great defect of our education today—a defect traceable through all the disquieting symptoms of trouble that I have mentioned—that although we often succeed in teaching our pupils "subjects," we fail lamentably on the whole in teaching them how to think: they learn everything, except the art of learning. It is as though we had taught a child, mechanically and by rule of thumb, to play "The Harmonious Blacksmith" upon the piano, but had never taught him the scale or how to read music; so that, having memorized "The Harmonious Blacksmith," he still had not the faintest notion how to proceed from that to tackle "The Last Rose of Summer." Why do I say, "as though?" In certain of the arts and crafts, we sometimes do precisely this—requiring a child to "express himself" in paint before we teach him how to handle the colors and the brush. There is a school of thought which believes this to be the right way to set about the job. But observe: it is not the way in which a trained craftsman will go about to teach himself a new medium. *He*, having learned by experience the best way to economize labor and take the thing by the right end, will start off by doodling about on an odd piece of material, in order to "give himself the feel of the tool."

THE MEDIAEVAL SCHEME OF EDUCATION

Let us now look at the mediaeval scheme of education—the syllabus of the Schools. It does not matter, for the moment, whether it was devised for small children or for older students, or how long people were supposed to take over it. What matters is the light it throws upon what the men of the Middle Ages supposed to be the object and the right order of the educative process.

The syllabus was divided into two parts: the Trivium and Quadrivium. The second part—the Quadrivium—consisted of "subjects," and need not for the moment concern us. The interesting thing for us is the composition of the Trivium, which preceded the Quadrivium and was the preliminary discipline for it. It consisted of three parts: Grammar, Dialectic, and Rhetoric, in that order.

Now the first thing we notice is that two at any rate of these "subjects" are not what we should call "subjects" at all: they are only methods of dealing with subjects. Grammar, indeed, is a "subject" in the sense that it does mean definitely learning a language—at that period it meant learning Latin. But language itself is simply the medium in which thought is expressed. The whole of the Trivium was, in fact, intended to teach the pupil the proper use of the tools of learning, before he began to apply them to "subjects" at all. First, he learned a language; not just how to order a meal in a foreign language, but the structure of a language, and hence of language itself—what it was, how it was put together, and how it worked. Secondly, he learned how to use language; how to define his terms and make accurate statements; how to construct an argument and how to detect fallacies in argument. Dialectic, that is to say, embraced Logic and Disputation. Thirdly, he learned to express himself in language—how to say what he had to say elegantly and persuasively. At the end of his course, he was required to compose a thesis upon some theme set by his masters or chosen by himself, and afterwards to defend his thesis against the criticism of the faculty. By this time, he would have learned—or woe betide him—not merely to write an essay on paper, but to speak audibly and intelligibly from a platform, and to use his wits quickly when heckled. There would also be questions, cogent and shrewd, from those who had already run the gauntlet of debate. It is, of course, quite true that bits and pieces of the mediaeval tradition still linger, or have been revived, in the ordinary school syllabus of today. Some knowledge of grammar is still required when learning a foreign language—perhaps I should say, "is again required," for during my own lifetime, we passed through a phase when the teaching of declensions and conjugations was considered rather reprehensible, and it was considered better to pick these things up as we went along. School debating societies flourish; essays are written; the necessity for "self-expression" is stressed, and perhaps even over-stressed. But these activities are cultivated more or less in detachment, as belonging to the special subjects in which they are pigeon-holed rather than as forming one coherent scheme of mental training to which all "subjects" stand in a subordinate relation. "Grammar" belongs especially to the "subject" of foreign languages, and essay-writing to the "subject" called "English"; while Dialectic has become almost entirely divorced from the rest of the curriculum, and is frequently practiced unsystematically and out of school hours as a separate exercise, only very loosely related to the main business of learning. Taken by and large, the great difference of emphasis between the two conceptions holds good: modern education concentrates on *teaching subjects*, leaving the method of thinking, arguing, and expressing one's conclusions to be picked up by the scholar as he goes along; mediaeval education concentrated on first *forging and learning to handle the tools of learning*, using whatever subject came handy as a piece of material on which to doodle until the use of the tool became second nature.

"Subjects" of some kind there must be, of course. One cannot learn the theory of grammar without learning an actual language, or learn to argue and orate without speaking about something in particular. The debating subjects of the Middle Ages were drawn largely from theology, or from the ethics and history of antiquity. Often, indeed, they became stereotyped, especially towards the end of the period, and the far-fetched and wire-drawn absurdities of Scholastic argument fretted Milton and provide food for merriment even to this day. Whether they were in themselves any more hackneyed and trivial then the usual subjects set nowadays for "essay writing" I should not like to say: we may ourselves grow a little weary of "A Day in My Holidays" and all the rest of it. But most of the merriment is misplaced, because the aim and object of the debating thesis has by now been lost sight of.

A glib speaker in the Brains Trust once entertained his audience (and reduced the late Charles Williams to helpless rage) by asserting that in the Middle Ages it was a matter of faith to know how many archangels could dance on the point of a needle. I need not say, I hope, that it never was a "matter of faith"; it was simply a debating exercise, whose set subject was the nature of angelic substance: were angels material, and if so, did they occupy space? The answer usually adjudged correct is, I believe, that angels are pure intelligences; not material, but limited, so that they may have location in space but not extension. An analogy might be drawn from human thought, which is similarly non-material and similarly limited. Thus, if your thought is concentrated upon one thing—say, the point of a needle—it is located there in the sense that it is not elsewhere; but although it is "there," it occupies no space there, and there is nothing to prevent an infinite number of different people's thoughts being concentrated upon the same needle-point at the same time. The proper *subject* of the argument is thus seen to be the distinction between location and extension in space; the *matter* on which the argument is exercised happens to be the nature of angels (although, as we have seen, it might equally well have been something else); the practical lesson to be drawn from the argument is not to use words like "there" in a loose and unscientific way, without specifying whether you mean "located there" or "occupying space there." Scorn in plenty has been poured out upon the mediaeval passion for hair-splitting; but when we look at the shameless abuse made, in print and on the platform, of controversial expressions with shifting and ambiguous connotations, we may feel it in our hearts to wish that every reader and hearer had been so defensively armored by his education as to be able to cry: *Distinguo.*

For we let our young men and women go out unarmed, in a day when armor was never so necessary. By teaching them all to read, we have left them at the mercy of the printed word. By the invention of the film and the radio, we have made certain that no aversion to reading shall secure them from the incessant battery of words, words, words. They do not know what the words mean; they do not know how to ward them off or blunt their edge or fling them back; they are a prey to words in their emotions instead of being the masters of them in their intellects. We who were scandalized in 1940 when men were sent to fight armored tanks with rifles, are not scandalized when young men and women are sent into the world to fight massed propaganda with a smattering of "subjects"; and when whole classes and whole nations become hypnotized by the arts of the spell binder, we have the impudence to be astonished. We dole out lip-service to the importance of education—lip-service and, just occasionally, a little grant of money; we postpone the school-leaving age, and plan to build bigger and better schools; the teachers slave conscientiously in and out of school hours; and yet, as I believe, all this devoted effort is largely frustrated, because we have lost the tools of learning, and in their absence can only make a botched and piece-meal job of it.

WHAT THEN?

What, then, are we to do? We cannot go back to the Middle Ages. That is a cry to which we have become accustomed. We cannot go back—or can we? *Distinguo.* I should like every term in that proposition defined. Does "go back" mean a retrogression in time, or the revision of an error? The first is clearly impossible per se; the second is a thing which wise men do every day. "Cannot"—does this mean that our behavior is determined irreversibly, or merely that such an action would be very difficult in view of the opposition it would provoke? Obviously the twentieth century is not and cannot be the fourteenth; but if "the Middle Ages" is, in this context, simply a picturesque phrase denoting a particular educational theory, there seems to be no a priori reason why we should not "go back" to it—with modifications—as we have already "gone back" with modifications, to, let us say, the idea of playing Shakespeare's plays as he wrote them, and not in the "modernized" versions of Cibber and Garrick, which once seemed to be the latest thing in theatrical progress.

Let us amuse ourselves by imagining that such progressive retrogression is possible. Let us make a clean sweep of all educational authorities, and furnish ourselves with a nice little school of boys and girls whom we may experimentally equip for the intellectual conflict along lines chosen by ourselves. We will endow them with exceptionally docile parents; we will staff our school with teachers who are themselves perfectly familiar with the aims and methods of the Trivium; we will have our building and staff large enough to allow our classes to be small enough for adequate handling; and we will postulate a Board of Examiners willing and qualified to test the products we turn out. Thus prepared, we will attempt to sketch out a syllabus—a modern Trivium "with modifications" and we will see where we get to.

But first: what age shall the children be? Well, if one is to educate them on novel lines, it will be better that they should have nothing to unlearn; besides, one cannot begin a good thing too early, and the Trivium is by its nature not learning, but a preparation for learning. We will, therefore, "catch 'em young," requiring of our pupils only that they shall be able to read, write, and cipher.

My views about child psychology are, I admit, neither orthodox nor enlightened. Looking back upon myself (since I am the child I know best and the only child I can pretend to know from inside) I recognize three states of development. These, in a rough-and-ready fashion, I will call the Poll-Parrot, the Pert, and the Poetic—the latter coinciding, approximately, with the onset of puberty. The Poll-Parrot stage is the one in which learning by heart is easy and, on the whole, pleasurable; whereas reasoning is difficult and, on the whole, little relished. At this age, one readily memorizes the shapes and appearances of things; one likes to recite the number-plates of cars; one rejoices in the chanting of rhymes and the rumble and thunder of unintelligible polysyllables; one enjoys the mere accumulation of things. The Pert Age, which follows upon this (and, naturally, overlaps it to some extent), is characterized by contradicting, answering back, liking to "catch people out" (especially one's elders); and by the propounding of conundrums. Its nuisance-value is extremely high. It usually sets in about the Fourth Form. The Poetic Age is popularly known as the "difficult" age. It is self-centered; it yearns to express itself; it rather specializes in being misunderstood; it is restless and tries to achieve independence; and, with good luck and good guidance, it should show the beginnings of creativeness; a reaching out towards a synthesis of what it already knows, and a deliberate eagerness to know and do some one thing in preference to all others. Now it seems to me that the layout of the Trivium adapts itself with a singular appropriateness to these three ages: Grammar to the Poll-Parrot, Dialectic to the Pert, and Rhetoric to the Poetic Age.

THE GRAMMAR STAGE

Let us begin, then, with Grammar. This, in practice, means the grammar of some language in particular; and it must be an inflected language. The grammatical structure of an uninflected language is far too analytical to be tackled by any one without previous practice in Dialectic. Moreover, the inflected languages interpret the uninflected, whereas the uninflected are of little use in interpreting the inflected. I will say at once, quite firmly, that the best grounding for education is the Latin grammar. I say this, not because Latin is traditional and mediaeval, but simply because even a rudimentary knowledge of Latin cuts down the labor and pains of learning almost any other subject by at least fifty percent. It is the key to the vocabulary and structure of all the Teutonic languages, as well as to the technical vocabulary of all the sciences and to the literature of the entire Mediterranean civilization, together with all its historical documents.

Those whose pedantic preference for a living language persuades them to deprive their pupils of all these advantages might substitute Russian, whose grammar is still more primitive. (The verb is complicated by a numberr of "aspects"—and I rather fancy that it enjoys three complete voices and a couple extra aorists—but I may be thinking of Sanskrit.) Russian is, of course, helpful with the other Slav dialects. There is something also to be said for Classical Greek. But my own choice is Latin. Having thus pleased the Classicists among you, I will proceed to horrify them by adding that I do not think it either wise or necessary to cramp the ordinary pupil upon the Procrustean bed of the Augustan Age, with its highly elaborate and artificial verse forms and oratory. Post-classical and mediaeval Latin, which was a living language right down to the end of the Renaissance, is easier and in some ways livelier; a study of it helps to dispel the widespread notion that learning and literature came to a full stop when Christ was born and only woke up again at the Dissolution of the Monasteries.

However, I am running ahead too fast. We are still in the grammatical stage. Latin should be begun as early as possible—at a time when inflected speech seems no more astonishing than any other phenomenon in an astonishing world; and when the chanting of "*Amo, amas, amat*" is as ritually agreeable to the feelings as the chanting of "eeny, meeny, miney, mo."

During this age we must, of course, exercise the mind on other things besides Latin grammar. Observation and memory are the faculties most lively at this period; and if we are to learn a contemporary foreign language we should begin now, before the facial and mental muscles become rebellious to strange intonations. Spoken French or German can be practiced alongside the grammatical discipline of the Latin.

In *English*, meanwhile, verse and prose can be learned by heart, and the pupil's memory should be stored with stories of every kind—classical myth, European legend, and so forth. I do not think that the classical stories and masterpieces of ancient literature should be made the vile bodies on which to practice the techniques of Grammar—that was a fault of mediaeval education which we need not perpetuate. The stories can be enjoyed and remembered in English, and related to their origin at a subsequent stage. Recitation aloud should be practiced, individually or in chorus; for we must not forget that we are laying the groundwork for Disputation and Rhetoric.

The grammar of *History* should consist, I think, of dates, events, anecdotes, and personalities. A set of dates to which one can peg all later historical knowledge is of enormous help later on in establishing the perspective of history. It does not greatly matter which dates: those of the Kings of England will do very nicely, provided that they are accompanied by pictures of costumes, architecture, and other "everyday things," so that the mere mention of a date calls up a very strong visual presentment of the whole period.

Geography will similarly be presented in its factual aspect, with maps, natural features, and visual presentment of customs, costumes, flora, fauna, and so on; and I believe myself that the discredited and old-fashioned memorizing of a few capital cities, rivers, mountain ranges, etc., does no harm. Stamp-collecting may be encouraged.

Science, in the Poll-Parrot period, arranges itself naturally and easily around collections—the identifying and naming of specimens and, in general, the kind of thing that used to be called "natural philosophy." To know the name and properties of things is, at this age, a satisfaction in itself; to recognize a devil's coach-horse at sight, and assure one's foolish elders, that, in spite of its appearance, it does not sting; to be able to pick out Cassiopeia and the Pleiades, and perhaps even to know who Cassiopeia and the Pleiades were; to be aware that a whale is not a fish, and a bat not a bird—all these things give a pleasant sensation of superiority; while to know a ring snake from an adder or a poisonous from an edible toadstool is a kind of knowledge that also has practical value.

The grammar of *Mathematics* begins, of course, with the multiplication table, which, if not learnt now, will never be learnt with pleasure; and with the recognition of geometrical shapes and the grouping of numbers. These exercises lead naturally to the doing of simple sums in arithmetic. More complicated mathematical processes may, and perhaps should, be postponed, for the reasons which will presently appear.

So far (except, of course, for the Latin), our curriculum contains nothing that departs very far from common practice. The difference will be felt rather in the attitude of the teachers, who must look upon all these activities less as "subjects" in themselves than as a gathering-together of *material* for use in the next part of the Trivium. What that material is, is only of secondary importance; but it is as well that anything and everything which can be usefully committed to memory should be memorized at this period, whether it is immediately intelligible or not. The modern tendency is to try and force rational explanations on a child's mind at too early an age. Intelligent questions, spontaneously asked, should, of course, receive an immediate and rational answer; but it is a great mistake to suppose that a child cannot readily enjoy and remember things that are beyond his power to analyze—particularly if those things have a strong imaginative appeal (as, for example, *Kubla Kahn*), an attractive jingle (like some of the memory-rhymes for Latin genders), or an abundance of rich, resounding polysyllables (like the *Quicunque vult*).

This reminds me of the grammar of *Theology*. I shall add it to the curriculum, because theology is the Mistress-science without which the whole educational structure will necessarily lack its final synthesis. Those who disagree about this will remain content to leave their pupil's education still full of loose ends. This will matter rather less than it might, since by the time that the tools of learning have been forged the student will be able to tackle theology for himself, and will probably insist upon doing so and making sense of it. Still, it is as well to have this matter also handy and ready for the reason to work upon. At the grammatical age, therefore, we should become acquainted with the story of God and Man in outline—i.e., the Old and New Testaments presented as parts of a single narrative of Creation, Rebellion, and Redemption—and also with the Creed, the Lord's Prayer, and the Ten Commandments. At this stage, it does not matter nearly so much that these things should be fully understood as that they should be known and remembered. Remember, it is material that we are collecting.

The Logic Stage

It is difficult to say at what age, precisely, we should pass from the first to the second part of the Trivium. Generally speaking, the answer is: so soon as the pupil shows himself disposed to Pertness and interminable argument (or, as a school-master correspondent of mine more elegantly puts it: "When the capacity for abstract thought begins to manifest itself"). For as, in the first part, the master faculties are Observation and Memory, so, in the second, the master-faculty is the Discursive Reason. In the first, the exercise to which the rest of the material was, as it were, keyed, was the Latin grammar; in the second, the key-exercise will be Formal Logic. It is here that our curriculum shows its first sharp divergence from modern standards. The disrepute into which Formal Logic has fallen is entirely unjustified; and its neglect is the root cause of nearly all those disquieting symptoms which we have noted in the modern intellectual constitution. Logic has been discredited, partly because we have come to suppose that we are conditioned almost entirely by the intuitive and the unconscious. There is no time to argue whether this is true; I will simply observe that to neglect the proper training of the reason is the best possible way to make it true. Another cause for the disfavor into which Logic has fallen is the belief that it is entirely based upon universal assumptions that are either unprovable or tautological. This is not true. Not all universal propositions are of this kind. But even if they were, it would make no difference, since every syllogism whose major premise is in the form "All A is B" can be recast in hypothetical form. Logic is the art of arguing correctly: "If A, then B"; the method is not invalidated by the hypothetical nature of A. Indeed, the practical utility of Formal Logic today lies not so much in the establishment of positive conclusions as in the prompt detection and exposure of invalid inference.

Let us now quickly review our material and see how it is to be related to Dialectic. On the *Language* side, we shall now have our vocabulary and morphology at our fingertips; henceforward we can concentrate on syntax and analysis (i.e., the logical construction of speech) and the history of Language (i.e., how we came to arrange our speech as we do in order to convey our thoughts).

Our *Reading* will proceed from narrative and lyric to essays, argument and criticism, and the pupil will learn to try his own hand at writing this kind of thing. Many lessons—on whatever subject—will take the form of debates; and the place of individual or choral recitation will be taken by dramatic performances, with special attention to plays in which an argument is stated in dramatic form.

Mathematics—algebra, geometry, and the more advanced kinds of arithmetic—will now enter into the syllabus and take its place as what it really is: not a separate "subject" but a sub-department of Logic. It is neither more nor less than the rule of the syllogism in its particular application to number and measurement, and should be taught as such, instead of being, for some, a dark mystery, and, for others, a special revelation, neither illuminating nor illuminated by any other part of knowledge.

History, aided by a simple system of ethics derived from the grammar of Theology, will provide much suitable material for discussion: Was the behavior of this statesman justified? What was the effect of such an enactment? What are the arguments for and against this or that form of government? We shall thus get an introduction to constitutional history—a subject meaningless to the young child, but of absorbing interest to those who are prepared to argue and debate. *Theology* itself will furnish material for argument about conduct and morals; and should have its scope extended by a simplified course of dogmatic theology (i.e., the rational structure of Christian thought), clarifying the relations between the dogma and the ethics, and lending itself to that application of ethical principles in particular instances which is properly called casuistry. *Geography* and the *Sciences* will all likewise provide material for Dialectic.

But above all, we must not neglect the material which is so abundant in the pupil's own daily life. There is a delightful passage in Leslie Paul's *The Living Hedge* which tells how a number of small boys enjoyed themselves for days arguing about an extraordinary shower of rain which had fallen in their town—a shower so localized that it left one half of the main street wet and the other dry. Could one, they argued, properly say that it had rained that day *on* or *over* the town or only *in* the town? How many drops of water were required to constitute rain? And so on. Argument about this led on to a host of similar problems about rest and motion, sleep and waking, *est* and *non est*, and the infinitesimal division of time. The whole passage is an admirable example of the spontaneous development of the ratiocinative faculty and the natural and proper thirst of the awakening reason for the definition of terms and exactness of statement. All events are food for such an appetite. An umpire's decision; the degree to which one may transgress the spirit of a regulation without being trapped by the letter: on such questions as these, children are born casuists, and their natural propensity only needs to be developed and trained—and especially, brought into an intelligible relationship with the events in the grown-up world. The newspapers are full of good material for such exercises: legal decisions, on the one hand, in cases where the cause at issue is not too abstruse; on the other, fallacious reasoning and muddleheaded arguments, with which the correspondence columns of certain papers one could name are abundantly stocked.

Wherever the matter for Dialectic is found, it is, of course, highly important that attention should be focused upon the beauty and economy of a fine demonstration or a well-turned argument, lest veneration should wholly die. Criticism must not be merely destructive; though at the same time both teacher and pupils must be ready to detect fallacy, slipshod reasoning, ambiguity, irrelevance, and redundancy, and to pounce upon them like rats. This is the moment when precis-writing may be usefully undertaken; together with such exercises as the writing of an essay, and the reduction of it, when written, by 25 or 50 percent.

It will, doubtless, be objected that to encourage young persons at the Pert Age to browbeat, correct, and argue with their elders will render them perfectly intolerable. My answer is that children of that age are intolerable anyhow; and that their natural argumentativeness may just as well be canalized to good purpose as allowed to run away into the sands. It may, indeed, be rather less obtrusive at home if it is disciplined in school; and, anyhow, elders who have abandoned the wholesome principle that children should be seen and not heard have no one to blame but themselves. The teachers, to be sure, will have to mind their step, or they may get more than they bargained for. All children sit in judgment on their masters; and if the Chaplain's sermon or the Headmistress's annual Speech-day address should by any chance afford an opening for the point of the critical wedge, that wedge will go home the more forcibly under the weight of the Dialectical hammer, wielded by a practised hand. That is why I said the teachers themselves would have to have undergone the discipline of the Trivium before they set out to impose it on their charges.

Once again, the contents of the syllabus at this stage may be anything you like. The "subjects" supply material; but they are all to be regarded as mere grist for the mental mill to work upon. The pupils should be encouraged to go and forage for their own information, and so guided towards the proper use of libraries and books for reference, and shown how to tell which sources are authoritative and which are not.

THE RHETORIC STAGE

Towards the close of this stage, the pupils will probably be beginning to discover for themselves that their knowledge and experience are insufficient, and that their trained intelligences need a great deal more material to chew upon. The imagination—usually dormant during the Pert Age—will reawaken, and prompt them to suspect the limitations of logic and reason. This means that they are passing into the Poetic Age and are ready to embark on the study of Rhetoric. The doors of the storehouse of knowledge should now be thrown open for them to browse about as they will. The things once learned by rote will be seen in new contexts; the things once coldly analyzed can now be brought together to form a new synthesis; here and there a sudden insight will bring about that most exciting of all discoveries: the realization that a truism is true.

It is difficult to map out any general syllabus for the study of Rhetoric: a certain free-dom is demanded. In literature, appreciation should be again allowed to take the lead over destructive criticism; and self-expression in writing can go forward, with its tools now sharpened to cut clean and observe proportion. Any child who already shows a disposi-tion to specialize should be given his head: for, when the use of the tools has been well and truly learned, it is available for any study whatever. It would be well, I think, that each pupil should learn to do one, or two, subjects really well, while taking a few classes in subsidiary subjects so as to keep his mind open to the inter-relations of all knowledge. Indeed, at this stage, our difficulty will be to keep "subjects" apart; for as Dialectic will have shown all branches of learning to be inter-related, so Rhetoric will tend to show that all knowledge is one. To show this, and show why it is so, is pre-eminently the task of the Mistress-science. But whether Theology is studied or not, we should at least insist that children who seem inclined to specialize on the mathematical and scientific side should be obliged to attend some lessons in the humanities and vice versa. At this stage, also, the Latin grammar, having done its work, may be dropped for those who prefer to carry on their language studies on the modern side; while those who are likely never to have any great use or aptitude for mathematics might also be allowed to rest, more or less, upon their oars. Generally speaking, whatsoever is *mere* apparatus may now be allowed to fall into the background, while the trained mind is gradually prepared for specialization in the "subjects" which, when the Trivium is completed, it should be perfectly well equipped to tackle on its own. The final synthesis of the Trivium—the presentation and public defense of the thesis—should be restored in some form; perhaps as a kind of "leaving examination" during the last term at school.

The scope of Rhetoric depends also on whether the pupil is to be turned out into the world at the age of sixteen or whether he is to proceed to public school and/or the univer-sity. Since, really, Rhetoric should be taken at about fourteen, the first category of pupil should study Grammar from about nine to eleven, and Dialectic from twelve to fourteen; his last two school years would then be devoted to Rhetoric, which, in this case, would be of a fairly specialized and vocational kind, suiting him to enter immediately upon some practical career. A pupil of the second category would finish his Dialectical course in his preparatory school, and take Rhetoric during his first two years at his public school. At sixteen, he would be ready to start upon those "subjects" which are proposed for his later study at the university: and this part of his education will correspond to the mediaeval Quadrivium. What this amounts to is that the ordinary pupil, whose formal education ends at sixteen, will take the Trivium only; whereas scholars will take both the Trivium and the Quadrivium.

THE TRIVIUM DEFENDED

Is the Trivium, then, a sufficient education for life? Properly taught, I believe that it should be. At the end of the Dialectic, the children will probably seem to be far behind their coevals brought up on old-fashioned "modern" methods, so far as detailed knowl-edge of specific subjects is concerned. But after the age of fourteen they should be able to overhaul the others hand over fist. Indeed, I am not at all sure that a pupil thoroughly proficient in the Trivium would not be fit to proceed immediately to the university at the age of sixteen, thus proving himself the equal of his mediaeval counterpart, whose precocity astonished us at the beginning of this discussion. This, to be sure, would make hay of the English public-school system, and disconcert the universities very much—it would, for example, make quite a different thing of the Oxford and Cambridge boat-race. But I am not here to consider the feelings of academic bodies: I am concerned only with the proper training of the mind to encounter and deal with the formidable mass of undigested problems presented to it by the modern world. For the tools of learning are the same, in any and every subject; and the person who knows how to use them will, at any age, get the mastery of a new subject in half the time and with a quarter of the effort expended by the person who has not the tools at his command. To learn six subjects without remembering how they were learnt does nothing to ease the approach to a seventh; to have learnt and remembered the art of learning makes the approach to every subject an open door.

It is clear that the successful teaching of this neo-mediaeval curriculum will depend even more than usual upon the working together of the whole teaching staff towards a common purpose. Since no subject is considered as an evil in itself, any kind of rivalry in the staff-room will be sadly out of place. The fact that a pupil is unfortunately obliged, for some reason, to miss the history period on Fridays, or the Shakespeare class on Tuesdays, or even to omit a whole subject in favour of some other subject, must not be allowed to cause any heart-burnings—the essential is that he should acquire the method of learning in whatever medium suits him best. If human nature suffers under this blow to one's professional pride in one's own subject, there is comfort in the thought that the end-of-term examination results will not be affected; for the papers will be so arranged as to be an examination in method, by whatever means.

I will add that it is highly important that every teacher should, for his or her own sake, be qualified and required to teach in all three parts of the Trivium; otherwise Masters of Dialectic, especially, might find their minds hardening into a permanent adolescence. For this reason, teachers in preparatory schools should also take Rhetoric classes in the public schools to which they are attached; or, if they are not so attached, then by arrangement in other schools in the same neighborhood. Alternatively, a few preliminary classes in Rhetoric might be taken in preparatory school from the age of thirteen onwards.

Before concluding these necessarily very sketchy suggestions, I ought to say why I think it necessary, in these days, to go back to a discipline which we had discarded. The truth is that for the last three hundred years or so we have been living upon our educational capital. The post-Renaissance world, bewildered and excited by the profusion of new "subjects" offered to it, broke away from the old discipline (which had, indeed, become sadly dull and stereotyped in its practical application) and imagined that henceforward it could, as it were, disport itself happily in its new and extended Quadrivium without passing through the Trivium. But the Scholastic tradition, though broken and maimed, still lingered in the public schools and universities: Milton, however much he protested against it, was formed by it—the debate of the Fallen Angels and the disputation of Abdiel with Satan have the tool-marks of the Schools upon them, and might, incidentally, profitably figure as set passages for our Dialectical studies. Right down to the nineteenth century, our public affairs were mostly managed, and our books and journals were for the most part written, by people brought up in homes, and trained in places, where that tradition was still alive in the memory and almost in the blood. Just so, many people today who are atheist or agnostic in religion, are governed in their conduct by a code of Christian ethics which is so rooted that it never occurs to them to question it.

But one cannot live on capital forever. However firmly a tradition is rooted, if it is never watered, though it dies hard, yet in the end it dies. And today a great number—perhaps the majority—of the men and women who handle our affairs, write our books and our newspapers, carry out our research, present our plays and our films, speak from our platforms and pulpits—yes, and who educate our young people—have never, even in a lingering traditional memory, undergone the Scholastic discipline. Less and less do the children who come to be educated bring any of that tradition with them. We have lost the tools of learning—the axe and the wedge, the hammer and the saw, the chisel and the plane—that were so adaptable to all tasks. Instead of them, we have merely a set of complicated jigs, each of which will do but one task and no more, and in using which eye and hand receive no training, so that no man ever sees the work as a whole or "looks to the end of the work." What use is it to pile task on task and prolong the days of labor, if at the close the chief object is left unattained? It is not the fault of the teachers—they work only too hard already. The combined folly of a civilization that has forgotten its own roots is forcing them to shore up the tottering weight of an educational structure that is built upon sand. They are doing for their pupils the work which the pupils themselves ought to do. For the sole true end of education is simply this: to teach men how to learn for themselves; and whatever instruction fails to do this is effort spent in vain.

T. S. Eliot

1888–1965

Where is the Life we have lost in living?
Where is the wisdom we have lost in knowledge?
Where is the knowledge we have lost in information?

"The Rock"

Thomas Stearns Eliot, modernist poet, playwright, literary and social critic, and editor, was born in St. Louis, Missouri. He earned his B.A. and M.A. at Harvard and studied philosophy at the Sorbonne and at Merton College, Oxford. At Harvard, he studied for a time with George Santayana and Irving Babbitt. His first poems appeared in print in 1917, but he supported himself for a time as a school teacher and as a clerk at Lloyds Bank in London. His most famous poems include *The Waste Land* (1922) and *Four Quartets* (1943). He was founding editor of the *Criterion*. In 1927, Eliot became a member of the Anglican Church and a British subject. His plays include *Murder in the Cathedral* (1935)—based on the martyrdom of Thomas à Becket—and *The Cocktail Party* (1949). He was awarded numerous honorary degrees as well as the Nobel Prize for Literature and the Order of Merit, both in 1948.

THE SELECTION

Eliot published his *Notes Towards the Definition of Culture* in 1948, drawing together and expanding several essays and radio talks from the close of World War II. His acknowledged debt to the work of Christopher Dawson is evident. The final chapter, "Notes on Education and Culture," is included here in its entirety (except for the final paragraph, which serves as a conclusion to the book as a whole). Like Albert Jay Nock, Eliot dared to question the democratic dogmas of the twentieth century as they related to higher education, especially the assumption that mere quantity and equality in mass education are self-evident goods and signs of a healthy society. Regarding the larger purpose of education, he wrote that "it would be a pity if we overlooked the possibilities of education as a means of acquiring *wisdom*; if we belittled the acquisition of *knowledge* for the satisfaction of curiosity, without any further motive than the desire to know; and if we lost our respect for *learning*."

from Notes Towards the Definition of Culture
Chapter 6: Notes on Education and Culture

During the recent war an exceptional number of books were published on the subject of education; there were also voluminous reports of commissions, and an incalculable number of contributions on this subject in periodicals. It is not my business, nor is it within my competence, to review the whole of current educational theory; but a few comments on it are in place, because of the close association, in many minds, between education and culture. What is of interest to my thesis is the kind of assumption which is made by those who write about education. The notes which follow comment on a few such prevalent assumptions.

1. THAT, BEFORE ENTERING UPON ANY DISCUSSION OF EDUCATION, THE PURPOSE OF EDUCATION MUST BE STATED.

This is a very different thing from defining the word "education." The Oxford Dictionary tells us that education is "the process of bringing up (young persons)"; that it is "the systematic instruction, schooling or training given to the young (and, by extension, to adults) in preparation for the work of life"; that it is also "culture or development of powers, formation of character." We learn that the first of these definitions is according to the use of the sixteenth century; and that the third use appears to have arisen in the nineteenth. In short, the dictionary tells you what you know already, and I do not see how a dictionary could do more. But when writers attempt to state the *purpose* of education, they are doing one of two things: they are eliciting what they believe to have been the unconscious purpose always, and thereby giving their own meaning to the history of the subject; or they are formulating what may not have been, or may have been only fitfully, the real purpose in the past, but should in their opinion be the purpose directing development in the future. Let us look at a few of these statements of the purpose of education. In *The Churches Survey Their Task*, a volume published in connexion with the Oxford Conference on Church, Community and State in 1937, we find the following:

> Education is the process by which the community seeks to open its life to all the individuals within it and enable them to take their part in it. It attempts to pass on to them its culture, including the standards by which it would have them live. Where that culture is regarded as final, the attempt is made to impose it on younger minds.

> Where it is viewed as a stage in development, younger minds are trained both to
> receive it and to criticise and improve upon it.
>
> This culture is composed of various elements. It runs from rudimentary skill and
> knowledge up to the interpretation of the universe and of man by which the com-
> munity lives. . . .

The purpose of education, it seems, is to transmit culture: so culture (which has not been
defined) is likely to be limited to what can be transmitted by education. While "education" is perhaps allowed to be more comprehensive than "the educational system," we
must observe that the assumption that culture can be summed up as skills and interpretations controverts the more comprehensive view of culture which I have endeavoured to
take. Incidentally, we should keep a sharp eye on this personified "community" which is
the repository of authority.

Another account of the purpose of education is that which sees it in terms of political
and social change. This, if I have understood him, is the purpose which fires Mr. H. C.
Dent. "Our ideal," he says in *A New Order in English Education*, "is a full democracy." Full
democracy is not defined; and, if full democracy is attained, we should like to know what
is to be our next ideal for education after this ideal has been realised.

Mr. Herbert Read gives his account of the purpose of education in *Education Through
Art*. I do not think that Mr. Read could see quite eye to eye with Mr. Dent, for whereas Mr.
Dent wants a "full democracy," Mr. Read says that he "elects for a libertarian conception
of democracy," which I suspect is a very different democracy from Mr. Dent's. Mr. Read
(in spite of *elects for*) is a good deal more precise in his use of words than Mr. Dent; so,
while he is less likely to confuse the hasty reader, he is more likely to confound the diligent
one. It is in electing for a libertarian conception of democracy, he says, that we answer
the question, "What is the purpose of education?" This purpose is further defined as "the
reconciliation of individual uniqueness with social unity."

Another kind of account of the purpose of education is the uncompleted account, of
which Dr. F. C. Happold (in *Towards a New Aristocracy*) gives us a specimen. The fundamental task of education, he tells us, is "training the sort of men and women the age
needs." If we believe that there are some sorts of men and women which are needed by
every age, we may remark that there should be permanence as well as change in education.
But the account is incomplete, in that we are left wondering who is to determine what are
the needs of the age.

One of the most frequent answers to the question "what is the purpose of education?"
is "happiness." Mr. Herbert Read gives us this answer too, in a pamphlet called *The Education of Free Men*, by saying that he knows of no better definition of the aims of education than that of William Godwin: "the true object of education . . . is the generation of
happiness." "The Government's purpose," said the White Paper which heralded the latest
Education Act, "is to secure for children a happier childhood and a better start in life."
Happiness is often associated with "the full development of personality."

Dr. C. E. M. Joad, showing more prudence than most of those who attempt to answer
this question, holds the view, which seems to me a very sensible one, that education has
a number of ends. Of these he lists three (in *About Education*, one of the most readable
books on the subject that I have consulted):

1. To enable a boy or girl to earn his or her living. . . .

2. To equip him to play his part as the citizen of a democracy.

3. To enable him to develop all the latent powers and faculties of his nature and so enjoy a good life.

It is a relief, at this point, to have presented to us the simple and intelligible notion that equipment to earn one's living is one of the purposes of education. We again note the close association between education and democracy; here also Dr. Joad is perhaps more prudent than Mr. Dent or Mr. Read in not qualifying his "democracy" by an adjective. "To develop all the latent powers and faculties" appears to be a variant of "the full development of personality": but Dr. Joad is sagacious in avoiding the use of that puzzling word "personality."

Some, no doubt, will disagree with Dr. Joad's selection of purposes. And we may, with more reason, complain that none of them takes us very far without getting us into trouble. They all contain some truth: but as each of them needs to be corrected by the others, it is possible that they all need to be adjusted to other purposes as well. Each of them needs some qualification. A particular course of education may, in the world in which a young person finds himself, be exactly what is needed to develop his peculiar gifts and yet impair his ability to earn a living. Education of the young to play their part in a democracy is a necessary adaptation of individual to environment if a democracy is what they are going to play their part in: if not, it is making the pupil instrumental to the accomplishment of a social change which the educator has at heart—and this is not education but something else. I am not denying that a democracy is the best form of society, but by introducing this standard for education, Dr. Joad, with other writers, is leaving it open to those who believe in some other form of society, which Dr. Joad might not like, to substitute (and so far as he is talking about education only, Dr. Joad could not confute them) some account like the following: "One of the purposes of education is to equip a boy or girl to play his or her part as the subject of a despotic government." Finally, as for developing all the latent powers and faculties of one's nature, I am not sure that anyone should hope for that: it may be that we can only develop some powers and faculties at the expense of others, and that there must be some choice, as well as inevitably some accident, in the direction which anyone's development takes. And as for the good life, there is some ambiguity in the sense in which we shall "enjoy" it; and what the good life is, has been a subject of discussion from early times to the present day.

What we remark especially about the educational thought of the last few years, is the enthusiasm with which education has been taken up as an instrument for the realisation of social ideals. It would be a pity if we overlooked the possibilities of education as a means of acquiring wisdom; if we belittled the acquisition of knowledge for the satisfaction of curiosity, without any further motive than the desire to know; and if we lost our respect for learning. So much for the purpose of education. I proceed to the next assumption.

2. THAT EDUCATION MAKES PEOPLE HAPPIER.

We have already found that the purpose of education has been defined as making people happier. The assumption that it *does* make people happier needs to be considered separately. That the educated person is happier than the uneducated is by no means self-evident. Those who are conscious of their lack of education are discontented, if they cherish ambitions to excel in occupations for which they are not qualified; they are sometimes discontented, simply because they have been given to understand that more education would have made them happier. Many of us feel some grievance against our elders, our schools or our universities for not having done better by us: this can be a way of extenuating our own shortcomings and excusing our failures. On the other hand, to be educated above the level of those whose social habits and tastes one has inherited, may cause a division within a man which interferes with happiness; even though, when the individual is of superior intellect, it may bring him a fuller and more useful life. And to be trained, taught or instructed above the level of one's abilities and strength may be disastrous; for education is a strain, and can impose greater burdens upon a mind than that mind can bear. Too much education, like too little education, can produce unhappiness.

3. That Education is something that everyone wants.

People can be persuaded to desire almost anything, for a time, if they are constantly told that it is something to which they are entitled and which is unjustly withheld from them. The spontaneous desire for education is greater in some communities than in others; it is generally agreed to be stronger in the North than in the South of England, and stronger still in Scotland. It is possible that the desire for education is greater where there are difficulties in the way of obtaining it—difficulties not insuperable but only to be surmounted at the cost of some sacrifice and privation. If this is so, we may conjecture that facility of education will lead to indifference to it; and that the universal imposition of education up to the years of maturity will lead to hostility towards it. A high average of general education is perhaps less necessary for a civil society than is a respect for learning.

4. That Education should be organised so as to give "equality of opportunity."[1]

It follows from what has been said in an earlier chapter about classes and elites, that education should help to preserve the class and to select the elite. It is right that the exceptional individual should have the opportunity to elevate himself in the social scale and attain a position in which he can exercise his talents to the greatest benefit of himself and of society. But the ideal of an educational system which would automatically sort out everyone according to his native capacities is unattainable in practice; and if we made it our chief aim, would disorganise society and debase education. It would disorganise society, by substituting for classes, elites of brains, or perhaps only of sharp wits. Any educational system aiming at a complete adjustment between education and society will tend both to restrict education to what will lead to success in the world, and to restrict success in the world to those persons who have been good pupils of the system. The prospect of a society ruled and directed only by those who have passed certain examinations or satisfied tests devised by psychologists is not reassuring: while it might give scope to talents hitherto

---

1. This may be called Jacobinism in Education. Jacobinism, according to one who had given some attention to it, consisted "in taking the people as equal individuals, without any corporate name or description, without attention to property, without division of powers, and forming the government of delegates from a number of men, so constituted; in destroying or confiscating property, and bribing the public creditors, or the poor, with the spoils, now of one part of the community, now of another, without regard to prescription or profession."—Burke, *Remarks on the Policy of the Allies*

obscured, it would probably obscure others, and reduce to impotence some who should have rendered high service. Furthermore, the ideal of a uniform system such that no one capable of receiving higher education could fail to get it, leads imperceptibly to the education of too many people, and consequently to the lowering of standards to whatever this swollen number of candidates is able to reach.

Nothing is more moving in Dr. Joad's treatise than the passage in which he expatiates on the amenities of Winchester and Oxford. Dr. Joad paid a visit to Winchester; and while there, he wandered into a delightful garden. One suspects that he may have got into the garden of the Deanery, but he does not know what garden it was. This garden set him to ruminating about the College, and its "blend of the works of nature and man." "What I see," he said to himself, "is the end-product of a long-continuing tradition, running back through our history, in this particular case, to the Tudors." (I cannot see why he stopped at the Tudors, but that was far enough to sustain the emotion with which his mind was suffused.) It was not only nature and architecture that impressed him; he was aware also of "a long tradition of secure men leading dignified and leisured lives." From Winchester his mind passed to Oxford, to the Oxford which he had known as an undergraduate; and again, it was not merely architecture and gardens upon which his mind dwelt, but also men:

> But even in my own time . . . when democracy was already knocking at the gates of the citadel it was so soon to capture, some faint aftermath of the Greek sunset could be observed. At Balliol, in 1911 there was a group of young men centring upon the Grenfells and John Manners, many of whom were killed in the last war, who took it for granted that they should row in the College boat, play hockey or rugger for the College or even for the University, act for the O.U.D.S., get tight at College Gaudies, spend part of the night talking in the company of their friends, while at the same time getting their scholarships and prizes and Firsts in Greats. The First in Greats was taken, as it were, in their stride. I have not seen such men before or since. It may be that they were the last representatives of a tradition which died with them. . . .

It seems strange, after these wistful reflections, that Dr. Joad should end his chapter by supporting a proposal of Mr. R. H. Tawney: that the public schools should be taken over by the State and used as boarding schools to accommodate for two or three years the intellectually abler secondary school boys from the ages of sixteen to eighteen. For the conditions over which he pronounces such a tearful valedictory were not brought about by equality of opportunity. They were not brought about, either, by mere privilege; but by a happy combination of privilege and opportunity, in the *blend* he so savours, of which no Education Act will ever find the secret.

5. THE MUTE INGLORIOUS MILTON DOGMA.

The Equality of Opportunity dogma, which is associated with the belief that superiority is always superiority of intellect, that some infallible method can be designed for the detection of intellect; and that a system can be devised which will infallibly nourish it, derives emotional reinforcement from the belief in the mute inglorious Milton. This myth assumes that a great deal of first-rate ability—not merely ability, but genius—is being wasted for lack of education; or, alternatively, that if even one potential Milton has been suppressed in the course of centuries, from deprivation of formal teaching, it is still worth while to turn education topsy-turvy so that it may not happen again. (It might be embarrassing to have a great many Miltons and Shakespeares, but that danger is remote.) In justice to Thomas Gray, we should remind ourselves of the last and finest line of the quatrain, and remember that we may also have escaped some Cromwell guilty of his country's blood. The proposition that we have lost a number of Miltons and Cromwells through our tardiness in providing a comprehensive state system of education, cannot be either proved or disproved: it has a strong attraction for many ardent reforming spirits.

This completes my brief list—which is not intended to be exhaustive—of current beliefs. The dogma of equal opportunity is the most influential of all, and is maintained stoutly by some who would shrink from what seem to me its probable consequences. It is an ideal which can only be fully realised when the institution of the family is no longer respected, and when parental control and responsibility passes to the State. Any system which puts it into effect must see that no advantages of family fortune, no advantages due to the foresight, the self-sacrifice or the ambition of parents are allowed to obtain for any child or young person an education superior to that to which the system finds him to be entitled. The popularity of the belief is perhaps an indication that the depression of the family is accepted, and that the disintegration of classes is far advanced. This disintegration of classes had already led to an exaggerated estimate of the social importance of the right school and the right college at the right university, as giving a status which formerly pertained to mere birth. In a more articulated society—which is *not* a society in which social classes are isolated from each other: that is itself a kind of decay—the social distinction of the right school or college would not be so coveted, for social position would be marked in other ways. The envy of those who are "better born" than oneself is a feeble velleity, with only a shadow of the passion with which material advantages are envied. No sane person can be consumed with bitterness at not having had more exalted ancestors, for that would be to wish to be another person than the person one is: but the advantage of the status conferred by education at a more fashionable school is one which we can readily imagine ourselves as having enjoyed also. The disintegration of class has induced the expansion of envy, which provides ample fuel for the flame of "equal opportunity."

Besides the motive of giving everyone as much education as possible, because education is in itself desirable, there are other motives affecting educational legislation: motives which may be praiseworthy, or which simply recognise the inevitable, and which we need mention here only as a reminder of the complexity of the legislative problem. One motive, for instance, for raising the age-limit of compulsory schooling is the laudable desire to protect the adolescent, and fortify him against the more degrading influences to which he is exposed on entering the ranks of industry. We should be candid about such a motive; and instead of affirming what is to be doubted, that everyone will profit by as many years of tuition as we can give him, admit that the conditions of life in modern industrial society are so deplorable, and the moral restraints so weak, that we must prolong the schooling of young people simply because we are at our wits' end to know what to do to save them. Instead of congratulating ourselves on our progress, whenever the school assumes another responsibility hitherto left to parents, we might do better to admit that we have arrived at a stage of civilisation at which the family is irresponsible, or incompetent, or helpless; at which parents cannot be expected to train their children properly; at which many parents cannot afford to feed them properly, and would not know how, even if they had the means; and that Education must step in and make the best of a bad job.[2]

Mr. D. R. Hardman[3] observed that:

> The age of industrialism and democracy had brought to an end most of the great cultural traditions of Europe, and not least that of architecture. In the contemporary world, in which the majority were half-educated and many not even a quarter-educated, and in which large fortunes and enormous power could be obtained by exploiting ignorance and appetite, there was a vast cultural breakdown which stretched from America to Europe and from Europe to the East.

This is true, though there are a few inferences which might be improperly drawn. The exploitation of ignorance and appetite is not an activity only of commercial adventurers making large fortunes: it can be pursued more thoroughly and on a larger scale by governments. The cultural breakdown is not a kind of infection which began in America, spread to Europe, and from Europe has contaminated the East (Mr. Hardman may not have meant that, but his words might be so interpreted). But what is important is to remember that "half-education" is a modern phenomenon. In earlier ages the majority could not be said to have been "half-educated" or less: people had the education necessary for the functions they were called upon to perform. It would be incorrect to refer to a member of a primitive society, or to a skilled agricultural labourer in any age, as half-educated or quarter-educated or educated to any smaller fraction. *Education* in the modern sense implies a disintegrated society, in which it has come to be assumed that there must be one measure of education according to which everyone is educated simply more or less. Hence *Education* has become an abstraction.

Once we have arrived at this abstraction, remote from life, it is easy to proceed to the conclusion—for we all agree about the "cultural breakdown"—that education for every body is the means we must employ for putting civilisation together again. Now so long as we mean by "education" everything that goes to form the good individual in a good society, we are in accord, though the conclusion does not appear to get us anywhere; but when we come to mean by "education" that limited system of instruction which the Ministry of Education controls, or aims to control, the remedy is manifestly and ludicrously inadequate. The same may be said of the definition of the purpose of education which we have already found in *The Churches Survey Their Task*. According to this definition, education is the process by which the community attempts to pass on to all its members its culture, including the standards by which it would have them live. The community, in this definition, is an unconscious collective mind, very different from the mind of the Ministry of Education, or the Head Masters' Association, or the mind of any of the numerous bodies concerned with education. If we include as education all the influences of family and

---

2. I hope, however, that the readerr of these lines has read, or will immediately read, *The Peckham Experiment,* as an illustration of what can be done, under modern conditions, to help the family to help itself.

3. As Parliamentary Secretary to the Ministry of Education, speaking on January 12, 1946, at the general meeting of the Middlesex Head Teachers' Association.

environment, we are going far beyond what professional educators can control—though their sway can extend very far indeed; but if we mean that Culture is what is passed on by our elementary and secondary schools, or by our preparatory and public schools, then we are asserting that an organ is a whole organism. For the schools can transmit only a part, and they can only transmit this part effectively, if the outside influences, not only of family and environment, but of work and play, of newsprint and spectacles and entertainment and sport, are in harmony with them.

Error creeps in again and again through our tendency to think of culture as group culture exclusively, the culture of the "cultured" classes and elites. We then proceed to think of the humbler part of society as having culture only in so far as it participates in this superior and more conscious culture. To treat the "uneducated" mass of the population as we might treat some innocent tribe of savages to whom we are impelled to deliver the true faith, is to encourage them to neglect or despise that culture which they should possess and from which the more conscious part of culture draws vitality; and to aim to make everyone share in the appreciation of the fruits of the more conscious part of culture is to adulterate and cheapen what you give. For it is an essential condition of the preservation of the quality of the culture of the minority, that it should continue to be a minority culture. No number of Young Peoples' Colleges will compensate for the deterioration of Oxford and Cambridge, and for the disappearance of that "blend" which Dr. Joad relishes. A "mass-culture" will always be a substitute-culture; and sooner or later the deception will become apparent to the more intelligent of those upon whom this culture has been palmed off.

I am not questioning the usefulness, or deriding the dignity of Young Peoples' Colleges, or of any other particular new construction. In so far as these institutions can be good, they are more likely to be good, and not to deliver disappointment, if we are frankly aware of the limits of what we can do with them, and if we combat the delusion that the maladies of the modern world can be put right by a system of instruction. A measure which is desirable as a palliative, may be injurious if presented as a cure. My main point is the same as that which I tried to make in the previous chapter, when I spoke of the tendency of politics to dominate culture, instead of keeping to its place within a culture. There is also the danger that education—which indeed comes under the influence of politics—will take upon itself the reformation and direction of culture, instead of keeping to its place as one of the activities through which a culture realises itself. Culture cannot altogether be brought to consciousness; and the culture of which we are wholly conscious is never the whole of culture: the effective culture is that which is directing the activities of those who are manipulating that which they *call* culture.

So the instructive point is this, that the more education arrogates to itself the responsibility, the more systematically will it betray culture. The definition of the purpose of education in *The Churches Survey Their Task* returns to plague us like the laughter of hyenas at a funeral. *Where that culture is regarded as final, the attempt is made to impose it on younger minds. Where it is viewed as a stage in development, younger minds are trained to receive it and to improve upon it.* These are cosseting phrases which reprove our cultural ancestors—including those of Greece, Rome, Italy and France—who had no notion of the extent to which their culture was going to be improved upon after the Oxford Conference on Church, Community and State in 1937. We know now that the highest achievements of the past, in art, in wisdom, in holiness, were but "stages in development" which we can teach our springalds to improve upon. We must not train them merely to receive the culture of the past, for that would be to regard the culture of the past as final. We must not impose culture upon the young, though we may impose upon them whatever political and social philosophy is in vogue. And yet the culture of Europe has deteriorated visibly within the memory of many who are by no means the oldest among us. And we know, that whether education can foster and improve culture or not, it can surely adulterate and degrade it. For there is no doubt that in our headlong rush to educate everybody, we are lowering our standards, and more and more abandoning the study of those subjects by which the essentials of our culture—of that part of it which is transmissible by education—are transmitted; destroying our ancient edifices to make ready the ground upon which the barbarian nomads of the future will encamp in their mechanised caravans.

Christopher Dawson

1889–1970

So long as the Christian tradition of higher education still exists, the victory of secularism even in a modern technological society is not complete. There is still a voice to bear witness to the existence of the forgotten world of spiritual reality in which man has his true being.

THE CRISIS OF WESTERN EDUCATION

Christopher Dawson, historian and Christian humanist, was born in Wales into an Anglo-Catholic family. He was educated at Winchester and at Trinity College, Oxford, where he studied modern history. In 1914 he converted to Roman Catholicism. His academic posts included appointments as lecturer in the History of Culture at University College, Exeter, and as the first holder of the Chauncey Stillman Chair of Roman Catholic Studies at Harvard University. He twice delivered the prestigious Gifford Lectures at the University of Edinburgh (1947–49). The formation of Western Christendom, primarily the role of religion in the development of culture, dominated his scholarly research and writing. He waged a tireless battle against modern materialism, secularism, totalitarianism, and nihilism, seeking a path back to the unity and continuity of Western civilization. He produced about twenty books, among them *Religion and Progress* and *Religion and the Rise of Western Culture*.

THE SELECTION

Dawson's *The Crisis of Western Education* (1961) marshals many of the authors and works represented in this anthology in order to provide a sharply focused overview of the classical and Christian tradition. It is the personal view of one historian, of course, but Dawson's diagnosis draws upon a lifetime of careful meditation on the strengths and weaknesses of Western civilization. Along with many other modern voices in the Great Tradition, Dawson speaks against the crude utilitarianism, vocationalism, and "centrifugal" specialization of the contemporary educational machine. Chapter 8, included here in its entirety, condemns the mass democratization of education and blames John Dewey (and his predecessor Rousseau) for making universal public education into a substitute church for promoters of an expansive, intolerant, secular religion. Like Eliot and Lewis, moreover, he seeks to rescue modern man from being "a provincial in time."

from The Crisis of Western Education
Chapter 8: Education and the State

Anyone who surveys the literature of modern education cannot help feeling discouraged by the thought of the immense amount of time and labor which has been expended with so little apparent fruit. Yet we must not forget that behind this smokescreen of blue-books and hand-books great forces are at work which have changed the lives and thoughts of men more effectively than the arbitrary power of dictators or the violence of political revolutions.

During the last hundred or two hundred years mankind has been subjected to a process which makes for uniformity and universality. For example, there is universal military service, there is universal suffrage and finally there is universal education. We cannot say that any one of these has caused the others, but they have all influenced one another and they are all presumably the expression of similar or identical forces operating in different fields.

Of these three examples I have given, universal suffrage is usually regarded as the most important. But it is less typical than the others because it is less compulsory. Indeed in the past the use of political suffrage has never been universal, even in societies in which every adult possessed the right to vote. Universal military service, on the other hand, has had less attention paid to it than it deserves. It is the earliest of the three and has its roots deepest in history. It is also the one in which the element of compulsion is strongest and most effective. In England, however, and still more in the United States and the Dominions, its introduction has been so long delayed that it is still regarded as an exceptional emergency measure and has not fully been assimilated by our society and culture.

There remains universal education, which is in fact the most universal of the three, since it has now extended all over the world. Moreover it goes deeper than the other two, since it is directly concerned with the human mind and with the formation of character. It is moreover a continually expanding force, for when once the State has accepted full responsibility for the education of the whole youth of the nation, it is obliged to extend its control further and further into new fields: to the physical welfare of its pupils—to their feeding and medical care—to their amusements and the use of their spare time—and finally to their moral welfare and their psychological guidance.

Thus universal education involves the creation of an immense machinery of organization and control which must go on growing in power and influence until it covers the whole field of culture and embraces every form of educational institution from the nursery school to the university.

Hence the modern movement towards universal education inevitably tends to become the rival or the alternative to the Church, which is also a universal institution and is also concerned directly with the human mind and with the formation of character. And in fact there is no doubt that the progress of universal education has coincided with the secularization of modern culture and has been very largely responsible for it.

In the philosophy of the Enlightenment which inspired the educational policy of the French Revolution and of Continental Liberalism, the Church and the influence of religion were regarded as powers of darkness that were responsible for the backward condition of the masses, and consequently the movement for universal education was a crusade of enlightenment which was inevitably anti-clerical in spirit. Even in England, as recently as 1870, Joseph Chamberlain could declare that "the object of the Liberal party in England, throughout the continent of Europe and in America has been to wrest the education of the young out of the hands of the priests, to whatever denomination they might belong."

In practice no doubt, universal education in England as in Germany and many other countries was the result either of a process of co-operation between Church and State or at least of some kind of *modus vivendi* between them. Nevertheless at best it was an unequal partnership: the fact that secular education is universal and compulsory, while religious education is partial and voluntary, inevitably favors the former and places the Church at a very great disadvantage in educational matters. This is not merely due to the disproportion in wealth and power of a religious minority as compared with the modern state. Even more important is the all-pervading influence of the secular standards and values which affects the whole educational system and makes the idea of an integrated religious culture seem antiquated and absurd to the politicians and the publicists and the technical experts who are the makers of public opinion.

Moreover we must remember that modern secularism, in education as in politics, is not a purely negative force. Today, as in the days of the Enlightenment and the Revolution, it has its ideals and its dogmas—we may almost say that it has its own religion. One of the outstanding exponents of this secular idealism in recent times was the late Professor Dewey, whose ideas have had a profound influence on modern American education, as I described in the last chapter.

Now Dewey, in spite of his secularism, had a conception of education which was almost purely religious. Education is not concerned with intellectual values, its end is not to communicate knowledge or to train scholars in the liberal arts. It exists simply to serve democracy; and democracy is not a form of government, it is a spiritual community, based on "the participation of every human being in the formation of social values." Thus every child is a potential member of the democratic church, and it is the function of education to actualize his membership and to widen his powers of participation. No doubt knowledge is indispensable, but knowledge is always secondary to activity, and activity is secondary to participation. The ultimate end of the whole process is a state of spiritual communion in which every individual shares in the experience of the whole and contributes according to his powers to the formation of "the final pooled intelligence," to use Dewey's expression, which is the democratic mind.

Now it seems to me obvious that this concept of education is a religious one in spite of its secularism. It is inspired by a faith in democracy and a democratic "mystique" which is religious rather than political in spirit. Words like "community," "progress," "life," and "youth," etc., but above all "democracy" itself, have acquired a kind of numinous character which gives them an emotional or evocative power and puts them above rational criticism. But when it comes to the question of the real significance and content of education we cannot help asking what these sacred abstractions really amount to. Do not the most primitive and barbarous peoples known to us achieve these great ends of social participation and communal experience no less completely by their initiation ceremonies and tribal dances than any modern educationalist with his elaborate programs for the integration of the school with life and the sharing of common experience?

The forefather of modem education, who was more consistent than his descendants, Jean Jacques Rousseau, would perhaps have approved of this, since he believed that civilization was on the whole a mistake and that man would be better without it. But the modern democrat usually has rather a naïve faith in modern civilization, and he wishes to accept the inheritance of culture, while rejecting the painful process of social and intellectual discipline by which that inheritance has been acquired and transmitted.

In this he differs from the Communist, who shares the same ideal of "participation" and the communalization of experience, but who has a very definite belief in the necessity of authority and social discipline and whose system of education is based not only on a common doctrine but also on a psychological technique for arousing faith and devotion.

The democrat, on the other hand, has no use for authority either in the State or in the school or in the sphere of cultural activity. But when it comes to the question of religious authority, the democrat and the Communist once more find themselves in agreement. As one of Dewey's supporters, Sidney Hook, has pointed out, the philosophy of Dewey, especially in education, is the enemy number one of "every doctrine which holds that man should tend to a supernatural end, in function of which he ought to organize his earthly life."

I have paid so much attention to Dewey's views because of the enormous influence he has had on American education and, through America, on educational ideas in the Far East and elsewhere. Moreover, his views are important because they state in a simplified and explicit form principles that have been taken for granted by liberal or democratic educationalists everywhere. The fact is that modern society was inevitably committed to something of this kind as soon as it abandoned the purely utilitarian conception of education which was characteristic of the English Radical reforms in the early nineteenth century. Henceforward universal education ceased to be considered as a means of communicating learning and became instead an instrument for creating a common mind. In this way universal education becomes the most important agent in the creation of the new secular religion of the state or the national community, which in democratic as well as totalitarian societies is replacing the old religion of the Church as the working religion of the modern world.

I do not, of course, mean to suggest that the democratic ideal is the same as the totalitarian one. For as I have already said with regard to Communism, totalitarian education, like the rest of the totalitarian way of life, is far more authoritarian and is the instrument of an exclusive and intolerant party ideology. The democratic ideal of education is, as

Dewey says, an education for freedom—for freedom of thought no less than for freedom of action—and he criticized the traditional forms of education because they retained the authoritarian principle alike in the relation of teacher to pupil and by imposing an absolute standard of culture which the uneducated are forced to accept and admire.

But for this very reason the traditional forms of religious education are the worst of all, because they are the most authoritarian and go furthest in asserting the existence of absolute truths and absolute moral standards to which the individual must conform. In this respect democratic educationalists like Dewey are at one with anti-Catholic propagandists like Mr. Blanshard. To the latter, it is precisely the Catholic attitude to public education which is the basis of his indictment. It is not that he objects to religion as such; for so long as religion is regarded as a private matter which only concerns the conscience and the feelings of the individual, it is a very good thing. But the moment that it attempts to create its own community of thought and to separate its adherents from the common mind of the democratic society and from the State school which is the organ of that common mind, it becomes an anti-social force which every good democrat must reject and condemn.

It is obvious that the whole question of the relations of education to State, Church, community and culture is inextricably involved with fundamental issues which cannot be avoided however we may try to do so. Neither secularism nor Christianity necessarily involves persecution. But both of them can easily become intolerant, and whether they are tolerant or intolerant they are inevitably and in every field irreconcilable with one another. On the one hand we have the secular view that the State is the universal community and the Church is a limited association of groups of individuals for limited ends. On the other there is the Christian view that the Church is the universal community and that the State is a limited association for certain limited ends. The philosopher and the theologian may say that both are perfect societies with their own rights and their proper autonomous spheres of action. But this is only true juridically speaking, not psychologically or morally. The Church is socially incomplete unless there is a Christian society as well as an ecclesiastical congregation, and the State is morally incomplete without some spiritual bond other than the law and the power of the sword. Ever since the loss of a living contact with the historic faith of Christendom modern society has been seeking to find such a bond, either in the democratic ideal of the natural society and its general will, or in the nationalist cult of a historic racial community, or in the Communist faith in the revolutionary mission of the proletariat. And in each case what we find is a substitute religion or counter-religion which transcends the juridical limits of the political State and creates a kind of secular Church.

It is, of course, true that this development has been almost entirely a continental one which finds its characteristic expressions in French revolutionary democracy, German nationalism and Russian communism. England and America, on the other hand, have always followed a different tradition, and their classical political doctrines in the past have been based on the older conception of a limited State which confined itself to certain specific activities and left the larger part of life as an open field for the free activity of individuals and independent organizations. Now in practice this Anglo-Saxon conception of the limited State was closely connected with a sectarian conception of the Church. Religion was active and influential, but it was not united. The dominant issue was not Church and State, but Church and sect, or State, Church and sect, so that in England the formal secularization of the State was not due to an anti-clerical attack on religious belief, but was the work of pious Nonconformists who were concerned above all with the defence of their own religious liberties and privileges.

All this has had an immense influence on the history of English education. For education is one of the forms of activity which traditionally lie outside the competence of a limited State. The fact that public education, as in the universities and the public schools, was Anglican was an inheritance from the Catholic past; and it depended not on education acts and government policy but on the foundation statutes of the educational institutions themselves, which were autonomous corporations, often very jealous of any interference by parliament or governments.

When elementary education was introduced in the nineteenth century it was regarded as the business of the Church of England and of the sects—a kind of extension of the old system of catechism classes and Sunday schools. Even an independent movement like Shaftesbury's Ragged Schools, which was undenominational, was nevertheless essentially religious and anti-governmental in spirit and opposed to any form of State control.

In England, therefore, and also in the United States, the victory of secular education has been due above all to interdenominational friction and jealousy, not to any conscious hostility to religion itself. But at the same time the whole relation of State and community has been changing, owing to the growing responsibility of the State for social and individual welfare and its increasing control of economic life. The continental conception of the State as an all-embracing community, a kind of secular church, has entered as it were by the back door and has gradually and inevitably destroyed the traditional conception of the limited State and drastically reduced the sphere of action of non-political organizations in education and social life generally. In some respects we are now worse off than the continental peoples, since there is no place in our traditions for the idea of a concordat as a kind of treaty between Church and State considered as two autonomous societies.

In the United States above all, the principle of the absolute separation of Church and State has been carried so far that it involves a refusal to recognize the Church as a corporate entity, so that anything of the nature of a concordat would be regarded as a violation of the Constitution. Similarly in the domain of public education, the principle of the separation of Church and State is now interpreted so rigorously as to ban any kind of positive Christian teaching from the school, with the result that the educational system inevitably favors the pagan and secularist minority against the Christian and Jewish elements who probably represent a large majority of the population.

Now this leads, on the one hand, to the propagation of that kind of substitute religion which I have already described as the established faith of the democratic state; and on the other hand, to the devaluation of traditional religion as unessential, non-vital, exceptional and perhaps even unsocial.

No doubt there are some American Protestants who are so convinced of the moral values of the democratic way of life that they tend to identify the democratic substitute religion with their own rather indefinite Christian tradition. One such Protestant educationalist asserts that "to call public education 'godless' betrays invincible ignorance, infinite prejudice and complete misunderstanding of what religion is about," since "the public school is more distinctly a faith of all the people than the Church"[1] itself.

I do not suppose that such utterances are representative of orthodox Protestant opinion. Certainly they would be rejected by every Catholic. Yet even Catholics are not immune from the pervasive influence of secularism in education. But this influence shows itself in two opposite ways. In so far as Catholics preserve their own schools and universities by great efforts and sacrifices, they are forced to devote so much energy to the mere material or technical work of keeping the system going that the quality of their teaching suffers. They become more concerned with the utilitarian need for practical results, as measured by the competitive standards set by the State or the secular educational system, than with the essential problem of the transmission of Catholic culture. And in the second place the strength and pervasiveness of secular culture forces Christians, Catholic as well as Protestant, to accept the sectarian solution, which acquiesces in the secularization of culture and social life and strives in compensation to maintain a strict standard of religious observance inside the closed doors of the conventicle and the home.

The most remarkable example of this system, applied with rigid consistency over a period of many centuries, is to be seen in the life of the Jewish community in the ghettos of Central and Eastern Europe. But the ghetto was, after all, a solution imposed from without, and it would never have existed without a certain amount of active persecution and a very strong element of racial prejudice and national self-consciousness. Where these factors exist among Christians, as for example in the case of the Irish mass immigration into Great Britain and the United States in the middle of the nineteenth century, we do get something like the formation of a Christian ghetto where a minority inspired by an intense religious patriotism lives its own spiritual life under the surface of a dominant hostile culture.

But there is no longer any room for a ghetto in the modern secular state. Both its tolerance and its intolerance are hostile to the existence of any such closed world. Under modern conditions the sectarian solution merely means that the religious minority abdicates its claim to influence the culture of the community. And the attempt to use religious education in order to enforce a rigid standard of religious practice in the midst of a secular culture only results in increasing the problem of "leakage." And thus we get a situation in which the Catholics who both practise and understand their religion are the minority of a minority, and the majority of the population are neither fully Christian nor consciously atheist, but non-practising Catholics, half-Christians and well-meaning people who are devoid of any positive religious knowledge at all.

Hence it is not enough for Catholics to confine their efforts to the education of the Catholic minority. If they want to preserve Catholic education in a secularized society, they have got to do something about non-Catholic education also. The future of civilization depends on the fate of the majority, and so long as nothing is done to counteract the present trend of modern education the mind of the masses must become increasingly alienated from the whole tradition of Christian culture.

But this is not inevitable. It need never have happened if Christians had not been so absorbed in their internal conflicts that they adopted a negative defensive attitude towards

---

1. C. H. Moehlman, *School and Church: The American Way* (New York: Harper, 1944).

the problem of national education as a whole. In England, at any rate, there has never been a time when public policy in education has been actively or consciously anti-Christian. Indeed some of the leading representatives of the Board of Education, like Matthew Arnold, were more fully aware of the dangers of secularization and the cultural importance of religious education than were the religious leaders themselves.

The situation has, of course, deteriorated considerably since Arnold's day, especially in the higher studies. Theology, which once dominated the university, has now been pushed from the center to the circumference and has become a specialism among an increasing number of specialisms, while the study of divinity as an integral part of the general curriculum of studies, which still survived in a vestigial form before World War I, has disappeared entirely. I do not suggest that it is possible, or perhaps even desirable, to restore it. What I do believe very strongly is that the time has come to consider the possibility of introducing the study of Christian culture as an objective historical reality into the curriculum of university studies.

Until a man acquires some knowledge of another culture, he cannot be said to be educated, since his whole outlook is so conditioned by his own social environment that he does not realize its limitations. He is a provincial in time, if not in place, and he almost inevitably tends to accept the standards and values of his own society as absolute. The widening of the intellectual horizon by initiation into a different world of culture was indeed the most valuable part of the old classical education.

The study of Christian culture would, I believe, provide a really effective substitute. It would initiate the student into a world that was unknown or at best half known, and at the same time it would deepen his knowledge of modern culture by showing its genetic relation to the culture of the past. No one denies the existence of a Christian literature, a Christian philosophy and a Christian institutional order, but at present these are never studied as parts of an organic whole. Yet without this integrated study it is impossible to understand even the development of the modern vernacular literature.

But how does this affect the question of Christian education? Obviously the academic study of Christian culture as an historical phenomenon is no substitute for religious education in the ordinary sense. What it might do, however, is to help to remove the preliminary prejudice against the Christian view of things which plays so large a part in the secularization of culture. The fact is that the average educated person is not only ignorant of Christian theology, he is no less ignorant of Christian philosophy, Christian history and Christian literature, and in short of Christian culture in general. And he is not ashamed of his ignorance, because Christianity has come to be one of the things that educated people don't talk about. This is quite a recent prejudice which arose among the half-educated and gradually spread upwards and downwards. It did not exist among civilized people in the nineteenth century, whatever their personal beliefs were. Men like Lord Melbourne and Macaulay could talk as intelligently about religious subjects as Gladstone and Acton. It was only at the very end of the century that Christianity ceased to be intellectually respectable and it was due not only to the secularization of culture but also to the general lowering of cultural standards that characterized the age.

Today there are signs of an improvement in this respect. Religion has come back into poetry and fiction, and there is once more a civilized interest in religious discussion. But this cannot go far unless religion is brought back into higher education, and this can only be achieved by giving the systematic study of Christian culture a recognized place in university studies.

A reform of this kind on the level of higher studies would inevitably penetrate the lower levels of secondary and primary teaching and by degrees affect the whole tone of public education. It is obviously difficult to improve the situation in the schools if the teachers have no knowledge of Christian culture and if the standard set by the university is a secular one. However, it is for the universities and the other centers of higher education to take the first step; and if they did so, there is little doubt that they would find plenty of support elsewhere, and that their initiation of the study of Christian culture would be most fruitful in results.

Michael Oakeshott

1901–90

> *To see oneself reflected in the mirror of the present modish world is to see a sadly distorted image of a human being; for there is nothing to encourage us to believe that what has captured the current fancy is the most valuable part of our inheritance, or that the better survives more readily than the worse. And nothing survives in this world which is not cared for by human beings.*

"Learning and Teaching"

Cambridge philosopher Michael Oakeshott was born into a middle-class English family in Chelsfield, Kent. His father was a Fabian socialist and friend of George Bernard Shaw. From 1912 to 1920, Oakeshott attended St. George's, Harpenden, where the headmaster exposed him to a heady mix of Kant and Hegel. He then studied at Gonville and Caius College, Cambridge, taking a degree in history, and continued at Cambridge for graduate work, also studying for at time at the universities of Tübingen and Marburg. Oakeshott was a fellow in history at Gonville and Caius from 1929 to 1951, lecturing and publishing extensively on political thought.

With the outbreak of World War II, Oakeshott joined the British Army, serving in an intelligence unit that helped target artillery. After the war, he returned to the academic life at Cambridge, founded the *Cambridge Journal* in 1947, taught briefly at Nuffield College, Oxford, and then was appointed University Professor of Political Science at the London School of Economics (LSE), where he remained until his retirement in 1967. Oakeshott was a private, apolitical man who shunned publicity and did not wish to found a school of thought. Some thought him aloof, while others recalled his gift for conversation and friendship. After retiring from the LSE, he spent the rest of his life in a simple cottage in Dorset.

Oakeshott distinguished himself as a leading authority on Thomas Hobbes. His published works include *Rationalism in Politics and Other Essays* (1962), *On Human Conduct*

(1975), and *The Voice of Liberal Learning* (1989). A conservative and skeptic, Oake-shott opposed the post–World War II collectivist state, the rationally planned society, and all forms of ideological reductionism and utopianism.

THE SELECTION

Oakeshott delivered his lecture "Learning and Teaching" in 1965. Though difficult to follow at points—especially in section 3—this lecture is an eloquent restatement of the ancient wisdom that education is not an abstraction but a shared activity between teacher and pupil, master and apprentice. Education is not training, but rather the "initiation of a pupil into the world of human achievement." Oakeshott returns to the old virtues of giving and receiving, of inheritance, reverence, and imitation. The teacher's task lies far beyond imparting a certain quantity of information to students (though that task is essential). The teacher, through his own example, imparts judgment. This transmitted inheritance "is implanted unobtrusively in the manner in which information is conveyed, in a tone of voice, in the gesture which accompanies instruction, in asides and oblique utterances, and by example."

"Learning and Teaching"

Even an amateur, like myself, when he fishes around in his head for some bright ideas, hopes to catch something. But nowadays fish don't come so easily; and I wish that what I have found to say on this topic did not look to me so shamefully dull. Let me, however, detain you a while with some clumsy thoughts on learning and teaching.

1

Learning is the comprehensive activity in which we come to know ourselves and the world around us. It is a paradoxical activity: it is doing and submitting at the same time. And its achievements range from merely being aware, to what may be called understanding and being able to explain.

In each of us, it begins at birth; it takes place not in some ideal abstract world, but in the local world we inhabit; for the individual it terminates only in death, for a civilization it ends in the collapse of the characteristic manner of life, and for the race it is, in principle, interminable.

The activity of learning may, however, be suspended from time to time while we enjoy what we have learned. The distinction between a driver and a learner-driver is not insignificant; a master-tailor making a suit of clothes is doing something other than learning to make a suit of clothes. But the suspension is, perhaps, never either decisive or complete: learning itself often entails practising what we have in some sense learned already, and there is probably a component of learning in every notable performance. Moreover, some activities, like intellectual enquiries, remain always activities of learning.

By learning I mean an activity possible only to an intelligence capable of choice and self-direction in relation to his own impulses and to the world around him. These, of course, are pre-eminently human characteristics, and, as I understand it, only human beings are capable of learning. A learner is not a passive recipient of impressions, or one whose accomplishments spring from mere reactions to circumstances, or one who attempts nothing he does not know how to accomplish. He is a creature of wants rather than of needs, of recollection as well as memory; he wants to know what to think and what to believe and not merely what to do. Learning concerns conduct, not behaviour. In short, these analogies of clay and wax, of receptacles to be filled and empty rooms to be furnished, have nothing to do with learning and learners.

I do not mean that the attention of a learner is focussed always upon understanding and being able to explain, or that nothing can be learned which is not understood; nor do I mean that human beings are uniquely predestined learners whatever their circumstances. I mean only that an activity which may include understanding and being able to explain within its range is different, not only at this point, but at all points in the scale of its achievements, from one to which this possibility is denied.

Teaching is a practical activity in which a "learned" person (to use an archaism) "learns" his pupils. No doubt one may properly be said to learn from books, from gazing at the sky or from listening to the waves (so long as one's disposition is that mixture of activity and submission we call curiosity), but to say that the book, the sky, or the sea has taught us anything, or that we have taught ourselves, is to speak in the language of unfortunate metaphor. The counterpart of the teacher is not the learner in general, but the pupil. And I am concerned with the learner as pupil, one who learns from a teacher, one who learns by being taught. This does not mean that I subscribe to the prejudice which attributes all learning to teaching; it means only that I am concerned here with learning when it is the counterpart of teaching.

The activity of the teacher is, then, specified in the first place by the character of his partner. The ruler is partnered by the citizen, the physician by his patient, the master by his servant, the duenna by her charge, the commander by his subordinates, the lawyer by his client, the prophet by his disciple, the clown by his audience, the hypnotist by his subject, and both the tamer and trainer by creatures whose aptitudes are of being tamed or trained. Each of these is engaged in a practical activity, but it is not teaching; each has a partner, but he is not a pupil. Teaching is not taming or ruling or restoring to health, or conditioning, or commanding, because none of these activities is possible in relation to a pupil. Like the ruler, or the hypnotist, the teacher communicates something to his partner; his peculiarity is that what he communicates is appropriate to a partner who is a pupil—it is something which may be received only by being learned. And there can, I think, be no doubt about what this is.

Every human being is born an heir to an inheritance to which he can succeed only in a process of learning. If this inheritance were an estate composed of woods and meadows, a villa in Venice, a portion of Pimlico and a chain of village stores, the heir would expect to succeed to it automatically, on the death of his father or on coming of age. It would be conveyed to him by lawyers, and the most that would be expected of him would be legal acknowledgement.

But the inheritance I speak of is not exactly like this; and, indeed, this is not exactly like what I have made it out to be. What every man is born an heir to is an inheritance of human achievements; an inheritance of feelings, emotions, images, visions, thoughts, beliefs, ideas, understandings, intellectual and practical enterprises, languages, relationships, organizations, canons and maxims of conduct, procedures, rituals, skills, works of art, books, musical compositions, tools, artefacts and utensils—in short, what Dilthey called a *geistige Welt*.

The components of this world are not abstractions ("physical objects") but beliefs. It is a world of facts, not "things"; of "expressions" which have meanings and require to be understood because they are the "expressions" of human minds. The landed estate itself belongs to this world; indeed, this is the only world known to human beings. The starry heavens above us and the moral law within, are alike human achievements. And it is a world, not because it has itself any meaning (it has none), but because it is a whole of interlocking meanings which establish and interpret one another.

Now, this world can be entered, possessed and enjoyed only in a process of learning. A "picture" may be purchased, but one cannot purchase an understanding of it. And I have called this world our common inheritance because to enter it is the only way of becoming a human being, and to inhabit it is to be a human being. It is into this *geistige Welt* that the child, even in its earliest adventures in awareness, initiates itself; and to initiate his pupils into it is the business of the teacher. Not only may it be entered only by learning, but there is nothing else for a pupil to learn. If, from one point of view, the analogies of wax and clay are inappropriate to learning, from another point of view the analogies of sagacious apes and accomplished horses are no less inappropriate. These admirable creatures have no such inheritance; they may only be trained to react to a stimulus and to perform tricks.[1]

There is an ancient oriental image of human life which recognizes this account of our circumstances. In it the child is understood to owe its physical life to its father, a debt to be acknowledged with appropriate respect. But initiation into the *geistige Welt* of human achievement is owed to the Sage, the teacher: and this debt is to be acknowledged with the profoundest reverence—for to whom can a man be more deeply indebted than to the one to whom he owes, not his mere existence, but his participation in human life? It is the Sage, the teacher, who is the agent of civilization. And, as Dr. Johnson said, not to name the school and the masters of illustrious men is a kind of historical fraud.

2

Now, most of what I have to say about learning and teaching relates to the character of what is taught and learned, and to the bearing of this upon the activities concerned; but there are two general considerations, one about the teacher and the other about the pupil, which I must notice first.

It is difficult to think of any circumstances where learning may be said to be impossible. Of course, in some conditions it will take place more rapidly and more successfully than in others; but, in principle, it does not depend upon any specifiable degree of attention, and it is not uncommon to find oneself to have learned without knowing how or

---

1. The horses I refer to are, of course, those of Elberfield. But it is, perhaps, worth recalling that the ancient Athenians delighted in the horse above all other animals because they recognized in it an affinity to man, and an animal uniquely capable of education. The horse had no *geistige* inheritance of its own, but (while other animals might be set to work) the horse was capable of sharing an inheritance imparted to it by man. And, in partnership with a rider (so Xenophon observed), it could acquire talents, accomplishments, and even a grace of movement unknown to it in its "natural" condition.

when it happened. Thus, the random utterances of anyone, however foolish or ignorant, may serve to enlighten a learner, who receives from them as much or as little as he happens to be ready to receive, and receives often what the speaker did not himself know or did not know he was conveying.

But such casual utterances are not teaching, and he who scatters them is not, properly speaking, a teacher. Teaching is the deliberate and intentional initiation of a pupil into the world of human achievement, or into some part of it. The teacher is one whose utterances (or silences) are designed to promote this initiation in respect of a pupil—that is, in respect of a learner whom he recognizes to be ready to receive what he has resolved to communicate. In short, a pupil is a learner known to a teacher; and teaching, properly speaking, is impossible in his absence.

This, of course, does not mean that "readiness to receive" is an easily discernible condition, or that it should be identified as the condition in which reception will come most easily. Jean Paul Richter's maxim that in teaching a two-year-old one should speak to him as if he were six, may be a profound observation. Nor does it mean that the relationship of teacher and pupil is emancipated from the latitudes and imprecisions common to all human relationships. Indeed, it is probably more subject to these imprecisions than any other relationship. What it means is that a teacher is one who studies his pupil, that the initiation *he* undertakes is one which has a deliberated order and arrangement, and that, as well as knowing what he designs to transmit, he has considered the manner of transmission. I once knew a wise man who, wishing to learn the art of the farrier, looked, not only for a man practised in the art, but for one accustomed to teaching, and he was gratified when he found a farrier who was also a teacher of boxing.

With regard to the pupil, there is a famous dilemma which has haunted reflection on education for long enough. Is learning to be understood as acquiring knowledge, or is it to be regarded as the development of the personality of the learner? Is teaching concerned with initiating a pupil into an inheritance of human achievement, or is it enabling the pupil to make the most or the best of himself? Like many such cruxes, this one points to what I believe to be a genuine discrepancy, but misinterprets it.

To escape from it we may recognize learning, not merely as the acquisition of knowledge, but also as the extension of the ability to learn, as the education and not merely the furnishing of a mind, as an inheritance coming to be possessed in such a manner that it loses its second-hand or antique character; and we may recognize teaching, not as passing on something to be received, nor as merely planting a seed, but as setting on foot the cultivation of a mind so that what is planted may grow. But the escape from the dilemma this affords us is imperfect; and, in any case, it is not an escape but a resolution we should be seeking.

What, I think, we must understand is that there is no discrepancy between a pupil succeeding to his inheritance of human achievement and his making the most of himself. "Self-realization" for human beings is not, of course, the realization of an exactly predetermined end which requires only circumstances favourable to this end in order that it should be achieved; but nor is this self an infinite, unknown potentiality which an inheritance of human achievement is as likely to thwart as to promote. Selves are not rational abstractions, they are historic personalities, they are among the components of this world of human achievements; and there is no other way for a human being to make the most of himself than by learning to recognize himself in the mirror of this inheritance.

A discrepancy, however, remains; but it is a discrepancy, not between the self and its world, but between learning and teaching. It is a divergence of point of view. For the pupil, to learn is not to endeavour to make the most of himself, it is to acquire knowledge, to distinguish between truth and error, to understand and become possessor of what he was born heir to. But to the teacher things must appear differently. Obliquely and upon a consequence he is an agent of civilization. But his direct relationship is with his pupil. His engagement is, specifically, to get his pupil to make the most of himself by teaching him to recognize himself in the mirror of the human achievements which compose his inheritance. This is the somewhat complicated manner in which he performs his work of initiation, and this is what distinguishes him from others who hand on the fruits of civilization; namely, that he has a pupil.

Now, to make a "civilization" available to a pupil is not to put him in touch with the dead, nor is it to rehearse before him the social history of mankind. Death belongs to nature, not *geist*; and it is only in nature that generation involves a process of recapitulating all earlier forms of life. To initiate a pupil into the world of human achievement is to make available to him much that does not lie upon the surface of his present world. An inheritance will contain much that may not be in current use, much that has come to be neglected and something even that for the time being is forgotten. And to know only the dominant is to become acquainted with only an attenuated version of this inheritance. To see oneself reflected in the mirror of the present modish world is to see a sadly distorted image of a human being; for there is nothing to encourage us to believe that what has captured current fancy is the most valuable part of our inheritance, or that the better survives more readily than the worse. And nothing survives in this world which is not cared for by human beings. The business of the teacher (indeed, this may be said to be his peculiar quality as an agent of civilization) is to release his pupils from servitude to the current dominant feelings, emotions, images, ideas, beliefs, and even skills, not by inventing alternatives to them which seem to him more desirable, but by making available to him something which approximates more closely to the whole of his inheritance.

But this inheritance is an historic achievement; it is "positive," not "necessary"; it is contingent upon circumstances, it is miscellaneous and incoherent; it is what human beings have achieved, not by the impulsion of a final cause, but by exploiting the opportunities of fortune and by means of their own efforts. It comprises the standards of conduct to which from time to time they have given their preferences, the pro- and con- feelings to which they have given their approval and disapproval, the intellectual enterprises they have happened upon and pursued, the duties they have imposed upon themselves, the activities they have delighted in, the hopes they have entertained and the disappointments they have suffered. The notions of "finished" and "unfinished" are equally inapplicable to it. It does not deliver to us a clear and unambiguous message; it speaks often in riddles; it offers us advice and suggestion, recommendations, aids to reflection, rather than directives. It has been put together not by designers but by men who knew only dimly what they did. It has no meaning as a whole; it cannot be learnt or taught in principle, only in detail.

A teacher, then, engaged in initiating his pupils into so contingent an inheritance, might be excused for thinking that he needed some assurance of its worth. For, like many of us, he may be expected to have a superstitious prejudice against the human race and to be satisfied only when he can feel himself anchored to something for which human beings are not responsible. But he must be urged to have the courage of his circumstances. This man-made inheritance contains everything to which value may be attributed; it is the ground and context of every judgment of better and worse. If there were a mirror of perfection which he could hold up to his pupils, he might be expected to prefer it to this home-made article. But there is no such mirror. He may be excused if he finds the present dominant image of civilized life too disagreeable to impart with any enthusiasm to his pupils. But if he has no confidence in any of the standards of worth written into this inheritance of human achievement, he had better not be a teacher; he would have nothing to teach.

But teachers are modest people, and we are likely to disclaim so large an engagement as initiating our pupils into the civilized inheritance of mankind. We do not pretend to hand on anything but scraps of that inheritance; and it does not escape us that the civilization we are directly concerned with is not alone in the world and that this is a further limitation of our activities. And all this constitutes a renewed recognition of the contingency of what we have to teach. But the important point here is that whether we are concerned with a relatively simple or (like ours) an exceedingly complex civilization, whether we are concerned with a small or a large part of it, and whether we are concerned with practical skills, with moral conduct or with large intellectual enterprises like philosophy or science), teaching and learning always relate to an historic inheritance of human achievement and that what is to be handed on and learned, known and understood, are thoughts and various "expressions" of thoughts.

3

Now, from one important point of view, all we can be said to know constitutes a manifold of different "abilities," different amounts of knowledge being represented in different degrees of ability, and every complex ability being a manifold of simpler abilities.

When an ability is recognized as an ability to do or to make something, and it is recognized to be significantly composed of physical movements, we usually call it a skill. Playing billiards and ploughing a field are skills; each may be enjoyed in different degrees and each may be seen to be a manifold of simpler skills. Thus the ability to plough entails the ability to manage the horse as well as the plough; and the ability to manage the horse entails the ability to manage the leads and the ability to make the appropriate noises.

Further, we are apt to extend this notion of skill to abilities not so significantly composed of physical movements. A navigator, a chairman or a painter may be said to be "skilful." But when we say this we usually mean that the abilities concerned in these activities are large and complex and that in this case they are enjoyed to only a limited extent: we mean that his ability runs to a *merely* skilful performance. And this draws attention to abilities which we do not normally call skills.

These are usually more complicated, less obviously concerned with doing and making and more obviously concerned with the performance of mental operations—like speaking, diagnosing, understanding, describing, explaining, etc. And the complex "abilities" denoted in the expressions engineer, Latin scholar, explorer, actor, surgeon, lawyer, army commander, physicist, teacher, painter, farmer, etc., are each manifolds in which simpler abilities are grouped and given a specific focus.

This conjunction, in a concept of "abilities," of what we know and the use we make of it, is not designed to prove anything, but merely to indicate the way in which we carry about with us what we may be said to know. What we are aware of is not a number of items of knowledge available for use, but having powers of specific kinds—the power of being able to solve a legal problem, or to understand a Latin inscription or to perform a surgical operation. What we know constitutes an equipment which we possess in terms of what it enables us to do or to understand. And the "pragmatism" which this way of thinking might seem to commit us to may be avoided if it is recognized that abilities are of different kinds and cannot be assimilated to one another—that (for example) the ability to understand and to explain cannot be assimilated to the ability to do or to make.

Now, these abilities of various kinds and dimensions which constitute what we may be said to know will be found to be conjunctions of what is called "information" and what I shall call "judgment."

The component of "information" is easily recognized. It is the explicit ingredient of knowledge, where what we know may be itemized. Information consists of facts, specific intellectual artefacts (often arranged in sets or bunches). It is impersonal (not a matter of opinion). Most of it is accepted on authority, and it is to be found in dictionaries, manuals, textbooks, and encyclopaedias. It is the appropriate answer to questions which ask: who? what? where? which? how long? how much? etc. Typical pieces of information are: the date of Shakespeare's death; of St. Paul's conversion; the average annual rainfall in Bournemouth; the ingredients of welsh rarebit; the specific gravity of alcohol; the age of consent; the atomic structure of nitrogen; the reasons given by Milton for favouring polygamy; the seating capacity of the Albert Hall.

Except in quizzes, where it is notoriously inert, information is a component of knowledge, and (unlike knowledge itself) it may be useful or useless. Useful information is composed of facts related to a particular skill or ability. There is no inherently useless information; there are only facts irrelevant to the matter in hand.

Some facts seem to convey detached pieces of information—"Mummy, Mrs. Smith wears a wig," "we cook on gas," "that is a bicycle," "this is a bassoon"—and they lose their inertness merely by reason of their place in a conversation. But the importance of information lies in its provision of rules or rule-like propositions relating to abilities. Every ability has its rules, and they are contained in that component of knowledge we call information. This is clearly the case with mathematical or chemical formulae, or with information like "glass is brittle," or "hemlock is poisonous"; but it is also the case with other items of information. A recipe tells me what ingredients I should use in making a dish, and one of the uses of knowing the seating capacity of the Albert Hall is that it tells me how many tickets I may sell.

But rules or rule-like propositions such as are supplied in pieces of information may be related to knowledge (that is, to a specific ability or skill) in either of two different ways. They may be items of information which must be known as a condition of being able to perform; or they may constitute the criterion by means of which a performance may be known to be incorrect, though here they are never the only means by which mistakes may be detected.

First, nobody could read or receive a message in morse unless he were correctly informed about the morse-code equivalents of the letters of the alphabet. This is information in the exact sense. It is a set of facts (specific intellectual artefacts), not opinions; it is stated in propositions; it is received on authority; it is capable of being forgotten and it needs to be recollected; and it appears in rules to be followed—rules which must be known and recollected as a condition of being able to perform.

Secondly, the grammar of a language may be said to constitute the criterion by which a performance may be known to be incorrect. It consists of facts, stated in propositions, and it appears as rules. But, while this information may obliquely promote a laudable performance, it is not necessary to it. A laudable performance is possible to somebody who never possessed this information, or to somebody who once had it but has now forgotten it. There are a number of things directly related to a performance which a person ignorant of these facts could not do; but among them is neither the ability to speak intelligently and to understand what is said in the language, nor the ability to detect mistakes. The rules, here, are observed in the performance and they are capable of being known. They are the criterion for determining an incorrect performance, but a knowledge of them is not a condition of a laudable performance.

There is, indeed, a third sort of rule-like proposition which, in order to distinguish it from other sorts, is often called a "principle." There are propositions which are advanced in order to explain what is going on in any performance; they supply what may be called its "underlying *rationale*." And, consequently, as I understand them, they are never components of the knowledge which constitutes the performance. They belong to a separate performance of their own—the performance of explaining a performance. Let me offer two examples of what I mean.

First, riding a bicycle is a skill which consists wholly of making the appropriate physical movements. In order to enjoy this skill certain information must have been acquired, and there may also be what could be called the "grammar" of the skill. But beyond all this, the skill may be said to be an exemplification of certain principles of mechanics. But these principles are utterly unknown to even the most successful cyclist, and being able to recite them would not help to be more proficient. They do not constitute a criterion. Their sole value is the contribution they may make to our understanding of what is going on. In short, they are unrelated either to learning or to practising the skill. They belong to a separate performance, the performance of explaining.

Secondly, moral conduct may be said to be the ability to behave well. Here, again, certain information must be known; and there may also be what could be called the "grammar" of moral conduct—the rules and rule-like propositions which constitute the criterion by means of which a performance may be known to be "incorrect." But, again, beyond all this there are, or may be, "principles" in terms of which what is going on in moral conduct may be understood and explained. Aristotle, for example, in the "principle of the Mean," formulated what he believed to be the "underlying *rationale*" of all good conduct. But a knowledge of this, or of any other such "principle," is not a condition of being able to behave well, nor does this principle constitute a criterion by means of which a performance may be known to be "incorrect." It is unrelated either to learning good conduct or to a good performance.

There is, then, as I understand it, a sort of information which is designed to explain a performance (and also to explain the rules of a performance), but which is never a component of the knowledge which constitutes the performance. And this, of course, is so even when the performance is itself a performance of understanding and explanation, as, for example, in history or in science.

But, to return from this not unnecessary digression; there is in all knowledge an ingredient of information. It consists of facts which may range from the recognitions and identifications in which knowledge of any sort emerges from indeterminate awareness, to rules or rule-like propositions which inform the skills and abilities in which we carry about what we may be said to know, and which are sometimes, but not always, expressly known and followed. This ingredient of information, however, never constitutes the whole of what we know. Before any concrete skill or ability can appear, information must be partnered by "judgment," "knowing *how*" must be added to the "knowing *what*" of information.

By "judgment" I mean the tacit or implicit component of knowledge, the ingredient which is not merely unspecified in propositions but is unspecifiable in propositions. It is the component of knowledge which does not appear in the form of rules and which, therefore, cannot be resolved into information or itemized in the manner characteristic of information.

That we enjoy such knowledge has seemed to some writers undeniable. They direct our attention, in the first place, to skills—that is, to abilities which are significantly composed of physical movements. We may know how to do something without being able to state explicitly the manner of acting involved. This, for example, appears to be the case in swimming, riding a horse, playing a fish, using a chisel, and in turning a bowl on a potter's wheel. And these writers point out, further, that we may recognize an action as being of a known kind without being able to specify how we recognized it; that we are able to discover similarities in things without being able to say what they consist of, or patterns without being aware of the elements they are composed of or the rules they exemplify; and that we may speak a language without knowing the rules we are following and even without those rules ever having been formulated.

All this, I think, is true. But what it suggests to me is that there are skills and abilities where what is known may lack certain sorts of informatory content (particularly the sort of information we call "the rules"), rather than that there is a "knowing *how*" which can be divorced from any "knowing *what*." And I have used "judgment" to distinguish "knowing *how*" from "information" because I think "knowing *how*" is an ingredient of all genuine knowledge, and not a separate kind of knowing specified by an ignorance of rules.

Facts, rules, all that may come to us as information, itemized and explicit, never themselves endow us with an ability to do, or to make, or to understand and explain anything. Information has to be used, and it does not itself indicate how, on any occasion, it should be used. What is required in addition to information is knowledge which enables us to interpret it, to decide upon its relevance, to recognize what rule to apply, and to discover what action permitted by the rule should, in the circumstances, be performed; knowledge (in short) capable of carrying us across those wide open spaces, to be found in every ability, where no rule runs. For rules are always disjunctive. They specify only an act or a conclusion of a certain general kind and they never relieve us of the necessity of choice. And they never yield more than partial explanations: to understand anything as an example of the operation of a rule is to understand it very imperfectly.

"Judgment," then, is not to be recognized as merely information of another sort; its deliverances cannot be itemized, they cannot be specified in propositions, and they are neither remembered nor forgotten. It is, for example, all that is contained in what has been called "the unspecifiable art of scientific inquiry" without which "the articulate contents of scientific knowledge" remain unintelligible.

And if we are obliged to retreat a little from the notion of an entirely independent "knowing *how*" (because every ability has an ingredient of fact, recognized as fact and specifiable in propositions), I do not think we can avoid recognizing what I have called "judgment" as a partner, not only in those abilities we call skills, but in all abilities whatever, and, indeed, more particularly in those abilities which are almost exclusively concerned with mental operations.

The connoisseurship we recognize to belong to the knowledge entailed in riding a horse, for example, or in transmitting or receiving a message in the morse code, has its counterpart elsewhere. Indeed, the further we go from manual and sensual skills the larger becomes the place occupied by this component of knowledge. Whatever its place in tea-tasting and in the diagnosis of disease, its place in art and literature, in historical, philosophical, or scientific understanding is almost immeasurably greater.

It is represented, for example, in the so-called *divinatio* of the textual critic in which a corrupt reading is detected and an emendation suggested. It is what comes into play where the information to be got from the collation of mss. and recension stops. It is all that goes beyond the point where critical rules and methods leave off, and all that is required to drag appropriate precepts from these rules. It is what escapes even the most meticulous list of the qualities required for practising the craft of the textual critic.

A similar ingredient appears in the practical relationships of human beings. The moral and legal rules which set out in propositional form the recognized rights and duties, and the prudential maxims which give some flexibility to those rules, constitute only a small part of the knowledge comprised in the ability to live a civilized life. The precepts themselves require interpretation in respect of persons and circumstances; where there is a conflict between precepts, it cannot be resolved by the application of other rules. "Casuistry," as it has been said, "is the grave of moral judgment."

In short, in every "ability" there is an ingredient of knowledge which cannot be resolved into information, and in some skills this may be the greater part of the knowledge required for their practice. Moreover, "abilities" do not exist in the abstract but in individual examples: the norms by which they are recognized are afterthoughts, not categorical imperatives. And each individual example has what may be called a style or idiom of its own which cannot be specified in propositions. Not to detect a man's style is to have missed three-quarters of the meaning of his actions and utterances; and not to have acquired a style is to have shut oneself off from the ability to convey any but the crudest meanings.

What, then, is significant is not the observation that one may know how to speak a language without knowing the rules one is following, but the observation that until one can speak the language in a manner not expressly provided for in the rules, one can make no significant utterance in it. And of course, by a language I do not mean merely Latin and Spanish, I mean also the languages of history, philosophy, science, and practical life. The rules of art are there, but they do not determine the practice of the art; the rules of understanding are there, but they do not themselves endow us with understanding. They set limits—often telling us only what not to do if we wish to speak any of the languages of our civilization; but they provide no prescription for all that must go on in the interval between these limits.

4

The inheritance of human achievements into which the teacher is to initiate his pupil is knowledge; and (on this reading of it) knowledge is to be recognized as manifolds of abilities, in each of which there is a synthesis of "information" and "judgment." What bearing has this view of things upon the activities of learning and teaching—learning which is succeeding to the inheritance, and teaching which is deliberately initiating a pupil into it? I doubt very much whether there are any practical conclusions to be drawn from it for either learners or teachers; but I think it may have some virtue as part of an attempt to understand what is going on in learning and teaching.

It suggests, first, that what I have called the two components of knowledge ("information" and "judgment") can both be communicated and acquired, but cannot be communicated or acquired separately—at least, not on separate occasions or in separate "lessons." This, I think, is certainly true in respect of all the more important abilities and passages in the inheritance, and it is not seriously qualified by the observations that it is possible to communicate and acquire inert information, and that there are some skills in which the component of information is minimal.

But, secondly, it suggests that these two components of knowledge cannot be communicated in the same manner. Indeed, as I understand it, the distinction between "information" and "judgment" is a distinction between different manners of communication rather than a dichotomy in what is known; and for me it springs from reflecting upon teaching and learning rather than from reflecting upon the nature of knowledge. Thus teaching may be said to be a twofold activity of communicating "information" (which I shall call "instructing") and communicating "judgment" (which I shall call "imparting"); and learning may be said to be a twofold activity of acquiring "information" and coming to possess "judgment."

And the rest of what I have to say concerns this distinction and the understanding it may give of what is going on in learning and teaching.

All teaching has a component of instruction, because all knowledge has a component of information. The teacher as instructor is the deliberate conveyor of information to his pupil.

The facts which compose information are specific, impersonal, and mostly to be taken on trust; they are also apt to be hard, isolated, arbitrary, and inert. They may be stored in encyclopaedias and dictionaries. Their immediate appeal is not to the pupil's desire to understand, but to his curiosity, his desire not to be ignorant—that is, perhaps, to his vanity. And this desire not to be ignorant is, for the most part, satisfied by knowing things in terms of their names and by knowing the signification of words and expressions. From his earliest years the pupil has been used to making such discoveries for himself; he has become accustomed to distinguishing in an elementary way between fact and not-fact—without, of course, knowing the rules he is observing in doing so. And, for the most part, he is used to doing all this as part of the process of coming to be at home in the world he inhabits. Thus, when he falls into the hands of an instructor, he is already familiar with the activity of acquiring information, particularly information of immediate use.

Now the task of the teacher as instructor is to introduce his pupil to facts which have no immediate practical significance. (If there were no such facts, or if they composed an unimportant part of our inheritance, he would be a luxury rather than a necessity.) And, therefore, his first business is to consider and decide what information to convey to his pupil. This may be decided by circumstances: the Sergeant-Instructor does not have to consider whether or not he shall inform his class about the names and uses of the parts of the Bren-gun. But, if it is not decided by such circumstances as these, it is something which falls to the teacher as instructor to consider. What part or parts of our inheritance of information shall be transmitted to his pupil?

His second task is to make the information he has to convey more readily learnable by giving it an organization in which the inertness of its component facts is modified.

The organization provided by an immediate application to the practical life of his pupil is spurious; much of the information he has to convey has no such application and would be corrupted by being turned in this direction. The organization provided by a dictionary or an encyclopaedia is not designed for learning but for the rapid discovery of items of information in response to a recognition of specific ignorance. And the organization of information in terms of the modes of thought, or languages, which are the greatest achievements of civilization, is much too sophisticated for the beginner. In these circumstances, what we have settled for, and what the instructor may be expected to settle for, is the organization of information in terms of the more or less arbitrarily distinguished "subjects" of a school or university curriculum: geography, Latin, chemistry, arithmetic, "current affairs," or what-not. Each of these is an organization of information and not a mode of thought; but each permits facts to begin to reveal their rule-like character (that is, their character as tools to be used in doing, making, or understanding) and thus to throw off some of their inertness. Moreover, there is, I think, some positive advantage in devising, for pedagogical purposes, special organizations of information which differ from the significant modes of thought of our civilization. For these modes of thought are not themselves organizations of information; and when one of them appears as a school "subject"—as, for example, "philosophy" in the curriculum of a *lycée*—its character is apt to be misrepresented. No great harm may be thought to come from representing "geography" or even "Latin" as information to be acquired, but there is something odd about "philosophy" when it appears as the ability (for example) to remember and rehearse the second proof for the existence of God or what Descartes said about dreams.

There are, I think, two other tasks which obviously fall to the teacher as instructor. First, he has to consider the order in which the information contained in each of these somewhat arbitrary organizations of facts shall be transmitted to his pupil. It is this sort of consideration which goes into devising a syllabus, writing a textbook, or composing the programme of an instructing machine. And second, he has to exercise his pupil in this information so that what has been acquired may be recognized in forms other than those in which it was first acquired, and may be recollected on all the occasions when it is relevant. That is, the instructor has not only to hear his pupils recite the Catechism, the Highway Code, the Capes and Bays, the eight-times multiplication table, and the Kings of England, but he has also to see that they can answer questions in which this information is properly used. For the importance of information is the accuracy with which it is learned and the readiness with which it can be recollected and used.

Nevertheless, our inheritance of information is so great that, whatever devices the instructor may use to modify its inertness, much of it must be acquired with only the dimmest notion of how it might be used. No doubt it would be a good thing (as Lichtenberg said) if we could be educated in such a way that everything unclear to us was totally incomprehensible; but this is not possible. Learning begins not in ignorance, but in error. Besides, in acquiring information we may learn something else, other and more valuable than either the information itself or perceiving that it is something to be used. And to understand what this is we must turn from "information" to "judgment," from the activity of "instructing" to the activity of "imparting."

Now, something of what I mean by "judgment" has begun to appear whenever the pupil perceives that information must be used, and perceives the possibility of irrelevance. And something of this is imparted in the organization of information itself; although these organizations are apt to give a restrictive impression of relevance. It is clear that this is not itself information; it cannot be taught in the way in which information may be conveyed, and it cannot be learned, recollected, or forgotten in the way in which information may be learned, recollected, and forgotten. But it is clear, also, that this is only an intimation of "judgment," for there is much more to be noticed which no mere organization of information can impart. To perceive that facts are rules or tools, to perceive that rules are always disjunctive, and never categorical, is one thing; to have acquired the ability to use them is another.

"Judgment," then, is that which, when united with information, generates knowledge or "ability" to do, to make, or to understand and explain. It is being able to think—not to think in no manner in particular, but to think with an appreciation of the considerations which belong to different modes of thought. This, of course, is something which must be *learned*; it does not belong to the pupil by the light of nature, and it is as much a part of our civilized inheritance as the information which is its counterpart. But since learning to think is not acquiring additional information it cannot be pursued in the same way as we add to our stock of information.

Further, "judgment" may be *taught*; and it belongs to the deliberate enterprise of the teacher to teach it. But, although a pupil cannot be explicitly instructed in how to think (there being, here, no rules), "judgment" can be taught only in conjunction with the transmission of information. That is to say, it cannot be taught in a separate lesson which is not (for example) a geography, a Latin or an algebra lesson. Thus, from the pupil's point of view, the ability to think is something learned as a by-product of acquiring information; and, from the teacher's point of view, it is something which, if it is taught, must be imparted obliquely in the course of instruction. How this is done is to be understood from considering the character of what has to be imparted.

"Judgment," the ability to think, appears first, not in merely being aware that information is to be used, that it is a capital and not a stock, but in the ability to use it—the ability to invest it in answering questions. The rules may have been mastered, the maxims may be familiar, the facts may be available to recollection; but what do they look like in a concrete situation, and how may a concrete situation (an artefact or an understanding) be generated from this information? How does Latin grammar appear in a page from

Cicero (whence, indeed, it was abstracted) and how can it be made to generate a page of genuine Latin prose? What do the copybook maxims look like in moral conduct observed, and how can they be made to generate conduct? These are the facts, but what conclusions do they authorize or forbid? This is the literature—the articulate contents, for example, of current knowledge about magnetic effects—but how does a pupil learn to speak the language in which it is written down: the language of science? How does he acquire the connoisseurship which enables him to determine relevance, which allows him to distinguish between different sorts of questions and the different sorts of answers they call for, which emancipates him from crude absolutes and suffers him to give his assent or dissent in graduate terms?

But learning to think is not merely learning how to judge, to interpret, and to use information; it is learning to recognize and enjoy the intellectual virtues. How does a pupil learn disinterested curiosity, patience, intellectual honesty, exactness, industry, concentration, and doubt? How does he acquire a sensibility to small differences and the ability to recognize intellectual elegance? How does he come to inherit the disposition to submit to refutation? How does he, not merely learn the love of truth and justice, but learn it in such a way as to escape the reproach of fanaticism?

And beyond all this there is something more difficult to acquire, but more important than any of it; namely, the ability to detect the individual intelligence which is at work in every utterance, even in those which convey impersonal information. For every significant act or utterance has a style of its own, a personal idiom, an individual manner of thinking of which it is a reflection. This, what I have called style, is the choice made, not according to the rules, but within the area of freedom left by the negative operation of rules. We may listen to what a man has to say, but unless we overhear in it a mind at work and can detect the idiom of thought, we have understood nothing. Art and conduct, science, philosophy, and history, these are not modes of thought *defined* by rules; they exist only in personal explorations of territories of which only the boundaries are subject to definition. To have command over the languages of our civilization is not to know the rules of their grammar, but to have the opportunity of a syntax and a vocabulary, rich in fine distinctions, in which to think for oneself. Learning, then, is acquiring the ability to feel and to think, and the pupil will never acquire these abilities unless he has learned to listen for them and to recognize them in the conduct and utterances of others.

Besides information, then, this is what has to be learned; for this (and not the dead weight of its products) is the real substance of our inheritance—and nothing can be inherited without learning. And this is what the teacher has to "impart" to his pupil, together with whatever information he chooses to convey.

It cannot be *learned* separately; it is never explicitly learned and it is known only in practice; but it may be learned in everything that is learned, in the carpentry shop as well as in the Latin or chemistry lesson. If it is learned, it can never be forgotten, and it does not need to be recollected in order to be enjoyed. It is, indeed, often enough, the residue which remains when all else is forgotten; the shadow of lost knowledge.

It cannot be *taught* separately; it can have no place of its own in a timetable of a curriculum. It cannot be taught overtly, by precept, because it comprises what is required to animate precept; but it may be taught in everything that is taught. It is implanted unobtrusively in the manner in which information is conveyed, in a tone of voice, in the gesture which accompanies instruction, in asides and oblique utterances, and by example. For "teaching by example," which is sometimes dismissed as an inferior sort of teaching, generating inflexible knowledge because the rules of what is known remain concealed, is emancipating the pupil from the half-utterances of rules by making him aware of a concrete situation. And in imitating the example he acquires, not merely a model for the particular occasion, but the disposition to recognize everything as an occasion. It is a habit of listening for an individual intelligence at work in every utterance that may be acquired by imitating a teacher who has this habit. And the intellectual virtues may be imparted only by a teacher who really cares about them for their own sake and never stoops to the priggishness of mentioning them. Not the cry, but the rising of the wild duck impels the flock to follow him in flight.

When I consider, as in private duty bound, how I first became dimly aware that there was something else in learning than the acquisition of information, that the way a man thought was more important than what he said, it was, I think, on the occasion when we had before us concrete situations. It was when we had not an array of historical "facts," but (for a moment) the facts suspended in an historian's argument. It was on those occasions when we were made to learn by heart, not the declension of *bonus* (which, of course, had to be learned), but a passage of literature, the reflection of a mind at work in a language. It was on those occasions when one was not being talked to but had the opportunity of overhearing an intelligent conversation.

And if you were to ask me the circumstances in which patience, accuracy, economy, elegance, and style first dawned upon me, I would have to say that I did not come to recognize them in literature, in argument, or in geometrical proof until I had first recognized them elsewhere; and that I owed this recognition to a Sergeant gymnastics instructor who lived long before the days of "physical education" and for whom gymnastics was an intellectual art—and I owed it to him, not on account of anything he ever said, but because he was a man of patience, accuracy, economy, elegance, and style.

Eric Voegelin

1901–85

The climate of our universities is certainly hostile to the life of reason, but not every man is agreeable to having his nature deformed by the "climate" or, as it is sometimes called, the "age." There are always young men with enough spiritual instinct to resist the efforts of "educators" who pressure for "adjustment."

"ON CLASSICAL STUDIES"

The German political philosopher Eric Voegelin was born in Cologne but moved to Vienna as a child. He attended the University of Vienna, earning a doctorate in political science in 1922. His education did not end there, however. He studied constitutional law at Berlin and Heidelberg and classics at Oxford, undertook further work in the United States at Columbia, Harvard, and Wisconsin, and in Paris at the Sorbonne on his way back to Vienna. In the 1930s, he opposed the rise of Nazi totalitarianism and racial ideology, concerned particularly with the dehumanizing spiritual evil underlying it. He devoted much of his scholarly career to analyzing and exposing the religious, "gnostic" spiritual deformation at the heart of the crisis of the modern West. He embraced the classical and Christian tradition in philosophy and rejected the Enlightenment's distorted views of human nature, knowledge, and the meaning of history. After Nazi Germany's forced unification with Austria in 1938, Voegelin fled to Switzerland and then to the United States. He taught briefly at Harvard, Bennington College in Vermont, and the University of Alabama before settling at Louisiana State University, where he profoundly influenced a generation of American conservatives. In 1958 he returned to Europe to teach political science at the University of Munich, and in 1969 he came back to the United States to join the Hoover Institution at Stanford University. He retired in 1974 but continued to write and publish extensively.

THE SELECTION

Voegelin's essay "On Classical Studies" appeared in *Modern Age* in 1973. It was written toward the end of the wave of student revolts that had erupted on campuses in America and Europe in 1968. He blamed the professors more than the students for the unrest, believing that they were simply reaping the consequences of the nihilism they had sowed in their students' souls. Voegelin points out the gulf between classical and modern understandings of man, philosophy, and society. Despite his grim diagnosis, he writes in hopeful expectation that the "climate of opinion" can and will change, that with intellectual courage and proper diligence academia will reconnect with man's true nature. Voegelin employed a highly specialized language in his scholarship, and readers may want to consult the glossary at the end of Michael P. Federici's *Eric Voegelin: The Restoration of Order*. By "metalepsis" (as in "metaleptic reality"), Voegelin means "the participation of both the divine and the human in consciousness." By "noesis" (adj., "noetic"), Voegelin indicates "the activity of nous [the divinely created intellect] that differentiates reality."[1]

"On Classical Studies"

A reflection on classical studies, their purpose and prospects, will properly start from Wolf's definition of classic philology as the study of man's nature as it has become manifest in the Greeks.[2]

The conception sounds strangely anachronistic today, because it has been overtaken by the two closely related processes of the fragmentation of science through specialization and the deculturation of Western society. Philology has become linguistics; and the man who manifested his nature in the Greek language has become the subject matter of specialized histories of politics, literature, art, political ideas, economics, myth, religion, philosophy, and science. Classical studies are reduced to enclaves in vast institutions of higher learning in which the study of man's nature does not rank high in the concerns of man. This fragmentation, as well as the institutional reduction, however, are not sensed as a catastrophe, because the "climate of opinion" has changed in the two hundred years since Wolf's definition. The public interest has shifted from the nature of man to the nature of nature and to the prospects of domination its exploration opened; and the loss of interest even turned to hatred when the nature of man proved to be resistant to the changes dreamed up by intellectuals who want to add the lordship of society and history to the mastery of nature. The alliance of indifference and hatred, both inspired by *libido dominandi*, has created the climate that is not favorable to an institutionalized study of the nature of man, whether in its Greek or any other manifestation. The protagonists of the Western deculturation process are firmly established in our universities.

Still, the end of the world has not come. For "climates of opinion," though they last longer than anyone but their libidinous profiteers would care, do not last forever. The

---

1. Michael P. Federici, *Eric Voegelin: The Restoration of Order* (Wilmington, DE: ISI Books, 2002), 225, 227.
2. Friedrich August Wolf (1759–1824) created the science of "philology." The work on which his fame still rests is the *Prolegomena ad Homerum* (1795).

phrase was coined by Joseph Glanvill (1636–1680); it received new currency when Alfred North Whitehead resumed it in his *Science and the Modern World* (1925); and following the initiative of Whitehead, the changes of this modern climate ever since the seventeenth century have become the subject of Basil Willey's perceptive and extensive *Background* studies, beginning in 1934. Through Whitehead's, as well as through other initiatives, we know by now what the problem is; Whitehead has stated it flatly: "Modern philosophy has been ruined." More explicitly I would say: The life of reason; the ineluctable condition of personal and social order, has been destroyed. However, though these statements are true, one must distinguish between the climate of opinion and the nature of man. The climate of our universities certainly is hostile to the life of reason, but not every man is agreeable to having his nature deformed by the "climate" or, as it is sometimes called, the "age." There are always young men with enough spiritual instinct to resist the efforts of "educators" who pressure for "adjustment." Hence, the climate is not static; through the emotionally determined constellation of opinions of the moment there is always at work the resistance of man's nature to the climate. The insight into this dynamics underlies the studies of Willey. As a matter of fact, neither the changes in the climate from indifference to hostility, nor the concomitant waning of institutional support for the life of reason, nor the fanatically accelerated destruction of the universities since the Second World War, could prevent the problem of the climate from being recognized, articulated, and explored in the light of our consciousness of human nature. The reflections in which we are engaged here and now are as much a fact in the contemporary situation as the notorious "climate." The freedom of thought is coming to life again, when the "climate of opinion" is no longer a massive social reality imposing participation in its partisan struggles, but is forced into the position of a pathological deformation of existence, to be explored by the criteria of reason.

This is the setting in which the question of classical studies must be placed. On the one hand, there is a powerful climate of opinion in our universities opposed to accord them any function at all, because classical studies inevitably represent the nature of man as it has become manifest in the Greeks. On the other hand, there are undeniable symptoms of the climate cracking up and the nature of man undeformed reasserting itself. If this movement toward a restoration of reason should gain sufficient momentum to affect the institutional level, classical studies would become an important factor in the process of education. I shall reflect on the two points in this order—though some disorder may creep in as we are dealing not with alternatives belonging to the past but with an ongoing process.

The effort of the Greeks to arrive at an understanding of their humanity has culminated in the Platonic-Aristotelian creation of philosophy as the science of the nature of man. Even more than with the Sophistic of their times the results are in conflict with the contemporary climate of opinion. I shall enumerate some principal points of disagreement:

I. *Classic*: There is a nature of man, a definite structure of existence that puts limits on perfectibility. *Modern*: The nature of man can be changed, either through historical evolution or through revolutionary action, so that a perfect realm of freedom can be established in history.

2. *Classic*: Philosophy is the endeavor to advance from opinion (*doxa*) about the order of man and society to science (*episteme*); the philosopher is not a philodoxer. *Modern*: No science in such matters is possible, only opinion; everybody is entitled to his opinions; we have a pluralist society.

3. *Classic*: Society is man written large. *Modern*: Man is society written small.

4. *Classic*: Man exists in erotic tension toward the divine ground of his existence. *Modern*: He doesn't; for I don't; and I'm the measure of man.

5. *Classic*: Man is disturbed by the question of the ground; by nature he is a questioner (*aporein*) and seeker (*zetein*) for the whence, the where to, and the why of his existence; he will raise the question: Why is there something, why not nothing? *Modern*: Such questions are otiose (Comte); don't ask them, be a socialist man (Marx); questions to which the sciences of world-immanent things can give no answer are senseless, they are *Scheinprobleme* (neopositivism).

6. *Classic*: The feeling of existential unrest, the desire to know, the feeling of being moved to question, the questioning and seeking itself, the direction of the questioning toward the ground that moves to be sought, the recognition of the divine ground as the mover, are the experiential complex, the *pathos*, in which the reality of divine-human participation (*metalepsis*) becomes luminous. The exploration of the metaleptic reality, of the Platonic *metaxy*, as well as the articulation of the exploratory action through language symbols, in Plato's case of his myths, are the central concern of the philosopher's efforts. *Modern*: The modern responses to this central issue change with the "climate of opinion."

In Locke the metaleptic reality and its noetic analysis are transformed into the acceptance of certain "common opinions" which still bear an intelligible relation to the experience from which they derive. The reduction of reality to opinion, however, is not deliberate; Locke is already so deeply involved in the climate of opinion that his awareness for the destruction of philosophy through the transition from *episteme* to *doxa* is dulled. *Cf.* Willey's presentation of the Lockean case.

Hegel, on the contrary, is acutely aware of what he is doing when he replaces the metaleptic reality of Plato and Aristotle by his state of alienation as the experiential basis for the construction of his speculative system. He makes it explicitly his program to overcome philosophy by the dialectics of a self-reflective alienated consciousness.

In the twentieth century, the "climate of opinion" has advanced to the tactics of the "silent treatment." In a case like Sartre's, metaleptic reality is simply ignored. Existence has the character of meaningless *facticité*; its endowment with meaning is left to the free choice of man. The choice of a meaning for existence falls with preference on the opinion of totalitarian regimes who engage in mass murder, like the Stalinist; the preference has been elaborated with particular care by Merleau-Ponty. The tactics of the "silent treatment," especially employed after the Second World War by the "liberation rabble," however, make it difficult to decide in individual cases whether the counterposition to metaleptic reality is deliberate, or whether the *libido dominandi* is running amok in a climate of opinion that is taken for granted, without questioning, as ultimate reality. On the whole, I have the impression that the consciousness of a counterposition is distinctly less alive than it still was at the time of Hegel. Philosophical illiteracy has progressed so far that the experiential core of philosophizing has disappeared below the horizon and is not even recognized as such when it appears in philosophers like Bergson. The deculturation process has eclipsed it so thoroughly by opinion that sometimes one hesitates to speak even of an indifference toward it.

7. *Classic*: Education is the art of *periagoge*, of turning around (Plato). *Modern*: Education is the art of adjusting people so solidly to the climate of opinion prevalent at the time that they feel no "desire to know." Education is the art of preventing people from acquiring the knowledge that would enable them to articulate the questions of existence. Education is the art of pressuring young people into a state of alienation that will result in either quiet despair or aggressive militancy.

8. *Classic*: The process in which metaleptic reality becomes conscious and noetically articulate is the process in which the nature of man becomes luminous to itself as the life of reason. Man is the *zoon noun echon*. *Modern*: Reason is instrumental reason. There is no such thing as a noetic rationality of man.

9. *Classic*: Through the life of reason (*bios theoretikos*) man realizes his freedom. *Modern*: Plato and Aristotle were fascists. The life of reason is a fascist enterprise.

The enumeration is not even remotely exhaustive. Everybody can supplement it with juicy items gleaned from opinion literature and the mass media, from conversations with colleagues and students. Still, they make it clear what Whitehead meant when he stated that modern philosophy has been ruined. Moreover, the conflicts have been formulated in such a manner that the character of the grotesque attaching to the deformation of humanity through the climate of opinion becomes visible. The grotesque, however, must not be confused with the comic or the humorous. The seriousness of the matter will be best understood if one visions the concentration camps of totalitarian regimes and the gas chambers of Auschwitz, in which the grotesqueness of opinion becomes the murderous reality of action.

The climate of opinion is unfavorable to classical studies; and the institutional power of its representatives in the universities, the mass media, and the foundations must not be underrated. Nevertheless, cracks in the establishment become noticeable. In particular, the international student revolt has been an eye-opener. Even the spiritually and intellectually underprivileged who live by the bread of opinion alone have become aware that something is wrong with our institutions of higher learning, though they do not quite know what. Could it be perhaps the professors and not the war in Vietnam? With grim amusement have I watched the discomfiture of assorted leftist professors in Frankfurt and Berlin when their students turned against them, because the professors did not go along when their "critical theory" (a euphemism for irrational, nihilistic opining) was translated by the students into uncritical violence; and the same spectacle is provided in America by the liberal professors who suddenly become conservative, when a lifetime of strenuous effort to ruin the minds of one generation of students after another has at last borne fruit and the minds are really ruined. An incident from my own teaching practice will illuminate the critical point: In the mid-1960s I gave a course in classical politics at a major university. All went well as long as the students believed they were offered the customary fare of information on Plato's "opinions." An uproar ensued when they found out that philosophy of politics was to be taken seriously as a science. The idea that some propositions concerning the order of man and society were to be accepted as true, others to be rejected as false, came as a shock; they had never heard of such a thing before. A few actually walked out of the course; but the majority, I am glad to report, stayed on, they became enchanted by Plato, and at the end they profusely expressed their gratitude to have at last learned of an alternative to the drivel of opinions they were routinely fed. But I do not want to go more deeply into this aspect of the matter. It will be sufficient to state that the students have good reasons to revolt; and if the reasons they actually advance are bad, one should remember that the educational institutions have cut them off from the life of reason so effectively that they cannot even articulate the causes of their legitimate unrest.

By the irrational violence of the attack, the revolt could expose the flabbiness and emptiness of the institutionalized climate and its personnel, but one should not expect the life of reason to emerge from the confrontation of two vacua. More important than the spectacular events is the quiet erosion of the climate through the historical sciences. The nature of man can be deformed by the dominant opinions—the other day I heard a well-intentioned but helpless colleague cry out in anguish: Our world is fragmented!—but it is indestructible and finds ways to reassert itself. The metaleptic reality that is brushed aside as stuff and nonsense if it claims in public to be the primary concern of man has deviously crept in again under the respectable cover of comparative religion, comparative literature, the history of art, the science of the myth, the history of philosophy, intellectual history, the exploration of primitive symbolisms in ethnography and anthropology, the study of ancient civilizations, archaeology, and prehistory of Hinduism, Islam, and the Far East, of Hellenistic mystery religions, the Qumran texts, and gnosticism, of early Christianity and the Christian Middle Ages, and last but not least of classical studies. In the cultural history of Western society, the splendid advance of the historical sciences has become the underground of the great *resistance* to the climate of opinion. In every one of the fields enumerated, we find the men who devote their life to it, because here they find the spiritual integrity and wholeness of existence which on the dominant level of the universities has been destroyed. No critical attack on the insanity of the "age" can be more devastating than the plain fact that men who respect their own humanity, and want to cultivate it as they should, must become refugees to the Megalithicum, or Siberian shamanism, or Coptic papyri, to the petroglyphs in the caves of the Ile-de-France, or to the symbolisms of African tribes, in order to find a spiritual home and the life of reason. Moreover, this underground has become the refuge not only for scholars but also for the more sensitive students, as one can ascertain by browsing for an hour in a college bookstore; the nature of man asserts itself even if these poor fellows, deprived of proper guidance, grope for support in such exotica as the I-Ching.

Under the historical cover, thus, the substantive knowledge concerning the nature of man is present in our universities. Thanks to the phantastic enlargement of the historical horizon in time and space that has occurred in the present century, this knowledge has even become more comprehensive and penetrating than at any other time in the history of our universities. At the same time it has become more easily accessible to everybody—I have only to compare the difficulties of access in the 1920s, when I was a student, with the present plethora of paperbacks. This formidable presence, however, is slow to develop into a formative force in our institutions of higher learning. One of the reasons for this odd state of things will become apparent from an incident, a few years ago, at a conference on comparative religion: One of the participants broke the great taboo and flatly put it to his confrères that the subject matter they were treating was irrelevant by the standards of opinion to which most of them seemed to adhere; sooner or later they would have to make up their mind whether the science of comparative religion was an occupational therapy for persons otherwise unemployable, or whether it was a pursuit of the truth of existence which its subject matter substantively contained; one could not forever explore "religious phenomena," and pretend to their importance, without unreservedly professing that man's search for the divine ground of his existence, as well as the revelatory presence of God in the motivation of the search, constituted his humanity; in brief, he confronted them with the question of truth implied in their admirable achievements as historians. Not everybody present was pleased by such tactlessness. The historical cover, thus, is a sensible device as long as it secures a degree of freedom for the life of reason in institutions which are dominated by an essentially totalitarian climate, but it is in danger of becoming itself a part of the climate, as this incident shows, if the cover is used to sterilize the content, preventing it from becoming effective in our society. The cover will then degenerate into the ideology of historical positivism.

The advance of the historical sciences concerning the nature of man in its various manifestations has arrived at a critical juncture: in retrospect from a future historical position, will it be the massive basis for a restoration of the life of reason or will it be an interesting last gasp of reason, exhaled by little men who did not have the courage of their convictions, before the totalitarian climate strangled it off for a long time to come?

Assuming the first alternative to be realized, classical studies will have an important function in the process, for in its Greek manifestation man's nature has achieved the luminosity of noetic consciousness and developed the symbols for its self-interpretation. The Greek differentiation of reason in existence has set critical standards for the exploration of consciousness behind which nobody is permitted to fall back. This achievement, however, is not a possession forever, something like a precious heirloom to be handed on to later generations, but a paradigmatic action to be explored in order to be continued under the conditions of our time. But at this point I must stop, for the great question how that is to be done cannot be answered by jotting down a program; concrete action itself would be necessary; and as the Greek manifestation of man's nature covered the range of a civilization, that feat cannot be performed here and now. Hence, I shall conclude these reflections with the designation of two general areas in which no major advance of science beyond its present state seems possible without recourse to, and continuation of, the Greek noetic effort.

I. If anything is characteristic of the present state of the historical sciences, it is the discrepancy between the mountains of material information and the poverty of their theoretical penetration. Whenever I have to touch on problems of the primitive myth or the imperial symbolism of Egypt, of Israelite prophetism, Jewish apocalypse, or Christian gospels, of Plato's historical consciousness compared with that of Deutero-Isaiah, of the Polybian ecumenic consciousness compared with that of Mani, of magic or hermetism, and so forth, I am impressed by the philosophical and text-critical work done on the sources but feel frustrated because so little work is done to relate the phenomena of this class to the structure of consciousness in the sense of noetic analysis.

2. One of the great achievements of the Greek struggle, both against the older myth and the Sophistic climate of opinion, for insight into the order of man's existence is the exploration of existential deformation and its varieties. Again, very little is done to explore this achievement, to develop it further, and to apply it to the modern phenomena of existential deformation. We do not even have a good study on "alienation," though this very topical subject ought to stir up any classical scholar to voice what he has to say about it on the basis of the sources he knows best.

Sources and Permissions

Aeneas Silvius

From The Catholic University of America studies in Medieval and Renaissance Latin Language and Literature, Vol. XII. *Aeneae Silvii, De Liberorum educatione*, a translation with an Introduction, Copyright © 1940. A Dissertation. By Brother Joel Stanislauss Nelson, F.S.C., M.A., St. Mary's College, Winona, MN. Reprinted by permission from The Catholic University of America Press, Washington, DC.

Alcuin

Selection from Charlemagne's "Capitulary of 787" taken from F. V. N. Painter, ed. *Great Pedagogical Essays: Plato to Spencer*. New York: American Book Company, 1905, pp. 156–57.

Selections from Alcuin's letters reprinted from Arthur F. Leach, *Educational Charter and Documents 598 to 1909*. Cambridge: Cambridge University Press, 1911, pp. 11–21.

Thomas Aquinas

Selection from *On the Teacher* taken from *Selected Writings* by Thomas Aquinas, edited and translated with an introduction and notes by Ralph McInerny (Penguin Classics, 1998). Copyright © Ralph McInerny 1998.

"Letter to Brother John" from Vernon J. Bourke, *Aquinas' Search for Wisdom*. Milwaukee: The Bruce Publishing Company, 1965, "The Roots of Wisdom," pp. 17–18.

Leonardo Bruni

Reprinted from *The Humanism of Leonardo Bruni, Selected Texts*, translations and introductions by Gordon Griffiths, James Hankins, and David Thompson. Medieval and Renaissance Texts and Studies, in conjunction with The Renaissance Society of America, Binghamton, NY: The Renaissance Society of America, Copyright © 1987. Used by permission of The Renaissance Society of America, The City University of New York.

Edmund Burke

From *Letter to Member of the National Assembly,* in *The Works of the Right Honorable Edmund Burke*. Fifth edition. Vol. IV. Boston: Little, Brown, and Company, 1877, pp. 23–34.

John Calvin

Selection from *The Institutes of the Christian Religion* taken from John T. McNeill, ed., *Calvin: The Institutes of the Christian Religion, in Two Volumes*. Translated by Ford Lewis Battles. London: SCM Press, 1960.

Commentary on Titus from John Calvin, *Commentaries on the Epistles to Timothy, Titus, and Philemon*. Translated from the original Latin by the Rev. William Pringle. Edinburgh: Printed for the Calvin Translation Society, 1865, pp. 300–301.

Cassiodorus

From *Cassiodorus: Institutions of Divine and Secular Learning and On the Soul*. Translated with notes by James W. Halporn and introduction by Mark Vessey. Liverpool: Liverpool University Press, Copyright © 2004. Reprinted by permission from Liverpool University Press.

Christine de Pizan

From Christine de Pizan, *The Book of the Body Politic*, edited and translated by Kate Langdon Forhan. Cambridge: Cambridge University Press, Copyright © 1994. Reprinted with the permission of Cambridge University Press.

John Chrysostom

Reprinted from M. L. W. Laistner, *Christianity and Pagan Culture in the Later Roman Empire*. Copyright © 1951 by Cornell University. Used by permission of the publisher, Cornell University Press.

Cicero

Selection from *Pro Archia Poeta* reprinted by permission of the publishers and the Trustees of the Loeb Classical Library from *Cicero: The Speeches*, with an English translation by N.H. Watts, from Loeb Classical Library. Cambridge, MA: Harvard University Press, Copyright © 1961, by the President and Fellows of Harvard College. The Loeb Classical Library is a registered trademark of the President and Fellows of Harvard College.

Selection from Book I of *De Oratore* reprinted by permission of the publishers and the Trustees of the Loeb Classical Library from *Cicero: De Oratore, in two volumes, I, Books I, II*, with an English

Clement of Alexandria

Edward Copleston

Christopher Dawson

T. S. Eliot

Thomas Elyot
From Thomas Elyot, *The Book Named the Governor*. Edited with an introduction by S. E. Lehmberg. London: Everyman's Library, 1962, "Book I," pp. 28–40, 45–47, 50.

Erasmus
Selection from *The Antibarbarians* taken from *Collected Works of Erasmus, Literary and Educational Writings 1, Antibarbari/Parabolae*. Volume 23. Edited by Craig R. Thompson. University of Toronto Press, Copyright © 1978. Reprinted by permission from University of Toronto Press.

Selection from *On Education for Children* taken from *Collected Works of Erasmus, Literary and Education Writings 4, De Pueris Instituendis/De Recta Pronuntiatione*. Volume 26. Edited by J.K. Sowards. University of Toronto Press, Copyright © 1985. Reprinted by permission from University of Toronto Press.

Selection from *The Education of a Christian Prince* reprinted from Erasmus, *The Education of a Christian Prince with the Panegyric for Archduke Philip of Austria*, translated by Neil M. Cheshire and Michael J. Heath, translated by Lisa Jardine. Copyright © 1997. Reprinted with the permission of Cambridge University Press.

Gregory the Great
From *The Homilies of Saint Gregory the Great on the Book of the Prophet Ezekiel*. Translated by Theodosia Gray. Etna, CA: Center for Traditionalist Orthodox Studies, Copyright © 1990. Reprinted by permission from Saint Palamas Monastery.

Hugh of St. Victor
From *The Didascalicon of Hugh of St. Victor: A Medieval Guide to the Arts*, edited by Jerome Taylor. Copyright © 1991, Columbia University Press. Reprinted with permission of the publisher.

Isocrates
All selections reprinted by permission of the publishers and the Trustees of the Loeb Classical Library from *Isocrates, in three volumes, II*, with an English translation by George Norlin, from Loeb Classical Library. Cambridge, MA: Harvard University Press, Copyright © 1982, by the President and Fellows of Harvard College. The Loeb Classical Library is a registered trademark of the President and Fellows of Harvard College.

Jerome
All selections from Jerome, Letters XXII, LXX, and CVII, in Philip Schaff and Henry Wace, eds., *A Select Library of Nicene and Post-Nicene Fathers of the Christian Church*, 2d series, Vol. VI. Edinburgh: T & T Clark/Grand Rapids, MI: Eerdmans, 1989, pp. 35–36, 149–51, 190–91, 195.

John of Salisbury
Selection from the *Policraticus* reprinted from *Frivolities of Courtiers and Footprints of Philosophers*, edited by Joseph B. Pike, by permission of the University of Minnesota Press. Copyright © 1938.

Selection from the *Metalogicon* taken from *The Metalogicon of John of Salisbury: A Twelfth-Century Defense of the Verbal and Logical Arts of the Trivium*. Translated with an Introduction and Notes by Daniel D. McGarry. Berkeley, CA: University of California Press, 1955, "Book I," pp. 64–72; "Book III," p. 167; "Book IV," p. 276.

C. S. Lewis

From *The Grand Miracle*, by C. S. Lewis. Copyright © C. S. Lewis Pte. Ltd. 1970. Extracts reprinted by permission.

Martin Luther

Reprinted by permission from *Luther's Works Vol. 45* edited by Walther I. Brandt, Copyright © 1962 Fortress Press. Used by permission of Augsburg Fortress.

Rhabanus Maurus

From F. V. N. Painter, ed. *Great Pedagogical Essays: Plato to Spencer*. New York: American Book Company, 1905, "Education of the Clergy," pp. 159–68.

Philip Melanchthon

From Philip Melanchthon, *Orations on Philosophy and Education*, edited by Sachiko Kusukawa, translated by Christine F. Salazar. Cambridge: Cambridge University Press, Copyright © 1999. Reprinted with the permission of Cambridge University Press.

John Milton

From *The Prose Works of John Milton: With a Biographical Introduction by Rufus Wilmot Griswold*. Vol. 1. Philadelphia: John W. Moore, 1847.

Paul Elmer More

From Paul Elmer More, *Aristocracy and Justice: Shelburne Essays, Ninth Series*. Boston: Houghton Mifflin Company, 1915, "Academic Leadership," pp. 41–67.

John Henry Newman

From John Henry Newman, *The Idea of a University, Defined and Illustrated*. London: Longmans, Green, and Co., 1898, "Discourse V, Knowledge its Own End," pp. 99–123; "Christianity and Letters," pp. 256–65.

Albert Jay Nock

From Albert Jay Nock, *The Theory of Education in the United States*. New York: Harcourt, Brace and Company, 1932, "VI," pp. 47–57; "VII," pp. 58–71.

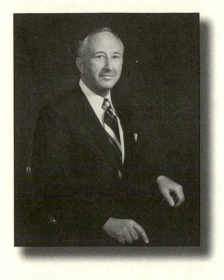

Publisher's Note: In Honor of Charles H. Hoeflich

ISI Books is pleased to publish *The Great Tradition: Classic Readings on What It Means to Be an Educated Human Being* in honor of Charles H. Hoeflich. His unwavering commitment to the promotion of wisdom and virtue—the noblest ideals and ends of both liberal education and Western civilization, and the special preoccupations of the writers anthologized in this volume—has played a crucial role in shaping the work of the Intercollegiate Studies Institute and enhancing its effectiveness. A graduate of the University of Pennsylvania, and chairman emeritus of the Univest Corporation, Mr. Hoeflich is a founding and still-active member of ISI's board of trustees, which he has served as chairman and secretary-treasurer. His name will be forever linked to the work of the Intercollegiate Studies Institute, along with those of Frank Chodorov, Henry Regnery, and E. Victor Milione, through his formal designation by ISI's board of trustees as Secretary-Treasurer Emeritus. In recognition of Mr. Hoeflich's vital institutional leadership, ISI also has named its highest award the Charles H. Hoeflich Lifetime Achievement Award.